The SAGE

Gov

Edited by
Mark Bevir

Los Angeles | London | New Delhi
Singapore | Washington DC

Introduction and editorial arrangement © Mark Bevir 2011
Chapters © contributors 2011

First published 2011

SAGE Publications Ltd
1 Oliver's Yard
55 City Road
London EC1Y 1SP

SAGE Publications Inc.
2455 Teller Road
Thousand Oaks, California 91320

SAGE Publications India Pvt Ltd
B 1/I 1 Mohan Cooperative Industrial Area
Mathura Road
New Delhi 110 044

SAGE Publications Asia-Pacific Pvt Ltd
33 Pekin Street #02-01
Far East Square
Singapore 048763

Library of Congress Control Number: 2010920019

British Library Cataloguing in Publication data

A catalogue record for this book is available from the British
Library

ISBN 978-1-44627-042-4

Typeset by Glyph International Ltd, Bangalore, India
Printed in India at Replika Press Pvt Ltd
Printed on paper from sustainable resources

Contents

Preface and Acknowledgments

The SAGE Handbook of Governance completes what I think of as a set of texts prepared for SAGE in an attempt to illuminate the contours and shadows of the vast literature that has arisen recently and rapidly on governance. *Key Concepts in Governance* (2009) used an overview of the literature on governance as a setting for discussions of 50 concepts that are prominent in discussions of governance. It is a textbook companion for students at all levels. While *Key Concepts* may serve as a reference work, that role falls primarily to the more extensive *Encyclopedia of Governance* (2007). The *Encyclopedia* offered a one-stop point of reference for anyone interested in any aspect of governance, whether they are a student, a researcher, a practitioner, or an everyday citizen. *Public Governance* (2007) is a four-volume collection of leading scholarly articles on theories of governance, public sector reform, public policy, and democratic governance. It provides researchers and students with easy access to some of the most influential and discussed articles in the field. I might be tempted to call it a collection of classic articles were the literature on governance not so current. Finally, this *Handbook of Governance* brings together an international cast of specialists to offer an authoritative overview of current scholarship. The *Handbook* provides a clear guide to advanced topics, cutting edge research, and future agendas.

Each of these SAGE texts provides an overview of governance studies as a whole. Indeed, these texts are a conscious attempt to forward my particular view of governance studies. In all these texts, I suggest that 'governance' refers to new theories of social coordination and new worlds of collective action, and, more controversially, I suggest that the new worlds arose in part because people acted on formal and folk versions of the new theories. This latter suggestion reflects my commitment to interpretive theory. If we are fully to explain a form of governance, we have to refer to the meanings and stories that are embodied in it; we have to interpret the beliefs and theories that have led people to act so as to create and maintain it. I hope that the *Handbook* will improve people's understanding of the world in which we live, the ideas that have made that world, and alternative ideas by which we might remake the world.

I would like to thank everyone at SAGE who has helped to produce the whole set of texts on governance. Lucy Robinson initially contacted me in 2004 to suggest that I edit an *Encyclopedia of Governance* for SAGE, and she later convinced me to do both the set on *Public Governance* and the *Key Concepts* book. David Mainwaring became the editor responsible for *Public Governance* and *Key Concepts*. He then raised the possibility of a *Handbook* and oversaw its creation. Throughout, Lucy and David were encouraging, responsive, and patient. I am most grateful.

Mark Bevir

List of Contributors

Kamran Ali Afzal is a career civil servant with the Government of Pakistan and has served in a range of administrative and policymaking positions over the past 16 years. His most recent assignment was with the finance department of the provincial government of the Punjab, where he was responsible for medium-term financial planning, drafting annual budgetary proposals, expenditure monitoring, and fiscal reforms. Currently a PhD candidate at the University of Melbourne, he is studying the relationship between public sector accountability and resource allocation. His areas of interest include comparative public policy, governance, government accountability structures, public finance, and social development.

Mark Bevir is a Professor in the Department of Political Science, University of California, Berkeley. He is the author of *The Logic of the History of Ideas* (1999), *New Labour: A Critique* (2005), *Key Concepts in Governance* (2009), and *Democratic Governance* (2010), and the co-author, with R.A.W. Rhodes, of *Interpreting British Governance* (2003), *Governance Stories* (2006), and *The State as Cultural Practice* (2010).

Lisa Blomgren Bingham is the Keller-Runden Professor of Public Service at Indiana University's School of Public and Environmental Affairs, Bloomington. Together with Rosemary O'Leary, she co-edited *The Promise and Performance of Environmental Conflict Resolution* (2003), *Big Ideas in Collaborative Public Management* (2008), and *The Collaborative Public Manager* (2009). She is an elected Fellow of the National Academy of Public Administration. Her current research examines dispute systems design and the legal infrastructure for collaboration, dispute resolution, and public participation in governance.

Hok Bun Ku is Associate Professor in the Department of Applied Social Sciences at the Hong Kong Polytechnic University and program leader of MSW (China). He is Deputy Director of the China Research and Development Network and executive editor of *China Journal of Social Work*. He has been involved in China's rural development for about 15 years and has written extensively on topics related to rural development, cultural politics, participatory design, social exclusion and marginality, and social work education. His most recent English-language book is *Moral Politics in a South Chinese Village: Responsibility, Reciprocity and Resistance* (2003). His Chinese-language books include *Fe/male Voices: A Practice of Feminist Writing* (2008), *The Stories of Pingzhai Village: The Practice of Culture and Development* (2007), *Practice-Based Social Work Research in Local Chinese Context* (2007), *Rethinking and Recasting Citizenship: Social Exclusion and Marginality in Chinese Society* (2005), *Research, Practice and Reflection of Social Work in Indigenous Chinese Context* (2004), and *Social Exclusion and Marginality in Chinese Societies* (2003).

Anthony B.L. Cheung is the President of The Hong Kong Institute of Education, Chair Professor of Public Administration and Director of the Centre for Governance and Citizenship. Professor Cheung has published extensively on privatization, civil service and public sector reforms, Asian administrative reforms, and government and politics in Hong Kong and China. His recent books are *Governance for Harmony in Asia and Beyond* (with Julia Tao *et al.*, 2010), *Governance and Public Sector Reform in Asia: Paradigm Shift or Business As Usual?* (co-edited, 2003), and *Public Service Reform in East Asia: Reform Issues and Challenges in Japan, Korea, Singapore and Hong Kong* (2005). Professor Cheung serves as a Member of Hong Kong's Executive Council and Chairman of the Consumer Council. He was the founder of the policy think-tank SynergyNet.

Robert K. Christensen is Assistant Professor in the School of Public and International Affairs at the University of Georgia. At the institutional level, he is interested in courts and their relationship to public/nonprofit organization outcomes. At the behavioral level, he is interested in the impact of pro- and anti-social attitudes/actions on public and nonprofit work groups and organizations. His work appears in such journals as *Administration & Society*, *Journal of Public Administration Research and Theory*, *Nonprofit Management and Leadership*, and *Public Administration Review*.

Steven Cohen is the Executive Director of the Earth Institute at Columbia University and Founder, Professor, and Director of the Master of Public Administration in Environmental Science and Policy Program at Columbia University's School of International and Public Affairs (SIPA). He is also a consultant and former policy analyst for the US Environmental Protection Agency. He is the author of *The Effective Public Manager* (1988) and *Understanding Environmental Policy* (2006). He has co-authored several books, including *Total Quality Management in Government* (1993), *Tools for Innovators: Creative Strategies for Managing Public Sector Organizations* (1998), *Strategic Planning in Environmental Regulation* (2005), and *The Responsible Contract Manager* (2008). Dr Cohen is also a columnist for *The Huffington Post* and has written extensively on public management innovation, ethics, and environmental policy.

Mark Considine is the Dean of the Faculty of Arts at the University of Melbourne and former Director of the Centre for Public Policy. He is a past winner of the American Educational Research Association's Outstanding Publication Award and in 2000 received the Marshall E. Dimmock Award for the best lead article in *Public Administration Review* (with co-author Jenny M. Lewis). His latest book (with Jenny M. Lewis and Damon Alexander) is *Networks, Innovation and Public Policy: Politicians, Bureaucrats and the Pathways to Change inside Government* (2009). His research areas include governance studies, comparative social policy, employment services, public sector reform, local development, and organizational sociology.

Janet V. Denhardt is a Professor and Doctoral Program Director in the School of Public Affairs at Arizona State University. Her research focuses on leadership, civic engagement, and governance. She has authored 10 books, including: *The New Public Service* (2007), *The Dance of Leadership* (2006), *Managing Human Behavior in Public and Nonprofit Organizations* (2009), *Public Administration: An Action Orientation* (2009), and *Street-Level Leadership* (1998). Her work has also appeared in *Public Administration Review*, *Administration & Society*, *American Review of Public Administration*, and *Journal of Public Administration Research and Theory*.

Robert B. Denhardt is a Regents Professor, the Coor Presidential Chair, and Director of the School of Public Affairs at Arizona State University. He is a Past President of the American Society for Public Administration and a Fellow of the National Academy of Public Administration. He has published 21 books, including *The Dance of Leadership* (2006), *The New Public Service* (2007), *Managing Human Behavior in Public and Nonprofit Organizations* (2009), *Public Administration: An Action Orientation* (2009), and *Theories of Public Organization* (2009).

Bas Denters is Professor of Public Governance at the Institute for Innovation and Governance Studies (IGS) of the University of Twente. His main research areas are local and regional governance, and issues of participation and representation in urban democracy. He is Overseas Editor of *Local Government Studies*, Convenor of the Standing Group on Local Government and Politics of the European Consortium for Political Research and Member of the Board of the European Urban Research Association. He has published in *Acta Politica*, *Environment & Planning*, *European Journal of Political Research*, *Local Government Studies*, *Public Administration*, and *Urban Affairs Review*. Relevant book publications include *The Rise of Interactive Governance and Quasi-Markets: A Comparison of the Dutch Experience with the Developments in Four Western Countries* (co-edited with O. van Heffen, J. Huisman and P.J. Klok, 2003), and *Comparing Local Governance: Trends and Developments* (co-edited with L.E. Rose, 2005).

Marian Döhler is Professor of Public Policy and Administration at Leibniz University, Hannover, and currently serves as Director of the Institute of Political Science. He has published four monographs on health policymaking and public administration. His articles have appeared in journals such as *Politische Vierteljahresschrift*, *Governance*, and *West European Politics*. He is co-editor of the peer-reviewed journal *der moderne staat* for which he is editing a special issue on regulation. His current research is about regulatory agencies, science and politics, managing public sector organizations, and the lawmaking process.

Keith Dowding is the Director of Research, College of Arts and Social Sciences, and Research Professor in the School of Politics and International Relations, Research School of Social Sciences at the Australian National University in Canberra. He has published widely on topics as diverse as public administration and public policy, urban politics, comparative politics, British politics, social and rational choice theory, and political philosophy. He recently edited (with Ken Shepsle and Torun Dewan) the four-volume *Rational Choice Politics* (2009). He is a Fellow of the Academy of Social Sciences, Australia and has been co-editor of the *Journal of Theoretical Politics* since 1996.

William B. Eimicke is the Executive Director of the Picker Center for Executive Education in the School of International and Public Affairs at Columbia University. He recently returned to Columbia University after serving three years as Deputy Fire Commissioner of New York City. Eimicke first started working with the New York City Fire Department in 2002 when he served as Faculty Director of the Fire Officers Management Institute (FOMI), a custom-designed leadership and management training program for fire and EMS personnel supported by Columbia. Previously, he served as the Director of Fiscal Studies for the New York State Senate, Assistant Budget Director for the City of New York, and Deputy Commissioner of the New York City Department of Housing Preservation and Development. He also served as New York Governor Mario Cuomo's Deputy Secretary for Policy and Programs as well as the

Housing Czar for New York State. Eimicke also served on Vice President Gore's Reinventing Government team.

Henrik Enroth is Assistant Professor at Linnaeus University, Sweden. He earned his PhD at Stockholm University and has been a Visiting Scholar at the Department of Political Science at the University of California, Berkeley. His research interests include the conceptual and theoretical development of the social sciences, and the history of political ideas. Specifically, he has devoted his research to twentieth-century conceptions of politics and political inquiry, and he is currently working on a book on the conceptual challenges facing a global political science, tentatively titled *A New Framework for Political Analysis*. Recent publications include a critical analysis of the pluralist legacy in modern political discourse, forthcoming in *Contemporary Political Theory*, and a contribution to *The SAGE Encyclopedia of Political Theory* (2010).

Anders Esmark is Associate Professor in the Department of Society and Globalisation, Roskilde University. His research interests include public administration, democratic theory, and the interplay between politics and media. Recent writings on governance include 'The Functional Differentiation of Governance: Public Governance beyond Hierarchy, Market and Networks' (*Public Administration*, 2009), 'Good Governance in Network Society: Reconfiguring the Political from Politics to Policy' (with Henrik Bang, *Administrative Theory & Praxis*, 2009),' and contributions to *Theories of Democratic Network Governance* (edited by Eva Sørensen and Jacob Torfing, 2007) and *Democratic Network Governance in Europe* (edited by Martin Marcussen and Jacob Torfing, 2007).

Thomas Hale is a PhD candidate in the Department of Politics at Princeton University. His research focuses on global problems and the institutions to govern them, particularly efforts to solve transnational dilemmas democratically. He is the co-editor of the forthcoming *Handbook of Innovation in Transnational Governance*.

Ian Hall is a Senior Lecturer in International Relations at Griffith University, Brisbane. He is the author of *The International Thought of Martin Wight* (2006) and the editor (with Lisa Hill) of *British International Thinkers from Hobbes to Namier* (2009). He has published a number of articles on the history of international thought, international relations theory, diplomacy, and international security in – amongst others – *British Journal of Politics and International Relations*, *Government and Opposition*, *International Affairs*, *Millennium: Journal of International Studies*, and *Review of International Studies*. He has just completed a new book called *The Dilemmas of Decline: British Intellectuals and World Politics* and is currently working on projects on global governance, public diplomacy, and the rise of India.

M. Shamsul Haque is Professor in the Department of Political Science at the National University of Singapore. His current research interests include contemporary issues and problems related to public administration, the state and governance, development theory and policy, and the environment and sustainability. He has authored and edited several books. His articles on these issues have appeared in peer-reviewed journals such as *Public Administration Review*, *Administration & Society*, *Governance*, *International Political Science Review*, *International Journal of Public Administration*, and *International Review of Administrative Sciences*. He is the editor of the *Asian Journal of Political Science*.

Carolyn J. Heinrich is the Director of the La Follette School of Public Affairs, Professor of Public Affairs, Affiliated Professor of Economics, and a Regina Loughlin Scholar at the

University of Wisconsin-Madison. Her research focuses on education and human capital development, social welfare policy, public management, and econometric methods for program evaluation. She works directly with governments at all levels and internationally in her research. She is the author of more than 50 peer-reviewed publications to date, including four co-authored/edited books. In 2004, she received the David N. Kershaw Award for distinguished contributions to the field of public policy analysis and management by a person under the age of 40.

Bob Jessop is Distinguished Professor of Sociology and Co-Director of the Cultural Political Research Centre at Lancaster University. He is best known for his contributions to state theory, critical political economy, welfare state restructuring, and theories of governance failure and metagovernance. He has published 17 books, 26 edited volumes, and over 300 journal articles and book chapters. His books include *The Capitalist State* (1982), *Nicos Poulantzas* (1985), *Thatcherism: A Tale of Two Nations* (1988), *State Theory* (1990), *The Future of the Capitalist State* (2002), *Beyond the Regulation Approach* (2006, co-authored with Ngai-Ling Sum), and *State Power: A Strategic-Relational Approach* (2007). He is currently working on the crisis of crisis-management in relation to the global financial and economic crisis with a three-year ESRC Professorial Fellowship (2010–13).

Petri Koikkalainen is University Lecturer of Political Science at the University of Lapland in Rovaniemi. His research interests include political theory and the history of political thought. Recently, he has studied the development of modernist social sciences after World War II with their implications on public policy and governance. He has published on topics that range from the Anglo-American debate about the 'end of ideology' during the 1950s (in, for example, *History of Political Thought*, 2009) to the modernization of the Finnish North (for example, 'Narratives of Progress in the Politics of Urho Kekkonen and the Agrarian League', in Linjakumpu and Wallenius (eds.), *Progress or Perish*, forthcoming). During 2009–10 he is the editor of *Politiikka*, the quarterly journal of the Finnish Political Science Association.

Wai Fung Lam is Associate Professor and Head of the Department of Politics and Public Administration at the University of Hong Kong. His research has evolved around institutional analysis, common-pool resource management, irrigation management in Asia, public governance, and policy process and dynamics. He is the author of *Governing Irrigation Systems in Nepal: Institutions, Infrastructure, and Collective Action* (1998), and a co-editor of *Asian Irrigation Systems in Transition: Responding to the Challenges Ahead* (2005). He has published in major international journals, including *Governance, International Review of Administrative Sciences, Journal of Institutional Economics, Policy Sciences, Voluntas*, and *World Development*.

Patrick Le Galès is CNRS Research Professor in Politics and Sociology at Sciences Po in Paris and part-time Professor of European Politics at King's College, London. He works on urban governance, comparative public policy, the restructuring of the state, and local and regional economic development. He won the UNESCO/ESRC Stein Rokkan prize for comparative research in 2002 and the French Political Science/Mattei Dogan prize for excellence in research in 2007. Among his publications in English are *Regions in Europe the Paradox of Power* (1998), *Local Industrial Systems in Europe, Rise or Demise?* (1999), *European Cities, Social Conflicts and Governance* (2002), and *The Changing Governance of Local Economies in Europe* (2003). He was an editor of the Palgrave series *Developments in French Politics*, Vols. 3 and 4. He edited a special issue of *Governance* entitled 'Policy Instruments and Policy

Changes', 2007 (with P. Lascoumes). His forthcoming book (with F. Faucher King) is *The New Labour Experiment* (2010).

Laurence E. Lynn, Jr is Sid Richardson Research Professor at the LBJ School of Public Affairs, University of Texas, Professor of Public Management at the Manchester Business School, and the Sydney Stein Jr Professor of Public Management Emeritus at the University of Chicago. His research is concerned with public management theory and research methods. His most recent books are *Public Management: Old and New* (2006), *Madison's Managers: Public Administration and the Constitution* (with Anthony M. Bertelli, 2006), and a textbook, *Public Management: A Three Dimensional Approach* (with Carolyn J. Hill, 2008). For lifetime contributions to public administration research and practice, he has received the John Gaus, Dwight Waldo, Paul Van Riper, and H. George Frederickson Awards.

Michael McGuire is Professor in the School of Public and Environmental Affairs at Indiana University–Bloomington. He is the co-author (with Robert Agranoff) of *Collaborative Public Management: New Strategies for Local Governments* (2003), which received the 2003 Louis Brownlow Best Book Award from the National Academy of Public Administration. His work on public management networks, collaboration, leadership, and intergovernmental relations in the policy areas of economic development, emergency management, and rural development has been published in numerous journals, including *Public Administration Review, Journal of Public Administration Research and Theory, The Leadership Quarterly, Public Performance and Management Review, Disasters*, and others.

Peter McLaverty is a Reader in Public Policy at the Robert Gordon University, Aberdeen, Scotland, and a former head of the Department of Public Policy. Dr McLaverty has published widely in academic journals such as *Journal of Political Ideologies, Democratization, International Political Science Review, Urban Studies,* and *Government and Policy*. He is the editor of *Political Participation and Innovations in Community Governance* (2002) and his main research interests are the theory and practice of democracy and public participation. For a number of years, he was convenor of the UK Political Studies Association Participatory and Deliberative Democracy Specialist Group.

James Meadowcroft is a Professor in the School of Public Policy and Administration and in the Department of Political Science, at Carleton University in Ottawa. He holds a Canada Research Chair in Governance for Sustainable Development. His research focuses on reforms to structures and processes of governance as political systems manage environmental issues. He has published a number of articles and books dealing with the politics of the environment and sustainable development, including *Implementing Sustainable Development* (co-edited with William Lafferty, 2000), the first full-length international study of how governments in industrialized countries responded to the sustainable development agenda. Recent contributions include work on public participation, sustainable development partnerships, planning for sustainability, national sustainable development strategies, environmental governance, socio-technical transitions, and sustainable energy policy. His volume *Caching the Carbon: The Politics and Policy of Carbon Capture and Storage* (co-edited with Oluf Langhelle) was published by Edward Elgar in 2009. He has also served as co-editor of *International Political Science Review* and as associate editor of the *Journal of Political Ideologies*.

Pippa Norris is the McGuire Lecturer in Comparative Politics at the John F. Kennedy School of Government, Harvard University, where she has taught since 1992. She also served recently on leave from Harvard as the Director of the Democratic Governance Group at the United Nations Development Program in New York. Her research compares public opinion and elections, democratic institutions and cultures, gender politics, and political communications in many countries worldwide. She has published almost 40 books, including most recently *Driving Democracy: Do Power-Sharing Institutions Work?* (2008), *Cosmopolitan Communications: Cultural Diversity in a Globalizing World* (2009, with Ronald Inglehart), and *Public Sentinel: News Media and the Governance Agenda* (edited, 2010). She has also served as an expert consultant for many international bodies, including the UN, UNESCO, NDI, the Council of Europe, International IDEA, the World Bank, the National Endowment for Democracy, the Afghanistan Reconstruction Project, and the UK Electoral Commission. Her work has been published in more than a dozen languages.

B. Guy Peters is Maurice Falk Professor of American Government at the University of Pittsburgh and Distinguished Professor of Comparative Governance at the Zeppelin University, Friedrichshafen. His work is primarily in governance, institutional theory, and comparative public policy and administration. He is currently co-editor of the *European Political Science Review*. His recent publications include *Policy Coordination in Seven Industrial Democracies* (with Geert Bouckaert and Koen Verhoest) and *Debating Institutionalism* (with Jon Pierre and Gerry Stoker, 2008).

Phyllis R. Pomerantz is Visiting Professor of the Practice of Public Policy at the Duke Center for International Development, Sanford School of Public Policy, Duke University. She has also held a series of senior appointments at the World Bank, including Country Director for Mozambique and Zambia, and Chief Learning Officer. Her research and teaching center on international aid effectiveness and poverty reduction. She is the author of various articles and reports. Recent works include *Aid Effectiveness in Africa* (Lexington Books, 2004), 'A Little Luck and a Lot of Trust: Aid Relationships and Reform in Southern Africa' in I. Gill and T. Pugatch (eds), *At the Frontlines of Development* (World Bank, 2005), and 'International Relations and Global Studies: The Past of the Future?', *Global-e* (August 2008).

Rod Rhodes holds a joint appointment as Professor of Government in the School of Government at the University of Tasmania and Distinguished Professor of Political Science at the Australian National University. He is also Professor Emeritus, University of Newcastle (UK). He is the former Director of the UK Economic and Social Research Council's 'Whitehall Programme' (1994–9), and of the Research School of Social Sciences at the Australian National University (2007–8). He is the author or editor of some 30 books, including. *The State as Cultural Practice* (co-author, 2010), *Comparing Westminster* (co-author, 2009), *Observing Government Elites* (co-editor, 2007), *The Oxford Handbook of Political Institutions* (co-editor, 2006, paperback 2008), and *Governance Stories* (co-author, 2006, paperback 2007). He is Treasurer of the Australasian Political Studies Association, life Vice-President of the Political Studies Association of the United Kingdom, and a Fellow of the Academy of Social Sciences in both Australia and Britain. He is editor of *Public Administration*, 1986–2011.

Fumihiko Saito is a Professor in the Faculty of Intercultural Communication, Ryukoku University, Japan. Dr Saito published *Decentralization and Development Partnerships: Lessons from Uganda* (2003) and edited *Foundations for Local Governance: Decentralization in Comparative Perspective* (2008). He has also published books in Japanese covering international development studies and participatory development. In recent years, he has been co-leading a comparative research project examining the complex interfaces between local governance reforms and sustainable development in selected countries in both developed and developing worlds.

Gunnar Folke Schuppert holds a Research Professorship on 'New Modes of Governance' at the Social Science Research Center, Berlin (WZB) and is Director of the WZB-Rule of Law Center. His main publications are *Verwaltungswissenschaft* (2000), *Staatswissenschaft* (2003), and *Politische Kultur* (2008) as well as *The Europeanisation of Governance* (2006) and *Global Governance and the Role of Non State Actors* (2006) as editor.

Jefferey M. Sellers is Associate Professor of Political Science, Geography and Public Policy at the University of Southern California. He is author of *Governing from Below: Urban Regions and the Global Economy* (2002) and co-editor of *Metropolitanization and Political Change* (2005) and *The Political Ecology of the Metropolis* (forthcoming). He has also authored or co-authored dozens of articles, book chapters, and papers on comparative urban politics, decentralization, law and society, urban geography, territorial identity, legal studies, and public policy.

Anne-Marie Slaughter is the Bert G. Kerstetter '66 University Professor of Politics and International Affairs at Princeton University. She is presently on leave, serving as Director of Policy Planning for the United States Department of State. She was Dean of the Woodrow Wilson School of Public and International Affairs at Princeton University, 2002–9. She came to the Wilson School from Harvard Law School where she was the J. Sinclair Armstrong Professor of International, Foreign, and Comparative Law, and Director of the International Legal Studies Program. She is also the former President of the American Society of International Law, is a Fellow of the American Academy of Arts and Sciences, and has served on the board of the Council on Foreign Relations. Drawing from this rich interdisciplinary expertise, she has written and taught broadly on global governance, international criminal law, and American foreign policy. Her most recent book is *The Idea That Is America: Keeping Faith with Our Values in a Dangerous World* (2007). She is also the author of *A New World Order* (2004), in which she identified transnational networks of government officials as an increasingly important component of global governance. She has been a frequent commentator on foreign affairs in newspapers, radio, and television. She was also the convener and academic co-chair of the Princeton Project on National Security, a multi-year research project aimed at developing a new, bipartisan national security strategy for the United States, and was a member of the National War Powers Commission.

Andy Smith is Research Professor at the SPIRIT Research Centre in Bordeaux. He is a specialist in public policy analysis and political economy, with a particular interest in European integration. His recent publications have been focused upon what he calls 'the Politics of Industry', both in general (*Industries and Globalization*, 2008, co-edited with Bernard Jullien) and particularly in the case of wine (*Vin et Politique*, 2007, co-written with Jacques de Maillard and Olivier Costa). His current research is centred upon the extent to which industries in Europe are governed either at the scale of the European Union, or at that of the WTO ('How Does the WTO Matter to Industry?', *International Political Sociology*, June 2009).

Mary Tschirhart is Professor of Public Administration at North Carolina State University. Professor Tschirhart writes about management and leadership of public and non-profit organizations. Her most recent research examines collaborative systems and cross-sector dynamics, resulting in publications on self-regulatory programs, workforce inclusion, and resource-sharing dynamics in networks. She is Director of the Institute for Nonprofit Research, Education, and Engagement at North Carolina State and formerly served as Director of the Alan K. Campbell Public Affairs Institute at Syracuse University. She is on the board of the International Research Society for Public Management, and formerly served on the board of the Association for Research on Nonprofit Organizations and Voluntary Action and as the Division Chair for the Public and Nonprofit Division of the Academy of Management.

Angelina W.K. Yuen-Tsang is Head of the Department of Applied Social Sciences and Associate Vice-President of The Hong Kong Polytechnic University where she has served since 1986. Her research interests and areas of specialism are mainly on social support networks and community care, social work education, social work practice in China, corporate social responsibility, and occupational social work. In recent years, her research focus has been on the indigenization of social work education and practice in the Chinese Mainland. She is a key player in social work education in the international arena. She has been President of the International Association of Schools of Social Work (IASSW) since July 2008.

Governance as Theory, Practice, and Dilemma

Mark Bevir

The word 'governance' is ubiquitous. The World Bank and the International Monetary Fund make loans conditional on 'good governance'. Climate change and avian flu appear as issues of 'global governance'. The European Union issues a White Paper on 'Governance'. The US Forest Service calls for 'collaborative governance'. What accounts for the pervasive use of the term 'governance' and to what does it refer? Current scholarship offers a bewildering set of answers. The word 'governance' appears in diverse academic disciplines including development studies, economics, geography, international relations, planning, political science, public administration, and sociology. Each discipline sometimes acts as if it owns the word and has no need to engage with the others. Too little attention is given to ways of making sense of the whole literature on governance.

At the most general level, governance refers to theories and issues of social coordination and the nature of all patterns of rule. More specifically, governance refers to various new theories and practices of governing and the dilemmas to which they give rise. These new theories, practices, and dilemmas place less emphasis than did their predecessors on hierarchy and the state, and more

on markets and networks. The new theories, practices, and dilemmas of governance are combined in concrete activity. The theories inspire people to act in ways that help give rise to new practices and dilemmas. The practices create dilemmas and encourage attempts to comprehend them in theoretical terms. The dilemmas require new theoretical reflection and practical activity if they are to be adequately addressed.

SCOPE AND ORGANIZATION

The *Handbook of Governance* reflects the breadth of a concept of governance as all of theory, practice, and dilemma. Governance in all these different guises stands in contrast to elder concepts of the state as monolithic and formal. For a start, theories of governance typically open up the black box of the state. Policy network theory, rational choice theory, and interpretive theory undermine reified concepts of the state as a monolithic entity, interest, or actor. These theories draw attention to the processes and interactions through which all kinds of social interests and actors combine to produce the policies, practices, and effects that define current patterns of governing. In addition, the relationship of state and society changed significantly in the late twentieth century. New practices of governance find political actors increasingly constrained by mobilized and organized elements in society. States and international organizations increasingly share the activity of governing with societal actors, including private firms, non-governmental organizations, and non-profit service providers. The new relationship between state and society admits of considerable variation, but it is an international phenomenon. New practices of governance extend across the developed and developing world, and they are prominent among strategies to regulate transnational flows and govern the global commons. Finally, current public problems rarely fall neatly in the jurisdictions of specific agencies or even states. Governance thus poses dilemmas that require new governing strategies to span jurisdictions, link people across levels of government, and mobilize a variety of stakeholders.

Governance draws attention to the complex processes and interactions that constitute patterns of rule. It replaces a focus on the formal institutions of states and governments with recognition of the diverse activities that often blur the boundary of state and society. Governance as theory, practice, and dilemma highlights phenomena that are *hybrid* and *multijurisdictional* with *plural stakeholders* who come together in *networks*.

Many of the ideas, activities, and designs of governance appear unconventional. A distinctive feature of the new governance is that it combines established administrative arrangements with features of the market. Governance arrangements are often *hybrid* practices, combining administrative systems with market mechanisms and non-profit organizations. Novel forms of mixed public–private or entirely private forms of regulation are developing. For example, school reform often now combines elder administrative arrangements (school districts, ministries of education) with quasi-market strategies that are meant to give parents greater choice (charter schools, voucher systems).

Another distinctive feature of governance is that it is *multijurisdictional* and often transnational. Current patterns of governance combine people and institutions across different policy sectors and different levels of government (local, regional, national, and international). Examples include varied efforts to regulate food standards and safety. International food safety standards are set in Rome by *Codex Alimentarius* – a joint body of the World Health Organization and the United Nation's Food and Agriculture Organization; however, if the USA imports fish from China, the presumption is that Chinese officials at the national and local level enforce these standards. The practice of regulating food safety operates simultaneously at international, national, and local levels.

A third distinctive feature of governance is the increasing range and *plurality of stakeholders*. Interest groups of various sorts have long been present in the policymaking process. Nonetheless, a wider variety of non-governmental organizations are becoming active participants in governing. One reason for the pluralization of stakeholders is an explosion of advocacy groups during the last third of the twentieth century. Another reason is the increasing use of third-party organizations to deliver state services. Arguably, yet another reason is the expansion of philanthropists and philanthropic organizations, both of which are becoming as prominent as they were in the nineteenth century. For example, the Gates Foundation has both mounted a multicity effort to reform urban school districts and embarked on a massive public health campaign in developing countries. The increasing range and variety of stakeholders has led to the emergence and active promotion of new practices and institutional designs, including public–private partnerships and collaborative governance.

Yet another distinguishing feature of governance reflects and responds to the fact that governing is an increasingly hybrid, multijurisdictional, and plural phenomenon. Scholars have called attention to the way that governing arrangements, different levels of governance, and multiple stakeholders are linked together in *networks*. Environmental scientists have shown how natural areas like watersheds or estuaries are often governed by networks of stakeholders and government agencies. Scholars of urban politics have called attention to the way urban, suburban, and exurban areas get organized in broader regional networks. International relations scholars have noted the increasing prominence of inter-ministerial networks as ways of governing the global commons. More recently, policymakers, often influenced by theories from the social sciences, have begun actively to foster networks in the belief that they provide a uniquely appropriate institutional design with which to grapple with the new governance. Joined-up governance and whole-of-government approaches are widespread in states such as Australia and Britain, in policy sectors such as Homeland Security, and in transnational and international efforts to address problems such as failed states.

So, the *Handbook of Governance* concentrates on the theories, practices, and dilemmas associated with recognition of the extent to which governing processes are hybrid and multijurisdictional, linking plural stakeholders in complex networks. A concern with the new theories, practices, and dilemmas of governance informs the main themes that recur throughout the individual chapters. The contributors generally focus on:

- The new theories of coordination that have drawn attention to the presence or possibility of markets and networks as means of coordination.
- The new practices of rule that have risen since the 1970s, especially the apparent growth of markets and networks.
- The dilemmas of managing and reforming hybrid patterns of rule that combine aspects of market, network, and hierarchy.

Even when a chapter title refers to a broader topic, the essay itself focuses on the relation of that topic to the theories, practices, and dilemmas of governance. For example, the chapters in the first section on theories of governance concentrate on how these theories illuminate new practices of governance and/or how they have been modified in response to the dilemmas posed by the new governance.

The very organization of the *Handbook of Governance* reflects an emphasis on the connections between governance as theory, practice, and dilemma. Few scholars sufficiently recognize the extent to which the new governance is a product of new formal and folk theories that led people to see and act differently. The first section of the *Handbook* focuses on those theories in the social sciences that arose and prospered in the twentieth century, transforming our understanding of society and politics. Many of these theories challenged the older idea of the state as a natural and unified expression of a nation based on common ethnic, cultural, and linguistic ties and possessing a common good. Many of them made people more aware of the role of pressure groups, self-interest, and social networks in the policy process. Later, toward the end of the twentieth century, some of these theories then inspired attempts to reform the public sector and develop new policy instruments. Certainly, the new public management owed a debt to rational choice and especially principal–agent theory, while joined-up governance drew on developments in organizational and institutional theory. The second section of the *Handbook* examines the changing practices of governance. Public sector reforms have transformed practices of governance across diverse levels and in diverse territories. The reforms have given rise to complex new practices that rarely correspond to the intentions of the reformers. What does the state now look like? What role do non-governmental organizations play in the formation and implementation of policies and the delivery of services? The final section of the *Handbook* explores some of the dilemmas that this new governance poses for practitioners.

GOVERNANCE AS THEORY

The twentieth century witnessed the rise of all kinds of new, and often formal, approaches to social science. These theories led people to see the world differently and then to remake the world. No doubt few people bother to think about social life in terms of the formal models of rational choice. But a folk recognition of the largely self-interested nature of action, even the action of public officials, spread far more widely. Moreover, as it spread, so political actors increasingly tried to introduce reforms to deal with self-interest – to mitigate its adverse consequences, to regulate it and keep it within limits, or to harness it to improve efficiency. In this way, new theories inspired both the recognition and the active formation of apparently new features of governance. Equally, of course, social science theories have often struggled to catch up with some of the apparently improvised changes in governance. The reader might even want mentally to rearrange the *Handbook* to trace a progression not from theoretical innovations to the practices these theories inspired, but from the rise of the new governance to attempts to comprehend it in theoretical terms; that is from Sections III and II to I, rather than from I to II and III.

So, the chapters in Section I on theories of governance play a dual role: on the one hand, they introduce the reader to some of the general ways of thinking that have helped to inspire the recognition and formation of the new governance; on the other, they show how theories that may have been designed for other uses have since been modified to accommodate the new governance.

Pluralists have long challenged reified concepts of the state. Empirically they point to the complex interactions, processes, and networks that contribute to governing. In addition, more radical and normative pluralists challenge mainstream concepts of sovereignty and argue for a greater dispersal of authority to diverse social organizations. In Chapter 2, Henrik Enroth discusses the pluralism of policy network theory as it

impacts governance. Policy network theory rose out of an earlier pluralism, with its attempts to disaggregate the state and focus on groups. Some policy network theorists have recently adopted anti-foundational, nominalist perspectives that have led them to pay more attention to meanings and to decenter even the concept of a group. Networks appear as undifferentiated parts of a social life characterized by contests of belief as they inform diverse actions. Enroth presses forward with this nominalist perspective, asking how it modifies our grasp of interdependence, coordination, and pluralism.

The dramatic rise of rational choice theory provided another powerful challenge to elder, reified concepts of the state. In Chapter 3, Keith Dowding discusses the ways rational choice influenced both the understanding and practice of governance. Rational choice theory is an organizing perspective or methodology that builds models of how people would act if they did so in accord with preferences having a certain formal structure. This perspective gave rise to theories about the non-predictability of politics, the problems of commitment, the hazards of principal–agent relations, and conflicts in democracies. Dowding shows how these rational choice theories inspired worries about the welfare state. Public choice in particular then inspired some of the managerial reforms associated with the new governance. Interestingly, Dowding also suggests that rational choice provides a critical perspective on just those reforms. Contemporary practices of governance rely too greatly on the superficial support public choice theory gave to choice and markets. Policy actors should pay more attention to rational choice analyses of the chaos and instability associated with weak institutions.

Chapter 4 looks at interpretive theories of governance. Interpretive theories reject the lingering positivism of most other approaches to governance. Social life is inherently meaningful. People are intentional agents capable of acting for reasons. Indeed, social scientists cannot properly grasp or explain actions apart from in relation to the beliefs of the actors. Many interpretive theorists conclude that social explanations necessarily involve recovering beliefs and locating them in the context of the wider webs of meaning of which they are a part. Governmentality, post-Marxism, and social humanism all share a concern with meanings and their contexts. Typically, these interpretive theories lead to a more decentered view of governance. Governance consists of contingent practices that emerge from the competing actions and beliefs of different people responding to various dilemmas against the background of conflicting traditions. Similarly, interpretive theory often challenges the idea of a set of tools for managing governance. Interpretive theorists are more likely to appeal to storytelling. Practitioners orientate themselves to the world by discussing illustrative cases and past experiences. They use stories to explore various possible actions and how they might lead the future to unfold.

Robert Christensen and Mary Tschirhart look, in Chapter 5, at organization theory. They distinguish four broad categories of organizational theories, depending on whether they concern the micro or macro level and whether they are deterministic or voluntaristic. Micro-level theories concentrate on individual organizations. Voluntaristic micro-level theories focus on strategic choices. They treat action as constructed, autonomous, and enacted. They generally explain the behavior of an organization in terms that echo the micro-level views of rational choice and interpretive theory as examined in the previous two chapters. In contrast, other forms of organizational theory either avoid clear micro-level assumptions or take a much more deterministic view of behavior. These forms of organizational theory overlap with the institutional and systems theories considered in the next two chapters. Deterministic micro-level theories inspire system-structural views. Macro-level approaches concentrate on populations or communities of organizations. The more deterministic macro-level theories take a natural selection view.

Voluntaristic macro-level theories focus on collective action.

In Chapter 6, Guy Peters discusses three institutionalist theories of governance. Normative institutionalism focuses on the role of values, symbols, and myths in defining appropriate actions for individuals and thereby shaping institutions. Rational choice institutionalism uses the assumptions of rational choice theory to understand institutions and to design better ones. Historical institutionalism stresses the persistence of path-dependent rules and modes of behavior. Institutionalists have pondered the dilemmas of entrenching the new governance that increasingly relies on networks to link public sector and other actors. They have drawn attention to the importance of institutionalizing a new network by developing its culture and inner functioning. And they have highlighted the need for a new network to develop effective relationships with its political environment. Institutionalists have also tried to explain the rise of the new governance. Institutions can be treated here as dependent or independent variables. Typically, as dependent variables, institutions appear as, for example, responses to dilemmas and challenges in a changing environment. As independent variables, different institutions might help explain, for example, varied patterns of governance, decision-making, and even good decisions. Yet Peters argues that a fuller account of how institutions explain aspects of governance must evoke a micro theory such as that associated with either rational choice or interpretive theory.

Anders Esmark uses Chapter 7 to discuss systems theory. Systems theorists conceive of coordination as a property of systems. General systems theory explores the abstract principles of organized complexity, asking how systems produce or exhibit order and coordination at the level of the whole. Social systems theory uses the language and ideas of general systems theory to study interactions, organizations, and societies. Typically, systems theorists locate the rise of the new governance within a more general narrative about modernity. Modernity consists of increased functional differentiation: over time, society increasingly develops discrete organizations to fulfill ever more specialized functions. The new governance of markets and networks consists of ever increasingly specialized and differentiated organizations performing discrete tasks. These specialized organizations are often autopoietic or self-governing. Systems theory characteristically explores issues of metagovernance, such as if it is possible to govern these self-governing organizations, how states try to do so, and how we might do so.

In Chapter 8, Bob Jessop argues that the theory and practice of metagovernance emerged as a response to governance failure. The failings of hierarchy led to public sector reforms intended to advance marketization. The failings of these reforms then led to an expansion of networks. But networks too fail, especially if communication among the relevant actors is distorted. So, on one level, metagovernance consists of appropriate responses to the characteristic failings of the different modes of governance. It responds to bureaucratic failure with meta-control and meta-coordination, to market failure with meta-exchange, and to network failure with meta-heterarchy. On another level, however, metagovernance involves rearticulating the nature and balance of different modes of governance. It relies on institutional design and the governmentality of subjectivities to create and sustain particular modes of governance. Jessop concludes by suggesting that metagovernance itself is necessarily incomplete and subject to failure. Policy actors should adopt a satisfying approach, deliberately cultivating a flexible set of responses, a critical self-reflexive awareness of their goals and projects, and a willingness to aim at success while knowing failure is more likely.

Jeff Sellers looks at governance in the context of state–society relations in Chapter 9. The new governance poses dilemmas for older approaches that treat state and society as mutually exclusive categories and the state in particular as monolithic and integrated.

Work on governance often shows how the state now rules with and through social actors. Sometimes it also presents a disaggregated image of the state as composed of diverse actors, meanings, and practices across various spatial and functional domains. Sellers then draws attention to some new analyses of state–society relations associated with the study of governance. Analyses of the state often highlight local, multilevel, and transnational practices. Analyses of society often rely on a bottom-up perspective that highlights the agency of social groups in community initiatives and the way firms and other groups treat the state as a resource. So, the interactions between state and society are increasingly complex and diverse. Instead of the older dichotomy between state and society, studies of the new governance highlight issues such as subnational and sectoral variation, multilevel and transnational configurations, the impact of specific institutions and policy instruments, and the feedback effects of policy outcomes.

In Chapter 10, Patrick Le Galès explores policy instruments. Policy instruments are the techniques or mechanisms by which actors seek to rule. The new governance consists of a shift in policy instruments away from planning and command and control towards contractual relations, standards, performance indicators, and regulation. Work on governance often traces this shift in policy instruments, or advocates specific policy instruments as solutions to current dilemmas. Much of it treats policy instruments as natural, debating their relative effectiveness under varied circumstances. In contrast, Le Galès highlights a broader sociological approach to policy instruments. Max Weber, Michel Foucault, and other social theorists have long interested themselves in the nature, causes, and effects of rationalities and technologies of governing. Policy instruments are technical means of organizing social relations by entrenching meanings, beliefs, and knowledge. For example, legislative and regulatory instruments generally promote the relations associated with a guardian state, economic and fiscal instruments entrench a redistributive state, and incentive-based instruments promote a mobilizing state. New rationalities and technologies inform new practices of governance.

Phyllis Pomerantz devotes Chapter 11 to debates on governance in development theory. Governance often refers to the rise of markets and networks in the public sector. The contrast is between bureaucratic or hierarchic institutions and governance conceived as markets and networks. Development theorists use governance somewhat differently to discuss the importance of political institutions for economic growth, where these political institutions include older forms of the state as well as networks. Their contrast is between the market and governance conceived as political institutions. As Pomerantz shows, discussions of governance reflect a consensus that development depends on state and market, not just market. The key theoretical innovation here was the new institutional economics. Neoliberalism, the Washington Consensus, and structural adjustment created new practices, but these practices failed to deliver the intended prosperity. The new institutional economics helped explain this failure by highlighting the importance of political institutions to growth and even the proper operation of markets. Governance thus emerged as a development agenda based on promoting things such as the rule of law, government capacity, decentralization, accountability, and democracy.

Increasingly public sector reforms are responsive to governance indicators. Pippa Norris discusses the theory and practice of measuring democratic governance in Chapter 12. Governance indicators should be valid, reliable, and legitimate. Validity depends on their accurately reflecting the concepts to which they relate. Reliability requires that they are consistent and that they use replicable data sources. Legitimacy depends on their construction being transparent and done with the involvement of relevant stakeholders. Norris then looks at the leading measurements of democratic governance, including

Freedom House's Gastil index, Polity Project's approach to constitutional democracy, and the World Bank's own governance indicators. One way to assess these elite measurements is to compare them with independently-generated measurements including mass public opinion polls. Norris herself compares them with citizen's opinions as revealed by the World Values Survey 2005–7. She concludes by advocating a pluralist recognition that different measurements may be suited to different purposes.

GOVERNANCE AS PRACTICE

Theories have little meaning apart from practices. Typically, theories are attempts to make sense of practices, and guides to the actions by which we forge practices. Section II explores governance as practice. New public sector reforms and patterns of rule have been the main topics of discussion in works on governance. They have inspired the shifts in theorizing explored in Section I. Equally, however, the reforms and resulting patterns of rule emerged in part precisely because people acted on beliefs such as those associated with rational choice theory. Scholars have noted the role of neoclassical economics in inspiring the greater reliance on market structures, and the role of principal–agent theory in inspiring aspects of the new public management. Yet many of the beliefs and traditions embedded in the reforms are less formal and less tied to grand theories or schemes. Folk versions of the new theories appeared in business and other areas of society, inspiring new practices and *ad hoc* responses to all kinds of issues, and public sector reform often then borrowed piecemeal from these other areas of society. Reformers appeared to be (and perhaps felt themselves to be) less driven by a clear set of theoretical commitments than groping for plausible responses to apparently new constraints and dilemmas. Nonetheless, of course, their conception of the constraints and dilemmas, their instincts as to what did and did not constitute an appropriate response, and the examples found in other areas of society all reflected their prior theories.

Much of the current interest in the idea of a new governance stems from the impact of public sector reforms since the 1980s. Neoliberal reforms spread markets and new managerial practices, fragmenting service delivery, and creating quasi-markets and hybrid organizations. Later reforms have often been attempts to address the dilemmas thrown up by marketization and managerialism without returning to an elder hierarchic bureaucracy. The chapters in Section II typically explore the nature, extent, diversity, and consequences of these varied public sector reforms.

Public sector reforms have given rise to a host of new designs and practices – from privatization through public–private partnerships to global public policy networks. The spread of these practices inspires questions about the relationship between state and society. Some scholars see new governance as a result or a cause of the decline of the state. Others see it as an adaptation of the state to increasing societal complexity. What is the scope and limits of the state's authority? What role does the voluntary sector play? How does governance occur in areas where the state lacks effective control or where there is no state?

Together with Rod Rhodes, I review the changing state in Chapter 13. We trace three waves of governance and the oscillating fortunes of the state therein. The first wave of governance evoked a world in which state power is dispersed among a vast array of spatially and functionally distinct networks composed of all kinds of public, voluntary, and private organizations with which the center interacts. The state appeared to be being hollowed out. The second wave of governance accepted the shift from bureaucracy to markets and networks but disputed it led to any significant dispersal of state authority. The state has simply changed the way it exercises its authority, adopting new tools for the

same old ends. The state concentrates now on metagovernance – an umbrella concept that describes the characteristic role and policy instruments of the state in contemporary governance. Rhodes and I then go on to challenge these first two waves of governance by appealing to a third wave, based on interpretive theory. We argue governance is constructed differently by many actors working against the background of diverse traditions. We challenge the state as a bewitching reification that simplifies and obscures the diversity and contingency of concrete political activity.

In Chapter 14, Laurence Lynn discusses the persistence of hierarchy. Whereas there have been changes in the state, we should be cautious of overstating the extent to which new practices of governance have spread or even the extent to which when they spread they displace older hierarchic structures. As Lynn shows, discussions of new practices often draw heavily on the spread of new theories about markets, networks, deliberative democracy, and e-governance. These theories generally combine conceptual, empirical, and normative elements. Empirical claims about changes need to be distinguished from conceptual arguments about the nature of governance. The empirical evidence offers a kaleidoscopic picture of diverse practices changing in complex and contested ways. It offers little support to grand claims about a social logic driving a more or less uniform transformation in governance. Hierarchy remains pervasive, not only in bureaucratic institutions but also within newer institutional forms. Hierarchy persists in part because of its importance for accountability and so liberal representative democracy.

Steven Cohen and William Eimicke discuss contracting out in Chapter 15. There is nothing intrinsically new about public sector organizations entering contracts with non-governmental actors. However, the dramatic spread of contracting out is one of the most noticed features of the new governance. The new governance has seen contracting out arise not only as a means of delivering services but also as a means of building complex networks of actors. Contracting out can enable public sector organizations to get goods, services, and expertise that their in-house staff cannot provide. However, as Cohen and Eimicke argue, the spread of contracting out reflected the rise of ideologies and theories that were overtly anti-government and pro-market. Contracting out is also a response to dilemmas associated with information technology, flexible production, and globalization. The spread of contracting now, in turn, poses dilemmas for the theory and practice of governance. Here Cohen and Eimicke consider the dilemmas of eliciting bids, framing contracts in suitable language, monitoring and managing performance, and maintaining ethical standards and clear lines of accountability.

Chapter 16 turns to public management. Carolyn Heinrich begins by discussing the gradual and confused emergence of a distinction between public administration and public management. Public management reflects the impact of new theories highlighting the informal processes and activities in organizations. Public management is the process of allocating and using public resources. The study of public management recognizes the enduring importance of laws and structures, but it also examines informal cultures and the craft or skilled practice by which cultures, processes, and structures are steered. In many ways, governance draws on this shift toward public management. In particular, the new public management (NPM) encouraged new practices of governance. NPM tried to make the culture of the public sector more like that of private companies by changing structures, incentives, and norms. It embraced marketization and also things such as performance pay, customer service, and output-based budgeting. NPM thus contributed greatly to the broad shift from direct service provision by government to more complex patterns of governance incorporating markets, networks, and private and voluntary sector actors.

Anthony Cheung looks specifically at budgeting and finance in Chapter 17. Cheung traces the rise of new practices, from the program planning budgeting system favored by many Keynesian welfare states in the 1960s and 1970s to cutback management in the 1980s and budgeting for results since the 1990s. The new practices were responses to a range of dilemmas that preoccupied policy actors in the 1970s: dilemmas such as fiscal stress, declining production, and government overload. The main features of the reforms included devolution of authority, on-line budgets, freedom to manage, central targets, multi-year budgeting, public service agreements, and, of course, various forms of commercialization such as contracting out and user charging. Cheung traces the pattern of reform across OECD and Asian states. The reforms were bold, but implementing them proved difficult. In practice, budgetary decisions are often divorced from performance evaluation and so dominated by political bargaining, central budgeting agencies have often tried to retain control thereby thwarting devolution, and legislative scrutiny remains focused on inputs. Hybrid budgeting regimes now cloak older forms of central control, concerns with distributional effects, and fiscal stability in managerialist garb.

Like contracting out, public–private partnerships transform the interplay between the state, business, and civil society. In Chapter 18, Gunnar Schuppert explains that these partnerships rely on horizontal modes of cooperation for the collaborative provision on public services. Typically, partnerships differ from contracting out in that they embody joint decision-making and production, not a principal–agent relationship. Yet while partnerships are a type of network, the literature on partnerships gives a more distinctly managerial focus to discussions of governance as and through networks. This managerial focus may reflect the reasons why states establish public–private partnerships within their territory. Domestic partnerships are all about reducing public spending. They are ways of ensuring cutbacks and seeking efficiency. In contrast, transnational partnerships often have more normative origins. Transnational and international partnerships often seek to promote trade, justice, and a sustainable environment.

Andy Smith looks at multijurisdictional regulation in Chapter 19. The new practices of governance often cover different levels, policy domains, and actors. No doubt we have been made increasingly aware of multijurisdictional coordination by the rise of theories about networks. Yet policy actors have also deliberately fostered such multijurisdictional patterns of policymaking and regulation to address transnational and wicked problems. The European Union exemplifies the rise of new ways of regulating transnational issues. Joined-up governance and whole of government agendas exemplify the turn to multijurisdictional practices as a way to address wicked problems such as welfare dependency and aid to fragile states. Smith tracks the ideas that have inspired these practices and by which people have then tried to and made sense of them. He traces and extends a shift from discussions of multilevel to multijurisdictional governance and from coordination to regulation.

In Chapter 20, Bas Denters looks at changing practices and dilemmas of local governance. Local governance, like the new governance more generally, has become increasingly polycentric, involving a greater variety of policy actors. The changing nature of local governance typically poses democratic and functional challenges. From a democratic perspective, a more polycentric system can restrict the leading historical forms of representation. From a functional or managerial perspective, a more polycentric system restricts the scope for hierarchic coordination and control. Nonetheless, the reforms of local governance have differed from country to country. Systems of local government vary in their capacity, autonomy, and size, generally according to their relationship to other levels of governance, and this variety influences the extent to which they confront democratic and functional

challenges. Denters illustrates the variety by studying the cases of Sweden, the Netherlands, Germany, the USA, the UK, and France.

Chapter 21 explores the role of nongovernmental organizations (NGOs) in the new governance. Shamsul Haque defines NGOs as legally constructed and recognized groups with durable and formal structures incorporating paid staff. NGOs are broadly autonomous from both the state and the private sector. They aim to serve the public interest through a non-profit orientation towards humanitarian purposes. Scholars disagree on whether NGOs typically collaborate or compete with the state, and on whether the state is dominant, NGOs are dominant, or the two are co-equal. Despite these different viewpoints, most scholars agree that NGOs have become increasingly important because of the rise of the new governance. Marketization and contracting out created an increased demand for NGOs to play a role in governance. New NGOs appeared, and older ones expanded and changed. Generally, NGOs did not merely spread; they also became more commercial in their activities and outlooks. The growing role of NGOs in governance has been both lauded and condemned. Advocates of NGOs have long associated them with social inclusion and participation. Critics argue they have proved ineffective, and are often corrupt and undemocratic.

Non-governmental organizations play a role in many transnational networks. Anne-Marie Slaughter and Thomas Hale examine transnational and transgovernmental networks in Chapter 22. These networks sustain regular and purposive interactions among policy actors from diverse states, thus often spanning domestic and international spheres. Many allow domestic policy actors to relate directly to their counterparts in other states without having to pass through older diplomatic channels. They facilitate the exchange of information, the enforcement of international treaties and rules, and the standardization of regulatory and other norms and laws. Slaughter and Hale suggest that transgovernmental networks have spread in response to dilemmas posed by increasing transnational flows and by globalization. Transgovernmental networks provide an important alternative or supplement to older approaches to international affairs. They expand the state's ability to address transnational issues, especially technical issues that require an expertise rarely found in foreign ministries. They are also generally more flexible and responsive than are diplomatic exchanges and international institutions.

Ian Hall and I turn to global governance more generally in Chapter 23. The term global governance flourished belatedly in the wake of discussions about governance and the changing nature of the state. Global governance is associated with a shift of focus towards processes and activities. It focuses on the role of diverse social actors as well as states in securing international order, and it allows that patterns of rule can arise without hierarchic institutions let alone an international sovereign power. Yet this novel focus can appear as a confusing mix of theoretical and empirical claims. A general theoretical orientation to processes and activities involving diverse actors gets confused with a more specific, empirical claim about the changing nature of international relations since the late twentieth century. The empirical claim suggests that while earlier ages had weak international institutions and strong sovereign states, the late twentieth century saw the rise of new times in which new actors and mechanisms became increasingly prominent. Hall and I argue that the theoretical lens, empirical claims, and consequent agendas of global governance are all connected to one another. They all emerged historically as the postwar era gave way to both neoliberal markets and new approaches to planning and networks.

GOVERNANCE AS DILEMMA

The changing nature of governance poses dilemmas for many older theories and practices. As the world changes, so responses to the world may need to change. Policy actors and citizens may need to devise new actions and perhaps ideals to deal with modes of governance that are increasingly hybrid and multijurisdictional, linking plural stakeholders in complex networks. I can put the same point differently by observing that the interaction of theory and practice continues apace: changes in the theories challenge our established ways of doing things, prompting us to adopt new actions in an attempt to remake the world, and changes in the practices often require us to rethink our beliefs and theories so as to make sense of the new worlds in which we find ourselves. Governance is, in this respect, a very practical concern. It is about activity – how people act, and how they might act more effectively and more justly. The ideas and actions by which people respond to dilemmas are the sources of new theories and new practices. The new theories and new practices create other dilemmas that lead people again to revise their ideas and actions. The practical activity of governing is continuous, as therefore is the process of reform. Governance is about the constantly shifting and contingent nature of practical political activity.

Currently governance presents us with a number of managerial and democratic dilemmas. From a managerial perspective, hybrid organizations with plural stakeholders in networks rarely exhibit the clear chains of command of hierarchic bureaucracies. Policymakers and others have struggled to find effective ways of acting in new settings. The fragmentation of governing can appear to make control, steering, and coordination increasingly elusive. Several of the chapters in Section III explore such issues, the ways practitioners have responded to them, and the ways in which practitioners might better respond to them. The chapters ask: How should public officials and citizens operate in the new environment of non-hierarchical, interlaced state–society interactions? Other dilemmas associated with governance are more obviously normative ones relating to democratic theory and social justice.

The involvement of non-state actors in policy-making and service delivery raises the question of whether the result is to deepen democracy or entrench private government. Accountability has become a widespread concern for new institutions and modes of participation. How have people responded to worries about ethics, legitimacy, inclusion, and justice? How might they better respond to such worries?

In Chapter 24, Kamran Ali Afzal and Mark Considine tackle accountability and the more general issue of legitimacy. The nature of legitimacy depends in part on how a society conceives of it. Democratic societies historically have conceived legitimacy as entwined with accountability. Bureaucrats are responsible to elected politicians, who in turn must give an account of themselves to citizens. The legitimacy of the public sector thereby derives from its being ultimately an expression of the will of the people or at least answerable to the people. Public sector officials can be answerable in terms of legal rules, professional norms, and personal moralities. The new practices of governance generally appear to pose dilemmas for accountability and legitimacy so conceived. Markets and networks break up clear lines of accountability. The complex patterns of the new governance make it difficult to determine who is responsible for what, let alone to hold them accountable. Afzal and Considine explore these dilemmas and responses to them. They highlight an agenda in which legitimacy depends on assigned goals and standards, transparent outcomes, knowable consequences, practices of review, answerability for failure, and the revision of programs.

Democracy is, of course, as much about participation as legitimacy. Indeed, participation may be essential to legitimacy and even accountability. As Lisa Bingham argues in Chapter 25, while collaborative governance is a vague term, it includes most attempts to enhance effective participation within the new governance. Collaborative governance focuses on the dilemmas of promoting practices in which state actors can achieve policy goals in partnership with stakeholders and the public, and especially by encouraging the public actively to involve themselves in the policy process. Typically, it emphasizes shared, negotiated, and deliberative decision-making. Bingham shows how collaborative governance might operate throughout the policy stream. Upstream in the policy process, collaboration overlaps with deliberative and participatory democracy. Midstream in the policy process, it overlaps with network management and engagement with civil society and the stakeholders within it. Downstream in the enforcement of policy, collaborative governance overlaps with innovations deriving from alternative forms of resolving disputes and conflict. Bingham concludes by drawing attention to the importance of designing appropriate institutions and building legal infrastructures in order to further develop collaborative approaches to governance.

Peter McLaverty uses Chapter 26 to consider upstream innovations in political participation. He suggests that the rise of governance alongside the decline of public participation in historic forms of politics has contributed to scholars and practitioners experimenting with other forms of participation. These forms of participation supplement those associated with representative institutions. They include deliberative mechanisms and co-governance initiatives as well as consultation exercises. The deliberative mechanisms cover citizens' juries, consensus conferences, deliberative opinion polls, and deliberative mapping. Typically, they aim to improve the quality of public opinion. They usually produce advice for policymakers, not decisions. In contrast, co-governance initiatives typically give citizens a direct and structured input into decision-making. They include participatory budgeting, appointing citizens to partnership boards, citizens' assemblies, and referenda. Finally, consultation exercises include public meetings, opinion surveys, planning for real, and standing forums. McLaverty argues that while these forms of participation can improve democracy, they may get captured by unrepresentative elites and they may pose challenges for other democratic values such as equality.

Chapters 27 and 28 shift attention to the problems and innovations facing collaborative governance midstream in the policy process. In Chapter 27, Janet and Robert Denhardt explore the dilemmas that the new governance poses for leadership. Public officials need new theories and practices of leadership. Historically, leadership has been conceived in hierarchical terms that rely at least tacitly on the possibility of coercion. In hierarchies, leadership generally depends on power and position; leaders use their power and position to develop organizational visions, manage operations, exert control, and overcome resistance to change. Now, the new governance poses dilemmas for this approach to leadership. Today, we need new concepts and practices of leadership better suited to the requirements of network governance. In the new governance, leaders increasingly find themselves having to manage and sustain cooperative relations and common purposes across multiple organizations over some of which they may have little authority. New imperatives of leadership include fostering collaboration, building resilience and adaptive capacity, resolving ethical concerns through dialogue, and engaging citizens.

Michael McGuire tackles the specific problems of network management in Chapter 28. He focuses on institutional and organizational perspectives. Network management is the attempt to influence other actors and thus the network. Diverse policy actors may need or try to manage networks. They may want to promote their individual goals or the goals of their home organizations, or simply to enhance the general effectiveness or intrinsic value of the network and its processes. Network management is usually directed towards one of a range of features of networks, including more effective decision-making, the promotion of trust, and the distribution of power. Network managers usually influence decisions, trust, and power

by means of a series of overlapping activities: they activate people and resources; they frame roles and issues; they mobilize people and specific behaviors; and they synthesize the results. No single individual need perform all these activities in linear succession. Rather, these activities normally depend on various people who sustain the relevant processes over time to sustain and modify the network.

Many of our democratic values relate not only to participation but also to justice and inclusion. As Petri Koikkalainen argues in Chapter 29, social inclusion overlaps not only with justice but also with community and cohesiveness. After World War II, many states promoted social inclusion by expanding welfare services. In the 1970s, the crisis of the state cast doubt on both the viability and desirability of the welfare state. The new governance emerged in tandem with a range of new theories and policies designed to address issues of social inclusion. Neoliberals turned to markets, even arguing that employment was the key way by which people became responsible and involved in society. Institutionalists respond by appealing to participation in social and economic networks based on trust. Their theories helped to inspire policies designed to activate people and connect them in partnerships, often involving public sector actors. Communitarians emphasized the importance of adherence to a shared set of core values embodied in a way of life. Their theories led to attempts to transform the grassroots of governance in families, neighborhoods, schools, and towns.

In Chapter 30, Angelina Yuen-Tsang and Hok Bun Ku look at capacity building. They note the breadth and vagueness of the concept of capacity building and the varied contexts in which it is used. Capacity building typically refers to attempts to foster democratic and accountable governance by strengthening civil society and especially the knowledge, abilities, and relationships among citizens. The concept of capacity building rose out of liberation theology and Marxist theories of literacy. To some extent, these roots encouraged a problem-centered approach; attempts to build capacity focused on overcoming the obstacles people confront. Today, however, there is a greater focus on building on the strengths people already have. The general aim is to empower people by working with micro- and mezzo-level institutions. Sometimes this aim is itself seen as a route to development. Here the idea is that enhancing the capabilities of citizens and their local organizations might ensure that socioeconomic policies are more inclusive and appropriate. Yuen-Tsang and Ku illustrate the nature and advantages of a capacity building approach by reference to community development work in a Chinese village in Yunnan province.

Fumihiko Saito examines the role and prospects of decentralization in Chapter 31. Decentralization appeals across the political spectrum as a possible response to various dilemmas that have become increasingly prominent since the 1970s. One dilemma is the problem of legitimacy discussed by Afzal and Considine (see Chapter 24). Other dilemmas include the greater demands that citizens make of governments, the heterogeneous nature of these demands, transnational flows, and globalization. Decentralization offers the promise of greater legitimacy and efficiency. Decentralized institutions may encourage participation and foster ethnic harmony and national unity. They may get better information, be more responsive, and find it easier to raise revenues. All these benefits, however, are open to doubt. Moreover, as Saito argues, decentralization can take different forms. Typologies of decentralization distinguish, for example, between deconcentration, devolution, and delegation. Deconcentration involves transferring service delivery from central agencies to local offices. Devolution involves transferring power, decision-making, and financial responsibility from central governments to subnational ones. Delegation can have a closer association with NPM, referring to the transfer of administrative responsibilities to private and voluntary sector actors. Empirical research suggests that these different types of decentralization foster legitimacy and efficiency only as part of a larger reform agenda including socio-economic reform.

In Chapter 32, Wai Fung Lam discusses the particular problem of governing the commons. Garret Hardin described the problem memorably. He postulated a common field on which ranchers graze cattle. The ranchers all have an interest in restricting grazing to maintain the fertility of the field. But each individual rancher hopes that the others restrict grazing while they themselves add further animals. Each rancher seeks to avoid the shared costs of restricting grazing while reaping the individualized benefits of adding more animals. The result is a tragedy of the commons: the field loses fertility. Lam traces the changing response to the problem of managing common pool resources. Initially, scholars and practitioners emphasized the importance of benevolent state action. Later, they turned to market approaches based on various systems of property rights. Yet, Lam argues, the dichotomy of bureaucratic state or free market proved unhelpful. Ethnographic and interpretive studies of practice combined with theories of bounded rationality to open up new perspectives. In particular, new approaches to institutional design turned from panaceas to studies of what rules worked well in what settings. These approaches typically promote things like connections between individual and collective interests, forms of interdependence, shared mental models, effective use of information, and multilevel approaches to problem solving.

As public managers increasingly find themselves managing networks rather than hierarchic bureaucracies, so the state increasingly seeks legal control through regulation. In Chapter 33, Marian Döhler explores the rise of regulation as a mode of governance. Historically, regulation was used to correct perceived market failures. In the 1960s and 1970s regulation was used to promote competition and the interests of consumers in industrial sectors such as air traffic and telecommunications. Yet the rise of the new governance included new theories and practices of regulation. For example, the Chicago School used economic reasoning to point to the apparent shortcomings of regulation and helped to inspire neoliberals to call for reduced regulation and a rolling back of the state. Equally, however, the attempt to roll back the state led to an expansion of networks and transnational interactions, many of which seemed to need regulation. The result is an expanded realm of regulation that addresses not only particular industrial sectors but also problems that cut across sectors. Some commentators even talk of a new regulatory state.

The *Handbook of Governance* concludes with Chapter 34 by James Meadowcroft on sustainable development. Sustainable development denotes a cluster of normative concerns, including the protection of the natural environment, public participation in environmental decision-making, the needs of the poor, and justice to future generations. Sustainability and governance are conceptually and historically entwined. Rising worries about sustainability inspire and require new theories of governance. The environmental movement pioneered several of the policy instruments most closely associated with the practice of the new governance. Today, sustainable development poses many of the main dilemmas of government in an especially acute form. How can we simultaneously build integration, measurement, partnerships, and reflexivity in policymaking? In addition, the advocates of sustainable development often remind us of the continuing importance of hierarchic state authorities intervening to redistribute wealth and regulate social action. Meadowcroft argues that approaches to sustainable development, notably the transition approach and the adaptive management perspective, often focus on policy and process. We might pay more attention to the socioeconomic and political context of sustainability – moving beyond an expansionist economy, rethinking the welfare state, and reforming representative democracy.

CONCLUSION

The term 'governance' has risen to prominence in the last 30 years as a way of describing and explaining changes in our world. It has become a prominent topic across the social sciences, and a major concern for political and non-profit actors. Typically, the new governance refers to changes in the nature and role of the state since the last quarter of the twentieth century. The state has become increasingly dependent on organizations in civil society and more constrained by international linkages. On the one hand, the public sector in many states has shifted away from bureaucratic hierarchy and toward markets and networks; governance thus captures the ways in which patterns of rule operate in and through groups within the voluntary and private sector. On the other hand, states have become increasingly embroiled with transnational and international settings as a result of the internationalization of industrial and financial transactions, the rise of regional blocks, and concerns over problems such as terrorism and the environment; governance thus captures the formal and informal ways in which states have attempted to respond to the changing global order.

A vast literature has arisen on governance and the changing nature of the state and other forms of rule. The literature includes contributions from the leading theories in the contemporary social sciences, including rational choice, institutionalism, and interpretive theory. The literature describes, explains, and evaluates trends in public sector reform, including marketization, public management, and multijurisdictional coordination. The literature explores the effect of these trends on diverse practices of rule, including local government, the changing state, and global governance. The literature raises practical issues about how practitioners can manage these changing patterns of rule: What types of leadership are appropriate? How can policymakers manage networks? How can we act collectively to preserve common goods? Finally, the literature raises ethical and political questions about good democratic governance: Can legitimacy still derive from clear lines of accountability? How can we promote social inclusion and participation? How can we preserve the environment for future generations? The *Handbook of Governance* aims to reflect and extend these literatures, but in its very organization it also emphasizes three things:

- The new governance rose in large part because new theories have led us to recognize the long-standing role of self-interest and networks, and because these new theories inspired reforms that often heightened the role of markets and networks in ruling practices.
- Practices of governance characteristically blur the boundaries between public and private, blending features of state, market, and community; and they blur the boundaries between levels of government and between states, forging multijurisdictional and transnational patterns.
- The new governance poses significant dilemmas for our current administrative and democratic practices, requiring us to develop new forms of public action and perhaps new political ideals.

Theories of Governance

Policy Network Theory

Henrik Enroth

INTRODUCTION: POLICY NETWORKS AND THE LANGUAGE OF GOVERNANCE

Today it is widely believed that we live in a world of networks, a world in which policy-making and governance are 'only feasible within networks, providing a framework for the efficient horizontal coordination of the interests and actions of public and private corporate actors, mutually dependent on their resources' (Börzel, 1998: 262–3). Governance, in this brave new world, involves a plurality of actors interacting in networks that cut across the organizational and conceptual divides by means of which the modern state has conventionally and all too conveniently been understood: notably, the distinction between state and civil society, and the distinction between public and private sectors.

If we accept this view of the world, policy network theory is an analytical, critical, and – for want of a better word – emancipatory enterprise. Theories of policy networks point to an alleged mismatch between received concepts and theories of governing, on the one hand, and what is taken to be the current realities of governance, on the other. A high degree of complexity and functional and sectoral differentiation in society and politics are presented as indubitable facts, while it is also stated or implied that these facts have been covered over or misrendered by outdated concepts and theories. While critics have remained unconvinced by 'pointless theorizing about policy networks' (Dowding, 2001: 102), the point of theorizing about policy networks has usually been to liberate us from such concepts and theories, making us perceive more clearly the conditions under which we are governed, and pointing in the direction of more sustainable forms of governance. *Governing Complex Societies*, the title of a book by two prominent scholars in the field (Pierre and Peters, 2005), supposedly calls for more complexity in governance than has hitherto been allowed, or as Rod Rhodes has pithily put it in what could be a slogan for the entire field, 'messy problems need messy solutions' (1997a: 21).

Insofar as there is relative agreement today on the existence and nature of this messy world of networks, such agreement is quite recent. Unquestionable as all this might seem today, only two decades ago talk of policy networks did not necessarily imply belief in a 'distinct new governing structure' (Adam and Kriesi, 2007); its recent adoption – or abduction – into the language of governance to one side, the policy network concept has long been used to describe and analyze 'different types of empirically possible patterns of interaction among public and private actors in policy-specific subsystems' (Adam and Kriesi, 2007: 130; cf. Börzel, 1998). So, there were policy networks before there was governance, or better, there were concepts and theories of policy networks before there was a language of governance, a language in which the term 'governance' is often used as shorthand for 'self-organizing, interorganizational networks characterized by interdependence, resource exchange, rules of the game and significant autonomy from the state' (Rhodes, 1997a: 15).

This chapter seeks to assess the past, present, and prospects of policy network theory by unpacking the generic policy network concept around which the field has been formed and transformed. Admittedly, there is no shortage of reviews and overviews of policy network theory. Assessing the state of the art has even become a thriving subgenre (see, for example, Freeman and Parris Stevens, 1987; Jordan, 1990; Rhodes, 1990; Jordan and Schubert, 1992; van Waarden, 1992; Klijn, 1997; Börzel, 1998; Thatcher, 1998; Mayntz, 2003; Adam and Kriesi, 2007). The range of perspectives, research interests, theoretical and methodological options, and empirical findings are all well covered in the literature. But the same cannot be said about the core concept that informs research, irrespective of perspective. Therefore, here, I approach policy networks and the theories devoted to them by way of the concept used to describe and analyze policy networks in the language of governance, rather than treat policy networks as empirically given in the world to which that concept is supposed to refer.

The reason for this take on the field is simple: concepts are the most fundamental tools of the trade in any academic discipline or field, and the best way to evaluate concepts is usually not to debate their match or mismatch with the world, which is the scantily clad empiricism of most policy network theory. Instead, the best way to evaluate concepts is to ask whether or not they are adequate for whatever task we want to use them for. In the present case that appears not to be the case, insofar as students of policy networks today may want to expand their field of inquiry to cover a broad range of policymaking phenomena not only within but also beyond the nation-state framework handed down with received concepts and theories. The problem, I suggest, is not that the policy network concept has come to cover too much, or the 'ever-increasing ambitions' that allegedly follow with the gradual extension of the scope of this concept (Thatcher, 1998: 390), but rather that it still encompasses too little, in the sense that it is premised on a nation-state model of politics no longer reflected by research interests in the field, let alone in the social sciences generally. While policy network theory is arguably best seen as part of a long and broad pluralist legacy in modern political discourse, it still remains statist in its implications for empirical, theoretical, and normative inquiry.

In the first and second sections, I trace the career of the policy network concept in influential varieties of policy network theory, past and present. This chronicle is far from original and necessarily selective, covering three odd decades. In the third section I then unpack what I take to be the main components of the generic policy network concept with which these theories have left us: *interdependence; coordination*; and *pluralism*. These notions have become a hard core of the policy network concept in all varieties of policy network theory, subject to different interpretations but without which the concept would be difficult to make out or make sense of. The fourth section offers some suggestions as to what arguably needs to be done with the policy network concept today in order for policy network theory to remain a fruitful form of political inquiry in the immediate future, beyond the nation-state framework within which the field has evolved.

DISCOVERING POLICY NETWORKS, CIRCA 1978–1990

For present purposes the story about policy network theory began in the late 1970s with two largely independent transatlantic developments, both part of a general shift in focus in political research in the twentieth century, from formal hierarchy and jurisdiction to informal constellations of power and interest. In America in the 1970s, a sizeable literature emerged on 'subgovernments', 'subsystems', or 'iron triangles', essentially synonymous terms designating 'clusters of individuals that effectively make most of the routine decisions in a given substantive area of policy' (Ripley and Franklin, 1984: 10; Freeman and Parris Stevens, 1987). With no discerniable influence from overseas, the term 'policy community' came to serve a similar purpose in British research on public services, signifying a stable network of actors sharing interests and attitudes in relation to a specific policy issue or area (Jordan, 1990: 327).

In an explicit critique of the iron triangle metaphor, Hugh Heclo argued in an influential essay in 1978 that American policymaking was in fact less a matter of 'closed triangles of control' and more a matter of relatively open and flexible 'issue networks', whose composition and ambitions were relative to the issues at hand. An issue network, Heclo explained, 'is a shared-knowledge group having to do with some aspect (or, as defined by the network, some problem) of public policy' (1978: 103). Heclo's image implied that policymaking was 'fragmented' in a more or less ad hoc manner, rather than 'segmented' into relatively permanent, cohesive triangles involving members from departments, interest groups, and congressional committees. Echoing the conclusion of Robert Dahl's pluralist classic *Who Governs?* (1961), he noted that '[r]ather than groups united in dominance over a program, no-one, as far as one can tell, is in control of the policy and issues' (Heclo, 1978: 102; cf. Jordan, 1990: 329).

These Anglo-American literatures left latter-day students of policy networks with a conceptual legacy within which much of the debate in the field still moves. First, the policy network concept came to cover a continuum along which different kinds of network can be plotted according to their relative cohesion, inclusion, and permanence, ranging from cohesive and stable policy communities to loosely integrated and ad hoc issue networks in declining order (see Rhodes, 1986; Bevir, 2009: 156). This continuum is largely a consequence of the different research interests, empirical cases, and concepts that precariously coexisted in these early literatures, and it has left a lasting imprint, not least as conceptual ambiguity between different conceptions of policy networks (cf. Börzel, 1998).

Secondly, in the early literatures, network interaction was typically conceived of as interpersonal rather than interorganizational, the networks studied being supposedly composed of individuals rather than of organizations. Soon, however, policy network theory took a decisive turn from the former to the latter position; at least since the early 1990s a conception of policy networks as interorganizational has been dominant, a dogma that only now appears to be loosening. In a recent volume where several contributions cross over from network governance into Foucauldian studies of governmentality and back, the editors suggest that whether policy networks are best seen as interpersonal or interorganizational should be an empirical rather than a conceptual question (Sörensen and Torfing, 2007: 11).

The legacy of early policy network theory has also influenced current notions of what networks are, and what is going on within and between them. In the 1970s terms such as 'clusters' or 'groups' were often used synonymously with 'networks', with no perceived difference between these labels. But as soon as Heclo and others made the move from subsystems or policy communities to more loosely integrated issue networks, the group concept became an awkward presence in the field. When we speak of groups we tend to assume that their members join together on the basis of shared interests or identities in order to act collectively on the latter, or at least that a sense of shared interest or identity will evolve among the group members in the course of interaction, an assumption that runs through the successive phases of our pluralist legacy (for an analysis, see Enroth, forthcoming).

Networks, on the other hand, seem to be a different and less communal matter. In networks we typically expect to find actors with interests or identities of their own, interacting not necessarily on the basis of anything they share with other actors, save the mere condition of interaction and whatever we believe that entails. Rather, actors interact in networks because network interaction is presumably facilitating or even necessary in order for them to pursue their own objectives. Under the name of interdependence, this has been a defining feature of policy networks since the 1980s and 1990s when British, German, and Dutch scholars systematically put the concept to empirical use.

ANALYZING POLICY NETWORKS, CIRCA 1990–2010

So much for the prehistory of policy network theory. Let us now turn to more recent developments. The following subsections trace the changing ambitions in the field, in roughly chronological order, from typologies of policy networks to various efforts at explanation, management, understanding, interpretation, and normative revaluation.

Typologizing policy networks: the Anglo-governance school

What is known as the Anglo-governance school has, arguably like no other approach to policy networks, 'formed into an authoritative theory of how new methods of governing society have emerged' (Marinetto, 2003: 592). Its chief proponent, Rod Rhodes, has

noted that in Britain '[p]olicy networks changed after 1979', changes summed up terminologically as a turn from 'government' to 'governance'. 'Functional policy networks based on central departments […] expanded to include more actors, most notably from the private and voluntary sectors. The institutions of the state were fragmented' (1997a: 45). Reflecting this fragmentation of the research object, Rhodes has described policy networks in terms of 'the structural relationship between political institutions' at different levels. This is the embryo of his later insistence that the policy network concept is best construed as a 'meso-level' concept, designating 'the variety of linkages between the centre and the range of sub-central political and governmental organizations' (1997a: 36–37).

The essence of those linkages is interdependence, which Rhodes has referred to as the 'explanatory motor' in policy network theory; mutual dependence on decentralized and asymmetrically distributed resources is the reason 'why different levels of government interact', as well as the explanation for 'variations in the distribution of power within and between networks' (1997a: 9). A policy network, on this view, is thus 'a cluster or complex of organizations connected to one another by resource dependencies', and network interaction is a 'game' in which the participants 'manoeuvre for advantage' (Rhodes, 1997a: 37). These are the essentials of what Rhodes has described as 'a broadly neo-pluralist argument' to the effect that 'power is structured in a few competing elites, which includes the private government of public policy by closed policy networks' (Rhodes, 2007: 1250).

As in earlier varieties of British pluralism, this approach to policy networks 'does not manifest a great deal of concern with the coordination of public services. Whether at a practical or a theoretical level, it has not sought to prescribe' (Rhodes, 1990: 308). But it has certainly sought to describe. From the early 1980s through the 1990s policy network theory in Britain progressed – if that is indeed the word – more than anything through creation, critique, and revision of typologies of policy networks. Critique and revision went with the territory, as it were, since, as Rhodes and David Marsh have noted, 'no policy area will conform exactly' to any given list of characteristics in any given typology, which for them underscores 'the need to retain the term "policy networks" as a generic description' (Rhodes and Marsh, 1992: 187).

The fact that typologies of policy networks cannot aspire to be empirically exhaustive made sure that typologizing was likely to go on as long as it seemed reasonable to use the policy network concept to chart empirical variations in public–private and state–society interactions in different policy areas. Predictably, new cases provided new variations, prompting new typologies. A quaint illustration of this self-perpetuating logic is Rhodes's erstwhile habit of refering to and revising his own publications on 'the Rhodes typology' in the third person. The typologies that resulted from these efforts did much to pave the way for subsequent attempts at explanation and understanding as well as normative assessment, but as Rhodes has recently remarked, in hindsight 'typologies of networks have become deeply uninteresting' (2007: 1249). With only slight oversimplification, it could be claimed that the Anglo-governance school and its forerunners in Britain successfully redescribed governmental policymaking, so that others could devote their attention to analyzing what is now, almost across the board, construed as a distinct new governing structure.

and to rational choice theory. Fritz Scharpf and Renate Mayntz and their colleagues at the Max Planck Institute have made much of blending the two. For them, as for Rhodes, contemporary policymaking is marked by the prevalence of networks and by interdependence between network actors, creating conditions where cooperation is dearly needed yet delicate. 'Networks', Mayntz has observed, 'typically emerge where power is dispersed among agents in a policy field, but where cooperation is necessary for the sake of effectiveness'. Hence the key question addressed by this variety of policy network theory: 'the problem of how to agree on an effective solution without shifting the costs this implies on to outsiders' (2003: 31).

Thus construed, policy network theory is essentially about the nature and conditions of strategic action in institutional contexts that shape the perceptions, preferences, and interactions of the network participants. Policy network theory is a systematic and formalized 'search for mechanisms that real-world actors could rely upon to increase their ability to predict each other's strategic choices' (Scharpf, 1991: 294). It seeks to identify the rules of the game that shape network interaction, and to account for the games network actors play in accordance with those rules (Marin and Mayntz, 1991; Scharpf, 1997). As Bevir has remarked, it is 'arguable' that this approach differs from the Anglo-Governance school 'mainly in the extent to which it uses formal game theory to analyze and explain rule-governed networks' (2009: 159).

Explaining policy networks: the Max Planck Institute

The most influential bid when it comes to explaining policymaking in and through networks is probably to refer to institutional theory and game theory. In retrospect it seems all but inevitable that empirical attention to policy networks would be wedded both to the 'new institutionalism' as it evolved in organizational analysis and political science,

Managing policy networks: the governance club

The members of the 'governance club' research program at Erasmus University, Rotterdam, likewise approach policy networks in terms of strategic action among public and private actors under conditions of interdependence. Here, too, we find the pluralist assumption that no one actor involved in any given policymaking process 'possesses the power to determine the strategies of the other actors', and that '[t]he government is no longer seen as occupying a superior position to other parties, but as being on equal footing with them' (Kickert et al., 1997: 9). And here, too, the strategies of network participants are analysed as contingent on the network itself, since '[p]roblems, actors and perceptions are not chance elements of policy processes but are connected with the interorganizational network within which these processes occur' (Klijn, 1997: 16). A policy network thus construed is 'an interaction system reproduced by concrete games', but as such it also 'shapes the context of new games'. A game, in turn, is 'an interaction between the strategies of interdependent actors' (Klijn and Teisman, 1997: 103). It is the main objective of this variety of policy network theory to analyse such games in order to facilitate the management of policy networks (see Klijn and Teisman, 1997: 105–12).

The most obvious difference between Rhodes's Anglo-governance school and the Dutch governance club is the latter's managerial perspective, the task being precisely to prescribe where Rhodes has explicitly foresworn such an ambition (cf. Rhodes, 1997b: xiii–xiv). The research program of Walter Kickert, Erik-Hans Klijn, Joop Koppenjan and associates treats policymaking through networks not simply as an empirical datum with which we have been confronted and in the face of which we can seemingly only acquiesce, but as a novel condition calling for new forms of coordination between new policy actors. Network management, however, is not a matter of top-down steering, but a question of how to make the games network actors play run more smoothly in the apparent absence of an umpire. This means that an aspiring network manager – typically a governmental actor – needs to be able to 'handle complex interaction settings and work out strategies to deal with the different perceptions, preferences and strategies of the various actors involved' (Kickert et al., 1997: 11). Ironically, then, the work of the governance club restates an old statist question about policy coordination in a language of governance that explicitly denies not only the efficacy but also the possibility of central steering. The question here is 'how governance and public management can take shape in situations in which central steering is not possible' (Kickert and Koppenjan, 1997: 35).

Understanding policy networks: a dialectical approach

Launching a critique of the above approaches, David Marsh and Martin Smith have introduced what they refer to as a 'dialectical approach' to policy networks, indebted to the structuration theory of Anthony Giddens. Existing approaches, according to Marsh and Smith, have neglected that treating policy networks as an explanatory variable properly involves three 'dialectical relationships': between structure and agency; between a given policy network and its surrounding context; and between a given policy network and the policy outcomes generated by the network, past and present. A dialectical relationship, on this view, is 'an interactive relationship between two variables in which each affects the other in a continuing iterative process' (Marsh and Smith, 2000: 5). Policy network theory thus construed involves 'looking at the institutionalization of power relations both within the network and within the broader socio-economic context' (Marsh and Smith, 2000: 7). In alleged contrast to other varieties of policy network theory, this leads Marsh and Smith (2000, 11) to conclude that

- 'the formation of the network is affected by a combination of external factors and the decisions of agents';
- 'policy outcomes are the product of the interaction between agents and structures';
- 'change in the network is the product of an interaction between context and networks';
- 'outcomes affect the network'.

Not everybody, however, has been convinced by the novelty of the dialectical approach of Marsh and Smith. 'Who are they kidding?', Keith Dowding responded in an acerbic critique, pointing out – accurately – that the three interactive relationships identified by Marsh and Smith have in fact been noted in much or most existing literature on policy networks (Dowding, 2001: 99). Dowding's response and Marsh and Smith's response to his response amounted to a heated but futile exchange not about substance – since there was no real disagreement on matters of substance, as even the interlocutors allowed – but about method and visions of social inquiry. As such, this exchange is not without interest, reflecting as it does the old clash between explanation and understanding in the social sciences, a clash forever reiterated in new contexts in virtually identical guise.

In the present context there has been an intensified criticism during the past decade of what has been presented as a lingering positivism in the above varieties of policy network theory, best replaced, critics have argued, by post-positivist or interpretative approaches. The exchange between Marsh and Smith and their critics may thus be seen as symptomatic of a general trend in the field, ostensibly a move away from substantive differences about policy networks and governance to differences of a methodological and epistemological kind. With policy networks now generally seen as indicative of a new governing structure, seemingly indubitable, old battles have subsided, as Rhodes and others have noted. With history in mind, this development evokes how mid-century political scientists successfully translated once controversial pluralist visions of politics into seemingly incontrovertible common sense, on the basis of which methodological and epistemological matters could be safely debated without putting the pluralist position itself at peril (see Gunnell, 2004: 219–52).

Decentering policy networks: an anti-foundational approach

An influential recent move in this process is the anti-foundational or decentered approach to policy networks introduced and elaborated by Mark Bevir, Rod Rhodes, and others. An anti-foundational approach to policy networks, Bevir and Rhodes have told us, attends to 'the social construction of policy networks through the capacity of individuals to create meaning' (Rhodes, 2000: 78). On this view, 'how the people we study actually see their position and their interests inevitably depends on their theories, which might differ significantly from our theories' (Bevir, 2003: 204). Policy networks thus construed are socially constructed by virtue of the 'contingent beliefs' on the basis of which actors interact in them, beliefs formed 'against the background of traditions' and transformed 'in response to dilemmas' (Bevir and Richards, 2009a, 2009b).

A tradition in this context is 'a set of theories, narratives, and associated practices that people inherit', and a dilemma arises 'when a new belief […] stands in opposition to their existing ones, thereby forcing a reconsideration of the latter' (Bevir, 2003: 210). It is the task of policy network theory to reconstruct the interaction in policy networks by recovering and unpacking the beliefs of actors in terms of the traditions they inherit and the dilemmas they face and seek to resolve in and through interaction with other network participants.

This approach explicitly rejects the ambition to explain interaction in policy networks and the policy that results from such interaction in terms of institutional or structural factors allegedly conditioning or even determining agency; an anti-foundational or decentered approach to policy networks seeks to explain network interaction and policy solely in terms of the beliefs of the network participants, against the background of traditions and in the face of dilemmas. The critical view of existing explanatory ambitions in the field also implies a critical view of existing ambitions to manage policy networks, notably the efforts of the governance club. For one thing, managing networks is not, according to this approach, the prerogative of the state alone, since 'there are various participants in markets and networks, all of whom can seek to manage them for diverse purposes' (Bevir, 2003: 217). For another thing, and more fundamentally, the decentered theory of policy networks of Bevir and Rhodes rejects 'the very idea of a set of techniques or strategies for managing governance' (Bevir, 2003: 216). Policy advice, from this perspective, is best delivered by telling 'stories that enable listeners to see governance afresh' (Bevir and Rhodes, 2007: 85; Rhodes, 2007: 1257).

Revaluating policy networks: participation and accountability

Simultaneous with the linguistic or interpretative turn in policy network theory, there has been an unmistakable normative revaluation of policy networks during the past two decades or so, making what was not so long ago perceived as democratically dubious seem more conducive to democratic participation and political accountability. In the words of prominent members of the governance club, early policy network theory tended to conceive of policy networks as 'synonymous with the resistance of vested interests standing in the way of effective and democratically legitimized problem solving and policy innovation'. Many latter-day contributions, by contrast, have paid more attention to 'the potentials of the concept of policy networks for public problem solving and societal governance' (Kickert, Klijn, Koppenjan, 1997: 2; Rhodes, 1997a: 58, 197–200; Bang, 2003; Bevir, 2003; Bevir and Rhodes, 2006: 68; Sörensen and Torfing, 2007).

Policy networks, on this recent view, 'allow citizens to express more nuanced preferences in a more continuous way than they can when restricted to electing representatives', and governance 'opens up new possibilities of participation and devolution in democracy' (Bevir, 2003: 217). Thus, the rise and spread of policy networks is not only or even mainly inimical to democracy but also an 'opportunity' to 'reimagine' or 'redefine' it (Bevir, 2003: 217–18). Rhodes has explicitly pointed out the 'normative implications'

of his approach, leading him in the direction of a 'republican' theory of democracy that emphasizes 'local ownership and a degree of independence from central government', qualities held to be 'defining features' of network governance (Rhodes, 2007: 1257). This vision seems to come close to the ideals of participatory democracy, especially in its pluralist varieties. Paul Hirst's 'associative democracy' is one such theory of relevance in the present context. According to Hirst, however, contemporary governance is marked not so much by loosely knit networks as by 'large hierarchically controlled institutions on both sides of the public-private divide'. Such institutions can only be rendered more democratic by 'devolving as many of the functions of the state as possible to society', turning organizations 'from top-down bureaucracies into constitutionally ordered democratically self-governing associations' (Hirst, 2000: 28), a vision very much in the spirit of G.D.H. Cole and other British pluralists around the turn of the last century.

John Dryzek has similarly drawn out the implications of his work on discursive democracy for policy network theory. According to him, networks may – ideally – function as sites for 'engagement across discourses in the public sphere', a kind of engagement which may in turn 'influence more formal authority structures' as well as 'be intrinsically valuable in its constitution and reconstitution of social relationships' (Dryzek, 2007: 271). Following Iris Marion Young, Dryzek refers to this as 'inclusive political communication', meant to 'connect the particular to the general' (Dryzek, 2007: 268). Of course, as Dryzek himself acknowledges, there can be no guarantees that policy networks will in fact allow for engagement across discourses rather than remain stuck within the particular by putting a premium on a single, hegemonic discourse as a 'low-cost way of coordinating the actions of members of a network' (Dryzek, 2007: 272).

What is immediately striking about these and similar visions of network democracy is that they are just that: visions, begging questions about how alleged democratic potential is to be actualized. Yet to remind ourselves of the importance of asking about the point, the point here is not so much description as prescription, giving normatively more forceful accounts of policy networks than those hitherto on offer. The recent revaluation of policy networks is best understood as a response to what Hirst has called 'the ad hoc pluralization of political authority' (2000: 24): i.e. an uneasy feeling that the alleged turn from government to governance has put cherished democratic values in peril.

In keeping with the entrenched fear of faction and self-interest in Western political thought, networks are, as Jon Pierre has put it, often 'assumed to cater almost exclusively to the interests of those actors that participate in the network, a scenario which raises questions about the long-term legitimacy of such governance instruments' (2000: 245). Today, by contrast, it has been suggested that 'political theorists and central decision makers to an increasing extent tend to view governance networks as both an effective and legitimate mechanism of governance' (Sörensen and Torfing, 2007: 4). So, on an upbeat reading of recent developments in policy network theory, policy networks now help to address the very problems they have long been thought to cause or exacerbate – problems such as societal fragmentation, deficits in democratic participation and political accountability, and a declining public sphere.

UNPACKING THE POLICY NETWORK CONCEPT

Whether aimed at description, explanation, management, understanding, interpretation, or revaluation, the above varieties of policy network theory all share the same generic policy network concept, a concept which these approaches have significantly shaped as well as been shaped by. To summarize, at a minimum in this literature, policy networks are characterized by:

- *Interdependence* – network participants are mutually dependent on each other's resources in order to realize their objectives;
- *Coordination* – network participants need to act jointly in order to realize shared objectives;
- *Pluralism* – networks are relatively autonomous vis-à-vis other networks and the state.

Before we consider what arguably needs to be done with the policy network concept today, we need to take a closer look at each of these conceptual components as they have been fashioned and refashioned in the above theories.

Interdependence

Interdependence is commonly construed as mutual resource dependence, meaning simply that the actors in a network are believed to be dependent on each other's resources – whatever resources – in order to realize their objectives (Bevir, 2009: 114). This notion of interdependence is implied by the narrative of societal complexity and functional differentiation that is integral to most if not all theories of policy networks. Strategic action based on interdependence has become the standard account of what keeps networks together, and as we have seen, network interaction has frequently, and more or less metaphorically, been described as 'games real actors play', as 'bargaining', or 'negotiation' (Dowding, 1995; Rhodes, 1997; Scharpf, 1997). Klijn has even suggested that '[i]nterdependencies cause interactions between actors, which create and sustain relation patterns' in policy networks (1997a: 31).

Even if we generously take 'cause' to mean something like 'is a condition of', 'interdependencies cause interactions' nevertheless seems an awkward way of unpacking the dynamics of policy networks. It is difficult to envision a situation in which actors in a policy network act strategically based on their interdependence with other actors in the network without first having come to perceive their interdependence as such, through interaction. So, this must be a two-way street: if interdependence may be construed as a condition of interaction in networks, then network interaction seems to be a condition of interdependence as well, a point in fact acknowledged by Klijn himself. Interdependence, he has also pointed out, 'is something actors discover in interaction and which is changed in interaction' (1997: 31).

For Bevir and Rhodes in their recent collaborative efforts, as for others who have taken a linguistic and interpretative turn in the study of policy networks, interdependence is more about communicative than strategic action. On this view, interdependence is contingent on the beliefs and interactions of 'situated agents' in networks, and is thus what actors make of it in the policy networks in which they interact (Bevir and Richards, 2009a). Interdependence is never, on this view, objectively given by the structure of the network or the institutions in which network participants interact, let alone by societal complexity or political differentiation in general; this is a point well made in relation to the governance club and others who find it difficult to account for intersubjective – as distinct from supposedly objective – aspects of interdependence.

Still other scholars have argued that 'there might be other reasons for the development and existence of networks than interdependence between actors' (Hoff, 2003: 45). Cited examples include a perceived need among actors to reach a common understanding on policy issues or to pool resources in order to implement policy; initiatives from public authorities; legal and financial incentives; and the intended or unintended diffusion of norms relevant for public policy (Hoff, 2003: 45; Triantafillou, 2007: 190–4). It is far from clear that these indeed constitute counter-evidence against interdependence as the explanatory motor in policy network theory, yet the point of suggesting that they do is clear: namely, to point beyond strategic action as the sole conceivable dynamic in policy network interaction. This brings us to our next conceptual component.

Coordination

'Coordination', Bevir has explained in an introduction to key concepts in governance, 'occurs whenever two or more policy actors pursue a common outcome and work together to produce it' (2009: 56–57). Coordination is not a given in policy networks, but rather, as Bevir has put it, 'both a driving force of governance and one of its goals' (2009: 56). This is a matter of what we make of network interaction. Simply put, the more the participants in policy networks are believed to be able to coordinate their own interactions the less we need to worry about coordination as a condition for interaction, and the less we need to worry about 'network management', or 'metagovernance', and whether and how such practices might involve the state.

If we take network interaction to be essentially about strategic action under conditions of interdependence, then nothing much seems certain about coordination. Whether and to what extent the actors in a given network are capable of coordination would seem to be a purely empirical question, turning on negotiation, compromise, and alignment of the respective objectives with which the actors enter the network. But not so fast. Some degree of cooperation would seem to be implied in the very notion of interdependence, without which, again, it seems difficult to make sense of the policy network concept. Yet in order for cooperation to be in some sense successful, and in order for shared objectives to emerge out of the process of network interaction, it would seem that something more is required. Just what this 'more' is has long been a sticking point in policy network research, just as it has long been a sticking point in the various forms of new institutionalism, and just as it was a persistent sticking point in earlier forms of pluralism.

Here we should note the prevalence in policy network theory of trust as a lubricant in network interaction. If, on the standard account, interdependence is the explanatory motor in policy network theory, and strategic action provides the dynamic in network interaction, then, still on the standard account, '[t]he medium of coordination appears indeed to be something like trust in the context of interdependence' (Bevir, 2009: 59; cf. Lane and Bachman, 1998; Klijn & Edelenbos, 2007). Facilitating and debilitating conditions of network interaction have also been broached in terms of the relative degree of conflict and consensus in policy networks, since the possibility of conflict between network actors with objectives of their own seems omnipresent, while at the same time at least relative consensus on objectives seems necessary in order for the network to persist and actually produce policy. As Sörensen and Torfing have noted, '[t]here is a permanent risk that conflicts between network actors will reduce or even destroy the self-regulating capacity of a governance network' (2007: 170). As always with conflict and consensus, the consensus view seems to be that we need a bit of both. Joop Koppenjan has argued that networks that suffer from 'excessive consensus' will tend towards 'the systematic suppression or exclusion of problems, interests, parties and innovations', while, on the other hand, excessive conflict may result in network disintegration (2007: 150; cf. Peters, 2007).

Theorists who opt for communicative rather than strategic action tend, justifiably or not, to make less of a problem of coordination, assuming that policy networks go it alone. And conversely, those who do believe that network interaction is tantamount to strategic action tend to doubt that policy networks can, or indeed should, go it alone when it comes to coordination between network participants. As Klijn and Jurian Edelenbos have succinctly put it, 'most of the time, self-steering will not be enough. Since we are dealing with autonomous actors, each with their own perception of the problem and their own chosen strategy, we need to address the question of collective action'. For Klijn and Edelenbos, addressing the question of collective action means that 'cooperation and the coordination of actors require more active

and deliberate managerial strategies' (2007: 200). The question of what such active and deliberate managerial strategies might be, and whether such strategies are at all viable and desirable, brings us to our next, intimately related point: the question of the nature and role of the state in policy network theory.

Pluralism

To many students of policy networks, where state actors participate in policy networks, 'they are a very special and privileged kind of participant' (Mayntz, 2003: 31). Rather than being simply a player among others, pluralist-style, the state ultimately sets the rules of the game for network interaction by furnishing the legal and organizational framework within which networking takes place. Policy networks thus inevitably go about their business in 'the shadow of hierarchy', to contribute to the dissemination of Fritz Scharpf's rampant metaphor, the reception and use and abuse of which in the field deserves an essay of its own (Scharpf, 1994).

For others, however, network management is very much an away game for state actors, since coordination is 'difficult to promote at a distance', whereas, on the other hand, direct involvement in policy networks requires state actors to play 'by the horizontal rules inherent in network governance', thus obtaining influence only 'with reference to the resources that they put into the network, and not [...] on the basis of their formal hierarchical authority vis-à-vis the network' (Sörensen and Torfing, 2007: 170–1). Drawing out the pluralist implications of these observations, Rhodes has argued in *Understanding Governance* that the state in contemporary governance thus 'becomes a collection of interorganizational networks made up of governmental and societal actors with no sovereign actor able to steer or regulate' (Rhodes, 1997a: 57).

With the state described entirely in terms of networks, it is but a short step to the claim – sustained by the critical and emancipatory thrust in the language of governance – that the state was in fact always a network of networks. In a classic pluralist move a number of theorists have argued that we are now, with the benefit of hindsight, in a position to see that 'that is what nation states have always been, formal sovereignty disguising the complex of organizations and actors within the state' (Hirst, 2000: 25). Or, as Bevir and Rhodes have remarked, 'the notion of a monolithic state in control of itself and civil society was always a myth', a myth that 'obscured the reality of diverse state practices that escaped the control of the center because they arose from the contingent beliefs and actions of diverse actors at the boundary of state and civil society' (2007: 89; Bevir and Richards, 2009a).

I believe these statements are indicative of a shift during the past decade, from a concern with the state's capacity to govern policy networks to a concern with its identity as a governing subject. In 2000, Jon Pierre noted in an introduction to an authoritative volume that 'the state's capacity to impose its will on society has become challenged by cohesive policy networks' (2000: 1). Today many seem to question the composition and even the existence of a unitary 'will' that might be ascribed to 'the state' as a unitary subject. And if the identity of the state as a governing subject seems less than clear, the same must be said about society as an object of governance. The very meaning of the distinction between state and society seems an open question in the field today, with policy networks supposedly criss-crossing the interface.

Yet a delicate consensus nevertheless seems to have developed to the effect that talk of 'the decline of the state' is overstated or premature. Rhodes, an erstwhile proponent of this notion, has lately granted critics that 'the traditional instruments of government co-mingle, compete and conflict with the new instruments of governance to variable effect' (2007: 1253), a picture that might be compared with his assessment in *Understanding Governance* (cf. Mayntz,

2003: 32). Similarly, Pierre and Peters have argued that 'networks, in order to be effective, must be connected to government organizations responsible for making policy', since networks without such connections 'are most unlikely to have any real influence over policy' (Pierre and Peters, 2005: 78).

Occasionally, and on variously functionalist assumptions, coordination in and through policy networks is even made to look very much like state governing by proxy, in a situation in which conventional forms of governing through hierarchy no longer seem effective. 'Through network governance', Tanja Börzel and Diana Panke have argued, 'governments can mobilize resources in situations where they are widely dispersed among public and private actors at different levels of government, international, national, regional, and local' (2007: 157). Similarly, policy networks can be seen as means of reclaiming the state's will and ability to govern in the wake of a neoliberal penchant for markets as the primary means of coordination in society and politics in general. Again Rhodes is a fine example. 'Governance', he has explained, 'is part of the fight back', allowing us to give an account of 'the unintended consequences of corporate management and marketization', 'a response, therefore, to the perceived weaknesses of marketization' (2000: 54).

Judging from the current state of policy network theory, then, the state seems to face quite a challenge: namely, to 'regulate networks and other self-regulating actors without reducing their space for manoeuvering in any radical way' (Sörensen and Torfing, 2007: 169), that is, network management as pampering. Jan Kooiman anticipated this challenge already in 1993 when he called for 'a state that governs in other, more apt ways', seeking 'to influence social interactions in such ways that political governing and social self-organization are made complementary' (1993: 256). Needless to point out, this complementarity still remains to be achieved, as it remains to make good sense – empirically, theoretically, and normatively – of the notion that this entity called 'the state' is still very much in place in the world, albeit transformed into so many networks networking with other networks.

RECONCEPTUALIZING POLICY NETWORKS

To recapitulate the story so far, our generic policy network concept has come to designate the following: mutual resource dependence among network actors, objectively given or intersubjectively perceived; strategic or communicative action as a consequence of interdependence; governmental actors in networks are either on a par with other actors as a consequence of mutual resource dependence, or in a privileged position to influence or even determine the rules of the game in network interaction; as a consequence of the prevalence of networks in policymaking, the state is itself best seen as a network of networks, rather than as a system of formal hierarchies. This is the hard core of the policy network concept that is today widely believed to signify a new governing structure in Western societies in general.

What is striking, and somewhat surprising, about all the varieties of policy network theory reviewed here is that in spite of frequent talk of governance as a distinct new governing structure, the policy network concept remains confined to its nation-state origins. As Mayntz has perspicaciously pointed out, at the global level, in contrast to the regional level paradigmatically illustrated by the European Union, we can no longer readily picture a policy process 'with its input and output aspects', since 'there exists no identifiable steering subject, and no institutionalized framework containing the object of steering'; that is, there is no state within the institutions of which policy is made and no easily identifiable society for which policy is made. This state–society constellation has provided, throughout the developments chronicled here, the general framework within which the policy network concept has made sense and within which it has been put to use. As Mayntz has concluded from her observation, in order for a theory of governance to encompass phenomena at a global level, 'governance' would have to be construed 'in the widest sense as basic modes of coordination, because only in that case is the concept not tied to the existence of some sort of a political control structure' (2003: 34–5).

Of course this is a conceptual, not an empirical point. Clearly not all governance is global governance, nor do all policy networks have transnational, let alone global, connections. Yet as policy issues and areas increasingly cut across the divide between the domestic and the international, just as policy networks have long been thought to cut across the divides between state and society and public and private, the prospects of the field turn largely on the will and ability of its researchers to go mobile, to conceptualize policy networks in such a way as to transcend not only the particular national contexts in which the concept has been put to empirical use (see Rhodes, 2007: 1258) but also the entire nation-state framework within which policy network theory evolved as part of the pluralist legacy in modern political discourse. Mayntz has hinted that that would point in the direction of 'an altogether new field' (2003: 38). Perhaps. However, the future of the field as we know it arguably depends on whether policy network theory can revisit, unpack, and rethink the policy network concept as it has been handed down to us. I would like to conclude with a few tentative suggestions as to what that might entail, based on the observations above.

First, we should turn the pluralist approach on its head. Instead of starting with the state and disaggregating it into its constituent networks, top-down, as it were, we should start by positing, for analytical purposes, a global, territorially undifferentiated social space as the most basic setting for human intercourse. Then, instead of individuating units of analysis in that global space by reference to existing geopolitical boundaries or political institutions, we should define our units of analysis in terms of an indefinite plurality of wills to govern, emanating from a broad variety of actors, individual and collective, in a broad variety of contexts, ranging from the kind of 'everyday makers' studied by Henrik Bang and his colleagues (Bang, 2003), to social movements, new and old, to corporations, associations, organizations, and institutions in what used to be known as state and civil society. These heterogeneous wills to govern may then, in turn, be aggregated into networks, bottom-up, insofar as the actors involved interact under conditions of interdependence, and policy results from their interactions.

Secondly, we should then conceptualize the state and hierarchies in general as being, themselves, networks (cf. Bevir and Richards, 2009a: 12). This suggestion is far from original; variations on this theme have reverberated in academic political discourse at least since the 1920s. This is not to deny relevant differences between formal hierarchies and networks, but it is to insist that in both cases, as in most other cases we encounter in the social sciences, we are dealing with interdependent – rather than simply independent or dependent – actors and the interactions between them. Much would be gained, then, from abandoning the specious notion that human interaction is ever wholly independent or dependent. The typology independent–interdependent–dependent should be taken for what it is: less an accurate representation of different forms of human interaction, and more a conceptual-*cum*-rhetorical device that helped scholars in organization theory carve out a network approach to the study of organizations, unmistakably distinct from what was then described as the conventional approaches to markets and hierarchies (Powell, 1990).

Thirdly, following Bevir and Rhodes, we should then conceive of interdependence not as something objectively given but as something intersubjectively created and recreated in interaction. As I have already suggested above, in the absence of actors perceiving

their interdependence as such it is difficult to think of the actors in question as constituting a network, as opposed to a crowd, a mob, or something similarly indistinct. Networks thus construed would still be premised on interdependent action, but interdependence should arguably be conceptualized in as non-committal a fashion as possible, simply as mutually enabling and constraining conditions of action, conditions that arise from the sheer fact of interaction but may be construed differently by individual actors as well as by observers. This makes the nature and degree of interdependence relative both to the perceptions of the actors involved and to the concepts, theories, and research interests of students of policy networks, which is precisely the point.

Fourthly, this would have consequences for our understanding of network autonomy as well. Autonomy could then no longer be equated with 'insulation from state power', as Peter Triantafillou has aptly noted has tended to be the case in much literature on policy networks. Instead network autonomy might then be construed, pithily, as the ability to do something, rather than anything (Triantafillou, 2007: 190), meaning simply that network autonomy arises from the enabling and constraining interactions between networks and their surroundings, including other networks, just as interdependence arises from the enabling and constraining interactions between actors within networks.

Fifthly, and perhaps most daunting, we would need a notion of the policy process that would not presuppose either established political institutions or territorially defined societies. As Marten Hajer and Hendrik Wagenaar have remarked, whatever 'new spaces of politics' we may need to reckon with today in the study of policy networks will 'initially exist in an institutional void' (2003: 9). David Easton, presupposing both political institutions and territorial societies, once explained that his concept of political system was intended to encompass 'all those kinds of activities involved in the formulation and execution of social policy' (1953: 129).

That might be a start, allowing us to get 'process' at least provisionally out of the way by making the existence and nature of institutions for policymaking subordinate or secondary to the existence of interaction from which policy results.

'Policy' itself might be trickier. One challenge would be to pluralize popular qualifiers such as 'public' and 'social', having these signify not singular predefined spheres or territorially demarcated domains, but human populations affected by policy in each actual case. The question of scope would then be an open empirical question, to be settled after the fact, rather than by reference to territorially demarcated societies. What would likewise be an open empirical question, rather than an object of wishful thinking, is the potential of policy networks thus construed for democratic participation and political accountability.

CONCLUSION: POLICY NETWORKS BEYOND THE NATION-STATE FRAMEWORK?

Clearly these suggestions are at least as contentious as anything I have reviewed in this chapter. I offer them not under the illusion, and certainly not in the hope, that they will be universally accepted, but as a way of prompting or provoking debate about what I take to be some of the most pressing yet also disregarded conceptual issues in the field. In all varieties of policy network theory to date the selling point of the policy network concept has been its supposed match with the current realities of policymaking: its capacity to address, better than its rivals, the conditions under which we are being governed. In the words of Rhodes, this concept 'directly confronts, even mirrors, the administrative and political complexity of advanced industrial societies' (1990: 313). What has happened lately, as the policy network concept has been turned into a centerpiece in the language of governance, is that complexity now seems territorially and institutionally unbound; the conditions 'confronted' or 'mirrored' by the concept are no longer obviously confined to what is going on within nation-states. What has yet to happen is a conceptual revision, taking these ostensible changes into account. If this chapter might contribute in any way to such an effort, then much has been gained.

ACKNOWLEDGMENT

I want to thank Mark Bevir, Andreas Duit, Malin Henriksson, and Alexandra Segerberg for their help and valuable comments on earlier versions of this chapter.

REFERENCES

Adam, Silke and Kriesi, Hanspeter (2007) 'The Network Approach', in Paul A. Sabatier (ed.), *Theories of the Policy Process*. Boulder, CO: Westview Press.

Bang, Henrik P. (2003) 'A New Ruler Meeting a New Citizen: Culture Governance and Everyday Making', in Henrik P. Bang (ed.), *Governance as Social and Political Communication*. Manchester: Manchester University Press.

Bevir, Mark (2003) 'A Decentered Theory of Governance', in Henrik P. Bang (ed.), *Governance as Social and Political Communication*. Manchester: Manchester University Press.

Bevir, Mark (2009) *Key Concepts in Governance*. London: Sage.

Bevir, Mark and Rhodes, R.A.W. (2006) 'The Life, Death, and Resurrection of British Governance', *Australian Journal of Public Administration* 65(2): 59–69.

Bevir, Mark and Rhodes, R.A.W. (2007) 'Decentered Theory, Change, and Network Governance', in Eva Sörensen and Jacob Torfing (eds), *Theories of Democratic Network Governance*. Basingstoke: Palgrave Macmillan.

Bevir, Mark and Richards, David (2009a) 'Decentering Policy Networks: A Theoretical Agenda', *Public Administration* 87(1): 3–14.

Bevir, Mark and Richards, David (2009b) 'Decentering Policy Networks: Lessons and Prospects', *Public Administration* 87(1): 132–41.

Börzel, Tanja A. (1998) 'Organizing Babylon: On the Different Conceptions of Policy Networks', *Public Administration* 76(2): 253–73.

Börzel, Tanja A. and Panke, Diana (2007) 'Network Governance: Effective and Legitimate?', in Eva Sörensen and Jacob Torfing (eds), *Theories of Democratic Network Governance*. Basingstoke: Palgrave Macmillan.

Dahl, Robert A. (1961) *Who Governs? Democracy and Power in an American City*. New Haven, CT: Yale University Press.

Dowding, Keith (1995) 'Model or Metaphor: A Critical Review of the Policy Network Approach', *Political Studies* 43(1): 136–58.

Dowding, Keith (2001) 'There Must Be End to Confusion: Policy Networks, Intellectual Fatigue, and the Need for Political Science Methods Courses in British Universities', *Political Studies* 49(1): 89–105.

Dryzek, John S. (2007) 'Networks and Democratic Ideals: Equality, Freedom, and Communication', in Eva Sörensen and Jacob Torfing (eds), *Theories of Democratic Network Governance*. Basingstoke: Palgrave Macmillan.

Easton, David (1953) *The Political System: An Inquiry into the State of Political Science*. New York: Alfred A. Knopf.

Enroth, Henrik (forthcoming) 'Beyond Unity in Plurality: Rethinking the Pluralist Legacy', *Contemporary Political Theory* 10.

Freeman, J. Leiper and Parris Stevens, Judith (1987) 'A Theoretical and Conceptual Reexamination of Subsystem Politics', *Public Policy and Administration* 2(1): 9–24.

Gunnell, John G. (2004) *Imagining the American Polity: Political Science and the Discourse of Democracy*. University Park, PA: the Pennsylvania State University Press.

Hajer, Marten and Wagenaar, Hendrik (2003) *Deliberative Policy Analysis: Understanding Governance in the Network Society*. Cambridge: Cambridge University Press.

Heclo, Hugh (1978) 'Issue Networks and the Executive Establishment', in Anthony King (ed.), *The New American Political System*. Washington, DC: American Enterprise Institute for Public Policy Research.

Hirst, Paul (2000) 'Democracy and Governance', in Jon Pierre (ed.), *Debating Governance: Authority, Steering, and Democracy*. Oxford: Oxford University Press.

Hoff, Jens (2003) 'A Constructivist Bottom-Up Approach to Governance: The Need for Increased Theoretical and Methodological Awareness in Research', in Henrik P. Bang (ed.), *Governance as Social and Political Communication*. Manchester: Manchester University Press.

Jordan, Grant (1990) 'Sub-Governments, Policy Communities, and Networks: Refilling the Old Bottles?', *Journal of Theoretical Politics* 2(3): 319–38.

Jordan, Grant and Schubert, Klaus (1992) 'A Preliminary Ordering of Policy Network Labels', *European Journal of Political Research* 21(1–2): 7–27.

Kickert, W.J.M. and Koppenjan, J.F.M. (1997) 'Public Management and Network Management: An Overview', in W.J.M. Kickert, E.-H. Klijn and J.F.M. Koppenjan (eds), *Managing Complex Networks: Strategies for the Public Sector*. London: Sage.

Kickert, W.J.M., Klijn, E.-H. and Koppenjan, J.F.M. (1997) 'Introduction: A Management Perspective on Policy Networks', in W.J.M. Kickert, E.-H. Klijn and J.F.M. Koppenjan (eds), *Managing Complex Networks: Strategies for the Public Sector*. London: Sage.

Klijn, E.-H. (1997) 'Policy Networks: An Overview', in W.J.M. Kickert, E.-H. Klijn and J.F.M. Koppenjan (eds), *Managing Complex Networks: Strategies for the Public Sector*. London: Sage.

Klijn, E.-H. and Edelenbos, J. (2007) 'Meta-Governance as Network Management', in Eva Sörensen and Jacob Torfing (eds), *Theories of Democratic Network Governance*. Basingstoke: Palgrave Macmillan.

Klijn, E.-H. and Teisman, G.R. (1997) 'Strategies and Games in Networks', in W.J.M. Kickert, E.-H. Klijn and J.F.M. Koppenjan (eds), *Managing Complex Networks: Strategies for the Public Sector*. London: Sage.

Kooiman, Jan (1993) 'Findings, Speculations, and Recommendations' in Jan Kooiman (ed.), *Modern Governance: New Government–Society Interactions*. London: Sage.

Koppenjan, Joop F. M. (2007) 'Consensus and Conflict in Policy Networks: Too Much or Too Little?' in E. Sörensen and J. Torfing (eds), *Theories of Democratic Network Governance*. Basingstoke: Palgrave Macmillan.

Lane, C. and Bachman, R. (1998) *Trust within and between Organizations: Conceptual Issues and Empirical Applications*. Oxford: Oxford University Press.

Marin, B. and Mayntz, R. (eds) (1991) *Policy Networks: Empirical Evidence and Theoretical Considerations*. Boulder, CO: Westview Press.

Marinetto, Mike (2003) 'Governing beyond the Center: A Critique of the Anglo-Governance School', *Political Studies* 51(3): 592–608.

Marsh, David and Smith, Martin (2000) 'Understanding Policy Networks: A Dialectical Approach', *Political Studies* 48(1): 4–21.

Mayntz, Renate (2003) 'New Challenges to Governance Theory', in Henrik P. Bang (ed.), *Governance as Social and Political Communication*. Manchester: Manchester University Press.

Peters, B. Guy (2007) 'Virtuous and Vicious Circles in Democratic Network Governance', in Eva Sörensen and Jacob Torfing (eds), *Theories of Democratic Network Governance*. Basingstoke: Palgrave Macmillan.

Pierre, Jon (2000) 'Introduction: Understanding Governance', in Jon Pierre (ed.), *Debating Governance: Authority, Steering, and Democracy*. Oxford: Oxford University Press.

Pierre, Jon and Peters, B. Guy (2005) *Governing Complex Societies: Trajectories and Scenarios*. Basingstoke: Palgrave Macmillan.

Powell, Walter W. (1990) 'Neither Market Nor Hierarchy: Network Forms of Organization', *Research in Organizational Behavior* 12(2): 295–336.

Rhodes, R.A.W. (1986) *The National World of Local Government*. London: Allen & Unwin.

Rhodes, R.A.W. (1990) 'Policy Networks: A British Perspective', *Journal of Theoretical Politics* 2(3): 293–317.

Rhodes, R.A.W. (1997a) *Understanding Governance: Policy Networks, Governance, Reflexivity, and Accountability*. Buckingham: Open University Press.

Rhodes, R.A.W. (1997b) 'Foreword', in W.J.M. Kickert, E.-H. Klijn and J.F.M. Koppenjan (eds), *Managing Complex Networks: Strategies for the Public Sector*. London: Sage.

Rhodes, R.A.W. (2000) 'Governance and Public Administration', in Jon Pierre (ed.), *Debating Governance: Authority, Steering, and Democracy*. Oxford: Oxford University Press.

Rhodes, R.A.W. (2007) 'Understanding Governance: Ten Years On', *Organization Studies* 28(8): 1243–64.

Rhodes, R.A.W. and Marsh, David (1992) 'New Directions in the Study of Policy Networks', *European Journal of Political Research* 21(1–2): 181–205.

Ripley, R. and Franklin G. (1984) *Congress, the Bureaucracy, and Public Policy*. Homewood, IL: Dorsey.

Scharpf, Fritz (1991) 'Games Real Actors Could Play: The Challenge of Complexity', *Journal of Theoretical Politics* 3(3): 277–304.

Scharpf, Fritz (1994) 'Games Real Actors Could Play: Positive and Negative Coordination in Embedded Negotiations', *Journal of Theoretical Politics* 6(1): 27–53.

Scharpf, Fritz (1997) *Games Real Actors Play: Actor-Centered Institutionalism in Policy Research*. Boulder, CO: Westview Press.

Sörensen, Eva and Torfing, Jacob (2007) 'Introduction: Governance Network Research: Towards a Second Generation', in Eva Sörensen and Jacob Torfing (eds), *Theories of Democratic Network Governance*. Basingstoke: Palgrave Macmillan.

Thatcher, Mark (1998) 'The Development of Policy Network Analyses: From Modest Origins to Overarching Frameworks', *Journal of Theoretical Politics* 10(4): 389–416.

Triantafillou, Peter (2007) 'Governing the Formation and Mobilization of Governance Networks', in Eva Sörensen and Jacob Torfing (eds), *Theories of Democratic Network Governance*. Basingstoke: Palgrave Macmillan.

van Waarden, Frans (1992) 'Dimensions and Types of Policy Networks', *European Journal of Political Research* 21(1–2): 29–52.

3

Rational Choice Theory

Keith Dowding

WHAT IS RATIONAL CHOICE THEORY?

Rational choice theory is not a theory of how society or governing processes work. It is a methodology or organizing perspective (Greenleaf, 1983; Gamble, 1990: 405) that generates questions about the social world and provides some standard techniques for answering those questions. Those methods include the axiomatic formal modelling techniques of social choice theory and formal modelling in game theory. Rational choice theory also includes less formal but still analytic verbal models. Rational choice in political science shares these techniques with economics, which provides its intellectual heritage. It assumes that individuals can order their preferences over states of the world (or 'objects') with the base relation 'R'. We define an 'R' relation as one where the agent either prefers the first alternative to the other or is indifferent between them, and it can be read as 'at least as good as'. Rational choice theory is then defined by three conditions concerned with preferences which are required for rationalizing or interpreting the behaviour of agents. Preferences must be reflexive, complete and transitive. The first condition means for any alternative x within a domain A an individual i either prefers or is indifferent between x and itself (for all $x \in$ A, $x\, R_i\, x$).[1] The second condition, completeness, is that any item in domain A must enter into the preference ordering so that for all alternatives $x, y \in$ A, either $x\, R_i\, y$ or $y\, R_i\, x$ (or both) (in other words either individual i prefers y to x or is indifferent between them). The final condition means for any triple of alternatives $x, y, z \in$ A, if $x\, R_i\, y$ and $y\, R_i\, z$, then $x\, R_i\, z$ (which means that if i weakly prefers x to y and to z, then i must weakly prefer x to z). These conditions allow for the weak axiom of revealed preference (WARP) which enables rationalization, interpretation and explanation of behaviour (see Austen-Smith and Banks, 1999: 1–24). Roughly speaking, with a further continuity assumption, the ordinal preferences of rational choice theory can be turned into cardinal representations and agents modelled as utility maximizers (see, for example, Binmore, 2007: 121–127). Whereas rational choice theory is an interpretative strategy, and the three conditions allow for rationalizing, utility maximizing is a further predictive step which is not always justified (see, for example, Ross, 2005).

As an organizing perspective and a way of analysing politics, rational choice does not make any specific recommendations about governance structures; it does not have *a* theory of governance or *a* theory about new modes of service delivery. Indeed any argument or account of the state, if it follows a coherent and logical structure, can be represented in the terms of formal theory. If that formal theory demonstrates that some conclusions drawn from less formal or analytic accounts do not in fact logically follow, then the formalization adds something. Otherwise, it is just for show. Rational choice can be used to model problems in new forms of governance and help provide normative justification (or critique) for them, as indeed it has done for old forms.

PUBLIC CHOICE AND CONSTITUTIONAL POLITICAL ECONOMY

Two branches of rational choice theory – public choice theory and constitutional political economy – have been associated with ideas concerned with modern theories of governance. Both can be traced back to James Buchanan's and Gordon Tullock classic and seminal work *The Calculus of Consent* (1962), and are associated with specific journals: *Public Choice* founded (in 1965) and edited for many years by Tullock, and *Constitutional Political Economy*, founded in 1990. Both these branches of rational choice (especially public choice theory) are associated with specific normative claims about the organization of the state. These claims specifically involve the *normative* assumption that agents should be modelled as self-interested material utility maximizers, and were used to critique the traditional welfare economics that assumed the state was a black box that could be modelled as a benevolent dictator directing resources to promote human welfare as specified by welfare various theorems (Besley and Coate, 2003). The task of welfare economics was simply to define and provide the basis for that welfare promotion; public choice brought back politics into the economic analysis of state welfare, albeit in a specific economic form.

Public choice and constitutional political economy insist that we must assume all state actors are materially self-interested and then design our institutions to ensure welfare gains notwithstanding. Those in this tradition are impressed by Adam Smith's 'invisible hand' argument to the effect that the self-interest of producers in competition will lead to overall welfare, and accept without question the two fundamental theorems of welfare economics: first, that each Walrasian equilibrium is Pareto efficient, at least if consumers are locally non-satiated; secondly, any Pareto-efficient allocation not on the boundary of the attainable set is a Walrasian equilibrium provided preferences satisfy the appropriate convexity and continuity assumptions. Armed with these and acceptance of Pareto efficiency as a normative tool by which to judge outcomes, public choice writers (and to a lesser extent constitutional political economists) judge markets always to be superior to other collective solutions. They do recognize that some markets may fail and thus require government to step in, although they do not think that government is likely to do so efficiently, according to Tullock's (1994) dictum: where there are no externalities, the market is good and the government mediocre; where there are externalities, the market is bad and the government is still mediocre. They argue that market failures are rare, and most government interventions occur due to rent-seeking by specific groups in society or through state predation.

Public choice theory and to a large (though not exclusive) extent constitutional political economy operate with a strong material self-interest assumption in additional to the standard utility maximizing. This leads the analysis to assume that groups are out to exploit each other, and state actors are trying to exploit the community. Public choice tends to analyse political processes to highlight these tendencies, whereas constitutional political economy is a normative programme about effective design to ensure welfare maximization.

In more recent years alternative strategies for examining constitutional procedures that rely not upon self-interest but on more complex utility functions have been utilized within the constitutional political economy tradition led by a former Buchanan collaborator Geoffrey Brennan and his collaborators (Brennan and Lomasky, 1993; Brennan and Hamlin, 2000, 2002, 2008; Brennan and Pettit, 2004; Eusepi and Hamlin, 2006).

Public choice theory grew up in the 1960s and 1970s alongside general concerns about the expansion of the state, budget deficits, stagflation and various peripheral analyses of the modern ungovernability of the state and its inexorable rise (e.g. Birch, 1975; Crozier et al., 1975; King, 1975) and inefficiencies caused by the political-business cycle. The political-business cycle is the idea that governments make spending promises to particular groups, fed by the rent-seeking discussed above, and general welfare promises to the community, which cause fiscal problems solved after the election by higher taxes. Such governmental manipulation ensures an economic upturn prior to an election and inflationary problems immediately afterwards (Nordhaus, 1975; Frey, 1997). This leads either to the overexpanding state or to a boom–bust cycle. Despite a great deal of econometric research, the political-business cycle has never been conclusively demonstrated although its existence might depend upon institutional factors (Schultz, 1995). Nevertheless, these ideas feed into the ideology of restricting the growth of the state and retracting its overall size. It was argued that responsibilities needed to be returned from the state to individual citizens and non-government market and community agencies in order to make the state governable once more. In economic terms, Thatcherism and Reaganomics imply reducing state activity and regulation. New governance forms are not a necessary consequence of New Right economics, but are a natural extension of it. To equate the public choice approach to new governance with rational choice theory is to

ignore the latter's major components. I will argue in fact that while we can see the ideological influence of public choice theory on new governance, new governance ideas are based upon an incoherent rendition of public choice theory, and rational choice analysis of new governance is likely to be highly critical.

ANALYSING POLITICS

In the subsections that follow I analyse some of the major findings in rational choice related to governance issues. Many of these issues are based on problems inherent in democracy, oversight procedures and governance issues.

The general non-predictability of politics

Social choice theory is normative and concerns how a set of individuals such as a legislature or a committee, or society as a whole should determine their collective choice. Given our account of well-defined preferences, and the collection of agents $N = \{1,2,\dots, n\}$ and the alternatives, $A = \{x, y, z, w,\dots\}$ then a decision rule, f, maps a profile of individual preferences, $(P_1, P_2,\dots, P_n)$, into a group preference ordering, P_G that must be transitive and complete. The social choice question is what rule f should be used to aggregate such individual preferences into a group preference?

Arrow proposes a small set of minimally demanding normative criteria and considers which rules would satisfy them, discovering that there is no such rule (Arrow, 1951/1963). Arrow's Theorem demonstrates that there is no decision rule that produces a rational collective ordering from rational individual orderings that allow any rational individual preferences over the domain A (universal domain); respects unanimity among the agents (the Pareto principle); ensures collective preferences over any specific pair of alternatives exclusively are based on the individual preferences over that pair (independence of irrelevant alternatives);[2] and is not dictatorial (non-dictatorship). The fundamental lesson of Arrow's theorem is that there is no such thing as an ordinal social welfare function that respects his conditions. In political science the theorem is usually interpreted to mean that there is no perfect aggregation rule or voting system (Riker, 1982; Nurmi, 1998; 1999). Social choice has examined how to overcome Arrow's theorem; an early and important result from Duncan Black (1948) shows that certain restrictions on individual preferences (relaxations of 'universal domain') *will* yield consistent group preferences. Black shows that if individual preferences are *single-peaked* (for a definition, consult Black, 1948 or Shepsle and Bonchek, 1997: 83–91), then majority-rule voting yields transitive and complete group preferences and, moreover, they reflect the preferences of the *median voter* – this constitutes the median voter theorem (MVT).

The MVT has been used extensively to produce predictions over collective decision domains. The MVT relies upon preferences lining up in a single dimension. In some contexts this might be an acceptable abstraction, but in others it is not. An important set of results in *n*-dimensions, however, demonstrates that any winning bundle of policies can be beaten by another bundle using the same preferences and voting rules (McKelvey, 1976, 1979; Schofield, 1978; McKelvey and Schofield, 1986). This suggests to some that politics should be chaotic (Riker, 1982). A large part of rational choice in this domain has been devoted to explaining stability, largely by showing how legislative rules constrain decisions into fewer dimensions (Kadane, 1972; Shepsle, 1979; Shepsle and Weingast, 1981, 1987); how political parties constrain the set of voters and policies on offer (Cox and McCubbins, 1993; Aldrich, 1995; Laver and Shepsle, 1996); or how other institutional rules also constrain the possibilities.[3] Essentially these approaches

constrain the set of choices sufficiently for the MVT to obtain in some form.

Yet another research programme developed from Arrow suggests that voting systems are inherently manipulable and thus the results cannot be trusted (Gibbard, 1973; Satterthwaite, 1975; Riker, 1982). Together these sets of results have suggested to some people that modern democracies are inherently flawed in certain ways and do not produce efficient or normatively acceptable outcomes. This might be alternatively expressed by Churchill's aphorism that democracy is the worst form of government – apart from all the rest.[4] Either way round, rational choice is largely based on analysing the difficulties of governing from an underlying normative perspective that leads to questions about inefficiencies in governing procedures and how these might be ameliorated. It is from this perspective that rational choice models comment upon new forms of governance.

The general lesson from the instability results for new governance techniques is that the growth of decentralized markets and networks within the core of the state is likely to lead to greater instability of policies. With fewer constraints than seen in more hierarchical systems and greater difficulties in bundling policies in single dimensions, implementation strategies might be subject to greater change and generate instability.

Commitment problems

Another research programme within rational choice theory concerns commitment problems. Cooperation between agents for collective benefits should be expected where agents can see those benefits, can see others can see those benefits, and can see others do their part in securing those benefits. Given other interests and constraints on time, agents may not always work to secure collective benefits. This 'free rider' or collective action problem was popularized in the modern literature by Mancur Olson (1965/1971). Collective action problems can be seen as a form of commitment problem. Commitment problems occur whenever there is doubt that an agent will keep to a contract as made. Rational choice models have suggested that the rise of the modern capitalist state was predicated upon monarchs' solving the commitment problem with subjects with regard to raising revenue through borrowing (North and Weingast, 1989). Essentially, if one actor is more powerful than the others, why should this leviathan not simply renege on any agreements? Olson (1993, 2000) gives one answer: that the leviathan will extract what it can from its subjects but provide protection from other predators. This account mirrors in an externalist form the original Hobbesian answer that the leviathan provides protection for each against all others.

Under new governance arrangements commitment problems need to be solved through network links and repeated interactions and exchanges. Resource transfers will be increasingly subject to pressures without strict authority relationships. Such problems create greater transactions costs (Williamson, 1996) which might be solved through the development of corporate cultures and practices (Kreps, 1990) or more generally trust relationships (Ben-Ner and Putterman, 1998). Such relations need to develop over time and one problem for new governance relationships has been the constant shifting of responsibilities, agencies and actors within new governance structures. This can fracture trust relations and allow neither the emergence of trust nor of corporate culture. This has caused increasing problems of implementation and strategy in many policy sectors.

Principal–agent models

Agency problems are similar to commitment problems. Principal–agent theory suggests delegation occurs when the agent has time, information or skills that the principal lacks (Kiewiet and McCubbins, 1991; Aghion and Tirole, 1997). So voters use politicians as their agents, elected politicians use bureaucrats as their agents, and so on. Three different agency problems exist: (1) the basic agency problem or agency rent; (2) adverse selection; and (3) moral hazard.

The basic agency problem occurs when the agent does not carry out his activities efficiently. It can emerge because of asymmetric information or hidden action. The agent knows the principal cannot always directly observe what he is doing. The agent might shirk through lack of effort or skills; or he might efficiently act on his own policy preferences (Bressler-Gonen and Dowding, 2009). Agent-shirking and policy-shifting thus constitute two broad categories within the basic agency problem.

Adverse selection can be illustrated by Gresham's law that bad money drives out good. When money was composed of real silver, people with coins had an incentive to shave them slightly before exchanging them. Given the likelihood that a coin is shaved, merchants would not exchange as much for it in return as for an unshaved coin. Holders of unshaved coins then have an incentive to shave them before using them. Bad money drives out good. In agency terms adverse selection generally occurs because those least qualified for a job are those most eager to attain it. At whatever level of remuneration, those least qualified are likely to gain the most comparative advantage over their current position and so be keener to attain it. Thus, those most likely to stand for elected office would not be those the public would most like to see standing – they are likely either to be hungry for power or to have strong policy preferences which might not be shared by the public. To get elected they will tend to hide both these qualities.

Moral hazard is a term first used in banking and insurance in the eighteenth century and reintroduced into the economics of risk by Kenneth Arrow in the 1960s (Arrow, 1971). In Arrow's sense moral hazard occurs where the act of making a contract itself creates perverse incentives. The very act of taking out insurance means that the insured will not act as carefully with regard to her property or her health since she is insured against damage to either. Thus if one is insured against personal injury, one might take greater risks. If one is insured against household burglary, one will spend less on door and window locks.

Moral hazard occurs in politics: for example, where elected politicians take greater risks than the public would like for re-election purposes. When the governing party is low in popularity polls, the government has an incentive to try to seize the agenda with new policy initiatives. To enhance re-election chances, they might create risky policies that have not been thought through properly or that might appeal to certain sections of the public. Foreign wars have been favourite tactic, of course, as Henry IV on his deathbed advises his unpopular wastrel son:

> ... Therefore, my Harry,
> Be it thy course to busy giddy minds
> With foreign quarrels, that action hence borne out
> May waste the memory of the former days.
> (Shakespeare *King Henry IV Part II*, Act IV, Scene V, l. 212–15)

The nature of the electoral contract makes such devices even more tempting and can create perverse incentives.

Rational choice theory has extensively analysed governance issues in terms of all three types of agency problems. Basic agency problems suggest that elected politicians need to provide oversight of agencies. Early crude models of bureaucracy such as Niskanen (1971, 1994; see Dowding, 1995: ch. 4 for a critique) assumed complete informational asymmetry between politicians and bureaucrats such that the latter could maximize their budgets up to the point of legislator indifference. Later literature concerns the type of monitoring procedures that are appropriate in given issue-domains (McCubbins and Schwartz, 1984; Bendor et al., 1987; Banks and Weingast, 1992; Huber and Shipan, 2002). For example, where there are strong

legislatures such as in the USA, committees can provide strong oversight. This might be 'fire alarm' oversight based on signals from dissatisfied client groups, or 'police patrol' regular oversight procedures (McCubbins and Schwartz, 1984). The former is usually more efficient: legislation can help groups gain access to information, shifting costs away from Congress and also allowing congressmen to gain greater credit for righting faults and for changing policies as well as enforcing old ones. In systems with strong executives such as the UK, parliamentary oversight, while still existing, is much weaker, only producing reports for the executive to respond to. However, within strong executives internal procedures also provide oversight, procedures increasingly strengthened with perceived governance problems from the 1970s. This explains the strengthening of the centre, around the Prime Minister and also the Treasury, which now operates line-by-line oversight of departmental business. Even as policy is dispersed through a greater number of agencies, the informational problems illustrated by the basic agency problem will lead to greater control at the centre of government (Dowding, 1995).

In order to overcome informational asymmetry, politicians can enfranchise and empower groups they wish to satisfy, and create agencies constrained by broad legislative guidelines. In doing so, politicians attempt to ensure their policy preferences are implemented even after they are no longer in power (McCubbins et al., 1987). The amount of discretion that might be given to bureaucrats within the scope of legislation relates to the basic agency problem with hidden information (Horn, 1995; Epstein and O'Halloran, 1999a, 1999b; Huber and Shipan, 2002). Here discretion is given to bureaucrats by the way legislation is framed. The more detailed the legislation the less discretion bureaucrats are allowed. Fiorina (1982) argues that legislators prefer to delegate to bureaucrats where the policy has dispersed benefits and concentrated costs, and to legislate in more detail when the benefits are concentrated and the costs dispersed. So they shift blame and take credit. The standard line that has emerged is that politicians will write less detailed legislation and so give bureaucrats more discretion according to certain parameters. These include:

- The less skilled or professional politicians are, the less detailed they are likely to make legislation. Unless ideologically driven, politicians lacking the information of bureaucrats will have weaker preferences over specific policy instruments than their agents and so will give discretion to bureaucrats to deliver services that the public want. There is little economic literature on this problem since in economic literature preferences are usually assumed to be well formed.
- The more risky the legislative intent – that is, the less informed politicians are about the precise consequences of their legislative proposal (the basic agency problem with hidden information) – the more discretion bureaucrats will have.
- The more stable the government – that is, the stronger its belief that it will stay in power for a long period of time – the greater the discretion it will give to bureaucrats on the assumption that more detailed direction can be given in the future.

The degree and type of monitoring are thought to depend largely upon the strength of politicians' policy preferences. To the extent that legislation is an electoral response to demands from the public or pressure groups, elected politicians are happy to allow monitoring to follow a 'fire alarm' policy. If bureaucrats implement policy incompetently, the public or pressure groups will alert politicians, who may then choose to intervene. To the extent that legislation is designed to secure the policy preferences of the politicians themselves, they are more likely to follow a 'police patrol' monitoring regime that entails having in place regular procedures to ensure their wishes are being carried out (McCubbins and Schwartz, 1984; Lupia and McCubbins, 1994). The problem is that the latter form of monitoring is much more costly than the first. Both forms concern the transfer of information about the actions of the knowledgeable player to the player lacking

information, who can then act to try to shift the actions of the agent in the direction the principal desires. These models are usually described as the basic agency problem with hidden actions – that is, the problem is getting bureaucrats to act as the politician desires.

The legal system can also be involved in these considerations. Landes and Posner (1975) argue that while judges might be considered politically neutral in the sense they are constrained by legislation and precedent, judicial decisions reflect the past successes of pressure groups in framing legislation in the first place. Judges sustain the intentions of the original legislators and they show counter-intuitively that an independent judiciary that provides greater legislative permanency allows politicians to extract larger rents from their clientele groups.

But if bureaucratic implementation is problematic, an agency might bias implementation to its own ends. Direct legislation may also be interpreted by the court. So legislators face bureaucratic and judicial uncertainty. Delegation might also avoid inefficient logrolls. Epstein and O'Halloran (1999b) examine the trade-off between the distributional and informational effects of different organizational designs to examine congressional delegation. They argue that variations in the preferences of the committee, the median congressional voter, and the executive cause Congress to choose different forms of delegation. They conclude that Congress delegates (a) when conflict between the Congress and the President is low, (b) when committees are preference outliers, and (c) when policy issues have uncertain outcomes. Thus, divided government will have more direct legislation with procedural gridlock and less discretion for agencies; unified government gives the executive more discretion.

In systems where the executive is stronger, the same theoretical considerations apply, although here direct control can be applied. Where agencies are thought to have their own policy preferences, politicians have an incentive to reorganize and politically appoint new heads in an attempt to solve policy-shifting; however, political appointees might be less able to deal with their own agency problems within a given bureau. Solving policy-shifting can increase agent-shirking, especially if monitoring is reduced because politicians trust their appointees (Bressler-Gonen and Dowding, 2009).

Conflicts in democracy

Olson (1965/1971) applies his collective action argument to the formation of pressure groups, arguing that the degree to which a group organizes depends upon its size, the asymmetry of interests among its members, and the ability of leaders to sanction members. As a consequence, larger more diffuse interests are harder to organize and so public goods for them will be undersupplied. Supply will be more responsive to smaller more concentrated interests, producing bias against the pluralist picture of the state (Olson, 1982).

Similarly Stigler (Stigler and Friedland, 1962; Stigler, 1971) examines state regulation of industry, asking whom it serves. He argues that regulation is an industry demand to create barriers to entry and provide monitoring and supervision of cheaters on industry's collective interests. Government in effect became a cartel organizer. Stigler's original models ignored consumers, as they were thought to face too great a collective action problem. Peltzman (1976) adds voters, arguing that price rises caused by Stigler's capture model would only be equal to the point where votes gained per dollar of price increase just equalled the votes lost from consumers. What is important in these early Chicago studies of regulation is that, contrary to Olson's argument, regulation is efficient: that is, any transfer from consumers to producers would be carried out in the most efficient manner.

Completely divergent results come from the Virginia school, which argues that rent-seeking activity by industries seeking monopoly rents are always inefficient (Tullock, 1967, 1990; Krueger, 1974). Such political activity is always thought to be wasteful since it could be used more productively elsewhere. Inefficiencies result both from the expenditure of resources in gaining the transfer, and in the resulting privileges the transfer involves. Tullock argues, however, that further inefficiencies will result from the use of resources to police protection. Krueger (1974) estimates these losses in terms of the difference in expenditure on rent-seeking and price of goods compared to the same output under a free-market economy. Becker (1983) and Wittman (1989, 1995) argue that the informational asymmetry the rent-seeking model requires will not last for ever: citizens will make enquiries and vote for politicians who make efficient transfers.

Coate and Morris (1995) show conditions under which these efficiencies and inefficiencies will emerge. Politicians make transfers to special interests to gain rewards, but can either make these efficiently (morally good politicians) or disguise them (morally bad politicians) by making them appear to enhance public welfare too. Since public projects have stochastic benefits, citizens receive noisy signals over whether the projects are simple transfers to special interests or serve the public interest. They show that if all politicians are identical and known to be so, then transfers are efficient. However, the existence of good and bad politicians can lead both to disguise transfers – the one to reward rent seekers and the other so as not to appear to be bad politicians.

ANALYSING GOVERNANCE

Rational choice theory when applied normatively – that is, when it is applied to failures in government or recommendations for superior governance forms – uses the concept of efficiency extensively. Efficiency in this context can be broken down into two components. Productive (or technical) efficiency describes the relationship between inputs and outputs: the higher the output relative to the input, the more technically efficient are productive techniques. Allocative efficiency describes the relationship between supply and demand: roughly speaking, we can say that the greater the number of people who receive the type and level of service they want, the more efficient is the allocation. Measuring either type of efficiency is problematic and such measures vary. All too often technical efficiency is measured by simply looking at costs without considering variation in the output. Spending less on a given service only measures greater efficiency if the same level of service is provided. Spending cuts do not necessarily result in efficiency gains. Allocative efficiency is usually measured by examining satisfaction as revealed through citizen surveys, but these are rather blunt instruments.

Public choice has defended breaking up hierarchical government structures with several arguments. First they see competition between units as bringing productive and allocative gains. If there is choice between service providers, the citizens or consumers can go to those they prefer. The service providers can also offer variation in services which, given heterogeneity of wants, will increase allocative efficiency. Where markets and quasi-markets obtain, there can also be productive efficiencies as costs will be forced down (Le Grand and Bartlett, 1993). Thus there are two processes involved in the public choice celebration of diversity in public services: one driven by competition (Reifschneider, 2006), and the other simply by diversity itself – having a wider choice means that more people can be satisfied.

One branch of public choice analysis that celebrates competition is still hierarchicalist and 'rational'. Another that fits better with new governance is non-hierarchicalist and is 'arational'. Both are promoted by writers who analyse lower tiers of government – federal structures or local government. Fiscal federalism is very much a 'rationalist' structure where it is argued that the nature of government services in terms of technical conditions such as scope, jointness supply and non-excludability should determine both what level of government should supply these services and what level should set tax rates. Fiscal federalism suggests there are natural levels of governmental unit and the central state should only allocate resources across lower units for specific welfare reasons (Oates, 1972, 1998; Bureau and Champsaur, 1992; Allsop et al., 1995; Breton, 1996; Blackorby and Brett, 2000). Fiscal federalism suggests a strong separation of competencies, making each tier responsible for both providing services and collecting taxes. This reduces the 'flypaper effect' where money sticks where it hits and intergovernmental grants tend to increase output rather than decrease local input (Oates, 1979; Hamilton, 1983, Schneider, 1989, Ch. 6). To a large degree this 'rationalist' form of organization runs counter to the more complex delivery modes of new governance.

New governance has complicated and interlocking forms of delivery that cut across both the public and private sectors. These ideas fit more broadly with the 'polycentric' urban approach of the Bloomington school (Bish, 1971; Bish and Ostrom, 1973; McGinnis, 1999; Oakerson, 1999). Polycentricity is not simply fragmented government but a mélange of both single-purpose and multi-purpose authorities with formally independent but often overlapping powers. The idea is that service-supply follows demand and the mixture should reflect this. These models tend to ignore transaction costs and assume costless formation and change processes of the pure market models. Across the developed world new public management practices have been increasingly adopted in local governments. Privatization, contracting-out, franchising, 'agencification', the introduction of 'quasi-' and 'internal markets', the idea of the 'entrepreneurial spirit' allowing public managers the initiatives to go outside of Weberian rule-following practices, all have major effects upon the efficient provision of services (Kolderie, 1983; Schneider, 1989; Osborne and Gaebler, 1992; Pollitt et al., 1998). Sets of small-scale local governments may contract out a given service to the same major company for large-scale technical efficiency gains. Conversely, a consolidated government can contract out services to a set of small competing companies for technical efficiency gains through competition.

In reality there is little public choice analysis of these complex governance relationships. However, the pro-market and competition stance of public choice might give some purported justification. The competitive market argument requires that there is genuine choice and genuine competition between agencies. Market competition might enhance efficiency if good agencies thrive and bad ones go out of business. Such competition requires that agencies directly compete and that there is a selection mechanism between agencies – in genuine competition that mechanism is driven by profits. The competitive mechanism is also driven by consumer choice, and choice requires not only product differentiation but also information. Finally, we might add that even if there is competition and choice between suppliers, that only drives the mechanism of efficiency if the choices of consumers provide a strong enough signal for providers to respond accordingly.

Contracting out services where public agencies buy services from the private sector (or other public agencies) can provide such efficiencies, especially where the product or service resembles a normal market for private goods or monopsonist buyer of services. However, that market is between public agencies and their suppliers and not between agencies and the public. Without pricing at the point of delivery, choices between agencies by members of the public do not necessarily provide the signals necessary for efficient market response. For example, while it seems clear from some evidence that households do respond to the tax-service packages offered by competing jurisdictions within metropolitan areas (Dowding et al., 1994; John et al., 1995), the only attempt to measure both the demand and supply side suggests that the signals are too weak and too noisy to enable competition (Dowding and Mergoupis, 2003). Furthermore, where the signals would be strong enough – where there is choice between schools, for example – governments are too risk averse to allow genuine full choice that would lead to some schools becoming oversubscribed and overcrowded while poor schools would become undersubscribed and either thereby better (since class size would reduce) or close if they became unsustainable. Clearly, parents would not be happy with massively oversubscribed schools or with the reality of the differentials between schools being reduced. Nevertheless, the equilibrium situation might create diversity in type of schooling. In reality, government does not allow overcrowding, and has to force diversity through central state-driven incentives. Governments, for good reasons, do not have the guts to allow real competition here.

Indeed, choice in many areas does not feed competition at all, but is justified in terms of its value in itself (for a defence, see Le Grand, 2007; for a critique, see Dowding and John, 2009; for a theoretical overview of the issue, see Dowding and van Hees, 2009). The informational requirements of genuine choice are often missing: agencies do not actually directly compete, whereas apparently competing agencies subcontract services to the same large provider. Thus 'competing' hospitals use the same agency to provide their nursing staff or cleaners; the same surgeons might operate in different hospitals, and so on. The multiplicity of different agencies also leads to massive complexity that does not lead to rational citizen choice, rather, they get served by whatever agency they can find to deliver to them.

It is true that rational informed choice by all consumers is not required to generate genuine market choice. As long as there are enough switchers from one provider to another, or those providers *believe* that there are switchers and have the correct information about what people want (through surveys of customers perhaps), then competitive efficiency might be driven. However, there is little evidence that such competition does occur through new governance arrangements, and where there is some evidence it tends to be in areas of relatively simple government services which truly resemble a market.

Indeed, the complexity of new governance arrangements might feed precisely the opposite conclusions from public choice analysis. The greater the number of agencies and complexity of service arrangements, the harder it is for citizens to make informed judgements. Outside of simple hierarchical rational forms of administrative structures lines of accountability are less clear and the political mechanisms of ensuring efficiency are blurred. As governments try to use choice (market exit) mechanisms they reduce political (voice) mechanisms, with the former driving out the latter (Hirschman, 1970). Dowding and John (2008) provide evidence that such effects do occur. Rent-seeking by agencies becomes greater as they compete for government resources, spending more of their resources on rent-seeking activity and lessening direct consumer provision. As citizen satisfaction decreases, government then turns to central mechanisms, regulation and central directives to try to keep complaints down. Furthermore, government problems are compounded by the trumpeting of the new governance structures as bringing better services, raising expectations which then feed satisfaction levels as much as any 'objective' or 'real' standards in service provision.

CONCLUSIONS

What does rational choice theory tell us about new governance techniques of networks and markets? The public choice and constitutional political economy schools seems to provide some superficial justification for them. They defend markets and in some variants celebrate

the diversity and complexity of these new institutional arrangements. Rational choice analysis, however, has revealed the chaos and instability that result when policies are formed without institutional structures that narrow the broad set of possibilities. It has specified the strategic possibilities that individuals and groups can utilize when they understand aggregation mechanisms better than others do. Rational choice theory warns of the dangers of regulation when agencies capture the regulators for their own interests, and the inefficiencies and inequities that result because the mobilization problems facing some groups are greater than those facing others. Multiplying agencies and networks also enables greater opportunities for rent-seeking activities, and they also increase the complexity of principal–agent relationships, making accountability and oversight more problematic. All of these factors make the rational choice approach critical of new governance systems. They are not completely critical. Economic arguments suggest that markets do work well in some contexts and specify the conditions where we should expect markets to be superior. Furthermore, where policy communities are relatively small, collective action and coordination problems are substantially reduced. Here, new governance relationships might work well and continued interaction amongst network partners produces allocative and productive efficiencies.

Where coordination is problematic and subject to the strains noted, positive rational choice models predict that the response to the instabilities and chaos that will proceed from networks will be recentralized command. As is well known in the policy literature, central command that ignores the network channels faces compliance problems. Perhaps the difficulties are simply a standard problem within public administration that is captured in agency models: getting the right balance between direction and discretion for agents providing public services is not easy and is itself subject to both welfare and political considerations.

NOTES

1   From the preference relation R (weak preference), the preference relations P (strictly prefers) and I (indifferent between) can be defined. Subscript i stands for the individual and lower-case letters for 'social states' or objects. The upper-case letter A stands for the set of alternatives.

2   This condition ensures the function f is ordinal. Relaxing it allows us to avoid Arrow's result; this brings questions about interpersonal comparisons of utility – see Fleurbaey and Hammond (2003) and Dowding (2009).

3   Another solution is to dismiss Arrow's condition of universal domain and assume more homogeneous cultures where Arrow-like problems are very unlikely to arise (Regenwetter et al., 2006).

4   For a critique of this 'Rochester school' interpretation, see Mackie (2003), and for a commentary, see Dowding (2007). For a rather different line of critique, see Dowding and van Hees (2008).

REFERENCES

Aghion, P. and Tirole, Jean (1997) 'Formal and Real Authority in Organizations', *Journal of Political Economy* 105(1): 1–29.

Aldrich, John H. (1995) *Why Parties? The Origin and Transformation of Party Politics in America*. Chicago: Chicago University Press.

Allsopp, C., Davies, G. and Vines, D. (1995) 'Regional Macoeconomic Policy, Fiscal Federalism and European Integration', *Oxford Review of Economic Policy* 11(2): 126–44.

Arrow, Kenneth J. (1951/1963) *Social Choice and Individual Values,* 1st/2nd edn. New Haven, CT: Yale University Press.

Arrow, Kenneth J. (1971) *Essays on the Theory of Risk Bearing*. Chicago: Markham.

Austen-Smith, David, and Banks, Jeffrey S. (1999). *Positive Political Theory I*. Ann Arbor, MI: University of Michigan Press.

Banks, Jeffrey, and Weingast, Barry (1992). 'The Political Control of Bureaucracies under Asymmetric Information', *American Journal of Political Science* 36(2): 509–24.

Becker, Gary (1983) 'A Theory of Competition among Pressure Groups for Political Influence', *Quarterly Journal of Economics* 98: 371–400.

Ben-Ner, Avner and Putterman, Louis (eds) (1998) *Economics, Values and Organization*. Cambridge: Cambridge University Press.

Bendor, Jonathan, Taylor, Serge and van Gaalen, Roland (1987) 'Politicians, Bureaucrats and Asymmetric Information', *American Journal of Political Science* 31: 796–828.

Besley, Timothy and Coate, Stephen (2003) 'On the Public Choice Critique of Welfare Economics', *Public Choice* 114: 253–73.

Binmore, Ken (2007) *Playing for Real: A Text on Game Theory*. Oxford: Oxford University Press.

Birch, Anthony H. (1975) 'Overload, Ungovernability and Delegitimation: The Theories and the British Case', *British Journal of Political Science* 14: 135–60.

Bish, Robert L. (1971) *The Political Economy of Metropolitan Areas*. Chicago: Markham.

Bish, Roger L. and Ostrom, Vincent (1973) *Understanding Urban Government*. Washington, DC: American Enterprise Institute.

Black, Duncan (1948) 'On the Rationale of Group Decision-making', *Journal of Political Economy* 56: 23–34.

Blackorby, C. and Brett, C. (2000) 'Fiscal Federalism Revisited', *Journal of Economic Theory* 92(2): 300–17.

Brennan, Geoffrey, and Hamlin, Alan (2000) *Democratic Devices and Desires*. Cambridge: Cambridge University Press.

Brennan, Geoffrey, and Hamlin, Alan (2002) 'Expressive Constitutionalism', *Constitutional Political Economy* 13: 299–311.

Brennan, Geoffrey, and Hamlin, Alan (2008) 'Revisionist Public Choice Theory', *New Political Economy* 13(1): 22–33.

Brennan, Geoffrey, and Lomasky, Loren (1993) *Democracy and Decision: The Pure Theory of Electoral Preference*. Cambridge: Cambridge University Press.

Brennan, Geoffrey and Pettit, Philip (2004) *The Economy of Esteem*. Oxford: Oxford University Press.

Bresler-Gonen, Rotem and Dowding, Keith (2009) 'Shifting and Shirking: Political Appointments for Contracting Out Services in Israeli Local Government', *Urban Affairs Review* 44(6): 807–31.

Breton, Albert (1996) *Competitive Governments: An Economic Theory of Politics and Public Finance*. Cambridge: Cambridge University Press.

Buchanan, James M. and Tullock, Gordon (1962) *The Calculus of Consent*. Ann Arbor, MI: Michigan University Press.

Bureau, D. and Champsaur, P. (1992) 'Fiscal Federalism and European Economic Unification', *American Economic Review* 82(2): 88.

Coate, Stephen and Morris, S. (1995) 'On the Form of Transfers to Special Interests', *Journal of Political Economy* 103(5): 1210–35

Cox, Gary and McCubbins, Mathew (1993) *Legislative Leviathan: Party Government in the House*. Berkeley, CA: University of California Press.

Crozier, Michael, Huntingdon, Samuel and Watanuki, Joji (1975) *The Crisis of Democracy*. New York: New York University Press.

Dowding, Keith (1995) *The Civil Service*. London: Routledge.

Dowding, Keith (2007) 'Can Populism Be Defended? William Riker, Gerry Mackie and the Interpretation of Democracy', *Government and Opposition* 41(3): 327–46.

Dowding, Keith (2009) 'What is Welfare and How Can We Measure It', in H. Kincaid and D. Ross (eds), *The Oxford Handbook of Philosophy of Economics*. Oxford: Oxford University Press.

Dowding, Keith and John, Peter (2008) 'The Three Exit, Three Voice and Loyalty Framework: A Test with Survey Data on Local Services', *Political Studies* 56(2): 288–311.

Dowding, Keith and John, Peter (2009) 'The Value of Choice in Public Policy', *Public Administration* 87(2): 219–233.

Dowding, Keith, and Mergoupis, Thanos (2003) 'Fragmentation, Fiscal Mobility and Efficiency', *Journal of Politics* 65(4): 1190–207.

Dowding, Keith and van Hees, Martin (2008) 'In Praise of Manipulation', *British Journal of Political Science* 38(1): 1–16.

Dowding, Keith and van Hees, Martin (2009) 'Freedom of Choice', In P. Anand, K. Suzamura and P.K. Pattanaik (eds), *Oxford Handbook of Rational and Social Choice*. Oxford: Oxford University Press.

Dowding, Keith, John, Peter and Biggs, Stephen (1994) 'Tiebout: A Survey of the Empirical Literature', *Urban Studies* 31(4–5): 767–97.

Epstein, David, and O'Halloran, Sharyn (1999a) 'Asymmetric Information, Delegation, and the Structure of Policy-Making', *Journal of Theoretical Politics* 11(1): 37–56.

Epstein, David, and O'Halloran, Sharyn (1999b) *Delegating Powers: A Transactions Cost Politics Approach to Policy Making under Separate Powers*. Cambridge: Cambridge University Press.

Eusepi, G, and Hamlin, Alan (eds) (2006) *Beyond Conventional Economics: The Limits of Rational Behaviour in Political Decision-Making*. Cheltenham: Edward Elgar.

Fiorina, Morris (1982) 'Legislative Choice of Regulatory Forms: Legal Process or Administrative Process?', *Public Choice* 39: 33–71.

Fleurbaey, Marc and Hammond, Peter J. (2003) 'Interpersonally Comparable Utility', in S. Barbera,

P.J. Hammond and C. Siedl (eds) *Handbook of Utility Theory*, Vol. 2, Dordrecht: Kluwer.

Frey, Bruno S. (ed.) (1997) *Political Business Cycles*. Cheltenham: Edward Elgar.

Gamble, Andrew (1990) 'Theories of British Politics', *Political Studies* 38(3): 404–20.

Gibbard, Allan (1973) 'Manipulation of Voting Schemes: A General Result', *Econometrica* 41(4): 587–601.

Greenleaf, W.H. (1983) *The British Political Tradition*. Vol. 2 London: Routledge.

Hamilton, Bruce W. (1983) 'The Flypaper effect and Other Anomalies', *Journal of Public Economics* 22: 347–61.

Hirschman, Albert O. (1970) *Exit, Voice and Loyalty: Responses to Decline in Firms, Organizations and States*. Cambridge, MA: Harvard University Press.

Horn, Murray J. (1995) *The Political Economy of Public Administration*. Cambridge: Cambridge University Press.

Huber, John D. and Shipan, Charles R. (2002) *Deliberate Discretion? The Institutional Foundations of Bureaucratic Autonomy*. Cambridge: Cambridge University Press.

John, Peter, Dowding, Keith and Biggs, Stephen (1995) 'Residential Mobility in London: A Micro-level Test of the Behavioural Assumptions of the Tiebout Model', *British Journal of Political Science* 25: 379–97.

Kadane, Joseph B. (1972) 'On the Division of the Question', *Public Choice* 13: 47–54.

Kiewiet, Roderick D. and McCubbins, Mathew (1991) *The Logic of Delegation*. Chicago: University of Chicago Press.

King, Anthony. (1975) 'Overload: Problems of Governing in the 1970s', *Political Studies* 23: 284–96.

Kolderie, Ted (1983) 'Rethinking Public Service Delivery', in B. H. Moore. (ed.), *The Entrepreneur in Local Government*. Washington, DC: International City Management Association.

Kreps, Daniel M. (1990) 'Corporate Culture and Economic Theory', in J.E. Alt and K. Shepsle (eds), *Perspectives on Positive Political Economy*. Cambridge: Cambridge University Press.

Krueger, Anne O. (1974) 'The Political Economy of the Rent-Seeking Society', *American Economic Review* 64(3): 291–303.

Landes, William M. and Posner, Richard A. (1975) 'The Indepedent Judiciary in an Interest-Group Perspective', *Journal of Law and Economics* 18: 875–901.

Laver, Michael and Shepsle, Kenneth A. (1996) *Making and Breaking Governments: Cabinets and Legislatures in Parliamentary Democracies*. Cambridge: Cambridge University Press.

4

Le Grand, Julian (2007) *The Other Invisible Hand: Delivering Public Services through Choice and Competition*. Princeton, NJ: Princeton University Press.

Le Grand, Julian and Bartlett, Will (eds) (1993) *Quasi-Markets and Social Policy*. Basingstoke: Macmillan.

Lupia, Arthur and McCubbins, Mathew (1994) 'Learning from Oversight: Fire Alarms and Police Patrols Reconstructed', *Journal of Law, Economics, and Organisation* 10: 96–125.

McCubbins, Mathew and Schwartz, Thomas (1984) 'Congressional Oversight Overlooked: Police Patrols versus Fire Alarms', *American Journal of Political Science* 28: 165–79.

McCubbins, Mathew, Noll, Roger and Weingast, Barry (1987) 'Administrative Procedures as Instruments of Political Control', *Journal of Law, Economics and Organization* 3: 177–243.

McGinnis, Michael D. (ed.) (1999) *Polycentricity and Local Public Economies: Readings from the Workshop in Political Theory and Policy Analysis*. Ann Arbor, MI: Michigan University Press.

Mackie, Gerry (2003) *Democracy Defended*. Cambridge: Cambridge University Press.

McKelvey, Richard D. (1976) 'Intransitivities in Multi-dimensional Voting Models and Some Implications for Agenda Control', *Journal of Economic Theory* 12: 472–82.

McKelvey, Richard D. (1979) 'General Conditions for Global Instransitivities in Formal Voting Models', *Econometrica* 47: 1084–111.

McKelvey, Richard D. and Schofield, Norman (1986) 'Structural Instability of the Core,' *Journal of Mathematical Economics* 15: 179–98.

Niskanen, William A. (1971) *Bureaucracy and Representative Government*. Chicago: Aldine Press.

Niskanen, William A. (1994) *Bureaucracy and Public Economics*. Aldershot: Edward Elgar.

Nordhaus, William D. (1975) 'The Political Business Cycle', *Review of Economic Studies* 42(2): 169–90.

North, Douglass C. and Weingast, Barry R. (1989) 'Constitutions and Commitment: The Evolution of Institutions Governing Public Choice in Seventeenth-Century England', *The Journal of Economic History* 49(4): 803–32.

Nurmi, Hannu (1998) *Rational Behaviour and the Design of Institutions*. Cheltenham: Edward Elgar.

Nurmi, Hannu (1999) *Voting Paradoxes and How to Deal with Them*. Berlin: Springer-Verlag.

Oakerson, Ronald J. (1999) *Governing Local Public Economies: Creating the Civic Metropolis*. Oakland, CA: ICS Press.

Oates, William E. (1972) *Fiscal Federalism*. New York: Harcourt Brace.

Oates, William E. (1979) 'Lump-Sum Grants Have Price Effects.' in P. Mieszkowski and W.H. Oakland, (eds), *Fiscal Federalism and Grants-in-Aid*. Washington, DC: The Urban Institute.

Oates, William E. (ed.) (1998) *The Economics of Fiscal Federalism and Local Finance*. Cheltenham: Edward Elgar.

Olson, Mancur (1965/1971) *The Logic of Collective Action: Public Goods and the Theory of Groups* 1st/2nd edn. Cambridge, MA: Harvard University Press.

Olson, Mancur (1982) *The Rise and Decline of Nations: Economic Growth, Stagflation, and Social Rigidities*. New Haven, CT: Yale University Press.

Olson, Mancur (1993) 'Dictatorship, Democracy and Development', *American Political Science Review* 87(3): 567–76.

Olson, Mancur (2000) *Power and Prosperity: Outgrowing Communist and Capitalist Dictatorships*. New York: Basic Books.

Osborne, David and Gaebler, Ted (1992) *Reinventing Government: How the Entrepreneurial Spirit is Transforming the Public Sector*. New York: Penguin.

Peltzman, Sam (1976) 'Toward a More General Theory of Regulation', *Journal of Law and Economics* 29(3): 211–40.

Pollitt, Christopher (1998) 'Managerialism Revisited', in B.G. Peters and D.J. Savoie (eds), *Taking Stock: Assessing Public Sector Reforms* Montreal: McGill-Queens University Press.

Regenwetter, Michel, Grofman, Bernard, Marley, A.A.J. and Tsetlin, Ilia M. (2006) *Behavioral Social Choice: Probabilistic Models, Statistical Inference, and Applications*. Cambridge: Cambridge University Press.

Reifshneider, Alexandra Petermann (2006) *Competition in the Provision of Local Public Goods*. Cheltenham: Edward Elgar.

Riker, William H. (1982) *Liberalism against Populism: A Confrontation between the Theory of Democracy and the Theory of Social Choice*. San Francisco: W.H. Freeman and Co.

Ross, Don (2005) *Economic Theory and Cognitive Science: Microexplanation*. Cambridge, MA: MIT Press.

Satterthwaite, Mark (1975) 'Strategy Proofness and Arrow's Conditions: Existence and Correspondence Theorems for Voting Procedures and Social Welfare Functions', *Journal of Economic Theory* 10(2): 187–217.

Schneider, Mark (1989) *The Competitive City: The Political Economy of Suburbia*. Pittsburgh, PA: University of Pittsburgh Press.

Schofield, Norman (1978) 'Instability of Simple Dynamic Games', *Review of Economic Studies* 45: 575–94.

Schultz, Kenneth A. (1995) 'Politics of the Business Cycle', *British Journal of Political Science* 25: 79–99.

Shepsle, Kenneth (1979) 'Institutional Arrangements and Equilibrium in Multidimensional Voting Model', *American Journal of Political Science* 23: 27–59.

Shepsle, Kenneth A. and Bonchek, Mark S. (1997) *Analyzing Politics: Rationality, Behavior and Institutions.* New York: W.W. Norton and Co.

Shepsle, Kenneth and Weingast, Barry R. (1981) 'Structure-Induced Equilibrium and Legislative Choice', *Public Choice* 37(3): 503–19.

Shepsle, Kenneth and Weingast, Barry R. (1987) 'The Institutional Foundations of Committee Power', *American Political Science Review* 81: 86–108.

Stigler, George J. (1971) 'The Theory of Economic Regulation', *Bell Journal of Economics and Management Science* 2(2): 3–21.

Stigler, George J. and Friedland, Claire (1962) 'What Can Regulators Regulate? The Case of Electricity', *Journal of Law and Economics* 5(3): 1–16.

Tullock, Gordon (1967) 'The Welfare Costs of Tarriffs, Monopolies and Theft', *Western Economic Journal* 5(3): 224–32.

Tullock, Gordon (1990) 'The Costs of Special Privilege', in J.E. Alt and K.A. Shepsle (ed), *Perspectives on Positive Political Economy.* Cambridge: Cambridge University Press.

Tullock, Gordon (1994) 'Is Public Choice Inherently Anti-Socialist'. Public debate: LSE.

Williamson, Oliver E. (1996) *The Mechanisms of Governance.* New York: Oxford University Press.

Wittman, Donald (1989) 'Why Democracies Produce Efficient Results', *Journal of Political Economy* 97(6): 1395–424.

Wittman, Donald (1995) *The Myth of Democratic Failure: Why Political Institutions are Efficient.* Chicago: University of Chicago Press.

Interpretive Theory

Mark Bevir

All kinds of social scientists show an interest in meanings. Institutionalism, systems theory, and rational choice theory have all inspired studies of the role of ideas in governance. However, interpretive approaches to governance are about more than studying meanings. They are mainly about a theoretical agenda that highlights the intentionality of actions, practices, and social life. Interpretive theory has a different vision of social science from other approaches to governance.

So, this chapter is not about the role of ideas in governance; it is about interpretive theory. Interpretive theorists believe that meanings are constitutive of actions. They imply that we cannot properly discuss actions and practices apart from the intentionality of actors. People act on beliefs, thus, social scientists can explain actions only by appealing to the beliefs of the actors. Any other supposed cause can influence the way people act only indirectly through their beliefs and wants. Consequently, to grasp the reasons for which someone acted is not just to understand their action but also to give the only proper explanation of their action. Interpretive social scientists do not assume that reasons for action are always conscious and rational. Sometimes they talk of meanings, discourses, and languages, rather than beliefs and reasons,

precisely to suggest that people are not always aware of the reasons for their action let alone in control of these reasons. Nonetheless, almost all interpretive social scientists believe that governance arises out of actions laden with meanings.

The first section of this chapter discusses the contrast between interpretive theory and positivist and modernist alternatives. The second section considers the different varieties of interpretive theory. The third section asks how interpretive theory changes our understanding of governance, especially changes in the state since the late twentieth century. This chapter then ends by exploring the implications of interpretive theory for policymaking.

INTERPRETATION VS POSITIVISM

The dazzling achievements of the natural sciences have exerted an enormous pressure on the social sciences to model themselves on the former. Positivists believe that we should study the natural and social worlds in the same way. Initially, in the nineteenth century, positivists wanted to exclude appeals to supernatural causes. They argued that humans were part of nature, and so open to empirical study using a scientific method based on the rigorous collection and sifting of facts. Later, by the middle of the twentieth century, positivists began to argue that the social sciences should search for causal and predictive explanations akin to those in the natural sciences (Ayer, 1967; Hempel, 1942). This positivism suggests that the social sciences study fixed objects with observable and, to some extent, measurable properties. Social scientists explain these objects by general laws, albeit general laws that assign probabilities to different outcomes.

Philosophers have increasingly turned against positivism. They argue the intentional nature of action requires an interpretive social science, aiming for historical understanding (*verstehen*). This defense of interpretation appears in the hermeneutic tradition, starting with the work of Wilhelm Dilthey (1976) at the turn of the twentieth century, and extending more recently to philosophers such as Hans-Georg Gadamer (2002) and Paul Ricoeur (1976). A similar defense of interpretation also now dominates anglophone philosophy, following the leads provided by Ludwig Wittgenstein (2001), Alasdair MacIntyre (1969), and Charles Taylor (1971).

Interpretive theorists argue that social science cannot take natural science as a model. Human life is intentional and historical in ways that set it apart from the rest of nature. I will explore intentionality and historicity and show they apply to social scientists as well as those they study.

Intentionality

Consider the intentional nature of social life. Some positivists argue that we confirm explanations by their fit with observations, and meanings are irrelevant because we cannot observe them (Skinner, 1938; Watson, 1924). Few social scientists still believe in this strong positivism. Most accept that agents act for reasons of their own, where these reasons may be irrational or unconscious. Today what divides positivist and interpretive theorists is

the role they give to meanings in explaining actions. Positivists want meanings to drop out of these explanations. They argue that to give the reasons for an action is merely to redescribe that action. If we want to explain an action, they add, then we have to show how it – and so agents' reasons – conforms to a general law referring to social facts (Ayer, 1967).

Interpretive theorists refuse to let meanings drop out of explanations in the social sciences. They argue that meanings are constitutive of human action. Thus, as Clifford Geertz claimed, social science is 'not an experimental science in search of law but an interpretive one in search of meaning' (1973: 5). Positivists often respond by saying that social science concerns structures such as traffic jams that are unintended consequences of actions. However, structures such as traffic jams scarcely undermine interpretive theory. Most of what social scientists want to know about traffic jams comes down to intentional actions. To explain why people are driving when and where they are, we need to know whether they intend to go to work, a sports game, shopping, or visiting relatives. Alternatively, we may explore the meanings that define the social practices to which their beliefs refer. Why do people believe that driving to work is better than using public transport? All such questions concern intentionality. An account of traffic jams that ignored intentionality would be thin and inadequate. It would tell us only in purely physical terms that a traffic jam arose because a given number of people tried to drive cars along a stretch of road of given dimensions. It would tell us nothing about the actions that had these physical results. It would not tell us why these people were driving their cars or why the roads were as they were.

The centrality of meanings in social science reflects the fact not only that actions are intentional but also that these meanings are holistic. Social scientists can properly explain people's beliefs only by placing them in a wider web. They cannot reduce beliefs to social facts since the content of a belief depends on its place among other beliefs. Social science needs contextual explanations.

Interpretive theory draws here on holistic theories of meaning. The idea of a hermeneutic circle entails meaning holism: Gadamer wrote, 'as the single word belongs in the total context of the sentence, so the single text belongs in the total context of a writer's work' (2002: 291). Semiotics treats signs as getting content from their place within a system of signs (Peirce, 1998; Saussure, 1966). Analytic and post-analytic philosophers often argue that concepts refer only in webs of belief or language games (Quine and Ulian, 1970; Wittgenstein, 2001). Most philosophers now agree that we explain beliefs by reference to wider webs, not by reference to objective categories such as social class or institutional position, and not by construing meanings as 'independent variables' in naturalist forms of explanation.

Historicity

Let us turn now to the historicity of human action. When positivists let meanings drop out of their explanations, they point to classifications, correlations, and regularities that hold across various cases. Even when they renounce the ideal of a universal theory, they still regard historical contingency and contextual specificity as obstacles that need to be overcome in the search for cross-temporal and cross-cultural regularities. Positivists characteristically search for causal connections that bestride time and space. They try to control for all kinds of variables to arrive at parsimonious explanations.

Interpretive theorists argue that the role of meanings in social life precludes ahistorical explanations. However, we should be careful how we phrase what is at issue here. Interpretive theorists have no reason to deny that we can make general claims that cover diverse cases. Rather, they object to two specific features of positivist generalizations.

First, interpretive theorists deny that general statements are a uniquely powerful form of social knowledge. To the contrary, they consider statements about the unique and contingent features of social life to be as valuable as general statements. Generalizations often deprive our understanding of social life: of what is most distinctly and significantly human about it.

Secondly, interpretive theorists reject the claim that ahistorical generalizations can not explain particular cases. Such generalizations are mere descriptions. Just as we can say various objects are red without explaining anything else about them, so we can say various countries are democracies without explaining any other feature they have in common. Interpretive theorists reject explanations of actions that rely on transhistorical generalities because they think that actions are inherently contingent.

Most philosophers now argue that the social sciences use languages assuming choice and contingency and so are incompatible with the forms of explanation found in the natural sciences (Davidson, 1980). In this view, the intentionality of actions means that to explain them we must invoke the reasons of the actors in a way that implies the actors could have reasoned and acted differently. Actions are the products of decisions, not the determined outcomes of general laws. Thus, social science needs narrative explanations that work by unpacking the contingent and particular conditions of actions and events, rather than by searching for transhistorical models, classifications, or correlations.

Reflexivity

Interpretive theory emphasizes the intentional and contingent nature of action, which applies to social scientists as well as the objects they study. Also, social scientists come to hold particular webs of belief against the background of contingent traditions.

Positivists usually treat the situatedness of the social scientist as an obstacle to be overcome in creating proper knowledge. They want social scientists to abstract themselves from their historical perspectives, arguing that social scientists can produce valid scientific knowledge only if they divest themselves of their prejudices. In contrast, interpretive theorists deny the possibility of abstracting ourselves from our prior webs of beliefs. They suggest that social science always takes place from within particular linguistic, historical, and normative standpoints. The questions social scientists ask and the concepts they use always reflect their existing webs of belief.

The situatedness of the social scientist makes the study of governance dialogical. Positivists construe explanation as a unidirectional subject–object relationship. Their neglect of the constitutive role of meanings leads them to think of the social scientist as the only agent involved in crafting explanations. The objects of social science are just that – passive objects. In contrast, interpretive theorists think of explanation as involving a dialogue between social scientists and those they study. Social science involves an interaction in which scholars respond to the interpretations of the actors they study. This interaction with the beliefs of social actors always has the potential to send out ripples through their own beliefs, altering their understanding of their research agenda, the traditions in which they work, or their normative commitments.

VARIETIES OF INTERPRETATION

Interpretive theory stands in opposition to the lukewarm positivism that still dominates the study of governance. Yet, interpretive theory is not monolithic. This section introduces some of the varieties of interpretive theory. Table 4.1 provides a brief outline. These varieties are neither mutually exclusive nor cover all there is of interpretive theory: they merely show diversity.

Governmentality

Michel Foucault's essay on governmentality first appeared in English in 1978 in a collection of essays, *The Foucault Effect: Studies in Governmentality*, edited by Graham Burchell, Colin Gordon, and Peter Miller (Foucault, 1991). Many Anglo-Foucauldians had been attracted to Althusser's theory of social control, and this theory also influenced Foucault (Resch, 1992; Stedman Jones, 1996). Foucault used structuralist and poststructuralist ideas to imply the distinctions between madness and sanity or sickness and health were products of particular epistemes, not neutral or rational accounts of an independent reality (Foucault, 1989, 1973). He suggested the role of institutions such as asylums and clinics was not the scientific and humanitarian promotion of health, but rather to control and normalize deviant individuals. Governmentality takes a similar approach to governance.

Anglo-Foucauldians often deny that Foucault provided a theory of governance. They take him instead to have sketched out a mode and field of inquiry. The mode of inquiry is genealogies of the power/knowledge that underlie current practices. These genealogies

Table 4.1 Varieties of interpretation

	Governmentality	Post-Marxism	Social humanism
Historical background			
(i) Key thinkers	(i) Structural Marxism; Foucault	(i) Sasussurean lingustics; Gramsci	(i) Idealism; the New Left
(ii) Key concept	(ii) Social control	(ii) Hegemony	(ii) Traditions and dilemmas
Theoretical themes	Power/knowledge	Semiotic code – relations among signifiers	Agency situated in cultural practices
Empirical focus	Technologies of power as ways of making subjects	Collective identities, especially of gender, race, and sexuality	Elite narratives and popular resistance
Example	Barry, Osborne and Rose (1996)	Griggs and Howarth (2000)	Bevir and Rhodes (2003, 2006)

reveal the contingency of modern governance, undermining any idea that it is neutral or unavoidable. The field of inquiry directs us away from an excessive focus on the state and toward the study of the diverse ways subjects are normalized. This field of inquiry includes the diffuse ways in which government and social power impact on populations. It draws attention to the ways discourses and technologies shape conduct to certain ends. As Nikolas Rose explains, 'the state now appears simply as one element – whose functionality is historically specific and contextually variable – in multiple circuits of power, connecting a diversity of authorities and forces, within a whole variety of complex assemblages' (Rose, 1999: 5).

The literature on governmentality portrays governance as composed of various technologies that have arisen as liberalism passed through welfarism into neoliberalism. Nineteenth century liberalism was less a rejection of state intervention than a positive political rationality by which to manage complex societies and economies. Liberalism tried to produce its preferred outcomes through interactions in society and the economy. Welfare states arose because of changes in this liberalism. Modern industrial society produced new social problems, and liberalism then tried to guarantee the security of the economy and state by responding to these social problems with new technologies that collectively formed the welfare state. In this view, public housing, unemployment insurance, and nationalized health care appear as technologies of power that normalize subjects. Finally neoliberalism arose as a response to problems in welfarism. The welfare state and Keynesianism seemed unproductive interferences with market relations, and new rationalities arose to correct them. Neoliberalism consists of governmental technologies that actively foster competitive market relations, simultaneously shifting responsibility to the individual and increasing social efficiency. Under neoliberalism 'it was the responsibility of political government to *actively* create the conditions within which entrepreneurial

and competitive conduct is possible' (Barry, Osborne and Rose 1996: 10).

Anglo-Foucauldians also extend Foucault's concern with the ways, seemingly neutral, that scientific discourses fix particular subjectivities (Rose, 1999). They describe liberalism, welfarism, and neoliberalism as composed of policies that seek to normalize subjects by drawing on technical discourses from disciplines such as medicine, social science, statistics, and public health. Initially, liberalism did not try to manage individual morality so much as guarantee the security of economic relations. Then, in the middle of the nineteenth century, liberal governments began to regulate the morals of particular parts of the population, with institutions such as the poorhouse disciplining people with perceived pathologies of character. In the twentieth century, the welfare state and Keynesianism arose as technologies by which experts tried to govern subjectivities to manage pathologies made visible by new social statistics. Finally, neoliberalism has brought an individualization of responsibility. Where the welfare state embodied a collectivist ethos, neoliberalism makes individuals responsible for their own conduct. Neoliberalism promotes freedom understood as personal choice while using psychology to create new forms of control. Psychological technologies increasingly influence how individuals think about their lives, including sex, consumption, work, and health. These technologies get individuals to discipline themselves to use their freedom to make responsible choices. Individuals analyze and improve their lives in ways that benefit themselves, the community, and the state.

Post-Marxism

Post-Marxists change Antonio Gramsci's idea of hegemony by infusing it with poststructuralist themes. In *Hegemony and Socialist Strategy*, Ernesto Laclau and Chantal Mouffe analyze discourses in terms of the quasi-structural properties of signs, and they trace the properties of these discourses and signs to a quasi-structural psychology drawn from Jacques Lacan. Laclau and Mouffe dissociate Marxism from foundationalism and essentialism. They reject theories that privilege the economic over the ideological and social class over discursively constructed identities. Gramsci used hegemony to refer to class domination through ideology, suggesting bourgeois hegemony explains why the workers consent to capitalism and so why there has not been a revolution. In contrast, Laclau and Mouffe use hegemony to dismiss social theories based on economic and class analysis. In their view, 'the search for a "true" working class and its limits is a false problem, and as such lacks any theoretical or political relevance' (Laclau and Mouffe, 1985: 84).

Laclau and Mouffe think of a discursive formation as 'a configuration, which in certain contexts of exteriority can be *signified* as a totality' (Laclau and Mouffe, 1985: 106). Their language and approach stem from the linguistics of Ferdinand de Saussure (1966). Saussure argued the link between a signified (or concept) and a signifier (or word) is arbitrary. Any signifier can evoke any signified provided only that it differs from other signifiers. The value of any signifier comes solely from relations of difference in a system of signs. Poststructuralists often suggest the relation between concepts and reality is similarly arbitrary: concepts gain meaning only from the relations of difference among them.

A Saussurean legacy appears in three prominent features of Laclau and Mouffe's idea of discourse. First, Laclau and Mouffe dismiss concerns with the relationship of discourses to any extra-discursive reality. Sometimes they imply the world, including class antagonisms, is a product of discourses. At other times they allow for an extra-discursive reality while contending that only signs in existing discourses can be grasped. Secondly, Laclau and Mouffe stress the constitutive role of relations of difference both within and between discourses. They imply that in any given discourse a binary structure governs identities, and all discourses are defined by opposition to an excluded other. Thirdly, Laclau and Mouffe dismiss agency. They argue that discourses define what individuals can say and do. And they analyze discourses in terms of structural relations among signs, not the ways agents use language.

Laclau and Mouffe tie their concept of discourse to Lacan's psychoanalytic theory. In their account, the subject desires 'fullness', conceived as psychological stability based on integrating the self with the other. Yet, this desire for fullness is thwarted by a primordial 'lack' since there is always doubt whether the 'other' has recognized the self. This lack means the other gets blamed for blocked identity. A quasi-structural antagonism between self and other is thus integral to identity formation.

According to Laclau and Mouffe, the same quasi-structural logic applies to discourses. On the one hand, discourses exhibit a logic of equivalence: they try to integrate many views into one worldview, stressing commonalities in contrast to another. On the other hand, discourses exhibit a logic of difference: they are constituted by an antagonism to the other – an antagonism that always limits the extent to which they can achieve integration. The interplay between equivalence and difference in discourses sets up hegemonic struggles.

Most applications of post-Marxism concentrate on discourses connected with identities of gender and race. There is little work addressed to governance. One exception is Griggs and Howarth's (2000) analysis of the campaign against Manchester Airport's second runway. They think of interests and identities as social constructs. In their case study of the runway, they ask how local village residents and direct action protestors overcame a collective action problem. Their explanation has three elements. First, there was strong group identity in that all were affected by the environmental costs of the runaway. Secondly, there was a social network and political entrepreneurs. There was a strong and activist, conservationist tradition in the villages. The leaders of the several associations could call on the support of professional people and so lower the costs of the campaign. Thirdly, new political identities emerged – 'the Vegans and the Volvos'. Middle-class protestors saw democratic channels as unreliable and so supported more radical forms of protest. This alliance worked because: the pro-runway campaign used heavy-handed tactics and stigmatized residents and protestors alike; the media saw residents and eco-warriors as fighting a common foe; and local political entrepreneurs played policy brokering and support roles. Yet, the protestors lost. The eco-warriors moved on to the next protest site. The residents split over whether to mount a national-level campaign or concentrate on the public inquiry.

Social humanism

Social humanism arose in part as the New Left reworked idealist themes in opposition to positivist philosophy and orthodox Marxism. Philosophers such as Benedetto Croce had turned to radical historicism, implying that beliefs and actions are contingent since the moment of choice is open. Croce influenced other philosophers who opposed positivism and modernist empiricism. R.G. Collingwood remained a rare champion of historicism as logical positivism swept through Oxford (Collingwood, 1940, 1946; Rubinoff, 1996). Later, Taylor drew on idealism, phenomenology, and historicism to challenge behavioralism (1964, 1971). Typically, these philosophers moved from the idealist ideas of mind, teleology, and unity towards ones of action, contingency, and diversity, while still espousing vitalist analyses of action and placing agency and freedom in social contexts.

Post-idealists such as Taylor and MacIntyre were also part of the New Left. Other figures in the New Left drew on Croce's historicism, often by Antonio Gramsci, to break with determinism and economism. E.P. Thompson

and Raymond Williams (1961; also see Dworkin, 1997) granted autonomy to human agency, consciousness, and culture, while still seeing them as sites of the contradictions and conflicts associated with capitalism. Yet, while Williams made culture a prominent concern for the New Left, the rise of cultural studies owed much to Stuart Hall and his work as Director of the Centre for Contemporary Cultural Studies at the University of Birmingham. Hall followed the New Left in thinking of culture as a form of expression also found in the everyday life of subordinated groups. Yet, Hall changed the New Left's appeals to lived experience. Williams described cultures of resistance as responses to experiences of the brutal realities of capitalism. Hall paid more attention to the way ideological traditions framed people's experiences (Hall and Jefferson, 1993). He did not return to the old view that ideologies represented a false consciousness that hid the reality of the class struggle. He just insisted that ideology was a site of struggle for social change.

Social humanists explore the conflicting ideologies and traditions found in modern governance. They show how several different traditions contribute to governing practices. Governments may promote policies inspired by a particular tradition. Yet, other actors typically develop and fulfill these policies in accord with beliefs inspired by other traditions. These actors, whether intentionally or unintentionally, draw on diverse cultures to resist the governing stories. For example, John Clarke argues that narratives of choice are particular not universal, and service providers and citizens are skeptical of official narratives (Clarke, 2007). His interviews in policy areas such as policing and health reveal popular resistance to the appropriateness of 'consumer' and 'choice' as identities. Service providers and service users alike believe the idea of choice sits uneasily alongside values such as equity. Citizens resist the language of choice and shopping as inappropriate for policing and health care.

Social humanists highlight the diverse nature of governance. In doing so, they imply that governmentality and post-Marxism may adopt too monolithic an analysis of governance. Governmentality theorists, with their debt to ideas of social control, focus on official discourses and policies, paying little attention to local levels. Social humanists, with their debt to the idea of traditions of resistance, explore the diverse ways in which street-level bureaucrats and citizens practice governance in their everyday lives. The focus thus shifts from the discourse of policymakers to the fractured and diverse processes by which discourses and policies become actions.

INTERPRETING GOVERNANCE

The different varieties of interpretive theory all highlight the intentional and contingent nature of action in a way that has relevance to the study of governance. Yet, social humanism has inspired more work on governance than has post-Marxism or governmentality. Post-Marxism and governmentality often seem more interested in discourses or official documents than in the administrative arrangements and policies of modern states and societies. Nonetheless, social humanists have developed and applied theories of networks and governance across various levels of government, policy sectors, and comparative cases (Bache and Catney, 2008; Bevir and Rhodes, 2003, 2006; Bevir and Richards, 2009; Bevir and Trentmann, 2007; Bevir, Rhodes and Weller, 2003; Clark and Gains, 2007; Craig, 2006; Dinham and Lowndes, 2008; Dudley, 2003; Finlayson, 2008; Irazabal, 2005; Jose, 2007; Monro, 2006; Morrell, 2006; Orr, 2005; Rhodes et al., 2007; Richards and Smith, 2004; Stoker, 2006; Wood et al., 2008; Yi-Chong and Weller, 2007).

Rethinking governance

Interpretive theory encourages us to examine the ways individuals act on their beliefs to create, sustain, and modify governance. Interpretive theory also insists that these beliefs do not simply reflect people's allegedly given interests or institutional locations. Rather, people reach the beliefs they do by changing an inherited tradition to respond to dilemmas. Because we cannot read-off people's beliefs from knowledge of social facts about them, we have to explore both how traditions prompt them to adopt certain beliefs and how dilemmas prompt them to change traditions. A tradition is a set of theories, stories, and associated practices people inherit that then forms the background against which they hold beliefs and perform actions. A dilemma arises for people when a new belief, often itself an interpretation of an experience, stands in opposition to their existing ones, thereby forcing a reconsideration of the latter.

Different people draw on different traditions to reach different beliefs about a pattern of governance. Often their beliefs include some about the failings of existing arrangements. When their understanding of these failings conflicts with their existing beliefs, the failures pose dilemmas for them. The dilemmas then push them to reconsider their beliefs and so the traditions that inform those beliefs. Crucially, because people confront these dilemmas against the background of diverse traditions, there arises a political contest over the nature of the failings and the solutions to them. Exponents of rival positions seek to promote their particular ideas and policies. This contest often leads to reforms of governance – reforms that thus arise as a contingent product of a contest of meanings in action. The reformed pattern of governance then displays new failings, posing new dilemmas, and producing competing proposals for reform. There is another contest over meanings, a contest in which the dilemmas are often significantly different, and the traditions have been modified in response to the previous dilemmas. Of course, while we can distinguish analytically between patterns of governance and a contest over reforms, we rarely can do so temporally.

Rather, governing continues during the contests, and the contests occur largely within practices of governing. Governance thus consists of a complex and continuous process of interpretation, conflict, and action that produces ever-changing patterns of rule.

Interpretive theory transforms our understanding of governance at the global, national, and local levels. We might begin by examining how diverse state traditions have led to different interpretations and practices of governance. We could ask if the Danish emphasis on local government and popular participation promotes efforts to keep changing, and perhaps multiplying, markets and networks under democratic control. We could ask whether the Germanic tradition, with its emphasis on the importance of a legal framework to official action, encourages attempts to control markets and networks at the center while remaining tolerant of their diversity at other levels. If we found continuity, we would not assume we could explain it by a vague appeal to institutional patterns. Instead we would unpack institutional patterns by reference to political conflicts and compromises between groups inspired by diverse beliefs. In the German case, for example, we might explore the alternative interpretations of the country's postwar development offered by a liberal tradition, a tradition of social partnership, and a radical democratic and environmentalist tradition.

What difference does it make?

An interpretive theory of governance differs from both the neoliberal narrative and that of governance as networks. It encourages us, first, to understand governance as political contests based on competing beliefs and, secondly, to explain these beliefs by reference to traditions and dilemmas. In doing so, it points toward novel perspectives on questions that recur in discussions of governance.

Is governance new?
Social scientists sometimes suggest the rise of markets or networks in the public sector represents a new epoch. Their skeptical critics argue that markets and networks are not new, even that governance is no different from government. In reply to such skeptics, proponents of governance have accepted that neither markets nor networks are new while insisting that both of them are now noticeably more common than they used to be (Rhodes, 1997: 46–61). The debate about the novelty of governance thus ends with the facile and no doubt impossible task of counting markets and networks in the past and present.

Interpretive theory casts new light on this facile debate. For a start, interpretive theory encourages us to treat hierarchies and markets as meaningful practices created and constantly recreated through contingent actions informed by diverse webs of belief. Governance is not new in that it is an integral part of social life. We find the allegedly special characteristics of networks in hierarchies and markets as well as governance. For example, the rules and commands of a bureaucracy do not have a fixed form but rather are constantly interpreted and made afresh through the creative actions of individuals as they come across always slightly novel circumstances. Also, competition in markets depends on the contingent beliefs and interactions of interdependent producers and consumers who rely on trust and diplomacy as well as economic rationality to make decisions. Once we stop reifying hierarchies and markets, we find that many of allegedly unique characteristics of networks are ubiquitous in social organization.

However, interpretive theory also encourages a shift of focus from reified networks, now recognized as an integral part of political life, to the beliefs of political actors and the stories told by political scientists. Governance is new in that it marks and inspires a significant change in these beliefs and stories.

Is governance a vague metaphor?
Skeptics who say governance is nothing new often go on to denounce the concept as

uninformative and inelegant. Peter Riddell has said, for example, 'every time I see the word "governance" I have to think again what it means and how it is not the same as government'. He complains, 'terms such as "core executive", "differentiated polity" and "hollowed out executive" have become almost a private patois of political science' (Riddell, nd). Presumably we should defend concepts when they provide more accurate and fruitful ways of discussing the world. Yet Riddell opposes the concept 'governance' not because he thinks it inaccurate but because it lacks clarity. To respond to his concerns, we might ask, what gives clarity to a concept?

Interpretive theory implies that concepts get their meaning from their location in a web. All concepts are vague when taken on their own. Governance may gain clarity from related ideas such as the hollow state and core executive. Yet, elder concepts – such as, for example, the Westminster Model – gain clarity from ideas such as the unitary state and cabinet government. No doubt people who are unfamiliar with concepts such as the hollow state will benefit from having them plainly related to processes such as a decline in state authority. Equally, however, people who are unfamiliar with the concept of a unitary state might benefit from having it plainly related to the fusion of a single transnational authority or the contrast provided by federal systems.

Although the terminology of governance can sound metaphorical, we need not worry about this. It is metaphorical only in that it applies novel names, such as the hollow state, to processes and practices we can unpack in more familiar terms, such as the erosion of the authority of the state. What is more, most concepts begin as metaphors in just this sense. They begin as novel names such as "loyal opposition" for familiar processes and practices. Only later do they acquire a familiarity such that they no longer have the unsettling effect they once did.

Is governance uniform?
Neoliberals portray governance as composed of policies, such as marketization and the new public management, which are allegedly unavoidable outcomes of global economic pressures. Institutionalists argue that these neoliberal policies do not have uniform outcomes; rather, the effects of the policies vary across states according to the content and strength of existing practices. Interpretive theory suggests, in addition, that the pressures are not given as brute facts, but constructed as different dilemmas from within various traditions. Interpretive theory suggests the policies a state adopts are not necessary responses to given pressures, but a set of perceived solutions to one particular set of concerns.

By raising the possibility of diversity of inputs and policies as well as outputs, interpretive theory may prompt us to wonder again about the idea of 'new governance'. 'The new governance' typically refers to a set of shared inputs, policies, and outputs tied to economic and technological developments since about 1970. Once we challenge the necessity and commonality of not only the outputs but also the inputs and policies, we may reject both the dichotomy between governance and government, and the attempt to use the idea of the new governance to explain developments in particular states. The worth of the idea of the new governance will depend on empirical studies that explore the ways in which different states have remade their public sectors. How similar have been their conceptions of the relevant dilemmas, the policies they have adopted, and the results of these policies? How far have different state traditions fed through into diverse inputs, policies, and outputs?

How does governance change?
Neoliberals can unpack change in terms of the self-interest of actors. Network theorists, in contrast, often use an institutionalism that remains ambiguous about the nature of change. To avoid the need to interpret beliefs and desires, institutionalists often reduce individual behavior to the following of rules that make up institutions, but, of course, if individuals merely follow rules, they cannot

be the causes of change. To explain change, therefore, institutionalists often appeal to external factors (Marsh and Rhodes, 1992). But external factors can bring about change in an institution only if they lead appropriate individuals to modify their behavior, and we can explain why individuals do this only by interpreting their beliefs and desires.

Interpretive theory reminds us that external factors influence networks and governance only through the ways they are understood by the relevant actors. No doubt change can be of varying extent. But interpretive theory implies it is continuous in that it is built into the nature of action. Change occurs as individuals interpret their environment in ways that lead them constantly to alter their beliefs. We can explain change as arising from the contingent responses of individuals to dilemmas.

Is governance failure unavoidable?

The neoliberal narrative of governance relies heavily on the idea that hierarchy has failed. The problems of inefficiency and overload justify calls for the new public management and marketization. The narrative of governance as networks similarly relies on the idea that the neoliberal reforms have failed because they ignored the need for trust, diplomacy, and accountability in the public sector. Some advocates of governance as networks present networks as the solution to the failings of bureaucracy and markets. There is an extensive literature on the conditions under which networks thrive (Lowndes and Skelcher, 1998; Powell, 1991). Other governance scholars argue that networks typically create problems of their own: they are closed to outsiders, unrepresentative, and relatively unaccountable, and they can serve private interests as well as being difficult to steer and inefficient (Rhodes, 1997: Chap. 3). Perhaps no governing structure works for all services in all conditions. Governance failure is unavoidable.

Interpretive theory complements and challenges this account of governance failure. A focus on contingent meanings provides us with one way of understanding why all forms of governance fail. The workings of a policy or institution depend on the ways various actors interpret the relevant directives. Because these responses are inherently diverse and contingent, reflecting the traditions and agency of the relevant individuals, the center cannot have prior knowledge of the way any policy or institution will work. Thus, the unexpected pervades governance. All policies are subject to unintended consequences that prevent them from fulfilling their purpose.

Here too, interpretive theory shows the diverse beliefs and preferences of the actors in a network. Many debates on governance failure blithely take government aims as their yardstick. Positivists typically aim to improve the chances of a policy's success in terms defined by the state. Yet civil servants and citizens can deliberately try to prevent policies having the effects the state intends. From their standpoint, policy failure may be a success.

CONCLUSION: IMPLICATIONS FOR POLICYMAKING

Interpretive theory provides a distinct account of governance that highlights intentionality and historicity. To end, we might note how a self-reflexive awareness of intentionality and historicity also alters our approach to governance as a practical program of policymaking. Interpretive theory points here to advice for practitioners. Policy-orientated work on governance usually tries to improve the capacity of the state to manage markets and networks. It treats markets and networks as objectified structures that governments try to manipulate using suitable tools (Salamon, 2002). In contrast, interpretive theory challenges the idea of a set of tools for managing governance. If governance is made differently, contingently, and continuously, we cannot have a tool kit for managing it. Statistics, models, and claims to expertise all have a place in policymaking, but we should not become too preoccupied with them. They are just narratives about how people have acted and may react given our sense of their beliefs and desires. No matter what rigor or expertise we bring to bear, all we can do is tell a story and judge what the future might bring. Interpretive theory suggests, therefore, that policymakers learn by telling stories and listening to them. The fate of policies depends on how civil servants, citizens, and others respond to them from within all sorts of traditions. The management of networks is in large part about trying to understand and respond to the beliefs of those one hopes to influence.

Here, interpretive theories of governance overlap with interpretive, argumentative, narrative, and storytelling approaches to policy analysis (Fischer and Forester, 1993; Hajer and Wagenaar, 2003; Roe, 1994; Yanow, 1999). Interpretive theory encourages 'those approaches to examining policy that emphasize how the initiation, contestation, adoption, implementation, and evaluation of any policy are shaped by the discursive, narrative, symbolic practices which socially construct our understanding of problems, methods of treatment and criteria of success' (Schram, 1993: 252).

Interpretive policy analysis is, moreover, a prominent part of the lived experience of many policy actors. Storytelling and dialogue are common not among policymakers. In public and private organizations, managers use stories to gain and pass on information, to inspire involvement, and as a repository of the organization's institutional memory. As Rein suggests (1973: 74–5), policy advice often uses 'illustrative stories, or accounts from past experience, which suggest how the future might unfold if certain actions were taken'. The task of the policy analyst 'is to invent objectively grounded normative stories, to participate in designing programmes of intervention based upon them and to test the validity of stories that others commend'.

Theories of governance are often abstract. Sometimes it is good to bring them down to earth. Many policy advisers accept that the art of storytelling is an integral part of their work. Phrases such as: 'Have we got our story straight?', 'Are we telling a consistent story?', and 'What is our story?' abound. The basis for much advice is the collective memory of the agency – its traditions, if you will. Advisors explain past practice and events to justify recommendations for the future. In short, interpretive theory is not an example of academic whimsy. It reflects both an explicit epistemology and the everyday practice of policymakers.

REFERENCES

Ayer, A. (1967) 'Man as a Subject for Science', in P. Laslett and W. Runciman (eds), *Philosophy, Politics and Society*, 3rd Series. Oxford: Basil Blackwell.

Bache, I. and Catney, P. (2008) 'Embryonic Associationalism: New Labour and Urban Governance', *Public Administration* 86: 411–28.

Barry, A., Osborne, T. and Rose, N. (1996) 'Introduction', in A. Barry, T. Osborne and N. Rose (eds), *Foucault and Political Reason*. London: UCL Press.

Bevir, M. and Rhodes, R. (2003) *Interpreting British Governance*. London: Routledge.

Bevir, M. and Rhodes, R. (2006) *Governance Stories*. London: Routledge.

Bevir, M. and Richards, D. (eds) (2009) *Decentring Policy Networks*. A special issue of *Public Administration* 88/1.

Bevir, M. and Trentmann, F. (eds) (2007) *Governance, Consumers, and Citizens: Agency and Resistance in Contemporary Politics*. Basingstoke: Palgrave Macmillan.

Bevir, M., Rhodes, R. and Weller, P. (eds) (2003) *Traditions of Governance: History and Diversity*. A special issue of *Public Administration* 81/1.

Clark, K. and Gains, F. (eds) (2007) *Constructing Delivery: Implementation as an Interpretive Process*, a special issue of *Critical Policy Analysis* 1/2.

Clarke, J. (2007) ' "It's Not Like Shopping": Citizens, Consumers, and the Reform of Public Services', in M. Bevir and F. Trentmann (eds), *Governance, Consumers, and Citizens: Agency and Resistance in Contemporary Politics*. Basingstoke: Palgrave Macmillan.

Collingwood, R. (1940) *An Essay on Metaphysics*. Oxford: Clarendon Press.

Collingwood, R. (1946) in T. Knox (ed.), *The Idea of History*. Oxford: Clarendon Press.

Craig, D. (2006) 'Community Well-Being Strategy and the Legacies of the New Institutionalism and New Public Management in Third Way New Zealand', in L. Bauld, K. Clarke and T. Maltby (eds), *Social Policy Review: Analysis and Debate in Social Policy*. Bristol: Policy Press.

Davidson, D. (1980) *Essays on Actions and Events*. Oxford: Clarendon Press.

Dilthey, W. (1976) *Selected Writings*, ed. and trans. H. Rickman. Cambridge: Cambridge University Press.

Dinham, A. and Lowndes, V. (2008) 'Religion, Resources, and Representation: Three Narratives of Faith Engagement in British Urban Governance', *Urban Affairs Review* 43: 817–45.

Dudley, G. (2003) 'Ideas, Bargaining and Flexible Policy Communities: Policy Change and the Case of the Oxford Transport Strategy', *Public Administration* 81: 433–58.

Dworkin, D. (1997) *Cultural Marxism in Postwar Britain: History, the New Left, and the Origins of Cultural Studies*. Durham, NC: Duke University Press.

Finlayson, A. (2007) 'Characterizing New Labour: The Case of the Child Trust Fund', *Public Administration* 86: 95–110.

Fischer, F. and Forester, J. (eds) (1993) *The Argumentative Turn in Policy Analysis and Planning*. Durham, NC: Duke University Press.

Foucault, M. (1973) *Birth of the Clinic: An Archaeology of Medical Perception*. London: Tavistock.

Foucault, M. (1989) *Madness and Civilization: A History of Insanity in the Age of Reason*. London: Routledge.

Foucault, M. (1991) 'Governmentality', in G. Burchell, C. Gordon and P. Miller (eds), *The Foucault Effect: Studies in Governmentality*. London: Harvester Wheatsheaf.

Gadamer, Hans-Georg (2002) *Truth and Method*. New York: Continuum.

Geertz, C. (1973) *The Interpretation of Cultures: Selected Essays*. New York: Basic Books.

Griggs, S. and Howarth, D. (2000) 'New Environmental Movements and Direct Action Protests: The Campaign against Manchester Airport's Second Runway', in D. Howarth, A.J. Norval and Y. Stavrakakis (eds), *Discourse Theory and Political Analysis*. Manchester: Manchester University Press.

Hajer, M. and Wagenaar, H. (eds) (2003) *Deliberative Policy Analysis: Understanding Governance in the Network Society*. Cambridge: Cambridge University Press.

Hall, S. and Jefferson, T. (eds) (1993) *Resistance through Rituals: Youth Subcultures in Post-war Britain*. London: Routledge.

Hempel, C. (1942) 'The Function of General Laws in History', *Journal of Philosophy* 39: 35–48.

Irazabal, C. (2005) *City Making and Urban Governance in the Americas: Curitiba and Portland*. London: Ashgate.

Jose, J. (2007). 'Reframing the "Governance" Story', *Australian Journal of Political Science* 42: 455–70.

Laclau, E. and Mouffe, C. (1985) *Hegemony and Socialist Strategy: Towards a Radical Democratic Politics*. New York: Verso.

Lowndes, V. and Skelcher, C. (1998) 'The Dynamics of Multi-Organisational Partnerships: An Analysis of Changing Modes of Governance', *Public Administration* 76: 313–33.

MacIntyre, A. (1969) 'A Mistake about Causality in Social Science', in P. Laslett and W. Runciman (eds), *Philosophy, Politics and Society*, 2nd Series. Oxford: Basil Blackwell.

Marsh, D. and Rhodes, R. (1992) *Policy Networks in British Government*. Oxford: Clarendon Press.

Monro, S. (2006) 'New Institutionalism and Sexuality at Work in Local Government', *Gender, Work, and Organization* 14: 1–19.

Morrell, K. (2006) 'Policy as Narrative: New Labour's Reform of the National Health Service', *Public Administration* 84: 367–85.

Orr, K. (2005) 'Interpreting Narratives of Local Government Change under the Conservatives and New Labour', *British Journal of Politics and International Relations* 7: 371–85.

Peirce, C. (1998) 'Pragmatism', in *Essential Peirce: Selected Philosophical Writings*, Vol. 2: *1893–1913*. Bloomington, IN: Indiana University Press, pp. 398–433.

Powell, W. (1991) 'Neither Market Nor Hierarchy: Networks of Organization', in Thompson, G., Frances J., Levacic, R. and Mitchell, J. (eds), *Markets, Hierarchies and Networks: The Coordination of Social Life*. London: SAGE.

Quine, W. and Ullian, J. (1970) *The Web of Belief*. New York: Random House.

Rein, M. (1973) *Social Science and Public Policy*. Harmondsworth: Penguin Books.

Resch, R. (1992) *Althusser and the Renewal of Marxist Social Theory*. Berkeley, CA: University of California Press.

Rhodes, R. (1997) *Understanding Governance*. Buckingham: Open University Press.

Rhodes, R., P. 't Hart, and Noordegraaf, M. (eds) (2007) *Observing Government Elites: Up Close and Personal*. Basingstoke: Palgrave Macmillan.

Richards, D. and Smith, M. (2004) 'Interpreting the World of Political Elites', *Public Administration* 82: 777–800.

Ricoeur, P. (1976) *Interpretation Theory: Discourse and the Surplus of Meaning*. Fort Worth: Texas Christian University Press.

Ridell, P. (nd) 'Portrait of the Whitehall Programme', Unpublished ms.

Roe, E. (1994). *Narrative Policy Analysis: Theory and Practice*. Durham, NC: Duke University Press.

Rose, N. (1999) *Powers of Freedom: Reframing Political Thought*. Cambridge: Cambridge University Press.

Rubinoff, L. (1996) 'The Relation between Philosophy and History in the Thought of Bendetto Croce and R. G. Collingwood', *Collingwood Studies* 3: 137–72.

Salamon, L. (ed.) (2002) *The Tools of Government: A Guide to the New Governance*. Oxford: Oxford University Press.

Saussure, F. (1966) *Course in General Linguistics*, trans. W. Baskin, ed. C. Bally and A. Sechehaye. New York: McGraw-Hill.

Schram, S.F. (1993) 'Postmodern Policy Analysis: Discourse and Identity in Welfare Policy', *Policy Sciences* 26: 249–70.

Skinner, B. (1938) *The Behavior of Organisms: An Experimental Analysis*. New York: Appleton-Century.

Stedman Jones, G. (1996) 'The Determinist Fix: Some Obstacles to the Further Development of the Linguistic Approach to History in the 1990s', *History Workshop* 42: 19–35.

Stoker, G. (2006) 'Public Value Management: A New Narrative for Networked Governance?' *American Review of Public Administration* 36: 41–57.

Taylor, C. (1964) *The Explanation of Behaviour*, London: Routledge.

Taylor, C. (1971) 'Interpretation and the Sciences of Man', *Review of Metaphysics* 25(1): 3–51.

Watson, J. (1924) *Behaviorism*. New York: Norton.

Williams, R. (1961) *The Long Revolution*. London: Chatto and Windrus.

Wittgenstein, Ludwig (2001) *Philosophical Investigations*. Malden, MA: Blackwell.

Wood, J., Flemming, J. and Marks, M. (2008) 'Building the Capacity of Police Change Agents: The Nexus Policing Project', *Policing and Society* 18: 72–87.

Yanow, D. (1999) *Conducting Interpretive Policy Analysis*. London: SAGE.

Yi-Chong, X. and Weller, P. (2007) 'To Be, but Not To Be Seen: Exploring the Impact of International Civil Servants', *Public Administration* 86: 35–51.

5

Organization Theory

Robert K. Christensen and Mary Tschirhart

INTRODUCTION

This chapter discusses a variety of classic organization theories that address governance, directly or indirectly. We review core perspectives and debates in organizational theory (originally framed by Graham Astley and Andrew Van de Ven in 1983) that remain relevant today. The Astley and Van de Ven framework serves as a device for categorizing these theories and illuminating similarities and differences in organization theory approaches. Our contribution is to utilize this categorization scheme to explore how classic organization theories inform an understanding of governance. We illustrate the application of organization theory to governance with examples from the public policy and public administration literatures. Our approach pays particular attention to what each category of theories implies for the study of governance in public administration.

DEFINING GOVERNANCE

There are numerous definitions and usages of the term *governance*. As Lynn, Heinrich and Hill (2000: p 234–5) explain, the term may refer to 'organizational structures, administrative processes, managerial judgment, systems of incentives and rules, administrative philosophies or combinations of these elements.' Governance may be discussed in the context of organizations, policy regimes, networks, and other units of analysis. We defer to Mark Bevir's definition of governance, restated here so it is fresh on the mind of the reader of this *Handbook*: 'Governance refers to theories and issues of social coordination and the nature of all patterns of rule. More specifically, governance refers to ... theories and practices of governing and the dilemmas to which they give rise' (Ch.1). 'Governance in all [of its] guises stands in contrast to elder concepts of government and the state as rather monolithic and formal institutions' (Ch.1). Admittedly, this is a broad conceptualization, but we think it is one that is critical to our overlay of organizational theories onto the governance literature.

PURPOSE OF THE CHAPTER

Most of the classic theories of organization initially developed when the state was viewed monolithically, i.e. hierarchically/centrally (Frederickson and Smith, 2003). The field of organization studies has adapted to address the fundamental dynamics of governance in a public sector and multi-sector context. In part, this recognizes a formative/adaptive dynamic between theory and reality reflected in Astley and Van de Ven's observation that 'organization theory not only reflects organizational reality, it also produces that reality' (1983: 269) and the editor's own view that 'theories that may have been designed for other uses have since been modified to accommodate the governance' (Ch.1).

CHAPTER ORGANIZATION

First, we provide a brief synopsis of classic theories of organization, classified according to the Astley and Van de Ven (1983) framework. Secondly, we review the debates implicit in the resulting categories. As part of this section, we explain how the debates of organizational theory can be articulated to be more specific to issues of governance. Finally, we use illustrative works to demonstrate how contemporary scholars are employing organization theory to enrich our understanding of governance. We show how modern public administration scholars are tackling the key debates of organization theory under a governance approach and suggest that the core questions underpinning these debates remain open.

Rather than exhaustively catalogue the development and nuances of every strand of organization theory relative to governance (a task we might recommend but do not ourselves undertake), we provide a more focused examination of the main perspectives and debates that capture multiple theories. Furthermore, because our approach is intentionally focused on implications for governance, we provide limited attention to when organization theories were introduced and the context surrounding their development. We also are not comprehensive in our

review of single theories, nor do we completely inventory all the theories fitting under particular perspectives. Other chapters in this *Handbook* examine specific theories in greater depth.

CLASSIC ORGANIZATION PERSPECTIVES

There are numerous devices for categorizing organization theories. For example, Scott and Davis (2006) sort them into rational, natural, and open system perspectives. Briefly, they note that some scholars have approached the examination of organizational behavior assuming that actors are rational pursuers of goals (rational system theorists), or part of collectives with common interests that may be informally structured (natural system theorists), or coalitions of shifting interests that develop goals through negotiations that are strongly influenced by the environment (open system theorists). As another example of categorical schemes, Christensen, Laegreid, Roness and Rovik (2007) differentiate among instrumental, cultural, and myth perspectives. In their categorization scheme, their 'denoted instrument' (instrumental) approach is consistent with the rational perspective in which there is an assumption of goal-setting and strategic pursuit of goals after alternatives are assessed. The cultural perspective stresses history and traditions as a source of informal norms and values which shape behavior. The myth perspective focuses on broad environmental 'recipes' that embody beliefs about the design and function of organizations.

Our choice of a categorization scheme for this chapter is from Astley and Van de Ven (1983). Their approach sets up two contrasts. The first is between voluntaristic and deterministic assumptions about human nature and organizational constraints. The second contrast is in level of analysis, macro versus micro. Within these broad contrasts are a cluster of theories that, while sharing some characteristics, are different in other respects. Astley and Van de Ven argue that all organizational theories can be placed into this framework. We adapt their table (Table 5.1) and offer brief descriptions of each of the perspectives, noting the early theorists who help define and broaden each perspective.

Natural selection view

The natural selection view takes a macro-level deterministic perspective. Early representatives of this view include Hannan and Freeman (1977), initial framers of population ecology.

Hannan and Freeman argue that organizations have limits to how much they can adapt to external exigencies given their placement in niches that determine access to resources. The neo-institutional approach shares this orientation in its focus on environmental forces shaping organizations. DiMaggio and Powell (1983) gave us the concept of coercive, mimetic, and normative demands to which organizations react. Meyer and Rowan (1977) were among the first theorists to explore how organizational behavior is influenced by existing values and norms within institutional domains. Early industrial economics (e.g. Caves and Porter, 1977) focused our attention on economic and technical

Table 5.1 Astley and van de Ven's categorization framework for organization theory perspectives

	Deterministic orientation	Voluntaristic orientation
Macro level (populations and communities of organizations)	**Natural selection view** Examples of theoretical schools: population ecology, industrial economics	**Collective action view** Examples of theoretical schools: human ecology, political economy, pluralism
	Structure: environmental competition and carrying capacity predefine niches. Organization is economically and technically determined	Structure: communities or networks of semi-autonomous partisan groups that interact to modify or construct their collective environment, rules, options. Organization is collective action-controlling, liberating, and expanding individual action.
	Assumptions about behavior: Random, natural of economic, environmental selection	Assumptions about behavior: reasonable, collectively constructed and politically negotiated
	Manager role: inactive	Manager role: interactive
Micro level (individual organizations)	**System-structural view**	**Strategic choice view**
	Examples of theoretical schools: structural functionalism, contingency theory	Examples of theoretical schools: contemporary decision, strategic management
	Structure: roles and positions are hierarchically arranged for efficiency in achieving function	Structure: people and their relationships organized and socialized to serve the choices and purposes of people in power.
	Assumptions about behavior: determined, constrained, and adaptive	Assumptions about behavior: constructed, autonomous, and enacted
	Manager role: reactive	Manager role: proactive

Source: adapted from Astley and Van de Ven (1983).

conditions which constrain organizational movement between markets and reduce strategic volition. Coase (1937), Williamson (1975), and Chandler (1977) helped develop the transactions costs approach, arguing that the environment, rather than management, determines organizational change and survival due to costs associated with resource exchanges.

Collective action view

Schools under the collective action view take a macro-level look with the assumption that behavior is largely voluntaristic. The focus here is on networks of symbiotically interdependent yet semi-autonomous organizations. The environment in which these organizations operate is constructed or modified through their interactions. One of the earliest advocates of a human ecology viewpoint, Hawley (1950), advocated that the effects of the natural environment can be mediated through purposive collective action. Through collaborations and networks, interdependent organizations can develop norms, rules, and compromises (Commons and Parsons, 1950). Negotiation is a key feature in the collective action view and its importance is forwarded in the early work of Benson (1975) who focuses on political activity affecting organizational change and survival.

System-structural view

The system-structural view focuses on the micro level of individual organizations and assumes strong determinism. We see the role of environments shaping organizations in structural functionalism, early systems theory (e.g. Pondy and Mitroff, 1979), and contingency theory (Lawrence and Lorsch, 1967). Also under this label, classical management (e.g. Fayol, 1949) and theories of bureaucracy (e.g. Blau and Scott, 1962) emphasize impersonal mechanisms that affect organizations. From the system-structural perspective, it is the managers' role to fine tune structural and technical mechanisms, such as bureaucratic layering and standardization, to keep the components of the organizational machine functioning in an effective and efficient manner. The field of organizational studies is largely founded around system-structural understandings and they still inform many organizational design principles used today.

Strategic choice view

One of the currently most active organization theory perspectives is that of strategic choice with its micro-level, voluntaristic approach. These theories give attention to how organizations can change the environmental conditions under which they operate. Organizations can be designed to take advantage of resources in the environment (see Child, 1972). In contrast to the system-structural emphasis on self-regulating systems, here we see political negotiation and enactment ideas in play. Individuals have the opportunity to construct their worlds. A variety of scholars inspired areas of study under the strategic choice umbrella, including Feldman and March (1981) for symbolic studies, Weick (1979) for phenomenology studies, and Goffman (1961) for interaction studies.

Organization Theory Debates and Their Relevance to Governance

In examining how organization theory is relevant to governance, we probe what Astley and Van de Ven (1983) characterized as the central debates in organization theory. They offered six questions, each answered differently depending on the theoretical perspective taken. Our approach in this section is to engage an overarching debate rather than explicitly review answers to each of the questions. We begin with highlights of the relevance of each question to understanding the governance of public service configurations. Readers may see additional applications of each question to specific strands of the governance literature. Astley and Van de Ven's (1983: 245–6) questions are:

1 Are organizations functionally rational, technically constrained systems, or are they socially constructed, subjectively meaningful embodiments of individual action?

This question speaks directly to the deterministic–voluntaristic debate. Applying it specifically to the topic of governance, we can ask whether governance systems allow for true empowerment. Do we control government or does it operate fairly independently out of its own momentum? Some of the literature on government red tape captures the sense that individual-initiated proactive change is difficult and that rules and structure come to have a life of their own, constraining innovation and choice. The public management reform movement attempted to instill a culture where individual workers felt empowered to take control of their workplaces and introduce changes to improve efficiency and effectiveness. Strategies to create this change in mindset, and case studies suggesting it is possible, offer a view that governance may be socially constructed, where individuals who believe they are empowered can change the established systems that affect their work tasks.

2 Are changes in organizational forms explained by internal adaptation or by environmental selection?

Organizations and governance systems die, though their life spans tend to be much longer in government than in the private sector. When they do die, is it from uncontrollable environmental pressures that shrink the resources available to them? Can we see whole public sector niches withering away, as we do in some of the population ecology cases focused on private business industries? When governmental units are closed or radically changed, was active decision-making from individuals in authority in those units the reason, or was their demise inevitable given environmental conditions? These questions point to a debate about what

explains the seemingly experimental forms of governance in operation today such as public–private partnerships and stakeholder involvement in issue analysis and decision-making. Scholars differ in their views on whether or not the governance forms we see today are a product of evolutionary action in which less effective forms died out due to environmental pressures. Scholars with a more voluntaristic view argue that what we see today as popular or emergent governance forms come from strategic decisions to reject old models not environmental selection.

3 Is organizational life determined by intractable environmental constraints, or is it actively created through strategic managerial choices?

Relative to public administration, this question gets to a key point of the politics administration dichotomy. Can you insulate the management core from the political environment? Many public administration scholars blend voluntaristic and deterministic factors in their models of policy and management outcomes. Is this blending appropriate if it implies contrary assumptions about the nature of human and organizational behavior? Astley and Van de Ven's question also speaks to the issue of self-steering or self-organizing networks. Rational actors may create properties of networks, but over time do the organizing mechanisms in place replace strategic decision-making in guiding network structures, rules, and outcomes? Is momentum created that shuts off or reduces the possibility of active interventions to switch to new governance models?

4 Is the environment to be viewed as a simple aggregation of organizations governed by external economic forces, or as an integrated collectivity of organizations governed by its own internal social and political forces?

There are many governance questions related to the will of the collective that are informed by classic organization theories. We use this question to direct readers' attention to the role of special interest groups that can work together to affect decisions. Some governance scholars, primarily those drawing from a political science tradition, focus on power dynamics in decision-making, emphasizing that to understand governance, we need to understand who within policy networks or policy communities has power and access to decision-makers. Scholars within the intergovernmental relations field also tend to focus on social and political dynamics, providing models of deliberation processes rather than deterministic environmental forces. They suggest that governance involves the process of combining value judgments and institutions involved in addressing social problems.

5   Is organizational behavior principally concerned with individual or collective action?

This question squarely lays out issues of level of analysis. Applying it to the governance literature we can ask if it is more helpful to focus on characteristics of individual human actors, decision-making units, organizations, networks, or policy communities to shed light on governance philosophies, processes, structures, outcomes, and other variables of interest. We can find policy group studies and social network analyses that lay out interrelationships among actors in a governance network. They suggest that actors are interdependent, and that it is important to understand how organizations and individuals collaborate and cooperate as collective actors. Other governance scholars are concerned with individual experience: for example, predicting motivations, personal satisfaction, and sense of efficacy of citizens with opportunities for involvement in decision-making. The stability of the set of actors involved in decision-making situations can affect the choice of level of analysis. As stability of a decision-making network increases, there may be more opportunity for institutional characteristics and collective action to come into play.

6   Are organizations neutral technical instruments engineered to achieve a goal, or are they institutionalized manifestations of the vested interests and power structure of the wider society?

Not all organizational theorists believe that individuals act to pursue their goals or even that organizational goals are known and accepted by those designated as responsible for their pursuit. To whom or what are governance systems accountable, especially given challenges in identifying goals and their pursuit? Klijn (2008b) argues that European researchers have placed more effort than American researchers on the horizontal accountability systems affecting vertical governance systems. This argument ties into Astley and Van de Ven's question by suggesting that there can be winners and losers in governance. Our assumptions about whether or not rational strategic pursuit of goals occurs and can be successful, given environmental factors, effects governance research questions and theoretical models. Some researchers may approach governance as a neutral tool that can be used strategically to achieve goals, whereas others may see it as an instrument for the most advantaged members of a society that is an inevitable reflection of existing power structures.

DETERMINISM AND VOLUNTARISM: ORGANIZATION THEORY IN GOVERNANCE RESEARCH

Some chapters in this book explore specific organization theories and may provide potential insight into one or more of the six questions above. Our goal, however, is to offer a broader perspective on the connection of organization theory and governance. To make our perspective more concrete, and to enhance insights related to the six questions, collectively, we focus on a general theme common to each point of inquiry: namely, are individuals and their created institutions autonomous, proactive, self-directing agents or are there structural deterministic properties of the context within which governance unfolds?

As we selectively assess the governance literature, we are primarily interested in how authors approach the voluntarism–determinism question that runs through each of Astley and Van de Ven's six questions. Our purpose is not to provide an exhaustive annotated bibliography of the organizational theory literature, but rather to illustrate with a range of examples how modern public administration scholars researching governance have addressed a major ongoing theme in organization theory.

Our methodology in identifying examples is fairly straightforward. We primarily used keyword searches of four top US and international public administration journals, *Public Administration Review, Public Management Review, Journal of Public Administration Research and Theory,* and *Journal of Policy Analysis and Management,* to identify articles that focus on governance, organization theory and/or a specific aspect of organization theory (e.g. transaction costs and population ecology). We also did keyword searches in databases of scholarly articles using 'governance' and 'organizational theory.' Our choice of examples identified through these searches is driven by our intent to overlay the determinism–voluntarism organization theory debate on studies of governance with an eye towards future research that might examine more nuanced questions. We preface our review by noting that many of the articles reviewed here do not fall into clean divisions between deterministic and self-directional organization theories. Instead, we primarily found work that seems to fall across a range between these poles. We emphasize this fact by including a 'middle-ground' category that highlights governance work employing a hybrid of deterministic/voluntaristic approaches.

Deterministic governance

In searching the literature, we easily found authors who have applied organization theories to governance questions. Many of these authors employ theorizing that lies primarily in what Williamson (1975) termed

new institutional economics. Richter (2005) and Karna (2009) note that these more deterministic-range theories include, among others, transaction costs, public choice, new institutional economics of history, and new institutionalism of political science and sociology. Karna (2009: 15) observes that this family of theories can simultaneously fit both the micro and macro levels of analysis, but is clearly 'in the deterministic category on orientation dimension.'

Several governance-focused meta-analyses or assessments of the field (Boyne et al., 2003; Forbes and Lynn, 2005; Hill and Lynn, 2005) use public choice-based theories to motivate their processing of the literature. At least by Karna's (2009) standard we might think of this work as primarily deterministic. For example, Hill and Lynn (2005) and Forbes and Lynn (2005) review domestic and international research that evaluates the link between management and public sector governance outcomes. Their analytical framework, the 'logic of governance' is based on assumptions or tenets of public choice theory: 'authority to administrative officers and organizations and the maintenance of appropriate political control over those officers and organizations' (Forbes and Lynn, 2005: 562). Admittedly, their framework entertains many avenues of voluntaristic behavior, such as managerial/administrative discretion behavior. Nevertheless, even these voluntaristic components are circumscribed in public choice theory's deterministic view of delegated authority (i.e. deterministic political environment) and fixed individual utility functions (i.e. rational self-interest).

In their work on contracting, Brown and Potoski (2003) draw upon two deterministic-type organization theories and apply them to governance arrangements. Their study uses transaction costs and neo-institutional theories to frame and probe their investigation of whether governments produce public goods and services internally or externally, i.e. contracting. Based on transaction costs theory they find empirical evidence that management costs (based on monitoring, asset specificity, goal congruence, and specificity of service measurement) influence public service governance configurations (Brown and Potoski, 2003). They also find mixed support for neo-institutional hypotheses. Institutional factors (form and age of government) show some correlation with the decision to jointly or internally produce public goods and services, while city age (industrial vs post-industrial) reveals no such correlation. Brown and Potoski's (2003: 447, 465) conclusions perhaps do too little to recognize the deterministic assumptions of the theories they used, but the authors do entertain that transaction costs and institutional dynamics affect governments' service production choices, including their structure, operation, and their success.

Amirkhanyan, Kim and Lambright's (2008) study of nursing home outcomes and governance arrangements across sectors implicitly emphasizes another set of deterministic theories. Amirkahanyan et al. use goal attainment theory as a point of departure to explore how theories of organizational ownership (e.g. public, private, non-profit) influence organizational performance. Based on public goods theory and contract failure theory (largely new institutional economics approaches), they conclude that environment (sectoral ownership) matters to and even determines organizational outcomes.

Reviewing theoretical approaches to metropolitan governance, Lowery (2000) argued that public-choice theories are less useful to explain metropolitan organization fragmentation and consolidation than conceptual approaches using transactions costs models that emphasize economic forces determining behaviors. Lowery concludes (2000: 73) that, 'just as the advent of firms facilitated the reduction of transactions costs by moving from spot to long-term employment contracts (Williamson 1975), consolidated governments reduce the transactions costs bearing on the adoption of regionally focused policies by relying on democratic choice rather than intergovernmental agreements.' In short, Lowery's work on metropolitan governance applies one of the key questions in organization theory: Are collectives opportunistic or deterministic? In concluding that a transaction costs model may better describe metropolitan governance arrangements, Lowery picks up Williamson's (1975) own argument that the 'shift from markets to hierarchies is explained as a triumph of the interests of the economic "system" as a whole over the opportunistic tendencies of its constituent members' (Astley and Van de Ven, 1983: 255).

A middle ground? Determinism and voluntarism

While many neo-institutional governance studies draw upon deterministic theories, we say again that we do not detect a bright line between deterministic and voluntaristic theories to support a conclusion that there is no place for a 'mixed' approach. For example, Helfstein's study of governance draws heavily from institutional approaches to organization, but he implicitly warns against reliance on any one view of organizations. His recent piece (Helfstein, 2009) utilizes neo-institutional theory, particularly work that stems from Coase (1960) on transaction costs, to further our understanding of terrorist organizations. Cautioning against a preoccupation with viewing terrorist organizations through a network-based, rational model of organization (i.e. voluntaristic approaches to organization theory), Helfstein reminds readers of the relevance of non-market structures and transaction costs. He observes (2009: 733) that terrorist organizations using market *and* non-market structures, including "hybrid structures" are evidence of transaction costs shaping organization structure and footprint. In keeping with the neo-institutional approach, Helfstein also finds some potential applicability of organization isomorphism (DiMaggio and Powell, 1983) with respect to terrorist organizations.

Very explicit attempts to merge voluntaristic with deterministic approaches are offered by Christensen and Laegrid (Christensen and Laegrid, 2001) and Hartley et al. (2002). Christensen and Laegrid address new public management with what they call a 'transformative perspective' that considers how governance is developed in an evolutionary manner shaped by national political-administrative history, culture, and traditions, and also through instrumental actions taken by leaders to pursue collective goals. Hartley et al. draw from Scott's (2001) model to explain change in governance structures through institutional and organizational processes. The model incorporates multiple levels of analysis, with more deterministic approaches generally used for the more macro levels and voluntaristic approaches generally used more at the micro level. Hartley and Scott draw from many classic organizational theorists, including but not limited to Weick (1995), Brunsson (1985), DiMaggio and Powell (1983), and Pugh and Hickson (1976). In their comprehensive review of organizational theories of change, Hartley et al. even discuss postmodernist approaches.

Additional insight into hybrid approaches comes from Herzog's (1993) survey of city managers' personal theories of organization. Herzog (1993: 439) observes that 'classical schools of organization thought ignored theories about politics and conflict in support of insular governance: a belief that government should avoid things that would subtract it from rationality.' While the majority of practitioners in Herzog's study 'agreed that politics should be divorced from their positions and that internal politics should be eliminated … most city managers disagreed that conflict should be avoided' and that managers should interact with their external environments by engaging local and professional players and serving as community leaders (1993: 439, 444). Herzog concludes that there is some support, at least from practitioners, for a model of organization based on limited instrumental rationality, which we view as a mix of deterministic and voluntaristic elements.

Another example of conflict among deterministic–voluntaristic theories is Provan and Kenis's (2008) study of how modes of networks further our understanding of governance. Without other context, a network approach to organization may seem most at home in the voluntaristic, collective action quadrant of Astley and Van de Ven's schema. However, scholars (e.g. Provan and Kennis, 2008; Kilduff and Tsai, 2003) point out several other modes of networks in governance arrangements: some are deterministic (e.g. 'serendipitous' networks), some are more voluntaristic ('goal-directed networks'). In keeping with what is seemingly a more hybrid approach, Provan and Kenis (2008: 248) conclude by recommending that scholars 'broaden their focus, moving away from describing network activities and behaviors, or focusing on how organizations function within networks [and] examine whole networks in greater depth, including how they are governed.'

Voluntaristic governance

In her study of professional accountability systems of public librarians, Bundt (2000) uses agency theory (Eisenhardt, 1989) as a point of departure to explore how stewardship theory (Davis et al., 1997) may explain governance structures. Departing from the organizational conclusions of agency theory that focus on agent shirking and self-interest, Bundt (2000: 760) finds evidence of strategic stewardship—agents 'motivated by broader organizational interests … and the good of the organization.' Bundt concludes that governance structures to ensure accountability can reasonably rely on coincidence between librarians' interests and the interests of the organization. This approach hints, more than most others from the U.S. literature, that individual behavior is not necessarily prescribed by fixed individual utility functions or set environmental conditions.

Klijn (2008a) characterizes a stream of the European research on governance networks as focused on complex, strategic decision-making. An emphasis in this litera-ture is on understanding the role and motiva-tions of a diverse array of actors (e.g. Sørensen and Torfing, 2003, 2007; Van Gils and Klijn, 2007; Voets and De Rynck, 2006). Decision and power theories, which have assumptions of voluntaristic action, are the foundation for much of this work. Klijn (2008b) argues that Europeans tend to focus more on the representation of stakeholder interests and involvement in governance net-works than American scholars, who he char-acterizes as having a managerial bias focused more on efficiency than stakeholder values and power. This may explain why we see much more of an individual actor focus in the European research, and with it more volun-taristic assumptions.

Some voluntaristic theorists place a strong emphasis on goals. The challenge of finding shared goals in governance networks may help explain why we find limited attention to goal pursuit in the governance literature. There is often not a clear hierarchy and struc-ture of goals to be followed in governance networks (e.g. Agranoff and McGuire, 2003; Kickert et al., 1997). However, some scholars have drawn our attention to goal-directed governance networks focusing on the ability for strategic, coordinated action (Provan and Kenis, 2008).

Some theorists suggest that more attention in the governance research should be placed on collaborative leadership of interorganiza-tional relationships (Connelly, 2007). Scholars focused on voluntaristic action in interorganizational systems draw our atten-tion to opportunistic behavior in which lead-ers choose to pursue individual rather than collective interests, increasing the likelihood of failure of the systems. In this vein, empir-ical research findings are growing on the importance of trust in and by these leaders, what leaders can bring related to social capi-tal, and willingness to collaborate and work within participative systems. Hood (2007) provides a glimpse into blame-avoidance. While Hood's agency, presentational, and policy strategies for blame-avoidance are for

public management generally, they can be specifically applied to governance systems. Research focused on individual factors suggests that interpersonal and personal incentive constructs based on voluntaristic assumptions should not be neglected in understanding effects on governance structures.

CONCLUSION

In this chapter we have raised and discussed six classic organization theory questions (Astley and Van de Ven, 1983). We interpret these questions to motivate important consid-erations and inquiries relative to governance research and practice. For example:

- Should governance systems allow for true empowerment? Do we control government or does it operate fairly independently out of its own momentum?
- To what extent are individuals and institutions involved in governance systems accountable for industry and organizational declines and deaths?
- Actors may influence or create properties of networks but do the extant organizing mecha-nisms replace, over time, strategic decision-making in guiding network structures, rules, and outcomes?
- Does governance involve the process of combin-ing value judgments and institutions involved in addressing social problems?
- Are there more or less opportunities for insti-tutional characteristics and collective action to come into play as governance structures and decision-making networks stabilize?
- To whom or what are governance systems accountable, especially given challenges in identifying goals and their pursuit?

While these questions have direct implica-tions for governance research and practice, our purpose in raising them is to illustrate how governance can be fundamentally con-nected to organization theory. As such, our primary focus has been on the overarching theme of deterministic versus voluntaristic behavior raised in Astley and Van de Ven's six questions. While we do not comprehensively catalogue how/whether governance research has exploited individual strands of organization theory (see other chapters in this book), our purpose has been to explore how this broad tension in organization theory has informed our understanding of governance to date and leaves us with unanswered questions.

Sampling a variety of leading US and European journals, we found that much of the contemporary governance literature falls along a spectrum between employing wholly deterministic and voluntaristic approaches. Whereas governance research that draws heavily on neo-institutional economics indicates certain levels of organizational determinism, even among these we found examples of hybrid, or mixed utilization of organizational determinism and voluntarism. At a minimum, this suggests to us that governance scholars have opened themselves up to the theoretical pluralism represented in the broader population of organization theories.

We recognize that our sample is limited and that our interpretation of included studies is open to debate. These limitations notwithstanding, we encourage scholars to continue to draw upon organization theory to inform their work. As the field develops the concept and practice of governance, we encourage recognition of the implicit assumptions about environmental and organizational determinism and voluntaristic behavior. Perhaps in relaxing dyadic assumptions (internal or external direction), governance scholars might further develop and illuminate models of governance.

REFERENCES

Agranoff, R. and McGuire, M. (2003) *Collaborative Public Management: New Strategies for Local Governments*. Washington, DC: Georgetown University Press.

Amirkhanyan, A.A., Kim, H.J. and Lambright, K.T. (2008) 'Does the Public Sector Outperform the Nonprofit and For-Profit Sectors? Evidence from a National Panel Study on Nursing Home Quality and Access', *Journal of Policy Analysis and Management* 27(2): 326–53.

Astley, W.G. and Van de Ven, A.H. (1983) 'Central Perspectives and Debates in Organization Theory', *Administrative Science Quarterly* 28(2): 245–73.

Benson, J.K. (1975) 'Interorganizational Network as a Political-Economy', *Administrative Science Quarterly* 20(2): 229–49.

Blau, P.M. and Scott, R. (1962) *Formal Organizations*. San Francisco: Chandler.

Boyne, G.A., Farrell, C., Law, J., Powell, M. and Walker, R.M. (2003) *Evaluating Public Management Reforms: Principles and Practice*. Buckingham, UK: Open University Press.

Brown, T.L. and Potoski, M. (2003) 'Transaction Costs and Institutional Explanations for Government Service Production Decisions', *Journal of Public Administration Research and Theory* 13(4): 441–68.

Brunsson, N. (1985) *The Irrational Organization: Irrationality as a Basis for Organizational Action and Change*. New York: Wiley.

Bundt, J. (2000) 'Strategic Stewards: Managing Accountability, Building Trust', *Journal of Public Administration Research and Theory*, 10(4): 757–78.

Caves, R.E. and Porter, M.E. (1977) 'Entry Barriers to Mobility Barriers – Conjectural Decisions and Contrived Deterrence to New Competition', *Quarterly Journal of Economics* 91(2): 241–61.

Chandler, A.D. (1977) *The Visible Hand: The Managerial Revolution in American Business*. Cambridge, MA: Belknap Press.

Child, J. (1972) 'Organizational Structure, Environment and Performance – Role of Strategic Choice', *Sociology – the Journal of the British Sociological Association* 6(1): 1.

Christensen, T. and Laegrid, P. (2001) 'New Public Management: The Effects of Contractualism and Devolution on Political Control', *Public Management Review* (1): 73–94.

Christensen, T., Laegreid, P., Roness, P.G. and Rovik, K.A. (2007) *Organization Theory and the Public Sector*. London: Routledge.

Coase, R. (1937) 'The Nature of the Firm', *Economica* 4(16): 386–405.

Coase, R.H. (1960) 'The Problem of Social Cost', *The Journal of Law and Economics* 3(1): 1.

Commons, J.R. and Parsons, K.H. (1950) *The Economics of Collective Action*. New York: Macmillan.

Connelly, D.R. (2007) 'Leadership in the Collaborative Interorganizational Domain', *International Journal of Public Administration* 30: 1231–62.

Davis, J.H., Schoorman, F.D. and Donaldson, L. (1997) 'Toward a Stewardship Theory of Management', *The Academy of Management Review* 22(1): 20–47.

DiMaggio, P. and Powell, W. (1983) 'The Iron Cage Revisited: Institutional Isomorphism and Collective Rationality in Organizational Fields', *American Sociological Review* 48: 147–60.

Eisenhardt, K.M. (1989) 'Agency Theory: An Assessment and Review', *The Academy of Management Review* 14(1): 57–74.

Fayol, H. (1949) *General and Industrial Management.* London: Pitman.

Feldman, M.S. and March, J.G. (1981) 'Information in Organizations as Signal and Symbol', *Administrative Science Quarterly* 26(2): 171–86.

Forbes, M. and Lynn, L.E., Jr (2005) 'How Does Public Management Affect Government Performance? Findings from International Research', *Journal of Public Administration Research and Theory* 15(4): 559–84.

Frederickson, H.G. and Smith, K.B. (2003) *The Public Administration Theory Primer.* Boulder, CO: Westview.

Goffman, E. (1961) *'Encounters, Two Studies in the Sociology of Interaction.* Indianapolis, IN: Bobbs-Merrill.

Hannan, M.T. and Freeman, J. (1977) 'Population Ecology of Organizations', *American Journal of Sociology* 82(5): 929–64.

Hartley, J., Butler, M.J.R. and Bennington, J. (2002) 'Local Government Modernization: UK and Comparative Analysis from an Organizational Perspective', *Public Management Review* 4(3): 387–404.

Hawley, A.H. (1950) *Human Ecology: A Theory of Community Structure.* New York: Ronald Press Co.

Helfstein, S. (2009) 'Governance of Terror: New Institutionalism and the Evolution of Terrorist Organizations', *Public Administration Review* 69(4): 727–39.

Herzog, R.J. (1993) 'Building Practitioner-Held Theory Through Triangulation', *Journal of Public Administration Research and Theory* 3(4): 431–56.

Hill, C.J. and Lynn, L.E., Jr (2005) 'Is Hierarchical Governance in Decline? Evidence from Empirical Research', *Journal of Public Administration Research and Theory* 15(2): 173–95.

Hood, C. (2007) 'What Happens When Transparency Meets Blame-Avoidance', *Public Management Review* 9(2): 191–210.

Karna, A. (2009) 'Revisiting New Institutional Economics as a Meta-Paradigm'. Available at SSRN: http://ssrn.com/abstract=1145982.

Kickert, W.J.M., Klijn, E.H. and Koppenjan, J.F.M. (1997) *Managing Complex Networks: Strategies for the Public Sector.* London: Sage.

Kilduff, M. and Tsai, W. (2003) *Social Networks and Organizations.* London: Sage.

Klijn, E.H. (2008a) 'Complexity Theory and Public Administration: What Is New; Key Concepts in Complexity Theory Compared to Their Counterparts in Public Administration Research', *Public Management Review* 10(3): 299–317.

Klijn, E.H. (2008b) 'Governance Networks in Europe: An Assessment of Ten Years of Research on the Theme', *Public Management Review* 10(4): 505–25.

Lawrence, P.R. and Lorsch, J.W. (1967) *Organization and Environment; Managing Differentiation and Integration.* Boston: Division of Research, Graduate School of Business Administration, Harvard University.

Lowery, D. (2000) 'A Transactions Costs Model of Metropolitan Governance: Allocation versus Redistribution in Urban America', *Journal of Public Administration Research and Theory* 10(1): 49–78.

Lynn, L.E., Jr., Heinrich, C.J. and Hill, C.J. (2000) 'Studying Governance and Public Management: Challenges and Prospects', *Journal of Public Administration Research and Theory* 10(2): 233–61.

Meyer, J. and Rowan, B. (1977) 'Institutionalized Organizations: Formal Structure as Myth and Ceremony', *American Journal of Sociology* 83: 340–63.

Pondy, L.R. and Mitroff, I.I. (1979) 'Beyond Open Systems Models of Organization'. in L.L. Cummings and B.M. Staw (eds), *Research in Organizational Behavior.* Vol. 1. Greenwich, CT: JAI Press.

Provan, K.G. and Kenis, P. (2008) 'Modes of Network Governance: Structure, Management, and Effectiveness', *Journal of Public Administration Research and Theory* 18(2): 229–52.

Pugh, D. and Hickson, D. (1976) *Organization Structure in Its Context: The Aston Programme.* Fairborough: Saxon House.

Richter, R. (2005) 'The New Institutional Economics: Its Start, its Meaning, its Prospects', *European Business Organization Law Review (EBOR)* 6(02): 161–200.

Scott, W.R. (2001) *Institutions and Organizations,* (2nd ed). Thousand Oaks; CA: Sage.

Scott, W.R. and Davis, G.F. (2006) *Organizations and Organizing: Rational, Natural and Open Systems Perspectives.* Englewood Cliffs, NJ: Prentice Hall.

Sørensen, E. and Torfing, J. (2003) 'Network Politics, Political Capital and Democracy', *International Journal of Public Administration* 26(6): 609–34.

Sørensen, E. and Torfing, J. (2007) *Theories of Democratic Network Governance*. New York: Palgrave Macmillan.

Van Gils, M. and Klijn, E.H. (2007) 'Complexity in Decision-Making: The Case of the Rotterdam Harbour Expansion: Connecting Decisions, Arenas and Actors in Spatial Decision-Making', *Planning Theory and Practice* 8(2): 139–58.

Voets, J. and De Rynck, F. (2006) 'Rescaling Territorial Governance: A Flemish Perspective', *European Planning Studies* 14(7): 905–22.

Weick, K.E. (1979) *The Social Psychology of Organizing*, (2nd edn). Reading, MA: Addison-Wesley.

Weick, K.E. (1995) *Sensemaking in Organizations*. Thousand Oaks, CA: Sage.

Williamson, O. (1975) *Markets and Hierarchies*. New York: Free Press.

6

Institutional Theory

B. Guy Peters

INTERPRETATIONS OF GOVERNANCE

Governance has become one of the most commonly used terms in political science, but it is also a contested concept (see Pierre, 2000). Other chapters in this *Handbook* discuss the various interpretations of governance in detail but here I focus on governance as a generic concept for the attempts of the state, and its allies in the private sector, to steer the economy and society: i.e. governance involves making decisions and utilizing resources in order to alter conditions in society.

This conception of governance bears many resemblances to public policy studies, but also has important differences. First, the governance approach is focused on establishing societal goals and then mobilizing the resources necessary to reach those goals. Although we may hope the goals will be set in a democratic manner, that is not a necessary condition for the logic of steering. The emphasis on steering toward collective goals also includes the political process of selecting goals within the domain of governing, Governance also tends to be more inclusive by both including a wider array of actors and by considering general patterns of policymaking rather than focusing on a single policy issue at a time.

Thus, governance emphasizes drives toward creating more consistent and coordinated policies, while also recognizing the need to steer within the individual policy sectors.

Many interpretations of governance tend to privilege one set of actors or another in the process of governing. For example, although governance traditionally would have been equated with government, some approaches have equated governance, or 'new governance' in the terminology used here, with the domination of social actors and the weaknesses of government (see Rhodes, 2007). The assumptions behind the new governance approach are that the conventional institutions of government are no longer capable of providing effective steering on their own and must be supplemented, or supplanted, by social actors. By taking a more generic approach, however, we then pose the empirical question of what actors are actually involved, and in what mix, in the processes of governing.

The steering conception of governing also stresses the capacity of governance systems to adapt to changing circumstances within their environment. `If the governing institutions are open to information from that environment then it should be able to create more effective governance. The steering conception of governance implies some continuous inter-action with the environment and finding appropriate mechanisms for integrating social actors and their perspectives into the governance process. Without such inter-actions and strong feedback mechanisms the capacity to steer effectively is diminished substantially. Thus, governance must con-form to many of the ideas about cybernetic governance that Karl Deutsch (1965) advanced some decades ago.

This integration then becomes a means of reconciling approaches to governance that depends on social actors to more inclusive conceptions of governance concentrating on steering. That said, however, the extent of the integration of social actors, and the manner in which they are integrated, provides a basis for comparison of political systems (see Peters, 2004). Likewise, it provides a means of com-paring policy sectors within a single govern-ance system, given that the differences among policy areas may be greater than the differ-ences among political systems (Freeman, 1985; Howlett and Lindquist, 2004). Thus, governance should be seen as a useful approach to comparative political analysis, and not as a generic process in which 'one size fits all'.

LINKING INSTITUTIONS TO GOVERNANCE

The roots of political science, and especially comparative politics, lie in study of institu-tions. Much of the study of institutions has been grounded in the description and analy-sis of formal institutions, generally in a legal-istic and manner (Apter, 1965; Peters, 2001). Although supplanted to some extent by more individualistic approaches to politics, as the-oretical developments in institutionalism have progressed, the study of institutions has returned to prominence. In all institutional studies, however, the assumption is that insti-tutions do matter. In terms of governance, the assumption is that the nature of institutions

will influence the capacity of the political system to govern effectively

If one begins to think about governance as inherently involving social actors, then the role of institutions in creating opportunities for that involvement becomes crucial. More traditional forms of institutionalism would provide relatively little opportunity for such interaction. Thus, institutions are significant not only for the manner in which they make decisions internally but also for the way in which they can promote democratic interac-tions with social actors (Sorenson, 2005). That interactive characteristic, in turn, emphasizes the need to move beyond exam-ining just the usual differences between presidential and parliamentary institutions (Schmidt, 2003; Roller, 2006) to consider a wider range of institutional arrangements.

Further, we also need to think about the social actors and their networks, as well as corporatist arrangements, as forms of institu-tions (see Peters, 2001: Ch. 6). They have all the features of institutions, e.g. regularity of behavior, some normative structure, a capac-ity (if perhaps limited) for imposing rules and generating compliance. Then, if we accept the fundamental premise in institu-tional analysis that the relevant environment of institutions is composed of other institu-tions, then the presence of formal institutions define the limits of action for these socially-based institutions, and vice versa.[1]

Varieties of institutionalism

To this point I have been discussing institu-tionalism in a rather undifferentiated manner, other than to make the distinction between traditional descriptive studies and more ana-lytic approaches. The first step in discussing the linkage of institutionalism and govern-ance is to specify the nature of institutional-ism and to identify the varieties of approaches. Although there can be a wide range of such approaches, I will focus attention on three of the most important of these, and their rele-vance for governing. Explicating each of the approaches fully would require a more extensive treatment than is possible here, but a relatively brief description can provide the basis for understanding their capacity to contribute to understanding governing.

The first of the approaches to consider is the *normative* institutionalism, which has served as the foundation for the resurgence of institutional theory in political science. This version of institutionalism is usually associated with the work of March and Olsen (1989), and has deep roots in the sociological study of organizations and institutions (Selznick, 1984). The basic argument of the normative approach, as the name implies, is that the behavior of institutions, and the individuals who comprise them, is shaped by a 'logic of appropriateness' that is composed of values, symbols, methods and routines that an individual learns as a member of the institution.

From the more normative perspective on institutions, the logical function of an institution is to create and sustain values among its members. As noted above, in this version of institutionalism the values of individual members are assumed to be shaped by institutions. This notion does not offer a very satisfying explanation of where those values have been created in the first instance, but it does provide an explanation of their capacity to maintain directions of policy. The internal socialization processes within institutions not only shape decisions but also tend to shape the values and subsequent behaviors of the members.

The principal alternative to the normative version of institutionalism is *rational choice* institutionalism. Although it contains several strands or approaches, the rational choice version of institutionalism employs the same assumptions of individual rationality and utility that rational choice as an approach to political science does more broadly (see Ericksson, 2009). The basic assumption is that individuals act within institutions in order to maximize their own personal interests. With those strong exogenous preferences that individuals bring into the institution, the designers of those institutions can achieve their intentions simply by creating the right combination of incentives and disincentives.

The above said, rational choice theorists argue that institutions are designed in order to solve a number of problems that cannot be solved solely by individuals acting alone. For example, the classic problem of the commons arises because individuals pursue their own interests, and in the process may produce consequences that harm everyone (see Ostrom, 2000). In addition, institutions are able to produce equilibrium in situations in which individual maximizing behavior would produce disequilibrium (Riker, 1980). In order to produce these more positive outcomes, institutions are conceptualized as manipulating incentives (positive and negative) to which the individuals respond in predictable ways.[2]

Rational choice institutionalism has provided one of the more important linkages between structures and processes. In particular, the logic of *veto points* and *veto players* within institutions defines the capability of institutions to make decisions and to implement them effectively. The more independent decisions that must be made, and the more individuals there are who must make those decisions, the more difficult it is to govern.[3] For example, a presidential regime with autonomous branches of government has greater difficulty in making decisions than does a parliamentary regimes, especially parliamentary regimes controlled by a simple party.

Historical institutionalism is the third major approach to institutional theory. The basic logic of historical institutionalism is that once policies are adopted and organizations are created those structures will persist until some major event – a punctuation in the equilibrium – occurs. This approach to institutionalism is derived from similar arguments in economics that were designed to explain how suboptimal solutions to problems persist even when superior solutions are available (David, 2007). In more political terms, institutions are maintained through the positive feedback that the participants receive from the existence of the policy outputs: again, even if superior options may exist.

Historical institutionalism appears to reinforce the usual critique of institutional theory – i.e. it is incapable of explaining change, That is, however, an overstatement of the persistence found in historical institutional theory. First, institutions as a whole are more open to change than is usually thought, and indeed they may contain within themselves the sources of change (Olsen, 2009). Further, although change within historical institutionalism may not be overt, there are a number of ways in which change may occur more gradually (Streeck and Thelen, 2007). Finally, change may occur in well-established institutions provided there are alterative ideas that can motivate the change (Peters, Pierre and King, 2005).

For the historical institutionalist perspective, the processes that have been institutionalized tend to push toward maintaining the current policies and programs of the structures. In many ways the logic is an extreme version of the normative version of institutionalism in which values and symbols are used to maintain existing patterns of behavior. The dynamic of that maintenance is not always as clear as in the normative version and the emphasis is on describing the path dependency as much as on the logic of action involved.[4]

Although there are some important differences among the approaches to institutions, there are also some common characteristics, and those common characteristics have a number of important implications for governance. Perhaps most importantly, institutional approaches to political life emphasize routinization and uniformity, and tend to favor stability over change (but see below). Thus, institutional approaches to governance will emphasize the predictability of policy responses within governance. Each of the approaches places a slightly different emphasis on these fundamental aspects of institutions, but each approach carries some of the fundamental traits of institutions.

Perhaps the principal manner in which institutions influence governance is that institutions represent the interaction of structures and processes for governing. We usually think of institutions in terms of structure, but the institutions can also be described in terms of basic processes through which decisions are made. Governing is about making decisions, and institutions define the ways in which those decisions are made. For example, law is one of the most basic institutions in society, and electoral laws tend to shape the number of political parties that are in parliament and in turn the nature of the government – majority or coalition, and what type of coalition – that is formed after the election (Taagepera and Shugart, 1989).

THE NEW GOVERNANCE

In contemporary views of governance the most important linkages among actors may be between actors within the public sector and actors coming from outside, whether from the market or from civil society. The linkages may present special challenges for governance as they may involve actors with different goals and different values about the policy problems they are addressing. What these linkages may require, therefore, is the creation of a distinct set of institutional arrangements so that the patterns of interaction between state and society can be routinized and made more predictable.

Arguably the first element of making this linkage will be to institutionalize the network itself, prior to linking it with the more formalized actors within the public sector. Whether they are produced by autonomous action or they are the product of strategic action from the public sector, networks will face several challenges as they are created and institutionalized. These are components of the 'liability of newness' (Stinchcombe, 1965) that any nascent organization will face. The first challenge (Boin and Goodin, 2007) that the network will face is developing its own internal culture and internal manner of functioning. Given that most of these organizations tend to be formed without any specific template and perhaps without individual leaders who can devote full-time to managing the structure, this routinization of activities will be difficult. That said, as these are meant to be relatively informal structures, these demands might not be so great as they would be for a business or even for one of the constituent organizations of a network.

Boin and Goodin were concerned primarily with the managerial elements of making a new organization function, but for networks there is a second and more subtle element. A network needs to establish internal values and a sense of belonging to the network. This challenge is, of course, analogous to Selznick's conception of institutionalization. The need to create these values may be greater for networks than for more formalized institutions because of their less formal nature, and their general inability to provide incentives for membership other than the moral, solidary benefits of belong and attempting to influence policy.[5] If networks are to fulfill their potential for bringing together potentially disparate social and economic interests, there must be a means of building common values, not the least of which is the benefits (intrinsic and extrinsic) of involvement with the network.

The second challenge that a new organization or network will have to overcome is establishing effective relationships with the political environment. Networks need to legitimate their role in governance and to secure a legitimate place within the processes of governing. This task is somewhat easier in societies with a history of corporatist and corporate pluralist forms for interest intermediation, in which the role of social actors has already been legitimated. The assumption for organizations operating in these societies is that their involvement with the public sector is a natural aspect of their being an organization with some policy relevance. That said, many corporatist arrangements were dominated by state actors, so the shift toward greater inequality and indeterminacy might still need some legitimation.

The above discussion is premised on an assumption that networks are indeed new, although some may have been in existence for some time and are only adapting their behavior to become more a part of governance. To some extent this adaptation on the part of existing structures should be easier, given that the initial challenges of institutionalization will all have been overcome. There should be some regular pattern of interaction as well as some shared meaning among the members that are necessary to maintain it. As a functioning organization, such a network should be able to transform its performance to cope with the new tasks, but they will require some deinstitutionalization, and then reinstitutionalization of its activities.

Although the existing networks may have the simple virtue of existing, that does not mean that they will necessarily have the capacity to adjust to changing pressures coming from their involvement with making policy. As noted, some members may be involved in network activities more for social reasons than for purposive reasons and may find the need for the network to play a more political role to be distasteful or at least unnecessary. Thus, these members must adopt different values or cease participating in the network. Further, the network structures may not have been able to achieve any effective level of institution on the criteria developed by Huntington (1968) to understand institutionalization. In particular, the networks may not have any effective autonomy from their members, nor indeed autonomy from the parts of the public sector with which they work.

Although the majority of the literature on the subject focuses on institutionalization, we also need to remember that there is a parallel process of deinstitutionalization. Institutions are rarely stable, but rather go through continuing movements to higher or lower levels of institutionalization. The deinstitutionalization of existing patterns of governance can be the means of producing change within the public sector, and of adjusting to new governance requirements arising within the environment. Further, as we will discuss below, that deinstitutionalization can also be the means of producing higher levels of cooperation and coordination among institutions and organizations.

ALTERNATIVE USES OF INSTITUTIONALISM

Institutions are used in a variety ways in contemporary political analysis. The variable treatment of institutions is also apparent when we begin to discuss them within the context of governance. Institutions represent solutions for the social and economic problems encountered in governing. The most important use of institutions, however, is to provide explanations for the decisions being made in governance. Understanding both aspects of institutionalism helps to explicate the importance of institutions in governing.

Institutions as the dependent variable

The first importance of institutions for understanding, and perhaps explaining, governance is that institutions represent responses to challenges in the environment, and represent mechanisms for managing those challenges. Rational choice institutionalism in particular recognizes the need to overcome collective action problems and to develop mechanisms for making individual behavior more predictable. Given that rational choice theorists begin with an assumption about the source of individual behavior, they can predict more readily the likely outcomes of any particular choice of institutions. In particular, there is an assumption that a particular set of institutional design choices will produce certain patterns of outcomes. Other versions of institutionalism will not be so sanguine about the capacity of institutional designers to make the right choices.

Beginning with a relatively open conception of governance, we can also argue that patterns of interaction among the actors in governance processes tend to produce institutions. This is true if we consider only the formal institutions associated with the state, and it is also true if we consider interactions between formal and informal actors in governance (see Helmke and Levitsky, 2004). For example, the use of networks of social actors may begin as a highly informal means of creating legitimacy for decisions and/or for garnering the expertise available from those social actors, but over time the interactions between state and society become regularized and become a regular component of the governance process.

The process of institutionalization therefore must be understood as a central component creating the capacity for governing. In particular, if the routines established for making decisions and governing cannot be maintained, then those processes cannot be successful for any substantial period of time, nor extend beyond an immediate small group. In normative institutional theory, institutionalization is conceptualized as infusing a structure with values, so that the structure is more than merely mechanical (Selznick, 1984). The conception of institutionalization is less clear in the rational choice and historical approaches, although in the former compliance with rules appears crucial.[6]

Institutions as the independent variable

Institutional patterns are usually considered to shape the governance capabilities of the public sector and its associates in the private sector. Much of the logic of comparative politics has been to assume that formal institutional arrangements can explain how governments work. In relatively simple views of institutions, formal, legal structures are more important than are the individuals who populate the institutions and organizations, whereas much of contemporary political science emphasizes the decisions of individuals within the structures. Even some contemporary versions of institutional theory (see Weaver and Rockman, 1994) have used relatively descriptive characterizations of institutions in an attempt to explain governing.

But what do institutions explain? We have been arguing throughout this chapter that institutions can explain governance, but what about governance. There appear to be several dependent variables related to governing that can be explained, at least in part, through institutional configurations. The capacity to provide those explanations will depend in part on the version of institutionalism being applied, but all versions to some extent will assist in understanding some aspects of governing.

The identification of these dependent variables returns to the initial discussion of what is governance. From the most generic notion of steering, it is important first that those actors responsible for governing – public, private or more likely a mixture of the two spheres – be capable of making decisions. Therefore, the most basic consideration is the extent to which institutional arrangements facilitate or inhibit decision-making. For example, the analysis of veto players coming from rational choice institutionalism addresses this point specifically.

A second consideration in governance is not only that decisions are made but also they are of high-quality. Rather obviously, this raises another definition question – What is a high quality decision? A huge literature has arisen on 'good governance', but that term generally means different things to different people. For example, some of the good governance literature concentrates on reducing corruption and improving transparency in governing. Another component is concerned more with making decisions that can objectively 'solve' the policy problems to which they are addressed. Good governance may also have several political dimensions: one would be the extent to which the decision-making process is open and democratic; another would be a *political*

assessment of the success of the decisions made, regardless of their objective success in reaching goals.[7]

Making decisions

To some extent institutional structures should contribute to making decisions, at least when compared with some state of nature lacking rules or procedures. In particular, institutional rules provide means of mapping a set of preferences into a decision, even when those preferences are opposed. Having decision rules agreed upon in advance, even if a simple majority voting rule, enables decisions to be made when their absence, as in some network or informal governance arrangements, may not. This fundamental virtue of decisions has been emphasized by the rational choice version of institutional theory (Buchanan and Tullock, 1962), although other variations of rational choice (Tsebelis, 2000).

The normative version of institutional theory adds to the contrast of an institutional structure with some state of nature by providing means of reducing the degree of conflict over goals and over decisions. If the institutionalization process is successful and the members of the institution are inculcated with relatively common values and goals, the conflicts over decisions will be minimized. Few institutions are so successful as to create a uniform set of values, and there will be conflicts over means if there are no conflicts over ends. Even that conflict, however, will tend to be mitigated by the routines and symbols of an institution. The historical version of institutionalism contains some of the same assumptions as the normative version. The path dependency central to the model is to a great extent a function of creating and maintaining a set of ideas that justify the maintenance of the existing pattern, and that also make reaching decisions relatively easy, if not automatic.

Although all three versions provide some explanations for the capacity to make decisions, their explanations are rather different. The normative institutionalism would provide an answer similar to that coming from organization theory – the capacity to make decisions depends on the routinization of practices within the structures and the availability of common decision-premises among the members. The answer provided by historical institutionalism would be much the same, with the path dependency of decisions tending to facilitate decisions and remove potential conflicts.

Rational choice institutionalism would provide serval different answers. One would be based on rules, with the availability of rules and compliance with them facilitating decisions. Institutional rules can be used to overcome decision-making situations that otherwise would produce unstable decisions, or no decisions at all. The analysis of veto points and players within institutions provides a means of comparing the likelihood of a decision, with institutional arrangements, with the most vetoes being less likely to make decisions. Those vetoes would be especially likely to inhibit making innovative decisions (see below; see also Scharpf, 1988)

Making good decisions

Understanding whether decisions being made are good decisions, and the role of institutions in determining that quality, is more difficult. Again, some of the problems are definitional, and we need to think carefully about what constitutes good governance and good decisions. For the purposes of this chapter, I will argue that good governance decision-making has four basic attributes:

1   Suitability – the decisions taken must correspond with the nature of the problem being addressed. That is, the nature of policy problems must be matched by the design of the instruments used (see Peters and Hoornbeek, 2007). The suitability of a governance decision may be affected by issues such as the scale of the problem and the time frame (short term or chronic). This criterion is sometimes discussed as policy solutions being isomorphic with the problems being addressed.
2   Robustness – the decisions taken should be effective in a range of circumstances. Governing and policymaking must cope with uncertainty, and effective governance involves constructing arrangements that can cope with that uncertainty. Some policy areas within the public sector are more affected by uncertainty than others, and hence this criterion needs to be considered differently when one is examining defense versus, for example, pensions.[8]
3   Innovation – good governance also involves the capacity to innovate. Innovation in turn will require means of identifying new problems and finding new solutions to those problems. This capacity is to some extent in contrast to the routinized policymaking capacity usually associated with governance, but may be increasingly important as the environment becomes more turbulent (Duit and Galaz, 2008).
4   Content – This is a more normative criterion. Although we tend to praise institutions as means of producing decisions, we may also want to enquire about the normative content of the institutions. For example, some institutional structures may be very effective in implementing corrupt practices; thus, one requirement for understanding the contribution of institutions to good governance would be to have a relatively detailed understanding of the institutions themselves. Thus, patterns of behavior such as clientelism have many institutional characteristics, but they do not contribute to creating what most people would consider good governance.

As already noted, the general assumption has been that well-institutionalized governance systems would be better at making these types of decisions than would less institutionalized systems. For example, Samuel Huntington (1968) argued in terms of developing political systems that institutionalization was crucial not only for order but also for effective governing more generally. The failed states literature (Bates, 2008) has continued in that style of arguing, stressing the need to institutionalize effective institutions for governance. Likewise, the good governance literature from the World Bank and other international organizations has emphasized values such as the rule of law and reliability that depend upon institutionalization.

An important danger for effective governance, however, may lie in the *over-institutionalization* of governance arrangements as well as in their inadequate institutionalization. If we consider institutions as a special class of organizations,[9] and apply organization theory, then much of that literature stresses the dangers of rigidity within highly structured organizations. Indeed, within notions of institutionalization, e.g. creating common values and routinization, there are the seeds of difficulties in making robust and innovative decisions.

There are some dangers of over-institutionalization in all three versions of institutional theory being discussed here. This possibility is perhaps most evident in historical institutionalization given that path-dependent responses are an almost automatic response, perhaps without serious deliberation about alternatives.[10] Likewise, in normative versions of institutionalism, having dominant routines and common values creates something like a 'groupthink' ('t Hart, 200x) within the structure so that relatively few alternatives may be considered when designing a response to a perceived problem.

The perception and identification of issues are important for understanding how institutions respond to circumstances in their environment. When institutions confront governance challenges a well-institutionalized, or over-institutionalized, structure they will tend to perceive those challenges as examples of the challenges which they also have coded into their organizational DNA, and therefore often attempt to 'solve' the wrong problems. Again, this is a common problem identified in organization theory but the same problem is perhaps more likely to arise within institutions.

For governance, as opposed to decision-making for individual organizations, the tendency of institutions and organizations to persist in their well-worn paths presents greater difficulties than it might for the individual organizations. As already noted, governance involves creating more or less coherent patterns of policy within a domain in order to create consistent patterns of steering. Therefore it is important to consider a range of policies and decisions rather than considering them individually when thinking about governance. Decisions by individual organizations and institutions therefore require effective coordination if there is to be effective governance (see Peters, 2004, forthcoming), and institutionalization may inhibit that coordination.

The framing and reframing literature (see Schon and Rein, 1994; also Bardach, 1999) points to some of the perils of overly-institutionalized structures for governance. The argument in this literature is that many policy problems remain unsolvable, or remain 'solved' in suboptimal ways, because the organizations involved force some closure over their own conceptions of policy and hence over their ability to cooperate with other organizations that may be important for governing within a policy area, Even when institutions or organizations might be thought to have a great deal in common, the institutionalization of their individual value sets may inhibit effective governance.

The principal arguments concerning the possible over-institutionalization of governance arrangements applies to historical and normative versions of institutionalism. In those cases, rigidity arises from common values and routinization. For rational choice institutionalism, some of the same dysfunctions may also be observed. Whereas the source of over-institutionalization in the other versions of institutionalism tends to be values and routines, in rational choice approaches the problems appears to be the rigidity of rules. One of the presumed virtues of the rational choice approach to institutions is that it can be designed easily by changing rules (Calvert, 1995).

The argument which emerges from this consideration of linking the quality of governance with institutions is that the relationship may not be linear; it is more likely to be U-shaped. It is clear that very low levels of institutionalization are incapable of providing effective governance. A range of literatures from comparative politics make that very clear. It also seems, however, that structures may become overly institutionalized, blocking innovation and tending to replicate the same decisions time and time again regardless of the circumstances. To some extent, over-institutionalization may be an advantage, as policy issues become more complex and levels of uncertainty increase. At least the governance institutions can provide some response to the problem regardless of the circumstances, but in terms of providing any high-quality governance the answers may not be desirable.

How do they explain?

It should be apparent at this point that institutional theory does have some capacity to explain the ability of governance systems to make steering decisions, and to some extent the quality of the decisions that are being made. What may be less clear is how do those institutions actually shape the behavior and explain the decisions that are made. Several basic building blocks of social theory (see Mayntz, 2004) appear to be involved in that process, although much of institutional theory, and governance, lacks a strong micro-level foundation to make that explanation (Stoker, 2008). All institutions to some extent rely on authority, but they may also involve other mechanisms. The existence of another instrument is most evident in rational choice institutionalism that depends on utility maximization for much of its explanation. Both the normative and historical versions of institutional theory depend upon processes of learning, and responding to feedback (Pierson, 2000).

In much of contemporary political science, and institutional theory, there are at least two alternative conceptions of the micro-foundations of political behavior. Perhaps the dominant approach is rational choice, which assumes that individuals are rational political actors who will act to maximize their individual utility and will use institutions as arenas within which they will pursue those personal goals. The assumption of the rational choice approach is that we can explain outcomes of (all) political processes by understanding the utility-seeking behavior of the individual participants in those processes (but see Ericksson, 2009).

Interpretative social science provides an alternative to rational choice perspectives. This perspective assumes that we cannot understand individual behavior unless we understand the ways in which individuals attach meanings to the social and political settings in which they are functioning. In terms of governance, Bevir and Rhodes (2003) have demonstrated that governance can be understood through the informal networks and relationships that surround all policy areas, and government as a whole. The various actors involved in these interactions bring with them various interpretations, and these aggregate into traditions that shape policymaking in various areas (see also Painter and Peters, 2010).

There may, however, be a third micro-approach that arises in the study of institutions, and this is social learning. In normative institutionalism, individuals become part of the institution by learning the symbols, values, and routines of that institution, and then internalize those values. Once those values are learned, the individual is expected to comply with the normative structure of the institution, and that it turn will influence if not determine the behavior of the institution as a whole. And the norms about appropriate behavior will also shape the governance activities of the institution.

At a very general level, institutions explain governance choices by placing constraints on the actions of individuals within them. As already noted, those constraints may be normative or they may be more structural. That said, institutions also provide opportunities for making governance decisions and involve ranges of actors in making those decisions. Again, we need to inquire about which institutions and what their nature is rather than providing any general institutional explanation of decisions. These decisions then contain some interaction of the values and interests of the decision-makers, the structural and normative constraints imposed by the institution, and the characteristics of the decision situation.

CONCLUSION: IS INSTITUTIONALISM A THEORY OF GOVERNANCE?

The above discussion has raised a number of questions about the capacity of institutional theory to function as a theory of governance, but does all of that add up to a theory of governance? The simplest answer, albeit an unsatisfying one, is 'yes and no'. As an advocate of institutionalism, I would like to given an unequivocal 'yes' answer but find that I cannot. Institutionalism provides a good place to begin an analysis of governance but it does not necessarily provide a complete explanation of the phenomena.

Institutions do provide an excellent place to begin the analysis of decisions made in governing societies, but do not generally provide a complete answer to those questions. To be able to understand how institutions are able to steer society, we also need to understand how the individuals within them function and how they also shape the institutions, at the same time that they are being shaped by those institutions. Further, we need to understand how institutions interact with other institutions to create a functioning governance system. A great deal of the analysis of institutions focuses on individual organizations but their interactions may be more important in providing governance.

As noted above, institutions and institutionalization are not just empty vessels with rules and formal structures: they also possess values and ideas about governing. Therefore, to understand their contribution to governance requires moving beyond simple conceptions of institutions to a more complex understanding that involves much of the content within the institutions. Further, institutionalism, or the various versions of institutionalism, may require a more explicit understanding of the micro-foundations of behavior within the institutions and the linkage of individuals and the institutions, Structure remains important but some closer attention to agency is still required.

NOTES

1 The familiar argument about the 'shadow of hierarchy' can be extended to allow for a 'shadow of society'. (see Peters, 2009).

2 This assumption also emphasizes that in rational choice models, institutions can be designed readily, while in the other versions design is less predictable.

3 The idea of 'clearance points' developed by Pressman and Wildavsky (1974) to describe implementation is an analogous concept.

4 There are notable exceptions, e.g. Streeck and Thelen (2005).

5 These categories of organizational incentives come from Etzioni (1975) and Clark and Wilson (1961).

6 The path dependency argument in historical institutionalism implies the existence of an institutionalized pattern of behavior.

7 Although one might think they would be, these two dimensions are often not correlated (see Bovens, 't Hart and Peters, 2000).

8 This is not to imply that there are not important policy issues in pensions, but rather given that the number of potential pensioners in a society is quite predictable there is less uncertainty about the demand.

9 This may be a somewhat suspect assumption, especially for more amorphous institutions such as the law. The literature differentiating institutions and organizations has several different dimensions, not all of which would support this assumption (see Khalid, 199x). That said, however, a great deal of analytic leverage can be gained by thinking about institutions in organizational terms.

10 This is perhaps too much of a stereotype of the historical institutionalism. In later versions of the approach there is a good deal of attention to the ways in which institutions can and do change.

REFERENCES

Apter, D.E. (1965) 'Introduction', in H. Eckstein and D.E. Apter (eds), *Comparative Politics*. New York: Free Press.

Bates, R. (2008) 'State Failure', *Annual Review of Political Science* 11: 3–19.

Bevir, M. and Rhodes, R.A.W. (2003) *Interpreting British Government*. London: Routledge.

Boin, A. and Goodin, R.E. (2007) 'Institutionalizing Upstarts: The Demons of Domestication and the Benefits of Recalcitrance', *Acta Politica* 42: 40–57.

Bovens, M.A., 't Hart, P. and Peters, B.G. (2000) *Success and Failure in Public Governance*. Cheltenham: Edward Elgar.

Buchanan, J. and Tullock, G. (1962) *The Calculus of Consent*. Ann Arbor, MI: University of Michigan Press.

Calvert, R.L. (1995) 'The Rational Choice Theory of Institutions: Implications for Design', in D. L. Weimer (ed.), *Institutional Design*. Boston: Kluwer.

David, P.A. (2007) 'Path Dependence, Its Critics and the Quest for Historical Economics', in G. M. Hodgson (ed.), *The Evolution of Economic Institutions*. Cheltenham: Edward Elgar.

Deutsch, K.W. (1965) *The Nerves of Government*. New York: Free Press.

Duit, A. and Galaz, V. (2008) 'Governance and Complexity – Emerging Issues for Governance Theory', *Governance* 21: 311–35.

Ericksson, L. (2009) *What Can Rational Choice Do?* Basingstoke: Palgrave.

Freeman, G. (1985) 'National Styles and Policy Sectors: Explaining Structured Variation', *Journal of Public Policy* 5: 467–96.

Grafstein (1992) *Institutional Realism: Social and Political Constraints on Rational Actors*. New Haven, CT: Yale University Press.

Helmke, G. and Levitsky, S. (2004) 'Informal Institutions and Comparative Politics', *Perspectives on Politics* 2: 725–40.

Howlett, M. and Lindquist, E. (2004) 'Policy Analysis and Governance: Analytic and Policy Styles in Canada', *Journal of Comparative Policy Analysis* 6: 225–49.

Huntington, S.P. (1968) *Political Order in Changing Societies*. New Haven, CT: Yale University Press.

Kesselman, M. (1970) 'Overinstitutionalization and Political Constraint', *Comparative Politics* 3: 21–44.

March, J.G, and Olsen, J.P. (1989) *Rediscovering Institutions: The Organizational Basis of Politics*. New York: Free Press.

Mayntz, R. (2004) 'Mechanisms in the Analysis of Social Macro-Phenomena', *Philosophy of Social Sciences* 34: 237–59.

Oliver, C. (1992) 'The Antecedents of Deinstitutionalization', *Organization Studies* 13: 563–88.

Olsen, J.P. (2009) 'An Institutional Approach to the Institutions of Democratic Governance', *European Political Science Review* 1: 3–32.

Ostrom, E. (1990). *Governing the Commons: The Evolution of Institutions of Collective Action*. Cambridge: Cambridge University Press.

Painter, M.A. and Peters, B.G. (2010) *Administrative Traditions and Administrative Reform*. London: Palgrave Macmillan.

Peters, B.G. (2001) *Institutional Theory in Political Science: The New Institutionalism*. London: Continuum.

Peters, B.G. (2004) 'Governance and Comparative Politics', in J. Pierre (ed.), *Debating Governance*. Oxford: Oxford University Press.

Peters, B.G. (2009) 'Governing in the Shadows'. Unpublished paper, European Collegoim, Free University of Berlin.

Peters, B.G. (2010) 'Institutional Explanations of Corruption', in P. Van et al. *The Good Cause*.

Peters, B.G. (forthcoming) *Managing Horizontal Government*. Lawrence, KS: University of Kansas Press.

Peters, B.G. and Hoornbeek, J.A. (2007) 'Policy Problems and Policy Instruments', in P. Eliadis, M. Hill and M. Howlett (eds), *Designing Government*. Montreal: McGill-Queens University Press.

Peters, B.G. and Pierre, J. (2010) 'Simple Answers to Complex Questions', *Global Economic Change*, forthcoming.

Peters, B.G., Pierre, J. and King, D.S. (2005) 'The Politics of Path Dependency: Political Conflict in Historical Institutionalism', *Journal of Politics* 67: 1275–300.

Pierre, J. (2000) *Debating Governance*. Oxford: Oxford University Press.

Pierson, P. (2000) 'Increasing Returns, Path Dependence and the Study of Politics', *American Political Science Review* 94: 251–67.

Pressman, J.L. and Wildavsky, A. (1974) *Implementation*. Berkeley, CA: University of California Press.

Primo, D.M. (2007) *Rules and Restraint: Government Spending and the Design of Institutions*. Chicago: University of Chicago Press.

Rhodes, R.A.W. (2007) 'Understanding Governance: Ten Years On', *Organization Studies* 28: 1243–64.

Riker, W.H. (1980) 'Implications from the Disequilibrium of Majority Rule for the Study of Institutions', *American Political Science Review* 74: 432–46.

Roller, E. (2005) *The Performance of Democracies: Political Institutions and Public Policies*. Oxford: Oxford University Press.

Scharpf, F.W. (1988) 'The Joint-Decision Trap: Lessons from German Federalism and European Integration', *Public Administration* 66: 239–78.

Schmidt, M.G. (2002) 'Political Performance and Types of Democracy: Findings from Comparative Studies', *European Journal for Political Research* 41: 147–63.

Schon, D.A. and Rein, M. (1994) *Frame Reflection: Solving Intractable Policy Disputes*. Cambridge, MA: MIT Press.

Selznick, P. (1984) *Leadership in Administration: A Sociological Interpretation,* rev. edn. Berkeley, CA: University of California Press (1st edn 1947).

Sorenson, E. (2006) 'The Democratic Anchorage of Governance Networks', *Scandinavian Political Studies* 28: 195–218.

Stereeck, W. and Thelen, K. (2005) *Beyond Continuity: Institutional Change in Advanced Political Economies.* Oxford: Oxford University Press.

Stoker, G. (2009) 'The Micro-foundations of Governance: Why Psychology Rather than Economics Could be the Key to Better Intergovernmental Relations'. Paper presented to Conference on Local Governance and Intergovernmental Relations in the West Indies.

Taagepera, R. and Shugart, M. (1989) *Seats and Votes: The Effects and Determinants of Electoral Systems.* New Haven, CT: Yale University Press.

't Hart, P., Stern, E.K. and Sundelius, B. (1997) *Beyond Groupthink: Political Group Dynamics and Foreign Policy-Making.* Ann Arbor, MI: University of Michigan Press.

Tsebelis, G. (2000) *Veto Players: How Political Institutions Work.* Princeton, NJ: Princeton University Press.

Weaver, R.K. and Rockman, B.A. (1994) *Do Institutions Matter?* Washington, DC: The Brookings Institution.

7

Systems Theory

Anders Esmark

SYSTEMS THEORY AND GOVERNANCE RESEARCH

In this chapter, I discuss the main implications of the systems theoretical approach to the core issues of the recent debate on governance, such as the limits and possibility of steering and coordination, the rise of markets and networks in public governance, and metagovernance and the role of the state. I distinguish between two strands of systems theory: (1) general systems theory and cybernetics and (2) sociological systems theory. Whereas general systems theory and cybernetics have had considerable impact on the governance debate, sociological systems theory has not yet received quite the same level of attention. I shall briefly clarify the relation between the two strands of thought before outlining the structure of the chapter.

General systems theory and cybernetics

In the words of Ludwig von Bertalanffy, widely recognized as the originator of general systems theory, systems theory is a 'science of wholeness' (1968: 37). The ontological stance implied by this somewhat vague characterization is that the whole constitutes a level of reality in its own right, displaying characteristics that cannot be identified on the level of individual parts or the sum of those of parts. A system, in this sense, is a whole defined by the existence of relations among a number of elements that constitute a boundary between an entity and its outside. General systems theory harbours strong interdisciplinary ambitions, including 'systems of any kind: physical, technological, biological, ecological, psychological, social or any combination of those' (Heyligen and Joslyn, 2001: 156). In spite of this apparent interdisciplinary ambition, contributions at the level of general systems theory display a strong preference for the scientific language of formal science, such as mathematics and logic, and the natural and technical sciences. An important aspect of general systems theory is its close affinity with cybernetics. In general, cybernetics can be defined as the science of 'control and communication' (Wiener, 1948) or 'co-ordination, regulation and control' (Ashby, 1999). Cybernetics focuses specifically on the potentials for steering and controlling systems embedded in various forms of (self-)organization, relying on concepts such as input and output, feedback loops, requisite variety, adaptation, goal-directedness, control mechanisms, etc. (Heyligen and Joslyn, 2001). For the purposes of the governance debate, general systems theory and cybernetics can be treated as virtually indistinguishable.

Sociological systems theory

Although this tradition has deeper roots, I focus here on the work of German Sociologist Niklas Luhmann. Parts of Luhmann's work can be seen as contributions to general systems theory and cybernetics, but his engagement with this strand of thinking is mainly a precursor to sociological analysis and discussion. Thus, Luhmann showed little interest in rigidly maintaining the formal and technical ambitions of general systems theory, opting rather to employ general systems theory as just one source among many in order to provide a more adequate socio-logical analysis of modernity. Luhmann was a sociologist above all else. His basic motivation was the quintessential macro-sociological quest for insights into the fundamental structures and dynamics of society (Luhmann, 2005). Methodologically speaking, Luhmann more or less considered himself a historian, thinking, as he stated 'mostly in historical terms' (1991). This somewhat neglected historical dimension of Luhmann's work has recently been made the subject of more careful scrutiny (Buskotte, 2006).

The chapter proceeds as follows. First, I discuss the theory of steering and control suggested by general systems theory and cybernetics, focussing on the so-called 'autopoietic' paradigm and the concept of self-governance. Secondly, I survey the macro-sociological analysis of constitutive traditions of governance suggested by Niklas Luhmann's work on functional differentiation, contrasting his approach with the conventional macro-sociology of state, market, and civil society widely applied in governance research. Thirdly, I discuss the implications of functional differentiation for the transformation of public governance, distinguishing between the application of new governance mediums and scripts by government organizations and the issue of network proliferation. Finally, I turn to the issue of metagovernance and the role of state as seen from the systems theoretical perspective.

THE GOVERNANCE OF SELF-GOVERNANCE: STEERING PESSIMISM OR ADVANCED LIBERAL GOVERNMENT?

General systems theory and cybernetics have had a considerable impact on governance studies, even to the extent that a 'socio-cybernetic' school of governance studies is included in Rhodes' widely used inventory of governance research (1997: 50, 2000: 54). The cybernetic approach to governance studies has been pursued most systematically by Andrew Dunsire (1986, 1990, 1993, 1996) and taken up by a number of Dutch governance scholars (Kickert, 1993a, 1993b; Kooiman, 1993, 2000, 2003; Schaap, 2007). Additionally, the general systems theory and cybernetics approach has been used in a more eclectic fashion by other contributions to the current governance debate (Jessop, 1998, 2000, 2002; Kaufmann, Majone and Ostrom, 1986; Mayntz, 1993, 2003; Rhodes, 1997; Scharpf, 1993, 1997) and related debates in organizational sociology (Hernes and Bakken, 2003), planning theory (Chettiparamb, 2007) and public administration (Brans and Rossbach, 1997).

Most of these contributions to the governance debate are based more or less explicitly on the 'autopoietic' paradigm within general systems theory and cybernetics. The concept of autopoiesis was introduced by the biologists Humberto Maturana and Francisco Varela (1980) and later applied to social systems by Stafford Beer (1985), Gareth Morgan (1986) and Niklas Luhmann (1984, 1986, 2002). In a fashion not untypical of debates within general systems theory, the application of autopoiesis to social systems has been criticized by those insisting on the primacy of its biological connotations (Varela, 1981). Bracketing the issue of whether the applications of autopoiesis and related concepts to social systems are formally correct from the perspective of general systems theory, the concept of autopoiesis basically suggests that a system is its own output: an autopoietic system produces itself rather than something else, the latter being the defining trademark of allopoietic systems. Moreover, autopoietic systems are recursive, meaning that such systems reproduce themselves within themselves. By implication, any operation or event within an autopoietic system is conditioned solely by the recursive reproduction of the system itself, rather than by circumstances outside of the system.

From a governance perspective, the core idea of the autopoietic paradigm is the notion of *self-governance*. The central concept of autopoiesis, literally meaning self-creation, has given rise to a host of related concepts such as self-organization, self-reference and self-steering. In each case, the prefix 'self' suggests that any state or event within the system is caused by the system itself. The basic idea can also be coined in terms of autonomy. An autopoietic system is completely autonomous in the sense that it maintains a distinction between system and environment that establishes the relation between the inner world of the system and the outer world of its environment – including other systems. The relation between system and environment is always a product of the system itself. An autopoietic system is only operational, which is the same as saying that it only exists, insofar as it maintains a boundary between itself and its environment and acts upon this distinction. As such, any autopoietic system enjoys radical autonomy.

Conventional cybernetics to some extent perceives systems mechanically, i.e. as more or less calculable algorithms connecting input with output, and output once again with input through feedback mechanisms subject to regulation by external control devices. Such systems are not self-creating, but can be perceived rather as servomechanisms with a potential for automated self-corrections according to set values under the supervision of an external controller. Autopoietic systems, however, cannot be described adequately as mechanisms: they do not operate according to the logic of automated self-corrections, but are self-steering in the sense that they remain in control of their own values as well as the variety of possible responses to their chosen values. Systems that are self-creating in a strict sense clearly retain a capacity to change their operations in a manner that cannot simply be considered automated self-correction, but constitutes self-steering in a much more fundamental sense. By the same token, autopoietic systems are self-controlling: they act as their own primary controller.

When applied to governance studies, the autopoietic paradigm suggests a reorientation of a number of key issues and assumptions according to the logic of self-governance. The self-governing capacity of social systems is seen as a crucial dynamic underlying a host of problems and potentials currently experienced by government organizations in their pursuit of more efficient instruments of steering, coordination and control. The most apparent result of the autopoietic paradigm in this respect is a significant level of mistrust in the possibility of steering and planning from the outside (Aasche and Verschraegen, 2008; Chettiparamb, 2007; Hernes and Bakken, 2003). The radical autonomy of autopoietic systems suggests that such systems can be governed only imperfectly or not at all from the outside. The basic problem of inducing changes in a system from the outside, or changing the behaviour and/or perceptions of other actors in more conventional terms, is confronted by the self-governing capacity of the targeted system.

Such 'steering pessimism' is often explained by reference to the notion of systemic closure (Schaap, 2007), referring to the well-established distinction between open and closed systems within general systems theory and cybernetics. Open systems, on the one hand, to the kind of input/output mechanisms capable of self-correction through feedback envisioned by conventional cybernetics. Autopoietic systems, on the other hand, are usually conceived as being closed since they do not react to external stimuli in the straightforward sense suggested by the input/output model, but operate according to their own logics and values within a boundary rigidly maintained by the system itself. Strictly speaking, nothing crosses the boundary of an autopoietic system: the system only reacts to the environment in the sense that the system operates on the basis of a distinction between itself and its environment, thus determining its own environment as part and parcel of systemic reproduction.

The systemic closure of autopoietic systems certainly does merit a substantial level of steering pessimism, highlighting the inadequateness of modern 'semantics' on planning and steering and the 'limits of steering' (Luhmann, 1997a). On the other hand, the notion of systemic closure is sometimes overstated: the fact that autopoietic systems determine their own environment does not exclude them from specifying events and circumstances in the environment that can be related to internal operations of the system. Although autopoietic systems do not receive input in the way suggested by the mechanical input/output model, they none the less create their own input as part of the process of system reproduction. The reality of such input, although subject to the process of autopoietic reproduction, introduces a certain level of openness in the system. Luhmann described this dual nature of autopoietic systems through the distinction between operational closure and cognitive openness: although systems remain closed on the level of operations, they remain cognitively open in their reproduction of the distinction between system and environment. In Luhmann's view at least, the autopoietic paradigm therefore involves a rejection of the traditional opposition between closed and open systems (1986) in favour of an interpretation of systemic closure as a condition for systemic openness (1984: 25).

Interpreted in this way, the autopoietic paradigm suggests a more nuanced perspective on contemporary governance than one-sided steering pessimism. The self-governance of autopoietic systems is not based solely on systemic closure, but in equal measure on the cognitive openness of such systems. By the same token, self-governance does not imply an outright rejection of steering from the outside. The key proposition of the autopoietic paradigm is rather that steering from the outside always involves steering of self-steering, or *governance of self-governance*. This relation of governance to self-governance can also be defined as second-order governance: the self-governance of a particular system constitutes first-order governance, making any attempt to govern the system from the outside an instance of second-order governance. The core proposition of systems theory, thus understood, is that second-order governance is fundamental to any exercise of government. Correspondingy, a vital theme for the systems theoretical research agenda is the various ways in which strategies and instruments of government pursue governance of self-governance, and in particular the level of sophistication displayed in approaching the self-governing nature of the subjects of government.

Government strategies and instruments may approach self-governance as an obstacle; as something to be subdued or at least thoroughly restricted. Such strategies, which would typically include conventional forms of sovereign rule and bureaucracy, may be conceived as relatively crude in their approach to self-governance. They do not, however, simply negate self-governance. In the final instance, autopoiesis and self-governance can of course be disrupted and negated by external intervention. But in systems theoretical terms, this would be the same as the destruction of the targeted system. In a manner not unlike Foucault's distinction between violence (or coercion) and power, systems theory distinguishes between systemic destruction and steering based on the self-steering capacity of the subject of steering (Esmark and Triantafillou, 2009).

At the other end of the spectrum, we find strategies and instruments that approach self-governance rather as something to be nurtured and enhanced, such as those identified by current debates on the rise of network governance and metagovernance (Kickert, Klijn and Koppenjan, 1997; Koppenjan and Klijn, 2004). According to this view, government strategies and instruments aimed at subduing or restricting self-governance are to a considerable extent being replaced by alternative ways of governing that seek to increase the efficiency of governance by strategically nurturing self-governance and pursuing 'steering at a distance'. According to this line of argument, self-governance still poses a challenge that limits the range of suitable governance instruments, but, in contrast to outright steering pessimism, debates on network governance and, in particular, network management have proposed that governance techniques that enhance and utilize the potentials of self-governance provide a viable and potentially highly efficient form of governance.

A similar line of argument, albeit from a decidedly more critical perspective, has been presented by governmentality studies and writings on 'advanced liberal government' (Rose, 1999). The essential structure of such advanced liberal government is the 'conduct of conduct', mirroring the kind of second-order governance suggested by the notion of governance of self-governance. In contrast to steering pessimism, as well as more optimistic and technocratic, but mainly technocratic concerns about the potentials of network management, governmentality studies remain highly critical of current governance strategies and instruments, which are seen rather as overly efficient, sophisticated and even intrusive in their capacity to extract resources from self-governing subjects of steering (Bang and

Esmark, 2009). The dispute between steering pessimism and the image of an intrusive and highly efficient 'advanced liberal government' can and should not be settled here, but will remain a question for future research. It will, however, also be a recurring theme in the remainder of this chapter.

A MACRO-SOCIOLOGICAL VIEW OF GOVERNANCE: BEYOND HIERARCHY, MARKET AND NETWORKS?

Whereas general systems theory and cybernetics constitutes an established 'school' of governance research, sociological systems theory has had a more limited impact. The major contribution of sociological systems theory, which is more or less to say the work of Niklas Luhmann, is to provide a historical account of the dominant governance traditions of modern society, and to some extent also the way government organizations relate to such traditions. As such, sociological systems theory engages the core proposition of a substantial portion of governance research: that public governance has changed substantially in recent decades through increased reliance on market instruments and, in particular, the strategic formation and utilization of networks. Network proliferation and the rise of a 'network paradigm' in public governance is seen by the bulk of governance research as a historically significant addition to the conventional state tradition based on hierarchy and bureaucracy as well as the market tradition of governance.

Luhmann does not engage this historical narrative of public governance directly, but rather provides a rich analysis of the historical era of modernity that challenges the basic assumptions of governance research on the level of macro-sociology. It is hardly controversial to claim that contributions to the field of governance research are rarely concerned explicitly with macro-sociological inquiry as such. Nonetheless, they almost invariably make use of the macro-sociological distinction between hierarchy, market and networks in the historical narrative about the transformation of public governance. The primary contribution of Luhmann's approach to this dimension of governance research is an alternative analysis of the constitutive traditions of governance in current society, equating such traditions with the major function systems of a functionally differentiated (world) society.

In macro-sociological terms, the distinction between hierarchy, market and networks can be interpreted as a variation on the distinction between state, market and civil society, which has served as the dominant image of modernity since the birth of sociology. Current governance research is certainly not the first to apply this distinction in political and administrative science. Previous variations include hierarchy, market and negotiation (Dahl and Lindblom, 1953), politics, market and persuasion (Lindblom, 1977), hierarchy, market and relational contracts (Williamson, 1985) and hierarchy, market and solidarity (Offe, 1984; Streeck and Schmitter, 1985), as demonstrated convincingly by Helmut Willke (1998: 88). The distinction between hierarchies, markets and networks used almost univocally in current governance research basically continues this tradition (Bevir and Rhodes, 2003; Jessop, 2003; Kettl, 2002; Kickert, Klijn and Koppenjan, 1997; Koppenjan and Klijn, 2004; Mayntz, 2003; Rhodes, 1997, 2000; Scharpf, 1993; Sørensen and Torfing, 2007.

Although state and hierarchy are not strictly synonymous, the two terms, together with the concept of bureaucracy, are used more or less interchangeably to describe a broad 'state tradition' of steering and coordination in the governance debate. The notion of governance based on the market mechanism is used more or less invariably in governance debates. The relation between the networks and civil society is perhaps less straightforward, but most definitions of the network tradition of governance nonetheless retain the essential attributes of civil society. Although the concept of networks was originally inspired by organizational sociology and work on

inter-organizational networks, the broad network tradition of governance is often defined in terms of cultural and communicative attributes traditionally seen as the province of civil society, such as dialogue or solidarity (Jessop, 2003: 102), reflexive rationality (Bang, 2003; Torfing, 2007), a culture of reciprocity and utilization of trust as a medium of exchange (Bevir and Rhodes, 2003: 55; Considine and Lewis, 2003: 133).

Conceptual variation notwithstanding, the macro-sociology of state, market and civil society is, in other words, proposed implicitly or explicitly as an exhaustive analysis of the basic modes or traditions of steering and coordination available to government organizations and other actors. Sociological systems theory, however, rejects that the distinction between state, market and civil society can be considered a viable analysis of current society, let alone modernity as such. If anything, the distinction falls under the province of normative theory in the sense that it reiterates the traditional concern for original and 'organic' community in sociology, also recognizable in the cultural and communicative attributes assigned to the network tradition of governance. As such, the distinction is imbued with a certain preference for civil society vis-à-vis the state and market, sometimes reframed as 'lifeworld' vs 'system'. Luhmann, however, attached little value to the category of civil society and its opposition to state and market, be it as normative theory or as an actual empirical and historical account of modern society.

Modern society, according to Luhmann's alternative account, is not simply divided into state, market and civil society, but is subject to a much more pervasive *functional differentiation* between function systems such as the political system, law, economy, science, family, religion, health, mass media, education, art, etc. (Luhmann 1997b: 145). Modernity, in other words, can be interpreted as a historical era throughout which functional differentiation gradually constitutes itself as the primary form of societal differentiation. Luhmann initially declared that the onset of functional differentiation is 'hard to date', being subject to historical traces reaching back well into the fourteenth and fifteenth centuries, but none the less comes to the conclusion that stratified society had decidedly given way to a society defined primarily by functional differentiation during the latter third of the eighteenth century (1997b: 734).

Sociology has of course always been concerned with the issue of functional differentiation, but the primacy and pervasiveness of functional differentiation suggested by Luhmann set his analysis apart from the tradition, as does his refusal to lament this development according to the conventional sociological schematics of differentiation vs integration. The best indicator of Luhmann's break with traditional sociological reasoning is probably his proposition that modernity implies the gradual substitution of societies in the plural for society in the singular. In the historical era of modernity, there is only one society: a world society fundamentally decomposed into the global function systems of politics, law, economy, science, etc. Stratification and other forms of differentiation such as territorial segmentation and centre – periphery relations obviously persists in modern society, but the core of Luhmann's analysis is that these and other forms of differentiation become secondary to functional differentiation throughout modernity. As such, Luhmann can basically be seen as the most preeminent historian of functional differentiation.

By and large, Luhmann wrote a volume on each of the major function systems of society, tracing the genesis and subsequent consolidation of the system in question historically, and summarized the findings in his magnum opus *Die Gesellschaft der Gesellschaft* (1997b). The notion of a functionally differentiated world society and the implied rejection of state, market and civil society is of course an empirical claim that could not be proven beyond dispute by Luhmann himself in his very extensive oeuvre. For the same reason, the following is limited to highlighting the main implications for governance research, based on the proposition that the notion of a functionally differentiated world society is a reasonably sound claim under the usual rules of macro-sociological and historical observation.

The main implication of Luhmann's analysis for governance research is that the broad and encompassing modes of governance in modern society are constituted through the process of functional differentiation. Thus understood, the prevailing traditions of governance in contemporary society are constituted by the governance mediums and programmes of the aforementioned function systems, including not only the political system and the legal system but also the economy, science, family, religion, education, health, art, etc. The interpretation of function systems as basic and encompassing traditions of governance in modern society refers, in the final instance, to the governance function of their so-called symbolically generalized mediums. Elaborating on Parsons' theory of 'interaction mediums', Luhmann relates each function system to a specific symbolically generalized medium of communication that defines the particular culture and communicative rationality of the system in question.

Luhmann also describes such mediums as governance mediums (Luhmann, 1997b: 363; see also Willke, 1998: 142). The governance function of the symbolically generalized mediums is 'fulfilled through the combination of fixed preferences and variable conditions' (Luhmann, 1997b: 363, italics in original). This distinction between fixed preferences and variable conditions refers to the so-called code of symbolically generalized mediums and the programmes related to this code. The code is the simple binary preference structure of the medium in question, such as ruler/ruled in the case of political power, lawful/unlawful in the case of law, loved/unloved in the case of love, etc., whereas programmes refer to the variability of the specific '(…) semantic apparatus that attaches itself to the code in question' (Luhmann, 1997b: 362). On the one hand, programmes refer to discourses and genres such as party programmes, legal sources, scientific publications, religious revelations, etc. On the other hand, it also designates scripts, procedures, norms and roles as pursued in sociological and organizational research, i.e. '(…) a complex of conditions for the correctness (and thus the social acceptability) of behaviour' (Luhmann, 1984: 317).

Function systems facilitate steering and coordination through the combination of a specific governance medium and variable scripts and programmes constituted in relation to that medium. Rather than state and market, the list of governance traditions identified by such an analysis includes a political function system based on the medium of sovereignty, a legal system based on the medium of law and an economic system based on the medium of money. Although the three systems do resemble the established inventory of state and market traditions of governance, they also differ crucially from these. Most importantly, function systems operate according to the communicative logic of their constitutive medium rather than the organizational dynamics of hierarchy, bureaucracy and the self-regulating market mechanism associated with state and market in current governance research (for a more comprehensive elaboration of this argument, see Esmark, 2009).

Moving beyond the political system, the system of law and the economic system, the distance between the systems theoretical approach and the macro-sociology of state, market and civil society becomes even more pronounced. In the systems theoretical analysis, the concept of civil society has no empirical value: it is seen purely as a category of normative theory. What is usually considered civil society is itself decomposed in a number of function systems. By the same token, the idea of network tradition of governance explicitly or implicitly reaffirming the attributes of civil society is deeply problematic. In its place, sociological systems theory suggests an open-ended list of other systems such as the scientific system,

family, religion, education, mass media, health, etc. On the macro-level of analysis, the governance mediums and programmes of these systems provide functionally equivalent responses to the basic challenge of steering and coordination, which is dependent neither on the attributes of civil society nor on the organizational dynamics of networks (Esmark, 2009).

THE TRANSFORMATION OF PUBLIC GOVERNANCE: NETWORK PROLIFERATION AND BEYOND

The macro-level analysis suggested by sociological systems theory is clearly not an argument about recent historical transformation. Rather the opposite: Luhmann vehemently resisted the idea that the historical era of modernity has somehow come to an end, opting instead for the claim that the basic outline of the functionally differentiated world society has remained unchanged from its inception to the present day (1997b; 1998). The historical narrative of Luhmann's macro-level analysis is not about recent rupture or transformation, but rather the increasing pervasiveness of functional differentiation throughout the entire historical era of modernity. Nevertheless, the systems theoretical analysis does not reject the possibility of a substantial reorientation of government action towards new traditions of governance within the rather stable structures of the functionally differentiated world society.

The systems theoretical analysis does, however, suggest some vital modifications of the conventional interpretation of current changes in public governance as a matter of network proliferation and orientation towards markets and a network paradigm of governance. Neither state, nor market or networks constitute distinct traditions of governance at the macro level of analysis, which is to say that they do not constitute function systems. Whereas certain aspects of the state and market traditions of governance can be retraced in the array of function systems, the notion of a network tradition of governance and the underlying concept of civil society are rejected rather straightforwardly by the systems theoretical analysis. If we accept that the constitutive and encompassing traditions of governance in modern society can reasonably be equated with the function systems uncovered in the systems theoretical analysis, the notion of a broad network tradition of governance has to be abandoned.

This is not to say that networks are excluded from the systems theoretical analysis altogether, though. In addition to function systems, sociological systems theory identifies two other major types of social systems: interaction systems and organizations. In his principal work on the general theory of social systems, Luhmann provided an overall typology of systems that included machines, physical systems, psychic systems and social systems (1984: 16). Luhmann never made any serious attempts to include machines or physical systems in his work, but invested his efforts in the case of social systems, which he further divided into *interaction systems*, *organizations* and *societies*, the latter being inseparable from the pervasive differentiation between function systems in the case of the functionally differentiated world society. The addition of other types of social systems to this list is of course an empirical question, and Luhmann did consider new social movements a potential innovation in this respect (1997b: 847), but the basic typology of systems was never substantially revised.

Within this typology of social systems, networks can (for all intents and purposes) be considered equal to interaction systems. Interaction systems are based on the actual presence of actors in the same physical location or contact mediated by communication technology (Luhmann, 1997b: 813). Interaction systems are modeled on the conventional micro-sociological concept of networks as a primary social morphology, basically requiring nothing but emergent relations among a set of actors. In this sense, the systems' theoretical concept of interaction systems is relatively aligned with the micro-level concept of network utilized in social network analysis. Luhmann would probably be the first to acknowledge such conceptual kinship and makes no claim to groundbreaking originality when it comes to organizations either. Organizations are defined as systems facilitating the communication of decisions, and in particular collective decisions (1997b: 826), essentially reframing insights from organizational sociology and the conventional understanding of organizations as solutions to the problem of collective action.

Correspondence with micro-sociology and organizational sociology notwithstanding, systems theory is particularly insistent on rigidly distinguishing between the disparate realities of different social systems. Function systems, organizations and interaction systems are mutually exclusive, autopoietic systems. Correspondingly, the relation between government organizations and the governance traditions comprised by function systems should be distinguished carefully from the relation between government organizations and interaction systems/networks. Insofar as the state and other government organizations increasingly utilize networks strategically in public governance, which clearly seems a reasonable proposition with considerable empirical backing, such a development pertains only to the relation between organizations and interaction systems. It does not, in the terms of sociological systems theory, pertain directly to the relation between government organizations and the traditions of governance comprised by function systems.

Network proliferation may be a probable and even highly likely scenario, but should none the less be seen as empirically distinct from an equally or more important historical dynamic less scrutinized by governance research: the adoption of governance mediums, programmes and scripts from function systems such as the economy, science and the family by government organizations. No one, least of all Luhmann, will deny that there are strong historical links between certain organizations and specific function systems. The selection of a primary function based on the orientation towards a particular symbolically generalized medium and the appropriation of a number of related programmes, standards and scripts are part and parcel of the history of any modern organization (Luhmann, 1997b: 841). In the case of government organizations, a process of 'co-evolution' with the political and legal function systems is evident (Luhmann, 2000: 189).

Such links and co-evolution notwithstanding, the relation between function systems and organizations is clearly also historically contingent and variable. Although primary functions are still evident in most cases, organizations no longer remain firmly rooted within a particular function system, but increasingly operate within various function systems. Organizations have become increasingly mobile in relation to the overarching function systems: the number and nature of the mediums, programmes and scripts utilized in the pursuit of more efficient steering and coordination have become highly variable, subject to organizational choice in a functionally differentiated world society. Government organizations may have been historically coupled to the communicative rationality and specific programmes, standards and scripts of the political system and later the legal system, but there is no a priori reason to assume that other mediums and programmes cannot be utilized in the strategies and instruments of public governance.

For pragmatic reasons, only a few brief examples of this dynamic can be included here. A first example would be the adoption of programmes and scripts from the scientific system through evaluation techniques and the advent of evidence-based policymaking based on data compilation and analysis, knowledge centres, semi-public think-tanks and the submission of public policy to 'peer review'. Another example would be the tendency of a number of modern management techniques widely applied in government organizations to emulate scripts and procedures of the modern family and the education system, interpreting the subjects of such governance techniques as family members or students engaged in processes of self-development and learning rather than public servants or citizens. Similarly, the 'mediatisation' of the political system widely discussed in political communication studies can be interpreted as the adoption of routines and procedures from the system of mass media and the aesthetic values in processes of public governance (Esmark, 2009).

METAGOVERNANCE AND THE ROLE OF THE STATE

The reorientation of public steering and coordination to new traditions of governance calls into question the role of the state, or government, organizations in general. The current wave of governance research was initially sparked by an interpretation of current transformations as a development from 'government to governance', suggesting a weakening or 'hollowing out' of the state (Rhodes, 1997). More recent contributions, however, tend rather to suggest a change in the overall role and form of the state, prompted by the orientation towards new governance traditions and the adoption of new governance instruments and techniques. Various definitions of the emerging state have been offered, but a recurring theme in most definitions is the increased tendency of government organizations to act as 'metagovernors', i.e. to adopt instruments and techniques of steering and coordination based on what I previously labelled second-order governance or governance of self-governance.

In the terms of general systems theory and cybernetics, the concept of metagovernance is based on Ashby's 'law of requisite variety', which suggests that the steering of a particular system always requires the capacity to match the complexity of that system (Jessop, 2003). The more common definition of metagovernance, however, is intrinsically linked to the concept of networks, interpreting metagovernance roughly as the strategic nurturing, guidance and management of networks (Koppenjan and Klijn, 2004; Sørensen and Torfing, 2007). Metagovernance, in the latter definition, emphasizes the role of government organizations in creating networks and/or guiding existing networks as a way to coordinate and 'collibrate' heterogeneous sources of knowledge and extract otherwise inaccessible and disparate resources required to solve contemporary policy problems.

Similar arguments have been made in systems theoretical analyses of the 'ironic state' (Willke, 1992) and a 'supervision state' acting through 'decentralised context steering' (Willke, 1997, 2003). In contrast to the notion of the state as a metagovernor, however, neither the increased use of networks nor the adoption of governance mediums and programmes from other function systems can be seen as a historical transition towards a more reflexive state relying on second-order governance in contrast to earlier less reflexive forms of first-order governance. By the same token, the interpretation of advanced liberal government and the 'conduct of conduct' as a historically specific era following less advanced forms of rule, are inherently problematic from a systems theoretical perspective.

The governance of self-governance, according to the systems theory analysis, may be variable to the extent that steering from the outside can be pursued with varying degrees of latitude for the self-governing capacity of the targeted system. But in the final instance, the governance of self-governance defines any instance of steering from the outside. The (historical) particularity of second-order governance suggested by the concepts of metagovernance and advanced liberal government alike, by implication, remains problematic from a systems theoretical perspective. Metagovernance is completely endemic to government action. Regardless of the tradition of governance applied, and regardless of the extent the network organization is utilized, government action directed at the behaviour of others (which is to say operations of other systems in the vocabulary of systems theory) will conform to the basic structure of the governance of self-governance. The particularity of the current role of state, in other words, lies not in the orientation towards metagovernance as such, but rather in the way the governance of self-governance is conducted.

In one if his more provocative moments, to political scientists at least, Luhmann dismissed the state as a 'semantic trick' needed to keep the political system going (2000). A less provocative interpretation is that the state still constitutes a manifest reality at the level of organizations, insofar as government organizations limited in various ways by the territorial segmentation of state borders are obviously still part of world society. The most fundamental problem of public governance or government action in general, against this background, derives from the fact that the organizational reality of states is completely enveloped by the functional differentiation between mutually exclusive function systems. The state offers no possibility of unity above or beyond functional differentiation. The most important dynamic in the transformation of the role and function of government, in other words, is the challenges provided by the increasing pervasiveness of functional differentiation.

This image of state organizations operating within a functionally differentiated world society corresponds well with the problems often highlighted in current public policy debate, such as negative externalities, the dispersion of knowledge and resources, fragmentation, conflicting demands and in particular 'wicked problems'. Although functional differentiation can indeed be said to result in such challenges, it should be noted that Luhmann's analysis does not lend itself easily to functionalist explanations, interpreting network proliferation as a 'functional response to the increasingly fragmented, complex and dynamic character of society' (Torfing, 2007: 8). Within this line of argument, functional differentiation is interpreted mainly as a matter of increased fragmentation, complexity and change, explaining network proliferation. Although Luhmann is sometimes included among the sources of such arguments, the interpretation of current society in terms of fragmentation,complexity and accelerated changes is mainly the trademark of general systems theory and cybernetics rather than sociological systems theory.

Even though some of Luhmann's earlier work did entail a rather simple stimulus–response model of increased complexity and semantic responses (1980), the analysis of functional differentiation is based explicitly on a rejection of such 'semantics of increasing differentiation' (Luhmann, 1997b: 615). Luhmann's point is not that modern society is becoming increasingly fragmented, but simply that it is defined by a particular kind of primary differentiation, in contrast to other forms of differentiation. Similarly, functional differentiation is not seen to imply increased complexity as such, but rather an increased potential for managing and accommodating complexity. Function systems may be mutually exclusive, which certainly produces problems of coordination, but the totality of function systems does not amount to a particularly complex society.

Interpreting current society simply in the terms of fragmentation, complexity and accelerated changes essentially disregards the substance of functional differentiation and the reality of function systems pursued in Luhmann's analysis. As a result, the changes in the relation between government organizations and the traditions of governance comprised by function systems is excluded from view, as is the notion that networks are not necessarily a functional response to increased differentiation. Whether public governance in the face of functional differentiation is best served by the use of formal organizations or by networks depends on the context. The creation of networks rather than the addition of more formal organizations may indeed prove an attractive option, but there is no inherent reason to assume that

formal organizations could be preferable in other cases.

CONCLUSION – A TENTATIVE AGENDA FOR FUTURE RESEARCH

Systems theory has earned a reputation of being highly abstract and theoretical. I have tried to show throughout the above that the reputation is largely underserved, in particular in the case of sociological systems theory. Luhmann's work might be macro-sociological and hence beyond the scope of indisputable empirical proof (we are dealing with an analysis of world society, after all), but he pursued his thesis rather consistently through historical analysis. Nonetheless, the systems theoretical approach to governance research still leaves a lot of empirical questions unanswered. I conclude by highlighting a few of these.

1 *Impotence vs omnipotence of public steering and regulation.* The standard interpretation of the autopoietic paradigm as a critique of conventional theories of steering, planning and administration still has substantial merit, although the case is sometimes overstated. The insights of governmentality studies and the debate on advanced liberal government provide an interesting counter-image to such steering pessimism. The structural identity of second-order governance and 'conduct of conduct' makes the concerns about the overly efficient and even deceptive character of current governance regimes voiced by governmentality studies highly relevant to the systems theoretical analysis. The diverging images are of course partly the result of the methodological difference between approaches concerned with improving regulatory efficiency and more critical approaches (Bevir, 2006), but such differences notwithstanding, the tension between the two assessments of current governance effects provides a vital theme for future empirical research.

2 *The instruments, techniques and implications of new governance traditions.* I have

outlined the array of governance traditions suggested by the systems theoretical analysis in a very broad manner and substantiated the claim about the adoption of scripts and programmes in public governance only by a few brief examples. The exact mechanisms involved in this development and the instruments and techniques of governance emulating procedures from various function systems constitute a research agenda in its own right. Pursuing the question in detail could involve any number of case studies, targeting specific policy fields, which may mix scripts and procedures from various function systems, or procedures from specific function systems, which may spread across various policy fields. Such an agenda should not be pursued only on the macro level of Luhmann's own analysis, but rather on the level of specific strategies and instruments of government (Esmark and Triantafillou, 2009), as well as the everyday interpretations and practical experiences of the governors and the governed alike (Bevir and Rhodes, 2006; Bevir, Rhodes and Weller, 2003).

3 *Networks vs formal organization.* Rigidly insisting on the disparate realities of function systems, organizations and interaction systems highlights a choice between formal organizations and networks not to be confused with a choice between state, market and networks. Systems theory tells us little about how to make such choices, however. A vital issue for future research is determining the conditions under which networks are actually preferable in public governance vis-à-vis relying on agencies or other types of formal organization. Existing research tends to assume that networks are privileged by default through very general references to broad societal trends and conditions. A systems theoretical approach challenges such assumptions about the necessity of network governance, suggesting instead research designs that could shed light on the implications of choosing between networks and formal organizations and perhaps even compare the two types of institutional framework for public governance.

REFERENCES

Aasche, K.V. and Verschraegen, G. (2008) 'The Limits of Planning: Niklas Luhmann's Systems Theory and the Analysis of Planning and Planning Ambitions', *Planning Theory,* 7(3): 263–83.

Ashby, W.R. (1999/1957) *An Introduction to Cybernetics.* London: Chapman & Hall.

Bang, H. (ed.) (2003) *Governance as Social and Political Communication.* Manchester: Manchester University Press.

Bang, H. and Esmark, A. (2009) 'Good Governance in Control Society: Reconfiguring the Political from Politics to Policy', *Administrative Theory and Praxis* 31(1): 7–37.

Beer, S. (1985) *Diagnosing the System for Organizations.* London: John Wiley & Sons.

Bertalanffy, L.V. (1968) *General Systems Theory.* New York: George Braziller.

Bevir, M. (2006) 'Democratic Governance: Systems and Radical Perspectives', *Public Administration Review* May/June 2006: 426–36.

Bevir, M. and Rhodes, R.A.W. (2003) *Interpreting British Governance.* London: Routledge.

Bevir, M. and Rhodes, R.A.W. (2006) *Governance Stories.* London: Routledge.

Bevir, M., Rhodes, R.A.W. and Weller, P. (2003) 'Traditions of Governance – History and Diversity', *Public Administration* 81(1): 1–19.

Brans, M. and Rossbach, S. (1997) 'The Autopoiesis of Administrative Systems: Niklas Luhmann on Public Administration and Public Policy', *Public Administration* 75: 417–39.

Buskotte, F. (2006) *Resonanzen für Geschichte: Niklas Luhmanns Systemtheorie aus geschichtswissenschaftlicher Perspektive.* Münster: LIT.

Chettiparamb, A. (2007) 'Re-conceptualizing Public Participation in Planning: A View through Autopoiesis', *Planning Theory* 6(3): 263–81.

Considine, M. and Lewis, J. (2003) 'Enterprise Goverenance: The Frontline Bureaucrat in Australia, the Netherlands, New Zealand and the United Kingdom', *Public Administration Review* 63(2): 131–40.

Dahl, R.A. and Lindblom, C.E. (1953) *Politics, Economics and Welfare.* New York: Harper and Brothers.

Dunsire, A. (1986) 'A Cybernetic View on *Guidance, Control and Evaluation in the Public Sector*', in F.X. Kaufmann, G. Majone and V. Ostrom (eds), *Guidance, Control and Evaluation in the Public Sector* Berlin: de Gruyter; pp. 327–49.

Dunsire, A. (1990) 'Holistic Governance', *Public Policy and Administration* 5(1): 4–19.

Dunsire, A. (1993) 'Modes of Governance', in J. Koimann, (ed.), *Modern Governance*. London: Sage; pp. 21–35.

Dunsire, A. (1996) 'Tipping the Balance – Autopoiesis and Governance', *Administration and Society* 28(3): 299–334.

Esmark, A. (2009) 'The Functional Differentiation of Governance – Public Governance beyond Hierarchy, Market and Networks', *Public Administration* 87(2): 351–71.

Esmark, A. and Triantafillou, P. (2009) 'A Macro-Level Perspective on the Governance of Self and Others'. in P. Triantafillou, and E. Sørensen (eds), *The Politics of Self-Governance*. Farnham: Ashgate; pp. 25–43.

Hernes, T. and Bakken, T. (2003) 'Implications of Self-reference: Niklas Luhmann's Autopoiesis and Organization Theory', *Organization Studies* 24(9): 1511–36.

Heyligen, F. and Joslyn, C. (2001) 'Cybernetics and Second Order Cybernetics', in R.A. Meyers (ed.), *Encyclopedia of Physical Science & Technology*. New York: Academic Press; pp.155–70.

Jessop, B. (1998) 'The Rise of Governance and the Risk of Failure', *International Social Science Journal* 50(15): 29–45.

Jessop, B. (2000) 'Governance Failure', in Stoker, G. (ed.), *The New Politics of Local British Governance*. Basingstoke: Macmillan.

Jessop, B. (2002) *The Future of the Capitalist State*. Oxford: Polity Press.

Jessop, B. (2003) 'Governance and Meta-governance: On Reflexivity, Requisite Variety and Requisite Irony', in H. Bang (ed.), *Governance as Social and Political Communication*. Manchester: Manchester University Press; pp.101–17.

Kaufmann, F.X., Majone, G. and Ostrom, V. (eds) (1986) *Guidance, Control and Evaluation in the Public Sector*. Berlin: de Gruyter.

Kettl, D.F. (2002) *The Transformation of Governance*. Baltimore: Johns Hopkins University Press.

Kickert, W. (1993a) 'Complexity, Governance and Dynamics: Conceptual Explorations of Public Network Management', in J. Koimann (ed.), *Modern Governance*. London: Sage; pp.191–205.

Kickert, W. (1993b) 'Autopoiesis and Science of (Public) Administration: Essence, Sense and Nonsense', *Organization Studies* 14(2): 261–78.

Kickert, J.M.W, Klijn, E. and Koppenjan, J.F.M. (eds) (1997) *Managing Complex Networks – Strategies for the Public Sector*. London: Sage.

Kooiman, J. (ed.) (1993) *Modern Governance*. London: Sage.

Kooiman, J. (2000) 'Societal Governance: Level, Modes and Orders of Social–Political Interaction', in J. Pierre (ed.), *Debating Governance*. Oxford, Oxford University Press; pp.138–64.

Kooiman, J. (2003) 'Activation in Governance', in H. Bang, (ed.), *Governance as Social and Political Communication*. Manchester: Manchester University Press; pp. 79–101.

Koppenjan, J.F.M and Klijn, E. (2004) *Managing Uncertainties in Networks; A Network Approach to Problem Solving and Decision-making*. London: Routledge.

Lindblom, C. (1977) *Politics and Markets*. New York: Basic Books.

Luhmann, N. (1980) *Gesellschaftsstruktur und Semantik*. Frankfurt am Main: Suhrkamp.

Luhmann, N. (1984) *Soziale Systeme*, Frankfurt am Main: Suhrkamp.

Luhmann, N. (1986) 'The Autopoiesis of Social Systems', in F. Geyer, and J. Zouwen, (eds), *Sociocybernetic Paradoxes*. London: Sage; pp.172–92.

Luhmann, N. (1991) 'Ich denke primär historisch – Religionssoziologische Perspektiven (interview with D. Pollack)', *Deutsche Zeitschrift für Philosophie* 39(9): 937–56.

Luhmann, N. (1997a) 'Limits of Steering', *Theory, Culture & Society* 14(1): 41–57.

Luhmann, N. (1997b) *Die Gesellschaft der Gesellschaft*. Frankfurt am Main: Suhrkamp.

Luhmann, N. (1998) *Observations on Modernity*. Palo Alto, CA: Stanford University Press.

Luhmann, N. (2000) *Die Politik der Gesellschaft*. Frankfurt am Main: Suhrkamp.

Luhmann, N. (2002) *Einführung der Systemtheorie*. Heidelberg: Carl-Auer.

Luhmann, N. (2005) *Einführung in die Theorie der Gesellschaft*. Heidelberg: Carl-Auer.

Maturana, H.R. and Varela, F.J. (1980/1973) *Autopoiesis and Cognition: The Realization of the Living*. Boston: Boston Studies in the Philosophy of Science (42).

Mayntz, R. (1993) 'Governance Failure and the Problem of Governability', in J. Koimann (ed.),*Modern Governance*. London: Sage; pp. 9–20.

Mayntz, R. (2003) 'New Challenges to Governance Theory', in H. Bang (ed.), *Governance as Social and Political Communication*. Manchester: Manchester University Press; pp. 27–41

Morgan, G. (1986) *Images of Organization*. London: Sage.

Offe, C. (1984) *Contradictions of the Welfare State*. Cambridge, MA: MIT Press.

Rhodes, R.A.W. (1997) *Understanding Governance – Policy Networks, Governance, Reflexivity and Accountability*. Buckingham: Open University Press.

Rhodes, R.A.W. (2000) 'Governance and Public Administration', in J. Pierre (ed.), *Debating Governance*. Oxford: Oxford University Press; pp. 54–90.

Rose, N. (1999) *Powers of Freedom*. Cambridge: Cambridge University Press.

Schaap, L. (2007) 'Closure and Governance', in M. Marcussen, and J. Torfing, (eds), *Democratic Network Governance in Europe* Basingstoke: Palgrave/Macmillan; pp. 111–133.

Scharpf, F.W. (ed.) (1993) *Games in Hierarchies and Networks: Analytical and Empirical Approaches to the Study of Governance Institutions*. Frankfurt am Main: Campus.

Scharpf, F.W. (1997) *Games Real Actors Play – Actor-Centered Institutionalism in Policy Research*. Boulder, CO: Westview Press.

Streeck, W. and Schmitter P.C. (eds.) (1985) *Private Interest Government. Beyond Market and State*. London: Sage.

Sørensen, E. and Torfing, J. (2007) 'Theoretical Approaches to Metagovernance', in E. Sørensen, and J. Torfing, (eds), *Theories of Democratic Network Governance*. Basingstoke: Palgrave Macmillan; pp. 169–82.

Torfing, J. (2007) 'Introduction: Democratic Network Governance', in M. Marcussen, and J. Torfing, (eds), *Democratic Network Governance in Europe*. Basingstoke: Palgrave Macmillan; pp. 1–25.

Varela, F.J. (1981) 'Describing the Logic of Living', in M. Zeleny (ed.), *Autopoiesis: A Theory of Living Organization*. New York: North Holland Publishers; pp. 36–48.

Wiener, N. (1948) *Cybernetics or Control and Communication in the Animal and the Machine*. Cambridge, MA: John Wiley & Sons.

Williamson, O.E. (1985) *The Economic Institutions of Capitalism. Firms, Markets and Relational Contracting*. New York: Free Press.

Willke, H. (1992) *Ironie des Staates: Grundlinien einer Staatstheorie polyzentrischerGesellschaft*. Frankfurt am Main: Suhrkamp.

Willke, H. (1997) *Supervision des Staates*. Frankfurt am Main: Suhrkamp.

Willke, H. (1998) *Systemtheorie III – Steuerungstheorie*. Stuttgart: Lucius & Lucius.

Willke, H. (2003) *Heterotopia*. Frankfurt am Main: Suhrkamp.

8

Metagovernance

Bob Jessop

Whereas governance is a familiar but fuzzy notion with a long history, the concept of metagovernance is fresher and somewhat more focused. It was introduced independently in the mid-1990s by several West European scholars interested in problems of complexity, governance, and governance failure and has since been integrated into several theoretical and policy paradigms. It has been defined as, *inter alia*, the organization of self-organization, the regulation of self-regulation, the steering of self-steering, the structuring of the game-like interaction within governance networks, and interaction among actors to influence parameter changes to the overall system.[1] In its most basic and general (but also most eclectic) sense, it denotes the governance of governance. Despite its importance in certain theoretical as well as policy paradigms, the term hardly surfaces in the leading journal, *Governance*,[2] and is rarely mentioned explicitly even in very recent surveys of research on governance (e.g. Benz et al., 2007; Bevir, 2007; Kjaer, 2004; Lütz, 2006; for exceptions, see Bell and Hindmoor, 2009; Sørensen, 2006; and some chapters in Sørensen and Torfing, 2007). This chapter aims to compensate for this neglect. Thus it traces the background to interest in metagovernance and its association

with governance failure, identifies some pre-theoretical antecedents that have often gone unremarked, notes possible meanings of metagovernance and locates them within a typology of modes of governance, notes the strong practical orientation of contemporary interest in metagovernance, and, in a critical and contrarian spirit, explores some implications of metagovernance failure for theoretical and policy analysis.

FROM GOVERNANCE TO METAGOVERNANCE

The notion of metagovernance is obviously supervenient on that of governance. Although it is not part of my remit to explore or explain the revival of theoretical and practical interest in governance in the 1980s and 1990s,[3] it is important to note that it was related to the growing perception of the problems generated in this period by a combination of state and market failure and/or by a decline in social cohesion in the advanced capitalist societies. This was reflected in notions such as governmental overload, legitimacy crisis, steering crisis, and ungovernability. It prompted theoretical and practical interest in the potential of coordination through self-organizing heterarchic networks and partnerships and other forms of reflexive collaboration. Most of the early studies of governance were concerned with specific practices or regimes oriented to specific objects of governance, linked either to the planning, programming, and regulation of particular policy fields or to issues of economic performance. Concern with problems of governance and the potential contributions of metagovernance followed during the mid-1990s and the nature and dynamics of metagovernance have since won growing attention. This is illustrated neatly in Figure 8.1, reproduced from Meuleman (2008: 73). It shows

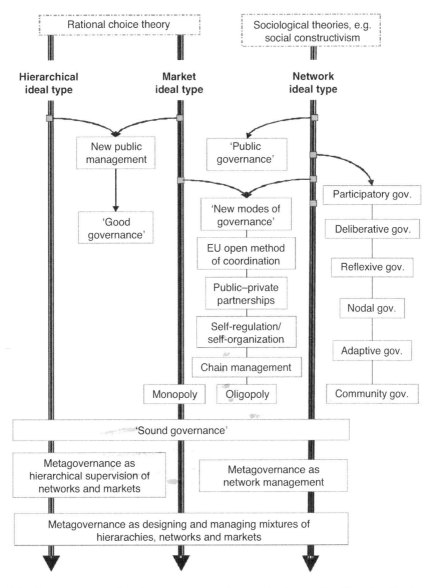

Figure 8.1   Governance and metagovernance: a 'conceptual crowd' addressing the 'new modes of governance' (From Meuleman 2008: 73, Figure 5)

some significant routes to interest in metagovernance in different theoretical traditions (rational choice vs sociological) and with respect to the three most commonly identified modes of governance (market, hierarchical, and network). Of particular interest in this figure is the implicit distinction between first-, second-, and third-order governance, to which I will return below, as well as the key role it accords to reflexivity, deliberation, and normative commitments in second- and third-order governance – which are also the two main sites of metagovernance.

Whereas some scholars and practitioners explicitly refer to metagovernance, many other terms have been used to denote or connote this phenomenon. This terminological variety is linked in part to the relatively 'pre-theoretical' and eclectic nature of work on governance and metagovernance, to the diversity of theoretical traditions with which more rigorous work is associated, to the different political traditions and tendencies that have shown interest in governance, to the great heterogeneity of the subjects and objects of governance and, *a fortiori*, of metagovernance, and to the challenges involved in translating theoretical reflections on governance and metagovernance into policy paradigms and, indeed, commercial consultancy in the public, private, and third sectors. For present purposes, governance refers to the structures and practices involved in coordinating social relations that are marked by complex, reciprocal interdependence, and metagovernance refers in turn to the coordination of these structures and practices (cf. Jessop 1995, 1997, 1998). I later distinguish between first- and second-order metagovernance in terms of whether coordination concerns one mode of governance or a combination thereof (cf. Kooiman, 1993). Before elaborating on these definitions and exploring some of their implications, I will review some pre-theoretical or tangential approaches to these phenomena.

It is important to note that there are significant historical precursors to the recent idea of metagovernance as well as some close contemporary equivalents. Among its antecedents we can mention Greek and Roman notions of a balanced constitution; the medieval and Renaissance 'mirror of princes' literatures on the art of government; various notions of 'police' (policey or *Polizei*)[4] concerned with the structures and practices that would help to promote a sound political economy, good governance, and state security; and such political principles of statecraft and diplomacy as the mixed constitution at home and the maintenance of international balance of power abroad. These traditions have survived in different forms. In addition, newer theoretical paradigms have turned their attention from governance (or its equivalents) to metagovernance for their own reasons, at different times, and in their own ways. An influential contemporary analogy is Foucault's approach to governmentality as 'the conduct of conduct' (1991), especially as developed by the Anglo-Foucauldian school of governmentality studies (see Miller and Rose, 2008).

An important contemporary precursor of the concept of metagovernance was the work of the second-generation critical theorist, Claus Offe, who drew on empirical research in the 1970s on market and state failure in vocational training (1975a) to develop a more general account of the problems involved in three main forms of public policymaking. He concluded that each of these forms – namely, rule-based bureaucratic decision-making, goal-oriented public planning, and participatory governance – had its own distinctive merits, limits, and vulnerabilities (Offe, 1975b). Bureaucratic routines were unsuited for complex public programmes requiring the mobilization of diverse resources and commitments (e.g. 'wars on poverty', a space programme). Yet purposive action is often made difficult by an absence of clear-cut, uncontroversial, and operationalizable goals and of a stable economic and political environment as well as by the problems facing the state in winning acceptance of the social and fiscal costs required for effective planning. In turn, democratic participation tends to generate demands that are inconsistent with capital accumulation and is also prone to politicize the process of administration. Offe noted that different modes of policymaking are better for some purposes than others and that, as policy objectives change, so does the preferred mode of policymaking. Matters are nonetheless complicated because even the most appropriate form has its own problems and will generate problems in turn. This raised the crucial question of how the state manages to survive in the face of the resulting tendency towards state failure. Offe's answer was that the state survives through a continual *fuite en avant*: i.e. in this context, an escape from an emerging crisis in one mode of governance by moving onto another mode of policymaking that is also likely to fail. This depends on a certain flexibility within the state such that it can escape the contradictions linked to one policymaking mode by changing policy objectives, adopting another mode from the existing repertoire, or, more generally, by modifying the relative weight of objectives and modes of policymaking to maintain at least the appearance of political success (1975b). This analysis clearly anticipated later studies on the nature of state failure, the role of metagovernance or collibration (see below), and the most appropriate way to respond to metagovernance failure. But its concern with the basic contradictions involved in the capital relation and the problems in governing that relation that derive from the separation of the economic and political spheres within a capitalist social formation systems has been largely neglected in later work on governance (see below).

Some of the earliest contemporary reflections on metagovernance emerged in work on the challenges of guiding the operations of relatively closed, self-organizing systems and/or coordinating interdependent systems of cooperative behaviour. Continental European work on 'autopoietic' (self-constituting, self-reproducing, and self-referential) systems illustrates the first theoretical paradigm; the latter is associated with 'socio-cybernetic' analyses of the interaction between observed

social systems and the systems that observe them. I consider these cases in turn.

First, in the 1980s, some German researchers argued that functional differentiation in modern social formations had created a complex ecology of self-organizing but interdependent social subsystems. Each of these 'autopoietic' subsystems has its own form of calculation (code) and mode of operation (programme). As such, these systems are resistant both to external control exercised by one subsystem that is superordinate to the others and to integration into a single, all-embracing horizontal network of coordination. Nevertheless, the material interdependence of these self-organizing subsystems also implied that a purely laissez-faire approach could (or would) lead to crises of societal integration and social cohesion (e.g. Braun, 1993; Luhmann, 1984; Teubner, 1984, 1985). This encouraged the conclusion that, while such entities could not be controlled through direct intervention from the outside, it might be possible to steer them 'at a distance' by modifying the environment in which a given self-referential, self-organizing system operated. For example, whereas economic actors may engage in illegal activities if they believe it would be profitable to ignore legal prohibitions, they may well respond to financial incentives and penalties. Influential concepts in this regard are *dezentrierte* or *dezentrale Kontextsteuerung* (decentred context steering) and societal guidance (see Glagow and Willke, 1983; Willke, 1988). Success in this regard was said to depend on an adequate, albeit necessarily incomplete, understanding of the *sui generis* dynamic of the system to be guided so that any measures taken would serve as positive system-modifying perturbations rather than being dismissed as trivial irritations or leading to the disintegration of the targeted subsystem. These grand metatheoretical concerns were initially less marked in Anglo-American work on governance in this period. Instead the latter type of work focused on more immediate and substantive problems of effective policymaking or issues of (neo-)corporatism. As later Anglo-American work moved from critique and problem-solving to *sui generis* theorization, however, its research agenda also integrated broader systems' theoretical concerns.

One of the two authors most often cited as the originator of the term 'metagovernance' is the Dutch scholar, Jan Kooiman, who belongs to a broader national tradition of sociocybernetic inquiry (e.g. Kickert et al., 1997; Klijn and Edelenbos, 2007; Meuleman, 2008; see also Deutsch, 1963). Interested in the problems that states faced in governing complex societies, he drew on sociocybernetics to explore state–society interactions not only in terms of automatic cybernetic mechanisms but also in terms of conscious guiding actions (Kooiman, 1993; 2003). Rather than assuming that the state stands over and against society, he viewed governments as cooperating with key societal actors to guide societal development. Accordingly, he stressed the need for requisite variety among modes of government–society interactions that range from hierarchical governance (top-down intervention) through co-governance (joint action) to self-governance (societal self-organization without government interference). Whereas Kooiman recognized that each mode has its own specific properties, he argued that they also interact to produce hybrid, or mixed, patterns of governance (Kooiman, 2003: 7). He further noted the importance for effective governance of cultivating the capacity to reflect on, and rebalance, the mix among these modes in response to changes in the challenges and/or opportunities that exist at the interface of market, state, and civil society. Governing in modern society requires an interactive perspective concerned to balance social interests and facilitate the interaction of actors and systems through self-organization, co-arrangements, or more interventionist forms of organization. Thus, for Kooiman, the key problem is how best to 'strike a balance' among different kinds of actors and steering mechanisms at the micro, meso and macrolevels of society.[5] He distinguished first-, second-, and third-order governing in this regard. First-order

governing is directly oriented to problem-solving and, for Kooiman, comprises the ensemble of governance forms ranging from hierarchy to self-governance; it is evaluated in terms of its effectiveness. Second-order governing occurs when attempts are made to modify the institutional conditions of problem-solving when they seem outdated, dysfunctional or harmful to governance and is evaluated in terms of legitimacy. Third-order governance, which Kooiman also calls metagovernance, involves efforts to change the broad principles that affect how governance occurs and to give it a clear normative rationality. Thus, it refers to the governance of governance and/or of governors by modifying the material or normative framework in which first- and second-order governing activities are pursued. It is judged in terms of moral responsibility (Kooiman, 2000; 2002; 2003).

About the same time, Andrew Dunsire introduced the notions of co-libration and 'collibration' to refer to what others term metagovernance. Although this has not yet become a standard term in the field, it has become more frequent and, as I will argue below, is especially apt for third-order governance (or metagovernance in its most precise sense). His 1993 lecture at the Max Planck Institute of Social Research (the home of the so-called Cologne School of Governance, on which, see next two pages) described collibration as a 'useful mode of state intervention' that enabled the state to secure some influence when faced with the growth of functional systems (such as law, economy, education, politics, and health) marked by operational closure and self-referentiality that made it hard for the state (or any other outside force) to regulate such systems. The result, other things being equal, was growing regulatory failure. Dunsire identified four main responses to this situation: (1) government subsidies that depended on compliance; (2) public–private partnerships and other forms of corporatist intermediation; (3) reflexive forms of law that require attention to the circumstances and consequences of their implementation; and (4) the use of various measures to indirectly influence the balance of forces. Each mechanism is said to transform in its own way the self-referentiality of functional systems from a problem into an asset that can be used to steer modern societies. But each also creates its own problems and must therefore be used reflexively and incrementally, monitoring effects and engaging in further rounds of intervention. Arguing that this useful set of tools lacks a general name, Dunsire initially proposed a phrase inspired by cybernetics: namely, 'selective inhibition of opposed maximisers' (1978, 1986). Later, and more elegantly, Dunsire referred to co-libration, i.e. the action of contributing with others to equilibration and, to 'collibration', a process that involves the state in 'the manipulation of balancing social tensions, the controlled shifting of a social equilibrium, the fine tuning of an oscillation of near-equal forces' (1993: 11). When this is successful, an unstable equilibrium of compromise (to use a Gramscian rather than Dunsirean phrase) is established within which the state can continue to exercise some influence (see Dunsire 1993, 1996; Gramsci, 1971).

The Cologne School has undertaken many studies of *Steuerung* (steering)[6] and has developed thereby a distinctive approach to the problems of governing functionally differentiated, organizationally dense and complex societies. Its leading figures recognized that these problems involved both the *Steuerungsfähigkeit* (steering capacity) of governing subjects and the *Steuerbarkeit* (governability) of the objects to be governed (Mayntz, 2003: 29; cf. 1993). Whereas these problems can lead to 'steering pessimism' (for example, in the work of Niklas Luhmann), the Cologne School was more optimistic, influenced, perhaps, by specific examples of successful administrative reform and the overall record of neo-corporatism in Germany in promoting economic development and sustaining a high-waged, high-tech, globally competitive 'Modell Deutschland'. Two key figures in developing these ideas were Renate

Mayntz and Fritz Scharpf who co-directed the Institute at Cologne for many years. A distinctive feature of this school is its actor-centred institutionalism, i.e. its interest in how the interaction between micro- and meso-level actors and institutional factors shapes the possibilities of effective governance. Indeed, Mayntz (2004) later emphasized that the actor-centred political steering (*Steuerung*) approach to policymaking was quite distinct from the governance (*Regulierung*) approach, which is more institutionalist and deals with regulatory structures combining public and private, hierarchical and network forms of action coordination. In this spirit, the Cologne School explored how to (re-)design the interaction between institutions and actors to improve the chances of overcoming policy problems. This is yet another way in which the topic of metagovernance (or, in this context, metasteering) has emerged.

For example, Scharpf once observed that:

> [c]onsidering the current state of theory, it seems that it is not so much increasing disorder on all sides that needs to be explained as the really existing extent, despite everything, of intra- as well as inter-organizational, intra- as well as inter-sectoral, and intra- as well as international, agreement and expectations regarding mutual security. Clearly, beyond the limits of the pure market, hierarchical state, and domination-free discourses, there are more – and more effective – coordination mechanisms than science has hitherto grasped empirically and conceptualized theoretically (Scharpf, 1993: 57, my translation).

He identified in particular the role of networks and added that their effectiveness could be enhanced 'by virtue of their "embeddedness" within hierarchical structures' (1993) or, put differently, through 'negotiated self-coordination where actual negotiations are embedded within hierarchical organisation' (1994). The idea that networking or self-regulation in the shadow of hierarchy could be more effective than either mode on its own anticipates the notion of metagovernance (see also Mayntz and Scharpf, 1995). Despite the influence of this approach, Mayntz later identified three crucial deficits: its methodological national-ism; its selective focus on domestic politics and policies; and, above all, its concern with policy effectiveness. The third of these defi-cits, which also characterizes many other approaches to governance and metagovern-ance, is evident in its concern with 'the output and outcome of policy processes, neglecting the input side of policy formation and the relationship between both' (Mayntz, 2003: 32). She also noted that the problems to be solved and/or crises to be managed were seen as shared, societal problems (Mayntz, 2001). Generalizing this observa-tion, we could say that studies of governance tend to focus on specific collective decision-making or goal-attainment issues relative to specific problems without asking how these problems are socially and discursively con-structed (cf. Jessop, 1995). For Mayntz, this bias leads students and practitioners of gov-ernance to neglect the problems generated by asymmetric power relations and domination. She therefore asked whether it is possible and, if so, worthwhile, to produce a single macro-theory that integrated the problem-solving approach with a concern about power asymmetries (Mayntz, 2001). This is a key question to which we will return.

The other scholar identified as the initiator of the current notion is the present author, whose analysis is grounded in critical theories of the state and political economy together with theories of autopoie-sis and context-steering (Jessop, 1990) and subsequent empirical research on local governance and private–public partnerships. Metagovernance was introduced to describe a counter-tendency to the shift from govern-ment to governance: namely, the shift from government to metagovernance, i.e. the 'organization of the conditions of self-organization' (Jessop, 1997). Later work has seen a more complex typology of modes of coordination of complex reciprocal interde-pendence (or governance in the broad sense); identified different forms of governance failure; considered different forms of metago-vernance in response to the different forms of governance failure, and argued that metagovernance in turn was prone to failure (Jessop, 2002, 2003). Some of these ideas are elaborated below.

MODES OF GOVERNANCE

The approach to governance and metagover-nance proposed in this chapter involves three analytical steps: first, identify the broad field of coordination of complex reciprocal inter-dependence with which governance practices are concerned; secondly, provide a narrow definition that identifies the *differentia speci-fica* of governance within this broad field; and, thirdly, distinguish forms of metagover-nance that correspond to these broad and narrow meanings. The literature on govern-ance identifies several forms of coordination of complex reciprocal interdependence, with three being especially prominent: *ex post* coordination through exchange (e.g. the anar-chy of the market); *ex ante* coordination through imperative coordination (e.g. the hierarchy of the firm, organization, or state); and reflexive self-organization (e.g. the heter-archy of ongoing negotiated consent to resolve complex problems in a corporatist order or horizontal networking to coordinate a com-plex division of labour). 'Governance' in the narrow sense is most commonly equated with the third form of coordination. Occasionally a fourth form of coordination is identified: namely, solidarity based on unconditional commitment to others (e.g. loyalty within small communities or local units or across imagined communities in times of crisis).

Governance as reflexive self-organization can be distinguished from exchange and imperative coordination in terms of its basic operational rationale and its institutional logic. Market exchange is characterized by a procedural rationality that is purely formal, *ex post*, and impersonal and oriented to the efficient allocation of scarce resources to competing ends. It prioritizes an endless 'economizing' pursuit of profit maximization.

Imperative coordination has a substantive rationality. It is goal-oriented, prioritizing 'effective' pursuit of successive organizational or policy goals. In contrast, reflexive self-organization is concerned to identify mutually beneficial joint projects from a wide range of possible projects, to redefine them as the relevant actors attempt to pursue them in an often turbulent environment and monitor how far these projects are being achieved, and to organize the material, social, and temporal conditions deemed necessary and/or sufficient to achieve them. It does not require actors to accept substantive goals defined in advance and from above on behalf a specific organization (e.g. a firm) or an imagined collectivity (e.g. the nation). Instead it has a substantive, procedural rationality that is concerned with solving specific coordination problems on the basis of a commitment to a continuing dialogue to establish the grounds for negotiated consent, resource sharing, and concerted action. To distinguish such an approach from the anarchy of the market and the hierarchy of command, governance in this narrow sense is often referred to as *heterarchic*.

The fourth form of coordination involves a relatively unreflexive, value-oriented rationality that is premised on unconditional reciprocal commitment and loyalty. This does not preclude processes through which such solidarity and mutual trust are established and reproduced (e.g. falling in love, coming to identify with fellow members of an imagined national – or other – community, or developing an even broader identification with humankind). Nonetheless, a thick form of unreflexive, unconditional support that covers many fields of social action is typically confined to small units (e.g. a couple or family) and, the larger the unit, the thinner and less intense does solidarity tend to become. Eventually it changes into more unilateral forms of 'trust' in the expertise of skilled practitioners providing goods and services that their clients cannot provide themselves (on trust and its failure, see Adler, 2001; Fukuyama, 1995; Gambetta, 1988; Luhmann, 1979; Misztal, 1996; Nooteboom, 2002).

MODES OF GOVERNANCE FAILURE AND METAGOVERNANCE RESPONSES

The growing interest in metagovernance is closely linked to (but not solely explicable in terms of) recognition that, like market exchange and imperative coordination, heterarchic governance is prone to failure. It is not a magic bullet that overcomes the problems of market and state failure without creating its own problems. Instead, each form of coordination of complex reciprocal interdependence has a distinctive primary form of failure together with typical secondary forms of failure (see Table 8.1). Market failure occurs when markets fail to allocate scarce resources efficiently in and through pursuit of monetized private interest. State failure in turn occurs when state managers cannot attain substantive collective goals determined on the basis of their political divination of the public interest (for a useful review of arguments about both kinds of failure, see Wallis and Dollery, 1999). Reflexive forms of governance were once seen as a 'third way' that could avoid both market and state failure and the tendency for switching between them. But they are also prone to fail – albeit for different reasons, in different ways, with different effects – with the result that governance failure has now become a topic of research. In addition, solidarity has its limits as a generalized mechanism, whatever potential it might have in small-scale social units, local groups, and tight-knit communities of fate (cf. Adler, 2001; Nooteboom, 2002).

In this regard it is tempting to agree with Malpas and Wickham (1995) that all efforts at governance are bound to fail to a greater or lesser degree – provided that we recognize, as I have noted above, that different forms of governance fail in different ways. This general propensity is due both to the general problem of 'governability'; the question of

Table 8.1   Modalities of governance

	Exchange	Command	Dialogue	Solidarity
Rationality	Formal and procedural	Substantive and goal-oriented	Reflexive and procedural	Unreflexive and value-oriented
Criterion of success	Efficient allocation of resources	Effective goal attainment	Negotiated consent	Requited commitment
Typical example	Market	State	Network	Love
Stylized mode of calculation	Homo economicus	Homo hierarchicus	Homo politicus	Homo fidelis
Spatio-temporal horizons	World market, reversible time	Organizational space, planning	Re-scaling, path-shaping	Any time, anywhere
Primary criterion of failure	Economic inefficiency	Ineffectiveness	'Noise', 'talking shop'	Betrayal, mistrust
Secondary criterion of failure	Market inadequacies	Bureaucratism, red tape	Secrecy, distorted communication	Co-dependency, asymmetry

whether a socially and discursively constituted object of governance could ever be manageable given the complexity and turbulence of the material, social, and spatio-temporal conditions in which it is embedded, and to particular issues of 'governability' associated with particular objects and agents of governance, with particular modes of coordination of reciprocal interdependence, and with problems of unacknowledged conditions of action and unanticipated consequences. This is particularly problematic where the objects of governance are liable to change and/or the environment in which they are embedded is turbulent, making strategic learning difficult (see Dierkes et al., 2001; Eder, 1999; Haas and Haas, 1995). A final consideration is that, in many cases, the appearance of successful governance depends on the capacity to displace and/or defer some of the unwanted effects of basic contradictions and dilemmas beyond the specific spatio-temporal horizons of a given set of social forces. Thus, an important aspect of governance success is the discursive and institutional framing of specific spatio-temporal fixes within which governance problems appear manageable because certain ungovernable features manifest themselves elsewhere (on spatio-temporal fixes, see Jessop, 2006).

If we consider exchange, hierarchy, heterarchy, and solidarity as four forms of

first-order coordination, responses to their respective forms of failure can be considered as second-order phenomena. Where these responses involve efforts to improve the performance of a given mode, they can be seen as examples of the metagovernance of that mode. Such efforts to redesign each coordination mechanism may focus directly on the mechanism itself and/or on its facilitating conditions. Thus, corresponding to the four basic, first-order modes of governance, we can identify four basic, second-order modes of metagovernance. In brief, and respectively, these involve: redesigning markets, constitutional innovation and design, changing the composition of networks and re-articulating networks of networks, and 'therapeutic' interventions oriented to restoring loyalty, trust, and commitment. In turn, efforts to rebalance the relative importance of different forms of governance correspond to third-order governance or what Dunsire calls collibration.

Briefly elaborating on these arguments, second-order governance (or first-order metagovernance) in response to market failure can be termed 'metaexchange', which involves the reflexive redesign of markets (e.g. for land, labour, money, commodities, knowledge) and/or the reflexive reordering of relations among two or more markets (or submarkets) by altering their operation, nesting, overall articulation, embedding in non-market relations or institutions, and so on. Likewise, the failure of imperative coordination can lead to 'metaorganization' – the reflexive redesign of organizational authority structures (e.g. Beer, 1990), the creation of intermediating organizations, the reordering of hierarchical inter-organizational relations, the management of organizational ecologies (i.e. the organization of the conditions of organizational evolution in conditions where many organizations coexist, compete, cooperate, and co-evolve), and the promotion of new policy rhetorics to justify new approaches (cf. Fischer, 2009; Hood, 1998). Next, in response to governance failure in its narrow sense, i.e. the failure of self-organizing networks, inter-organizational partnerships based on negotiation, or the heterarchic steering at a distance of inter-systemic relations, we can talk of 'metaheterarchy' (on network management, see Jones et al., 1997; Sørensen and Torfing, 2009). This involves the reflexive organization of the conditions of reflexive self-organization by redefining the framework in which heterarchy (or reflexive self-organization) occurs and can range from providing opportunities for 'spontaneous sociability' (Fukuyama, 1995; see also Putnam, 2000) through various measures to promote networking and negotiation to the introduction of innovations to promote 'institutional thickness' (Amin and Thrift, 1995). Van Bortel and Mullins (2009) distinguish three forms of metagovernance in this context: network design, to shape the organizational form of networks; framing, to define their goals, material conditions, and narrative rationale; and participation by metagovernor(s) in network operations, to influence network activities and outcomes. To this list, Sørensen, Torfing and Fotel (2009) add network management, which is concerned with smoothing network operations and making them more efficient and effective.[7] Lastly, at least for present purposes, there is metasolidarity: this involves forms of therapeutic action, whether spontaneous or mediated through therapeutic

intervention, to repair or refocus feelings of loyalty and unconditional commitment.

These responses are best described as involving second-order governance or, shifting perspective, first-order metagovernance. But there is no need to stop here. For there is another level of responses: one that, if it were not too confusing, could be called 'meta-metagovernance'. Better options are third-order governance (à la Kooiman) or second-order metagovernance; and, best of all, in part because of its etymological roots as well as its conceptual precision, is Dunsire's suggestion of 'collibration'. This can be defined for present purposes as the judicious re-articulating and rebalancing of modes of governance to manage the complexity, plurality, and tangled hierarchies found in prevailing modes of coordination with a view to achieving optimal outcomes as viewed by those engaged in metagovernance. In this sense it also means the organization of the conditions of governance in terms of their structurally-inscribed strategic selectivity, i.e. the asymmetrical privileging of different modes of coordination and their differential access to the institutional support and the material resources needed to pursue reflexively-agreed objectives.

Collibration is no more the preserve of one actor or set of actors than it is confined to one site or scale of action. Instead, it should be seen, like the various first-order forms of coordination of complex reciprocal interdependence and the various second-order forms of metacoordination, as fractal in character: i.e. as taking self-similar forms in many different social fields (on fractal relations, see, classically, Mandelbrot, 1982).

That said, now and for the foreseeable future, governments do play a major and increasing role in all aspects of metagovernance in areas of societal significance, whether these are formally private or public. This is especially true during periods of crisis that threaten system integration and/or social cohesion. They get involved in redesigning markets, in constitutional change and the juridical re-regulation of organizational forms and objectives, in organizing the conditions for networked self-organization, in promoting social capital and the self-regulation of the professions and other forms of expertise, and, most importantly, in the collibration of different forms of first-order governance and metagovernance. This role means that networking, negotiation, noise reduction, and negative as well as positive coordination often occur 'in the shadow of hierarchy' (Scharpf, 1994: 40).

For example, states at different levels provide the ground rules for governance and the regulatory order in and through which governance partners can pursue their aims; ensure the compatibility or coherence of different governance mechanisms and regimes; act as the primary organizer of the dialogue among policy communities; deploy a relative monopoly of organizational intelligence and information in order to shape cognitive expectations; serve as a 'court of appeal' for disputes arising within and over governance; seek to rebalance power differentials by strengthening weaker forces or systems in the interests of social cohesion and/or system integration; take material and/or symbolic flanking and supporting measures to stabilize forms of coordination that are deemed valuable but prone to collapse; contribute to the meshing of short-, medium- and long-term time horizons and temporal rhythms across different sites, scales, and actors, in part to prevent opportunistic exit and entry into governance arrangements; try to modify the self-understanding of identities, strategic capacities, and interests of individual and collective actors in different strategic contexts and hence alter their implications for preferred strategies and tactics; organize redundancies and duplication to sustain resilience through requisite variety in response to unexpected problems;[8] and also assume political responsibility in the event of governance failure in domains beyond the state (based in part on Jessop, 2002: 219; see also Bell and Hindmoor, 2009).

An additional aspect concerns the role of the state itself within metagovernance, because state managers typically monitor the effects of governance failure and attempts at metagovernance on their own capacity to secure social cohesion in divided societies. In addition, the state reserves the right to open, close, juggle, and re-articulate governance not only in terms of particular functions but also from the viewpoint of partisan and global political advantage. This can often lead state managers into self-interested action to protect their particular interests rather than to preserve the state's overall capacity to pursue an (always selective and biased) consensual interpretation of the public interest and to promote social cohesion.

Metagovernance involves not only institutional design but also the transformation of subjects and cultures. Whereas there has been much interest in issues of institutional design appropriate to different objects of governance, less attention has been paid by governance theorists to reforming the subjects of governance and their values. Yet the neoliberal project, for example, clearly requires attempts to create entrepreneurial subjects and demanding consumers, aware of their choices and rights as well as needing actions to shift the respective scope and powers of the market mechanism and state intervention. This is an area where Foucauldian students of governmentality offer more than students of governance. They have been especially interested in the role of power and knowledge in shaping the attributes, capacities, and identities of social agents and, in the context of self-reflexive governance, in enabling them to become self-governing and self-transforming (cf. Miller and Rose, 2008). This raises important questions about the compatibility of different modes of governance insofar as this involves not only questions of institutional compatibility but also the distribution of the individual and collective capacities needed to pursue creatively and autonomously the appropriate strategies and tactics to sustain contrasting modes of governance.

THE SUCCESS (AND FAILURE) OF METAGOVERNANCE IN THE SHADOW OF HIERARCHY

Given the tendency for first-order governance to fail, whether due to lack of governance capacities or the inherent ungovernability of the objects of governance, we can conjecture that metagovernance and collibration are also prone to fail. This conjecture is more plausible where the relevant objects of governance and metagovernance are complicated, interconnected, and, perhaps, internally and/or mutually contradictory and where any impression of effective governance and metagovernance to date has depended on displacing certain governance problems elsewhere and/or on deferring them into a more or less remote future. This could well be one source of the 'steering optimism' as opposed to pessimism that one finds in the governance and metagovernance literatures – especially when such temporary spatio-temporal fixes are reinforced by the capacity to engage in *fuite en avant* to produce new fixes. In contrast, 'steering pessimism' tends to look at the underlying long-term structural obstacles to effective governance and metagovernance and that, by virtue of the simplification of the conditions of action, so often lead to the 'revenge' of problems that get ignored, marginalized, displaced, or deferred. This sort of simplification is evident in attempts to define problems as societal in scope and as requiring consensual governance solutions rather than as conflictual effects of exploitation, oppression, or discrimination that can be solved only by addressing fundamental patterns of domination (cf. Mayntz 2001, 2003). This is reinforced by the normative assumptions that inform policy paradigms focused on governance, governance failure, and metagovernance – where the emphasis is on different forms of cooperation that obviate the need for antagonism and violence. In this sense, prolonged resort to organized coercion tends to be excluded from governance policy paradigms other than as a clear sign of governance failure.

Overall, considered from the viewpoint of their policy implications, this analysis of governance failure suggests three principles for metagovernance practices:

1 Deliberate cultivation of a flexible repertoire (requisite variety) of responses. This involves recognition that complexity excludes simple governance solutions and that effective governance often requires a combination of mechanisms oriented to different scales, different temporal horizons, etc., that are appropriate to the object to be governed. In this way strategies and tactics can be combined and rebalanced to reduce the likelihood of governance failure in the face of turbulence in the policy environment and changing policy risks.
2 A reflexive orientation about what would be an acceptable policy outcome in the case of incomplete success, to compare the effects of failure/inadequacies in the market, government, and governance, and regular reassessment of the extent to which current actions are producing desired outcomes.
3 Self-reflexive 'irony' such that the participants in governance recognize the likelihood of failure but then continue as if success were possible. The supreme irony in this context is that the need for irony holds not only for individual attempts at governance using individual governance mechanisms but also for metagovernance using appropriate metagovernance mechanisms.

Regarding the first principle, requisite variety involves informational, structural, and functional redundancies in governance practices and is necessitated by the complexity of their objects. As initially introduced into cybernetics, the law of requisite variety states that, in order to ensure that a given system has a specific value at a given time despite turbulence in its environment, the controller or regulator must be able to produce as many different counteractions as there are significant ways in which variations in the environment can impact on the system (Ashby, 1956). This principle has major implications for governance but, as specified, it is essentially static. In a dynamic and changing world the inevitable forces of natural and/or social entropy would soon break down any predefined control mechanism established using this concept. Because of the infinite variety of perturbations that could affect a system in a complex world, one should try to maximize its internal variety (or diversity) so that the system is well prepared for any contingencies. Thus it is better to reformulate the law as follows. To minimize the risks of metagovernance as well as governance failure in a turbulent environment, maintain a broad and flexible spectrum of possible responses so that the governance mix can be modified as the limits of any one mode become evident. While this requirement might seem inefficient from an economizing viewpoint because it introduces slack or waste, it also provides major sources of flexibility in the face of failure (Grabher, 1994). This involves the monitoring of mechanisms to check for problems, resort to collibrating mechanisms to modulate the coordination mix, and a commitment to the reflexive, negotiated re-evaluation of objectives. Moreover, because different periods and conjunctures as well as different objects of governance require different kinds of policy mix, the balance in the repertoire will need to be varied as circumstances change.

The second principle reflexivity, involves the ability and commitment to uncover and make explicit to oneself the nature of one's intentions, projects, and actions and their conditions of possibility, and, in this context, to learn about them, critique them, and act upon any useful lessons that have been learnt. Complexity requires that a reflexive observer recognizes that she cannot fully understand what she is observing and must therefore make contingency plans for unexpected events. In relation to governance, this involves inquiring in the first instance into the material, social, and discursive construction of possible objects of governance and reflecting on why this rather than another object of governance (or the policy problems with which it is associated) has (have) become hegemonic, dominant, or simply taken-for-granted. It also requires thinking critically about the strategically selective implications

of adopting one or other definition of a specific object of governance and its properties, *a fortiori*, of the choice of modes of governance, participants in the governance process, and so forth (on these particular issues, see Larmour, 1997). It requires monitoring mechanisms, modulating mechanisms, and a willingness to re-evaluate objectives. And it requires learning about how to learn reflexively. There is a general danger of infinite regress here, of course, but this can be limited, provided that reflexivity is combined with the first and third principles.

Finally, given 'the centrality of failure and the inevitability of incompleteness' (Malpas and Wickham, 1995: 39), the third principle highlights respect for what can be defined as 'the law of requisite irony' in approaching governance and metagovernance. Irony is required to avoid the temptations of fatalism, stoicism, opportunism, and cynicism in tackling the often daunting problems of governance in the face of complex, reciprocal interdependence in a turbulent environment. Fatalism leads to inaction, stoicism rests on passive resignation in the pursuit of familiar routines, opportunism is expressed in avoiding or exploiting the consequences of failure for self-interested motives, and cynicism leads to the stage management of appearances to claim success in the face of failure. Cynicism is the realm of symbolic politics, accelerated policy churning (to give the impression of doing something about intractable problems), and the 'spin doctor' – the realm of 'words that work but policies that fail'. This is particularly evident in the highly mediatized world of contemporary politics. In contrast to these other responses to the prospects of failure, the ironist is a sceptic. If one is likely to fail, one can at least choose one's preferred form of failure. This is irony in the Rortyan sense but it has a public, not private, form. Rortyan irony primarily concerns a contrast between public confidence about the permanency and validity of one's vocabulary of motives and actions and private doubt about their finality and apodicticity (Rorty, 1989: 73–4). Translated into the public domain of self-reflexive, deliberative governance and metagovernance, this could be expressed in terms of the need to combine 'optimism of the will' with 'pessimism of the intelligence'. The ironist accepts incompleteness and failure as essential features of social life but acts as if completeness and success were possible. She must simplify a complex, contradictory, and changing reality in order to be able to act – knowing full well that any such simplification is also a distortion of reality and, what is worse, that such distortions can sometimes generate failure even as they are also a precondition of relatively successful interventions to manage complex interdependence. The only possibility open for political ironists, then, is to stand apart from their political practices and at the same time incorporate this awareness of their ironic position into the practice itself. Thus, the public ironist is more romantic than cynical, committed to continuing public dialogue rather than a privatized world of laissez-penser, and also opposes passive resignation and opportunistic behaviour. For the law of requisite irony entails that those involved in governance choose among forms of failure and make a reasoned decision in favour of one or another form of failure. In this respect it is important to note that, in contrast to cynics, ironists act in 'good faith' and seek to involve others in the process of policymaking, not for manipulative purposes but in order to bring about conditions for negotiated consent and self-reflexive learning. In line with the law of requisite variety, moreover, they must be prepared to change the modes of governance as appropriate. But for good philosophical reasons to do with empowerment and accountability, they should ideally place self-organization at the heart of governance in preference to the anarchy of the market or the top-down command of more or less unaccountable rulers. In this sense, self-reflexive and participatory forms of governance are performative – they are both an art form and a life form. Like all forms of governance they are constitutive of their objects

of governance but they also become a self-reflexive means of coping with the failures, contradictions, dilemmas, and paradoxes that are an inevitable feature of life. In this sense participatory governance is a crucial means of defining the objectives as well as objects of governance as well as of facilitating the co-realization of these objectives by reinforcing motivation and mobilizing capacities for self-reflection, self-regulation, and self-correction.

CONCLUSIONS

This chapter has distinguished a set of first-order variants concerned with the reflexive redesign of individual modes of governance (such as markets, hierarchies, networks, and solidarities) and a set of second-order metagovernance practices concerned with the collibration, or rebalancing, of different forms of governance and their metagovernance. Metagovernance comprises a complex array of more or less reflexive social practices concerned with the governance of social relations characterized by complex, reciprocal interdependence. Interest in the topic has grown in step with recognition, even among its strongest advocates, of the limits of heterarchy (self-organization) as a solution to the failure of other forms of governance (such as the anarchy of the market or the hierarchy of command) (cf. Peters, 2008). It is always hard for critical scholars to engage with governance and metagovernance because of the normative bias in the definition of governance problems and governance solutions. Although there is a theoretical literature on governance and metagovernance (especially in the fields of critical political economy and governmentality studies), most research on governance is concerned with organizational and/or policy issues in the private, third, and public sectors and connected to irenic modes of problem solving. This is especially clear in current concerns with 'democratic network governance' and 'good governance'. This has discouraged, as Renate Mayntz has noted, inquiries into the grounding of 'societal problems' in economic and political domination (see above) and, as I have argued in my own contributions to the critique of political economy, serious neglect of the extent to which the sources of governance failure are deeper rooted than issues of cognitive capacities, the discursive framing of problems, institutional design, the tools of governance, or the willingness to engage in co-governance. These are fundamental questions that must be integrated into the governance research agenda and that require more work on the theoretical assumptions rather than policy implications of interest in governance and metagovernance.

Failure to address these issues is part of the explanation for the messiness of this field. For it is located uneasily at the interface of competing theoretical paradigms, their translation (and simplification) into policy paradigms, and the efforts of experts and consultants to market specific approaches and panaceas. They are also complicated by the strategic dilemmas involved in metagovernance design and the basic contradictions that often characterize specific objects of governance. For these reasons it is also a highly contested field, with significant ideal and material interests at stake, and one with major implications for the role of the national territorial state as the addressee of demands to act as 'metagovernor' in the last resort. When this is combined with the growing complexity and turbulence of world society, governance and, *a fortiori*, metagovernance are deeply problematic practices. This is why I have argued that metagovernance and, above all, collibration require a degree of romantic public irony if they are to stand some chance of success in producing a less conflictual, unequal, and unjust society. This leads to one final concluding remark: the continuing temptation to reduce disinterested *theoretical* work on governance and metagovernance into interested *policy-driven* work

risks throwing the whole notion of metagovernance into disrepute. Nonetheless, in the light of my preceding remarks, these threats to the theoretical paradigm should not be approached fatalistically or cynically but in the same ironic spirit that is appropriate to metagovernance as practice.

NOTES

1   The first two definitions are relatively commonplace and obvious; on the third, see van Bortel and Mullins (2009); on the fourth, see Bovaird (2005).

2   This observation is based on an 'all text' search of the complete index at the journal website, 20.09.2009. The same holds for the new journal, *Regulation & Governance*, which was first published in 2006.

3   For an earlier review, see Jessop (1995).

4   'Police', 'policey', or *Polizei* concern the governance of conduct in ways that will enable those in charge of 'affairs of state' to produce an orderly 'state of affairs' in a given state's territory. This is an issue much debated in early doctrines of statecraft and discussed more recently in Foucault's work on governmentality.

5   This balance will vary in the light of specific sectoral problems.

6   *Steuerung* is the main German equivalent of governance, a term derived from the medieval Latin word, *gubernantia*, In turn, this is related to the Greek word for steering, piloting, or guiding.

7   Sørensen, Torfing and Fotel (2009) explicate these principles as follows: (1) network design, which endeavours to determine the scope, character, composition, and institutional procedures of networks; (2) network framing, which seeks to define the political goals, fiscal conditions, legal basis, and discursive storyline of networks; (3) network management, which attempts to reduce tensions, resolve conflicts, empower particular actors, and lower the transaction costs by providing different kinds of material and immaterial inputs and resources; and (4) network participation, which aims to influence the policy agenda, the range of feasible options, the decision-making premises, and the negotiated outputs and outcomes.

8   One implication of this is that one should not be too hasty in destroying alternative modes of coordination – for they may need to be reinvented in one or another form in response to particular forms of coordination failure. This lesson is being relearnt in the current financial crisis.

REFERENCES

Adler, P.S. (2001) 'Market, Hierarchy, and Trust: The Knowledge Economy and the Future of Capitalism', *Organization Studies* 12 (2): 215–34.

Amin, A. and Thrift, N. (1995) 'Globalisation, Institutional "Thickness" and the Local Economy', in P. Healey et al. (eds), *Managing Cities: The New Urban Context.* Chichester: John Wiley; pp. 91–108.

Ashby, W.R. (1956) *Introduction to Cybernetics.* London: Chapman & Hall.

Beer, S. (1990) 'Recursion Zero: Metamanagement', *Systems Practice* 3(3): 315–26.

Bell, S. and Hindmoor, A. (2009) *Rethinking Governance. The Theory of the State in Modern Society.* Cambridge: Cambridge University Press.

Benz, A., Lütz, S., Schimank, U. and Simonis, G. (eds) (2007) *Handbuch Governance: Theoretische Grundlagen und Empirische Anwendungsfelder.* Wiesbaden: Verlag für Sozialwissenschaften.

Bevir, M. (ed.) (2007) *Encyclopedia of Governance.* London: Sage.

Bovaird, T. (2005) 'Public Governance: Balancing Stakeholder Power in a Network Society', *International Review of Public Administrative Sciences* 71: 217–28.

Braun, D. (1993) 'Zur Steuerbarkeit funktionaler Teilsysteme: Akteurtheoretische Sichtweisen funktionaler Differenzierung moderner Gesellschaften', *Politische Vierteljahresschrift*, *Sonderheft* 24.

Deutsch, K.W. (1963) *The Nerves of Government: Models of Political Communication and Control.* New York: Free Press.

Dierkes, M., Antal, A.B., Child, J. and Nonaka, I. (eds) (2001) *Handbook of Organizational Learning and Knowledge.* Oxford: Oxford University Press.

Dunsire, A. (1978) *Control in a Bureaucracy.* Oxford: Martin Robertson.

Dunsire, A. (1986) 'A Cybernetic View of Guidance, Control and Evaluation in the Public Sector', in F.-X. Kaufmann et al., (eds), *Guidance, Control and Evaluation in the Public Sector.* Berlin: de Gruyter, pp. 327–46.

Dunsire, A. (1993) 'Manipulating Social Tensions: Collibration as an Alternative Mode of Government Intervention'. Köln: Max-Planck-Institut für Gesellschaftsforschung, http://www.mpi-fg-koeln.mpg.de/pu/dp93-97_en.asp#1993, accessed 19.08.2009.

Dunsire, A. (1996) 'Tipping the Balance: Autopoiesis and Governance', *Administration & Society* 28(3): 299–334.

Eder, K. (1999) 'Societies Learn and Yet the World is Hard to Change', *European Journal of Social Theory* 2(2), 195–215.

Fischer, F. (2009) *Democracy and Expertise: Reorienting Policy Inquiry.* Oxford: Oxford University Press.

Foucault, M. (1991) 'Governmentality', in G. Burchell, C. Gordon, and P. Miller (eds), *The Foucault Effect. Studies in Governmentality.* London: Routledge; pp. 87–104.

Fukuyama, F. (1995) *Trust: The Social Virtues and the Creation of Prosperity.* New York: Free Press.

Gambetta, D. (ed.) (1988) *Trust: Making and Breaking Cooperative Relations.* Oxford: Blackwell.

Glagow, M. and Willke, H. (eds) (1987) *Dezentrale Gesellschaftssteuerung: Probleme der Integration polyzentristischer Gesellschaft.* Pfaffenfeiler: Centaurus.

Grabher, G. (1994) *Lob der Verschwendung.* Berlin: Edition Sigma.

Gramsci, A. (1971) *Selections from the Prison Notebooks.* London: Lawrence & Wishart.

Haas, P.M. and Haas, E.B. (1995) 'Learning to Learn: Improving International Governance', *Global Governance* 1(4): 255–85.

Hood, C. (1998) *The Art of the State: Culture, Rhetoric and Public Management.* Oxford: Oxford University Press.

Jessop, B. (1990) *State Theory: Putting Capitalist States in Their Place.* Cambridge: Polity Press.

Jessop, B. (1995) 'The Regulation Approach, Governance and Post-Fordism: Alternative Perspectives on Economic and Political Change?' *Economy and Society* 24(3): 307–33.

Jessop, B. (1997) 'The Governance of Complexity and the Complexity of Governance', in A. Amin and J. Hausner, (eds), *Beyond Markets and Hierarchy: Interactive Governance and Social Complexity*, Chelmsford: Edward Elgar; pp. 111–47.

Jessop, B. (1998) 'The Rise of Governance and the Risks of Failure: The Case of Economic Development', *International Social Science Journal* 155: 29–46.

Jessop, B. (2002) *The Future of the Capitalist State.* Cambridge: Polity Press.

Jessop, B. (2003) 'Governance and Meta-governance. On Reflexivity, Requisite Variety, and Requisite Irony', in H.P. Bang (ed.), *Governance as Social and Political Communication*, Manchester: Manchester University Press, Press; pp. 101–16.

Jessop, B. (2006) 'Spatial Fixes, Temporal Fixes, and Spatio-temporal Fixes', in N. Castree and D. Gregory, (eds), *David Harvey: a Critical Reader.* Oxford: Blackwell; pp. 142–66.

Jones, C., Hesterly, W.S. and Borgatti, S. (1997) 'A General Theory of Network Governance: Exchange Conditions and Social Mechanisms', *Academy of Management Review* 22(4): 911–45.

Kickert, W.J.M., Klijn, E.H. and Koppenjan, J.F.M. (eds) (1997) *Managing Complex Networks: Strategies for the Public Sector*. London: Sage.

Kjaer, A.M. (2004) *Governance*. Cambridge: Polity Press.

Klijn, E-H. and Edelenbos, J. (2007) 'Meta-governance as Network Management', in E. Sørensen and J. Torfing, (eds), *Theories of Democratic Network Governance*. Basingstoke: Palgrave Macmillan; pp. 199–214.

Kooiman, J. (1993) 'Governance and Governability: Using Complexity, Dynamics and Diversity', in Kooiman, J. (ed.), *Modern Governance: New Government–Society Interactions*. London: Sage, pp. 35–48.

Kooiman, J. (2000) 'Societal Governance: Levels, Models, and Orders of Social-Political Interaction', in J. Pierre (ed.), *Debating Governance: Authority, Steering, and Democracy*. Oxford: Oxford University Press; pp. 138–64.

Kooiman, J. (2002) 'Activation in Governance', in H. Bang, (ed.), *Governance, Governmentality and Democracy*. Manchester: Manchester University Press.

Kooiman, J. (2003) *Governing as Governance*. London: Sage.

Larmour, P. (1997) 'Models of Governance and Public Administration', *International Political Science Review* 63(4): 383–94.

Luhmann, N. (1979) *Trust and Power*. Chichester: Wiley.

Luhmann, N. (1984) *Soziale Systeme: Grundriß einer allgemeinen Theorie*, Frankfurt: Suhrkamp.

Lütz, S. (2006) *Governance in der politischen Okonomie. Struktur und Wandel des modernen Kapitalismus*. Wiesbaden: Verlag für Sozialwissenschaften.

Malpas, J. and Wickham, G. (1995) 'Governance and Failure: On the Limits of Sociology', *Australian and New Zealand Journal of Sociology* 31(3): 37–50.

Mandelbrot, B. (1982) *The Fractal Geometry of Nature*. New York: W.H. Freeman.

Mayntz, R. (1993) 'Governing Failures and the Problem of Governability: Some Comments on a Theoretical Paradigm', in J. Kooiman, (ed.), *Modern Governance: New Government–Society Interactions*. London: Sage; pp. 9–20.

Mayntz, R. (1997) *Soziale Dynamik und politische Steuerung. Theoretische und methodologische Überlegungen*. Frankfurt: Campus.

Mayntz, R. (2001) 'Zur Selektivität der steuerungstheoretischen Perspektive', Köln: Max Planck Institut für Gesellschaftsforschung. http://www.mpi-fg-koeln. mpg.de/pu/workpap/wp01-2/wp01-2.html, accessed 27/09/2009.

Mayntz, R. (2003) 'New Challenges to Governance Theory', in H. Bang, (ed.), *Governance as Social and Political Communication*. Manchester: Manchester University Press; pp. 27–40.

Mayntz, R. (2004) 'Governance Theory als fortentwickelte Steuerungstheorie?', Köln: Max Planck Institut für Gesellschaftsforschung. http://www.mpi-fg-koeln.mpg.de/publikation/workpap/wp04-1/wp04-1.html, accessed 27/09/2009.

Mayntz, R. and Scharpf, F.W. (eds) (1995) *Gesellschaftliche Selbstregulierung und politische Steuerung*. Frankfurt: Campus.

Meuleman, L. (2008) *Public Management and the Metagovernance of Hierarchies, Networks and Markets: The Feasibility of Designing and Managing Governance Style Combinations*. Heidelburg: Springer.

Miller, P. and Rose, N. (2008) *Governing the Present. Administering Economic, Social and Personal Life*. Cambridge: Polity Press.

Misztal, B. (1996) *Trust in Modern Societies. The Search for the Bases of Social Order*. Cambridge: Cambridge University Press.

Nooteboom, B. (2002) *Trust. Forms, Foundations, Functions, Failures and Figures*. Cheltenham: Edward Elgar.

Offe, C. (1975a) *Berufsbildungreform. Eine Fallstudie über Reformpolitik*, Frankfurt: Suhrkamp.

Offe, C. (1975b) 'The Theory of the Capitalist State and the Problem of Policy Formation', in L.N. Lindberg, R. Alford, C. Crouch and C. Offe, (eds), *Stress and Contradiction in Modern Capitalism*, Lexington: D.C. Heath; pp. 125–44.

Peters, B.G. (2008) 'The Two Futures of Governing: Decentering and Recentering Processes in Governing', Vienna: Institut für Höhere Studien.

Putnam, R.D. (2000) *Bowling Alone: the Collapse and Revival of American Community*. New York: Simon & Schuster.

Rorty, R. (1989) 'Private Irony and Liberal Hope', in *Contingency, Irony, and Solidarity*. Cambridge: Cambridge University Press; pp. 73–95.

Scharpf, F.W. (1994) 'Games Real Actors Could Play: Positive and Negative Co-ordination in Embedded Negotiations', *Journal of Theoretical Politics* 6(1): 27–53.

Sørensen, E. (2006) 'Metagovernance. The Changing Role of Politicians in Processes of Democratic

Governance', *American Review of Public Administration* 36(1): 98–114.

Sørensen, E. and Torfing, J. eds (2007) *Theories of Democratic Network Governance*. Basingstoke: Palgrave Macmillan.

Sørensen, E. and Torfing, J. (2009) 'Making Governance Networks Effective and Democratic through Metagovernance', *Public Administration* 87(2): 234–58.

Sørensen, E., Torfing, J. and Fotel, T. (2009) 'Democratic Anchorage of Infrastructural Governance Networks: the Case of the Femern Belt Forum', *Planning Theory* 8(3): 282–308.

Teubner, G. (1984) 'Autopoiesis in Law and Society: A Rejoinder to Blankenburg', *Law and Society Review* 18(2): 291–301.

Teubner, G. (1985) 'After Legal Instrumentalism? Strategic Models of Post-regulatory Law', *International Journal of the Sociology of Law* 12(4): 375–400.

van Bortel, G. and Mullins, D. (2009) 'Critical Perspectives on Network Governance in Urban Regeneration, Community Involvement and Integration', *Journal of Housing and the Built Environment* 24: 203–19.

Wallis, J. and Dollery, B. (1999) *Market Failure, Government Failure, Leadership and Public Policy.* Basingstoke: Palgrave Macmillan.

Willke, H. (1988) 'Staatliche Intervention als Kontextsteuerung', *Kritische Vierteljahresschrift für Gestezgebung und Rechtswissenschaft* 3: 214–29.

9

State–Society Relations

Jefferey M. Sellers

As an area of inquiry, state–society relations spans history from the emergence of states as a form of governance in medieval and early modern Europe (Ertman, 1997) to the alternative trajectories of economic development in contemporary developing countries (Evans, 1995; Kohli, 2004). Two fundamental concepts have defined this field. First, state–society relations is partly about the state itself. Despite the notorious elusiveness of 'stateness', and the fluctuating fortunes of this concept (Nettl, 1968; Levi, 2002), it has remained useful to identify a set of common organizational, administrative, legal, territorial and sociocultural attributes of public authority. Secondly, in contrast with purely statist accounts, state–society relations as a field focuses on the interactions and interdependency between the state and society. Among a range of theoretical perspectives, scholars in the field have converged around a broadly similar conclusion that society provides crucial elements of support for a state to be effective, and that a state is critical to collective action in society (Haggard, 1990; Evans, 1995; Migdal, 2001; Kohli, 2002).

From its origins in the Weberian tradition of political sociology, work on state–society relations has inherited several propensities. Regardless of its specific focus, it shares a predilection for large-scale generalizations about the state and its relation to society. Conceptions of the state itself, bearing the imprint of traditional European state forms, continue to portray it as a hierarchical, Weberian bureaucratic apparatus (Kohli, 2002). Consistent with this view of the state, analysts in the field have characteristically presumed a sharp analytical distinction, if not always an actual separation, between the state and society. In comparative studies that have sought to generalize about encompassing contrasts and similarities among nation-states, these approaches to state–society relations remain largely hegemonic.

This chapter demonstrates how these traditional approaches have proven increasingly inadequate to capture the realities of state–society relations. Not only in developed countries but also increasingly beyond them, a variety of trends have progressively altered the Weberian state and the overall patterns of state–society relations that accompanied it. Societal influences on the state have also grown, diversified and assumed new forms. The social imaginaries that have linked states with national societies may gradually be changing as well. Work in numerous fields, from public policy and public administration to local governance, political culture, and economic sociology, reveals important dimensions of state–society relations that can rarely be fully grasped by means of the traditional state–society dichotomy.

This emerging work points to a need for more sophisticated approaches to state–society relations. The traditional state–society dichotomy has given way to more nuanced, more complex conceptualizations of relations between state and society. Predominantly state-centered approaches have increasingly yielded to approaches that give greater attention to society and its dynamics. The changing understandings of the micro-level relations between society and the state will ultimately necessitate a wider rethinking of macro-level generalizations about state–society relations. Improved empirical understandings can eventually furnish the basis for more sophisticated normative critiques of existing practice, and more effective, more democratic policies and institutions.

This chapter is divided into three sections. The first section outlines the traditional approaches that still largely dominate the study of state–society relations, and developments since the 1970s that have called these approaches into question. The second section surveys the variety of approaches to state–society relations that a diverse array of contemporary disciplines have brought to bear. A final section outlines a number of promising alternative approaches that have begun to shed new light on the shifting state–society divide.

TRENDS IN STATE–SOCIETY RELATIONS: BEYOND THE WEBERIAN STATE

A full overview of the trends in contemporary state–society relations worldwide lies beyond the scope of the present chapter. Although theoretical assertions about the direction of these shifts have proliferated, the harder task of describing the overall character of these shifts empirically remains to be accomplished. This chapter focuses instead on two pervasive assumptions in accounts of state–society relations, and a range of developments that have increasingly undermined them. One of these assumptions takes state and society as dichotomous, mutually exclusive categories. The other holds the aggregation of state–society relations throughout a nation-state into an integrated, macro-level view as inherently unproblematic.

The cornerstone of the state–society dichotomy is a unitary notion of the state itself. In an influential essay, Peter Nettl outlined what this view of the state entails (1968). In this formulation, the state is an institutionalized collective power superordinate to other organizations that is sovereign vis-à-vis other states, autonomous or distinct from the rest of society, and identified socioculturally with a national collectivity.[1] This view of the state builds on Continental European legal theories with roots in the absolutist state, and on empirical conceptions developed by Marx, Weber, and Hintze. Where such an autonomous state is present, there is also an analytically distinct society. In many state–society accounts, social forces and social ties contribute to the autonomy of the state. Yet the corporate, civic, cultural, and other social elements of society are not to be mistaken with the state itself.

Thirty years after a prominent call to 'bring the state back in' (Skocpol, Rueschmeyer and Evans, 1979), this traditional view remains a predominant one in much of the literature on state–society relations. Even many accounts of state-building in the United States, described by Nettl himself as a country of low 'stateness,' highlight elements of hierarchy and autonomy in US institutions (Skowronek, 1982; Jensen, 2008; King and Lieberman, 2008). Leading analysts of state–society relations in developing countries such as Evans (1995), Migdal (1988, 2001), and Kohli (2004) continue to rely on this Weberian conception of the state even as their analyses demonstrate limits to its autonomy and authority.

A second element implicit in this dichotomy reflects a wider problem in the traditional understanding of both state and society. Work on state–society relations has generally taken the problem of aggregating patterns of institutions and practices as unproblematic. To treat the state as a single starting point for the analysis of relations between government and society, however, requires an approach to summing up patterns of institutions and informal practices that neglects a profound, practically irreducible diversity. Actual modern states encompass dozens of institutionally distinct policy sectors with highly diverse organizational architectures, from delivery of welfare services to environmental regulation to macroeconomic management. The institutional reality of a state is a matter of vertical as well as sectoral diversity. The multiple institutional tiers with some amount of autonomy in most contemporary states range from the nationally elected leaders at the heights of the state to the local officials who deliver local services. Alongside this vertical diversity, there is also territiorial diversity. Configurations of state policies, institutions, and actors may assemble in very different ways in one region or locality than in another. In the analysis of state–society relations, the even greater diversity of civil society compounds this challenge of aggregation.

Among its many meanings, the term 'governance' captures a variety of ways in which society is not simply acted upon by the state, but has actively shaped the actions of and outcomes of state activity. The recent trends that many analysts have characterized as a shift from government to governance (Peters and Pierre, 1998) aggravate the difficulties of aggregation inherent in the state–society dichotomy. A broad shift in this direction has been particularly evident in parts of Western Europe, where bureaucracies and state policies over the first half of the twentieth century maintained comparative autonomy from societal influences.

In Western Europe as elsewhere, however, even accounts of state–society relations prior to the 1970s pointed to elements of governance that had long been present. Parties and democratic elections linked voters to policymaking.

Corporatist interests of organized labor and capital exercised regular influence on the processes and substance of policy (Schmitter, 1974). In the United States, accounts of the legislative process found a pluralist universe of interest groups (Truman, 1967) or an iron triangle (McConnell, 1966). Analyses of urban politics portrayed it as the product of leadership and the distribution of public and private political resources (Dahl, 1962), or as the assertion of power by an élite that spanned public and private realms (Hunter, 1954). In developing countries too, work on clientelism had already pointed to intricate ties between society and the state.

Since the 1960s the shifts in government and policymaking as well as in the actions and influence of societal actors have brought about new complexity to relations across the state–society divide. These shifts have introduced new dynamics of interdependence between state and society, and contributed to growing ambiguity in the state–society distinction itself.

In part, these shifts trace to changes in institutions and policymaking processes:

- In numerous sectors of policy, sector-specific regimes of regulation have given rise to separate spheres of relations between societal and official stakeholders.
- Expansion of environmental and consumer regulation has mobilized both specialized groups and interests representing diffuse and activist citizen constituencies, and business and economic lobbies representing corporate interests.
- Policymakers have engaged a third sector of non-state organizations like non-profits and charities in the delivery of social services (Anheier and Seibel, 1990; Salomon and Aneier, 1997), and a variety of public–private partnerships (Heinz, 1993)
- Decentralization of important policies and other decisions has opened new local channels of state–society relations (United Cities and Local Governments, 2008). Increasingly, governance strategies in a range of policy sectors have revolved around efforts to incorporate regional and local participation in arrangements to conserve ecosystems or implement environmental policy (Mazmanian and Kraft, 2001; Layzer 2008),

or to pursue local social and economic agendas (Sellers, 2002a).

- In response to privatization of public companies and services, new regulations have sought to compensate for deficiencies in unregulated markets (Vogel, 1998), or regional and local interventions to replace national ones (Snyder, 1998).
- State regulation has itself taken new, more flexible forms that also deploy market mechanisms. Cap-and-trade systems that allow market exchange of rights to emit carbon dioxide or sulfur dioxide, taxes that impose penalties on carbon emissions, and voluntary green certification systems employ markets themselves as means to accomplish state ends more effectively as well as more efficiently (Rosenbaum, 2005: 130–70).
- Other new mechanisms have provided for public and stakeholder participation in policy. Institutionalized opportunities for citizens and groups representing interests have expanded in a wide range of contexts, from environmental impact procedures to public hearings in the ordinary administrative process, to new rights to challenge the state through courts (Cain, Dalton and Scarrow, 2006).

Societal changes have not only grown out of these shifts in states and policymaking but also helped drive them. A voluminous literature has linked them to shifts in capitalism, such as a growing imperative of competition for regional advantage (Brenner, 2004; Crouch et al., 2004) or the growth of advanced services into the leading edge of advanced industrial economies (Sassen, 1991; Sellers, 2002a). Jessop (1993) has argued that a 'Shumpeterian workfare state' oriented toward promoting regional and local competition for employment has increasingly supplanted the Keynesian welfare state as the effective model of economic policy for advanced industrial countries.

Since the 1960s, surveys throughout the developed world have documented the growth of 'cognitive mobilization' in popular attitudes toward politics (Dalton, 1984). Larger proportions of mass publics have adopted more active stances toward choices about party affiliations and have expressed willingness to participate in politics beyond the simple act of voting (Dalton, 2006: 47–50; 2008). Broad-based social movements around environmental issues, civil rights, and social justice, and on both sides of such controversial issues as abortion, help to account for these broad shifts.

Many of these shifts have been incremental, and many trace their origins back to periods before the era of governance. Their cumulative effects nonetheless suggest an ongoing sea change in state–society relations, particularly in developed countries. Increasingly since the 1960s, the focus of research on state–society relations has been on strategic analysis of these shifts, and ways to further engineer state–society dynamics. The logic of the Weberian state, like that of Weber's concept of bureaucracy, was that of a self-contained, integrated organization. Formal, hierarchical organization was the path to the most effective, most efficient form of state. As governance has replaced government as the guiding concept, institutions and policies have increasingly been understood and ultimately crafted around state–society relations as well as around the state. Market incentives among societal actors, effective practices to implement policies, and responsiveness to the concerns of policy stakeholders and citizens now often play as important a role as internal bureaucratic considerations in shaping policy within the state.

Considerable evidence suggests that the spread of ideas about policy and the ways it should be crafted have been one of the most powerful drivers of these institutional, economic, and social shifts (Derthick and Quirk, 1985; Hall, 1986; Blyth, 2002). An increasingly professionalized, internationalized class of policy experts has diffused such innovations in state–society relations as the new public management and local participatory reforms.

For the same reasons that the cumulative impact of these shifts on state–society relations remains difficult to discern, it is also hard to ascertain the full dimensions of the global variations in these trends. Among developed countries, the state–society relations of distinctive capitalist political economies, welfare states, systems of interest intermediation, and party systems have persisted even in the face of common trends. Shifts toward privatization, deregulation, and welfare retrenchment, for instance, have on the whole proceeded further in liberal market economies and liberal welfare states (e.g. Lane, 1997b; Feigenbaum, Henig and Hammett, 1999). The social democratic welfare states and corporatist systems of Nordic countries have often introduced mechanisms to enhance accountability and participation as an alternative to marketization (Lane, 1997a).

Among developing countries, where economic development is a pervasive, pressing concern, the problem of building effective states has kept the focus of the comparative literature more on the state–society dichotomy. Evans (1995) and Kohli (2004), for instance, examining a range of developing and transitional countries, show that effective state institutions and policies have generally played a critical role in successful cases of economic development. Informal state–society ties, often loosely characterized in such terms as clientelism, particularism or corruption, have been a pervasive influence on the implementation of state policy and the capacities of the state in developing countries (Van de Walle, 2001; Manzetti, 2003; Kitschelt and Wilkinson, 2007).

Still, similar shifts in state–society relations to those among developed countries are also taking place in the developing world. Partial or full privatization, often linked to a growing foreign investment in domestic economies and infrastructure, has played a major role in the economic strategies of developing countries from Latin America to China (Murillo, 2002; Tunç, 2005). In recent decades, decentralization across the developing world has enhanced the place of regional and local state–society relations in wider systems (United Cities and Local Governments, 2008). A growing literature reveals such new innovations as citizen participation in local budgeting and city planning (De Sousa

Santos, 1989), participatory arrangements for service provision (Berry, Portney and Thomson, 1993), and institutions for private and public stakeholder participation in resource management (Agarwal and Ribot, 1999; Abers and Keck, 2009). Especially in postcolonial countries and among indigenous communities, legal pluralism has enabled traditional community forms of authority and decision-making to persist beyond or even with the sanction of the institutions and laws of the state (Tamanaha, 2000; van Cott, 2000).

Despite these shifts, especially in comparative work on the state–society relations of developing countries, the state–society dichotomy dominates the leading analytical frameworks. In one influential account (Migdal, 2001), a 'strong state' is what makes the difference for effective policy. But a 'strong society' is crucial to building an effective state. Similarly, Evans (2002) points to the 'synergies' between states and societal groups as the crucial element for understanding state–society relations. This insistence on broad state–society distinctions can even be seen in such critical treatments as Scott's (1998) sweeping critique of statist approaches to policymaking and policy-relevant knowledge.

Whether in developing or developed countries, this state–society dichotomy itself has proven to be an unsuitably blunt instrument for scrutiny of relations between states and societies. Part of the reason lies in the way such concepts as 'state' and 'society' flatten crucial dimensions of nation-states that need to be distinguished for their consequences for relations with society to be understood. Retrenchment of welfare states and privatization, for instance, has followed different trajectories depending on the structure of distinct welfare sectors as well as differences in nation-state structures (Pierson, 1994; Murillo, 2002). Local and regional regimes of territorial governance also differ widely among places even under the same matrix of national policies and institutions (Sellers, 2002a; Navarro Yáñez, Magnier, and Ramírez 2008). Only in relatively exceptional circumstances, such as the similar local configurations of influence in social policy and economic development in Nordic countries (Sellers and Kwak, 2011) or the national introduction of decentralization and marketization in New Zealand in the 1990s, have state–society relations followed patterns that can be considered uniformly national in scale. In specific domains, such as the sector of telecommunications policy (Thatcher, 2004) or the territorial context of local governance in Europe (Heinelt, Sweeting, Getimnis, 2005), subnational practices have converged even as macro-level national institutional differences have persisted.

Similarly, analysis of governance across the state-divide consistently points to actors, forces, and mechanisms that the state–society dichotomy remains insufficient to capture. In a suggestive analysis of river basin governance in Brazil, Abers and Keck (2009) show that dynamics of informal networks among prominent individuals and experts have been more critical to successes of environmental governance in Brazil than either formal or informal institutions. Although their analysis demonstrates what Evans has termed 'state–society synergies', effective governance was not the product of a state that achieved autonomy from civil society. Instead, it emerged from networks of activists in civil society which ultimately mobilized state authority. The state–society relationship itself was less decisive for governance and its consequences than the politics of the activist groups and networks. Societal actors rather than the state effectively dictated the dynamics of governance.

A growing array of studies focused on state–society relations in developing countries have also pointed to the crucial role of joint governance arrangements within local society, or local societal initiatives and institutions, for effective governance (Agarwal and Ribot, 1999; Shaw, 2005; Tsai, 2006). A shift away from the traditional state–society distinction has been even more evident in studies of developed countries, as researchers have sought to explain such diverse arenas of

state–society relations as local governance, capitalist institutions, and social movements. Accounts in these domains regularly portray state authority as fragmented, subject to mobilization by societal as well as state actors, and only one set of resources among many.

In developing as well as developed countries, analysts in diverse fields have settled on modes of analysis that disaggregate the state, that focus on subnational sectoral or territorial units of analysis, and that place the burden of explanation on factors beyond either the state itself or the state–society divide. Subsequent sections will examine the variety of perspectives that researchers have brought to bear to understand these patterns, and sketch promising directions for future analysis.

ALTERNATIVE EMPIRICAL APPROACHES TO STATE–SOCIETY RELATIONS

No unified consensus has emerged around an agenda for the study of state–society relations. Instead, a variety of disciplines from anthropology to law to political science have adopted various approaches to the state and its interface with society. Although state–society relations rather than either the state or society comprises the central focus for all of these approaches, the largest portion of work in public administration, public policy, and comparative politics has retained a perspective centered on the actors and institutions of the state. Other lines of research, from a variety of other disciplinary and interdisciplinary perspectives, have sought to develop society-centered approaches to understanding state–society dynamics. The differences among these accounts are often rooted as much in different normative questions as in contrasting empirical contentions about how the relationship between state and society should be understood. Each of these contrasting approaches exhibits characteristic limitations as an account of state–society relations.

The advantages and disadvantages of each depend on its approach to aggregating patterns of state–society relations as well as its perspective on the state–society divide.

Approaches to state–society relations in the contemporary literature may be classified along two broad dimensions. On the one hand, these accounts have differed in whether they primarily adopt a viewpoint of policymakers within the state itself, or the viewpoint of ordinary citizens, groups or organizations in society. In an analytically distinct set of contrasts, these accounts can also be distinguished by whether they focus on the 'top-down' view of actors and institutions at the top of either state or societal hierarchies, or a 'bottom-up' perspective of those on the lower rungs of state and societal organizations.

Statist approaches retain much of the focus on the state that was a hallmark of the emphasis of early institutionalism on governmental institutions and the officials within them (e.g. Friedrich, 1963), as well as behavioralist work on political élites (e.g. Aberbach, Putnam and Rockman, 1981) and structuralist theories about the autonomy of the state from class structures (e.g. Poulantzas, 1973). In contrast with most of this work, state-centered approaches in the contemporary literature generally pay closer attention to the substance of policymaking, and to the interplay of relations between society and the state. Alongside such social science disciplines as economics, sociology, and political science, new applied professional fields like public administration and public management have reinforced statist approaches to state–society relations.

State-centered accounts persist in the presumption of traditional institutionalism that state–society relations can best be understood from the perspective of officials or other actors within the state. The affinities with the old institutionalism are clearest when the perspective is that of those at the highest levels of state hierarchies. Work on political élites or national leaders, and on executive–legislative relations more generally,

often clearly reflects this perspective. 'New institutionalist' work on state–society relations has largely retained this top-down state-centered perspective on the relation between the state and society. Skowonek's focus on the agency exercised by the US president (1993), and the contributions in Steinmo, Thelen and Longstreth (1992), exemplify how this work has illuminated policymaking at the heights of the state. Much of more recent attempts to analyze policymaking reflect a similar analytical focus. Thus, institutionalist work on public management reform continues to stress the centrality of organizations or their leaders in adopting innovations (Pollit and Bouckaert, 2004; Barzelay and Gallego, 2006). Similarly, approaches to regulation such as that of Ayres and Braithwaite (1992) look to firm and societal dynamics, but analyze them from the standpoint of the strategies of élite policymakers. Hall (2005) has called for more searching inquiries into the ways that policies and institutions of the state affect the motivations and potential for collective action of societal groups. Even as these accounts shift the focus of empirical inquiry beyond the circle of élite policymakers, the analytical focus remains on lines of causation from the heights of the state into civil society.

With the array of shifts in the state and state–society relations, however, it has become increasingly clear that this top-down perspective fails to capture a large component of the state and what it does. In an era of increasingly complex state activity, an expanding line of research has incorporated a disaggregated conception of the state and its relations with society. Accounts adopting a bottom-up approach to state–society relations that remains centered on the state itself have sought to reconceptualize relationships within the state in ways that capture these additional dimensions.

Work before the 1970s had already begun to develop accounts of state–society relations that stressed the role of the local state (Tiebout, 1956; Dahl, 1962; Kesselman, 1966). Studies of implementation, although still framed from the perspective of higher-level policymakers, showed a variety of local institutional and social conditions at the local level to be crucial to the success or failure of policy (Wildavsky and Pressman, 1974; Mazmanian and Sabatier, 1989). Accounts of multilevel or layered governance have gone a step further. Work in this vein demonstrates that lower as well as higher levels in state hierarchies have played important roles in policy and governance, and analyzes the interplay between levels. Marks and Hooghe's comparative analysis of two different varieties of multilevel governance (2005), for instance, highlights contrasts between models based on functional divisions between policy sectors and on hierarchies of territorial divisions between general purpose governments. Ostrom's framework for institutional analysis (Ostrom et al., 1994) focuses on formal organization and rules at multiple levels of the state as a source of governance.

Other work has shifted the locus of analysis to conceptualizations that span the multilevel state as well as civil society, but has retained a focus on officials and state policies. Rather than formal institutions of the state, the advocacy coalition framework elaborated by Sabatier and his colleagues (Sabatier, 1988; Sabatier and Jenkins-Smith, 1993) has shifted the focus to institutionalized policies and coalitions that form around contested alternatives in processes of policy and implementation. Similarly, frameworks that look to networks of organizations and interests at multiple levels, and which have increasingly been employed to account for patterns of governance in Europe (Ansell, 2006), incorporate participation by governments at a variety of levels and informal dynamics of interaction.

A further line of state-centered analysis has focused on state–society relations at the local or regional level. Studies of governance at the city level often stress the fluidity of state–society relationships and the critical role of coalition-building across the state–society divide. Much of the work in this vein, however, from Dahl's account of politics in

the city of New Haven, Connecticut (1962), to Stone's analysis of an urban regime in the city of Atlanta, Georgia (1989), has taken as its starting point the actions and initiatives of local political leaders. In such accounts, as in other state-centered ones, the object of empirical analysis remains how far the mayor is able to carry out the agenda he or she has set out to accomplish. Applied analyses of state–society relations in the field of public management and leadership, such as Moore (1995), have elaborated this perspective explicitly. In this work, the main point of the analysis is to discern how public officials can act as policy entrepreneurs to bring elements of state and society together.

Alongside either type of state-centered approach, a variety of literatures since the 1970s have also developed society-centered accounts of governance across the state–society divide. Accounts of this kind have most often appeared in disciplines like sociology or economics, which focus less exclusively on the state than political science, or in cross-disciplinary fields like public policy, education, and urban studies. Society-centered approaches mark a new departure not only from state-centered approaches with societal elements, such as accounts of interest intermediation, but also from structuralist accounts of classes, regions or aggregated economic interests. In contrast with both state-centered perspectives and structuralist accounts, these accounts of state–society relations look to the agency in society. Groups, individuals, and institutions beyond the state comprise the main analytical focus, either as a potentially decisive influence on processes and outcomes or as the main concern for purposes of understanding the consequences of governance. Just as state-centered approaches have increasingly acknowledged the importance of society, society-centered approaches can rarely jettison state actors and institutions as an important element in explanation. In society-centered accounts, however, the state remains a disaggregated, contingent institution open to influence from without.

Since organizational hierarchies remain a common feature of society as well as the state, society-centered accounts encompass a variety of top-down as well as bottom-up approaches. For instance, studies of private or market governance in such processes as international standard-setting for industries generally focus on initiatives and relationships among peak organizations (Mattli and Büthe, 2003). In comparative national political economy, Hall and Soskice (2001) shifted the focus for comparative analysis of capitalism away from the state, as such, to the institutions of the economy itself. The distinction they draw between liberal market capitalism and coordinated market capitalism, however, turns primarily on contrasts between national institutions for corporate governance, industrial relations, education and training, and interfirm relations. As a result, most of the research that has applied this framework has focused primarily on the leadership of national business, labor, and other organizational representatives in the crafting of these institutions (e.g. Mares, 2003; Thelen, 2004). Similarly, work on social movements has frequently dealt with their relations to the state. When these accounts focus on states, and treat the movements as unitary actors, the focus often narrows to the movement leaders themselves (e.g. Khagram, Riker and Sikkink, 2002; Tarrow, 2005).

Most frequently, however, society-centered approaches to the analysis of state–society relations have proceeded from the disaggregated perspective of individuals and communities. This societal perspective from the bottom-up approach offers a vantage point from which to assess the wider impact of the state and its policies in society. Simultaneously, this starting point enables an inquiry into what difference citizens, workers, neighborhoods, or other small-scale groups and individuals have made for policy and implementation. Within this general approach, distinct lines of research have adopted a range of alternative views of what it means to center analysis of the state and public policy around the vantage point of society.

One of the approaches focuses on collective action or community-based governance at the regional, local or neighborhood level. Analyses of social capital in the USA, Italy, and India have suggested that more organized, more participatory local civic groups can enhance the effectiveness and responsiveness of governance (Putnam, 1993, 2000; Varshney, 2002). Accounts of urban governance at the level of neighborhoods or school districts also point to organization and mobilization at the community level as being critical to enable effective local policymaking and neighborhood representation (Fung, 2004; Stone, 2005). In a different vein, Ostrom's analysis of effective arrangements to solve the problem of the commons in a wide range of local contexts (1990) demonstrates how institutional arrangements beyond the state, such as local cooperative arrangements for the governance of grazing land or forests, can be made to work through such mutually agreed-up mechanisms. Similarly, arrangements within specific firms and industries within coordinated capitalist systems of countries like Germany foster interpersonal and interorganizational dynamics of trust that can be crucial to the operation of the wider institutional system (Herrigel, 1996; Culpepper, 2003).

A second approach has examined individuals, families or firms who confront the state and employ it as a resource. In the US law and society literature, such authors as Edelman, Uggen and Erlanger (1999) or Barnes and Burke (2006) have investigated how firms, other organizations, and citizens have carried out legal norms beyond the formal reaches of state authority. Work on legal mobilization has also explored how legal institutions offer opportunities for ordinary citizens and local groups to contest state decisions (Sellers, 1995). In accounts of social capital like Putnam's work on the USA and Italy, the scope of the analysis also extends to everyday interactions within families or among individuals. In such accounts, organized forms of social capital in formal associations are inextricable from sociability within families or in friendships (1993, 2000). A number of accounts of relations among neighbors in both urban and rural settings portray interpersonal dynamics rather than any aspect of the state as the crucial element in governance (Crenson, 1983; Ellickson, 1994).

Table 9.1 summarizes the distinctive emphases of these approaches. Throughout these bodies of work, the interplay and interdependency between state and society remain consistent themes. Whether the approach to this interdependence is state-centered or society-centered makes an important difference in the conclusions authors reach about these themes. The emergence of both society-centered and bottom-up accounts has helped to highlight empirical gaps in more traditional state-centered approaches. State-centered approaches can easily lapse into similar mistakes as earlier institutional or élitist accounts that looked primarily to governmental actors and institutions. When the analysis starts with state actors, and concentrates on elaborating their role, it is all too easy to attribute them more power than they actually hold to set agendas or shape the outcomes from policy. The influence of societal actors and pressures, whether from dominant class interests or from the pressures of social movements, may seem invisible by

comparison with the choices of state actors. Influences on the outcomes from policy beyond actions within the state are also more difficult to discern.

A society-centered perspective enables both a clearer view of the consequences from policy and a better understanding of the social sources of state activity. In an era of growing and increasingly articulated state–society interactions, this perspective has become indispensable to a full understanding of the state itself. A society-centered perspective, however, can obscure critical influences from the state. Often these influences are indirect and only become evident from comparative analysis. Skocpol (2004), for instance, has plausibly argued that changes in the nature of the US state over the twentieth century can account for the decline in social capital that Putnam has observed. As increasingly, a centralized array of policies in specialized policy subsectors have replaced the decentralized, less specialized arrangements of the early twentieth-century US state, the networks of local civic associations from the early to mid-twentieth century have declined. A new generation of specialized, mass-membership advocacy organizations has replaced them. Society-centered analyses focused on everyday relationships between citizens and the state have

Table 9.1 Approaches to state–society relations

Approach	State-centered	Society-centered
Top-down	National institutions (Skowronek, 1982; Stéinmo, Thelen and Longstreth, 1992)	National capitalist institutions (Hall and Soskice, 2001)
	Political élites (Aberbach, Putnam and Rockman, 1981)	International standard-setting (Mattli and Büthe, 2003)
	Institutional effects on collective capacities (Hall, 2005)	
	National development policies (Haggard, 1990; Evans, 1995; Kohli, 2004)	
Bottom-up	Implementation studies (Wildavsky and Pressman, 1974; Mazmanian and Sabatier, 1981)	Local and regional economies (Culpepper, 2003)
	Multilevel governance (Marks and Hooghe, 2005)	Law and society (Edelman, Uggen and Erlanger, 1999; Barnes and Burke, 2006)
	Local leadership analyses (Dahl, 1962; Stone, 1989)	Social capital (Putnam, 2000)
	Local public management (Moore, 1995)	Ecosystem-based governance (Layzer, 2008)
		Social movement-based governance (Stone, 2005; Hochstetler and Keck, 2007)

encountered even greater difficulty sorting out agency from the background of state influences. This problem has been especially notable for accounts that focus on everyday interactions between the state and society. Law and society scholars, for instance, have struggled to delineate how the shadow of the law shapes the perceptions and incentives of citizens, and have neglected to capture the ways that power relationships can shape and reshape state policy (Sellers, 2007). Yet even society-centered accounts focused on local or national governance among organized groups must take account of the multiple ways that differences between state traditions and policymaking institutions influence the strategies and even the agendas of societal actors (Sellers, 2002b).

The choice between top-down or bottom-up approaches entails an analytically distinct set of alternatives not to be confused with the distinction between state and society. Two interconnected problems make it difficult to reconcile top-down and bottom-up approaches. The first problem arises out of the divergent ways the two approaches aggregate the myriad of individual local decisions of taxpayers, voters, workers, or small firms in society, or individual officials within the state, into wider patterns. Top-down approaches, following the conventions of macro-level social science, characteristically start from generalizations about local states, local societies or both. This approach probabilistically ascribes uniform behaviors to individuals, or looks to organizations and representatives who speak for them in the political process to act on their behalf. Such an approach need not discount bottom-up processes, but it flattens the individual agency of actors in a way that makes it difficult to understand them properly. Within the state, top-down accounts may mistake responses to pressures from constituencies or influences from local states as exercises of leadership. Within society, they can mistake the positions of leaders or organizations as the expression of more ambivalent or more contingent societal mobilization. Backward mapping from

outcomes of environmental or economic development decisions often reveals important local influences on the results from policy that a top-down account would not have discovered (Sellers, 2002a).

In a mirror image of the difficulties with the top-down approach, a bottom-up approach faces the need to take account of influences from the heights of institutions and organizations on individuals. Cross-national comparison, for instance, demonstrates a wide range of ways that national contexts influence the goals and means of local social and environmental movements (Sellers, 2002b). Contestation, deliberation, and interest intermediation at the heights of states or other organizations can remain impenetrable from a bottom-up perspective. Moreover, the qualitative case study methodology that is often best suited to exploring the individual motivations and relationships faces inherently greater difficulties of aggregation from the local level than at the heights of organizational hierarchies. Every micro-level action of the US President has a broad macro-level significance that a single neighborhood activist, a local government or a small regulated firm lacks. As a result, findings from bottom-up approaches in such fields as urban governance, law and society studies, and environmental policy are often more open to challenge as reliable general explanations.

The layered character of governance (Thelen, 2004) further complicates the relationship between bottom-up and top-down approaches. Within both the state and other social, political, and economic institutions, governance arrangements take place in a variety of nested settings that inevitably alter the relation between lower and higher levels of analysis. Especially in federal states, territorial and functional disaggregation have long meant that macro-level generalizations about state–society relations at the national level could not simply be arrived at through aggregation of organizations and relations at the local or provincial level. The sectoral disaggregation and decentralization of the state adds further layers to this complexity.

Parallel trends in the economy and society, such as the decentralization of firm governance and shop-floor relations (Culpepper, 2003), reinforce the importance of state–society relations at the local and regional levels.

Multilevel analyses that adopt an explicit focus on multiple levels of policymaking and their interplay provide a way to bridge the difference between levels. Studies in this vein have drawn connections between local and national dynamics in such specific arenas of US federal policy as urban development (Mollenkopf, 1983) and metropolitan issues (Weir, Ronengerude and Ansell, 2009), and in Europe between transnational and local arrangements (Börzel, 2002). This work highlights the need to recognize the complexity of the feedback loops between state–society relations at different levels of state hierarchies. Feedback from lower levels can decisively influence not only the aggregate patterns of state–society relations but also governance at the national level itself. Yet even multilevel analysis has not been able to resolve the tensions among the four alternative approaches to state–society relations. Multilevel accounts themselves may adopt widely different emphases, from a top-down approach that uses local examples (e.g. Mollenkopf) to a bottom-up approach that starts from local cases (Weir, Ronengerude and Ansell, 2009).

Multilevel analyses, and more generally hybrid approaches, hold considerable promise for advances beyond the shortcomings of each approach. Yet no single integrated approach is likely to resolve the inherent analytical tensions between macro and micro analysis as well as between the perspectives of state and society. As strategies of governance shift more toward reliance on societal actors, society-centered approaches will gain in validity. As decentralization, flexibility, and local responsiveness predominate, bottom-up approaches must supplement top-down ones. The optimal mix of approaches differs with both the policy sectors and the aspect of state–society relations under study. The choices

also have normative implications. A society-centered, bottom-up approach, for instance, will be more likely to clarify the possibilities for movements of citizens to organize to attain power. A top-down approach is more likely to be instructive about the possibilities for those who obtain power to enact effective policies.

PATTERNING BEYOND THE STATE–SOCIETY DIVIDE

As the recent study of state–society relations has focused increasingly on interactions between societal and state actors in joint processes of governance, it has advanced debates about the subject in several ways. In place of assumptions that the state remains somehow autonomous from the exercise of agency by societal actors, the interplay and interdependence between state and society has become established as conventional social science wisdom. Alongside aggregated, nation-centered approaches to the analysis of the state, a diverse set of literatures has emerged to scrutinize governance across the state–society divide in the subnational sectoral and territorial settings where it most often occurs. In supplementing both hierarchical and state-centered accounts, contemporary work in state–society relations has revealed previously unexamined sources of agency both outside the state and at the lower levels of state hierarchies. Although these shifting understandings partly reflect changes in practices of governance since the 1960s, the shifts in understandings about state–society governance have also given impetus to governance reforms.

As the diversity of state–society relationships has become clear and the changes in those relationships have increasingly recast the state–society divide, it has become clear that there is a need for reformulated approaches to the patterning of state–society relations. Recent innovations, partly driven by empirical studies as well as technocratic fashion, contributed to a world of state–society relations that increasingly eludes the traditional conceptual categories and even the methodologies of established social science. Institutions like the executive, the legislature, the bureaucracy, and federalism, and even established typologies of interest intermediation, can only partly capture the new dynamics. If the aim of understanding state–society relations is partly to craft better institutional mechanisms for more representative processes and more effective policy, then this need for better empirical accounts also has a normative dimension (e.g. Heller, 2000; Fung, 2004). But no normative critique or proposal to improve state–society relations can dispense with the need for reliable empirical generalizations about actual practice.

In place of traditional organizational divides and national institutions, patterns are emerging around dimensions of state–society relations that had previously received little attention. As the field continues to develop, several types of patterns offer promising prospects for future work:

1 *Subnational sectoral variation across countries*. As governance arrangements place growing emphasis on responsiveness and the effectiveness of policy, Lowi's observation that 'policy shapes politics' (1979) has taken on added significance. Agendas specific to different types of policy now regularly shape the roles that governments as well as societal actors play in governance, and the shape of governance networks. Only recently have a number of cross-sectoral studies begun to explore the difference that these agendas make for the involvement and influence of different types of officials and societal interests in processes of governance (Heinelt, Sweeting and Geimnis, 2005; Sellers and Kwak, 2011). This work suggests that in some sectors, such as local economic development policy, state–society relationships have been similar across countries. In others, such as welfare services, important national differences persist. Cross-national comparative studies have tended to focus on a single domain of policy within different countries (e.g. welfare policy, environmental policy, economic policy). As a result, the consistent consequences of differences in policy sectors for state–society relations, and the relations between sectoral and national institutional differences for state–society relationships, remain underexamined and undertheorized.

2 *Multilevel territorial configurations*. Along with processes of governance themselves, patterns of state–society relations have also increasingly organized around places. As theorists of 'joined-up' governments in the UK (Bogdanor, 2005), or 'administrative conjunction' in the USA (Frederickson, 1999), have noted, policy problems themselves often converge upon places. Efforts to remedy pollution or conserve ecosystems have frequently centered around coordinated governance arrangements among a variety of stakeholders concerned with a particular region (Mazmanian and Kraft, 2001; Layzer, 2008). Similarly, urban governance often amounts to what Pinson (2009) calls 'governance by project', taking its shape from an array of state and societal influences that converge at the level of a city. The governance of metropolitan regions can place through any number of intergovernmental and state–society channels, including multiple levels of government and diverse sectors of policy with a common focus on the region (Sellers, 2009). Analyses of how the territorial politics of formations like these at multiple levels of states, and the role that societal elements play in local governance as well as in higher-level policy, promises to cast new light on a dimension that has increasingly become a focus of governance.

3 *Effects of specific mechanisms to institutionalize state–society interaction*. Although institutions remain important, new types of institutions have emerged to regulate intergovernmental and state–society relations. Institutional arrangements like mechanisms for interlocal cooperation within metropolitan areas (Feiock, 2004; Sellers and Hoffmann-Martinot, 2008), regional resource management in developing countries (Abers and

Keck, 2009), cross-level cooperation in European multilevel governance (Ansell, 2006), participatory budgeting (Nylen, 2002), information release (Fung, Graham and Weil, 2007) or neighborhood participatory institutions (Berry, Portney and Thomson, 1993) need to be understood in terms of their consequences for the role of societal actors in governance. For a macro-level view, a full analysis of individual mechanisms also requires attention to their contribution to wider systems of state–society relations, and to the configurations of state and societal influences that contribute to their introduction.

4 *State-societal configurations in processes of governance*. In more contingent, more open-structured contexts of state–society relations, even effective policymaking by state officials may depend on processes of mobilization and institution-building that resemble the construction of a successful social movement (Stone, 2005). Studies of local education reform in the USA (e.g. Stone, 2001), and of environmental policy in Brazil (Hochstetler and Keck, 2007), show how mobilization by societal movements and experts that ultimately penetrate the state can play a critical role in effectuating policy change. As accounts of 'network governance' suggest (Jones, Hesterly and Borgatti, 1997), what links these formations can rarely be fully captured through formal organizations alone. Theoretical and empirical work on diverse institutional and social contexts of state–society relations should yield increasingly robust accounts of how these formations work.

5 *Policy outcomes and state–society feedback*. One of the approaches that work in public policy has taken to improving governance has been to devote more systematic attention to outcomes from policy. Closer examination of outcomes, through such methods as 'backward mapping' from societal processes to policy decisions (Elmore, 1979), also has the potential to deepen understandings of state–society relations. Shifts in societal interests and movements over time are often a consequence of the feedback

effects from earlier policies and institutions (Pierson, 1993). Tracing the causal chains between policy and politics in this way, such as between changing settlement patterns and mass opinion about urban policy (Mollenkopf, 1983), can illuminate underlying connections between state actions and societal change.

6 *Social classes, ethnicity, and their effects*. Wider patterns of social privilege and disadvantage remain a persistent influence on public policy. Some accounts have contended that new forms of state–society relations have diminished the influence of race and class on policy and politics (Clark and Hoffmann-Martinot, 1998). It seems more likely that the shifts in modes of state–society relations have altered the mechanisms of social class and racial influence in ways that still sometimes reward social and economic privilege. In local development policy, for instance, citizen and business mobilization around environmental issues and economic development in some cities of the USA and France has reinforced the biases of local governance against the most disadvantaged neighborhoods. Elsewhere, especially in northern Europe, greater local participation has worked to the advantage of marginalized groups in social policy (Sellers, 2002a). In developing world cities like Sao Paulo, opposition from a growing constituency of middle- and upper-class auto owners have often undermined initiatives to restrict vehicle pollution (Hochstetler and Keck, 2007).

The turn toward governance as a guiding approach to practice and an explicit focus of analysis and prescription has left the state–society dichotomy of increasingly limited utility for understanding state–society relations. As long as the state and society remain institutionally distinct, the difference between them will continue to play some role in analysis of governance. But the new informal as well as formal mechanisms of state–society interaction have increasingly required new conceptual approaches to the state–society divide, and altered methods applied to them. The flexibility, versatility, and responsiveness inherent in these mechanisms make it likely that patterns of state–society relations will become more contingent as well as more complex. More fine-grained units of analysis than the nation-state, and approaches to macro analysis based on closer attention to micro-level dynamics, will be necessary to capture these shifts. The challenge for the twenty-first century will be to devise new, refined reformulations that can capture these patterns within the broader critical perspective that social science can also provide.

NOTE

1 A further element of the state noted by Nettl – its role as an actor in international relations – lies beyond the scope of this essay.

REFERENCES

Aberbach, Joel, Putnam, Robert and Rockman, Bert (1981) *Politicians and Bureaucrats in Western Democracies*. Cambridge, MA: Harvard University Press.

Abers, Rebecca and Keck, Margaret (2009) 'Mobilizing the State: The Erratic Partner in Brazil's Participatory Water Policy', *Politics and Society* 37(2): 289–314.

Agarwal, Arun and Ribot, Jesse (1999) 'Accountability in Decentralization', *Journal of Developing Areas* 33(4): 473–502.

Anheier, Helmut K. and Seibel, Wolfgang (eds) (1990) *The Third Sector*. Amsterdam: Walter de Gruyter.

Ansell, Chris (2006) 'The Networked Polity: Regional Development in Western Europe', *Governance* 13(3): 303–33.

Ayres, Ian and Braithwaite, John (1992) *Responsive Regulation*. Oxford: Oxford University Press.

Barnes, Jeb and Burke, Thomas F. (2006) 'The Diffusion of Rights: From Law on the Books to Organizational Rights Practices', *Law and Society Review* 40(3): 493–523.

Barzelay, Michael and Gallego, Raquel (2006) 'From "New Institutionalism" to "Institutional Processualism"', *Governance* 19(4): 531–57.

Berry, Jeffrey, Portney, Kent and Thomson, Ken (1993) *The Rebirth of Urban Democracy*. Washington, DC: Brookings Institution.

Blyth, Mark (2002) *Great Transformations*. New York: Cambridge University Press.

Bogdanor, Vernon (ed.) (2005) *Joined–Up Government*. Oxford, UK: Oxford University Press.

Börzel, Tanya (2002) *Shaping States and Regions*. Cambridge: Cambridge University Press.

Brenner, Neil (2004) *New State Spaces*. Oxford: Oxford University Press.

Cain, Bruce, Dalton, Russell J. and Scarrow, Susan (eds) (2006) *Democracy Transformed? Expanding Political Opportunities in Advanced Industrial Democracies*. Oxford: Oxford University Press.

Clark, Terry N. and Hoffmann-Martinot, Vincent (eds) (1998) *The New Political Culture*. Boulder, CO: Westview.

Crenson, Matthew (1983) *Neighborhood Politics*. Cambridge, MA: Harvard University Press.

Crouch, Colin, Le Galès, Patrick, Trigilia, Carlo and Voelzkow, Helmut (eds) (2004). *Changing Governance of Local Economies*. Oxford: Oxford University Press.

Culpepper, Pepper D. (2003). *Creating Cooperation: How States Develop Human Capital*. Ithaca, NY: Cornell University Press.

Dahl, Robert (1962) *Who Governs?* New Haven, CT: Yale University Press.

Dalton, Russell (1984) 'Cognitive Mobilization and Partisan Dealignment in Advanced Industrial Democracies', *Journal of Politics* 46(1): 264–84.

Dalton, Russell (2006) *Citizen Politics*. Washington, DC: CQ Press.

Dalton, Russell (ed.) (2008) 'Citizenship Norms and the Expansion of Political Participation', *Political Studies* 56: 76–98.

Derthick, Martha and Quirk, Paul (1985) *The Politics of Deregulation*. Washington, DC: Brookings Institution Press.

De Sousa Santos, Boaventura (1989) 'Participatory Budgeting in Porto Alegre', *Politics and Society* 26(4): 461–510.

Edelman, Lauren, Uggen, Christopher and Erlanger, Howard (1999) 'The Endogeneity of Legal Regulation: Grievance Procedures as Rational Myth', *American Journal of Sociology* 105(2): 406–54.

Ellickson, Robert (1994) *Order Without Law*. Cambridge, MA: Harvard University Press.

Elmore, Richard (1979) 'Backward Mapping', *Political Science Quarterly* 94(4): 601–16.

Ertman, Thomas (1997) *Birth of the Leviathan*. Cambridge: Cambridge University Press.

Evans, Peter (1995) *Embedded Autonomy*. Princeton, NJ: Princeton University Press.

Evans, Peter (ed.) (2002) *Toward Sustainable Cities?* Berkeley, CA: University of California Press.

Feigenbaum, Harvey, Henig, Jeffrey and Hammett, Chris (1999) *Shrinking the State*. New York: Cambridge University Press.

Feiock, Richard (2004) *Metropolitan Governance*. Washington, DC: Georgetown University Press.

Feiock, Richard (2004) 'Rational Choice and Regional Governance', *Journal of Urban Affairs* 29(1): 47–63.

Frederickson, George (1999) 'The Repositioning of American Public Administration', *PS: Political Science & Politics* 32: 701–11.

Friedrich, Karl (1963) *Man and His Government*. New York: McGraw-Hill.

Fung, Archon (2004) *Reinventing Urban Democracy*. Princeton, NJ: Princeton University Press.

Fung, Archon, Graham, Mary and Weil, David (2007) *Full Disclosure: The Perils and Promise of Transparency*. New York: Cambridge University Press.

Haggard, Stephen (1990) *Pathways from the Periphery*. Ithaca, NY: Cornell University Press.

Hall, Peter (1986) *Governing the Economy*. Oxford: Oxford University Press.

Hall, Peter (2005) 'Public Policy-Making as Social Resource Creation' *APSA-CP* 16(2): 1–4.

Hall, Peter and David Soskice (2001) 'Introduction', in Peter Hall and David Soskice (eds), *Varieties of Capitalism*. Oxford: Oxford University Press.

Heinelt, Hubert, Sweeting, David and Getimnis, Panagiotis (eds) (2005) *Legitimacy and Urban Governance*. London: Routledge.

Heinz, Werner (ed.) (1993) 'Public Private Partnership – ein neuer Weg zur Stadtentwicklung? [Public–Private Partnership – A New Path to Urban Development?]. Stuttgart, Germany: Verlag W. Kohlhammer.

Heller, Patrick (2000) 'Degrees of Democracy: Some Comparative Lessons from India', *World Politics* 52: 484–519.

Herrigel, Gary (1996) *Industrial Constructions: The Sources of German Industrial Power*. New York, NY: Cambridge University Press.

Hochstetler, Kathryn and Keck, Margaret (2007) *Greening Brazil*. Durham, NC: Duke University Press.

Hunter, Floyd (1954) *Community Power Structure*. Chapel Hill, NC: UNC Press.

Jensen, Laura (2008) 'Politics, History and the State of the State' *Polity* 40(3): 321–5.

Jessop, Bob (1993) 'Towards a Schumpeterian Workfare State?' Preliminary Remarks on Post-Fordist Political Economy, *Studies in Political Economy* (40): 7–40.

Jones, Candace, Hesterly, William and Borgatti, Stephen (1997) 'A Theory of Network Governance' *The Academy of Management Review* 22(4): 911–45.

Kesselman, Mark (1966) *The Ambiguous Consensus*. New York: Knopf.

Khagram, Sanjiv, Riker, James and Sikkink, Kathryn (eds) (2002) *Restructuring World Politics: Transnational Social Movements, Networks and Norms*. Minneapolis, MN: University of Minnesota Press.

King, Desmond and Lieberman, Robert (2008) 'Finding the American State: Transcending the "Statelessness" Account' *Polity* 40(3): 368–78.

Kitschelt, Herbert and Wilkinson, Steven (eds) (2007) *Patrons, Clients and Policies*. Cambridge: Cambridge University Press.

Kohli, Atul (2002) 'State, Society and Development' in Ira Katznelson and Helen Milner (eds), *Political Science: The State of the Discipline*. New York: Norton; pp. 84–117.

Kohli, Atul (2004) *State-Directed Development*. New York: Cambridge University Press.

Lane, Jan-Erik (1997a) 'Public Sector Reform in the Nordic Countries', in Jan-Erik Lane (ed.), *Public Sector Reform*. London: Sage; pp. 188–208.

Lane, Jan-Erik (1997b) 'Conclusion', in Jan-Erik Lane (ed.), *Public Sector Reform*. London: Sage; pp. 301–7.

Layzer, Judith (2008) *The Environmental Case*. Cambridge, MA: MIT Press.

Levi, Margaret (2002) 'The State of the Study of the State', in Ira Katznelson and Helen Milner (eds), *Political Science: The State of the Discipline*. New York: Norton; pp. 33–55.

Lowi, Theodore (1979) *The End of Liberalism*. New York: Norton.

Manzetti, Luigi (2003) 'Political Manipulations and Market Reforms Failures', *World Politics* 55: 315–60.

McConnell, Grant (1966) *Private Power and American Democracy*. New York: Knopf.

Mares, Isabela (2003) *The Politics of Social Risk*. Cambridge: Cambridge University Press.

Marks, Gary and Hooghe, Liesbet (2003) 'Unraveling the Central State, but How?' Types of Multi-Level Governance. *American Political Science Review* 97(2): 233–43.

Mattli, Walter and Büthe, Tim (2003) 'Setting International Standards: Technical Rationality or the Primacy of Power?', *World Politics* 56(1): 1–42.

Mazmanian, Daniel A. and Kraft, Michael E. (2001) *Toward Sustainable Communities*. Cambridge, MA: MIT Press.

Mazmanian, Daniel and Sabatier, Paul (eds) (1989) *Implementation and Public Policy*. University Press of America.

Migdal, Joel (1988) *Strong Societies and Weak States*. Princeton, NJ: Princeton University Press.

Migdal, Joel (2001) *State in Society: Studying How States and Societies Transform and Constitute Each Other*. New York: Cambridge University Press.

Mollenkopf, John (1983) *The Contested City*. Princeton, NJ: Princeton University Press.

Moore, Mark (1995) *Creating Public Value*. Cambridge, MA: Harvard University Press.

Murillo, M. Victoria (2002) 'Political Bias in Policy Convergence: Privatization Choices in Latin America' *World Politics* 54(4): 462–93.

Navarro Yáñez, Clemente, Magnier, Annick and Ramírez, M. Antonia (2008) 'Local Governance as Business-Government Cooperation', *International Journal of Urban and Regional Research* 32(3): 531–47.

Nettl, J.P. (1968) 'The State as a Conceptual Variable', *World Politics* 20: 559–92.

Nylen, William R. (2002) 'Testing the Empowerment Thesis', *Comparative Politics* 34(2): 127–45.

Ostrom, Elinor (1990) *Governing the Commons*. Cambridge: Cambridge University Press.

Ostrom, Elinor, Gardner, Roy and Walker, James (1994) *Rules, Games and Common-pool Resources*. Ann Arbor, MI: University of Michigan Press.

Peters, Guy and Pierre, Jon (1998) 'Governance Without Government', *Journal of Public Administration Research and Theory* 8(2): 223–43.

Pierson, Paul (1993) When Effect Becomes Cause: Policy Feedback and Political Change. *World Politics* 35: 595–628.

Pierson, Paul (1994) *Dismantling the Welfare State?* Cambridge: Cambridge University Press.

Pinson, Gilles. (2009). *Gouverner par Projet*. Paris: Presses de Sciences Po.

Pollit, Christopher and Bouckaert, Geert (2004) *Public Management Reform: A Comparative Analysis*. Oxford: Oxford University Press.

Poulantzas, Nico (1973) *Political Power and Social Classes*. London: Sheed and Ward.

Putnam, Robert (1993) *Making Democracy Work*. Princeton, NJ: Princeton University Press.

Putnam, Robert (2000) *Bowling Alone*. New York: Simon & Schuster.

Rosenbaum, Walter A. (2005) *Environmental Politics and Policy*. Washington, DC: CQ Press.

Sabatier, Paul (1988) 'An Advocacy Coalition Model of Policy Change and the Role of Policy-Oriented Learning Therein', *Policy Sciences* 21: 129–68.

Sabatier, Paul and Jenkins-Smith, Hank C (eds). (1993) *Policy Change and Learning: An Advocacy Coalition Approach*. Boulder, CO: Westview Press.

Salamon, Lester and Anheier, Helmut K. (1997) *Defining the Nonprofit Sector: A Comparative Analysis*. Manchester, UK: Manchester University Press.

Sassen, Saskia (1991) *The Global City*. Princeton, NJ: Princeton University Press.

Scott, James (1998) *Seeing Like a State*. Oxford: Oxford University Press.

Sellers, Jefferey (1995) 'Litigation as a Local Political Resource', *Law and Society Review* 29(3): 475–516.

Sellers, Jefferey (2002a) *Governing from Below: Urban Regions and the Global Economy*. New York: Cambridge University Press.

Sellers, J. M. (2002b). 'The Nation-State and Urban Governance: Toward Multilevel Analysis', *Urban Affairs Review* 37: 611–41.

Sellers, Jefferey (2007) 'Urban Governance and Sociolegal Studies: Mapping an Interdisciplinary Frontier', *Canadian Journal of Law and Society* 22(2): 245–8.

Sellers, Jefferey (2009) 'Metropolitan Inequality and Governance: An Analytical Framework'. Paper presented at American Political Science Association Annual Meeting, Toronto.

Sellers, Jefferey and Hoffmann-Martinot, Vincent (2008) 'Metropolitan Governance', in United Cities and Local Governments (eds), *World Report on Decentralization and Local Democracy*. Washington, DC: World Bank; pp. 259–83.

Sellers, Jefferey and Kwak, Sun-Young (2011) 'State and Society in Local Governance: Lessons From a Multilevel Comparison', *International Journal of Urban and Regional Research*.

Shaw, A. (2005) 'Peri-Urban Interface of Indian Cities: Growth, Governance and Local Initiatives', *Economic and Political Weekly* 129–36.

Skocpol, Theda (2004) *Diminished Democracy*. Norman, OK: University of Oklahoma Press.

Skocpol, Theda, Rueschmeyer Dietrich, and Evans, Peter (eds) (1979). *Bringing the State Back In*. Cambridge: Cambridge University Press.

Skowronek, Stephen (1982) *Building a New American State*. New York, NY: Cambridge University Press.

Skowronek, Steven (1993) *The Politics Presidents Make*. Cambridge, MA: Harvard University Press.

Snyder, Richard (1998) *After the State Withdraws: Neoliberalism and the Politics of Reregulation in Mexico*. Berkeley, CA: University of California Press.

Steinmo, Sven, Thelen, Kathleen and Longstreth, Frank (eds) (1992) *Structuring Politics*. Cambridge: Cambridge University Press.

Stone, Clarence (1989) *Regime Politics*. Lawrence, KS: University of Kansas Press.

Stone, Clarence (2005) 'Looking Back to Look Forward: Reflections on Urban Regime Analysis', *Urban Affairs Review* 40(3): 309–341.

Stone, Clarence (2001) *Building Civic Capacity: The Politics of Reforming Urban Schools*. Lawrence, KS: University of Kansas Press.

Tamanaha, Brian Z. (2000) 'A Non-Essentialist Version of Legal Pluralism', *Journal of Law and Society* 27(2): 296–321.

Tarrow, Sidney (2005) *The New Transnational Activism*. New York: Cambridge University Press.

Thatcher, Mark (2004) 'Varieties of Capitalism in an Internationalized World: Domestic Institutional Change in European Telecommunications', *Comparative Political Studies* 37(7): 751–80.

Thelen, Kathleen (2004) *How Institutions Evolve*. Cambridge: Cambridge University Press.

Tiebout, Charles (1956) 'A Pure Theory of Local Expenditures', *The Journal of Political Economy* 64(5): 416–24.

Truman, David (1967) *The Governing Process*. New York: Knopf.

Tsai, Kellee (2006) 'Adaptive Informal Institutions and Endogenous Institutional Change in China', *World Politics* 59: 116–41.

Tunç, Hakan (2005) 'Priviatization in Asia and Latin America' *Studies in Comparative International Development* 39(4): 58–86.

United Cities and Local Governments (2008) *World Report on Decentralization and Local Democracy*. Washington, DC: World Bank.

Varshney, Ashutosh (2002) *Ethnic Conflict and Civic Life*. New Haven, CT: Yale University Press.

Van Cott, Donna Lee (2000) 'A Political Analysis of Legal Pluralism in Bolivia and Colombia', *Journal of Latin American Studies* 32: 207–34.

Van de Walle, Nicolas (2001) *African Economies and the Politics of Permanent Crisis, 1979–1999*. Cambridge: Cambridge University Press.

Vogel, Steven J. (1998) *Freer Markets, More Rules*. Ithaca, NY: Cornell University Press.

Weir, Margaret, Rongerude, Jane and Ansell, Christopher (2009) 'Collaboration Is Not Enough: Virtuous Cycles of Reform in Transportation Policy', *Urban Affairs Review* 44: 455–89.

Wildavsky, Aaron and Pressman, Jeffrey (1974) *Implementation*. Berkeley, CA: University of California Press.

10

Policy Instruments and Governance

Patrick Le Galès

INTRODUCTION

Much of the debate on governance is either concerned with the question of conceptualization in relation to different theoretical traditions (see the previous chapters of the *Handbook*) or with the characterization of modes of governance often centred on networks.

This chapter, by contrast, deals with the ways through which governance is operationalized, i.e to come back to classic questions associated with governance and government alike: not just who governs but how governments and various actors involved in governance processes operate. This is not a new idea. Foucault, in particular, made the point about the importance of governmental activities to understanding change of governmentality and the theme was central for N. Rose and P. Miller when they started their long-term research project on governmentatility.

However, to raise this issue is to underline that the governance research agenda is historically related to the 1970s research about public policy failures, which is well represented by the work of Pressman and Wildavsky (1973). The question was whether complex societies were becoming ungovernable or if, at the very least, governments were

less and less able to govern society through the administration, taxes and laws.

Ever since, this debate has led to a dynamic governance research domain organized around the following questions:

- Can government govern, steer or row (Peters, 1997)
- Do governments always govern?
- What do they govern, and how?
- What is not governed?
- Can we identify dysfunctions of governments over time?
- Can groups or sectors escape from governments (Mayntz, 1993)?
- Who governs when governments do not govern (Favre, 2005)?
- Can governance replace government or will governance failure replace government failures (Jessop, 2003)?
- How does government and governance operate?
- What does it mean to govern complex societies (Peters and Pierre, 2005)?

As shown in this *Handbook*, governance can be defined in different ways but a distinctive line of research has made close links with public policy implementation. Government failures and public policy failures have been associated both with the limits of governmental actors in a context characterized by myriads of actors operating at different levels, but also with the failures of classic tools mobilized by governments to govern, i.e. taxes and laws. In a seminal paper on governance and government failures, the German sociologist Renate Mayntz (1993) explicitly linked the governance question to the search for new policy instruments. In Canada and the USA, public policy scholars such as M. Howlett and L. Salamon have developed important research projects on policy instruments and new forms of governance.

This chapter argues that the question of the policy instrument is central to the conceptualization and the understanding of changing forms of governance. However, it aims to disconnect this research question from the naive identification of 'new policy instruments' and 'new governance', a reification that was particularly strong in the European context of the 'new Europe' of the 'new millennium' and in the search in the USA for 'new policy instruments'. The point is also to avoid the functionalism often associated with choice of policy instruments.

We therefore argue that the focus on the public policy dimension of governance and its operationalization, i.e. the choice of policy instruments, is a fruitful avenue to demonstrate and interpret changing forms of governance.

Following Hood (1986), Hall (1993) and Linder and Peters (1990), public policy instruments are defined sociologically as

> A device that is both technical and social, that organizes specific social relations between the state and those it is addressed to, according to the representations and meanings it carries. It is a particular type of institution, a technical device with the generic purpose of carrying a concrete concept of the politics/society relationship and sustained by a concept of regulation (Lascoumes and Le Galès, 2007: 5).

Policy instruments embody particular policy frames and represent issues in particular ways. They are a form of power. Rarely neutral devices, they produce specific effects. The impact of an instrument is independent of the aims ascribed to it or the objective pursued.

Instruments structure public policy and modes of governance according to their own logic.

The chapter first reviews the policy instrument literature in relation to the question of governance and governmentality. I then argue that a political sociology of policy instruments is particularly useful to contribute to the conceptualization of governance and to identify changing modes of governance. The policy instrument approach provides some empirical substance to characterize different modes of governance. I then argue that in mobilizing, in particular in the British case, the choice of policy instruments reveals the development of two modes of governance in the making. To use Bourdieu's metaphor, one might contrast a left democratic version promoting negotiation, and more deliberative making of the general interest and a right mode of governance using indicators, standards and technical instruments to centralize and promote a more market-oriented society. In other words, the use of policy instruments to understand governance suggests both the development of depoliticized formulas in 'the new governance' and the strenghthening of powerful mechanisms for the control and direction of behaviours.

GOVERNANCE AND POLICY INSTRUMENTS: NEW POLICY INSTRUMENTS FOR NEW MODES OF GOVERNANCE?

In different types of polity, at different levels, the proliferation of actors and coordination instruments in an ever-increasing number of sectors has brought out a new paradigm: 'the new governance', or 'new negotiated governance', in which public policies are less hierarchized, less organized within a sector demarcated or structured by powerful interest groups at the risk of denying the interplay of social interests and of masking power relations. The state itself is increasingly differentiated. It seems to be a series of enmeshed agencies, organizations, flexible rules, and negotiations with an increasing number of actors. Public policy is characterized by ad hoc or contingency arrangements and enmeshed networks, randomly by a proliferation of actors, multiple aims, heterogeneity, cross-linking of issues and changes in the scales of reference territories. The capacity for direction of the state is subject to challenge; it seems to be losing its monopoly and is less the centre of political processes or of conflict regulation. At the same time, scholars identify logics of state expansion and recentralization (Gamble, 1993; Jacobs and King, 2009).

To understand the dynamics of governance in this historically precise context, Lascoumes and Le Galès (2007) have suggested focusing precisely on policy instruments and instrumentation in order to document change over time. In the past, policy instruments were not a central domain of interest for governance scholars and hardly more so for those working on regulations. Policy instruments were analysed in a rather functionalist way to understand some minor processes of policy changes. By contrast, over the last two decades the question of policy instruments has been very closely linked to the developments of modes of governance. To be more precise, the question of 'new policy instruments' has been associated with the making of 'new governance', if possible in order to innovate for the 'new millennium'. Empirical research in different policy domains has identified significant change in the choice of policy instruments, both in the USA and Europe, in different policy sectors. In other words, innovations in policy instruments has become significant up to the point where it was suggested that the rise of new policy instruments might be an indicator of a 'new governance' in the making. Indeed, what accounts for the transition from 'old' command and control to 'new' market-friendly policy instruments? How, if at all, do 'new' instruments differ from the 'old', and to what extent have they overcome the contradictions and unintended impacts of more traditional instruments?

Classically, the question of policy instruments has been studied in order to analyse public administration and policy change, as in the work of Dahl and Lindblom on economic policy (1953). It was also used in the critical management research of the 1980s and in the sociology of science. The work of Christopher Hood stands out as the reference in the field. In his classic book '*The Tools of Government*' (1986), rewritten as '*The Tools of Government in the Digital Age*' (with H. Margetts, 2007), which is seen as a contribution to the public policy implementation literature, Hood's analysis is mainly concerned with information-gathering and behaviour-modifying activities of governments. The analysis provided a generic classification to develop comparison over time and sectors. In the public policy literature, the use of policy instruments was also developed to understand the change in the provision of services, the rise of automatic instruments to avoid blame (Weaver, 1989), to improve policy implementation (Bertelmans-Videc, Rist and Vedung, 1998) or to identify public policy change. The creation of a public policy instrument may serve to reveal a more profound change in public policy – in its meaning, in its cognitive and normative framework, and in its results. Writers of the various neoinstitutionalist persuasions have all turned towards highlighting institutional reasons for obstacles to change and tendencies towards inertia. Peter Hall first revived the question of public policy change when he identified different dimensions of change in this area, differentiating between reform objectives, instruments, and their use or their parameters: this led him to hierarchize three orders of public policy change (Hall, 1993). Thus, he situated instruments at the heart of his analysis of public policy change. Although a good deal of the literature proved quite functionalist, Linder and Peters (1989, 1990) moved towards a more political analysis of the choice of instruments and their impacts.

This chapter does not aim to provide a sophisticated review of the policy instrument literature (see Hood, 2007a) but rather to see how research questions associated with governance brought in the policy instruments dimension.

Four examples of research projects developed over at least a decade bear witness to this development.

First, in 1984, a political scientist, Fritz Scharpf and a sociologist, Renate Mayntz, established the Max Planck Institute for the Study of Societies in Cologne. For nearly two decades, that centre has analysed emerging forms of governance in Europe. In Kooiman's classic book on governance, Renate Mayntz (1993) stressed the failure of the German state to govern various groups. Influenced by Luhman, she analysed the capacity of groups and sectors to differentiate and to create their own rules in order to escape, to avoid the pressure of law and taxation. She therefore framed a 'governance' agenda, calling for the mobilization of new policy instruments, more based upon negotiation, which would give back some governance capacity to the state. She has therefore emphasized the need for policy instruments that can increase or re-establish the capacity of governments to govern, steer, guide or pilot (see also Mayntz, 2006). This discussion echoes classic themes in public policy research, not least the emphasis on implementation failure. A parallel project was also underway at the Erasmus University of Rotterdam, with Jan Kooiman and his group analysing the dynamics of networks in complex societies and the logics of governance (Kooiman, 1993, 2003). Policy instruments were less central here, except to control and orientate policy networks.

In addition to the question of who governs – as well as to questions of who guides, who directs society, who organizes the debate about collective aims – there is now the question of how to govern increasingly differentiated societies. States are parties to multinational regional logics of institutionalization, to diverse and contradictory globalization processes, to the escape of some social groups and to economic flows, and to

the formation of transnational actors partly beyond the boundaries and injunctions of governments. Enterprises, social mobilizations and diverse actors all have differing capacities for access to public goods or political resources beyond the state – the capacities for organization and resistance that, in the 1970s, brought about the theme of the ungovernability of complex societies. This literature has reintroduced the issue of instruments, through questions about the management and governance of public subsystems of societies and policy networks (Kickert et al., 1997; Rhodes, 1997).

On the other side of the Atlantic, L. Salamon (1981) pioneered a programme of research on the tools of governments, focusing on the role of third-sector organizations in government. Various scholars in Canada (*The choice of governing instrument group* 1982), M. Howlett (1991, 1995) and in the USA (in particular, Linder and Peters, 1989) contributed to the thinking about policy instruments and the design of new forms of governance. Howlett has in particular emphasized the logic of what he calls the 'first generation studies of policy instruments', which look at policy choice in a very limited way, in terms of efficiency in particular.

Secondly, policy instruments have been especially important in the literature on the transformation of the state in the late twentieth century as a consequence of processes of public sector reform, the technological revolution, and devolution, as well as globalization and Europeanization. They have become an important focus as traditional methods of command-and-control have given way to more flexible and inclusive modes of state–citizen interaction, also in relation to privatization processes (Salamon, 2002). Salamon and his colleagues have focused on governance mechanisms beyond the state and the rise of the state acting through others, in an indirect way. That has given rise to this link between new policy tools and a new governance paradigm stressing the capacity of non-state actors to participate in governance as a process. It promotes a normative view of governance in which public policies are less hierarchized, and less organized within a sector demarcated or structured by powerful interest groups (e.g. urban policy, environmental policy, new social policies or the negotiation of major infrastructures) – at the risk of denying the interplay of social interests and of masking power relations. Over and above deconstructing this issue (as well as the limits of government and failures of reform), research into government and public policies has highlighted the renewal of public policy instruments either for the development of depoliticized formulas in 'the new governance' or through fostering powerful mechanisms for the control and direction of behaviours.

This normative view about the 'new governance' has sometimes been criticized as the 'enchanted land' of negotiated governance where questions of power and domination more or less evaporate. Salamon's massive edited volume in 2002, 'The Tools of Government: A Guide to the New Governance', is a key achievement of that group, providing a rather large and encompassing definition of policy tools and making a brave claim about the rise of a 'new governance' paradigm.

Thirdly, scholars of the European Union (EU) have used instruments as an organizing concept, sometimes as equivalent to new modes of governance. The EU White paper on 'Governance' was marginalized in policy terms but raised an interesting intellectual debate (Commission of the European Communities, 2001). Always searching for an adequate characterization of the EU as a political beast, EU scholars have in particular noticed the rise of new policy instruments in a number of domains, seen as evidence of a 'new EU governance' in the making (Zito, Radaelli and Jordan, 2003). This is particularly the case in research on EU environmental policy, where scholars have been especially attentive to changing modes of governance (Knill and Lenschow, 2000; Jordan and Lenschow, 2008; Halpern, 2010).

This instrument-oriented research has been focused mainly on 'new' instruments and directed at the debate about 'new governance' or 'new' modes of governance. This literature developed in the early late 1990s and early 2000s in response to the series of EU initiatives launched with the declared intention of transforming EU governance and giving integration a new dynamic, despite the growing influence of the member states. As is usually the case, they did not produce the results that were anticipated, but they did attract considerable scholarly attention, with authors excited by innovation, new modes of governance and the functioning of a 'new' enlarged Europe in the 'new' millennium. Major EU-wide research project including 'NEWGOV' (website: http://www.eu-newgov.org/) attempted to characterize the EU governance.

In this world, soft law and new policy instruments appeared to flourish. Attempts to involve representatives of civil society in EU decision-making were seen as promising avenues to deal with the so-called 'democratic deficit' (Smisman, 2006; Steffek et al., 2007), and although the White Paper on Governance itself had a limited impact, new policy instruments carried the promise of making the EU more transparent and more participatory. Particular attention was directed towards networked instruments and networks, which were emblematic of the new approach (see, for example, Jordan and Schout, 2006). The research had the contradictory impact of different policy instruments and the rise of what is often called new modes of governance as a response to the coordination problems raised by the use of new policy instruments. 'New Modes of Governance' comprise ranges of policy instruments, which are combined. Most policy instruments advocated by the EU have to combine, somewhat uneasily with existing policy instruments at a different level, thus creating issues of sedimentation and contradictions, and opening new avenues for coordination mechanisms (Kassim and Le Galès, 2010).

Because the EU is a polity in the making, the choice of policy instruments is particularly central to define the characteristics of its public policymaking and to map out some mechanisms of institutionalization. In that context, some instruments of coordination and rationalization were supposed to characterize the 'new governance' paradigm, i.e. without power relations. In the case of the open method of coordination, an instrument to coordinate various policy domains in EU countries without constraints, Dehousse (2004) has decisively shown that the instrument is the policy: i.e. the choice of the instrument is explained by the need to be seen to do something concerning the governance of the EU without political agreements about the goals.

GOVERNANCE, GOVERNMENTALITY AND POLICY INSTRUMENTS

The question of policy instruments has to be disentangled from that of a new governance paradigm. The most positivist, sometimes naïve and normative tone of some of the literature has to be contested. To start with, the question is not so new and should be embedded within a broader literature.

Interest in policy instruments is not new. As Hood (2007: 128), reminds us:

> Debating alternative possible ways of keeping public order, enforcing laws, or collecting revenue is a classical concern of political thought. In the Enlightenment era, discussion of effective instruments of policy was a central concern of European 'police science' from the early policy science literature of the 1530s.

In fact, social scientists studying the state and government have long taken an interest in the issue of the technologies of government, including its instruments – Weber and Foucault, for instance. Max Weber pioneered this interest, in his analysis of forms taken by the exercise of power, when he made the creation of bureaucracies a major indicator of the degree of rationalization of societies.

Through this emphasis on the importance of devices that embody a formal legal rationality in the development of capitalist societies, he gave an autonomous role to the material technologies of government (Weber, 1978), whereas classic theories had centred mainly on the sovereignty and legitimacy of those who govern. In seeing public policy instruments as a technique for domination, he was also offering an early problematization of their role.

Michel Foucault took up this subject in his own way and pointed out the importance of what he called the 'technical procedures' of power – that is, the 'instrumentation' – as a central activity in 'the art of governing' (Senellart, 1995).

For Foucault, the central issue was not the democratic or authoritarian nature of the state; nor did it relate to the essence of the state or to its ideology, factors which legitimize or fail to legitimize it. He looked through the opposite end of the telescope, taking the view that the central issue was that of the statization of society – that is, the development of a set of concrete devices, practices through which power is exercised materially. He proposed a study of the forms of rationality that organize powers. Analysing practices, he stressed that the exercise of discipline was at least as important as constraint. Contrary to the traditional concept of an authoritarian power functioning through handing down injunction and sanction, he proposed a disciplinary concept that was based on concrete techniques for framing individuals, allowing their behaviours to be led from a distance.

In a 1984 text, he formulated his programme for the study of governmentality as follows. This approach:

> Does not revolve around the general principle of the law or the myth of power, but concerns itself with the complex and multiple practices of a 'governmentality' that presupposes, on the one hand, rational forms, technical procedures, instrumentations through which to operate, and, on the other, strategic games that subject the power relations they are supposed to guarantee to instability and reversal. (Foucault, 1984)

In other words, the question of policy instruments is central in Foucault's analysis of governmentality. He contributed to the renewal of thinking on the state and governmental practices by shunning the conventional debates of political philosophy about the nature and legitimacy of governments, devoting himself instead to their materiality, their policies and their modes of acting. In his reflections on the political, he put forward the question of the 'statization of society' – that is, the development of concrete devices, instruments, practices functioning more through discipline than constraint, and framing the actions and representations of all the social actors.

The legacy of this thought has been remobilized, in the contemporary period, to account for changes in modes of government/governance and the making of new forms of neoliberal governmentality (Miller and Rose, 2008). Focusing on policy instruments is a way to link sociological analysis of forms of rationalization of power to the public policy tradition that is looking at new linkages between public authorities and economic and social actors in an internationalized context, for means of regulation and governance.

The question of policy instruments is therefore central for the governmentality tradition of research revived in particular in the UK around Rose and Miller as much as for the governance research agenda. This raises the delicate question of conceptualizing and differentiating goverance and governmentality. This would require a more detailed discussion that is made perilous by the fact that the conceptualization of both governmentality and governance are not stabilized. Without too much of theoretical syncretism and at the risk of confusion, it makes sense to argue that some questions are part of a parallel research agenda, e.g. policy instruments. The main problem derives from the fact that Foucault never wrote a clear book on governmentality, that several conceptions have developed over time, and that the publication of some of his key texts (lectures in the

Collège de France) is pretty recent and hence has caused confusion amongst governmentality scholars, in particular Anglo-Saxon and French scholars. As is also well known, scholars are innovative when using important thinkers in creative ways with or without being absolutely loyal to the original. Lascoumes (2008) has in particularly argued that three conceptions of governmentality have been developed by Foucault over time.

First, Foucault uses the term 'governmentality' in 1984 but already, in *Surveiller et Punir*, published in 1975 (translated as *Disciple and Punish*; Foucault, 1977), Foucault elaborates an original conception of politics, the art of governing, and the conduct of conducts. In this book, the long chapter about 'discipline' deals with the different places where 'discipline' is exercised beyond prison: for instance, in the army, hospitals, schools and convents. He studies the normalization of discipline practices within the army, both to train individuals and to organize collective action.

Secondly, in 1984 and for a few years, Foucault developed his thinking about governmentality in a series of conferences and lectures based upon his reworking of the writings of the cameral sciences (the science of police): i.e. the concrete organization of society that took shape in France and Prussia in the seventeenth and eighteenth centuries that combined a political vision based on the philosophy of *Aufklärung* (Enlightenment) with principles that claimed rationality in administering the affairs of the city (Senellart, 1995). This rationality was gradually displaced by populationist concern for the happiness of populations, combining dimensions of public order, well-being and culture. The individuals and populations as collective entities were to be rationally disciplined in order to promote the well-being of the population, its reproduction, pacified social relations and economic productivity. Economics became as important as military science for state power. In that sense, the cameral sciences were the melting-pot of contemporary public policies.

Thirdly, in the *History of Sexuality* and the work developed about biopolitics, Foucault seems to be willing to go beyond his image of critical thinker only dealing with social control and constraints placed upon individuals. By contrast, the concept of governmentality becomes more centred upon individuals and the production of individuality, even if the collective dimension does not disapear. He stresses the 'subjectivation' process: i.e. how subjects invest and act in various situations to make sense of their existence. He also progressively analyses how public authorities (with the health world in particular), encourage subjects to be responsible for themselves, to think reflectively and to modify their behaviour – to self-regulate. This new form of governmentality (biopolitics) is seen as a postmodernist form of government at distance, where self disciplined subjects change their conducts in relation to assimilated norms and legitimate behaviours promoted by state organizations.

Those three related but slighly different conceptualizations open a large research agenda which bears some resemblance, for some limited issues to the question raised in terms of governance. In particular, the focus on the activities of the state, the understanding of power as a relation and the conception of politics, including various actors beyond the state, is quite important. Although a more precise analysis remains to be done, it is worth remembering that the UK-original 'governmentality' line of research developed in particular by Rose was informed by numerous exchanges with public policy scholars and in particular Hood. This strand of research on governmentality focuses on the second and third elements in particular and has led to interesting insights about biopolitics and neoliberal governmentality in the UK. Inspired by Foucault, Miller and Rose in London began in the second half of the 1980s to undertake a series of research on the question of governmentality. Following Fourquet classic analysis of French public accounting (1980) and the programme of the Sociology of Sciences particularly developed

by Callon and Latour (1981), their programme of research included in particular the analysis of what they call technologies to shape the conducts, social and economic activities in accounting or management. They used Callon and Latour's idea of 'government at a distance' to focus on the material side of governmentality, i.e. the instruments making interventions possible. In a recent introduction to their work, they make the following comment: 'We took the idea of instruments broadly, to include not only actual instruments – tools, scales, measuring devices and so forth – but also the ways of thinking, intellectual techniques, ways of analyzing oneself, and so forth, to which they were bound' (Miller and Rose, 2008: 11). Rationalities could only become operationable through the instruments to act upon conducts. This has progressively led these authors to consider the making of a neoliberal governmentality or ways of governing liberal advanced democracies based upon three ideas:

1 A new relation between expertise with knowledge accumulated in management tools and calculating techniques.
2 A new pluralization of 'social technologies' and the 'deassembling' of governmental activities.
3 A new spefication of the subject of government.

For the purposes of this chapter, it suffices to concentrate on one dimension informed by Foucault's discussion of governmentality but also by the developments of the conceptualization in terms of governance, i.e. policy instruments and instrumentation.

A POLITICAL SOCIOLOGY OF POLICY INSTRUMENTS[1]

The focus on policy instruments specifically directs attention to the mechanisms of rule and the relationship between government and the governed. At the macro level, research on instruments has afforded insights into the changing dynamics of state intervention.

In the twentieth century, for example, the growth of the state was accompanied by the development and diversification of public policy instruments and by the accumulation of programmes and policies across an ever-broadening range of activities. At the micro level, it problematizes policy choice and policy change. It has been a key concept in debates concerning changing modes of governance, ungovernable societies and regimes of govermentality. However, it is crucial to focus on the instrumentation process, i.e. the logic of the choice of instruments, and to stop taking for granted instruments as neutral devices.

Instrument-focused research has made an interesting contribution to a series of important debates and has illuminated understanding of key developments and processes with respect to the modern state. However, much of the literature is dominated by an approach that restricts the insights of an instruments perspective. This functional approach has four main deficiencies:

1 It assumes that instruments are natural. Instruments are treated as though they are readily available, at the disposal of government, needing only to be selected from a toolkit or chosen from a repertoire. The only question is which particular instrument is best for the job.
2 The key concern relating to instruments is their effectiveness. Research on policy implementation, for example, has focused principally on the effects of a particular instrument and a wider reflection on whether the correct instrument has been chosen for the purpose.
3 Insofar as the new governance is concerned, the search for instruments is pragmatic in aim. The task is either to find an alternative to the traditional instruments, whose limitations have been acknowledged by governments and reported by numerous works on implementation failures, or to design meta-instruments (usually a form of better coordination) that will make the traditional instruments more effective, whether through planning, organizational reconfiguration, framework agreements or networks.
4 Analyses often take as their point of departure either the importance of particular policy networks or the autonomy of certain subsectors

of society. However, the problem with this particular approach is that it tends to conflate the choice and combination of instruments (a question that properly belongs to instrument-centred research) with the management or regulation of networks, which is a distinct organizational question.

More recent scholarship has seen the emergence of an alternative to the functional approach. The political sociology conception of policy instruments developed by Lascoumes and le Galès (2004, 2007), following Linder and Peters (1990) or Salamon's conclusion (2002), retains the same focus on the mechanisms of rule and the relationship between government and the governed, but it broadens and deepens the scope of enquiry considerably. Crucially, however, and corresponding with the four elements of the functional approach outlined above, it insists on the importance of the power dimensions that underlie the choice of instruments; re-conceptualizes instruments as institutions that require composition or construction rather than readily available objects; suggests that effectiveness is not the only or even the main criterion that governs instrument selection; and holds that the extent to which an instrument is effective is only one among several potentially significant aspects of instrument use and often not the most important.

In other words, policy instruments are important to understand governance, but, from a sociological point of view, it is more interesting to focus on public policy instrumentation. This refers to the set of problems posed by the choice and use of instruments (techniques, methods of operation, devices) that allow government policy to be made material and operational. It encompasses the processes by which instruments are selected and operationalized. Policy instrumentation involves not only understanding the reasons that lead to the decision to opt for or to retain one instrument rather than another but also consideration of the effects produced by these choices. Public policy instrumentation is therefore a means of orienting relations

between political society (via the administration) and civil society (via its administered
subjects), through intermediaries in the form
of devices that combine technical (measuring, calculating, the rule of law, procedure)
and social components (representation,
symbol). In most political systems, this
instrumentation is expressed in a more or less
standardized form – a requirement for public
policy – and combines obligations, financial
relations (for example, tax deductions or economic assistance) and methods of learning
about populations (for example, statistical
observations).

This conceptualization contrasts sharply
with the understanding that is explicit or
implicit in the functional approach. In the
traditional literature, the choice of tools
and their modes of operation are treated
superficially to the extent that their meaning
is unexplored – governing *means* making
regulations, taxing, entering into contracts,
or communicating – or as if the questions
it raises (the properties of instruments, justifications for choosing them, and their applicability) are secondary issues, merely part of
an established process without any autonomous meaning. In the sociological approach,
they are laden with meaning, carry implications for social and political interaction,
and have effects independent of intended
goals. Two further implications follow. The
first implication is that policy instrumentation is a major issue in public policy, since it
reveals a (fairly explicit) theorization of the
relationship between the governing and the
governed. Every instrument constitutes a
condensed form of knowledge about social
control and ways of exercising it. Secondly,
for government élites, the debate on instruments may be a useful smokescreen to hide
less respectable objectives to depoliticize
fundamentally political issues, to create a
minimum consensus on reform by relying on
the apparent neutrality of instruments presented as modern, whose effects in practice
are felt permanently.

Public policy instrumentation is therefore
a means of orienting relations between

political society (via the administrative executive) and civil society (via its administered
subjects), through intermediaries in the form
of devices that mix technical components
(measuring, calculating, the rule of law, procedure) and social components (representation,
symbol). This instrumentation is expressed
in a more or less standardized form – a
required passage for public policy – and
combines obligations, financial relations
(tax deductions, economic aid) and methods
of learning about populations (statistical
observations).

It is therefore possible to argue that the
instrumentation of public policy is a major
issue for governance as it reveals the implicit
conceptualization of the relationship between
government and the people. Public policy
instruments are a form of power. Instruments
are not neutral: they structure public policies
and their outcomes; they have impacts on
their own, independent from the policy goals;
and they structure the modes of governance.
Policy changes can partly be explained by
their instruments as disconnected from their
goals: public policy is a sedimentation of
instruments. Choice and combination of policy
instruments contribute to the understanding of
the making of modes of governance.

With the exception of the seminal contribution of Hood (1986, 2007), many recent
contributions on policy instruments (Linder
and Peters, 1990; Salamon, 2002; Howlett,
2005; Lascoumes and Le Galès, 2007) take
policy instruments as institutions, since they
partly determine the way in which the actors
are going to behave; they create uncertainties
about the effects of the balance of power;
they will eventually privilege certain actors
and interests, and exclude others; they constrain the actors, while offering them possibilities; and they drive forward a certain
representation of problems. The social and
political actors therefore have capacities for
action that differ widely according to the
instruments chosen. Once in place, these
instruments open new perspectives for use or
interpretation by political entrepreneurs,
which have not been provided for and are

Table 10.1   Typology of policy

Type of instrument	Type of political relations	Type of legitimacy
Legislative and regulatory	Social guardian state	Imposition of general interest by mandated elected representatives
Economic and fiscal	Redistributive state	Socioeconomic efficiency
Agreement- and incentive-based	Mobilizing state	Seel direct involvement
Information- and communication-based	Audience democracy	Explain decisions/accountability
De facto and *de jure* standards/Best practices	Competitive mechanisms	Mixed: scientific/technical and/or pressure of market mechanisms

difficult to control, thus fuelling a dynamic of institutionalization. The instruments partly determine what resources can be used and by whom. Like any institution, instruments allow forms of collective action to stabilize, and make the actor's behaviour more predictable and probably more visible. From this angle, instrumentation is really a political issue, since the choice of instrument – which, moreover, may form the object of political conflicts – will partly structure the process and its results. Taking an interest in instruments must not in any way justify the erasure of the political. On the contrary, the more public policy is defined through its instruments, the more the issues of instrumentation risk raising conflicts between different actors, interests and organizations. The most powerful actors will be induced to support the adoption of certain instruments rather than others.

Finally, working from Hood's classic work (1986), Lascoumes and Le Galès (2004) have suggested a typology of policy instruments (Table 10.1).

Classic instruments are *taxes and laws* and relate more clearly to the classic conception of representative democracy. By contrast, the three last categories of instrument in Table 10.1 represent what is commonly associated with the rise of 'new' policy instruments. They have in common the fact that they offer less interventionist forms of public regulation, taking into account the recurrent criticisms directed at instruments of the 'command and control' type. In this sense, they lend themselves to organizing a different kind of

political relations, based on communication and consultation, and they help to renew the foundations of legitimacy.

Agreement- and incentive-based instruments

This mode of intervention, often linked to charters, partnership or contracts has become generalized in a context strongly critical of bureaucracy – because of its cumbersome, yet abstract nature, and the way it reduces accountability. In societies with growing mobility, motivated by sectors and subsectors in search of permanent normative autonomy, only participatory instruments are supposed to be able to provide adequate modes of regulation. A framework of agreements, with the incentive forms linked to it, presupposes a state in retreat from its traditional functions, renouncing its power of constraint and becoming involved in modes of ostensibly contractual exchange, mobilizing and enrolling resources and actors. The central questions of autonomy of wills, of reciprocity of benefits, and of sanction for non-observance of undertakings are rarely taken into account.

Information- and communication-based instruments

These instruments form part of the development of what is generally called 'audience democracy' or 'democracy of opinion' – that is, a relatively autonomous public space in the political sphere traditionally based on representation. The growing use of information and communication instruments that correspond to situations in which information or communication obligations have been instituted, is a particular concept of the political. It is conceptualized by Manin (1997) as audience democracy, what is called the second age of democracy.

De jure *and* de facto *standards instruments*

These instruments organize specific power relations within civil society between economic actors (competition–merger) and between economic actors and NGOs (consumers, environmentalists, etc.). They are based on a mixed legitimacy that combines a scientific and technical rationality, helping to neutralize their political significance, with a democratic rationality based on their negotiated development and the cooperative approaches that they foster. They may also allow the imposition of objectives and competition mechanisms and exercise strong coercion.

Most modes of governance combine several of these policy instruments. However, in different sectors, at different levels, the combination will be different and more or less stable over time and hence a particular characteristic of modes of governance more or less organized by command and control, standards, or negotiation and partnership.

POLICY INSTRUMENTS AND MODE OF GOVERNANCE: THE LEFT AND THE RIGHT HAND

This last section of the chapter deals with two set of issues:

1 Do new policy instruments matter?
2 What does the use of different policy instruments tell us about modes of governance in the making.

The answer to the first question requires some serious and systematic empirical work over time. Kassim and Le Galès project on the policy instruments of the EU (2010)

show that in the number of policy domains which are taken into consideration (agriculture, environment, gender, regional policy, security, assessment, open method of coordination), the focus on new policy instruments does not make sense. In most cases, 'old' classic policy instruments have of course not disappeared and they have a long-term important impact in every domain, including the much heralded case of environment. Using systematic database of policy instruments over three decades in three countries and the EU, Halpern (2010) decisively shows that linking new policy instruments to the making of a new governance of the environment sector does not hold (Jordan, 2005, an argument very similar to that of Salamon). By contrast she shows both the long-term influence of classic policy instruments and the extent to which the introduction of new policy instruments is combined to the old one and makes sense as such. Instead of focusing on this policy instrument mix (Howlett et al., 2005), one is likely to be victim of the fascination for the 'new' instrument and the 'new governance'.

The point being made, i.e. it does not make sense to focus only on the rise of new policy instruments, is the development of those instruments likely to tell us anything about the making of new modes of governance?

I would like to argue that the systematic introduction in different sectors, in different contexts, of mobilizing instruments on the one hand, and norms and indicators on the other, points to the making of two very different modes of governance – one could say, the left hand and the right hand of the state (mimicking a famous Bourdieu's phrase about *la main droite et la main gauche de l'Etat*). This also echoes some of the ideas that Peters (2008) has expressed on the future of governing: i.e. the simultaneous development of new public management and centralizing tendencies together with forms of negotiated governance.

First, one of the distinctive transformation of modes of governance is related to the rise and rise of those policy instruments requiring the mobilization of various actors and groups for the construction of the collective good, and the implementation of public policies. Agreements, charters and contracts reveal a different conceptualization of the state aiming at mobilizing different actors and their resources. This mode of intervention has become generalized in a context strongly critical of bureaucracy – of its cumbersome yet abstract nature, and of the way it reduces accountability (Salamon, 2002). The interventionist state is therefore supposed to be giving way to a state that is a prime mover or coordinator, non-interventionist and principally mobilizing, integrating and bringing coherence. This echoes a view of a democracy of protest, of collective actors. In the USA and in the EU all organizations want to become political actors. But what is an actor? Who knows (Meyer, 2000)? This profound uncertainty both constrains and facilitates mobilization within groups and organizations to attain the status of actor and to gain recognition as such by others, thus marking a strong dependence on outside models of legitimation. More generally, the actors mobilize to gain recognition as actors. Internal mobilization towards this status meets outside injunctions and produces a dynamic system driven by all sorts of models and norms.

In many cities for instance, governance is not just organized by coalitions such as urban regimes (Stone, 1989). Protest can limit the implementation of projects decided by an urban growth coalitions (Logan and Molotch, 1987). Overcoming implementation failure often requires a long process of consultation, of enrolment of different groups, of local construction of the general interest, of deliberation, of contracts, of partnerships of charters to stabilize the relationship between various actors, including state actors among others, to define common goals and instruments to reach them, hence making more likely the desired outcomes of a mode of governance. Instruments have also a life of their own and, once in place, sometimes significantly contribute to the outcome (Bezes, 2007; Lascoumes, 2009; Jacquot, 2010).

In many countries, in different sectors, the systematic introduction of those mobilizing policy instruments is giving rise to modes of governance characterized by negotiation between various groups, the 'enchanted land of governance', leading to the normative view of a deliberative democracy, free of conflicts, markets inequalites and power relations.

A second development, which has attracted less interest except in the UK points to the rise of policy instruments based upon norms, standards, performance indicators, management instruments and the rise of a new bureaucracy in particular to 'govern at a distance', including networks and agencies. This leads to profound changes of behaviour and allows a remarkable come back of state élite to govern and to constrain various groups in society. The New Labour experiment in the UK is probably one of the most remarkable examples of this new governance in the making (and its failures) (Moran, 2003; Bevir, 2005; Hood, 2007b; Faucher-King and Le Galès, 2010).

For the Blair and Brown teams, the invention that is 'New Labour' served to demonstrate the distance they had put between themselves and previous Labour governments and the unions. They promised to regenerate the declining public sector and provide better services, challenge the excesses of competition, and offer protection for employees and workers. They committed themselves to principles of management and responsibility, democratization of public agencies, performance indicators, and a valorization of associations and the 'third sector'. Several authors have shown the debt the New Labour project owns to ideas about communitarianism, social inclusion and even to the rise of neo-institutionalism. Bevir, taking an interpretative standpoint, in particular argues that New Labour was a kind of social democratic approach to questions and issues brought to the fore by the New Right. New Labour developed discourse of partnership, joined-up governance, inspired by new institutionalism. Many policy instruments developed in that framework make sense in that line of thinking by contrast to market rationality advocated by the Right and based upon micro economics.

However, this is only one part of the story. Another part of the New Labour project is the continuity of the market-making society promoted by Mrs Thatcher and the new Right and legitimized by the massive use of economics, rational choice and micro economics in particular, determining policy instrumentation, i.e. choice of instruments characterizing New Labour governance.

The Thatcher governments centralized and reformed the state, and destroyed traditional social structures (including at the heart of the British establishment, in the organization of the City, or in the legal and medical professions), social solidarities, and institutions. They encouraged actors to behave like egoistic, rational individuals. Establishing rewards and penalties makes it possible to pilot changes in individual and organizational behaviour. According to Max Weber, the 'bureaucratic revolution' changes individuals 'from without' by transforming the conditions to which they must adapt (Le Galès and Scott, 2008). Bureaucracy is a force for social change, for the destruction of traditional social systems and the creation of new systems, with all that that entails in terms of violence and resistance. Bureaucratic rationalization is wholly compatible with modernization of the economy. It makes behaviour more predictable and helps create social order organized on the basis of calculation and efficiency.

The bureaucratic revolution initiated by Margaret Thatcher was at the heart of New Labour's strategy for modernizing Britain. New Labour wanted to put consumers of public services at the centre of public services and, to the maximum possible extent, limit the influence of producers – in particular, the public sector unions, which were regarded as one of the most conservative forces in the country. Transformation of the mode of governing – that is, incessant, sometimes contradictory reform of the public sector – was the badge of the Blair governments.

It took the form of autonomy for the basic units of public management (schools, hospitals, social services), but flanked by a battery of statistical measures, indicators, and objectives for results or improvements in performance.

The New Labour team elected in 1997 was largely won over to the rather vague thesis of 'new public management' inspired by public choice economics. This resulted in the application of the principles of rational choice and classical microeconomics to public management, sometimes by transferring the recipes of private management to public management. Blair and Brown clearly understood that a redefinition of the rules of political action (in the direction of the regulatory state) went hand in hand with an increase in controls. While part of the traditional bureaucracy was dismantled and subjected to market mechanisms, the core executive gained in independence. The new government did not intend to reconsider the framework of public management left by the Conservatives. The inheritance was adopted, mobilized and consolidated by New Labour, whose action can be characterized as follows:

- indicators for good public management extending beyond performance were developed for the precise piloting of public action
- according to the social model of neoclassical economists, individuals respond to stimulation
- the delivery of public policy combined public and private partners in flexible ways
- priority was given to delivery and the definition of objectives
- Power was centralized in order to initiate reforms, monitor delivery, and make government action coherent
- the inspiration for reforms no longer derived from the senior civil service, but from think-tanks, experts, consultants, academics, and foreign experience (essentially the USA).

New Labour systematized a way of steering government on the basis of performance objectives, league tables, and strict financial control. These developments revealed their credence in the magical powers of synthetic indicators to bring about rapid changes. Moreover, this was one of the characteristics of New Labour management: radical reforms were conducted through a proliferation of indicators and a rapid redefinition of targets and programmes. In their eyes, the social world was malleable, reactive and dynamic. Under pressure, it reacts forthwith to commands for mobilization from the masters of the moment. One cannot but be surprised by the extraordinary ambition of piloting society through such indicators and the discrepancy as regards service provision to the population. Thus, as early as 1998 the government announced the creation of 300 performance objectives for all departments. Each of them might make for newspaper headlines! These objectives were bound up with the resources allocated by the Treasury; each of its objectives was then divided up into dozens or hundreds of specific indicators by area. In view of the importance of the rhetoric of modernization, New Labour made it a point of pride to mobilize every 'modern' technique, not just the latest managerial fashions but also the systematic production of aggregate indictors thanks to increasingly sophisticated new technologies. They promoted the development of e-government with enthusiasm. Following the example of the managerial software used in large firms to know the activity of different units in real time, they generalized the activity of reporting from agency or unit heads to the lowest level.

In line with Polanyi's argument on fear and hunger, systems of rewards and sanctions were gradually put in place. In universities, schools, hospitals, and local governments, the development of ranking based upon aggregated indicators was associated to constraining system of rewards (such as 'earned autonomy' in terms of budget) and sanctions. The disciplining effect over time, over several years, was remarkable as individuals and organizations alike learned the rules of the game, anticipated the effects, learned to cheat with the rules (Hood, 2007b) and the rules became progressively naturalized. The routinization of league tables legitimated

penalties – that is, closure of a school, a department or a hospital. The same approach prevailed in numerous areas of public action: primary and secondary education, higher education, the environment, social services, and so on. The logic of the audit and inspection progressively led to more standardization, with the 'managerial' dimension getting the upper hand over the more political dimension of administration; the pressure on workforces was increasingly strong. Strategic priorities, the needs of local populations and political choices were set aside, in favour of competition to obtain the maximum score, which counted as political and professional success.

Thus, the culture of the audit, which derived from firms, was gradually transferred to all areas of British public life and affected political parties, associations and charitable organizations alike (Power, 1997). While the government decentralized public service provision, and encouraged the participation of the voluntary sector in managing public services, it combined this decentralization with new quid pro quos. All sectors were henceforth subject to an assessment of their performance and procedures. The illusion of the total 'inspectability' of society betrayed the influence of the utilitarianism of the philosopher Jeremy Bentham. But the proliferation of audits eroded trust in the professional ethic and sense of public service. Social control of this kind contradicts the idea that everyone acts in good faith and destroys trust in the competence of social actors.

The audit has become natural in British society. Control is now present at all levels of social and political life. It transfers the management of uncertainty, especially economic uncertainty, from political authorities to individuals. The constant invocation of individual responsibility, which is the quid pro quo of the logic of multiplying the choices offered to the citizen-consumer, aids the internalization of controls and the adoption of individualistic strategies that rupture existing solidarities or loyalties. Summoned to take responsibility for the costs of their choices, individuals cannot be the counter-powers formerly represented by groups. When the audit does not yield satisfactory results, it is rarely the audit itself that is called into question, but instead the skills of the auditors. The whole of society is affected: political parties, agencies, schools, and associations.

Indicators of performance are great policy instruments for government because they can change the indicators relatively easily. On the basis of the British case, even constant modification of instruments can be seen as significant, in that this obliges the actors to adapt all the time, 'running along behind' instruments that are constantly changing in the name of efficiency and rationality. This instrumentalization of the instrumentation considerably increases the degree of control by central élites and marginalizes the issue of aims and objectives even further – or at the very least, euphemizes them. From this angle, public policy instruments may be seen as revealing the behaviours of actors, with the actors becoming more visible and more predictable through the workings of instruments (an essential factor from the point of view of the state's élites).

Policy instruments are not neutral; they condense some form of political power and technique. They have effect of their own but, as for other types of institutions, creative use by various actors produce unintended effects. The instrumentation process reveals political logic and some characteristics of modes of governance. At times, it may be quite central to understand this dimension and one can argue that modes of governance can be transformed by technical instruments and their use. The focus on policy instruments and the activities within governance is not the whole story to understand modes of governance but it's a fruitful way to analyse some of it and the implicit power dimension, beyond the goals and the discourses.

ACKNOWLEDGEMENT

This chapter owes much to the Policy Instruments and Instrumentation project that I have run at Sciences Po with Pierre Lascoumes and now Charlotte Halpern. Some of the developments are directly taken from working notes and papers written with Pierre Lascoumes, whom I also thank for his precise analysis of Foucault. I thank Mark Bevir for incisive and constructive comments on the first draft of this chapter.

NOTE

1 This section develops arguments made by Lascoumes and Le Galès (2004, 2007) and Halpern and Le Galès, 2008).

REFERENCES

Bertelmans-Videc, M.L, Rist, R.C. and Vedung, E. (1998) *Carrots, Sticks and Sermons, Policy Instruments and Their Evaluation.* New Brunswick, Canada: Transaction Books.

Bevir M. (2005) *New Labour, A Critique:* London, Routledge.

Bezes, P. (2007) 'Cutting Public Service Wages with a Low-Profile Instrument: A Technical and Genealogical View of the French Policy of Economic Stringency', *Governance* 20(1).

Callon, M. and Latour, B. (1981) 'Unscrewing the Big Leviathan; or How Actors Macrostructure Reality and How Sociologists Help Them To Do So?', in A. Cicourel (ed.), *Advances in Social Theory and Methodology: Toward an Integration of Micro and Macro-Sociologies.* London: Routledge and Kegan Paul.

Commission of the European Communities (2001) *European Governance.* A White Paper, COM 428.

Dahl R. and Lindblom C. (1953) *Politics, Economics and Welfare.* New York: Harper & row.

Dehousse, R. (2004) La Méthode Ouverte de Coordination, Quand l'Instrument Tient Lieu de Politique', in P. Lascoumes and P. Le Galès (eds), *Gouverner par les Instruments.* Paris: Presses de Sciences Po.

Faucher-King, F. and Le Galès, P. (2010) *The New Labour Experiment.* Stanford, CA: Stanford University Press.

Favre, Pierre (2005) *Comprendre le Monde pour le Changer, Épistémologie du Fait Politique.* Paris: Presses de Sciences Po.

Foucault, M. (1977) *Discipline and Punish*, Harmondsworth: Penguin.

Foucault, M. (1984) L'usage des plaisirs.

Fourquet F. (1980) *Les Comptes de la puissance*. Paris: Encres.

Gamble, A. (1993) *The Free Market and the Strong State*. Basingstoke : Palgrave Macmillan.

Hall, P. (1993) 'Policy Paradigm, Social Learning and the State', *Comparative Politics* 25(3): 275–96.

Halpern, C. (2010) 'The Politics of Environmental Policy Instruments', *West European Politics* 1(1).

Halpern, C. and Le Galès P. (2008) 'Public Policy Instrumentation in the EU', Working Paper, New Modes of Governance Project, Policy Brief, No. 32.

Hood, C. (1986) *The Tools of Government*. Chatham: Chatham House.

Hood, C. (2007a) 'Intellectual Obsolescence and Intellectual Makeovers: Reflections on The Tools of Government after Two Decades', *Governance* 20(1): 127–44.

Hood, C. (2007b) 'Public Service Management by Numbers: Why Does It Vary? Where Has It Come From? What Are the Gaps and the Puzzles?' *Public Money and Management* 27(2): 95–102.

Hood, C. and Margetts, H. (2007) *The Tools of Government in the Digital Age*. Oxford: Oxford University Press.

Howlett, M. (1991) 'Policy Instruments, Policy Styles, and Policy Implementations, National Approaches to Theories of Instrument Choice', *Policy Studies Journal* 19(2): 1–21.

Howlett, M. (1995) *Inquiring Public Policy*. Oxford: Oxford University Press.

Howlett, M., Eliadis, P and Hill, M. (2005) *Designing Government: From Instruments to Governance*: Montreal: McGill Queens University Press.

Jacobs, L. and King D. (eds) (2009) *The Unsustainable American State*. Oxford: Oxford University Press.

Jacquot, S. (2010) 'The Paradox of Gender Mainstreaming. The Unanticipated Effects of New Modes of Governance in the Gender Equality Domain', *West European Politics* 1.

Jessop, B. (2003) 'Governance and Meta-governance: On Reflexivity, Requisite Variety and Requisite Irony', Online paper, Department of Sociology, Lancaster University: http://www.comp.lancs.ac.uk/sociology/jessop/governance-metagovernance.

Jordan, A., Rüdiger, K.W. and Zito, A. R. (2005) 'The Rise of "New" Policy Instruments in Comparative Perspective: Has Governance Eclipsed Government?', *Political studies* 33, 477–496.

Jordan, A.J. and Lenschow, A. (eds.) (2008) *Innovation in Environmental Policy? Integrating the Environment for Sustainability*. Cheltenham: Edward Elgar.

Jordan, A.J. and Schout, J.A. (2006) *The Coordination of European Governance*. Oxford: Oxford University Press.

Kassim H. and Le Galès P. (eds) (2010) 'Exploring Governance in a Multilevel Polity: A Policy Instruments Approach', *West European Politics* 33(1): 1–21.

Kickert, W., Klijn, E.H. and Koppenjan, J. (1997) *Managing Complex Networks*. London: Sage.

Knill, C. and Lenschow, A. (ed.), (2000). *Implementing European Environmental Policy: New Directions and Old Problems*. Manchester: Manchester University Press.

Kooiman, J. (ed.), (1993) *Modern Governance*. London: Sage.

Kooiman, J. (2003) *Governing as Governance*. London: Sage.

Lascoumes P. (2008) 'De l'Art Militaire à la Gouvernementalité … en Passant par les Disciplines', in F. Chauvaud et al., (eds), *Michel Foucault: Savoirs, Dominations, Sujets*. Rennes: Presses Universitaires de Rennes.

Lascoumes, P. (2009) 'Gli Strumenti dell'azione Pubblica, Indicatori di Cambiamento', P. Lascoumes and P. Le Galès (eds), *Gli Strumenti per Governare*. Milan: Bruno Mondadori.

Lascoumes, P. and Le Galès, P. (eds) (2004) *Gouverner par les Instruments*. Paris: Presses de Sciences Po.

Lascoumes, P. and Le Galès, P. (2007) 'From the Nature of Instruments to the Sociology of Public Policy Instrumentation', *Governance, Understanding Public Policy through Its Instruments* 20(1): 1–21.

Le Galès, P. and Scott, A. (2008) 'Une Révolution Bureaucratique Britannique? Autonomie Sans Contrôle ou "freer markets, more rules', *Revue Française de Sociologie* 49(2): 301–30.

Linder, S. and Peters, G. (1989) 'Instruments of Government: Perceptions and Contexts', *Journal of Public Policy* 9(1): 35–58.

Linder, S. and Peters, G. (1990) 'The Designs of Instruments for Public policy', in S. Nagel (ed.), *Policy Theory and Policy Evaluation*. Westport, (Co): Greenwood Press, pp. 103–19.

Logan, J. and Molotch, H. (1987) *Urban Fortunes. The Political Economy of Place*. Berkeley, CA: University of California Press.

Manin, B. (1997) *The Principles of Representative Government*. Cambridge, Cambridge University Press.

Mayntz, R. (1993) 'Governing Failures and the Problem of Governability', in J. Kooiman (ed.), *Modern Governance*. London: Sage.

Mayntz, R. (2006) 'From Government to Governance: Political Steering in Modern Societies', in Dirk Scheer and F. Rubik (eds), *Governance of Integrated Product Policy*. Aizlewood Mill: Greenleaf Publishing, pp. 18–25.

Meyer, J. (2000) 'Globalization. Sources and Effects on States and Societies', *International Sociology* 15(2): 233–48.

Miller, P. and Rose, N. (2008) *Governing the Present*. Cambridge: Polity Press.

Moran, M. (2003) *The British Regulatory State*. Oxford: Oxford University Press.

Moran, M. (2003) 'The British Regulatory State: High Modernism and Hyper-innovation', Oxford: Oxford University Press.

Peters, G. (1997) 'Shouldn't Row, Can't Steer, What's a Government to Do', *Public Policy and Administration* 12(2): 51–61.

Peters, G. (2008) 'The Two Futures of Governing: Decentering and Recentering Process in Governing', Working Paper 114, Political Science Series, Institute for Advanced Studies, Vienna.

Peters, G. and Pierre, J. (2005) *Governing Complex Societies*. Basingstoke: Palgrave Macmillan.

Power, M. (1997) *The Audit Culture, Rituals of Verification*. Oxford: Oxford University Press.

Pressman, J. and Wildavsky, A. (1973) *Implementation*. Berkeley, CA: University of California Press.

Rhodes, R.A.W. (1997) *Understanding Governance*. Basingstoke: Palgrave Macmillan.

Salamon, L.M. (ed.) (1989) *Beyond Privatisation. The Tools of Government Action*. Washington, DC: Urban Institute.

Salamon, L.M. (ed.) (2002) *The Tools of Government: A Guide to the New Governance*. New York: Oxford University Press.

Senellart, M. (1995) *Les Arts de Gouverner*. Paris: Seuil.

Smisman, S. (ed.) (2006) *Civil Society and Legitimate European Governance*. Cheltenham: Edward Elgar.

Steffek, J, Kissling, C. and Nanz, P. (eds) (2007) *Civil Society Participation in European Governance, a Cure for the Democratic Deficit?* Basingstoke: Palgrave Macmillan.

Stone, C. (1989) *Regime Politics, Governing Atlanta, 1946–1988*. Lawrence, KS: University Press of Kansas.

Weaver, K. (1989) 'Setting and Firing Policy Triggers', *Journal of Public Policy* 9(3): 307–36.

Weber, M. (1978) *Economy and Society*, Berkeley: The University of California Press.

Zito, A., Radaelli, C. and Jordan, A. (eds.) (2003) 'New Policy Instruments in the European Union: Better Governance or Rhetorical Smoke?', *Public Administration* 81: 3 (theme issue): 509–606.

11

Development Theory

Phyllis R. Pomerantz

INTRODUCTION

Following World War II competing theories sought to explain how and why economic development takes place. For awhile now, the theoretical framework has narrowed. Mainstream development theory has settled into the neoclassical economic tradition, albeit with variations.

In contrast to the narrowing of economic development theory, the meaning of development has grown wider. Originally, development was virtually synonymous with national income increases. Access to social services and employment, including for the poor, were added in the 1970s and 1980s. More recently, absence of fear, along with reduced vulnerability and powerlessness, has been incorporated into the definition (World Bank, 2000).

Within this context, the role of governance has evolved. For much of the past 60 years, mainstream economic development theory has tended to relegate governance issues to the 'back burner'. This has changed. Since the 1990s, governance has assumed a central and controversial role in development thought and practice.

Governance's prominence in development discourse does not imply agreement over what the concept means. Governance outside of the development context usually refers to the rise of markets and networks as part of public sector policymaking and coordination. In development theory, governance does not include the rise of markets. Instead, the focus is on public institutions – hierarchical, bureaucratic organizations, as well as networks and formal and informal rules – how they function, and especially, their relationship to markets and economic growth.

In one recent definition, 'Governance refers to the manner in which public officials and institutions acquire and exercise the authority to shape public policy and provide public goods and services' (World Bank, 2007: 3).[1] Factors such as government capacity and effectiveness, clear rules, transparency, accountability and probity, citizens' participation, human rights and civil liberties, and how governments are chosen and exercise power all come under the 'big tent' of governance in the development context. However, there is disagreement over which elements are included, which are the most important, what constitutes 'good governance', and how much it matters for economic growth.

The chapter begins with a brief recap of development in the postwar period through the 1980s. The chapter then goes on to the 1990s, when both theory and experience converged to elevate governance to a central concern. Growing academic research was accompanied by an increasingly contentious governance dialog between aid recipients and donors. The new century witnesses an extensive debate on development policy, aid effectiveness, and governance. After reviewing the principal unsettled issues in that debate, the chapter concludes with some thoughts on how to move the governance and development agenda forward.

THE POSTWAR DECADES

The aftermath of World War II unleashed demands for independence among the colonies of European nations. Undeterred by low incomes and levels of physical and human capital, the newly independent nations were buoyed by optimism and convinced they would rapidly develop. A new branch of economics, development economics, shared their optimism.

According to the early theories, economic growth was largely a function of capital accumulation. Developing countries needed to expand investment either through domestic savings or foreign investment, borrowing, or aid. Against the backdrop of the Cold War, nations garnered assistance from either the Soviet or Western camps or both. The rise of the Soviet Union as an economic power challenged Western models of development. State-led development and centralized planning seemed attractive, even for nations not adopting the socialist model. Dependency theory reinforced the role of the state in economic development, with import substitution spurred on by government protection, subsidies, or direct investment. Big infrastructure projects served as symbols of modernity.

There was little preoccupation with what is now associated with governance. Capacity constraints were viewed as short term and manageable. There was support for consultancies or twinning arrangements; training programs, including graduate study abroad;

and expatriate technical assistance with line responsibilities. The task and project orientation of governments and foreign aid agencies meant that there were few systematic attempts to build sustainable public sector capacity (Nunberg, 2007: 63–4).

As the 1970s unfolded, economic difficulties waylaid many countries. Exogenous shocks such as the 1973 oil crisis, coupled with domestic policy decisions, arrested economic progress. Income inequality and poverty were on the increase in developing countries. This, in turn, led to a questioning of the capital-intensive, industrial-biased development model. A new focus on agriculture and the rural poor was ushered in by then World Bank President Robert McNamara. 'New-style' integrated rural development projects targeted the poor and incorporated infrastructure, agricultural services, and social sector support within a single project framework. Many of the projects ran into implementation difficulties and were criticized as too complex. In reality, they merely mirrored the complexity of the development and administrative challenges faced by the governments on a national scale.

THE ERA OF STRUCTURAL ADJUSTMENT

At the start of the 1980s, many developing economies were reeling from another oil crisis, a collapse in commodity prices, and the poor performance of the 'new-style' projects. Government policies – from overvalued exchange rates to big government spending and borrowing, to protection of import-substitution industries, to urban-biased agricultural pricing policies – were seen to be worsening the crisis. Far from the state being the engine of economic growth, it began to seem more like the brake.

What ensued was a return to neoclassical economic thought where markets play a predominant role in development and are viewed as more efficient allocative mechanisms than governments. Several different strains of development theory coexisted during the 1980s. These ranged from the market as the pivot of socioeconomic and even political life, with a heavily proscribed role for formal government, to more government-friendly theories. The latter took issue with the 'less government, the better' view that came to be known as 'market fundamentalism'. In contrast to market fundamentalism, government was needed to provide an enabling environment for markets, supply a limited range of public goods, and correct market failures and imperfections (J. Williamson, 2000: 255–6).

Independent of the strain, policy change was paramount. It was assumed that the appropriate institutions to support the policies were there or could be put into place. The 'first generation' reforms were largely 'stroke of the pen', approved by senior government officials. Many of the reforms, for example, changes in exchange rates or tariffs, did not require elaborate institutional support.

Despite scant attention to governance in the initial stages of structural adjustment, the reforms had an important impact on governance. Foremost, structural adjustment changed the relative power between governments and markets. Budget deficit reduction and privatization shrunk governments and weakened their capacity. Deregulation, interest rate liberalization, and trade reforms increased activity in the marketplace. A second effect was to cast some attention on civil service reform. The thrust of civil service reform, especially in the early 1980s, was *not* related to the capacity to govern, but to reducing the fiscal deficit by containing the public wage bill. In the event, the impact of the programs, whether on cost, size, or efficiency of the civil service, was small at best (Nunberg and Lindauer, 1994: 239).

A third effect of structural adjustment was the insertion of aid donors, especially the international financial institutions (IFIs), into the national policy arena. The IFIs viewed their work – and their policy conditions – as providing support to reformers and strengthening the governments' ability to govern.

Many saw the IFI role differently. Accepting policy conditionality designed elsewhere was seen as weakening the autonomy and authority of the recipient governments (Kapur and Webb, 2000).

The results of structural adjustment were disappointing. While macroeconomic stabilization was more or less achieved, growth stagnated in Latin America and Africa. There were different explanations for the reforms' failure to propel growth. Whether the critiques focused on a too limited role for governments (versus markets), the substance of specific policies, the pace and sequencing of reform, the lack of government capacity and/or commitment, or the policies' impact on the poor, the inherent weakness of many governments became transparent in the face of the donors' insistence on policy changes.

The inability or unwillingness of many governments to articulate their own, often divergent views, governments' scant maneuvering room, given the size of fiscal deficits and external debts, the lack of in-depth knowledge – or even worse, a lack of concern – about conditions on the ground, particularly for the poor, the dearth of capacity to carry out reforms, and the failure to involve, or sometimes even inform, critical stakeholders all pointed to a crisis of political authority in many developing countries.

Ensuing political instability in parts of Africa, along with the disintegration of the Soviet Union, posed challenges to the international community. They also presented opportunities for regime change: no wonder 'good governance' became the rallying cry of the 1990s.

THE 1990s – GOOD GOVERNANCE: THE MISSING INGREDIENT

The emerging role of institutions and 'good governance'

The preoccupation of the 1990s with governance was not only the result of structural adjustment and unfolding political events. There was a unique convergence of experience and theory as development economists became influenced by the New Institutional Economics (NIE). North's seminal work, *Institutions, Institutional Change and Economic Performance*, asserted that institutions, understood broadly as the formal and informal 'rules of the game in a society', 'are the underlying determinant of long-run performance of economies' (1990: 3, 107). Institutions are created to reduce uncertainty in a world of imperfect knowledge and 'subjective perceptions' (North, 1990: 9). Institutions influence expectations and behavior by providing (or withholding) information and decreasing (or increasing) risk.

These functions are not without costs. Transaction costs directly influence economic decisions. They also influence the choice of institutional arrangements (the demand side). Even more fundamentally, transaction costs are part of the explanation for institutional change, which, in turn, impacts long-run economic performance. Gradual shifts in technology or factors of production, as well as exogenous shocks, can change transaction costs and institutional choice. Fundamental institutional changes, such as changes in culture and norms, take a long time. Other reforms, such as in contracts and organizations, are easier and occur more frequently. Institutional reform – large and small – impacts economic performance.

Institutions are also subject to supply side constraints. Institutional change is 'path dependent': 'Path dependence means that history matters. We cannot understand today's choices…without tracing the incremental evolution of institutions' (North, 1990: 100). Path dependence, in essence, limits the possibilities for scope and speed of institutional change. There are also issues associated with collective action: free riding (the ability to benefit without contributing); principal–agent problems (where the interest and actions of the 'agent' do not align with those of the 'principal'); and 'the tragedy of the commons' and 'prisoners' dilemmas' (where rational individual choices impede cooperation and reduce benefits). All of these can negatively impact incentives and economic growth.

However, it is possible to overcome collective action problems. For example, smaller groups, with longer histories and homogeneous origins, who possess better information and complementary goals, are more likely to cooperate (Olson, 1965; Lin and Nugent, 1995). The state can also play a fundamental role in overcoming collective action problems and fostering growth.

As a result of NIE analyses, economists began highlighting the role of institutions in promoting growth by either lowering transaction costs or facilitating collective action. Championing property rights; enforcing contracts; promoting innovation; and providing public goods were just a few of the ways that institutions were seen to facilitate and complement markets. In contrast, in traditional neoclassical economics 'transactions were often assumed to be costless, relevant information freely available, and governments ready and willing to undertake socially beneficial projects…' (Lin and Nugent, 1995: 2303). Up until NIE, 'neoclassical economics was dismissive of institutions' (O. Williamson, 2000: 595).

NIE broke new ground in economic development theory by using institutional analysis. For example, using NIE, it was possible to theoretically postulate the circumstances under which autocrats would promote economic growth or democracies would fail to prosper (Olson, 1997). '… NIE … relaxes some of the strong assumptions of traditional economics with respect to the motivations of, and the information available to, individual decision-makers, and it widens the scope of economics to include political phenomena and the evolution of institutions' (Clague, 1997: 2). With NIE, markets and institutions became interdependent, and institutions became important factors in economic development.

In the ensuing literature, there are many definitions of institutions and governance. Some authors (O. Williamson, 2000: 597; Hyden et al., 2004: 2) consider governance as a subset of a broader institutional context. Among development practitioners and most economists, there is little differentiation between the concepts of institutional reform and improving governance. Economists generally refer to a narrower definition of institutions, what Lin and Nugent term 'institutional arrangements', which more closely approximates many of the definitions of governance. (Lin and Nugent, 1995: 2307).

The term 'governance' was seldom employed in the development context prior to the late 1980s. 'Good governance' has since become 'a mantra for development professionals' (Grindle, 2007: 553). Some definitions emphasize process, others performance measures or institutional structures. Some are analytical, others normative. Some virtually equate governance and government, while others emphasize the role of non-governmental organizations. Some focus on legitimacy and specific forms of acquiring political authority, for example, 'free and fair elections' (Grindle, 2007: 556–7).

Complementing the World Bank definition concerning the selection and execution of political authority, the following are frequently mentioned as part of the 'governance agenda' in the development context:

- Rule of law, regulatory authority, accountability, transparency, probity and anti-corruption.
- Government capacity, leadership, organization, institutional structure, scope, and effectiveness.
- Decentralization, voice, participation, strengthening of civil society and social capital.
- Democracy, free and fair elections, civil liberties and human rights, freedom of the press.
- A subset of the global governance agenda – the accountability, transparency, probity, organization, legitimacy, and effectiveness of IFIs.

The new interest in governance swirled around a number of topics. Some of the debate was back to 'first principles': the role of markets versus states in economic development.

Much of the East Asian success came with state activism, and there was a renewed appreciation of the complementarity between states and markets. Even if markets were the primary engines of growth, governments were needed to provide critical public goods and support private transactions. Also, some recommended policy reforms in the wake of ineffective or corrupt governments could actually make things worse (Stiglitz, 2003). So the markets versus states debate evolved into the embrace of markets *and* states.

As research proceeded, a correlation was established between higher income levels and better governance and stronger institutions (Aron, 2000; Acemoglu et al., 2001). A key question was whether institutions and good governance drove economic development or whether economic development led to better institutions and governance. There was renewed debate on whether democracy was a prerequisite for development. With the publication of Sen's influential *Development as Freedom* (1999), for some, the concept of development became inextricably entwined with democratic ideals. Many began to doubt the 1960s' wisdom that democracy was a luxury many developing nations could not afford (Huntington, 1968). The debate would gain intensity in the new century.

Decentralization was another issue that attracted attention. Decentralization was seen by some as a solution for the ills of the illegitimate, overstretched, unresponsive and incompetent state (Bardhan, 2002: 185). Local decision-making seemed to offer the chance to involve citizens and ease ethnic tensions. It could counterbalance centralized power and improve outcomes using local knowledge. Yet, there was also the possibility that decentralization could diffuse accountability, accentuate regional disparities, and weaken government performance. Decentralization's likely impact appeared linked to the probabilities for corruption and élite capture of public resources at various levels of government (Bardhan, 2002: 194). Hence, decentralization's contribution to improving governance depended on the circumstances.

Research on corruption also revived interest in its impact on economic development. Earlier scholars had suggested that, in certain circumstances, corruption could promote growth by circumventing or overturning bad government decisions and policies or by cutting through excessive 'red tape' (Leff, 1964; Huntington, 1968). Others concluded that corruption was harmful to development (Rose-Ackerman, 1978). Studies in the 1990s attempted to either model the effects of corruption, specify the circumstances under which it flourishes, or demonstrate its impact on economic growth (Shleifer and Vishny, 1993; Mauro, 1995; Bardhan, 1997). The evidence on the *relative importance* of corruption as a brake on economic development remained mixed.

In a later section, some of these debates will be revisited. Despite the absence of definitive answers to many governance and growth-related questions, donors began incorporating governance concerns into policy and funding decisions.

Putting theory into practice – aid and governance

Conditionality

By the mid-1990s, governance was a central topic for leading aid agencies. Many agencies were still pursuing structural adjustment and policy-based lending, so they added governance conditionality. For the IFIs, conditionality related to privatization, transparency, and institutional reform became commonplace. Since many reforms were no longer 'stroke of the pen', the conditions became a series of process steps, and the number of conditions increased during the 1990s compared with the earlier period (Koeberle and Malesa, 2005: 49).[2]

The World Bank, in its Articles of Agreement, was prohibited from taking the type of political regime and other political considerations into account. It limited its actions in the field of governance to accountability, transparency, rule of law, and government efficiency and effectiveness (World Bank, 1992). Bilateral donors did not face similar restrictions and began conditioning part of their financial support on a host of governance concerns related to the carrying out of 'free and fair elections'. These included, among others, voter registration procedures, campaign restrictions and treatment of the opposition, and constitutional amendments curbing electoral competition. The extent of civil society participation, freedom of speech and the press, and respect for human rights also became part of the bilateral aid dialog.

Donors had previously considered corruption 'too hot to handle'. That changed markedly when James Wolfensohn, then President of the World Bank, bluntly declared: 'And let's not mince words: we need to deal with the cancer of corruption' (1996: 50). Following this, corruption became an integral part of the governance agenda. The aid community supported actions such as the strengthening of audit institutions, the revamping of public procurement, and the establishment of 'independent' anti-corruption commissions. Deregulation and cutting bureaucratic 'red tape' were also viewed as helpful in reducing opportunities for corruption (World Bank, 1997: 104–9).

Harmonization among aid donors – always an issue – was particularly elusive on governance. Aid recipients complained that different donors insisted on different conditions and that expectations varied from country to country, with larger and richer countries subject to less rigorous conditionality. Most considered expectations too high and time-frames too short. Donors emphasized the expectations of home constituencies loathe to provide aid to unaccountable and corrupt governments (Kapur and Webb, 2000; Pomerantz, 2004).

By the mid-1990s, the 'governance dialog' became difficult in most countries, with four main 'irritants'. The first, mentioned above, was the reality of 'mixed messages', with different donors giving priority to different aspects of reform. The second source of discord was recipients' perception that bilateral insistence on specific political governance measures was an infringement upon national sovereignty. A third area of disagreement was the strategy to strengthen civil society and involve non-governmental organizations (NGOs) in aid-funded programs. Governments viewed this less as a complement to their efforts and more as an attempt to substitute or circumvent them. The fourth 'irritant' was a perceived disproportionate attention to corruption. The idea that much of Africa's woes can be attributed to corruption permeates donor thinking and Western media reporting until the present time (Botchwey, 2005: 266–7; Hyden, 2007: 16754). Recipient country officials attempted – without much success – to place corruption within the broader context of pervasive poverty and capacity constraints.

Selectivity

The addition of governance-related conditions – coupled with disappointing growth performance in Africa and Latin America – was a pivotal factor in the mounting criticism of conditionality and aid effectiveness. Towards the end of the 1990s, the World Bank came out with new theory and evidence that aid works best in a good policy environment. *Assessing Aid* challenged the use of conditionality in the absence of strong support within countries. 'Efforts to "buy" policy improvements in countries where there is no movement for reform… have typically failed' (World Bank, 1998: 3).

Assessing Aid argued instead for increased *selectivity* based on sound policies and institutions (World Bank, 1998: 12). While its supporting evidence has since been contested (Easterly et al., 2004), it influenced aid discussions and shifted the behavior of some donors. A few countries, for example, Sweden, narrowed their list of priority aid recipients, with governance criteria figuring prominently. In 1998, the World Bank revised its CPIA (Country Performance and Institutional Assessment), which helps guide country funding allocations, to include social

policies and governance. Currently, 5 of the 16 criteria in the CPIA are directly related to governance. Although much of US foreign aid is determined using other criteria, in 2004, the Millennium Challenge Corporation (MCC) was established with a specific charge to operate based on country selectivity. The MCC uses governance indicators among its threshold criteria.

Critics of selectivity charged that the strategy 'made the poor pay twice', since the poor were disadvantaged by living in a country with weak governance and policies and then cut off from meaningful foreign assistance. Meanwhile, others questioned whether greater selectivity was even being applied (Easterly and Pfutze, 2008: 41–2).[3]

Measurement

The spotlight on governance spawned new interest in its measurement. Freedom House's country ratings related to political rights and civil liberties became more widely known and used. Transparency International's (TI) Corruption Perceptions Index, started in 1995, ranks countries according to their perceived corruption. It became influential in aid circles. This was followed by Kaufmann et al., who in 1996, devised a set of six indicators to measure governance performance over time. The Worldwide Governance Indicators (WGI) – voice and accountability, political stability and absence of violence, government effectiveness, regulatory quality, rule of law, and control of corruption – are widely used by academics and policymakers.

The WGI have faced methodological criticism (Arndt and Oman, 2006; Kurtz and Schrank, 2007a, 2007b). Kurtz and Schrank point to systematic perceptual and sample selection biases in the methodology based partly on business surveys. The first source of bias is that business interests may not equate with the public interest. For example, business owners may not consider increased taxation as a sign of government effectiveness. Policy preferences get confused with effectiveness measures. Secondly, perceptions of governance competence and probity may be colored by other factors. For example, governments experiencing economic growth are more likely to be viewed as comparatively more effective and efficient (2007a: 542–3). While the Kurtz and Schrank criticisms have been contested (Kaufman et al., 2007a, 2007b), renewed criticism of the indicators has come from the World Bank's own Development Research Group. That study concluded that the six indicators do not capture different aspects of governance and that each reflects only broad governance perceptions. Similarly, TI's index may be a broad indicator of perceptions about governance rather than a corruption measure per se (Langbein and Knack, 2008).

These methodological concerns go beyond interesting academic debate. The WGI are used in policy and funding decisions. Studies conclude that the use of the indicators by policymakers (and academics) may be 'limited' (Langbein and Knack, 2008: 4) or ill-advised (Kurtz and Schrank, 2007a: 552).

TODAY'S KEY QUESTIONS AND DEBATES

At the turn of the century, the questions posed by the academic community surrounding governance were multiplying, the governance dialog was a difficult one within aid partnerships, and some of the intellectual basis for aid decisions appeared to be on uncertain ground.

Rethinking aid, development, and governance at the international level

Early in the new century, the adoption of the eight Millennium Development Goals to be achieved by 2015 highlighted the need for more aid *and* increased aid effectiveness. A formal link among development, aid, and governance was forged in the Monterrey Consensus emerging from the 2002 UN International Conference on Financing for Development. In essence, donors pledged more aid, and recipients, better governance.

A new aid and development model surfaced, based on country ownership, donor alignment with government priorities, and harmonization among donors. At three High-Level Forums (Rome, Paris, Accra) within the decade, it became clear that implementation hinged not only on improved *recipient governance* but also on the quality of individual and collective *donor governance*. Fragmentation, limited client responsiveness, unclear strategies, cumbersome processes, duplication, and competition for staff and 'good projects' were recognized as hampering donor effectiveness and contributing to governance problems in aid-dependent countries.

There were other international initiatives aimed at improving governance in developing countries. The New Economic Partnership for African Development (NEPAD) established a Peer Review Mechanism, where African countries could voluntarily submit to a governance review. The Kimberly Process (KP), to stem the flow of 'conflict' diamonds, and the Extractive Industries Transparency Initiative (EITI), to set global accountability and transparency standards for companies and governments involved in extractive industries, are private–public partnerships aiming to reduce conflict and corruption. There have also been unprecedented efforts to track and return money stolen by corrupt governments.

There were other developments. China, with an interest in oil, metals and minerals, and funds for both aid and investment – and strict non-interference policies in other nations' domestic affairs – gave African countries needed finance *without* governance-related 'dialog' or preconditions. Private foundations became increasingly important as aid providers (Kharas, 2007). Armed with a private sector mentality, the foundations tended to focus more on getting things done and less on longer-term institution-building and governance concerns. At the World Bank, there was an emphasis on combating corruption in World Bank–financed projects. Several high-profile cases came to light, and the World Bank published, after much internal debate, a new strategy on anti-corruption and governance. Nonetheless, it was far from clear that significantly more resources were being directed towards governance-related activities (Nunberg, 2007: 78–82). By 2008, the worldwide financial crisis and economic recession changed the focus of international development concern. Helping economies to weather the storm became the predominant theme uniting industrial and developing countries.

The development community's principal unsettled debates on governance

There was a dawning, and perhaps disappointed, realization that improving governance was *not* the 'silver bullet' it had appeared to be in the 1990s (Rodrik, 2006: 977–80). Key questions surrounding governance and economic development remain unresolved.

Institutions, governance and economic growth

A fairly broad consensus has evolved that there *is* a relationship between governance and economic growth. Disagreement persists about the direction of the causality and the relative importance of governance and institutions in the growth process.

In the early 2000s, research found a strong causal effect from institutions on incomes (Acemoglu et al., 2001). This was followed by work proclaiming the primacy of institutions in determining income levels (Rodrik et al., 2004). Others went even further: '... a country that improves its governance from a relatively low level to an average level could almost triple the income per capita of its population in the long term ...' (Kaufman, 2005: 41). For a time, it looked like the 'silver bullet' had been found.

Not everyone agreed. The primacy argument was vigorously disputed:

> ... endogeneity means that nothing is the primary cause. Institutions are not a deeper cause than the supply of factors or technology: institutions, to reiterate may determine the supply of factors and their use, but these factors, in turn, affect growth and future wealth, which affect the evolution of institutions (Przeworski, 2004: 184).

Another view, espoused by Jeffrey Sachs, was that while institutions were important, increased aid and investment were the critical factors in overcoming poverty and improving governance (2003).

Harking back to earlier political science a number of scholars concluded that improved governance was likely the result of economic growth and *not* vice versa. 'Our evidence suggests ... countries that emerge from poverty, accumulate human and physical capital under dictatorships, and then, once they become richer, are increasingly likely to improve their institutions' (Glaeser et al., 2004: 298); and 'Our chapters show that, in many ways, institutional development is a consequence, rather than a cause, of economic development' (Chang, 2007: 13).

Those who could be regarded as 'institutions fundamentalists' began to temper their views, perhaps cautioned by the zeal with which policymakers translated theory into practice and aid conditions.

> While there is relatively strong evidence showing that the *broad cluster of institutions* – comprising economic, political, and legal aspects – are essential for long-run economic development, we must be modest and admit that we are still at the beginning of the process of understanding how exactly specific aspects of institutions influence economic outcomes (Acemoglu, 2008: 2; see also, Hyden et al., 2004: 193, 202; Rodrik, 2006: 979, 2008b: 19).

Support has emerged for a more contextually specific relationship between governance and development. Collier in *The Bottom Billion* notes:

> Good governance and policy help a country to realize its opportunities, but they cannot generate opportunities when none exist, and they cannot

defy gravity. Even the best governance and policies are not going to turn Malawi into a rich country [and] ... being the most corrupt country on earth has not prevented Bangladesh from adopting fairly reasonable economic policies and from growing (2007: 65–6).

'Good enough', 'just enough, 'must-have' governance

If good governance, at least in certain development scenarios, is important for economic growth, then the question is what is 'good enough governance' or 'just enough governance' (Grindle, 2004, 2007; Fukuyama, 2008: 33). Enthusiasm for good governance among the development community quickly led to a long list of desirable characteristics. One study, for example, defined a governance framework with six arenas (civil society, political society, government, bureaucracy, economic society, judiciary) and six basic principles (participation, fairness, decency, accountability, transparency, and efficiency), leading to 36 indicators (Hyden et al., 2004: 189). An analysis of the World Bank's *World Development Reports* showed the expanding governance agenda. 'In the 1997 report, developing countries were advised to pay attention to 45 aspects of good governance; by 2002, the list had grown to 116 items' (Grindle, 2004: 527).

That analysis defined 'good enough governance' as 'a condition of minimally acceptable governance performance and civil society engagement that does not significantly hinder economic and political development and that permits poverty reduction initiatives to go forward' (Grindle, 2004: 526). The answer may be contextually specific, but frameworks exist that can help practitioners determine what, when, how and how fast to proceed. A more contextual approach to institutional reform has gained increasing favor: '...[D]ealing with the institutional landscape in developing countries requires a second-best mindset. In such settings, a focus on best-practice institutions not only creates blind spots, leading us to overlook reforms that might achieve the desired ends at lower cost, but can also backfire' (Rodrik, 2008a: 100–1).

Yet there is far from a consensus on what is 'second best' or 'minimally acceptable' and, ironically, if the concept of 'good enough governance' is good enough:

> A 'good enough' approach to improving governance, that concentrates on strengthening executive capacity, might seem appropriate in a weak or failing state. But by skirting round such essentially political issues as voice and accountability it could end up reinforcing executive autonomy of society. If political power continues to reside in the hands of an unrepresentative minority then the prospects for good governance and pro-poor development will probably both remain fragile and uncertain (Burnell, 2008: 308).

In a similar vein, Carothers cautions against the 'sequencing fallacy', arguing that autocrats generally cannot be relied on for rule of law and state-building, and that there is a limit to how far they will go even if 'enlightened' (2007).

Thus, attention has returned to the relationship between democracy and economic growth. Earlier, democracy, with its clamor of competing interest groups, was considered somewhat antagonistic to rapid economic growth (Huntington, 1968). More recent views echo this (Djankov et al., 2003). There is concern that democratization could provoke increased disorder: 'With the loss of public revenues, governments became more predatory. With the loss of their political monopolies, they became less secure ..., many governments in Africa were tempted to abandon their role as guardian and to embrace the role of predator ...' (Bates, 2008: 121). The impressive Chinese growth performance, while most democracies in Africa and Latin America stagnated through the 1990s, underlined the view that democracy was far from being a 'must have' for economic growth.

Refuting the view that democracy is detrimental to growth, one influential study examined the experiences of 135 countries between 1950 and 1990:

> ... we did not find a shred of evidence that democracy need be sacrificed on the altar of development. The few countries that developed spectacularly during the past fifty years were as

likely to achieve that feat under democracy as under dictatorship ... . But these findings also imply that the recently heralded economic virtues of democracy are yet another figment of the ideological imagination. Democracy has other virtues, but at least with regard to the growth of total economies, political regimes are not what matters (Przeworski et al., 2000: 271).

Yet, according to the same study, per capita incomes grow faster in democracies because democracies have lower population growth rates, and democracies are more likely to exist and survive in higher-income countries. A meta-analysis of 84 studies on democracy and growth similarly concludes that 'available empirical evidence does not support the notion that developing countries need to forego civil liberties and political freedom in order to enjoy faster economic growth' (Doucouliagos and Ulubasoglu, 2008: 79). While finding no direct effect of democracy on economic growth, it found *indirect* positive effects through impacts on human capital formation and levels of economic freedom, inflation, and political stability (Doucouliagos and Ulubasoglu, 2008: 77).

A high-level Commission on Growth and Development studied 13 developing countries with sustained growth episodes to identify common characteristics. Among other factors, it highlighted the importance of 'committed, credible, and capable governments' and 'policymakers [who] understood that successful development entails a decades-long commitment, and a fundamental bargain between the present and the future' (2008: 26). It emphasized the need for policymakers to be trusted and noted that different types of regimes could provide the necessary leadership.

The Commission's statements highlight the problems in defining 'must-have governance' or 'good-enough governance'. Aside from democracy, there are other elements that might be considered as essential to good governance – even a scaled-back, 'good enough' governance. These include: leadership, trust and other cultural norms associated with Western democracies, and corruption control.

There is a long-standing reflection on how much leaders matter. Looking at leadership transitions due to accidents or natural causes, Jones and Olken found that leaders' death led to substantial changes in growth (both good and bad) in autocratic regimes, but not in democratic ones (2005: 837). Further research into leaders' role in economic growth and governance reform could be useful since the examples of 'toxic leaders' damaging growth prospects are indisputable: for example, Mugabe in Zimbabwe and Mubutu in Zaire.[4] Yet, the definition of effective leadership in the development context is likely to be as contested as the concept of good governance itself.

Others would point to trust and other cultural norms associated with Western, market-based economies as essential to the governance 'package' for economic growth. 'A nation's well being, as well as its ability to compete, is conditioned by a single, pervasive cultural characteristic: the level of trust inherent in the society' (Fukuyama, 1996: 7). Cultural norms and values are also considered by some as a major factor explaining economic disparities among nations (Harrison and Huntington, 2000). If correct, the practical implications are far from evident.

Finally, new analyses tried to refine the causes and consequences of various forms of corruption, including its impact on economic growth (Blackburn et al., 2006; Rose-Ackerman, 2007). The majority view has swung in favor of corruption hurting economic growth. However, the precise impact has been difficult to measure and appears highly variable, depending on the type of corruption, its predictability, and country and regional context (Smith, 2007).

Aid and governance

Many development economists continue to be optimistic that aid, properly designed, can have a beneficial impact on economic development and, more narrowly, on governance (Kaufmann, 2005: 43; Sachs, 2005; Collier, 2007: 184). Yet, there is little evidence that governance-related aid has worked. An evaluation found that the World Bank's 'work on governance became explicit and more systematic' in the second half of the 1990s (World Bank, 2006: 7). Activities included: developing and using governance indicators in country allocations; public sector and judicial reform; more attention to financial management and procurement; community-driven development (CDD) to 'circumvent corrupt governments'; developing a category of countries with 'severe governance problems'; and focusing on fraud in Bank-supported projects and within the Bank itself (World Bank, 2006: 7–8). The review concluded '… governance indicators had shown no significant improvement since the mid-1990s; the variety of institutional and process reforms had been slow, insufficient, or circumvented; and CDD appeared "unable to stem corruption" (World Bank, 2006: 9–11).

Another review by several development research agencies, found little systematic evidence of what works in two key governance areas: democracy promotion and anti-corruption efforts. The review, while supporting donor involvement, was clear that past efforts were ill-advised. 'What donors do need to back off from is the kind of involvement in country governance that stem[s] from conditionality, selectivity or the search for strong fiduciary guarantees' (Overseas Development Institute et al., 2008: vii).

Yet, there are also views that most donors resist political conditionality or selectivity and that aid has had the effect of propping up weak and corrupt regimes (Van de Walle, 2005). A related argument is that aid works much like the 'natural resource curse', generating corruption, rent-seeking, and conflict, thereby reducing the rate of growth (Djankov et al., 2006). In addition to those effects, aid can also adversely affect governance by generating high transaction costs for the government, 'poaching' qualified government staff, and reducing tax receipts (Brautigam and Knack, 2004). Another study found evidence that in countries that receive more aid, governance-dependent industries grow more slowly. The hypothesis is that aid reduces the incentives to improve government capacity

and accountability, weakening the institutional environment, including rule of law, and specifically, contract enforcement (Rajan and Subramanian, 2007).

Caution has become the watchword in governance interventions:

> The principle is *nonintervention*. Don't reward bad governments by working through them, but don't try to boss them around or overthrow them either (Easterly, 2006: 157).

Similarly:

> There are thus grave limitations to the ability of external powers to create demand for institutions and therefore limitations on the ability to transfer existing knowledge about institutional construction and reform to developing countries. These limitations suggest that IFIs, international donors, and the NGO community more broadly should be cautious about raising expectations for the long-term effectiveness of its new 'capacity-building' mantra (Fukuyama, 2004: 39).

Global governance and economic development

Among the contested aspects of global governance linked to economic development is the debate over the governance structures and legitimacy of the World Bank and the International Monetary Fund (IMF). The dominance of industrialized countries in the governance of the institutions has called into question their legitimacy vis-à-vis their clients – middle- and low-income countries. Some countries do not question the legitimacy per se of the arrangements, but want more of a say given their emerging economic importance. Others support fundamentally changing the governance structure so that *stakeholders* (as opposed to *shareholders*) have a predominant role. Arguably, the IMF and the World Bank have been the development trendsetters in the postwar period. Challenges to their legitimacy could profoundly affect the intellectual and policy landscape for development, including attitudes towards governance. It remains to be seen if the debate will result in 'symbolic' reform (such as allowing non-US and non-European citizens at the helm of the institutions) or more substantive reform.[5]

MOVING FORWARD

Debates on governance and economic development have enlivened and complicated an already cluttered field of theoretical conjecture. Initially, the focus was more on the high-level question of the role of markets versus states. While not entirely resolved, there has been a convergence towards 'markets *and* states' as the key governance framework for economic development, with the relative importance of each varying across nations and time periods. Consequently, preoccupation has shifted to the relationships among governance, aid, and economic growth.

Debate goes on, with several promising avenues for research. More importantly, there are a few areas – methodological and substantive – where 'caution flags' need to be raised.

Methodological approaches and measurement tools

Much of the recent research on governance, aid, and economic growth has been based on large-sample, multi-country, multivariable regression analysis. While perversely fascinating, the results of these studies, taken together, are not consistent, conclusive or particularly helpful for policymaking. Varying definitions and development objectives, problems of endogeneity, directions of causality and country-specific characteristics create complexity and 'noise'. In addition, at all levels, attribution problems are formidable (Bourguignon and Sundberg, 2007). This suggests that a different methodological approach might bear more fruit.

Measurement tools such as the WGI and TI's Corruption Perceptions Index also have been subject to methodological criticism. Both sets of indicators have been perceived as helpful in publicizing governance and corruption issues, 'naming and shaming' the worst offenders. How effective this has been is open to doubt: there has been no overall improvement in scores over time (Kaufman et al., 2008: 20). More concerning is the use of the indicators in performance criteria linked to aid decisions and cross-country research.

It may be time to return to the 'old-fashioned approach' of using fieldwork and case studies at the national and subnational levels to analyze 'the governance deficit' and the dynamics between growth and specific governance aspects. There has been a new emphasis on randomized impact evaluation using experimental or quasi-experimental designs. This is helpful in bringing back a focus on 'what works' and may assist in pinpointing governance/growth linkages, if they exist, at the project level. However, the usefulness of randomized evaluations is probably confined to testing alternative design strategies in project settings. Broad policy questions like the ones discussed are not amenable to this type of evaluation. Also, even at the project level, there can be ethical, efficiency, and opportunity cost concerns (Banerjee, 2007; Bourguignon and Sundberg, 2007: 318; Goldin et al., 2007).

The case-by-case approach is time-consuming. Also, if one accepts governance as a contextually-specific, interlocking system, most findings will not be easily portable. Nonetheless, if some of the resources were redirected from other approaches, an impressive body of knowledge – and perhaps some robust conclusions, building theory from the ground up – could emerge relatively quickly.

A final comment, more procedural than methodological: there is a communications gap between academics and practitioners on the subject of governance and economic development. Nuanced and caveated academic findings were transformed into simplified policy prescriptions and put into practice prematurely. This manifested itself, for example, in the international aid community's embrace of governance reforms and conditionality in the latter half of the 1990s. The gap has narrowed, but still exists. There is also the perennial distance between political scientists and economists. Unless the disciplines come together, there is little hope of meaningful progress in resolving, or at least better understanding, the principal unsettled questions.

Simplicity is overrated

The search for a 'silver bullet' to bring about economic development and poverty reduction continues. While intellectually tempting, there are dangers in simplicity.[6]

Shrinking substance and 'institutional engineering'
For a time, bad governance was embraced as the primary cause of economic stagnation. In effect, economic development was reduced to a matter of governance. In turn, bad governance was reduced to corruption by a segment of the donor community (Hyden, 2007: 16754). A symptom of this is that the World Bank's 2007 strategy needed to make the point that 'Governance and corruption are not synonymous'. Przeworski, in his critique of the primacy of institutions in economic development, notes: 'This theoretical claim has practical, policy, consequences: it licenses institutional engineering. If different institutions generate different outcomes, then one can stick any institution into any historical condition and expect that it would function in the same way it has elsewhere' (2004: 166). When it comes to economic development and governance, looking for simple formulaic answers across countries has not been helpful (Rodrik, 2006; Chang, 2007).

Avoiding simplistic constructs does not grant, however, a license to overcomplicate with elaborate frameworks that attempt to capture all possible variations of governance across countries. The contextual concept of 'good enough governance' may frustrate theory but improve practice.

Overlooking the mundane
An evaluation of World Bank-supported public sector reform between 1999 and 2006 found: 'Performance usually improved for public financial management, tax administration, and transparency, but not usually for civil service. Direct measures to reduce corruption – such as anticorruption laws and commissions – rarely succeeded' (World Bank, 2008: xiii). Civil service reform and anti-corruption campaigns capture headlines. Improved expenditure management, auditing, and accounting rarely get public notice. Routinizing the latter set may prove critical to the public sector's ability to foster economic development.

Leaving aid out of it
Aid has become so entwined in development that it is impossible to leave aside donor governance issues. It is a relatively recent phenomenon for donors to admit that their own governance issues (poor accountability, transparency, and coordination) hamper aid effectiveness. More analysis, beyond the anecdotal, of aid practices and donor governance issues is needed.

Ignoring new developments
Globalization has brought new challenges, actors, and aid modalities. Providing global public goods (GPGs) is an increasing challenge (International Task Force, 2006). There is a fairly complex relationship between GPGs and economic development at the country level. There are instances of complementarity between supplying GPGs and aiding development (for example, containing the spread of HIV/AIDS in Africa). There are also instances where providing GPGs involves short-term trade-offs with income-producing activities and/or distorts country development priorities (for example, preserving large tracts of tropical forests or prioritizing polio eradication over more prevalent 'poor country' diseases). Also, GPGs have spawned single-purpose global programs. Some have impressive results, but many global programs are not well integrated into country planning, increase the coordination burden on governments and donors, and focus on short-term

results rather than longer-term capacity and governance issues (World Bank, 2004).

There are also new actors on the development scene, including private foundations, NGOs, public–private partnerships, and transnational corporations. The new players 'up the ante' for governments, demanding new capabilities, increased transparency, and a greater voice for non-governmental actors. For weak governments, this multiplies their governance challenges. On the other hand, the new actors have the potential to create new networks, coalitions, and pathways that could substitute or complement traditional government and market institutions, bolstering economic development. Whatever the ultimate impact, the new stakeholders cannot be ignored.

Finally, new modalities of finance and aid are influencing governance in developing countries. China's financial assistance, with its non-interference policy, is providing alternatives to governments at odds with traditional donors' views on governance and economic policies. Traditional donors are also innovating with increased use of sector-wide approaches and general budget support. Both modalities are reliant on a country's own systems and institutions. Budget support, in particular, has the potential to redirect government accountability away from donors and towards citizens. However, the potential for misuse, along with possible donor involvement in government budget decisions, could have an opposite effect, weakening overall governance. The new modalities' impact on governance remains to be seen.

CONCLUSION

Moving forward on the governance and economic development agenda is no easy task. Academics and practitioners have come a long way from the time when governance was virtually ignored in development thinking.

An important relationship between governance and economic development is now accepted. Beyond that, much remains unsettled. Meaningful progress will depend on:

- shifting methodological approaches;
- acquiring deep contextual knowledge;
- factoring in new developments;
- regaining an appreciation for the inherent complexities of governance and economic development in their own right and in relation to each other.

It turns out that there are no 'silver bullets' – just plenty of hard work ahead.

NOTES

1 In other World Bank-sponsored governance work, the Worldwide Governance Indicators (WGI), the most recent definition of governance is:

> We define governance broadly as the traditions and institutions by which authority in a country is exercised. This includes the process by which governments are selected, monitored and replaced; the capacity of the government to effectively formulate and implement sound policies; and the respect of citizens and the state for the institutions that govern economic and social interactions among them (Kaufmann et al., 2008: 7).

2 According to Koeberle and Malesa (2005: 53), only 15–18% of conditions associated with World Bank adjustment lending in 1990–98 were explicitly for public sector management. However, there were institutional and governance conditions in specific sectors, making the actual percentage of this type of conditionality higher.

3 In contrast to Easterly's general conclusions, Bermeo (2008), reviewing bilateral aid, found evidence of greater selectivity, based on governance and economic policy indicators, in aid allocations to economic infrastructure and production sectors.

4 The term 'toxic leader' is from Lipman-Blumen (2005).

5 There is a growing literature on World Bank and IMF reform (see, for example, Woods, 2006 and Birdsall, 2006). The Brookings Institution and IMF websites carry analyses of proposals and reforms.

6 Sachs has made the point that development economics needs to heed some of the lessons of clinical medicine: Lesson 1 is *'the human body is a*

complex system'; Lesson 2 is *complexity requires a differential diagnosis*' (Sachs, 2005: 74–81).

REFERENCES

Acemoglu, Daron (2008) 'Interactions between Governance and Growth: What World Bank Economists Need to Know', in Douglass North, Daron Acemoglu, Francis Fukuyama and Dani Rodrik, *Governance, Growth and Development Decision-making.* Washington, DC: The World Bank, pp. 1–7.

Acemoglu, Daron, Johnson, Simon and Robinson, James A. (2001) 'The Colonial Origins of Comparative Development: An Empirical Investigation', *The American Economic Review* 91(5): 1369–401.

Arndt, Christiane and Oman, Charles (2006) *Uses and Abuses of Governance Indicators.* Paris: Development Center of the Organization for Economic Co-operation and Development.

Aron, Janine (2000) 'Growth and Institutions: A Review of the Evidence', *World Bank Research Observer* 15(1): 99–135.

Banerjee, Abhijit Vinayak (2007) *Making Aid Work.* Cambridge, MA: MIT Press/Boston Review.

Bardhan, Pranab (1997) 'Corruption and Development: A Review of Issues', *Journal of Economic Literature* 35(3): 1320–46.

Bardhan, Pranab (2002) 'Decentralization of Governance and Development', *Journal of Economic Perspectives* 16(4): 185–205.

Bates, Robert H. (2008) *When Things Fell Apart: State Failure in Late Century Africa.* New York: Cambridge University Press.

Bermeo, Sarah Blodgett (2008) 'Foreign Aid, Foreign Policy, and Development: Sector Allocation in Bilateral Aid'. Princeton University, Department of Politics.

Birdsall, Nancy (2006) *Rescuing the World Bank: A CGD Working Group Report and Selected Essays.* Washington, DC: Center for Global Development.

Blackburn, Keith, Bose, Niloy and Haque, M. Emranul (2006) 'The Incidence and Persistence of Corruption in Economic Development', *Journal of Economic Dynamics and Control* 30(12): 2447–67.

Botchwey, Kwesi (2005) 'Changing Views and Approaches to Africa's Development', in Timothy Besley and Roberto Zagha (eds), *Development Challenges in the 1990s: Leading Policymakers Speak from Experience.* New York: Oxford University Press and the World Bank. pp. 261–70.

Bourguignon, Francois and Sundberg, Mark (2007) 'Aid Effectiveness – Opening the Black Box', *American Economics Review* 97(2): 316–21.

Brautigam, Deborah and Knack, Stephen (2004) 'Foreign Aid, Institutions, and Governance in Sub-Saharan Africa', *Economic Development and Cultural Change* 52(2): 255–85.

Burnell, Peter (2008) 'Governance and Conditionality in a Globalizing World' in Peter Burnell and Vicky Randall (eds), *Politics in the Developing World,* 2nd edn. Oxford: Oxford University Press. pp. 291–311.

Carothers, Thomas (2007) 'The "Sequencing" Fallacy', *Journal of Democracy* 18(1): 13–27.

Chang, Ha-Joon (ed.) (2007) *Institutional Change and Economic Development.* Tokyo: United Nations University Press.

Clague, Christopher (1997) 'Introduction' and 'The New Institutional Economics and Economic Development' in Christopher Clague (ed.), *Institutions and Economic Development: Growth and Governance in Less-Developed and Post-Socialist Countries.* Baltimore: Johns Hopkins University. pp. 1–36.

Collier, Paul (2007) *The Bottom Billion: Why the Poorest Countries Are Failing and What Can Be Done About It.* Oxford: Oxford University Press.

Commission on Growth and Development (2008) *The Growth Report: Strategies for Sustained Growth and Inclusive Development.* Washington, DC: World Bank.

Djankov, Simeon, Glaeser, Edward, La Porta, Rafael, Lopez-de-Silanes, Florencio and Schleifer, Andre (2003) 'The new comparative economics', *Journal of Comparative Economics* 31(4): 595–619.

Djankov, Simeon, Montalvo, Jose G. and Reynal-Querol, Marta (2006) 'Does Foreign Aid Help?', *Cato Journal* 26(1): 1–28.

Doucouliagos, Hristos and Ulubasoglu, Mehmet Ali (2008) 'Democracy and Economic Growth: A Meta-Analysis', *American Journal of Political Science* 52(1): 61–83.

Easterly, William (2006) *The White Man's Burden: Why the West's Efforts to Aid the Rest Have Done So Much Ill and So Little Good.* New York: Penguin Press.

Easterly, William and Pfutze, Tobias (2008) 'Where Does the Money Go? Best and Worst Practices in Foreign Aid', *Journal of Economic Perspectives* 22(2): 29–52.

Easterly, William, Levine, Ross and Roodman, David (2004) 'Aid, Policies and Growth: Comment', *American Economic Review* 94(3): 774–80.

Fukuyama, Francis (1996) *Trust: The Social Virtues and the Creation of Prosperity.* New York: Free Press.

Fukuyama, Francis (2004) *State-Building: Governance and World Order in the 21st Century*. Ithaca: Cornell University Press.

Fukuyama, Francis (2008) 'What Do We Know About the Relationship between the Political and Economic Dimensions of Development' in Douglass North, Daron Acemoglu, Francis Fukuyama and Dani Rodrik *Governance, Growth and Development Decision-making*. Washington, DC: World Bank. pp. 25–34.

Glaeser, Edward L., La Porta, Rafael, Lopez-de-Silanes, Florencio and Shleifer, Andrei (2004) 'Do Institutions Cause Growth?', *Journal of Economic Growth* 9(3): 271–303.

Goldin, Ian, Rogers, F. Halsey, and Stern, Nicholas (2007) [untitled], in Banerjee, Abhijit Vinayak, *Making Aid Work*. Cambridge, MA: MIT Press/ Boston Review. pp. 29–38.

Grindle, Merilee S. (2004) 'Good Enough Governance: Poverty Reduction and Reform in Developing Countries', *Governance: An International Journal of Policy, Administration, and Institutions* 17(4): 525–48.

Grindle, Merilee S. (2007) 'Good Enough Governance Revisited', *Development Policy Review* 25(5): 553–74.

Harrison, Laurence E. and Huntington Samuel P. (eds) (2000) *Culture Matters: How Values Shape Human Progress*. New York: Basic Books.

Huntington, Samuel P. (1968) *Political Order in Changing Societies*. New Haven; CT: Yale University Press.

Hyden, Goran (2007) 'Governance and Poverty Reduction in Africa', *Proceedings of the National Academy of Sciences of the United States of America* 104(43): 16751–6.

Hyden, Goran, Court, Julius and Mease, Kenneth (2004) *Making Sense of Governance: Empirical Evidence from 16 Developing Countries*. Boulder, CO: Lynne Rienner.

International Task Force on Global Public Goods (2006) *Meeting Global Challenges: International Cooperation in the National Interest*. Stockholm, Sweden.

Jones, Benjamin F. and Olken, Benjamin A. (2005) 'Do Leaders Matter? National Leadership and Growth Since World War II', *The Quarterly Journal of Economics* 120(3): 835–64.

Kapur, Devesh and Webb, Richard (2000) *Governance-Related Conditionalities of the International Financial Institutions*, G-24 Discussion Paper 6. New York and Geneva: United Nations.

Kaufmann, Daniel (2005) '10 Myths about Governance and Corruption', *Finance and Development* 42(3): 41–3.

Kaufman, Daniel, Kraay, Aart and Mastruzzi, Massimo (2007a) 'Growth and Governance: A Reply', *The Journal of Politics* 69(2): 555–62.

Kaufman, Daniel, Kraay, Aart and Mastruzzi, Massimo (2007b) 'Growth and Governance: A Rejoinder', *The Journal of Politics* 69(2): 570–2.

Kaufman, Daniel, Kraay, Aart and Mastruzzi, Massimo (2008) *Governance Matters VII: Aggregate and Individual Governance Indicators 1996–2007*. Washington, DC: World Bank.

Kharas, Homi (2007) 'The New Reality of Aid'. Paper presented at the Brookings Blum Roundtable. Washington, DC: Brookings Institution.

Koeberle, Stefan and Malesa, Thaddeus (2005) 'Experience with World Bank Conditionality', in Stefan Koeberle, Harold Bedoya, Peter Silarszsky and Gero Verheyen (eds), *Conditionality Revisited: Concepts, Experiences and Lessons*. Washington, DC: World Bank. pp. 45–56.

Kurtz, Marcus J. and Schrank, Andrew (2007a) 'Growth and Governance: Models, Measures, and Mechanisms', *The Journal of Politics* 69(2): 538–54.

Kurtz, Marcus J. and Schrank, Andrew (2007b) 'Growth and Governance: A Defense', *The Journal of Politics* 69(2): 563–9.

Langbein, Laura and Knack, Stephen (2008) *The Worldwide Governance Indicators and Tautology: Causally Related Separable Concepts, Indicators of a Common Cause, or Both?* Policy Research Working Paper 4669. Washington, DC: World Bank.

Leff, Nathaniel H. (1964) 'Economic Development through Bureaucratic Corruption', *The American Behavioral Scientist* 8(2): 8–14.

Lin, Justin Yifu and Nugent, Jeffrey B. (1995) 'Institutions and Economic Development', in J. Behrman and T.N. Srinivasan (eds), *Handbook of Development Economics, Volume III*. Netherlands: Elsevier. pp. 2301–70.

Lipman-Blumen, Jean (2005) *The Allure of Toxic Leaders*. New York: Oxford University Press.

Mauro, Pablo (1995) 'Corruption and Growth', *Quarterly Journal of Economics* 110(3): 681–712.

North, Douglass C. (1990) *Institutions, Institutional Change and Economic Performance*. Cambridge: Cambridge University Press.

Nunberg, Barbara (2007) 'Generational Shifts in International Governance Assistance: The World Bank and State-Building After 911', *International Journal of Economic Development* 9(1&2): 59–110.

Nunberg, Barbara and Lindauer, David L. (1994) 'Conclusion: The Political Economy of Civil

Service Pay and Employment Reform', in David L. Lindauer and Barbara Nunberg (eds), *Rehabilitating Government: Pay and Employment Reform in Africa*. Washington, DC: The World Bank. pp. 238–44.

Olson, Mancur (1965) *The Logic of Collective Action*. Cambridge, MA: Harvard University Press.

Olson, Mancur (1997) 'The New Institutional Economics: The Collective Choice Approach to Economic Development', in Christopher Clague (ed.), *Institutions and Economic Development: Growth and Governance in Less-Developed and Post-Socialist Countries*. Baltimore: Johns Hopkins University. pp. 37–64.

Overseas Development Institute, Christian Michelsen Institute, Economic and Social Research Foundation, and Center for Democratic Development (2008) *Good Governance, Aid Modalities and Poverty Reduction: From Better Theory to Better Practice – Final Synthesis Report*. Research project (RP-05-GG) of the Advisory Board for Irish Aid.

Pomerantz, Phyllis R. (2004) *Aid Effectiveness in Africa: Developing Trust between Donors and Governments*. Lanham, MD: Lexington Books.

Przeworski, Adam (2004) 'The Last Instance: Are Institutions the Primary Cause of Economic Development?', *European Journal of Sociology* 45(2): 165–88.

Przeworski, Adam, Alvarez, Michael E., Cheibub, Jose Antonio and Limongi, Fernando (2000) *Democracy and Development: Political Institutions and Well Being in the World, 1950–1990*. New York: Cambridge University Press.

Rajan, Raghuram and Subramanian, Arvind (2007) 'Does Aid Affect Governance?', *American Economic Review* 97(2): 322–7.

Rodrik, Dani (2006) 'Goodbye Washington Consensus, Hello Washington Confusion? A Review of the World Bank's Economic Growth in the 1990s: Learning From a Decade of Reform', *Journal of Economic Literature* 44(4): 973–87.

Rodrik, Dani (2008a) 'Second-Best Institutions', *American Economic Review: Papers and Proceedings* 98(2): 100–4.

Rodrik, Dani (2008b) 'Thinking about Governance' in Douglass North, Daron Acemoglu, Francis Fukuyama and Dani Rodrik Governance, *Growth and Development Decision-Making*. Washington, DC: World Bank. pp. 17–24.

Rodrik, Dani, Subramanian, Arvind and Trebbi, Francesco (2004) 'Institutions Rule: The Primacy of Institutions over Geography and Integration in Economic Development', *Journal of Economic Growth* 9(2): 131–65.

Rose-Ackerman, Susan (1978) *Corruption: A Study in Political Economy*. New York: Academic Press.

Rose-Ackerman, Susan (ed.) (2007) *International Handbook on the Economics of Corruption*. Cheltenham: Edward Elgar.

Sachs, Jeffrey (2003) 'Institutions Matter, but Not for Everything', *Finance and Development* 40(2): 38–41.

Sachs, Jeffrey (2005) *The End of Poverty: Economic Possibilities for Our Time*. New York: Penguin Press.

Sen, Amartya (1999) *Development as Freedom*. New York: Random House.

Shleifer, Andrei and Vishny, Robert W. (1993) 'Corruption', *The Quarterly Journal of Economics* 108(3): 599–617.

Smith, B.C. (2007) *Good Governance and Development*. New York: Palgrave Macmillan.

Stiglitz, Joseph E. (2003) *Globalization and Its Discontents*. New York: W.W. Norton.

Van de Walle, Nicolas (2005) *Overcoming Stagnation in Aid-Dependent Countries*. Washington, DC: Center for Global Development.

Williamson, John (2000) 'What Should the World Bank Think about the Washington Consensus?', *The World Bank Research Observer* 15(2): 251–64.

Williamson, Oliver E. (2000) 'The New Institutional Economics: Taking Stock, Looking Ahead', *The Journal of Economic Literature* 38(3): 595–613.

Wolfensohn, James D. (1996) '"People and Development" Address to the Board of Governors at the Annual Meetings of the World Bank and the International Monetary Fund', in World Bank (2005), *Voice for the World's Poor: Selected Speeches and Writings of World Bank President James D. Wolfensohn, 1995–2005*. Washington DC: World Bank. pp. 45–54.

Woods, Ngaire (2006) *The Globalizers: The IMF, the World Bank, and Their Borrowers*. Ithaca, NY: Cornell University Press.

World Bank (1992) *Governance and Development*. Washington, DC: World Bank.

World Bank (1997) *The State in a Changing World*. World Development Report 1997. New York: Oxford University Press.

World Bank (1998) *Assessing Aid: What Works, What Doesn't and Why*. New York: Oxford University Press.

World Bank (2000) *World Development Report 2000/2001: Attacking Poverty*. New York: Oxford University Press.

World Bank (Operations Evaluation Department) (2004) *Addressing the Challenges of Globalization: An Independent Evaluation of the World Bank's Approach to Global Programs.* Washington, DC: World Bank.

World Bank (Independent Evaluation Group) (2006) *Governance and Anti-Corruption: Ways to Enhance the World Bank's Impact,* Evaluation Brief 2. Washington, DC: World Bank.

World Bank (2007) *Strengthening World Bank Engagement on Governance and Anticorruption.* Washington, DC: World Bank.

World Bank (Independent Evaluation Group) (2008) *Public Sector Reform: What Works and Why?* Washington, DC: World Bank.

12

Measuring Governance

Pippa Norris

The third-wave era since the early 1970s has been remarkable for the spread of democratic goverance and human rights in many societies around the globe. Freedom House (2009) estimate that the number of liberal democracies doubled from the early 1970s until 2000. During the last decade, however, progress slowed to a sluggish and uncertain pace (Puddington, 2009). It is premature and unduly pessimistic to claim that a 'reverse' wave or 'democratic recession' is occurring, as some observers believe (Diamond, 2008), but multiple challenges continue to limit further progress in democratization. Fragile electoral democracies have been undermined by inconclusive or disputed election results, partisan strife, recurrent political scandals, and military coups (Kapstan and Converse, 2008; Fish and Wittenberg, 2009). These issues, always difficult, have been compounded in recent years by the aftermath of the global financial crisis, which generated worsening economic conditions, falling employment and wages, and the largest decline in world trade for 80 years. Even before this downturn, in the world's poorest societies, democratic governance faced particularly severe obstacles in delivering basic public services to their citizens. The United Nations (UN, 2008)

reports enduring and deeply- entrenched poverty for the bottom billion in the least-developed nations, raising doubts about whether the world can achieve the Millennium Development Goals by 2015, as planned. In fragile or post-crisis societies, the struggle to reduce conflict, build sustainable peace, and strengthen the capacity and legitimacy of democratically- elected states cannot be underestimated (Doyle and Sambanis, 2006). In this complex and difficult environment, it would be naïve to assume that the third-wave era of democratization continues to advance steadily. It has become even more vital to understand the conditions which underpin regime change, as well as the underlying processes and policies leading towards the advance and consolidation of democratic governance.

An important issue arising from these developments concerns how we measure changes in the quality of democratic governance. Recent years have seen a burgeoning array of approaches and indicators designed for this purpose.[1] Quantitative indicators are particularly valuable to provide an initial check-up of democratic health, where a country is compared against cross-national standards. Is voter turnout in the USA and the UK particularly low – or relatively high?

Is the proportion of women in elected office in India, Bangladesh, and Pakistan a cause for celebration – or concern? In Ghana, Malawi, and Benin, is the quality of human rights, the transparency of government information, and the rule of law all relatively positive or negative compared with other sub-Saharan African societies? Political indicators are now widely used to evaluate needs, to highlight problems, and to monitor the effectiveness of policy interventions.

The idea of political indicators is far from new; some of the earliest, which became widely adopted in the academic and policy research communities, were developed to measure the state of civil liberties and political rights by Freedom House in 1972, as well as the Polity I data collection by Ted Robert Gurr and Harry Eckstein focusing upon patterns of democratic and autocratic regime change. But this enterprise has rapidly expanded. During the last decade, literally dozens of indicators, of varying quality and coverage, became widely available to gauge the quality of democracy in general, as well as multiple measures of 'good governance', human rights, corruption, women's empowerment, civic engagement, social capital, and many other related issues (UNDP, 2007). During recent decades, the range of public opinion surveys monitoring these issues has also grown substantially in scope and reach (Norris, 2008a). In the process, important gains in the level of conceptual sophistication, methodological transparency, scope, and geographic coverage of all these measures have occurred.

These developments raise many important and complex questions. In particular, do indicators based on mass or élite evaluations of the quality of democratic governance coincide? If there is congruence, this increases our confidence in the reliability of both estimates. Where mass and élite assessments diverge, however, which source provides the most legitimate, valid, and reliable benchmark for scholars and practitioners? What are the reasons for any divergence, such as measurement error, and which source

is preferable? Élite evaluations are commonly assumed to be 'correct' and where mass evaluations differ, the public is usually assumed to be mistaken, unaware, ill-informed, or simply misguided in their judgments. Yet for policymakers, in some circumstances, the legitimacy derived from professionally-conducted public opinion polls makes these preferable indicators of the health of democratic governance.

To consider these issues, the first section of the chapter outlines the criteria of validity, reliability, and legitimacy which are useful standards for evaluating indicators of democratic governance. A series of élite-level indicators are compared against equivalent measures in cross-national public opinion surveys. The élite-level indicators are chosen to represent some of the most widely- cited cross-national measures commonly used by scholars and policy analysts. They each have broad cross-national scope and a lengthy time-series, with data based on annual observations classifying regimes worldwide (Munck, 2009). These include the Kaufmann–Kraay measures of 'good governance' (KK good governance), created by the World Bank Institute, and widely adopted in the development community. We also compare Freedom House's index of liberal democracy and the Polity IV project's assessment of constitutional democracy, the élite-level Transparency International's (TI) Corruption Perception Index, and CIRI's Human Rights Index. Public opinion is derived from equivalent items measured by representative surveys at mass level, as contained in the fourth and fifth waves of the World Values Survey.

The second section of the chapter compares élite-level and public evaluations of the quality of democratic governance. The results demonstrate that these evaluations of democracy often diverge. Closer agreement between mass and élite evaluations can be found concerning certain indicators of 'good governance' and human rights, although judgments also differ on some other dimensions. Some of the difference between mass and élite can be attributed to measurement errors;

the equivalent survey items may not prove equivalent to the élite-level indicators, and the élite indicators ranking countries also have large margins of error. But the extent of the mass–élite divergence across multiple indicators suggests that the contrasts cannot be dismissed as simply the product of measurement error.

The third section of the chapter, the conclusions and implications, considers the implications of these findings and how the results should be interpreted. Where there is divergence between mass and élite, it is usually assumed that the élite indicators based on 'expert' judgments are usually more informed and accurate, and the public evaluations must therefore be mistaken, unaware, or ignorant. After all, accurate judgments about the quality of democracy or the state of corruption in a country often require processing and evaluating complex technical information, and it may be that the public is simply unaware of the true situation. Delli Carpini and Keeter (1996) documented numerous examples where the American public lacks awareness about technical policy issues, as well as the limited knowledge that most citizens display about political events, institutions, and people, even in long-established democracies and highly- educated post-industrial societies.

Instead of assuming that expert indicators always provide the 'correct' measurement, however, this study concludes, more agnostically, that no single best measure or indicator of democratic governance exists for all purposes; instead, as Collier and Adcock (1999) suggest, specific choices are best justified pragmatically by the theoretical framework and analytical goals used in any study. The most prudent strategy is to compare the results of alternative indicators at both mass and élite levels, including those available from cross-national public opinion surveys, to see if the findings remain robust and consistent irrespective of the specific measures employed for analysis. If so, then this generates greater confidence in the reliability of the results, since the main generalizations hold irrespective of the particular measures which

are used. If not, then we need to consider how far any differences in the results can be attributed to the underlying concepts and methodologies which differ among these measures. The available élite-level indicators are relatively blunt instruments for assessing the quality of democracy and for diagnosing specific problems of concern within any particular state. For policymakers, élite-level indicators also suffer from certain problems of legitimacy, which may limit their use politically. By contrast, public opinion surveys are likely to prove more politically legitimate, nuanced, and useful to diagnose, monitor, and strengthen the quality of democratic governance across and within many states worldwide.

INDICATORS MONITORING THE HEALTH OF DEMOCRATIC GOVERNANCE

Given the existence of a growing range of indicators of the health of democratic governance, how can they be evaluated? Three criteria – validity, reliability, and legitimacy – are particularly important considerations.

Valid empirical measures accurately reflect the analytical concepts to which they relate. The study of the origin and stability of democratic regimes requires attention to normative concepts in democratic theory, as well as to the construction of appropriate operational empirical indicators. Other indicators that are often used, such as those concerning corruption, human rights, rule of law, and government effectiveness, also involve complex theoretical concepts. Invalid empirical measures may miss the mark by producing unconvincing inferences: for example, if the operational indicators fail to capture important aspects of the underlying concept.

Reliable empirical measures prove consistent across time and place, using data sources which can be easily replicated to allow scholars to build a cumulative body of research. Scientific research makes its procedures public and transparent, including the steps involved in selecting cases, gathering data, and performing analysis. For Karl Popper (1963), the classic hallmark of the scientific inquiry is the process which subjects bold conjectures to rigorous testing, allowing strong claims to be refuted, if not supported by the evidence. While repeated confirmations cannot prove inductive probabilities, attempts to refute findings can advance the body of scientific knowledge. Scientific progress arises from successive attempts to prove ourselves wrong. This process requires reliable empirical measures that are easily open to replication in cumulative studies conducted by the scientific community.

In addition to these common scientific standards, for practitioners and policymakers the *legitimacy* of measures is also important, especially concerning sensitive issues such as the quality of democratic governance, human rights, and corruption. The use of indicators by the international development community raises concern about who decides upon the rankings, whether the results are ideologically biased, and how they are constructed. Legitimacy is strengthened by transparency in the construction and measurement of indices and benchmarks, ownership of the

process by national stakeholders, and the inclusion of a wide diversity of viewpoints in any evaluative process. Conversely, measures may be regarded by the development community and by local officials as less trustworthy and legitimate if the process by which they are generated is closed and opaque, if evaluations are conducted by outside experts (especially if limited to those based in the global North), and if only a few experts drawn from one sector make the assessments.

How far do the available empirical indicators meet the criteria of validity, reliability, and legitimacy? The range of diagnostic tools currently available to assess the health of democratic governance in any country is arrayed as ideal types in the analytical classification illustrated in Figure 12.1. This typology distinguishes between *public* assessments, based on either in-depth deliberative audits or more representative public opinion polls, and *élite* evaluations, based on either 'expert' surveys or composite indices (combining a range of different expert surveys with élite judgments and/or using official statistics).

Public assessments include the democratic audit approach, pioneered by International IDEA (Beetham et al., 2002) and David Beetham (1999, 2004), which represents the

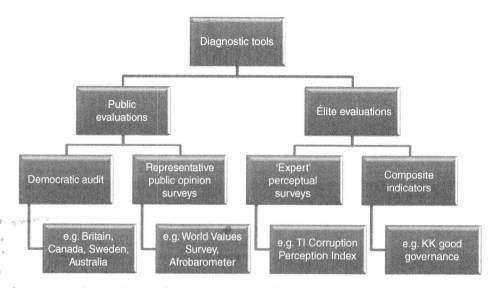

Figure 12.1 Diagnostic tools for assessing the quality of democratic governance.

most in-depth qualitative method. Through this approach, multiple stakeholders and groups within each country deliberate about the state of the state, as exemplified by the Canadian, Swedish, and Australian versions. The audit approach has generated important debates in many countries and contributed towards major political and constitutional reforms, as in the UK. Audits have now been used in more than 18 states worldwide, including newer democracies exemplified by Mongolia. The audit approach is not appropriate for every context, however, as it requires certain conditions for deliberation to operate, including freedom of expression and tolerance of dissent, a rich civil society with inclusive voices from multiple stakeholders, and the necessary resources to engage in this process.

Public assessments of the state of democracy include the growing array of national and cross-national public opinion surveys which have been burgeoning in many societies (Norris, 2008a), illustrated in Table 12.1. Major cross-national and time-series surveys of public opinion include the Euro-barometer and related European Union (EU) surveys (which started in 1970), the European Election Study (1979), the European Values Survey and the World Values Survey (1981), the International Social Survey Programme (1985), the global barometers (1990 and various), the Comparative National Elections Project (1990), the European Voter and the Comparative Study of Electoral Systems (1995), the European Social Survey (2002), the Transatlantic Trends survey (2002), the Pew Global Attitudes project (2002), and the

Table 12.1 Key features of the cross-national series of public opinion surveys

Series	Series started (i)	Frequency	Total nations (latest survey) (ii)	Data downloadable (iii)	Coordinating organization	Online resources
Euro-barometer and related studies	1970	Biannual	27	Public archives	Directorate General Press & Comms, European Commission	Organizing and reports: http://europa.eu.int/comm/public_opinion/ Data and continuity guides from ZUMA Cologne archive: www.gesis.org/en/data_service/eurobarometer
European Values Survey/ World Values Survey	1981–1983	Approx. 5 years	92	Public archives	Ronald Inglehart, Institute of Social Research, University of Michigan	Organizing and data; www.worldvaluessurvey.org/
International Social Survey Programme (ISSP)	1985	Annual	38	Public archives	Secretariat: Bjørn Henrichsen, Norwegian Social Science Data Services (NSD), Bergen	Organizing: www.issp.org/ Data and continuity guide from the ZUMA Cologne archive: www.gesis.org/en/data_service/issp/
Comparative Study of Electoral Systems (CSES)	1996–2001	Module every 5 years	31	Public archives	Secretariat: David Howell, ISR, University of Michigan. Chair: Ian McAllister, ANU	Organizing and data: http://www.cses.org

(Continued)

Table 12.1 *(Cont'd)*

Series	Series started (i)	Frequency	Total nations (latest survey) (ii)	Data downloadable (iii)	Coordinating organization	Online resources
Comparative National Election Project	1990	Irregular	19	Public archives	Richard Gunther, Ohio State University	Organizing and data: http://www.cnep.ics.ul.pt/
Global barometers, including:						http://www.globalbarometer.net/
New Europe Barometers	1991	Irregular	16		Richard Rose, CSPP, Aberdeen University	www.cspp.strath.ac.uk
Afrobarometer	1999	Annual	18	Public archives	Michael Bratton (Michigan State), Robert Mattes (IDASA, SA) and Dr E. Gyimah-Boadi (CDD Ghana)	www.afrobarometer.org
Latino barometer	1995	Annual	18	Tables only	Marta Lagos, MORI, Santiago	www.latinobarometro.org
Asian barometer	2001	Annual	17		Yun-han Chu, Taiwan	www.eastasiabarometer.org http://www.asianbarometer.org/
Arab barometer	2005	Annual	5		Mark Tessler, University of Michigan	http://arabbarometer.org/
The European Social Survey (ESS)	2002	Biennial	21	Public archives	Roger Jowell, Center for Comparative Social Surveys, City University	Organizing: http://naticent02.uuhost.uk.uu.netData from the Norwegian archive: http://ess.nsd.uib.no.
Transatlantic Trends Survey	2002	Annual	13	Public archives	German Marshall Fund of the United States and the Compagnia di San Paolo	http://www.transatlantictrends.org
The Pew Global Attitudes Project	2002	Irregular	54	Via website	Andrew Kohut, Director, The Pew Research Center for the People & the Press	http://pewglobal.org/
Gallup International *Voice of the People*	2002	Annual	60	Only tables released	Meril James, Secretary General, Gallup International	www.voice-of-the-people.net/

Notes: (i) In some cases there were often pilot studies and forerunners, such as the European Community Study, but this date is the recognizable start of the series in its present form. (ii) The number of countries included in each survey often varies by year. (iii) If not deposited in public archives or directly downloadable, access to some data may be available from the surveys' organizers on request, but there might also be charges for access.

Gallup World Poll (2005). These allow a representative sample of the general public to express their views about the quality of democracy in their own country, as well as to assess the performance of their government leaders, institutions, and policies, confidence in government institutions and satisfaction with democracy, patterns of participation and civic engagement, and changes in social and political values.

Among the élite indices, some composite measures have drawn heavily upon expert surveys, sometimes in combination with official national statistics and surveys of public opinion. Composite measures are exemplified by the World Bank Institute's six indicators of good governance, developed by Daniel Kaufmann and his colleagues (2003, 2007). Others have relied solely upon aggregate national data, exemplified by the Inter-Parliamentary union's database on the proportion of women in national parliaments, used to evaluate gender equality in elected office; International IDEA's dataset on electoral turnout worldwide since 1945, to document trends in voter participation, and CIRI's human rights index, monitoring national ratification and implementation of major international conventions and treaties.[2] Where reliable official statistics are collected and standardized, these indices facilitate global comparisons across states and over time.[3]

There are now numerous approaches to measure democracy; one review noted almost four dozen separate indicators of democratic performance, differing in their geographic and temporal scope (Foweraker and Krznaric, 2000; Munck and Verkulian, 2002). Which of these should be compared? We can set aside the indicators which are restricted in the number of states they cover, the frequency of the measures, or the years to which they apply. Publicly- available indicators which are widely used in the comparative literature reflect the prevailing consensus among researchers. Using these criteria produces a selected list of five standard élite indicators of democratic governance, each reflecting differing conceptions of the essential features. Table 12.2 summarizes the key dimensions of each.

Table 12.2   Selected élite indicators and measures of democratic governance

	Liberal democracy (i)	Constitutional democracy (ii)	Good governance (iii)	Corruption Perception Index (iv)	Human Rights (v)
Source	Freedom House	Polity IV	Kaufmann–Kraay	Transparency International	Cingranelli–Richards
Core attributes	Political rights and civil liberties	Democracy and autocracy	Six dimensions of 'good' governance	Perceptions of corruption	Measures practices in 13 types of human rights
Measurement of attributes	Continuous 7-point scales for each	Continuous 20-point scale	Each is presented as continuous scales	Continuous global ranking	Continuous scales
Annual observations	1972 to date	1800 to 1999	1996 to date	1995 to date	1981–2006
Main strengths	Comprehensive scope	Extended time-period	Comprehensive global coverage	Comprehensive	Replicability, allows disaggregation
Main weaknesses	Problems of conflation and measurement	Exclusion of mass participation; aggregation problems	Composite indicators poorly related to concepts; large margins of error	Aggregates 14 sources using different concepts and measures	Data is derived mainly from US State Department reports

Sources: Freedom House (2007) *Freedom in the World 2007.* Washington, DC: Freedom House. www.freedomhouse.org; Monty Marshall and Keith Jaggers (2003). *Polity IV Project: Political Regime Characteristics and Transitions, 1800–2003. http://www.cidcm.umd.edu/inscr/polity/;* Tatu Vanhanen (2000) 'A New Dataset for Measuring Democracy, 1810–1998', *Journal of Peace Research* 37(2): 251–65; Jose Cheibub and Jennifer Gandhi (2004) 'A Six-fold Measure of Democracies and Dictatorships', unpublished paper presented at the 2004 Annual Meeting of the American Political Science Association.

Freedom House: liberal democracy

One of the best known measures of liberal democracy, and one of the most widely used in the comparative literature, is the Gastil index of civil liberties and political rights produced annually by Freedom House. The measure has been widely employed by practitioners: for example, its results are incorporated into the benchmark data employed by the US Millennium Challenge Account to assess the quality of governance and award aid in poorer societies. It has also been employed by many comparative scholars (Diamond, 1996; Barro, 1999; Inglehart and Welzel, 2005). Freedom House, an independent think tank based in the United States, first began to assess political trends in the 1950s, with the results published as the Balance Sheet of Freedom. In 1972, Freedom House launched a new, more comprehensive annual study called *Freedom in the World*. Raymond Gastil developed the survey's methodology, which assigned ratings of their political rights and civil liberties for each independent nation-state (as well as for dependent territories) and then categorized them as free, partly free, or not free. The survey continued to be produced by Gastil until 1989, when a larger team of in-house survey analysts was established. Subsequent editions of the survey have followed essentially the same format, although more details have recently been released about the coding framework used for each assessment.

The index monitors the existence of political rights in terms of electoral processes, political pluralism, and the functioning of government. Civil liberties are defined by the existence of freedom of speech and association, rule of law, and personal rights. The research team draws upon multiple sources of information to develop their classifications based on a checklist of questions, including 10 separate items monitoring the existence of political rights and 15 on civil liberties. These items assess the presence of institutional checks and balances constraining the executive through the existence of a representative and inclusive legislature, an independent judiciary implementing the rule of law, and the existence of political rights and civil liberties, including to reasonable self-determination and participation by minorities, and the presence of free and fair election laws. Each item is allocated a score from 0 to 4 and each is given equal weight when aggregated. The raw scores for each country are then converted into a 7-point scale of political rights and a 7-point scale for civil liberties, and in turn these are collapsed to categorize each regime worldwide as either 'free', 'partly free', or 'not free'. As a result of this process, Freedom House (2009) estimates that out of 193 nation-states, roughly two-thirds or 119 (62%) could be classified as electoral democracies. The emphasis of this measure on a wide range of civil liberties, rights, and freedoms means that this most closely reflects notions of liberal democracy. The index has the advantage of providing comprehensive coverage of nation-states and independent territories worldwide, as well as establishing a long time-series of observations conducted annually since 1972. The measure is also comprehensive in its conceptualization and it is particularly appropriate for those seeking an indicator of liberal democracy.

Despite these virtues, the index has been subject to considerable criticism on a number of methodological grounds (Munck and Verkulian, 2002). The procedures used by the team of researchers employed by Freedom House lack transparency, so that scholars cannot double-check the reliability and consistency of the coding decisions, or replicate the results. The questions used for constructing the index often involve two or three separate items within each subcategory, allowing ambiguous measurement and aggregation across these items. The process of compositing the separate items is not subject to systematic factor analysis, so it remains unclear whether the items do indeed cluster together into consistent scales of political rights and civil liberties. Moreover, since the index contains such a broad range of indicators, this also makes it less valuable as an analytical tool useful for policymakers (Mesquite et al., 2005).

Polity IV: constitutional democracy

Another approach commonly used in the comparative and international relations literature is the classification of constitutional democracy provided by the Polity project. This was initiated by Ted Robert Gurr (1974) and it has evolved over the past three decades. The latest version, Polity IV, provides annual time-series data in country-year format covering 161 countries from 1800 to date.[4] Coders working on the Polity IV project classify democracy and autocracy in each nation-year as a composite score of different characteristics relating to authority structures. Democracy is conceived of conceptually as reflecting three essential elements: the presence of institutions and procedures through which citizens can express preferences about alternative policies and leaders; the existence of institutionalized constraints on the power of the executive; and the guarantee of civil liberties to all citizens (although not actually measured). The classification emphasizes the existence or absence of institutional features of the nation-state. By contrast, autocracies are seen as regimes which restrict or suppress competitive political participation, in which the chief executive is chosen from within the political élite, and, once in office, leaders face few institutional constraints on their power. The dataset constructs a 10-point democracy scale by coding the competitiveness of political participation (1–3), the competitiveness of executive recruitment (1–2), the openness of executive recruitment (1), and the constraints on the chief executive (1–4). Autocracy is measured by negative versions of the same indices. The two scales are combined into a single democracy–autocracy score, varying from −10 to +10. Polity has also been used to monitor and identify processes of major regime change and democratic transitions, classified as a positive change in the democracy–autocracy score of more than 3 points.

The Polity IV scores provide an exceptionally long series of observations stretching over two centuries, as well as covering most nation-states worldwide. The provision of separate indices for each of the main dimensions allows scholars to disaggregate the components. The emphasis on constitutional rules restricting the executive may be particularly valuable for distinguishing the initial downfall of autocratic regimes and the transition to multiparty elections. Unfortunately the democracy–autocracy score also suffers from certain important limitations. Polity IV emphasizes the existence of constraints upon the chief executive as a central part of their measure. Yet this does not distinguish restrictions on the executive arising from democratic checks and balances compared to those due to other actors, such as the power of the military or economic élites. Although more information is now released in the user's codebook, the processes which the Polity team uses to classify regimes continue to lacks a degree of transparency. Moreover, although acknowledging the importance of civil liberties as part of their overall conceptualization of democracy, Polity IV does not actually attempt to code or measure this dimension.

Good governance

The last decade has also seen a proliferation of alternative indicators which have sought to operationalize the related but distinct notion of 'good governance' and its components. The World Bank has used assessments of government performance when allocating resources since the mid 1970s. Focusing at first on macroeconomic management, the assessment criteria have expanded to include trade and financial policies, business regulation, social sector policies, the effectiveness of the public sector, and transparency, accountability, and corruption. These criteria are assessed annually for all World Bank borrowers. Among these, the issue of corruption has moved towards the center of the World Bank's governance strategy, as this is regarded as a fundamental impediment towards reducing poverty. Many of the available indicators of good governance, political risk, and corruption are based on perceptual assessments, using expert surveys and subjective judgments. These may prove unreliable for several reasons, including reliance upon a small number of national 'experts', the use of business leaders and academic scholars as the basis of the judgments, variations in country coverage by different indices, and possible bias towards more favorable evaluations of countries with good economic outcomes. Nevertheless in the absence of other reliable indicators covering a wide range of nation-states, such as representative surveys of public opinion, these measures provide some of the best available gauges of good governance.

The most ambitious attempt to measure all the dimensions of 'good governance' concerns the indices generated by Kaufmann–Kraay and colleagues for the World Bank Institute. The Kaufmann–Kraay indicators (also known as 'The Worldwide Governance Indicators') are some of the most widely- used measures of good governance. Compiled since 1996, these composite indices measure the perceived quality of six dimensions of governance for 213 countries, based on 31 data sources produced by 25 organizations. The underlying data are based on hundreds of variables and reflect the perceptions and views of many types of 'experts' as well as mass survey respondents on various dimensions of governance. The World Bank does not generate these separate assessments; rather, it integrates them into composite indices. The measures specify the margins of error associated with each estimate, allowing users to identify a range of statistically likely ratings for each country.

The Worldwide Governance Indicators measure the quality of six dimensions of governance:

- *Voice and accountability*: the extent to which a country's citizens are able to participate in selecting their government, as well as freedom of expression, freedom of association, and free media.
- *Political stability and absence of violence*: perceptions of the likelihood that the government will be destabilized or overthrown by unconstitutional or violent means, including political violence and terrorism.
- *Government effectiveness*: the quality of public services, the quality of the civil service and the degree of its independence from political pressures, the quality of policy formulation and implementation, and the credibility of the government's commitment to such policies.
- *Regulatory quality*: the ability of the government to formulate and implement sound policies and regulations that permit and promote private sector development.
- *Rule of law*: the extent to which agents have confidence in and abide by the rules of society, and in particular the quality of contract enforcement, the police, and the courts, as well as the likelihood of crime and violence.
- *Control of corruption*: the extent to which public power is exercised for private gain, including both petty and grand forms of corruption, as well as 'capture' of the state by élites and private interests.

One problem, unfortunately, is that the core concept of 'good governance' contains a number of distinct dimensions, it is often overloaded and conflated with multiple meanings and measures, and it remains under-theorized compared with the work on democratic governance (Brinkerhoff and Goldsmith, 2005). As Grindle (2004, 2007) has argued, the 'good governance' agenda is poorly- focused, over-long and growing ever longer, depending upon the emphasis given to nostrums for reform.

Corruption

Related well-known attempts to monitor several aspects of 'good governance' include the Corruption Perception Index (CPI), generated annually since 1995 by Transparency International. This is based on expert assessments. The CPI is a composite index, making use of surveys of business people and assessments by country analysts. Fourteen sources are used in the construction of the CPI: for example, from the Economist Intelligence Unit, the Asian Development Bank, and the World Economic Forum. All sources generally apply a definition of corruption such as the misuse of public power for private benefit – e.g. bribing of public officials, kickbacks in public procurement, or embezzlement of public funds – but the exact definition and measures vary among sources. The CPI is to be credited with collecting, integrating, and disseminating data on this sensitive topic, which is particularly difficult to gauge through official statistics and related sources. The dataset has been widely used, generating a burgeoning literature on the causes and consequences of corruption.

Human rights

Lastly, the Cingranelli-Richards (CIRI) Database monitors a range of human rights, such as civil liberties, women's rights, and state repression.[5] The dataset contains standards-based quantitative information for a wide range of internationally- recognized human rights, covering 191 countries from all regions of the world. The data set contains measures of government human rights practices, not human rights policies or overall human rights conditions (which may be affected by non-state actors). It codes physical integrity rights – the rights not to be tortured, summarily executed, disappeared, or imprisoned for political beliefs – as well as civil liberties such as free speech, freedom of association and assembly, freedom of movement, freedom of religion, and the right to participate in the selection of government leaders, workers rights, and women's rights.

COMPARING PUBLIC OPINION AND ÉLITE INDICATORS

How do we evaluate each of these approaches to monitoring the quality of democratic governance? There is debate about the most appropriate criteria used to measure the core concepts, the weighting which should be given to separate components, the reliability of the coding procedures used by different researchers, and the way that these indicators should be translated into regime typologies. Élite indices come under particularly strong challenge from states which regularly rank close to the bottom on these measures. One approach to evaluation is to see whether the élite indicators are related to similar but independently- generated measures. In practice, despite all the differences in the construction of these indices, it is striking that the two alternative élite measures of democracy correlate strongly with each other (Collier and Adcock, 1999; Elkins, 2000). For comparison, the Polity IV scale of democracy–autocracy was recoded to a positive 20-point scale, and the Freedom House index was recoded so that a score of 1 represented the least democratic regimes, while a score of 7 represented the most democratic. The Freedom House rating of liberal democracy was strongly and significantly related to the Polity IV score ($R = 0.904**$). An examination of the trends since 1972 (Norris, 2008b) documented by each of these indicators also shows considerable agreement among the series, and among other indices of democracy, despite differences in their conceptualization, measurement, and time periods.

This suggests that there is an underlying élite-level consensus about historical developments in democracy, generating confidence about the reliability and robustness of measures. Yet it remains possible that systematic bias may affect all these measures, where similar data sources and reference works are used to construct these scales, or if subjective evaluations of each country by experts are influenced by the results published by other élite indices. It is important to see how far these élite indicators coincide with the public's perception of the quality of governance in each society. If there is a strong correlation, this increases confidence in the estimates, and suggests that the élite measures which have been constructed reflect the underlying views of citizens in each state. This would greatly strengthen their legitimacy and undermine the charge that the indices reflect 'Western' values rather than universal standards. If, on the other hand, there are sharp discrepancies between public views of the health of democratic governance and the élite indicators, then this suggests a more complex picture which requires careful elaboration and interpretation.

Evidence of attitudes and values from public opinion in many different societies is available from many cross-national surveys of public opinion. Here the study draws upon the fifth wave of the World Values Survey (WVS-5), which covers a wide range of countries from all major cultural regions, as well as democratic and autocratic regimes. The World Values Survey is a global investigation of sociocultural and political change. This project has carried out representative national surveys of the basic values and beliefs of the publics in more than 90 independent countries, containing over 88% of the world's population and covering all six inhabited continents. It builds on the European Values Surveys, first carried out in 22 countries in 1981. A second wave of surveys, in 41 countries, was completed in 1990–91. The third wave was carried out in 55 nations in 1995–96. The fourth wave, with 59 nation-states, took place in 1999–01. The fifth wave was completed in 2005–7.[6]

The WVS survey includes some of the most affluent market economies in the world, such as the United States, Japan, and Switzerland, with per capita annual incomes as high as $40,000; together with middle-level industrializing countries including Taiwan, Brazil, and Turkey, as well as poorer agrarian societies, exemplified by Uganda, Nigeria, and Vietnam, with per capita annual incomes of $300 or less. Some smaller nations have populations below one million, such as Malta, Luxembourg, and Iceland, while at the other extreme almost one billion people live in India, and over one billion live in China. The survey contains older

democracies such as Australia, India, and the Netherlands, newer democracies including El Salvador, Estonia, and Taiwan, and autocracies such as China, Zimbabwe, Pakistan, and Egypt. The transition process also varies markedly: some nations have experienced a rapid consolidation of democracy during the 1990s. The survey also includes some of the first systematic data on public opinion in many Muslim states, including Arab countries such as Jordan, Iran, Egypt, and Morocco, as well as in Indonesia, Iran, Turkey, Bangladesh, and Pakistan. The most comprehensive coverage comes from Western Europe, North America, and Scandinavia, where public opinion surveys have the longest tradition, but countries are included from all world regions, including Sub-Saharan Africa. This study draws primarily on the fourth and fifth wave of the survey, reflecting the contemporary state of democratic governance.

Mass and élite evaluations of democracy

We can start by comparing the relationship between public evaluations of the state of democracy in their own country with the Freedom House and Polity IV élite indicators of democracy. The public was asked to evaluate the state of democracy in their own country on a 10-point scale, based on the following question in the 2005–7 WVS: *'How democratically is this country being governed today? Again, using a scale from 1 to 10, where 1 means that it is "not at all democratic" and 10 means that it is "completely democratic", what position would you choose?'*

The comparison of public and élite evaluations in 2005, presented in Table 12.3, shows no significant relationship across the 37–41 nations under comparison. To double-check the results, the study also compared the Freedom House and the Polity IV élite measures of democracy with public satisfaction with the performance of democracy in the 1999–2000 WVS, using an alternative

Table 12.3 Correlation between public and élite evaluations of democracy

Élite evaluations	Public evaluations of state of democracy, 2005–07			Public satisfaction with democracy, 1999–2000		
	R	Sig.	N	R	Sig.	N
Liberal democracy 2006 (FH)	0.240	0.130	41			
Constitutional democracy 2006 (Polity IV)	0.093	0.585	37			
Liberal democracy 2000 (FH)				0.064	0.646	54
Constitutional democracy 2000 (Polity IV)				0.000	0.998	51

Note: Public evaluations of democracy in 2005–07 are the mean national scores derived from the fifth wave of the World Values Survey (Q163): *'How democratically is this country being governed today? Again, using a scale from 1 to 10, where 1 means that it is "not at all democratic" and 10 means that it is "completely democratic"*, what position would you choose?'

Public evaluations of democracy in 1999–2000 are the mean national scores derived from the fourth wave of the World Values Survey (Q168): *'On the whole are you very satisfied, rather satisfied,* not very satisfied or not at all satisfied with the way democracy is developing in our country?'

The table presents the simple correlation coefficient (*R*), its significance (Sig.), and the number of nations (*N*) under comparison.

Sources: FH – Freedom House (2007) *Freedom in the World 2007.* Washington, DC: Freedom House. www.freedomhouse.org; Polity IV – Monty Marshall and Keith Jaggers (2006) *Polity IV Project: Political Regime Characteristics and Transitions, 1800–2006. http://www.cidcm.umd. edu/inscr/polity/.*

4-point scale, but this test also failed to detect any significant correlations. Figure 12.2 explores the pattern in greater detail for the Freedom House data by showing the clusters of countries on both mass and élite indicators. In the top-right quadrant, there is considerable agreement between the public and the Freedom House evaluation, where citizens in countries as varied as Sweden, Mali, Ghana, and Canada gave high marks to the state of democracy in their own country, as did Freedom House. In a couple of countries, notably Ethiopia and Russia, the negative judgments of Freedom House and the public also coincided. But there were many nations located in the top-left quadrant, where Freedom House gave the country a positive rating for liberal democracy, but where citizens were more critical, including in many of the post-Communist nations such as Poland, Slovenia, Romania, Bulgaria, and Ukraine. In these nations, the institutions of multi-party elections have become established over successive contests and yet the public does not express a relatively high evaluation of the state of democracy. And there are also some

important outliers in the bottom-right quadrant, where citizens in both China and Vietnam expressed very positive evaluations of the state of democracy, while Freedom House proved far more critical of the civil liberties and political rights under these regimes. We need to consider and interpret the reasons for these outliers and this issue will be discussed in the final section.

Good governance and corruption

How do the Kaufmann-Kraay indices relate to public opinion? Table 12.4 compares the simple correlation between the public's evaluation of the state of democracy in their own country in the 2005–7 wave of the WVS against the six Kaufmann–Kraay measures plus a summary good governance index created by adding these separate items into one composite measure.

Here some significant relationships are evident: in particular, public evaluations of democracy were positively correlated with the Kaufmann–Kraay indicators of

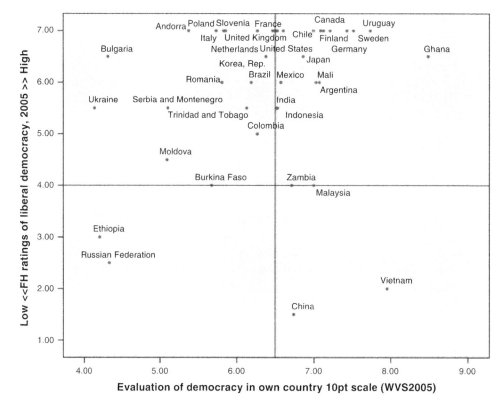

Figure 12.2   Comparison of mass and élite evaluations of democracy.

Notes: Freedom House rating of liberal democracy, 2005 (7-point scale of civil liberties and political rights with the score reversed, so that more democratic = high). World Values Survey 2005–07 Q163: *'How democratically is this country being governed today? Again, using a scale from 1 to 10, where 1 means that it is "not at all democratic" and 10 means that it is "completely democratic"*, what position would you choose?'

Sources: Freedom House www.freedomhouse.org; World Values Survey 2005–07.

Table 12.4   Correlation between public evaluations of democracy and the Kaufmann–Kraay indicators of 'good governance'

	Correlation with public evaluations of democracy	Sig. (2-tailed)	No. of countries
Political stability	0.442**	0.004	40
Rule of law	0.398*	0.011	40
Government effectiveness	0.388*	0.013	40
Corruption	0.377*	0.017	40
Voice and accountability	0.281	0.087	40
Government regulatory quality	0.279	0.081	40
Summary good governance index	0.383*	0.015	40

Notes: Public evaluations of democracy are the mean national scores derived from the World Values Survey 2005–07 (Q163): *'How democratically is this country being governed today? Again, using a scale from 1 to 10, where 1 means that it is "not at all democratic" and 10 means that it is "completely democratic"*, what position would you choose?' The Kaufmann–Kraay good governance indicators, 2006, are from the World Bank Institute.

Sources: Daniel Kaufmann, Aart Kraay, and Massimo Mastruzzi (2007) *Governance Matters VI: Aggregate and Individual Governance Indicators, 1996–2006.* Washington, DC: The World Bank, Policy Research Working Paper. www.worldbank.org

political stability, rule of law, government effectiveness, and corruption, although the correlation of public opinion with measures of government regulatory quality and voice and accountability were not significant at the conventional cut-off level $(P > 0.05)$. It requires further investigation, however, to establish more precisely whether these correlations are actually related to each other, or merely spurious. For example, more affluent countries could plausibly have both better governance and also greater public satisfaction with the state of democracy. One way to make a more precise comparison is to contrast the public's attitudes towards corruption

in their own society against the Transparency International (TI) élite perceptions of the level of corruption within each country. There are two items in the World Values Survey, relating to ethical standards, concerning whether it was ever thought justifiable to cheat on taxes and on whether it was ever thought justifiable to take a bribe, both of which allow us to explore this issue.

Figures 12.3–12.5 present the results of the comparisons. A weak but insignificant relationship was found between the public's view of the justifiability of taking a bribe and cheating on taxes and the TI Corruption Perception Index by élites. The scatter-plot

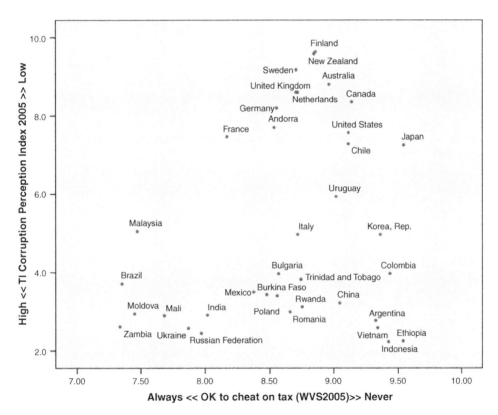

Figure 12.3   Comparison of the TI Corruption Perception Index with the public's attitudes towards tax-paying.

Notes: World Values Survey 2005–07 Q200–201: *'Please tell me for each of the following statements whether you think it can always be justified (1), never be justified (10), or something in-between, using this card … . Cheating on taxes if you have a chance … . Someone accepting a bribe in the course of their duties.'*

Sources: World Values Survey 2005–07; Transparency International Corruption Perception Index 2005 based on expert surveys. http://www.transparency.org/policy_research/surveys_indices/cpi

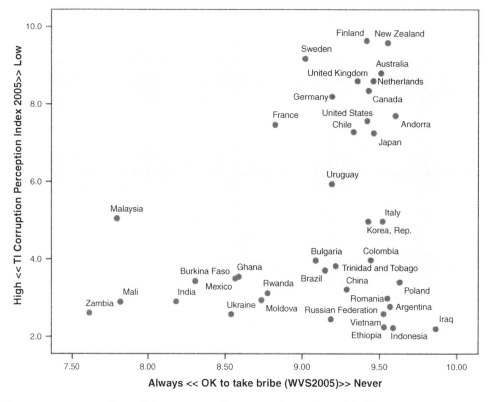

Figure 12.4   Comparison of the TI Corruption Perception Index with the public's attitudes towards bribe taking.

Notes: World Values Survey 2005–07 Q200–201: *'Please tell me for each of the following statements whether you think it can always be justified (1), never be justified (10), or something in-between, using this card … . Someone accepting a bribe in the course of their duties.'*

Sources: World Values Survey 2005–07; Transparency International 'Corruption Perception Index 2005'.

reveals two clusters of countries. In one cluster, exemplified by Finland, New Zealand, the UK, and Australia, ethical standards are high according to both indicators. The public believes that it is never or rarely justifiable to take a bribe or to cheat on taxes, and TI's CPI index classifies these countries as relatively clean. But among the countries which the CPI expert index ranks as higher in corruption, the general public displays a wide diversity of moral views. In some of these societies the public reports that it is never or rarely thought appropriate to take a bribe or to cheat on taxes, such as Argentina, China, Vietnam, and Indonesia, ranging across the spectrum to cultures which are more tolerant towards

these acts, such as Zambia, Mali, and Mexico. Therefore while mass and élite judgments coincide among the 'cleanest' states, there is only a weak mass and élite correspondence in perceptions in societies regarded by élites as problematic for corruption.

Lastly, what of human rights: Is there a stronger linkage between the élite indices provided by CIRI and the public's evaluation of the state of human rights in their own country? Table 12.5 presents the comparison. The results reveal a significant level of agreement between the élite and the public's views of the most extreme and dramatic cases of human rights abuses, involving disappearances and extrajudicial killings (see Figure 12.6).

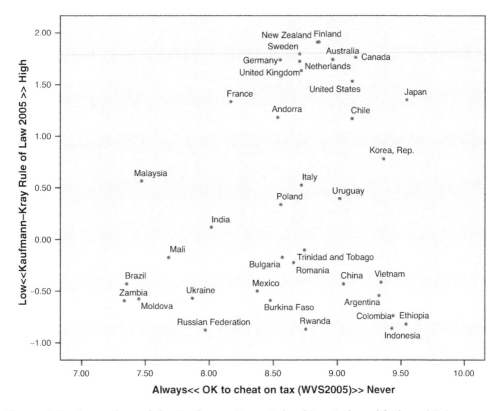

Figure 12.5   Comparison of the Kaufmann–Kraay Rule of Law Index with the public's attitudes towards tax-paying.

Notes: World Values Survey 2005–07 Q200–201: *'Please tell me for each of the following statements whether you think it can always be justified (1), never be justified (10), or something in-between, using the card … . Cheating on taxes if you have a chance … . Someone accepting a bribe in the course of their duties.'*

Sources: World Values Survey 2005–07; Kaufmann–Kraay Rule of Law Index 2005 (WBI).

Table 12.5   Correlation between mass and élite (CIRI) evaluations of human rights

	Correlation	*Sig. (2-tailed)*	*No. of countries*
Physical Integrity Index	0.433*	0.012	33
Disappearances	0.545**	0.001	33
Extrajudicial killings	0.353*	0.044	33
Political imprisonment	0.306	0.084	33
Torture	0.219	0.222	33
Empowerment Index	0.264	0.144	32
Freedom of association	0.111	0.537	33
Freedom of movement	0.305	0.084	33
Freedom of speech	0.154	0.392	33
Political participation	0.264	0.138	33

(Continued)

Table 12.5   (Cont'd)

	Correlation	Sig. (2-tailed)	No. of countries
Freedom of religion	0.129	0.473	33
Worker's rights	0.259	0.146	33
Women's economic rights	0.423*	0.017	33
Women's political rights	0.451**	0.008	33
Women's social rights	0.361	0.043	32

Note: Public evaluations of human rights in each country in 2005–07 are the mean
national scores derived from the fifth wave of the World Values Survey (Q164): '*How
much respect is there for individual human rights nowadays in this country? Do you
feel there is … . A great deal of respect for individual human rights (4), Fairly much
respect (3), Not much respect (2), or No respect at all (1)?*'

Sources: David L. Cingranelli and David L. Richards (2004). *The Cingranelli-Richards
(CIRI) Human Rights Database Coder Manual.* http://ciri.binghamton.edu/; World Values
Survey 2005–07.

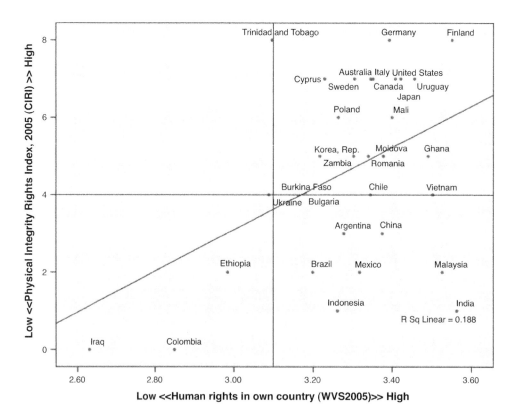

Figure 12.6   Comparison of mass and élite evaluations of human rights.

Notes: World Values Survey 2005–07 Q: 164: How much respect is there for individual human rights nowadays in this
country? Do you feel there is: '*A great deal of respect for individual human rights (4), Fairly much respect (3), Not much
respect (2)*, or No respect at all (1)?'

Sources: David L. Cingranelli and David L. Richards (2004). *The Cingranelli-Richards (CIRI) Human Rights Database Coder
Manual.* http://ciri.binghamton.edu/; World Values Survey 2005–07.

Countries such as Germany, Finland, and Canada were seen as highly respectful of human rights, according to both the public and the élite evaluations, while, by contrast, some states, notably Iraq, were ranked low by both. There is also a significant link between mass and élite perceptions of the state of human rights in their country and of women's economic, political, and social rights. By contrast, the other élite evaluations, especially those reflecting basic civil liberties such as freedom of speech and association, were not significantly correlated with the public's evaluation of their own country's respect for human rights.

CONCLUSIONS AND IMPLICATIONS

The comparison presented in this chapter presents somewhat complex results. First, on evaluations of the state of democracy, it is apparent that there is no significant relationship between the mass and élite assessments. This is particularly evident in the one-party Communist states of China and Vietnam, but this is also true in many post-Communist societies with freedom of expression, where many citizens proved highly critical of the state of their democracy, compared with the evaluations given by the Freedom House and Polity IV. Secondly, the indicators of good governance showed greater congruence between public and élite evaluations. The more rigorous test, however, came from the comparisons about perceptions of corruption, where there was some agreement between the public and élite judgments in the top-ranked states, but no consensus among the countries ranked low by TI's CPI. Lastly, on human rights, public and élite evaluations were in agreement on the worst types of abuses of physical integrity, and the state of women's rights, but no agreement between the public and élite evaluations of civil liberties.

Where there is divergence between mass and élite, it is often assumed that the élite indicators based on 'expert' judgments are usually 'correct' or 'accurate'. This assumption implies that public evaluations expressed through representative surveys must therefore be mistaken, unaware, or simply ignorant. There are many reasons why public perceptions may be mistaken: accurate judgments about the quality of democracy or the state of corruption in a country requires the capacity to process and evaluate complex technical information, and the public may simply be unaware of the 'true' situation. Delli Carpini and Keeter (1996) documented numerous examples of public ignorance concerning factual judgments about complex policy issues, such as estimates about levels of government spending, changes in crime rates, or the risks arising from climate change, although the United States has well-educated publics, widespread access to information, and open political debate in the free press. Moreover, in autocracies with the most restrictive regimes, information is commonly manipulated, restricted, and censored. In states where freedom of speech is limited, survey respondents may be unwilling or unable to express their true feelings about politically-sensitive issues, such as the state of human rights or levels of democracy. Fear of intimidation by government authorities could deter respondents from answering social surveys honestly or openly. Furthermore, enduring cultural attitudes towards the state of democratic governance could lag behind the regime transitions which occurred during the third wave of democracy. Élite perceptions may also be based on similar standards, but the judgments of international élites, such as experts in regional non-governmental organizations (NGOs), foreign journalists, and comparative scholars, could provide a more accurate cross-national perspective. For all these reasons, it is often assumed that élite judgments provide more accurate estimates.

Yet we can conclude, more agnostically, that no single best measure or indicator of democratic governance exists for all purposes. In particular, due to a 'ceiling' effect, many of the élite indicators are often limited in their capacity to distinguish among contemporary states which score relatively well according to the data. Élite indices often suffer from a substantial margin of error. They are also commonly insufficiently nuanced and precise to provide rich insights into underlying problems *within* each country, still less to provide reliable guidance to what programs and policies work most effectively in any particular case. In this regard, it may be more helpful to turn to alternative approaches, including the burgeoning range of contemporary social survey resources which are now covering more and more parts of the globe. Allowing the public to express its own views about how their democracy works – or fails to work – is important as an avenue of expression and participation, as a way to guide policy priorities, as well as being one of the many ways in which polls can serve the public good.

NOTES

1 The University of Goteborg's Quality of Governance Institute, http://www.qog.pol.gu.se/
2 CIRI. Human Rights Data Project. http://ciri.binghamton.edu/
3 The Quality of Governance dataset, the University of Goteborg: http://www.qog.pol.gu.se/
4 Polity IV http://www.systemicpeace.org/polity/polity4.htm
5 *The Cingranelli-Richards (CIRI) Human Rights Database Coder Manual.* http://ciri.binghamton.edu/
6 The World Values Survey, http://wvs.isr.umich.edu/wvs-samp.html.

REFERENCES

Barro, Robert J. (1999) 'Determinants of Democracy', *Journal of Political Economy* 107(6): 158–83.
Beetham, David (1999) 'The Idea of Democratic Audit in Comparative Perspective', *Parliamentary Affairs* 52(4): 567–81.
Beetham, David (2004) 'Freedom as the Foundation', *Journal of Democracy* 15(4): 61–75.
Beetham, David, Bracking, Sarah, Kearton, Iain, and Weir, Stuart. (2002) *International IDEA Handbook on Democracy Assessment.* The Hague: Kluwer Law International.

Brinkerhoff, Derick W. and Goldsmith, Arthur A. (2005) 'Institutional Dualism and International Development: A Revisionist Interpretation of Good Governance', *Administration and Society* 37(2): 199–225.
Collier, David and Adcock, Robert (1999) 'Democracy and Dichotomies: A Pragmatic Approach to Choices about Concepts', *Annual Review of Political Science* 1: 537–65.
Collier, Paul (2007) *The Bottom Billion.* New York/Oxford: Oxford University Press.
Delli Carpini, Michael and Keeter, Scott (1996) *What Americans Know about Politics and Why It Matters.* New Haven, CT: Yale University Press.
Diamond, Larry (1996) *Developing Democracy: Toward Consolidation.* Baltimore: Johns Hopkins University Press.
Diamond, Larry (2008) *The Spirit of Democracy: The Struggle to Build Free Societies throughout the World.* New York: Times Books.
Doyle, Michael and Nicholas Sambanis (2006) *Making War and Building Peace.* Princeton, NJ: Princeton University Press.
Elkins, Zachary (2000) 'Gradations of Democracy? Empirical Tests of Alternative Conceptualizations', *American Journal of Political Science* 44(2): 293–300.
Fish, M. Steven and Wittenberg, Jason (2009) 'Failed Democratization.' In: Christian W. Haerpfer, Patrick Bernhagen, Ronald Inglehart and Christian Welzel (eds), *Democratization.* Oxford: Oxford University Press.
Foweraker, Joe and Krznaric, Roman (2000) 'Measuring Liberal Democratic Performance: An Empirical and Conceptual Critique', *Political Studies* 48: 759–87.
Freedom House (2009) *Freedom in the World 2009.* Washington, DC: Freedom House. www.freedomhouse.org.
Grindle, Merilee S. (2004) 'Good Enough Governance: Poverty Reduction and Reform in Developing Countries', *Governance* 17(4): 525–48.
Grindle, Merilee S. (2007) 'Good Enough Governance Revisited', *Development Policy Review* 25(5): 553–74.
Gurr, Ted Robert (1974) 'Persistence and Change in Political Systems', *American Political Science Review* 74: 1482–504.
Inglehart, Ronald and Welzel, Christopher (2005) *Modernization, Cultural Change, and Democracy: The Human Development Sequence.* New York: Cambridge University Press.
Kapstein, Ethan B. and Converse, Nathan (2008) *The Fate of Young Democracies.* New York: Cambridge University Press.

Kaufmann, Daniel, Kraay, Aart, and Mastruzzi, Massimo (May 2003) *Governance Matters III: Governance Indicators 1996–2002*. Policy Research Working Paper: Washington, DC: The World Bank.

Kaufmann, Daniel, Kraay, Aart and Mastruzzi, Massimo (2007) *Governance Matters VI: Aggregate and Individual Governance Indicators, 1996–2006*. Policy Research Working Paper: Washington, DC: The World Bank.

Mesquita, Bruce Bueno De, Downs, G.W. Smith, Alistair and Cherif, F.M. (2005) 'Thinking Inside the Box: A Closer Look at Democracy and Human Rights', *International Studies Quarterly* 49(3): 439–57.

Munck, Geraldo L. (2009) *Measuring Democracy*. Baltimore, MD: Johns Hopkins University Press.

Munck, Geraldo L. and Verkuilen, Jay (2002) 'Conceptualizing and Measuring Democracy: Evaluating Alternative Indices', *Comparative Political Studies* 35(1): 5–34.

Norris, Pippa (2008a) 'The Globalization of Comparative Public Opinion Research.' In: Neil Robinson and Todd Landman (eds), *Sage Handbook of Comparative Politics*. London: Sage.

Norris, Pippa (2008b) *Driving Democracy: Do Power-sharing Institutions Work?* New York: Cambridge University Press, Chapter 3.

Popper, Karl (1963) *Conjectures and Refutations*. Oxford: Clarendon Press.

Puddington, Arch (2008) 'Freedom in Retreat: Is the Tide Turning? Findings of Freedom in the World 2008'. Washington, DC: Freedom House (www.freedomhouse.org).

Puddington, Arch (2009) 'Freedom in the World 2009: Setbacks and Resilience', *Freedom in the World, 2009*. Washington, DC: Freedom House. http://www.freedomhouse.org/uploads/fiw09/FIW09_OverviewEssay_Final.pdf

UNDP (2007) *Governance Indicators: A Users' Guide*, 2nd edn. Oslo: UNDP. http://www.undp.org/oslocentre/flagship/governance_indicators_project.html.

United Nations (2008) *The Millennium Development Goals Report 2008*. New York: United Nations.

Practices of Governance

13

The Stateless State

Mark Bevir and R.A.W. Rhodes

INTRODUCTION

The study of politics has long concentrated on the state as a sovereign authority; as 'a set of institutions with a dedicated personnel', which wields 'a monopoly of authoritative rule making within a bounded territory' (Hay, Lister and Marsh, 2006: 8). This notion of the state arose gradually and contingently during the Renaissance and Reformation, culminating in the great texts of Bodin and Hobbes (see Skinner, 1978). However, once the idea of the state as sovereign authority had arisen, it proved to be remarkably powerful and resilient. It inspired political actors to remake the world in its image, most famously in the Treaty of Westphalia, which enshrined it as a principle of international relations. Moreover, as it became more and more entrenched in political life, so many students of politics began to take it for granted, treating it as a natural development and object for study.

In this chapter, we do not provide either a historical review of the origins and development of the state (see Hall and Ikenberry, 1989; Skinner, 1978; Tilly, 1975) or a survey of the extensive and varied literature on social science theories of the state (see Dunleavy and O'Leary, 1987; Hay, 1996; Hay, Lister and Marsh, 2006; Jessop, 2000, 2007a). Rather, we focus on recent developments in analysing the state: namely, the various claims there has been a change in the pattern and exercise of state authority from government to governance; from a hierarchic or bureaucratic state to governance in and by networks. We identify three waves in the literature discussing the changing state, from network governance to metagovernance and on to decentred governance and its post-foundational move to the stateless state.

The literature on network governance studies the institutional legacy of neoliberal reforms of the state. Network governance is associated with the changing nature of the state following the public sector reforms of the 1980s. The reforms are said to have precipitated a shift from a hierarchic bureaucracy toward a greater use of markets, quasi-markets and networks, especially in the delivery of public services. The effects of the reforms were intensified by global changes, including an increase in transnational economic activity and the rise of regional institutions such as the European Union (EU). The resulting complexity and fragmentation are such that the state increasingly depends on other organizations to secure its intentions and deliver its policies.

Network governance evokes a world in which state power is dispersed among a vast array of spatially and functionally distinct networks composed of all kinds of public, voluntary and private organizations with which the centre now interacts. The network governance literature offers a compelling picture of the state; indeed Marsh (2008b: 738) is concerned it 'may be becoming the new orthodoxy' (see also Kerr and Kettell, 2006, 13). We will decentre this first-wave approach to network governance, examining the work of the Anglo-governance school.

The second-wave of network governance accepted the shift from bureaucracy to markets to networks but disputed it led to any significant dispersal of state authority. It focused on metagovernance or 'the governance of government and governance' (Jessop 2000: 23, Jessop, 2007b). Metagovernance is an umbrella concept that describes the role of the state and its characteristic policy instruments in network governance. Given that governing is distributed among various private, voluntary and public actors, and that power and authority are more decentralized and fragmented among a plurality of networks, the role of the state has shifted from the direct governance of society to the 'metagovernance' of the several modes of intervention and from command and control through bureaucracy to the indirect steering of relatively autonomous stakeholders. We also decentre 'bringing the state back in (yet again)' (Jessop 2007a: 54).

We then argue for a third-wave narrative of 'decentred governance' that challenges the idea there are inexorable, impersonal forces driving a shift from government to network governance. To decentre is to focus on the social construction of a practice through the ability of individuals to create, and act on, meanings. It is to unpack a practice into the disparate and contingent beliefs and actions of individuals (Bevir and Rhodes 2003: Ch. 4). We argue that governance is constructed differently by many actors working against the background of diverse traditions. In effect, we pronounce the death of the Anglo-governance school, of metagovernance, and of the state. We argue, in their place, for the analysis of the various traditions that have informed the diverse policies and practices by which élite and other actors have sought to remake the state.

Finally, we explore the implication of this shift to a narrative of decentred governance. We challenge a craving for generality that characterizes the earlier waves of governance and define governance as a series of family resemblances, none of which need be always present. There is no list of general features or essential properties that are supposed to characterize governance in every instance. Rather, there are diverse practices composed of multiple individuals acting on changing webs of beliefs rooted in overlapping traditions. Patterns of governance or state authority arise as the contingent products of diverse actions and political struggles informed by the beliefs of agents as they arise against a backcloth of traditions. We discuss the new research topics prompted by this conception of the stateless state (Abrams, 1988).

THE FIRST-WAVE OF GOVERNANCE: THE ANGLO-GOVERNANCE SCHOOL

Social scientists typically describe network governance as consisting of something akin to a differentiated polity characterized by a hollowed-out state, a core executive fumbling to pull rubber levers of control, and, most notably, a massive growth of networks. Of course, people define governance in all kinds of ways. Nonetheless, social scientists typically appeal to inexorable, impersonal forces, to logics of modernization, such as the functional differentiation of the modern state or the marketization of the public sector, to explain the shift from hierarchy to governance by markets and especially networks. Indeed, neoliberal reforms did not lead to markets but to the further differentiation of policy networks in an increasingly hollow state. Social scientists typically use a concept of differentiation here to evoke specialization based on function. They offer a modernist empiricist account of network governance.[1] They treat governance as self-organizing, inter-organizational networks; as a complex set of institutions and institutional linkages defined by their social role or function. They make any appeal to the contingent beliefs and preferences of agents largely irrelevant.[2]

The Anglo-governance school

In Britain, the first-wave of governance narratives challenges the long-standing Westminster model, claiming to capture recent changes in British government in a way the Westminster model did not. The Anglo-governance school starts with the notion of policy networks or sets of organizations clustered around a major government function or department. These groups commonly include the professions, trade unions and big business. So, the story continues, central departments need the cooperation of such groups to deliver services. They allegedly need their cooperation because British government rarely delivers services itself; it uses other bodies to do so. Also, there are supposed to be too many groups to consult, so government must aggregate interests; it needs the legitimated spokespeople for that policy area. The groups in turn need the money and legislative authority that only government can provide.

Policy networks are a long-standing feature of British government; they are its silos or velvet drainpipes. The conservative government of Margaret Thatcher sought to reduce their power by using markets to deliver public services, bypassing existing networks and curtailing the 'privileges' of professions, commonly by subjecting them to rigorous financial and management controls. But these corporate management and marketization reforms had unintended consequences. They fragmented the systems for delivering public services, creating pressures for organizations to cooperate with one another to deliver services. In other words, marketization multiplied the networks it aimed to replace. Commonly, packages of organizations now deliver welfare state services. First-wave governance narratives thus concentrate on the spread of networks in British government. They tell us not only that fragmentation created new networks but also that it increased the membership of existing networks, incorporating both the private and voluntary sectors. They also tell us the government swapped direct for indirect controls, so that central departments are no longer either necessarily or invariably the fulcrum of a network. The government can set the limits to network actions: after all, it still funds the services. But it has also increased its dependence on multifarious networks.

The Anglo-governance school conceives of networks as a distinctive coordinating mechanism notably different from markets and hierarchies and not a hybrid of them. They associate networks with characteristics such as interdependence and trust. In their view, trust is essential because it is the basis of network coordination in the same way that commands and price competition are the key mechanisms for bureaucracies and markets, respectively (see also: Frances et al., 1991: 15; Powell, 1991). Shared values and norms are the glue that holds the complex set of relationships in a network together. Trust and reciprocity are essential for cooperative behaviour and, therefore, the existence of the network (see, for example, Kramer and Tyler, 1996). With the spread of networks there has been a recurrent tension between contracts on the one hand with their stress on competition to get the best price and networks on the other with their stress on cooperative behaviour.

According to the Anglo-governance school, multiplying networks means that core executive coordination is modest in practice. It is largely negative, based on persistent compartmentalization, mutual avoidance and friction reduction between powerful bureaux or ministries. Even when cooperative, anchored at the lower levels of the state machine and organized by specific established networks, coordination is sustained by a culture of dialogue in vertical relations and by horizontal integration. In this view, coordination is rarely strategic, so that almost all attempts to create proactive strategic capacity for long-term planning have failed (Wright and Hayward, 2000). The Anglo-governance school explain New Labour's reforms as an attempt to promote coordination and strategic oversight and combat both Whitehall's departmentalism and the unintended consequences of managerialism.

So, the Anglo-governance school tells us a story of fragmentation confounding centralization as a segmented executive seeks to improve horizontal coordination among departments and agencies and vertical coordination between departments and their networks of organizations. An unintended consequence of this search for central control has been a hollowing out of the core executive. The hollowing out of the state suggests the growth of governance has further undermined the ability of the core executive to act effectively, making it increasingly reliant on diplomacy. The state has been hollowed-out from above by, for example, international interdependence, and from below by, for example, marketization and networks, and sideways by agencies. Internally, the British core executive was already characterized by baronies, policy networks and intermittent and selective coordination. It has been further hollowed-out internally by the unintended consequences of marketization, which fragmented service delivery, multiplied networks and diversified the membership of those networks. Externally, the state is also being hollowed-out by membership of the EU and other international commitments.

THE SECOND-WAVE: METAGOVERNANCE

Critics of the first-wave characteristically focus on the argument the state has been hollowed-out. For example, Pierre and Peters (2000: 78, 104–5, and 111) argue that the shift to network governance could 'increase public control over society' because governments 'rethink the mix of policy instruments'. As a result 'coercive or regulatory instruments become less important and ... "softer" instruments gain importance', for example, steering through brokerage. In short, the state has not been hollowed-out but reasserted its capacity to govern by regulating the mix of governing structures such as markets and networks and deploying indirect instruments of control.

Metagovernance refers to the role of the state in securing coordination in governance and its use of negotiation, diplomacy and more informal modes of steering. It suggests the state now steers and regulates sets of organizations, governments and networks rather than rowing by directly providing services through state bureaucracies. These other organizations undertake much of the work of governing; they implement policies, they provide public services, and at times they even regulate themselves. The state governs the organizations that govern civil society, the governance of governance. Moreover, the other organizations characteristically have a degree of autonomy from the state; they are often voluntary or private sector groups or they are governmental agencies or tiers of government separate from the core executive. So the state cannot govern them solely by the instruments that work in bureaucracies.

Nonetheless, there are several ways in which the state can steer the other actors involved in governance (see, for example, Jessop 2000, 23–4; 2007b). First, the state can set *the rules of the game* for other actors and then leave them to do what they will within those rules; they work 'in the shadow of hierarchy'. So, it can redesign markets, reregulate policy sectors, or introduce constitutional change, Secondly, the state can try to steer other actors using *storytelling*. It can organize dialogues, foster meanings, beliefs and identities among the relevant actors, and influence what actors think and do. Thirdly, the state can steer by the way in which it distributes *resources* such as money and authority. It can play a boundary spanning role, alter the balance between actors in a network; act as a court of appeal when conflict arises; rebalance the mix of governing structures; and step in when network governance fails. Of course, the state need not adopt a single uniform approach to metagovernance. It can use different approaches in different settings at different times.

This summary implies much agreement about metagovernance. In fact, Sørensen and Torfing (2007: 170–80) identify four approaches to metagovernance: interdependence, governability, integration and governmentality. Interdependence theory focuses on the state managing networks using a more sophisticated, indirect tool kit (Rhodes, 1997b). Governability theory stresses that metagovernance and network management occur in the shadow of hierarchy (Scharpf, 1997). Integration theory stresses the formation and management of identities (March and Olsen, 1989). Governmentality theory focuses on the regulation of self-regulation; on the norms, standards and targets that set the limits to networks (Barry, Osborne and Rose, 1996). This categorization is odd. Proponents of integration theory and governmentality never talk of metagovernance, although some of their ideas are relevant, whereas integration theory lumps together strange bedfellows. Nonetheless, distinguishing these approaches helps to identify the differences over the extent and form of state intervention and control.

Proponents of interdependence theory would argue that manipulating the rules of the game allows the state to keep much control over governing without having to bear the costs of direct interference. Proponents of governability theory stress the resources the state has at its disposal for metagovernance. They argue the state can easily deploy these resources to manage other policy actors. Proponents of integration theory argue the viewpoints and interests of different actors are so diverse that managing identities is the core task: for example, storytelling about best

practice and successful cooperation and coordination. Storytelling can create coherent social and political meanings and identities that soften the tensions among competing viewpoints and interests. Proponents of governmentality theory identify the complex of rules, norms, standards and regulatory practices that extend state rule more deeply into civil society by regulating the ways in which civil society self-regulates. Accountancy, performance management and other management techniques are not just ways of achieving the '3Es' of economy, efficiency and effectiveness. They are also ways of measuring, approving, appraising and regulating the beliefs and practices of network actors (and, for examples, see McKinlay and Starkey, 1998). Of course, the approaches are not mutually exclusive; state actors deploy a different mix of approaches in different contexts.

Common ground

For all their different emphases and the debate between the several proponents, the first two waves of governance share much common ground. First, proponents of metagovernance take for granted the characteristics of network governance. They accept that states are becoming increasingly fragmented into networks based on several different stakeholders, and the dividing line between the state and civil society is becoming more blurred because the relevant stakeholders are private or voluntary sector organizations. So, Jessop (2000: 24) concedes 'the state is no longer the sovereign authority ... [it is] less hierarchical, less centralised, less *dirigiste*'. There is a shared modernist empiricist description of the characteristics of network governance.

Secondly, the analysis of metagovernance not only recognizes non-state actors by granting them the power to self-regulate but also distinguishes them from the state, so creating the space for the state to exert macrocontrol over their self-regulation. The state governs the other actors involved in governance. In other words, metagovernance heralds the return of the state by reinventing its governing role. This return to the state opens opportunities for policy advice on the practice of metagovernance. The two waves share a common concern with providing advice on network governance. Both assume the role of the state is to manage, directly and indirectly, the networks of service delivery. For example, Part III of Sørensen and Torfing (2007; Chs 10–12) on 'metagovernance' is devoted to such topics as governing the performance of networks, institutional design and network management, and the possibilities for public authorities to shape network outputs. They are not alone.[3]

Thirdly, both narratives rely on a reified notion of structure. The proponents of first-wave governance are self-confessed modernist empiricists with a reified notion of structure rooted in an explicit social science theory of functional differentiation. The proponents of metagovernance also continue to claim that the state is a material object, a structure, or a social form. They draw on critical realist epistemology and such notions as 'emergence' and 'mechanisms' ostensibly to guard against the charge of reification (see, for example, Jessop, 2007a). Their position is flawed and has a closer affinity to modernist empiricism than they realize or care to admit.

Modernist empiricists rely on reified concepts such as institution, structure, state formation and system to offer explanations that transcend time and space. They appeal to ideal types, institutions and structures as if they are natural kinds. Rational choice theory challenges the reifications and raises the issue of microtheory. Modernist empiricists can respond in three ways. First, they could adopt the third-wave decentred approach. They could view social life solely as activity, reject reifications, and avoid rational choice theory by emphasizing contingency. They don't like this route because they have to give up their ideas about expertise, science and some varieties of socialism (and often all three). Secondly, they can recast their reifications as if they were consequences of rational actors behaving more or less as rational choice theory suggests. This response is common in the USA but not with critical realists in the UK. They prefer to appeal to structure, emergence and mechanism. They claim these concepts do not involve reification but they avoid the micro-level questions that would show how they avoid reification. Thus, they often shift back and forth between using the old reifications of modernist empiricism and paying some kind of lip-service to the kind of micro theories associated with rational choice or the decentred approach. For example, McAnulla (2006) argues that structures are emergent or temporal mechanisms rather than reifications, but never explains how these structures differ from practices, or how they determine individual actions without passing through intentional consciousness. He provides no clear account of why agents can't change emergent structures. The structure emerges from actions, so presumably if all the relevant people change their actions, they will stop producing that structure, so changing it. The emergent structures are better understood as practices. They consist simply of what a bundle of people do and the unintended consequences of these actions.

Of course, structure can be used as a metaphor for the way activity coalesces into patterns and practices. But the metaphors have a bewitching effect. People treat them as real, reified entities; the fate of David Marsh (2008a) in his analysis of the British political tradition. In short, critical realism and the analysis of metagovernance all too often rely on the reifications of modernist empiricism and first-wave governance.

The idea of the state as a structure is useful only if we unpack it into the specific notions of tradition, dilemma, practice and unintended consequence. First, the state might refer to traditions, i.e, inherited webs of belief that influence what people do. Secondly, the state might refer to a subset of dilemmas, i.e., to intersubjective views about the way the nature of the world precludes or impels certain actions. Thirdly, the state might refer to cultural practices, where although these practices arise from people's actions, they then confront other people as if objective social facts. Finally, the state might refer to the intended and unintended consequences of meaningful actions, although, of course, to explain such consequences, we would have to refer to the actions and the meanings (or intentionality) they embodied.

Finally, both waves seek to provide *comprehensive* accounts of governance. Social scientists typically aim to provide a general account of what network and metagovernance looks like and why it does so. For example, network governance is often characterized by the shift from bureaucratic hierarchies to multiplying networks. This defining feature is then said to explain other characteristics of network governance such as the need for indirect 'diplomatic' styles of management, and the search for better coordination through joint ventures, partnerships and holistic governance. Defining network and metagovernance by one or more of its essential properties, such as multiplying networks, implies these properties are general and characterize all cases of governance. So, we will find governance in its new guise if and only if we find a spread of networks. Moreover, these essential properties explain the most significant features of network and metagovernance.

A comprehensive account of governance makes sense, even as a mere aspiration, only if governance has some essence. We should seek a comprehensive account only if the way to define and explain network and metagovernance is to find a social logic or essential property that is at least common to all its manifestations and ideally even explains them. But why would we assume that network and metagovernance has one or more essential features?

The search for comprehensive accounts arises from a preoccupation with the natural sciences. However, even if appropriate in the natural sciences, it is counter-productive in the human sciences. Human practices are not governed by social logics or law-like regularities associated with their allegedly essential properties. They arise instead out of the contingent activity of individuals. Therefore, when we

seek to explain particular cases of governance, we should do so by reference to the contingent activity of the relevant individuals, not to a social logic or law-like regularity. We should explain practices, including cases of governance, using narratives that unpack the contingent actions that embody beliefs informed by contested traditions and dilemmas. The contingent nature of the links between traditions and their development undermines the possibility of a comprehensive account that could relate any one practice to a specific set of social conditions as opposed to a historical process. If we explore these possibilities, we will adopt a decentred approach that refutes the narratives of previous waves.

THE THIRD-WAVE: DECENTRING THE CHANGING STATE[4]

Decentred Theory

A decentred account of the changing state explores the institutions of the state as the contingent meanings that inform the actions of the individuals involved in all kinds of practices of rule. First-wave narratives of the changing state focus on issues such as the objective characteristics of policy networks and the oligopoly of the political market place. They stress power-dependence, the relationship of the size of networks to policy outcomes, and the strategies by which the centre might steer networks. The second-wave of narratives about the changing state focus on the mix of governing structures such as markets and networks and deploying various instruments of control such as changing the rules of the game, storytelling and changing the distribution of resources. In contrast to these comprehensive, reified views of governance, a decentred approach focuses on the social construction of patterns of rule through the ability of individuals to create meanings in action.

A decentred approach draws on interpretive theory to change our conception of the state. It encourages us to examine the ways in which patterns of rule, including institutions and policies, are created, sustained and modified by individuals. It encourages us to recognize that the actions of these individuals are not fixed by institutional norms or a social logic of modernization, but, to the contrary, arise from the beliefs individuals adopt against the background of traditions and in response to dilemmas.

A decentred approach highlights the importance of beliefs, practices, traditions and dilemmas for the study of the changing state (see Bevir and Rhodes: 2003, 2006, 2010). Any existing pattern of rule will have some failings. Different people will have different views about these failings, since the failings are not simply given by experience but rather constructed from interpretations of experience infused with traditions. When people's perceptions of the failings of governance conflict with their existing beliefs, the resulting dilemmas lead them to reconsider beliefs and traditions. Because people confront these dilemmas against the background of diverse traditions, there arises a political contest over what constitutes the nature of the failings and what should be done about them. This contest leads to a reform of governance. The reformed pattern of rule poses new dilemmas, leading to a further contest over meanings and policy agendas. All these contests are governed by laws and norms that prescribe how they should be conducted. Sometimes the relevant laws and norms have changed because of simultaneous contests over their content and relevance. Yet while we can distinguish analytically between a pattern of rule and a contest over its reform, we rarely can do so temporally. Rather, the activity of governing continues during most contests, and most contests occur partially in local practices of governing. What we have, therefore, is a complex and continuous process of interpretation, conflict and activity that produces ever-changing patterns of rule.

This decentred approach prompts us to adopt narrative explanations. We cannot explain network and metagovernance adequately by using allegedly objective social processes or locations. We can explain governance using narratives. Narratives are a form of explanation that works by relating actions to the beliefs and desires that produce them. They depend on the conditional connections between beliefs, desires and actions. In narratives, pointing to conditional connections that relate people, ideas and events to one another explains actions and practices. So, to explain the different and changing patterns of rule, we need to understand the beliefs and practices of the actors against the background of particular traditions and in response to specific dilemmas. In short, we have to adopt an actor-centred or bottom-up approach to explaining any pattern of rule.

A decentred account of the changing state represents, therefore, a shift from institutions to meanings in action, and from social logics to narratives. The first-wave narrative of network governance reduces the diversity of governance to a social logic of modernization, institutional norms, or a set of classifications or correlations across networks. Its proponents tame an otherwise chaotic picture of multiple actors, creating a contingent pattern of rule through their diverse understandings and conflicting actions. The second-wave of metagovernance compounds this mistake by reinventing the state's capacity to control. The third-wave narrative decentres the changing state to show how governance arises from the bottom-up as conflicting beliefs, competing traditions, and varied dilemmas give rise to diverse practices. It replaces aggregate concepts that refer to objectified social laws with narratives that explain actions by relating them to the beliefs and desires that produce them.

What does this decentred approach tell us about governance? We have two answers. First, we offer a definition of governance as a series of family resemblances that does not crave generality and aspire to comprehensiveness because none of the resemblances need be always present. Secondly, we point to some of the distinctive research topics that spring from a decentred approach. Our concern with diverse and contingent meanings encourages a focus on such new empirical topics as rule, rationalities and resistance.

Defining governance

A decentred approach to the changing state contrasts sharply with comprehensive accounts that seek to unpack the essential properties and social logic of network and metagovernance. Neither the intrinsic rationality of markets, nor the path dependency of institutions, decides patterns of governance. Rather, patterns of governance are explained as the contingent constructions of several actors inspired by competing webs of belief and associated traditions. A decentred approach explains shifting patterns of governance by focusing on the actors' own interpretations of their actions and practices. It explores the diverse ways in which situated agents are changing the boundaries of state and civil society by constantly remaking practices as their beliefs change. Because we cannot explain cases of network and metagovernance by reference to a comprehensive theory, we cannot define governance by its key features. Rather, we can define it only for particular cases. However, the absence of a comprehensive theory of network and metagovernance also implies there need be no feature common to all the cases to which we would apply the term. It is futile to search for the essential features of an abstract category that denotes a cluster of human practices. Worse still, the search for allegedly common features can lead political scientists to dismiss the particular cases which are essential to understanding the abstract category. When we provide a definition or general account of governance, it should be couched as a set of family resemblances.

Wittgenstein (1972a) famously suggested that general concepts such as 'game' should be defined by various traits that overlapped and criss-crossed in much the same way as do the resemblances between members of a family – their builds, eye colour, gait, personalities.

He considered various examples of games to challenge the idea that they all possessed a given property or set of properties – skill, enjoyment, victory and defeat – by which we could define the concept. Instead, he suggested the examples exhibited a network of similarities, at various levels of detail, so they coalesced even though no one feature was common to them all.[5]

We do not master such family resemblances by discovering a theory or rule that tells us precisely when we should and should not apply it. Our grasp of the concept consists in our ability to explain why it should be applied in one case but not another, our ability to draw analogies with other cases, and our ability to point to the criss-crossing similarities. Our knowledge of 'governance' is analogous to our knowledge of 'game' as described by Wittgenstein. It is 'completely expressed' by our describing various cases of governance, showing how other cases can be considered as analogous to these, and suggesting that we would be unlikely to describe yet other cases as ones of governance.

Some of the family resemblances that characterize governance derive from a focus on meaning in action and so apply to all patterns of rule. A decentred approach highlights, first, a more diverse view of state authority and its exercise. All patterns of rule arise as the contingent products of diverse actions and political struggles informed by the varied beliefs of situated agents. First-wave narratives of network governance suggest the New Right's reinvention of the minimal state and the more recent rediscovery of networks are attempts to find a substitute for the voluntaristic bonds weakened by state intervention (Harris, 1990). A decentred approach suggests that the notion of a monolithic state in control of itself and civil society was always a myth. The myth obscured the reality of diverse state practices that escaped the control of the centre because they arose from the contingent beliefs and actions of diverse actors at the boundary of state and civil society. The state is never monolithic and it always negotiates with others.

Policy always arises from interactions within networks of organizations and individuals. Patterns of rule always traverse the public, private and voluntary sectors. The boundaries between state and civil society are always blurred. Transnational and international links and flows always disrupt national borders. In short, state authority is constantly remade, negotiated and contested in widely different ways within widely varying everyday practices.

A decentred approach suggests, secondly, that these everyday practices arise from situated agents whose beliefs and actions are informed by traditions and expressed in stories. In every government department, we can identify departmental traditions, often embodied in rituals and routines. They might range from specific notions of accountability to the ritual of the tea lady. Actors pass on these traditions in large part by telling one another stories about 'how we do things around here', and about what does and does not work. For example, British civil servants are socialized into the broad notions of the Westminster model, such as ministerial responsibility, as well as the specific ways of doing things around here; they are 'socialized into the idea of a profession', and learn 'the framework of the acceptable' (Bevir and Rhodes 2006: Ch. 7). Governance is not any given set of characteristics. It is the stories people use to construct, convey and explain traditions, dilemmas, beliefs and practices.

A decentred approach might also help to highlight a third family resemblance that characterizes British governance but might not be found in patterns of rule in other times or places. In Britain, the reforms of the New Right and New Labour have brought about a shift from hierarchy to markets to networks. While this shift is widely recognized, a decentred approach suggests, crucially, that it takes many diverse forms. For the police, the shift from hierarchy to markets to networks poses specific dilemmas. They know how to rewrite the rulebook, manage a contract or work with neighbourhood watch, but they struggle to reconcile these ways of working,

believing they conflict and undermine one another (Bevir and Rhodes, 2006: Ch. 9). For doctors, the equivalent shift poses different dilemmas: the key issue is how to preserve the medical model of health and medical autonomy from managerial reforms that stress hierarchy and financial control (Bevir and Rhodes, 2006: Ch. 8).

A fourth family resemblance is that the central state has adopted a less hands-on role. Its actors are less commonly found within various local and sectoral bodies, and more commonly found in quangos concerned to steer, coordinate and regulate such bodies. Once again, a decentred approach suggests, crucially, that such steering, coordination and regulation take many diverse forms. In Britain, the pre-eminent example is 'joining-up' as the government seeks to devise policy instruments that integrate both horizontally across central government departments and vertically between central and local government and the voluntary sector (Bevir, 2005: 83–105).

A decentred approach highlights the resemblances that contribute to a general characterization of governance and a more specific characterization of governance in Britain. Nonetheless, it disavows any logic to the specific forms that governance takes in particular circumstances. So, a decentred approach resolves the theoretical difficulties that beset earlier waves or narratives of the changing state. It avoids the unacceptable suggestion that institutions fix the actions of individuals in them rather than being products of those actions. It replaces unhelpful phrases such as path dependency with an analysis of change rooted in the beliefs and practices of situated agents. Yet it allows political scientists to offer aggregate studies by using the concept of tradition to explain how people come to hold beliefs and perform practices.

New research topics

A decentred approach to the state rejects both comprehensive theory and the related idea that the state is a material object or emergent structure or social form. We reject the claim that the *preexistence* [of social forms] implies their *autonomy* as possible objects of scientific investigation; and their *causal efficacy* confirms their *reality* (Jessop, 2005: 42). We offer a stateless theory in the sense that we reject the idea of the state as a pre-existing causal structure that can be understood independently of people's beliefs and practices. Studying the changing state is not about building formal theories; it is about telling stories about other people's meanings; it is about narratives of their narratives. As Finlayson and Martin (2006: 167) stress, the object of analysis is not the state but 'a diverse range of agencies, apparatuses and practices producing varied mechanisms of control and varied forms of knowledge that make areas or aspects of social life available for governmental action'. A decentred approach leads us to new narratives of such practices and knowledge, which we explore as rule, rationalities and resistance.

Rule – élite narratives

Decentred theory suggests that political scientists should pay more attention to the traditions against the background of which élites construct their worldviews, including their views of their own interests. Moreover, the central élite need not be a uniform group, all the members of which see their interests in the same way, share a common culture, or speak a shared discourse. Our decentred approach suggests that political scientists should ask whether different sections of the élite do not draw on different traditions to construct different narratives about the world, their place within it, and their interests and values. In Britain, for example, the different members of the central élite are inspired by Tory, Whig, liberal, and socialist narratives. The dominant narratives in the central civil service used to be the Whig story of the generalist civil servant, spotting snags and muddling through. It has been challenged by

a liberal managerial narrative that sees civil servants as hands-on, can-do managers trained at business schools not on the job. But the traditions coexist sometimes separately but sometimes bumping into one another to create dilemmas. Thus, civil servants continue to believe in the Westminster model of ministerial accountability to parliament, a centralizing idea, even as they decentralize decision-making in line with managerial notions (see, for example, Rhodes, 2007; Rhodes and Fawcett, 2007).

Rationalities

Central élite may construct their world using diverse narratives but they also turn to forms of expertise for specific discourses. Nowadays, different traditions of social science influence public policy. Our decentred approach draws attention to the varied rationalities that inform policies across different sectors and different geographical spaces. Rationalities refer here to the scientific beliefs and associated technologies that govern conduct; it captures the ways in which governments and other social actors draw on knowledge to construct policies and practices, especially those that regulate and create subjectivities. Britain, like much of developed world, has witnessed the rise of neoliberal managerial rationalities using a technology of performance measurement and targets that spread far beyond the central civil service to encompass the control of localities. Kelly (2006: 615, 617) describes how the UK's Audit Commission acts as a metagovernor of local authorities for the New Labour government. It ensures that 'the regulatory regime is embedded in the everyday operations and actions of local government practitioners'. It espouses the notion of the well-run authority and it works 'with other inspectorates and professional auditing bodies to maintain professional standards and also to share best practice'. It sets auditors' fees, and standards, and monitors the work of the auditors (see also

Power, 1994). It is one of those varied agencies employing indirect mechanisms of control and knowledge (for other examples see Dean and Hindess, 1998; McKinlay and Starkey, 1998; Miller and Rose, 2008: Ch. 2).

Resistance

When political scientists neglect agency, they can give the impression that politics and policies arise exclusively from the strategies and interactions of central and local élites. Yet other actors can resist, transform and thwart the agendas of élites. Our decentred approach draws attention to the diverse traditions and narratives that inspire street-level bureaucrats and citizens. Policy cultures are sites of struggles not just between strategic élites, but between all kinds of actors with different views and ideals reached against the background of different traditions. Subordinate actors can resist the intentions and policies of élites by consuming them in ways that draw on their local traditions and their local reasoning. For example, street-level police officers are often influenced by organizational traditions that encourage them to set priorities different to those of both their superior officers and élite policymakers. For example, combating crime is seen as the core of police work, not the 'touchy-feely' areas of community policing. The new police commissioner may want to set an example, cause a stir, or otherwise ginger up the troops but the troops know he or she will be gone in a few years and there will be a new commissioner with new interests and priorities (see, for example, on community policing, Fleming and Wood, 2006; and on other street-level bureaucrats, see Lipsky, 1979; Vinzant and Crothers, 1998).

CONCLUSIONS

In sum, network governance was the modernist empiricist story of the changing state

that described the shift from hierarchy to markets to networks. A decentred approach brings about the death of this first-wave narrative, because we argue there is no single account or theory of contemporary governance, only the differing constructions of several traditions. We also announce the death of the second-wave of metagovernance not only because it relies on modernist-empiricist assumptions but also because it argues for a top-down narrative of state regulation and control. There is no necessary logical or structural process determining the form of network governance or the role of the 'central state' in the metagovernance of governance. The intrinsic rationality of markets, the path dependency of institutions, and the state's new toolkit for managing both the mix of governing structures and networks do not explain patterns of governance and how they change.

The third-wave analysis of decentred governance announces the arrival of the stateless state. It argues that the state arises out of the diverse actions and practices inspired by varied beliefs and traditions. The state, or pattern of rule, is the contingent product of diverse actions and political struggles informed by the beliefs of agents rooted in traditions. Our approach seeks to explain social life by reference to historical meanings, infusing the beliefs and practices of individual actors. It encourages political scientists to decentre concepts such as state, institution, power and governance and focus on the social construction of a practice through the ability of individuals to create and act on meanings. It is to unpack a practice into the disparate and contingent beliefs and actions of individuals. It is to reveal the contingent and conflicting beliefs that inform the diverse actions that constitute any domain of social life. It involves challenging the idea that inexorable or impersonal forces, norms, or laws define patterns and regularities in the social world. Instead, it implies the social world in general and the state in particular are constructed differently by many actors inspired by different ideas and values.

Our stories construct and reconstruct the stateless state.

NOTES

1 Modernist–empiricism treats institutions such as legislatures, constitutions and policy networks as discrete, atomized objects to be compared, measured and classified. It adopts comparisons across time and space as a means of uncovering regularities and probabilistic explanations to be tested against neutral evidence (see Bevir, 2001).

2 It would use too much space to provide supporting quotations, but the point is well made in, for example, Marinetto's 2003 discussion of the 'Anglo-Governance School'. For specific examples, see Rhodes (1988, 1997a, 2000), Richards and Smith (2002), Smith (1999), and Stoker (2000, 2004).

3 There is an extensive literature on managing networks, collaboration and partnerships, including Agranoff (2007), Agranoff and McGuire (2004), Ferlie et al. (2005), Goss (2001), Koppenjan and Klijn (2004), Perri et al. (2002), Salamon (2002), and Stoker (2004).

4 Although they arrive at this point by a different route to ours, post-structuralism in the guises of governmentality and discourse analysis also stresses the constructed nature of the state and governance: see, for example, Barry, Osborne and Rose (1996), Burchell (1991), Dean (1998 , 2007: Ch. 2), Dean and Hindess (1998), Finlayson and Martin (2006, 2008), Howarth, Norval and Stavrakakis (2000), and Miller and Rose (2008: Ch. 3). They also favour research on rule, rationalities and resistance. On the differences with our approach, see Bevir and Rhodes (2010: Ch. 2 and 3).

5 In his preliminary sketch of his discussion of games, Wittgenstein (1972b: 17–20) explicitly contrasts this position with a 'craving for generality' he ascribes to inappropriate attempts to model all knowledge on natural science.

REFERENCES

Abrams, P. (1988) 'Notes of the Difficulty of Studying the State', *Journal of Historical Sociology* 1(1): 58–89.

Agranoff, R. (2007) *Managing within Networks: Adding Value to Public Organizations*. Washington, DC: Georgetown University Press.

Agranoff, R. and McGuire, M. (2004) *Collaborative Public Management: New Strategies for Local Governments*. Washington, DC: Georgetown University Press.

Barry, A., Osborne, T. and Rose, N. (eds) (1996) *Foucault and Political Reason*. London: UCL Press.

Bevir, M. (2001) 'Prisoners of Professionalism: On the Construction and Responsibility of Political Studies', *Public Administration* 79(2): 469–89.

Bevir, M. (2005) *New Labour: A Critique*. London: Routledge.

Bevir, M. and Rhodes, R.A.W. (2003) *Interpreting British Governance*. London: Routledge.

Bevir, M. and Rhodes, R.A.W. (2006) *Governance Stories*. London: Routledge.

Bevir, M. and Rhodes, R.A.W. (2010) *The State as Cultural Practice*. Oxford: Oxford University Press.

Burchell, G. (ed.) (1991) *The Foucault Effect: Studies in Governmentality*. Chicago: Chicago University Press.

Dean, M. (1998) *Governmentality: Power and Rule in Modern Society*. London: Sage.

Dean, M. (2007) *Governing Societies*. Berkshire: Open University Press.

Dean, M. and Hindess, B. (eds) (1998) *Governing Australia: Studies in Contemporary Rationalities of Government*. Cambridge: Cambridge University Press.

Dunleavy, P. and O'Leary, B. (eds) (1987) *Theories of the State*. Houndmills, Basingstoke: Macmillan.

Ferlie, E. Lynn, L.E. and Pollitt, C. (eds) (2005) *The Oxford Handbook of Public Management*. Oxford: Oxford University Press.

Finlayson, A. and Martin, J. (2006) 'Post-Structuralism', in C. Hay, M. Lister and D. Marsh (eds), *The State: Theory and Issues*. Houndmills, Basingstoke: Palgrave Macmillan, pp. 155–71.

Finlayson, A. and Martin, J. (2008) '"It Ain't What You Say … "': British Political Studies and the Analysis of Speech and Rhetoric', *British Politics* 3(4): 445–64.

Fleming, J. and Wood, J. (eds) (2006) *Fighting Crime Together. The Challenges of Policing and Security Networks*. Sydney: UNSW Press.

Frances, J., Levacic, R., Mitchell, J. and Thompson, G. J. (1991) 'Introduction', in G. Thompson, J. Frances, R. Levacic, and J. Mitchell (eds), *Markets Hierarchies and Networks: The Co-ordination of Social Life*. London: Sage, pp. 1–19.

Goss, S. (2001) *Making Local Governance Work*. Houndmills, Basingstoke: Palgrave Macmillan.

Hall, J.A. and Ikenberry, G.J. (1989) *The State*. Milton Keynes: Open University Press.

Harris, J. (1990) 'Society and State in Twentieth Century Britain', in F.M.L. Thompson (ed.), *The Cambridge Social History of Britain 1750–1950*.

Volume 3. *Social Agencies and Institutions*. Cambridge: Cambridge University Press, pp. 63–117.

Hay, C. (1996) *Re-stating Social and Political Change*. Buckingham: Open University Press.

Hay, C, (2002) *Political Analysis: A Critical Introduction*. Houndmills, Basingstoke: Palgrave Macmillan.

Hay, C. Lister, M. and Marsh, D. (eds) (2006) *The State: Theory and Issues*. Houndmills, Basingstoke: Palgrave Macmillan.

Howarth, D., Norval, A.J. and Stavrakakis, Y. (eds.), (2000) *Discourse Theory and Political Analysis*. Manchester: Manchester University Press.

Jessop, B. (1990) *State Theory: Putting Capitalist States in Their Place*. Cambridge: Polity.

Jessop, B. (2000) 'Governance failure', in G. Stoker (ed) *The New Politics of British Local Governance*. Houndmills, Basingstoke: Macmillan, pp. 11–32.

Jessop, B. (2005) 'Critical Realism and the Strategic-Relational Approach', *New Formations* 56(1): 40–53.

Jessop, B. (2007a) *State Power*. Cambridge: Polity.

Jessop, B. (2007b) 'Governance and Metagovernance: On Reflexivity, Requisite Variety, and Requisite Irony', in M. Bevir. (ed.), *Public Governance*. Volume 1. *Theories of Governance*. London: Sage, pp. 230–45.

Kelly, J. (2006) 'Central Regulation of English Local Authorities: An Example of Meta-governance?' *Public Administration* 84(3): 603–21.

Kerr, P. and Kettell, S. (2006) 'In Defence of British Politics: The Past, Present and Future of the Discipline', *Journal of British Politics* 1: 1, 3–25.

Koppenjan, J.F.M. and Klijn, E.H. (2004) *Managing Uncertainties in Networks: A Network Approach to Problem Solving and Decision Making*. London: Routledge.

Kramer, R.M. and Tyler, T. (eds) (1996) *Trust in Organizations: Frontiers of Theory and Research*. London: Sage.

Lipsky, M. (1979) *Street-level Bureaucracy*. New York: Russell Sage Foundation.

McAnulla, S. (2006) 'Challenging the New Interpretivist Approach: Towards a Critical Realist Alternative', *British Politics* 1(1): 113–38.

McKinlay, A. and Starkey, K.P. (eds) (1998) *Foucault, Management and Organization Theory: From Panopticon to Technologies of Self*. London: Sage.

March, J.G. and Olsen, J.P. (1989) *Rediscovering Institutions*. New York: Free Press.

Marinetto, M. (2003) 'Governing Beyond the Centre: A Critique of the Anglo-Governance School', *Political Studies* 51(3): 592–608.

Marsh, D. (2008a) 'Understanding British Government: Analysing Competing Models', *British Journal of Politics and International Relations* 10(2): 251–68.

Marsh, D. (2008b) 'What is at Stake? A Response to Bevir and Rhodes', *British Journal of Politics and International Relations* 10(4): 735–9.

Miller, P. and Rose, N. (2008) *Governing the Present: Administering Economic, Social and Personal Life*. Cambridge: Polity.

Moran, M., Rein, M. and Goodin R.E. (eds) (2006) *The Oxford Handbook of Public Policy*. Oxford: Oxford University Press.

Perri 6, Leat, D., Seltzer, K. and Stoker, G. (2002) *Towards Holistic Governance. The New Reform Agenda*. Houndmills, Basingstoke: Palgrave.

Pierre, J. and Peters, B.G. (2000) *Governance, Politics and the State*. Houndmills, Basingstoke: Macmillan.

Powell, W. (1991) 'Neither Market nor Hierarchy: Network Forms of Organization', in G. Thompson, J. Frances, R. Levacic and J. Mitchell (eds) *Markets, Hierarchies and Networks: The Coordination of Social Life*. London: Sage, pp. 265–76.

Power, M. (1994) *The Audit Explosion*. London: Demos.

Rhodes, R.A.W. (1988) *Beyond Westminster and Whitehall*. London: Unwin-Hyman.

Rhodes, R.A.W. (1997a) *Understanding Governance*. Buckingham and Philadelphia: Open University Press.

Rhodes, R.A.W. (1997b) 'It's the Mix That Matters: From Marketisation to Diplomacy', *Australian Journal of Public Administration* 56(2): 40–53.

Rhodes, R.A.W. (ed.) (2000) *Transforming British governance*. Two volumes. London: Macmillan.

Rhodes, R.A.W. (2007) 'The Everyday Life of a Minister: A Confessional and Impressionist Tale', in R.A.W. Rhodes, Paul 't Hart and M. Noordegraaf (eds), *The Ethnography of Government Elites: Up Close and Personal*. Houndmills, Basingstoke: Palgrave-Macmillan, pp. 21–50.

Rhodes, R.A.W. and Fawcett, P. (2007) 'Central Government', in Anthony Seldon, (ed.), *Blair's Britain 1994–2007*. Cambridge: Cambridge University Press, pp. 79–103.

Richards, D. and Smith, M.J. (2002) *Governance and Public Policy in the UK*. Oxford: Oxford University Press.

Salamon, L.M. (ed.) (2002) *The Tools of Government: A Guide to the New Governance*. Oxford: Oxford University Press.

Scharpf, F.W. (1997) *Games Real Actors Play. Actor-Centred Institutionalism in Policy Research*. Boulder, CO: Westview Press.

Skinner, Q. (1978) *The Foundations of Modern Political Thought*. Two volumes. Cambridge: Cambridge University Press.

Smith, M. J. (1999) *The Core Executive in Britain*. London: Macmillan.

Sorsensen, E. and Torfing, J. (2007) 'Theoretical Approaches to Metagovernance', in E. Sorsensen and J. Torfing (eds), *Theories of Democratic Network Governance*. Houndmills, Basingstoke: Palgrave-Macmillan, pp. 169–82.

Stoker, G. (ed.) (2000) *The New Politics of British Local Governance*. London: Macmillan.

Stoker, G. (2004) *Transforming Local Governance*. Houndmills, Basingstoke: Palgrave Macmillan.

Tilly, C. (ed.) (1975) *The Formation of National States in Western Europe*. Princeton, NJ: Princeton University Press.

Vinzant, J.C. and Crothers, L. (1998) *Street-Level Leadership: Discretion and Legitimacy in Front-Line Public Service*. Washington, DC: Georgetown University Press.

Wittgenstein, L. (1972a) *Philosophical Investigations*. Translated by G. Anscombe. Oxford: Basil Blackwell.

Wittgenstein, L. (1972b) *The Blue and Brown Books*. Oxford: Blackwell.

Wright, V. and Hayward, J. (2000) 'Governing from the Centre: Policy Co-ordination in Six European Core Executives', in R.A.W. Rhodes (ed.), *Transforming British Government*. Volume 2. *Changing Roles and Relationships*. London: Macmillan, pp. 27–46.

14

The Persistence of Hierarchy

Laurence E. Lynn, Jr

INTRODUCTION

Hierarchical governance in advanced democracies is being replaced by collaborative arrangements among public and private organizations: so goes a popular narrative within public administration, one of many narratives that constitute a discourse of transformation in state–society relations. While these narratives vary by the nationality of their authors and by how authors interpret what they perceive as significant change, scholars on both sides of the Atlantic have been claiming that revolutionary advances in information and communication technologies, a public policy agenda of rapidly increasing complexity, and more engaged civil society actors distrustful of government have inaugurated an era, often characterized as 'the new governance', that, to some, is approaching 'governance without government'. If not obsolete, traditional institutions of hierarchical control, public bureaucracies, are, in this view, partnering with and becoming subordinate to a wide variety of consociational arrangements empowered and largely controlled not by government but by civil society.

This new governance discourse emerged late in the twentieth century concurrently with the more robust and popular discourse celebrating the advent of a 'new public management' (NPM). The central NPM claim was that hierarchical, rule-bound governance was giving way to institutional arrangements featuring market-like competition and choice among entities, public and private, that provide publicly- financed services. While the new governance narrative has outlasted NPM as a theme of transformist arguments, administrative technologies that mimic the incentives of competitive markets are now widely accepted by policymakers as legitimate tools of government, if not of the new paradigm many advocates foresaw.

Post-hierarchical narratives also incorporate other themes and logics, including, for example, revolutionary advances in interpersonal communication and societal access to information – digital-era governance – and post-industrial developments in direct democracy. Some of these narratives proceed from a critical theory perspective and promote non-instrumental conceptions of governance based on post-rational, non-oppressive, deliberative, and self-liberating institutions and altogether different principles of democratic legitimacy than those associated with traditional representative institutions, even in their transformed versions.

A strong-minded group of dissenters contests these narratives, arguing that public bureaucracies remain essential to the effective functioning of representative democracy. Changes in the technologies and practices of governance, they insist, extend and elaborate but do not replace traditional principles of democratic delegation and control. Although posing new problems of accountability, these adaptations are, in this counter-narrative, responsive to the increasing interdependence of governments and civil society as they confront complex new and emerging policy challenges. So long, however, as public policies depend on authority and resources provided through representative institutions, these dissenters argue that hierarchically- ordered administration structures reflecting the rule of law will remain at the heart of liberal representative governance.

These kinds of claims and counterclaims raise two basic questions. First, how and to what extent is hierarchical governance actually being transformed, if it is? What kinds of evidence support, or might support, various narratives either of adaptation or of transformation? Secondly, why is transforming change occurring, if indeed it is? Hierarchy and bureaucratic government have emerged and been elaborated over thousands of years, surviving dynastic change, wars, dramatic economic transformations, and the revolutionary emergence of popular democracy. If we are arriving at public administration's equivalent of 'the end of history', why is that happening now?

This chapter explores these questions. The next section briefly reviews the logic of narratives, claiming the emergence of networks, markets and a variety of other institutions that are said to be replacing hierarchical governance. Following is an assessment of the evidence supporting these claims. Then, rationales for hierarchy, in particular, bureaucracy, are discussed in the context of contemporary liberal representative governance. Then, the relative strengths of the contending arguments are appraised, with the conclusion that hierarchy almost certainly will persist in twenty-first century governance and beyond.

LOGICS OF TRANSFORMATION

The general post-hierarchical claim is that new patterns of rule that have emerged or have been visible since the 1990s deviate from traditional forms of hierarchical delegation and control to an extent that justifies a reappraisal of how contemporary societies are being, will be, and should be, governed. The argument is that citizens have become impatient with and distrustful of government and are exercising their sovereignty to seize authority from political and administrative élites and create more democratic structures of governance.

According to a comprehensive analysis of post-hierarchical claims by Johan Olsen (2006: 6), the predominant criticism of traditional hierarchy is that

> Rules are followed too slavishly or that public administration should be organized and staffed according to non-bureaucratic principles, administrators should act according to a different ethos and code of conduct, or there should not be public intervention at all. Complaints that a law is badly administered are then mixed with criticism of the content of the law and a principled opposition to the primacy of representative government. Such criticism is often part of a conflict over organizational and normative principles, worldviews, symbols, and legitimacy, where the aim is to change the institutional identity and power of public administration . . .

Olsen continues:

> What started as an attack on 'bureaucracy' and its inefficient, costly, and rigid internal organization and operations has since the late 1970s developed into a criticism of the role of public administration; the possibility and desirability of government shaping society; the power balance between institutions and between actors; and the relevance and functionality of jurisdictional boundaries, including those of the territorial state.

Bearing out Olsen's point, Angela Eikenberry asserts that '[t]here is wide agreement among scholars and practitioners that political systems around the world are transforming from hierarchically organized, unitary systems of *government* to more horizontally organized, relatively fragmented systems of *governance*' (Eikenberry 2007: 193 [italics in original]; cf. Sorenson, 2002). Claims that hierarchy as a form of social organization is and ought to be waning are of even older vintage (cf. Bennis, 1966; Hummel, 1977; Marini, 1971; Thayer, 1973). Lester Salamon said in 1989 that the American welfare state 'is not run by the state at all, but by a host of nongovernmental "third parties"' (Salamon, 1989: xv). Linda Dicke asserted in her 1998 entry in the *International Encyclopedia of Public Policy and Administration* that

> [g]iven the changes in many contemporary organizations in terms of the nature of duties and responsibilities expected from employees (which has widened) and the distinction between the relationships of roles among workers (which has narrowed), it is unlikely that the tall vertical structures of the modern age will ever be as popular again. (Dicke, 1998: 1065)

The most widely discussed of these new patterns of rule have been, in their shorthand versions, 'markets' and 'networks'. But, as noted earlier, claims concerning emerging new patterns of rule include, as well, several other themes that may acknowledge networks and markets, and even elements of hierarchy, but are based on different logics of transformation. These logics include direct or participatory democracy, digital-age redistributions of control over information, and postmodern conceptions of state–society–individual relations. These perspectives are briefly discussed in turn.

Markets

Beginning in the 1970s in the United States and Europe, economic recessions, fiscal scarcity, demographic change, immigration and concerns about the financial appetite of the welfare state gave impetus to public policies emphasizing government retrenchment and increased efficiency through imitating the incentive structures of the private sector (Lynn, 2006). The logic of this 'new public management' is that the administrative state is replaced by a 'political economy' in which purposeful actors – policymakers, public managers, consumers of public services – make choices among alternatives created by competitive processes in the light of their costs and consequences (Hughes, 2003). Holding agencies accountable for compliance with hierarchically- ordered rules inhibits flexibility, creativity, and responsiveness to changing contexts and technologies. Such accountability should, therefore, be replaced by performance measurement and management. Policies, programs, and organizations should be evaluated in terms of measurable outputs and outcomes, with managers 'liberated' from regimes of constraints to identify the strategies and tools most likely to produce strong, measurable performance.

Networks and the new governance

A competing view of the same period of change is that 'networked forms of governance increasingly [are] replac[ing] hierarchical arrangements as the vehicles through which public programs are designed and delivered' (Balla, 2008: 347). Those who proclaim the ascendancy of network governance see it as 'a corrective to the conventional view of politics and government as centered on formal-constitutional institutions (Marinetto, 2003: 598–9). They argue, according to Olsen, that 'no single political center can legitimately claim to represent the public and the common good, issue commands, and expect compliance. Attempts to command are likely to generate withdrawal of cooperation, noncompliance, and a loss of trust' (Olsen, 2006: 7). In an analysis of the new governance literature in Europe, Erik-Hans Klijn concludes that the term governance refers to governance networks: i.e. to government's 'relationships with other actors and the process of handling complex decisions and implementation processes' (Klijn, 2008: 510–11).

Deliberative democracy

Some scholars advocate the replacement of hierarchical public administration by 'deliberative' or 'direct' democracy: reliance on various means of consulting and empowering citizens who are affected by administrative decision-making. Jon Elster defines deliberative democracy as 'decision making by discussion among free and equal citizens' (Elster, 1998: 1). Linda and Peter deLeon (2002) urge academics and practitioners to promote 'citizen (and public employee) participation' within public organizations: i.e. means for ensuring that citizens and employees have direct influence over organizational decisions that affect them. According to Amy Gutmann and Dennis Thompson, deliberative democracy is the only acceptable conception of politics under the circumstances of reasonable pluralism, because it consists of the political minimum that all reasonable persons, who disagree on comprehensive doctrines, can agree is 'a basis on which those who morally disagree can cooperate.' In deliberative democracy, citizens and public officials are 'committed to making decisions that they can justify to everyone bound by them' by giving and deliberating on reasons that can be accepted by others (Gutmann and Thompson, 1996: 93, quoted by Herr, 2008: 27).

Digital-era governance

A number of other scholars see information technology as having the potential to transform politics and governance at global, national, and local levels, although both controversy and skepticism infuse debates about the nature of this potential (Kamarck and Nye, 2002). The general idea is that the reduced costs and increased availability of information and dramatic improvements in the ease and speed of communications are already altering patterns of economic and administrative interdependence, power relationships, and the relationships of individuals and institutions in ways that diffuse power and undermine traditional hierarchical forms of authority. According to Patrick Dunleavy and his colleagues (Dunleavy et al., 2006), for example, revolutionary advances in information technology have brought about 'changes in management systems and in methods of interacting with citizens and other service-users in civil society in the underpinning and integrating of current bureaucratic adaptations' whose effects are felt 'via a wide range of cognitive, behavioral, organizational, political, and cultural changes that are linked to information systems, broadly construed' (Dunleavy et al., 2006: 468). The Internet, Jane Fountain argues (2001: 82), is 'a catalyst for the formation of inter-organizational networks by providing a cheap, powerful infrastructure for communication and shared information . . . . The decentralization of information sources and exchanges is fostering new types of community and different roles for government.'

The postmodern state

Postmodernist thinking is also having its influence on public administration. 'Post' comes after modern: i.e. after bureaucracy, after hierarchy, and after the industrial era. The postmodern organization may be defined as that comprising a networked set of diverse, self-managed, self-controlled teams with many centers of coordination that fold and unfold according to the requirements of the tasks (Boje and Dennehy, 1993). Peter Bogason has noted (Bogason, 2005: 236) that while 'many facets of life are thoroughly modern' – he refers to rationalization, centralization, specialization, bureaucratization, and industrialization – 'some trends indicate that things could be different, and if trends are indicative of future conditions, then society will in the longer run [tend toward] the decentralization, individualization, and internationalization of public-regarding institutions.' The unit of analysis will no longer be the organization or the individual but 'organizations in their societal and cultural context' and the 'integration of diverse arenas' of knowledge (Boje and Dennehy, 1993: 32).

WEIGHING THE EVIDENCE

Is hierarchy actually losing favor among policymakers and public managers as an instrument of policy implementation and expenditure control? Is public bureaucracy as an institutional expression of representative democracy yielding to other, non-representative expressions of democratic values? To what extent are changes in governance that can be documented intentional and to what extent 'unintended consequences' of faulty policy designs?

Evaluating the various claims and narratives of change and transformation is difficult because their scientific/empirical, conjectural/hopeful, and normative/theoretical dimensions are conflated: transformation is, or at least might be, and surely ought to be, occurring. Many such narratives are vulnerable to the charges that (1) the status quo they depict is a caricature of reality, and (2) evidence has been selected to support a preconceived thesis based on caricature. Olsen notes (2006: 14) that 'what recent reformers present as universal diagnoses and prescriptions for public administration are in fact partial, time- and space-bound interpretations.' For the most part, the various narrators talk past each other, neither engaging nor refuting the arguments of critics in a rigorous way.

The ideological influence on various narratives of transformation is often noted. Observes Dennis Thompson, '[s]ome of the claims of deliberative theory are not empirical.' The claim that deliberative democracy is more legitimate because it respects the moral agency of the participants, for example, is, he says, 'inherent in the process, not a consequence of it' (Thompson, 2008: 498). In a similar vein, Paul du Gay says that one of the most prominent arguments against bureaucracy is that reducing it is necessary to increasing personal liberty (du Gay, 2005).

Of postmodern narrators, Meier and Hill (2005: 59) note that they are

> strongly opposed to empirical research unless that research is based on subjective methods that are unlikely to transfer from one scholar to the next. As a result, the approach can be charged with presenting bureaucratic stereotypes, . . . rejecting any efforts to determine if their views represent a significant portion of the world.

No attempt will be made here to engage ideological claims on behalf of the various modes of governance. The discussion that follows comments instead on the extent, quality, and implications of the evidence that might be adduced on behalf of anti-bureaucratic narratives.

What should we know?

As a point of departure, it is useful to outline the kinds of evidence which might substantiate claims that a new form or new forms of governance are emerging, for whatever reason and with whatever consequences. How might changes in the boundary between the state and civil society be verified? Accompanying an authentic transformation might be, for example, the following changes.

- Significant reductions in the proportion of human services resources flowing through governments and thus subject to legislative authorization and appropriation processes.
- Evidence of both devolution and deregulation of administration, such as removing governmental hands from the steering wheel (for example, a reduction in the number of pages of applicable regulations or instances of language changes that reassign 'steering authority' to non-governmental or hybrid entities).
- Evidence of changes in agency enforcement strategies: not lax enforcement, but increased reliance on non-coercive, voluntary, and negotiated enforcement across significant swaths of public responsibility.
- A growing chorus of voices from stakeholders – both from public program administrators and from their private sector agents and other civil society institutions – that government has become less

intrusive, that street-level professionals are feeling more empowered and less burdened by red tape, and that local priorities are being given greater weight in street-level practice.

- A strengthening of interest group and citizen involvement and influence at all levels of policy-making and bargaining over program features.
- Shifts of interest group lobbying and advocacy from higher to lower levels of government and from targeted political action to broader forms of social mobilization.
- An increasing number and coverage (of individuals and households) by alternative, non-traditional service delivery arrangements: i.e. evidence that more aspects of well-being for more people are in non-governmental hands.
- Reduction in the extent of co-optation of the charitable non-profit sector by government as public resources and guidance are replaced by civil society resources.

It might even be the case that civil society institutions themselves – for example, foundations, fund-raising associations, and large non-governmental organizations (NGOs) – are relinquishing their own authority over priorities and methods of implementation in favor of greater community and grassroots control.

For the most part, little effort has been made to assemble these kinds of evidence. The main exceptions are the data on contracting and third-party participation in service delivery collected by NGO researchers and data on contracting published by some national governments and analyzed by scholars. The worldwide database of governance indicators maintained by the World Bank is promising but little analyzed outside the World Bank itself and the development community, and comprehensive analyses such as the Organization for Economic Co-operation and Development's Modernising Government (OECD, 2005) are seldom cited in narratives of transformation.

One reason for the lack of effort to gather evidence is, as noted earlier, the ideological basis of reform promotions. As Olsen notes (2006: 8),

> There has been little felt need to examine assumptions about the extent and consequences of administrative reform because so many reforms have been driven by strong ideological convictions or even a doctrinaire faith in what is the ideal organization and role of public administration in the economy and society.

Also, those with ideological commitments to new patterns of governance may be more interested in demonstrating how they can work. Says Eikenberry, for example, '[s]tudies on network governance have focused primarily on how to build and manage effective networks in order to improve service delivery and increase the production of public goods, not on the effects of network governance on democracy or social justice/equity issues' (Eikenberry, 2007: 193; cf. O'Toole and Meier, 2004a).

What do we know?

As noted earlier, the various narratives of transformation include synoptic but usually subjective interpretations of developments in administrative policy and practice; examples and cases of how transformation is occurring; official reports, evaluations, and other literature that purports to document change; and selected citations of academic research. Evidence of different kinds on behalf of transformative claims are often combined; edited volumes in particular do this (e.g. Bevir et al., 2003; Kooiman, 1993; Salamon, 2000). Christopher Pollitt and Geert Bouckaert note that, for some, 'the crucial evidence is the growth of a new community of discourse' (Pollitt and Bouckaert, 2004: 137); transformation is occurring because a growing number of responsible experts say it is. The resulting pictures are often kaleidoscopic: fragmentary, disparate, often contradictory, and of dubious quality.

More reliable evidence is available, however.

Evidence from scientific studies

Enlightening evidence of what might be happening in the administration of representative democracies can be found in systematic studies of particular propositions or hypotheses found in academic literature. While such studies cover a very wide variety of governance issues, two are worth noting as examples.

The virtues of networks   Networks have been an especially popular subject of empirical research. Mark Considine and Jenny Lewis, for example, 'sought to turn the vague reform rhetoric of various countries at the leading edge of change [Australia, Britain, the Netherlands, and New Zealand] into testable propositions about the way real officials should work in the new systems' (Considine and Lewis, 2003: 132). A sample of over 1000 individuals engaged in governance in the four countries was surveyed concerning 'two sequential propositions: (1) the strength of commitment to the traditional bureaucratic or procedural model of governance; and (2) the strength of . . . new models of governance' (133). They concluded that 'enterprise governance' – i.e. NPM-style governance – and network modes of governance 'now operate as norms in practice, *in addition to* the older form of bureaucratic or procedural organization, in reform-minded countries' (138, italics added). Perhaps the most important conclusion, the authors say, 'is that the less well developed, and hitherto poorly theorized idea of a network orientation, is nevertheless a meaningful concept' in administrative practice (138).

Based on their review of research literature, Meier and Hill (2005) argue that, in general, the distinction between networks and hierarchies is less significant in practice than in theory. They cite as evidence a series of studies of mental health networks by Brinton Milward and Keith Provan (2000), which find that 'those networks that develop long term relationships that mimic the stability of bureaucracy actually perform better than those that remain more fluid.' Meier and Hill also note that O'Toole and Meier (2004b), in their studies of network relationships within and among school districts, find that 'stability of personnel and management, both traits more associated with bureaucracy than networks, were strongly and positively

correlated with higher performance on a wide variety of organizational outputs and outcomes.' Networks may, in Meier and Hill's view (2005: 62), 'be more effective to the degree they take on bureaucratic traits.'

According to Eikenberry, many scholars 'show that networks can exacerbate rather than alleviate inequality in the political process' (2007: 194). Similarly, Rouban (1999) notes, based on several investigations, that 'networks are not necessarily democratic and more often create communities than they do citizens . . . [D]ecentralization procedures have not always led to more local democracy' (2) but may strengthen local elites. Compromise between political edicts and competitive markets 'requires original and diversified administrative models' (3), says Rouban, such as a more sociological model (cf. Kooiman, 2003) that 'emphasizes partnership between administrative agents and users in the production of social services' (3).

In her analysis of literature on the determinants of inter-organizational relationships, Christine Oliver (1990) included among the potential determinants what she termed 'asymmetry', 'the potential to exercise power or control over another organization or its resources' (243). 'The contention that organizational efforts to control interdependencies predict relationship formation also is fortified by the assumption that relationship formation necessitates the loss of decision-making latitude and discretion, a consequence to which organizations are purported to have a particular aversion' (244), a phenomenon, she says, that is noted repeatedly in the literature. She continues (247):

> The enforcement of a joint program by a higher authority may . . . engender conflict and asymmetry. Compliance with the laws and standards of a governing body may improve an organization's legitimacy in the public eye or it may increase the organization's centrality in a network. In contrast, organizations that are constrained by several mandated relations may possess less attributed influence or reduced feelings of power. Therefore, the need to comply with constraints from above may interact with other contingencies in determining relationship formation.

In a similar spirit, based on their analysis of the literature, Carolyn Hill and Lynn (2005) argue that accomplishing the goals of collaboration requires the selection of appropriate governance arrangements, which may range from resource-sharing agreements and informal leadership to centralizing of functions and formal agreements subject to enforcement. '[W]hen there is a mismatch between governance mechanisms and provider motivations, one of these two results – collaborative failure or goal displacement – is likely; the collaborative effort will experience unanticipated difficulties and the likelihood of failure' (C. Hill and Lynn, 2005: 75).

In a study of the formation of integrated health services networks, Nolan and Zuvekas (2001) found that

> Networks are facing similar challenges: 1) developing trust among partners; 2) maintaining momentum; 3) being realistic with goal setting and achieving such goals; 4) organizing the network, agreeing on organizational form and leadership; 5) obtaining data from network participants. Certain environmental elements (e.g., political, geographic, population size and make-up, managed care market, state health care financing decisions) contribute to the degree of success achieved by a network. (116)

Their research implies that, paradoxically, the emergence of trust among collaborators, often thought to be a substitute for hierarchy, may be a reason why hierarchical mechanisms necessary for efficiency can function well.

In summary, collaborations may obscure both formal and informal governance arrangements or understanding that reflect or create power differentials and hierarchy and that can either strengthen or weaken the collaboration.

Engaging citizens Studies of direct democracy and citizen participation reveal numerous contradictions between claims and realities (Lynn, 2002). One study of how well community service organizations meet community needs concluded: 'From a broader policy standpoint, our findings question the ability of community service organizations to identify and respond to community needs'

(Markham et al., 1999: 176). A survey of research on neighborhood-representing organizations found 'a low level of both participatory and representative democracy' in such organizations (Cnaan 1991: 629). According to another study, citizen initiatives that restrict civil rights experience far greater success than citizen initiatives in general (Gamble, 1997). Finally, winners and losers in political contests express different levels of satisfaction with democratic institutions: winners preferring majoritarian government, losers preferring consensual processes (Anderson and Guillory, 1997).

In summary, findings concerning citizen involvement in governance are widely varying, and highly qualified by contextual factors. Findings range from benefits such as 'social learning', better agency-public relations, and better alignment of agency and citizen interests to costs such as increased divisiveness, the displacement of reason by passion and persistence, and heightened distrust of and respect for public officials. Empirical research does not support a presumption that the pursuit of self-interest will yield to shared understandings and the accommodation of differences. Indeed, the opposite may be the result.

Research on managerialist reforms

Similar contradictions emerge in research on managerialist reforms. James Thompson (2000) attempted to summarize the accomplishments of the Clinton Administration's National Performance Review. He notes that 'NPR incorporates a diverse set of interventions directed toward the achievement of multiple objectives' (509). First, he summarized and classified the objectives of the NPR as of first, second, and third order of importance: of first-order importance were downsizing, reducing administrative costs, and reforming administrative systems; of second-order importance were decentralizing authority within agencies, empowering front-line workers, and promoting cultural change in agencies; of third-order importance were improving the quality of public services and improving the efficiency of agency work procedures.

Thompson conducted a broad review of the results of NPR in terms of satisfying these objectives based on survey research conducted by a US government personnel agency.

> A broad conclusion, is that while some success has been achieved with regard to lower, first-order goals, only limited progress has been made toward critical, higher, second- and third-order reinvention objectives. Thus, downsizing and cost reduction objectives have been substantially achieved . . . . but there is no evidence of any significant, systemic improvement in quality of services or culture. (Thompson, 2000: 510).

Mixed results were also the finding of a study of the New Steering Model, an NPM-style reform in German local government (Kuhlmann et al., 2008: 860).The authors conclude that

> A comprehensive 'paradigm shift' from the Weberian bureaucracy to a managerial NSM administration has not occurred. Many local authorities tend to implement new structures and instruments only formally, without using them in a 'managerial' way. Rather, they seek to make these instruments fit into the traditional bureaucracy. Public administrations in Continental Europe still have no solution how to make managerialism match with their prevailing legalist 'rule of law' culture.

In general,

> 'Knowledge of what works and what does not tends to be heavily context-dependent. That is to say, a technique or organizational structure which succeeds in one place may fail in another. There is no set of general tools that can be transferred from one jurisdiction to another, all around the world, with confidence that they will work well every time'. (Pollitt, 2002)

Elsewhere Pollitt notes that 'cases where there is unmistakable evidence of management reform producing more effective government action are rare' (2000: 194). In later work, Pollitt and Bouckaert (2004) identify four levels of results by which reforms can be evaluated: operational results, process results,

improvements in organizational/institutional capacity, and progress towards a goal. Efforts to draw conclusions from available evidence are difficult, Pollitt and Bouckaert say, because '[t]here is often contradictory information and an ambiguous, changing reality' (104).

Of particular interest in reform-oriented research is the analysis of governance reforms in Anglophone and European states by Bevir et al. (2003). They ask: 'What is the plot of our story?' The complex plot comprises twelve points. Notable among them is the following: 'the beliefs and practices of elite actors [engaged in reform] originate in the traditions they have inherited. They construct issues or dilemmas out of experiences infused with these traditions' (2003: 202). Further, '[g]overnance is constructed differently and continuously reconstructed so there can be no one set of tools' (203). Moreover, specific reforms have different meanings in different countries; new governance in the Netherlands will differ from new governance in the UK. There is 'no universal process of globalization driving public sector reform' (203). The primary élites, moreover, remain central government agencies.

In summary, one might well conclude that obtaining unambiguous measures of performance is conceptually almost impossible. There are too many politically- significant things to measure in a complex administrative reform, and these measures, if obtainable, are likely to be highly interrelated. Even more important, it may be impossible to develop any kind of meaningful causal understanding of the important factors contributing to measured performance.

Evidence from multilevel research

To improve causal understanding, recent research has analyzed governance in terms of how multiple levels of policymaking and administration interact to produce the outputs and outcomes of public policies and programs (C. Hill and Lynn, 2005; M. Hill and Hupe, 2008; Smith, 2003). Carolyn Hill and Lynn (2005), for example, have used a multilevel 'logic of governance' to evaluate over 800 published studies that explore such interactions. They found that 'the vast majority of studies adopt a top-down perspective on governance. . . . Influence is modeled as flowing downward from legislation and management toward treatments and consequences' (C. Hill and Lynn, 2005: 179). They conclude that 'conjectures by hundreds of investigators in specialized domains [are] that the interesting questions of administration and management concern the effects of hierarchical interactions more than of horizontality' (189). In a study that replicated the Hill and Lynn research but with published studies using non-US data, Melissa Forbes and Lynn (2005) concluded that '[e]vidence based on international data suggests, as do American studies, that different levels of governance influence one another, that is, that the organization of governance impacts what, how, and for whom public services are provided' (568).

These findings have been further replicated in studies by Melissa Forbes, Hill and Lynn (2006) and by Robichau and Lynn (2009). Robichau and Lynn, following an analysis of 300 recently published research studies, concluded that 'the presumption is warranted that implementation is generally hierarchical; influences flow downward through a chain of delegation to the retail level of service delivery' (24). In one such published study, for example, Peter May and Søren Winter (2009) seek to explain the extent to which 'street-level bureaucrats emphasize actions that reflect higher level policy goals' (3) in reformed Danish employment programs. The authors found that 'higher level political [attention by relevant municipal politicians to employment issues] and managerial [supervision, communicating specific goals] influence the policy emphases of frontline workers' (16). In another such study, Roderick, Jacobs, and Bryk found 'strong evidence that [student] achievement in promotional gate grades increased after the institution of [the Chicago public school system's] accountability policy' (350), with the implication that hierarchically- imposed performance standards and measures strongly affect behavior at subordinate levels of administration.

Evidence from international organization research

Recent years have seen a proliferation of country indices that rank or assess countries according to some measure (Bandura, 2006). The most comprehensive such effort is the World Bank's Worldwide Governance Indicators (WGI) database covering 212 countries and territories and measuring six dimensions of governance. The indicators are based on hundreds of specific and disaggregated individual variables measuring various dimensions of governance taken from 33 data sources provided by 30 different organizations. These include: voice and accountability; political stability and absence of violence; government effectiveness; regulatory quality; rule of law; and control of corruption. The data reflect the views on governance of public sector, private sector, and non-governmental experts, as well as thousands of citizen and firm survey respondents worldwide. The aggregate indicator for voice and accountability for the United States, for example, is based on data from the Economist Intelligence Unit, Freedom House, the World Economic Forum Global Competitiveness Survey, the Global Integrity Index, the Gallup World Poll, the Cingranelli-Richards (CIRI) Human Rights Database, the International Budget Project, the Open Budget Index, the Political Risk Services International Country Risk Guide, the Reporters Without Borders Press Freedom Index, the Institute for Management and Development World Competitiveness Yearbook, and the Global Insight Business Conditions and Risk Indicators.

The approach thus implies that, properly understood, 'governance' has multiple dimensions and that a transformation of governance would imply multi-dimensional change. In an analysis of trends during the period 1998 to 2008, Daniel Kaufmann, Aart Kraay and Massimo Mastruzzi conclude to the contrary that 'there is little evidence of significant (or quantitatively important) changes in world averages of governance over the past decade' (Kaufmann et al., 2009: 23). For advanced liberal democracies such as the USA, UK, and Germany, there was no significant change in the six aggregate indicators and even some selective deterioration between 1998 and 2008.

The OECD also conducts comparative analyses of governance in member countries. One such analysis observed that

[a]cross the OECD area, the liberalisation of domestic markets and international trade, coupled with the introduction of regulatory management tools, has led to a profound reformulation of the state's role in the economy. Scholars have labeled this trend the 'rise of the regulatory state'. . . . A vital factor behind this change has been the creation of a host of new institutions – oversight bodies, regulatory agencies, administrative courts and ombudsman commissions – to manage newly liberalized markets. These specialised agencies have developed a host of tools to develop evidenced-based policies and to enforce economic regulations. (OECD 2009a)

Another OECD study documented countries' uses of 'agencies, authorities, and other autonomous bodies' (OECD, 2002). According to the report, 'it is probably impossible to draw conclusions across countries on the criteria for establishing bodies that are legally separate or not from the state. In public law, awarding the status of legal person *does not usually affect the political responsibility or accountability of the minister* for the activities of such a body' (10, italics added). But, the report notes, 'there is wide agreement that the large majority of government tasks can be carried out within ministerial departments, and, that the default organisational form should be subsidiary bodies that belong to government ministerial departments but benefit from some managerial flexibility'(10).

Yet another OECD study addressed issues raised by the rise of the regulatory state. An assessment of barriers to administrative simplification notes that '[g]overnments are facing increasing and changing challenges and, in response, regulatory activities multiply red tape' (OECD, 2009b: 6). The list of barriers is impressive, ranging from lack of political support to legal complexity and lack of the requisite skill and capacity. Approaches to overcoming them include, although are not restricted to, a variety of hierarchical tools: 'whole of government' reform strategies, making institutions accountable, evidence-based prioritization, and training.

The general conclusion of such comparative analyses might well have been provided by Jan Kooiman, a progenitor of the governance-as-networks perspective, who concedes that 'the state is still very much alive' (Kooiman, 2003: 130). Although new modes of government, with the state as a participant, are 'on the agenda', he says, 'the state is perfectly capable of giving with one hand and taking with the other.' As Olsen argues (2006: 13), the notion infusing transformist narratives that transformation is inevitable and that it will converge on a new paradigm 'is not supported by empirical observations.'

If the best evidence does not support narratives of transformation, the question arises as to why, in principle, hierarchy should persist in a dramatically changing world?

HIERARCHY AND REPRESENTATIVE DEMOCRACY

In the context of democratic governance, hierarchy is a 'pattern of rule', a means of coordinating social activity through the mechanism of the rank ordering of authority within a society. In pre-democratic times, rank was typically imposed by force or fiat. The American and European popular revolutions established the principle that 'the people' are the ultimate source of authority, and the rule of law they authorize is the primary institution for defining and enforcing ordered rule. Paradoxically, the hierarchical institutions of premodern dynasties continued to flourish in elaborated form as emperors and monarchs were replaced by presidents, prime ministers, parliaments, and courts, even as nations were shaken by wars, violent social movements, and economic upheaval. Hierarchical arrangements were evidently indispensable to post-tribal societies desiring security and material goods.

Two contrasting, albeit complementary, perspectives on hierarchy are found in the literature: hierarchy as a rationalized instrument of authority and hierarchy as an institutional expression of liberal democratic principles of accountability, i.e. as a system of ordered rule regarded as legitimate by citizen sovereigns.

Hierarchy as instrument

Hierarchy is a way of organizing and carrying out the work of complex social systems (Simon, 1962; Williamson, 1996). In this light, hierarchy is an instrument, a mechanism, or a tool of governance whose key attributes are independent of the substantive content of public policies or the particulars of national institutions. From an instrumental perspective, policymakers analyze the characteristics of activities to be undertaken in pursuit of public purposes and choose instruments that are most appropriate to their realization.

The instrumental view has several expressions. Olsen notes (2006: 12) that Max Weber 'viewed bureaucratic structure as malleable – a rationally designed tool, deliberately structured and restructured in order to improve the ability to realize externally determined goals.' Early organization theorists conceptualized hierarchy as an administrative technology, a means whereby managers controlled output (Gerwin, 1979; Gillespie and Mileti, 1977; Jelinek, 1977). Oliver Williamson has derived three generic 'discrete structural alternatives' – hierarchies, markets, and hybrid forms of organization – from applying transaction cost economics to characteristics of the specific activities to be coordinated or organized (Williamson, 1996). From a more political perspective, Lester Salamon has identified 13 distinct 'tools of government' – hierarchical agencies are termed 'direct government' – whose consequences can be evaluated along four dimensions: coerciveness, directness, automaticity, and visibility (Salamon, 2000, 2002). In all such instrumental approaches, hierarchy as a mechanism for coordination and control of productive activity is preferred to other mechanisms, such as markets or networks, under certain circumstances.

Hierarchy and bureaucracy should not be confused with one another. Hierarchy is a necessary but not sufficient condition for bureaucracy. Bureaucracy is the most elaborate form of hierarchically- ordered rule and reflects not only the organization of power within societies but also the characteristics and complexity of the activities which polities authorize to be undertaken in their name. As has already been suggested and will be discussed later in this chapter, *hierarchy* may emerge even in consociational arrangements, and, indeed, may contribute in important ways to their success.

When is hierarchically- ordered bureaucracy an appropriate tool of governance? In general, when all relevant concerns of parties to a transaction, including the consequences of uncertainty, can be defined in explicit, contractible terms – i.e. in the form of complete contracts covering all contingencies – then arms-length exchange relationships, or markets, are more efficient than hierarchy. Reciprocity can be reasonably guaranteed by all parties' agreeing to the terms of exchange. When uncertainty and ambiguity make it impossible to write contracts that cover all possible contingencies of concern to the parties, then incomplete forms of contracting, and in particular employment contracts, can be more efficient. Hierarchical arrangements such as bureaucracies in principle afford more flexibility in controlling outputs and ensuring that reciprocity is achieved and enforced across tasks and over time.

Hierarchy as institution

An institution may be defined as an organization infused with durable values. Institutionalization is the process by which the members of an organization 'acquire values that go beyond the technical requirements of organizational tasks' (Thoenig, 2003: 129). In another expression of this concept, institutionalization is 'the emergence of orderly, stable, socially integrating patterns out of unstable, loosely organized, or narrowly technical activities' (Selznick, 1994: 232, quoted by Fountain, 2001: 92). Thus, the importance of institutionalized values is that they constitute a unifying source of meaning and purpose that formal structures of authority and assignments of responsibility cannot provide by themselves.

Weber also viewed bureaucracy in broad historical and institutional terms. Where the rule of law prevails, Weber argued, the following familiar principles govern: business is conducted on a continuous basis, there is a well-defined division of labor, authority is hierarchical, officials have neither an ownership interest in organizational resources nor property rights in their positions, and business is conducted on the basis of written documents (Bendix, 1960: 424). These principles are the basis for what is termed the 'ideal-type' bureaucracy and, as well, for caricatures of bureaucracy as inflexible and inward-looking, ill-suited to changed circumstances.

This caricature is to misunderstand Weber, however. According to Olsen (2006: 4–5),

> Weber observed the possibility that beliefs in a legitimate order will govern organized action but also that human behavior can be guided by utility, affinity, and traditions . . . . Orders could be interpreted differently. There could be contradictory systems of order . . . . Bureaucrats had interests and power of their own, and the distinction between politics and administration could be hard to uphold in practice. As a result, there was a potential tension among elected officials, bureaucrats, and citizens, and the causal chain from a command to actual compliance could be long and uncertain.

Thus, as with the instrumental perspective, bureaucracies as actual institutions exhibit much greater variety than is suggested by the Weberian ideal type.

As an institution of democratic governance, bureaucracy is, in Paul du Gay's expression, 'a diversely formatted organizational device' (du Gay, 2005: 1). The reason for this diversity is that, as Weber suggested, the process of bureaucratization varies across countries and jurisdictions within countries and, as well, across time. As Olsen (2006: 3) summarizes an extensive literature, bureaucratizatrion as 'the emergence and growth of bureaucratic forms.' It follows, Olsen argues, that bureaucracy must be analyzed as a political institution, not just as an instrument, and in its actual contextualized forms, not its ideal type. Olsen expands on the notion of the institutionalization of bureaucracy (2006: 3–4):

> Administration is based on the rule of law, due process, codes of appropriate behavior, and a system of rationally debatable reasons. It is part of society's long-term commitment to a Rechtsstaat and procedural rationality for coping with conflicts and power differentials. Bureaucracy, then, is an expression of cultural values and a form of governing with intrinsic value . . . . As a partly autonomous institution, bureaucracy has legitimate elements of non-adaptation to leaders' orders and environmental demands.

THE LOGIC OF PERSISTENCE

Without doubt, the institutional expressions of liberal democratic governance are evolving as the ends and means of public policy in national and global contexts become more complex and politically controversial. Many new administrative tools and technologies, the products of necessity and innovation, are becoming available to policymakers and public managers.

The evidence summarized in the preceding section does not, however, sustain an argument that the role of the state in democratic governance is diminishing in importance. Accountability to duly- constituted authority may be more difficult to achieve, but it has not been abandoned by policymakers as obsolete. This conclusion does not imply that political and administrative élites are stifling the kinds of changes favored by civil society élites and by citizens in their roles as taxpayers and voters. Nor does it imply that inertia reigns. The explanation for the persistence of hierarchy is a logic of path-dependent institutional evolution constrained by the principle of accountability to the rule of law. Although this explanation can be contested, as will be noted below, its validity cannot simply be dismissed.

Accountability in representative democracy

The persistence of a non-democratic institution, public bureaucracy, in mature liberal democracies might appear paradoxical. Where obtaining the consent of the governed is a meaningful, operational reality, why should citizens and those they elect to represent them consent to an arrangement of authority that is so regularly the object of complaint and criticism?

The straightforward answer is that bureaucracy produces positive results. As Meier and Hill (2005: 65) put it:

> The persistence of bureaucracy and hierarchy in the light of the numerous critiques clearly demonstrates that hierarchy must perform some vital function . . . . The reason is simple, accountability. Although it takes many forms, one of the basic building blocks of modern governance is accountability. Hierarchy is the default option in creating accountability systems – A is accountable to B for performing task C. To the extent that policymakers seek to create governance systems that can be held accountable, we are likely to see hierarchy as a basic principal [sic]. That practical notion has not changed since the time of Weber's writings.

Likewise, Olsen argues (2006: 19) that bureaucracy is

> A tool for legislators and representative democracy and is positively related to substantive outcomes that are valued in contemporary democracies, by some more than others. The juridification of many spheres of society, human rights developments, increased diversity, lack of common overriding goals, and renewed demands for public accountability

may furthermore contribute to a rising interest in the legal/bureaucratic aspects of administration and governing.

There are ironies in this logic. James Morone (1990; cf. Nelson, 1982) shows how popular longing for 'more democracy' is translated into the institutions of the modern administrative state, including the use of delegation, hierarchy, rules, specialization, merit and neutral competence, consultation, and due process. Although far from coherent, occasionally oppressive, and sometimes ill-suited to a changing world, such institutions are intended to secure the benefits of democracy. In America, public administration's founders fully understood this in arguing that transparent, politically responsible administration of public policies and functions, despite the dangers inherent in bureaucracy, is a primary means of implementing rule by the people. In a similar vein, Du Gay vigorously contests the view that hierarchical rule is inimical to personal liberty; indeed, he argues (2005: 54), bureaucracy is essential to securing liberty:

> The uniqueness of the public administration as a form of governmental institution lies in the extent of bureaucratic constraints permeating it. These constraints are intrinsic to the practice of liberal state administration. They are not by-products that can be removed at will to produce fresher, cleaner, faster, shinier public sector management.

Thus, hierarchy, as institutionalized in real-world bureaucracies, is endogenous to representative democracy. Bureaucracy persists because it is essential to administration that is accountable for serving public interests (Aucoin, 1997; Dahl and Lindblom, 1953; du Gay, 2000; Goodsell, 1983; Meier, 1997; Peters and Pierre, 2003). A fortiori, hierarchy is arguably essential to (the essence of) liberal democratic governance, in which the sovereign people and their representatives will, in one way or another, sooner or later, insist on accountability on the part of those who act in their name using resources appropriated from them. It is better that such accountability be institutionalized in rule-governed hierarchies than in loose, unaccountable, possibly unstable arrangements of an indeterminate localism.

An imperfect institution

The logic of persistence is best understood as an imperfect expression of democratic ideals. Weber himself noted that '[t]he final result of political action often, even regularly, stands in incomplete inadequate and often even paradoxical relation to its original meaning' (Weber, 1970: 117, quoted by Olsen, 2006: 5). Such departures from the ideal have been characterized in many ways: as 'authority leakage' (Downs, 1967), as 'pathologies' (Bozeman, 2000), as collective action problems inside bureaucracies (Dunleavy, 1992), as 'nonmarket failure' (Wolf, 1988), and as 'dilemmas' (Miller, 1992). Olsen (2006: 4–5) argues that 'public administration is never a fully developed bureaucracy. There are fluid and overlapping organizational principles, and the functioning, emergence, growth, and consequences of bureaucracy depend on a variety of factors.' Realistically conceived, in other words, the bureaucratic instrument is anything but static or uncompromised.

While the so-called pathologies of actual bureaucracies can be invoked as a *casus belli* for advocates of post-hierarchical transformation, they can also motivate the search for ways of achieving greater accountability and democratic control of the administrative state. Victor Thompson argued long ago that bureaucracy's virtues obscure its shortcomings. The need for productivity and control, he argued, are inimical to creativity (V. Thompson, 1965). Anticipating contemporary preoccupations with bureaucratic failure, Thompson said that this defect might be ameliorated by perfecting the instrument through, for example, 'increased professionalization, a looser and more untidy structure, decentralization, freer communications, project organization when possible, rotation of assignments, greater reliance on group processes, attempts at continual restructuring, modification of the

incentive system, and changes in many management practices.' With prescience, Thompson observed that 'bureaucratic organizations are actually evolving in this direction' (1965).

More recently, the likely prospect has been limned by Olsen (2006: 17):

> Rather than a linear trend, there may be contradictory developments, cycles, reversals, breakdowns, and transformations. If so, students of public administration are given an opportunity to explore the shifting legitimacy and importance of different forms, their changing relations and interactions, and the conditions under which each is likely to decline or rise in importance. A general lesson seems to be that the Enlightenment-inspired democratic belief in administrative design, learning, and reform in the name of progress is tempered by a limited human capacity for rational understanding and control, making reformers institutional gardeners rather than institutional engineers.

In Olsen's view, transformations may be subtle: authority and position power may continue to exist but may be invoked less often, and only after extensive consultation. Distributions of authority and of influence may be more notable, the underlying hierarchy less visible.

Is hierarchy inevitable?

Viewing democracy as an aspect of modernity, Fred Riggs (1997) has argued that top-down, monarchic authority was replaced with bottom-up representation: dominated subjects were replaced by free citizens able to participate in governance, choose their governors, and hold them accountable through periodic elections. But, Riggs says, '[i]t has never been easy in even the most democratic countries for the organs of representative government to sustain effective control over their bureaucracies' (1997: 350), and it became more difficult as those bureaucracies were being rationalized in order that they might approach industrial reliability and efficiency. Attempts at democratic control, as Riggs also notes, only undermine the effectiveness of administrative action, ensuring a fundamental tension between them.

It is not altogether beyond the realm of possibility that civil society institutions, governing élites, and other stakeholders might come to the view, perhaps provoked by a crisis of performance, that the inevitable tensions between representative democracy and non-representative bureaucracy should be ameliorated by redrawing the state–society boundary so as to enlarge the sphere of civil society, a political preference which would come to be accepted by policymakers and judges, through a long process of deliberation and litigation, as consistent with democratic constitutions and therefore legitimate. American bureaucracy, after all, had to overcome the ingrained 'pre-bureaucratic' practices of the nineteenth century clerkship state and the legal profession's adherence to the non-delegation doctrine. A logic of persistence is not a logic of inevitability.

The abandonment of hierarchy would, therefore, require a substantial modification, if not outright repudiation, of representative institutions, a reconstitution that does not yet appear to be even remotely in prospect in mature democracies. If anything, the problems emergent in the twenty-first century are placing even greater demands on central institutions, national and international, for leadership in arranging coordinated, purposeful action. The more plausible proposition is that we are witnessing an expansion of the array of tools democracies use to accomplish their purposes and, as well, new forms of hierarchy. Not less bureaucracy and fewer rules, but different kinds of bureaucracy and more sophisticated rules, are the likely prospect. The logic of hierarchy's persistence, then, is a logic of the continued evolution of a fundamentally useful institution of representative democracy.

REFERENCES

Anderson, Christopher J. and Guillory, Christine A. (1997) 'Political Initiatives and Satisfaction with Democracy: A Cross-National Analysis of Consensus and Majoritarian Systems', *American Political Science Review* 91(1): 66–81.

Aucoin, Peter (1997) 'The Design of Public Organizations for the 21st Century: Why Bureaucracy Will Survive in Public Management', *Canadian Public Administration* 40 (2): 290–306.

Balla, Steven J. (2008) 'The Enigmatic Bureaucracy–Democracy Nexus', *Journal of Public Administration Research and Theory* 18: 345–47.

Bandura, Romina (2006) 'A Survey of Composite Indices Measuring Country Performance: 2006 Update', UNDP/ODS Working Paper. Office of Development Studies United Nations Development Programme, New York.

Bendix, Reinhard (1960) *From Max Weber: An Intellectual Portrait*. Berkeley, CA: University of California Press.

Bennis, Warren (1966) 'The Coming Death of Bureaucracy', *Think Magazine* November/December: 30–5.

Bevir, M., Rhodes, R.A.W. and Weller, P. (2003) 'Comparative Governance: Prospects and Lessons', *Public Administration* 81(1): 191–210.

Bogason, Peter (2005) 'Postmodern Public Administration', in E. Ferlie, L E. Lynn, Jr. and C. Pollitt (eds), *The Oxford Handbook of Public Management*. New York and Oxford: Oxford University Press; pp. 234–56.

Boje, David and Dennehy, Robert (1993) *Managing in the Postmodern World*. Dubuque, IA: Kendall Hunt.

Bozeman, Barry (2000) *Bureaucracy and Red Tape*. Upper Saddle River, NJ: Prentice-Hall.

Cnaan, Ram A. (1991) 'Neighborhood-Representing Organizations: How Democratic Are They?', *Social Service Review* 73(4): 614–34.

Considine, Mark and Lewis, Jenny M. (2003) 'Bureaucracy, Network, or Enterprise? Comparing Models of Governance in Australia, Britain, the Netherlands, and New Zealand', *Public Administration Review* 60(2): 131–40.

Dahl, R.A. and Lindblom, C.E. (1953) *Politics, Economics, and Welfare: Planning and Politico-economic Systems Resolved into Basic Social Processes*. New York: Harper Torchbooks.

deLeon, Linda and deLeon, Peter (2002) 'The Democratic Ethos and Public Management', *Administration & Society* 34(2): 229–50.

Dicke, Linda A. (1998) 'Hierarchy', in Jay M. Shafritz (ed.), *International Encyclopedia of Public Policy and Administration*. Boulder, CO: Westview Press; pp. 1061–5.

Downs, Anthony (1967) *Inside Bureaucracy*. Boston, MA: Little, Brown.

du Gay, Paul (2000) *In Praise of Bureaucracy: Weber – Organization – Ethics*. Milton Keynes, UK: Open University Press.

du Gay, Paul (2005) 'Bureaucracy and Liberty: State, Authority, and Freedom', in Paul du Gay (ed.), *Values of Bureaucracy*. Oxford: Oxford University Press; pp. 41–61.

Dunleavy, Patrick (1992) *Democracy, Bureaucracy and Public Choice*. Englewood Cliffs, NJ: Prentice-Hall.

Dunleavy, Patrick, Margetts, Helen, Bastow, Simon and Tinkler, Jane (2006) 'New Public Management is Dead – Long Live Digital-Era Governance', *Journal of Public Administration Research and Theory* 16: 467–94.

Eikenberry, Angela M. (2007) 'Symposium – Theorizing Governance beyond the State', *Administrative Theory & Praxis* 29(2): 193–7.

Elster, Jon (1998) 'Introduction', in J. Elster (ed.), *Deliberative Democracy*. New York: Cambridge University Press; pp. 1–18.

Forbes, Melissa, and Lynn, Laurence E., Jr (2005) 'How Does Public Management Affect Government Performance? Findings from International Research', *Journal of Public Administration Research and Theory* 15(4): 559–84.

Forbes, Melissa K., Hill, Carolyn J. and Lynn, Laurence E., Jr (2006) 'Public Management and Government Performance: An International Review', in George Boyne, Kenneth Meier, Laurence O'Toole Jr. and Richard Walker (eds.), *Public Services Performance: Perspectives on Measurement and Management*. Cambridge: Cambridge University Press; pp. 254–74.

Fountain, Jane E. (2001) *Building the Virtual State: Information Technology and Institutional Change*. Washington, DC: Brookings Institution.

Gamble, Barbara S. (1997) 'Putting Civil Rights to a Popular Vote', *American Journal of Political Science* 41(1): 245–69.

Gerwin, Donald (1979) 'The Comparative Analysis of Structure and Technology: A Critical Appraisal', *The Academy of Management Review* 4(1): 41–51.

Gillespie, D.F. and Mileti, D.S. (1977) 'Technology and the Study of Organizations: An Overview and Appraisal', *Academy of Management Review* 2: 7–16.

Goodsell, C.T. (1983) *The Case for Bureaucracy: A Public Administration Polemic*, 2nd edn. Chatham, NJ: Chatham House Publishers.

Gutmann, Amy and Thompson, Dennis (1996) *Democracy and Disagreement*. Cambridge, MA: Harvard University Press.

Hall, Thad E. and O'Toole, Laurence J., Jr (2000) 'Structures for Policy Implementation: An Analysis of National Legislation, 1965–66 and 1993–94', *Administration and Society* 31: 667–86.

Herr, Ranjoo Seodu (2008) 'Cultural Claims and the Limits of Liberal Democracy', *Social Theory and Practice* 34: 25–48.

Hill, Carolyn J. and Lynn, Laurence E., Jr (2005) 'Is Hierarchical Governance in Decline? Evidence from Empirical Research', *Journal of Public Administration Research and Theory* 15: 173–95.

Hill, Michael and Hupe, Peter (2008) *Implementing Public Policy*, 2nd edn. London: Sage.

Hughes, Owen E. (2003) *Public Management and Administration*, 3rd edn. New York: Palgrave Macmillan.

Hummel, Ralph P. (1977) *The Bureaucratic Experience*. New York: St. Martin's Press.

Jelinek, M. (1977) 'Technology, Organizations, and Contingency', *Academy of Management Review* 2(1): 17–26.

Kamarck, Elaine Ciulla and Nye, Joseph S., Jr (eds) (2002) *Governance.Com: Democracy in the Information Age*. Washington, DC: Brookings Institution Press.

Kaufmann, Daniel, Kraay, Aart and Mastruzzi, Massimo (2009) 'Governance Matters VIII Aggregate and Individual Governance Indicators 1996–2008', Policy Research Working Paper 4978. Washington, DC: The World Bank.

Klijn, Erik-Hans (2008) 'Governance and Governance Networks in Europe: An Assessment of Ten Years of Research on the Theme', *Public Management Review* 10: 505–25.

Kooiman, Jan (ed.) (1993) *Modern Governance: New Government–Society Interactions*. London: Sage.

Kooiman, Jan (2003) *Governing as Governance*. London: Sage.

Kuhlmann, Sabine, Bogumil, Jörg and Grohs, Stephan (2008) 'Evaluating Administrative Modernization in German Local Governance: Success or Failure of the "New Steering Model"?', *Public Administration Review* 68(5): 851–63.

Lynn, Laurence E., Jr (2002) 'Democracy's "Unforgiveable Sin"', *Administration & Society* 34(4): 447–54.

Lynn, Laurence E., Jr (2006) *Public Management: Old and New*. London and New York: Routledge.

Lynn, Laurence E., Jr (2008) 'The 2007 John Gaus Lecture: New Frontiers of Public Administration: The Practice of Theory and the Theory of Practice', *PS: Political Science and Politics* XLI: 3–9.

Marinetto, M. (2003) 'Governing beyond the Centre: A Critique of the Anglo-Governance School', *Political Studies* 51: 592–608.

Marini, Frank (1971) *Toward a New Public Administration*. Scranton, PA: Chandler Publications.

Markham, William T., Johnson, Margaret A. and Bonjean, Charles M. (1999) 'Nonprofit Decision Making and Resource Allocation: The Importance of Membership Preferences, Continuity Needs, and

Interorganizational Ties', *Nonprofit and Voluntary Sector Quarterly* 28(2): 152–84.

May, Peter J. and Winter, Søren C. (2009) 'Politicians, Managers, and Street-Level Bureaucrats: Influences on Policy Implementation', *Journal of Public Administration Research and Theory* 19(3): 453–76.

Meier, K.J. (1997) 'Bureaucracy and Democracy: The Case for More Bureaucracy and Less Democracy', *Public Administration Review* 57(3): 193–9.

Meier, Kenneth J. and Hill, Gregory C. (2005) 'Bureaucracy in the Twenty-first century', in E. Ferlie, L.E. Lynn, Jr. and C. Pollitt (eds), *The Oxford Handbook of Public Management*. New York and Oxford: Oxford University Press; pp. 51–71.

Miller, Gary J. (1992) *Managerial Dilemmas: The Political Economy of Hierarchy*. New York: Cambridge University Press.

Milward, H. Brinton and Provan, Keith G. (2000) 'Governing the Hollow State', *Journal of Public Administration Research and Theory* 2: 359–79.

Morone, James A. (1990) *The Democratic Wish: Popular Participation and the Limits of American Government*. New York: Basic Books.

Nelson, Michael (1982) 'A Short, Ironic History of American National Bureaucracy', *The Journal of Politics* 44: 747–78.

Nolan L. and Zuvekas A. (2001) 'Challenges to Early Development of Integrated Service Delivery Networks and Keys to Success: Lessons Learned from the Community Integrated Services Initiative', Academy for Health Services Research and Health Policy Meeting. *Abstracts of Academy of Health Services Research Health Policy Meeting* 18: 116.

OECD (2002) *Distributed Public Governance: Agencies, Authorities and Other Government Bodies*. Paris: OECD.

OECD (2005) *Modernising Government: The Way Forward*. Paris: OECD.

OECD (2008) *Public Management Reform and Economic and Social Development*. Paris: OECD.

OECD (2009a) *Overcoming Barriers to Administrative Simplification Strategies: Guidance for Policy Makers'*. Paris: OECD.

OECD (2009b) *Reviews of Regulatory Reform: China, Defining the Boundary between the Market and the State*. Paris: OECD.

Oliver, C. (1990) 'Determinants of Inter-organizational Relationships: Integration and Future Directions', *Academy of Management Review* 15: 241–55.

Olsen, Johan P. (2006) 'Maybe It Is Time to Rediscover Bureaucracy', *Journal of Public Administration Research and Theory* 16(1): 1–24.

O'Toole, L.J. and Meier, K.J. (2004a) 'Desperately Seeking Selznick: Cooptation and the Dark Side of

Public Management in Networks', *Public Administration Review* 64: 681–93.

O'Toole, Laurence J., Jr and Meier, Kenneth J. (2004b) 'Public Management in 40 Intergovernmental Networks: Matching Structural Networks and Managerial Networking', *Journal of Public Administration Research and Theory* 14: 469–95.

Peters, B.G. and Pierre, J. (eds) (2003) *Handbook of Public Administration*. London: Sage.

Pollitt, Christopher (2000) 'Is the Emperor in His Underwear? An Analysis of the Impacts of Public Management Reform', *Public Management* 2(2): 181–99.

Pollitt, Christopher (2002) 'Public Management Reform: Reliable Knowledge and International Experience'. Paper supporting presentation to OECD Global Forum on Governance, London School of Economics, 2–3 December 2002. At: http://idbdocs.iadb.org/wsdocs/getdocument.aspx?docnum=623671. Accessed 28 July 2009.

Pollitt, Christopher and Bouckaert, Geert (2004) *Public Management Reform: A Comparative Analysis*, 2nd edn. New York and Oxford: Oxford University Press.

Power, Michael (2005) 'The Theory of the Audit Explosion', in Ewan Ferlie, Laurence E. Lynn Jr and Christopher Pollitt (eds), *The Oxford Handbook of Public Management*. Oxford and New York: Oxford University Press; pp. 326–44.

Riggs, Fred W. (1997) 'Modernity and Bureaucracy', *Public Administration Review* 57: 347–53.

Robichau, Robbie Waters and Lynn, Laurence E., Jr (2009) 'Public Policy Implementation: Still the Missing Link', *Policy Studies Journal* 37(1): 21–36.

Roderick, Melissa, Jacob, Brian A., and Bryk, Anthony S. (2002) 'The Impact of High-Stakes Testing in Chicago on Student Achievement in Promotional Gate Grades'. *Educational Evaluation and Policy Analysis* 24(4): 333–57.

Rouban, Luc (1999) 'Introduction: Citizens and the New Governance', in Luc, Rouban, (ed.), *Citizens and the New Governance: Beyond the New Public Management*. Amsterdam: IOS Press; pp. 1–5.

Salamon, Lester M. (ed.) (1989) *Beyond Privatization: The Tools of Government Action*. Washington, DC: The Urban Institute Press.

Salamon, Lester M. (2000) 'The New Governance and Tools of Government Action: An Introduction', *Fordham Urban Law Journal* 28: 1611–74.

Salamon, Lester M. (ed.) (2002) *The Tools of Government: A Guide to the New Governance*. New York and Oxford: Oxford University Press.

Selznick, Philip (1994) *The Moral Commonwealth: Social Theory and the Promise of Community*. Berkeley, CA: University of California Press.

Simon, Herbert A. (1962) 'The Architecture of Complexity', *Proceedings of the American Philosophical Society* 106: 467–82.

6, Perri, Leat, Diana, Seltzer, Kimberly and Stoker, Gerry (2002) *Towards Holistic Governance: The New Reform Agenda*. New York: Palgrave.

Smith, Andy (2003) 'Multi-level Governance: What It Is and How It Can Be Studied', in B. Guy Peters and Jon Pierre (eds), *Handbook of Public Administration*. London: Sage; pp. 619–28.

Sørensen, E. (2002) 'Democratic Theory and Network Governance', *Administrative Theory & Praxis* 24: 693–720.

Thayer, Frederick (1973) *An End to Hierarchy! An End to Competition!* New York: New Viewpoints.

Thoenig, Jean-Claude (2003) 'Institutional Theories and Public Institutions: Traditions and Appropriateness', in B.G. Peters and J. Pierre (eds), *Handbook of Public Administration*. London: Sage; pp. 127–37.

Thompson, Dennis F. (2008) 'Deliberative Democratic Theory and Empirical Political Science', *Annual Review of Political Science* 11: 497–520.

Thompson, James R. (2002) 'Reinvention as Reform: Assessing the National Performance Review', *Public Administration Review* 60(6): 508–21.

Thompson, Victor A. (1965) 'Bureaucracy and Innovation', *Administrative Science Quarterly* 10(1): 1–20.

Weber, M. (1970) 'Politics as a Vocation', in H.H. Gerth and C. Wright Mills (eds), *From Max Weber: Essays in sociology*. London: Routledge and Kegan Paul; pp. 77–128.

Williamson, Oliver E. (1996) *The Mechanisms of Governance*. New York and Oxford: Oxford University Press.

Wolf, Charles, Jr (1988) *Markets or Governments? Choosing Between Imperfect Alternatives*. Cambridge, MA: MIT Press.

15

Contracting Out

Steven Cohen and William Eimicke

WHAT IS CONTRACTING AND WHY IS IT GROWING?

Contracting defined

The formal definition of a contract is simple: 'An agreement between two or more parties, especially one that is written and enforceable by law' (Answers.com, 2004). A contract specifies the good or service being procured, and typically includes information about price, schedule, and the definition and amount of the service or product being delivered. While the definition of a contract might be quite simple, as Phillip Cooper notes: 'great latitude is left to the contracting parties to an agreement to have the tools to fashion and implement it. Negotiations resulting in a meeting of minds are the dominant dynamic in most contracting' (2003: 13).

This chapter focuses on contracts between government and non-governmental entities and the role of the government contract manager. Government contracting has expanded substantially over the past three decades and has taken on ideological baggage, often associated with shrinking the size of government, lower pay, job losses, and outsourcing of jobs to other countries. At the same time, government has been a major purchaser of goods and services in the marketplace for hundreds of years, buying everything from weapons, uniforms, airplanes, and ships to paper, soap, light bulbs, and paper clips.

Public administration scholars pay particular attention to the relationship between government and its typically non-governmental contract partner. While the contractor is non-governmental, the product or service they provide through their contract is generally perceived as public and the government is held accountable for outcomes. As Jeffrey L. Brudney and his colleagues (2005: 394) describe it:

> Despite the apparent heterogeneity of the privatization concept and the various methods for achieving privatization, in the U.S. context especially, this term is usually taken to mean government 'contracting out' or 'outsourcing' with a for-profit firm, a non-profit organization, or another government to produce or deliver a service. Although the job of delivering services is contracted out, the services remain public, funded mainly by taxation, and decisions regarding their quantity, quality, distribution, and other characteristics are left to public decision makers (compare Boyne 1998: 475; Ferris 1986: 289) (Brudney et al., 2005).

Central to Brudney's definition is the notion of public control, funding and decision-making. The government is the principal and the contractor is simply the agent. Our definition of contracting leaves no ambiguity about the power relationship we see in government contracting. We understand that those who implement policy hold the power to define policy through administration, but that any exercise of this power by the contractor does not eliminate or diminish in any way government's responsibility for the actions of contractors.

The make or buy decision and managing organizations

There is nothing new about government carrying out its responsibilities through contracts. Don Kettl makes this point in recounting George Washington's complaints about the shoddy uniforms supplied to his revolutionary troops by private contractors. At the same time, many observers believe that the nature and impact of government contracting has changed significantly since revolutionary times. Stephen Goldsmith and William D. Eggers discuss the evolution from simple contracting for goods and services, to contracting as a means of establishing and maintaining complex inter-organizational networks:

> In service contract networks, governments use contractual arrangements as organizational tools. Contractor and subcontractor service agreements and relationships create an array of vertical and horizontal connections as opposed to simple one-to-one relationships. Such networks are prevalent in many areas of the public sector, including health, mental health, welfare, child welfare, transportation and defense (2004: 69).

In this view, contracting is a part of the organization's very culture and what Phillip Selznick termed the 'distinctive competence' of the network is indistinguishable from that of the organization. In fact, one key dimension of the value added by the organization is its ability to manage the network it has established. Indeed, Peter Drucker has predicted that by the middle of the twenty-first century most of the work in many organizations will

be done by persons not employed by the organization – contractors (1999).

The make-or-buy decision helps define an organization's effort towards identity and distinctive competence. An organization may decide that to adequately focus on their core mission, they must contract out non-core functions. This non-core work still needs to get done but it is now done by workers from the contractor organization.

Organizations contract when a needed good or service cannot be provided by in-house staff. A related reason to contract is to access distinct competence that is available in the marketplace, such as cutting-edge technology, an environmental expert, legal or financial specialists. Contracting can be used to create competition and thereby reduce the cost and/or improve the quality of a desired good or service.

Contracting can be used to access a particular expertise in a geographic location where in-house specialists are not available. A temporary surge in work might dictate the use of contract staff rather than hiring permanent employees. The need to act quickly in an emergency might also dictate the use of contractors.

Government organizations may decide to contract for reasons other than management efficiency or effectiveness. In the aftermath of the taxpayer revolts that began in California in the 1970s, a strong anti-government movement developed in the United States that advocates reducing public employment and privatizing as much of the economy as possible. For example,

> The 1970s witnessed an anti-bureaucratic mood that sought to limit the bureaucracy's power through various budgetary approaches, reorganizations, reforms, and spending limitations such as California's Proposition 13. Though not without efficacy and utility, overall, such approaches are inadequate to the task. They must be augmented by an effort to maximize the political representativeness of public bureaucracy (Krislov and Rosenbloom, 1981: vii).

In many cases, this 'contracting to downsize' is really an illusion as the displaced public workforce has been replaced with a contractor workforce, often located across the street or down the block; sometimes, it is the same worker paid more or less to do the same work he or she did for the government. Anti-government leaders will nevertheless trumpet their achievement of 'substantially reducing government headcount'.

Contracting can also be used to weaken the power of public employee unions and to achieve reductions in pension and benefit costs. Similarly, contracting is used to weaken or even eliminate civil service rules and protections. Taken together, all of these 'ideological' reasons to contract can be used to reduce cost and the obligation of government to public employees.

Government leaders also use contracting to build bridges to key constituencies and neighborhoods. For health and human services, it has been increasingly common to contract with local non-profit organizations to provide services previously provided by government social workers, child and elder care workers, and healthcare professionals. A related reason for these contracts may be to avoid direct government responsibility for difficult or failing services such as job training and placement, drug treatment, prison re-entry, homeless services, low-income housing, and even elementary and secondary education.

Why outsourcing is increasing

Government contracting has been growing for the past quarter of a century, coinciding with an international movement toward privatization ignited by Margaret Thatcher and Ronald Reagan. The supply of available contractors has increased dramatically over that time, aided by the rapid expansion of the Internet and related concepts of 'e-commerce' and 'e-government'. In the wake of this expansion of supplies and contract utilization, contract management must work to develop systems to ensure that contractors deliver the best possible goods and services at the lowest possible price.

We expect that the current trend toward greater outsourcing and increased organizational specialization in the private sector will influence government management for the foreseeable future. Perhaps even more important for government managers, effective management in an era of increased technical, economic, and social complexity requires additional contracting. Particularly in the current constrained fiscal environment, sophisticated public managers must master 'make-or-buy' decision-making to focus their organization on core competencies and simultaneously to more with less.

In government, contracting is a highly regulated activity. There are rules on advertising, the bidding process, and the steps that must be taken to review a bid. Once a contract is awarded, there are rules governing the ethics of interaction between government and contractor. Even as governments around the world expand their investments and purchasing in the market place to stimulate their economies, they must be mindful of the performance and ethical risks. For example, President Obama demanded unprecedented requirements of transparency and accountability in contracts funded by the American Recovery and Reinvestment Act of 2009 (US GAO, 2009). Three distinct report systems were put in place: one to the Vice President's Task Force; one to the agency letting the contract; and one to the Office of Management and Budget.

Despite these regulatory constraints, government must find a way to get contractor personnel to meet high performance standards. Incentives must be provided to obtain desired behavior from contractor staff. As Goldsmith and Eggers (2004) point out, communication through both formal and informal channels is essential to the efficient and effective functioning of government service providers and their contract partners. Communication and informal contact, in particular, may be difficult in an environment designed to prevent corruption and the appearance of impropriety.

Contracting has been increasing all over the world. As Barbara Romzek and

Jocelyn Johnston have observed, 'Governments at all levels have expanded the range of services they deliver through contracts – from traditional "make-or-buy" decisions for defense weaponry, highway construction and fleet purchases, to contracting for the ongoing provision of specialized social services' (2005: 436).

Adoption of the 'new public management', or NPM, varies across nations. For instance,

Traditional public administration persists in the Commission of the European Union (EU) and Germany. The aims and results of NPM differ. In the UK, NPM aimed to create the minimalist state. In Norway, it aimed to protect the state. The language of NPM obscures differences. Distinctiveness lies in the package not in the parts but there is no uniform, agreed upon package. Finally, the meaning of NPM has changed; for example, in Australia the early focus was corporate management but it gave way to a focus on contracting (Bevir, Rhodes and Weller, 2003).

Several factors may influence public sector modernization; they include '"path dependency" (or "historical traditions, cultural norms and established practices"); political mobilization by advocacy coalitions of administrative and political elites; the institutionalization of such coalitions; and influential meta-organizations and institutions that produce knowledge' (Bevir, Rhodes and Weller, 2003). Reform in Western Europe is characterized by the following: 'continuous adjustment; responses to specific political crises; pragmatic structural change; reform as its own cause; and comprehensive programmes' (Bevir, Rhodes and Weller, 2003).

Australia and the Netherlands have contracted out typical government services such as welfare. These contracts are referred to as 'relational contracts' because more than just commercial considerations are at stake; they include commitments to more general values (Finn, 2008). More specifically,

The Australian Job Network (JN) was created in 1998 and, in a decade, made the transition from 'radical experiment' to established institution. Its design changed as policymakers adapted the model

to secure greater efficiencies, to deal with unanticipated effects and, through successive 'welfare reforms', to redefine services to 'activate' more working age benefit claimants. The evidence suggests the JN delivers more job outcomes for half the cost of the previous system (Finn, 2008).

Performance in general has improved with contracting, but not without producing a myriad of complications. Contracting has improved participants' short-term job prospects minimally, by 5–10 percent. 'The cost-efficiency gains attributed to the Dutch and Australian models appear significant, but relatively little is known about the extent to which these gains have been offset by high transaction costs for the purchaser, providers and service users' (Finn, 2008). Futhermore,

Securing the delivery of government objectives through contracts is prone to the same implementation problems experienced in public sector delivery systems. Contracting out poses further challenges because it fragments programme responsibility among multiple contractors, changes the relationship between those who design policy and those who deliver front-line services, and blurs lines of responsibility and accountability (Finn, 2008).

Lobbying has also increased alongside of contracting: 'Providers have emerged as a distinct interest group and powerful lobbying force, with direct access to senior civil servants and ministers' (Finn, 2008). With this political backdrop, contracting is only set to increase in the near future.

Lower-cost technology of information, communication, and rapid, low-cost transportation make 'production location' more flexible

The expanded use of contracts is related to the dramatic expansion in the availability of extremely low-cost voice communication and information-sharing virtually anywhere in the world. Workers can share documents, financial officers can receive invoices and pay them electronically, and inspectors can transmit reports and video instantaneously from the site of the customer interface to the handheld of the CEO. For example, it is often said that Proctor and Gamble virtually runs the section of Wal-Mart stores where its products are sold. Multiple organizations can operate as one from disparate sites to serve customers.

In New York City, a Police Department operator answers a 911 call from a sick citizen, forwards the call with critical information to an FDNY (Fire Department of New York City) ambulance dispatcher who sends the nearest FDNY or private ambulance to bring the critically ill person to the nearest public or non-profit hospital. Billing and payment for the FDNY ambulance service is handled by FDNY civilian staff, an outside billing firm and/or city/state/federal Medicaid/Medicare public employees.

Similarly, ever larger air transports and cargo ships can carry goods from one side of the world to the other rapidly and at relatively low cost. Fresh Dover sole can be caught off the coast of England in the morning and served in a Manhattan restaurant that evening. It can make economic sense to ship water from Fiji to a New York City deli and sell it for profit at a price that is only slightly higher than Poland Spring water from Maine. Overnight shipping of documents, books, and other small, light items is almost taken for granted. Distance, time, and cost are less and less an obstacle to contracting as a tool to accomplish the work of an organization, be it public, private or non-profit.

The ideology of globalization and our global economy

In our view, it was large-scale, vertically-integrated bureaucratic hierarchies that enabled the economies of scale and mass production needed for the wealth-generating machine we called industrialization. For the first half of the twentieth century this model worked, and to some extent, it works today. However, as technology developed (satellite communications, the Internet, superhighways, containerized shipping on huge cargo ships, air freight, super and personal computers, cell phones, bar codes), a global economy

developed which rewards organizational specialization and discourages vertical integration.

The make-or-buy calculus has changed. We now live in the post-industrial information age with much higher standards of efficiency, effectiveness, and customer service. Customers expect excellent goods and services promptly and at a good price. They are much less willing to accept slow, non-responsive organizations – as General Motors learned the hard way in 2009. New models of organizational efficiency are emerging, out of necessity and by design. For Margaret Thatcher, Ronald Reagan, and the anti-government advocates, the model was privatization – the smaller the government the better. For Osborne and the reinventers, the model was innovation – streamlined and more effective government (Osborne and Hutchinson, 2004). Today, we see increased emphasis on contracting out and a broader strategy of managing public services through networks. Contracting out and network management are not synonymous, but our view is that networks include both informal and contractual linkages. We consider the contractual links as equivalent to the steel frame of a bridge – the key relationships upon which the informal and non-contractual relationships are built.

Globalization and advancements in communication, transportation, and technology have created problems and demand that are larger than generally experienced only a few decades ago. Goldsmith and Eggers (2004) use the example of homeland security to illustrate that dealing with terrorism requires global scope and cooperation and simultaneously customized, local response capacity. This new network management 'bears less resemblance to a traditional organization chart than it does to a more dynamic web of computer networks that can organize or reorganize, expand or contract, depending on the problem at hand' (Goldsmith and Eggers, 2004: 8). The relationship between the various government and private organizations in efforts dealing with terrorism are not always defined entirely by contracts, but in some instances are in the interest of the private sector to perform. For example, a private firm's security force and its practices are a clear part of the network of organizations delivering homeland security services, even though they may have no contractual relationship with government. Information exchange between security forces can be critical, but is not provided in exchange for fees in a formal relationship, but in exchange for goodwill that might later result in reciprocity.

What management challenges does contracting present? Formal and legal relationships

Crafting RFPs and eliciting bids

Governments use a variety of methods to select contractors. The most common techniques are a sealed bid and a request for proposal (RFP). A sealed bid is used when the product or service is relatively easy to define, is widely available in the marketplace, and both the unit cost and total contract amount are modest (total purchases of less than $100,000). Since quality is assumed to be standard, the sealed bid is awarded to the lowest bidder. The sealed bid must be received by a specific deadline. All bids are opened in public and recorded. The contract is awarded to the lowest bidder that also meets all the specifications of the bid.

Requests for proposals, or RFPs, are used for purchases of higher amounts ($100,000 or more) and/or when the product or service is technical, approaches vary widely or the government is not exactly sure about the best approach. The RFP will set out what problem it seeks to solve or need it seeks to meet and then ask those interested in bidding to tell them what they think is the best approach, balancing price and level of performance. As government contracts out more services and requires complex technological solutions, the RFP is being used ever more frequently.

To avoid charges of favoritism and to enable intelligent choices among what might be significantly different proposals, RFPs should include a predetermined scoring system, informing bidders how their proposals will be judged. The government agency must also assemble a team of knowledgeable staff to independently score the proposals and a predetermined methodology to choose among the bidders with the highest scores. RFP price quotes can be negotiated after submission but the government agency involved must take care to ensure that fairness is assured, in fact and in terms of appearance.

Negotiated or sole source contracting is generally discouraged in the public sector because the appearance of favoritism is so hard to avoid. Sole source contracting may be used when there is only one supplier of an essential commodity or service – a medical device, a weapons system, a medication or a special security system – or in an emergency circumstance such as a flood or terrorist attack where lives are at risk. A negotiated contract might also be used when a delay in acquiring the product or service might result in substantial cost over-runs for a larger construction project or weapons system.

To ensure the widest possible distribution of its notices of solicitation, governments may develop lists of bidders. Organizations interested in competing for government business fill out an enrollment application and are placed on a mailing or email list so that they automatically receive notification of solicitations for government contracts. In certain circumstances, where work is complicated, technical, and predictable, government agencies may develop pre-qualified lists of vendors. Pre-qualified lists might apply for construction projects, auditing, maintenance and repair, road work, and snow removal.

Governments may also make special provisions to ensure that small locally based businesses and businesses owned by minorities and women have access to public contracts. These provisions may include preference for subcontracts from larger contracts, exemption from bonding requirements, prompt payment guarantees, and technical assistance. Government wants to buy the highest quality at the lowest possible price but it may also want to ensure that the local citizens and businesses that provide its taxes and revenues have a reasonable chance to participate in the business opportunities provided by their government. Governments that are fully committed to a transparent and competitive contracting process will reach out to a broad range of stakeholders concerning the decision to contract and in assessing the efficacy of contracts after they are awarded.

Developing contract language that maintains management prerogatives

When a service is being contracted for the first time, it is difficult for the staff working on the RFP (or on the actual contract) to develop contract provisions that anticipate all the tasks involved in the work and all of the problems that may arise. Sometimes specifications in the RFP or the contract do not permit critical tasks to be performed. While contracts must provide a vendor with some predictability, there are a number of techniques that government can use to retain discretion over contract provisions and contractor work.

One very common technique is to use a task-order, mission contract. This large-scale, multipurpose contract provides a general description of the contract's anticipated tasks, but does not release funding until a government client writes a specific task-order directing the firm to perform particular tasks. Another practice for dealing with this problem is to let a short-term 'trial' contract with explicit provisions for early and rapid renewal. Both of these techniques are useful as the organization learns more about the work being contracted out. As this learning occurs, the contract can get more specific. In the long run, it is best to translate these learning experiences into standard operating procedures and clearly delineated tasks, incentives, and expected outputs and outcomes.

Other techniques for improving an RFP or contract include a request for qualifications or request for information from prospective vendors. These requests to firms to either provide a demonstration of capability or evidence of qualifications can be used to narrow the field or develop the additional information needed in order to draft an appropriate RFP. Another strategy is to find one organization to work with and use a sole source procurement to pay that firm. Through this method the government can obtain some of the firm's time to learn more about how to define and measure the service being contracted. If this sole source technique is used, it may be necessary to prohibit this firm from competing on the final contract, in order to avoid conflicts of interest.

Managing performance

Effective contract management requires a range of management tools. Some of those tools relate to contract provisions that provide resources to government contract managers. What we mean by resources are contract clauses that provide managers with:

- the ability to define and shape the work of contractors;
- the flexibility to make mid-course corrections;
- the ability to obtain frequent and audited measures of contractor performance;
- methods for systematically providing performance-based incentives and disincentives – particularly financial bonuses and penalties.

We are strongly attracted to the use of incentive clauses in contracts. Incentives work best when they are rewards for the accomplishment of specific, verified performance measures. For example, when a firm that is installing subway tracks completes the work a month ahead of time, it is given a bonus for every day the project comes in ahead of schedule. In fact, an even better technique links a similar penalty clause to late completion. The point of an incentive is that it is only useful if it inspires the specific changes in behavior that improves organizational performance. If it doesn't motivate change or motivates the wrong change, it fails.

Managers should experiment with different forms of incentives, and attempt to determine the independent impact of the incentive on performance. One problem with bonuses is that if they are given too easily, they are soon seen as a type of base pay and people come to rely on and expect them. When that happens, their impact on performance is significantly reduced.

Designing and implementing performance measures

Performance measurement is critical to contract management – 'contractual relationships with private and non-profit firms provide the surest way to punish poor performance: contract termination' (Cohen and Eimicke, 2000: 102). A properly designed performance management system can help a public manager decide whether it makes more sense to contract or to perform the task in-house. If contracting is the decision, then performance management can help make the best choice among competing contractors. An effective, real-time performance measurement system can allow contract managers and contractors to recalibrate resource allocations, assignments, and strategy. If the measures are accurate and focused on the outcomes that matter to those served, the metrics can be used to modify contractor behavior.

Performance contracts need not be extremely complicated but that does not mean they are easy to design or employ effectively. At a minimum, performance contracts must include objective performance standards, rewards for superior performance and penalties for failure to meet a minimum baseline (Osborne and Hutchinson, 2004: 180–1). In terms of rewards, contractors can share in savings achieved for the government, receive a portion of revenues increased, and/or be rewarded for high customer/citizen satisfaction or delivering the product or service more quickly than anticipated. Conversely, they can be punished for failing to meet contract minimum requirements.

We recognize that contractors will use their influence with elected officials to 'cut red tape' and minimize the 'interference of rule-driven bureaucrats'. Politically connected contractors will try to avoid complying with contract provisions they previously agreed to but now find 'onerous' and use friendly legislators and staff to apply pressure to government contract managers and monitors. And, when contract renewal time rolls around the contract manager is sure to receive many phone calls and emails from elected officials and 'interested citizens' expressing unbridled support for even the worst-performing contractor. Involving a broad range of stakeholders throughout the contract process is always a good idea and it becomes particularly valuable in these circumstances. The effective contract manager can draw on the unbiased feedback from a wide range of knowledgeable and involved stakeholders to resist political pressure to renew a poorly performing contractor.

The reality that 'better' may not always be 'cheaper' necessitates that the public contract manager choose the proper mix of metrics to use when soliciting and awarding government contracts, particularly in the field of human services. For-profit firms may appear cheaper, but non-profits may be better able and more willing to make sure they really help the hard to serve and those most in need. Unfortunately, studies comparing the performance of for-profits and non-profits in terms of quality and cost are limited and inconclusive (Frumkin, 2002: 14; Sanger, 2003).

Public program and contract managers should consider factors other than cost when setting criteria for contractor selection. Points should be awarded for documented past success in delivering quality outcomes, as measured by other governments, customers, and/or independent third parties. In fields where success has been difficult to achieve – foster care, substance abuse treatment, and prisoner reentry, for example – points could be awarded for innovative approaches that might lead to new best practices (Frumkin, 2002: 16). Government can also break up the workload into large and small assignments; divide the workload by geography and give preference to some community-based providers; reward experience in the field and in the community; and/or reward collaborations between for-profit and non-profit providers.

This challenge of ensuring contractor performance is relatively simple when purchasing goods such as office supplies, computers or even food services. What makes government contracting so complex today is that human services such as child care, elder care, job training, education, and even security services – generally considered the core functions of the public sector – care now being contracted out to for-profit and non-profit companies. Finding the right contractor is complicated by potentially conflicting objectives for government contracting – cheaper may not be better or faster and better may not be either faster or cheaper.

Finding the right contractor begins with reaching consensus among a broad range of stakeholders on the objectives for the services to be contracted. Next, the effective contractor manager must find appropriate methods to measure contractor performance. Finally, the contractor manager must identify effective incentives and penalties to ensure that the contractor achieves the desired outcomes.

ETHICS AND ACCOUNTABILITY

Contracting and democratic accountability

When we discuss contractor accountability, we need to ask the question: Accountable to what or who? We believe that the answer to that question is: 'Accountable to the system of democratic representation and its elected officials.' Accountability is not simply intended as a means of punishing representatives for taking wrong positions, but more importantly, it should encourage representatives to be responsive to the needs of those they represent. The difficulty with the accountability position is that this notion of

providing stimulation for right behavior does not necessarily follow from the definition of accountability. Representation is an ongoing activity, not merely a set of mechanical or formal structures.

The accountability view of representation leaves a measure of power in the hands of the represented. According to this view, if the representative is willing to be elected to office only once, he (she) can do as he (she) pleases. Hence, the power relationship can be described as follows: in the short run, the representative is in the dominant position, but due to their ultimate veto, the represented have the last word and in the long run hold greater power. Clearly, the represented hold greater power in this view of representation than in the authorization view. Nonetheless, the public's leverage is periodic and latent rather than continuous and present.

The role of the unelected bureaucracy makes the issue of contractor accountability all the more difficult. As Carl Friedrich once observed, 'the core of modern government… [is] a functioning bureaucracy' (1937: 44). Put another way, the major actors operating at the heart of the American political system are unelected officials. This has been extended to networks of public and private unelected officials in an increasingly complex set of market and non-market-based relationships (Olsen, 2005). The presence of unelected government and non-governmental players is a difficult notion to reconcile with a theory of governance that maintains that government ought to be democratic, or of and by the people. The problematic nature of citizen linkage to unelected officials is addressed in part through direct communication between the public and the bureaucracy. It is also addressed through the strong sense of responsibility and public ethics that is typical in the American public service. This internal norm in government is a deeply ingrained element of government's organizational culture. Perhaps some of these same communication techniques and a sense of public ethics can inform private contractors of public preferences and inspire them to pay attention to them. However, contractor behavior should be even more constrained than the acts of unelected government officials, since whatever actions they take must be approved or at least known by government officials.

When Rudolph Giuliani was mayor of New York City, a contractor with the City's human resources administration placed a young girl into foster care who died at the hands of her guardian. Initially, the mayor attempted to assign blame to the contractor. While the contractor was at fault, the media and the public held the mayor accountable. He came to agree with this position and created a new agency exclusively focused on foster care. This agency reengineered the foster care contracting system with new reporting requirements, more effective management controls, and better procedures for quality control.

We believe that the overall probability of ensuring real accountability is lower when government contracts a function. When life and death issues are involved and higher levels of accountability are required, contracting should be avoided. Most of the time, such extreme accountability is not needed and the issue then becomes one of establishing a set of performance indicators and management processes adequate to ensuring appropriate contractor performance.

The danger of fraud and conflicts of interest

It is critical that government officials avoid both the reality and appearance of conflicts of interest. It is not enough to respond to an investigation or attack. Government officials must think through their past interactions and those of people they are close to, and anticipate potential conflicts of interest.

A number of techniques have been developed to reduce the possibility of conflicts of interest. Sealed, competitive bidding is one such technique. So, too, is the use of panels of officials to review proposals and select winning bids. Panels can include people from outside the agency to ensure greater independence and objectivity. Still, the best technique is vigilance and sensitivity on the part of government officials involved in contracting.

A common understanding of corruption in government is the use of a public position for private gain. Corruption and unethical behavior associated with contracting usually involves compromising the public interest for private benefit (Gray and Kaufmann, 1998: 1). The World Bank describes administrative corruption as 'the intentional imposition of distortions in the prescribed implementation of existing laws, rules and regulations to provide advantages to either state or non-state actors as a result of the illegal transfer or concentration of private gains to public officials' (2005: 2). A simple example is when a contractor pays a bribe to influence a person with the authority to award, renew, or change the terms of an existing contract. In such a circumstance, both parties may be acting illegally or at least unethically – offering and/or paying a bribe by one party and soliciting and/or accepting the bribe by the second party.

A related category of corruption is often characterized as the 'revolving door' where a contractor has the capacity to 'trade' career opportunities for the contracting agent or members of their families in return for assistance in winning the contract. Whether it just looks bad or is the result of an explicit quid pro quo, most organizations seek to monitor the behavior of its employees regarding the award of contracts and future employment of those employees. Many governments and non-profit organizations have explicit laws or regulations limiting the right of former employees to work for an organization that received contracts during their public employment. A common limit lasts for one year after separation from the contracting organization (see, for example, Corporation for Public Broadcasting, 2004: 5).

In complicated contracting situations such as the outsourcing of a large information technology operation or the operation of a sewage treatment plant or waste treatment facility, the government may hire a third-party expert to advise them. It is not unusual for these third-party experts to have financial relationships with some of the bidders for the contract. These experts may even have a financial interest in the outcome of the transaction, directly or indirectly. These relationships may not be easily identified. Therefore, it is essential that the government invest in extensive due diligence to ensure that their hired advisors receive only payments for their analysis and advice, and demonstrate affirmatively that they have no other financial interest in the transaction (Sclar, 2000: 121).

Because government may be unsure of exactly how to fully specify what needs to be in the contract, they may leave aspects of the contract's requirements open or only generally defined. Contractors will often take advantage of the vagueness, requiring additional payments to do what is not explicitly required in the contract (Savas, 2005: 33). This failure to fully define what is required could be the result of genuine uncertainty, but it could also be due to incompetence or could be a deliberate act to enable a favored vendor to reap the benefits from the changes required after the contract is signed.

Political considerations can corrupt the contracting process in the public sector. The decision to contract rather than perform a service with in-house staff can be the result of political influence. Campaign contributors may convince an elected official to bid out services without any analysis justifying the decision (Clynch, 1999: 2). Career public servants may be pressured by political appointees to award contracts to those who have supported the current party or person in power. The connected contractor might even be very qualified and experienced. The problem is the distortion of an objective, merit-based selection process to meet other objectives.

Corruption can also occur among the contract seekers, with or without the knowledge of the contracting agency. Contractors cooperate to take turns or divide territories, submitting deliberately inflated bids for the contracts or districts that are not 'theirs' and winning with comfortably 'fat' bids in the areas 'given' to them. Large contractors and contractors associated with organized crime can intimidate legitimate, honest competitors out of the competition (Sclar, 2000: 48).

More broadly, there is corruption by incompetence. Many government agencies are contracting on a massive scale without necessarily instituting equally dramatic changes in their hiring and training practices. As Goldsmith and Eggers note, 'Managing a portfolio of provider networks is infinitely different than managing divisions of employees' (2004: 22). Governments that view contracting as a means of off-loading management headaches and that do not invest in staff and training for proper oversight can expect waste, complaints, and scandal.

Some rules that must apply to public employees in the contracting process cannot apply to their private sector partners. For example, the American Society for Public Administration's Code of Ethics suggests that public officials should not realize undue personal gain in the performance of their official duties. In the private sector, a key motivating tool is additional compensation for behaviors creating additional profit for the firm. This creates a conflict of interest.

Corrupt and/or improper contract decisions can result because the officials making those decisions have not been trained in contract solicitation, evaluation, design or implementation. Many government employees assigned to the contracting process were not originally hired for that task and subsequently receive no training for a complicated and demanding assignment. Rigorous training of those assigned to contract management could help limit corruption and lead to better contracts and contract outcomes (Institute of Public Administration, 2005: 1–7).

Techniques for detecting and discouraging violations of public ethics

To determine the ethical standards for government contractors, we must first establish the rules that government officials dealing with contractors should follow. Laws and regulations covering compensation, gifts, bidding procedures, equal opportunity and discrimination, and disclosure must be reviewed and assessed to determine the potential applicability to contractors. Ethical standards, laws, and regulations should be part of the contracting process from the outset, should be part of the negotiation of contract terms, and should be reflected explicitly in the contract document and operating procedures.

Perhaps not surprisingly, Transparency International argues that transparency is an effective mechanism to prevent corruption (2005: 1–2). Contract solicitations, evaluations, and selections that are as open as possible to all potential bidders, to media observers, interested advocates, and the general public, are more likely to be fair, well-analyzed, and properly awarded. Transparency has its limits, however. Intelligent but corrupt officials and their contract partners may be able to keep their illicit behavior secret. The contract may be so technical that observers may not be interested or able to effectively monitor the process. Or, to ensure fairness or for security reasons, some processes cannot be completely transparent.

Whether it is gifts or bribes, annual financial disclosure filing requirements can be a check on the trading of contracts for personal financial gain. As part of that filing, federal income tax returns can be required. While the completely dishonest person will falsify all documents, the deterrent of multiple chances of discovery and multiple levels of penalties (tax fraud) may keep others from yielding to temptation.

Similarly, there are laws in many places seeking to limit the negative effects of the revolving door between public contracting offices and their contractors. To further discourage improper behavior, we could enact laws prohibiting members of the Senior Executive Service (and similarly situated high-level administrative policymakers at the state and local level) and political appointees from seeking employment with contractors benefiting from their policymaking or rule-making for at least a year or two upon leaving public service. We could also prohibit former government employees from working in a different division or subsidiary of the division of the company benefiting from their public contracting decision (POGO, 2004: 4).

Other methods of limiting the impact of conflicts of interest include recusals, waivers, divestiture, and trusts (US Office of Government Ethics, 2005: 5). Recusal requires a public official to withdraw from participation in a contracting decision where there might be personal gain, or benefit to a family or close associate. Waivers can be used on a case-by-case basis to enable officials to participate in a decision where they may have an interest, but only where that interest is not substantial, very indirect, and is mitigated by its disclosure. Divestiture can enable an official to eliminate a potential conflict by selling the property that creates the potential conflict. Trusts can manage assets for public officials while they are in a decision-making position such that their actions have no relationship to gains or losses in their investment portfolio.

Stronger laws to protect or even to encourage civil servants aware of corrupt practices might also lead to a better contracting process. Those on the inside of the process are most likely to know about corruption in the contracting process, yet these potential whistleblowers are often subordinates of those engaging in the corrupt practices. And the superiors who they might be implicating are often politically connected to the chief executive and/or legislative leaders. There must be a secure process that encourages and enables those with concerns about corrupt practices to share what they know with enforcement officials without risking their job or creating a chilling environment for those trying to do their jobs honestly.

First, the contracting agency can educate bidders on the laws and regulations governing the contracting process and what constitutes ethical behavior. Agency personnel can also exhort and advocate the proposition that private contractors of the government should become guardians and protectors of the public trust. This moral conscience role can be accomplished more effectively if the private contractor is located in or close to the government agency they are serving. Effective public managers will learn to 'manage by wandering around' (Peters and Waterman, 1982) their own offices and those of their contractors, reinforcing the reality that these private firms are acting in the public service.

Secondly, in RFPs, the government agency can award points to contractors that have a track record of ethical behavior, have strong corporate codes of ethics, and can document a history of rewarding ethical behavior and punishing corrupt behavior on their own. The contract document itself should articulate ethical standards and behaviors and include enforcement mechanisms for violations. The contract could even require the contractor to report overtures for corrupt behavior coming from public employees.

Thirdly, the contract can specify incentives or bonus payments for meeting ethical standards and stiff penalties for violations. Contract renewals can be conditioned on the meeting of ethical requirements. Violations of certain provisions can even specify that the contractor is blacklisted from bidding on all future public contracts for a number of years, or even forever.

Finally, the public agency should independently monitor the behavior of the contractor to ensure ethical behavior. This can be done with agency employees or a third party, such as a private accounting firm, that can be hired to serve as a monitor. While potentially expensive, an outside monitor can help to preserve a positive working relationship between agency and contractor personnel and eliminate the possibility that agency personnel might try to deliberately sabotage the contractor. Inspectors General should also be established as a self-guided investigators of potentially corrupt practices.

Ultimately, it is the responsibility of the public manager to ensure that ethical standards are understood and observed. To do so, public managers will need to develop a set of skills that are helpful in managing internal hierarchies but are essential to effective management of a network of outside contractors.

Public network managers must become expert consumers of information technology and performance management tools, so that they can effectively monitor the activities of off-site contractors and provide incentives for ethical behaviors and penalties for actions that do not meet government standards. Clearly, there must be performance measures for ethical behavior and those measures must be highlighted as critically important to the private contractors.

Unethical behavior by government officials, alone and in partnership with private contractors, has occurred since the founding of the United States and will no doubt be with us as long as we are a nation. The increase in government contracting increases the risk of unethical behavior. We believe the risk is worth the reward of better government services at a lower price. Government is already doing a better job of managing these networks of service providers and ensuring the ethical behavior of its own employees and those of its contractors. It remains one of the great challenges for public managers in the twenty-first century, but with proper training, attention, and application of the proper management tools, it is a challenge that we believe can be met.

CONCLUSIONS: CONTRACT MANAGEMENT AND EFFECTIVE, ACCOUNTABLE PUBLIC MANAGEMENT

We do not believe that representative democracy is compromised by the presence of contractors working for unelected government officials. To the extent that contracted work enhances government's capacity and performance, it connects representatives to a more effective and efficient administrative system. In a formal sense, policy decisions flow from elected leaders to unelected government officials and from these public officials to private organizations under contract to the government. The reality, of course, is that contractors are in direct communication with elected leaders. Contractor behavior is influenced by contractor perceptions of the policy intent of elected leaders. Contractors lobby and make campaign contributions to influence those policies. The policy intent of these elected representatives is mediated and made operational by regulations, guidance, and contract provisions developed by unelected officials. All of these factors influence the behaviors that make the policy pronouncements of elected leaders real.

The increase in government contracting over the past several decades presents additional challenges to accountable, representative government. However, these challenges are part of a series of changes in modern times arising from new technology, globalization, and cultural shifts in the world. Contracting, properly managed, should not impair accountability and representative democracy. Poorly managed, contracting can pose significant threats.

Effective contract management requires skill at using all the tools of traditional and innovative management. Effective public managers understand human resource, financial, organizational, information, performance, strategic, political, and media management. They also acquire experience with quality management, benchmarking, reengineering, and team management.

The responsible contract manager must do more. In addition to deploying those tools in problem-solving, today's responsible public manager must learn how to elicit contract bids that result in appropriate and well-priced services and goods. They must learn to monitor contractor performance, and write contracts that allow them to perform this monitoring function. Contract managers must learn how to develop informal networks that reach deep into contractor organizations, just as they have done within their own organizations.

ACKNOWLEDGEMENT

Several sections of this chapter are based on work previously published in the *Responsible Contract Manager: Protecting the Public Interest in an Outsourced World*, Cohen, S. and Eimicke, W., Georgetown University Press, Washington, DC, 2008.

REFERENCES

Answers.com. (2004) Contract. http://www.answers.com/topic/contract (accessed 30 September, 2005).

Bevir, M., Rhodes, R.A.W. and Weller, P. (2003) 'Traditions of Governance', *Public Administration* 81(1).

Boyne, George A. (1998) 'Bureaucratic Theory Meets Reality: Public Choice and Service Contracting in U.S. Local Government', *Public Administration Review* 58(5): 475.

Brudney, J.L., Fernandez, S., Ryu, J.E. and Wright, D.S. (2005) 'Exploring and Explaining Contracting Out: Patterns among the American States', *Journal of Public Administration Research and Theory* 15(3): 393–419.

Clynch, Edward (1999) 'Contracting and Government: Some Further Thoughts', *Public Administration and Management: An Interactive Journal* 4(2). http://pamij.com/99_4_2_Clynch.html

Cohen, Steven and Eimicke, William (2000) 'The Need for Strategic Information Systems Planning when Contracting Out and Privatizing Public Sector Functions', in G. Gason (ed.), *Handbook of Public Information Systems*. New York: Marcell Decker.

Cohen, Steven and Eimicke, William (2008) *Responsible Contract Manager: Protecting the Public Interest in an Outsourced World*. Washington, DC: Georgetown University Press.

Cooper, Phillip J. (2003) *Governing by Contract: Challenges and Opportunities for Public Managers*. Washington, DC: CQ Press.

Corporation for Public Broadcasting (2004) *Code of Ethics and Business Conduct for Employees of the Corporation for Public Broadcasting.* Washington, DC: Office of the General Counsel.

Drucker, Peter (1999) *Management Challenges for the 21st Century.* New York: Harper Business Press.

Ferris, J.M. (1986) 'The Decision to Contract Out: An Empirical Analysis', *Urban Affairs Quarterly* 22(2): 289.

Finn, Dan (2008) *The British 'Welfare Market,' Lessons from Contracting Out Welfare to Work Programmes in Australia and the Netherlands.* Joseph Rowntree Foundation. http://www.jrf.org.uk/sites/files/jrf/2306-welfare-unemployment-services.pdf

Friedrich, Carl J. (1937) *Constitutional Government and Politics.* New York: Harper and Brother.

Frumkin, Peter (2002) *Service Contracting with Nonprofit and For-profit Providers: On Preserving a Mixed Organizational Ecology.* Washington, DC: Brookings Institution Press.

Goldsmith, Stephen and Eggers, William D. (2004) *Governing by Network: The New Shape of the Public Sector.* Washington, DC: Brookings Institution Press.

Gray, Cheryl W. and Kaufmann, Daniel (1998) 'Corruption and Development'. *Finance and Development* 35(March): 7–10.

Institute of Public Administration (2005) Government Integrity. www.theipa.org/programs/eac.html (accessed 29 November, 2005).

Krislov, Samuel and Rosenbloom, David H. (1981) *Representative Bureaucracy and the American Political System.* New York: Praeger.

Olsen, Johan P. (2005) 'What's New about the New Public Management? Administrative Change in the Human Services', *Public Administration Review* 65(6): 713–27.

Osborne, David and Hutchinson, Peter (2004) *The Price of Government: Getting the Results We Need in an Age of Permanent Fiscal Crisis.* New York: Basic Books.

Peters, Thomas and Waterman, Robert (1982) *In Search of Excellence.* New York: HarperCollins.

Project on Government Oversight (PDGO) (2004) 'The Politics of Contracting'. http://www.pogo.org/p/contracts/c/co-040101-contractor.html.

Romzek, Barbara S. and Johnston, Jocelyn M. (2005) 'State Social Services Contracting: Exploring the Determinants of Effective Contract Accountability', *Public Administration Review* 65(4): 436–49.

Sanger, M. Bryna (2003) *The Welfare Marketplace: Privatization and Welfare Reform.* Washington, DC: The Brookings Institution.

Savas, E.S. (2005) *Privatization in the City: Successes, Failures, Lessons.* Washington, DC: CQ Press.

Sclar, Elliott D. (2000) *You Don't Always Get What You Pay for: The Economics of Privatization.* Ithaca, NY: Cornell University Press.

US GAO (2009) *American Recovery and Reinvestment Act: GAO's Role in Helping to Ensure Accountability and Transparency.* Washington, DC: GAO-09-453T.

Transparency International (2005) 'Preventing Corruption in Public Contracting'. http://www.corisweb.org/article/archive/322.

United States Office of Government Ethics (2005) 'Impartiality in Performing Official duties'. http://www.usoge.gov/pages/common_ethics_issues/common_ethics_issues_pg2.html#Anchor–Impartiali-23629 (accessed 28 December, 2005).

World Bank (2005) 'Glossary of Key Civil Service Terms', *Administrative & Civil Service Reform.* http://web.worldbank.org/WBSITE/EXTERNAL/TOPICS/EXTPUBLICSECTORANDGOVERNANCE/0,,contentMDK:20201644~pagePK:210058~piPK:210062~theSitePK:286305,00.html.

16

Public Management

Carolyn J. Heinrich

INTRODUCTION

Ongoing debate about the distinctions, or lack thereof, between public management and public administration, and increasingly, governance, begs an upfront discussion of the definition of public management and its relationship to public administration and governance. A thoughtful review of this discourse in the literature could easily fill an entire chapter, and prominent scholars have published seminal works on this subject that could not be adequately apprised here (see, for example, Hood, 1989, 1991; Lynn, 1996, 2003, 2006). Instead, I begin by highlighting important conceptual differences between public *administration* and public *management* and follow with a more extensive discussion of contemporary conceptions of public management and a description of important changes in the guiding principles, structures, processes, and statecraft of public management, including the new public management (NPM) reforms. I next consider alternative assessments of the impact of NPM reforms, and the chapter concludes with a discussion of future directions and ongoing challenges in the study and practice of public management.

WHAT IS PUBLIC MANAGEMENT?

Early definitions of public administration did not distinguish between *management* and *administration*, using one to define the other; nor was the primacy of either established (Lynn, 2005). Stoked by the works of Goodnow (1900), White (1926) and others, debate over the central features of public administration intensified in the twentieth century, leading up to the report of the President's (Brownlow) Committee on *Administrative Management* (1937) and its accompanying volume of papers (Gulick and Urwick, 1937). The Brownlow report articulated the following basic underpinnings of public administration: a separation between politics and *administration*; neutral competence or the delegation of power within hierarchical structures to managers with "administrative expertise'; administrative efficiency built into the structure of government*;* executive authority, and control by *administrative* law. Administrative principles set forth in France and Germany at this time were highly consistent, similarly embracing the politics–administration dichotomy, the formulation of rules (based on scientific study) to enhance efficiency, and a highly structured approach to administrative law (Lynn, 2006).

In his 1933 writings for President Hoover, Leonard White first introduced the term 'the New Management,' yet subsequent administrative reforms still reflected little conceptual distinction between administration and management and continued with a 'scientific managerialism' emphasis. The First (1947–49) and Second (1953–55) Hoover Commissions, for example, strongly adhered to the idea that 'management research technicians' should advise policy and executive agency decisions. The series of reforms that followed in the 1960s and 1970s, including the Planning Programming Budgeting System (PPBS), Zero-Base Budgeting (ZBB), and management by objectives (MBO), promoted the application of technical and legal expertise in objective, 'systems analysis' of the efficiency of public programs. These reforms were readily embraced by other central governments as well, including the adoption of PPBS by Canada's Department of National Revenue, the Netherlands in its Government Accounts Act of 1976, and by the Department of Education and Science in England.

The 1970s ultimately became a watershed time in both the study and practice of public administration and management. Works such as Guttman and Willner's *The Shadow Government* (1976: xii) were among the first to call attention to significant changes in how the federal government was managing its responsibilities and accomplishing its goals through an 'invisible bureaucracy' of private, for-profit, and non-profit firms that were increasingly contracted to 'suggest, shape, and even implement much governmental policy in both its narrowest and broadest sense.' A decided shift away from an emphasis on hierarchical (tight, rule-based supervisor–subordinate relationships) and legal (compliance-oriented, external oversight) approaches to management and accountability was taking place, moving toward looser professional and political mechanisms that were more likely to defer to experts guided

by professional norms and broad parameters for performance outcomes (O'Toole, 1997; Romzek, 1998; Milward and Provan, 2000; Kettl, 2002). Leading scholars in the new public policy schools were simultaneously arguing for more emphasis on the political roles of public managers in traditional executive functions such as agenda setting, control and strategic management of resources, and political positioning and steering (Moore, 1995; Lynn, 1996).

Although continuity was evident in the managerial aspects of newly emerging conceptions of public management, interest in normative questions of the field intensified, such as: How is accountability to the public upheld in the context of complex governance arrangements that obscure sector lines? Lynn (1998), a foremost scholar in setting the intellectual agenda of public management, argued that long-standing public *administration* questions about the roles of executives, policy analysts, policy experts, and managers in priority setting and policy implementation could not be effectively addressed in isolation of contemporary public *management* questions about the roles of institutions, administrative structures, incentives, and accountability for government performance. At the same time, a strong case has yet to be made that a distinctive disciplinary perspective or intellectual tradition of public management has emerged. 'Public administration has become public management, and public management has become public administration,' states Moynihan (2007: 149), and Lynn (2006: 10) comments that for some, 'public management is nothing more than traditional public administration with a fashionable new label ... .' But what may, perhaps, be truly novel is an expanded tolerance for a diversity of theories and perspectives, as scholars explore new applications of theory and models to grasp and explain new public management challenges associated with decentralization and devolution, privatization and contracting out, and networks and other "hybrid" or collaborative arrangements for achieving public goals.

Defining public management

Many definitions of public management have been offered in the literature, some varying appreciably in their conceptual depth. Rather than discussing and comparing a large number of them, I briefly discuss a conceptual definition set forth by Lynn (2003, 2006) and elaborated by Hill and Lynn (2009) in their textbook, which brings together key elements common to many other definitions in a reasonably tight and coherent way. At first glance, their formal definition of public management comes across as particularly generic: 'the process of ensuring that the allocation and use of resources available to the government are directed toward the achievement of lawful public policy goals.' But in elaborating three core dimensions of public management – structure, culture, and craft – both the richness and utility of this conceptual definition for research and practice become apparent.

Enduring importance of structure

Structure is the component that most clearly embodies traditional public administration principles. For all the urgent discussion of a shift away from administrative structures to 'tools' of governance (Salamon, 1989) and of the 'de-bureaucratization' of authority, one is hard-pressed to find a theoretical or empirical work that rejects an important role for 'formal and lawful delegations of authority and specific responsibility to designated officials and organizations …' to advance the achievement of public goals (Hill and Lynn, 2009: 139). This conceptualization of structure encompasses modern-day governance tools such as networks and 'quangos' (quasi-autonomous, non-governmental organizations) and diverse sources of delegated authority such as statutes, executive orders, lawful rules and regulations and court decisions, as well as internal sources (e.g. managerial decisions and directives). Thus, while their definition is specific in its reference to *formal* authority, it is also applicable to 'loosely coupled' organizations that rely more on horizontal or collaborative ties in carrying out the business of government.

Most network theorists, for example, emphasize the interdependent, relational, and non-subordinate aspects of these organizing arrangements, yet it is practically impossible to find a description of a network that is devoid of a vertical or *hierarchical* line of delegated authority. In an ongoing study of networks for the delivery of mental health services in Arizona, Milward et al. (2010) identify very clear, hierarchical relationships that grant authority for network operations, starting with the Arizona Department of Health Services Division of Behavioral Health Services that contracts with community-based organizations or private firms to govern the mental health services system. These intermediary organizations, known as Regional Behavioral Health Authorities (RBHAs), in turn contract with networks of service providers to deliver a full range of behavioral healthcare services. The contracts, between the state and the RBHAs and the RBHAs and their provider networks, have explicit structural features (e.g. a term for re-bidding, payment conditions and other rules governing service delivery) that both direct and shape service provision and client outcomes. In their study of different levels of network management in more than 100 English local government units, Walker, O'Toole and Meier (2007) distinguished between network structures and network behavior (or 'networking') and likewise concluded that in addition to the managerial choices of individual network actors, 'hierarchy matters' importantly in determining network initiation and networking interaction patterns and functioning.

Recognizing the role of culture

Whereas structure was central to traditional public *administration*, culture – the 'informal aspects of organization,' such as values, beliefs, shared norms, ethics, and individual motives (Hill and Lynn, 2009: 192) – was a relatively neglected feature. Diverging from the administrative management perspective, the early, renowned writings of organization theorist Chester Barnard (1938) urged more attention to the integral role of incentives, norms, and the 'social character' of organizations (relative to clear channels of hierarchical authority and rule-based processes), yet they had little immediate influence on subsequent reforms or prevailing conceptions of skillful public administration. In this regard, the rise of organizational culture as an essential and influential element in effective government functioning, both in shaping the decisions of public managers and as a feature that public managers can mold, was a significant contribution of evolving theories of public management in the 1970s and 1980s.

In fact, the NPM reforms that followed were as much about cultural change as they were about structural transformation and new tools of government action. The bold efforts of the Thatcher government and Reagan administration in initiating reforms to increase government efficiency were palpably focused on changing both organizational incentives and individual employee motives in ways that mimicked the private sector: for example, promoting organizational values such as transparency and accountability for results and rationally linking employee efforts to their pay and other rewards for improving organizational performance. Moynihan and Pandey (2005: 425) describe this type of cultural change as realignment toward a 'mission-based culture,' i.e. 'one that frames for employees a focus on results rather than a procedural approach toward work.' Such changes, they suggest, were so pervasive in the last two decades of the twentieth century as to have ushered in a new era of 'government by performance management' (p. 422).

Cultivating craft

The third element of Hill and Lynn's (2009) conceptual definition of public management – craft, or 'skilled practice' – is described by Lynn (2006) as an 'intentional departure' from traditional public administration perspectives on managerial roles, which saw

managers as relying exclusively on formal authority and impartially applying the laws of the state. A managerial craft perspective focuses instead on individual public managers' need to draw on leadership and entrepreneurial capabilities, political and strategic management skills, as well as their technocratic competencies in responding to challenges and opportunities they face in governing. At the same time, the most constructive views of managerial craft recognize that managers operate within institutional settings, with their formal (structural) and informal (cultural) attributes, that both facilitate and frustrate their leadership and entrepreneurial efforts, and indeed, demand creative managerial talent to advance organizational goals. The increasing devolution of important federal government responsibilities to state and local governments and third-party organizations has exacerbated the need for managerial craft, particularly, when there is ambiguity in the authorizing legislation or mandate that allows for substantial judgment on the part of managers in shaping and implementing public policy.

The importance of understanding the role of craft in government outcomes is argued convincingly in Brodkin's (2007) study of welfare policy reforms. She suggests that although there is considerable focus on formal policy that is written into law, as in the 1996 welfare reforms, the 'less glamorous but fundamental challenge lies in the seemingly mundane functions of administration' that give social policies their 'practical legal meaning' as they are translated into practice (p. 2). Discretionary judgments that are 'more art than science' are particularly critical in social services provision, such as recognizing barriers to self-sufficiency and deciding if a single mother is capable of full-time work, or trying to determine how an agency's limited resources can best be used to support client efforts to meet work and family responsibilities. The 1980s NPM reforms championed discretion by devolving more authority to state and county welfare agencies, some of which subsequently contracted with private sector agencies to encourage use of innovative strategies and incentives. Despite their promise to change the compliance-oriented welfare office culture, however, Brodkin concludes that institutional barriers – inadequate funding, a lack of professional skills among staff, and other limits to organizational capacity – impeded the success of welfare reform and contributed to new problems, such as gaming of performance measures and other malfeasant practices to reduce welfare caseloads (e.g. indifference, 'red tape' or excessive proceduralism, etc.).

From public management to governance

To the extent that there are real differences, conceptually and practically, between public administration and public management, the term *governance* may make them less relevant, having come into fashion as a more intellectually inclusive concept that encompasses both, as well as a wide range of governing arrangements. Indeed, a recent article in the *American Economic Review* on governance and economic activity points out that in the 1970s, the word governance is mentioned in the economics literature just five times; by the end of 2008, it had appeared 33,177 times (Dixit, 2009). Broadly construed, governance is the exercise of authority, public or private, "concerned with creating the conditions for ordered rule and collective action" (Milward and Provan, 2000: 360). Governance thus comprises both formal and informal relationships, with public and private agents, in what Lynn, Heinrich and Hill (2001: 7) describe as 'regimes of laws, rules, judicial decisions, and administrative practices that constrain, prescribe, and enable the provision of publicly supported goods and services.'

For some, governance is the continuation and broadening of public management trends that are transforming government as we know it, changing the structures through which state and society engage (from horizontal to vertical, tightly-controlled to dispersed and relational, public to private), while at the same time presenting new challenges for democratic control, representation, and accountability. George Frederickson (2005: 283) suggests that this is what Harlan Cleveland had in mind when he first argued in the 1970s that people want 'less government and more governance,' i.e. more decentralized, consultative power-sharing in new public–private configurations. For others, Frederickson notes, 'governance is the new public management' (p. 7).

THE NEW PUBLIC MANAGEMENT AND RELATED REFORMS

In descriptively (and retrospectively) mapping the amalgamation of managerial reforms and related institutional changes that were sweeping across the United States, the United Kingdom, Canada, Australia, New Zealand, and elsewhere in Europe, Hood (1991: 3) introduced the term 'New Public Management' as a loose, 'shorthand name' for 'a set of broadly similar administrative doctrines' that were dominating bureaucratic reform agendas in many developed countries as early as the 1970s. The impetus for these reforms, alluded to in the preceding discussion, included increasing public demands for a more efficient or 'business-like' government, the corresponding development of new public–private partnerships through devolution and contracting out of public service responsibilities to local 'quasi-public' and private partners and networks of organizations, and the ensuing expectations for a more responsive, 'customer-oriented' service delivery approach and for more information and evidence on government performance.

The substantial number of differing characterizations of NPM in the literature reflects, in part, the varying circumstances (political, institutional, and economic) that shaped the nature of these reforms in different contexts and countries and the confluence of many different public management reforms emerging in the final decades of the twentieth century. For example, both Margaret Thatcher and Ronald Reagan came into their roles in a period of serious economic recession with explicit agendas to reduce the size of government, and both were ideologically oriented toward market principles and the belief that increasing the role of the private sector would bring about significant efficiencies in the public sector. The Thatcher government launched the Financial Management Initiative (FMI) in 1982 to improve UK public sector financial management through the devolution of responsibility for budget and financial controls and corresponding changes in institutional rules and procedures. Australia initiated the Financial Management Improvement Program at the same time with the same basic goals. In New Zealand, a 'thermostat-like' system of managerial control was designed, in which managers were given clear objectives and the freedom to manage, along with quality information to enable them to make more efficient resource allocation decisions (Norman and Gregory, 2003). As Barzelay (2001: 69) explains, in each of these cases, 'the policy problem was defined in terms of organizational inefficiency, and the policy stream was stocked with ideas about how to change the administrative systems of government, especially in financial management.'

The UK Next Steps Initiative, one of the most visible and salient of NPM reforms, followed in 1998 with the central objective of 'mimicking corporate management' (Lynn, 2006: 118). Departments in the UK government were given the option to restructure as executive agencies, led by chief executives with fixed-term contracts who reported directly to ministers. Other facets included more discretionary control accorded to decentralized units, increased flexibility in hiring, and the use of rewards and other private sector management tools to improve efficiency and performance (Hood, 1991). Simultaneously, New Zealand was developing a comprehensive system for strategic planning, outputs-based budgeting, accrual accounting, and performance indicators, and both the UK and New Zealand reforms were viewed as a catalyst for the introduction of similar systems worldwide (Norman, 2002).

The crest of the US NPM reforms made less of a splash, in part because the major elements described above had been gradually working their way into public management practice, even before Reagan's reform efforts and the 'Reinventing Government' initiative that followed. The Reagan administration accelerated the already-growing trend toward decentralized and devolved (third-party) responsibility for public services provision, aggressively increasing the use of revenue-sharing, user fees and competitive, performance-based contracting in public programs. The Job Training Partnership Act (JTPA) of 1982, for example, introduced what is still regarded as one of the most highly developed public sector performance management systems, including mandatory performance measures and standards, accounting and performance reporting rules, and monitoring and rewarding/sanctioning of agency performance. In effect, the underpinnings for the Reinventing Government platform advanced by the Clinton administration had been largely established by the time the influential work of Osborne and Gaebler (1992) and the report of Clinton's National Performance Review formalized these themes and principles into a "movement" to improve government performance.

The emphasis on performance management in subsequent initiatives was pervasive, and other elements of public management reforms at this time – reducing 'red tape,' empowering individuals and organizations to streamline processes and develop new partnerships with devolved decision-making, and incentivizing innovation – were likewise directed at 'getting results.' The 1993 Government Performance and Results Act (GPRA) took these reform efforts government-wide. Continuing today, federal agencies are required under GPRA to establish performance goals, measures, and plans, to provide evidence of their performance relative to targets, and to report their results annually to the public. In addition, the Program Assessment Rating Tool (PART) introduced by George W. Bush in 2002 sought to take these processes a step further by linking federal program dollars to rigorous proof of results achieved. Moynihan and Pandey (2005: 422) note that 'whether classified as New Public Management (NPM) or reinvention,' a core assumption of these global reform movements was that 'changes in management systems could and should be made in ways that enhanced performance.'

Assessing NPM and other public management reforms of recent decades

NPM has been described as a doctrine – a set of arguments about how the government should be managed – and yet scholars differ considerably in their views of the central doctrinal content of NPM, and the extent to which the core ideas are *new*. Hood and Jackson (1991) identified no less than 99 different administrative doctrines, tracing the origins of NPM tenets such as transparent management, pay for performance, and private sector involvement in public service provision as far back as Jeremy Bentham's writings of the late eighteenth and nineteenth centuries. Moynihan (2006) argues, however, that these subcomponents of NPM would not have achieved the same degree of prominence without their simultaneous implementation in the NPM benchmark countries. He shows how the interdependence of these elements is key to what is new about the NPM – authority is devolved and managers are empowered with flexibility to achieve goals, but only in conjunction with more highly developed, formal systems of accountability that focus on results produced.

Of course, doctrine, fashionable principles or a new ideology of how to manage are one thing, and the successful implementation of organizational change and new management tools and reforms that translate into measurable improvements in government performance are another. For example, in his empirical study of Dutch 'quangos,' which were extolled for their flexibility, Bertelli (2006) noted the trade-off between two NPM features, accountability and autonomy. Although 'quangos seem to be the answer to the problem of agency design in the New Public Management era,' he observed (p. 240), as the Dutch quangos became more autonomous, the challenges to ensuring their accountability to the public grew. Yet paradoxically, the quangos in his study with the most task discretion and least legal liability were also the *least* likely to publicly report spending priorities and financial performance, suggesting that a key component of NPM, accountability for results, was falling short in practice.

Governance by networks has likewise been described as well-suited to solving difficult public management problems through the freedom it accords employees from rule-driven processes and the opportunities for experimentation, innovation, and sharing of best practices in collaborative relationships (O'Toole, 2000; Kamarck, 2002). Local governments and their non-governmental partners, it is argued, are better able to identify and respond to the diverse preferences, values, and needs of citizens and to facilitate new channels for citizen participation. This has also been articulated as governing *with* society instead of *above* society (Klijn, 2005), an idea with particular relevance for social services delivery, which has seen some of the greatest growth in third-party involvement but also heightened concern about the impacts of these governance changes on vulnerable constituencies (Salamon, 1989; Rivlin, 1992).

An example of this, and perhaps a 'poster child' for networked government success, is the Florida Department of Children and Families (DCF), which recruited more than 2400 community partners – a mix of government and non-governmental organizations, including local workforce development centers, county public health offices, senior citizen centers, food banks, libraries, faith-based organizations, and others – to help connect constituents with benefits (welfare, Medicaid, and food stamps). Participation as a community partner is voluntary, and partners specify the scope of services that they would like to offer, within guidelines established by DCF. DCF supports these informal networks by providing training and program support, organizing quarterly community partners meetings to increase networking, and serving as a central repository for partner information and the sharing of best practices. The *ACCESS Florida* model – recognized in 2007 with an Innovations in American Government Award for having increased access points to DCF benefits by 1500%, while simultaneously cutting service costs by almost 30%, reducing DCF staff by 43%, and achieving a 95% customer satisfaction rate – has been replicated in state governments throughout the United States.

It is also important to point out, though, that the drivers of innovation in the Florida DCF were primarily internal, and program control has stayed squarely with the state government and its regional offices. Despite the considerable downsizing, traditional lines of hierarchy and control are largely intact, and even as DCF cultivated its extensive network of community-based partners, it was careful to protect its authority and control in the critical function of eligibility determination. This has allowed the program to avoid one of the trade-offs most frequently discussed in the literature: i.e. between flexibility and innovation and the constitutional values of equity, transparency, and accountability, which have been steadfastly associated with traditional bureaucratic structures and their central control mechanisms. As Sheila Seuss Kennedy (2006) cautioned, freedom from rule-driven processes frequently blurs the boundaries of government's legal responsibilities and may undercut the role and efficacy of the courts in protecting and supporting citizens' constitutional rights

and privileges. The state's role in the success of the DCF network is also consistent with O'Toole and Meier's (2004) finding that networking efforts generally pay bigger 'dividends' if the government is an important source of resources for inter-organizational management and networking.

Other public management scholars have shown, however, that the bureaucratic process controls that were supposed to be replaced by flexibility and 'freedom to manage' were not only retained in many cases but also were intensified or formalized in the course of NPM reforms (Light, 1993; Pollitt et al., 1999). Dunleavy et al. (2006: 470–1) reported that New Zealand's pioneering NPM structural reforms 'left a country of 3.5 million people with over three hundred separate central agencies and forty tiny ministries, in addition to local and health service authorities,' and a degree of administrative fragmentation that contributed to its dismal economic performance. Quasi-government agencies in the United Kingdom and elsewhere were likewise beginning to see the burdens of costly and duplicative separate management hierarchies for comparable functions, leading the OECD (2004) to criticize the growing number of autonomous arm's-length public bodies impeding effective policy action. Christopher Hood and Guy Peters (2004: 271) described this as 'a new form of Tocquevillian paradox, with the unintentional production in many domains of bureaucratic activity of a style even more rules based and process driven than the "traditional" forms of public bureaucracy that NPM was meant to supplant.'

Indeed, for all of the scholarly stocktaking, intellectual dueling, and labeling of transformations of governance, there is still comparatively little rigorous empirical evidence of substantial changes in public management and improvements in government outcomes. In a 2010 symposium in the *Journal of Public Administration Research and Theory*, an assembly of scholars conducting theoretical and empirical public management research set as their goal to engage some of the focal questions about these governance changes and to sharpen the discussion by bringing new empirical evidence to bear on key arguments and assertions in the ongoing debate about the effects of recent public management changes. What is the evidence, Heinrich, Lynn and Milward (2010) ask, that government control and democratic responsiveness are loosening or slipping away as a result of these changes? Is the public sector drifting into a 'state of agents,' with widely dispersed and diluted government authority and ineffectual accountability? Or is there a growing chorus of public managers and their private sector agents who are singing the praises of a less intrusive government that has left them more empowered and less burdened by hierarchical structures and official rules? Or alternatively, has little changed in practice, so that the essential nature of government today is simply a new configuration (with more players and more tools) in mostly the same institutional settings? Of course, questions about the implications of public management changes for government performance, which is especially challenging to measure in contexts where it relies largely on third parties to carry out core functions and responsibilities, are also critical.

Evidence (or the lack thereof) on public management changes

Few dispute that there has been a steady, long-term transformation away from direct service provision by government to increasingly central roles for third parties, and the symposium contributors affirm that *how* the government arranges for them to perform their roles has important implications for what is accomplished. In their study of relational contracting, Bertelli and Smith (2010) show how both vertical and horizontal forms of control can simultaneously exist and be effectively managed, including in the face of unexpected contingencies or shocks to these relationships. They suggest that while the growth in third-party governance may "stretch" traditional lines of authority and accountability, bureaucratic control firmly continues, in part through the use and effective management of relational contracts in the public sector. Milward et al. (2010) confirm this finding in their comparative analysis of the evolution of two community mental health networks contracted with the State of Arizona, which both operate under the same set of rules but are governed through alternative network forms. Resources flow into these two networks hierarchically from federal, state, and county sources, and contracts and informal vertical relationships determine their allocation in the mental health system. Although they find distinct differences in the contracting behavior between the two networks, the informal relationships in each grew to resemble one other as the networks matured over time, leading them to conclude that the sector of the governing organization mattered little in the provision of quality services.

At the same time, the symposium contributors consistently find that there is considerable room for improvement in the level of oversight the government exercises in its relationship with third-party agents. Even if they are not engaging directly in service provision, governments play a far more vital role than just funding the services, and the organizational structures and incentives they establish to promote service quality, efficiency, and effectiveness importantly shape service outcomes. In their study of changes in US affordable housing policy that devolved authority from federal to lower levels of government and opened the door for the use of multiple policy instruments to encourage private developers to produce affordable housing, Elizabeth Graddy and Raphael Bostic (2010) explore the consequences of these policy changes for public authority and housing policy effectiveness. They conclude that coherent statewide plans, whether generated by the judiciary or the legislature, were essential to effectively overcome local resistance to affordable housing development. Yet in many states, there is no mechanism for enforcement by regional or state-level authorities to ensure the local production of affordable units, and no tracking of the production of these units. They suggest that this decentralized approach to affordable housing policy oversight not only generates little information with which to assess compliance but also likely perpetuates underprovision of affordable housing.

Chris Skelcher (2010) describes how these challenges to democratic policymaking and accountability are likewise growing in complexity in the European Union (EU), with the evolution of new supranational institutions and governance networks and partnerships that are accorded a high degree of autonomy in their specific jurisdictions. These partnerships and governing networks have horizontal dimensions, involving the interaction of actors around individual programs, and vertical dimensions that facilitate cooperation between programs across member states, as well as linkages to the EU that are mediated by regional and national governments. Thus, contrary to the tidy hierarchical structure that the theory of representative democracy assumes (i.e. linking elected representatives, public managers, third-party providers, and citizens), the resulting multilevel governance system mixes different tiers of government (with differing levels of capacity and control) in networks that formulate policy and deliver services through interactions with private sector and civil society actors. In earlier work, Rhodes (1994) expressed concern about these developments for EU member states, suggesting they are ceding functions and the reins of democratic accountability to the EU and its autonomous governing units and thereby risking a crumbling of the state. As Lynn (2006: 144) elaborates, 'the shift of responsibility for public service delivery to more distant and autonomous agents excludes or minimizes constitutionally authorized forms of accountability,' which may imperil traditional public service values such as equity, transparency, and responsiveness to the public interest. Others, however, such as Olsen (2003), downplay the role of NPM in

the EU and suggest that the member states have largely resisted administrative impositions and the transfer of state responsibilities to the EU.

At the core of these issues concerning administrative control, democratic accountability, and responsiveness to the public is the question as to whether these new governance tools are mostly *supplementing* or *supplanting* more traditional public administration structures and levers of control. Thus far, the empirical evidence appears to suggest that there is more supplementing than supplanting: i.e. this is not a 'bold new era of the hollow state' (Rhodes, 1994: 149). This is not to say that there was not ever a risk of hollowed-out public management capacity, however, as there are case examples of governments reversing course and taking back control of essential functions, and a growing recognition by scholars and practitioners of the need to retain or strengthen government management capacity in the context of long chains of delegation and multifaceted governance arrangements (Kettl, 1993; Hefetz and Warner, 2004). Indeed, it is in these areas where I think the frontiers of public management research lie: How can we better organize and manage these complex, multilevel, third-party governance arrangements and more accurately measure their performance outcomes so as to achieve accountability for results?

ONGOING CHALLENGES AND FUTURE DIRECTIONS IN PUBLIC MANAGEMENT

Public sector efforts to advance performance management may turn out to be one of the most far-reaching and enduring facets of NPM reforms. Performance management is now a goal or function of most governmental and non-governmental organizations, and many governments worldwide are also attaching higher stakes to the achievement of performance outcomes through the use of performance-contingent pay, organization-wide performance bonuses, and competitive performance-based contracting. That said, as it stands today, performance management probably falls into the category of NPM-related reforms that Christopher Hood and Guy Peters (2004: 272) have described as 'triumph of hope over experience' – we repeatedly introduce performance management reforms, despite recurring disappointments in their usefulness and effectiveness.

In his extensive studies of New Zealand's performance management system, described as one of the most advanced in the world, Richard Norman (2002) interviewed senior public managers and public servants in a cross-section of 27 public service organizations about their views on the desirability and effectiveness of performance management. Although, as he notes, interviewees were unvaryingly in favor of key principles and goals of these reforms, such as transparency and accountability, they differed considerably in their overall assessments of their value and effectiveness. In analyzing the interview data, he distinguished three categories of perspectives that I think capture more generally the major (and diverse) views of performance management in government today:

- 'true believers,' who think performance management has not gone far enough, and that more emphasis on outcomes and better measures of them is needed
- 'pragmatic skeptics,' who see performance management as 'part of a new game of public management,' taking the objectives and measures 'with a grain of salt' and reading between the lines in looking at performance reports
- 'active doubters,' who see the processes of performance management as burdensome routines that are 'more form than substance' and miss the meaning in what is essentially political, 'relationship-based work' (p. 622).

Lack of confidence in the performance information being collected affected the views of public managers in each of these groups, but their reactions were also influenced by their roles: i.e. politician vs public servant; an agency manager under the gun to produce vs an advisor to performance management system design; cabinet ministers vs chief executives, etc.

In designing and implementing public sector performance management systems, we have unfortunately given far more attention to structure than we have to culture or craft. In successive attempts to implement pay-for-performance schemes, governments have emphasized technical systems and incentives that will result in more business-like organizations focused on 'bottom line' outcomes, with the expectation that they will significantly improve the performance of employees and their organizations (Hood and Peters, 2004). An OECD study (2005) based on nearly 1000 interviews of public managers in 11 agencies and 5 countries reported that many have felt more constrained in their ability to decide on and reward good performers, in part because of the necessary standardization of performance measures across governmental units, but also because systems were not well understood or accepted by managers. In addition, probably because of the standardization and adherence to performance management system rules, the OECD study did not find any evidence of bias in the distribution of performance awards, yet only one in three public managers thought the distribution was equitable and appropriate. In her study of the implementation of GPRA, Beryl Radin (2000) similarly concluded that rather than freeing public managers to focus on results, performance requirements under GPRA have increased administrative constraints, elevated conflict among multiple levels of program management, and engendered distrust between agencies and legislators about gaming of measures. The 'skeptics' and 'doubters' in Norman's study (2002) probably got it right in suggesting that missing from these system design efforts has been attention to relationships, informal processes, and leadership roles in motivating performance.

Frontiers in contracting and performance management

In light of the significant challenges that governments worldwide have experienced in monitoring and managing third-party governance arrangements and measuring government performance, what are the next frontiers in both research and practice in these areas? One area that will continue to be critical is government contracting, both internal and external and formal and informal (or relational). Broadly conceptualized, a public manager can arrange an internal contract with government employees that fully specifies their job tasks and performance goals and expectations, or the government can establish a contract with a third party that similarly defines the primary work tasks, expected outcomes, and other aspects of the exchange relationship (e.g. price, quality, quantity, residual rights of control, etc.). Performance-based contracts can likewise be internal, such as the pay-for-performance schemes that have been widely used or tried in government, or external, such as contracts with third parties that make at least some part of their compensation contingent on performance.

One of the more recently developing areas of contracting, mentioned earlier, is relational contracting. Relational contracts may be arranged between organizations (horizontal), as well as within an organization (vertical) between managers and employees. The core of the relational contract is built on trust and cooperation – i.e. the mutual desire of both parties to continue the relationship – and thus, it typically does not involve any third-party enforcement (such as the courts). Relational contracts may develop alongside of and enhance or expand the arrangements specified in a formal contract, which in the context of the increasingly complex, multilevel governance arrangements described by Hood, Skelcher, and others, offers an alternative approach to knottier lines of administrative control and more inflexible tools of performance accountability that

might otherwise be employed. Another advantage of the relational contract identified by Bertelli and Smith (2010) is its explicit acknowledgement of the social and political institutions and informal rules and norms that inevitably shape contractual exchanges.

In a case study of the Coast Guard's contractual exchanges with a private consortium to upgrade and integrate its entire fleet of air and sea assets (known as the Deepwater project), Brown, Potoski and Van Slyke (2010) illustrate the public management challenges involved in a highly complex, multi-layered set of formal and relational contracting arrangements between the government and its non-governmental partners, in circumstances characterized by limited information and unanticipated economic and political contingencies. They describe three contractual layers that specified the terms of exchange and the process by which the Coast Guard and the contracting firm would collaborate in the design and production of the Deepwater products. One of these contractual layers was a pledge, invoking 'partnership' language, to engage in cooperative strategies for navigating the contract complexities and working toward a set of products that would satisfy the needs and expectations of the Coast Guard. In effect, the contract design, with both formal and relational features, left a wide scope for discretion and either cooperative or opportunistic behavior on the part of both partners. Although Brown, Potoski and Van Slyke find that both parties were disappointed with the contract outcomes, they argue that because these types of complex contracts are prone to renegotiation, the prospect of a long-term relationship leaves the door open to more cooperative strategies to cultivate norms of reciprocity and trust and the possibility of future success.

Indeed, contract and incentive system designers typically will not know in advance all of the ways in which the structural, cultural, and craft aspects of a given system will interact to influence individual and organizational responses to the incentives established by the contract specifications and performance requirements. Inevitably, distortions generated by imperfect performance measures and incomplete contracts will become known, as will the responses of workers or third-party agents, which are likely to depend on their roles and level of intrinsic motivation or identification with organizational goals, as well as their rate of learning about how their actions influence measured performance (Heinrich and Marschke, 2010). Thus, even if a government has designed a contract or performance management system that initially suggests shrewd attention to formal and informal aspects of organizational functioning and a strong correlation between performance measures and desired outcomes, over time, its effectiveness may decline as pragmatic-skeptic types learn how to game the measures and other limitations of the measures and system design become known. Public managers therefore need to appreciate and confront the evolutionary dynamic that is inherent in most contracting and performance management relationships with a willingness to renegotiate and to modify or discard contract and performance management features as their effects become known.

At times, though, an early step in the wrong direction in a contracting relationship will not be salvageable, or difficulties in contract specification, monitoring, or failures of government management or market capacity will require governments to pull back or 'contract back in' (Hefetz and Warner, 2004). In their study of contracting out of welfare services provision to for-profit firms, Dias and Maynard-Moody (2007) noted that performance-based contracting was advanced as an 'antidote' for organizational problems in welfare bureaucracies. As their research showed, however, requirements for meeting contract performance (job placement) goals and profit quotas stirred up tensions between managers and workers with different philosophies about the importance of meeting performance goals vs meeting client needs. For firm managers, the easiest way to meet job placement goals and make a profit was to

minimize the time and effort line staff devoted to each client, given the extensive individualized and sometimes emotional interactions that caseworkers had with clients. The managers therefore assigned larger caseloads to front-line staff to allow less individual time with clients, triggering an 'ideological war' with the public service-oriented staff that subsequently led to 'enduring and debilitating organizational problems' and failure on both sides to achieve the program goals (p. 199). Their study also provides an example of how a relational contract that recognized the role of professional norms and other aspects of culture in welfare services may have been preferred to the formal, performance-based contracting system that was used with these for-profit firms.

Recent work by Moynihan (2008) also suggests a way forward in performance management system design that might bring 'pragmatic skeptics' and 'active doubters' on board with continued efforts to measure and monitor performance. Moynihan sets forth an 'interactive dialogue model of performance information use' that involves the assembly and use of performance information as a form of 'social interaction' (p. 95). His approach assumes that performance information is ambiguous, subjective, and incomplete, and that context, institutional affiliation, and individual beliefs will affect its use, thereby challenging the rational suppositions underlying most performance management reforms to date. In addition, while most performance management reforms have emphasized the potential 'instrumental benefits' of performance management, such as increased accountability and transparency of government outcomes, Moynihan suggests that elected officials and public managers have been more likely to realize the 'symbolic benefits' of creating an impression that 'government is being run in a rational, efficient and results-oriented manner' (p. 68). He argues convincingly for the cultivation and use of strategic planning, learning forums, dialogue routines, and related approaches to more effective use of performance information and encourages the view that documentation of performance is not an 'end' but rather a means for engaging in policy and management change.

Evolving governance structures and tools and enduring issues of accountability

Increasing expectations for accountability for results have also amplified concerns about the limited control of governments, in light of the growing complexity of government structures and blurring of sector lines in alternative governance arrangements. In their study of US environmental policy and performance, for example, Kraft, Stephen and Abel (2011) describe a complicated array of policies that mandate the use of specific technologies and require achievement of new standards of environmental protection and community health. They point out that approximately 15,000 pages of federal regulations provide instructions for companies and other entities covered by laws – e.g., the Clean Air Act, Clean Water Act, Toxic Substances Control Act, Superfund and others that apply to the approximately 40,000 stationary air sources, 90,000 facilities with water permits, 425,000 hazardous waste facilities, 400,000 underground injection wells, and 173,000 drinking water systems – with some specifying in excruciating detail which chemicals are to be managed and how, and others delineating requirements for reporting, inspections, and penalties associated with the rules and violations of them. In addition, in response to criticism that US environmental policy has become excessively bureaucratic, inefficient, and lacking in incentives for compliance, new (mostly voluntary) alternatives to federal regulation have also been advanced, paralleling the public management reform efforts discussed above. These include voluntary public–private partnerships, greater use of market incentives and information disclosure, performance-based flexible regulation, and

collaborative processes open to citizen participation.

Information disclosure policies are one of the rapidly proliferating new governance tools, from campaign finance reforms to food and drug product labeling to school report cards and carbon footprint calculators, intended to promote transparency and accountability by empowering citizens with information that they can use to exert public pressure for change and bring about performance improvements. Although the Environment Protection Agency (EPA) credits its information disclosure programs with sharp and efficient reductions in the release of toxic chemicals, Kraft, Stephen and Abel's research argues against *replacing* federal regulation with non-regulatory policies. That is, these governance tools may be effective supplements for strengthening federal monitoring and accountability efforts, but they are not adequate to supplant traditional 'command and control' structures. They note that the compilation and dissemination of environmental performance information is costly, and it is frequently difficult to accurately calculate values for reporting in the required form. It appears, furthermore, that the information is not well understood by the public, and that it is at best an imperfect proxy for what people really want to know about the risks of toxic chemicals to their health. Thus, while some companies have made visible progress in better managing their use of chemicals through voluntary tools and coordinated strategies such as these, the results thus far in terms of improving accountability and environmental performance have been too uneven to move to dismantle the long-standing environmental policy regime, as costly and complex as it is.

These experiences with environmental policy reflect what is happening more widely in twenty-first century governance today, perhaps most evident in the recent crisis in the public and private financial management sectors. There is indeed an ongoing transformation of governance that is creating new challenges for public managers who address complex problems and public needs that require coordination across multiple levels of government and non-governmental, contracted entities and the use of new tools of governance to meet public responsibilities (Kettl, 2002). At the same time, after more than three decades of coming to terms with and adapting to these public management changes, it is time to ease back on the alarmist characterizations of these trends and the language that suggests our institutions are failing us. In his most recent book, *The Next Government of the United States*, Kettl (2009) provides examples where he suggests that 'no one was in charge' (p. 12) and 'no one is fully accountable for anything government does' (p. 125) and that we face 'exceptionally dangerous' problems with a government that is 'increasingly handcuffed' by the separation of powers and limited capacity for tackling 'big, inescapable, wicked problems' (p. 95). Kettl's tendency to focus on well-known public management breakdowns, such as the Federal Emergency Management Agency's failure in Hurricane Katrina, and to draw sweeping conclusions about a fragmented and fumbling public sector, distorts our image of government effectiveness, akin to the nightly news which is more likely to focus on the accidents and shocking crimes of the day rather than all of the beneficial and productive acts of society that occurred.

One of the lessons of Kraft, Stephen and Abel's study and the symposium articles discussed here is that the traditional, centralized elements of government structure – i.e. the formal and lawful delegations of authority and specific responsibility to designated officials and organizations, be they 'first,' 'second' or 'third' parties – continue to be key and powerful in shaping government action and outcomes. Even in contexts where non-governmental agencies with loosely defined boundaries are doing the primary work of government – mental health services, affordable housing, the integration of national defense assets, etc. – research shows that one can trace and find the lines of hierarchy and control intact, and, for the most

part, serving the essential purposes of allocation of authority, financial support, specification of expectations for performance, provision for monitoring and oversight, and a conduit for democratic accountability. In this light, it is not surprising that the Obama administration's early response to the first serious financial crisis of the twenty-first century has consisted of a significant tightening of government control and re-centralization of power and decision-making authority in the executive branch. And thus, while I concur with Kettl that recent experiences suggest that ensuring accountability will continue to be one of the greatest challenges of government today, I would also argue that there are probably more successes than failures to observe in governments innovating, trying, modifying, and re-evaluating their use of new and old tools of governance as they struggle to evolve and better manage in a rapidly changing, information-inundated, and globalizing society.

Dunleavy and colleagues (2006: 468) recently declared that 'the intellectually and practically dominant set of managerial and governance ideas of the last two decades, new public management (NPM), has essentially died in the water,' with the reversal of some key reform components. Contrary to their 'one step forward, two steps back' perspective, I would argue that if one adopts the organizational learning perspective suggested by Moynihan (2008), we have, in fact, learned a great deal through the variety of experiences of governments worldwide in attempting to implement a relatively unique convergence of reform efforts and new governance tools aimed at improving government performance and accountability. Although there have clearly been failures, or at least dashed expectations of perhaps inflated ideas of the extent to which basic elements of government would change, we have also come to better appreciate the role of traditional administrative structures and principles in guiding how we handle the new governance tools and complex third-party governance arrangements that are surely here to stay. Dunleavy et al. add that 'even analysts sympathetic to NPM have been driven to acknowledge that it is "middle-aged",' a characterization I do not dispute. Rather, I would instead point out some of the benefits that come with middle age, such as patience, wisdom, and reason drawn from experience, both successes and failures, in attempting bold change.

REFERENCES

Barnard, Chester (1938) *Functions of the Executive.* Cambridge, MA: Harvard University Press.

Barzelay, Michael (2001) *The New Public Management.* Berkeley, CA: University of California Press.

Bertelli, Anthony (2006) 'Governing the Quango: An Auditing and Cheating Model of Quasi-Governmental Authorities', *Journal of Public Administration Research and Theory* 16(2): 239–261.

Bertelli, Anthony and Smith, Craig (2010) 'Relational Contracting and Network Management', *Journal of Public Administration Research and Theory:* i21–i40.

Brodkin, Evelyn Z. (2007) 'Bureaucracy Redux: Management Reformism and the Welfare State', *Journal of Public Administration Research and Theory* 17(1): 1–17.

Brown,T.L. and Van Slyke, D.M (2010) 'Contracting for Complex Products', *Journal of Public Administration Research and Theory:* i41–i58.

Dias, Janice Johnson and Maynard-Moody, Stephen (2007) 'For-Profit Welfare: Contracts, Conflicts, and the Performance Paradox', *Journal of Public Administration Research and Theory* 17(2): 189–211.

Dixit, Avinash (2009) 'Governance Institutions and Economic Activity', *The American Economic Review* 99(1): 5–24.

Dunleavy, Patrick, Margetts, Helen, Bastow, Simon and Tinkler, Jane (2006) 'New Public Management is Dead–Long Live Digital-Era Governance', *Journal of Public Administration Research and Theory* 16(3): 467–94.

Frederickson, George F. (2005) 'Whatever Happened to Public Administration? Governance, Governance Everywhere', in Ewan Ferlie, Laurence E. Lynn, Jr and Christopher Pollitt (eds), *The Oxford Handbook of Public Management.* Oxford: Oxford University Press; pp. 282–304.

Goodnow, Frank J. (1900) *Politics and Administration: A Study in Government.* New York: The MacMillan Company.

Graddy, Elizabeth and Bostic, Raphael (2010) 'The Role of Private Agents in Affordable Housing', *Journal of Public Administration Research and Theory:* i81–i99.

Gulick, Luther and Urwick, Lyndall (eds) (1937) *Papers on the Science of Administration.* Institute of Public Administration, New York.

Guttman, Daniel and Willner, Barry (1976) *The Shadow Government.* New York: Pantheon Books.

Hefetz, A. and Warner, M. (2004) 'Privatization and Its Reverse: Explaining the Dynamics of the Government Contracting Process', *Journal of Public Administration Research and Theory* 14(2): 171–90.

Heinrich, Carolyn J. and Marschke, Gerald R. (2010) 'Incentives and Their Dynamics in Public Sector Performance Management Systems', *Journal of Policy Analysis and Management* 29(1): 183–208.

Heinrich, Carolyn J., Lynn, Laurence E., Jr and Milward, H. Brinton (2010) 'A *State of Agents*? Sharpening the Debate and Evidence over the Extent and Impact of the Transformation of Governance,' *Journal of Public Administration Research and Theory:* i59–i80.

Hill, Carolyn J. and Lynn, Laurence E., Jr (2009) *Public Management: A Three-Dimensional Approach.* Washington, DC: CQ Press.

Hood, Christopher (1989) 'Public Administration and Public Policy: Intellectual Challenges for the 1990s', *Australian Journal of Public Administration* 48(4): 346–58.

Hood, Christopher (1991) 'A Public Management for all Seasons?' *Public Administration* 69 (1): 3–19.

Hood, Christopher and Jackson, Michael W. (1991) 'The New Public Management: A Recipe for Disaster?', *Canberra Bulletin of Public Administration* 64: 16–24.

Hood, Christopher and Peters, Guy (2004) 'The Middle Aging of New Public Management: Into the Age of Paradox?', *Journal of Public Administration Research and Theory* 14(3): 267–82.

Kamarck, Elaine (2002) 'The End of Government as We Know It', in John D. Donahue and Joseph S. Nye, Jr. (eds), *Market Based Governance: Supply Side, Demand Side, Upside and Downside.* Washington, DC: Brookings Institution Press; pp. 227–63.

Kennedy, Sheila Seuss (2006) 'Holding "Governance" Accountable: Third-Party Government in a Limited State', *The Independent Review* XI(1): 67–77.

Kettl, Donald F. (1993) *Sharing Power: Public Governance and Private Markets.* Washington, DC: Brookings Institution Press.

Kettl, Donald F. (2002) *The Tranformation of Governance: Public Administration for Twenty-First Century America.* Baltimore, MD: Johns Hopkins University Press.

Kettl, Donald F. (2009) *The Next Government of the United States: Why Our Institutions Fail Us and How to Fix Them*. New York: W.W. Norton & Co.

Klijn, Erik-Hans (2005) 'Networks and Inter-organizational Management: Challenging, Steering, Evaluation, and the Role of Public Actors in Public Management', in Ewan Ferlie, Laurence E. Lynn, Jr and Christopher Pollitt (eds), *The Oxford Handbook of Public Management*. Oxford: Oxford University Press; pp. 257–81.

Kraft, Michael E., Stephen, Mark and Abel, Troy D. (2011) *Coming Clean: Information Disclosure and Environmental Performance*. Cambridge, MA: MIT Press.

Light, Paul C. (1993) *Monitoring Government: Inspectors-General and the Search for Accountability*. Washington DC: Brookings Institution Press.

Lynn, Laurence E., Jr (1996) *Public Management as Art, Science, and Profession*. Chatham, NJ: Chatham House.

Lynn, Laurence E., Jr (1998) 'The *New Public Management*: How to Transform a Theme into a Legacy', *Public Administration Review 58(3)*: 231–7.

Lynn, Laurence E., Jr (2003) 'Public Management', in Guy Peters and Jon Pierre (eds), *Handbook of Public Administration*. London: Sage; pp. 14–24.

Lynn, Laurence E., Jr (2005) 'Public Management: A Concise History of the Field', in Ewan Ferlie, Laurence E. Lynn, Jr and Christopher Pollitt (eds), *The Oxford Handbook of Public Management*. Oxford: Oxford University Press; pp. 27–50.

Lynn, Laurence E., Jr (2006) *Public Management Old and New*. New York: Routledge.

Lynn, Laurence E., Jr, Heinrich, Carolyn J. and Hill, Carolyn J. (2001) *Improving Governance: A New Logic for Empirical Research*. Washington, DC: Georgetown University Press.

Milward, H. Brinton and Provan, Keith G. (2000) 'Governing the Hollow State', *Journal of Public Administration Research and Theory* 10(2): 359–79.

Milward, H. Brinton, Provan, Keith G. and Fish, Amy (2010) 'Governance and Collaboration: An Evolutionary Study of Two Mental Health Networks', *Journal of Public Administration Research and Theory*: i125–i141.

Moore, Mark H. (1995) *Creating Public Value: Strategic Management in Government*. Cambridge, MA: Harvard University Press.

Moynihan, Donald P. (2006) 'Managing for Results in State Government: Evaluating a Decade of Reform', *Public Administration Review* 66(1): 78–90.

Moynihan, Donald P. (2007) 'Public Management by the Book', *Journal of Public Administration Research and Theory* 17(1): 149–53.

Moynihan, Donald P. (2008) *The Dynamics of Performance Management: Constructing Information and Reform*. Washington DC: Georgetown University Press.

Moynihan, Donald P. and Pandey, Sanjay K. (2005) 'Testing How Management Matters in an Era of Government by Performance', *Journal of Public Administration Research and Theory* 15(1): 421–39.

Norman, Richard (2002) 'Managing through Measurement or Meaning? Lessons from Experience with New Zealand's Public Sector Performance Management Systems', *International Review of Administrative Sciences* 68(4): 619–28.

Norman, Richard and Gregory, Robert (2003) 'Paradoxes and Pendulum Swings: Performance Management in New Zealand's Public Sector', *Australian Journal of Public Administration* 62(4): 35–49.

Olsen, Johan P. (2003) 'Towards a European Administrative Space?' *Journal of European Public Policy* 10: 506–31.

Organization for Economic Cooperation and Development (2004) *Modernising Public Sector Employment*. Paris, France; OECD Policy Brief.

Organization for Economic Cooperation and Development (2005) *Performance-related Pay Policies for Government Employees*. Paris, France: OECD.

Osborne, David and Gaebler, Ted (1992) *Reinventing Government: How the Entrepreneurial Government is Transforming the Public Sector*. Reading, MA: Addison-Wesley.

O'Toole, Lawrence (1997) 'Implementing Public Innovations in Network Settings', *Administration & Society* 29(2): 115–38.

O'Toole, Lawrence J. (2000) 'Different Public Managements? Implications of Structural Context in Hierarchies and Networks', in Jeffrey Brudney, Laurence J. O'Toole Jr and Hal G. Rainey (eds), *Advancing Public Management*. Washington, DC: Georgetown University Press; pp. 19–32.

O'Toole, Lawrence J. and Meier, Kenneth J. (2004) 'Public Management in Intergovernmental Networks: Matching Structural Networks and Managerial Networking', *Journal of Public Administration Research and Theory* 14(4): 469–94.

Pollitt, Christoper, Girre, Xavier, Lonsdale, Jeremy, et al. (1999) *Performance or Compliance? Performance Audit and Public Management in Five Countries*. Oxford: Oxford University Press.

President's Committee on Administrative Management (1937) 'Administrative Management in the Government of the United States,' Senate document 8, 75th Congress, 1st session. Washington, DC: United States Government Printing Office.

Radin, Beryl A. (2000) 'The Government Performance and Results Act and the Tradition of Federal Management Reform: Square Pegs in Round Holes?' *Journal of Public Administration Research and Theory* 10(1): 11–35.

Rhodes, Richard A. (1994) 'The Hollowing Out of the State: The Changing Nature of the Public Service in Britain', *Political Quarterly* 65(2): 138–51.

Rivlin, Alice M. (1992) *Reviving the American Dream: The Economy, the States, and the Federal Government.* Washington, DC: Brookings Institution Press.

Romzek, Barbara S. (1998) 'Where the Buck Stops: Accountability in Reformed Public Organizations',

in Patricia W. Ingraham, James R. Thompson and Ronald P. Sanders (eds), *Transforming Government: Lessons from the Reinvention Laboratories.* San Francisco, CA: Jossey-Bass; pp. 193–219.

Salamon, Lester (1989) *Beyond Privatization: The Tools of Government Action.* Washington, DC: The Urban Institute Press.

Skelcher, Christopher (2010) 'Fishing in Muddy Waters: Principals, Agents, and Democratic Governance in Europe', *Journal of Public Administration Research and Theory:* i161–i175.

Walker, Richard M., O'Toole, Laurence J. and Meier, Kenneth J. (2007) 'It's Where You Are That Matters: The Networking Behaviour of English Local Government Officers', *Public Administration* 85(3): 739–56.

White, Leonard D. (1926) *Introduction to the Study of Public Administration.* New York: Macmillan.

17

Budgeting and Finance

Anthony B.L. Cheung

INTRODUCTION

Politics is about 'who gets what, when, [and] how' (Lasswell, 1936). In public governance, the process of policymaking determines such distributional (and redistributional) outcome. As Dye put it,

> Public policy is whatever governments choose to do or not to do. Governments do many things. They regulate conflict within society; they organize society to carry on conflict with other societies; they distribute a great variety of symbolic rewards and material services to members of the society; and they extract money from society, most often in the form of taxes. (2002: 1)

The more governments have grown and extended into the economic and social life of the populace, the greater the impact of public policymaking on the well-being of ordinary citizens – as marked, for example, by the rise of the welfare state in the last century, and the growing interventionism of the government in the market in light of the recent global financial crisis.

Public budgeting is about the allocation of financial resources to support specific government activities and public purposes/tasks; as well as an expression both of current policy preferences of government and of past policy commitments. It is thus not simply an accounting process. Its importance lies in three major aspects: resource allocation; the satisfaction of social and political demands; and the securing of political and social support. Politically, it seeks to satisfy social and political demands, in accordance with the government's political priorities and partisan orientation. Socially, it serves as a vehicle to grant and deny privileges and distribute burdens and benefits to individuals and businesses, e.g. through direct provision of goods and services, entitlements, transfer payments, and other policy handouts. Economically, it provides fiscal policy instruments to influence the growth and productive capacity of the economy, thereby affecting the well-being of the community at large and different social sectors. As a planning document, it coordinates the mobilization of public resources within an overall government expenditure plan indicating what programmes and activities will be supplied, at what levels, and with what intended results. Legally, it confers the rights, responsibilities, powers and administrative parameters for the regulation of public expenditure.

Conventional literature has long recognized the budgeting process as a political process, whether in terms of incremental bureaucratic politics or legislative politics – e.g. Wildavsky (1964, 1986), Helco and Wildavsky ([1974] 1981), and Rubin (1990). Such work, however, mostly focused on the institutional politics of the previous budgetary mode operated in incremental bargaining whether in the bureaucratic or legislative arena. Different approaches to budgeting represent different philosophical perspectives on the role of the state and the features of governance. For example, the traditional 'night watchman' state emphasized economy and control, while a welfare state would go for programme expansion and transfer payments to meet planned targets and forecasted demands. Since the 1980s, the trends of privatization and contractization have spurred new initiatives in the management of public finances through commercialization, contracting out, outsourcing, and public–private partnership (PPP) in the provision of public goods and services.

Many people tend to think budget and finance is mostly about tools and techniques. However, as Miller pointed out, at least three rival views of financial management could be found among public financial management texts, mirroring some of the basic theoretical variations within public administration (Miller, 1994). The first group of texts builds within an applied macro- and micro-economics framework (the Economics view), describing or prescribing the utility maximizing behaviour of budgetary players (controllers, requesters, claimants, politicians, citizens), their inter-relationships and public choice rules and mechanisms. The second and third groups of texts employ a framework from public administration's traditional study of institutions, focusing on either the 'Accounting view' (management control, cost control) or 'Budget Execution view' (institutional rules and interactions). In practice, all three dimensions coexist. Governments and public organizations have to work to both organizational and financial goals, where the former emphasizes utility maximization criteria (whether economic, political or social), and the latter is measured in real money and liquidity

terms (Miller, 1994: 213). Table 17.1 gives a gist of the three views.

POSTWAR EVOLUTION OF BUDGETARY APPROACHES

The traditional budget was considered a housekeeping instrument for a minimal government. Over the past century, public budgeting had evolved from a traditional line-item input-oriented model to an output-oriented, performance-geared budgeting model. After World War II, many governments had moved into more state intervention in the economy and provision of public goods. This was even more so in socialist systems where the state took control of economic and social production through central planning and distribution. The postwar economic boom and the rise of a welfare state in many Western developed economies had fuelled an expansionist, and planning- and growth-oriented public finance approach. Since the 1960s government spending in the Organization for Economic Co-operation and Development (OECD) area had escalated by about 50 per cent relative to gross domestic product (GDP), from 28 per cent in 1960 to more than 40 per cent in 1990 (OECD, 1995: 12); social security and related transfers had more than doubled from 7 per cent of GDP to 15 per cent (1995: 12).

As the postwar boom gradually faded in the 1970s, lower economic growth rates had become the norm in most industrialized countries; for example, the OECD's average annual changes in real GDP between 1960–73 and 1991–93 had slowed down from 5.2 per cent to 1.2 per cent (OECD, 1995: 9, Table 17.1). This, together with demographic shifts and rising old-age dependency ratios, resulted in sharpened awareness of the need for budgetary adjustments. From the 1980s onwards, under the pressure of economic fluctuations and fiscal restraint, a new 'financial management' paradigm has taken seat, emphasizing macro- and micro-budgetary adaptations (Schick, 1986b, 1988). Many Western governments had

Table 17.1   Three views of financial management

Economics	Accounting	Budget Execution
Focuses on choices made by self-interested individual actors: bureau chief, department head, budget director, comptroller, financial manager, politician or citizen	Focuses on institutions: finance office, budget office, comptroller's office, or all three	Focuses on institutions: finance office, budget office, comptroller's office, or all three
	Views individual choices as mediated by institutional arrangements such as structures, rules or traditions	Views individual choices as mediated by institutional arrangements such as structures, rules or traditions
Describes or prescribes the utility-maximizing behaviour of all of these individuals and groups in relationship to each other	Involves mainly management control, dominated by accounting rules	Institutional rules and sequential process in legislature as well the executive branch significantly affect individual choices and social behaviours
		Management control, budgeting rules as well as political interaction involved
Values and methods Classic utility maximization, cost–benefit analysis, public choice economics	*Values and methods* Cost minimization and control	*Values and methods* Programme planning and performance
Control through voting systems that approximate the unanimous view of the population, e.g. tax polls, constitutional limits on budget	*Control* through normative procedures institutionalized through professionalization and external pressure	*Control* either through majoritarianism and top-down budgeting or through legislative-interest group pluralism

Source: Based on Miller (1994).

resorted to capping public expenditure through various financial management reforms such as devolution, performance contracts and commercialization, and 'budgeting for results' (OECD, 1995; Schick, 1990). As a result of pragmatic political considerations, however, fiscal consolidation was achieved largely through reduced government consumption and the curtailment of subsidies, rather than a restructuring of transfer payments (OECD, 1995: 13). The several stages of budgetary reforms can be illustrated by Table 17.2.

Table 17.2   Evolution of budgetary reforms

Budgetary reform	Main reform issues	Reform orientation
Performance budgeting (War time–1960s in USA)	Focuses on management of inputs and outputs; incremental in policymaking style	Efficiency-oriented
Planning–Programming–Budgeting System (PPBS) (1960s and 1970s)	Focuses on rational planning, entailing inputs, outputs, effects and alternatives; systemic in policymaking style	Policy-oriented
Zero-based budgeting (ZBB) (1976–1980 in USA)	Short-lived experiment focusing on policy prioritization	Decision-making oriented
Cutback management (1980s)	Efficiency reviews, cost-cutting exercises, cash-limits, privatization and contracting out	Efficiency-oriented
Budgeting for results (1990s–current)	Performance indicators, output targets and evaluation	Decision-making oriented (control over total spending and efficiency in resource management)

Postwar growth

Postwar prosperity and growth had facilitated the shift of emphasis from 'tight control over spending' to expansionary budgeting. The objective of budgeting was transformed from that of 'financial control' to that of 'an annual opportunity to obtain goods and services'. The growth of government was perceived to be legitimate and even desirable as the role of the state shifted to that of public service provider. In the new era of state intervention and expansion, it was generally accepted that more public spending could lead to more benefits and better societal well-being because it was believed that, given sufficient resources, the state could deal with most social problems. The budget had thus become an important fiscal policy vehicle to achieve the state's wider objectives in social reforms. Within a buoyant economy with progressive taxation, the government was also able to finance its expansion with increased tax revenue, thus facilitating 'policy without pain'. Budgetary politics took the form of *distributive* politics in which everyone could and expected to get something extra. There was greater emphasis on programme planning and multi-year budgeting, with a concurrent critique of traditional budgeting characterized by an 'incremental' approach whereby the pre-existing basis was not disputed, and negotiation and attention focused on increases to be provided over the previous year's appropriations (or consensus) (Wildavsky, 1964).

The criticism of traditional input-oriented incremental budgeting in the 1960s gave rise to budget innovations such as performance budgeting, 'Planning–Programming–Budgeting' (PPB) in the 1960s and 1970s, and zero-base budgeting (ZBB) in the late 1970s. These innovations were grounded in a rational approach to decision-making that linked objectives to policy programmes and resource allocation. The main effort was to render budgeting more systematic, analytic and planning-oriented. For example, multi-year budgeting was a device to forward-commit government expenditures (i.e. to commit future 'increments') assuming continuous growth trends. Whereas Wildavsky regarded programme budgeting, PPB and multi-year budgeting as anti-incremental innovations in the technical and procedural sense, such an interpretation was only premised on a narrow conception of incrementalism as 'small steps' budgeting; if incrementalism was interpreted as growth-oriented budgeting, then the postwar innovations, including PPB, were very much in accord with the expansionist spirit of the times (Schick, 1986a), to facilitate fiscal consensus and political stability. Budgeting for growth was further reinforced by the rise of entitlements and the 'indexing' of state benefits which rendered the bulk of the budget determined more by outside factors than internal bidding efforts within the budgetary process. Off-budget expenditures such as credit guarantees, and tax subsidies and relief, had also strengthened the growth tendency. In the past, appropriations by the legislature were intended to limit government expenditure. With the new incremental budgeting, however, appropriations enabled executive agencies to 'legitimately' spend more and more.

Constraints on budgetary choices

As the modern budget evolved, it had been made increasingly subject to some general constraints irrespective of the political and ideological colours of the government in office. These included: past decisions and ongoing commitments and the resulting expectations from the public and spending agencies; changes in demographic conditions leading to increased spending on demographically indexed 'entitlements' (there being a time gap between demographic changes and changes in social policy); economic considerations (e.g. growing demands for government support and services as the economy declined and weakened the government's capacity to supply); political and electoral constraints; and resistance from established interests which had benefitted from the prevailing budgetary decisions.

More specifically, on the expenditure side, constraints took the form of statutory requirements, debt-servicing commitments, contractual commitments (e.g. ongoing public works projects, civil service pay and conditions, pensions), difficulty to cut staff or reduce staff-related expenditures because of redundancy and/or industrial relations considerations, and resistance to cut existing expenditure from interests built around existing expenditures and activities. Hence the freedom of manoeuvre was mainly limited to new expenditure, with such normality only broken in times of severe external events (e.g. fiscal crisis or political change). On the revenue side, there were limitations in the sources of income (due to political, electoral considerations). Economy-related income was affected by economic fluctuations, and the scope for adjusting fees and charges as a means to avoid cuts in the level of activity in a period of restraint was equally limited.

Budgetary adaptations to cope with fiscal stress

By the late 1970s, the increasing costs of production, demographic changes as well as the decline in productivity in the industrialized nations had led to economic slowdown and an accumulation crisis of the capitalist state. There was also government overloading due to unrestrained expansion and the proliferation of fiscal entitlements and 'uncontrollable' expenditure items built into the welfare state. As a result, a budget crisis in the form of the rise of public debts and continuous budget deficits began to emerge, causing increasing conflicts between state and public service demanders on the expenditure side, and between state and taxpayers on the revenue side. The political New Right had escalated its attack on the state, calling for cutbacks in spending, privatization, and rolling back the frontier of the public sector. This, coupled with the concurrent rise of supply-side economics, had eroded the postwar Keynesian consensus. Initially, governments

had resorted to increased public borrowing and some waste-cutting efforts (such as finding efficiency savings) in order to buy time. When this proved to be futile and it was realized that economic difficulties were to stay for long, governments had to ultimately turn to an overhaul of the role and functions of the state through privatization, downsizing and retrenchment, commercialization and user-charging, contracting out and outsourcing, and other public sector reforms. Such reform attempts were facilitated by the rise of Rightist (in the UK and USA) or right-wing social democratic governments (such as in France and Australia). Constitutional-legal limitations were also used in some cases (as in the USA at the state level) to cap government expenditure – such as the need for referendum approval for tax increases, the requirement for balanced budget, and linking public expenditure to economic performance.

According to Schick (1986b, 1988), both macro-budgetary and micro-budgetary adaptations were used during the 1980s in industrialized nations to cope with fiscal stress. Macro measures referred to those relating to the management of total expenditure. These included: fiscal norms and targets to restrain expenditure either in real terms or relative to gross national product (GNP)/GDP; disaggregation of fiscal norms into specific targets and guidelines for particular sectors and review of programme and spending plans in light of such targets; imposition of ceilings; use of baselines to achieve cutback objectives (with baseline budgeting refocusing budgetary negotiations on where and how to retrench); the conversion of multi-year budgeting from a planning to control process; and the use of budget pre-preparation techniques to strengthen the conservation function of budgeting.[1] Micro measures referred to internal mechanisms to control expenditure on particular programmes or in particular agencies. These included: cutback budgeting and the re-emphasis of cash budgeting (e.g. cash limits); withdrawing central control of details of expenditure and allowing reallocation of resources within spending departments;

shift from policy reviews to efficiency reviews; closer monitoring of budget execution to promote compliance with cutback decisions; and tightening financial controls through management initiatives such as financial management accountabilities, financial devolution, performance measurement, contracting out and private sector financing.

PATTERN OF BUDGETARY REFORMS SINCE THE 1980s

Overall, international budgetary and financial management reforms have followed a common pattern since the 1980s, the features of which can be identified as follows, albeit with variations among countries:

- Devolution of authorities
- One-line budget
- Year-end flexibilities (carryovers, forward borrowings)
- Efficiency dividends and surplus retention
- Departmental autonomy – such as 'Next Steps' agencies; 'agencification'; corporate entities
- Freedom to manage and accountability for results
- Central targets (budget pre-preparation) coupled with 'budgeting for results'
- Multi-year budgeting and spending reviews
- Baseline review (of expenditure)
- Public service agreements – service agreements and framework documents, linking budget decisions to planned targets and performance results
- Commercialization: privatization, contracting out, PPP, user charging, and market-based mechanisms
- Accrual accounting and greater use of financial information.

OECD budgetary reforms

The OECD countries are widely regarded as the pioneers in budgetary and financial management reforms since the 1980s. By then it was widely realized that the traditional compliance-oriented budgetary system had significant limitations – such as complex restrictions, diminished allocative and operational efficiency, and limited responsibility for results. The emerging political consensus was now in favour of a more flexible budgetary management regime. Owing to new reform measures, better budgetary practices, privatization, targeted spending freezes or reductions in certain sectors, budget deficits began to narrow. The OECD-wide general government deficit had declined during the 1990s – from 5 per cent of GDP in 1993 to 1.8 per cent in 1997, returning to balance or surplus in member countries by 2000 (Blondal, 2003). From the 1980s, significant financial management reforms were notably undertaken in the Anglo-Saxon family of developed countries. For illustration, Table 17.3 gives a summary of these reforms in the UK, Australia and New Zealand.

In general, OECD countries have sought to 'modernize' their budget management system to achieve three objectives: to make it more responsive to priorities, more outcome-oriented, and more marketized in order to enhance the effectiveness of public spending programmes (Ball, 2002; OECD, 1995, 2003).

In making the budgetary process more responsive to priorities, there have been more legislative requirements to impose fiscal discipline: such as the European Union (EU) Growth and Stability Pact; the US Gramm–Rudman Acts of 1985 and 1987 (aiming at balanced budget) and Budget Enforcement Act of 1998; New Zealand's Fiscal Responsibility Act 1994; and Australia's Charter on Budget Honesty. A longer time frame is adopted in the budget process, through multi-year and medium-term budgeting, global targets, expenditure monitoring and control, and evaluations of medium-term budget frameworks. An effective medium-term framework can provide useful information on overall fiscal policy targets, costs of existing programmes, and implications of current decisions on future budgets. Measures are adopted to improve the reliability of forecasts, such as regular review of the assumptions and assessments of economic conditions. There is now more attention to fiscal risks,

Table 17.3 Summary of financial management reforms in the UK, Australia and New Zealand from the 1980s

Country	Reforms
United Kingdom (UK)	<ul><li>End-of-year flexibilities since 1983</li><li>Financial Management Initiative (FMI) in early 1980s – to emphasize performance results and resource management accountability</li><li>'Next Steps' agencies (from 1987) – to restructure blocks of service delivery work in departments into executive agencies, each headed by a chief executive operating outside the core structure, while the ministerial departments would concentrate on policy advice to ministers, contract government work to agencies through framework agreements, and coordinate resource allocation to agencies</li><li>Compulsory market testing (1991)</li><li>Control Total (mid-1990s) – 3-year spending plans</li><li>New Budgetary Framework (1997, when New Labour came to power), comprising:<ul><li>Code for Fiscal Stability (1997): (a) the golden rule – borrow only to invest; (b) the sustainable investment rule – net debt as stable percentage of GDP</li><li>Total Managed Expenditure (TME) = Departmental Expenditure Limits (DEL) + Annually Managed Expenditure (AME), where DEL is determined by biennial Spending Reviews, set 3 years ahead (negotiated between Treasury and departments); and AME is based on demand-led items not subject to firm limits</li><li>Public Service Agreements (PSA) between Treasury and spending departments</li><li>Performance targets under PSA – specific, quantified, and measurable</li></ul></li><li>From Privatization (1980s to 1990s) to PFI (Private Finance Initiative) (early 1990s), then to PPP (Public–Private Partnership)</li></ul>
Australia	<ul><li>Forward Estimates (late 1970s to 1980s)</li><li>Portfolio Budgeting (1980s) – ministers empowered to adjust priorities and funding across organizations within their portfolio</li><li>Financial Management Improvement Program (FMIP) (1983) – managing for results, devolution of controls and financial autonomy</li><li>PMB (Program Management & Budgeting) (1987) – linking expenditure decisions to objectives and programme results</li><li>Running Costs System (1987–88):<ul><li>Single appropriation for total running costs</li><li>Carryovers to next year and borrowings from next year allowed</li><li>Efficiency dividends (1987–88) (target percentage for improving efficiency) – to replace traditional across-the-board cuts</li></ul></li><li>'Reforming the Australian Public Service' (1993) – to improve efficiency and effectiveness, and to 'run the state like a business'</li><li>Resources agreements – more flexible funding</li><li>Programme evaluation</li><li>Corporate planning</li><li>Commercialization</li><li>User charging – 'user pays'; user choice</li><li>Accrual accounting</li></ul>
New Zealand	<ul><li>New policy to introduce full user-charging by phases (1985)</li><li>State-Owned Enterprises Act (1986) – to transfer trading activities of government organizations into state corporate structures with full commercial objectives, rights and responsibilities, including needs to pay taxes and dividends to government</li><li>State Sector Reform Act (1988) – to redefine relationship between ministers and permanent heads of departments who were re-designated as chief executives appointed on 5-year contracts and appraised according to outputs and results</li><li>Public Finance Act (1989) – contractual management and separation of purchasing and ownership interests within government</li><li>Public spending framework – removes input controls; managers accountable for results:<ul><li>Clarifying objectives and outputs-oriented</li><li>Freedom to manage (managerial freedom plus accountability)</li><li>Better information for managers (accrual accounting)</li></ul></li><li>Key Results Areas (KRAs) – to link broad goals and expenditure decisions</li><li>Market-based mechanisms, pricing tools, user charges, and quasi-markets (for education and health)</li><li>Programme goals – SMART (Specific, Measurable, Achievable, Relevant, Timed)</li><li>Multi-year appropriations</li><li>Value for Money exercises – review of baseline expenditure</li></ul>

such as 'backdoor' expenditures consisting of entitlements and tax expenditures, and off-budget expenditures (off-budget funds, direct loans, guarantees, and PPPs). Top-down budgeting techniques like budget pre-preparation and pre-set spending limits have become common. Budget transparency is also emphasized, e.g. the 'OECD Best Practices for Budget Transparency', which covers budget reports, specific disclosures, and integrity.

Most governments have sought to embrace financial management practices geared towards outcomes. The new 'budgeting for results' model comprises several elements: namely, the new performance budgeting; outcome-based evaluation; performance contracts; performance targets, benchmarks and measurement; and performance auditing. In practice, there were varied stages of progress among different OECD countries along the 'results' chain – with some countries only monitoring activities and outputs, some evaluating outcomes without output indicators, and some doing both (Perrin, 2002). Accrual accounting has been adopted by some countries in full (such as Australia, New Zealand and the UK) or for specific transactions. However, there is greater acceptance of accruals for financial reporting than for budgeting purposes. All countries now allow agencies to freely carry over the operating expenditures from one year to the next. Through interest-bearing accounts, government agencies now have the incentive to reduce the need for cash and become aware of the need for better cash management practices.

Australia, New Zealand, UK, Canada and most Nordic countries are increasing their flexibility in this area. Capital charges are imposed on agencies' asset holdings (so that there are now no *free* assets) and internal markets are created to spur some competition for the provision of goods and services. Central input controls have been relaxed, through: the consolidation of various budget lines into a single appropriation (one-line budget) for all operating costs; end-of-year flexibility; use and transfer of funds among budget categories and between fiscal years;

retention of all or some revenue raised from user charges; decentralization of personnel management functions (including pay administration and collective bargaining with staff unions); and decentralization of common services provisions. Although input controls relaxation is essential for the overall success of the reform process, all governments have also found it necessary to maintain an adequate level of central fiscal control to ensure compliance and stabilization.

Market signals have been imported into government operations so as to enhance the effectiveness of public spending. Measures include: benchmarking for selected services (e.g. hospital care, education); 'targeting' provision of merit goods and transfer payments; contracting out public sector activities; liberalization of public procurement markets; user charging; use of 'vouchers' to distribute merit goods and services to customers as the means of entitlement; managing public infrastructure projects by cost–benefit analysis, PPP and private sector financing; and greater use of 'corporatization' (e.g. New Zealand) and privatization (e.g. UK, New Zealand, Germany and France).

Budgetary reforms in Asian countries

OECD-type reforms have also spread to Asia. Hong Kong and Singapore are arguably the pioneers of financial management reform. Since the 1980s, both have pursued a similar series of extensive reforms, resulting in greater devolution of financial powers to ministries/ bureaus and departments, through inter-departmental charging, the amalgamation of line items, and greater management flexibilities at the operating levels of public service delivery under macro-funding caps (Cheung, 2006; Jones, 2005). Reforms in Hong Kong began with the amalgamation of line items, inter-departmental charging, abolition of 'block vote' arrangements for internal 'supplier' departments of common services, and the gradual devolution of financial authorities from the central budget agency (the Finance Branch of Government Secretariat) to policy bureaus and departments. In the 1990s output-budgeting presentation was adopted in the form of Controlling Officer's Reports containing performance indicators and results, baseline budgeting was introduced, and self-financing and self-accounting 'trading funds' were established. At the turn of the century, to cope with fiscal stringency following economic recession, an Enhanced Productivity Programme, efficiency savings, 'Save & Investment' accounts, and one-line budgets in the form of 'operating expenditure envelopes' were consecutively implemented.

In Singapore, inter-departmental charging and a block vote budgeting (lump-sum allocation) system were introduced quite early on, followed by 'Budgeting for Results' and performance measurement in the mid-1990s. There had also been a corresponding process of devolution of resource accountability from the Ministry of Finance to ministries and departments, which, by the late 1990s, were turned into 'autonomous agencies' with substantial autonomy in prioritizing programmes, apportioning financial and other resources, and making delivery decisions. They were either 'piece-rate funded' or 'macro-funded' (Jones, 2001: 144–50). Current features of the budgeting system include: baseline operating budgets; surplus retention and revenue retention (known as 'net budgeting' to refer to budget allocation net of committed revenue level); Reinvestment Fund; and overall and sectoral budget ceilings, operating block budgets and total block budgets under the *Budgeting 21* programme.

Japan and South Korea, though member countries of OECD, have somewhat differed from their Western counterparts by retaining a more traditional and centralized mode of budgeting and financial management, and were laggards in reform compared to Hong Kong and Singapore. According to Tanaka (2003) the Japanese budgetary process had been top-down and control-based, with expenditure management oriented towards legal and procedural compliance rather than

performance assessment. Accounting in the public sector was also complicated and less transparent. As the economy sank into a serious downturn in the 1990s, national deficits and debts began to rise rapidly. The Fiscal Structural Reform Act passed in 1997 was ground breaking as it aimed at: reducing fiscal deficit down to 3 per cent of GDP and reducing and then ceasing special deficit-covering bond issues; setting three-year spending ceilings and spending reduction targets in major budget categories; achieving a negative growth in general account budget; scaling down long-term plans; and conducting fiscal management that would reduce the gross debt burden to below 50 per cent of GDP. These reforms introduced the concept of multi-year budgeting, spending targets and individual spending limits set for a host of programmes (Savage, 2000). Although the outbreak of the Asian Financial Crisis had subsequently forced the government to put fiscal consolidation plans on hold, new reform momentum was picked up in 2002 when 'Reference Estimates' were introduced to project medium-term fiscal balance in line with the Report on Structural Reform and Medium-term Economic and Fiscal Perspective. From April 2002, under the 2001 Policy Evaluation Act, all ministries, agencies and independent administrative institutions started to introduce a policy evaluation system with the results informing the budgeting process, as an effort to introduce some form of performance-based programme budgeting (Kudo, 2003).

In South Korea, budgetary and financial management had also long been highly controlled by the centre, with undue complexity and fragmentation in the budget structure because of the proliferation of non-conventional expenditures and the low level of efficiency in the management of financial resources (Ha, 1997, 2004). It was only following the outbreak of the 1997 Asian Financial Crisis that the government was driven into extensive public management reforms. A White Paper on Government Reform emphasized scaling down the size of the public sector through privatization, deregulation, and introducing market principles into the operation of government (Ha, 2004). Budgetary and financial management reforms were introduced to facilitate results-oriented budgeting, more efficient government spending, and more transparent and accountable financial management. Measures included: the simplification and consolidation of budget structure; adoption of tax expenditure budgets; accounting and budgetary reforms (such as accrual accounting, performance and multi-year budgeting); and flexible financial management (e.g. carryovers, total operational expenditure system or one-line budget, budget savings incentive scheme, performance measurement and evaluation) (Ha, 2004). A new Ministry of Planning and Budgeting was established in 1999 to take charge of budget allocation.

IMPLEMENTATION PROBLEMS

Despite these bold attempts to reform the financial management system in many countries, some major problems have been encountered in implementation. Performance measurement and evaluation has proved to be difficult to achieve: fiscal incentives for 'good' performance are still limited, and there is insufficient information on outcomes. In practice, budget decisions are often *divorced* from performance evaluation so that public budgeting is still essentially a political bargaining process. Market-based mechanisms are difficult to apply to some public sector work, such as social services. There have been ongoing tensions between the central budget agency (CBA, such as the Treasury and Ministry of Finance) and spending departments, resulting in the 'control vs devolution' paradox. Legislative scrutiny of the budget has remained very much inputs-oriented, since budgetary politics tend to focus on bids for resource inputs from various claimants. Commercialization of public operations requires a change of skills such as

contract writing, without which there will be overdependence on or even reverse capture by the private for-profit contractors. The critical question is whether budgeting has really become 'less' political (thus 'more' managerial), *or* it is still as political as before (e.g. over the negotiation of Public Service Agreements with the Treasury and of performance targets and measurements between the controllers and spenders).

Evaluating performance

The new financial management model champions 'managing for performance', which implies a results-oriented culture focused on: delivering the services the community needs; a public service which is trained and equipped to deliver quality service; continuous improvement in services; and reinvented notions of 'value for money'. This is very often easier said than done. In reality there is a limit to performance measurement and to linking it to financial allocation decisions and rewards. Performance measurement is *both* a science and an art. As science, measurement is subject to methodological, cognitive and technical constraints and prejudice. As art, it has to be the 'art of the possible' – accommodating bureaucratic negotiations and the limitations of management culture in the organization, which explains why performance measurement is often implemented among government organizations in a somewhat indeterminate and flexible context. In most systems, performance results and performance indicators do not play any key role in annual budget allocation decisions, which have remained politically dirven.

Devolution

Devolution is an expressed objective of the new financial management. Decentralized budgeting and control is mainly pursued through the process of contracting, whether internal (by delegating more authority and

control to line managers) or external (by contracting out to private service providers).
There remain, however, contentions over
what is to be decentralized to line departments and what should still be kept firmly
under central Treasury control (e.g. civil service pay system, investment and procurement
policies, and public service targets). Questions
remain as regards: the balance between competing objectives of uniformity versus difference (what can be devolved to managers and
what measures to be used to ensure uniformity); the degree to which performance can be
measured and monitored; and the process of
negotiation over resources and results (what
is to be devolved and the exchange of control
over resources for accountability on results).
CBAs may resist moves to devolve because
of organizational inertia, the long-standing
tradition of hierarchical accountability, and
the fear of loss of control among Treasury
bureaucrats ('departments will take the money
and run'). All this has fed into a new form of
neo-Treasury control that creeps into the
system through the back door.

Legislative scrutiny and audit

Financial management reform has called for
a role transformation of the legislature and
central audit institutions. The legislature is
used to handling incremental budgets – it
imposes ceilings, requires balanced budget
and approves borrowings. Traditionally it
approved department spending through annual
appropriations. Such appropriations, however, were not effective in regulating demand-
determined expenditure and in controlling
expenditure on long-term commitments. The
typical parliamentary model gives a dominant
role to the executive and bureaucrats in budgetary matters and a limited role to the legislature. Under budgetary reform, there is likely
to be a weakening of conventional parliamentary control as the general trend is to reduce
the number of line items in the budget and to
vote appropriations in broad frames (e.g.
blocks or portfolios in Australia and Finland),

and as controls over virement and transfer of
funds between votes are lifted.

In terms of audit, external audit agencies
are moving from traditional spending and
integrity audits towards performance or 'value
for money' audits. Such a move may entail
large-scale organizational change – involving
mission, professional identities, procedures
and working styles. Among OECD countries,
while nearly all conduct efficiency audit, only
one-half, two-thirds, and one-fourth are
engaged in performance effectiveness audit,
performance management capacity audit, and
performance information audit, respectively
(Barzelay, 1997). The prevalent practice of
efficiency audit may imply that many governments still resist institutional change that
favours organizational autonomy. Moving
towards performance management further
poses the risk of an excessive judgmental
focus on unbalanced reports and compliance
of rules.

IMPACT OF REFORMS ON
TRADITIONAL TREASURY POWER

The new financial management reforms are
premised on the 'new public management'
(NPM) logic of letting managers free to manage
and of management by outputs and outcomes
(Hood, 1991; Lane, 2000; Lynn, 2006) – to
the extent that managers can mobilize and
organize various financial, human and organizational resources within agreed budgets and
policy frameworks and are only accountable
for organizational and policy performance as
measured by agreed targets and performance
indicators. A new mode of budgetary relationships has thus emerged, operating within
a 'principal–agent' regime (Lane, 2005), geared
towards the negotiation of contracts and performance targets. Along with the new budgetary reforms, there have been suggestions of a
retreat from the previously entrenched doctrine
of Treasury Control in favour of decentralizing and restructuring budgetary control and
management – proportedly reducing the

detailed direct controls of the CBA (budget controllers) over spending departments (OECD, 1997: 13). Traditional Treasury power was built upon two pillars: detailed line-item control sustained by the use of cumbersome rules and procedures and process scrutiny at various levels of the organizational hierarchy; as well as top-down and centrally driven processes of 'incremental' bureaucratic and political bargaining (Wildavsky, 1964, 1986). Under the current reforms, a new mode of resource accountability is supposed to be driven by systems of performance contracts and framework agreements. During this shift, the CBA as principal employs new instruments to ensure performance by executive agencies – such as strategic and operational plans, performance measures and targets, performance contracts, decoupling service delivery from policymaking, new accountability rules and annual reports, greater evaluation and audit, and financial inducements and sanctions (OECD, 1997: 12).

Demise of treasury power?

Schick (2001: 10) saw the new culture of budget reform as in conflict with the traditional function of the CBA as a central command and control post within government, which specified the items of expenditure, monitored compliance with regulations, enforced budget conformity and imposed top-down interventions as appropriate. Financial and budget management reforms are thus not only a matter of relaxing one or another restriction but also about reshaping the operations of public institutions and the behaviours of those working in them (i.e. budgetary actors either as budget conservers, or as demanders, claimants and spenders). Management reform ultimately leads to process change, behavioural adjustments and institutional reconfiguration, resulting in new forms and norms of CBA–departments relationships, with significant power consequences. As the current wave of budgetary reforms unfolds in a simple divestiture of

financial control, the CBA's power in theory risks being hollowed out, as 'doing so would destroy the discipline on which all budgeting rests' (Schick, 2001: 9). A CBA operating in 'a devolved environment that shifts decision making authority with respect to the particulars of public expenditure from central institutions to line agencies, and from headquarters in these agencies to subordinate units and fields' (Schick, 2001: 10) would be turned into more nominal guardians of the public purse vis-à-vis the rising autonomy of ministries and departments.

However, the expected demise of Treasury or CBA power has not proven to be the case just because of budget reforms. For one thing, budgetary relationships seem less dependent on the new 'budgeting for results' mode of contractual management, which has not really taken off, as explained later. Besides, resource allocation is largely determined by a strategy of budget capping, with the CBA opting for macrocontrol in lieu of microcontrol, which at best only has a marginal effect on the balance of power between the budget controllers and budget spenders. In other words, new strategies have evolved on the part of the CBA to reinvent its Treasury power as it *games* with the spending departments. In the UK, for example, the Treasury owes its pre-eminent position to the early recognition, back in the 1660s, of its role as 'the office with responsibility for all financial questions' and 'the power of the purse brought with it a voice in all decisions of policy and administration' (Chapman, 1997: 161). After World War II, it had accumulated control and influence over the economy and was subsequently charged with pioneering new management methods and techniques. Despite the recent reforms, the British Treasury has continued with its traditional responsibilities for expenditure control and advice on good government practice and accountability, amid changes in management thoughts and approaches. Thain and Wright's (1995) study of Treasury–departments relations during the 1970s to 1990s found that, while the Treasury was not able to stop new initiatives like the Next Steps reform which gave more resource management autonomy to departments, 'it was able to insert a degree of caution about the need to balance value-for-money with the need for the continued control of expenditure' (1995: 82). Under New Labour's modernizing government project, the Treasury has gained undue influence over government priorities through its steering role in policy reviews. The balancing (and rebalancing) of Treasury–departments relationships is also shaped by the politico-economic context within which the budget is negotiated, and by the development and operation of the decision-making system, i.e. 'the rules of the game', and the prevailing 'administrative culture' (Thain and Wright, 1995: 535).

Experience among OECD countries shows there are both 'strong' and 'weak' Ministries of Finance in the reform era. Budget formulation entails essentially two stages – at the beginning of the cycle as the Finance Minister sends out target numbers or guidelines to spending departments, and at the end of the cycle as he conveys the final proposal (allocation decisions) to spending departments (OECD, 2005: 35–6). A 'weak' Finance Minister will not be able to impose his proposal on spending ministers unilaterally, whereas a 'strong' Finance Minister can, with at best an appeal procedure to the Prime Minister or President. Indeed, as Schick (2001: 12) too argued, 'devolution of operations must be accompanied by centralization of policy making' in order to reflect government policy priorities and coherence. Hence a strong CBA can still thrive, depending on the prevailing institutional environment within core government. Under the old system of detailed line-item control, economy and efficiency were achieved through the CBA's close scrutiny and control of expenditure inputs (in particular personnel expenditure). The new devolved system, though expecting the CBA to withdraw from involvement in most of the details of expenditure and to give spending departments greater operational discretion within a capped budget, still

requires the latter to exercise self-discipline and expenditure control. Ideally, though, the two opposite approaches would still work for the same purpose (Schick, 2001: 24).

Rebalancing relationships

By refocusing on macro control and system monitoring, using resource allocations to reflect central priorities but allowing ministerial/departmental reallocations, and requiring spending departments to conform to centrally promulgated efficiency measures, the CBA still has a strong capacity to impose and enforce aggregate budgetary discipline to maintain fiscal stability throughout government. Wanna, Jensen and Vries observed that CBA power remains very much alive and well:

> Behind all the new jargons of public management, some fundamental aspects of CBA life are still evident. The 'Treasury Knights' of the UK Treasury are still in place; their standing and influence remains a perennial feature of the British state. In Denmark, the 'light blue shirts' are alive and well, while the 'suits' in Canberra still act as if they rule the roost. . . . Hence, CBAs remain powerful organizations, ... Increasingly [their] power derives from its arguments and quality of advice. (2003: 269)

It is true that the CBA is being pulled in two directions – one for budgeting to become integrated into financial management through closer links with accounting, auditing and output measurement; and the other for the CBA to become the policymaking centre of government (OECD, 1997: 35), which causes confusing relationships with operating departments. However, it is also clear that the CBA is not merely an accounting and spending control organization: its power goes beyond the strict boundary of budgeting and financial management, well into the policy centre of government.

Among OECD countries the current wave of reforms aims more at changing managerial behaviour than rationalizing budgetary choice. Whereas budget officials want performance measures and other related information available when they allocate resources, they do not actually allocate according to performance because they doubt if the state-of-the-art performance measurement is sufficiently advanced to justify an explicit cause–effect linkage of resources and results.

> In theory, the budget should be one of the principal means by which performance measures affect public policy. It should not be difficult to devise a performance-based budget system in which each increment of resources is directly linked to a planned increment in output. . . . Yet the governments examined [i.e. Australia, France, New Zealand, Sweden and United Kingdom] have not closely linked performance and budgeted resources, preferring instead an arrangement in which data on actual or expected results is just one of several influences on the budget . . . . The expectation is that past results will feed into future budget decisions, but [neither Australia nor Sweden] formally allocates resources on the basis of performance. In the United Kingdom, . . . the direct impact [of performance information] on the budget may be *more apparent than real*. (OECD, 1997: 23–4, emphasis ours)

This author's own research into the new budgetary system in Hong Kong and Singapore also confirms that despite reforms featuring devolved management and an emphasis on performance outputs, the system remains in essence not much of a deviation from the historical path of central control, fiscal stability, and concern for distributional politics or economic development, as the case may be.[2] Financial management reforms have been implemented largely because they are considered more cost-effective ways to achieve such key government goals, within the new fiscally volatile environment.

'Budgeting for results' may be in the rhetoric, but is in practice only a façade. For example, budget envelopes in Hong Kong are determined on the basis of the *historical* estimates of departments, which have captured previous consensus and compromise between budget requesters and reviewers. In Singapore, budget caps (the annual 'block budgets') are pegged to a pre-agreed percentage of GDP – in other words, general economic performance – rather than any detailed evaluation of ministerial/agency performance; and should the economy continue to grow, there will be *de facto* incremental budgeting. The actual interactions between the CBA and ministries/departments are thus still guided by pragmatic and mutually accommodating behaviours not so dissimilar to traditional budgetary incrementalism.

A NEW HYBRID REGIME OF BUDGETARY POLITICS

A new hybrid form of budgetary politics may be emerging within the reformed budget systems, which is rooted in traditional incrementalism but features new managerialist wrappings as the additional means to legitimize budget demands. Neo-Treasury control has also been reinvented which, though displaying different control mechanisms, still keeps strong aggregate fiscal discipline as the ultimate goal, thereby requiring and ensuring a strong CBA role one way or the other. The new control mechanisms can be contrasted with the traditional ones as shown in Table 17.4.

Table 17.4   Reconstitution of treasury control in reformed budget systems

New budgetary regime	Traditional budgetary regime
• Control by budget caps	• Control by line items (detailed expenditure)
• Control by fiscal targets, supplemented by budgeting-for-results (but procedural and regulatory controls remain)	• Control by process and procedures (detailed regulation), based on scrutiny of inputs
• Control by benchmarks and baseline (but baseline still essentially linked to historical base)	• Control by negotiation (as increments on top of historical base)
• Control by managerial culture – the politics of performance measurement	• Control by bureaucratic politics (incremental politics)

Under the new, alternative, model for achieving fiscal stability and sustainability, the objectives of the CBA lie primarily in: macro expenditure control; fiscal policy as overriding, accompanied by other related fiscal goals (such as deficit reduction); and the avoidance of moral hazard of the spenders (hence the imposition of new rules and constraints) and of information asymmetry (hence not to unduly rely on performance/results evaluation, the validity of which remains problematic and the transaction costs of which are just too high). As to the spending ministries and departments, their primary objective is still budget maximization rather than performance optimization. Hence they would pay greater attention to political incrementalism, and would spend in order to get more next year in a reinvented fiscal regime that still emphasizes historical spending levels; in the process they would find that it pays to follow the rules and regulations imposed by the CBA. Such budgetary motives and behaviours on the part of the CBA and ministries/departments are no different from those prevailing under the old budgetary regime.

In conclusion, budgetary reforms have not materially altered the basic functions of budgeting, which ensures a key role for the CBA as part of the policymaking centre of government. Fiscal discipline and stability, in line with government goals, remain a strong force which inhibits the logic of budgetary devolution from really weakening and eroding CBA power. Budgeting for results, though rational in the new NPM appeal, has not obviated the need for playing the budgetary political game.

NOTES

1   As opposed to budget preparation that tends to be a decentralized, bottom-up process in which spending agencies press their claims, budget pre-preparation is directed from the center in a top-down flow of information and instructions to ensure conformance with pre-set limits. Pre-preparation is therefore a 'rationing' rather than a 'requesting' process.

2   Based on this author's research in 2003–05, supported by a grant from the Hong Kong Research Grants Council (Project No. CityU 1063/02H).

REFERENCES

Ball, I. (2002) 'Modern Financial Management Practices', *OECD Journal of Budgeting* 2(2): 49–76.

Barzelay, M. (1997) 'Central Audit Institutions and Performance Auditing: A Comparative Analysis of Organizational Strategies in the OECD', *Governance* 10(3): 235–60.

Blondal, J.R. (2003) 'Budget Reform in OECD Member Countries: Common Trends', *OECD Journal of Budgeting* 2(4): 7–25.

Chapman, R.A. (1997) *The Treasury in Public Policymaking.* London: Routledge.

Cheung, A.B.L. (2006) 'Budgetary Reforms in Two City States: Impact on Central Budget Agency in Hong Kong and Singapore', *International Review of Administrative Sciences* 72(3): 341–61.

Dye, T.R. (2002) *Understanding Public Policy,* 10th edn. Upper Saddle River, NJ: Prentice-Hall.

Ha, Y.-S. (1997) 'Public Finance and Budgeting in Korea under Democracy: A Critical Appraisal', *Public Budgeting and Finance* 17(1): 56–73.

Ha, Y.-S. (2004) 'Budgetary and Financial Management Reforms in Korea: Financial Crisis, New Public Management, and Fiscal Administration', *International Review of Administrative Sciences* 70(3): 511–25.

Helco, H. and Wildavsky, A. [1974] (1981) *The Private Government of Public Money.* London: Macmillan.

Hood, C. (1991) 'A Public Management for All Seasons?', *Public Administration* 69(1): 3–19.

Jones, D.S. (2001) 'Budgetary Policy in Singapore', in L. Low and D.M. Johnston (eds), *Singapore Inc.: Public Policy Options in the Third Millennium.* Singapore: Times Media Private Limited; pp. 131–56.

Jones, D.S. (2005) 'Recent Changes in the Financial Management of the Singapore Civil Service: The Adoption of Resource Accounting, Internal Charging and Revenue Retention', in Anthony B.L. Cheung (ed.), *Public Service Reform in East Asia: Reform Issues and Challenges in Japan, Korea, Singapore and Hong Kong.* Hong Kong: The Chinese University Press; pp. 105–24.

Kudo, Hiroko (2003) 'Between the "Governance" Model and the Policy Evaluation Act: New Public Management in Japan', *International Review of Administrative Sciences* 60(4): 483–504.

Lane, J.-E. (2000) *New Public Management.* London: Routledge.

Lane, J.-E. (2005) *Public Administration and Public Management: The Principal–Agent Perspective.* London: Routledge.

Lasswell, H.D. (1936) *Politics: Who Gets What, When, How.* Cleveland, OH: Meridian Books.

Lynn, L.E., Jr (2006) *Public Management: Old and New.* London: Routledge.

Miller, G.J. (1994) 'What Is Financial Management? Are We Inventing a New Field Here?', *Public Administration Review* 54(2): 209–13.

OECD (Organization for Economic Co-operation and Development) (1995) *Budgeting for Results: Perspectives on Public Expenditure Management.* Paris: OECD.

OECD (1997) *Modern Budgeting.* Paris: OECD.

OECD (2003) 'Part VI – Enlarging the Cost Effectiveness of Public Spending', *OECD Economic Outlook* 74: 161–75.

OECD (2005) *Reallocation: The Role of Budget Institutions.* Paris: OECD.

Perrin, B. (2002) 'Implementing the Vision: Addressing Challenges to Results-Focused Management and Budgeting'. Presented to the OECD Meeting on 'Implementation Challenges in Results Focused Management and Budgeting', Paris.

Rubin, I.S. (1990) *The Politics of Public Budgeting.* Chatham, NJ: Chatham House.

Savage, James D. (2000) 'A Decade of Deficits and Debt: Japanese Fiscal Policy and the Rise and Fall of the Fiscal Structural Reform Act of 1997', *Public Budgeting and Finance* 20(1): 55–84.

Schick, A. (1986a) 'Incremental Budgeting in a Decremental Age', in F.S. Lane (ed.), *Current Issues in Public Administration,* 3rd edn. New York: St. Martin's Press.

Schick, A. (1986b) 'Macro-budgetary Adapations to Fiscal Stress in Industrialized Democracies', *Public Administration Review* 46(2): 124–34.

Schick, A. (1988) 'Micro-budgetary Adapations to Fiscal Stress in Industrialized Democracies', *Public Administration Review* 48(1): 523–33.

Schick, A. (1990) 'Budgeting for Results: Recent Developments in Five Industrialized Countries', *Public Administration Review* 50(1): 26–34.

Schick, A. (2001) 'The Changing Role of the Central Budget Office', *The OECD Journal on Budgeting* 1(1): 9–26.

Tanaka, Hideaki (2003) 'Fiscal Consolidation and Medium-term Fiscal Planning in Japan', *OECD Journal on Budgeting* 3(2): 105–37.

Thain, C. and Wright, M. (1995) *The Treasury and Whitehall: The Planning and Control of Public Expenditure, 1976–1993.* Oxford: Clarendon Press.

Wanna, J., Jensen, L. and Vries, J.d. (eds) (2003) *Controlling Public Expenditure: The Changing Roles of Central Budget Agencies – Better Guardians?* Northampton, MA: Edward Elgar.

Wildavsky, A. (1964) *The Politics of the Budgetary Process.* Boston: Little Brown.

Wildavsky, A. (1986) *Budgeting: A Comparative Theory of Budgetary Processes.* Boston: Little Brown.

18

Partnerships

Gunnar Folke Schuppert

When the topic 'partnerships' shows up on the contemporary governance agenda most people think immediately of public–private partnerships (PPPs): PPPs are extremely popular, they enjoy a positive image and they fit neatly into discussions about administrative reform. Administrators all over the world like PPPs. Using them is a sign of a modernizing bureaucracy, and that they are taking advantage of an organizational arrangement which represents a win–win situation: the private partner is carrying out his business and making profits; the public partner improves the provision of public services by bringing together the specific capacities and capabilities of state and non-state actors.

While there may be a 'public love affair' with PPPs, a full assessment of their utility requires answers to certain crucial questions that are often neglected in the public discussion of PPPs: Is there really a fair sharing of risk between the public and private partners? How can an intelligently designed contract ensure an ongoing win–win situation in complex partnerships? What are realistic exit options for the public partner if the 'know-how' (and the procedural knowledge) are monopolized by the private actor? One should bear these questions in mind, and I will address them in the third part of this chapter.

Another danger to a full understanding of PPPs is this: when reading the literature about PPPs it can be observed that the discussion is too narrow from the very beginning, concentrating immediately on the practical aspects and neglecting the theoretical background. This chapter aims to avoid this danger, and will therefore start with a section called 'Partnerships in Context' before moving on to PPPs themselves. The second section will discuss partnerships in the light of possible institutional choices. The third section will look in more detail at selected problems with PPPs. The final section – the appropriate place for an overview – will look at partnerships in the broader context of the phenomenon of increasing 'co-production' of statehood in different fields of public policy.

PARTNERSHIPS IN CONTEXT

Partnerships in governance discourse

In this chapter governance means the various institutionalized modes of social coordination used to produce and collectively implement binding rules, or to provide collective goods. This conceptualization closely follows the understanding of governance that is widespread within the social sciences (Mayntz, 2004; Schuppert and Zürn, 2008; Risse, 2010). Governance consists of both structural ('institutionalized') and process ('modes of social coordination') dimensions. Accordingly, governance covers direction by the state ('governance by government'); governance via cooperative networks of public and private actors ('governance with government'); as well as rule-making by non-state actors or self-regulation by civil society ('governance without government'; Czempiel and Rosenau, 1992; Grande and Pauly, 2005; Zürn, 1998).

Within this capacious governance concept most scholars focus on the *non-hierarchical* and *non-state-centered* forms of governance, which (often taking place in the 'shadow of hierarchy') are frequently labeled 'new modes' of governance as shown in Table 18.1.

Looking at Table 18.1 and the mainstream of the governance literature, *partnerships* fit extremely well into the governance discourse. Public–private partnerships are by definition organizational arrangements with a *sector-crossing* or *sector-blurring* character, and are thus a most suitable candidate for the label 'new mode of governance'. It is therefore no surprise that a specific term for governance by partnerships has been found

– 'collaborative governance' – a term which already has a well-recognized place in the governance discourse (see Freeman, 1997; Donahue and Zeckhauser, 2006).

However, I prefer instead the concept of *sector-crossing governance* to make clear that the specific 'institutional competence' of partnership arrangements is rooted in the combination of the capabilities of state and non-state actors.

Coming back to Table 18.1, and especially to the shaded areas on the right-hand side, I would like to point out that 'partnerships' should be understood in this chapter to mean not only PPPs in a narrow sense – from building roads and prisons to collaborative provision of public services – but also as the whole range of cooperation by state and non-state actors, as illustrated in Figure 18.1.

This broader definition of partnerships, includes the four governance modes of:

- cooptation
- delegation
- co-regulation
- self-regulation in the shadow of hierarchy.

It is also on the whole compatible with the 'international governance' discourse. Börzel and Risse (2005) suggest distinguishing between four types of PPPs in the transnational arena (Table 18.2).

Table 18.1 ('New') modes of governance

Actors involved/steering modes	State actors only	State and non-state actors	Non-state actors only
Hierarchical Top-down (threat of) sanctions	• Modern nation-state • Supranational institutions (EU, partly WTO) • Protectorates and international trusteeships		• For example, warlords in markets of violence
Non-hierarchical Positive incentives; bargaining; non-manipulative persuasion (learning, arguing, etc.)	• Intergovernmental bargaining • Institutional problem-solving	• Delegation of public functions to private actors • Public–private networks and partnerships	• Private interest governance/ private regimes • Private–private partnerships (e.g. NGOs–firms)

Shaded area = 'new' modes of governance.
Source: Risse (2010: 8).

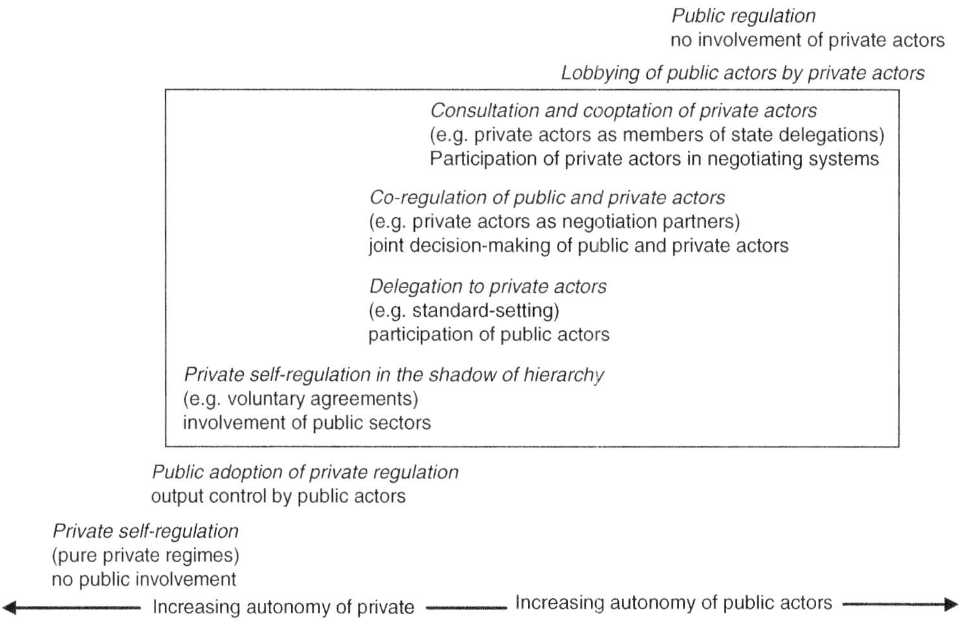

Figure 18.1 The realm of public–private partnerships (from Börzel and Risse, 2005).

Table 18.2 PPPs according to type and purpose

Type/purpose	Rule setting	Rule implementation	Service provision
Cooptation	Human rights regimes	UN human rights system	UN development agencies
Delegation	International Standardization Organization (ISO)	Executive outcomes	Humanitarian and development aid sectors
Co-regulation	International Labor Organization (ILO)	Various emission trading schemes of climate change Regime	UNAIDS
Self-regulation in the shadow of hierarchy	Safe Harbor Agreement	Global Compact	Rating agencies?

Partnerships as part of the 'new interplay' between the state, business, and civil society

In writing about a 'new interplay' between the state, business, and civil society, I use a term coined by Klaus Dieter Wolf (2008) to describe emerging new patterns of global governance. There are two basic assumptions underpinning this 'new interplay concept' which I largely share (Schuppert, 2008):

The first point is that it is helpful from an analytical perspective if we understand

partnerships as *a distinct mode of interaction*, as Table 18.3 suggests.

In the same vein – and also drawing on the shift from government to governance – Ulrika Mörth (2009) in her article 'The market turn in EU governance', proposes a distinction of the following two systems of authority (Table 18.4).

The second assumption is that the interplay can be described as a 'new' interplay because it embodies the shifting roles of the three main actors: the state is moving from an 'authority monopolist to an authority

Table 18.3 Types of interaction embedded in the context of the shift from government to governance

Organizational form	Pluralist	Corporatist	Partnership
Relationship of the state with business and civil society	Different societal lobbies compete to influence public policy decisions taken by the state	Institutionalized ('incorporated') participation by major associations in consensual formulation and implementation of public policy decisions	Various forms of horizontal deliberative cooperation in governance networks. Collaborative provision of public services by PPPs, etc.

Source: Bressel, N. and Wolf, K. D., Forest certification as a political regulation concept in the context of global governance, in: Dietrich Burger, Jürgen Hess and Barbara Lang (eds.), *Forest Certification: An innovative instrument in the service of sustainable development?*, Deutsche Gesellschaft fürTechnische Zusammenarbeit (GTZ), pp. 187–194.

Table 18.4 Two systems of authority

	Government	Governance
Modes of regulation	Hard law Public law	Soft law Private law
Regulators	Public actors	Public and private actors
Democratic model	Representative and state-centric	Deliberative and societally-based
Democratic reforms	Hierarchy and parliamentarization	Open structures and network-building

Source: Morth (2009)

manager' (Zangl and Genschel, 2008); in the business domain we see an ever-increasing 'public role for the private sector' (Haufler, 2001); and the changing role of the last group of actors can best be summed up by the semantic shift from the term 'third sector' (Anheier and Seibel, 1990) to what is now called 'civil society'.

Ulrika Mörth describes the changing landscape of governance as follows (Mörth, 2009: 103):

> PPPs can ... be characterized neither as markets nor as hierarchies. Contracting involves bargaining and reciprocity and not domination by one part. They can instead be characterized as a relational form of social organization based on trust and on a rather long-term commitment in which legitimacy and other noncommercial values play an important role for the private enterprises (Linder, 2002). It is therefore surprising that partnerships often are treated in the literature as fairly straightforward affairs ... . They are seldom analyzed as a reflection of a more general transformation of changed borders between business, state and civil society (Sahlin-Andersson, 2006). Indeed, PPPs are about complex legal and economical arrangements but underneath they are much more about how new demands on the three spheres have emerged ... . Modern states are placing more emphasis on the 'use of authority, rules and standard-setting,

partially displacing an earlier emphasis on public ownership, public subsidies, and directly provided services' (Jordana and Levi-Faur, 2004: 8).

PARTNERSHIPS AND INSTITUTIONAL CHOICE

Institutional choice – an overview

Policymaking is about making choices – choosing the instruments that best suit a certain public policy (instrumental choice); choosing the 'right' organizational form or type of agency for implementing the policy in question (institutional choice); and – last but not least – choosing the appropriate regulatory regime, especially for the governance of partnerships (regulatory choice). To make the 'good choices' essential for effective public administration a certain amount of theoretical reflection is needed – as Donahue and Zeckhauser (2006) have pointed out with regard to 'collaborative governance':

> Good governance requires choosing the right implementation model as well as the right ends. The richer the repertoire of alternative models, the

more important is analytic work to guide the assignment of tasks. As government increasingly shares the collective-action stage with private actors, both for-profit and not-for-profit, addressing this assignment problem – who should do what? – becomes both more complex and more consequential.

These tough choices *have* to be made: the state and its administration are more than ever under considerable political and financial stress, which forces public service providers to search for intelligent reactions. Christoph Reichard (2006) has visualized this 'stress' on choice-making in a challenge-and-response diagram (Figure 18.2).

To respond to this challenge, Figure 18.3 provides a *variety of organizational possibilities* (after Reichard, 2006).

Thinking in terms of *delivery modes* we can make the distinction given in Figure 18.4.

Sector-crossing institutional arrangements: contracting out, PPPs and networks

Before looking at public–private partnerships in more detail, it seems useful to say a few words about the differences and similarities between three types of *sector-crossing*

institutional arrangements (contracting out, PPPs, and networks).

Contracting out and PPPs

At first glance, contracting-out (this term is also used here as a synonym for 'functional privatization') and public–private partnerships seem to be very similar: in both cases, the partners come from different sectors and their collaboration is governed by contracts, but at a second glance the differences are considerable, as Table 18.5 shows.

PPPs and networks

On the surface, PPPs and networks seem to be organizational arrangements with very similar functions: both are instruments for sector-crossing implementation of public policy and their main advantages can be seen in their 'institutional capacity' to bring together the contributions of state and non-state actors for a common goal. PPPs bring the 'entrepreneurial spirit' into the public sector; networks function as a bridge between actors from the private, public, and third sector. However, if we investigate a little deeper the differences are considerable – not in the sense that both types could not be (to a certain extent) interchangeable (there are

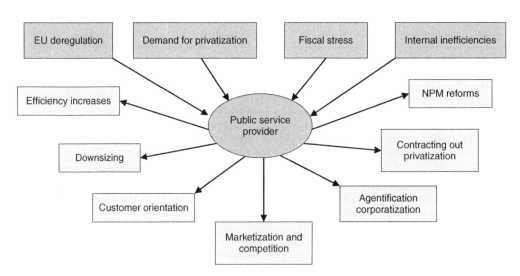

Figure 18.2   Challenges and reactions of public service providers (from Reichard 2006: 39)

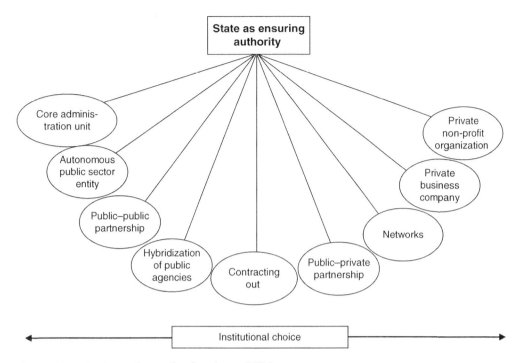

Figure 18.3   Variety of organizational possibilities

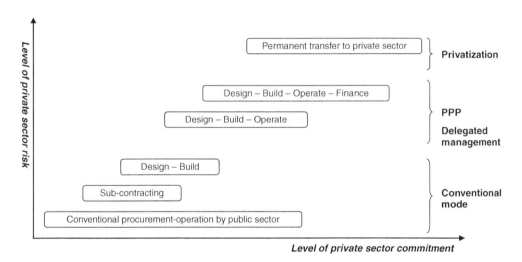

Figure 18.4   Delivery modes (from Government of Québec, 2004: 10)

a lot of examples at the transnational level), but in terms of the *different perspectives dominating the perception of both govern-ance structures*. PPP practice and research focuse on a *managerial perspective*, whereas the extremely rich literature on networks is about a *new mode of governance beyond market and hierarchy*, which charac-terizes the emergence of a post-statist network-society.

As far as public–private partnerships are concerned, it might be useful to have a look

Table 18.5   A comparison between contracting-out arrangements and partnerships

Contracting out	Partnerships
Government and company (or consortium) are involved in a principal–agent relationship	Government and company (consortium) are involved in joint decision-making and production
Government defines the problem, specifies the solution, and selects a private company that can produce results in a cost-efficient way	Both parties are involved in joint processes early on in order to develop joint products that contribute to both their interests
Benefits of contracting out arrangements especially relate to efficiency (quicker and cheaper)	Benefits of partnership arrangements especially relate to increasing effectiveness (synergy and enrichment of output)
Keys to success are unambiguous definitions of goals, projects, rules of tendering, rules of selection, and rules of delivery	Keys to success are an interweaving of goals, establishing rules for ongoing interaction, developing rules, and tailor-made assignments concerning joint effort and production commitments
Based on the principles of project management, because there is a clear principle, clear goals, and well-defined project specifications	Based on the principles of process management because the joint goals, the art of financing, realization, and utilization remain subject to joint decision-making
Contractual transparency regarding rules of tendering, selection, delivery, and rules of inspection are crucial for a good relationship	Mutual trust is crucial for lasting relationships between partners who maintain their own interest, ways of working, accountability, and financing principles

Source: Klijn and Teisman (2000: 86).

at the management course papers which are used at the Hertie School of Governance in Berlin, the only professional public policy school in Germany. The most important dimensions of PPPs are listed as:

- Participation: two or more parties involved, of which one is a public body.
- Relationship: *an enduring relationship and collaboration.*
- Resources: each party makes a value and resource contribution (money, property, authority, reputation).
- Sharing: PPPs involve a *sharing of responsibilities* and risk to outcomes in the collaborative framework.
- Continuity: a framework contract underpins the partnership, which sets out the 'rules of the game' and provides the partners with some certainty.

The following six points are mentioned as important aspects of managing contracts:

- care in make/buy decisions and vendor selection;
- a *'balanced' contract*: not too detailed but covering major performance issues, based on mutual trust;

- careful reflection of the three involved groups (values/institutions/markets);
- risk calculation and reduction: maintaining some in-house capacity, adequate termination of contract arrangements, risk assessment;
- *regular and effective monitoring of results*; including citizen feedback (e.g. user groups, surveys);
- *effective distribution of accountability* between purchaser and provider (ensuring responsibility = purchaser, providing responsibility = provider).

In contrast to this very managerial perspective on PPPs as an instrument for providing public services, we can draw out of the huge literature on networks (for an overview, see Börzel, 1998) seven characteristic elements of network governance (Kenis et al., 2008):

1   Policy networks are based on *bargaining processes* between corporate actors, and on the exchange of material and political resources.
2   The dominant control mechanism is *reputation*. If a network partner does not comply with and stick to the results of the bargaining process, its

reputation will be damaged and this will result in an erosion of trust.

3   In contrast to coordination by markets, *collective aims and purposes* are possible; this is a precondition for networks to function as instruments of governance.

4   *Decision-making is multilateral* – all the actors try to find a common solution.

5   Therefore, relations in networks are predominantly *horizontal relations*.

6   Network actors are focused on the solution of common problems, which function with a pooling of resources as a *method of integration*.

7   Networks are characterized by *functional differentiation*, i.e., network actors have different functions and roles, following their own logic of action, and bringing with them (as network inputs, so to speak) different forms of knowledge and skills.

If we want to summarize these points, it seems that all agree with the finding that partnerships rely to a considerable extent on trust, as pointed out by Klijn and Teisman (2000: 97–8):

> Trust is important in partnerships. Trust, however, not only depends on the specific process itself, but also on the stability of the network in which partnerships are developed and the type of rules that are at work. If a network is dominated by the rule that autonomy is important, it will be difficult to develop partnerships. The actors will not be inclined to exchange information and ideas and will tend to focus on their own ambitions and goals.

They therefore recommend – strongly stressing the similarity of networks and PPPs – the strategies in Table 18.6 for improving trust-building.

Regardless of whether these proposed strategies are well-chosen, what we can learn from these proposals is that governance of partnerships is very complex; what is needed are government structures which not only foster effective provision of public goods in a managerial sense but also which organize partnerships to promote mutual learning and so encourage the mutual exchange of ideas and perspectives.

PUBLIC–PRIVATE PARTNERSHIPS: WHY AND HOW?

Reasons for establishing PPPs

In the literature on PPPs, we find in nearly every article a list of the pros and cons of PPPs, often reflecting the particular view of the author. In a survey mainly of summaries of workshop sessions, as well as the scientific literature, Detlef Sack (2009: 175) recently presented a list of characteristics which are most frequently associated with PPPs.

Characteristics of PPPs

- Relationship between public budget and PPPs   39
- Relationship between efficiency and PPPs   39
- Appropriate sharing of risks   25
- Relationship between innovation and PPPs   18
- Improving the continuity of public services   18
- PPPs rely on mutual partnership   15
- PPPs reflect the concept of the "slim state"   8

Table 18.6   Network constitution strategies for public–private partnerships

Strategy	Aim
Add new actors/change distribution of means over different actors	Break the closed character of the networks in order to generate a wider field for formation of partnerships
Reframe the themes and beliefs in a network by introducing alternatives	Establish new ideas and transform inflexible thinking in order to facilitate the search for quality
Change rules of behavior towards: • conflict regulation • evaluation/benefits • positions	Establish rules that facilitate partnering and also generate a common approach concerning how to behave in partnerships

Source: Klijn and Teisman (2000: 98).

- PPPs should be under public oversight   7
- PPPs are in contact with local self-government   6
- PPPs express citizens' engagement   6
- PPPs increase the plurality of services   5
- PPPs change a concept of 'Daseinsvorsorge' (service publique)   4
- PPPs reflect the concept of the 'activating state'   3
- PPPs lead to more competition   3

This picture is quite clear. *Domestic PPPs* in the field of public services are about money – reducing public spending – and efficiency. That is it.

The picture is quite different if you look at the *transnational or global level*, where we can witness an increasing number of *global partnerships*. These are termed public–private partnerships, but have a more network-like structure and have aims which have little to do with management of cutbacks or improvements in efficiency. These PPPs (examples taken from Kaul, 2006) aim at:

- strengthening worldwide social and environmental responsibility;
- pioneering new markets;
- promoting global technical standards;
- advancing the frontiers of the insurance market (the African Trade Insurance Agency);

- making essential private goods affordable for all (global funds to fight AIDS, tuberculosis, and malaria);
- promoting the fight against poverty in research and development (The Medicines for Malaria Venture).

Typologies of PPPs

Again we have to make a clear distinction between domestic PPPs involved in the provision of public services, and global PPPs which are mainly engaged in poverty reduction and sustainable development.

We can distinguish between three types of domestic PPPs:

- *organizational PPPs*, which are based on company law contracts, mostly as companies with limited liability;
- *contractual PPPs*, which are based on private law contracts;
- *self-committing network-like PPPs*.

An analytical look at their internal governance structures leads to the typology in Table 18.7.

On a global level, Kaul (2006) distinguishes between three basic types of *global PPPs*.

Table 18.7 Typology of domestic PPPs

	Organizational PPPs (I)	Contractual PPPs (II)	Self-committing network-like PPPs (III)
Actors involved	Public agencies and private companies	Public agencies, private firms and third-sector organizations	Public agencies, private firms and third-sector organizations
Number of actors	Low (2–5)	Low (2–3)	Medium (5–15)
Coupling of actors	Close contractual coupling creating a common organization	Close contractual coupling with a principal–agent relation	Loose close coupling relying on informal mutual commitment
Task description	Product-oriented, more comprehensive	Product-oriented, more specific	Price-oriented, more comprehensive
Profit and risk-allocation	Symmetric	Symmetric	Symmetric
Management	Public–private	Private	Public–private
Criteria for evaluation	Mutual development	Fixed in advance	Mutual development
Mix of modes of governance	Cooperation	Cooperation/hierarchy	Cooperation/competition

Source: adapted partly from Sack (2009: 165).

- *Business ventures*, seeking mainly private gain that would accrue to at least one or all of the partners (the term 'private gain', when accruing to a public partner, i.e. a government agency, refers to organizational benefits, such as cost-savings).
- *Double bottom-line ventures*, seeking to combine private returns on investments with social- or public-interest goals, such as enhanced energy or water provision in poorer countries.
- *Social ventures*, pursuing as a primary objective such public-interest concerns as poverty reduction, communicable disease control, and sustainable development.

With this basic distinction as a starting point, Kaul (2006) presents the overview given in Table 18.8 of the internal structures of global PPPs.

How to get a PPP to work: the case of Québec

In order to better meet the population's needs and provide quality services at lower cost, the Québec government encourages PPPs when they clearly offer greater added value for the public funds invested. To ensure a fruitful combination of more effective public services and the safeguarding of the public interest, the government of Québec has established a special PPP Agency, the 'Agence des partenariats public-privé' to approve all PPP projects in which a public body wants to engage. As a guideline for the 'PPP project approval process' the government has published the diagram shown in Figure 18.5 (Government of Québec, 2004), which shows in a very convincing way the steps necessary to ensure that a PPP really works.

An extremely important step has turned out to be No. 4, the procurement process. Under the influence of European Community law and the jurisdiction of the European Court of Justice, procurement law has developed into an "imperialistic" branch of law, claiming that all choices concerning the private partner of a PPP fall under the regime of procurement laws.

Risk sharing in public–private partnerships

Setting up a PPP is a complex endeavor, especially if the projects are ambitious, like

Table 18.8 Typology of global public–private partnerships

Venture class	Partnership type/ purpose	Nature of partnership product	Legal status of partnership agency	Main sources of financing
	Trading comparative advantage	Private good	For-profit/non-profit	Payments for services, reassignment of rights to collect revenue
	Pioneering new institutions (notable new markets)	Private good/ group good	For-profit	Cost-sharing contributions from partners
	Defining rules/setting standards	Group good	Non-profit	Fees, charges
	Advancing the frontiers of markets	Private good/ national public good	For-profit	Equity and other capital, guarantees
	Brokering 'affordable price' deals	Merit good	Non-profit	Differential contracting/ patenting, purchase guarantees
	Leveraging R&D	Merit good/private good	Non-profit	Donations, differential patenting
	Managing for strategic results	Merit good	Non-profit/unit of intergovernmental organization	Donations

Source: From Kaul (2006: 40).

Galileo at the European level (see Mörth, 2009) or the Toll-Collect-System in Germany. Budäus and Grüb (2008) – two of the foremost experts on PPPs in Germany – have recently presented a *phase model of PPPs at work* (Figure 18.6), marking the decisive *point of no return*, after which the public partner has to concern itself with additional costs and the technical problems of implementation.

If this model mirrors – as it seems to – the reality of complex PPPs quite well, it is of utmost importance to develop an efficient

risk management plan, which requires a high degree of expertise and skill from the public partner. To facilitate this, Budäus and Grüb suggest as a governance instrument for PPPs a *transparency report* (Figure 18.7).

OUTLOOK: FROM PARTNERSHIPS TO CO-PRODUCTION OF STATEHOOD

It is useful to sometimes leave the narrow world of the OECD countries and look at

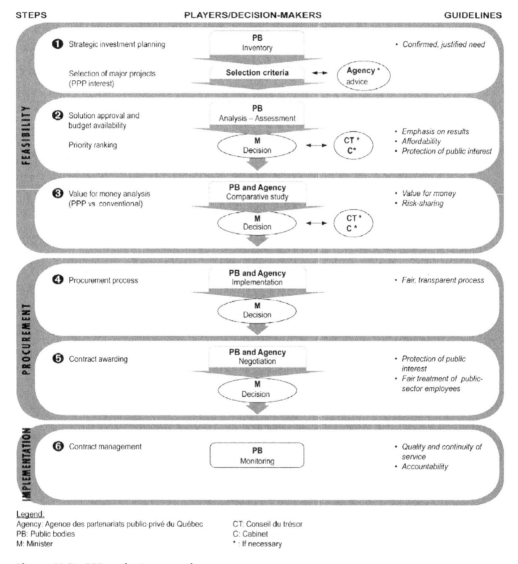

Figure 18.5 PPP project approval process

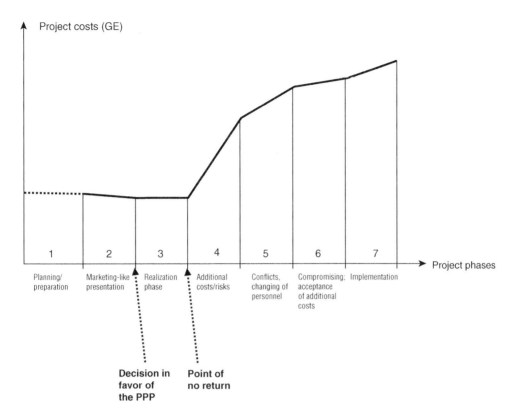

Figure 18.6 Phase model of PPPs at work

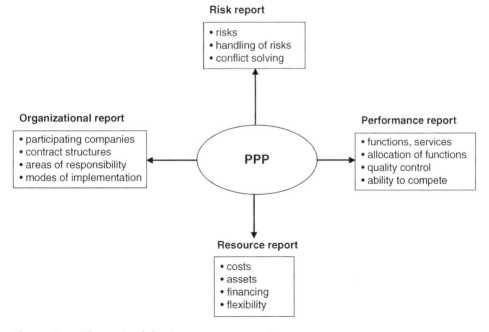

Figure 18.7 Elements of the transparency report

governance problems in areas of limited state-hood (weak states, failing states, etc.). This quite different world of governance con-fronts scholars with the empirical reality that the provision of statehood by a multitude of actors can be observed in many post-conflict and low-income countries, and that the local elites use the 'outsourcing of statehood' as a very helpful strategy. One of the best experts in this field – Christoph Zürcher – comments on this reality as follows (2007: 14 ff.):

> I depart from the notion that statehood is provided solely by the state. I suggest that we *think of statehood as a product* which is produced by the state in association with other actors. There are examples abundant when states outsource – intentionally or not – the provision of basic func-tions to external actors. It is sufficient to think of who provides security in Afghanistan or Tajikistan, domestic authority in Kosovo or Bosnia, or public services in Mozambique or Burundi. There are also international institutions and organizations in place to assume these functions – think of the UN tran-sitional administration, the international forces in Afghanistan, or of the World Bank's suggestion to set up so-called ISAs (Independent Service Authorities) in low-income countries under stress (LICUS). ISAs would provide basic services, being independent from government and acting like wholesale contractors with multiple channels for retail provision. In essence, ISA is the outsourcing of basic state services to a private, donor-funded organization.

The message of these interesting observa-tions is that we can and should look at *state-hood as a product*. If statehood is regarded as a product, we can think about: the required *quality of the product* and how it can be improved; the *production process* which leads to the 'output of statehood'; and – last but not least – the variety of actors who con-tribute as *co-producers* to the final product. If we take this point of view, we can examine different policy fields and ask if we find forms of co-production in

- the field of a classic state monopoly, the *provi-sion of security* (private military companies, community police, etc.);
- the field of *welfare* (non-profit organizations and charities as reliable partners of the welfare state; Salamon, 1987);

- the field of *law making* (standard setting committees, etc.);
- the field of *infrastructure* (PPPs at every corner).

We could easily continue with these exam-ples. The point that I want to make is that understanding statehood as a product with a variety of actors involved in the process of production might help to over-come the often too-narrow managerial perspective on partnerships; instead, PPPs should be looked at in the broader context of changing statehood and changing patterns of governance.

REFERENCES

Anheier, Helmut K. and Seibel, Wolfgang (eds), (1990) *The Third Sector: Comparative Studies of Non-Profit Organizations*. Berlin/New York: De Gruyter.

Börzel, Tanja A (1998) 'Organizing Babylon – on the Different Conceptions of Policy Networks', *Public Administration* 76: 253–73.

Börzel, Tanja and Risse, Thomas (2005) 'Public–Private Partnership. Effective and Legitimate Tools of Transnational Governance?', in Edgar Grande and Louise W. Pauly (eds), *Complex Sovereignty: Reconstituting Political Authority in the Twenty-First Century*. Toronto: University of Toronto Press, pp. 195–216.

Budäus, Dietrich and Grüb, Birgit (2008) 'Public Private Partnership (PPP): Zum aktuellen Entwicklungs- und Diskussionsstand', in Hartmut Bauer, Christian Büchner and Frauke Brosius-Gersdorf (eds), *Verwaltungskooperation. Public Private Partnerships und Public Public Partnerships*. Potsdam: Universitätsverlag Potsdam, pp. 33–50.

Czempiel, Ernst-Otto and Rosenau, James (eds), (1992) *Governance Without Government: Order and Change in World Politics*. Cambridge: Cambridge University Press.

Donahue, John D. and Zeckhauser, Richard J. (2006) 'Public–Private Collaboration', in Michael Moran, Martin Rein and Robert E. Goodin (eds), *The Oxford Handbook of Public Policy*. Oxford: Oxford University Press, pp. 496–526.

Freeman, J. (1997) 'Collaborative Governance in the Administrative State', *UCLA Law Review* 45: 1–99.

Government of Québec (2004) *Public–Private Partnerships Framework Policy*. Québec.

Grande, Edgar and Pauly, Louis W. (eds), (2005) *Complex Sovereignty. Reconstituting Political Authority in the Twenty-First Century*. Toronto: Toronto University Press.

Haufler, Virginia (2001) *A Public Role for the Private Sector. Industry Self-Regulation in a Global Economy*, Washington, DC: Carnegie Endowment for International Peace.

Jordana, Jacint and Levi-Faur, D. (eds), (2004) *The Politics of Regulation – Institutions and Regulatory Reforms for the Age of Governance*. Cheltenham, UK: Edward Elgar.

Kaul, Inge (2006) 'Exploring the Policy Space Between Market and States: Global Public–Private Partnerships', in Inge Kaul and Pedro Conceicao (eds), *The New Public Finance: Responding to Global Challenges*. Oxford, Oxford University Press.

Kenis, Patrick, Nölke, Andreas and Raab, Jörg (2008) 'Transnationale Politiknetzwerke. Institutionenkultur jenseits des Nationalstaates', in Dieter Gosewinkel and Folke Schuppert (eds), *Politische Kultur im Wandel von Staatlichkeit*. Berlin: WZB-Jahrbuch 2007, Ed. Sigma, pp. 163–80.

Klijn, Erik-Hans and Teisman, Geert R. (2000) 'Governing Public–Private Partnerships. Analyzing and Managing the Processes and Institutional Characteristics of Public–Private Partnerships', in Steven P. Osborne (ed), *Public–Private Partnership. Theory and Practice in International Perspective*. London: Routledge Chapman & Hall, pp. 84–104.

Linder, Stephen (2002) 'Coming to Terms with the Public–Private Partnership: A Grammar of Multiple Meanings', in Pauline Vaillancourt Rosenau (ed), *Public–Private Policy Partnerships*. Cambridge, MA: MIT Press.

Mayntz, Renate (2004) 'Governance im modernen Staat', in Arthur Benz (ed), *Governance – Regieren in komplexen Regelsystemen*. Wiesbaden: VS Verlag für Sozialwissenschaften, pp. 65–76.

Mörth, Ulrika (2009) 'The Market Turn in EU Governance – The Emergence of Public–Private Collaboration', *Governance: An International Journal of Policy, Administration, and Institutions* 22: 99–120.

Reichard, Christoph (2006) 'New Institutional Arrangements of Public Service Delivery', in Christoph Reichard, Riccardo Mussari and Soren Kupke (eds), *The Governance of Services of General Interest between State, Market and Society*. Berlin: Wissenschaftsverlag, pp. 35–48.

Risse, Thomas (forthcoming) 'Governance in Areas of Limited Statehood: Introduction and Overview', in: Thomas Risse and Ursula Lehmkuhl (eds), *Governance Without a State? Policies and Politics in Areas of Limited Statehood*. New York: Columbia University Press.

Sack, Detlef (2009) *Governance und Politics. Die Institutionalisierung Öffentlich-Privater Partnerschaften in Deutschland*. Baden-Baden: Nomos.

Sahlin-Andersson, Kerstin (2006) 'Corporate Social Responsibility: A Trend and a Movement, but of What and for What?', *Corporate Governance* 6: 595–608.

Salamon, Lester (1987) 'Partners in Public Service: The Scope and Theory of Government – Non-profit Relations', in W.W. Powell (ed), *The Non-Profit Factor. A Research Handbook*. New Haven, CT: Yale University Press, pp. 99–117.

Schuppert, Gunnar Folke (2008) 'Was ist und wie misst man Wandel von Staatlichkeit?', *Der Staat* 47: 325–58.

Schuppert, Gunnar Folke and Zürn, Michael (eds), (2008) *Governance in einer sich wandelndenWelt, PVS – Politische Vierteljahresschrift. Sonderheft 41*. Wiesbaden: VS Verlag für Sozialwissenschaften.

Wolf, Klaus Dieter (2008) 'Emerging Patterns of Governance: The New Interplay between the State, Business and Civil Society', in Andreas Scherer and Guido Palazzo (eds), *Handbook of Research on Global Corporate Citizenship*. Cheltenham: Edward Elgar, pp. 225–48.

Zangl, Bernhard and Genschel, Philipp (2008) 'Metamorphosen des Staates–vom Herrschaftsmonopolisten zum Herrschaftsmanager', *Leviathan* 36: 430–54.

Zürcher, Christoph (2007) 'When Governance meets Troubled States', in Marianne Beisheim and Gunnar Folke Schuppert (eds), *Staatszerfall und Governance*. Baden-Baden: Nomos. pp. 11–27.

Zürn, Michael (1998) *Regieren jenseits des Nationalstaates. Globalisierung und Denationalisierung als Chance*. Frankfurt/Main: Suhrkamp.

19

Multijurisdictional Regulation

Andy Smith

INTRODUCTION

Since the early 1980s, the rise of 'the multi' in political analysis has been concomitant to the spread of 'governance' throughout much of the world. More precisely, if one considers that governance encapsulates significant change in the relationship between political, administrative, collective and private actors (Rhodes, 1997), the qualification 'multi' has frequently been attached to this term in order to capture what is generally seen as an increase in the institutionalized overlap of decision-making arenas. In turn, these arenas purport to set and implement rules which cover different scales of public intervention that either surpass that of the nation-state or determine the politics that takes place within it (Sassen, 2007). The European Union (EU) is the most obvious, recent and structured example of a governance entity which incorporates multiple scales of governance. But it is important to consider that even within long-established nation-states, for instance Canada, governing through and across multiple decision-making levels is not necessarily new. Instead, the novelty of this subject is to be found in two directions.

First, empirically the intensity and density of governance that encompasses several scales of formal authority has certainly increased since the 1970s. In particular, this has meant that practitioners in public authorities, interest groups and large firms have had to adapt to a world within which power tends strongly to be shared and exercised in different ways than hitherto. As the rest of this volume has consistently shown, over the last 30–40 years governing through networks has come to dominate contemporary governance. This particular chapter is specifically concerned with the increases in the overlapping of governance arenas that this trend has also entailed.

Secondly, from the point of view of social science analysis, examining the multi-scaled dimension of contemporary governance challenges the concepts, questions and research methods which for decades had been framed in terms of the 'centre–periphery relations' of sovereign states. In a world where national capitals are no longer necessarily the sites within which governance is centralized, thinking in terms of its plural *loci* enables research to avoid *a priori* and often outdated assumptions about the holding of power. Instead, it encourages a focus upon empirical enquiry into power's actual distribution. In developing this claim, this chapter also seeks to further substantiate the second major theme of this *Handbook* which concerns the importance of coordination within contemporary politics. More precisely, by examining the multi-organizational and multi-scale networks of actors through which such coordination takes place, this volume's contention that power in today's world is fundamentally interdependent will be further pursued.

Over the last 30 years, changed patterns of governance and their increasing overlap have constituted a significant challenge for both practice and analysis. This chapter endeavours to set out how social science research has sought to capture the causes and consequences of these changes by focusing upon the 'multijurisdictional' dimension of contemporary governance in three sections. First, a set of key terms for studying this subject will be introduced, discussed and defined. Secondly, using this vocabulary, case studies of public sector reform entailing multiple jurisdictions will be presented as both illustration of multijurisdictional governance and as a means of exploring its causes and consequences. Thirdly, through identifying and comparing a certain number of traits that seem to be recurrent when governance is multijurisdictional, suggestions for reflection and future research will be proposed.

STUDYING MULTIJURISDICTIONAL REGULATION

When social scientists encounter something they consider 'new', their initial reaction is often to borrow words from everyday speech in order to qualify it. Initially, such terms serve the useful purpose of flagging the subject as meriting empirical study and, therefore, worthy of funding in order to do so! However, as most existing publications on governance across multiple jurisdictions clearly testify, two such 'commonsense' notions – 'levels' and 'coordination' – are of much less value when one actually sits down to design research that is rigorous, comparative and cumulative.

Instead, concepts developed and grounded within established social science theories give empirical enquiry much greater analytical purchase.

From the multi-level to the multijurisdictional

The first term that needs conceptualizing in this way concerns what the prefix 'multi' is used to qualify. Most existing publications on governance that are interested in coordination across scales between a plurality of public, collective and private bodies have been centred upon 'levels' of governance. This section describes their key term 'Multi-level governance', highlights its analytical problems and instead presents the first building block for an alternative perspective around the concept of jurisdiction.

The term multi-level governance was originally defined by specialists of the EU as a form of decision-making that is linked to 'a polity-creating process in which authority and policymaking influence are shared across multiple levels of government – subnational, national, and supranational' (Marks, Hooghe and Blank, 1996: 342). The initial aim of the term multi-level governance was thus to describe the sharing of decision-making amongst actors representing different constituencies and holding a variety of political resources (Smith, 2003). Subsequently, however, multi-level governance has often been accorded the status of a theory of European integration or, more generally still, of globalized politics. Indeed, many political scientists have come to use multi-level governance as a 'conceptual umbrella' (Bache and Flinders, 2004; Gualini, 2004: 33) under which a consensus has been rallied against 'intergovernmentalist' approaches to European integration (Moravcsik, 1993) and realist approaches to international relations (both of which depict the politics that takes place between countries as driven by 'powerful' and 'unitary' nation-states such as France or the United Kingdom).

Recent research has shown that multi-level governance can and should be critiqued from a number of angles (Carter and Smith, 2008). The only one focused upon here is that behind this term lies an ontology of politics as being fundamentally cleaved by 'levels' of governance. The central thesis concerning the underlying political logic of multi-level governance is one of 'friction' between central and regional 'levels' of national governance (Marks, Nielsen, Ray and Salk, 1996: 44). This 'friction' has been used to explain 'subnational mobilization' which, the argument goes, has taken the form of regional authorities seeking power by 'evading' the central state in order to act autonomously at the EU level in general, and this by allying themselves with the European Commission in particular.

A first problem with this ontology of public authority in contemporary Western Europe as a 'game' of multiple levels is that it conceptualizes the EU's key organizations, its member states and all its regions as three deeply different types of actor. All actors working for 'supranational' bodies such as the Commission are grouped together, just as all 'regions' are assumed to share the same interest and strategy of action. As shown by studies which highlight heterogeneity within the Commission (Robert, 2004) and between regions such as Scotland and Aquitaine (Smith, 2008), this vision of empirical reality bears little or no relation to the way practitioners represent their daily engagement within the EU. Indeed, reasoning in terms of levels makes analysis disincarnated and, ultimately, actor-less. From this flawed starting point, multi-level governance then characterizes the interactions between representatives of its three types of actor as being fundamentally structured around a contest between an alliance of the European Commission and the regions on the one hand, and member state governments on the other. Again, not only is this depiction of EU politics rarely borne out by solid empirical research but also it encourages interpretation of this politics that fails to specify how actors work within it and how their actions have causal effects.

A second problem with reasoning in terms of levels is that it considers the most important cleavages within politics to be between different territories of government. If the issue of territory does indeed remain essential for political analysis (Carter and Smith, 2008), thinking in terms of 'levels' overlooks one of the principal finding of sociologies of the state and of public-policy analysis about where contemporary politics is mostly played out: around the deeply sectoral cleavages which, since the end of the nineteenth century, have structured the societies and political spaces of the Western world (Schmitter, 1974; Jobert and Muller, 1987; Hollingsworth, Schmitter and Streeck, 1994). Indeed, not only do sectors constitute the principal lines of differentiation within societies and their respective states but also for decades sectoral governance has crossed territorial boundaries, thereby provoking tension, institutionalized divisions of competence and/or partial compromise solutions.

Consequently, if one begins analysis instead by reasoning about governance while keeping firmly in mind the importance of sectors that straddle different patterns of scales of authority, the term level can be abandoned in favour of another that better captures the struggles for power that take place within sectoral spaces of governance. The proposal made thus far by a handful of social scientists[1] and taken up here is to adopt the concept of 'jurisdiction' that is so central to specialists of the law and adapt it to fit with social science questions and research techniques. According to legal scholars such as Ian McLeod, jurisdiction means both the power to hear a case and the geographical area which is subject to the power of a court (2006: 127). In other words, jurisdictions delimit authority to rule (here defined in terms of legal competence) and the territorial frontiers of that rule. From the perspective of the discipline of law, the term multijurisdictional is now frequently used in publications on issues ranging from drug task forces in the USA (Cardenas, 2002) to competition law in the EU. Indeed, to cite a specialist of the latter subject (Cseres, 2007), here 'the central query is whether the same rules applied in a multiple variety of institutions can result in uniform and consistent law application as well as in equal gains and losses for the jurisdiction'.

Although specialists of governance within political science have in common this interest in studying authority, territorial frontiers and their increasing overlap, they share neither the positivism of a legal specialist's line of questioning nor, at least as yet, the very term multijurisdictional. The first and general reason for this is that most contemporary political scientists are more interested in understanding how politics takes place than in making judgements of it. The second more specific reason political scientists distance themselves from the posture of most academic lawyers is that for four decades now, studies of policy implementation have shown that analysts should never expect policy to be implemented in the same way in different jurisdictions, nor precisely as its legislator intended (Pressman and Wildavsky, 1973).

Bearing these epistemological and ontological points firmly in mind, the concept of jurisdictions can nonetheless be usefully translated and imported into social science as an antidote to the imprecise thinking and research inspired by the notion of 'levels'. To do so, three aspects of a social science definition of jurisdictions initially need highlighting before being further developed below.

1 Jurisdictions will be envisaged as applying to policy sectors rather than to polities or political territories as a whole. In this way one can better understand why, for example, the US Federal Government has sole jurisdiction for making rules for the US Army but that jurisdiction over education policy is shared with state and local authorities, and is thus multijurisdictional.
2 The competence of a jurisdiction (i.e. its right to rule) will be seen as always liable to be contested. Whereas lawyers tend to maintain that disputes over jurisdiction are settled by the courts, such contestation is framed here as a permanent process that is only ever provisionally stabilized, and

this through political activity which may or may not involve the judiciary.
3 Issues of competence will be framed here as being inseparable from the legitimacy of a jurisdiction's frontiers. Again, we consider that the latter is constantly rather than episodically challenged during the making of sectoral policies and laws – as is the legitimacy of the actors who reproduce or seek to change them.

From coordination to regulation

An important means of thinking about multijurisdictional governance is to reflect upon the daily coordinating tasks it strongly tends to encompass. These tasks include the efficient and equitable sharing of information, 'joining-up' organizations across jurisdictions and avoiding duplication – in short, 'making sure that the left hand knows what the right is doing'. For this reason, the operation of networks of public, collective and private actors is clearly an essential part of this governance (Rhodes, 1997). For example, specialists of the European Union have rightly highlighted the density and character of interactions between national ministries and each member state's 'Permanent Representation' which impacts upon how policy positions are defended in the Council of Ministers (Kassim et al., 2001). However, as social science has increasingly come to underline (Pierre, 2000), around these functional 'coordinating' tasks a series of more fundamental challenges to the accountability and legitimacy of public action are also raised, tackled or avoided (for example, who should decide about the UK's position on policing during EU negotiations).

The challenge for research is thus to get away from the limited and functionalist focus upon 'coordination' favoured by specialists of public management who consider this process can be evaluated in terms of a universalist and apolitical definition of 'efficiency'. Instead, one needs to begin reasoning here from the hypothesis that the configuration of a sector is never the result of functionally determined 'efficiency'. Rather, each pattern of sectoral governance is the sedimented consequence of rules which have regularized behaviour around stable and legitimate institutions that generally prevent unpredictable acts on the part of the organizations it concerns, e.g. governments, interest groups and firms (Fligstein and Choo, 2005: 61). In other words, even if the sustainability of the rules which structure daily conduct within sectors are of course linked to functional issues (e.g. producing and selling consumer goods or providing health services), their durability is above all a political construction. It follows that the critical condition for the stability of a sector is the capacity of certain actors to impose and maintain a division of authority that rests upon justifications which are generally accepted by the practitioners concerned.

In order to grasp this constant process of institutionalization which both shapes the external frontiers of a sector and the politics that goes on within it, this chapter therefore suggests abandoning the term 'coordination' in favour of the concept of 'regulation'. Defined as the making and implementation of a set of stabilized rules which transform potentially anarchic functional processes (e.g. inter-firm competition) into durable and 'secure' ones (Jessop and Sum, 2006), the concept of regulation enables and encourages research to focus upon:

- the frontiers that are given to rules, as well as the eligibility of the actors who make and implement them
- contestations of these frontiers which, over time, contribute to change or stasis in the regulation of a sector.

Put from the point of view of practitioners, over the last 30 years, a major challenge for reformers has frequently been to re-regulate sectors by establishing frontiers for their rules which are no longer nation-state specific. More precisely, this process of institutionalizing regulatory change needs studying as both one of the setting of rules and also of their legitimation, i.e. making them socially and politically accepted (Lagroye, 1985).

MULTIJURISTDICTIONAL REFORMS: CASE STUDIES

In order to illustrate the points made above, this section presents three examples of recent attempts to reform governance by changing multijurisdictional regulation. The first concerns the EU's competition policy, the second the Scotch whisky industry and the third the governance of aquaculture in Canada.

Multijursidictional regulation supreme? The 2004 reform of EU competition policy

Throughout the contemporary world, competition policy ostensibly creates 'a level playing field' for firms that produce goods or services. It does so through sets of 'anti-trust' rules that restrict behaviour such as price-fixing or inter-firm collusion (cartels), by constraining the creation of monopolies through mergers or takeovers and by outlawing 'unfair' public intervention in markets ('state aids'). On paper, the EU has possessed a common competition policy since the early 1960s. In reality, however, this policy only began to systematically take effect in the 1990s. Indeed, over the period 1985–92 many specialists consider that competition policy came to be the EU's most 'supranational' field of action (Cini and McGowan, 2009). An EU-wide jurisdiction was built with the European Commission, and more specifically its Commissioner and Directorate General for Competition (DG Competition), as its sole 'judges'. What this meant in practice was that firms seeking to undertake a merger, or public authorities wishing to distribute a subsidy, had to notify the Commission and receive its approval.

This system certainly encouraged the spreading of a single approach to competition policy throughout the EU. Indeed, many observers consider that it caused a significant reduction in anti-trust activities, monopolies and state aids. However, by the end of the

1990s actors within the Commission and representatives of business began to see the notification system as too slow and, therefore, out of step with contemporary commercial activity. After several years of consultation and negotiation, the EU's Council of Ministers and the European Parliament (EP) decided to introduce a radical reform which formally and explicitly made EU competition policy multijurisdictional. Starting with a key regulation adopted in 2003 (1/2003), the 'decentralization' of EU competition law and policy has been channelled through the creation of a formalized European Competition Network (ECN). As Lehmkuhl suggestively describes: 'The music of European Competition Law will in future be performed by an orchestra of national competition authorities plus the European Commission rather than by the Commission as a soloist' (2009: 103). In briefly describing the ECN, what it appears to have done since 2004 and some impacts in the member states, a line of questioning about its power dynamics will be developed. Indeed, perhaps the best way into this line of enquiry is to discover what the ECN changes for representatives of the Commission. Within this network is it a *primus inter pares* or the dominant actor? To paraphrase Lehmkuhl (2009: 103), and using ongoing research findings (Montalban, Ramirez-Perez, and Smith; 2009), the question explored here is does the ECN constitute a shift from hierarchy to cooperation within the multiple jurisdictions through which inter-firm competition is now regulated?

The ECN is essentially a grouping of four forums for exchange, debate or negotiation:

- a biannual meeting of the general directors of competition authorities from each of the member states and of DG Competition
- an ECN Plenary of liaison officials in the network and the ECN unit in DG Competition
- working groups of officials from each competition authority who exchange information and views on issues such as sanctions, leniency programmes and multijurisdictional mergers
- sector-specific subgroups of more specialized officials.

As for the roles and activities of the ECN, they fall into three categories. The first is to serve as a conduit for information between DG Competition and national competition authorities. This most often seems to entail the Commission issuing 'Guidelines' and notices. Indeed, by June 2007 the Commission had issued 20 such documents. Although legally non-binding, they do appear to be having significant impacts upon behaviour and role perceptions within national authorities. Moreover, from the point of view of Commission officials, guidelines and notices present the added advantage of not requiring consultation or negotiation in the Council or the EP. For the moment at least then, most communication of 'information' appears to flow 'down' from DG Competition to its national 'partners', rather than feed up in the opposite direction.

The second role of the ECN is to oblige all its members to notify the network as a whole, and therefore DG Competition, whenever it is preparing to make a decision which might affect cross-border trade within the single market. This obligation is formally intended to encourage the establishment of common views on individual cases. However, interviews within the French national competition agency (*Le Conseil de la Concurrence*) in 2007 and 2008 suggest that the effects of this obligation to notify are even more far reaching. Indeed, according to senior officials from this organization, its transformation into an independent *Autorité de la Concurrence* in January 2009, and in particular the reinforcement of its investigatory powers that this has entailed, owes much to the role this body now plays in the ECN. Indeed, in the words of one interviewee, this change 'consecrates the slow but structural evolution' of the logic of action of this organization from that of a court, to that of an independent agency.

The third and final role played by the ECN is much less formal but also more pervasive: to encourage the development and deepening of a European-wide community of competition law and policy specialists. The most tangible vectors of this phenomenon are the funding, designing and provision of training on the one hand and, on the other, the organization of conferences and other modes of communication. Although systematic research has yet to be devoted to this subject, it certainly does seem that the ECN fosters the development of an EU-wide 'epistemic community' of lawyers and civil servants specialized in competition policy who tend strongly to frame this policy and the issues it raises in similar ways.

In summary, the 2004 reform of EU competition policy appears strongly to have institutionalized the multijurisdictional regulation of this extremely important field of public action throughout the 27 member states of this international region. Information and reporting channels have been built or rebuilt, while attempts have been made to clarify the respective competence of the EU-wide and national jurisdictions. However, examining this subject around the concept of regulation does reveal that actors from the Commission appear nevertheless to have retained a great deal of power within the ECN. Indeed, if multijurisdictional regulation now exists, it still appears to be dominated by the staff of the Commission, their framing of competition and their logic of action. Over the coming years, new research will hopefully reveal more about their legitimacy, particularly if other members of the ECN seek to reshape the hierarchy of this policy area's jurisdictional landscape.

A multijurisdictional sector meets polity change: Scotch whisky and British devolution

Industries tend strongly to be regulated sectorally and, at least today, through configurations of actors and institutions that are highly multijurisdictional (Jullien and Smith, 2008). The Scotch Whisky industry provides a clearcut illustration of this point because it is regulated through arenas with overlapping jurisdictions that concern four scales of governance: Scotland, the UK, the EU and the World Trade Organization (WTO). By synthesizing analysis presented in full elsewhere (Smith, 2010), this section unpacks this particular form of multijurisdictional regulation through recounting the preparation and adoption of legislation to recodify in a single law a number of the industry's key institutions. Initial plans for this legislation emerged in 2003 from conflict between rival distillers. In the short term, this dispute was settled within the industry's main collective action group: the Scotch Whisky Association (SWA). However, its longer-term resolution also entailed enlarging the issue as part of the implementation of EU and WTO legislation. For the next four years, many actors considered that the best site for providing institutionalized regulation of this problem was the Scottish Parliament (SP). Ironically, however, since the election of a Scottish National Party (SNP) led Scottish Government (SG) in May 2007, plans for a symbolically charged 'Scottish Scotch Whisky Act' have been dropped in favour of a UK statutory instrument. From the point of view of multijurisdictional regulation, the case illustrates how the regulatory 'frontiers' proposed in the polity-changing Scottish devolution settlement left open many questions to be negotiated sector by sector. Moreover, our analysis also shows that negotiations in fact took place in a regional–national–EU–WTO space where jurisdictions have remained decidedly 'fluid' to the end. Through unpacking successively the three parts to this story, the aim here is above all to tease out the relationship between the multijurisdictional regulation sites of a sector, polity change and political action undertaken as a consequence of both.

Until 2003, the jurisdictions that concerned the whisky industry had been stable for many years. The deepening of the EU, the creation of the WTO and, more specifically, the adoption of its Trade Related Aspects of Intellectual Property Rights (TRIPS) agreement in 1994, had all led the industry's protagonists to adjust their political work, but not to change it radically. However, in 2003 the relative serenity of Scotch's institutional order disappeared overnight because of a dispute sparked by its biggest player: the multinational drinks company *Diageo*. This dispute began because of a decision taken within this company regarding *Cardhu*, one of its leading brands of malt whisky. Until then, Diageo had complied with industry convention which required that a 'single malt whisky' should be entirely produced in one distillery. Lacking stocks to supply a rapidly growing Spanish market, managers of Diageo decided to produce more *Cardhu* by blending it with other malts, altering the labelling from 'single malt' to 'pure malt', but otherwise not drawing the consumer's attention to this change in production method. This provoked an immediate reaction from other distillers who were dismayed that this action would undermine the cachet and premium attached to malt whisky.

However, the issue had much wider ramifications because its initial resolution (Diageo stopped its new labelling practices) also entailed the setting up of an internal SWA working group charged with revising a wider range of the industry's rules. The report of this group led the SWA to propose to codify in law five categories of Scotch Whisky, but also to legislate over three other issues (the use of regional names as geographical indications, a requirement that all Scotch be wholly matured in Scotland and the prohibition of exporting single malts until bottled and labelled). However, one major element of uncertainty remained: Which public authorities should prepare and adopt the new legislation?

From the viewpoint of formal legitimacy and past practice, the most obvious jurisdiction for developing this legislation was the UK. First, previous whisky acts had been set within and through this jurisdiction. Secondly, the devolution settlement did not clearly assign competence for legislation concerning this industry to the SP and SG. Although some responsibility for food and drink issues had been devolved, the proposed Whisky Act did not neatly fall within this category of public action. However, despite these reasons for legislating 'in London', a decision was taken within the SWA to attempt to legislate

'in Edinburgh' through a 'Scottish Scotch Whisky Act'. The 'efficiency' of legislating by using the formal resources of Scottish devolution was put forward as a major reason for this choice, but many stakeholders also more fundamentally saw this as an issue of legitimacy: *'the Scottish Parliament is a natural home for this'* (Interview, May 2006).

However, from mid 2006 to early 2007, negotiations with the UK civil service about proposed legislation became bogged down and eventually ground to a halt. Scotland's then Labour-dominated ministers chose not to override uncertainty over this aspect of devolution by demanding the right to legislate. Revealingly, it was only after the election to government in May 2007 of politicians from the SNP–a party committed to 'independence for Scotland' – that a choice of jurisdiction was made. Ironically, this choice was to abandon a Scottish Scotch Whisky Act in favour of a UK statutory instrument. Analysis of this radical and counter-intuitive shift highlights two major jurisdictional uncertainties that remained when the SNP came to power.

The first concerned the breadth of the proposed legislation and how this should be problematized. The issue of whisky categories was initially presented by the SWA as a food and drink issue and, therefore, within the devolved competence of the Scottish Parliament. However, officials in the UK's Department of Environment, Food and Rural Affairs (DEFRA) framed these issues instead in terms of trade and the European single market; both competences that had been 'reserved' to the UK government.

A second uncertainty concerned the issue of whether the devolution settlement of the late 1990s could and should be reopened to discussion and, possibly, be changed. Here, in their advice to Ministers, officials in the Scottish Government consistently represented this uncertainty as a reason for caution and, in the end, for choosing the technocratic solution of a depoliticized UK statutory instrument.

In summary, the deepening and accumulation of these uncertainties led to a transformation in the commonly- held representation of a Scottish Scotch Whisky Act from being 'an opportunity' to being 'a risk'. Networks of actors specialized in regulating the Scotch Whisky industry closed ranks and convinced generalist politicians that they should choose a technocratic route to legislation which did not openly challenge a trans-sectoral multi-jurisdictional settlement. Indeed, implicitly, they sought to keep future options for sectoral regulation open by deliberately maintaining the fundamental ambiguity of the devolution settlement.

Multijurisdictional regulation meets intersectoral conflict: Canadian aquaculture

Having grown throughout the world at nearly 9 per cent per year since the 1970s, aquaculture has often been seen as a major part of the answer to food shortages in general and that of proteins in particular (Culver and Castle, 2008: 1). However, over the last 15 years this fast-expanding sector has also fuelled ongoing contestations about the way food is produced and the negative externalities this can engender for the environment, coastal areas and human health. From the point of view of students of governance, such debates and conflict are of great interest, especially because as a 'new' industry, aquaculture is largely structured by regulation that has been created and adopted almost from scratch.

For the purposes of this chapter, the case of the world's sixth biggest aquaculture producer – Canada – is of even more interest because within this federal polity the sector's regulation has been both multijurisdictional and highly controversial. On one level, the plurality of actors involved and the heatedness of debates appears curious. Federal government regulation is legitimated by the 1867 Constitution Act, which accorded it jurisdiction over sea coasts, navigation, the rights of 'First Nations peoples' and environmental protection. Meanwhile provincial governments possess constitutionally- protected

jurisdiction over property rights and economic development – thus, over the licensing of fish farms and the provision of subsidies to them. Moreover, Canada has frequently been described as a polity where governance by consensus is the norm. Notwithstanding such factors, specialists of this subject area recently have come to the conclusion that 'the jurisdictional tangle that has emerged in the sector has proved to be a considerable obstacle to the sustainable development of the aquaculture industry' (Rayner and Howlett, 2007: 58). How has this situation occurred in a country with an enormous coastline, a failing 'capture' fishing industry and close proximity to the lucrative US market?

The explanation put forward here privileges the non-emergence of mechanisms and actors for building and implementing genuinely multijurisdictional regulation in this sector. To explain this absence, the emergence and growth of aquaculture in Canada will first be traced, before briefly analysing the type of regulation it has thus far given rise to.

When looking at the history of this sector, the first thing to bear in mind is that fishing has always been of major importance to First Nations peoples. Today the first consequence of this 'tradition' is that they often see themselves as 'stewards or even owners' of the wild fish (Shepert, 2008: 205) that swim in the coastal waters in which most Canadian aquaculture takes place. The second consequence is that some such peoples, encouraged by environmentalist allies such as 'The Salmon Aquaculture Review', see themselves as having jurisdiction over these waters. Given that Canada's federal government has responsibility both for these peoples and environmental protection, one can better understand how its representatives have often been extremely cautious in developing Canada-wide policies that could be seen as encouraging the expansion of aquaculture. Likewise, one can also comprehend why provincial governments charged with developing their respective economies have also discouraged federal legislation in order to retain autonomy to grant licences to fish farms without consulting First Nations groups (Shepert, 2008: 206).

As aquaculture has expanded, this underlying tension has been exacerbated by highly publicized scientific uncertainties regarding the 'waste footprint' of this industry upon both local water columns and, consequently, upon wild fish. More precisely, the residues of feedingstuffs and medicines administered to farmed fish, along with the waste of these animals, have been criticized for damaging water quality. Although such damage has rarely been proven, opponents of aquaculture have politicized this issue to such an extent that in the late 1990s the province of British Columbia decided to announce a moratorium upon new fish farming activity.

Is this then simply a question of a 'wicked' or 'unsolvable' public problem where governance must attempt the impossible of squaring a circle formed by 'the need' to develop a new, lucrative industry and the 'requirements' of environmental and property right protection? Here Rayner and Howlett (2007) propose instead a more interesting and less fatalistic interpretation that, in combining insights from organizational sociology with public policy analysis, speaks strongly to our subject of multijurisdictional regulation. First, they reject the popular thesis that 'nothing has been done to resolve this problem' because, as they underline, since 1984 successive attempts to develop an integrated and nation-wide policy have been undertaken. Secondly, they underline that very early on federal government institutionalized a crucial decision by making aquaculture the responsibility of a Department of Fisheries and Oceans that has continued to be 'captured' by the constituencies of wild and sports fishing. Thirdly, they criticize the provinces' main policy instrument – licencing applications – as inadapted to the requirements of ongoing monitoring and evaluation. Finally, and more generally, Rayner and Howlett claim that years of activity without open public debate about the strengths and problems of aquaculture

has led to a 'legitimation crisis' (2007: 56). This means that now even measured discussion between policy specialists is highly difficult to set up.

In summary, this particular case of multijurisdictional regulation provides illuminating examples of both the types of conflict this form of governance often has to deal with and, in particular, the problems that are added to this challenge when intersectoral disputes are at issue.

RECURRENT TRAITS AND ISSUES

As the preceding case studies begin to show, multijurisdictional regulations frequently feature a number of similar characteristics which merit identification and analysis. Just as importantly, if not more, this type of governance also tends to raise a comparable range of issues over which many actors and social commentators take normative views. Without abandoning the objectivity of social science, these will also be listed and discussed.

Similar traits, common trajectories or convergence?

One means of comparing modes of multijurisdictional regulation across sectors and polities is to go beyond the simple description of their similarities or differences by questioning whether they reflect common trajectories or convergence.

A first means of answering this question is to examine the procedures and practices multijurisdictional regulation appears to engender. First, as our three case studies testify, this type of regulation demands high levels of interorganizational consultation. EU competition specialists have systematized this process the most through their use of questionnaires and obligatory information sharing. Less formalized consultation appears to be just as institutionalized, however, around the regulation of the Scotch whisky industry. Even in the domain of Canadian aquaculture, where conflict is rife, consultation appears to constantly being attempted. Secondly, and more revealingly, some cases of multijurisdictional regulation use the law or legally binding instruments more frequently than do others. This has been the case for Scotch whisky, where the Devolution Concordats (Bulmer et al., 2002) have played an important role, but also for EU competition policy where a regulation provides the basis for institutionalized coordination throughout this international region. In contrast, in Canadian aquaculture the law is if anything an obstacle to multijurisdictional regulation.

A second means of examining the question of convergent multijurisdictional regulation is to discover whether new organizations have been set up to foster it. This is clearly the case in many instances not dealt with in depth here. For example, the creation of the WTO and agencies such as the European Medicines Agency provide clear illustrations of this point. In our own case studies, however, multijurisdictional regulation has not given rise to entirely new organizations but has instead caused existing bodies to modify their respective practices.

This observation spills over into a third and final area of potential convergence around the question of multijurisdictional regulation that concerns the individual actors engaged in this process. Our case studies suggest that this form of regulation demands certain skills (e.g. the mastery of English, interpersonal management) and *savoir faire*. More fundamentally still, as our cases from the EU and Scotland underline, 'acting multijurisdictionally' often also encourages actors to undergo processes of resocialization during which their organizational allegiances shift and become more open.

Biases and normative issues

In a multijurisdictional world, regulations built upon common understandings of issues and fairly achieved compromises are clearly desirable. But is this what most such regulations achieve? Two sets of existing scholarship tend to suggest that in reality multijurisdictional regulation suffers instead from considerable bias.

The first instance of this concerns the tendency of such regulations to negotiate settlements on the basis of least common denominator solutions which, moreover, tend to result in neoliberal policy outcomes. For example, numerous international trade law specialists highlight three types of intrinsic partiality within the WTO's dispute settlement procedures. The first concerns developing countries. Many specialists highlight substantial variations in power which stem from the different capacity of rich and poor states to finance delegations in Geneva and legal representation (Kapoor, 2004: 529). The second concerns the WTO's tendency to prioritize 'market access' above other political goals such as the protection of public health. Consequently, the WTO is seen as a problematical driver of regulatory reform because it 'tends to treat regulatory differences as undesirable obstacles' (Piciotto, 2003: 385). Finally, and more fundamentally still, critical scholars of world trade's legalization identify a WTO bias against value-based decision-making in favour of technocratic processes and methods. Certain researchers underline that legalistic reasoning runs counter to the search for optimal solutions through diplomacy. Alter, for example, highlights that WTO panels tend strongly to follow legalistic procedures, which contrast with preceding GATT (General Agreements on Tariffs and Trade) panels where 'legal rulings did not run roughshod over politically sensitive issues' (2003: 790–1). Similarly, Piciotto regrets that within WTO negotiations notions of 'fair competition' and 'equal treatment' are never interpreted in terms of 'substantive issues and value judgements' (2003: 378).

A second type of bias concerns the lack of public deliberation which often appears to correlate with multijurisdictional regulation. Here the way the EU is governed provides a wide range of examples which seem to validate this hypothesis. As many studies have shown (Radaelli, 1999; Robert, 2004), in order to reach agreement over policies that entail Europe's multiple jurisdictions, the dominant logic of action tends to be technocratic (i.e. based on expertise and negotiations behind closed doors) rather than political (where values-based arguments are made in public settings). Indeed, even European parliamentarians tend strongly to engage in multijurisdictional regulation using technocratic rather than political lines of argumentation. Put more generally, this form of regulation raises deep questions about the contemporary role of the public organizations through which democracy and accountability is ostensibly ensured, in particular parliaments and local assemblies. More widely still, multijurisdictional regulation presents a challenge for the very notion of public deliberation and participation in politics.

of actors, including university teaching staff, charged with training today's and tomorrow's representatives of such stakeholders. In short, the rise of 'the multi', alongside that of networked and coordinated governance, merits deep reflection amongst both a range of practitioners and those whose job it is to advise and train them.

Meanwhile, from the point of view of social science analysis, this chapter has endeavoured to show that multijurisdictional regulation also constitutes a considerable challenge for theories, concepts and methods. The answer proposed here is not to invent ad hoc terms or borrow from positivist management studies. Instead, it has been argued that analysis can best be deepened by reinvesting in strong social science concepts, such as regulation and institutions. These both enable interdisciplinary exchange (e.g. between political scientists and legal anthropologists: von Benda-Beckmann et al., 2005), and the cumulative confrontation of research findings and questions.

CONCLUSION

This chapter has sought to show that the deepening of multijurisdictional jurisdiction constitutes one of the principal characteristics of the two new patterns of rule that have been underlined throughout this *Handbook*: the spread of networked governance and the increased importance of coordination within contemporary politics. Although this has yet to be comprehensively inventoried, the findings of a wide swathe of social science research strongly indicate that since the early 1980s, and throughout most of the world, contemporary governance has increasingly cut across the jurisdictions of public organizations and formal political authority. As the case studies presented above indicate, this 'social fact' represents a considerable change for the public, collective and private stakeholders who endeavour to act within multijurisdictional policymaking and implementation environments. Indeed, it therefore also constitutes a considerable challenge for the variety

ACKNOWLEDGEMENT

1   The editor of this volume himself, Mark Bevir, is one of the social scientists alluded to. Indeed, the term 'multijurisdictional' was first suggested to the author by M. Bevir. I take the opportunity here of thanking him for this suggestion and, more generally, for his helpful comments on a first draft of this piece.

REFERENCES

Alter, K. (2003) 'Resolving or Exacerbating Disputes? The WTO's New Dispute Resolution System', *International Affairs* 79 (4): 783–800.

Bache, I. and Flinders, M. (eds) (2004) *Multi-level Governance*. Oxford: Oxford University Press.

von Benda-Beckmann, F., von Benda-Beckmann, K. and Griffiths, A. (eds) (2005) *Mobile People, Mobile Law. Expanding Legal Relations in a Contracting World*. Aldershot: Ashgate.

Bulmer, S., Burch, M., Carter, C., Hogwood, P. and Scott A. (2002) *European Policy-Making under*

Devolution: Transforming Britain into Multi-Level Governance. London: Palgrave.

Cardenas, G.C. (2002) *An Assessment of the Multijurisdictional Drug Task Forces in Texas: A Case-Study*. Texas State University – San Marcos.

Carter, C. and Smith, A. (2008) 'Revitalizing Public Policy Approaches to the EU: Territorial Institutionalism, Fisheries and Wine', *Journal of European Public Policy* 15 (2): 263–81.

Cini, M. and McGowan, L. (2009) *Competition Policy in the European Union*, 2nd edn. Basingstoke: Palgrave-Macmillan.

Cseres, K. (2007) 'Multijurisdictional Competition Law Enforcement: the Interface between European Competition Law and the Competition Laws of the New Member States', *European Competition Journal* 3(2): December.

Culver, K. and Castle, D. (eds) (2008) *Aquaculture, Innovation and Social Transformation*. New York: Springer.

Fligstein, N. and Choo, J. (2005) 'Law and Corporate Governance', *Annual Review of Law and Social Science* 1: December.

Gualini, E. (2004) *Multi-level Governance and Institutional Change*. Aldershot: Ashgate.

Hollingsworth, J., Schmitter, P. and Streek, W. (eds) (1994) *Governing Capitalist Economies*. Oxford: Oxford University Press.

Jessop, B. and Sum, N. (2006) *The Regulation Approach and Beyond*. Cheltenham: Edward Elgar.

Jobert, B. and Muller, P. (1987) *L'Etat en Action. Politiques Publiques et Corporatismes*. Paris: Presses Universitaires de France.

Jullien, B. and Smith, A. (eds) (2008) *Industries and Globalization: The Political Causality of Difference*. London: Palgrave.

Kapoor, I. (2004) 'Deliberative Democracy and the WTO', *Review of International Political Economy* 11(3): 522–41.

Kassim, H., Menon, A., Peters, G. and Wright, V. (eds) (2001) *The National Co-ordination of EU Policy. The European Level*. Oxford: Oxford University Press.

Lagroye, J. (1985) 'La Légitimation', in M. Grawitz and J. Leca (eds), *Traité de Science Politique*. Paris: Presses Universitaires de France.

Lehmkuhl, D. (2009) 'Cooperation and Hierarchy in EU Competition Policy', in I. Tömmel and A. Verdun (eds), *Innovative Governance in the European Union*. Boulder, CO: Lynne Rienner.

McLeod, I. (2006) *Key Concepts in Law*. Basingstoke: Palgrave.

Marks, G., Hooghe, L. and Blank, K. (1996) 'European Integration from the 1980s: State-Centric versus Multi-Level Governance', *Journal of Common Market Studies* 34(3): 341–78.

Marks, G., Nielsen, F., Ray, L. and Salk, J. (1996) 'Competencies, Cracks and Conflicts: Regional Mobilization in the European Union', in G. Marks, F. Scharpf, P. Schmitter and W. Streeck (eds), *Governance in the European Union*. London: Sage; pp. 40–63.

Montalban, M., Ramirez-Perez, S. and Smith, A. (2009) 'EU Competition Policy Revisited: Economic Doctrine and European Political Work'. Paper presented to the biannual conference of the Society for Advanced Economics, Paris, July.

Moravcsik, A. (1993) 'Preferences and Power in the European Community: A Liberal Intergovernmental Approach', *Journal of Common Market Studies* 31(3): 473–524.

Piciotto, Sol (2003) 'Private Rights vs. Public Standards in the WTO', *Review of International Political Economy* 10(3): 377–405.

Pierre, J. (ed.) (2000) *Debating Governance: Authority, Steering, Democracy*. Oxford: Oxford University Press.

Pressman, J. and Wildavsky, A. (1973) *Implementation*. Berkeley, CA: University of California Press.

Radaelli, C. (1999) *Technocracy in the European Union*. London: Longman.

Rayner, J. and Howlett, M. (2007) 'Caught in a Staples Vise: The Political Economy of Canadian Aquaculture', *Policy and Society* 27(1): 49–69.

Rhodes, R. (1997) *Understanding Governance*. Milton Keynes: Open University Press.

Robert, C. (2004) 'Doing Politics and Pretending Not to. The Commission's Role in Distributing Aid to Eastern Europe', in A. Smith (ed.), *Politics and the European Commission. Actors, Interdependence, Legitimacy*. London: Routledge.

Sassen, S. (2007) 'The Places and Spaces of the Global: An Expanded Analytical Terrain', in D. Held and A. McGrew (eds), *Globalization Theory. Approaches and Controversies*. Cambridge: Polity Press; pp. 179–105.

Schmitter, P. (1974) 'Still the Century of Corporatism?', *Review of Politics* 36.

Shepert, M. (2008) 'Oral History and Traditional Ecological Knowledge', in K. Culver and D. Castle, (eds), *Aquaculture, Innovation and Social Transformation*. New York: Springer; pp. 205–20.

Smith, A. (2003) 'Multi-level Governance: What It Is and How to Study It', in M. Painter, (ed.), *Handbook on Public Administration*. London: Sage.

Smith, A. (2008) 'Territory and the Regulation of Industry: Examples from Scotland and Aquitaine', *Regional and Federal Studies* 18(1): 37–53.

Smith, A. (2010) 'Industries as Spaces for the Politics of Territory: The Case of Scotch Whisky', *Regional and Federal Studies*, 20(3): 389–407.

20

Local Governance

Bas Denters

In academic circles the term (local) govern-ance came into fashion in the middle of the 1990s. Before that date the term was hardly used, either in political science or in the field of public administration.[1] One of the first signs of the concept's advent in the field of local government and politics was the organization of a workshop on *The Changing Local Governance of Europe at the European Consortium of Political Science's Joint Sessions* in Bordeaux (1995). In a paper presented at this workshop, Gerry Stoker, now a leading academic in the field, quotes William Hampton (as cited in Stoker, 1995: 2), who somewhat hesitantly suggests that '[p]erhaps we should adopt "governance" or some other phrase, to dis-tinguish the emerging pattern from the dis-appearing world of democratic local government'. In the years that have passed since then it is obvious that – notwithstand-ing Hampton's reluctance – 'governance' is now generally accepted as a convenient conceptual tool to characterize contempo-rary patterns of collective decision-making and collective action in the local public domain.

IS THERE A SHIFT TOWARDS LOCAL GOVERNANCE?

Initially the focus in the fast-growing litera-ture on local governance was on conceptual issues – 'What is the meaning of the term local governance?' – and on the empirical question, 'Is it appropriate to characterize changes in local public decision-making as a shift from government to governance?'

Conceptually, 'governance' is an umbrella concept that covers a wide range of phenom-ena (Pierre and Peters, 2000: 14). Notwith-standing the existence of numerous different definitions, there is a more or less common understanding that the term (local) govern-ance refers to a more or less *polycentric* system in which a *variety* of actors are engaged in local *public decision-making pro-cesses* (Stoker, 2000: 3; Leach and Percy-Smith, 2001: 2–5; Van Kersbergen and Van Waarden, 2001: 24–5; Benz, 2004).[2] Three elements in this definition require further explanation. First, *polycentricism* refers to a constellation where there is not a single uni-tary actor, but a multitude of relatively auton-omous players in the field. Relations between actors in systems of (local) governance are not characterized by purely hierarchical relations. Secondly, (local) governance is typically about relations between a *variety* of actors that come from different domains of political and socioeconomic life. In the governmental domain, actors may come from different tiers of government (e.g. supranational, national, regional and local) or they may be quasi-governmental functional bodies. But, typically, governance networks are also comprised of non-governmental actors, from the corporate sector, third sector or civic associations. Thirdly, there are a variety of *mechanisms* for public decision-making in processes of (local) governance: in addition to traditional bureaucratic and political mechanisms like hierarchy and (majority) voting, decisions can also be based on competition or negotiations (Pierre and Peters, 2000: 14–22; Leach and Percy-Smith, 2001: 5; Benz, 2004: 20).

Empirically, the early years of local governance research were characterized by a concern with the question of whether changes in local public decision-making could for good reasons be characterized as a move from government to governance and the subsequent question about the reasons for any such changes.[3] Several efforts were made to map out changes in local political arenas. At the beginning of the new millennium, Peter John (2001) undertook an ambitious comparative analysis of local political change in 15 Western European countries on six dimensions of governance and concluded that countries like the Netherlands, Germany and Spain were moving on a rather similar reform trajectory to the UK. He observed that the emergence of governance is not a unique UK phenomenon but that 'governance practices have diffused and emerged across mainland Europe' (John, 2001). John also observed that 'governance takes various forms according to country and locality' (John, 2001: 175). These basic conclusions were corroborated in Denters and Rose's *Comparing Local Governance* (2005a). In this edited volume, various authors mapped the continuities and

changes in 12 selected Western countries. On the basis of this material, the editors concluded:

> If contemporary local political arenas are contrasted with the prevalent model of local government in the Western world of the early 1980s, three major changes are to be observed:
>
> - a widespread adoption of NPM and public-private partnerships;
> - involvement of organized local associations, interest groups and private actors in policy partnerships; and
> - introduction of new forms of citizen involvement. (Denters and Rose, 2005c: 261)

These changes indicate an increasing influence of non-governmental actors in public decision-making. This shift from local government to local governance, however, by no means implies that governance takes place without government. It means a redefinition of local government's role in local public affairs rather than a wholesale retreat of local government (Denters and Rose, 1995c: 253; Pierre and Peters, 2000; Stoker, 2004: 193). As Pierre and Peters (2000: 12) have argued: 'although governance relates to changing relationships between state and society and a growing reliance on less coercive policy instruments, the state is still the centre of considerable political power'. And therefore it is appropriate to 'look at governance as processes in which the state plays a leading role'.

Moreover, Pierre and Peters (2000: 29) also argue that 'the role that government plays in governance is a variable and not a constant' and therefore – depending on varying paths of change – both the prominence and the nature of government's role in governance will vary. The changes in local governance observed by John (2001) and Denters and Rose (2005c) confirm this general observation. Denters and Rose concluded that the three above changes in subnational politics in the Western world vary from one country to another. This conclusion, however, also requires some refinement. Whereas trends towards the introduction of new public management (NPM) and public–private partnerships (PPPs) are rather uniform, there seems to be great variety in patterns of

involvement of citizens and private organizations (from the corporate and third sector).

On the basis of these and similar other
studies, there is a consensus that it is indeed
appropriate to characterize contemporary
systems of Western local policymaking and
public service delivery in terms of 'governance', where public decision-making concerning local issues increasingly takes place
in the context of multi-agency networks that
cross traditional jurisdictional boundaries
(both vertical, across levels of government,
and horizontal, between different local governments) and cut across the public–private
divide. In Central and Eastern Europe (CEE)
the picture is more diffuse. Swianiewicz
(2005: 123) concludes that although

> 'local politicians in at least some of the CEE coun-
> tries (Poland, Hungary, the Czech Republic) have
> been attracted by the idea of the shift from tradi-
> tional government to the wider concept of govern-
> ance, and by management styles identified often
> with the New Public Management'

One should nevertheless be aware that the
conditions for the implementation of 'local
governance' practices are different from
those in the West:

> 'There are, for example, limited resources in the
> hands of local business men, the relative weakness
> of NGOs, and a limited market of suppliers of
> contracted out services' (2005: 123).[4]

THE CONSEQUENCES OF NEW PATTERNS OF GOVERNANCE

More recently, a natural move to a new set of
questions in the local governance literature
can be observed. These questions pertain to
the consequences of the shift towards governance. A main issue in the literature is what
the shift from local government to local governance has meant for two related classical
functions of local government.

On the one hand, from a *democratic perspective*, the locality was seen as an accessible arena for meaningful public participation.[5]
Typically, 'the accessibility of local government is greater and the opportunities for an

active political role are more varied than they
are at the central government level' (Stoker,
1996: 16; see also, for example, Sharpe,
1970; Dahl and Tufte, 1973: 41–65; Wilson
and Game, 1994: 36–8). Moreover, it has also
been argued that local affairs 'are more
within reach of the citizen's mind than others'
and therefore local political involvement may
be seen as 'a very important factor in "making
democracy work"' (Schumpeter, 1979: 260;
see also De Tocqueville, 1990: 68; J.S. Mill,
1993: 376–90; Beetham, 1996: 33; Vetter,
2002). This might be seen as a good in its
own right, but it could also contribute to local
government's potential for democratic responsiveness. Widespread participation provides
policymakers with extensive information that
makes it easier to better gear local policies
and services to the preferences of the citizenry (Dahl and Tufte, 1973: 13–15).

From a *managerialist or functional perspective*, local government also allows for
more effective and integrated public policies
and services. This argument has a dual meaning. On the one hand, in a decentralized
polity, local authorities on the basis of their
supposedly superior knowledge of specific
local conditions (genius of place) are capable
of developing more effective policies and
providing better services (Oates, 1999: 1123).
Moreover, small-scale public organizations
may also be less vulnerable to the excessive
departmentalism that allegedly haunts
national governments (e.g. Kavanagh and
Richards, 2001), and may function as a 'com-
pendious, horizontal co-ordinating agency
which can gather together the separate vertical services coming down from the centre
and adjust their content and character to the
particular needs of each community'(Sharpe,
1970: 167).

Both these justifications for local government implicitly or explicitly assume the
existence of a model of local government that
rests on two main pillars:

- From a democratic perspective, local government
  rests on the primacy of popularly elected officials
  (oftentimes a directly elected council) who are

responsible for translating local inputs (needs and demands) into authoritative decisions that provide the framework for the work of executive leaders and local government officers (Denters, 2005: 423). In this system voting in local elections and other more direct forms of active political engagement provide channels for local political activism and channels through which citizens can voice their needs and demands.

• From a functional perspective, local government is conceived as a form of territory-based multi-functional governance (Wollmann, 2003: 103), where local government's responsibilities cover a broad range of policies and services.

The trend of functional fragmentation that is – as will be discussed below – inherent in the shift from government to governance is problematic from both angles. *Democratically,* functional fragmentation considerably reduces the scope for traditional forms of political participation and mechanisms for securing responsiveness.[6] *Functionally,* the relocation of many traditional local government responsibilities also reduces the scope for traditional hierarchical coordination of local policies and services and local governments' integrative potential.

The remainder of this contribution will show how and to what extent recent developments have changed local governance and how local governments in a number of Western countries[7] have reacted to the dual challenge inherent in the trend of functional fragmentation.

LOCAL GOVERNANCE IN SIX COUNTRIES

As stated above, local authorities are still likely to play a major role in governing localities, even though in many countries the position of local government in local governance has changed. The capacity of localities for self-governance to a considerable degree depends on the relations of their governments with other levels of governance. Systems of local governance are typically embedded systems. In a recent contribution Sellers and Lidström (2007) have characterized the intergovernmental relations of local government systems in terms of two main dimensions. First of all, these authors classify systems of local governance in terms of:

• The capacity of local government: this is defined by Sellers and Lidström as a combination of politico-administrative capacity (indicators: constitutional protections on local autonomy; corporate representation of local government; local government employment as percentage of public employment) and fiscal capacity (indicators: local government expenditure as percentage of public expenditure; and local tax revenues as percentage of total tax revenue).

• The supervision of local government: defined as a combination of politico-administrative supervision (indicators: local government supervisory officials; supra-local appointment of local executive; supra-local control of governmental form; trans-local civil service) and fiscal supervision (indicators: grants as percentage of local revenue; local tax autonomy; supervision of local borrowing). The relative strength of local government is stronger the less its operations are subject to supervision by other governments.

In addition to these characteristics, the average size of municipal governments was included in the Table 20.1. Population size is often seen as a factor that positively affects the local system's functional capacity and its capacity for autonomy and independence (Dahl and Tufte, 1973: 110–36; see also Wollmann, 2008: 293).[8]

If one defines the institutional strength of local governments in relation to these three factors, a number of marked differences between various countries are observable. At one extreme, the relatively large-scale Swedish municipalities combine a strong fiscal and politico-administrative position vis-à-vis the central state with a moderate degree of central supervision of local operations. At the other extreme, the French and the British local authorities combine a weak fiscal and politico-administrative position with limited local discretion due to an extensive central supervision of local governments.

Table 20.1   Systems of local governance in six Western democracies

	Sweden	Netherlands	Germany	USA	UK	France
Capacity*	Strong (1.99)	Moderate (1.07)	Moderate (1.00)	Moderate (0.90)	Weak (0.75)	Weak (0.60)
Freedom of supervision*	Moderate (1.02)	Weak (0.74)	Weak (0.74)	Strong (1.62)	Weak (0.77)	Weak (0.71)
Size of local government**	Large (30.827)	Large (32.466)	Small (6.100)	Small (6.000)	Very large (125.000)	Small (1.640)

*Based on Sellers and Lidström (2007), Tables 3 and 4 (rankings assigned by BD). Both these composite measures are summarized in scales with a range between 0 and 2, where a score of 2 indicates the highest degree of local capacity or freedom of supervision; the Sellers–Lidström original scaling was reversed for the supervision indicator, so that a maximum score indicates minimal supervision.

**Size data are based on Rose and Ståhlberg (2005; Sweden); Denters and Klok (2005; Netherlands); Wollmann (2008; Germany); US Census Bureau (2002; USA); Wollmann (2008; UK: average of size districts and unitary authorities/ county boroughs); and Borraz and Le Galès (2005; France).

Whereas the weakness of the French 'communes' is further accentuated by the small size of its municipalities, the weakness of British local governments is exacerbated by the gargantuan size of its 'oversized' municipalities (Wollmann, 2008: 299–301). The other local government systems take positions in between these two extremes.

Sweden

Swedish local governance systems are embedded in an intergovernmental context that creates favourable conditions for vigorous local collective action (see Table 20.1). In this context the Swedish communes may be seen as the prototype of multipurpose government where local responsibilities cover a broad range of policies and services and where the ultimate political power rests with a council of directly elected citizen representatives (Wollmann, 2004: 647). The Swedish municipalities were traditionally built on a model in which both the provision and the delivery of local (social) services were done 'in house', under the direction of the council and by local government employees (Wollmann, 2008: 37). In the 1990s, under the influence of the new public management (NPM) movement, EU liberalization policies and budgetary pressures, this model of in-house production, came under

increasing pressure. In 1991 a new Local Government Act explicitly gave municipalities the powers to contract out local government services to private or quasi-governmental agencies (Wollmann, 2004: 649). This has resulted in an increasing number of municipalities, which have transferred responsibilities for social services to organizations in the corporate and the third sector. Moreover, many municipalities have hived off municipal utilities (e.g. provision of electricity, water and waste disposal; Wollmann, 2008: 39). Nevertheless, there is a consensus that the reception of NPM prescriptions in Sweden, as elsewhere in Scandinavia, has at best been limited (John, 2001: 104; Wollmann, 2004: 650; Rose and Ståhlberg, 2005: 95).

Facing challenges

This leads to the conclusion that the functional fragmentation that is oftentimes considered as characteristic for the shift from government to governance has only had a limited impact on local governance arenas in Sweden. If there are problems of functional fragmentation they appear to come from central government's departmentalism rather than from a shift towards governance (Wollmann, 2008: 257). This does not imply, however, that the system did not undergo any changes.

The main pillar of Swedish local democracy and *civic participation* in local affairs is the election of the municipal councils. In addition to forms of democratic participation that are common in any democratic system (petitioning, contacting politicians and administrators and taking part in a demonstration), the Swedish national government in 1991 introduced the option for advisory local referendums. These referendums are either initiated by the council or by request of 5 per cent of the electorate (Loughlin, 1999: 289). In an effort to compensate for possible negative effects of the municipal amalgamation reforms of the 1970s, municipalities were also given the possibility of setting neighbourhood councils. Because citizen interest in these councils was low, most of these councils, however, have since been abolished. Another reform, the introduction of new forms of user democracy, appears to have been more successful. About 90 per cent of Swedish municipalities have one or more user boards in domains such as primary and secondary education, child day-care facilities and homes for the elderly (Rose and Ståhlberg, 2005: 96; Wollmann, 2008: 71). Finally, in 2002 the Swedish national parliament passed a bill aimed at increasing citizens' influence between elections. The act aimed at encouraging councils to introduce additional channels for citizen participation: for example, the right for citizens to put topics on the agenda of the municipal council, the introduction of citizen panels, and advisory boards as well as the use of E-participation (Montin, 2005: 128).

In terms of their capacity to develop an effective and integrated approach for complex local problems, Swedish municipalities were traditionally well equipped. Recent developments appear to have had only a limited impact on the degree of fragmentation in local governance arenas. The main responsibilities for integration rest with the council's executive committee and its chairman. This chairman, who is a full-time professional politician, may be seen as the council's 'political leader' or 'mayor' (Bäck, 2005: 83; Montin, 2005: 118), but in essence executive political leadership is collective rather than

personal. If one has to characterize the Swedish situation, it probably come closest to what Davies (2002: 316) has called *governance by (local) government*. On the one hand, the coordinating capacity of the municipality is rather strong; on the other hand, the disintegration that was the result of a rather modest shift towards governance was rather limited. In the Swedish context, the primacy in the local governance arena rests with the municipal executive, which makes its policies without intensive interactions with local economic élites and civil society.

Netherlands

Dutch local governance takes place in a situation in which relatively large municipalities with considerable politico-administrative and financial resources have the capacity to act authoritatively in local governance arenas. In a formal sense, local government's room for manoeuvre is restricted by national legislation and a relatively strict supervisory regime. The local governance arenas in which local governments have to operate took their basic shape in the interbellum period and in the 1950s and 1960s when the Dutch welfare state was developed. During these years, responsibilities for the execution of various welfare state programmes (in housing, social services and social assistance) were typically delegated to local third-sector organizations. This resulted in a highly segmented system of 'private governments' (Denters and Klok, 2005). In the 1970s the powers of municipalities to regulate and supervise these organizations were increased, but in the Dutch case in-house production of local public services remained the exception rather than the rule. This is a clear difference between the Dutch and the Swedish case. In addition to the provision by third-sector organizations, municipalities – under the influence of NPM doctrines – have also contracted out the production of services and the exploitation of facilities to private firms and to inter-municipal corporations and used forms of contract management to introduce more business-like management methods in the organization of the local public bureaucracy (Van Thiel, 2002). All this has further fragmented the traditionally patchy organizational ecology of Dutch local governance. In such a context, effective governance requires good working relations with other governments, and organizations in the corporate and third sector are crucial for getting things done locally.

Facing challenges

As in other countries, the increasing complexity of local governance arenas implies challenges for citizen participation and for the development of integrated (joined-up) approaches to complex local problems. Periodic council elections remain the most important channel for *local political participation* in the Netherlands. Although some municipalities have occasionally used advisory referendums, this form of direct democracy is no regular feature of Dutch local democracy. Citizen participation on public services and policymaking was extended in two directions. In the domain of *public services*, new forms of user democracy were introduced. Many organizations (e.g. housing associations, primary and secondary schools, welfare departments and homes for the elderly) have adopted user boards and similar devices to allow interested citizens to voice their opinions. Sometimes such forms of participation were put in place as a result of national statutory obligations; in other cases the initiative for such institutions came from the organizations themselves. Moreover, in many cities, service delivery was deconcentrated to neighbourhood-based service units in order to enhance responsiveness. In the domain of *public policymaking*, municipalities have widely adopted practices of interactive policymaking. This refers to public decision-making processes in which interested citizens and other stakeholders (social organizations, business firms, public independent boards) are given the opportunity to participate in the decision process. In many municipalities these interactive schemes

are combined with a neighbourhood approach.

Access to such interactive arenas is increasingly important, because local collective action more progressively takes shape in such interactive settings. These local interactive arenas are of crucial importance in developing *coordinated approaches to complex problems* like sustainable development, social inclusion and revitalizing deprived neighbourhoods. Because the relations between the partners in such contexts are predominantly non-hierarchical, collective decisions are made on the basis of mutual agreement. These forms of collective decision-making are not only found in the early stages of the policy process but also during the implementation stage in teams of street-level bureaucrats employed by a variety of local and regional organizations. These local networks are oftentimes embedded in a quasi-hierarchical setting. In several policy areas, however, municipalities and national government have used covenants to reach mutual agreements that provide local authorities with more discretion and additional funding to pursue shared objectives (Denters, Van Heffen and De Jong, 1999).

To strengthen the executive branch of Dutch municipal government all executive powers were concentrated in the hands of the Board of Mayor and Aldermen (BMA). As in Sweden, the executive powers were not put in the hands of a (directly elected, strong) mayor but transferred to a collegial body. At the same time the supervisory and scrutiny powers of the council in its relation to the board were strengthened, in order to reinforce the democratic accountability in local government (Denters and Klok, 2003; Denters, Klok and Van der Kolk, 2005; De Groot, 2009).

The Dutch response to the contemporary local governance challenges could probably be best described as *governance by (municipal) partnerships*.[9] In this model the primacy in the local governance arena rests with the municipal executive, which makes its policies in close interaction with a variety of partners from the local corporate and third sector and other governments (from various levels: subnational, national and EU).

Germany

Like their Dutch counterparts, German municipalities command considerable politico-administrative and financial resources and are rather heavily restricted in their capacity to act independently by national legislation and a relatively strict supervisory regime. The average size of German municipalities is much smaller than in the Netherlands. There are, however, substantial size differences within Germany (Wollmann, 2008: 54). Of old, German municipalities are multipurpose governments that have a wide variety of responsibilities: most of the implementation of federal and state legislation and programmes takes place on the municipal level (Wollmann, 2008: 49). In states with typically small municipalities, many of these tasks are performed by means of inter-municipal cooperation.

According to Wollmann (2008: 51–2), local government in Germany, traditionally, left much of the provision of local social services to the local third sector. The role of the municipalities was enabling and facilitating rather than hierarchically directing. In the 1990s, under the influence of NPM doctrines, the principles of marketization and competitive tendering were introduced into German local government; service delivery by private firms became an increasingly popular alternative for provision by third-sector organizations. In the domain of public utilities' EU competitiveness policies, many municipalities have privatized their public utility departments (Wollmann, 2008: 52). Such developments have resulted in an organizational fragmentation in local governance arenas and in an erosion of the traditional primacy of the political institutions of municipal government.

Facing challenges

First, the shift from government to governance asks for new ways to allow citizens to participate and voice their opinions in public service provision and public policymaking. In the domain of German *public services*, the adoption of NPM was primarily seen as a tool to 'bring about an economically efficient administration' (Wollmann, 2003: 97) and was essentially conceived as a new form of intra-organizational resource management. This stands in contrast to the approach in the Netherlands, where after an initially similar approach, the focus shifted to a more external approach, in which responsiveness to citizens and clients prevailed. In the *policymaking domain*, Germany has opted for the introduction of electoral reforms by introducing referendums and initiatives rather than forms of participatory governance by including citizens in policy networks (like the Dutch interactive policy arenas). In the wave of political reforms following German reunification in the 1990s, the nature of German local democracy was drastically transformed from a model of party democracy (without referendums and with an indirectly elected mayor) to a system based on a model of citizen democracy (with referendums and with a directly elected mayor; Vetter, 2009: 127–31). The introduction of directly elected mayors in combination with the direct democratic instrument of recall referendums provide strong mechanisms for citizens to hold the mayor to account and to be responsive to local political opinion (Wollmann, 2005: 36).

The introduction – in the local government systems of most German states – of a directly elected mayor is also seen as a promising way to secure joined-up government. Although Wollmann concedes that in the light of the available evidence it is not possible to reach well-founded conclusions on the impact of the introduction of directly elected mayors, he nevertheless argues, that it:

> seems plausible that by installing the mayor as a democratically legitimated and politically accountable political as well as executive leader increases the capacity of local government for proactive policymaking and coordinated action [...] and has the opportunity to become the key local networker and to exercise a pivotal role in horizontal as well

as vertical co-ordination of the German cities (Wollmann, 2005: 41).

In facing the challenges of local governance, Germany – like Sweden – seems to have adopted a model that is probably closer to the *governance by local government* mode (Davies, 2002: 316). An important difference with the Dutch case is the more-detached, less-interventionist role of central and state governments.

USA

US local governments combine considerable fiscal and politico-administrative capacity with a high degree of local discretion, which is the result of a lenient supervisory regime. These potential ingredients for a vigorous system of local governance are, however, undermined by the fragmentation of its local government system. This fragmentation is perhaps best illustrated by the fact that the USA is probably the only country on the globe that has a *Census of governments*. According to the most recent of these censuses, in 2007 there were 89,476 local governments in the country. More than half (56 per cent) of these governments are special purpose authorities, comprising so-called school districts (14,561), and special districts (37,381) with limited functional responsibilities for water management, sewer systems, parks, pollution control, etc.

About 44 per cent of US local governments can be characterized as general or multi-purpose authorities. These multi-purpose authorities are typically small. In 2002 the average size of US general purpose local governments was around 6000 inhabitants, and 82 per cent of the municipalities had less than 5000 population (US Census Bureau, 2002). This shows that to a large extent local government in the USA does not mirror the ideal typical pattern of a territorially integrated multi-purpose unit of government, governed by a directly elected popular assembly: rather, the system is characterized by a considerable degree of functional specialization.

The numerical dominance of single-purpose units is not the only sign of the importance of functional differentiation as an organizational principle of US local government. Functional differentiation is also of key importance in the organization of many US multi-purpose governments. In many of these, voters not only elect representatives (councillors) who define the main policies and oversee the efficient operation of government but also vote for a variety of executive officials (e.g. a mayor, a sheriff, a controller, and a treasurer/tax collector).

This system of fragmented local governance is part of the US historical heritage and clearly predates the contemporary shift from government to governance in the rest of the Western world. But this does not imply that the rise of governance has left the urban political landscape in US cities untouched. The prevalent functional fragmentation of local government was further increased by the NPM-inspired 'reinventing government' movement, which propagated the use of systems of performance management and the privatization of public services (Savitch and Vogel, 2005: 225–6). Traditionally, this US system was also characterized by close links between local government and the business community (Elkin, 1987). The heavy reliance of US local governments on locally raised taxes as a source of revenue has been a major factor that contributed to this close link between local government and the corporate sector. Traditionally, this collaboration took place in the context of chambers of commerce or downtown partnerships. Currently, many US cities use Public Benefit Corporations as a vehicle for PPPs in urban development (Savitch and Vogel, 2005: 223).

Facing challenges
In a way, the US system could be characterized as 'governance avant-la-lettre'. Recent developments, if anything, have further accentuated the traditional fragmentation of the traditional US systems of local governance. US localities have a long history of coping with the challenges faced elsewhere;

therefore, it is interesting to see which channels US towns and cities have provided for public participation and how they have coped with the challenge of providing integrated policies in such a fragmented system.

Of old, the US polity offers a vast array of channels for *public participation*, including elections for a wide variety of governments and governmental offices (both legislative and executive), referendums, initiatives and rights to recall elected officials.[10] In addition to these various forms of voting, there are a variety of other forms of civic participation. These include government-initiated efforts to create opportunities for consulting citizens and soliciting their advice (e.g. neighbourhood advisory commissions and community boards), for the co-production of public services (e.g. citizen and user boards and block watch programmes) and for community control (e.g. neighbourhood associations and school boards).[11]

The main challenge facing US local government is the *integration* of policy initiatives in the light of a high degree of fragmentation. In the context of the USA, such integrative efforts are not to be expected from either the federal or the state governments and, as stated before, the local governance arenas are highly fragmented. Savitch and Vogel (2005: 222–3) argue that increasingly the role of 'dealing with the centrifugal nature of local government and providing a mechanism to centralize influence' falls to mayors. This rise of mayoral leadership is especially evident in the large cities where the governance challenges are most daunting. This type of mayoral leadership is embedded in a form of regime governance, or in other words, mayoral leadership is embedded in a system of *governance by regime* (Davies, 2002: 316), based on a close cooperation between the mayor, business élites and other community actors. This state of affairs is at least partly the result of US local governments' dependency on resources from the local corporate and the third sector (rather than on grants provided by central government). It is for this reason that Clarence

Stone (2005) has entitled a recent essay about the role of American mayors '*Institutions counts but resources decide*'. In this essay, Stone also concludes that in the highly fragmented US arenas, mayoral leadership 'rests on informal proclivities to cooperate more than on formal authority to issue mandates and send executive orders' (2005: 193).[12]

UK

In the last three decades local government in the United Kingdom has been radically transformed. During the 1980s and 1990s the traditional model of multi-purpose local government units responsible for both the provision and in-house production of local public services was largely abandoned. This was the result of two central government policies. First, Whitehall initiated the establishment of numerous quasi non-governmental organizations (*quangos*). These quangos, that were headed by centrally appointed or indirectly elected officials, were given the responsibility for a wide variety of local public services that were previously controlled by local authorities (Wilson, 2005: 162) and were also made responsible for the 'formulation, implementation and delivery of local public policies' (Wilson, 2005: 162).

Secondly, Whitehall also introduced compulsory competitive tendering for the services remaining in the hands of local authorities. To improve service quality and efficiency, local authorities were forced to consider the option of contracting out service production rather than using the traditional model of in-house production (Wilson, 2005: 164–5). In combination, these two initiatives resulted in a spectacular fragmentation of local government's control over policymaking and service delivery. This has resulted in a situation where the direction of local policies and services by a single directly elected local council and a bureaucratic, rule-driven local public bureaucracy was replaced by a system in which there is 'virtually no field of local-decision-making where local government is able to operate on its own' and where for every function there is 'a mixed range of partners from freestanding agencies to various partnerships' (Stoker, 2004: 15).

Facing challenges

In this new constellation, two challenges emerged for British local government. First, the question was how citizen participation and responsiveness could be accommodated in the new system. Initially, under the Conservative governments of Thatcher and Major, citizen participation was primarily defined in terms of consumer empowerment in the provision and production of *local public services*. Citizen's charters were an important instrument to this end. These documents specify both procedural rights of proper treatment and substantive rights to high-quality and low-cost services (Barnes et al., 1999: 121; see also Prior, Stewart and Walsh, 1995: 22–47). Moreover, consumer empowerment also opened new ways of active involvement of citizens in user groups (e.g. Barnes et al., 1999; Ranson et al., 1999). Under the subsequent Labour government, the focus shifted towards forms of *community involvement*, beyond ballot box participation. In addition to traditional modes of engagement (e.g. public hearings and other meetings) and the consumerist forms of participation introduced previously, innovative forms of civic involvement were introduced, including forums, citizen panels, interactive websites, issue forums and citizen juries (Lowndes et al., 1998; Stoker, 2004: 108–25). The character of most of these new channels for public participation is advisory, respecting the democratic primacy of the directly elected council. Different from the German reforms, there were no proposals to introduce decisive referendums and initiatives to give people a direct say over policy decisions.

The need to provide for an integrated approach to the solution of complex community problems provided a second challenge. In reaction to this, two important initiatives were developed. First, there was an attempt at strengthening local executive leadership. The traditional committee system was widely replaced by a leader–cabinet model.[13] This model would allow for more clearly defined political leadership, that would

> facilitate the expression of voice in diverse communities and reconcile differences, develop shared visions and build partnerships to ensure their achievement. Leadership in these new circumstances is not about seizing control of the state machine; it is about building coalitions, developing networks and steering in a complex environment. (Stoker, 2004: 139).

Secondly, a commitment to *partnerships* is a key element in coordinating the efforts of a variety of actors to approach complex community problems. Rather than setting up a 'bonfire of local quangos' (Stoker, 2004: 158), the new Labour government initiated the idea of partnerships in urban regeneration and service delivery to ensure an integrated community-oriented approach to local governance challenges. Stoker lists no less than 17 of these central-government-initiated local partnerships and argues that New Labour has 'further contributed to complexity through its sustained drive to encourage partnerships' (2004: 160–2). Moreover, the nature of central–local partnerships diverted considerable resources to efforts in setting up new organizations, preparing bids for central grants and providing information for accountability purposes, rather than addressing the substantive problems (Sullivan and Skelcher, 2002: 25–32; Stoker, 2004: 162–3).

There is some uncertainty as to the effects of these centrally orchestrated efforts to set up local partnerships. On the one hand, they may be interpreted as steps towards an 'over-centralized set of mechanisms for stimulating joined up governance'; on the other hand, it is also argued that 'a joined up agenda is not necessarily a centralizing one' (Stoker, 2004: 173). Because of the central role of Whitehall, the mode of governance in the UK could best be characterized as a form of *governance in multi-level partnerships*, wherein there is a key role for non-local actors and more specifically central government (cf. Davies, 2002: 316).

France

As is evident from Table 20.1, France is a highly centralized country, where municipalities (*communes*) are relatively weak. In the development of the French welfare state, the municipalities, not in the least because of their often lilliputian scale, did not play a major role. The main beneficiary of the decentralization reforms of the 1980s were the *départements* rather than the *communes* (Borraz and Le Galès, 2005; Wollmann, 2008: 44). To overcome their size-induced weak functional capacity, French municipalities have frequently resorted to inter-municipal forms of cooperation. Over the years, this has resulted in a hodgepodge of collaborative arrangements. Many of these were oriented toward a single purpose (or a small range of related purposes) rather than a multi-sectoral purpose, and the territorial scale of these arrangements was also primarily dictated by sector-specific rather than general considerations.

The scope of local government was not only reduced by the dislocation of local responsibilities to these inter-municipal bodies but also by the privatization of local public utilities and public services to private providers. These private firms could offer the technical competences and financial resources that many *communes* were lacking (Borraz and Le Galès, 2005).

Facing challenges

These developments first of all called for a reconsideration of the traditional democratic infrastructures. In the domain of *public services*, there has been an increasing demand for stricter controls over public services, especially those provided by utility firms (Borraz and Le Galès, 2005: 20). In 2002, new national legislation forced all municipalities with more than 10,000 inhabitants and inter-municipal bodies with more than 50,000 inhabitants to establish advisory boards for local public services that were either provided by a municipal or a non-municipal corporation (Borraz and Le Galès, 2005: 25;

Wollmann, 2008: 73). In addition to these formal structures, in many places public opinion surveys were used to better identify citizens' needs and preferences (Hoffmann-Martinot, 2003: 174).

Notwithstanding changes, French local democracy remains essentially a representative democracy where the periodic election of the municipal council and the mayor is the crucial event. The mayor is very much the cornerstone of French local government. Although in a formal sense it is the council that selects and holds the mayor (as head of the municipal executive) to account, it is in fact the mayor who draws up the electoral list of candidates for his party and thus more or less co-opts the council (Kerrouche, 2005: 152). In the policymaking domain, the mayor therefore remains the single most important office-holder. There have been some reluctant attempts to reform this system. National legislation enacted in 2003, for example, has provided the opportunity for organizing binding municipal referendums. These referendums, however, can only be initiated by the mayor and require approval by a majority of the municipal council. Another example of democratic reforms induced by national legislation was the 2002 legislation that forced the cities with more than 80,000 inhabitants to set up neighbourhood councils. The law provides municipal councils in these municipalities with wide discretion in deciding over the competencies and the composition of the neighbourhood councils. Therefore, it remains to be seen whether this reform will bring about major changes (Hoffmann-Martinot, 2003: 175). In addition to these top-down reforms, municipalities and local citizen groups have also initiated democratic reforms. An important channel for citizen-initiated collective action is provided by the many locally- based voluntary associations (Borraz and Le Galès, 2005: 25).

Mayoral leadership is also crucial in establishing *coherence in local governance*. The mayor holds a dominant position by (a) controlling the council (majority); (b) being at the pinnacle of the – oftentimes small – executive branch (c) by establishing links of the locality to other tiers of government through the accumulation of local, regional and national mandates (Hoffmann-Martinot, 2003: 166–8).

The role of the mayors is important in at least two domains. First, French national government has initiated a number of 'new' policy initiatives aimed at making subnational governments together with other local and supra-local actors responsible for an integrated approach to complex local social and environmental projects (Borraz and Le Galès, 2005: 17). Potentially, mayors are well positioned to bring together partners in such cooperative arenas. Borraz and Le Galès (2005: 18), however, are sceptical about the actual success of such contracts and partnerships. Although each of these initiatives aims to provide a framework for coordinating efforts of various partners, there is now a dazzling multiplicity of such policy initiatives, each with a different approach and changing partners. Borraz and Le Galès (2008: 15) conclude, however, that only the stronger (larger) municipalities 'may be able to achieve some coherence and develop a mode of integrated governance for the whole area' but fear that elsewhere 'extensive confusion is the norm'.

Mayors of these larger cities are also becoming increasingly important in newly emerging inter-municipal arenas. In 1999, national government undertook an effort to establish new, consolidated inter-municipal cooperative arenas. Many tasks requiring joint decision-making and coordination that are well beyond the administrative capacity of (small) municipal governments were transferred to these new inter-municipal entities (*communautées*). The governors of these *communautées* are elected by the councils of the municipalities in the region. Many of these units are now chaired by mayors of the central cities in the region.

In the highly centralized French polity, local governance very much takes place in the shadow of hierarchy. Although contracts and partnerships are common arrangements to establish coordination amongst different

governments, and in relations between governmental and non-governmental actors (similar to the situation in the Netherlands), the centre of gravity in these collaborative arrangements is on the supra-local level. Competent, agile mayors of especially central cities in regions may play a powerful role in such governance arenas (John and Cole, 1999). Although there are clear differences between the French and the British situation (especially relating to the strong position of French mayors; cf. John and Cole, 1999), it seems appropriate to characterize the French mode of local governance as *governance in multi-level partnerships*, wherein there is a key role for non-local actors.

CONCLUSIONS

From the mid 1990s onwards, the term local governance became increasingly popular to describe changes in local politics and government. Initially the question was whether governance – as a catchword for a tendency towards multi-actor and multi-level policymaking – provided an adequate description of the nature of collective decision-making in local political arenas in modern democratic societies. Gradually a consensus emerged, according to which it was indeed appropriate to characterize Western systems of local policymaking and public service delivery in terms of 'governance', where public decision-making concerning local issues increasingly takes place in the context of multi-agency networks that cross traditional jurisdictional boundaries (both vertical, across levels of government, and horizontal, between different local governments) and cut across the public–private divide. To a lesser degree, similar trends were found in countries in Central and Eastern Europe.

More recently, there has been a shift of attention in the local governance literature to another set of questions, pertaining to the possible effects of such shifts towards governance for (a) the potential of local systems for democratic participation and responsiveness and (b) the capacity to provide joined-up approaches to complex local problems. On the basis of an analysis of six countries (Sweden, Germany, the Netherlands, USA, UK and France) it was concluded that:

- The fragmentation of decision-making powers that is to a greater or lesser extent characteristic for contemporary systems of local governance poses challenges in both the democratic (participation and responsiveness) and the functional (securing an integrated, joined-up approach to cross-cutting, complex issues) domain.
- In facing the democratic challenge, some countries have opted for an innovation of consultation and co-decision mechanisms and/or forms of consumer participation (UK, Netherlands, France and Sweden), while others have also resorted to forms of plebiscitary democracy, like citizen-initiated, decisive referendums and initiatives and the direct election of the mayor. Traditionally, this has been the case in many places in the USA, but recently Germany has also taken this democratic reform route.
- In facing the functional challenge, there has been a general tendency towards the strengthening of the executive branch of local government. In some countries this was done by means of a reinforcement of the position of collegial executive leadership (Sweden, Netherlands and UK), whereas other countries have relied more on the option of strong mayoral leadership (Germany, USA and France).
- In addition to the strengthening of the executive branch of local government, local governments remain a more or less important player in networks of governance. The strength of local government actors in these networks is to a considerable extent dependent on historic national patterns of central – local relations (path-dependent). This has resulted in rather different governance regimes: governance by local government (Sweden and Germany); governance by municipal networks (Netherlands); governance by regime (USA); and governance by multi-level partnerships (UK and France).

An important question for future local governance research is how such differences, both between countries (with different governance regimes) and within these countries (between, for example, units of different size or in different states), affect the democratic (input) and the functional (output) legitimacy of local governments.

NOTES

1 In the index to *A New Handbook of Political Science* (Goodin and Klingemann, 1996) there is not a single reference to the term governance, whereas the second edition of the *Handbook of Public Administration* (Perry, 1996) lists but one single reference to this phrase.

2 In this definition the term 'local' refers to the territorial community that is defined by the political jurisdiction in a particular national political system that is closest to the citizen.

3 Typically the explanatory question about the antecedents of the changes in local governance has been answered by pointing to general trends in the broader context of local governance. Denters and Rose (2005b), for example, have pointed to the possible impact of the socioeconomic environment (urbanization, globalization, Europeanization) and the political environment (individual modernization, declining social capital). In a rather similar vein, others have pointed to these and more or less similar developments (e.g., John, 2001: 9–14; Pierre and Peters, 2000: 50–69). Specific research on how these general trends affect changes in local governance in different countries (cross-nationally) and differences in developments within countries is conspicuous by its absence.

4 See also: Coulson and Campbell (2006) and the other contributions in a special issue of *Local Government Studies on Local Government in Central and Eastern Europe.*

5 Another set of issues has to deal with another classic function of local government: namely, as an important institutional check on domination by one centre of government (dispersion of power). An important set of issues in the study of consequences of the shift from government to governance pertains to its effects on the distribution of powers in intergovernmental relation. This contribution will set this issue aside (for a discussion of such issues; see Goldsmith, 2005).

6 In addition to changes in the scope of the mechanisms for participation and representation, the traditional mechanisms were also increasingly problematic because citizen's orientations to their local governments have changed as a consequence of the emancipation of citizens (see Denters and Rose, 2005b: 5–6).

7 The reason for this focus on Western systems is twofold. Methodologically, it is rewarding to focus

on these systems, because in Western countries the shift from government to governance has been most pronounced, and therefore these systems are the locus par excellence to study the potential impact of this development. More pragmatically, information about Western systems is more readily available in English or German scientific publications (the two foreign languages that I am best able to comprehend).

8 At the same time, an excessively large scale may also have a negative effect on the opportunities for citizen participation and reduce the system's responsiveness to citizen demands and needs (Dahl and Tufte, 1973: 41–109).

9 Cf. Davies (2002: 316). This type of partnership is to be distinguished from Davies 'governance by (multilevel) partnership', which refers to central government dominated partnerships, in the UK and the French case. The word 'municipal' has been added to make clear that municipalities are a key actor in such local networks.

10 See Dalton and Gray (2003: 34) and Scarrow (2003: 48).

11 See, for example, Ross and Levine (1996: 217–47, 262–64) and Berry, Portney and Thomson (1993).

12 This is also the reason why in this respect the distinction between different models of local government (council manager vs strong mayor model) is only of limited importance; see Stone (2005) and Svara (2005).

13 Actually, municipalities could choose from a number of alternative model, some of them allowing for a direct election of the mayor. In England and Wales, however, more than 80 per cent of the local authorities opted for the leader and cabinet model (Rao, 2005: 50). In this model, the council elects a leader who is seconded by a cabinet of councillors (either appointed by the leader or elected by the council).

REFERENCES

Bäck, H. (2005) 'The Institutional Setting of Political Leadership and Community Involvement', in M. Haus, H. Heinelt and M. Stewart (eds), *Urban Governance and Democracy. Leadership and Community Involvement*. London: Routledge; pp. 65–101.

Barnes, M., Harrison, S., Mort, M., Shardlow, P. and Wistow, G. (1999) 'The New Management of Community Care: User Groups, Citizenship and Co-production', in G. Stoker (ed.), *The New Management of British Local Governance*. Houndmills: Macmillan; pp. 112–27.

Benz, A. (2004) 'Einleitung: Governance – Modebegriff oder nützliches sozialwissenschaftliches Konzept?', in A. Benz (ed.), *Governance – Regieren in komplexen Regelsystemen: Eine Einführung*. Wiesbaden: VS Verlag für Sozialwissenschaften; pp. 11–28.

Berry, J.M., Portney, K.E. and Thomson, K. (1993) *The Rebirth of Urban Democracy*. Washington, DC: The Brookings Institution.

Beetham, D. (1996) 'Theorising Democracy and Local Government', in D. King and G. Stoker (eds), *Rethinking Local Democracy*. Houndmills: The Macmillan Press. pp. 28–49.

Borraz, O. and Le Galès, P. (2005) 'France: The Intermunicipal Revolution', in B. Denters and L.E. Rose (eds), *Comparing Local Governance: Trends and Developments*. Houndmills: Palgrave; pp. 12–28.

Coulson, A. and Campbell, A. (2006) 'Into the Mainstream. Local Democracy in Central and Eastern Europe', *Local Government Studies* 32(5): 543–62.

Dahl, R.A. and Tufte, E.R. (1973) *Size and Democracy*. Stanford, CA: Stanford University Press.

Dalton, R.J. and Gray, M. (2003) 'Expanding the Electoral Marketplace', in B.E. Cain, R.J. Dalton and S.E. Scarrow (eds), *Democracy Transformed? Expanding Political Opportunities in Advanced Industrial Democracies*. Oxford: Oxford University Press; pp. 23–43.

Davies, J.S. (2002) 'The Governance of Urban Regeneration: A Critique of the "Governing without Government" Thesis', *Public Administration* 80(2): 301–22.

Denters, B. (2005) 'Squandering Away Thorbecke's Legacy? Some Considerations on Recent Dutch Local Government Reforms', in H. Reynaert, P. Delwit, K. Steyvers and J.-B. Pilet (eds), *Revolution or Renovation? Reforming Local Politics in Europe*. Brugge: Van den Broele; pp. 421–44).

Denters, B. and Klok, P.J. (2003) 'A New Role for Municipal Councils in Dutch Local Democracy?', in N. Kersting and A. Vetter (eds), *Reforming Local Government in Europe: Closing the Gap between Democracy and Efficiency*. Opladen: Leske + Budrich; pp. 65–84.

Denters, B. and Klok, P.-J. (2005) 'The Netherlands: In Search of Responsiveness', in B. Denters and L.E. Rose (eds), *Comparing Local Governance: Trends and Developments*. Houndmills: Palgrave. pp. 65–82.

Denters, B. and Rose, L.E. (eds) (2005a). *Comparing Local Governance: Trends and Developments*. Houndmills: Palgrave.

Denters, B. and Rose, L.E. (2005b) 'Local Governance in the Third Millennium: A Brave New World?', in B. Denters and L.E. Rose (eds), *Comparing Local Governance: Trends and Developments*. Houndmills: Palgrave; pp. 1–11.

Denters, B. and Rose, L.E. (2005c) 'Towards Local Governance?', in B. Denters and L.E. Rose (eds), *Comparing Local Governance: Trends and Developments*. Houndmills: Palgrave; pp. 46–62.

Denters, S.A.H., Heffen, O.v. and Jong, H.M.d. (1999) 'An American Perestroika in Dutch Cities? Urban Policy in the Netherlands at the End of a Millennium', *Public Administration* 77: 837–53.

Denters, B., Klok, P.-J. and Kolk, H. v. d. (2005) 'The Reform of the Political Executive in Dutch Local Government', in R. Berg and N. Rao (eds), *Transforming Political Leadership in Local Government*. Houndmills: Palgrave Macmillan; pp. 15–28.

Elkin, S.L. (1987) *City and Regime in the American Republic*. Chicago: The University of Chicago Press.

Goldsmith, M. (2005) 'A New Intergovernmentalism?', in B. Denters and L.E. Rose (eds.), *Comparing Local Governance: Trends and Developments*. Houndmills: Palgrave; pp. 228–45.

Goodin, R.E. and Klingemann, H.D. (eds) (1996) *A New Handbook of Political Science*. Oxford: Oxford University Press.

Groot, M.d. (2009) 'Democratic Effects of Institutional Reform in Local Government: The Case of the Dutch Local Government Act 2002'. Unpublished PhD, University of Twente, Enschede.

Hoffmann-Martinot, V. (2003) 'The French Republic, One yet Divisible?', in N. Kersting and A. Vetter (eds), *Reforming Local Government in Europe: Closing the Gap between Democracy and Efficiency*. Opladen: Leske + Budrich; pp. 157–82.

John, P. (2001) *Local Governance in Western Europe*. London: Sage.

John, P. and Cole, A. (1999) 'Political Leadership in the New Urban Governance: Britain and France Compared', *Local Government Studies* 25: 98–115.

Kavanagh, D. and Richards, D. (2001) 'Departmentalism and Joined-Up Government', *Parliamentary Affairs* 54(1): 1–18.

Kerrouche, E. (2005) 'The Powerful French Mayor. Myth and Reality', in R. Berg and N. Rao (eds), *Transforming Local Political leadership*. Houndmills: Palgrave; pp. 150–67.

Kersbergen, K.v. and Waarden, F.v. (2001) *Shifts in Governance: Problems of Legitimacy and Accountability*. The Hague: MAGW Social Science Research Council.

Leach, R. and Percy-Smith, J. (2001) *Local Governance in Britain*. Houndmills: Palgrave.

Loughlin, J.E.A. (1999) *Regional and Local Democracy in the European Union*. Committee of the Regions, Luxembourg.

Lowndes, V., Stoker, G., Pratchett, L., et al. (1998). *Enhancing Public Participation in Local Government: A Research Report*. London: Department of the Environment, Transport and the Regions.

Mill, J.S. (1993) *Utilitarianism, On Liberty, Considerations on Representative Government, Remarks on Bentham's Philosophy*. London: Everyman Library.

Montin, S. (2005) 'The Swedish Model. Many Actors and Few Leaders', in R. Berg and N. Rao (eds), *Transforming Local Political Leadership*. Houndmills: Palgrave; pp.116–30.

Oates, W.E. (1999) 'An Essay on Fiscal Federalism', *Journal of Economic Literature* 37(3): 1120–49.

Perry, J.L. (ed.) (2006) *Handbook of Public Administration*, 2nd edn. San Francisco: Jossey-Bass Publishers.

Pierre, J. and Peters, B.G. (2000) *Governance, Politics and the State*. Houndmills: Macmillan.

Prior, D., Stewart, J. and Walsh, K. (1995) *Citizenship: Rights, Community and Participation*. London: Pitman.

Ranson, S., Martin, J., McKeown, P. and Nixon, J. (1999) 'The New Management and Governance of Education', in G. Stoker (ed.), *The New Management of British Local Governance*. Houndmills: Macmillan; pp. 97–111.

Rao, N. (2005) 'From Committees to Leaders and Cabinets. The British Experience', in R. Berg and N. Rao (eds), *Transforming Local Political Leadership*. Houndmills: Palgrave; pp. 42–58.

Rose, L.E. and Ståhlberg, K. (2005) 'The Nordic Countries: Still the Promised Land?', in B. Denters and L.E. Rose (eds), *Comparing Local Governance: Trends and Developments*. Houndmills: Palgrave; pp. 83–99.

Ross, B.H. and Levine, M.A. (1996) *Urban Politics: Power in Metropolitan America*, 5th edn. Itasca, IL: F.E. Peacock.

Savitch, H.V. and Vogel, R.K. (2005) 'The United States: Executive-Centred Politics', in B. Denters and L.E. Rose (eds), *Comparing Local Governance: Trends and Developments*. Houndmills: Palgrave; pp. 211–27.

Scarrow, S.E. (2003) 'Making Elections More Direct? Reducing the Role of Parties in Elections', in B.E. Cain, R.J. Dalton and S.E. Scarrow (eds), *Democracy Transformed? Expanding Political Opportunities in*

Advanced Industrial Democracies. Oxford: Oxford University Press; pp. 44–58.

Schumpeter, J.A. (1979) [1943] *Capitalism, Socialism and Democracy.* London: George Allen and Unwin.

Sellers, J.M. and Lidstrom, A. (2007) 'Local Government and the Welfare State', *Governance* 20(4): 609–32.

Sharpe, L.J. (1970) 'Theories and Values of Local Government', *Political Studies* 18: 153–74.

Stoker, G. (1995) *'Local Governance. A Conceptual Challenge'.* 23rd European Consortium of Political Research for Political Research Joint Sessions of Workshops. The Changing Local Governance of Europe. Bordeaux.

Stoker, G. (1996) 'Introduction: Normative Theories of Local Government and Democracy', in D. King and G. Stoker (eds), *Rethinking Local Democracy.* Houndmills: Macmillan; pp. 1–27.

Stoker, G. (2000) 'Introduction', in G. Stoker (ed.), *The New Politics of British Local Governance.* Houndmills: Macmillan; pp. 1–9.

Stoker, G. (2004) *Transforming Local Governance.* Houndmills: Palgrave Macmillan.

Stone, C. (2005) 'Institutions Count but Resources Decide. American Mayors and the Limits of Formal Structure', in R. Berg and N. Rao (eds), *Transforming Local Political Leadership.* Houndmills: Palgrave; pp. 180–94.

Sullivan, H. and Skelcher, C. (2002) *Working across Boundaries. Collaboration in Public Services.* Houndmills: Palgrave-Macmillan.

Svara, J.H. (2005) 'Institutional Form and Political Leadership in American City Government', in R. Berg and N. Rao (eds), *Transforming Local Political Leadership.* Houndmills: Palgrave; pp. 131–49.

Swianiewicz, P. (2005) 'Cities in Transition. From Statism to Democracy', in M. Haus, H. Heinelt and M. Stewart (eds), *Urban Governance and Democracy. Leadership and Community Involvement.* London: Routledge. pp. 102–28.

Thiel, S. van (2002) 'Lokale verzelfstandiging: trends, motieven en resultaten van verzelfstandiging door gemeenten', *Beleidswetenschap* 16(1): 3–31.

Tocqueville, A. de. (1990) *Democracy in America.* New York: Vintage.

US Census Bureau (2002) 2002 *Census of Governments, Volume 1, Number 1, Government Organization.* Vol. GC02(1)-1. Washington, DC: US Government Printing Office.

Vetter, A. (2002) 'Local Political Competence in Europe: A Resource of Legitimacy for Higher Levels of Government?', *International Journal of Public Opinion Research* 14(1): 3–18.

Vetter, A. (2009) 'Citizens versus Parties: Explaining Institutional Change in German Local Government, 1989–2008', *Local Government Studies* 35: 125–42.

Wilson, D. (2005) 'The United Kingdom: An Increasingly Differentiated Polity?', in B. Denters and L.E. Rose (eds), *Comparing Local Governance: Trends and Developments.* Houndmills: Palgrave; pp. 155–73.

Wilson, D. and Game, C. with Leach, S. and Stoker, G. (1994) *Local Government in the United Kingdom.* Houndmills: Macmillan.

Wollmann, H. (2003) 'German Local Government under the Double Impact of Democratic and Administrative reforms', in N. Kersting and A. Vetter (eds), *Reforming Local Government in Europe: Closing the Gap between Democracy and Efficiency.* Opladen: Leske + Budrich; pp. 85–112.

Wollmann, H. (2004) 'Local Government Reforms in Great Britain, Sweden, Germany and France: Between Multi-Function and Single-Purpose Organisations', *Local Government Studies* 30(4): 639–65.

Wollmann, H. (2005) 'The Directly Elected Executive Mayor in German Local Government', in R. Berg and N. Rao (eds), *Transforming Local Political Leadership.* Houndmills: Palgrave; pp. 29–41.

Wollmann, H. (2008) *Reformen in der Kommunalpolitik und -Verwaltung. England, Schweden, Frankreich und Deutschland im Vergleich.* Wiesbaden: Verlag für Sozialwissenschaften.

21

Non-governmental Organizations

M. Shamsul Haque

INTRODUCTION

In recent decades there has been an unprecedented global proliferation of non-governmental organizations (NGOs) at the local, national, and international levels with diverse missions, such as poverty eradication, human rights, environmental protection, gender equality, and so on. This worldwide expansion of NGOs has coincided with changes in the ideological, theoretical, and practical tenets of governance based on market-biased neoliberal assumptions, anti-welfare programs, business-friendly policies (e.g. deregulation and privatization), and neo-managerial structures and techniques (Hulme and Edwards, 1997a). For some scholars, the emergence and consolidation of such promarket agendas during the past three decades created an atmosphere that was against the role of the state and its bureaucracy, and popularized the role of non-state actors, including NGOs (Baccaro, 2001; Paul, 2000). In many Asian, African, and Latin American countries, NGOs have increasingly undertaken the role of delivering services and addressing a wide range of socioeconomic problems (Edwards and Hulme, 1996).

In line with this trend, the number of NGOs has significantly increased in both developed and developing nations. There are thousands of NGOs in advanced Western nations, accounting for a considerable proportion of their national employment. Many of these Western NGOs have networks and operations in other parts of the world and are therefore known as international NGOs (or INGOs). Between 1990 and 1995, employment in such INGOs increased by over 10 percent in Germany, 8 percent in France, and 30 percent in the UK (Anheier and Cho, 2005). According to one earlier estimate, the number of such INGOs is about 48,000, and some of them are very large, including Amnesty International, Oxfam, the Friends of the Earth, Save the Children, the Red Cross, etc. For example, the Friends of the Earth Federation has about one million members and 5000 local groups in around the world; Amnesty international has over 1.8 million members and subscribers in 140 countries and territories, and the International Union for the Conservation of Nature deals with 735 local NGOs and 112 government agencies, and it also has about 10,000 scientists and experts from more than 180 countries (Anheier and Cho, 2005).

However, the recent proliferation of NGOs has been more rapid and intensive in the developing regions. Depending on the sources of information, the number of NGOs in Asia, Africa, and Latin America varies from several hundred thousands to one million (Haque, 2002). Among many other factors, the diversion of foreign assistance from the state to the NGO sector has contributed greatly to this proliferation of NGOs in the developing world. For instance, the percentage of World-Bank-funded projects involving NGOs increased from 20 percent in 1989 to 47 percent in 1997; the percentage of USAID's (United States Agency for International Development) development assistance that went to NGOs or similar institutions increased to 37 percent by 2001; and during the past two decades NGOs from Western nations raised billions of dollars to finance national or local NGOs in developing countries (Gauri, 2003; Tvedt, 1998).

Owing to this proliferation of NGOs worldwide, there is greater academic interest in studying various dimensions and implications of these organizations. An expanding volume of research and literature can be found in the major social science disciplines and fields dealing with non-profit, non-government, or voluntary sector organizations (VSOs) around the world (Dollery, Wallis, and Crase, 2002). In addition to the existing development studies institutions, more specialized professional organizations have emerged, like the International Society for Third Sector Research and the Association for Research on Nonprofit Organizations and Voluntary Action (Lewis, 1998). There are also several academic journals, including *Nonprofit Management and Leadership*, *Nonprofit and Voluntary Sector Quarterly*, and *Voluntas: International Journal of Voluntary and Nonprofit Organizations*, which focus largely on NGO-type organizations.

There are some major factors contributing to the mushrooming growth of NGOs and the expanding range of academic studies and publications about them. As explained later in more detail, the move towards NGOs was shaped not only by the emergence of the promarket and anti-state neoliberal framework mentioned above but also it was advocated and made in the name of enhancing civil society and democracy, reaching the grassroots, and ensuring direct participation in decision-making (Hulme and Edwards, 1997a, 1997b; Kitsing, 2003). Gradually, it has almost become taken-for-granted that NGOs are symbols of social responsibility, empowerment, and morality, and thus, that they represent a form of ideological persuasion (Mercer, 2002; Tvedt, 1998). However, there are still limits to the study of NGOs and other VSOs in terms of the lack of established common concepts, an acceptable analytical framework, and an agreed theoretical consensus (Gidron, Kramer and Salamon, 1992a). In addition, according to Dollery, Wallis and Crase (2002), despite the proliferation of academic literature on the subject, there is still inadequate understanding of the relationship between these non-state organizations and the state. There are serious controversies regarding whether NGOs are more effective and efficient than state agencies in delivering services and whether NGOs can reach the poorest of the poor (Baccaro, 2001; Edwards and Hulme, 1996).

This chapter attempts to deal with these diverse issues and concerns; it provides a conceptual, analytical, and critical explanation. In particular, it first presents the prevailing conceptual and theoretical interpretations and their limits, and tries to offer a more satisfactory conceptual–theoretical framework. Secondly, it examines the recent rise of NGOs as an alternative mode of governance in relation to the emergence of the market-based neoliberal state (especially in terms of why NGOs have become a substitute for the public sector), how NGOs themselves have changed in line with business-oriented principles and norms, and the implications of such changes for the overall identity and role of NGOs. Thirdly, it evaluates the positive and negative outcomes of the work of NGOs, as reported or publicized by their advocates and critics, and offers a more objective procedural assessment that demonstrates the serious limitations of NGOs as an option for governance.

CONCEPTS AND THEORIES OF NGOs

There is considerable diversity in the interpretation and conceptualization of NGOs, depending on the conceptual framework (broad vs narrow), their national or regional contexts, sectoral identities, and the interpreter's academic background. As a result, some scholars have observed that 'NGOs are notoriously difficult to define' and that they have 'different meanings in different contexts' (Farrington and Lewis, 1993: 20, 31). For Martens (2002: 272, 277), 'NGOs have not yet sufficiently been defined,' 'many studies fail to offer any definition of the term NGO,' and 'the term NGO has been criticized for being the "rubbish bin" or "catch-all word" for everything that is simply not governmental.' The problem of definition is accentuated further by the existence of many less-genuine NGO-like organizations that are categorized as 'NGO pretenders'[1] by Richard Holloway (1997). Because of this ambiguity of definition, there is a need for a comprehensive analysis and understanding of the concept.

Conceptual analysis

There are various organizational terms similar to and often used interchangeably with NGO, including non-profit organization (NPO), voluntary sector organization (VSO), third sector organization (TSO), community-based organization (CBO), grassroots organization (GRO), informal sector organization (ISO), and civil society organization (CSO) (Haque, 2002; Holloway, 1997; Martens, 2002). However, there are some differences between these terms, and the concept of the NGO has certain distinctive factors that need to be clarified. While NGOs are supposed to be non-profit, in most countries, there are many NPOs without a mission to advocate or empower (e.g. museums, hospitals, universities), and which are not NGOs (Paul, 2000). While NGOs, like VSOs, often depend on voluntary workers and are devoted to charitable or philanthropic purposes, most NGOs also have regular employees and pursue activities beyond charity. NGOs are also similar to TSOs in terms of their location between and distinction from the government and private sectors, but there are many TSOs (including clubs and associations based on common identities and/or mutual interests of their members) that do not qualify as NGOs.

Similarly, most CBOs are engaged in addressing problems or serving the interests of their own members within a local community – they hardly follow the NGOs in aiming to serve overall society. There is also a distinction between GROs and NGOs – while GROs are small membership-based organizations usually without paid staff, NGOs are relatively large organizations with hired and paid professional staff working to reduce poverty, build capacity, empower people, and so on (Baccaro, 2001; Mercer, 2002). Compared to ISOs, which are autonomous, informal, and often ad hoc, NGOs are regulated, formal, and relatively durable organizations (Martens, 2002; Wagle, 1999). Finally, it is quite fashionable to consider NGOs as a part of civil society and to identify them as CSOs. But similar to the TSOs, with their broad scope mentioned above, the CSOs represent the third sector, they are quite wide-ranging (including foundations, community organizations, research organizations, grassroots entities, and voluntary initiatives), and many of them do not qualify as NGOs (Wagle, 1999). In addition, while many TSOs and CSOs often exist without legal standing and formal structures, NGOs are legal entities with formal organizational structures (Holloway, 1997; Kitsing, 2003).

Thus, in important ways, NGOs differ from the similar organizations (VSOs, TSOs, CBOs, GROs, ISOs, and CSOs) mentioned above. In particular, compared to these other categories, NGOs are more legal and formal entities with professional/skilled and paid staff, established organizational rules and structures, and the common goal of serving the public interest at the national and international levels (Martens, 2002: 282). However, in varying degrees, NGOs possess some of the major attributes of those similar organizational categories. More specifically, NGOs are usually created by private and voluntary initiatives, they are relatively autonomous from the state, and they are not owned and controlled by government, although they have to function in line with certain state regulations. NGOs are also separate from the business sector, they are non-profit organizations without any objective to make monetary gains, and their main purpose is to assist underprivileged and powerless groups and serve the public at large (Holloway, 1997; Wagle, 1999). Finally, although NGOs have paid permanent staff, like other similar organizations, they often use voluntary workers.

Thus, in their ideal form, *NGOs are organizations characterized by a certain legal basis of existence, a durable formal structure, hired and paid (non-government) staff, a private status with the purpose of serving the public interest, autonomy from the state and the private sector, a non-profit orientation, and the promotion of humanitarian goals* (Haque, 2002; Martens, 2002). The scope of NGO activities encompasses diverse sectors and areas, including public health, education and research, environmental protection, gender issues, social services, poverty eradication, and advocacy and politics. Local NGOs originate from and operate in both developed and developing countries to serve local people and communities in each nation, whereas international NGOs (mostly from developed nations) operate in many countries, have worldwide networks, and are often connected to local NGOs.

Theoretical interpretation

Beyond articulating the concept of NGOs, it is necessary to comprehend theoretical explanations of them. There are theoretical perspectives that tend to explain the importance of NGOs in terms of their economic, social, and political significance. For instance, it is argued that due to the failures of state intervention and market competition, the NGO sector represents a viable economic alternative for ensuring 'good governance' (Cross, 1997). In the social realm, due to the relative absence of information about and trust in the business sector, NGOs provide consumers with a better alternative for gathering adequate information and delivering more reliable or trustworthy goods. In terms of political significance, it is argued that NGOs play a crucial role in strengthening democracy by expanding and enhancing the realm of civil society (Mercer, 2002: 7).

However, the most common and comprehensive theoretical explanations are largely about the nature and structure of the relationship between NGOs and the state, especially with regard to the extent of their autonomy from state control and regulation (Cross, 1997). In this regard, although there are many theoretical frameworks, it is possible to discern five major frameworks or models (the government-dominant model, the third-sector-dominant model, the dual-track model, the collaboration model, and the competition model) to explain the nature of government–NGO relations.

First, for the *government-dominant model*, the government–NGO relationship is largely based on the dominant role played by the state in financing and providing goods and services, as is usually seen in the 'modern welfare state' (Gidron, Kramer and Salamon, 1992b). The services provided by NGOs are often specified by the state, which prescribes guidelines for service delivery and requires financial reporting and accountability from NGOs (Lyons, 2001).

Secondly, in opposition to this government-dominant model (which gives only limited autonomy to NGOs), the *third-sector-dominant model* allows NGOs to play a much greater role in funding and delivering services, and can be observed in countries where there is opposition to the state's welfare provisions (Dollery, Wallis and Crase, 2002).

Thirdly, in the *dual-track model,* the responsibility for financing and distributing services can be shared between the state and the NGO sector because the former is unable to deliver all services and serve all clients, and NGOs therefore play a necessary role in covering these services and clients (Dollery, Wallis and Crase, 2002).

Fourthly, in the *collaboration model,* the government–NGO relationship goes beyond the parallel or coexisting roles played by state agencies and NGOs: they both share responsibilities and work jointly to finance and deliver services based on mutual partnership (Gidron, Kramer and Salamon, 1992b).

Finally, and conversely to the collaboration model, the *competition* model explains government–NGO relations in terms of a zero-sum game or gain–loss situation between the state and the NGO sector: while both actors enjoy a certain independence from each other, they compete for resources and to deliver services (Gronberg, 1987). Such a situation may arise when certain advocacy NGOs develop an antagonistic relationship with the state and, thus, face government restrictions (Young, 2000).

The above conceptual analysis and theoretical interpretation constitute a generic ideal-type understanding of NGOs. Although the actual practices of NGOs may show some deviation from these conceptual and theoretical criteria, there should be a minimal consistency between the conceptual–theoretical frameworks and practical standards in order to claim or qualify an organization as an NGO. However, recent decades have witnessed considerable proliferation and reconfiguration of NGOs under the new market-driven governance, as discussed below.

GOVERNANCE AND NGOs: TRENDS AND LINKAGES

It is widely recognized that since the early 1980s, due to diverse national and global factors, the form of the state and the mode of its governance have drastically shifted in line with the neoliberal assumptions of market supremacy and the non-interventionist state, market-oriented policies (such as deregulation and privatization), neo-managerial measures (like corporatization and agencification), and so on. These relatively anti-state and market-driven trends in state formation, governance, and policy orientation caused the rolling back of the state and contraction of the public sector by transferring most government responsibilities and activities to non-state actors, including local and foreign private enterprises and investors, as well as national and global NGOs. These developments significantly affected the NGO sector in two ways: (1) they created greater demand to use NGOs as effective non-state alternatives and (2) they converted or transformed most NGOs themselves, in line with businesslike standards, structures, and motives.

Using NGOs for the new mode of governance

It has been observed that the current shift towards neoliberal belief in market-led solutions and state non-intervention has increased the prominence of non-state actors like NGOs in developing countries; it has increased their share of donor funds and expanded their role in providing services such as health, education, and agriculture (Commins, 1997; Lewis, 2004). Even in advanced capitalist nations like the USA, Australia, and the UK, the role of the voluntary sector has considerably increased, so that it delivers social services that used to be managed by the public sector (Austin, 2003; Dollery and Wallis, 2001). According to Rong (2008), as the emergence of promarket public management led to the rolling back of the welfare state and marginalized it to the role of mere facilitator or enabler, governments became increasingly dependent on 'third party' organizations (including NGOs) to carry out their social responsibilities, and they began to enhance the capacity of NGOs. It is now a common belief that 'NGOs have tremendous potential for enhancing the quantity and quality of delivering social sector services' (Sarker, 2005: 257). Thus, in addition to transferring state ownership, management, and service delivery to the private sector through measures like privatization and outsourcing, the transfer of government responsibilities to NGOs has increasingly become a desirable alternative. It is argued that NGOs are better at delivering cost-effective services, especially in reaching low-income families (Edwards and Hulme, 1996).

In line with this new trend towards a diminishing role for the state, a new framework of governance has emerged, based on multiple stakeholders (private, public and non-profit) – known as 'distributed,' 'networked,' or 'shared' governance – which underscores the roles played by all major actors (called 'partners in governance'), including NGOs (Choudhury and Ahmed, 2002: 562). More specifically, within market-led governance, while the business sector came to occupy an expanded and central space, the NGO sector became crucial for dealing with certain issues and concerns (e.g. the needs of low-income families) that could not be addressed by market forces (Sarker, 2005: 254).

In fact, the common social problems, such as poverty, illiteracy, and health care, were likely to be worsened by market-led reforms but overlooked by the business sector. Therefore, NGOs have become increasingly important under promarket governance in order to deal with these unavoidable problems. According to Robinson (1997: 61), the role of NGOs in providing social services has grown in response to the recent cutbacks in public spending on education, health, employment, etc. In reference to the use of NGOs to

disguise the hardship caused by promarket policies and reforms, Petras (1997) suggests that NGOs have become the 'community face' of neoliberalism.

Converting NGOs under the new governance

Owing to the influence of neoliberal atmosphere on overall governance, the nature of NGOs themselves has significantly changed in favor of such market-led ideological tendencies. Some authors have also mentioned that under the influence or pressure of external donors, many NGOs have increasingly embraced neoliberal policy options in choosing the areas of their service delivery and the nature of their transactions with clients (Tobin, 2005). In particular, compared to their original non-profit principles, most NGOs today are in the profit-making business. Similar to business corporations, many large NGOs have been commercialized – today they own and manage enterprises related to banking, the press, handicrafts, telecommunications, transport, cold storage, video libraries, real estate, internet services, and more (Paul, 2000; Sarker, 2005).

Most NGOs have replaced their earlier non-profit-making missions and social programs with profit-making activities like microfinance, which involves the provision of microcredit to their members or clients at high interest rates. In South Asia, in countries like Bangladesh, profit-making microfinance has become the dominant area or activity for most well-known NGOs, and such business-like ventures are often prescribed by international agencies like the World Bank (Charitonenko and Rahman, 2002; Sarker, 2005). Latin America has seen a similar expansion of microfinance as the primary activity of NGOs, which increasingly behave like commercial banks, having reduced or eliminated their previous non-profit social programs (Bell, 2006).

There is a growing tendency among NGOs to promote a market-oriented mindset among their poorer members and to treat them as customers (Hulme and Edwards, 1997b: 280). On the other hand, these NGOs have formed partnerships and expanded commercial joint ventures with many state agencies, business enterprises, and foreign investors, although such profit-motivated partnerships may create tension and marginalize members' participation (Jorgensen, 2006; Paoletto, 2000). Thus, there has been some redefinition and restructuring of relationships between NGOs and their poorer members, as well as between NGOs, state agencies, and private enterprises (Rong, 2008). Owing to this new trend for NGOs to be transformed into profit-making entities and to be used as contractors by the state and business sectors, there is concern that such NGOs are losing their original character and betraying the previous trust in them (Holloway, 1997).

In addition, and similar to recent neo-managerial reforms in the public sector, in most countries NGOs have experienced organizational and managerial changes drawn from business. In particular, NGOs have adopted commercial skills, principles of competition, managerial entrepreneurship, performance-based contracts, outcome targets, etc. (Rong, 2008; Sarker, 2005). Most NGOs try to comply with the quantitative performance targets and output standards that are usually set by their foreign donors (Sarker, 2005). Other managerial tools recently introduced in NGOs include efficiency measures, strategic planning, project evaluation, marketing techniques, etc. (Roberts, Jones and Hling, 2005). In line with the increasing use of managerial principles and tools in NGOs, courses and graduate degrees in NGO management are also offered (Roberts, Jones and Hling, 2005). In this regard, Roberts, Jones and Hling (2005: 1853) state: 'The overall managerialist imperative, in terms of the way an organization [NGO] is run and functions, can be summed up in the ubiquitous terms efficiency and effectiveness which are themselves captured by the more overarching concern for good governance'.

EVALUATING THE OUTCOMES FROM NGOs IN GOVERNANCE

There are significant controversies about the achievements and failures of NGOs. The advocates of NGOs identify many positive outcomes, including greater efficiency, grassroots connections, participatory management methods, democratic potential, poverty eradication, gender equality, and people empowerment. More specifically, compared to government agencies, NGOs are considered more efficient, transparent, and innovative (Cross, 1997) due to their closeness to people, less-hierarchical structure, and flexible managerial style. It is also argued that NGO staff are highly committed as they share some common humanitarian values and beliefs (Wagle, 1999). The other positive outcomes from NGOs are claimed to be their contribution to the democratization process and to democratic capacity building (Cross, 1997). Moreover, compared to other institutions, NGOs encourage bottom-up participation, especially with regard to the participation of the underprivileged and the powerless.

On the negative side, critics argue that NGOs have failed to reduce the number of poor people in Africa, Latin America, and South Asia (Temple, 2000). There is no solid evidence that NGOs can reduce poverty on a national scale. In addition, NGOs often oversimplify a complex issue like poverty and offer piecemeal solutions, and they play a conservative role in preserving class inequality, disaggregating or disuniting the poor, and reducing pressure for more fundamental reforms in favor of restructuring income and ownership (Edwards and Hulme, 1996; Tvedt, 1998). NGOs may also perpetuate the external dependence of a country by receiving financial aid from external donors and international agencies, and their strong alliance with such external actors may have an adverse impact on national sovereignty (Hulme and Edwards, 1997a: 14). The presence of too many NGOs not only causes functional overlap or duplication and waste of resources but it may also encourage governments of poor countries to avoid their own responsibility to provide welfare services to the poor and to use NGOs to cover up their own failure (Wagle, 1999).

The above brief discussion on the positive and negative outcomes from NGOs shows that there is no definitive conclusion about their actual contribution. A more objective assessment of NGOs can be made by evaluating their procedural features and principles, including leadership appointments, recruitment of staff, mode of decision-making, performance and accountability, rate of service charge or interest rate for loans, and so on. Unfortunately, most NGOs do not appear to be very fair in terms of these procedural criteria.

First, with regard to top leadership, there is no systematic process of leadership selection. Most NGOs are dominated by their founding charismatic leaders who are usually quite authoritarian, and who continue to hold the leadership position and become almost cult figures in their NGOs (Mercer, 2002: 13). These leaders are neither elected by NGO members or local people, nor selected and appointed by any neutral professional body, and thus the process is not based on a fair merit principle. Similar lack of proper recruitment and selection procedures can be observed in the middle and lower management of many NGOs. Some scholars have highlighted that in the process of recruiting staff, NGO leaders often use 'kinship and patronage networks' to ensure their loyalty (Sarker, 2005: 263).

Secondly, almost all major decisions in NGOs are made and/or approved by the top founding leaders through their 'personalized rule,' and there is a lack of adequate member participation in the decision-making process (Mercer, 2002: 14). Moreover, the decision-making process is often based on personal beliefs and interests rather than on rational organizational criteria.

Thirdly, there is a serious problem in ensuring the accountability of NGOs due to the absence of proper institutional measures. In democratic societies there are various legislative, executive, judicial, organizational,

and informal means to guarantee the public accountability of government agencies and employees, and there are regulatory means, established business principles, and the rules of the market to make business enterprises accountable to customers. But for NGOs, there is a relative lack of such accountability measures: they are not required to be legally answerable to the poor whom they try to serve, and they often do not have specific and clear performance standards against which they can be held accountable (Holloway, 1997). It has been pointed out by some authors that the local NGOs in developing countries are usually accountable externally to foreign donors and international NGOs that provide financial support, but they are hardly accountable internally to their local members or clients (Focus, 1997).

Fourthly, many NGOs are involved in providing microcredit or small loans to the poor, but the process of lending can be quite unfair. In countries like Bangladesh, for instance, some large NGOs claim to serve the underprivileged population by offering microcredit – these NGOs receive interest-free donations and low-interest loans from various sources, but they provide microcredit to the poor at very high interest rates (often more than 20 percent). Such 'banking for the poor' has become big business for these NGOs (Rady, 1999). In addition, in opposition to the traditional belief that NGOs are less likely to be involved in corruption, there are cases of rampant NGO corruption in many countries, especially due to the minimal scrutiny and monitoring of their financial transactions and procedures. In 2003 it was found that contracts worth 1.5 billion Euros were awarded annually from European Union funds to NGOs without adequate tendering measures (Kitsing, 2003). It has been pointed out that NGOs do not have public responsibility, but that they do have public resources (Holloway, 1997).

Finally, as mentioned above, in most countries NGOs have increasingly become involved in all sorts of profit-making commercial ventures and businesslike contracts or partnerships with private investors and state agencies, although these are against their characteristics of non-profit status and independence from the state and business sectors. What makes this new trend procedurally unfair is the fact that such profit-making ventures adversely affect their main goal of helping the poor (in terms of ensuring employment, equality, and empowerment), and create a corporate culture of high salaries and undue privileges for top NGO executives based on an exploitative relationship with poor NGO members. More importantly, NGOs receive undue privileges such as tax exemption, easy low-interest loans, duty-free imports, and so on, which is unfair to private sector enterprises without such privileges, and is incompatible with the principle of free and fair market competition. According to Holloway (1997), 'part of the problems of corruption of NGOs come when they start behaving more like businesses or more like governments.'

From the above discussion of the outcomes and implications of the role of NGOs in governance, it is clear that some serious concerns exist, and the academic advocacy of NGOs needs to be seriously reexamined. There are several critical studies that demonstrate that in many cases, NGOs have failed to reach 'the poorest of the poor,' and may even have contributed to the perpetuation of poverty and inequality (Edwards and Hulme, 1996; Klees, 1998). Critics also argue that in many developing countries, instead of enhancing civil society and democratization, NGOs may have undermined the emergence of strong civil society and democracy (Atarah, 2000; Farrington and Lewis, 1993). For Petras (1997), the language of 'popular power,' 'empowerment,' 'gender equality,' and 'sustainable development' is often co-opted by NGOs when collaborating with donors and state agencies. It should be noted, however, that there are admirable NGOs with genuine achievements, but most of these have also now changed, due to an increased level of bureaucratization, a concern for raising quick funds, and involvement in profit-making commercial activities (Farrington and Lewis, 1993; Holloway, 1997).

CONCLUDING REMARKS

This chapter has highlighted that in recent decades, although there has been a significant proliferation of NGOs in terms of their number, activities, resources, and academic studies and debates, there are still conceptual and theoretical controversies. After analyzing these conceptual and theoretical issues, the chapter has examined the significance of the role of NGOs in governance, and the positive and negative outcomes and implications of such a role. Despite claims about the merits and achievements of NGOs made by their proponents or advocates, there are some serious limitations and negative consequences arising from these organizations, especially in the current era of market-driven neoliberal governance. Thus, Bebbington and Riddell (1997: 114) oppose the claim that NGOs represent a better alternative to state bureaucracy, and they think that such rhetoric is 'little more than self-fulfilling prophecy.' In fact, there is a lack of systematic studies comparing NGO and government programs, and the evaluations often done by NGOs themselves cannot guarantee impartiality (Baccaro, 2001).

Several studies have concluded that there is no empirical evidence that NGOs perform better than the state and business sectors in terms of efficiency, cost, and quality of services (Edwards and Hulme, 1996). A recent comparative study of the government-promoted and NGO-initiated community forestry programs in India found that participants benefited more from government programs than NGO programs, that the affluent upper-class elite unduly influenced the projects, and that the lower-class participants fared better in government programs than in NGO programs (Baccaro, 2001). In this regard, Edwards and Hulme (1996) mention that if government ministries of health and education could receive the large subsidies from foreign donors that the NGOs have been receiving, over time these ministries could become more cost-effective in service delivery. Given the above claims and critiques, it is possible to identify certain remedial policy measures.

First, it is possible to restructure or rein-vent NGOs in order to overcome their limita-tions and adverse consequences. This strategy may include measures such as intensive scru-tiny and assessment of NGOs, abolition of fake NGOs or NGO pretenders, systematic selection of NGO leadership and other staff, strict regulation of NGO funding and trans-parency in their financial transactions, effec-tive control of the foreign sources of financial assistance and interaction,[2] prevention of profit-driven business ventures by NGOs, prohibition of excessive fees or interest rates charged to poor members, introduction of effective means to hold NGOs accountable to their clients,[3] and so on. All these measures would require the adoption of comprehensive legal provisions and effective regulatory institutions.

Secondly, since it is a great challenge to address some of the major limits of NGOs through their reform, there is a need to explore alternative institutional choices. One such choice is a viable system of decentral-ized and elected local self-government, which has most of the advantages claimed by NGOs (e.g. nearness to people, low transaction cost, localized and need-based services, and direct participation and interaction of the people). In India, for instance, the local government system (known as the *Panchayat* system) has provided greater opportunity for underprivi-leged low-caste citizens and powerless women to be elected and to express grievances. In addition, the system of representative local government has been one of the main compo-nents of democracy and public empowerment in Western countries. It might also resolve the innate problems of NGOs such as self-proclaimed paternalistic leadership, lack of internal institutional accountability, etc.

Thirdly, since the use and existence of NGOs have increasingly become an accepted reality, and they have certain advantages in addressing problems related to specific issues and groups, it may be more feasible to have a system of governance based on respon-sibilities shared among the major actors, including the national government, the local government, the business sector, the NGOs, and other self-help organizations at the com-munity or grassroots level. Which actors would undertake what responsibilities, manage what programs, and deliver what services should largely depend on the politi-cal, economic, and sociocultural contexts that vary considerably among nations. Thus, the sharing of responsibilities, programs, and services should be worked out by the major actors through dialogue and consensus.

The most critical factor for adopting any of the above measures, however, is the role played by the state. Despite the continuous negative campaign launched against the state and its bureaucracy during the recent decades of neoliberal reforms, the importance of the state's role in governance remains not only because of the need for the state's direct involvement in major domains or sectors of society but also because of its capacity to steer and coordinate the roles played by all other actors.[4] With regard to the significance of the state for the success of NGOs them-selves, Sanyal (1994: 48) mentions that 'without some form of state involvement, developmental efforts of NGOs, however well intentioned, cannot flourish.'

NOTES

1   Holloway includes in the list of such 'NGO pretenders' some amusing titles, including the Briefcase NGO (BRINGO), which represents just a briefcase carrying a well-written proposal; the Commercial NGO (CONGO), created by businesses to participate in bids and win contracts; the Criminal NGO (CRINGO), set up for a criminal goal like smug-gling; the Government-run and initiated NGO (GRINGO), created for countering real NGOs; the Party NGO (PANGO), used by defeated or banned political parties; the Mercenary NGO (MENGO), cre-ated to act as contractor for any funded develop-ment project; and My own NGO (MONGO), initiated and used by an individual as personal property often to satisfy his or ego; and so on (Holloway, 1997).

2   A closer scrutiny of such foreign funds and linkages is essential to reduce the possibility of cor-ruption and the unfair privileges NGOs receive from these external sources, and to ensure that their main

obligations are to their members rather than to foreign donors (Edwards and Hulme, 1996).

3   This accountability of NGOs should be to multiple stakeholders: 'downwards' to their beneficiaries, partners, supporters, and employees; and 'upwards' to the relevant government agencies, donors, and trustees (Edwards and Hulme, 1996).

4   It has been pointed out that each government has the 'ultimate responsibility' to deal with all national affairs, including those managed or addressed by NGOs (*Asiaweek*, 1996).

REFERENCES

Anheier, Helmut and Cho, Hyo-Je (2005) 'International NGOs as an Element of Global Civil Society: Scale, Expressions, and Governance'. Sixth Global Forum on Reinventing Government, 23–27 May, Seoul, South Korea.

Asiaweek (1996) 'Governments Should Accept NGOs as Partners', *The Asiaweek* December 13.

Atarah, Linus (2000) 'Development: Activists Debate Future of NGOs'. Inter Press Service, 30 August.

Austin, Michael J. (2003) 'The Changing Relationship between Nonprofit Organizations and Public Social Service Agencies in the Era of Welfare Reform', *Nonprofit and Voluntary Sector Quarterly* 32(1): 97–114.

Baccaro, Lucio (2001) *Civil Society, NGOs, and Decent Work Policies: Sorting Out the Issues*. Discussion Paper Series No. DP/127/2001. Geneva: International Institute for Labour Studies.

Bebbington, Anthony and Riddell, Roger (1997) 'Heavy Hands, Hidden Hands, Holding Hands? Donors, Intermediary NGOs and Civil Society Organisations', in David Hulme and Michael Edwards (eds), *NGOs, States and Donors: Too Close for Comfort*. New York: St. Martin's Press; pp. 107–27.

Bell, Shannon (2006) 'The Commercialization of Microfinance', *WCCN's Newsletter*, 22(4).

Charitonenko, S. and Rahman, S.M. (2002) *Commercialization of Micro-finance – Bangladesh*. Manila: Asian Development Bank.

Choudhury, Enamul and Ahmed, Shamima (2002) 'The Shifting Meaning of Governance: Public Accountability of Third Sector Organizations in an Emergent Global Regime', *International Journal of Public Administration* 25(4): 561–88.

Commins, Steven (1997) 'World Vision International and Donors: Too Close for Comfort?', in David Hulme and Michael Edwards (eds), *NGOs, States and Donors: Too Close for Comfort*. New York: St. Martin's Press; pp. 140–55.

Cross, John C. (1997) 'Development NGOs, the State and Neo-liberalism: Competition, Partnership or Co-conspiracy', in *Proceedings of the Fourth Annual AUC Research Conference*. Office of Graduate Studies and Research, The American University in Cairo, July 1997.

Dollery, Brian and Wallis, Joe (2001) *Economic Approaches to the Voluntary Sector: A Note on Voluntary Failure and Human Service Delivery*. Working Paper Series in Economics, No. 2001–16, December 2001. School of Economics, University of New England, Australia.

Dollery, Brian, Wallis, Joe and Crase, Lin (2002) *Public Policy Approaches to the Voluntary Sector*. Working Paper Series in Economics. School of Economics, University of New England, Australia.

Edwards, Michael and Hulme, David (1996) 'Too Close for Comfort? The Impact of Official Aid on Nongovernmental Organizations', *World Development* 24: 961–73.

Farrington, John and Lewis, David J. (eds) (1993) *Non-Government Organizations and the State in Asia*. London: Routledge.

Focus (1997) *The Changing Roles and Accountabilities of NGOs in the New World*. Discussion Paper, Focus on the Global South, Chulalongkorn University, Bangkok, Thailand (http://www.focusweb.org/focus/pd/roles/roledp.html).

Gauri, Varun (2003) *Location Decisions and Nongovernmental Organization Motivation: Evidence from Rural Bangladesh*. World Bank Policy Research Working Paper No. 3176. Washington, DC: The World Bank, December 2003.

Gidron, B., Kramer, R.M. and Salamon, L.M. (1992a) 'Preface', in B. Gidron, R.M. Kramer, and L.M. Salamon (eds), *Government and the Third Sector*, San Francisco: Jossey-Bass.

Gidron, B., Kramer, R.M. and Salamon, L.M. (1992b) 'Government and the Third Sector in Comparative Perspective: Allies or Adversaries', in B. Gidron, R.M. Kramer and L.M. Salamon (eds), *Government and the Third Sector*. San Francisco: Jossey-Bass.

Gronberg, K. (1987) 'Patterns of Institutional Relations in the Welfare State: Public Mandates and the Nonprofit Sector', *Journal of Voluntary Action Research* 16(1/2): 64–80.

Haque, M. Shamsul (2002) 'The Changing Balance of Power between the Government and NGOs in Bangladesh', *International Political Science Review* 23(4): 413–37.

Holloway, Richard (1997) 'NGOs: Losing the Moral High Ground – Corruption and Misrepresentation'.

Paper presented at Eighth International Anti-Corruption Conference, 7–11 September, Lima, Peru.

Hulme, David and Edwards, Michael (1997a) 'NGOs, States and Donors: An Overview', in David Hulme and Michael Edwards (eds), *NGOs, States and Donors: Too Close for Comfort*. New York: St. Martin's Press; pp. 3–22.

Hulme, David and Edwards, Michael (1997b) 'Conclusion: Too Close to Be Powerful, too Far from the Powerless?', in David Hulme and Michael Edwards (eds), *NGOs, States and Donors: Too Close for Comfort*. New York: St. Martin's Press; pp. 275–84.

Jorgensen, Mette (2006) 'Evaluating Cross-sector Partnerships'. Paper presented at the Conference on Public–Private Partnerships in the Post-WSSD Context, Copenhagen Business School, Copenhagen, Denmark, 14 August.

Kitsing, Meelis (2003) 'Behind Corruption: From NGOs to the Civil Society', *eumap.org* (Budapest), July. (http://www.eumap.org/journal/features/2003/july/behindcorruption)

Klees, Steven J. (1998) 'NGOs: Progressive Force or Neoliberal Tool?', *Current Issues in Comparative Education* 1(1).

Lewis, David (1998) *Bridging the Gap? The Parallel Universes of the Non-profit and Non-governmental Organisation Research Traditions and the Changing Context of Voluntary Action*. International Working Paper No. 1. London: Centre for Civil Society, London School of Economics.

Lewis, David (2004) 'On the Difficulty of Studying "Civil Society": NGOs, State and Democracy in Bangladesh', *Contributions to Indian Sociology* 38: 299–322.

Lyons, M. (2001) *Third Sector: The Contribution of Nonprofit and Cooperative Enterprises in Australia*. Sydney: Allen and Unwin.

Martens, Kerstin (2002) 'Mission Impossible? Defining Nongovernmental Organizations', *Voluntas: International Journal of Voluntary and Nonprofit Organizations* 13(3): 271–85.

Mercer, Claire (2002) 'NGOs, Civil Society and Democratization: A Critical Review of the Literature', *Progress in Development Studies* 2(1): 5–22.

Paoletto, Glen (2000) 'Public–Private Sector Partnerships: An Overview of Cause and Effect', in Yidan Wang (ed.), *Public–Private Partnership in the Social Sector: Issues and Country Experiences in Asia and the Pacific*. ADB Institute Policy Paper Series No. 1. Tokyo: ADBI Publishing.

Paul, James A. (2000) *NGOs and Global Policy-Making*. New York: Global Policy Forum, United Nations (http://www.globalpolicy.org/ngos/analysis/ anal00.htm).

Petras, James (1997) 'Imperialism and NGOs in Latin America', *Monthly Review* December.

Rady, Faiza (1999) 'Banking for the Poor', *Al-Ahram Weekly* (Cairo), August, No. 443: 19–25.

Roberts, Susan M., Jones, J. Paul and Hling, O. Fro (2005) 'NGOs and the Globalization of Managerialism: A Research Framework', *World Development* 33(11): 1845–64.

Robinson, M. (1997) 'Privatising the Voluntary Sector: NGOs as Public Service Contractors?', in David. Hulme and Michael. Edwards (eds), *NGOs, States and Donors: Too Close for Comfort*. New York: St. Martin's Press.

Rong, Tian (2008) 'New Public Management and Its Impact on NGOs in Hong Kong'. 8th International Conference of the International Society for Third Sector Research, Barcelona, Spain, 9–12 July.

Sanyal, Bishwapriya (1994) *Cooperative Autonomy: The Dialectic of State–NGOs Relationship in Developing Countries*. Geneva: International Institute for Labour Studies.

Sarker, Abu Elias (2005) 'New Public Management, Service Provision and Non-governmental Organizations in Bangladesh', *Public Organization Review* 5(3): 249–71.

Temple, Frederick T. (2000) 'Strategies to Alleviate the Woes of Pervasive Poverty', *The Independent* 10 May.

Tobin, Sarah A. (2005) *Microfinance in Neoliberal Times: The Experience of an Egyptian NGO*. MA Thesis, College of Arts and Sciences, University of South Florida.

Tvedt, Terje (1998) *Angels of Mercy or Development Diplomats?: NGOs & Foreign Aid*. Oxford: James Currey Publishers.

Wagle, Udaya (1999) 'The Civil Society Sector in the Developing World', *Public Administration and Management: An Interactive Journal* 4(4).

Young, D.R. (2000) 'Alternative Models of Government–Nonprofit Relations', *Nonprofit and Voluntary Sector Quarterly*, 29(1): 149–72.

22

Transgovernmental Networks

Anne-Marie Slaughter
and Thomas N. Hale

INTRODUCTION

Transgovernmental networks are informal institutions linking regulators, legislators, judges, and other actors across national boundaries to carry out various aspects of global governance. They exhibit 'pattern[s] of regular and purposive relations among like government units working across the borders that divide countries from one another and that demarcate the "domestic" from the "international" sphere' (Slaughter, 2004a). They allow domestic officials to interact with their foreign counterparts directly, without much supervision by foreign offices or senior executive branch officials, and feature 'loosely structured, peer-to-peer ties developed through frequent interaction rather than formal negotiation' (Raustiala, 2002, see also Risse-Kappen, 1995).

Transgovernmental networks occupy a middle place between traditional international organizations and ad hoc communication. They have emerged organically in response to the increasing complexity and transnational nature of contemporary problems, to which they are uniquely suited, challenging the distinction between domestic and foreign policy. They appear most commonly in the realm of regulatory policy – e.g. commercial and financial regulation, environmental protection – but also extend to judicial and even legislative areas of government.

This chapter discusses the form and function of transgovernmental networks and their growing role in international governance. The first section provides an overview of the evolution of networks. The second presents a typology and describes some prominent examples. The mechanisms through which transgovernmental networks operate are described in the third section, and issues pertaining to their legitimacy are treated in the fourth. The fifth section considers the skills bureaucrats operating in networks require, and the last section concludes by identifying questions for future research.

OVERVIEW OF TRANSGOVERNMENTAL NETWORKS[1]

Transgovernmental networks are everywhere, having proliferated into almost every area of government regulation. They have been used to address the leading problems of the day, ranging from high politics questions of national security and official corruption to more mundane issues such as common policies on airplane regulation. Legal scholars have identified and considered the implications of regulatory cooperation in tax, antitrust, food and drug, and telecommunications regulation.[2] Indeed, in the European Union (EU) alone, Sabel and Zeitlin have documented disaggregated forms of coordinative governance (which to them are network-like, but branded as examples of 'directly-deliberative polyarchy') in privatized network infrastructure, public health and safety, employment and social protection, other forms of regulation, and even rights-sensitive areas like the protection of race, gender, and disabled (Sabel and Zeitlin, 2006).

Transgovernmental networks have arisen in response to the complex governance challenges posed by increasing transnational interdependence. The phenomenon dates back at least to the 1970s, when Keohane and Nye noted the growing importance of 'transgovernmental' activities (Keohane and Nye, 1974). In 1972 Francis Bator testified before the US Congress, 'It is a central fact of foreign relations that business is carried on by the separate departments with their counterpart bureaucracies abroad, through a variety of informal as well as formal connections' (Keohane and Nye, 1974).

By the late 1990s, however, transgovernmental networks had increased so dramatically in degree as to amount to a difference in kind. As the latest intense wave of globalization has made international cooperation increasingly necessary on a range of issues – from the economy to the environment to policing – 'traditional' forms of diplomacy have sometimes proven cumbersome. By strictly bifurcating the international and domestic spheres, traditional diplomacy – conducted through foreign ministries, ambassadors, and international organizations – has been outstripped by the transnationality of many contemporary policy issues, which operate simultaneously the domestic and international realms.

By associating 'domestic' officials in networks that stretch between nations, transgovernmental networks perform three important functions.

First, they expand the state's capacity to confront transnational issues. So many areas of policymaking now require international coordination that foreign ministries alone are simply unable to handle the full portfolio of extra-national assignments. Similarly, domestic officials find they are unable to adequately fulfill their responsibilities without consulting and coordinating with foreign counterparts.

Second, and related to the first point, international cooperation now extends to many highly technical issues – e.g. financial regulation or environmental monitoring – in which foreign ministries simply lack expertise. The expanded scope and depth of contemporary interdependence sometimes necessitates technocratic responses that only specialized 'domestic' officials can provide.

Third, networks allow for flexibility and responsiveness in a way that traditional diplomatic channels and international institutions often do not, increasing efficiency. Because networks are not formal institutions, they can often reach outcomes with lower transaction costs than international institutions. Networks focus attention on information exchange, discussion, and coordination, avoiding many of the obstacles that inevitably draw out efforts to negotiate formal treaties or pass resolutions. Moreover, by bringing together the actual officials responsible for a certain policy area – as opposed to diplomats responsible for liaising with other countries – networks can also increase the efficiency of international coordination.

A TYPOLOGY OF TRANSGOVERNMENTAL NETWORKS

Transgovernmental networks can be categorized both by the relationships they establish and the functions they perform.

Transgovernmental relationships can be either horizontal or vertical. Networks between actors at the same level (e.g. judge-to-judge or regulator-to-regulator) are horizontal, and form the majority of trans-governmental networks. However, some vertical networks between supranational officials and national-level officials also exist. For example, in the European Union, supranational officials work closely with their domestic counterparts to ensure that EU policy is implemented in the national context. In this article we focus on the more common horizontal networks.

Beyond the horizontal–vertical distinction, networks can be grouped in three basic types: information networks, enforcement networks, and harmonization networks.

Horizontal information networks, as the name suggests, bring together regulators, judges, or legislators to exchange information and to collect and distill best practices. This information exchange can also take place through technical assistance and training pro-grams provided by one country's officials to another. The direction of such training is not always developed country to developing country, either; it can also be from developed country to developed country, as when US antitrust officials spent six months training their New Zealand counterparts.

Enforcement networks typically spring up due to the inability of government officials in one country to enforce that country's laws, either by means of a regulatory agency or through a court. But enforcement coopera-tion must also inevitably involve a great deal of information exchange and can also involve assistance programs of various types. Legislators can also collaborate on how to draft complementary legislation so as to avoid enforcement loopholes.

Finally, harmonization networks, which are typically authorized by treaty or execu-tive agreement, bring regulators together to ensure that their rules in a particular substan-tive area conform to a common regulatory standard. Judges can also engage in the equivalent activity, but in a much more ad hoc manner. Harmonization is often politi-cally controversial, with critics charging that the 'technical' process of achieving conver-gence ignores the many winners and losers in domestic publics, most of whom do not have any input into the process.

A few examples may prove instructive. Consider first an information network, the International Network for Environmental Compliance and Enforcement (INECE), which describes itself as a 'partnership among government and non-government compliance and enforcement practitioners from over 150 countries' (INECE, 2008). Founded in 1989, this network of some 4000 domestic environmental regulators allows participants to share experiences and best practices, to develop common standards, and to coordinate around transboundary issues. Originally a joint project of the US and Dutch environmental agencies, INECE has evolved into a global and increasingly insti-tutionalized organization. As it has grown, INECE has created a number of regional subnetworks which specialize in environ-mental enforcement problems particular to certain areas of the world. By creating a 'net-work of networks,' the organization has been able to grow rapidly while still providing tailored information to individual partners.

The International Competition Network (ICN) has followed a similar trajectory to INECE in the antitrust sphere. In the mid-1990s antitrust regulators felt that the grow-ing size and number of transnational corporations required coordinated responses from regulators across jurisdictions. After much consultation, in 2001 14 countries launched the ICN to provide 'competition authorities with a specialized yet informal venue for maintaining regular contacts and addressing practical competition concerns' with the hope of allowing 'a dynamic dia-logue that serves to build consensus and convergence towards sound competition policy principles across the global antitrust community' (ICN, 2008). The ICN does not make antitrust laws, but rather relies on working groups to develop recommendations and guidelines to specific problems that are then implemented by national regulators.

Enforcement networks are among the most important transgovernmental networks. Consider the realm of transnational policing. As countries have grown more interdependent, so have the darker sides of globalization, such as the drug trade, human trafficking, and transnational terrorism. Police and security agencies have had to adopt similarly transnational working procedures in order to confront these problems. The secondment of law enforcement officers to crime centers has become routine for many police agencies (Den Boer, 2005). Such officers are typically tasked with marinating contact between two jurisdictions, sharing information, and perhaps helping with extradition requests. When many jurisdictions are involved, these seconded officers can be thought of as ad hoc mini networks of police enforcers.

There are also more institutionalized policing networks. The Financial Action Task Force (FATF) is a 34-member network dedicated to fighting money laundering and to eliminating financial support for transnational terrorism. FATF was founded in 1989 through the G7, and is based at OECD (Organization for Economic Co-operation and Development) headquarters in Paris. FATF performs a number of functions, including developing standards countries should follow to limit money laundering, as well as regularly evaluating and critiquing countries' money laundering policies. Unlike many networks, FATF limits its membership to only those countries deemed sufficiently committed to the network's goals. This allowed the organization to adopt, for example, in the wake of the September 11 attacks, a more explicit focus on anti-terrorist financing. At the same time, the organization has also been criticized from some quarters as a tool of the G7 (Roberge, 2008).

Like enforcement networks, harmonization networks serve a regulatory role, but focus more on finding common standards than on facilitating cross-jurisdiction enforcement. The Basel Committee on Banking Supervision, one of the most prominent transgovernmental networks, was founded in 1974 by the central bank governors of the Group of Ten industrialized economies 'to enhance understanding of key supervisory issues and improve the quality of banking supervision worldwide … by exchanging information on national supervisory issues, approaches and techniques, with a view to promoting common understanding'. By the 1970s the need for greater coordination and centralized information exchange among central bankers had become apparent. Once created, the Basel Committee also took on a policymaking function by promulgating a global accord on capital adequacy standards (Basel I). In 1997 the Committee issued a 'Set of Core Principles for Effective Banking Supervision,' which its members have worked actively to promote in many other countries around the world.

By the 2000s, the Basel Committee had developed four subcommittees, one of which is a regular liaison to 16 supervisory authorities around the world as well as regional and international financial institutions. It also undertook an elaborate process of consultation to revise Basel I and issue new 'Basel II' standards for capital adequacy and other banking issues. The committee meets regularly with central bankers from important emerging markets, holds biannual international conferences of banking supervisors, circulates published and unpublished papers to banking supervisors around the world, and offers technical assistance on banking supervision in many countries.

Expanding even more, the Basel Committee Secretariat now acts as Secretariat to the 'Joint Forum' and the 'Coordination Group,' both entities created to foster cooperation among central bankers, insurance supervisors, and securities commissioners. The Bank for International Settlements, the 'traditional' international institution that hosts the Basel Committee and other regulatory networks, now describes itself in part as a 'hub for central bankers,' linking to central bank web-sites and related sources of information and expertise all over the world. It also provides secretariat functions for related organizations of financial regulators, such as the Financial Stability Forum and the International Organization of Insurance Supervisors. The result is nothing less than a new global financial architecture, but one created by informal networks rather than formal institutions.

Another important harmonization network is the International Conference on Harmonization of Technical Requirements for the Registration of Pharmaceutical Products (ICH). This network brings together both regulators and industry groups from the USA, Europe, and Japan in order to find common standards through which to approve new pharamaceutical products. The process is 'aimed at eliminating duplication in the development and registration process so that a single set of studies can be generated to demonstrate the quality, safety and efficacy of a new medicinal product' (Katsikas, 2007). In other words, the more these three jurisdictions can cooperate on the approval process, the less time and money each will have to spend approving new drugs. In some jurisdictions in Europe and in Japan the ICH guidelines have become legally binding. In other jurisdictions they guide policy, but must be implemented through national rule-making.

The proliferation of transgovernmental networks will continue and likely increase. Their informal nature has thus far foiled efforts to generate a comprehensive list of these organizations, and so scholars cannot say precisely how broad their impact is. However, calls for the expansion of these networks at the highest levels indicate they will grow even more important to multilateral cooperation in the future. To take just one example, the US Centers for Disease Control and Prevention (CDC) Director Julie Gerberding's experience with managing the SARS (severe acute respiratory syndrome) crisis affirmed the extreme difficulty of trying to manage a global crisis affecting hundreds

of agencies and authorities at different levels of national and international governance through a national hierarchy – the CDC itself (Gerberding, 2005). Faced with responsibility for a problem but lacking the authority to command all the necessary actors, Gerberding discovered that a networked approach was the only way to confront the global pandemic.

Beyond specific issues, a major study by the Brookings Institution on 'Managing Global Insecurity' recommends the expansion of the G8 to a G16, creating a leaders' network that would include developed and developing country leaders (Jones, 2008). The 2004 UN High Level Panel on Threats, Challenge and Change endorsed a similar proposal for a leaders' network of some 20 countries. The 'E-8' – a group of the largest polluters aimed at addressing climate change – is another proposal. From high politics to the more mundane realms of everyday technical cooperation, networks are necessary.

HOW TRANSGOVERNMENTAL NETWORKS WORK

The Basel Committee describes its own authority and role as follows:

> The Committee does not possess any formal supranational supervisory authority, and its conclusions do not, and were never intended to, have legal force. Rather, it formulates broad supervisory standards and guidelines and recommends statements of best practice in the expectation that individual authorities will take steps to implement them through detailed arrangements – statutory or otherwise – which are best suited to their own national systems. In this way, the Committee encourages convergence towards common approaches and common standards without attempting detailed harmonisation of member countries' supervisory techniques. (BIS, 2008)

That, in a nutshell, is how most transgovernmental networks, at least information networks, work. They have no formal legal authority, and instead operate through exchanging and distilling information and expertise. They are able to exploit the institutional benefits unique to the network form, which are produced in a variety of different ways.

First, on the informational level, networks serve as fora for experimentation and sharing, which leads to learning. As Powell puts it, networks are 'based on complex communication channels,' and so are able not only to communicate information but also to generate new meanings and interpretations of the information transmitted, thereby providing 'a context for learning by doing' (Powell, 1990). The mechanics of this kind of learning- and experiment-based governance have been explored in depth by Sabel and co-authors, principally in the domestic context (Sabel and Zeitlin, 2006). Indeed, these types of learning networks are an increasingly common feature of domestic governance in many countries (see, for example, Sørensen and Torfing, 2008). They are also important in many *private* transnational networks, like the United Nations Global Compact, which serves, in part, as a platform for multinational corporations to share methods for making their business practices more environmentally and socially sustainable (Ruggie, 2002). However, this 'wiki-government' remains underutilized in the realm of state-to-state relations (Noveck, 2008).

Secondly, regarding coordination, networks may provide a platform for mutual influence. In very few networks do participants have direct influence over one another. Instead, they must try to convince their counterparts to follow a certain course of action through argumentation and persuasion. Influence thus comes not solely from a nation's power or wealth, but rather from an actor's ability to earn the trust of his peers. Kal Raustiala finds that this process can lead to significant policy coordination (Raustiala, 2002). Looking at regulatory networks in the securities, competition, and environmental fields, Raustiala shows that transgovernmental networks serve as channels for 'regulatory export' from advanced nations to developing countries. Through technical advice and

example-setting, networks in each of these areas have served to strengthen regulatory capacity within and across states.

Thirdly, networks provide a way to coordinate actions across states without many of the transaction costs associated with international institutions or traditional diplomacy. Simply by providing a regularized environment in which relevant actors can interact with one another, networks lower the transaction costs of coordinating actions like enforcement or rule-making. The role of traditional international institutions in providing information and lowering the transaction costs of coordination is well established in international relations theory (Keohane, 1984). Networks bring many of the benefits of traditional organizations – e.g. information sharing, monitoring, the creation of focal points – without many of the costs, such as decreased autonomy, principal–agent dilemmas, or administrative burdens. Consequently, this lighter, more flexible form of institutionalism cannot achieve some of the deeper benefits of traditional institutions, such as allowing states to make credible, enforceable commitments to one another. Nor do they allow the state to delegate tasks to an international organization, because it is state officials themselves who comprise the network. Networks thus represent a distinct form of international cooperation from 'traditional' institutions.

Transgovernmental networks also suffer some deficiencies, of course, and are by no means the ideal institutional arrangement for every setting. The very flexibility that makes networks useful may also render them toothless when strong enforcement powers are necessary to sustain international cooperation. For example, it is difficult to imagine the World Trade Organization (WTO) functioning as a network. Formal rules and the possibility of enforcing those rules through the regulated withdrawal of trade concessions are necessary to make the parties agree to liberalization.

In general, we can identify several conditions under which transgovernmental networks are likely to be most or less useful. First, when interdependence is high, states will find networks useful means to coordinate around common policy. Conversely, in policy areas where states do not confront transnational problems, networks will offer little benefit. Secondly, networks forms of governance will be appropriate when the chief barriers to cooperation result from a lack of information about other states' policies or goals. For example, in anti-terror cooperation, information sharing is vital to enhance the effectiveness of law-enforcement officials in various countries. Thirdly, networks work best when states' interests align. Because networks are typically informal and voluntary, states have to want to exchange information; in other words, they must be able to gain some benefit from it. For many issues – like counter-terrorism – these benefits are clear. But when states want to keep information private – e.g. in an enforcement scenario, in which states may wish to be less than transparent about their compliance records – meaningful networks are unlikely to form.

DEMOCRATIC LEGITIMACY AND TRANSGOVERNMENTAL NETWORKS

Transgovernmental networks can be a normatively attractive form of global governance. Traditional international institutions and other forms of global governance are sometimes said to suffer from a 'democratic deficit.' Far removed from public pressure and electoral politics, international institutions like the World Bank or International Monetary Fund (IMF) – to cite two of the most prominent examples – have been accused of trampling the interests of marginalized peoples or poor countries to promote their preferred policies. Because transgovernmental networks are made from *national* officials, they are more closely linked to states and thus, in theory, bound by the same accountability mechanisms that control national governments.

By giving states a way to solve transnational problems directly, governmental networks elide a potential legitimacy problem that bedevils many other areas of global governance.

But while transgovernmental networks avoid the accountability concerns of delegating to international institutions, they can face legitimacy problems of their own (Slaughter, 2004b). To the extent they empower domestic officials to act without approval from their domestic superiors, networks may take power out of the hands of elected officials and put it into the hands of enterprising bureaucrats. This problem is reinforced by the technical nature of many transgovernmental networks. By bringing together experts and specialists from different countries, transgovernmental networks gain efficiency and capacity but may lose sight of potential trade-offs with other policy areas. For example, the US public interest organization Public Citizen has criticized harmonization networks – which seek to facilitate economic coordination – for being secretive and biased toward industry. Moreover, because they are not official government agencies but simply ad hoc transnational committees, they are shielded from the accountability guarantees enshrined in domestic administrative law (Slaughter, 2004a). Projects aimed at developing global administrative law could address some of these defects (Kingsbury et al., 2005). In other cases the participants in government networks have themselves realized the need for much greater transparency and participation (Barr and Miller, 2006). One of us has also called repeatedly for the creation of legislative networks to correspond to regulatory networks, to enhance national legislative oversight (Slaughter, 2004a). In EU member states, national parliamentarians serving on committees focused on EU affairs realized that they needed to network with one another quite independently of the EU Parliament. Legislators themselves often realize that they are being left out of the action. As transgovernmental networks grow, not only in their number but also in the number and types of tasks they are asked to undertake, mechanisms for increased accountability will grow with them.

MANAGING IN HORIZONTAL INSTITUTIONS

Transgovernmental networks require different approaches and skills from government officials than 'traditional' forms of international cooperation. Going forward, government leaders will have to think more about how to manage networks for maximum efficiency and impact. In the business literature much is made of 'orchestrating networks.' The Hong Kong-based Li and Fung Ltd., the largest sourcing company in the world, essentially links different partners at different times to produce different products around the world. Orchestration differs from management in a vertical organization. It purportedly 'requires a more fluid approach that empowers partners and employees, yet demands that control be maintained at the same time' (Fung, Fung and Wind, 2007). The aim is to unleash the kind of creativity and collaboration that produces Wikipedia while still maintaining quality control and enough discipline to ensure that holes get filled and new projects undertaken. Fung, et al. write about moving from a firm to a network, from control to empowerment, and from specialization to integration. Other business authors write about 'team leadership' and working within decentralized organizations where no one individual is really in charge (Barna, 2001). Indeed, the mantra of team leadership is 'strength through shared responsibility,' which is a way of describing collective responsibility for a common problem, a requirement for solving global problems like terrorism and climate change that cannot be contained within national borders.

It is of course not clear to what extent management practices in the business community will translate into the government arena. But as both national governments and international organizations adapt to operating in a networked world, it will be very important to understand the optimal functions for a small secretariat or 'central node' of a horizontal network and to know which functions are best allocated to traditional organizations and which are better handled by networks. Government officials can also learn from some of the large non-governmental organizations (NGOs); CARE, for instance, operates supply networks that in some ways resemble Li and Fung. They use information technology to identify individuals all over the world who can take part in disaster relief teams ready to be deployed at once.

Similarly, transgovernmental networks may force scholars to reconsider the way they believe influence operates between countries. In formal international institutions, a state's influence is often a function of its power vis-à-vis other states. Power relations are often even institutionalized in the laws governing an institution – consider the proportional voting system in the WTO or IMF or the permanent members of the UN Security Council, for example. Influence within a transgovernmental network is certainly also a function of state power, but may also include other factors. The goal of many networks is to share experience, deliberate over experiences, learn from colleagues, and coordinate action around 'best practices.' To become influential, an actor must win colleagues over to her point of view by means of her technical expertise, practical experience, or reasoned argument.

Conventional economic or diplomatic levers may play a role where national interests are directly at stake, but much of the work of transgovernmental networks falls outside the realm of competitive diplomatic wrangling. In this way networks favor a different set of skills and competencies than traditional institutions. Convincing one's peers of the rightness of a common course of action is qualitatively different from lobbying an interlocutor to do what you want him to do. While networks certainly include both kinds of interactions, their ability to highlight the former may broaden the range of successful cooperation beyond that available in traditional institutions.

CONCLUSION: QUESTIONS FOR FUTURE RESEARCH

There is no reason to believe that, given the continued and growing importance of transnational problems, government officials will not increasingly network with their counterparts abroad. Indeed, we imagine this form of governance will only grow in importance. We thus conclude by highlighting two questions for future research.

First is the question of how the *social* nature of networks affects their political functions. We have argued that networking is a form of creating and storing relational capital. But do the government officials who participate in networks also develop a common sense of values and norms? Most observers of transgovernmental networks – and most scholars of networks of all kinds – believe this kind of socialization is at least possible. In the transgovernmental context, such socialization can enhance trust and coordination between countries, thus making networks more effective. However, some observers have worried that socialization may also lead bureaucrats to place the values of the network over national interests, though no specific instances are cited in the literature. In general, socialization – the transfusion of norms, values, and identities amongst actors – is not well understood in the political literature. More research is needed to understand the mechanisms through which socialization might occur within transgovernmental networks, the relation between socialization and the operation of networks, and the conditions under which socialization does and does not occur.[3]

Secondly, what role will private organizations such as non-profit groups and corporations play in a world of networked governance? Local and domestic officials are increasingly working with private actors on subnational policy problems ranging from environmental protection to the provision of welfare benefits.[4] Indeed, some government officials see themselves not so much as regulators or service providers but rather as conveners and coordinators of a range of interests. Will these patterns also extend to the international realm? Public–private partnerships are now common place in global governance, and some take an explicitly network form.[5] The UN Global Compact, for example, brings UN agencies, environmental, labor, and human rights groups, as well as for-profit corporations, together to share ideas and create projects aimed at enhancing corporate social responsibility. While we have argued in this chapter that there is something unique about *government* networks, it is not implausible that the fluid and problem-solving approach such networks embody will lead them to interact with private actors more in the future.

NOTES

1 Parts of this section are drawn from Slaughter (2004a) and Slaughter and Zaring (2006).

2 A full list of references is given in Slaughter and Zaring (2006).

3 Wang, for example, finds little evidence that multilateral institutions have socialized Chinese foreign policy. Hongying Wang, 'Multilateralism in Chinese Foreign Policy: The Limits of Socialization', *Asian Survey* 40, No. 3 (2000). See, generally, Jeffery Checkels 'International Institutions and Socialization in Europe,' special issue of *International Organization* 59, 4 (Fall 2005).

4 Eva Sørensen and Jacob Torfing 2007.

5 See, for example, Jan Martin Witte and Wolfgang Reinicke, 'Business UNusual: Facilitating UN Reform through Partnerships,' Global Public Policy Institute, Berlin, 2005.

REFERENCES

Barna, George (2001) *The Power of Team Leadership: Finding Strength in Shared Responsibility.* Colorado Springs, CO: Waterbrook Press.

Barr, Michael and Miller, Geoffrey (2006) 'Global Administrative Law: The View from Basel', *European Journal of International Law* 17(1): 15–46.

Den Boer, Monica (2005) 'Cobweb Europe. Venues, Virtues and Vexations of Transnational Policing', in Wolfram Kaiser and Peter Starie (eds), *Transnational European Union. Towards a Common Political Space.* Abingdon: Routledge, pp. 191–209.

Fung, Victor K., Fung, William K. and Wing, Yoram (2007) *Competing in a Flat World: Building Enterprises for a Borderless World.* Upper Saddle River, NJ: Wharton Publishing.

Gerberding, Julie (2003) 'Faster … but Fast Enough? Responding to the Epidemic of Severe Acute Respiratory Syndrome', *New England Journal of Medicine* 348(20): 2030–1.

International Competition Network (ICN) (2008) *About the ICN.* Available from http://www.internationalcompetitionnetwork.org/index.php/en/about-icn.

International Network for Environmental Compliance and Enforcement (INECE) (2008) *About the International Network for Environmental Compliance and Enforcement.* Available from http://www.inece.org/.

Katsikas, Dimitrios (2007) 'The Politics of Hybrid Regulatory Governance: Interests, Power and Pharmaceutical Harmonization' Paper presented at the annual meeting of the International Studies Association 48th Annual Convention, Chicago.

Keohane, Robert O. (1984) *After Hegemony.* Princeton, NJ: Princeton University Press.

Keohane, Robert O. and Nye, Joseph S. (1974) 'Transgovernmental Relations and International Organizations', *World Politics* 27: 39, 43.

Kingsbury, Benedict, Krisch, Nico and Stewart, Richard (2005) 'The Emergence of Global Administrative Law', *Law and Contemporary Problems* 38: 3–4.

Noveck, Beth Simone. (2008). 'Wiki-Government', *Democracy* 7.

Powell, W. (1990) 'Neither Market nor Hierarchy: Network Forms of Organization', *Research in Organizational Behavior* 12: 325.

Raustiala, Kal (2002) 'The Architecture of International Cooperation: Transgovernmental Networks and the Future of International Law', *Virginia Journal of International Law* 43.

Risse-Kappen, Thomas (1995) *Bringing Transnational Relations Back In: Non-State Actors, Domestic Structures and International Institutions.* Cambridge: Cambridge University Press.

Roberge, Ian (2008) 'Financial Action Task Force', *Encyclopedia of Transnational Governance Innovation.* Available at www.etgi.co.uk.

Ruggie, John Gerard (2002) 'The Theory and Practice of Learning Networks: Corporate Social Responsibility and the Global Compact', *Journal of Corporate Citizenship* 5.

Sabel, C.F. and Zeitlin, H. (2006) 'Learning from Difference: The New Architecture of Experimentalist Governance in the European Union', in *ARENA Seminar,* University of Oslo.

Slaughter, Anne-Marie (2004a) *A New World Order.* Princeton, NJ: Princeton University Press.

Slaughter, Anne-Marie (2004b) 'Disaggregated Sovereignty: Toward the Public Accountability of Global Government Networks', *Government and Opposition* 39(2):159–90.

Slaughter, Anne-Marie and Zaring, David. (2006) 'Networking Goes International: An Update', *Annual Review of Law and Social Science* 2.

Sørensen, Eva and Torfing, Jacob (2008) *Theories of Democratic Network Governance.* New York: Palgrave Macmillan.

23

Global Governance

Mark Bevir and Ian Hall

The term 'global governance' is a product of the post-cold war era (Hewson and Sinclair, 1999: 3). It emerged in the late 1980s, notably in the pioneering work of James Rosenau (1987). But it did not enter common usage until the late 1990s. Its acceptance became clear in 1995 when the United Nations Commission on Global Governance published *Our Global Neighbourhood*, and when scholars created a journal titled *Global Governance*.

Global governance signals a particular interest in the management of transnational issues by international organizations and other non-state actors as well as by sovereign states (Cutler, 2003). It also can signal a particular focus on problems of efficacy, authority and accountability (Kahler and Lake, 2003). The term 'global governance' serves three main purposes:

- It recasts theoretical perspectives that dominate the study of international relations.
- It makes sense of seemingly new practices and the political responses they produced.
- It sets agendas for change in international institutions, states, and non-state actors in the practices of international relations.

Today, global governance refers to a diverse research programme and policy agenda. By 2005 scholars could reasonably argue that 'global governance' was a 'central orienting theme' in the theory and practice of international relations (Barnett and Duvall, 2005: 1). Global governance now challenges 'international relations' as the preferred moniker for understanding politics beyond the domestic. Discussions of global governance extend to all the main subfields, including international organization, international political economy, international regimes, international law, and international security studies. Proponents of global governance try to subsume the insights of these subfields into their own analyses and argue their approach improves our understanding of organizations, economics, regimes, law, and security. Discussions of global governance also extend to diverse policy actors. Global governance – and related ideas like 'good governance' – especially concern policymakers addressing development issues and global financial institutions like the International Monetary Fund (IMF) and the World Bank (Thomas, 2007).

So, global governance has a confusing variety of meanings. This chapter tries to bring order to the confusion. The first section examines the uses and controversies of global governance as a new theoretical lens, a new practice of international relations, and a new policy agenda. After that we offer a historical analysis of the rise of these uses of global governance in the late twentieth century.

THE MEANINGS OF GLOBAL GOVERNANCE

Global governance can refer to a new theoretical lens, a changed world, or a policy agenda. In this section, we consider each aspect of global governance.

New theories

At a general level, global governance offers a new theoretical lens through which to view international relations. This lens highlights the role of diverse social actors as well as states in securing patterns of rule at the transnational and global levels. It allows that patterns of rule can arise without hierarchic institutions, let alone an international sovereign power. The lens of global governance thus stands in contrast to older theories of international relations that privileged states and formal institutions such as the United Nations (UN). The older theories commonly presented international relations as an anarchical system or a society of states interacting by trade, war, and diplomacy. The defining feature of international relations was the absence of any effective world government controlling, regulating, and coordinating the actions of different states (Bull, 1977).

The term 'governance' alerts us to the possibility that governing can occur without an effective sovereign power (Stoker, 1998). Control can arise when actors internalize informal norms as well as when an external power imposes rules. Regulation can occur when actors monitor themselves as well as when an external power supervises them. Coordination can be the result of mutual adjustments among actors as well as hierarchic organization.

The term 'global governance' draws attention, therefore, to the diverse activities and processes that organize international relations. James Rosenau defines global governance as the 'systems of rule' that exist 'at all levels of human activity – from the family to the international organization – in which the pursuit of goals through the exercise of control has transnational repercussions' (Rosenau, 1995: 13). Global governance encompasses not only actions of states and international institutions but also the actions of non-governmental organizations (NGOs) and the processes associated with markets and networks that impact on transnational issues. Global governance shifts our focus from sovereign states in an anarchic international society to the creation, enforcement, and change of global 'systems of rule'.

Global governance also draws attention to the diverse objects that may be subject to rule in world politics. When older approaches concentrated on the anarchic nature of the international system, they implied the more or less sole aim of international relations was to prevent war. The point of international institutions was to secure peace (Keohane, 1988). In contrast, scholars now suggest that global governance can address all kinds of transnational problems in addition to the prevention and limitation of war. Others include managing the global commons, promoting development, and regulating global financial markets (Keohane, 2001: 2–3).

Global governance as theory is about shifting our focus from government as formal institutions to governing as a complex set of processes and activities. This theoretical lens is widespread; even some realists use the broad idea of global governance as anything that creates and enforces rules (Drezner, 2004; Sterling-Folker, 2005). Nonetheless, this broad idea of global governance is controversial. Many realists continue to believe the international system is just anarchic, so there can be no global governance (Waltz, 1999). Proponents of global governance respond by arguing traditional accounts of international relations are outdated. We have to turn to global governance if we are to respond adequately to changes in the world and to transform the practices of global politics (Rosenau and Czempiel, 1992; Held and McGrew, 2002).

New worlds

Much of the literature on global governance suggests the role of social actors, markets, and networks is a novel feature of international relations. Global governance can refer to new worlds of international relations. The theory of global governance is a general claim that possibly applies to international relations across the ages. Yet it gets confused with a more specific, empirical claim about the changing nature of international relations since the late twentieth century. The latter claim suggests that while earlier ages had weak international institutions and strong sovereign states, the late twentieth century saw the rise of new times in which new actors and mechanisms became increasingly prominent.

New actors and mechanisms of international relations allegedly emerged because of globalization. Globalization undermined the capacity and authority of states to exercise an exclusive and unchallenged power over their own territorial jurisdictions. Global governance is a response to this erosion of statism and territorialism. Scholars such as Jan Aart Scholte argue that, while the state may remain powerful, globalization nonetheless changed the state in five principal ways:

1 Empirical sovereignty – as opposed to the juridical form – effectively disappeared; the state is no longer the sole arbiter of what occurs in its borders.
2 The state was 'reoriented' to 'serve supraterritorial as well as territorial interests'.
3 'Public sector welfare guarantees' were degraded.
4 Globalization shifted the circumstances and uses of war from interstate to intrastate conflict.
5 'Multilateral regulatory arrangements' proliferated.

These five changes in the state led to 'multilayered' and 'privatised' governance.

Multilayered governance involves regulation by substate, state, and suprastate bodies with 'transborder' connections at each layer. Privatized governance includes 'business associations, NGOs, foundations, think-tanks and even criminal syndicates' (Scholte, 2000: 135, 143, 151).

Much of the literature on global governance develops or reacts against these arguments about how globalization changes states and international relations. Some scholars have drawn on the idea that globalization has weakened the state to expand the topics they study far beyond the analysis of the institutions that once were the main preoccupation of non-realist work in international relations. These scholars – especially in the United States – concentrate on the rules of global governance and the authority of those that make and enforce them (Kahler and Lake, 2003). They draw variously on mainstream theories of international institutions and regimes (Haggard and Simmons, 1987; Martin and Simmons, 1998), various branches of social constructivist theory (Hall 2008; and for discussion Adcock, Bevir and Stimson, 2007), and newer and less traditional approaches, such as those that explore the role of 'epistemic communities' or 'global civil society' (Adler and Haas, 1992; Lipshutz, 1992). These various influences facilitated a huge outpouring of work that examined actors other than states or international organizations. Much of this work looked at the changing perceptions of actors and the norms that shape their behaviour.

Other scholars of international relations react against accounts of global governance that suggest globalization weakened the state. They argue that state keeps its empirical sovereignty and the rise of multilayered and private governance does not signal a significant transformation in international relations. They think of the new global governance as a product of states adopting new means to secure the same old ends. The new networks have not displaced states; they are the tools of states (Krasner, 1991). For example, Daniel Drezner argues that when different states want different forms of regulation, the strong cajole the weak into complying with their preference. States only delegate regulatory authority to non-state actors when their interests converge. Then, Drezner argues, strong states prefer regulation by NGOs rather than international organizations, since 'NGOs plugged into public policy networks can have a comparative advantage in gathering information and harnessing the requisite technical expertise' (Drezner, 2004: 483). The states themselves keep final control: 'Governments can act like a board of directors: states devolve regime management to nonstate actors, while still ensuring that they can influence any renegotiation of the rules of the game' (Drezner, 2004: 483; Drezner, 2007).

Yet other scholars of international relations – especially in Europe – offer critical versions of the idea that states are the motive force behind the new global governance. This critical literature does not deny international relations have changed – as do the realists who argue the international system is just anarchic. Rather, the critics argue the changes are products of, for example, global capitalism, Western self-interest, or neoliberalism. They stress the interdependence, as they see it, of global governance, the good governance agendas advanced by global financial institutions and development agencies, and the democratization agenda favoured by liberals and neoconservatives (Thomas, 2000; Abrahamsen, 2004). Many of the critics also discuss sources of resistance to Western and neoliberal practices of global (and good) governance. They look especially to social movements in a nascent global civil society and sites of private authority in global governance (O'Brien et al., 2000; Cutler, 2003).

So, scholars paint three rather different portraits of the new world of global governance:

- some argue that globalization has radically reshaped states and institutions and introduced new actors
- others argue that traditional actors have simply begun to use new modes of governance

- yet others argue that any such changes have given control of global governance to actors with agendas detrimental to global welfare.

All three are open to dispute. Sceptics argue that even if international relations have been transformed, the results of global governance research have been 'extremely meagre' (Strange, 1996: 183, 199).

New agendas

A final aspect of the literature on global governance focuses on 'good governance' and other policy agendas. Some scholars welcome global governance as a necessary and desirable response to challenges that states, international institutions, and international agreements could not tackle properly (Keohane, 2001). Others oppose global governance as a malign project aimed at preserving and extending a Western neoliberal hegemony (Thomas, 2000).

The early policy discussions of global governance reflected the optimism of the immediate post-cold war period. Global governance seemed to represent an opportunity to set an agenda to address problems sidelined during the cold war, correct flaws in the architecture of international institutions, and meet emergent challenges. Global governance also embodied hopes for greater accountability and democracy in international relations. The authors of *Our Global Neighbourhood*, for example, contrasted the democratic potential of global governance with the possible concentration of power under a global government:

> We are not proposing movement towards a world government, for were we to travel in that direction we could find ourselves in an even less democratic world than we have – one more accommodating to power, more hospitable to hegemonic ambition, and more reinforcing of the roles of states and governments rather than the rights of people (Commission on Global Governance, 1995: xvi).

Our Global Neighbourhood looked to new forms of global governance to nurture a global civic ethic, strengthen global security, manage economic interdependence, reform the UN, and bolster the rule of law in international relations. The Commission's proposals were self-consciously internationalist and focused on intergovernmental institutions. The Commission may have wanted to involve 'non-governmental organizations ... citizens' movements, multinational corporations, and the global capital market', but it had a limited understanding of the role, power, and authority of these actors (Commission on Global Governance, 1995: 3). Again, the Commission mentioned the role of networks and markets in international relations, but it focused on adjusting the policies of nation-states to the capabilities of new actors. It concentrated on 'reforming and strengthening the existing system of intergovernmental institutions ... improving its means of collaboration with private and independent groups' (Commission on Global Governance, 1995: 4–5).

Later policy discussions have moved away from institutional and legal features of global governance. Most observers think a focus on these features is both too limited in ambition and, at the same time, too optimistic about the capacity of existing organizations to address transnational challenges (Diehl, 2001: 5). Their pessimism reflects the failures to reform the United Nations and the stalemate of the Doha Round of trade negotiations as well as the legitimacy and accountability gaps that bedevil the international institutions created in the postwar era (Zürn, 2004).

Discussions of UN reform have given way to ones about the potential of newer or more flexible forums, including the G8 and G20. Generally these reform agendas are statist, privileging the interests of states above those of non-state actors. The new agendas seek to make international institutions less formal and more responsive to member states. Similar agendas have risen for the IMF and the World Bank. Reformers want to make these organizations more accountable to those who contribute and receive funds. They want to improve the legitimacy of these organizations in the eyes of developing states, especially in selecting senior officials.

The European Union (EU) has adopted a more radical agenda. It has tried to bypass state governments and international institutions and build networks with non-state actors and civil society groups. This agenda relies on novel modes of 'public diplomacy' (Riordan, 2003; Wallström, 2008). For example, the 10th birthday of the EU witnessed extensive global efforts to promote the organization and its 'core messages' (European Commission, 2007). The aims of such public diplomacy include bolstering the EU's 'soft power', promoting its liberal democratic values, and creating 'partnerships' between states and non-European NGOs. The NGOs can play various roles in these partnerships. They can be the initiators of action, mediators between states and international agencies, joint managers of cooperative ventures, and even alternative leaders in forming policies (Cooper, 2002: 8–9). Such partnerships may yet challenge statist and institutionalist approaches to global governance.

THE ROOTS OF GLOBAL GOVERNANCE

Global governance remains a disputed term, covering a new theoretical lens, depictions of a new world, and varied policy agendas. One way to bring these disparate ideas together is by a historical account highlighting the links that led to their appearing concurrently in the global politics of the post-cold war period. We concentrate on how new theories led scholars to see the world differently and policy actors to make the world anew, and on how new worlds led scholars to rethink their theories and policy actors to modify their policies.

Forerunners

The sources of the current form of global governance, as well as global governance theories, lie in the late eighteenth and nineteenth centuries. One forerunner was the series of specialist agencies designed to manage the rules governing transnational flows, especially in communications technology (Murphy, 1994). Specialized agencies addressing transnational problems have a long pedigree, stretching back at least to the middle of the nineteenth century. These agencies were strictly functional in design, intended to regulate specific areas of concern, such as the transborder telegraph connections and postal services served by the International Telegraphic Union (1865) and Universal Postal Union (1874).

Another forerunner of global governance lies in the tradition of classical internationalism. Internationalists designed institutions to regulate the relations of states, advance a perpetual peace (Aksu, 2008), or forge a 'new world order' (Williams, 2007). They hoped to enforce international law, arbitrate disputes, and regulate transnational trade by promoting both international institutions and political reform within states, usually towards a republican or liberal democratic constitution (Halliday, 1988). Classical internationalism arguably had little impact on the practice of international relations until after the First World War. Then it inspired the League of Nations and the attempt to implant liberal democratic regimes in the new states of Central and Eastern Europe.

Between the two world wars, the specialized agencies were relatively successful in performing the functions for which they were designed. In contrast, the international institutions, particularly the League of Nations, glaringly failed to provide a forum for the peaceful resolution of disputes. Scholars and policymakers reacted to these experiences in ways that led to the foundations of global governance. The League had relied on a regular conference diplomacy combined with a commitment to collective security based on unanimity. Observers inferred that this approach to internationalism could not uphold peace and security. Many turned instead to a more Hobbesian version. The United Nations

Security Council (UNSC) is the flawed fruit of their doing so – a collective international sovereign without a world state. At least during the cold war, it provided neither government nor governance (Brierly, 1947).

Postwar settlement

Interwar experiences encouraged former internationalists and their critics to turn to theories such as federalism, functionalism, and planning theory. Federalists argued the problems of interstate war and the unequal distribution of wealth needed more dramatic actions than those proposed by internationalists. They called for the progressive creation of a world state by treaty, taking inspiration from the federalism of the American Founding Fathers and Immanuel Kant's 'Perpetual Peace'. They feared a war between the super powers might result in a world state imposed by force (Lloyd, 1949). Their goal was thus to replace the anarchy of international relations with a world government, albeit with a federal constitution, rather than a novel form of polity.

The functionalists rejected both classical internationalism and federalism. They drew their inspiration from the practical experience and relative success of specialized agencies, as well as anthropological and sociological theorists such as Talcott Parsons. David Mitrany was the most influential early functionalist working on international relations. In *A Working Peace System*, Mitrany (1943) argued that peaceful relations between states could emerge from functional agencies addressing discrete transnational problems. Functionalism promised 'peace by pieces'. Peace would arise as an effect of a series of agencies progressively reducing issues of conflict between states, turning political disputes into technical ones, and so binding states in ever-closer relations.

Functionalism overlapped with sympathy for an increased role for planning in international relations. Enthusiasts for planning argued that it was the 'planlessness of the liberal order' that had turned international relations in the first half of the twentieth century to 'anarchy'. They proposed 'a form of planning ... which will allow a maximum of freedom and self-determination' (Mannheim, 1940: 7). They wanted to replace the competition and conflict they believed characterized classical liberalism with long-term thinking and rational planning. Technocratic planning would remove the insecurity and irrationality of the constant turmoil of free markets.

The traditions of internationalism, federalism, functionalism, and planning theory all shaped the global governance that rose after the Second World War. Just as Hobbesian internationalism influenced the design of the UNSC, so a general internationalism inspired the design of the General Assembly. Federalism influenced the European Economic Community (EEC) (McKay, 1999), and the (not always successful) creation of postcolonial states with federal constitutions, such as Malaysia or Nigeria (Rothermund, 2006). The functionalist tradition also influenced the EEC and helped inspire various specialized agencies within and beyond the United Nations. Indeed, the postwar period saw the creation of some 70 new agencies between 1943 and 1970 (Murphy, 1994: 154–7). Finally, planning theory influenced international, regional, state, and specialist actors, many of whom fused it with ideas emerging from the new field of development theory. These forms of social science flourished especially in the institutions of the global financial order set up at Bretton Woods and among the Anglo-American expert policy community that created and upheld that order (see Ikenberry, 1993). These experts hoped to promote essentially liberal ends by intervening in ways defined by the knowledge associated with their social scientific theories (Gilman, 2007).

Crisis

The postwar period saw the rise of a hybrid structure of global governance that merged internationalism with traditions from the social sciences. This hybrid structure confronted several dilemmas in the 1970s. One dilemma was the rise of the South. The South questioned the legitimacy of the existing pattern of global governance. Its demands to redistribute wealth culminated in the Non-Aligned Movement's 1973 proposal for a New International Economic Order. The Third World proved adept at using the United Nations to voice grievances about the attitude of particular states, especially the United States, to issues such as global trade and global finance. Parts of Western opinion then became increasingly doubtful about the efficacy and desirability of international organization. Their doubts also fed on the paralysis of the UNSC during the cold war.

Another dilemma of the 1970s was the falling apart of the Bretton Woods system. The United States experienced inflationary pressures and worsening terms of trade. Large amounts of dollars gathered in Europe and Japan. Foreign-held dollars lost their value. Inflation spread to other industrialized economies. In 1971 the United States ended the convertibility of the dollar into gold. Global exchange rate mechanisms collapsed. Later, in 1973, the United States, the Europeans, and Japan agreed to formalize an arrangement in which their currencies floated freely in a deregulated market. But this arrangement did not restore stability and health to the global economy. Instead the West's reaction to the Arab–Israeli dispute, especially the United States' military aid to Israel during the Yom Kippur War of October 1973, prompted the Gulf states to place pressure on the West by increasing the price of oil. Rising oil prices aggravated the economic problems of the United States and Europe. The result was stagflation – a combination of high unemployment and high inflation.

Other dilemmas included the perception that economic and technological developments were making states ever more interdependent (Keohane and Nye, 1977). Yet another was that Third World states failed to develop their economies, despite extensive technical backing and direct aid from both the West and the Soviet Union. By the late 1970s and early 1980s, these various dilemmas had eroded the postwar consensus in the West about the best means of managing the global economy and international relations.

THE RISE OF MARKETS AND NETWORKS

The new global governance rose in response to the dilemmas of the 1970s. Scholars and policymakers responded to these dilemmas by turning to new theories and new practices that have defined new agendas. The best known of the new theories and practices is the shift from a classic internationalism to a neoliberalism that stressed markets. Other important new theories and practices stemmed from the shift from older forms of functionalism and planning theory to a greater emphasis on networks and partnerships.

Neoliberalism and markets

While some neoliberals claim to be merely reviving the ideas of Adam Smith, neoliberalism actually combines a specific cluster of new theories that arose out of neoclassical economics during the first half of the twentieth century. Many of these ideas stem from the critique of totalitarianism developed by the Austro-German school and especially Friedrich Hayek (1944). The Austro-Germans believed that planning and state action were inherently flawed. They argued that planners could not know and coordinate the subjective preferences of individuals; planning necessarily led to a misallocation of resources. They thought the impossibility of measuring and knowing subjective preferences meant planners would necessarily assign resources in accord with particular perspectives and judgements; planning necessarily handed resources to special interests, spreading corruption. The Austro-Germans championed

free markets as an alternative to planning. In their view, a decentralized price mechanism allowed for the inherently scattered and fragmented nature of knowledge. Each actor needs to know only his or her own preferences and to act on them. The market then ensures coordination among these actions. The role of the state is not to intervene in the economy, but merely to uphold the rule of law and so enable the market to work properly.

A neoliberal advocacy of free markets and a limited state also characterized the Chicago School of Economists, including Milton Friedman. The Chicago School added a distinctive stress on the quantity theory of money. It also began applying economic analysis to social relations. A leading example of the application of economic analysis is principal–agent theory – a theory that was by no means restricted to Chicago folk. Principal–agent theory models situations in which one actor (the principal) delegates work to another (the agent). It focuses on the dangers arising from the agents pursuing their own interests, as a rational economic actor, rather than those of the principals. For example, public officials may pursue private ends rather than the public good or the goals of their elected masters. Neoliberalism drew on principal–agent theory to recommend various market mechanisms and techniques of corporate management as ways of improving the efficiency of the public sector. Neoliberals called for greater competition, contracts, and targets.

Neoliberalism was a minority position until the 1970s. Its early exponents organized around Hayek to form the Mont Pelerin Society as early as 1947, but they had little impact on global governance. It was the dilemmas of the early 1970s that brought neoliberalism to the fore. Neoliberals had long rejected key principles of the postwar system of global governance, notably the emphasis on centralized, rational planning. They argued the economic crisis of the 1970s and early 1980s showed planning had failed to deliver stability and growth at both the national and global levels. They also argued that top-down, capital-intensive planning had failed to develop the newly independent underdeveloped countries – an argument that even their critics often accepted.

The neoliberal response was a call for markets, deregulation, and public sector reform. This response dramatically transformed domestic policy beginning with Chile and New Zealand but most prominently in the United States and the United Kingdom. In addition, neoliberalism had much impact on global financial institutions, in large part because of the powerful influence of the United States in forging what became known as the 'Washington Consensus'.

Neoliberals complained about the spiralling of Third World debt, much of which had been borrowed to pay for the large-scale projects that planners prescribed to kick-start economic development. The failure of these projects to achieve their goals – and indeed the loss of funds through mismanagement and corruption – prompted changes to lending practices and to Western attitudes to Third World development.

In 1980 the World Bank introduced 'structural adjustment loans' tied to neoliberal policy reforms. Normal investment loans had been disbursed against project expenditures. The new structural adjustment loans 'were nominally given to offset the transaction cost of adopting and implementing better policies and were disbursed as agreed reforms were undertaken' (Thomas, 2007: 732). In October 1985, the United States Treasury Secretary, James Baker, recommended this new stance on debt to the joint annual meeting of the IMF and the World Bank. He proposed a plan that allowed for debt restructuring in return for neoliberal reforms, such as tax cuts, privatizing state-owned enterprises, reducing trade barriers, and liberalizing investment rules. Baker proposed, 'first, and foremost, the adoption by principal debtor countries of comprehensive macroeconomic and structural policies to promote growth and balance-of-payments adjustment to reduce inflation' (Baker, 1986). Mexico was the first nation to participate. It joined the General Agreement on Tariffs and Trade (GATT) in 1986. By the end of 1988 it had reduced tariffs to a maximum of 20 per cent and an average of 10 per cent. Mexico also undertook aggressive privatization, with the number of state-owned enterprises falling from 1200 in 1982 to 500 in 1988. Later still, in March 1989, the then US Treasury Secretary, Nicholas Brady, announced his own successor to Baker's plan. The Brady plan differed from its predecessor in many ways, but it still used debt restructuring to promote neoliberal reforms. After the fall of the Berlin Wall, several ex-communist states introduced similar neoliberal reforms.

Neoliberal policies have faced much criticism (Logan and Mengisteab, 1993: 1–2). There is even debate over the degree to which the Washington Consensus and the shock therapy applied to post-communist economies were properly neoliberal (Williamson, 2003). The reforms certainly did not include every aspect of those President Reagan and Prime Minister Thatcher imposed on the United States and United Kingdom. However, they did include tax reform, deregulation, financial and trade liberalization, free-floating currencies, and extensive privatization. These reforms aimed to take the allocation of resources out of the hands of bureaucratic planners and give it to markets.

In addition, after 1989 the World Bank widened its approach to the domestic policies of states from 'structural adjustment' to 'good governance'. The new approach recognized that economic reform alone could not underpin development and that political reform was also required to stem corruption and misgovernment (World Bank, 1989). By 2005 almost half of the conditions imposed on the recipients of loans concerned public sector governance rather than macroeconomic reform (Thomas, 2007: 732).

During the first-half of the 1990s, neoliberal economics became just one part of a more general liberal revival in global governance. Liberalism was strengthened by a Third Wave of democratization; more than

60 states adopted liberal democratic forms of government (Huntington, 1991). Liberalism also appeared in the increasing activity and growing authority of the UNSC, a new humanitarianism, and the rise of a global civil society of NGOs, pressure groups, and other social actors. Countervailing developments in the late 1990s, however, have diminished liberal optimism. In particular, the failure to reform the United Nations and growing disquiet over the direction of the new humanitarianism – now widely denounced as a cover for Western neocolonialism (Bellamy, 2005) – cast doubt on the prospects for a purely liberal or neoliberal form of global governance. These doubts gave momentum to other approaches to global governance.

Planning, institutionalism, and networks

As neoliberalism began to falter, or at least lose some of its initial confidence, so revised versions of functionalism and planning theory began to reassert themselves. New forms of social science, including the new institutionalism and organizational theory, led people both to notice the increasing role of networks and actively to foster new types of partnership among states and between states and other actors. This return to planning theory and functionalism reflects the experiences and dilemmas of the 1990s and after. New dilemmas relating to terrorism, climate change, asylum-seekers, and the digital divide appear to be less about efficiency than about collective goods such as security and equity. Other dilemmas have risen from the unintended consequences of neoliberalism itself. Many observers believe neoliberal reforms fragmented governance, exasperating problems of coordination and steering (Hood and Peters, 2004). The neoliberal reforms threaten further to weaken fragile and failing states, whose main problems already include a lack of capacity. More generally, once services and other policies depend on diverse public and private actors, there is often a new need to coordinate and manage these actors.

During the 1970s planning theorists may have turned away from rational planning, but they rarely adopted neoliberal ideas. Instead, they developed new approaches to planning, including transactive planning, social learning theory, and communicative planning theory (Friedman, 1973; Forester, 1989; Healey, 1997). These approaches differed from rational planning in championing informal structures and wider participation. Planners had a more facilitative and less directive role. Planning occurred in networks based on partnerships and interactions with the community.

The shift from rational planning to more informal approaches appears in the rise of terms such as 'wicked problem' (Rittel and Webber, 1973; Conklin, 2006). Most definitions of a wicked problem refer to clusters of features such as:

- a problem of more or less unique nature
- the lack of any definitive formulation of such a problem
- the existence of multiple explanations for it
- the absence of a test to decide the value of any response to it
- all responses to it being better or worse rather than true or false
- and each response to it having important consequences such that there is no real chance to learn by trial and error.

Examples of wicked problems include pressing issues of global governance such as security, the environment, and world poverty. Planning theorists argue that wicked problems explain the failings of hierarchic bureaucracies: departmental silos undermine the coordination needed to address interrelated and intransigent problems. They suggest that wicked problems require more collaborative and innovative approaches, with agencies working across organizational boundaries both within and outside the state. Some planning theorists thus conclude that networks and partnerships are the way of dealing with wicked problems.

A similar turn to networks and partnerships took place among functionalists and institutionalists. These mid-level social scientists often responded to the challenge of rational choice by turning away from an old institutionalism they thought was too formal and legalistic, and towards a new institutionalism that was more receptive to informal norms and organizations, including networks and partnerships.[1] Many institutionalists accept neoliberal arguments about the inflexible and unresponsive nature of rational planning and bureaucratic hierarchies. However, instead of promoting managerialism and markets, they appeal to joined-up governance and networks (Bevir, 2005: 29–53). These institutionalists think networks are characteristically flexible and responsive structures that allow for the structured and yet informal environments in which social actors operate. They argue that competitiveness and efficiency derive less from markets and competition than from stable relationships characterized by mutual trust, social participation, voluntary associations, and even friendship. In their view, networks combine an enabling or facilitative leadership with greater flexibility, creativity, inclusiveness, and commitment.

Recent shifts in global governance reflect the turn to networks, joining-up, and public–private partnerships. One prominent example is international aid to fragile states. Before 9/11, debates about aid were conducted mainly in terms of underdeveloped states and their economic needs. Since the terrorist attacks, greater attention has been paid to fragile states and the wicked problems they confront. Fragile states are defined not just by poverty but also by related problems of weak governance and violent conflict. Donor states increasingly conceive of aid as requiring a 'whole of government' approach that sets out to address all these problems simultaneously. They argue that effective aid to fragile states depends on networks that combine actors and issues associated with foreign policy, security, and development. By 2005, Australia, Germany, the United Kingdom, and the United States had all established dedicated units to coordinate departmental efforts to aid reconstruction in fragile states. Several states were exploring novel funding arrangements to encourage greater interdepartmental collaboration.

These 'whole of government' approaches also took root in the Organization for Economic Co-operation and Development (OECD). In 2005 the Fragile States Group of the OECD Development Assistance Committee devised Principles for Good Engagement in Fragile States that highlighted the importance of developing coherent programs spanning administrative, economic, political, and security domains. The Group then set up a workstream, chaired by Australia and France, to devise a framework for an explicitly 'whole of government' approach (OECD, 2006).

The international community even appears to be moving toward support for a 'whole of government' approach to aid more generally. From February to March 2005 a high-level forum on Joint Progress Toward Enhanced Aid Effectiveness met in Paris. The forum brought together over a hundred countries as well as international institutions such as the African Development Bank, the Asian Development Bank, the European Bank for Reconstruction and Development, the OECD, the World Bank, and the United Nations Development Programme. The forum resulted in the Paris Declaration, calling for greater harmonization, alignment, and managing aid in relation to a set of monitorable indicators.

CONCLUSION

Global governance refers to a range of new theories, practices, and agendas associated with informal processes and activities of governing. These theories, practices, and agendas are interconnected. The new theories – neoliberalism and rational choice, and revised versions of planning theory and institutionalism – have changed the ways people see the world and inspired reform agendas that have contributed to the further spread of markets and networks. Recognition of the spread of markets and networks has inspired attempts to develop new theories of international relations and new agendas to regulate, control, and preserve transnational flows and the global commons. The agendas have generated theoretical controversy over how best to reform the world in which we now find ourselves.

To conclude, we should briefly note at least some of the diversity of the agendas on offer. This chapter has paid particular attention to theories and agendas that clearly influenced the changing pattern of international relations; however, the academic and policy communities abound with alternative reform agendas and visions of global governance.

In the 1940s and again in the 1970s and 1980s, demands for new approaches to global governance reflected concerns that existing arrangements could not meet the basic demands being made of them. The international system seemed unable to provide international peace and security, economic and financial stability, and the effective management of transnational problems. Today, by contrast, the demands for a new approach reflect less a belief that current arrangements are not working and more a belief that they are not legitimate in the eyes of their stakeholders or that they are insufficiently democratic (Scholte, 2002; Seabrooke, 2007). These beliefs inspire two main reform agendas.

One current reform agenda builds upon those mid-level social scientific approaches that emphasize the role of networks and partnerships. In practice, however, it can be harnessed to a number of different policies, from the extension of modified forms of neoliberalism to those of its opponents. This agenda concentrates on building legitimacy by institutional reform. Relevant proposals include rebalancing the voting rights of particular groups of states within the IMF. This agenda also seeks to build new networks around institutions and thereby involve civil society groups with interests in that institution's area of concern (Slaughter, 2005).

A second reform agenda goes far further in advocating change based on a return to classic internationalism. Cosmopolitan internationalists take their cue from Kant's plan for perpetual peace. They propose the progressive extension of cosmopolitan law into global governance underpinned by representative and democratic institutions. One version of this cosmopolitan vision consists mainly of top-down reforms (Held, 1995: 273; Zolo, 1997). Proposals include placing control of international institutions and functional agencies in the hands of boards that are statistically representative of their constituencies. Ultimately these reformers envisage an authoritative assembly – a fully democratized version of the UN General Assembly – with the power to make binding global law. Other cosmopolitans propose a more bottom-up process in which an emergent global civil society demands piecemeal changes in contemporary practices of global governance (Scholte, 2002).

NOTE

1 The narrative is complicated here by the existence of a distinctive rational choice institutionalism. In what follows, we use the term 'institutionalism' to refer solely to the sociological institutionalism and historical institutionalism with their debt to mid-level forms of social science such as functionalism. For a more detailed discussion and references, see Adcock, Bevir and Stimson (2007).

REFERENCES

Abrahamsen, Rita (2004) 'The Power of Partnerships in Global Governance', *Third World Quarterly* 25(8): 1453–67.

Adcock, Robert, Bevir, Mark and Stimson, Shannon (2007) 'Historicizing the New Institutionalism(s)', in Robert Adcock, Mark Bevir and Shannon Stimson (eds), *Modern Political Science: Anglo-American Exchanges since 1880.* Princeton, NJ: Princeton University Press; pp. 259–89.

Adler, Emanuel and Haas, Peter M. (1992) 'Epistemic Communities, World Order, and the Creation of a

Reflective Research Program', *International Organization* 46: 367–90.

Aksu, Esref (ed.) (2008) *Early Notions of Global Governance: Selected Eighteenth-Century Proposals for 'Perpetual Peace'*. Cardiff: University of Wales Press.

Baker, James (1986) 'Administration's Program for Sustained Growth Would Expand Loan Activity of Development Banks'. Speech, 12 April 2009.

Barnett, Michael N. and Duvall, Raymond (eds), (2005) *Power in Global Governance*. Cambridge: Cambridge University Press.

Bellamy, Alex J. (2005) 'Responsibility to Protect or Trojan Horse? The Crisis in Darfur and Humanitarian Intervention after Iraq', *Ethics & International Affairs* 19(2): 31–53.

Bevir, Mark (2005) *New Labour: A Critique*. London: Routledge.

Brierly, J.L. (1947) *The Covenant and the Charter*. Cambridge: Cambridge University Press.

Bull, Hedley (1977) *The Anarchical Society: A Study of Order in World Politics*. Basingstoke: Macmillan.

Commission on Global Governance (1995) *Our Global Neighbourhood*. Oxford: Oxford University Press.

Conklin, Jeff (2006) *Dialogue Mapping: Building Shared Understanding of Wicked Problems*. Chichester: Wiley.

Cooper, Andrew F. (2002) 'Like-Minded Nations, NGOs, and the Changing Pattern of Diplomacy within the UN System: An Introductory Perspective', in Andrew F. Cooper, John English and Ramesh Chandra Thakur (eds), *Enhancing Global Governance: Towards a New Diplomacy?* Tokyo: United Nations University Press; pp. 1–18.

Cutler, A. Claire (2003) *Private Power and Global Authority: Transnational Merchant Law in Global Political Economy*. Cambridge: Cambridge University Press.

Diehl, Paul (ed.) (2001) *The Politics of Global Governance: International Organizations in an Interdependent World*, 2nd edn. Boulder, CO: Lynne Rienner.

Drezner, Daniel W. (2004) 'The Global Governance of the Internet: Bringing the State Back In', *Political Science Quarterly* 119(3): 477–98.

Drezner, Daniel W. (2007) *All Politics Is Global: Explaining International Regulatory Regimes*. Princeton, NJ: Princeton University Press.

European Commission (2007) 'A Glance at EU Public Diplomacy at Work', online at http://europa.eu/50/around_world/images/2007_50th_anniv_broch_en.pdf

Forester, John (1989) *Planning in the Face of Power*. Berkeley, CA: University of California Press.

Friedman, John (1973) *Retracking America: A Theory of Transactive Planning*. Garden City, NY: Anchor Press.

Gilman, Nils (2007) *Mandarins of the Future: Modernization Theory in Cold War America*. Baltimore: Johns Hopkins University Press.

Haggard, Stephan and Simmons, Beth A. (1987) 'Theories of International Regimes', *International Organization* 41: 491–517.

Hall, Rodney Bruce (2008) *Central Banking as Global Governance: Constructing Financial Credibility*. Cambridge: Cambridge University Press.

Halliday, Fred (1988) 'Three Concepts of Internationalism', *International Affairs* 64(2): 187–98.

Hayek, Friedrich (1944) *The Road to Serfdom*. London: Routledge and Kegan Paul.

Healey, Patsy (1997) *Collaborative Planning: Shaping Places in Fragmented Societies*. Basingstoke: Macmillan.

Held, David (1995) *Democracy and the Global Order: From the Modern State to Cosmopolitan Governance*. Cambridge: Polity.

Held, David and McGrew Anthony (eds), (2002) *Global Transformations: Politics, Economics and Culture*. Cambridge: Polity.

Hewson, Martin and Sinclair, Timothy J. (eds) (1999) *Approaches to Global Governance Theory*. Albany, NY: SUNY Press.

Hood, Christopher and Peters, Guy (2004) 'The Middle Aging of New Public Management: Into the Age of Paradox?', *Journal of Public Administration Research and Theory* 14: 267–82.

Huntington, Samuel P. (1991) *The Third Wave: Democratization in the Late Twentieth Century*. Norman, OK: University of Oklahoma Press.

Ikenberry, G. John (1993) 'The Political Origins of Bretton Woods', in Michael D. Bordo and Barry J. Eichengreen (eds), *A Retrospective on the Bretton Woods System*. Chicago: University of Chicago Press; pp. 155–82.

Kahler, Miles and Lake David A. (eds) (2003) *Governance in a Global Economy: Political Authority in Transition*. Princeton, NJ: Princeton, University Press.

Keohane, Robert (1988) 'International Institutions: Two Approaches', *International Studies Quarterly* 32(4): 379–96.

Keohane, Robert (2001) 'Governance in a Partially Globalized World', *American Political Science Review* 95(1): 1–13.

Keohane, Robert and Nye, Joseph (1977) *Power and Interdependence: World Politics in Transition*. Boston: Little, Brown.

Krasner, Stephen D. (1991) 'Global Communications and National Power: Life on the Pareto Frontier', *World Politics* 43(3): 336–66.

Lipschutz, Ronnie (1992) 'Reconstructing World Politics: The Emergence of Global Civil Society', *Millennium: Journal of International Studies* 21(2): 389–420.

Lloyd, Wm Bross (1949) 'The United Nations and World Federalism', *The Antioch Review* 9(1): 16–28.

Logan, Ikubolajeh Bernard and Mengisteab, Kidane (1993) 'IMF–World Bank Adjustment and Social Transformation in Sub-Saharan Africa', *Economic Geography* 69(1): 1–24.

McKay, David (1999) *Federalism and the European Union: A Political Economy Perspective.* Oxford: Oxford University Press.

Mannheim, Karl (1940) *Man and Society in an Age of Reconstruction: Studies in Modern Social Structure*, trans. Edward Shils. London: Routledge and Kegan Paul.

Martin, Lisa L. and Simmons, Beth (1998) 'Theories and Empirical Studies of International Institutions', *International Organization* 52: 729–57.

Mitrany, David (1943) *A Working Peace System.* London: Royal Institute for International Affairs.

Murphy, Craig N. (1994) *International Organization and Industrial Change: Global Governance since 1850.* Cambridge: Blackwell.

O'Brien, Robert, Goetz, Anne-Marie, Scholte, Jan Aart and Williams, Marc (2000) *Contesting Global Governance: Multilateral Economic Institutions and Global Social Movements.* Cambridge: Cambridge University Press.

Organization for Economic Cooperation and Development (2006) *Whole of Government Approaches to Fragile States.* Paris: OECD.

Riordan, Shaun (2003) *The New Diplomacy.* Cambridge: Polity.

Rittel, Horst and Webber Melvin (1973) 'Dilemmas in a General Theory of Planning', *Policy Sciences* 4: 155–69.

Rosenau, James (1987) *Governance without Government: Systems of Rule in World Politics.* Los Angeles: Institute for Transnational Studies, University of Southern California.

Rosenau, James (1995) 'Governance in the Twenty First Century', *Global Governance* 1(1): 13–43.

Rosenau, James and Cziempel, Ernst Otto (1992) *Governance without Government: Order and Change in World Politics.* Cambridge: Cambridge University Press.

Rothermund, Dietmar (2006) 'Constitution Making and Decolonization', *Diogenes* 53(4): 9–17.

Scholte, Jan Aart (2000) *Globalization: A Critical Introduction*, 1st edn. Basingstoke: Palgrave.

Scholte, Jan Aart (2002) 'Civil Society and Democracy in Global Governance', *Global Governance* 8: 281–304.

Seabrooke, Len (2007) 'Legitimacy Gaps in the World Economy: Explaining the Sources of the IMF's Legitimacy Crisis', *International Politics* 44(2), 250–68.

Slaughter, Anne-Marie (2005) *A New World Order.* Princeton, NJ: Princeton University Press.

Sterling-Folker, Jennifer (2005) 'Realist Global Governance: Revisiting *Cave! Hic Dragones* and Beyond', in Alice C. Ba and Matthew Hoffmann (eds), *Contending Perspectives on Global Governance: Coherence, Contestation and World Order.* London: Routledge; pp. 17–38.

Stoker, Gerry (1998) 'Governance as Theory: Five Propositions', *International Social Science Journal* 50(155): 17–28.

Strange, Susan (1996) *The Retreat of the State: The Diffusion of Power in the World Economy.* Cambridge: Cambridge University Press.

Thomas, Caroline (2000) *Global Governance, Development and Human Security.* London: Pluto.

Thomas, M.A. (2007) 'The Governance Bank', *International Affairs* 83(4): 729–45.

Wallström, Margot (2008) 'Public Diplomacy and Its Rule in EU External Relations', online at http://europa.eu/rapid/pressReleasesAction.do?reference=SPEECH/08/494&format=PDF&aged=0&language=EN&guiLanguage=en

Waltz, Kenneth (1999) 'Globalization and Governance', *PS: Political Science and Politics* 32(4): 693–700.

Williams, Andrew (2007) *Failed Imagination? The Anglo-American New World Order from Wilson to Bush.* Manchester: Manchester University Press.

Williamson, John (2003) 'The Washington Consensus and Beyond', *Economic and Political Weekly* 38(15): 1475–81.

World Bank (1989) *Sub-Saharan Africa: From Crisis to Sustainable Growth.* Washington, DC: World Bank.

Zolo, Danilo (1997) *Cosmopolis: Prospects for World Government*, trans. David McKie. Cambridge: Polity.

Zürn, Michael (2004) 'Global Governance and Legitimacy Problems', *Government and Opposition* 39(2): 260–87.

Dilemmas of Governance

24

Legitimacy

Mark Considine and Kamran Ali Afzal

Public sector institutions in most advanced democracies have undergone unprecedented transformation over the past three decades or so, and no settlement of the process yet appears in sight. Many of these changes have also been seen in developing countries. This process of transformation has impacted forms of steering and coordination, methods of service delivery, and core assumptions about the rights of consumers and citizens. Broadly perceived, the change has moved these institutions away from a traditional Weberian structure towards those based upon corporate, market, and entrepreneurial mechanisms (Considine, 2002a; Rhodes, 1997). More recently, this process has seen the emergence of new types of network governance in which state agencies are found operating key functions through somewhat self-organizing arrangements comprising bureaucrats, private enterprises, not-for-profit agencies, community organizations, and even citizens themselves (Considine, 2005). For many scholars of political science and public administration, the new countenance of the public sector signifies a shift from 'government' to 'governance' that has rendered the distinction between the public and private sectors almost obsolete, and permanently altered the power relations between state and civil society.

There is, of course, nothing inevitable in the drive from hierarchies to markets to networks; nor can a claim be made for any one set of defining characteristics, central elements or classifiable structures of contemporary governance (Bevir and Rhodes, 2006a). Conventional public sector institutions continue to exert a powerful influence and the state remains both hierarchical and decisive in many domains, not least because security concerns have bolstered surveillance and coercion functions in many countries. Although it has a persuasive set of family resemblances to distinguish it, the new public management (NPM) is far from a cohesive theory of public administration and is better understood as a compilation of connected ideas adapted largely from private sector values and practices to improve public sector efficiency (Ferlie et al., 1996; Nolan, 2001; Peters, 2001). Public policy and service-delivery networks, too, exhibit many different shapes, forms and purposes, and cut across contemporaneously existing hierarchies and markets (Considine, 2002b, 2005; Considine and Lewis, 2003a). In fact, the contemporary governance structures of individual states tend to be distinctive,[1] and are largely produced by the interaction of state and local societal traditions, beliefs of élite actors, legacies of conquest and imperialism, and the nature of the dilemmas faced by states (Bevir and Rhodes, 2006a, 2006b).

And yet governance in the developed world – and under the influence of international organizations and financial agencies, even in the developing world – shows substantial similarity across states in terms of public sector objectives, trends and features. So prolific appears to be the influence of NPM theories and network structures that Considine and Lewis (2003b) find empirical evidence of three distinct, though coexisting, governance orientations amongst the bureaucracies of Australia, New Zealand, the United Kingdom, and Netherlands: procedural (or traditional) governance, enterprise governance, and network governance. Owing to this admixture of similarities and variations, it becomes useful to conceptualize the common characteristics of contemporary governance, following Bevir and Rhodes (2006b: 59), in terms of the 'family resemblances' metaphor: i.e. a set of shared traits, not all of which will always emerge. The common features in contemporary governance have been largely generated by common concerns on public sector performance that have, in turn, encouraged the adoption of NPM and network options for the organization and management of the public sector: the variations, on the other hand, have been produced by enduring state and societal traditions (for example, Pollitt and Bouckaert, 2004).

With the transformation in the role and structure of the public sector, the principles and philosophy sustaining the public sector paradigm have also undergone challenge and modification. This chapter focuses on the altered framework of public sector legitimacy in the face of the transformation of government to governance. The first section conceptualizes legitimacy and its traditional foundations in democratic forms of organization and governance; the second section reviews the probable effect of NPM-inspired reforms on public sector legitimacy; the third section focuses on the impact of governance traits produced by networks; the fourth section

identifies some approaches to reconstruct public sector legitimacy in the emerging 'new' governance structures; and the fifth section concludes the chapter.

LEGITIMACY AND ITS TRADITIONAL FOUNDATIONS

Legitimacy is a crucial requirement for public sector organizations since it is directly related to their acceptability, credibility, approval, and support both amongst citizens and other stakeholders, including foreign élites (Häikiö, 2007; Suchman, 1995). Because so much depends upon the interaction of state institutions and social structures (modes of social inclusion, etc.), legitimacy is always and everywhere a 'joint property' of a society and not just a characteristic of this or that public organization. Which is not to say that we should not pay attention to legitimacy failure by key agencies, such as public bureaucracies. We should. But we really need to see these in the context of the larger picture of social legitimacy before drawing conclusions of a systemic kind.

The assessment of legitimacy rests upon an understanding of the way a society frames the issue (Suchman, 1995; Weatherford, 1992), rendering a fixed definition of the term rather awkward, if not impossible. Certainly we cannot link legitimacy directly to democracy, since many non-democratic hierarchical and familial systems enjoy high levels of legitimacy among their members; but legitimacy in such governance systems is beyond the scope of this chapter. Not many scholars appear to have attempted a universal definition of legitimacy, even in the context of democracies, and most have restricted themselves to descriptions of the concept. For instance, in his well-noted organizational perspective, Maurer (1971) views legitimacy in terms of a justification for organizations to exist, which includes the questions of being socially responsible, and morally and legally accountable. Even Suchman's (1995: 574) definition[2] for legitimacy is broad: 'a generalized perception or assumption that the actions of an entity are desirable, proper, or appropriate within some socially constructed system of norms, values, beliefs, and definitions.' The critical aspect, however, is that the legitimacy of organizational structures is constructed within their socially determined environments, and not solely predicated on any objective abstractions or criteria that may be used to validate their existence. This construction of legitimacy holds as true for private sector enterprises as it does for public organizations, including the state itself as a political entity. But in the case of the public sector, the subjective environment in which legitimacy is created leads us directly to the citizens. Zürn (2004: 260) refers to this as the 'descriptive perspective' of legitimacy, and explains it as the 'societal acceptance of political decisions and political orders as well as the belief of the subjects of rule in legitimacy.' Buchanan and Keohane (2006: 405) term this understanding of legitimacy as its 'sociological sense'. We might think of this as the aspect of national character that helps frame the expectations that citizens have of their institutions and the boundaries set both explicitly and implicitly on the conduct of the state.

Traditional public sector institutional structures in democratic regimes derive their legitimacy from a number of sources, which include:

- democratic accountability through the parliament and other, auxiliary, channels;
- preserving cardinal public sector values, including the public interest;
- supporting a regime of formal rules and procedures to help shape positive interactions between individuals and groups.

These factors are taken up in some detail below.

Democratic accountability

In democratic theory, legitimacy derives from a definition of sovereignty that values effective representation of the citizenry in the executive and legislative branches of government. In this model, it is representation that provides accountability; but this on its own does not produce legitimacy. In addition, the framework of institutional rules and competencies establishes public confidence and stakeholder acceptance. Thus, within the ambit of these rules and competencies, representation and accountability become two countenances of the paradigm of democratic legitimacy: representation is the philosophical, and accountability the practical. Accountability operationalizes representation by providing the functional link that connects governments and public sector institutions with citizens, and thereby establishes the latter's sovereignty. The traditional public sector accountability framework can be viewed as a chain of institutionalized, mostly hierarchical, relationships structured around a broad spectrum of meaning, but centring on responsibility, obligation, and answerability for the use of public office, public resources, and formally delegated authority, both in the context of probity and performance. The framework also embodies a few lateral linkages, such as the accountability to courts of law, ombudsmen, and international treaties. For these reasons, the concept, characteristics and parameters of public sector accountability, as in the case legitimacy, may elude a precise definition, but in the standard works, as for instance Waldo (1956) and Wilson (1992[1887]), accountability is conceptualized as the obligation to be responsive to the legitimate interests of those affected by public policies, where the obligation to respond is embedded in legal or democratic rights.

However, as the focus of public sector accountability is mostly on its processes and outcomes rather than on its definition (Fearon, 1999), it is meaningful to focus on the relationships and conditions necessary for the existence of a legitimizing accountability mechanism to exist. Since the obligation to be responsive includes the duty of care and the responsibility to provide information on the utilization of public funds and the exercise of public authority to all individuals affected, including legislators, the issue of accountability constitutes the core of the larger issue of public agency (Considine, 2002a, 2005). In simple terms, an accountability relationship tends to exist between two individuals or entities when: (1) one of them is responsible and/or authorized to act on behalf of the other; and (2) the first actor, on whose behalf the second actor is performing, also has formal or informal authority to reward or punish the second actor on the basis of some predefined, preconceived or expected criteria or outcomes (Fearon, 1999). This relationship, in fact, delineates the principal–agent framework,[3] where the agent is responsible to act on behalf of the principal, in accordance with the principal's preferences or best interest. Nevertheless, being representative does not necessarily mean that the decisions of the citizens' representatives must always coincide with what the citizens want: representation also includes acting in the best interest of the citizens and the common good even when citizens may wish for something else[4] (Przeworski et al., 1999). The two possibilities are termed in the literature as 'mandate representation' and 'delegate representation' (Sørensen, 2002: 697): the former perception holds the will of the people paramount, while the latter gives precedence to their best interest. But then, representatives may not always have the citizens' best interest in mind while ignoring their aspirations. As Moore (1995: 31) explains succinctly, '[w]e have all become painfully aware of the folly and corruption that can beset the deliberations and choices of representative democratic institutions.' In such instances, accountability provides a powerful incentive for representatives to align their actions with citizens' wishes or their best interest.

It is important to note at this juncture that even though the objective of accountability as a tool of representative democracy is to futuristically induce agents to be responsive to the preferences of principals or act in their best interest (Maravall, 1999), its process is essentially retrospective in that it comprises only *ex post* assessment of agents' actions by principals (Cheibub and Przeworski, 1999). This apparent incongruity is reconciled by the fact that the imminence of accountability tends to create an incentive structure that aligns the interests of the agents with the interests of the principals – or what has been referred to as the 'deterrent effect' of accountability (Behn, 2001: 14). In this line of argument, however, democratic accountability appears to pose another conceptual hurdle. Representative democracy does not have any *legally binding* mechanism to ensure that citizens' representatives abide by citizens' wishes or best interest, or even by the promises that they themselves make during election campaigns (Przeworski et al., 1999).[5] But just as much as there is consensus amongst theorists as to representative democracy being the most conducive political form to ensure the implementation of citizens' wishes or best interest, there is broad acceptance that despite its shortcomings the election process embedded in representative democracy tends to be the best primary mechanism available to ensure that either the representatives implement citizens' preferences or act in their best interest.[6]

However, the accountability of only political representatives to citizens is not sufficient to sustain public sector legitimacy in democracies. The action of all public sector agencies must also be directed towards citizens' wishes or best interest. Although the ideal in the traditional public sector model remains the Wilsonian politics–administration dichotomy sustained by a neutral Weberian bureaucracy, it has long been recognized that bureaucracies do not limit themselves to the implementation of public policies and that they can and do affect public policy formulation itself (Behn, 1995, 2001; Moore, 1994; Waldo, 1948). Thus, the acknowledgement of the bureaucracy's role in public policy formulation reduces the question of the ability of citizens to align their representatives' preferences with their own to only one part of a bigger story. Fortunately, the structures of democratic accountability extend the control of citizens, through their representatives in legislatures, over non-representative public sector organizations also. This link in the chain of accountability is indirect and complex, but owing to the more formal procedures available to legislatures, as well as lesser information asymmetries, the ability of legislatures to control bureaucracies tends to be greater than the ability of citizens to control legislatures. In parliamentary democracy, the chain of political accountability runs from citizens to the legislature, to the cabinet[7] (or the 'executive' or 'government'), to ministers,[8] to senior bureaucrats,[9] to subordinate civil servants (Laver and Shepsle, 1999; Sinclair, 1995). The first link in the chain – the accountability of the legislature to the citizens – tends to be institutionalized by the election process. The second link – the accountability of the cabinet to the legislature – is institutionalized, in similar fashion, by the ability of the legislature to move a motion of 'confidence' or 'no confidence' with respect to an individual minister or the cabinet[10] (Laver and Shepsle, 1999). In presidential regimes, the legislature tends to have a weaker control over the executive as compared to parliamentary regimes, but because the executive is directly elected, it is also directly accountable to the citizens.

The third link in the chain is the control of the bureaucracy by the government, which is created by the institutionalized accountability of the heads of government departments (who in most cases are senior civil servants) to their ministers. The formal procedures of accountability range from transfers and demotions to public embarrassment and budget reductions, to disciplinary proceedings, investigations, and even dismissals from service (Dunn, 1999). The accountability of civil servants to the government, and through the government to the legislature and citizens, constitutes the political accountability of the bureaucracy, and lies at the very centre of democratic accountability (for example, Dunn, 1999 and Sinclair, 1995). Theorists such as Behn (2001), Halligan (2001) and Sinclair (1995) identify several other traditional forms of accountability, the more significant of which are administrative, legal, professional, and personal. Drawing from these theorists:

- Administrative accountability refers to the internal hierarchical relationships of responsibility and answerability of public functionaries in government departments as well as to the accountability of the departments themselves within the organizational structure of government. Administrative accountability also includes the answerability of public functionaries and organizations to external administrative institutions, such as the Ombudsman, the Auditor General, and parliamentary committees. Administrative accountability, in fact, defines the traditional form of institutional responsibility of public actors.
- Legal accountability is structured through formal laws, rules or codes of conduct, and refers to the answerability of all public actors before courts of law, statutory bodies or other legally empowered agencies.
- Professional accountability relates to civil servants' sense of responsibility emanating from loyalty to the value systems of their service cadre or profession. These value systems are expected to be adhered to by members of a cadre or profession voluntarily, but can be imposed by members' organizations where they exist.
- Personal accountability arises from the principles and moral values of public officials as individuals, and tends to be molded by the ethos and belief system of the society in which they live as well as by their organizational culture.

The latter forms of accountability (that is, other than political accountability) may not be so important in the context of their ability to *directly* align the objectives of public sector institutions with the objectives of the legislature, or of the legislature with those of the citizens, but they tend to be very important in the context of upholding the public interest and the common good. For instance, strong judicial systems can rein in aggrandizing governments and bureaucracies where control by elected representatives is seen to fail. Similarly, judicial systems can also induce legislatures, governments, and bureaucracies to act in the public interest where they are not doing so, or to protect civil rights and political liberties, and even to ensure free and fair elections.

Cardinal public sector values

In the classical construction, public sector institutions gain a large part of their legitimacy in being the guardians of the public interest and of public sector values. Many public sector organizations could lay claim to legitimacy simply as providers of collective goods, especially where markets have failed or have led to large externalities, but this reason alone has never been considered sufficient. In democracies, the legitimacy of public sector organizations in public provision can only be valid if they uphold cardinal public sector values such as societal welfare, distributive justice, fairness, equity, the protection of the public interest, and promotion of the common good (for example, Moore, 1995). The precise meaning and connotations of each of these values are, of course, normatively determined within the sociopolitical environment of any society, but their general understanding across states tends to be the same; and upholding these cardinal public sector values in decision-making, policy interventions, and service provision forms an integral part of the public sector's 'output' legitimacy (Skogstad, 2003: 956), as well as its 'moral legitimacy' (Suchman 1995: 579).

Formal rules and procedures

Traditional public sector organizations also derive legitimacy by adhering to a defined set of rules, codes, and procedures. The 'due processes' for public agencies are largely designed to establish probity and transparency in public sector operations, facilitate intra- and inter-agency oversight, promote a fair distribution of public benefits, and ensure a judicious exercise of public authority. Similarly, formulation of public

policies requires the adoption of certain mandatory processes, procedures, and consultations, as well as obtaining formal approvals at various levels. Often these rules and procedures have the direct or indirect approval of legislatures and, through them, of citizens.

Authors like Van Kersbebergen and Van Waarden (2004: 158) refer to these procedural aspects as 'input' legitimacy, which validates organizational operations and policy interventions on the basis of the observance of socially acceptable processes and 'rules-of-the-game'. For Suchman (1995), procedural legitimacy is also a part of moral legitimacy, and logically so – after all, the objective of rules and procedures is to produce fair and judicious outcomes. In this sense, the greater ideal of the rule of law appears to be an extension of procedural legitimacy, just as are the principle of separation of powers or the frameworks of institutional checks and balances for organizations exercising authority, particularly coercive authority. The politics–administration dichotomy and a neutral bureaucracy, too, reflect a commitment to ensuring compliance with rules and procedures. Indeed, in Weber's (1978) classical construction nothing seems to legitimize the exercise of public authority more than an adherence to the rules and norms valued by a society. Admittedly, no inefficient government, no matter how well-meaning, can be considered legitimate, and efficiency in production, especially in terms of the optimal utilization of resources, has always been a part of the public sector's input legitimacy. But whenever there is a *bona fide* trade-off between efficiency and considerations of procedural probity or transparency, the latter take precedence in the classical understanding of public sector legitimacy.

The new governance structures are, however, more efficiency-oriented, and the next two sections attempt to understand how the traditional foundations of legitimacy have been affected by the traits and trends produced by markets and networks.

THE IMPACT OF THE NEW PUBLIC MANAGEMENT

The changes in the public sector paradigm brought about by the new public management have challenged the traditional foundations of public sector legitimacy by affecting the accountability framework as well as by altering some of the values embodied in conventional public sector objectives, structures, and procedures. Moreover, by elevating the status of private providers of public services, NPM has sometimes weakened the claims of public servants to be the upholders of any special ethical or normative role in society. It is true that NPM reforms have also created new sources of legitimacy; but, on balance, public sector legitimacy appears to have been conflicted.

For many scholars of political science and public administration, NPM-inspired practices have depleted some core public sector competencies, leading to the 'hollowing out' of the state.[11] And the new hollowed-out state, according to these critics, is beset not only with depleted core competencies but also with depleted legitimacy. Under the NPM paradigm, performance and efficiency in terms of outputs and cost-minimization take precedence over considerations of procedural propriety (Beckett, 2000; Hedley, 1998), which in many spheres has compromised the moral legitimacy of the public sector drawn from following a defined set of rules, codes, and processes that are designed to uphold the conventional public sector values. The NPM discourse views such regulatory or procedural requirements as red tape, sources of organizational rigidity, and impediments to efficiency and output-based performance (Lane, 2000; Osborne and Gaebler, 1992; Walsh, 1995). Compounded further by the effects of initiatives like outsourcing policy advice, contracting-out service provision, decentralizing government authority, disaggregating public organizations, and devolving government functions to the private sector, the outcome has not only been a more horizontal and complex framework of

control, responsibility, and accountability but also, very often, a vague one (Christensen and Lægreid, 2001). The lines of accountability between citizen and legislature, or between minister and departmental secretary, or even between senior bureaucrat and field manager are now neither straight nor continuous because of the involvement of several other competing channels of responsibility (Ciborra, 1996; Considine, 2002a, 2005).

It should also be noted, however, that where NPM has increased the efficiency of programs it has helped rescue aspects of public service organization from claims that the older bureaucratic norms were more sensitive to local conditions and stakeholder concerns. In an age where business interests and economic performance is highly regarded by citizens and élites, finding a way to re-legitimize the state and its public organizations must be taken seriously. The question then becomes an empirical one from a legitimacy perspective. Those elements of NPM that increase responsiveness, tailoring of services, and efficiency may help drive stronger attachment of citizens and élites to key state institutions. Those that push services out to contractors who then care little for creating public value and only seek to maximize profits will have the opposite impact on legitimacy.

An effective accountability mechanism is crucial for the public sector from two distinct, but interrelated, aspects (Considine, 2005):

1 It is required to ensure that public policies and interventions achieve the purpose for which they are designed: this can be called the 'functional' aspect. And,
2 It tends to guarantee that public policies and interventions have some accepted moral standard: this can be termed as the 'ethical' aspect.

Under either consideration, effective accountability entails the ability to apportion responsibility to real actors, who may be individuals or organizations. Doing so, however, may not be simple or straightforward as it requires an ability to decipher the contribution of each actor to a public policy or program, or as Hardin (1996: 126) notes: '[w]ho is how much responsible for which part of what?' In the case of functional accountability, contributions need not be precisely identified as long as the anomalies can be understood and improvements made. But ethical accountability cannot be treated simply as an organizational issue: defaulting individuals need to be identified and sanctioned in commensuration with their role. From this vantage point, whereas both the organizational and individual form of contribution-identification may be possible in a traditional public sector setting, neither form appears achievable in the complexity created by overlapping vertical and horizontal domains and responsibilities.

Furthermore, in entrepreneurial governance the authority to hold people accountable derives not from formal rules or procedural requirements, but from contracts linking service providers to managers, and managers to government departments, and, unfortunately, the implementation of contract provisions is seldom as straightforward as that of rules and codes. Even the most skillfully worded contract clauses lend themselves to different interpretations, which are often used by defaulters to their advantage. Besides, the potential for interpretation allows for intervention by courts, ombudsmen and arbitration committees. All these factors lead to the diffusion of accountability as well as the dispersion of the authority to hold actors accountable. In addition, the increased interface between public officials and private enterprises in an environment of ineffective accountability has expanded the possibilities of collusion and corruption (Considine and Lewis, 1999). When responsibility cannot be traced back and appropriately sanctioned, accountability mechanisms lose their 'deterrent effect' or their ability to align the behavior of agents with the objectives of principals. It is not, then, very surprising that the public sector has lost much of its legitimacy because of NPM-inspired organizational structures and delivery systems. This may not be so

much a problem in the developed nations, but in the developing world, where even the integrity of judicial systems and quasi-administrative adjudicating forums is suspect, NPM-driven reforms have led to a further deterioration in governance.

Nevertheless, proponents of NPM lay claim to legitimacy in terms of improved public sector efficiency. Admittedly, NPM creates a strong culture of managerial accountability – the NPM variant of administrative accountability. Supported by quantitative techniques of evaluation, managerial accountability focuses on cost-effectiveness, output efficiency, results, and customer satisfaction, rather than institutional processes and formal procedures. But whether this type of legitimacy can be considered a substitute for the 'moral legitimacy' of the public sector remains questionable. It is not easy to reject the argument that the public sector cannot focus on efficiency alone, for public sector performance and outcomes must also be evaluated against core public sector values such as justice, fairness, and equity (Van Thiel and Leeuw, 2002), and an unqualified focus on quantification will always have the inherent danger of compromising public sector concerns for probity, traditional public sector values, and procedural transparency (Considine and Painter, 1997).

In some cases, NPM practices have also compromised the legitimacy derived from a neutrally competent bureaucracy. As noted earlier, although the politics–administration dichotomy was largely accepted as fiction even in the conventional public sector paradigm, the democratic accountability of the bureaucracy to citizens through their representatives in legislatures was believed to legitimize its position in a democracy (Bevir, 2006). More significantly, an absence of the politics–administration dichotomy did not mean that bureaucracies were also politically aligned: the role of bureaucracy in policy-making was always expected to be politically neutral and based on professional expertise. NPM-instigated reforms have, however, altered this legitimizing framework. Even though the new practices attempt to revive the politics–administration dichotomy as a theoretical foundation by assigning the steering part to politics and the rowing part to management (Osborne and Gaebler, 1992), they dispense with the ideal of bureaucratic neutrality, at least in the case of the upper echelons of the public services. Influenced by the theories of political control of bureaucracy,[12] NPM-inspired governments have attempted, not infrequently, to make bureaucracies more acquiescent by appointing politically selected heads of departments from career civil servants or even inducting them from the private sector. Margaret Thatcher, for instance, would pick senior civil servants on the basis of their ideological inclinations rather than their loyalty to the British norm of neutrality (Kingdom, 2000). Similar policies were adopted with respect to senior civil servants in a number of other Western democracies, including Australia and New Zealand (Boston et al., 1996; Laffin, 1996; O'Brian and Fairbrother, 2000).

Particularly problematic is NPM's vague assumption that the customer represents the citizen – a notion that is often evoked to legitimize NPM-infused public sector orientations. Suchman (1995: 578) classifies this form of narrow 'pragmatic legitimacy' as an 'exchange legitimacy' grounded in the self-interest of a particular group of beneficiaries. The customer focus in the public sector is useful to the extent that it provides incentives to public sector agencies to improve the quality of their services for clients, but customers cannot be equated with citizens, for citizens are the owners (Frederickson, 1992). This distinction has a crucial bearing on the question of public sector legitimacy. The final consumers of public policy and provision are not the clients of a public organization who derive only private value at the receiving end: it is the citizens through their representatives in government (Alford, 2002; Moore, 1995). It is the citizens who are the arbiters of the public value created by the public sector and decide what is valuable enough to be produced through this sector (Alford, 2002;

Moore, 1995). And it is the public value of public policies and programs, as determined by citizens, which is ultimately the source of public sector legitimacy, not the private value that these policies and programs may have for customers or direct beneficiaries. Both values will often move in the same direction, but it is not uncommon for the self-interest of a select group of customers of a public sector agency to diverge from considerations of the common good as assessed by citizens. In the latter eventuality, pragmatic legitimacy emanating from the customer can only detract from the legitimacy derived from considerations of the common good.

Thus, the only real contribution to public sector legitimacy of the NPM-generated set of family traits in contemporary governance structures appears to be the potential of the new practices to improve public sector performance by providing managerial and political accountability holders with some additional efficiency-gauging tools, and by enabling them, perhaps, to use the findings to improve outputs, decisions, and policies, or to develop better incentives to maintain or improve efficiency levels.

THE EFFECT OF NETWORKS

The new public management's approach to traditional public sector values has been viewed as a serious flaw by many an academic, politician, bureaucrat, and citizen alike, and a remedy appears to have been sought more recently in governance through networks structured upon the interdependence, cooperation, and reciprocal trust between an array of state and civil society actors (Considine, 2005). Network governance suggests a form of state coordination based upon pluricentric steering, which has expanded horizontal accountability even beyond enterprise governance, and has also rendered it much more complex. In the world of new governance, the public official is required both to fulfill the formal mandate of his office and to transcend the conventional public sector hierarchies and structures to forge cooperative, collaborative, and quasi-market arrangements with other state and non-state actors (Considine, 2002a, 2005). As the network of operators expands, so do the intricacies of the accountability relationships. In a framework of multidimensional agency power, accountability cannot be understood simply as compliance with rules and procedures, or as following a chain of hierarchical authority, or even as operating within a set of horizontal linkages. It is now more aptly understood in terms of navigational competence – or the appropriate utilization of authority to traverse across a vast domain of multiple relationships and multifaceted structures in the quest for the most advantageous route to achieving objectives (Considine, 2002a, 2005). Where the NPM model dismissed the neutral bureaucrat in favor of the entrepreneurial one, network governance requires a mediating and facilitating bureaucracy (Sørensen, 2002).

Commentators like Box (2002) suggest that the new role of bureaucracies as facilitators of collaborative action may be more legitimate than their traditional role structured within the notion of democratic accountability. While this might be true in some ways, common purposes as well as reliable accountability mechanisms are prerequisites for successful cooperation even in networks (Van Dijk and Winters-van Beek, 2009). And the assortment of vertical and horizontal relationships that networks produce can, in fact, make objectives ambiguous and render questionable the relevance of agency-based accountability (Considine, 2002a, 2005). To some extent, public sector accountability has always been multilayered, with actors being accountable within hierarchical chains of command, or before legislative committees and lateral legal or quasi-legal establishments, and even directly to the public. But until recently, the channels of accountability could be understood within the parameters of a single ministry or public organization's jurisdiction, where actors had

clear areas of responsibility and obligation. Entrepreneurial and network governance have, however, made organizational boundaries irrelevant in an intricate web of accountability, which is itself plagued with gaps and inconsistencies (Considine, 2002a, 2005). The diffused identities of public, private, and civil society actors and their overlapping mandates across loosely organized networks create potential for both confusion in, and evasion of, accountability linkages. It may not be possible to identify defaulting state actors, while in the case of private and third-sector actors an additional handicap may be the lack of accountability tools. Rhodes' (1997:5) lamentation that '[s]elf-steering interorganizational policy networks confound mechanisms of democratic accountability focused on individuals and institutions', therefore, comes as no surprise.

To complicate matters even more, supranational actors – for instance, the European Commission in the case of the European Union and institutions like the World Bank, International Monetary Fund (IMF) and several others in the case of the developing world – may become part of networks too. Such inclusion, as Van Kersbergen and Van Waarden (2004) suggest, may not only have an adverse impact on the ownership of policy objectives by national actors but also may further warp the framework of accountability and legitimacy. For instance, how far can ministers (or even public servants), as the same authors question, be held responsible for decisions flowing down from supranational authorities, and how far can they be answerable for actions taken by networks that often lie beyond their direct jurisdictions and which may comprise more private and civil society actors than public functionaries?

However, it is not that network accountability will necessarily be ineffective. Rather, it becomes a question of approach. Whereas in traditional governance, accountability can be seen as a legal strategy driven by compliance, and in enterprise governance as an economic strategy motivated by performance, in network governance it is a cultural strategy, or a matter of organizational convergence based on core public sector values (Considine, 2002a, 2005). Furthermore, although network governance may not be able to ground its legitimacy as much in accountability as traditional public sector structures do, it may still derive substantial legitimacy from its ability to 'join-up' and harmonize the objectives of several different actors: various levels of government; citizen, community, and civil society interests; private for-profit and not-for-profit organizations; and many other contributors. The caveat, however, is that the question of mandate and responsibility must be retained in the public domain (Considine, 2002a, 2005). Interestingly, in certain cases, even the inclusion of supranational actors can enhance public sector legitimacy. For instance, in aid-recipient countries, citizens often mistrust public officials with the grassroots utilization of aid. But when programs are implemented through networks that include donor and civil society representatives, issues of public confidence and trust tend to become much less serious.

From a related perspective, networks can also be viewed as the practical manifestation of participatory or deliberative democracy in governance structures, where the direct involvement of citizens and community organizations in networks – with public action becoming grounded in their participation and trust – can potentially enhance public sector legitimacy (Chambers, 2003; Papadopoulos, 2000; Skogstad, 2003). But then, even though a claim to legitimacy like this would appear to have very strong theoretical underpinnings, in practice it may be less inspirational. For example, as Häikiö's (2007) Finnish case study shows, citizens involved in networks may not always be motivated by considerations of the common good, but by their own personal interests. The possibility of élite or interest group capture, or the exclusion of the less-organized segments of society, or even the inclusion of unrepresentative and unaccountable groups, cannot be eliminated from networks either (Skogstad, 2003). Not only this, the new

governance forms have also created rivalry between legislative bodies, subnational government units, semipublic institutions, and networks over questions of representation, legitimacy, and authority (Sørensen, 2002). These rivalries, combined with a less-effective framework of institutional accountability and weaker formal checks on the exercise of authority brought about by entrepreneurial and network governance (Van Kersbergen and Van Waarden, 2004), have evidently indented overall public sector legitimacy.

THE WAY FORWARD

The paradigm of public sector legitimacy has changed, perhaps permanently, and in the process the conventional theoretical and systemic underpinnings of legitimacy have also been affected. The greatest challenge appears to have come from the unprecedented spread of accountability relationships along the horizontal axis of governance that are not only in themselves weak but also have, in many ways, disrupted the traditional vertical channels of accountability. It is obviously retrogressive to lament the weakening control of a legislature, prerogative of a minister, or authority of a civil servant, in upholding the public interest. Rather, it is now essential to accept and to understand the new dynamism of public sector governance and to devise structures and processes that strengthen its legitimacy. On one hand, the traditional sources of legitimacy, particularly accountability, need to be constantly bolstered in the rapidly evolving governance context, and on the other hand, as opportunities unfold, new sources of legitimacy will have to be incorporated. There can, of course, be no simple or standard answers, and the response of governments to emerging dilemmas will derive from both their historically embedded traditions and their particular governance traits.

Feedback and the learning experience of governments will, however, play the pivotal role in this process of restructuring and alignment. In organization theory, learning refers to the process through which systems absorb new information, and innovatively enhance their ability to adjust their activities to core values. Argyris and Schon's (1996) concept of double-loop learning is crucial for understanding this process. In this conceptualization, organizational systems learn both by understanding how to return to stability and by modifying the conditions of the state of stability itself in accordance with new information about their environment. The creative change remains legitimate as long as it incorporates core values and agreed principles, even where the action cannot itself be predicted specifically (Considine, 2005). Applying this understanding to the vertical and horizontal dimensions of accountability, simple feedback in terms of single-loop learning, yielding only correction of errors, will clearly not suffice. Network arrangements and NPM-inspired reforms have imposed multi-level complexity on governance structures, entailing a double-loop learning process. Consequently, accountability becomes the most important domain in the new governance paradigm, and it follows discursively, that to retain public sector legitimacy, definitions of accountability will have to be extended to incorporate the nature and extent of the double-loop or improvisation. If NPM and network governance have created shared mandates for institutions, and if governance now comprises not just public and quasi-public organizations but also their private and civil society appendages, then a cultural framework of obligations must also accompany the traditional chain of accountability. This would reflect the recognition of other actors in governance as co-sharers in a wider agency right, obligation or accountability for public sector intervention or provision (Considine, 2005). In fact, when accountability involves a multiplicity of actors and several pathways, it becomes more relevant to conceive of it as a 'chain of elements' that determines the responsiveness of individual and organizational actors to both functional and ethical standards. In this

context, we would need to concentrate on the following elements in the chain of accountability – subject again to the peculiarities of the evolving governance patterns of states, their traditions, and the dilemmas they confront – to create greater legitimacy for the public sector (Considine, 2005):

- *Assignability of goals and standards:* governments need to clearly identify the purpose and objective of public policies, programs, and interventions while devising them, including the nomination of the targeted beneficiaries.
- *Transparency of results:* programs and interventions must be open to scrutiny, and results publicized earnestly, which is necessary to enable citizens, legislatures, and courts to verify that governments are acting in accordance with their commitments and mandates, including taking responsibility for the actions of private and civil society actors associated with such public interventions.
- *Knowability of consequences:* unless it is possible for reasonable observers to see the link between program and outcome, it may not be possible to assign responsibility to any of the actors involved in the program for any fault in the performance of their functions.
- *Reviewability by supervisors and courts:* any citizen, client, or any individual or organization affected by a public intervention must be permitted to seek redress from some administrative or legal forum that is independent of the agencies formulating and implementing the intervention.
- *Answerability for failure:* defaulting individuals or organizations need to be held accountable and sanctioned in proportion to their responsibility, particularly where knowable errors or flaws lead to adverse outcomes, otherwise accountability may lose both its spirit and 'deterrent effect'; the process of enquiry and sanction must itself be transparent and open to scrutiny.
- *Revisability of programs:* for effective public sector accountability, it is also necessary that policies, programs, and interventions be open to revision, modification, and even rollback where they do not meet the accountability requirement.

The chain of elements will, of course, need to be given new formations and linkages in response to emerging public sector environments.

The vertical structure of accountability can be bolstered, for instance, by expanding the role of parliamentary committees and state auditors, and horizontal accountability can be improved by strengthening the supervisory role of networks' centers. However, given the diversity and intricacy in the horizontal spread of the new governance, improving horizontal accountability will be the more daunting task. The chains of horizontal accountability for market or competitive environments will also need to be different from those developed for collaborative and cooperative networks (Considine, 2005). Nevertheless, in both cases, effective rules, procedures, and structures will need to be devised to keep in the public domain the questions of mandate, responsibility, and the obligation to promote the public interest, or otherwise networks will, as Rhodes (2000: 61) asserts, 'resist government steering, develop their own policies and mould their environments.'

Hirst (2000: 29) proposes the idea of 'associative self-governance' structured on service provision through democratically organized, government funded and supervised, competitive, self-governing voluntary associations in which members have both voice and the right to exit and join other similar associations. According to Hirst (2000), since these organizations would be democratically constituted, and their governing bodies democratically elected, they would possess democratic legitimacy. This variant of network governance is appealing since it retains the questions of public interest and accountability (because of the public funding and supervision) ultimately in the public domain. But the idea may have several practical hurdles. For one, not all members will have equal voice and also it may not always be possible to prevent élite or pressure group capture of associations or avoid discord arising from vested interests. Furthermore, too much competition may fragment governance even more, apart from raising service costs because of small-scale operations. Similarly, even though members' exit option may

legitimize associations democratically, it may create too much uncertainty for associations to plan and invest, which are vital factors in efficient service provision. Nevertheless, the idea of associative governance yields important lessons for network governance. For instance, the least which networks can do to improve their legitimacy is to expand the opportunities for citizen participation and political debate in networks beyond élites and sub-élites (Bingham et al., 2005). Greater participation can, of course, lead to organizational indecisiveness (Skogstad, 2003), but it may be possible to counterbalance it through effective procedures of coordination, engagement, negotiation, and consensual decision-making.

Under the new modes of governance, the role of bureaucracies (large segments of which are employed on contract) as entrepreneurs, facilitators, coordinators, and mediators has increased along with the autonomy of the organizational structures in which they work, but, simultaneously, their role has also become less distinguishable from the contributions of the private and civil society actors operating in their domains (Sørensen, 2002). Since this poses serious challenges to accountability, particularly in its horizontal dimension, the new chains of accountability will need to incorporate special tools to hold bureaucracies accountable and to link them back to citizens, particularly for the responsibility to uphold the core public sector values and promote the common good. This may, nevertheless, need to be done without re-regulation or increasing bureaucratic discretion.

Given the nature of the public sector and its requirement to protect and promote the cardinal public sector values, it is unlikely that the horizontal dimension of governance will replace its vertical dimension. Output-based performance and cost-effectiveness can enhance public sector legitimacy, but not when they create accountability deficits or compromise public sector values. As Underhill (2003: 779–80) argues '[i]f market pressures bring democratically unacceptable results, they must be rethought and redesigned ... the *outcome* must be perceived as legitimate [emphasis original].' The crux of public sector legitimacy, then, is that market or network outcomes cannot be legitimate unless they are also democratically acceptable. In the multi-level and multi-domain governance structures what is, therefore, required is that one dimension of governance should serve as a check and balance for the other (Van Kersbergen and Van Waarden, 2004).

Furthermore, governance domains which deal with the regulation of the private sector or service provision through privatized state-owned (former) providers, and which in several instances have now become oligopolies or conglomerates, will need more than competition-enhancing tools to maintain a structure of checks and balances to protect the public interest (Van Kersbergen and Van Waarden, 2004). Greater procedural transparency and accountability will also be required (Majone, 1999). A structure of corporate governance can be considered legitimate when it leads not only to efficiency in production, but also to equity in distribution (Judge et al., 2008). If this standard of legitimacy is to be attained, the new tools will need to be more stringent than those currently viewed as permissible in the new governance paradigm. An even more strict approach will have to be adopted towards providers of financial services, particularly those with significant market power. The financial crisis in 2008 and the accompanying global recession reflect, in many ways, a failure of public accountability. The debacle has also clearly shown that the system of self-regulation or regulation through publically created independent agencies has much to be desired, and that the whole structure needs to be made more responsive to public sector values. Re-emphasizing professional ethics and an appeal to norms and morals, as Van Kersbergen and Van Waarden (2004) suggest, may also serve to improve the behavior of actors, and thereby enhance public sector legitimacy.

CONCLUSION

The state cannot retract from the cardinal principles of social justice, fairness, and equity; nor can it abdicate its responsibilities to work for the common good and to safeguard the public interest. For as long as this is true, any legitimate public sector governance structure must facilitate the realization of these ends. In the classical public sector paradigm, these objectives were understood to be achieved *inter alia* through representation, democratic accountability to citizens, and formal rules and codes of procedure. These underpinnings of public sector legitimacy have, however, been weakened over the recent decades by globalization, increased social complexity, and by some of the theories and practices of the new modes of governance. Nevertheless, it is not inevitable that the regard for output-based performance, or cost-efficiency, must also compromise considerations of the common good or devalue the ideal of social justice. Many tools offered by NPM and network structures can themselves be used to enhance the efficiency with which the traditional public sector objectives are achieved. After all, the Clinton–Blair 'third way' was largely structured upon these considerations: multi-agency collaboration; a 'new mixed economy' within the public sector; and 'utilizing the dynamism of markets but with the public interest in mind' (Giddens, 1998: 99–100).

In fact, it all appears to come down to a question of citizens' aspirations and how faithfully these hopes can be understood, aggregated, and implemented. Strengthening the legitimacy of the state involves renewed attention to the responsiveness of public institutions and their effectiveness in representing not only individual stakeholder demands but also some articulated narrative of the shared future of all those being represented. Each society will express this shared future differently. New policy input and implementation structures like markets and networks will continue to evolve in response to stakeholder pressures for change.

The need, from the perspective of legitimacy, is to recognize and accept such new developments and to devise formal arrangements to align them with core public sector values and structures. And in those cases where efficiency is a danger to legitimacy, a public discourse and clear institutional rules for protecting the reasonable aspirations of citizens will prove critical.

NOTES

1 For analyses of how contemporary governance structures vary across states see, for instance, Pollitt and Bouckaert (2004) and *Public Administration*, 2003, Volume 81, Issue 1.

2 Suchman's (1995: 574) definition of legitimacy is one of the more cited definitions in the literature.

3 Absorbed into political science from economic theory.

4 Such situations, though infrequent, may arise for instance when representatives, by virtue of their position, have access to information that citizens do not have.

5 As Manin (1995: 209–14, cited in Maravell, 1999: 156) notes, two binding mechanisms – imperative mandates and revocable representations – were discontinued at the end of the eighteenth century.

6 However, some theorists consider the accountability function performed by elections to be ineffective. For instance, Cheibub and Przeworski (1999) do not find any association between the economic performance of governments and subsequent electoral outcomes.

7 In terms of the principal–agent construct, the legislature is the principal and the cabinet is the agent.

8 Ministers are also responsible to the parliament in their individual capacities, which tends to make the accountability chain a little more direct.

9 In this case, the cabinet is the principal and the bureaucracy is the agent.

10 When moved by the government, the motion is referred to as a motion of 'confidence', and when moved by the opposition, it is referred to as a motion of 'no confidence'.

11 See, for instance, Rhodes (1994).

12 These theories emanated from the theories of public choice, which argue that bureaucracies are self-aggrandizing and motivated by selfish interests, rather than the public interest.

REFERENCES

Alford, J. (2002) 'Defining the Client in the Public Sector: A Social-Exchange Perspective', *Public Administration Review* 62(3): 337–46.

Argyris, Chris and Schon, Donald A. (1996) *Organizational Learning II: Theory, Method, and Practice*. Reading, MA: Addison-Wesley.

Beckett, J. (2000) 'The "Government Should Run Like a Business" mantra', *American Review of Public Administration* 30(2): 185–204.

Behn, R.D. (1995) 'The Big Questions of Public Management', *Public Administration Review* 55(4): 313–24.

Behn, Robert D. (2001) *Rethinking Democratic Accountability*. Washington, DC: Brookings Institution Press.

Bevir, M. (2006) 'Democratic Governance: Systems and Radical Perspectives', *Public Administration Review* 66(3): 426–36.

Bevir, Mark and Rhodes, Roderick A.W. (2006a) *Governance Stories*. New York: Routledge.

Bevir, M. and Rhodes, R.A.W. (2006b) 'The Life, Death and Resurrection of British Governance', *Australian Journal of Public Administration* 65(2): 59–69.

Bingham, L.B., Nabatchi, T. and O'Leary, R. (2005) 'The New Governance: Practices and Processes for Stakeholder and Citizen Participation in the Work of Government', *Public Administration Review* 65(5): 547–58.

Boston, Jonathan, Martin, John, Pallot, June and Walsh, Pat (1996) *Public Management: The New Zealand Model*. Auckland: Oxford University Press.

Box, R.C. (2002) 'Pragmatic Discourse and Administrative Legitimacy', *American Review of Public Administration* 32(1): 20–39.

Buchanan, A. and Keohane, R.O. (2006) 'The Legitimacy of Global Governance Institutions', *Ethics and International Affairs* 20(4): 405–37.

Chambers, S. (2003) 'Deliberative Democratic Theory', *Annual Review of Political Science* 6(1): 307–26.

Cheibub, José A. and Przeworski, Adam (1999) 'Democracy, Elections, and Accountability for Economic Outcomes', in A. Przeworski, S. Carol Stokes and B. Manin (eds), *Democracy, Accountability, and Representation*. Cambridge: Cambridge University Press; pp. 222–49.

Christensen, T. and Lægreid, P. (2001) 'New Public Management: The Effects of Contractualism and Devolution on Political Control', *Public Management Review* 3(1): 73–94.

Ciborra, Claudio U. (1996) *Teams, Markets, and Systems: Business Innovation and Information Technology*. Cambridge: Cambridge University Press.

Considine, M. (2002a) 'The End of the Line? Accountable Governance in the Age of Networks, Partnerships, and Joined-up Services', *Governance* 15(1): 21–40.

Considine, Mark (2002b) 'Joined at the Lip? What Does Network Research Tell Us about Governance?' in M. Considine (ed.), *Knowledge Networks and Joined-Up Government: Conference Proceedings*. University of Melbourne, Centre for Public Policy.

Considine, Mark (2005) *Making Public Policy: Institutions, Actors, Strategies*. Cambridge: Polity Press.

Considine, M. and Lewis, J. (1999) 'Governance at Ground Level: The Frontline Bureaucrat in the Age of Markets and Networks', *Public Administration Review* 59(6): 467–80.

Considine, M. and Lewis, J. (2003a) 'Networks and Interactivity: Making Sense of Front-line Governance in the United Kingdom, the Netherlands and Australia', *Journal of European Public Policy* 10(1): 46–58.

Considine, M. and Lewis, J. (2003b) 'Bureaucracy, Network, or Enterprise? Comparing Models of Governance in Australia, Britain, the Netherlands, and New Zealand', *Public Administration Review* 63(2): 131–40.

Considine, M. and Painter, M. (eds) (1997) *Managerialism and Its Critics: The Great Debate*. Melbourne: University of Melbourne Press.

Dunn, Delmer D. (1999) 'Mixing Elected and Nonelected Officials in Democratic Policy Making: Fundamentals of Accountability and Responsibility', in A. Przeworski, S. Carol Stokes and B. Manin (eds), *Democracy, Accountability, and Representation*. Cambridge: Cambridge University Press; pp. 297–325.

Fearon, James D. (1999) 'Electoral Accountability and the Control of Politicians: Selecting Good Types Versus Sanctioning Poor Performance', in A. Przeworski, S. Carol Stokes and B. Manin (eds), *Democracy, Accountability, and Representation*. Cambridge: Cambridge University Press; pp. 55–97.

Ferlie, Ewan, Ashburner, Lynn, Fitzgerald, Louise and Pettigrew, Andrew (1996) *The New Public Management in Action*. Oxford: Oxford University Press.

Frederickson, H.G. (1992) 'Painting Bull's-eyes around Bullet Holes', *Governing Magazine* October.

Giddens, Anthony (1998) *The Third Way: The Renewal of Social Democracy*. Cambridge: Polity Press.

Häikiö, L. (2007) 'Expertise, Representation and the Common Good: Grounds for Legitimacy in the Urban Governance Network', *Urban Studies* 44(11): 2147–62.

Halligan, John (2001) 'Accountability', in C. Aulich, J. Halligan and S. Nutley (eds), *Australian Handbook of Public Sector Management*. Crows Nest, NSW: Allen & Unwin; pp. 174–85.

Hardin, Russell (1996) 'Institutional Morality', in R.E. Goodin (ed.), *The Theory of Institutional Design*. Cambridge: Cambridge University Press; pp. 126–53.

Hedley, T.P. (1998) 'Measuring Public Sector Effectiveness Using Private Sector Methods', *Public Productivity and Management Review* 21(3): 251–8.

Hirst, Paul (2000) 'Democracy and Governance', in J. Pierre (ed.), *Debating Governance*. Oxford: Oxford University Press; pp. 13–35.

Judge, W.Q., Douglas, T.J. and Kutan, A.M. (2008) 'Institutional Antecedents of Corporate Governance Legitimacy', *Journal of Management* 34(4): 765–85.

Kingdom, John (2000) 'Britain', in J.A. Chandler (ed.), *Comparative Public Administration*. New York: Routledge; pp. 14–49.

Laffin, Martin (1996) 'The Bureaucracies Compared: Past and Future Trends', in P. Weller and G. Davis (eds), *New Ideas, Better Government*. St Leonards, NSW: Allen & Unwin; pp. 38–54.

Lane, Jan-Erik (2000) *The Public Sector: Concepts, Models, and Approaches*, 3rd edn. London: Sage. (1st edn, 1993; 2nd edn, 1995)

Laver, Michael and Shepsle, Kenneth A. (1999) 'Government Accountability in Parliamentary Democracy', in A. Przeworski, S. Carol Stokes and B. Manin (eds), *Democracy, Accountability, and Representation*. Cambridge: Cambridge University Press; pp. 279–96.

Majone, G. (1999) 'The Regulatory State and Its Legitimacy Problems', *West European Politics* 22(1): 1–24.

Maravall, José M. (1999) 'Accountability and Manipulation', in A. Przeworski, S. Carol Stokes and B. Manin (eds), *Democracy, Accountability, and Representation*. Cambridge: Cambridge University Press; pp. 154–96.

Maurer, John G. (1971) *Readings in Organization Theory: Open-System Approaches*. New York: Random House.

Moore, M.H. (1994) 'Public Value as the Focus of Strategy', *Australian Journal of Public Administration* 53(3): 296–303.

Moore, Mark H. (1995) *Creating Public Value: Strategic Management in Government*. Cambridge, MA: Harvard University Press.

Nolan, Brendan C. (ed.) (2001) *Public Sector Reform: An International Perspective*. New York: Palgrave.

O'Brian, J. and Fairbrother, P. (2000) 'A Changing Public Sector: Developments at the Commonwealth Level', *Australian Journal of Public Administration* 59(4): 59–66.

Osborne, David and Gaebler, Ted (1992) *Reinventing Government: How the Entrepreneurial Spirit is Transforming the Public Sector*. Reading, MA: Addison-Wesley.

Papadopoulos, Y. (2000) 'Governance, Coordination and Legitimacy in Public Policies', *International Journal of Urban and Regional Research* 24(1): 210–23.

Peters, B.G. (2001) *The Future of Governing*, 2nd edn. Lawrence, KS: University Press of Kansas. (1st edn, 1996)

Pollitt, Christopher and Bouckaert, Geert (2004) *Public Management Reform: A Comparative Analysis*, 2nd edn. Oxford: Oxford University Press. (1st edn, 2000)

Przeworski, A., Stokes, S.C. and Manin B. (eds) (1999) *Democracy, Accountability and Representation*. Cambridge: Cambridge University Press.

Rhodes, R.A.W. (1994) 'The Hollowing Out of the State: The Changing Nature of the Public Service in Britain', *The Political Quarterly* 65(2): 138–51.

Rhodes, Roderick A.W. (1997) *Understanding Governance: Policy Networks, Governance, and Accountability*. Buckingham, Philadelphia: Open University Press.

Rhodes, Roderick A.W. (2000) 'Governance and Public Administration', in J. Pierre (ed.), *Debating Governance*. Oxford: Oxford University Press; pp. 54–90.

Sinclair, A. (1995) 'The Chameleon of Accountability: Forms and Discourses', *Accounting, Organizations and Society* 20(2–3): 219–37.

Skogstad, G. (2003) 'Who Governs? Who Should Govern?: Political Authority and Legitimacy in Canada in the Twenty-first Century', *Canadian Journal of Political Science* 36(5): 955–73.

Sørensen, E. (2002) 'Democratic Theory and Network Governance', *Administrative Theory and Praxis* 24(4): 693–720.

Suchman, M.C. (1995) 'Legitimacy: Strategic and Institutional Approaches', *The Academy of Management Review* 20(3): 571–610.

Underhill, G.R.D. (2003) 'States, Markets and Governance for Emerging Market Economies: Private Interests, the Public Good and the Legitimacy of the Development Process', *International Affairs* 79(4): 755–81.

Van Dijk, Jan and Winters-van Beek, Anneleen (2009) 'The Perspective of Network Government: The Struggle between Hierarchies, Markets and Networks as Modes of Governance in Contemporary Government', in A. Meijer, K. Boersma and P. Wagenaar (eds), *ICTs, Citizens and Governance: After the Hype!* Amsterdam: IOS Press.

Van Kersbergen, K. and Van Waarden, F. (2004) '"Governance" as a Bridge between Disciplines: Cross-disciplinary Inspiration Regarding Shifts in Governance and Problems of Governability, Accountability and Legitimacy', *European Journal of Political Research* 43(2): 143–71.

Van Thiel, S. and Leeuw, F.L. (2002) 'The Performance Paradox in the Public Sector', *Public Performance and Management Review* 25(3): 267–81.

Waldo, Dwight (1948) *The Administrative State: A Study of the Political Theory of American Public Administration*. New York: Roland Press.

Waldo, Dwight (1956). *Perspectives on Administration*. Tuscaloosa, AL: University of Alabama Press.

Walsh, Kieron (1995) *Public Services and Market Mechanisms: Competition, Contracting and the New Public Management*. Houndmills, Basingstoke, UK: Macmillan.

Weatherford, M.S. (1992) 'Measuring Political Legitimacy', *American Political Science Review* 86(1): 149–66.

Weber, Max (1978) *Economy and Society: An Outline of Interpretive Sociology,* edited by G. Roth and C. Wittich. Berkeley, CA: University of California Press.

Wilson, Woodrow (1992[1887]). 'The Study of Administration', reprinted in J.M. Shafritz and A.C. Hyde (eds), *Classics of Public Administration,* 3rd edn. Pacific Grove, California: Brooks/Cole Publishing Company; pp. 11–24. (1st edn, 1978; 2nd edn, 1987).

Zürn, M. (2004) 'Global Governance and Legitimacy Problems', *Government and Opposition* 39(2): 260–87.

25

Collaborative Governance

Lisa Blomgren Bingham

During the final third of the twentieth century, the discourse about both government and conflict evolved. So-called 'wicked problems' such as environmental degradation, urban economic development, and public health all challenged the capacity of a single governmental unit operating in hierarchy. The traditional concept of the policy process entailed a single sovereign actor with legal jurisdiction over a substantive policy arena pursuant to a defined delegation of authority. However, hierarchy's command and control management strategies failed in the face of problems that could not be solved or solved easily by one entity acting alone (Bevir, this volume). Moreover, hierarchy failed entirely as an approach to global and transnational problems, i.e. those that cross the jurisdictional boundaries of nation-states.

These developments have given rise to the concept of governance rather than government. Governance entails activity among multiple actors with potentially overlapping jurisdiction. Fredrickson (1999: 702) observed that public administration is moving 'toward theories of cooperation, networking, governance, and institution building and maintenance' in response to the 'declining relationship between jurisdiction and public management' in a 'fragmented and disarticulated state.'

Kettl (2002a: 159) noted that the forces transforming governance are 'the diffusion of administrative action, the multiplication of administrative partners, and the proliferation of political influence outside government's circles.'

Governance suggests steering rather than top-down directing. In its contemporary usage, it means a process involving resources and strategic, often collaborative, relationships outside a single organization aimed toward achieving a public policy goal. Governance requires that participants use different skills from hierarchy. It requires coordination across multiple organizations and stakeholders from public, private, and non-profit sectors that combine in a network to address a common and shared problem (Bevir, 2006). Kettl (2002a: 163) pointed to the need for improved skills in negotiation and coordination. While understanding the use of hierarchy and authority, public administrators must also manage complex networks, rely more on interpersonal and inter-organizational processes, use information technology and performance management effectively, provide transparency, build human capital in terms of negotiation and coordination skills, provide channels for citizens to participate, and supply bottom-up accountability to the public

(Kettl, 2002a: 169–70). For governance, public managers need skills in negotiation, persuasion, collaboration, and enablement, which include activation, orchestration, and modulation skills (Salamon, 2002: vii).

There are multiple streams of literature that focus on the relationships among government, the public, and stakeholders in governance. The literature on collaboration in governance falls into two general categories:

- collaboration with and among organizations (collaborative public management or network governance, e.g. Agranoff and McGuire, 2003; see generally, O'Leary, Bingham, and Gerard, 2006; for a more detailed discussion, see McGuire, this volume)
- collaboration with the public (public participation, public involvement, and civic engagement, see generally, Roberts, 2008).

The concept of a network refers to more players than simply two parties in a bilateral contract. While contracting out work creates a formal legal relationship (for a more detailed discussion, see Cohen, this volume), this relationship is often absent in networks. Nevertheless, the notion of contract as a metaphor is appropriate; governance entails the blurring of public and private through the use of consensual agreements among network members. Governance may also involve the public through civic engagement and participatory decision-making or 'participatory governance,' which is the active involvement of citizens in government decision-making and may include deliberative democracy (for a more detailed discussion, see McLaverty, this volume).

The term 'collaborative governance' encompasses all these phenomena: forums for public deliberation, community problem-solving, and multi-stakeholder dispute resolution (Bingham, 2009, from which much of this discussion is drawn; Henton, Melville, Amsler, and Koppell, 2005). What distinguishes it from governance more generally is a focus on the process through which actors achieve policy goals in partnership with the public and stakeholders. Ansell and Gash (2008: 545) define collaborative governance as 'a type of governance in which public and private actors work collectively in distinctive ways, using particular processes, to establish laws and rules for the provision of public goods.' They argue that collaborative governance includes formal arrangements that imply organization and structure (Ansell and Gash, 2008: 546).

For the purposes of this chapter, collaborative governance includes collaboration with the broadest definition of partners within and outside government, meaning the general public, national, state, regional, and local government agencies, tribes, non-profit organizations, voluntary associations and other manifestations of civil society, business, and other non-governmental stakeholders.

Secondly, it includes collaboration across the broadest scope of government work in the policy process, not only establishing laws and rules but also practices for management and implementation. For this purpose, the phrase 'policy process' is defined as any action in developing, implementing, or enforcing public policy, including but not limited to identifying and defining a public policy issue, defining the options for a new policy framework, expanding the range of options, identifying approaches for addressing an issue, setting priorities among approaches, selecting from among the priorities, enacting law in the legislative branch, developing and adopting regulations in the executive branch, implementing solutions, project management, program evaluation, enforcing law and regulations through agency adjudication, and enforcing law and regulations through litigation in the judicial branch.

Thirdly, it includes collaboration through any method, model, or process that is deliberative and consensual as distinguished from adversarial or adjudicative, including but not limited to dialogue, public deliberation, deliberative democracy, public consultation, multi-stakeholder collaboration, collaborative public management, consensus-building, negotiation, and dispute resolution. Fourthly, it includes both in-person and online methods for collaboration.

Collaborative governance entails shared, negotiated, and deliberative consultation and decision-making. A principle of collaborative, or shared, governance is that expert policy analysts do not have exclusive or even the necessary information about public values and knowledge. Collaborative governance may occur at any stage of the policy process.

For the most part, the public administration literature does not look comprehensively across the policy continuum at the processes for collaboration (Bingham, Nabatchi, and O'Leary, 2005). More specifically, there is little work on the emergence of dispute resolution or deliberative democracy as social phenomena that relate to the evolution of collaborative governance, nor is there a satisfying synthesis of the diverse literatures examining its various forms or aspects (Bingham and O'Leary, 2006). We can advance our understanding of collaborative governance by examining the relationship among its various manifestations from the standpoint of their use in the policy process.

GOVERNANCE AND THE POLICY PROCESS

The evolution toward governance has begun to change the policy process at every jurisdictional level, whether local, regional, state, national, transnational, or global. At its most general, the policy process consists of stages in a dynamic system across a division among legislative, executive, and judicial powers. It is arbitrary to begin at any one point because these powers, or branches of government, react to each other continuously. For example, a national court may decide a controversial case that prompts legislation. The legislature may adopt a law that ends up in court. The executive branch, acting through administrative agencies, takes both quasi-legislative and quasi-judicial action. The legislative

branch may disagree with how the executive branch interprets and implements law; it may respond with new legislation. However, it is conventional to begin with identifying a policy problem in the legislative arena as part of a linear account.

Conflict can and will occur throughout the policy process. One helpful metaphor is the flowing stream. Upstream generally involves making policy through more legislative or quasi-legislative activity; midstream involves implementing, managing, and evaluating policy; and downstream involves enforcing policy through quasi-judicial or judicial action.

While the public sector has grappled with the evolution from government to governance, civil society has experienced parallel social phenomena of groups seeking more public and stakeholder voice. The processes for collaboration in governance provide opportunities for public and stakeholder voice.

Generally, processes upstream involve broader public participation among a larger number of people with less control over the ultimate decision or outcome; these may entail dialogue and deliberation. Midstream processes may entail both collaborative public management and public policy dispute resolution. These involve targeted stakeholder groups in more focused consultation with somewhat more influence on the outcome.

Downstream generally entails conflict resolution (alternative or appropriate dispute resolution, or ADR). It involves fewer participants and generally those with a legally cognizable stake in the outcome and shared decision-making authority.

However, there are exceptions at every stage of the policy continuum; moreover, practitioners are increasingly recognizing that it is important to design a sequence of processes to address a given policy issue across the continuum. For simplicity, the chapter will address the processes from upstream to downstream.

UPSTREAM IN THE POLICY PROCESS: DELIBERATIVE AND PARTICIPATORY DEMOCRACY

Upstream in the policy process includes legislative or quasi-legislative action up to the point of implementation. In a traditional conception of government instead of governance, a legislative body enacts legislation with limited public participation through, for example, committee testimony, written comment, or participants speaking briefly at public hearings. After the legislature acts, agencies engage in quasi-legislative activity aimed at filling in the details and establishing general standards of behavior for prospective or future application. Traditionally, agencies offer opportunities for public participation through notice and comment. Increasingly, agencies use focus groups and round tables. Most recently, they provide online means to comment or participate.

New forms of participation have included various models of dialogue, deliberation, and e-democracy. As a movement, deliberative democracy emerged during the past decade (for reviews, see Bohman and Rehg, 1997; Fung and Wright, 2003; Macedo, 1999). It is sufficiently new that there is no consensus about what to name it: terms include participatory governance (Fung and Wright, 2003), deliberation and dialogue (Forester, 1999), deliberative democracy (Gastil and Levine, 2005), and more broadly, collaborative governance (Freeman, 1997). This movement emerged in response to perceived failings in representative democracy with respect to conflict over public policy. Various manifestations of civil society (the non-profit and voluntary sector and citizen groups) pressed for more public participation. The movement sought more public deliberation, dialogue, and shared decision-making in governance to address conflict at the broader level of public policy. Recently, its advocates have argued government should take advantage of new technologies for human communication, including e-democracy and e-government (Noveck, 2009).

Central to each are notions of dialogue as contrasted with traditional adversarial processes of debate. In dialogue, participants engage in a reasoned exchange of viewpoints in an atmosphere of mutual respect and civility, in a neutral space or forum, with an effort to reach a better mutual understanding and sometimes even consensus. In debate, participants listen in an effort to identify weaknesses in the argument and score points in an effective counterargument. In dialogue, participants listen in an effort to better understand the other's viewpoint and identify questions or areas of confusion to probe for a deeper understanding. Deliberation is the thoughtful consideration of information, views, and ideas.

The underlying theory is that these processes promote a more civil public discourse, more collaborative policymaking among citizens, and narrow the adversarial policy gap. However, models of dialogue and deliberation vary across several dimensions. Professor Archon Fung (2006) suggests that dimensions include participants, authority, and modes of communication. The categories of participants include the diffuse public sphere, open self-selection, open targeted recruiting, random selection, lay stakeholders, professional stakeholders, elected representatives, and expert administrators. He describes types of authority as including personal benefits, communicative influence, advise and consult, co-governance, and direct authority. He identifies six modes of communication and decision-processes: participants listen as spectators, express preferences, develop preferences, aggregate and bargain, deliberate and negotiate, and deploy technique and expertise. Using these three dimensions, Professor Fung creates a 'democracy cube,' on which he maps different processes. There are a variety of models for dialogue and deliberation, including public conversations, deliberative town meeting forums, choice work dialogues, national issues forums, participatory budgeting, citizen juries, study circles, collaborative policymaking, and deliberative polling (Fishkin, 2009; see generally, Gastil and Levine, 2005).

Commentators have suggested that the quality of processes depends upon how well they satisfy three criteria: inclusiveness, deliberativeness, and influence (Carson and Hartz-Karp, 2005). Inclusiveness is defined as getting a broadly representative portion of the relevant community to participate; deliberativeness has to do with the quality of dialogue, information exchanged, and civility of the conversation among participants and decision-makers; and influence has to do with the impact of deliberation on policy and decision-making.

However, research on the outcomes of various models or their impact on policy is relatively new (for a more detailed examination of representative models and research on them, see McLaverty, this volume). Given its complexity, environmental governance has attracted more research (Durant, Fiorino and O'Leary, 2004). A recent meta-analysis found that, on average, best practices in public participation are associated with better results in terms of quality, legitimacy, and capacity (National Research Council, 2008: 75–93). However, this study defined public participation to include three different classes of agency activities: information exchange, involvement, and engagement (National Research Council, 2008: 113). While information exchange and involvement addressed conventional public comment and deliberative democratic processes, respectively, engagement included both collaborative public management and dispute resolution (National Research Council, 2008: 113; similarly, see Beierle and Cayford, 2002: 72 in distinguishing between fact finding or visioning and implementation; Thomas, 1995, 163–7). Not surprisingly given this broad range of process designs, researchers examining the experimental and quasi-experimental literature found variation along a number of dimensions, including breadth in terms of who is involved, timing in how early in the decision process the public participates, intensity in terms of the amount of time and effort, and influence over the ultimate decision (Beierle and Cayford, 2002: 76).

The open research issue is the relation of institutional design to outcome (see generally, Hajer and Wagenaar 2003; Renn, Webler, and Wiedemann 1995). A review of scholarship in environmental conflict resolution suggested possible criteria for assessing success upstream in dialogue and deliberation (Bingham, Fairman, Fiorino, and O'Leary, 2003). Indicators of process quality included socioeconomic representativeness, consultation and/or outreach with wider public, diversity of participants and views represented, integration of concerns, and information exchange (Bingham et al., 2003: 332–3). Indicators of outcome included incorporating public values, improving decision quality, resolving conflict, building trust, educating the public, mutual learning, effectiveness, efficiency and equity, cost avoidance, project/decision acceptability as legitimate, mutual respect, social capital, increased overall knowledge, increased individual stakeholder knowledge, identifying threats, goals, and management actions, adequacy of plan to achieve goals, and certainty of agreement on implementation (Bingham et al., 2003: 332–3).

MIDSTREAM IN THE POLICY PROCESS: COLLABORATIVE PUBLIC OR NETWORK MANAGEMENT

Midstream in the policy process, collaboration occurs largely in the executive branch, and includes rulemaking, implementation, program management and development, and program evaluation. These functions are both quasi-legislative and quasi-judicial. In this part of the continuum, there is wide variation in processes, including a mix of participatory governance, collaborative public management, and multi-party public policy dispute resolution or consensus-building processes. There is no strict boundary between upstream and midstream. Somewhere between the legislative act of adopting policy and the quasi-legislative work of implementing it, there is a shift from deliberation to agreement-seeking processes.

In general, there are independent literatures on collaborative public management (Agranoff and McGuire, 2003) and multi-party public policy dispute resolution (Carpenter and Kennedy, 1988; Gray, 1991; Susskind, McKearnan and Larmer, 1999). Moreover, these families of collaborative governance may differ in structure, context, and design on a number of dimensions, including jurisdictional boundaries, organizational boundaries, homogeneous or diverse partners, shared or different goals, voluntary or mandatory settings, legal mandates, the use of professional facilitators or neutrals, and the use of public participation or engagement (Bingham and O'Leary, 2008).

Collaborative public management

Public administration scholars distinguish among cooperation, coordination, and collaboration (Bryson and Crosby, 2008: 55–7). Cooperation is the absence of conflict; it is less formal, involves sharing information, may be short term, and presents little risk. Coordination is the orchestration of people toward a particular goal; it involves more formal and longer-term interaction, increased risk, and shared rewards. Collaboration, however, suggests a closer relationship; it suggests that participants 'co-labor.' It entails a new structure, shared resources, defined relationships, and communication. Collaboration also involves creating, enhancing, and building on social and organizational capital in pursuit of shared purposes. It is a dynamic evolving relationship.

The study of collaborative public management is an outgrowth of work in intergovernmental relations, privatization, devolution, and non-profit management (O'Leary, Gazley, McGuire and Bingham, 2009). It represents a shift in perspective; instead of viewing relations from the eyes of a single public manager working in hierarchy or engaged in a linear series of contractual and partnership arrangements, scholars of collaborative public management view the actors

from a distance in relation to each other (Bingham and O'Leary, 2008; O'Leary and Bingham, 2009).

In a comprehensive review of the literature, Gazley (2008) predicts that managers' motivation for intersectoral collaboration will vary as a function of sectoral-level, group-level, and individual-level variables. Sectoral-level variables include formal or informal structures, political constraints or incentives, and the independence of sectors. Social network or partnership variables include professional experience, training, or education, volunteerism, and collaborative experience. Institution or community variables include size or capacity, poverty or rural rate, shared funding, efficiency incentives, environmental uncertainty, regulatory constraints or incentives, and organizational age. Service sector or policy network variables include differences in constraints, incentives, norms, and practices by network or service sector. Individual variables include gender, ideology, and individual incentives or advantages. Thomson and Perry (2006) examined the process of collaboration. They found that antecedents of collaboration include high levels of interdependence, the need for resources and risk sharing, resource scarcity, a previous history of efforts to collaborate, a situation in which each partner has resources that the other partners need, and complex issues (Thomson and Perry 2006: 21). They argue that the process of collaboration is a function of five dimensions: two structural dimensions of governance and administration; organizational autonomy; and two social capital dimensions of mutuality and norms (Thomson and Perry 2006: 24).

To illustrate these variations, an agency may use collaboration in managing a watershed that crosses jurisdictional boundaries of federal, state, regional, local, and tribal governments (Leach, 2006). Concerned stakeholders may include multiple units and levels of government (local, county, state, and federal), various representatives from civil society such as non-profit environmental organizations, citizen groups representing users of natural resources, and the private sector. The agency may need to implement state and federal law through a permit for a particular land use or development in the watershed. Permitting or licensing sets future standards and involves defined actors with a specific history of past behaviors (emitting pollutants).

Collaboration occurs within and across organizations. A single organization may have multiple districts, units, or offices that need to collaborate, such as extension offices of a university with multiple campuses. Collaboration occurs within and across sectors. It includes cooperative management bodies, and other partnership arrangements. There are networks of agencies; for example, federal agencies coordinate on environmental conflict resolution and across the government on ADR. It also occurs between both homogeneous and diverse partners. Environmental groups may form a coalition among themselves; yet in a collaborative effort, they may work with putative private sector polluters; conflicting local, regional, state, and federal government agencies; and concerned citizen groups.

Collaboration occurs among those with shared and different goals. It does not nullify competition, and paradoxically it may yield conflict (Connelly, Zhang and Faerman, 2008). For example, higher education may band together to develop an alternative to an external ranking formula. However, each institution may seek to best the other in the quest for top applicants, and schools will still compete against each other for advances in reputation.

Collaboration also occurs when it is mandatory as well as when it is emergent or voluntary. States vary in mandating collaboration regarding community efforts to serve children and families (Page, 2008). Some states define through mandate which agencies must participate, while other states set goals with proportions of members representing certain categories. Still other states use an open-ended approach, allowing the networks to self-organize.

Collaboration occurs with large and small numbers of actors; more recently, collaborative networks have also engaged the public. For example, 59 different municipal authorities collaborated in Hamilton County, Ohio, to develop a plan for growth and development; they reached unanimous agreement on its outlines (www.americaspeaks.org). Their process included a deliberative democratic forum at which over a thousand residents discussed priorities and elements for the plan.

In lower-conflict settings, regional voluntary service coordination and collaboration may emerge voluntarily among local governments. Local neighborhood councils collaborate with city service agencies to enhance communication and responsiveness (Cooper, Bryer and Meek, 2006).

Collaboration also occurs with and without public participation. Emergency management planning in New Orleans prior to Hurricane Katrina involved representatives of local, state, and federal government and was largely limited to professionals (Kiefer and Montjoy, 2006). This engendered substantial criticism. Planning for the recovery now involves collaboration of local, state, and federal agencies and a series of large-scale, high-profile citizen forums and participation by elected officials. These are just a few examples of the wide variation of collaborative public management networks in practice.

Professor Carmen Sirianni documented how the Environmental Protection Agency (EPA) has been an innovative leader in collaborative governance (Sirianni, 2009). He described how EPA uses watersheds as a cognitive frame for civic organizing; sponsors conferences of the watershed movement; uses citizen advisory committees; hosts trainings, Web casts, and conferences; develops handbooks for planning conservation and management; provides matching grants; provides guides for deliberation in the form of community watershed forums; and enlists volunteers in monitoring performance; he termed these 'tools for democratic watershed collaboration' (Sirianni, 2009: 166). We have only begun to chart this new world of agencies using collaborative governance (De Souza Briggs, 2008).

Public policy dispute resolution and consensus-building

A related family of processes midstream includes public policy dispute resolution and consensus-building. These are agreement-seeking processes in which an impartial third party, often a mediator or facilitator, works with a group of citizens or network of stakeholders to build consensus around the elements of a specific plan, permit, or policy proposal. Collaboration has been occurring in planning and environmental settings for three decades (for an early meta-analysis of case studies by Gail Bingham, one of the founders of environmental mediation in the United States, see Bingham, 1986).

In public policy dispute resolution, typically a third party or neutral will engage in a conflict-assessment process before convening the stakeholder group in order to assess the feasibility of reaching consensus (Susskind, McKearnan and Larmer, 1999). The neutral generally uses techniques of interest-based bargaining or principled negotiation (Fisher, Ury and Patton 1991). This approach involves a focus on the interests of the parties rather than their adversarial positions. The mediator or facilitator may identify interests by asking problem-solving questions (who, what, where, why, how, why not) to get at the stakeholders' basic human and organizational needs. These will, most often, fall into one of five categories: (1) needs relating to security; (2) economic well-being; (3) belonging to a community, organization, or social group; (4) recognition; and (5) autonomy. Parties engage in brainstorming, a process through which they first generate a list of possible solutions. They next prioritize among these ideas, deliberate on them, and attempt to reach consensus. In the event of impasse, the stakeholders are encouraged to use objective criteria, moral and professional standards, and other sources in a reasoned exchange rather than threaten to use leverage or bargaining power.

In mediation, the neutral can assist the parties with this negotiation process by meeting with subgroups or individual stakeholders in caucus, a private confidential session (Moore, 2003). The mediator can also help the parties by using active listening techniques such as paraphrasing and restating, by framing and reframing issues and suggestions, helping them identify their best alternative to a negotiated agreement (BATNA), and reality-testing about what might happen if parties fail to reach an agreement. Facilitators may use many of these techniques, but do not define their task as assisting the parties in reaching an agreement. Instead, they foster an organized discussion; nevertheless, this discussion may produce a consensus.

This family of processes reveals more varieties of collaboration. Collaboration may occur in the formation of law. For example, an agency may convene stakeholders in negotiated rulemaking to collaboratively develop rules to implement public law. Collaboration occurs on highly contentious issues and on less controversial ones. The field of environmental conflict resolution is a testament to the use of collaboration on highly contentious issues such as natural resource allocation and development; cleanup of water, land, or air; and land use (see generally, Durant, Fiorino and O'Leary, 2004; O'Leary and Bingham, 2003).

Moreover, collaboration occurs with and without professional facilitators or mediators (Leach and Sabatier, 2003). Facilitated or mediated collaboration has occurred at highly polluted sites involving local, regional, state, and federal government, Native American tribes, non-profit organizations, environmental advocacy groups, and groups of local residents since the 1970s. It has also occurred in areas such as food safety, HIV/AIDS treatment, urban air quality, and dam decommissioning. In watershed management, some groups use professionals while others, instead, designate one member to chair meetings.

For example, an agency might use consensus policymaking or mediation with taxpayer associations or recreational users of a natural resource to agree on the permit terms. The permit may create a collaborative public

management network that oversees implementation of policy in the form of
the permit conditions over a protracted and
continuous period of time. In the Florida
Everglades, stakeholders collaborated to
resolve a conflict over the science of restoring the watershed and how to foster and
measure progress (www.ecr.gov).

For these various midstream uses of collaboration, measures of successful outcomes
might include positive net benefits, measurable objectives, cost-effective implementation, financial feasibility, fair distribution of
costs among parties, flexibility, incentive
compatibility, improved problem-solving
capacity, enhanced social capital, clear documentation protocols, reduction in conflict
and hostility, improved relations, cognitive
and affective shift, ability to resolve subsequent disputes, durable agreements, comprehensive or complete agreements, improvement
in party capacity, and improvement in
government decision-making (Bingham,
Fairman, Fiorino and O'Leary 2003: 332–3).
Some have argued that collaboration should
also be measured in terms of its impact on
the substantive policy goal, such as improving the environment (Bingham et al., 2003;
Koontz and Thomas, 2006).

DOWNSTREAM AND ENFORCING POLICY: CONFLICT RESOLUTION AND THE ADR MOVEMENT

Downstream stages in the policy process are
quasi-judicial or judicial action aimed at
determining rights and responsibilities among
a defined set of actors based on past events.
Traditionally, these processes include formal
and informal adjudication and informal government action. However, there is currently
widespread use of alternative dispute resolution (ADR). Some call it 'appropriate' dispute resolution, in response to criticism that
ADR exists independently from the justice
system and is thus not 'alternative' in all
cases. These processes include negotiation
(preferably interest-based and collaborative

rather than positional and competitive bargaining), mediation (negotiation with the
help of a third party with no decision-making
power), and arbitration (private judging).

ADR can be used for both executive
agency action and disputes within the jurisdiction of the judiciary. Generally, these
processes occur at the quasi-judicial or judicial end of the policy continuum in that they
assist specific identified disputants and are
retrospective in nature; they examine the
facts of past events that gave rise to the
dispute. The processes may either seek a
consensual and voluntary settlement agreement (mediation) or may provide disputants
with a decision that ends their conflict more
expeditiously than traditional agency or court
adjudication (varieties of arbitration).
Generally, ADR–and not deliberative or participatory democracy or collaborative public
management – is associated with downstream stages of the policy process.

The history of ADR in governance

ADR has a well-established history. These
processes are not new; they exist informally
in every culture throughout recorded
history, for example, in the work of village
elders and religious leaders. In the United
States, government institutions were not
sufficient to cope with waves of conflict
after World War II (Barrett, 2004). Various
new institutions evolved outside government
to meet this need, including private justice
systems for collective bargaining. The contemporary ADR movement emerged in large
part from these systems in labor relations;
philanthropies subsidized experiments applying them in new contexts, such as community
and neighborhood conflict. In theory, these
processes became civil society's way of
enhancing community, its problem-solving
capacity, social capital, and justice. The ADR
movement gave rise to community mediation
centers funded in part by the US Department
of Justice to address social unrest during
the 1960s. Civil society contributed to
dissemination of these processes in a variety

of ways. In the United States, philanthropic institutions such as the Ford, Carnegie, Rockefeller, and Hewlett Foundations, among others, funded the movement. Hewlett's contribution was central to the development of ADR in the United States.

During the 1970s and 1980s, the business community adopted ADR to reduce transaction costs in addressing conflict in commercial dealings. Supreme Court Chief Justice Warren Burger took up the cause in the federal courts. In Europe and the states made newly independent by the end of the cold war in the 1990s, these same philanthropies, together with the European Union, the American Bar Association and its Foundation, the Soros Foundation, the World Bank, and the United States Agency for International Development (USAID), among others, funded various training and efforts at ADR program development to strengthen the rule of law.

During the 1990s, ADR became institutionalized in many judicial systems, including both state and federal courts in the United States, and increasingly in Europe and other developed economies such as Australia. Under the Administrative Dispute Resolution Acts of 1996, United States federal executive branch agencies adopted policies implementing forms of dispute resolution (Senger, 2003). ADR is currently widely institutionalized in US federal agencies.

Varieties of dispute resolution in governance

ADR processes for public conflict resolution include both consensus-based and decisional processes. The foundation for consensus-based processes is principled or interest-based negotiation (Fisher, Ury and Patton, 1991); it is considered a form of ADR because it is different from traditional competitive or adversarial bargaining (see previous description). Additional consensus-based processes include conciliation, facilitation, and mediation. Conciliation is a term used when an agency attempts to negotiate a private settlement between two or more parties to a

dispute subject to the agency's jurisdiction. It historically also referred to mediation in the context of labor relations and collective bargaining, as in the Federal Mediation and Conciliation Service (FMCS). Facilitation is widely used in environmental conflict resolution, as previously described. This process is more commonly used in multi-party issues or for large groups and is considered less interventionist than mediation.

Mediation is the most widely used process in the federal government, particularly for federal employee disputes and procurement or federal contracting (Bingham and Wise, 1996; Nabatchi, 2007). In mediation, the third-party neutral assists the disputants in negotiating a voluntary settlement of their conflict. The military has used dispute resolution in its procurement contract relationships. The US Postal Service has the largest employment mediation program in the world as part of its administrative process for addressing complaints of employment discrimination (Bingham et al., 2009). A longitudinal evaluation of that program found a statistically significant decrease in formal complaints of discrimination correlated with implementation of mediation in each geographic district over an 18-month period. The US Environmental Protection Agency (EPA) has been a leading innovator in the use of mediation and other forms of dispute resolution (O'Leary and Raines, 2003). In both programs, researchers found high levels of satisfaction with the process and the mediators among disputants on both sides of conflict; moreover, most participants were satisfied with the outcome.

Dispute resolution also includes decision-based processes, such as fact-finding, mini-trials, and many varieties of arbitration (non-binding or advisory, rights and interest-based, and binding). Arbitration is private adjudication or private judging. Fact-finding is a form of advisory arbitration in which a third-party neutral conducts an informal evidentiary hearing to narrow disputed facts. Mini-trials are a form of advisory arbitration in which a third-party neutral conducts a more formal but still abbreviated evidentiary hearing and advises on disputed questions of law after which the disputants attempt to negotiate a settlement. Due to concerns about delegating government authority to private decision-makers, binding arbitration is much less prevalent in the United States federal government. Non-binding decision processes do not pose this problem. If advisory, arbitration represents a recommended decision for the parties. In the great majority of cases, parties comply with an advisory arbitration award. In the United States, binding arbitration is more final than a court decision; it can be overturned only on grounds of fraud, collusion, evident partiality, an incomplete or imperfect award, or refusing to hear evidence or postpone the hearing for good cause (Federal Arbitration Act, 9 U.S.C. §§ 1 et seq.).

Arbitration itself can be quasi-legislative or quasi-judicial. Interest arbitration is quasi-legislative; the arbitrator helps the parties write a contract for their future relationship. Sometimes, a downstream enforcement process, such as a complex piece of multi-party environmental litigation, will be transformed through the mechanism of a special master and a negotiated consent decree into an ongoing collaborative public management network for supervising an environmental cleanup. This is analogous to interest arbitration. Rights arbitration is quasi-judicial; the arbitrator determines rights under a textual standard from law or contract based upon a retrospective examination of facts.

Dispute resolution includes not only processes but also programs that give participants choices among a variety of processes. For example, ombudsperson programs use an in-house third-party neutral to assist people in handling conflict; these programs serve both employees within an agency and stakeholders or contractors outside the organization. Properly structured, these programs may contribute to systemic change.

There is substantial research on dispute resolution processes in the fields of social psychology, organizational behavior, political science, economics, planning, communications, education, labor, and industrial relations, among other fields (for reviews,

see Jones, 2004). One leading theory is that of procedural justice, which suggests that people will judge the outcome of a dispute process to be fair if they judge the process for reaching that outcome to be fair and if they are given opportunities for voice and respectful treatment (Lind and Tyler, 1988). Researchers have also identified interactional and interpersonal justice as frames for understanding disputant preferences for dispute resolution processes. Thus, for downstream uses, measures of successful outcomes include participant procedural justice, comparative satisfaction of different categories of disputants, reducing or narrowing issues, referrals, changes in disputant relationships, and voluntary use rates (Bingham et al., 2003: 332–3).

FUTURE RESEARCH DIRECTIONS FOR COLLABORATIVE GOVERNANCE

To advance our knowledge of collaborative governance, it is important to recognize that dialogue and deliberation, collaborative public management, multi-party public policy dispute resolution, consensus-building, and ADR are related approaches to the problems of networking and coordination posed by governance. Collaborative governance encompasses a wide array of models, designs, and contexts. The important questions for the future involve institutional design. How do we understand the varieties of structure and process found in collaborative governance? What impact do these have on outcomes?

Institutional analysis and design

Elinor Ostrom (2005) builds on earlier work (1990) to explore and explain the wide diversity of institutions that humans use to govern their behavior. Ostrom examines collaboration in governance of common pool resources. She attempts to identify an underlying set of universal building blocks and to provide a common vocabulary and syntax for researching institutions and how they function. She argues that these universal building blocks are in layers that one can analyze using the Institutional Analysis and Development (IAD) framework (Ostrom, 2005: 6). The simplest unit of analysis is the action situation. The action situation may be embedded within deeper layers; structures are nested (Ostrom, 2005: 11). To analyze an action situation, Ostrom uses seven categories of information:

> 1) the set of participants [single individuals or corporate actors]; 2) the positions to be filled by participants; 3) potential outcomes; 4) the set of allowable actions and the function that maps actions into realized outcomes [action-outcome linkages]; 5) the control that an individual has in regards to this function; 6) the information available to participants about actions and outcomes and their linkages; and 7) costs and benefits – which serve as incentives and deterrents – assigned to actions and outcomes. (Ostrom, 2005: 32)

These are the common structural components that represent the building blocks for all institutions at their most general level.

Once a researcher understands the initial action arena, she will often 'zoom out' (Ostrom, 2005: 15) to understand the outside variables that are affecting it; this is a two-stage process. First, the action arena now becomes a dependent variable subject to factors in three categories of variables: '1) the *rules* used by participants to order their relationships, 2) the attributes of the *biophysical world* that are acted upon in these arenas, and 3) the structure of the more general *community* within which any particular arena is placed' (Ostrom, 2005: 15–16). In the second stage of the analysis, the researcher will examine linkages between one action arena and others, either in sequence or at the same time.

These categories of information provide a means to examine varieties of structure, processes, and models for collaborative governance more systematically. Moreover, our understanding could benefit through a systematic comparison of institutions designed top-down with those that arise organically from the bottom-up, as in indigenous cultures managing forests and fisheries. The wide variety of collaborative processes and structures would benefit from a common frame for analysis.

Empirical approaches to examining collaborative governance

Ansell and Gash (2008) conducted a meta-analysis of 137 empirical case studies across policy sectors to develop a contingency model of collaborative governance. Their cases explicitly cross the silos of work on dialogue and deliberation, collaborative public management, and dispute resolution; they include all three process types. They identify critical variables that influence whether there will be successful collaboration. The starting conditions include the prior history of conflict or cooperation, incentives for or constraints on stakeholders to participate, and power, resource, and knowledge imbalances. They find that facilitative leadership and institutional design will both influence the collaborative process. Within the collaborative process itself, they argue that important factors include face-to-face dialogue, trust building, the development of commitment to the process, and development of shared understanding, which in turn create a dynamic process and intermediate outcomes that reinforce trust. Together, these factors influence ultimate outcomes.

Ansell and Gash focus upon institutional design in terms of process design and 'the basic protocols and ground rules for collaboration, which are critical for the procedural legitimacy of the collaborative process' (2008: 555). These include an open and inclusive process (one in which broad participation is actively sought), an exclusive forum (one that creates an incentive to participate), and clear ground rules and process transparency (which provide legitimacy). They indicate that consensus rules are less important, as they can lead to either least common denominator outcomes or stalemate. Lastly, they identify deadlines as an important feature of institutional design.

Legal infrastructure and collaborative governance

Another source of institutional design related to collaborative governance is law. Law may operate to facilitate or constrain collaboration. The term legal infrastructure has been used to refer to a combined system of constitutional, statutory, decisional, and administrative law, taken together with the available institutional enforcement and support mechanisms. Its most common use is in reference to efforts to develop the rule of law and viable protection of private property and investment in emerging democracies.

Statutes may lower the barriers to collaboration, for example, by authorizing public agencies to do anything together that they have power to do apart. One study shows that networks with express legislative authorization or charters are more likely to take action rather than simply share information (Agranoff, 2007). When experiments in collaboration are successful, states may then mandate collaboration as the preferred method to implement public policy (Ryu and Rainey, 2009). States have enacted mandates for accountability and managing for results in collaboration (Page, 2008). Legal mandates may provide collaborative public management networks with legitimacy that facilitates their work implementing policy (Provan, Kenis and Human, 2008). Law is an independent variable; it creates incentives, barriers, or obstacles to collaboration.

However, administrative and public law scholars generally address challenges to the legitimacy of the administrative state. In the US, these arise from the absence of any reference to administrative agencies in the Constitution, the combination of quasi-legislative, executive, and quasi-judicial functions in one agency potentially violating separation of powers, and the absence of direct accountability to the electorate. As a result, most legal scholarship addresses fundamental values of accountability, transparency, efficiency, participation, and recently, collaboration.

Legal scholars have recognized an evolution away from command-and-control hierarchy to the new governance. Professor Jody Freeman (1997, 2000) examines the private role in public governance across the policy continuum, finding that non-governmental actors engage in legislative and adjudicative roles and that public–private interdependence is a reality best understood as a set of negotiated relationships in policy-making, implementation, and enforcement. Importantly, she argues that institutional design should move away from the traditional legislative, executive, and judicial branches to an examination of alternative private institutions and stakeholders and the role they can effectively play in governance.

Administrative law scholars largely ignore the mismatch between the existing statutory framework for governance and collaboration. In the United States, legislators drafted the key federal and state statutes as legal infrastructure contemplating unilateral, command-and-control, hierarchical, and individual agency action. The relevant statutes largely address only questions of process from the individual agency perspective. They are silent on the substantive work of agencies, except with regard to judicial review for *ultra vires* agency action. They are silent on the structure of collaborative networks or other forms of collaborative public management. They may in places require public participation – e.g. notice and comment in rulemaking or public hearings – but they are largely silent as to the wide variety of models for collaborative governance in agency policymaking. Moreover, information is critical to collaborative governance; transparency laws do not reach the non-governmental organizations (NGOs) to whom responsibility for delivery of public services has devolved.

Collaborative governance involving the public is a key way to respond to some criticisms of networked and privatized government action. Public law is a tool for institutional design; it needs to provide a framework that authorizes collaboration, facilitates broader and more effective use, and preserves accountability to the rule of law and transparency in government.

CONCLUSION

Bevir (2006) documents the rise in the rhetoric of dialogue, participation, consensus, empowerment, and social inclusion in system governance. He suggests that the goals of system governance are efficiency and an effective social order through consensus on policy; however, it limits participation to recognized, organized, élite stakeholders in a consultative role, and does not allow citizens to make or implement policies.

On his first full day in office, President Barack Obama signed an executive memorandum on Open Government directing federal agencies to be more transparent, participatory, and collaborative (http://www.whitehouse.gov/the_press_office/TransparencyandOpenGovernment/). However, after almost a year, the Office of Management and Budget issued an Open Government Directive framed primarily in terms of posting machine readable datasets on government websites and providing the public with links for public comment (http://www.whitehouse.gov/open/). Coglianese (2006) is skeptical about the potential for broad, democratic participation in governance, particularly through means of new media; he cites empirical studies on electronic and negotiated rulemaking that suggest there has been no broad increase in meaningful engagement.

There is certainly the risk that public managers will adopt the language and rhetoric of collaborative governance and not the reality. Limited resources, an imperfect and ambiguous legal framework, and inadequate training in the essential skills of negotiation, collaboration, and dispute resolution together present substantial obstacles. Moreover, we lack systematic research regarding institutional design and its impact. There are various models for engaging the public and stakeholders across the policy continuum, but there is no comprehensive understanding of how these relate to each other, how they affect participants, or how they influence policy outcomes.

Nevertheless, collaborative governance has the potential to change the way that citizens and stakeholders interact with both elected representatives and public managers across the policy continuum through appropriate institutional designs. Given the complexity of current policy problems, simple command and control does not work. With the limits on public resources, government needs to leverage assistance from the private and non-profit sectors. Collaborative governance has emerged in response to these demands; the practices exist across the policy continuum. The question is how to design processes and institutions that allow us to collaborate meaningfully and well.

REFERENCES

Agranoff, R. (2007) *Managing within Networks: Adding Value to Public Organizations.* Washington, DC: Georgetown University Press.

Agranoff, R. and McGuire, M. (2003) *Collaborative Public Management: New Strategies for Local Governments.* Washington, DC: Georgetown University Press.

Ansell, C. and Gash, A. (2008) 'Collaborative Governance in Theory and Practice', *Journal of Public Administration Research and Theory* 18: 543–71.

Barrett, J. (2004) *A History of Alternative Dispute Resolution: The Story of a Political, Cultural, and Social Movement.* San Francisco, CA: Jossey-Bass.

Beierle, T.C. and Cayford, J. (2002) *Democracy in Practice: Public Participation in Environmental Decisions.* Washington, DC: Resources for the Future Press.

Bevir, M. (2006) 'Democratic Governance Systems and Radical Perspectives', *Public Administration Review* 66: 426–36.

Bingham, G. (1986) *Resolving Environmental Disputes: A Decade of Experience.* Washington, DC: Conservation Foundation.

Bingham, L.B. (2009) 'Collaborative Governance: Emerging Practices and the Incomplete Legal Framework for Public and Stakeholder Voice,' *Missouri Journal of Dispute Resolution* 2009(2): 269–325.

Bingham, L.B. and O'Leary, R. (2006) 'Conclusion: Parallel Play, not Collaboration: Missing Questions, Missing Connections', *Public Administration Review* 66(s1): 161–7.

Bingham, L.B. and O'Leary, R. (eds) (2008) *Big Ideas in Collaborative Public Management.* Armonk, NY: M.E. Sharpe.

Bingham, L.B. and Wise, C.R. (1996) 'The Administrative Dispute Resolution Act of 1990: How Do We Evaluate Its Success?', *Journal of Public Administration, Research and Theory* 6(3): 383–414.

Bingham, L.B., Fairman, D., Fiorino, D.J. and O'Leary, R. (2003) 'Fulfilling the Promise of Environmental Conflict Resolution', in R. O'Leary and L. B. Bingham, (eds), *The Promise and Performance of Environmental Conflict Resolution*. Washington, DC: Resources for the Future Press.

Bingham, L.B., Nabatchi, T. and O'Leary, R. (2005) 'The New Governance: Practices and Processes for Stakeholder and Citizen Participation in the Work of Government', *Public Administration Review* 65(5): 547–58.

Bingham, L.B., Hallberlin, C.J., Walker, D.A. and Chung, W.T. (2009) 'Dispute System Design and Justice in Employment Dispute Resolution: Mediation at the Workplace', *Harvard Negotiation Law Review* 14: 1–50.

Bohman, J. and Rehg, W. (eds) (1997) *Deliberative Democracy: Essays on Reason and Politics*. Cambridge, MA: MIT Press.

Bryson, J.M. and Crosby, B.C. (2008) 'Failing into Cross-sector Collaboration Successfully', in L.B. Bingham and R. O'Leary (eds), *Big Ideas in Collaborative Public Management*. Armonk, NY: M.E. Sharpe; pp. 55–78.

Carpenter, S.L. and Kennedy, W.J.D. (1988) *Managing Public Disputes: A Practical Guide to Handling Conflict and Reaching Agreements*. San Francisco, CA: Jossey-Bass.

Carson, L. and Hartz-Karp, J. (2005) 'Adapting and Combining Deliberative Designs', in J. Gastil and P. Levine (eds), *The Deliberative Democracy Handbook: Strategies for Effective Civic Engagement in the 21st Century*. San Francisco, CA: Jossey-Bass; pp. 120–38.

Coglianese, C. (2006) 'The Role of the Internet in Agency Decision Making: Citizen Participation in Rulemaking: Past, Present, and Future', *Duke Law Journal* 55: 943–68.

Connelly, D., Zhang, J. and Faerman, S. (2008) 'The Paradoxical Nature of Collaboration', in L.B. Bingham and R. O'Leary (eds), *Big Ideas in Collaborative Public Management*. Armonk, NY: M.E. Sharpe; pp. 17–35.

Cooper, T.L., Bryer, T.A. and Meek, J.M. (2006) 'Citizen-Centered Collaborative Public Management', *Public Administration Review* 66(s1): 76–88.

De Souza Briggs, X. (2008) *Democracy as Problem Solving: Civic Capacity in Communities across the Globe*. Cambridge, MA: MIT Press.

Durant, R.F., Fiorino, D.J. and O'Leary, R. (eds) (2004) *Environmental Governance Reconsidered: Challenges, Choices, and Opportunities*. Cambridge, MA: MIT Press.

Fisher, R., Ury, W. and Patton, B. (1991) *Getting to Yes*. New York, NY: Penguin Press.

Fishkin, J.S. (2009) *When the People Speak: Deliberative Democracy and Public Consultation*. Oxford: Oxford University Press.

Forester, J. (1999) *The Deliberative Practitioner: Encouraging Participatory Planning Processes*. Cambridge, MA: MIT Press.

Frederickson, H.G. (1999) 'The Repositioning of American Public Administration', *PS: Political Science and Politics* 32(4): 701–11.

Freeman, J. (1997) 'Collaborative Governance in the Administrative State', *University of California Los Angeles Law Review* 45: 1–98.

Freeman, J. (2000) 'The Private Role in Public Governance', *New York University Law Review* 75: 543–75.

Fung, A. (2006) 'Varieties of Participation in Complex Governance', *Public Administration Review* 66(S1): 66–75.

Fung, A. and Wright, E.O. (eds) (2003) *Deepening Democracy: Institutional Innovations in Empowered Participatory Governance*. London: Verso.

Gastil, J. and Levine, P. (eds) (2005) *The Deliberative Democracy Handbook: Strategies for Effective Civic Engagement in the Twenty-First Century*. San Francisco, CA: Jossey-Bass.

Gazley, B. (2008) 'Intersectoral Collaboration and the Motivation to Collaborate: Toward an Integrated Theory', in L.B. Bingham and R. O'Leary (eds), *Big Ideas in Collaborative Public Management*. Armonk, NY: M.E. Sharpe; pp. 36–54.

Gray, B. (1991) *Collaborating: Finding Common Ground for Multiparty Problems*. San Francisco, CA: Jossey- Bass.

Hajer, M. A. and Wagenaar, H. (eds) (2003) *Deliberative Policy Analysis: Understanding Governance in the Network Society*. Cambridge: Cambridge University Press.

Henton, D., Melville, J., Amsler, T. and Kopell, M. (2005) *Collaborative Governance: A Guide for Grantmakers*. Menlo Park, CA: The William and Flora Hewlett Foundation.

Jones, T.S. (ed) (2004) 'Conflict Resolution in the Field: Special Symposium', *Conflict Resolution in the Field: Special Symposium*, 22 Conflict Resolution Quarterly 3(4): 1–320.

Kettl, D.F. (2002a) *The Transformation of Governance: Public Administration for Twenty-First Century America*. Baltimore, MD: Johns Hopkins University Press.

Kettl, D.F. (ed.) (2002b) *Environmental Governance: A Report on the Next Generation of Environmental Policy*. Washington, DC: Brookings Institution Press.

Kiefer, J.J. and Montjoy, R.S. (2006) 'Incrementalism before the Storm: Network Performance for the Evacuation of New Orleans', *Public Administration Review* 66(S1): 122–30.

Koontz, T.M. and Thomas, C.W. (2006) 'What Do We Know and Need to Know About the Environmental Outcomes of Collaborative Management?', *Public Administration Review* 66(s1): 111–121.

Leach, W.D. (2006) 'Collaborative Public Management and Democracy: Evidence from Western Watershed Partnerships', *Public Administration Review* 66(S1): 100–10.

Leach, W.D. and Sabatier, P. (2003) 'Facilitators, Coordinators, and Outcomes', in R. O'Leary and L. B. Bingham, (eds), *The Promise and Performance of Environmental Conflict Resolution*. Washington, DC: Resources for the Future Press; pp. 148–72.

Lind, E.A. and Tyler, T.R. (1988) *The Social Psychology of Procedural Justice*. New York, NY: Plenum.

Macedo, S. (ed.) (1999) *Deliberative Politics: Essays on Democracy and Disagreement*. Oxford: Oxford University Press.

Moore, C. (2003) *The Mediation Process: Practical Strategies for Resolving Conflict*. San Francisco, CA: Jossey-Bass.

Nabatchi, T. (2007) 'The Institutionalization of Alternative Dispute Resolution in the Federal Government', *Public Administration Review* 67(4): 646–61.

National Research Council (2008) *Public Participation in Environmental Assessment and Decision Making*. Washington, DC: National Academies Press.

Noveck, B.S. (2009) *WIKI Government: How Technology Can Make Government Better, Democracy Stronger, and Citizens More Powerful*. Washington, DC: Brookings Institution Press.

O'Leary, R. and Bingham, L.B. (eds) (2003) *The Promise and Performance of Environmental Conflict Resolution*. Washington, DC: Resources for the Future Press.

O'Leary, Rosemary and Bingham, Lisa Blomgren (2007) *A Manager's Guide to Resolving Conflicts in Collaborative Networks*. Arlington, VA: IBM Center for the Business of Government.

O'Leary, R. and Bingham, L.B. (eds) (2009) *The Collaborative Public Manager*. Washington, DC: Georgetown University Press.

O'Leary, R. and Raines, S.S. (2003) 'Dispute Resolution at the U.S. Environmental Protection Agency', in R. O'Leary and L.B. Bingham (eds), *The Promise and Performance of Environmental Conflict Resolution*. Washington, DC: Resources for the Future Press; pp. 253–76.

O'Leary, Rosemary, Bingham, Lisa Blomgren and Gerard, Catherine (eds) (2006) 'Symposium on Collaborative Public Management', *Public Administration Review* 66(s1): 1–170.

O'Leary, R., Gazley, B., McGuire, M. and Bingham, L.B. (2009) 'Public Managers in Collaboration', in R. O'Leary and L.B. Bingham (eds), *The Collaborative Public Manager*. Washington, DC: Georgetown University Press; pp. 1–12.

Ostrom, E. (1990) *Governing the Commons: The Evolution of Institutions for Collective Action*. New York: Cambridge University Press.

Ostrom, E. (2005) *Understanding Institutional Diversity*. Princeton, NJ: Princeton University Press.

Page, S. (2008) 'Managing for Results across Agencies: Building Collaborative Capacity in the Human Services', in L.B. Bingham and R. O'Leary (eds), *Big Ideas in Collaborative Public Management*. Armonk, NY: M.E. Sharpe, pp. 138–61.

Provan, K.G., Kenis, P. and Human, S.E. (2008). 'Legitimacy Building in Organizational Networks', in L.B. Bingham and R. O'Leary (eds), *Big Ideas in Collaborative Public Management*. Armonk, NY: M.E. Sharpe; pp. 121–37.

Renn, O., Webler, T. and Wiedemann, P. (1995) *Fairness and Competence in Citizen Participation: Evaluating Models for Environmental Discourse*. Dordrecht, NL: Kluwer Academic Publishers.

Roberts, N.C. (2008) *The Age of Direct Citizen Participation*. Armonk, NY: M.E. Sharpe.

Ryu, J.R. and Rainey, H.G. (2009) 'Collaborative Public Management and Organizational Design: One-Stop Shopping Structures in Employment and Training Programs', in R. O'Leary and L.B. Bingham (eds), *The Collaborative Public Manager*. Washington, DC: Georgetown University Press; pp. 179–96.

Salamon, L. (ed.) (2002) *The Tools of Government: A Guide to the New Governance*. Oxford: Oxford University Press.

Senger, J.M. (2003) *Federal Dispute Resolution: Using ADR with the United States Government*. San Francisco, CA: Jossey Bass.

Sirianni, C. (2009) *Investing in Democracy: Engaging Citizens in Collaborative Governance*. Washington, DC: Brookings Institution Press.

Susskind, L., McKearnan, S. and Thomas-Larmer, J. (eds) (1999) *The Consensus-Building Handbook: A Comprehensive Guide to Reaching Agreement*. Thousand Oaks, CA: Sage.

Thomas, J.C. (1995) *Public Participation in Public Decisions: New Skills and Strategies for Public Managers*. San Francisco, CA: Jossey Bass.

Thomson, A.M. and Perry, J.L. (2006) 'Collaboration Processes: Inside the Black Box', *Public Administration Review* 66(s1): 20–32.

26

Participation

Peter McLaverty

Over the last 25 years or so, governments in a number of countries have made considerable efforts to increase the opportunities for members of the public to engage in political participation. A number of participatory mechanisms have been developed and applied. In this chapter, I will outline some of those mechanisms and analyse the climate within which the mechanisms have been implemented by governments. I will argue that the concern with political participation has been a consequence both of declining levels of public participation in traditional forms of politics and concerns which are associated with the idea of governance. More specifically, I will outline ideas associated with the development of governance and analyse how these ideas have influenced patterns of political participation and opportunities for public participation. Finally, I will consider the ways in which developments in public participation are related to conceptions of political legitimacy and ideas of democracy.

GOVERNANCE

There are differences between writers about the core features of governance and about whether different aspects of governance represent desirable developments. Over recent years, it is argued that in a number of states (and particularly in advanced capitalist countries) the power of central government has been reduced. Power has been dispersed geographically and socially. In some definitions, the state has moved from a position where it both controlled and acted itself, with the state now taking a steering role and non-state actors carrying out a rowing role (Osborne and Gaebler, 1992). In other words, the state is seen as acting strategically and relying on non-state bodies and actors to deliver the strategic objectives. This idea ties into the argument of Pierre and Peters (2000) that the moves to a system of governance do not necessarily represent the sidelining of government but rather represent new ways in which government strives to achieve its goals. Others see moves to governance as not only changing the activities of the state but also reducing the role of the government within society. Governance is seen as committing elected government ministers and government officials to work with others from outside government, with the growth of formal and informal networks and partnerships of various kinds (Rhodes, 1997, 2006).

Networks and partnerships can take a number of different forms. There are disagreements about whether the growth of networks and partnerships is a threat to democracy or an opportunity to enhance democracy. For some, the developments are seen as opening up opportunities for greater public participation, while for others, they are seen as part of the development of 'private governance' (Dingwerth, 2008). Whether networks and partnerships are an opportunity to enhance public participation would seem to depend on the nature of the network or partnership.

Supporters of the idea that networks and partnerships have participatory and democratic potential argue that the old or traditional system of government was insensitive to the demands and opinions of service users, citizens and the general public. The 'traditional' governmental system was seen as producer dominated and excessively bureaucratic. For some, this led to the waste of resources and the inefficient and ineffective provision of services. It was argued that the governmental system, and the public sector more generally, should be disrupted and fundamentally changed through a variety of different measures. In some critiques of traditional government, the answer to the problems of unresponsive, bureaucratic and producer-dominated public sector organizations was to introduce market or quasi-market innovations and for the public sector to learn from the private sector. This approach is commonly seen as resulting in measures associated with 'new public management' (such as performance management, the introduction of quasi-markets, privatization and a more managerial approach) (cf. Hood, 1991).

Such arguments did not preclude efforts to enhance public participation. The type of participation that was supported by these arguments was based more around empowering the people as consumers, rather than as democratic citizens. Even the more 'consumerist' approaches, however, recognized that market principles could not be applied directly and completely in many aspects of the public sector's activities (Flynn, 2007). At the other extreme, from the supporters of a market and consumerist approach, are those who see the idea of governance opening up the possibility for an expansion of participatory democracy. Writers supporting this approach see the geographical and social decentralization of control over neighbourhoods and services as offering a way forward to engage with the people, including social groups who have historically been marginalized from formal politics or who have played only a limited part in the more traditional methods of political participation.

Support for ideas of the decentralization of government and of public services can be traced back a long way. For theorists like J.S. Mill, people can learn the skills associated with democratic government from a direct involvement in running local government and engagement in worker cooperatives (Mill, 1975: 363–80; 1987; Williams, 1976: 335–8). The anarchist tradition has, of course, seen the decentralization of power and local control as essential to the exercise of personal autonomy and direct democracy (cf. Marshall, 1993). Anarchist ideas were not a basis for the actual developments associated with governance but arguments in favour of engaging people at the local level sometimes were.

While many of the writers who have supported participatory democracy have seen the basis for this form of democracy as arising from the 'bottom up' and being developed and controlled by active self-governing communities of various sorts, and not just geographical communities, many of those involved in promoting forms of participation associated with governance have engaged in 'top-down' approaches. In such approaches, participatory mechanisms have been instituted to help the governance process work more efficiently and to aid the process of political legitimation (cf. Bevir, 2006: 428). Some have argued that while élite driven, developments in governance have built on the expansion of activity in civil society (cf. Warren, 2008b). The development of new forms of public participation is seen as due, in part at least, to the ability of groups in civil society to generate effective opposition to public policy. This opposition means that policymakers want to incorporate interest groups into the policy process, not only to benefit from their knowledge and experience but also to help the policy process run more smoothly.

The commitments to decentralizing decision-making, in order to increase the power of public service users as individual consumers, which is associated with developments in governance, have sometimes led to new forms of collective participation. It has often proved very difficult to treat the users of public services as consumers in the way they would be treated in the private sector. Individualizing service provision has not proved possible in a number of public services around the world. Mechanisms have been developed, as a result, which aim to gauge the views of service users, sometimes along with those who fund services, so that service providers can gain important information and service users and those who fund services can influence service provision and delivery.

Moreover, as will be detailed in the next section, over recent decades there has been a decline in popular involvement in traditional forms of 'politics' in a number of countries. This decline has been seen by some as representing a serious problem for liberal democracies (cf. Dalton, 2004). Moves towards governance can be seen as, in part, a response to the declining popular involvement in formal politics. The move to governance has involved commitments to make politics more relevant and to address issues surrounding public dissatisfaction with formal politics. Although these commitments have been associated with an individualized, consumer-type approach, they have also resulted in the use of new mechanisms of public participation.

DEVELOPMENTS IN POLITICAL PARTICIPATION

The comparative research of Russell Dalton has shown evidence of a decline in public participation in traditional forms of politics. From analysis of surveys of opinions carried out in the biggest and longest-established OECD (Organization for Economic Co-operation and Development) countries, he argues that developments, in a number of areas, show that support for, and trust in, the political regimes and politicians across the countries surveyed declined between the mid 1970s and the late 1990s. Other research has shown that the number of voters turning out to vote at each parliamentary election, across the globe, represented 61 per cent of the voting age population in the period 1945–50. This figure rose to 62 per cent in the 1950s, 65 per cent in the 1960s, 67 per cent in the 1970s and 68 per cent in the 1980s but fell to 64 per cent in the 1990s. The percentage of registered voters who actually voted was fairly constant between the 1940s and the 1980s but dipped in the 1990s, from just under 80 per cent to under 70 per cent (International IDEA, 2009). This suggests a reasonably healthy picture.

However, Dalton (2006: 59) has argued that for what he terms 'the advanced industrial democracies', electoral turnouts have decreased in most cases and so too has electoral campaign activity. Moreover, if we take membership of political parties as an indicator of traditional political participation, we find that in Western Europe between 1980 and 2000 party membership fell by over 50 per cent in the United Kingdom, by nearly two-thirds in France and by 51 per cent in Italy. An exception is Germany where the decline was only 9 per cent (Mair and van Biezen, 2001: 12). Outlining the position in 20 European countries in 1998, 1999 or 2000, Mair and van Biezen (2001: 9) found that, with the exception of Austria where the percentage was 17.66 and Finland where it was 9.65, the percentage of the electorate who were party members was under 8 per cent in each of the 18 other countries. The mean average for the countries was 4.99 per cent. Between the 1980s and the end of the 1990s, 'Across all 13 long-established [European] democracies, membership levels in absolute terms have fallen by a staggering average of almost 35 per cent' (Mair and van Biezen, 2000: 13). Dalton (2004: 28, 30) summarizes the findings of research he has conducted into public opinion in OECD countries between the 1970s and the late 1990s, as follows: 'there is clear evidence for a general erosion in support for politicians and government in most advanced industrial democracies'. Specifically, his research found that, in nearly all the countries surveyed, there has been a decline in people's commitment to specific political parties (Dalton, 2004: 31–4). The decline in party affiliation has been connected to a decline in popular support for political regimes and the efficacy of parliaments (Dalton, 2004: 34–9). It is more difficult to gauge the extent of support for democratic values or for democracy as a form of government, as time series data, similar to that which enables comparisons of support for political parties and regimes and for the efficacy of parliaments, are not available across the OECD countries. However, Dalton argues that:

> To the extent that such data are available, they suggest that support for political rights and participatory norms have actually grown over the past generation. For instance, the available long-term data suggest that contemporary publics have become more politically tolerant during the post-war period. (2004: 40)

And the evidence suggests that, 'On average, more than three-quarters of the public feel that democracy is the best form of government even if it has its problems' (Dalton, 2004: 41).

The picture, therefore, seems to be mixed. On the one hand, in most of the countries researched, support for politicians (a belief that they work for the good of the people and are to be trusted), political regimes and the

efficacy of parliaments has declined, since the mid 1970s. There has also been a substantial decline in the membership of European political parties since the 1980s. On the other hand, there seems to have been an increase in popular support for democratic values and for democracy as a form of government. In other words, populations seem to support democracy and its values in the general, abstract sense, but they do not seem to think that governments, parliaments and politicians are doing a good job. As Dalton (2004: 47) puts it: 'Most people remain committed to the democratic ideal, if anything these sentiments have apparently strengthened as satisfaction with the actuality of democratic politics has decreased'.

It is against the background of declining participation in traditional types of politics, and the evidence of declining trust in political regimes, that interest in ideas of governance began to grow and governments began to look for new mechanisms of political participation. I will outline a range of participation mechanisms that have been used by different governments in an effort to increase public participation. Having outlined the mechanisms, in the following section, I will assess how they relate to developments associated with governance.

MECHANISMS OF PARTICIPATION

Most of the participation mechanisms that have been introduced over the last quarter century have been of a consultative nature. In other words, the outcomes of the mechanisms do not result directly in the making or implementation of public policy. The results do not threaten, nor should they be seen as an alternative to, traditional representative forms of democracy. Instead, they should be seen as a supplement to traditional forms of political representation. In a few cases, such as the use of citizens' assemblies and referendums, the mechanisms to be considered do give groups within the public control over policymaking but such examples, as we will see, are fairly unusual.

In his study for the Power Inquiry, *Beyond the Ballot*, Graham Smith (2005) outlines *57 Democratic Innovations from Around the World* (as his report is subtitled). The innovations he mentions are grouped around six headings: electoral innovations; consultation innovations; deliberative innovations; co-governance innovations; direct democracy innovations; and e-democracy innovations. A number of the mechanisms (or innovations), such as postal ballots, public opinion surveys, compulsory voting and reducing the voting age, will not be considered, as they either have not been widely applied or are of limited significance in understanding developments in political participation. Instead, I want to concentrate on the newer innovations that have attempted to take political participation in new directions. In particular, I intend to look at deliberative mechanisms, co-governance initiatives, mechanisms of direct democracy and some consultation exercises.

Deliberative mechanisms

Perhaps the biggest type of innovations introduced by public organizations in an effort to increase public participation relate to ideas of deliberation. Dryzek (2002: 1) has argued that

> The final decade of the second millennium saw the theory of democracy take a strong deliberative turn. Increasingly, democratic legitimacy came to be seen in terms of the ability or opportunity to participate in effective deliberation on the part of those subject to collective decisions. (Note that only the ability or opportunity to participate is at issue; people can choose not to deliberate.)

This turn in theory was connected to changes in practice in a number of countries. A number of deliberative mechanisms have been used in various countries. These include citizens' juries, deliberative opinion polls, consensus conferences and deliberative mapping.

The thinking behind the deliberative mechanisms is to move beyond the simple aggregation of people's current opinions. The idea that deliberation is crucial to politics can probably be traced back to Ancient Athens (the generally accepted home of democracy) but its importance was also stressed by the those like the eighteenth century British conservative Edmund Burke (Burke, 1854–56). For Burke, however, the deliberation that was desirable should take place between the people's elected representatives, within parliament. In the last 30 years or so there has been a move away from this élitist view of political deliberation to support for the idea that members of the public should engage directly in deliberation. While supporters of deliberation do not all agree on the form deliberation should take or the aims behind deliberation, academic writers on deliberation generally see it as related to ideas of reciprocity and a willingness among participants to move away from existing prejudices and be persuaded by the arguments of others (for example, Parkinson, 2003: 180–1). There are debates about whether the aim of deliberation should be for participants to reach a consensus, with most writers today rejecting the overriding importance of consensus (Dryzek, 2002). There are also debates about whether deliberation demands that participants try to achieve the common good or whether it is legitimate for participants to try to further their own interests through deliberation (a position supported, at least in part, by Mansbridge, 2003: 179–88). There is a belief that deliberation between members of the public can help participants to refine their opinions and adopt positions that more accurately reflect their considered views and contribute to better policymaking (Squires, 2002). There are, however, debates about the ways in which organized deliberation between members of the public should relate to policymaking in liberal, representative democracies and about the extent to which deliberative democracy is compatible with representative democracy (Dryzek, 2002; McLaverty and Halpin, 2008).

Citizens' juries can be traced back over 30 years to developments in the United States and Germany. The idea of citizens' juries, as such, was created at the Jefferson Center (2008). About the same time in Germany, Peter Dienel, at the University of Wuppertal, was developing the idea of planning cells, which are very similar to the concept of citizens' juries (Dienel, 1999). The original US citizens' juries were not directly connected to the public policy process but the German planning cells were. As they have developed, citizens' juries have been applied in a number of countries (besides the United States and Germany), including Australia, Britain, Denmark and Spain (Jefferson Center, 2008). The idea behind citizens' juries is that a small number of citizens, normally between 12 and 24, chosen by stratified random sampling, will come together for a number of days to consider a specific topic which has high relevance for public policy. They will hear evidence from specialists and experts on the topic, they will be able to question the 'witnesses' on their evidence and they will deliberate among themselves about what should be done, based on the evidence and information. In some cases, for example the Planning Cells in Germany, the participants will divide into smaller groups to help make deliberation easier and more rewarding, before coming back together as the full group. A facilitator, or facilitators, is used to try to ensure that the jury subscribes to the principles of deliberation.

The jurors produce a report with recommendations, based on their deliberation. It is generally the case that a consensus between the jurors is not needed and reports can include different recommendations, if the participants do not agree. What happens to the report will vary in different systems. It is unusual for a citizens' jury report to be automatically accepted and for its recommendations to be directly incorporated into public policy. In most cases, citizens' juries are a consultative mechanism, not a policy decision-making body. In Britain and Spain, the public body that commissioned the jury is often under an obligation to respond to the report and, if it intends to reject the report's recommendations, to give reasons to the jurors as to why it is doing so. There is evidence that jurors feel that engaging in a citizens' jury is worthwhile (Lowndes et al., 2001; O'Neill, 2003). There are questions about the ability of most citizens' juries to seriously influence public policy and about the role they should play in the policy process.

Consensus conferences have a number of similarities to citizens' juries. They have been widely used in Denmark and have also taken place in the Netherlands, New Zealand, Switzerland and the United Kingdom. Like citizens' juries, the participants in consensus conferences in Denmark are selected to be representative of the socio-demographic composition of the population but, unlike citizens' juries, are chosen from a list of volunteers. Participants are also expected to attend a number of meetings, before the conference takes place, where they will learn about the issues and be able to work out relevant questions (Smith, 2005: 42). As with citizens' juries, recommendations from consensus conferences are not binding on policymakers, though some have had an impact on legislation in Denmark.

A different kind of deliberative forum is represented by deliberative opinion polls. These were created by the US academic James Fishkin (1997). Members of deliberative opinion polls are chosen at random, with between 250 and 500 people taking part. The process starts with participants completing a questionnaire on a particular topic. Material on the topic to be considered is sent to participants before the event. The people then meet together for a few days (for example a weekend), where they hear evidence from witnesses, have the chance to question the witnesses and deliberate on the topic among themselves. At the end of the period, participants are asked to complete again the questionnaire they originally completed. The responses to the questionnaires before and after the deliberation can then be compared. Deliberative opinion polls have been held in a number of countries. Some deliberative opinion polls have been held online (Smith, 2005: 98). Unlike, citizens' juries and consensus conferences, deliberative opinion polls are more a mechanism for helping members of the public to refine their opinions, than a mechanism which helps the public to directly influence the public policy process.

Deliberative mapping is a newer mechanism than the ones outlined above. Unlike the other deliberative mechanisms mentioned, deliberative mapping aims to bring together members of the public and experts in a deliberative process (Smith, 2005: 43). Citizens, who are representative of the wider population in terms of socio-demographic criteria, meet, in the first part of the process, as a group. At this stage they learn about the problem, they agree a set of criteria to judge different options and score the options they are considering against the criteria. Specialists also give their opinions about the options, during individual interviews. The specialists and the citizens then meet together in a workshop. Finally, the citizens and the specialists re-evaluate the options. This is a relatively new mechanism and its use by public policymakers is in its early days.

Co-governance Innovations

The deliberative mechanisms outlined above are aimed not only at increasing public participation but also, and perhaps more importantly, they are aimed at improving the quality of public opinion. They are generally used to advise policymakers, rather than being direct public policy decision-making bodies. Co-governance innovations have a slightly different aim. The thinking behind co-governance is public bodies, or governance institutions, sharing power with the people. Co-governance mechanisms give members of the public a role in policymaking that goes beyond consultation or advice and involves a direct say in decision-making; they also usually give members of the public a direct role in agenda-setting. Generally

co-governance mechanisms are not one-off events but continue over time. Co-governance approaches can promote deliberation between participants but they do not always do so. Perhaps the most well-known form of co-governance innovation is participatory budgeting, as pioneered in Porto Alegre, Brazil in 1989. The aim behind this approach was to give members of the public a direct input, in a structured way, into the budget process of their city council. In outline, participatory budgeting, as originally developed in Porto Alegre, involved assemblies being established at neighbourhood level where citizens could decide on investment priorities and select some of their number to join decision-making bodies that made proposals on a budget for the whole city that was considered by the city legislature (Smith, 2005: 59). In a five-year period at the end of the 1990s, 8.4 per cent of the adult population said they had participated in the budgeting process within the previous five years. While the deliberative mechanisms mentioned earlier tend to be either one-off initiatives or the participants only take part over a fairly short time period, the participatory budgeting process is carried out annually and people can participate year after year if they so wish. Moreover, the activities and decisions of the people have a direct and structured input into the policy process (Ginsborg, 2008). Participatory budgeting has undergone development and has been extended from Brazil into a number of other Latin American countries and has been tried in other countries, such as Britain.

Another type of co-governance involves giving citizens places on partnership boards of one kind or another. In a number of countries, regeneration projects have been introduced, with the boards that control the implementation of the projects being made up, solely or in part, of people from the local community (Burton et al., 2004). In most cases, the budgets for these projects are determined by the government but, subject to oversight, the local boards are given control over the spending of the budget and the successful implementation of the project.

Members of the public are also in some cases given seats on other types of partnership board, such as those that are formed between different types of public service providers or between public and private sector organizations. These developments are often criticized for giving the appearance of democracy and legitimacy while largely ignoring the substance of democratic legitimacy and reflecting inequalities of power (Davies, 2007).

A third form of co-governance is the use of citizens' assemblies. Two citizens' assemblies have been used by two provinces in Canada to consider the question of which electoral system should be used in the province. In British Columbia, the assembly was set up in January 2004. The assembly operated for just short of a year, with its report being produced in December 2004 (Warren and Pearse, 2008). The assembly had 160 members who were selected at random, an independent chair, a man and a woman from each of the 79 electoral districts of the province and two Aboriginal members. Members of the assembly were paid a limited amount for their work. The assembly took evidence from a wide range of people and groups. Its recommendation was put to a referendum of the electors, where it failed to gain the required threshold level of support for reasons that do not concern us here (but see Warren, 2008a for an analysis of the reasons). What was fairly unique about this mechanism is that it gave the assembly almost complete control over the selection of the province's voting system (with the referendum as the only proviso to that control). It is unusual for governments (at any level of authority) to voluntarily give up control of a policy area, especially one, like the voting system, that will have considerable impact on elected representatives.

Mechanisms of direct democracy

The citizens' assembly idea is very close to a form of direct democracy and, indeed, the final method that determined the process in British Columbia (the referendum) is seen as one of the main mechanisms of direct democracy. Direct democracy can, of course, be traced back to Ancient Athens and is regarded by some as the purest form of democracy (cf. Ranciere, 2006). Direct democracy enables individuals to express individually their position on a specific issue or issues. Using direct democracy can be seen as giving decisions added legitimacy. The use of referendums is not particularly new. Referendums are widely used in Switzerland, where they have been part of the policymaking process for a number of years, and in parts of the United States (Qvortrup, 2005). The basic idea of the referendum is that the electorate is able to vote yes or no on a specific issue. Referendums can be advisory or binding (the government, etc., has to implement the referendum decision). They can also be introduced on the volition of the legislature or as a result of the citizens demanding a referendum, after getting a certain number of signatures on a petition, the so-called citizen initiative. The right of citizens to demand a referendum only applies in a small number of countries. The use of referendums has increased around the world in recent years and referendums have been held online, as have citizen initiatives (Smith, 2005: 99–100). Referendums are sometimes criticized for pandering to populism, for simplifying complex issues and for being open to manipulation by the press and the wealthy who have the resources to get their views across to the public which others lack (cf. O'Toole, 2008, analysing the Irish referendum on the European Union Lisbon Treaty).

Consultation innovations

Consultation exercises, such as public meetings and opinion surveys, have been used for a number of years to gauge the views of citizens and the users of public services. However, there are more recently established mechanisms of consultation that have been used to try to involve citizens in the policy process. Unlike co-governance initiatives, consultation exercises do not give members of the public a direct say in policymaking, nor generally do they involve members of the public in setting the agenda for consultations. The aim behind most consultations is for public institutions to collect information, ideas and opinions from members of the public and to use this data to help improve policymaking and implementation. Consultations can also be used with the aim of giving people a feeling that they have contributed to the public policy process and to help reduce the gap between the positions of public policymakers and the people. One consultation mechanism developed in recent years is Planning for Real, established by the Neighourhood Initiatives Foundation. It is often, though not exclusively, used in neighourhood regeneration schemes (Smith, 2005: 31). A model of the local community is devised and taken physically to different geographical parts of the neighbourhood. This is a mechanism that enables people to physically express through the use of option cards how they would like their local community to develop. The recommendations that people make are only advisory and people have no further direct input into decision-making.

Another consultation method that is widely used is standing forums, of one sort or another (Smith, 2005: 32–4). Forums made up of users of a specific service, or a sample that is representative of the population, have been established in a number of countries, at different territorial levels, and they can give the members the opportunity to discuss issues relating to the service, or the more general issues, and to feed through the outcomes of those discussions to policymakers. Forums can hold face-to-face meetings, communicate through the post or use the Internet for communication. Such forums are usually advisory and do not have decision-making powers. Forums can sometimes promote deliberation between members but do not always do so or aim to do so. Questions have been raised about their democratic content

and how they relate to issues of democratic legitimacy.

GOVERNACE AND DEVELOPMENTS IN PARTICIPATION

Having outlined a number of participation mechanisms that have been used by public policymakers in recent years, in this and the following sections, I will critically analyse those developments. The main concern of this analysis will be to consider the extent to which the innovations in participation are compatible with, and help to advance, democracy.

Ricardo Blaug (2002) has argued that there are two broad approaches to democracy. One approach sees democracy as essentially connected to ideas of representation and broadly associated with the institutions of liberal democracy. This conception of democracy he contrasts with another approach, which sees democracy as an ethical way of life that transcends the limited institutions of liberal democracy and permeates, or should permeate, all areas of society. The first approach, Blaug (2002: 104) terms incumbent democracy, the second, critical democracy (Blaug 2002: 105–6). The two approaches do not sit easily together.

Blaug (2002: 112–3) argues that where incumbent democracy, by which he means the leaders of governments at different geographical levels, try to increase the opportunities for public participation they do so on their terms and they end up controlling the participation process and the people who participate. Efforts to increase public participation usually involve governments trying to work with groups in civil society of various kinds. Such democratic engineering, Blaug (2002: 112) argues, results in what Habermas (1987) has termed 'colonization'. For Blaug (2002: 112) this process leads to the representatives of groups being separated from other group members and becoming part of one or more bureaucratic structures. Critical participation among group members is discouraged and incumbent democracy takes precedence over critical democracy.

In a not dissimilar vein, Bevir (2006) contrasts two approaches to participation. Systems governance is a top-down approach, where participation is developed through networks which are seen as a means of improving service delivery. Systems governance uses the language of radical democracy. Radical democrats, on the other hand, support a bottom-up position, which is a pluralist approach where power over aspects of governance is taken over by civil society associations and in which citizens are involved in actual public policymaking and implementation. Bevir is sceptical of efforts by policymakers to promote participation.

Of course, many academics, politicians and officials would not accept Blaug's characterization of democracy and would deny the whole 'colonization thesis'. Beetham (1993), for example, has argued that the distinction between a representative form of democracy and a participatory democracy is misplaced. He sees ideas associated with democracy as finding expression along a continuum. At one end of the spectrum is complete direct democracy, where all decisions are made by all participants (or what Beetham calls the 'collectivity'). At the other end is complete autocracy, where the people (or the members of the collectivity) have no say at all in policy- or decision-making. In reality, Beetham argues, democratic systems fall somewhere in between the two extremes. At the heart of most modern forms of democracy lies the election of representatives. The mechanisms that aim at promoting public participation, which were outlined earlier in the chapter, are an enhancement of the basic representative system. They are fully compatible with representative, parliamentary democracy but, none the less, in Beetham's view, represent useful efforts to expand public participation (Beetham, 2005). Beetham's argument is similar to that of Van Rooy (2004) who supports what she terms 'supplementary democracy'. In this argument, civil society organizations, or international non-governmental organizations (INGOs), would supplement the existing institutions of global governance. Under supplementary democracy, INGOs would influence the agenda of such institutions and supplement the activity of national governments at the global level. The involvement of national governments in international forums would provide a form of legitimacy based on the accountability of government ministers to their national electorates. However, for Van Rooy (2004), from a democratic perspective, this should be enhanced by the involvement of INGOs in different ways in helping to hold global policymakers accountable.

A number of global institutions have shown a willingness to work with (certain) INGOs. The European Commission (EC) and the European Union (EU) more generally has addressed its relationship with civil society organizations and considered what it expects from non-governmental organizations (NGOs) that work with the EC and other EU institutions (cf. Greenwood and Halpin, 2007). The United Nations (UN) has also reflected on how best to engage with civil society, forming a Panel of Eminent Persons on UN–Civil Society Relations that reported in 2004. The Panel's report argues that the engagement with NGOs 'could help the United Nations do a better job, further its global goals, become more attuned and responsive to citizens' (United Nations, 2004: 8). Similar debates have taken place within the World Trade Organization (WTO) about its relationship with civil society organizations (Mason, 2004). But on what basis can the involvement of civil society organizations in the process of governance, at whatever geographical levels, be justified or seen as legitimate?

LEGITIMACY

A central concept in political analysis is legitimacy. The broad idea of legitimacy is connected to an action, a process, a decision, an institution, or a political regime being justified. There have been a number of different approaches to the idea of legitimacy. For some, the main way to determine if legitimacy existed was whether the institution, action or whatever was being considered, was perceived to be legitimate. For example, a liberal democratic electoral system would be legitimate if a large proportion of the electorate voted. This approach can be found, for example, in the work of Lipset (1984: 88). He has argued that 'Legitimacy involves the capacity of its political system to engender and maintain the belief that the existing political institutions are the most appropriate for the society'. As we will see later, legitimacy can be seen as having other elements. This use of the concept, however, relates to the feeling among politicians that the falling turnout in elections, the decline in party political membership and falling political trust were symptomatic of a decline in political legitimacy. A widespread corollary of this was that new opportunities for the public to engage politically were seen as needed for regimes to regain political legitimacy. However, given that universal adult suffrage, voting in elections and mass engagement in political parties are seen as key factors that give liberal democratic regimes legitimacy, where would the new mechanisms of public participation gain their legitimacy?

One argument that has been used to try to show that the types of mechanisms outlined earlier are legitimate is based on the nature of the process or procedures that the mechanisms entail. So, for example, deliberative mechanisms, like citizens' juries, are seen as legitimate because they are based around procedures where all participants have an equal, or fair, opportunity to express their opinions, participants try to convince others of the validity of their positions through reasoned arguments, and power external to the jury and coercion are excluded. In short, citizens' juries are seen as expressing free, equal and informed decision-making, in line with key aims of democracy. Two different types of criticisms can be made against

this argument. One criticism is based around the importance of representation in any conception of democracy. Given that not everyone can participate, O'Neill (2001) argues that those involved in political decision-making should represent those who cannot participate. For O'Neill, a basic problem with the type of deliberative mechanisms outlined in this chapter is that the participants do not represent wider constituencies. The participants have no authorization from, or accountability to, a constituency. Moreover, because (generally speaking) only small numbers participate in deliberative mechanisms, it is argued that they are unrepresentative of those who are affected by the decisions made in these mechanisms (Kenyon et al., 2001). Those types of criticisms could also be applied to other mechanisms where members of the public are not representing non-participants.

Another criticism is that it is often unclear how the decisions made in deliberative institutions influence and feed into public policy decision-making. As consultative mechanisms, in many cases it is unclear how most of the innovative mechanisms outlined in this chapter relate to traditional methods of public policy decision-making or even how they influence ultimate policy outcomes. O'Neill (2001: 494), however, picking up on an argument advanced by Jacobs (1997: 224), sees one of the possible ways of overcoming the representation problem of deliberative mechanisms as an insistence 'upon a weaker role for such institutions within the democratic process, say to the formulation of options and possible recommendations, allowing for other forms of accountability to be retained in the decisionmaking process'.

A number of writers have argued that political legitimacy in a democracy is not just concerned with procedures or processes, it also demands a substantive element (for example, Estlund, 1997). Parkinson (2006: 23) argues that, 'The substantive grounds are of two kinds: the degree to which policy outcomes match the goals of the people affected, and the degree to which they achieve normatively justifiable or desirable ends'. Parkinson (2006: 23–4) argues that in a legitimate democracy, the ends of policy should be determined by the people, but he suggests that the ends would include freedom, justice, equality, along with meeting the emotional, physical and educational needs associated with individual autonomy. Some might question whether the mechanisms outlined in this chapter meet this requirement of legitimacy.

DEMOCRACY

Beetham (1993) sees the idea of democracy as underpinned by the principles of political equality and popular control. A number of other writers also see political equality as central to the idea of democracy and as bound up with the opportunity to participate in the political process (e.g., Dahl, 1989, 2006), while writers like Held (2006: 1–4), who view democracy as representing the rule of the people, also see the equal opportunity to participate in the political process as a crucial element of democracy. However, Parry and Moyser (1994: 44), while accepting that in measuring the extent of democracy 'the degree of popular political participation must constitute one of the indices', argue that we cannot simply 'conclude that the more the people participate in politics, the more democratic the system of government'. As they show in respect of Britain, participation in politics is uneven between social groups. Important issues for Parry and Moyser (1994: 57) are who participates, whether the views of those who participate are representative of wider populations and whether élite decision-makers respond to the outcomes of the participation. As they put it:

> There are at least two dimensions to the 'effectiveness' of participation. One would be the extent to which the most active participants are representative of the concerns of the mass of the inactive population. The second is the degree

to which the elite appear to respond to citizen participation.

Those points reflect the concerns of O'Neill about participation and about the impact of participation.

Parry and Moyser (1994: 56) also raise a point about the danger of devolved forms of participation, which are common in some forms of governance, providing the advantaged in society, and their well-entrenched and well-resourced groups, with the opportunity to protect their interests. 'To the degree that fairness requires uniformity of consideration and treatment, this can point in the direction of a significant measure of centralization. At the very least, the autonomy of devolved centres of decision-making must be constrained by some minimal constitutional rules' (Parry and Moyser, 1994: 57). For all its limitations and problems, universal adult suffrage, one person one vote, is based on clear ideas of equality. Of course, in practice, at least in the majority of countries where voting is not compulsory, there are differences between social groups in the levels of electoral participation. However, people have the same formal opportunity to participate, whereas, critics argue, in the type of mechanisms outlined in this chapter and associated with developments in governance, this very often is not the case. There are, of course, mechanisms that enshrine the idea of political equality such as the citizen assemblies used in Canada, where a referendum of the people ultimately decides the issue, and the referendum itself conforms to ideas of political equality. However, there are debates about the extent to which the referendum should be used within democracy.

For some writers, such as Weale (2000: 54–105), one of the benefits of representative democracy is that it enables a workable division of labour to be established. Engagement in politics, for Weale, is only one activity in which people want to participate. People have important priorities other than participating in politics and we should not make unreasonable demands on people's limited time when deciding what a workable democracy should contain. The implication of this argument is that the widespread use of referendums would represent too great an imposition on the public. An added argument against the use of referendums to decide some subjects is that many public policy issues are extremely complex and it is a travesty to reduce them to a yes or no decision in a referendum. Members of the general public cannot be experts in all areas of public policy, even with the best will in the world, and it is only sensible to leave some issues to be decided by a limited section of the public. If the people who ultimately make the decisions are elected by, and accountable to, the wider population, the principles of democracy are not undermined.

Where representatives from social groups or parts of a geographical community are selected to engage in participation exercises, as is often the case in partnership boards or where the providers of public services meet with representatives of local communities and service users, issues of the accountability of the representatives to the wider constituencies become particularly pertinent. Efforts to enhance political participation can often ignore crucial issues of political equality.

Dahl has argued that there are five criteria which stand at the heart of democracy: effective participation; equality in voting; gaining enlightened understanding; final control of the agenda; and inclusion (Dahl, 2006: 9; see also Dahl, 1989: 106–31). The relation of the initiatives to ideas of equality in voting and inclusion has been considered. However, it is also worthwhile seeing how the initiatives relate to the other criteria. Effective participation should relate not only to opportunities to participate and the relationship of non-participants to participants but also to the policy impact of the participation. If there is no clear, systematic mechanism by which the decisions reached can feed into ultimate policy decision-making, I would suggest that it is difficult to regard the participation as effective. This criticism can be levied at a number of the initiatives mentioned where there is no systematic

process for the decisions of the participants to be incorporated into the policy process. The deliberative initiatives are intended to help participants become more informed and to reach 'better' decisions. As such, they are compatible with, and indeed help to advance, Dahl's criterion of people gaining enlightened understanding. The same might be said about initiatives such as citizen assemblies and for community and user participation in partnerships and networks. It is not, however, necessarily true for referendums or citizen initiatives, neither of which inevitably leads to greater understanding among those who vote or sign petitions.

The question of who controls the agenda is one where most of the initiatives can come under criticism. In the deliberative mechanisms, participants are generally given a topic or subject that they have to deliberate about; similarly, in citizen assemblies and referendums the issue is one that is determined before the activity begins. The position may be more open with respect to partnerships and networks, where members of the public participate. In these initiatives, the members of the public who participate often have a chance to influence the agenda, though in some cases, the providers of public services or other members of the network will have either formal or affective control of the agenda (Burton et al., 2004). Citizen initiatives are, of course, a mechanism where members of the public determine the agenda.

CONCLUSION

Moves to governance have resulted in new forms and opportunities for public participation. A number of the new mechanisms have been considered in this chapter. The initiatives in participation have been associated with the development of policy networks, policy partnerships of various kinds, decentralization and a more consumerist and market-oriented approach to public services.

The innovations in participation have reflected declines in traditional forms of participation associated with representative democracy. The various mechanisms have different implications for who can participate, how they can participate and the impact the outcomes of the participation have for the public policy process.

On the whole, the innovations are a supplement to traditional representative democracy, rather than an alternative to representative democracy. A number of key critiques have been made of different mechanisms. At a fundamental level, some argue that the efforts of policymakers to promote participation can undermine the development of a radical democracy where the people control the process and are actively involved in policy decision-making. Among those who are not so sceptical in principle of efforts by policymakers to promote public participation, a key criticism is that a number of the mechanisms do not sit easily with ideas of political equality which are central to democracy. As we have seen, the problem of representation is raised in relation to deliberative mechanisms and might also be applied to other initiatives. How convincing is this critique? Most writers on democracy would accept that, taking the political system overall, it is crucial that the idea of political equality is embedded in the system. But, it can be argued, that does not necessarily mean that all elements of the political system have to enshrine political equality. Writers such as Saward (2003) and Parkinson (2006) have argued that a multiple of different mechanisms, some of which, for example, will be deliberative, some of which will be based on traditional representative mechanisms, should be combined in an overall democratic system. In this approach, it would not matter whether some mechanisms are not made up of 'representative' participants. This seems to me to be a strong argument, which also connects with a consideration of O'Neill.

However, if the 'representation' critique can in theory be answered, that does not mean that under systems of governance that have been developed, it is satisfactorily dealt with in practice. The mechanisms outlined are often applied in an ad hoc way and do not form a systematic effort to achieve an overall system of democracy that reflects the five key aspects identified by Dahl. Moreover, developments associated with governance, such as greater use of the private sector for the delivery of public services and the development of quasi-markets, do not increase the opportunities for greater democratic participation. The whole idea of treating the users of public services as consumers is seriously at odds with any commitment to extending democratic public participation. There is no denying that the mechanisms introduced do create enhanced opportunities for sections of the population to participate more fully in politics. But, given that participation levels in different sections of society tend to be unequal, if the enhanced opportunities for participation only result in those who already participate a great deal participating even more, while those who do not participate, or participate little, do not increase their participation, then one of the reasons for introducing the mechanisms will not have been fulfilled. This is obviously an empirical point and evidence on this matter from around the world is limited.

The fear that democrats have about the mechanisms is that, rather than dealing with the issue of under-representation by some social groups, they will accentuate inequalities in participation. Phillips (1999: 116–9), for example, argues that, for all their attractive features, deliberative mechanisms rarely address issues of who makes the final decision. If deliberative mechanisms are consultative then, Phillips argues, whatever efforts are made to ensure that their composition is socially representative, if nothing is done to make the final decision-making body socially representative, the promise of democracy – to institute self-government – will not be fulfilled. Similar arguments could be made about other of the mechanisms outlined, especially, but not solely, those that are consultative. Macpherson (1977) argued some time ago that a vicious circle operated in respect of participation in capitalist liberal democracies. Macpherson's view was that for greater public participation to be achieved, more equality is needed, but to gain more equality, greater public participation is needed. The problem was how to break into this circle. Since Macpherson wrote, inequality in many societies has increased and in some cases significantly (cf. Therborn, 2006). For those who hope to see an increase in public participation, and a more equitable social spread, working to reduce inequality may be as important as increasing the possibilities for participation.

REFERENCES

Beetham, David (1993) 'Liberal Democracy and the Limits of Democratization', in D. Held (ed.), *Prospects for Democracy: North, South, East, West*. Cambridge: Polity Press; pp. 53–73.

Beetham, David (2005) *Democracy: A Beginner's Guide*. Oxford: One World Publications.

Bevir, Mark (2006) 'Democratic Governance: Systems and Radical Perspectives', *Public Administration Review* 66(3): 426–36.

Blaug, Ricardo (2002) 'Engineering Democracy', *Political Studies* 50(1): 102–16.

Burke, Edmund (1854–56) 'Speech to the Electors of Bristol on Being Declared by the Sheriffs Duly Elected', in *The Works of the Right Honourable Edmund Burke*. Vol. 1. London: Henry G. Bohn; pp. 446–8.

Burton, Paul, Goodlad, Robina, Croft, Jacqui, et al. (2004) *What Works in Community Involvement in Area-Based Initiatives? A Systematic Review of the Literature*, Online Report 53/04. London: Home Office. Available at: http://www.homeoffice.gov.uk/rds/pdfs04/rdsolr5304.pdf Accessed 15 November 2005.

Dahl, Robert (1989) *Democracy and Its Critics*. New Haven, CT: Yale University Press.

Dahl, Robert (2006) *On Political Equality*. New Haven, CT: Yale University Press.

Dalton, Russell (2004) *Democratic Challenges, Democratic Choices: The Erosion in Political Support in Advanced Industrial Democracies*. Oxford, Oxford University Press.

Dalton, Russell (2006) *Citizen Politics: Public Opinion and Political Parties in Advanced Industrial Democracies*, 4th edn. Washington, DC: CQ Press.

Davies, Jonathan S. (2007) 'The Limits of Partnership: An Exit-Action Strategy for Local Democratic Inclusion', *Political Studies* 55(4): 779–800.

Dienel, Peter (1999) 'Planning Cells: The German Experience', in U. Khan (ed.), *Participation Beyond the Ballot. Box European Case Studies in State–Citizen Political Dialogue*. London: UCL Press; pp. 81–93.

Dingwerth, Klaus (2008) 'Private Transnational Governance and the Developing World: A Comparative Perspective', *International Studies Quarterly* 52(3): 607–34.

Dryzek, John (2002) *Deliberative Democracy and Beyond: Liberals, Critics, Contestations*. Oxford: Oxford University Press.

Estlund, David (1997) 'Beyond Fairness of Deliberation: The Epistemic Dimension of Political Authority', in J. Bohman and W. Rehg (eds), *Deliberative Democracy: Essays on Reason and Politics*. Cambridge, MA: MIT; pp. 173–204.

Fishkin, James (1997) *The Voice of the People*. Durham, NC: Duke University Press.

Flynn, Norman (2007) *Public Sector Management*, 5th edn. London: Sage. (1st edn, 1990)

Ginsborg, Paul (2008) *Democracy Crisis and Renewal*. London: Profile Books.

Greenwood, Justin and Halpin, Darren (2007) 'The European Commission and the Public Governance of Interest Groups in the European Union: Seeking a Niche between Accreditation and Laissez-faire', *Perspectives on European Politics and Society* 8(2): 189–210.

Habermas, Jürgen (1987) *The Theory of Communicative Action*. Vol. 2. Cambridge, MA: MIT Press.

Held, David (2006) *Models of Democracy*, 3rd edn. Cambridge: Polity Press. (1st edn, 1987)

Hood, Christopher (1991) 'A Public Management for All Seasons?'. *Public Administration* 69(1): 3–19.

International IDEA (2009) *Turnout Over Time*, Available at: http://www.idea.int/vt/survey/voter_turnout1.cfm Accessed 10 January 2009.

Jacobs, Michael (1997) 'Environmental Valuations, Deliberative Democracy and Public Decision-making Institutions', in J. Foster (ed.), *Valuing Nature*. London: Routledge; pp. 211–31.

Jefferson Center (2008) 'Citizens' Juries Process'. Available at: http://www.jefferson-center.org/index.asp?Type=B_BASIC&SEC={2BD10C3C-90AF-438C-B04F-88682B6393BE} Accessed 24 November 2008.

Kenyon, Wendy, Hanley, Nick and Nevin, Ceara (2001) 'Citizens' Juries: An Aid to Environmental Valuation?', *Environment and Planning C: Government and Policy* 19(4): 557–66.

Lipset, Seymour Martin (1984) 'Social Conflict, Legitimacy and Democracy', in W. Connolly (ed.), *Legitimacy and the State*. Oxford: Blackwell; pp. 88–103.

Lowndes, Vivien, Pratchett, Lawrence and Stoker, Gerry (2001) 'Trends in Public Participation: Part 2 – Citizens' Perspectives', *Public Administration* 79(2): 445–55.

McLaverty, Peter and Halpin, Darren (2008) 'Deliberative Drift: The Emergence of Deliberation in the Policy Process', *International Political Science Review* 29(2): 197–214.

Macpherson, C.B. (1977) *The Life and Times of Liberal Democracy*. Oxford: Oxford University Press.

Mair, Peter and van Biezen, Ingrid (2001) 'Party Membership in Twenty European Democracies, 1980–2000', *Party Politics* 7(1): 5–21.

Mansbridge, Jane (2003) 'Practice-Thought-Practice', in A. Fung and E.O. Wright (eds), *Deepening Democracy: Institutional Innovations in Empowered Participatory Governance*. London: Verso; pp. 175–19.

Marshall, Peter (1993) *Demanding the Impossible: A History of Anarchism*. Glasgow: Fontana.

Mason, Michael (2004) 'Representing Transnational Environmental Interests: New Opportunities for Non-governmental Organisation Access within the World Trade Organisation?', *Environmental Politics* 13(3): 566–89.

Mill, John Stuart (1975) *Considerations on Representative Democracy*, in *John Stuart Mill Three Essays*. Oxford: Oxford University Press.

Mill, John Stuart (1987) *Principles of Political Economy: With Some of Their Applications to Social Philosophy*. Fairfield, NJ: A.M. Kelley.

O'Neill, Claire (2003) 'Citizens' Juries and Social Learning: Understanding the Transformation of Preference'. PhD thesis, University of Luton.

O'Neill, John (2001) 'Representing People, Representing Nature, Representing the World', *Environment and Planning C: Government and Policy* 19(4): 483–500.

Osborne, David and Gaebler, Ted (1992) *Reinventing Government: How the Entrepreneurial Spirit Is Transforming the Public Sector*. New York: Plenum.

O'Toole, Fintan (2008) 'The Fear Factor Devastated Ireland's Flaccid Political Class', *Guardian* June 14.

Parkinson, John (2003) 'Legitimation Problems in Deliberative Democracy', *Political Studies* 51(1): 180–96.

Parkinson, John (2006) *Deliberating in the Real World: Problems of Legitimacy in Deliberative Democracy*. Oxford: Oxford University Press.

Parry, Geraint and Moyser, George (1994) 'More Participation, More Democracy?', in D. Beetham (ed.), *Defining and Measuring Democracy*. London: Sage; pp. 44–62.

Phillips, Anne (1999) *Which Equalities Matter?* Cambridge: Polity Press.

Pierre, Jon and Peters, B. Guy (2000) *Governance, Politics and the State*. Basingstoke: Palgrave Macmillan.

Qvortrup, Matt (2005) *A Comparative Study of Referendums*, 2nd edn. Manchester: Manchester University Press. (1st edn, 2002)

Rancière, Jacques (2006) *Hatred of Democracy*. London: Verso.

Rhodes, R.A.W. (1997) *Understanding Governance: Policy Networks, Governance, Reflexivity and Accountability*. Buckingham: Open University Press.

Rhodes, R.A.W. (2006) 'Policy Network Analysis', in M. Moran, M. Rein and R.E. Goodin (eds), *The Oxford Handbook of Public Policy*. Oxford: Oxford University Press; pp. 425–47.

Saward, Michael (2003) 'Enacting Democracy', *Political Studies* 51(1): 161–79.

Smith, Graham (2005) *Beyond the Ballot, 57 Democratic Innovations From Around the World*. London: The Power Inquiry.

Squires, Judith (2002) 'Deliberation and Decision Making: Discontinuity in the Two-track Model', in M.P. d'Entrèves (ed.), *Democracy as Public Deliberation: New Perspectives*. Manchester: Manchester University Press; pp. 133–56.

Therborn, Goran (2006) 'Meaning, Mechanisms, Patterns and Forces: An Introduction', in G. Therborn (ed.), *Inequalities of the World*. London: Verso; pp. 1–59.

United Nations (2004) *We the Peoples Civil Society, the United Nations and Global Governance. Report of the Panel of Eminent Persons on United Nations–Civil Society Relations*. New York: United Nations.

Van Rooy, Alison (2004) *The Global Legitimacy Game: Civil Society, Globalization, and Protest*. Macmillan: Palgrave.

Warren, Mark E. (2008a) 'Citizen Representatives', in M.E. Warren and H. Pearse (eds), *Designing Deliberative Democracy: The British Columbia Assembly*. Cambridge: Cambridge University Press; pp. 50–69.

Warren, Mark E. (2008b) 'Governance-driven Democratization'. Paper presented at the Interpretation in Policy Conference, University of Essex.

Warren, Mark E. and Pearse, Hilary (eds) (2008) *Designing Deliberative Democracy: The British Columbia Assembly*. Cambridge: Cambridge University Press.

Weale, Albert (2000) *Democracy*. Basingstoke: Palgrave.

Williams, Geraint (ed.) (1976) *John Stuart Mill on Politics and Society*. London: Fontana; pp. 335–8.

27

Leadership

Janet V. Denhardt and
Robert B. Denhardt

Scholars and practitioners now recognize that the design and implementation of public policy, or what some have called 'the steering of society' (Nelissen et al., 1999), no longer resides with a single governmental unit acting alone or in close concert with one or two others, but has been supplanted by complex governance networks composed of a plurality of actors, each bringing their own special interests, resources, and set of expertise. Consequently, studies have focused on definitions of network governance, typical structures of governance, the role of metagovernance schemes, and how new governance schemes might best incorporate norms of transparency and civic engagement (Bang, 2003; Goldsmith and Eggers, 2004; Hajer and Wagenaar, 2003; Heffen, Kickert and Thomassen, 2000; Kettl, 2002; Kickert, Klijn and Kooiman, 1993; Koppenjan, 1997; March and Olsen, 1995; Marin and Mayntz, 1991; Pierre and Peters, 2000; Rhodes, 1997; Sorensen and Torfing, 2008).

Interestingly, the literature on network governance has paid relatively little attention to management issues and even less attention to *leadership* in governance. For example, while contributors to the recent and significant

volume *Theories of Democratic Network Governance* (Sorensen and Torfing, 2008) casually mention the importance of 'effective leadership,' there is not even sufficient attention given to this topic for it to be listed in the book's index. In many ways, this is surprising. Certainly, scholars interested in leadership have explored the relationship between political leadership and policy development, and that would seem to be a topic of great interest to those concerned with network governance. Moreover, there is a vast body of literature that demonstrates that the quality of leadership within an organization affects the performance of that organization (see, for example, Avolio and Luthans, 2006; Avolio et al., 2004; Gardner et al., 2005; Ilies, Morgeson and Nahrgang, 2005; Walumbwa et al., forthcoming). For those interested in the effectiveness of networks, a similar interest in the relation between leadership and governance would seem appropriate.

We suggest that one reason for the relative lack of attention to leadership among students of network governance is that leadership is typically conceived of in hierarchical terms, whereas network governance is primarily conceived in non-hierarchical terms.

Contemporary governance transcends the organizational boundaries and traditional authority structures that are foundational to our traditional understanding of leadership. As long as leadership is conceived in terms of power and position, the study of leadership would seem irrelevant to studies of network governance, where power and position are far from clear.

Not only do governance problems transcend traditional boundaries and negate the possibility of leadership based on hierarchy but also they challenge our ability to rationally plan for the future. The most vexing problems faced in governance today are those that are simply unanticipated. In such cases, traditional conceptions of planning, strategy, and the implementation of preconceived plans are of little use. These circumstances demand that we rethink the roles of leaders and question the aims and purposes of leadership. Taken together then, contemporary network governance demands that leaders work across structures, levels of government, sectors, as well as other traditional geographic, and even cultural boundaries, to find creative ways of responding to stubborn, exquisitely complex, and largely unanticipated problems. In short, what does it mean to be a leader when no one is in charge and no one has a plan?

We consider this question by first exploring the movement in studies of network governance from a concern for structure, often hierarchical structure, to a concern for modes of operation that are necessarily far less hierarchical. Secondly, we note a similar movement in leadership studies from leadership being conceived as dependent on the power and position of a single individual located in a hierarchical structure to one that sees leadership as a function that exists in all groups and organizations. Thirdly, we outline what we argue are the four new imperatives of leadership in governance: (1) fostering collaboration; (2) building resilience and adaptive capacity; (3) resolving ethical concerns through dialogue; and (4) engaging citizens.

NETWORK GOVERNANCE

Early studies of the operations of networks in the public, non-profit, and for-profit sectors tended to focus on the question of how various structures contribute to or detract from the effective operation of networks. In a summary and elaboration of this work by Provan and Kenis (2008), three forms of network governance are postulated. The first and simplest form is *participant governance*, a case in which the network is governed by the participants themselves without an overarching governance structure. Participant-governed networks can be highly decentralized or highly centralized, and may be governed as a lead organization. The second form is called *lead organization-governed networks*. In these cases, the inefficiencies of shared governance give way to the necessity for one organization taking a lead role in the network. A third type of network governance is the *network administrative organization*. Here a separate administrative entity, either an individual or a formal organization, is set up to govern the network. Provan and Kenis (2008) argue that the success of a particular mode of network governance is related to issues of trust, size, goal consensus, and the nature of the task. While Provan and Kenis (2008) note that networks cannot assume hierarchy, there are many cases in which networks find it beneficial to move toward more hierarchical structures.

More recent theories of network governance tend to more explicitly specify the non-hierarchical nature of network governance in the formulation of public policy. Sorensen and Torfing define a governance network as:

> 1) a relatively stable horizontal articulation of interdependence, but operationally autonomous actors; 2) who interact through negotiations; 3) which take place within a regular to, normative, cognitive and imaginary framework; 4) that is self-regulating within limits set by external agencies; and 5) which contributes to the production of public purpose' (Sorensen and Torfing, 2008: 9).

Similarly, in the same volume, Borzel and Panke define network governance as 'the formulation and implementation of collectively binding decisions by the systematic involvement of private actors with whom public actors coordinate their preferences and resources on the voluntary (nonhierarchical) basis' (Borzel and Panke, 2008: 156). In any case, the interdependency characteristic of network governance means that relations among participants are horizontal rather than vertical and no one actor can use hierarchical power to dominate others without risking destruction of the network (Wachhaus, 2009).

Network governance then, by definition, depends on the negotiated interaction of multiple and often independent participants. And, since these networks are composed of voluntary participants, any one of which may withdraw at any time, an insistence on hierarchical command within the network may be exactly the wrong approach to maintaining its effectiveness. In networks, various public, private, and non-profit groups cooperate on a non-hierarchical basis in the development and often implementation of public policy. Consequently, non-traditional approaches to leadership that emphasize the building of trust and commitment to common purposes are essential to the effective operation of the network.

CHANGING NOTIONS OF LEADERSHIP

Traditional conceptions of leaders as executives who develop organizational visions, manage operations, exert authority and control, and overcome resistance to change are inadequate and even counterproductive to the leadership imperatives of network governance in the twenty-first century. What is the nature of the current context and how does it change how we think about leadership, the roles of leaders, and the values that guide them as they seek to work through

others to tackle the complex and fluid challenges of governance?

Most definitions of leadership draw on a long history of defining leadership in terms of the power and position held by the leader. The leader is the one who exercises control and power over others to move them in a direction they might otherwise not go. Or, the leader is the one who occupies a certain position or 'office' in a hierarchy. That is, the president is seen as the leader of the country or the chief executive officer (CEO) is seen as the leader of the corporation. Even James Macgregor Burns (1978), whose notion of 'transformational leadership' is probably the most sophisticated formulation of ethical leadership, struggles to sort out an authentic relationship between leaders and followers because, for Burns, leadership remains tied to the idea of power and position, which carries with it a presumption of the leader's being in a privileged position in relation to followers.

Contemporary governance calls into question the very foundations of leadership as it has been commonly studied and practiced. For example, many see 'creating a vision' as the essential act of leadership. Indeed, the necessity of leaders providing a vision has become so much a part of contemporary leadership folklore that potential leaders often begin their efforts to lead by fashioning a vision and then transmitting that vision to the group or organization: indeed, often imposing it on the group. Fundamentally, however, the imposition of a vision involves either the explicit or implicit exercise of power. In a governance network involving multiple organizations and interests, there will at least initially be many and competing visions about what should happen, with no one group or organization with the authority or power to impose its vision on the other participants.

We may intellectually recognize the limitations of traditional conceptions of leadership, but it is so deeply engrained in modern society that it is difficult to conceive of an alternative. We suggest two reasons for the traditional association of leadership with power and position. The first is that the *practice of leadership* is deeply rooted in patterns of military domination and the relationship between masters and slaves, patterns that lie deep in our history and remain a part of our collective consciousness even today (Denhardt, 1987). The second reason for the traditional association of leadership with power and position is that the *study of leadership* has grown primarily out of studies of political leadership and corporate management, both of which are inevitably tied to considerations of power and authority. As Rost (1991) puts it, 'The influence of the industrial paradigm on leadership theory and practice has been monumental and pervasive' (91). What is needed is nothing short of a paradigmatic shift in how we conceptualize and practice leadership.

This reconceptualization is urgently necessary if we are to begin to address the demands of governance across levels, sectors, and organizations. In addressing pressing societal problems that cut across boundaries, there is simply no structure of authority that applies. Representatives of organizations may have authority within their own organizations, but as participants in a governance process there is no common authority structure. Instead, a new basis of leadership must be established based on a different set of assumptions. As Bryson, Crosby and Stone (2006) point out, leadership is essential in maintaining the viability of a network or collaboration because participants cannot rely on clear-cut rules or easily enforced directions. Network members will have to resolve issues of who plays key roles in the network, including 'leadership' roles (Crosby and Bryson, 2005). But, to a far greater degree than in traditional hierarchical organizations, the process of leadership will be shared among many participants and will be more informal than formal.

Consequently, the skills needed for leadership in governance networks are not the traditional skills of top-down management (supervision, delegation, etc.) but a quite different set of skills. The role of leadership

becomes far different from creating and imposing a vision; it becomes one of engaging with the various groups that are or might become members of the network to bring forth a common vision in which all can share. We prefer an alternative definition of leadership, one we think is far better suited to leadership in governance: leadership occurs where one member of a group or organization stimulates others to more clearly recognize their previously latent needs, desires, and potentialities and to work together toward their fulfillment. Note that using this definition (1) moves us away from a reliance on power and position, (2) recognizes leadership as a process that must occur throughout groups, organizations, and networks, and (3) recognizes that leadership can and will move from individual to individual. In the next section, we will outline several implications of a new mode of leadership for network governance.

THE NEW IMPERATIVES OF LEADERSHIP

If traditional conceptions of leadership based on power and authority are a poor fit with modern governance, it is helpful to consider how we might think about the new purposes or aims of leadership in this context. While the traditional aims of leadership can be conceived of as control, production, and organizational goal attainment, we argue that the primary aims of leadership in governance are: (1) fostering collaboration, (2) building resilience and adaptive capacity, (3) resolving ethical concerns through dialogue, and (4) engaging citizens. These imperatives are not mutually exclusive, but rather mutually reinforcing interrelated ideas that outline the shape of leadership in contemporary governance.

Fostering collaboration

In a most fundamental sense, network governance is about collaboration – collaboration among groups, organizations, and jurisdictions that bring different strengths, weaknesses, capacities, and limitations to the table. For this reason, it is important to review what we know about collaboration in the governance process, and then examine approaches to leadership that foster collaboration as well as the specific skills required of collaborative leaders.

The term 'collaboration' has received considerable attention in the literature on public policy and administration since there are an increasing variety of collaborations involving public agencies. Indeed, one might say that the governance networks that are our focus here are an extension or reconceptualization of the notion of collaboration. In any case, the general literature on collaboration provides an easy entry point into discussion of collaboration in network governance. We find especially useful the special issue of the *Public Administration Review* (2006) on 'Collaborative Public Management.' For purposes of the symposium, the editors defined collaborative public management as the process of facilitating and operating in multiorganizational arrangements to solve problems that cannot be solved or easily solved by single organizations. 'Collaborative means to *co-labor*, to cooperate to achieve common goals, working across boundaries in multisector relationships. Cooperation is based on the value of reciprocity' (O'Leary, Gerard and Bingham, 2006: 7).

Thomson and Perry (2006) suggest five dimensions of collaboration that we might interpret as *challenges* facing any potential leader of a governance network. The first is what Thomson and Perry (2006) call the *governance dimension*: the requirement that parties must come together to jointly make decisions about the rules to govern their activities and develop structures through which power can be shared. Such processes imply that the collaboration or network lacks authoritative or hierarchical structures for decision-making and that all parties must recognize the legitimate interests of other parties in the relationship. As we have

already pointed out, this requirement places special strains on traditional conceptions of leadership. The second, the *administration dimension*, is necessary to put ideas into action and, in the best cases, requires 'clear roles and responsibilities, the capacity to set boundaries, the presence of concrete achievable goals, and good communication' (Thomson and Perry, 2006: 25). Doing so requires a combination of administrative structures and social capacities both of which take quite different forms from those in traditional hierarchies and require different leadership skills.

Third is the *autonomy dimension*: i.e. the process of reconciling individual and collective interests. Parties to a collaboration or network retain their own distinct identities and allegiances to their 'home' organizations, but must simultaneously contribute to the achievement of collective goals and objectives. Many scholars point to this circumstance as perhaps the most challenging to the maintenance of effective governance networks (Bardach, 1998; Tschirhart, Christensen and Perry, 2005; Vigoda-Gadot, 2003; Wood and Gray, 1991). When individual goals or self-interests conflict with goals of the collective, the maintenance of the network is extremely difficult. For this reason, one of the requisite skills of leaders in networks is that of arriving at agreement around a set of shared goals or directions (which is markedly different from the traditional idea of a leader creating and imposing a vision).

The fourth is the *mutuality dimension*, the idea that unless all parties receive mutual benefits from the collaboration either in terms of differing interests or shared interests the collaboration will not likely be maintained. In contrast to negotiation, which begins from differences, Thomson and Perry (2006) stress the importance of 'jointly identifying commonalities among organizations such as similarity of mission, commitment to the target population, or professional orientation and culture' (27). The *trust and reciprocity dimension* is the fifth and refers to the necessity of establishing conditions of mutual trust among partners to the collaboration and building of both short-term and long-term reciprocity, a willingness to contribute assuming that others will contribute as well. We argue that trust-building is a central leadership skill, especially in governance networks.

As we said earlier, these dimensions of network performance may be considered challenges to the management of networks or, perhaps even more so, challenges to leadership in networks. What are the specific skills that we might associate with leaders interested in fostering collaboration? McGuire (2006) suggests four such skills: activation, framing, mobilizing, and synthesizing.

- Activation is the process of identifying and bringing into the network the right people and the right resources needed to meet mutually-agreed-upon program goals and objectives.
- Framing has to do with facilitating agreement around leadership and administrative roles and structures, even though those may change and evolve rapidly over time.
- Mobilizing is concerned with gaining commitment to the joint undertaking and building support from those who are participating in the network as well as those outside.
- Finally, synthesizing involves engendering productive and purposeful interaction among all actors. This again includes facilitating relationships in order to build trust and promote information exchange.

We would argue that these skills, and others like them, are not merely management skills but are leadership skills. Yet, they are not the traditional skills associated with power and position. Fostering collaboration requires facilitation, negotiation, conflict resolution, trust-building, and related skills. Importantly, in a governance network, these skills will not be the skills of a particular person holding a particular position, and indeed may shift from person to person over time. Leadership in this sense is better viewed as a process, something that occurs within a group,

organization, or network, but is not the 'property' of any particular individual. Nevertheless, effective leadership will be essential to the success of the network.

What can leadership scholars tell us about such an approach to leadership? Several studies of leadership have focused on the collaboration as a central quality of the leadership process and a key skill of effective leaders in modern society. Jean Lipman-Blumen, for example, begins her study of *Connective Leadership* (1996) by describing the circumstances increasingly faced by leaders today entering what she calls 'the connective era,' an era marked on the one hand by interdependence and on the other by diversity. Politically and economically, she argues, we are living in an age in which a decision made in one country or one industry has the potential to affect important decisions in many other countries or many other industries. Everything seems connected to everything else. At the same time, however, society seems marked by diversity. Everywhere there are signs of distinctive identities and the assertion of individualism. These developments are paradoxical in their impact. Interdependence may drive some individuals and groups to seek the comfort of their own distinctive identity. But the assumption of distinctive identities may make the process of negotiating interdependencies more difficult.

According to Lipman-Blumen (1996), the connective era has important implications for leaders and for the process of leadership. Leaders no longer have the luxury of making independent, autonomous decisions and expecting that their wishes will be carried out. Leaders are confronted with shorter time frames in which speed and agility are essential. As we elaborate in the next subsection, the capacity to adapt and respond is more and more central to leadership. Finally, leaders must develop new skills in negotiation, dialogue, and conflict resolution in preference to the traditional skills of command and control.

The connective era that Lipman-Blumen describes is very much the world of networks and network governance:

> The identifying marks of the Connective Era can be seen at all levels of organizations and in all spheres of human activity: politics and government, business and industry, education and religion. Wherever we look, we see loosely structured global networks of organizations and nations tied to multiple subnetworks, living in a clumsy, federated world (and sharing space in the archetype of interdependences, the natural environment). These networks link all kinds of groups, with long chains of leaders and supporters who communicate, debate, negotiate, and collaborate to accomplish their objectives (Lipman-Blumen, 1996: 9).

Lipman-Blumen's connective leader exhibits many qualities that fit the situation in which leaders in the connective era find themselves. They must be highly attuned to the ethical considerations involved in working across organizational, even cultural boundaries. They must be respectful of the interests and objectives of others, while at the same time working to create common understandings and a common commitment to a course of action. They must build communities of interest. Similarly, they must support the development of leadership and responsibility in others, including former adversaries. Most of all, they must operate 'by joining their vision to the dreams of others; by connecting and combining, rather than dividing and conquering' (Lipman-Blumen, 1996: 17).

Their primary interest is connection and their primary skill is collaboration, though not the old form of collaboration that relies too often on 'consensus or nothing.' Instead, the connective leader is interested in bringing together individuals, groups, and organizations that the leader recognizes as important for the diverse gifts they bring. This type of leadership is not one that seeks compromise as a way of moving forward, but rather values diversity and individualism, and builds *patchworks of interests* that permit, even encourage creative solutions and positive actions to address mutual concerns. The connective leader has the capacity to move beyond the sometimes paralyzing desire for consensus to achieve active collaboration.

Adaptive capacity and resilience

The second imperative of leadership in network governance is to build the adaptive capacity and resilience of the system. This imperative is a fundamental departure from the traditional and largely dominant view that focuses on leaders as the managers of and catalysts for organizational change. For example, transformational leadership models, particularly as defined by Bass (1985) and Bass and Avolio (1993), argue that the primary function of leadership is to focus on and bring about significant organizational change. As Van Wart (2003) states, leaders are called transformational when they succeed in moving their organizations in new directions and achieving measurably better results and outcomes. In this model, the objective is to raise the follower's level of awareness and acceptance of goals designated by the leader, and find ways to convince followers to transcend their own self-interests for the sake of the team or organization. Or, as Pawar and Eastman (1997) put it, leaders 'create a dynamic organizational vision that often necessitates a metamorphosis in cultural values to reflect greater innovation' (83). Successful transformational leaders convince followers to give up their 'selfish' personal goals, and look beyond their own self-interest to accept and embrace the organizational interests as defined by the leader.

This conception of leadership is a poor fit for contemporary realities of network governance for a number of reasons. First, the focus is on 'the' organization, rather than a fluid network of actors. Secondly, as already noted, there is at least an implied measure of control within the hierarchical organization which would underlie the leader's efforts to convince or coerce followers to adopt the leader's vision and goals. Obviously, in network governance, the focus moves beyond a single organization and hierarchical controls. It is not a matter of convincing people to give up their 'selfish' goals for the organizational good. Rather, leadership in this context must recognize that different participants and organizations have legitimate and important goals that, though they may be inconsistent with one another, cannot simply be overridden in light of a particular individual's vision for the future. A leadership approach that recognizes diversity and yet achieves a degree of unity is obviously needed.

We question here whether it is sufficient or appropriate to simply focus on 'change' as the goal. As Glover, Friedman and Jones (2002) note, there is a difference between 'adaptive' change and 'maladaptive' change. Organizations change all the time, but it is possible, even common, to create change that is not adaptive for the organization: 'change is no guarantee of successful adaption ... . When change does not involve adaptation, the result may be only additional activity layered on top of an organizations culture, often creating a situation worse than the starting place' (Glover, Friedman and Jones, 2002: 19).

Moreover, we argue that, regardless of the outcome of a particular change effort or challenge, the nature of the *change process itself* can leave a system either more brittle and inflexible or more flexible and adaptive. The need to retain flexibility and adaptability is even more critical as we move from leadership in organizations to leadership in networks. Traditionally, we pay particular attention to the response of leaders to crisis and evaluate their effectiveness based on how well they can engineer recovery from a particular challenge or disaster. With traditional command-and-control approaches, we may recover from such challenges, but, too often, the organizations and networks involved in the governance process are left weakened, more rigid, and less adaptive in the end.

A key imperative of leadership in governance, then, is to find ways to address pressing problems while also building the capacity for long-term resilience. It is no longer enough to simply recover from disaster if the recovery process leaves us less able to cope with future problems. In meeting the challenges of governance, leaders can play a central role in building cross-organizational and intra-sectorial adaptative capacity. Resilience speaks not only to the efficacy of the solutions to problems but also to the relationships that are built, the communication that is fostered, and the common ground that is realized through the process.

Focusing on resilience rather than recovery allows us to recognize that the most difficult problems confronted by the governance system not only transcend organizational and sector boundaries but also cannot be anticipated. While it is possible to develop strategies and plans for what we think will happen, doing so does not help when the utterly unexpected occurs. The challenge is not only to govern across boundaries but also to cope with the unanticipated and unimagined. Leaders in governance need to address challenges in a way that retains and enhances the capacity of the system to not only address the problem at hand but also to respond adaptively in the future to problems that are not yet foreseen.

Horne and Orr define resilience as:

> A fundamental quality of individuals, groups, organizations, and systems as a whole to respond productively to significant change that disrupts the expected pattern of events without engaging in an extended period of regressive behavior. This robust response capability is a direct reflection of the richness of internal/external connections for physical, emotional and resource support in learning-alternative adaptive behavior (Horne and Orr, 1998: 31).

Resilience in ecological terms refers to the capacity of natural systems to recover from environmental stresses in a way that leads to system sustainability: i.e. 'the use of environment and resources to meet the needs of the present without compromising the ability of future generations to meet their own needs' (Berkes, Colding and Folke, 2003: 2).

This has interesting parallels to network governance in that if we only focus on the problem at hand, rather than considering the vitality and adaptability of the system or network itself, we may compromise our ability to meet future challenges. As Sutcliffe and Vogus put it, 'An entity not only survives/thrives by positively adjusting to current adversity, but also, in the process of responding, strengthens its compatibilities to make future adjustments' (Sutcliffe and Vogus, 2003: 97).

It is this adaptive capacity of the governance system, purposefully instilled over time, that provides the basis for coordinated social action and decision-making when complex and unanticipated challenges occur. Resilience and capacity are built by consistently practicing over time and across problem or issue areas the process of adapting to change, focusing on opportunities rather than past practices, using problems as experiments, and collaborating across organizations and sectors. In writing about individual organizations, Lengnick-Hall and Beck (2005) suggest that the way to build resilience is by overcoming 'just manageable' threats over time. We suggest that the same can be said about networks. The reliability and resilience of the system or network is enhanced by practice: by handling problems and challenges over time in a manner that fosters trust, relationships, and collaboration. Leaders can play a pivotal role in this regard by acting and thinking about adaptive capacity as more important and fundamentally more useful than organizational visions, plans, and short-term responses to crisis.

Traditional management practices that rely on control strategies can actually erode organizational capacity and resilience (Denhardt and Denhardt, 2009). As Sutcliffe and Vogus (2003) note, organizations under threat often respond by becoming more rigid and exerting more control. Doing so reduces the variety and complexity of information and narrows the number of possible responses to the problem. Even if they know, intellectually, that collaboration and participation are important, in times of crisis – when everything seems to be flying out of control – leaders can often revert to command-and-control strategies. One way to avoid doing so is to practice resiliency and adaptive behaviors *before* disaster strikes so that it becomes an ingrained behavioral and cultural pattern within the system.

Horne and Orr (1998) suggest that there are seven 'streams' of practical behavior that contribute to adaptability and resilience:

Community:	A shared sense of purpose and identity
Competence:	The capacity and skills to meet demands
Connections:	Relationships and linkages expand capacity and flexibility
Commitment:	Trust and goodwill
Communication:	Strong communication to make sense and derive order
Coordination:	Good timing to ensure alignment
Consideration:	Attention to the human factor

These behaviors are consistent with the view of leadership espoused by Heifetz in his book, *Leadership Without Easy Answers* (1994). He states that leadership is no longer about 'telling people what to do.' Instead, the purpose of leadership is to help a group, an organization, or a community in recognizing its own vision and then learn how to move in that direction. He illustrates the difference between these two views of leadership, contrasting the following two definitions of leadership: 'leadership means influencing the community to follow the leader's vision' versus 'leadership means influencing the community to face its problems' (Heifetz, 1994: 14). Heifetz argues that the latter view is better suited to contemporary realities and recognition that tasks of leadership are not merely getting a job done, but rather 'adapting' to new and unusual circumstances.

Once established, resilient systems tend to have a number of important characteristics:

- First, resilient systems are redundant. Redundancy or excess capacity allows the system to function even if one component fails.

- Secondly, resilient systems are robust in that they are vigorous and interactive.
- Thirdly, resilient systems are flexible in that they are experienced in and comfortable with experimentation rather than only relying on standard operating procedures.
- Fourthly, resilient systems are reliable in that they can depend on the availability and accuracy of data and working communication channels.
- Finally, resilient systems are characterized by strong relationships, respect, and trust (Denhardt and Denhardt, forthcoming).

In this context, the focus of leadership moves from control to collaboration, from organizational authority to shared leadership, from results to relationships, from short-term change to long-term capacity. The purpose is not only to design and manage a particular change project but also to exercise leadership in a manner that contributes to the adaptability and flexibility of the network. Some have called this approach 'adaptive management,' which is, in many ways, the antithesis of traditional command-and-control management strategies. It is based on the premise that change and variability are like experiments that allow organizations and systems to continuously learn and adapt.

The adaptive management approach originated in industrial operations theory in the 1950s, and, in the 1970s, arguments emerged that it should be used as the approach to managing natural resources (Johnson, 1999). Rather than traditional natural resource management practices that focused on human control and engineering, ecologists increasingly embraced the idea that ecosystems are characterized by great uncertainty, suggesting that 'control' strategies be replaced by approaches that treat natural resource management policies as 'experiments' from which information could be gained and practices modified. The adaptive management of natural resources is 'a series of linked iterative steps involving problem identification, collaborative brainstorming, model development, hypothesis testing, planning, experimentation, monitoring, evaluation and behavioral change' (Habron, 2003: 29).

Adaptive management refers 'to a structured process of "learning by doing" that involves much more than simply better ecological monitoring and response to unexpected management impacts' (Walters, 1997: 1).

The concept of adaptive management can also be applied to networked governance as a means to foster resilience, adaptability, and sustainability. As already noted, modern governance is characterized by fluidity, complexity, and unpredictability. Under such circumstances, a 'learn as you go' strategy allows the leadership to respond to new information and new challenges in a manner that protects the flexibility and adaptability of the system itself. Rather than working from a unilateral 'grand plan' that is 'sold' to others, participants in the network learn together based on their shared experience, drawing on expertise wherever it resides, and rely on existing relationships of trust and collaboration to try different approaches and see how they work. This not only increases the likelihood of creative and successful solutions to problems but also it is an approach that can help maintain, rather than constrict, innovation and flexibility. Adaptive management is also related to the key role that leaders and managers play in creating shared values and shaping culture. The difference here is that the shared values transcend organizational boundaries and interests to embrace the higher-level values of democracy, participation, civility, shared power, and collaboration.

Resolving ethical concerns through dialogue

The third imperative for leadership in governance is resolving ethical concerns through dialogue. The leadership of governance networks clearly involves ethical considerations, not only related to the substance of what the network is doing but also with respect to the process of leadership itself.

First, if we are concerned with the effectiveness of the leader, is ethical leadership – that which most effectively promotes the interests of one's 'home' group or that which enables the different groups and organizations involved in a network to work together, most effectively?

Secondly, if we ask whether the leader is pursuing the right goals, whose goals are to be pursued? How do we justify the choice of one set of goals over another? What are the standards of, say, justice and equity, by which we would judge one goal to be good and another bad? Are such standards the same or similar across different groups and organizations or across different cultures? And, how do we define the character of the leader, a definition that may differ from group to group and certainly from culture to culture?

Thirdly, there is the question of *how* leadership is carried out, especially the question of how leaders and followers relate to one another. Certainly some organizations and some societies tolerate or even justify much more hierarchical structures and processes than others. What happens when the culture of one participating group or organization brings a far different set of expectations about the relation between leaders and followers than those of other participants? What happens when an organization reflecting one culture acts in ways that are inconsistent with the norms of another culture represented in the collaboration? We would suggest that these questions, related to the relationship between leaders and followers, are foundational, in the sense that an answer to any of these questions will affect the way in which all other questions of ethical leadership are answered.

We may be aided in understanding this question by recent work in ethical theory. In her book *Moral Understandings*, Margaret Walker (1998) distinguishes two models of morality. The first, which she calls the *theoretical-juridical* model, includes utilitarian, contract, Neo-Kantian, or rights-based theories, all of which see 'morality as a compact, propositionally codifiable, impersonally action-guiding code with an agent, or as a compact set of law-like propositions that 'explain' the moral behavior of a well-formed moral agent' (Walker, 1998: 7–8). Presumably all such codes would be universal. (This is, incidentally, the approach found in most studies of leadership ethics.) The alternative, which will be especially salient to our concerns, Walker calls the *expressive-collaborative* model. 'This view prescribes an investigation of morality as a socially embodied medium of mutual understanding and negotiation between people over their responsibility for things open to human care and response' (Walker, 1998: 9).

Such an expressive-collaborative model is increasingly necessary today, because it is extremely difficult to find a specific moral code that applies in all, or even most situations. People have different ideas about what constitutes ethical behavior depending on their position in society, their cultural background, or the accepted practices of their groups, their organizations, or their communities. People find their interactions make sense within one frame of reference, but make no sense to those outside that frame. This is especially true when groups and organizations come together in network relationships.

'An expressive-collaborative model looks at moral life as a continuing negotiation *among* people, a practice of mutually allotting, assuming, or deflecting responsibilities of important kinds, and understanding the implications of doing so' (Walker, 1998: 60). The resolution of a moral problem then may not be an appeal to authority or even precedent but rather the interactive process of constructing a narrative, one which is not at all set at the beginning and only takes shape as the negotiation continues. The answer is not set in stone waiting to be discovered. Consequently, in Walker's words, 'the resolution of a moral problem may be less like the solution to a puzzle or the answer to a question than like the outcome of a negotiation' (Walker, 1998: 70).

This insight is aided by conceiving of ethical issues involving the creation and maintenance of a common narrative. Mark Johnson puts it this way: 'Our moral reasoning is situated within our narrative understanding.' He continues, 'Any adequate moral philosophy must give a central role to the narrative structure of experience and to the nature of the particular narratives that make up different moral traditions' (Johnson, 1993: 180, 198). The question is whether the narrative of a group is dictated by someone in a position of power or created through a group process. 'Some people have the authority or power to define the terms in which their own and other people's stories are to be officially narrated' (Addelson quoted in Walker, 1998: 125). This definition can occur either through the leader's establishing the normative culture of the group or promulgating actual codes of conduct that can be enforced within the group. One of the defining characteristics of the expressive-collaborative model would be the widespread involvement of all parties in a group or organization or network in developing the narrative of the group, including its likely stance on the major moral issues it faces, including the ethics of leadership.

This approach is well-suited to leadership in governance. Absent a hierarchical relationship between leaders and followers and a single organizational vision to guide action, an ongoing dialogue between participants in governance is imperative. As we are using the term, this dialogue bears many similarities to the term 'vision' that is so frequently invoked as the chief element of leadership practice today. However, there are two key differences.

First, traditionally, a vision is most often based on one organization's or even one individual's aspirations for the future based on a rational analysis of predicted future events and challenges. In the governance process, there will be competing visions and predictions. Unlike vision, the term 'dialogue' suggests an ongoing process of negotiating and framing priorities in an evolving set of circumstances that is dependent both on the nature of the problem and the characteristics and needs of the participants, but most importantly, on how the participation in the dialogue itself shapes and changes the values, priorities, and actions of the participants.

Secondly, a vision may simply be imposed on a group. But in these cases real leadership has not occurred. It has been replaced by 'bossism' or 'managerialism.' Dialogue, on the other hand, clearly results from a group process, one in which the network may be assisted in its work by a leader, but one in which both the leader and the group are engaged. The vision that emerges from this dialogue may provide the basis for one to lead and others to follow at a particular point in time. And, of course, at another moment, a different person or group may assume leadership in furthering the dialogue.

It may be helpful to think in terms of the potential leader engaging in a continuing conversation around the group's 'story' or 'narrative.' A narrative is a 'story' told by members of a group that gives an account of their past history and their expected future (Rhodes and Bevir, 2006). A narrative is usually highly symbolic and filled with metaphor. It evokes the emotions of group members and provides a 'center of gravity' for their work together. The potential leader must be fully sensitive, indeed quite respectful of the narrative of the group, because the leader, even one hoping to move the group in a new direction, first has to understand and connect with the shared history of the group. Any act of leadership must be grounded in the group or organization's 'past, present, and expected future.' Understanding the group's narrative early on is essential for the potential leader, because doing so engages the group in a way that typically generates interest and respect.

Building a conversation, the next and closely related step, means engaging members of the group or organization as well as others outside the group in an extended (indeed never-ending) dialogue about what the group should be doing and where the group should be going. The conversation can occur in a formal setting with most or all present, but is more likely something that will evolve through an endless set of individual discussions. In this process, the potential leader need not speak with everyone, but certainly those involved must fairly represent the group's nature and commitments and aspirations. The result is an expanded and indeed ever-expanding narrative.

Creating and facilitating dialogue calls for diffuse and shared leadership in which all participants in the dialogue share the responsibility for both content and process and play different roles at different times in the process. Leaders contribute their ideas and perhaps even argue for their acceptance. But the dialogue is constantly evolving, connected to but also apart from anything an individual leader can do. Nonetheless, a primary function of leadership in governance is the maintenance and elaboration of the group's narrative.

It is important to recognize that this dialogue should not commence when the situation becomes dire. The dialogue is an ongoing process, dealing with new and old, big and small problems. In this way, when new and complex challenges occur, the conversation and the evolving narrative is already in progress based on relationships and trust built over time. The dialogue may take on new urgency and even completely change focus, but the participants are already engaged and hopefully have learned to know and trust each other. They share a narrative structure that enables their active and resilient response to new situations.

In this process, especially in leadership in governance, the leader or leaders must assure that the conversation never becomes one-sided, that it remains multi-directional, with no single participant (especially the leader) dominating, either through power or even the force of elocution. The leader must be sure that all viewpoints are fully entertained and always remember that participants are free to engage (or withdraw) on their own terms. Over time, if a leader is able to build and maintain the trust of the group (something that is very fragile), then the leader may be

accorded a more significant role in shaping the dialogue. But if leadership becomes based on individual power and prerogative, then a collapse of the governance network will be likely.

Engaging citizens

Leadership in the public sector, whether focused on the organization, community, or the society as a whole, unavoidably involves normative and value-based questions. In addition to the ethical dimension of network governance, there are also higher-level ideals and norms related to the nature and role of citizenship that must be considered. Numerous scholars have argued for the centrality of democratic values, citizenship, and service in the public interest as the normative foundation of public administration (i.e. deLeon and Denhardt, 2000; Denhardt and Denhardt, 2007; Frederickson, 1996; King and Stivers, 1998; Schachter, 1997; Terry, 1995; Wamsley and Wolf, 1996). Whereas this literature has spawned an important and exciting dialogue about the normative foundations of public administration, these ideas have not been adequately integrated with our understanding of the responsibilities and scope of leadership in network governance. We argue that leadership in governance should explicitly address democratic norms and the role of citizens and citizenship in both formulating and realizing shared goals (Denhardt and Campbell, 2006). Although numerous scholars have called for the use of value-based leadership, they have not directly addressed the question of these democratic ideals (Block, 1993; Greenleaf, 1977; Heifetz, 1994; O'Toole, 1995; Terry, 1995).

While the involvement of citizens in governance may be implied in our discussions of collaboration and dialogue, we believe the importance of this leadership imperative deserves a separate emphasis. Given the already complex system of organizations and actors involved in networked governance, it may seem overwhelming to think about citizen engagement too. But, in at least some sense, citizenship is the glue that holds democratic governance together. Engaged citizens are not necessarily or even typically aligned with a particular organization's mission or goals. Rather, their expectation is for a broad network of organizations and groups to work together to meet their communities' needs *despite* this complex network of actors. Unburdened by organizational allegiance and standard operating procedures, they provide a perspective on societal problems and solutions that is both vitally necessary and not available any other way.

While this is a compelling reason in and of itself to focus on citizen engagement, it is also important to recognize that the challenges of contemporary society cannot be met by formal public or private organizational action. For public policy to 'work' in areas as broad ranging as environmental quality, education, public safety, health care, and many others, individual citizens must be actively engaged in both the design and implementation of public policy. Individual actions and choices have a profound effect on how organizational actions and policies are manifested in governance. Accordingly, citizen engagement is absolutely vital to solving the complex and intractable problems we face.

We are not referring here to the stilted and formal public hearings and other similar vehicles used in jurisdictions around the country to satisfy public meeting laws and public participation requirements. Rather, we are talking about the imperative of leadership to foster citizenship and citizen engagement in the broadest and most active sense. To quote Barber, the goal is to create communities of citizens 'who are united less by homogeneous interests than by civic education and who are made capable of common purpose and mutual action by virtue of their civic attitudes and participatory institutions' (Barber, 1984: 117). Democratic government depends on the development of an engaged, involved citizenry and a 'civil' society in which people work together to express their

personal interests in the context of the broader needs of the community (Putnam, 2000).

What is the role of leadership in this regard? This question has already been partly addressed in the preceding sections on collaboration, resilience, and dialogue. Fostering citizenship and citizen engagement, however, requires explicit attention to a number of additional factors.

First, the key to successful citizen engagement is for leaders to fundamentally rethink the meaning and role of citizens in governance. Public participation is not simply a procedural requirement. Citizen engagement is essential not only because it makes government work better but also because it is consistent with our values. Box (1998), Cooper (1991), Denhardt and Denhardt (2007), King, Feltey and O'Neill (1998), King and Stivers (1998), Thomas (1995), among others, remind us that government, very literally, belongs to the people. Furthermore, not only has contemporary government largely failed to facilitate meaningful citizen involvement, in many cases, governmental practices have actually thwarted attempts to build citizenship and citizen engagement. Accordingly, a key leadership function in networked democratic governance is to create arenas and opportunities for individuals to become responsible and engaged citizens.

Secondly, if it is to be meaningful, citizens should be involved in policy formulation, implementation, and evaluation. Too often, citizens are offered the opportunity to 'comment' on proposed public policies rather than to be engaged in shaping and evaluating public policy and organizational practices. Yet, examples abound of jurisdictions that have successfully and productively involved citizens in major planning efforts, public budgeting, performance evaluation, and a variety of other public functions and arenas (Denhardt and Denhardt, 2007). When there are strong networks of citizen interaction and high levels of social trust and cohesion, leaders can count on this 'stock' of social capital to build even stronger networks, to open new avenues for dialogue and debate, and to further educate citizens with respect to matters of democratic governance (Woolum, 2000).

Finally, leaders in networked governance bear a special responsibility to ensure that divergent voices are heard and respected in the process. Gardner states,

> 'In our system, the 'common good' is first of all preservation of a system in which all kinds of people can – within the law – pursue their various visions of the common good, and at the same time accomplish the kinds of mutual accommodation that make a social system livable and workable. (Gardener, 1991: 16)

The shared values of a community are important, but Gardner reminds us that, 'To prevent wholeness from smothering diversity, there must be a philosophy of pluralism, an open climate for dissent, and an opportunity for sub-communities to retain their identity and share in the setting of larger group goals' (Gardner, 1991: 16) To accomplish this, there is a need for 'diminishing polarization, for teaching diverse groups to know one another, for coalition-building, dispute resolution, negotiation and mediation' (Gardner, 1991: 16).

CONCLUSION

While there has been a surprising lack of attention to the leadership process in network governance, the process of leadership is clearly significant in affecting the structure and outcomes of such networks. We have suggested that traditional leadership models and practices, based on power and position and the assumptions of rational planning, are ill-suited to network governance. In contrast, we have argued that the primary aims of leadership in governance are (1) fostering collaboration, (2) building resilience and adaptive capacity, (3) resolving ethical concerns through dialogue, and (4) engaging citizens. Leadership in network governance will likely flow from person to person and

group to group over time, but these significant leadership functions must be maintained. Traditional leadership models simply do not fit the circumstances of network governance. Governance today *necessitates* new models of leadership.

REFERENCES

Avolio, Bruce J., Gardner, William L., Walumbwa, Fred O., et al. (2004) 'Unlocking the Mask: A Look at the Process by Which Authentic Leaders Impact Follower Attitudes and Behaviors', *Leadership Quarterly* 15(6): 801–23.

Avolio, Bruce J. and Luthans, Fred (2006) *The High Impact Leader: Moments Matter in Accelerating Authentic Leadership Development*. New York: McGraw-Hill.

Bang, Henrik P. (ed.) (2003) *Governance as Social and Political Communication*. Manchester: Manchester University Press.

Barber, Benjamin R. (1984) *Strong Democracy: Participatory Politics for a New Age*. Berkeley, CA: University of California Press.

Bardach, Eugene (1998) *Getting Agencies to Work Together: The Practice and Theory of Managerial Craftsmanship*. Washington, DC: Brookings Institution Press.

Bass, Bernard M. (1985) *Leadership and Performance beyond Expectations*. New York: Free Press.

Bass, Bernard M. and Avolio, Bruce J. (1993) 'Transformational Leadership: A Response to Critiques', in Martin M. Chemers and Roya Ayman (eds), *Leadership Theory and Research: Perspectives and Directions*. San Diego, CA: Academic Press; pp. 49–76.

Berkes, Fikret, Colding, Johan and Folke, Carl (eds) (2003) *Navigating Social–Ecological Systems: Building Resilience for Complexity and Change*. Cambridge: Cambridge University Press.

Block, Peter (1993) *Stewardship: Choosing Service Over Self-Interest*. San Francisco, CA: Berrett-Koehler.

Borzel, Tanja A. and Panke, Diana (2008) 'Network Governance: Effective and Legitimate', in Eva Sorensen and Jacob Torfing (eds), *Theories of Democratic Network Governance*. New York: Palgrave Macmillan.

Box, Richard (1998) *Citizen Governance: Leading American Communities into the 21st Century*. Thousand Oaks, CA: Sage.

Bryson, John M., Crosby, Barbara C. and Stone, Melissa Middleton (2006) 'The Design and Implementation of Cross-Sector Collaborations: Propositions from the Literature', *Public Administration Review* 66(1): 45–55.

Burns, James MacGregor (1978) *Leadership.* New York: Harper and Row.

Cooper, Terry L. (1991) *An Ethic of Citizenship for Public Administration.* Englewood Cliffs, NJ: Prentice-Hall.

Crosby, Barbara C. and Bryson, John M. (2005) *Leadership for the Common Good: Tackling Public Problems in a Shared Power World.* San Francisco: Jossey-Bass.

deLeon, Linda and Denhardt, Robert B. (2000) 'The Political Theory of Reinvention', *Public Administration Review* 60(2): 89–97.

Denhardt, Janet V. and Campbell, Kelly B. (2006) 'The Role of Democratic Values in Transformational Leadership', *Administration and Society* 38(5): 556–72.

Denhardt, Janet V. and Denhardt, Robert B. (2007) *The New Public Service: Serving, Not Steering,* 2nd edn. Armonk, NY: M.E. Sharpe.

Denhardt, Janet V. and Denhardt, Robert B. (2009) 'Building Organizational Resilience and Adaptive Management', in John Hall and John Reich (eds), *Handbook of Adult Resilience: Concepts, Methods and Applications.* New York: Guilford Publications.

Denhardt, Robert B. (1987) 'Images of Death and Slavery in Organizational Life', *Journal of Management* 13(3): 529–42.

Frederickson, H. George (1996) 'Comparing the Reinventing Government Movement with the New Public Administration', *Public Administration Review* 56(3): 263–70.

Gardner, John William (1991) *Building Community.* Washington, DC: Independent sector.

Gardner, William L., Avolio, Bruce J., Luthans, Fred, et al. (2005) '"Can You See the Real Me?" A Self-Based Model of Authentic Leader and Follower Development', *Leadership Quarterly* 16(3): 343–72.

Glover, Jerry, Friedman, Harris and Jones, Gordon (2002) 'Adaptive Leadership: When Change is Not Enough', *Organizational Development Journal* 20(2): 15–32.

Goldsmith, Stephen and Eggers, William D. (2004) *Governing by Network: The New Shape of the Public Sector.* Washington, DC: Brookings Institution Press.

Greenleaf, Robert K. (1977) *Servant Leadership: A Journey into the Nature of Legitimate Power and Greatness.* New York: Paulist Press.

Habron, Geoffery (2003) 'Role of Adaptive Management for Watershed Councils', *Environmental Management* 31(1): 29–41.

Hajer, Maarten A. and Wagenaar, Hendrik (eds) (2003) *Deliberative Policy Analysis: Understanding Governance in the Network Society.* Cambridge: Cambridge University Press.

Heffen, Oscar van, Kickert, Walter J.M. and Thomassen, Jacques J.A. (eds) (2000) *Governance in Modern Society: Effects, Change and Formation of Government Institutions.* Dordrecht: Kluwer Academic Publishers.

Heifetz, Ronald A. (1994) *Leadership Without Easy Answers.* Cambridge, MA: Harvard University Press.

Horne, John F. and Orr, John E. (1998) 'Assessing Behaviors that Create Resilient Organizations', *Employment Relations Today* 24(4): 29–39.

Ilies, Remus, Morgeson, Frederick P. and Nahrgang, Jennifer D. (2005) 'Authentic Leadership and Eudaemonic Well-Being: Understanding Leader–Follower Outcomes', *Leadership Quarterly* 16(3): 373–94.

Johnson, Barry L. (1999) 'Introduction to the Special Feature: Adaptive Management – Scientifically Sound, Socially Challenged?', *Ecology and Society* 3(1): 10. [online] http://www.ecologyandsociety.org/vol3/iss1/art10/

Johnson, Mark (1993) *Moral Imagination: Implications of Cognitive Science for Ethics.* Chicago, IL: University of Chicago Press.

Kettl, Donald F. (2002) *The Transformation of Governance: Public Administration for Twenty-First Century America.* Baltimore, MD: Johns Hopkins University Press.

Kickert, Walter J.M., Klijn, Erik-Hans and Koppenjan, Joop F.M. (eds) (1997) *Managing Complex Networks: Strategies for the Public Sector.* London: Sage.

King, Cheryl Simrell and Stivers, Camilla M. (1998) *Government Is Us: Public Administration in an Anti-Government Era.* Thousand Oaks, CA: Sage.

King, Cheryl Simrell, Feltey, Kathryn M. and Susel, Bridget O'Neill (1998) 'The Question of Participation: Toward Authentic Public Participation in Public Administration', *Public Administration Review,* 58(4): 317–26.

Kooiman, Jan (ed.) (1993) *Modern Governance: New Government–Society Interactions.* London: Sage.

Lengnick-Hall, Cynthia and Beck, Tammy (2005) 'Adaptive Fit versus Robust Transformation', *Journal of Management* 31(5): 1–20.

Lipman-Blumen, Jean (1996) *Connective Leadership: Managing in a Changing World.* Oxford: Oxford University Press.

McGuire, Michael (2006) 'Collaborative Public Management: Assessing What We Know and How We Know It', *Public Administration Review* 66(1): 33–43.

March, James G. and Olsen, Johan P. (1995) *Democratic Governance*. New York: Free Press.

Marin, Bernd and Mayntz, Renate (1991) *Policy Networks: Empirical Evidence and Theoretical Considerations*. Frankfurt-am-Main: Campus Verlag.

Nelissen, Nicolaas Johannes Maria, Bernel Mans-Videc, Marie-Louise (eds) (1999) *Renewing Government: Innovative and Inspiring Visions*. Utrecht: International Books.

O'Leary, Rosemary, Gerard, Catherine and Bingham, Lisa Blomgren (2006) 'Introduction to the Symposium on Collaborative Public Management', *Public Administration Review* 66(1): 6–9.

O'Toole, James (1995) *Leading Change: Overcoming the Ideology of Comfort and the Tyranny of Custom*. San Francisco: Jossey-Bass.

Pawar, Badrinarayan Shankar and Eastman, Kenneth K. (1997) 'The Nature and Implications of Contextual Influences on Transformational Leadership: A Conceptual Examination', *Academy of Management Review* 22(1): 80–109.

Pierre, Jon and Peters, B. Guy (2000) *Governance, Politics and the State*. New York: St. Martin's Press.

Provan, K.G. and Kenis, P.N. (2008) 'Modes of Network Governance: Structure, Management, and Effectiveness', *Journal of Public Administration Research and Theory* 18(2): 229–52.

Putnam, Robert D. (2000) *Bowling Alone: The Collapse and Revival of American Community*. New York: Simon and Schuster.

Rhodes, R.A.W. (1997) *Understanding Governance: Policy Networks, Governance, Reflexivity and Accountability*. Buckingham: Open University Press.

Rhodes, R.A.W. and Bevir, Mark (2006) *Governance Stories*. London: Routledge.

Rost, Joseph C. (1991) *Leadership for the Twenty-First Century*. Westport, CT: Praeger.

Schachter, Hindy Lauer (1997) *Reinventing Government or Reinventing Ourselves: The Role of Citizen Owners in Making a Better Government*. Albany, NY: State University of New York Press.

Sorensen, Eva and Torfing, Jacob (2008) 'Introduction: Governance Network Research', in Eva Sorensen and Jacob Torfing (eds), *Theories of Democratic Network Governance*. New York: Palgrave Macmillan.

Sutcliffe, Kathleen and Vogus, Timothy J. (2003) 'Organizing for Resilience', in Kim S. Cameron, Jane E. Dutton and Robert E. Quinn (eds), *Positive Organizational Scholarship*. San Francisco: Berrett-Koehler Publishers; pp. 94–110.

Terry, Larry D. (1995) *Leadership of Public Bureaucracies: The Administrative as Conservator*. Thousand Oaks, CA: Sage.

Thomas, John Clayton (1995) *Public Participation in Public Decisions: New Skills and Strategies for Public Managers*. San Francisco, CA: Jossey-Bass.

Thomson, Ann Marie and Perry, James L. (2006) 'Collaboration Processes: Inside the Black Box', *Public Administration Review* 66(1): 20–32.

Tschirhart, Mary, Christensen, Robert K. and Perry, James L. (2005) 'The Paradox of Branding and Collaboration', *Public Performance and Management Review* 29(1): 67–84.

Van Wart, Montgomery (2003) 'Public-Sector Leadership Theory: An Assessment', *Public Administration Review* 63(2): 214–28.

Vigoda-Gadot, Eran (2003) *Managing Collaboration in Public Administration: The Promise of Alliance Among Governance, Citizens, and Businesses*. Westport, CT: Praeger.

Wachhaus, Aaron (2009) 'Networks in Contemporary Public Administration: A Discourse Analysis', *Administrative Theory & Praxis* 31(1): 59–77.

Walker, Margaret Urban (1998) *Moral Understandings: A Feminist Study in Ethics*. New York: Routledge.

Walters, Carl (1997) 'Challenges in Adaptive Management of Riparian and Coastal Ecosystems', *Ecology and Society* 1(2): 1. online at http://www.consecol.org/ vol1/iss2/art1/

Walumbwa, Fred O. et al. (forthcoming) 'Authentically Leading Groups: The Mediating Role of Collective Psychological Capital and Trust', *Journal of Organizational Behavior*, in press.

Wamsley, Gary L. and Wolf, James F. (eds) (1996) *Refounding Democratic Public Administration: Modern Paradoxes, Postmodern Challenges*. Thousand Oaks, CA: Sage.

Wood, Donna and Gray, Barbara (1991) 'Toward a Comprehensive Theory of Collaboration', *Journal of Applied Behavioral Science* 27(2): 139–62.

Woolum, Janet (2000) 'Social Capital as a Community Resource: Implications for Public Administration.' Unpublished manuscript.

28

Network Management

Michael McGuire

Collective action across organizational, sectoral, and geographic boundaries for the purposes of public sector service production and delivery consists of an array of social and administrative interconnections. Such connections, variously referred to as collaborative partnerships, alliances, and, most vividly, networks, have been the subject of much research over the past few decades. Public management scholars, political scientists, sociologists, organizational theorists, and economists have studied multi-actor contexts, but these researchers often tend to speak past one another, resulting in different conceptualizations, interpretations, and many untested assumptions about networks (Huxham, 2003; Rethemeyer and Hatmaker, 2008). Furthermore, even in the midst of a lack of consensus about the usage of the term 'network' (Agranoff, 2007; Borzel, 1998), a more pressing matter has recently gained the attention of scholars and practitioners alike: managing the network. Issues of network performance (Chen, 2008; McGuire and Silvia, 2009; Meier and O'Toole, 2003), antecedents (Thomson and Perry, 2006), operations (Agranoff, 2007), and structure (Provan and Kenis, 2008) have emerged as fertile empirical territory.

Saint-Onge and Armstrong address the challenges faced by twenty-first century managers:

> The capability to effectively manage complex partnerships is growing in importance as organizations are reconfigured. Organizations are becoming more and more involved in complex value-creation networks, where the boundaries between one organization and another become blurred and functions become integrated. It's becoming a critical organizational and leadership capability to be able to create and leverage participation in network-designed and -delivered solutions (Saint-Onge and Armstrong, 2004: 191).

It is not enough simply to understand networks, but to also know how to leverage them to improve public sector operations. Network management is not a movement or fad. It has become the most fundamental component of public sector performance.

I have organized this chapter into five sections. The first section reviews three approaches to understanding what is meant by the term 'network.' It also offers examples of networks as a means to demonstrate the administrative levers available to the network manager. The next section discusses briefly the network manager (and managers), concluding that networks often have many different managers. It also discusses what network management is *not* about. The third section forms the heart of the chapter by examining the management of networks, both in terms of the 'targets' of management and the competencies needed for effective management. The penultimate section reviews various approaches to studying network management. The final section offers concluding remarks.

NETWORKS

Approaches

There are many different, general perspectives that inform our understanding of managing networks. Some have argued that the complex interaction between several actors can best be analyzed as if it were a game or series of games (Klijn and Teisman, 1997). Using the language of game theory, derived from a rational-choice approach to the study of interorganizational phenomena, the crux of this argument is that actors in a network employ strategies that contribute to (or hinder) the formation of a network and, subsequently, policy success. From this perspective, self-coordination among ostensibly autonomous actors is achieved through negotiated agreement (cooperative games) in structurally complex connected games (Scharpf, 1993), while each actor strategically calculates whether formation of and 'membership' in a network is beneficial. There is a continuous need for cooperation among actors in a network. However, given the level of uncertainty and complexity in network settings, there are significant impediments to cooperation and coordination (the classic problem of the free rider, for example), so network action must be 'induced and not simply expected' (O'Toole, 1993). Actors must perceive that they have the opportunity and the incentive to act cooperatively. Interdependency among functionally specialized organizations is one particularly strong incentive for participating in networks since interdependent actors, by definition, cannot achieve their goals on their own (Hertting, 2008). Therefore, managing networks is

equivalent to bringing to light such incentives for action and changing the perceptions of the actors to recognize these incentives; in essence, game management.

The limitations of explicitly employing game theoretic applications to multi-organizational settings have been explored elsewhere. Most of the criticisms are based in the belief that current formulations of rational-choice models are too simplistic to deal with the complexity of multi-organizational networks. Another compelling rejection of the rational-choice perspective of networks is based on the argument that networks are not simply fixed structures that some network actors can manipulate using the right tools and incentives to participate. If there are no such tools that can be used to manage networks, then modeling network relationships from the perspective of a 'game' is not appropriate. Instead, networks are constructed differently, contingently, and continuously by many actors 'against the background of diverse traditions' (Bevir and Richards, 2009: 3). This theory argues that a discussion of management techniques and strategies is not as useful as the stories that are told by network actors about how and why they acted as they did or will react given their own beliefs and perspectives. This interpretative approach to the study of and practice in networks relies on ethnographic analysis to explore meanings embedded in traditions, challenging the 'language of managerialism, markets and contracts, as well as the language of predictive social science' (Bevir and Richards, 2009: 13).

The more mainstream approach to the study of networks, and the one adopted in this chapter, is to focus the discussion on the network as a mechanism for achieving goals. I thus use the term network in this chapter to refer to an actual structure (as opposed to a metaphor or analytical tool) involving multiple nodes – agencies and organizations – with multiple linkages, ordinarily working on cross-boundary collaborative activities. It constitutes one form of collaborative activity for facilitating and operating multi-organizational arrangements to solve problems that cannot be solved, or solved easily, by using single organizations (Agranoff and McGuire, 2003a: 4). A public management network includes governmental and non-governmental agencies that are connected through involvement in a public policymaking and/or administrative structure through which information and/or public goods and services may be planned, designed, produced, and delivered (and any or all of the activities). Such network structures can be formal or informal, and they are typically intersectoral, intergovernmental, and based functionally in a specific policy or policy area. Officials from government organizations and agencies at federal, state, and local levels operate in structures of exchange and production with representatives from profit-making and not-for-profit organizations (Agranoff, 2007: 7–8; McGuire, 2003).

It should be noted that, contrary to some observers (Powell, 1990; Thompson, 2003), the very concept of the network is not easily distinguishable from other organizational forms, such as hierarchies and markets. There are 'hierarchical networks' that can be a product of hierarchical regulation (6 et al., 2006) or which require a command-and-control operation over a network (Moynihan, 2008). There are also market-oriented networks (Herranz, 2008). The network may be distinct in terms of many of its properties, functions, and operations, but other influences from single-organization principles to market-like coordination can also, in some circumstances, permeate the network. Also, Rhodes (2003) cautions us that the term 'network' holds different meanings for each respondent who participates in empirical research. So while theorists sort out the meaning of the term, so too do practitioners, who have various conceptions of a network.

Furthermore, not all networks are alike. Agranoff's (2007) typology of networks indicates that some networks have no authority, even to jointly program; they merely exchange information. Other types of networks involve information exchange combined with education that enhances the ability of the member

organizations to implement solutions, again at the individual organization rather than at network level. Another network type is involved in problem-solving approaches, albeit indirectly, as they blueprint strategies that are used by network members as these members directly approach client agencies. The most extensive type of network is known as an action network. Unlike the other three network types, action networks engage in collective action by formally adopting network-level courses of action and often delivering services.

Milward and Provan also offer a similar four-fold typology of networks based on distinguishing the purposes of networks (2006: 11). One type of network they discuss is an information diffusion network, whose central purpose is to share information across governmental boundaries. This is consistent with Agranoff's aforementioned information network. Another type of network is a service implementation network that governments fund to deliver services to clients, but that do not actually deliver the services. Joint production is the hallmark of this type of network. A third type of network is a problem-solving network. The purpose of this network is to solve a complex immediate problem-rather than build capabilities for dealing with future problems. Milward and Provan's fourth type of network is a community capacity building network, whereby the focus is to build social capital in a community of persons and organizations to better enable the actors to address future complex problems.

There are other ways of classifying networks beyond delineating the purposes of the network. 6 et al. argue that different types of networks – and the consequent management of the networks – can be distinguished according to five key features (6 et al., 2006). One typology is based simply on examining the characteristics of the organizations – the nodes – involved in the network, such as the number and types of organizations. Other ways to classify networks include recognizing the differences in structure, content, and function (or purpose). Finally, various institutional forces such as social norms, the degree of formality, and the stability of relationship patterns shape networks as well. These five variables or features 'can be thought of as key differentiators in the various descriptions and explanations of network forms' (6 et al., 2006: 32).

Yet another useful way to look at differences in network types involves a distinction between the value orientations of the organizations involved in the network (Herranz, 2008), resulting in three basic network 'ideal types' modeled after the three basic mechanisms of organizational control posited by Wilkins and Ouchi (1983):

- Community-based networks are characterized by a non-profit orientation and the underlying communitarian values associated with the civil society sector.
- Bureaucratic-based networks are characterized by the attributes associated with the public sector: legalism, procedural, and, for the most part, hierarchicall organization.
- Entrepreneurial-based networks are characterized by market sector organizational values.

Like the typologies discussed above, the three network types have implications for the style/type of management that occurs in each (Herranz, 2008).

There have been practical and normative concerns about the meaning of networks for American bureaucracy and democratic constitutional values. Some claim that the 'disarticulation' of the state through contracting by governments has 'hollowed out' agencies in the United States in the same way as it has many corporations (Frederickson, 1999; Milward, Provan and Else, 1993; Rhodes, 1997). Consultants and popular writers who would like to write off or eliminate governments' roles (Osborne and Gaebler, 1992; Osborne and Plastrik, 1997), argue that the state is weakening at the core (Keating, 1999), or fear that networking means a loss of accountability because governments are no longer the central steering actor in the policy process (Frederickson, 1997); they are not comfortable with the idea that networks may be supplanting bureaucracies. However, networks have not eclipsed or displaced the power or centrality of government agencies. The reality is that neither networks (or the for-profit and non-profit partners within them) nor government agencies dominate these partnerships. Thus, despite the very broad range of network activity in the United States, the 'ability [of nongovernmental actors] to influence the public agency domain is real but quite limited in scope ... accommodations are made, decisions are influenced, strategies are altered, resources are directed, intensive groups exert undue influence, and public responsibility is indirectly shared' (Agranoff, 2007: 219). While an interactive interdependency has emerged within networks crossing many boundaries, public agency–non-governmental organization connections seem to overlay the hierarchy rather than act as replacements for government action. In addition, not all government agency administrators are totally or to a high degree in the business of working in networks. With the exception of certain 'boundary spanners' who spend full-time in cross-agency work, many administrators spend as little as 15–20 percent of their total work time in collaborative activity, including participating in networks (Agranoff and McGuire, 2003a).

Network examples

One ideal example is the governing network for Metro High School in Columbus, Ohio, USA, which is a Science, Technology, Engineering, and Mathematics (STEM) school that educates approximately 100 students per grade. It is nearly impossible to be more 'networked' than Metro. Management of the school is both by government agencies and by non-governmental entities. Metro includes a governing body, the Educational Council, which is a non-profit organization formed in 1986 to foster cross-district programming and improve education through a confederation of 16 public school districts in Franklin County, Ohio. The school also includes a governance and advisory structure in the form of the Metro Partnership Group. This partnership is composed of representatives from the Battelle Center for Mathematics and Science Education Policy, an international science and technology organization that undertakes research and supports education; The Ohio State University; KnowledgeWorks, a school innovation foundation based in Ohio; and the Educational Council. The partnership is not divisionalized or specialized, and Metro as a network features consensus-based decision models. Its participants do experience role differentiation but operate with a fluid, participatory agreement-seeking orientation. Metro's operations extend well beyond the walls and staff of the school, involving the active learning and support activities of many partner resources and learning centers throughout the metropolitan area.

Networks and network management abound in local emergency management. Emergency managers face extraordinary challenges, both in number and severity, and as a result, they increasingly prepare for and respond to natural hazards and disasters through networks. For example, in California in the United States, an emergency collaborative network involving federal, state, and local officials, private agencies, and local representatives was established to address the outbreak of a deadly poultry-based disease (Moynihan, 2008). In contrast to Metro High School, management was considered to be both networked and 'hierarchical' in the sense that a command system was in place to administer the vast network. Indeed, a single actor often serves as the network manager in disaster response networks.

The recently adopted United States National Response Framework provides a clear endorsement of the idea of networks in emergency management (Department of Homeland Security, 2008). Indeed, creating networks is one of the main principles of the framework. It defines the duties of the local emergency manager as having the day-to-day authority and responsibility in their jurisdiction for overseeing emergency management programs and activities, but it also emphasizes that the emergency manager works collaboratively with other local agencies, which may include both non-profit and for-profit organizations. In a case study of the Fort Worth, Texas tornado that struck in 2000, McEntire (2002) found that networks grounded in an understanding of the resources and roles of the actors played an important part in achieving a largely successful response. Conversely, the breakdown of networks is at least partially to blame for the poor outcomes during Hurricane Katrina in 2005 (Kiefer and Montjoy, 2006).

THE NETWORK MANAGER

Who is the network manager? Or perhaps more accurately, who are the network managers? It is tempting to ascribe all network management to a single actor, typically the governmental representative in the network. Klijn and Koppenjan (2000) assert that one must avoid the presumption 'that governments are like other actors. Governments have unique resources at their disposal and work to achieve unique goals. They occupy a special position…' (Klijn and Koppenjan, 2004: 151). Sharpe long ago reminded us that 'government is not just another actor' (Sharpe, 1986). However, Kickert et al. worry about the top-down implications of the single actor model when, by definition, there are many actors in a network with different goals, positions, and strategies (Kickert et al., 1997: 183). Indeed, multiple, potentially competing managers exist in many networks (Agranoff and McGuire, 2003b).

Milward and Provan 'sort out' these different views by building a framework whereby there may be a designated, legitimate steerer *of* the network, but there are also managers *in* the network:

Managers of networks are concerned with the network as a whole. These are typically individuals who are charged with the task of coordinating overall network activities and, in general, ensuring that network-level goals are set, addressed, and attained. The goals and success of organizational members become secondary to the network as a whole. Managers in networks are individuals who represent their organization within the network. They are managers whose primary loyalty is to their organization, but who must work within a network context, addressing both organization- and network-level goals and objectives. These managers have split missions and, sometimes, split loyalties. (Milward and Provan, 2006: 18)

This distinction is consistent with that put forth by 6 et al. (2006), who distinguishes between governance of a network, which is designed to exercise control, regulation, inducement, incentive or persuasive influence over the whole network, and management within a network, which are activities carried out by individuals who are themselves actors in the network (6 et al., 2006: 5).

That steerer may be the government manager, but it may not be. Indeed, the steerer or single network manager may be an organization that exists solely to administer network processes (Provan and Kenis, 2008). The network manager is thus the person or persons who assume a network-level perspective, act strategically to effect interactions within the network, and undertake tasks and behaviors designed to achieve network-level goals, be they process- or outcome-oriented goals.

Before looking more closely at managing networks, it is necessary to point out what network management is *not*. First, network management should not be confused with managing contracts or outsourcing. The use of networks is not a type of privatization to the extent that a principal–agent relationship exists between payer and deliverer of a good or service. Networks can be created by contract or a series of contracts, but managing a human services network is fundamentally different from managing a contract with a solid waste company to pick up trash in a city. The latter involves the more technically-oriented capacities of determining whether to make or buy the good or service; bidding the

contract, selecting a provider, and negotiating a contract; and evaluating the contractor's performance (Brown et al., 2006). As I will show, managing in networks may include these capacities, but it will also far exceed them, at least in scope and number. Secondly, and similarly, management at the network level is not (usually) simply a series of dyadic relationships that are managed like a contract. Interactions are the heart of network processes, but network management occurs at the 'meta' level, or what Sorensen and Torfing call 'meta-governance' (2008: 15). Thirdly, as in single organizations, network management is not always organic, free flowing, and conflict-free. While this type of harmonious atmosphere may prevail in some cases, the reality can also be the opposite: acrimony, domination, disagreement over aims, difficulties in reaching agreement, and lack of ability to make solutions work. This is the other side of network management, so to speak, where real obstacles to network operations often prevent any level of collaborative success.

MANAGING NETWORKS

Network management is the strategic activity meant to influence the interaction of the nodes (actors). The purposes of the interactions may include achieving the goals of the individual actors (and their 'home' organizations) while simultaneously achieving network-level results. From this 'managerialist' perspective, adopting at least a minimal set of rules, providing coordinative tools, and working within a defined governance structure can increase the chances of success (and, by extension, lack of these can contribute to failure) (Rodriguez et al., 2007). This instrumental, administrative-oriented view of collaborative networks is the dominant theme in some discussions of network effectiveness (McGuire, 2002).

However, the goal achievement perspective of management may have less credence with network processes because objectives are more autonomous with no central authoritative coordinating actor (Klijn and Koppenjan, 2000). The use of *ex ante* formulated objectives is usually untenable because actors adapt their perceptions and objectives interactively, responding to other parties and to the environment. If certain parties do not participate in the interaction process, the chances are high that their interests and preferences will not be represented in the derived solution. As a result, network results also need to be considered by the '*ex post* satisfying' criterion (Klijn and Koppenjan, 2000: 148), based on the subjective judgment of network actors. It is both the 'significance and meaning of relationships and practices' that constitute the most desirable effectiveness assessments (Sydow and Windeler, 1998: 280).

Thus, network management also includes activities that enhance the intrinsic value of the process (Rodriguez et al., 2007). The process of facilitated network interaction itself has some intrinsic value to the people who participate in networks (Rodriguez et al., 2007: 178). The interactions and negotiations that constitute collaborative processes can socialize the actors to a new language that might be drawn on more successfully in future network involvement (Rodriguez et al., 2007: 184).

Network management targets

Decision-making

The most difficult of collaborative decisions and agreements are often not over money, but aimed at getting large, established partners to change a long-standing way of operating that is deeply entrenched in standards, regulations, and procedures. Effective networks make decisions by exploration, discussion, and ultimately consensus. The principle of 'soft guidance' by the multiple focal nodes is an accurate description of the way decisions are made and actions are taken (Windhoff-Hentier, 1992). Consensus is the desired mechanism

for making decisions. Most networks will not vote. Instead, if the network cannot reach complete consensus, then that time presumably is not the right one to reach agreement.

Certain preconditions should be in place to facilitate network-level decision-making. First, the commitment of participants in time is essential. Actors in a network commit a great deal of time for appraisal, design, concept building, and solidifying their relationships while laying the framework for the network's purpose. Social time together reinforces this. Secondly, in many cases, most of the actors generally do not know one another professionally before entering into a network relationship. The actors are thus brought together with a minimum of baggage and with the aim of lining up the key players. Thirdly, together, a network should exercise flexibility and let the project evolve rather than immediately imposing solutions. Task forces, committees, and 'design' teams can be created, which operate more informally, but they should also be consensus-oriented in making decisions. A succession sequence of problem emergence/problem delay/problem solution characterizes how an effective network anticipates challenges, even delaying the 'big' issues until putting together the multiple agreements and resources required for earlier, more pressing concerns.

However, some networks can overdose on consensus, knotting up proceedings and slowing down decision-making. Thus, a limitation faced by networks that inhibits their ability to move forward is the difficulty in getting other agencies to act unless there is total agreement by the network. Consensus-seeking can lead to protracted deliberative processes that consume excessive energy and resources but 'ultimately produce weak compromises, deadlocked decision making or non-implementation …' (Koppenjan, 2008). Majority rule is not the way that effective networks make decisions but the consensus that is needed to act is sometimes elusive or, at a minimum, takes a great deal of time. Countless person-hours are spent in task forces or work groups. Even when collaborative inertia (Huxham and Vangen, 2005) is somehow overcome, it nevertheless comes at the expense of protracted human relations processing, as partners try to respect the multidimensionality of network efforts. Consensus means letting everyone put their agenda on the table as networks unpack complex political, financial, technical, and regulatory issues. Issues often come to the table only after all the politics have been played, agreements established, and resources put in place. Networks that have high numbers of conflicting or potentially conflicting stakeholders tend to be more sensitive and risk aversive when it comes to the problem agenda, often leading to lowest common denominator types of decisions (Coglianese, 1999).

Trust

Trust exists at all levels of an effective network, meaning that managers of the networks and managers in the network, each with their different perspectives and lenses, must possess at least a minimal amount of trust in the other actors and in the network as a whole. In the absence of legal authority, actors join, remain, and work together in a network because of some element of trust (Agranoff and McGuire, 2001). It is in many ways an important glue that holds parties together transactionally. Trust may not necessarily require a harmony of beliefs, but rather mutual obligation and expectation (Sabel, 1993). However, it is difficult to know if trust exists a priori and to empirically assess its effect on the network (Brass et al., 2004). Trust can be based merely in acknowledging the significance of another organization (Zaheer et al., 1998), whereas others argue that trusting the behavior of individual participants in a network is paramount to network success (Ferguson and Stoutland, 1999). There is thus no general agreement about what a manager can do to build it, even though trust is linked to an entity's ability to make decisions and take actions based on those decisions.

Vangen and Huxham suggest that trust is built through a cyclical trust-building loop (Vangen and Huxham, 2003: 12). When there is no history of prior ties, partners must be willing to take some risk to initiate the collaboration and aim for realistic goals: i.e., the collaboration should first take small steps toward some modest level of achievement (Agranoff, 2003). Such success reinforces attitudes that the parties to the network can be trusted, which leads to riskier undertakings. The lesson for the public manager is that trust takes time to develop and that it grows as the network becomes successful. Networks may begin virtually 'trust-free,' but ultimately it becomes a necessary component of future success (McGuire, 2006).

There is general agreement that what should be done is consistent with the observation of Goldsmith and Eggers (2004), who mention that communication builds trust. Efforts to link and join people together should continue because new connections can lead to trust. Finally, it is important to remember that trust is often the most difficult to build at the implementation level. The costs in terms of resources such as money, time, and knowledge come out most directly at this level. Moreover, the costs that might be absorbed by larger network partners are more transparent among the connecting organizations. It is also clear that while common philosophies or working principles may be worked out at the managerial level, it does not follow that such understanding will automatically translate to the working level. Trust is thus multi-faceted and multi-level, and fostering it requires multiple managerial behaviors.

Power

It is important to recognize that power and influence in a network may be unequally distributed, even in effective networks. It is commonly assumed that the more the actors in a network are dependent upon one another for policymaking resources, the more equal the division of power in the network. However, not all networks are interdependent relationships based on reciprocity and mutual trust where self-interest is subservient to the network's common cause and consensus is built with ease (Koppenjan, 2008). Indeed, the norm is an amalgam of actors, each operating on behalf of both the network and his or her home organization. These dual interests may result in one actor attempting to satisfy both aims by wielding the ability to sanction another network actor (Bachmann, 2001) or by offering inducements to other network actors to come around to his or her way of thinking. Power is therefore a permanent feature of networks.

The widely accepted view asserts that power exists because some organizations (or a single organization) bring to the network an inordinate amount of resources; thus the organization's representative is able to exert undue influence over the other network members. From this perspective, the organizational representative has power over the other actors and can obstruct or dominate the network. Power is a relational concept; it involves at least two actors (Huxham and Beech, 2008). This dominant perspective focuses on gains and losses in the representative's power resources, viewing power in a network as a zero-sum game (Triantafillou, 2008). However, managing networks

> may constitute a plus-sum game if attention is directed to the devices, methods, and techniques of governing rather than the actors. By focusing rather narrowly on actors and their interactions with a network ... it becomes very difficult to bring to the fore those workings and effects of network governance that depend on a wide set of both legally binding and non-legally binding governing instruments. (Triantafillou, 2008: 197)

Power can be used not just as a force for promoting agency interests in preventing agreement, but also as a force for promoting facilitation of an agreement; both 'power over' as well as 'power to' exists (Agranoff and McGuire, 2001). Huxham and Beech extend this dichotomy by adding 'power for,' which relates to the involvement of parties who would otherwise not have a voice in network deliberative processes (Huxham and Beech, 2008: 562). Four dimensions of power

manifest themselves in networks: agency power, which is the power the partner brings to the agency; internal operational power related to the network's maintenance and operations; knowledge-based power, whereby the network's technical core assumes greater sway as a result of their specialized knowledge and information; and deliberative power that accrues from those primarily involved in affecting decisions, agreements, or courses of action. Power in networks can also be derived from the occupancy of important positions within network structures (Burt, 1992; Yan and Gray, 1994), through social network relationships (Kenis and Oerlemans, 2008), and by gaining access to and control over 'critical resources' (Knoke and Chen, 2008). Power can also be distributed among network champions, promoters, technical specialists, and network staff, where it exists (Agranoff, 2007).

Knowledge creation and management

Creating and managing knowledge is a core function of public sector networks. Indeed, the desire for knowledge leads agencies to seek network activity; it may bring the network into existence, but networks are also valuable in disseminating knowledge that can be used to solve problems. For example, a typical first response to policy uncertainty and ambiguity in networks is information collection (Koppenjan and Klijn, 2004). The information is often challenged by the various actors in the network, and new complexities are then raised as a new, shared form of knowledge is developed and implemented through affiliated organizations. Much like organizations, networks are 'a fluid mix of framed experiences, values, contextual information, and expert insight that provides a framework for evaluating and incorporating new experiences and information' (Davenport and Prusak, 2000: 5). Knowledge management is directed to identifying, extracting, and capturing knowledge in order to direct network actors toward accomplishing some goal (Newell et al., 2002: 16). Although not all networks are exclusively devoted to knowledge or its management, virtually all seek a collaborative form of explicit and tacit knowledge that supports their interorganizational missions (Agranoff, 2008). Managers of networks thus help network actors grow and learn as they steer knowledge toward problem solving.

Management behaviors and competencies

Managing networks is challenging because of the changing allocation of resources in the network structure over time. In many networks, managing is less a function of one person's ability to command and control and more a function of various persons who, over time, sustain the networked features. A conceptual model from Agranoff and McGuire (2001; McGuire, 2002) isolates four distinct sets of behaviors or phases of network management. The model components are described below.

The first category of behaviors undertaken by most network managers is *activation*, which may be the most important activity of managing networks. In general, activation refers to the set of behaviors employed for identifying and incorporating the persons and resources needed to achieve program goals. Selective activation (Scharpf, 1978) is based on correctly identifying necessary participants and other resources needed for the network. The skills, knowledge, and resources of these potential actors must be assessed and tapped.

The second network management behavior employed in networks helps frame the structure and the norms and values of the network as a whole. Managers do this *framing* by facilitating agreement on leadership roles, helping to establish an identity and culture for the network; assisting in developing a working structure for the network (e.g. committees, network 'assignments'), and altering the perceptions of participants to understand the unique characteristics of working with persons in contexts without organizational

mechanisms based on authority relations. Recent research suggests that framing behavior is more significant to the success of the network at the outset of the creation of the network, and may in fact be detrimental when employed in an established network (McGuire and Silvia, 2009)

In addition to activating and framing the network, managers must induce individuals to make and keep a commitment to the network. *Mobilizing* behaviors are used to develop support for network processes from network participants and external stakeholders. Publicizing the network's accomplishments, establishing and maintaining its legitimacy, and using incentives to motivate network participants are a few of the mobilizing behaviors undertaken by network leaders.

Finally, the model posits that managers employ *synthesizing* behaviors intended to create an environment and to enhance the conditions for favorable, productive interactions among network participants. One critical behavior of network management is to build relationships and interactions that result in achieving the network purpose. Synthesizing behaviors include facilitating and furthering interaction among participants, reducing complexity and uncertainty by promoting information exchange, and facilitating linkages among participants. Managers try to create and maintain trust among network participants as a means of building relationships and interactions that result in achieving the network purpose. Successful network management thus achieves collaboration between network participants while minimizing and removing informational blockages to cooperation.

Recent research (Agranoff et al., 2008) demonstrates that, as hypothesized by McGuire (2002), management through these four behaviors is recursive rather than linear. That is, activation and framing does not stop after a network was created, mobilization does not end with going public and garnering champions to the cause, and synthesizing is an ongoing struggle to keep ideas and practices fluid and information exchanged openly.

Rethemeyer and Hatmaker extend the application of these four network management behaviors by showing how network managers must be able to perform these behaviors 'across policy, collaborative, and fiscal networks within their home system as well as in adjacent systems' (Rethemeyer and Hatmaker, 2008: 641). Management is not an explicit function of just one person, and the actors in a specific network may also be actors in other networks simultaneously (Agranoff and McGuire, 2003b). Thus, activation, framing, mobilizing, and synthesizing are applicable categories of network management behaviors, but contrary to McGuire (2002), who offers propositions regarding the use of these behaviors by assuming a single manager, the application of such behaviors is more complex. Managers must be 'flexible enough to tailor their network management activities' (Rethemeyer and Hatmaker, 2008: 641) to the different interests of the manager's home network and other adjacent network systems.

Basing their work on previous case study research and their extensive work with networks around the United States, Milward and Provan suggest that five groups of tasks constitute network management:

- Management of accountability involves determining who is responsible for outcomes and 'rewarding and reinforcing compliance with network goals' (Milward and Provan, 2006: 19).
- Management of legitimacy includes publicizing network accomplishments and attracting resources as well as new members.
- Conflict management is carried out through mechanisms for resolving disputes and making decisions that reflect network-level goals.
- Management of design involves 'determining which structural governance forms would be most appropriate to success' (Milward and Provan, 2006: 22) and changing the structure when needed.
- Finally, managing commitment in a network includes getting 'buy-in' of the network, ensuring that network resources are distributed equally, and keeping network members informed.

Klijn and Edelenbos draw a distinction between process design and management and institutional design for describing various network management strategies. Process design involves agreements regarding the nature of the interaction process and the ground rules for participating in the network. The authors assert that there is no standard, all-encompassing design type for networks; it is situational. Process management includes the direct, hands-on application of the behaviors and tasks discussed above. Institutional design, on the other hand, is indirect. Such design strategies are typically focused on changing the formal and informal rules that 'influence, guide, and limit' the behavior of the network participants (Klijn and Edelenbos, 2008: 207). The strategies include changing the network composition, influencing network outcomes, and affecting network interactions.

Managing networks involves the range of decision-making activities such as resource acquisition, resource allocation, distribution and exchange, coordination, planning and strategy development, and collective sense-making (6 et al., 2006). Just as managing within single organizations requires a core of skill-based knowledge, a specific network management knowledge base is emerging (Agranoff and McGuire, 1999). For example, research in economic development found that skill areas include designing joint financing arrangements, negotiating joint strategies, implementing projects through a sequence of organizations (joint production), interagency negotiations, and multi-party contract development (Agranoff and McGuire, 2003). Studies in the environment demonstrate the importance of managing uncertainty in networks (Koppenjan and Klijn, 2004). And a study of emergency management indicates that significant differences exist between single agency and network leadership skills (Silvia and McGuire, 2010).

It's important to caution that managers cannot (and should not) control the interactions in a network; there are far too many diverse interactions (Klijn and Edelenbos, 2008). Facilitation, mediation, negotiation, intervention, and the ability to organize what are ostensibly self-organizing processes are better characterizations of the actions of a network manager. In many cases there is a central actor or actors in a network (Provan and Milward, 1995), but hierarchical principles of command and control do not apply in network settings.

So what are the skills or competencies needed for effective network management? For one, recognition of the problem and the persons needed to solve the problem. The ability to tap the skills, knowledge, and resources of others – money, technology, information, expertise, time, and other needed commodities – is perhaps the most critical management skill. The public manager needs to identify and include in the network needed expertise and resources to move a project forward. Public managers need to know who has access to information. It is important to identify the stakeholders from different entities and bring them into the support coalition (Agranoff and McGuire, 1999).

Similarly, the network should have some substantive knowledge of the issues/problems dealt with in the network (Klijn and Edelenbos, 2008). Network managers thus must be able to engage in what could be called transdisciplinary practice. A manager must know something about the work of different professions and occupations, and be ready to respond with this knowledge. In a fashion similar to project or matrix management in organizational settings, the boundaries of multiple disciplines merge as network participants work together on a product. Acquiring and utilizing knowledge from multiple disciplinary practices simultaneously can thus be critical to the success of a single project (Agranoff and McGuire, 1999).

A manager must also be able and ready to sell an idea/project, or a set of ideas/projects, to representatives of other organizations. Collaboration does not come automatically and the more the potential collaborators perceive demands on agency autonomy, power, and resources, the more resistance is likely to follow. The decision to join efforts thus requires persuasion that participation or partnering will be of mutual benefit and/or for a larger cause. Developing and maintaining a type of program rationale (Mandell, 1988), which is network-level shared meaning, is one way to mobilize support within the network. In this regard, visioning becomes an important network management competency (Gray, 2008).

STUDYING NETWORK MANAGEMENT

As in any field of social science inquiry, scholars employ a number of different approaches and methods in the study of public management networks. Whether the empirical research generates or tests hypotheses, uses qualitative or quantitative data, or employs small-n studies or large-n studies, the contributions made to our understanding of networks come from many different circles. The issue for network scholars in the twenty-first century is whether networks and their management constitutes so new a form of organization that non-traditional research is required.

One methodological technique for describing a network that has been around since the 1930s, but which still captures the allure of modern-day scholars (Berry et al., 2004), is the sociogram, which is a depiction of a network using a collection of nodes connected by lines. The utility of the sociogram is its ability to identify patterns of interaction in a network. More sophisticated analyses of network ties and connections can be performed. Social network analysis has become popular in private sector research as a means of revealing patterns of connectivity in specific functions and business units that cannot be adequately described with an organizational chart. The strength of the social network approach is that it can provide alternative explanations for why actors form ties while also explaining with whom the actors form ties (Kenis and Oerlemans, 2008: 305).

In other words, the advantage of social network analysis is sorting out 'who works with whom' and the scope of these connections, which offers a powerful way to describe a network.

Social network analysis can also be used a tool for providing valuable 'diagnostic' information about a network. For example, such analysis can allow researchers to decipher information flow and knowledge transfer, recognize blockages in communication, identify central people on whom a network may rely for expertise and knowledge, assess how a network is integrating the core members of the network (e.g. political, technical, financial), and determine whether the appropriate collaborations are occurring to support performance objectives (Cross and Parker, 2004). Social network analysis can isolate breakdowns in information flow – information bottlenecks – and identify untapped and valuable expertise in a network. It can expose excessive connectivity, revealing potential sources of power and influence and demonstrating who may have the largest hand in shaping the evolution of the network (Powell et al., 2005). Social network analysis can also reveal that even peripheral actors can exert some influence over network operations and outcomes (Stevenson and Greenberg, 2000). Although few analytical techniques offer such opportunities for empirically describing and explaining activity in a network, integrating the results of this type of analysis with fully specified models of network management and performance remains a challenge.

The study of networks may demand more grounded research deeper inside the black box than social network analysis can reach. It is important to point out that 'grounded' does not mean non-systematic and anecdotal. On the contrary, one example of the use of grounded theory is based on a 'qualitative but positivist systematic' comparative case analysis (Agranoff, 2007: 37). Others have used the comparative case method to draw conclusions regarding network structure and performance (Herranz, 2008; Imperial, 2005;

Provan and Milward, 1991, 1995). Qualitative research through comparative case studies can provide insight that quantitative research cannot offer (Agranoff and Radin, 1991). Models of network performance drawn from case studies can include accurate descriptions of the network, a thorough examination of the actions and interactions of network participants, a concern with network context, and, where relevant to the research, causal connections to outcomes. Observation of managerial behavior is another such mechanism for more accurately documenting how managers match behavior with environmental constraints, as is interviewing of managers (McGuire, 2002).

On the other hand, comparative case study analysis, even with a relatively large number of cases, is still not able to offer truly generalizable studies that large-n, quantitative studies can do. One way to move toward a greater understanding of the role of networks in program performance is to develop a general management model and then isolate those factors that are network-specific. Many scholars have tested a formal model developed by Meier and O'Toole (2003) with performance data from Texas public school districts. The variable conceptualized as 'network management' in the model is measured as the level of interaction between the primary network managers, the superintendents, and five (with subsequent analyses including eight) actors from the school districts' organizational environment. The researchers continually find that the frequency of interaction is positively related to school district performance: the greater the number of actors and interaction with whom the superintendents 'networked,' the higher the performance. However, in spite of these important findings, the weakness of large-n studies in general is the typically thin description of the measures of 'network' and 'management.' While it has been argued that a simple count of contacts and interactions is an appropriate measure of actual management behavior (Meier and O'Toole, 2005), there are still limitations to adding up dyadic contacts compared to viewing the network qua network as the primary unit of analysis.

So the preponderance of empirical research on public management networks has thus far been either small-n studies with strong measurement validity but perhaps lacking clear causal relationships between actions and effectiveness, or large-n studies that establish strong internal validity but lack the thick description that comparative case analyses can provide. With a few notable exceptions, these studies have been cross-sectional. While there have been many important contributions from the best of this research, the public management field must find a way to bridge the use of complete and accurate conceptualizations of a network with the network's activities, and in turn with its outcomes.

CONCLUSION

Network management is a field of study that offers a great deal of knowledge about management in such contexts, but it cries out for more empirical research. Its primary proposition is that networks need managers in order to be effective, but that the style of management needed is different than what is typically found in single agency settings. There is sufficient theory for asserting that proposition, but heretofore insufficient empirical verification of its utility. Thus, there are several important questions to be answered about managing in networks.

First, how do/should managers respond when the network 'hits a wall?' What are the barriers, the pulls and drags on network operations, and how can/do networks overcome them? Secondly, in what ways do networks grow and learn, and what is the role of the network manager in instigating that learning process? Thirdly, we have much to learn about developing the skills of the network manager. What can be 'borrowed' from traditional organization theorists (e.g. contingency management, principles of coordination)

and what is not applicable or useful? Fourthly, how can/should networks measure outcomes, as opposed to measuring effectiveness with purely process, output, or perceptual measures? Despite the prevalence of network examination, there is still considerable confusion over exactly what outcomes are actually achieved (Agranoff and McGuire, 2001; Provan and Sydow, 2008). Finally, what is the relationship between networks and government agencies? How do networks and bureaucracies function? There are clear political and legal limits on public networks, but such networks emerge despite these parameters. How do networks operate, sustain themselves, and sometimes succeed if they are so limited?

Among the most important issues that remain with regard to network management concerns the process of converting a network-generated, multi-agency solution into policy 'energy.' Too often, networks find reasonable solution approaches, but then run into political, financial, or legal barriers that prevent the next action step. Networks can attempt to overcome provisions of established public policy simply by attempting to change them, but that can be a convoluted process. A few solutions have been suggested: incorporating representative policymakers like state legislators into the network process, hoping for the efficacy of knowledge-based appeals, or lobbying on behalf of the network. In these very common situations, network-derived knowledge that is transformed into brokered consensus becomes, in effect, a step in the policy process, and one that may evolve over time (Koppenjan and Klijn, 2004). In order to fully understand how to manage networks, more must be known about how networks overcome such barriers and about the steps between network agreement and policy action.

REFERENCES

6, Perri., Goodwin, Nick, Peck, Edward and Freeman, Tim (2006) *Managing Networks of Twenty-first*

Century Organisations. New York: Palgrave Macmillan.

Agranoff, Robert (2003) *Leveraging Networks: A Guide for Public Managers Working across Organizations*. IBM Endowment for The Business of Government.

Agranoff, Robert (2007) *Managing within Networks: Adding Value to Public Organizations*. Washington, DC: Georgetown University Press.

Agranoff, Robert (2008) 'Collaboration for Knowledge: Learning from Public Management Networks', in Lisa Blomgren Bingham and Rosemary O'Leary (eds), *Big Ideas in Collaborative Public Management*. Armonk, NY: M.E. Sharpe; pp. 162–94.

Agranoff, Robert and McGuire, Michael (1999) 'Managing in Network Settings', *Policy Studies Review* 16(1): 18–41.

Agranoff, Robert and McGuire, Michael (2001) 'Big Questions in Public Network Management Research', *Journal of Public Administration Research and Theory* 11(3): 295–326.

Agranoff, Robert and McGuire, Michael (2003a) *Collaborative Public Management: New Strategies for Local Governments*. Washington, DC: Georgetown University Press.

Agranoff, Robert and McGuire, Michael (2003b) 'Inside the Matrix: Integrating the Paradigms of Intergovernmental and Network Management', *International Journal of Public Administration* 26(12): 1401–22.

Agranoff, Robert and Radin, Beryl A (1991) 'The Comparative Case Study Approach in Public Administration', in James L. Perry (ed.), *Research in Public Administration*. Vol. I. Greenwich, CT: JAI Press; pp. 203–31.

Agranoff, Robert, Hunter, Monica, McGuire, Michael, et al., (2008) *Metro High School: An Emerging STEM Community*. Columbus, Ohio: PAST Foundation.

Bachmann, Reinhard (2001) 'Trust, Power, and Control in Trans-organizational Relations', *Organization Studies* 22(2): 337–65.

Berry, Frances S., Brower, Ralph S., Choi, Sang Ok, et al., (2004) 'Three Traditions of Network Research: What the Public Management Research Agenda Can Learn from Other Research Communities', *Public Administration Review* 64(5): 539–52.

Bevir, Mark, and Richards, David (2009) Decentring Policy Networks: A Theoretical Agenda', *Public Administration* 87(1): 3–14.

Borzel, Tanja A. (1998) Organizing Babylon – On the Different Conceptions of Policy Networks', *Public Administration* 76(2): 253–73.

Brass, Daniel J., Galaskiewicz, Joseph, Greve, Henrich R. and Tsai, Wenpin (2004) 'Taking Stock of Networks and Organizations: A Multilevel Perspective', *Academy of Management Journal* 47(6): 795–817.

Brown, Trevor L., Potoski, Matthew and Van Slyke, David M. (2006) 'Managing Public Service Contracts: Aligning Values, Institutions, and Markets', *Public Administration Review* 66(3): 323–31.

Burt, Ronald (1992) *Structural Holes: The Social Structure of Competition*. Cambridge, MA: Harvard University Press.

Chen, Bin (2008) 'Assessing Inter-organizational Networks for Public Service Delivery: A Process-Perceived Effectiveness Framework', *Public Performance and Management Review* 31(3): 348–63.

Coglianese, Cary (1999) 'The Limits of Consensus', *Environment* 41(1): 28–33.

Cross, Rob and Parker, Andrew (2004) *The Hidden Power of Social Networks*. Boston, MA: Harvard Business School Press.

Davenport, Thomas H. and Prusak, Laurence (2000) *Working Knowledge: How Organizations Manage What They Know*. Boston, MA: Harvard Business School Press.

Department of Homeland Security (2008) *National Response Framework*. http://www.fema.gov/pdf/emergency/nrf/nrf-core.pdf Accessed 23 April, 2009.

Ferguson, Ronald F. and Stoutland, Sara E. (1999) 'Reconceiving the Community Development Field', in Ronald F. Ferguson and William T. Dickens (eds), *Urban Problems and Community Development*. Washington, DC: Brookings; pp. 33–75.

Frederickson, H. George (1997) *The Spirit of Public Administration*. San Francisco, CA: Jossey-Bass.

Frederickson, H. George (1999) 'The Repositioning of American Public Administration', *PS: Political Science and Politics* 32(4): 701–11.

Goldsmith, Stephen and Eggers, William D. (2004) *Governing by Network: The New Shape of the Public Sector*. Washington, DC: Brookings Institution Press.

Gray, Barbara (2008) 'Intervening to Improve Inter-Organizational Partnerships', in Steve Cropper, Mark Ebbs, Chris Huxham and Peter Smith Ring (eds), *The Oxford Handbook of Inter-Organizational Relations*. Oxford: Oxford University Press; pp. 664–90.

Herranz Jr, Joaquin (2008) 'The Multisectoral Trilemma of Network Management', *Journal of Public Administration Research and Theory* 18(1): 1–31.

Hertting, Nils (2008) 'Mechanisms of Governance Network Formation – A Contextual Rational Choice Perspective', in Eva Sorensen and Jacob Torfing (eds), *Theories of Democratic Network Governance*. London: Palgrave Macmillan; pp. 43–60.

Huxham, Chris (2003) 'Theorizing Collaboration Practice', *Public Management Review* 5(3): 401–23.

Huxham, Chris and Beech, Nic (2008) 'Inter-Organizational Power', in Steve Cropper, Mark Ebbs, Chris Huxham and Peter Smith Ring (eds), *The Oxford Handbook of Inter-Organizational Relations*. Oxford: Oxford University Press; pp. 555–79.

Huxham, Chris and Vangen, Siv (2005) *Managing to Collaborate: The Theory and Practice of Collaborative Advantage*. London: Routledge.

Imperial, Mark T. (2005) 'Using Collaboration as a Governance Strategy: Lessons from Six Watershed Management Programs', *Administration and Society* 37(3): 281–320.

Keating, Michael (1999) 'Regions and International Affairs: Motives, Opportunities, and Strategies', *Regional and Federal Studies* 9(1): 1–16.

Kenis, Patrick and Oerlemans, Leon (2008) 'The Social Network Perspective: Understanding the Structure of Cooperation', in Steve Cropper, Mark Ebbs, Chris Huxham and Peter Smith Ring (eds), *The Oxford Handbook of Inter-Organizational Relations*. Oxford: Oxford University Press; pp. 289–312.

Kickert, Walter J.M., Klijn, Erik-Hans and Koppenjan, Joop F.M. (1997) 'Managing Networks in the Public Sector: Findings and Reflections', in Walter J.M. Kickert, Erik-Hans Klijn and Joop F.M. Koppenjan (eds), *Managing Complex Networks*. London: Sage; pp. 166–91.

Kiefer, John J. and Montjoy, Robert S. (2006) 'Incrementalism before the Storm: Network Performance for the Evacuation of New Orleans', *Public Administration Review* 66(s1): 122–30.

Klijn, Erik-Hans and Edelenbos, Jurian (2008) 'Meta-governance as Network Management', in Eva Sorensen and Jacob Torfing (eds), *Theories of Democratic Network Governance*. London: Palgrave Macmillan; pp. 199–214.

Klijn, Erik-Hans and Koppenjan, Joop F.M. (2000) 'Public Management and Policy Networks: Foundations of a Network Approach to Governance', *Public Management* 2(2): 135–58.

Klijn, Erik-Hans and Teisman, Geert R. (1997) 'Strategies and Games in Networks', in Walter J.M. Kickert, Erik-Hans Klijn and Joop F.M. Koppenjan (eds), *Managing Complex Networks*. London: Sage; pp. 98–118.

Knoke, David and Chen, Xinxiang (2008) 'Political Perspectives on Inter-organizational Networks', in Steve Cropper, Mark Ebbs, Chris Huxham and Peter Smith Ring (eds), *The Oxford Handbook of Inter-Organizational Relations*. Oxford: Oxford University Press; pp. 441–72.

Koppenjan, Joop F.M. (2008) 'Consensus and Conflict in Policy Networks: Too Much or too Little?', in Eva Sorensen and Jacob Torfing (eds), *Theories of Democratic Network Governance*. London: Palgrave Macmillan; pp. 133–52.

Koppenjan, Joop F.M. and Klijn, Erik-Hans (2004) *Managing Uncertainties in Networks*. London: Routledge.

Mandell, Myrna (1988) 'Intergovernmental Management in Interorganizational Networks: A Revised Perspective', *International Journal of Public Administration* 11(4): 393–416.

McEntire, David A. (2002) Coordinating Multi-organisational Responses to Disaster: Lessons from the March 28, 2000, Fort Worth Tornado', *Disaster Prevention and Management* 11(5): 369–79.

McGuire, Michael (2002) 'Managing Networks: Propositions on What Managers Do and Why They Do It', *Public Administration Review* 62(5): 599–609.

McGuire, Michael (2003) 'Is It Really So Strange? A Critical Look At The "Network Management is Different from Hierarchical Management" Perspective', Paper Presented at the Seventh National Public Management Research Conference, Washington, DC.

McGuire, Michael (2006) 'Collaborative Public Management: Assessing What We Know and How We Know It', *Public Administration Review* 66(s1): 33–43.

McGuire, Michael and Silvia, Chris (2009) 'Does Leadership in Networks Matter? Examining The Effect Of Leadership Behavior On Managers' Perception Of Network Effectiveness', *Public Performance and Management Review* (forthcoming).

Meier, Kenneth J. and O'Toole, Laurence, J. Jr, (2003) 'Public Management and Educational Performance: The Impact of Managerial Networking', *Public Administration Review* 64(3): 363–71.

Meier, Kenneth J. and O'Toole, Laurence, J. Jr, (2005) 'Managerial Networking: Issues of Measurement and Research Design', *Administration and Society* 37(5): 523–41.

Milward, H. Brinton and Provan, Keith G. (2006) *A Manager's Guide to Choosing and Using Collaborative Networks*. IBM Center for The Business of Government.

Milward, H. Brinton, Provan, Keith G. and Else, Barbara A. (1993) 'What Does the "Hollow State" Look Like?, in Barry Bozeman (ed.), *Public Management: The State of the Art*. San Francisco, CA: Jossey-Bass: pp. 309–22.

Moynihan, Donald P. (2008) 'Combining Structural Forms in the Search for Policy Tools: Incident

Command Systems in U.S. Crisis Management', *Governance* 21(2): 205–29.

Newell, Sue, Robertson, Maxine, Scarbrough, Harry and Swan, Jacky (2002) *Managing Knowledge Work*. Hampshire: Palgrave.

Osborne, David and Gaebler, Ted (1992) *Reinventing Government*. Reading, MA: Addison-Wesley.

Osborne, David and Plastrik, Peter (1997) *Banishing Bureaucracy: The Five Strategies for Reinventing Government*. Reading, MA: Addison-Wesley.

O'Toole, Laurence J., Jr (1993) 'Multiorganizational Policy Implementation: Some Limitations and Possibilities for Rational-Choice Contributions', in Fritz W. Scharpf (ed.), *Games in Hierarchies and Networks: Analytical and Empirical Approaches to the Study of Governance Institutions*. Boulder, CO: Westview Press; pp. 27–64.

Powell, Walter W. (1990) 'Neither Market Nor Hierarchy: Network Forms of Organization', *Research in Organizational Behavior* 12: 295–336.

Powell, Walter W., White, Douglas R., Koput, Kenneth W. and Owen-Smith, Jason (2005) 'Network Dynamics and Field Evolution: The Growth of Interorganizational Collaboration in the Life Sciences', *American Journal of Sociology* 110(4): 1132–205.

Provan, Keith G. and Kenis, Patrick (2008) 'Modes of Network Governance: Structure, Management, and Effectiveness', *Journal of Public Administration Research and Theory* 18(2): 229–52.

Provan, Keith G. and Milward, H. Brinton (1991) 'Institutional-Level Norms and Organizational Involvement in a Service-Implementation Network', *Journal of Public Administration Research and Theory* 1(4): 391–417.

Provan, Keith G. and Milward, H. Brinton (1995) 'A Preliminary Theory of Interorganizational Effectiveness: A Comparative Study of Four Community Mental Health Systems', *Administrative Science Quarterly* 40(1): 1–33.

Provan, Keith G. and Sydow, Jorg (2008) 'Evaluating Inter-Organizational Relationships', in Steve Cropper, Mark Ebbs, Chris Huxham and Peter Smith Ring (eds), *The Oxford Handbook of Inter-Organizational Relations*. Oxford: Oxford University Press; pp. 691–716.

Rethemeyer, R. Karl and Hatmaker, Deneen M. (2008) 'Network Management Reconsidered: An Inquiry into Management of Network Structures in Public Sector Provision', *Journal of Public Administration Research and Theory* 18(4): 617–46.

Rhodes, Rod. A.W. (1997) *Understanding Governance: Policy Networks, Governance, Reflexivity and Accountability*. Buckingham, UK: Open University Press.

Rhodes, Rod A.W. (2003) 'Putting People Back into Networks', in Ari Salminen (ed), *Governing Networks*. Amsterdam: IOS Press; pp. 9–23.

Rodriguez, Charo, Langley, Ann, Beland, Francois and Denis, Jean-Louis (2007) 'Governance, Power, and Mandated Collaboration in an Interorganizational network', *Administration and Society* 39(2): 150–93.

Sabel, Charles F. (1993) 'Studied Trust: Building New Forms of Cooperation in a Volatile Economy', *Human Relations* 46(9): 1133–170.

Saint-Onge, Hubert and Armstrong, Charles (2004) *The Conductive Organization*. Amsterdam: Elsevier.

Scharpf, Fritz W. (1978) 'Interorganizational Policy Studies: Issues, Concepts, and Perspectives', in Kenneth Hanf and Fritz W. Scharpf (eds), *Interorganizational Policy Making*. London: Sage, pp. 345–370.

Scharpf, Fritz W. (1993) 'Games in Hierarchies and Networks: An Introduction', in Fritz W. Scharpf (ed.), *Games in Hierarchies and Networks: Analytical and Empirical Approaches to the Study of Governance Institutions*. Boulder, CO: Westview Press; pp. 7–23.

Sharpe, Laurence J. (1986) 'Intergovernmental Policy-Making: The Limits of Subnational Autonomy', in Franz-Xaver Kaufman, Giandomenico Majone and Vincent Ostrom (eds), *Guidance, Control, and Evaluation in the Public Sector*. Berlin: Walter de Gruyter; pp. 159–181.

Silvia, Chris and McGuire, Michael (2010) 'Leading Public Sector Networks: An Empirical Examination of Integrative Leadership Behaviors', *The Leadership Quarterly* 21(2): 264–277.

Sorensen, Eva and Torfing, Jacob (2008) 'Theoretical Approaches To Governance Network Dynamics', in Eva Sorensen and Jacob Torfing (eds), *Theories of Democratic Network Governance*. London: Palgrave Macmillan; pp. 25–42.

Stevenson, William B. and Greenberg, Danna (2000) 'Agency and Social Networks: Strategies of Action in a Social Structure of Position, Opposition, and Opportunity', *Administrative Science Quarterly* 45(4): 651–78.

Sydow, Jorg, and Windeler, Arnold (1998) 'Organizing and Evaluating Interfirm Networks: A Structuralist Perspective on Network Process and Effectiveness', *Organization Science* 9(3): 265–84.

Thompson, Grahame F. (2003) *Between Hierarchies and Markets: The Logic and Limits of Network Forms of Organization*. Oxford: Oxford University Press.

Thomson, Ann Marie and Perry, James L. (2006) 'Collaboration Processes: Inside the Black Box', *Public Administration Review* 66(s1): 20–32.

Triantafillou, Peter (2008) 'Governing the Formation and Mobilization of Governance Networks', in Eva Sorensen and Jacob Torfing (eds), *Theories of Democratic Network Governance.* London: Palgrave Macmillan; pp. 183–98.

Vangen, S. and Huxham, C. (2003) 'Nurturing Collaborative Relations: Building Trust in Interorganizational Collaboration', *Journal of Applied Behavioral Science* 39(1): 5–31.

Wilkins, Allen L. and Ouchi, William G. (1983) 'Efficient Cultures: Exploring the Relationship between Culture and Organizational Performance', *Administrative Science Quarterly* 28(3): 468–81.

Windhoff-Hentier, Andriene (1992) 'The Internationalization Of Domestic Policy: A Motor of Decentralization'. Paper Presented at the European Consortium for Political Research Joint Sessions, Limerick, Ireland.

Yan, Aimin and Gray, Barbara (1994) 'Bargaining Power, Management Control, and Performance in United States–China Joint Ventures', *Academy of Management Journal* 37(6): 1478–518.

Zaheer, Akbar, McEvily, Bill and Perrone, Vincenzo (1998) 'Does Trust Matter? Exploring the Effects of Interorganizational and Interpersonal Trust on Performance', *Organization Science* 9(2): 141–59.

29

Social Inclusion

Petri Koikkalainen

INTRODUCTION

The term 'social inclusion' may be used as broadly synonymous with very general notions such as unity, cohesion, civic engagement, togetherness, or bridging the gap between 'us' and 'the other'. But its meaning can also relate to much more carefully defined courses of action or policies that are designed to help in the active 'social inclusion' of identifiable disadvantaged groups into the wider society. It is the latter meaning rather than the first one that is characteristic of contemporary governance at the level of policies promoted by international organizations, governments and non-governmental organizations (NGOs).

What in today's public policy is handled under the rubric of social inclusion, would in the emerging welfare states of the 1960s and 1970s have been part of their general social policy. The aim was to improve the conditions of underprivileged groups by two main sorts of measures: first, by redistributing national income in order to narrow the socioeconomic gap between the rich and the poor; secondly, by providing public services, such as free education, that would narrow the gap that existed in terms of personal ability and opportunity. Such policies, it was thought, would guarantee a necessary level of cohesion in terms of both identity and economy.

Since the 1970s, however, the emphases of public policy have changed hand in hand with the theoretical ways of explaining social exclusion and inclusion. For the theorists of the so-called New Right (e.g. Nozick, 1974), cohesion and inclusion are for the most part spontaneous phenomena, which may emerge as a result of non-regulated interaction between free individuals. The state ought not to assume the task of maintaining social inclusion to itself, albeit at the level of maintaining a necessary level of public order. Recent communitarian and new institutionalist theorists have challenged this view. They have sought to bring such notions as *community, network* and *social capital* into discourses that were previously dominated by questions regarding the legitimacy of redistributive policies and the dichotomy between the state and the market. Aspects of all these influences can be traced in contemporary governance and public policy at its national, intergovernmental (e.g. the EU) as well as international (e.g. UN, OECD) level.

The term *social inclusion* rose to prominence in European social policy discourse during the 1980s. It emerged as a counter-concept to *social exclusion*, which denoted the inability of some persons or groups to take part in the mainstream functions of society, especially the labour markets. Thus, social inclusion is understood as a specific target-oriented policy that complements the services and incentives that are universally available for every citizen.

As a result, a shift of emphasis has occurred in the concepts and practices that are related to the goal of social cohesion. Social inclusion in its present meaning is not as much about securing an even distribution of material income as it is about achieving a tolerably even distribution of *opportunities* – equality in terms of agency, participation and memberships in beneficial networks. This has been characteristic especially for the British Blairite Third Way, as well as for New Zealand, Australia, Canada, and the New or Clintonite Democrats of the United States (Esping-Andersen, 1996: 15–18; Bevir, 2005: 37–53). Continental European and Scandinavian countries have responded in various ways, but in the public discourse on issues related to governance, the influence of the Third Way ideas is widely perceivable.

To get a fuller picture of the issue, however, one needs to look also at the theories behind the various policies that seek to explain the nature of the relevant human communities. In other words, should the 'socially included' individuals become members of a welfare state, functioning markets, beneficial networks, or a moral community defined by its shared values? Each of these possibilities is examined in the next section. Following that, examples of the contemporary uses of 'social inclusion' in public policy are provided. The chapter concludes with a review of the concept of social inclusion and the influence of the theoretical ideas as presented in the earlier sections.

SOCIAL INCLUSION IN THEORIES OF GOVERNANCE

The welfare statist model of social inclusion

Nordic countries (Sweden, Finland, Denmark, Norway, Iceland) arguably provide the Western model example of a universalist conception of social inclusion. The heyday of the 'Nordic welfare model' is often said to have lasted from the 1960s to the late 1980s. Before the late 1960s, the Nordic countries were not that dramatically different from countries like Germany or the Netherlands, which also developed extensive social policies in the form of income redistribution programmes. According to Esping-Andersen (1996: 10–11), the truly distinctive Nordic (especially Swedish) model 'came into being with the shift towards active labour market policies, social service expansion, and gender equalization in the 1970s and '80s. An important goal of these policies was to assist in the transfer of individuals from one life-course situation to another – say, from unemployment to work, or from work to parental leave and back. Strong investments in education were considered as the best means to produce a workforce that was both flexible and re-educable. During the 1970s and 1980s, exceptionally high numbers of women entered the workforce while unemployment figures remained relatively low.

Individuals confronted the welfare state mostly in the form of free or heavily subsidized day-care, schools, universities and medical treatment organized by the public sector, as well as in the rather generous financial benefits that were awarded in cases of retirement or temporary unemployment. One of the key assumptions of the Nordic model of social inclusion was, and still is, participation in the workforce. If one remains outside of the workforce for longer than the publicly-supported periods of transition, the benefits usually weaken substantially. The purpose of the 'social safety-net' was to ensure that if an individual's career choices proved untenable, the individual would get public support to regain membership in the productive mainstream of society. During the 1980s, the network of social services had grown so extensive that the Swedish Trade Union Confederation Landsorganisationen i Sverige (LO) declared that there was no need for the welfare state to grow in order to achieve the basic goals of social security and equality. That was, in effect, to admit that the welfare state was fully developed (Stephens, 1996: 44).

Despite the Nordic model's goal of full employment, the basic right to receive entitlements and services is based on citizenship, not personal contribution. Hence the model has been called institutional or universal (Esping-Andersen, 1990; Stephens, 1996). This has also been its main horizon of conceptualizing social inclusion. As long as there was simultaneous increase in equality and economic growth and almost full employment, 'social inclusion' – understood as the opposite of material or socioeconomic exclusion – came almost as a by-product. More than that, it has been a central assumption for the defenders of the model that 'social policy can create loyalties and social bonds, which in turn have important consequences for the distribution of power in society' (Kangas and Palme, 2005: 29). Hence it is possible to generate a '"virtuous circle" between democracy and social policy', which in turn would 'create and fortify a general feeling of inclusion' and produce precisely that kind of mutual trust that since the 1990s has also been termed 'social capital' (Kangas and Palme, 2005: 3, 50).

The Nordic countries have comparatively strong traditions of local self-governance, and perhaps even paradoxically, the welfare state with all its machinery for the administration of economic and human resources may be legitimized as a continuation of a traditionally rather egalitarian and independent society (Ervasti et al., 2008: 3–5).

This is supported by the historical fact that the origins of social aid and insurance were in late-nineteenth-century and early-to-mid-twentieth-century voluntary associations, cooperatives and popular movements, which later often, but not always, merged with the public agencies.

Hence 'civil society' and 'the state' typically permeate each other to the degree that 'it is often hard to say where the civil society ended and the public sector began', and even the words 'state' and 'society' may be used synonymously (Kangas and Palme, 2005: 19). During the expansion of the welfare state, central bureaucratic planning and tripartite corporatism[1] strengthened their role in regard to social policy and inclusion. More recently, there has been a counter-reaction, especially in the political right and centre, where the state is seen as too fostering and more responsibility for social inclusion is allocated to NGOs and voluntary associations. At the same time, parts of public services have been outsourced or privatized.

The discourse that has legitimized the institutional/universal welfare model has been, from the point of view of party ideologies, mostly social democratic. From the point of view of scientific disciplines, rationalistic planning discourse characteristic of social policy, macroeconomics and sociology has been more influential than for example moral philosophy, political science or management. If assessed through the categories of academic philosophy, the early origins of welfare economics and distributive justice were strongly utilitarian (Rescher, 1967: 8–12), but since the appearance of Rawls' *A Theory of Justice* (1971), it has been popular to discuss the welfare state in contractarian terms, employing such of Rawls' ideas as the veil of ignorance, the requirement of open access regarding all institutions that produce inequality, and the principle of allowing inequalities only under specific conditions so that also the worst-off individuals are among the ultimate beneficiaries (e.g. Kangas and Palme, 2005: 39–40).

The New Right critique against the welfare model

Broadly similar ideas prevailed in most Western countries from the 1950s to the '70s regarding the need of public services and redistributive social policy. The United Kingdom had been an early leading example of the welfare state, largely because of the inception in 1948 of the National Health Service. Reliance on the public sector appeared natural not only because of the huge government-led investments in postwar reconstruction but also as a result of governments' enhanced capability for action that they had developed during the wartime.

The main lines of the New Right or neoliberal[2] critique of the 'welfare model' are familiar to most. Macroeconomic Keynesianism was powerfully criticized from the early 1970s by such monetarist or supply-side economists as Milton Friedman, Alan Greenspan and Arthur Laffer, whose ideas would have a strong influence on policymaking[3]. As a result, the idea of the welfare state as the basis of collective identity and social inclusion also became increasingly criticized. The term 'welfare society', which has largely replaced 'welfare state' in daily political discussion, is descriptive, as it takes into account the increasing amount of private and third-sector service providers. But it is also politically convenient, since it avoids the statist or collectivist allusions of the term welfare state.

The philosophical and ethical critiques against the welfare state with its collectivism and excessive rationalism are also of interest. They began to emerge in the late 1940s and ranged from Michael Oakeshott's traditionalist conservative criticisms of the British planning ideology (1956) to the radical rationalist individualism of the American novelist and philosopher Ayn Rand (Rand, 1957; Rand and Branden, 1964); from the philosophical descriptions of the malaises of modern mass society by Hannah Arendt (1959) or Sheldon Wolin (1960) to the leftist, openly political critiques of the

commodification and instrumentalization of life by the likes of Herbert Marcuse (1964). They all perceived the 'welfare', 'collectivist' or 'capitalist' state as an impersonal organization that, despite its apparently 'neutral' nature, at least covertly played into the hands of some particular interests.

On the political right, the traditional conservative answer has been to describe social inclusion as resulting from adherence to a historically inherited form of life. The process of social inclusion takes place when individuals learn about the customs and institutions of their communities, come to appreciate what is worth preserving in them, make their life meaningful within such bounds – and exercise civic virtue by renewing and carefully revising their form of life when the need arises (e.g. Oakeshott, 1956; MacIntyre, 1981). In daily political discourse, such shorthand expressions as family, church and nation have epitomized the idea of a historically mediated institution or practice. They continue to exercise their influence in the conservative politics of most European and North American countries. Whereas according to traditional conservatives there is nothing wrong with the idea of the state taking care of its citizens' social inclusion, they think that the (social democratic) welfare state has simply done it in the wrong way.

The anti-collectivist wing of the political right, with its emphases on economic liberalism and individual rights, has emphasized quite different things. According to their view, the state should not meddle in exchanges that happen between free individuals. The government's interest in economic activity, and especially its attempts to improve the socioeconomic position of some individuals by redistributing money earned by others, should be very limited. The celebrity author and philosopher Ayn Rand presented a popularly influential early version of this doctrine in her philosophy of rational self-interest. She stated that government should be separated from economy as it was separated from religion in America almost 200 years earlier. According to Rand, government had no responsibility for the weaker socioeconomic position of some individuals. She opposed all forms of government-led social aid or inclusion, but she also thought that individuals' full economic liberty would lead to a much more affluent and qualitatively better society. 'If you do not regulate production and trade', she said after the publication of her best-selling novel *Atlas Shrugged*, 'you will have peaceful cooperation and harmony and justice among men' (Rand, 1959). Later libertarian philosophers and neoliberal economists (such as Alan Greenspan, who was Rand's writing associate for two decades) have often held similar, albeit not always equally radical positions in their subtler and academically better-received studies (Nozick, 1974: esp. footnote 3 on p. 306; Nozick, 1997).

Thus, the New Right or neoliberal solution to the problem of social inclusion has been twofold. First, it is not primarily the responsibility of the government to guarantee the cohesion of society or the social inclusion of individuals. The market itself, with its various transactions and incentives, is described as the natural model of all human relations. Therefore, a well-functioning market is also the best means to address the problem of 'social exclusion' that the welfare model has partly produced. The problem of the welfare state is that individuals become morally dependent on its money-providing agencies. What for social democrats is 'social inclusion' with a moral purpose is a form of corruption for libertarians. The tendency of expert bureaucracies and corporatist decision-making to treat individuals as a means to achieve some collective end will generate suppression of individuality, lack of spontaneity, and even hostility to exceptional talent. Moreover, to remain 'socially excluded' can be an individual choice that governments should respect.

The other side of the matter is, as the title of Nozick's *Anarchy, State, and Utopia* suggests, that there also is a utopian element in neoliberal thought that relates to social inclusion. This comes from the fundamentally liberal vision of spontaneous interchange of ideas and goods between free individuals. If the government puts an end to its fostering interventions, energies are released that will lead to the emergence of flourishing networks and communities. Although there can be no way of knowing beforehand how such associations would evolve, according to Nozick they would have the potential of containing 'a diversity of persons, with a diversity of excellences and talents, each benefiting from living with the others, each being of great use or delight to the others, complementing them' (Nozick, 1974: 306).

Network and trust: the new institutionalist solutions

The New Right views of society are in many respects symmetrical critiques of the welfare model: individualism instead of collectivism, markets instead of hierarchy, freedom of contract instead of regulation, and supply-side economics instead of Keynesianism. The welfare model was strong, perhaps particularly so in the Nordic countries, in its ability to equip superficially technocratic social and economic policies with essentially moral and ideological meanings. Even in its more institutionalized phases, social democracy was for a long time able to maintain an image of itself as a 'movement', a vehicle of carrying out principled and future-oriented politics while at the same time creating social bonds and a democratic atmosphere within the movement as well as in the wider society.

The New Right critiques of the welfare model have worked to undermine the credibility of the social democratic vision of progress and inclusion. With more than a little success, the welfarist idea of a democratic society has been portrayed as collectivism where state bureaucracy suffocates individual initiative. The New Right, however, has been more influential in its critique of the welfare model than in producing its own accounts of human sociability or social cohesion.

The new institutionalists have taken advantage of this weakness of the New Right. Politically, new institutionalism has often been close to the centre–left Third Way, such as New Labour in the UK and Clintonite or New Democrats in the USA. Theoretical origins for the new institutionalism are in the sociology of organizations, from where the ideas soon spread into management studies and administrative science. Granovetter argued in his famous article (1973) that a form of social interconnectedness that he called 'weak ties' is instrumental with regard to the functioning of organizations and networks. As opposed to 'strong ties', which are typical of such tight-knit institutions as the family or a religious congregation, weak ties develop in the more or less casual encounters that the conduct of our daily businesses is dependent on. Weak ties build social *networks*, structures that are legally informal and not in anyone's direct ownership, but can still involve high expectations regarding personal trust, obligation, reciprocity, and even friendship. According to the new institutionalists, the evolution of a functional network requires more than just the 'generalized morality' of the market, where the keeping of formal contracts is a sufficient guarantee of one's personal reputation (e.g. Granovetter, 1985: 489; Powell, 1990: 301).

Such ideas have provided the broad framework within which the new institutionalists have theorized social inclusion. The superiority of the network against pure markets, on the one hand, and a command-based hierarchy, on the other, is often explained in a narrative that contains elements of the following kind (Bevir, 2005: 39–40). Networks – or whatever we call those relatively stable patterns of social interaction that people engage in because of mutual interest and trust – are 'organic' social formations. Even in pure market situations or under rigid hierarchies, people generate relationships of exchange, trust and affection that go beyond the logic of the market or the bureaucracy. To understand why the market or the bureaucracy can sometimes be effective modes of

organization, one needs to understand them as networks of individuals who are bound together by social ties. This network is the true social fabric behind markets, bureaucracies and the civil society, and hence also the true basis of social inclusion. To grasp this 'human' dimension of life, the new institutionalists have included such concepts as participation, embeddedness, diplomacy and friendship in their vocabulary.

If the network is an organic mode of life, then it is also an inherently dynamic and creative one. If we look at how success has been achieved in science, business or art, the best solutions have usually emerged from more or less loose groups of individuals who possess shared interests while facing substantially less hierarchy than in a traditional bureaucracy. At the same time, they have more interpersonal encounters with each other than in pure market situations. The spontaneity and flexibility of the network gives it a superior ability to reorganize itself in response to the needs of the rapidly- changing economy, while at the same time it can contain remarkably high levels of trust, which in Powell's words is 'a remarkably efficient lubricant to economic exchange' (Powell, 1990: 305).

The new institutionalist reading of 'trust' arises from reciprocal relations between individuals who encounter each other in decision-making or exchange situations, and is hence close to economics and rational-choice theory. It is also precisely this mutual or reciprocal meaning of trust that is invoked in the recently very popular theories of *social capital* (e.g. Putnam, 2000). It may be worthwhile to note that the mainstream theories of representative government since the time of Locke have defined trust in a different way (see Laslett, 1960: 113–17): as a condition of legitimate *authority*, according to which governors are accountable to their electorate and must resign if trust is withdrawn.

New institutionalist theorists have often been more interested in explaining the emergence of flourishing human networks than in 'social inclusion' understood in the traditional socioeconomic sense. Nevertheless, the theoretical implications as well as the policy recommendations have been rather clear: the best way for an individual to avoid exclusion is by access to beneficial networks that are the chief means of getting jobs and otherwise improving one's socioeconomic condition.

The new institutionalist impetus can be traced in the various 'activating' policies that are designed to enhance the capacity of individuals to deal with the contingent situations of modern life, especially in the rapidly-changing labour market. Some new institutionalist policies attempt to strengthen civic participation and voting turnout, since active political participation is interpreted as a polity-level indicator of trust and social capital (Finnish Ministry of Justice, 2003). As mentioned earlier, 'active' social policy designed to improve individuals' labour market capabilities is not a wholly new institutionalist or Third Way invention, but was also part of the Nordic welfare model from the early 1970s. A key difference between these models is that whereas the traditional Nordic welfare policies chiefly relied on government in the creation of public services, socioeconomic benefits and even jobs, the new institutionalists have put more emphasis on the role of voluntary and informal networks and the third sector.

Community: an alternative form of social order?

Communitarianism as a philosophical movement evolved from critiques of the new normative liberal theories, such as the social liberalism of Rawls, or the libertarianism of Nozick, during the 1970s. If the disciplinary origins of the new institutionalism have been mainly in sociology, public administration and management, the most renowned communitarians, such as Alasdair MacIntyre, Charles Taylor, Michael Sandel, or Michael Walzer, have been moral philosophers. Sociologist Amitai Etzioni established the

Communitarian Network, the best-known American advocacy organization for the spread of communitarian ideas, in 1990 (see Etzioni, 1993). However, not all 'communitarians' have endorsed the actual policy implications of the label. What might be called a communitarian vision of social inclusion thus contains various and even conflicting elements. Common to them all is still their critique of certain aspects of 'modernity', most notably liberal individualism and the dependency-creating character of the welfare state.

The communitarian critiques of liberalism, as first epitomized by the works of MacIntyre (1981) and Sandel (1982), have sought to challenge the prominence of the state–individual dichotomy of 'traditional' political philosophy by introducing a set of concepts that are all pertinent to the theme of social inclusion: for instance, *morality*, *tradition*, *practice*, and *community*.

The broad thrust of the communitarian critique has been that the contemporary (welfare) state is not a suitable or sufficient model of social order, and that the liberal conception of 'individual' leads to too narrow descriptions of the human condition. For MacIntyre, the result of his philosophical critique of liberalism is a wholesale rejection of 'modern systematic politics, whether liberal, conservative, radical or socialist', for they all lack connection to the Aristotelian tradition of virtues, which for MacIntyre is the best attempt so far to capture the political nature of man, and which until the full onslaught of modernity was able to shape and regulate European political life (MacIntyre, 1981: 255). Regarding communities and inclusion, MacIntyre suggests the 'construction of local forms of community within which civility and the intellectual and moral life can be sustained through the new dark ages that are already upon us' (MacIntyre, 1981: 263). Such communities should reflect the philosophical notions of practice, virtue and tradition (MacIntyre, 1981: 187–9).

Taylor (1989, 1991) has not been equally critical of all aspects of modernity, but proposes a 'moral revival' based on the original modern 'ideal of authenticity' that enlightened the writings of such figures as Rousseau, Kant, Herder, Hegel and Marx. According to Taylor, the more recent 'malaises of modernity' have resulted from shallower readings of the ideal, which have overemphasized individuality and instrumental reason (Taylor, 1991: 2–9). Sandel (1996) has endorsed the civic republican tradition of American politics and proposed policies that lead to more effective 'character-formation' guided by public authorities in accordance with the republican ideals.

It is a shared communitarian view that some aspects of modernity seriously erode human communities, and that the state has not been able to repair the loss with its well-meaning programmes of social welfare and inclusion. The communitarian answer to the problem of social inclusion (although they might not choose to talk about 'social inclusion') has not been framed through formal membership in political institutions such as the state, but through adherence to a shared set of core values or substantial morality. Such values or morality, in turn, require a community of people to sustain them.

For the more practically oriented communitarian thinkers and activists, family, neighbourhood, congregation, town and school are models of community where the actions of individuals are guided by shared values. For Robert N. Bellah et al. in their famous sociological study (1985), the American small town with its religious and republican traditions was an obvious point of reference. Intellectuals of the Communitarian Network, such as Etzioni, have often invested their hope on 'restoring communities' at the grassroots level that can bring back 'the moral voice' and a 'sense of obligation' to the lives of individuals (Etzioni, 1993: 1–3). The emphasis on strong local communities has borne some resemblance to the social capital theory initiated by Robert Putnam, but communitarians often stress that it is not enough just to form networks or associations

around bowling or choir music: in addition, communities should be informed by substantial moralities that can deal with wider aspects of life (Etzioni, 1997: 96).

Communitarian thinkers often present strong overall criticisms against the welfare policies of the 1960s to 1980s. These also frequently mediate a recognizable feeling of a generational conflict. The following words by Etzioni could have been written by many a communitarian or conservative intellectual:

> We require a general *shoring up of our moral foundations*. Since the early sixties, many of our moral traditions, social values, and institutions have been challenged, often for valid reasons. The end result is that we live in a state of increasing moral confusion and social anarchy. (Etzioni, 1993: 11–12, emphasis in original)

For Etzioni, the good society

> is not first and foremost one of law-and-order, but one based on shared moral values that the members affirm .... For the same reasons, the main social body is not the state (or even the polity) and the main actors are not citizens, but the body is the society (as a community of communities) and the actors are members in it. (Etzioni, 1997: 140–1).

The philosophical and sometimes fundamental critiques of modernity distinguish communitarians from the network theorists, who otherwise stress the importance of social bonds. Not surprisingly, some communitarians have found common ground with traditionalist social conservatives.

POLICY APPLICATIONS

Social inclusion is a 'strategic' policy concept that emerged during the 1980s in response to studies that demonstrated the existence of the phenomenon of *social exclusion*. According to most sources, the concept was first used in France during the 1970s. *Exclusion sociale* described the disabled, single parents and the uninsured unemployed, *les exclus*, who were not only disregarded by the social insurance system, but also otherwise marginalized in society (Hayes et al., 2008: 4; Silver, 1994). In Italy, *esclusione sociale* has since 2000 been a legal concept that describes poverty combined with social marginalization. One of the first steps taken by the European Union (then the European Community) to address a related problem was its Community Action Programme to Foster the Economic and Social Integration of the Least Privileged Groups, initiated in 1989. In the UK, the terms social exclusion and social inclusion became prominent in 1997, when Tony Blair's Labour government established its Social Exclusion Unit (SEU). The unit was based in the Cabinet Office and it reported directly to the Prime Minister. Achieving social inclusion was one of the government's 'joined-up policies for the joined-up problems'. In 1997 social exclusion was officially defined as:

A shorthand label for what can happen when individuals or areas suffer from a combination of linked problems such as unemployment, poor skills, low incomes, poor housing, high crime environments, bad health and family breakdown. (UK Social Exclusion Unit, 1997)

The majority of the contemporary definitions of social inclusion target particular disadvantaged groups, who can be below the standards of the majority of the population in multiple different respects. The target-specific character of the concept may be the reason why 'social inclusion' has in the Scandinavian countries with their traditionally universalist social policies been a less prominent and more vaguely defined goal than on the Continent or in the UK. For example, the Swedish and Finnish official equivalents of the term social inclusion, *social delaktighet* and *sosiaalinen osallisuus* (Swedish Government Offices, 2008; Finnish Ministry of Social Affairs and Health, 2008), convey the meaning of 'taking part' in the social whole, but they do not express the idea of a *process* of inclusion of particular disadvantaged groups as clearly. Nevertheless, the 'Nordic model' has also been revised as

a result of external pressures and internal changes of ideology. Nowadays, it is common to perceive social policy as a 'social investment' that aids in the emergence of beneficial networks and the inclusion of the most disadvantaged individuals within them. As the programme of the incoming Finnish centre–right government put it in 2007, 'Social services and aid should target people in greatest need of assistance' (Finnish Government, 2007).

Regarding the changes in actual social policy, the New Zealand's free market reforms during the late 1980s were an important example to many countries in Europe and elsewhere. The philosophy behind the New Zealand reforms was that of economic liberalism, with 'the general scarcity of resources' as its starting point. The purpose of economic and social policy was to 'align the interests and actions of individuals with those of the nation', thus encouraging 'greater efficiency, equity or liberty' (NZ Treasury, 1987: 1–2). The relationship between government and the individual was defined as a *partnership*, where government has a role in 'providing leadership, in explaining clearly the need for changes', while 'the responsibility of deciding whether to accept change and to proceed to the construction of new, superior societal arrangements lies with the individuals' (NZ Treasury, 1987: 5).

Regarding social inclusion, the New Zealand policies emphasized the importance of a well-functioning and flexible labour market, reflecting 'the fact that the economy is composed of individuals pursuing their own interests, and that the inevitable constraints on exchange prevent the full achievement of social goals' (NZ Treasury, 1987: 6). The goal also was to ensure that tax money is spent carefully 'where the need is greatest', mainly to guarantee access to social services to the poor and to redistribute income so that the most disadvantaged individuals are not 'forced to lead mean and squalid lives' (NZ Treasury, 1987: 7). The goal of the market-oriented or New Right reforms also more generally has been to shift the emphasis of social policy from universal citizenship-based entitlements to target-specific and means-tested policies.

The new institutionalist models of social inclusion have combined elements of market-oriented reforms with the desire to maintain at least some key aspects of a welfare society. Terms such as 'the third sector', 'network', 'partnership' and 'social capital' have climbed high on the contemporary agenda of governance in national governments, international organizations and NGOs. It is not an exaggeration to attribute a key role here to the UK New Labour Party. Its famous 1997 election manifesto promised a 'country in which people get on, do well, make a success of their lives … a society where we do not simply pursue our own individual aims but where we hold many aims in common and work together to achieve them' (UK Labour Party, 1997).

The precise nature of the Blairite ideology has been much debated, but at least it was a genuine departure from old Labour socialism. In making the departure, Blair and his advisors relied on ideas the theoretical background of which was for the most part in the new institutionalism and communitarianism (Bevir, 2005). Such themes were prominent as early as in the 1997 election programme, including 'partnership not conflict', 'stakeholder economy', the personal responsibility of the unemployed 'to take up the opportunity', and a 'sensible balance between rights and duties' (UK Labour Party, 1997). Combating social exclusion takes place in four key dimensions, according to a recent UK definition:

- *consumption*: the capacity to purchase goods and services;
- *production*: participation in economically and socially valuable activities;
- *political engagement*: involvement in local or national decision-making; and
- *social interaction*: integration with family, friends and community. (Burchardt et al., 2002)

As we can observe, *participation*, *involvement* and *integration* have largely replaced such traditional policy goals as income redistribution

or progressive taxation. Moreover, and as the new institutionalist theories would suggest, networks such as family, friends and community are now at the centre of attention. Here one can also observe the close linkage between the contemporary practices of social inclusion and the theoretical notion of social capital, which according to a recent Australian policy briefing can be defined as 'the networks of social relations that are characterised by norms of trust and reciprocity that facilitate cooperative behaviour and build a cohesive society' (Hayes et al., 2008: 5).

The British SEU, being moved to the Department of Communities and Local Government in 2002, was disbanded and transferred to a smaller Social Exclusion Task Force in the Cabinet Office in 2006. Now its tasks focus on the most deprived people, including hard-to-reach children and families. These changes 'reflected concern that Social Exclusion Unit programs had failed to reach some of the poorest, most isolated and vulnerable families' (Hayes et al., 2008: 11). In Australia, Kevin Rudd's government (Australian Labor Party) established a Social Inclusion Unit (SIU) in the Department of the Prime Minister and Cabinet in 2007 and an Australian Social Inclusion Board in 2008. Deputy Prime Minister Julia Gillard is also Australia's first Minister for Social Inclusion since 2007. These are probably the most prominent official uses so far of the term 'social inclusion'.

Other countries have designed and implemented policies of social inclusion with various degrees of enthusiasm. The European Union established what is presently known as the EU Social Protection and Social Inclusion Process in 2000 in order to make 'a decisive impact on eradicating poverty by 2010' (EUROPA, 2008: Social Inclusion). The process was formally launched within the second of the three pillars of the EU Lisbon Strategy (2000): *modernising the European social model, investing in people and combating social exclusion*. The general context of social inclusion policy was the transition to a knowledge economy by making investments in education and training and conducting an active policy for employment in order to achieve an 'active and dynamic welfare state'. (EU Lisbon Strategy, 2000) The closely- related concept 'social protection' describes 'the risks of inadequate incomes associated with unemployment, illness and invalidity, parental responsibilities, old age or inadequate income following the loss of a spouse or parent'. Together, social inclusion and social protection contribute to the EU's strategic goal of 'sustained economic growth, more and better jobs, and greater social cohesion' (EUROPA, 2008).

Following a mid-term review of the Lisbon Strategy in 2005, it was decided that the social inclusion measures should be more clearly focused on economic growth and jobs. These were perceived as the main prerequisites of Europe's prosperity. The instrument of the EU Social Protection and Social Inclusion Process is called 'The Open Method of Coordination'. The member states have agreed to identify their particular problems in the fields of social protection and inclusion and to promote their best policies to alleviate them, while it is the duty of the European Commission to provide monitoring and peer reviews and to otherwise coordinate the national strategies. In 2008, the member states submitted their latest National Strategy Reports on Social Protection and Social Inclusion (2008–2010), the implementation of which is reported annually. The reports concentrate on the labour market situation, education, pensions, health issues and child poverty under the general framework of economic competitiveness, jobs and social cohesion.

The North American commentators on social inclusion usually acknowledge the European origins of the concept. The term is not as established as it is in Europe or Australia, and its uses may be slightly different; for instance, the Center for Social Inclusion (CSI) based in New York defines its mission as to 'achieve a fair distribution of the benefits and burdens of public policy to dismantle structural racism, which creates and perpetuates racially identifiable poverty and social exclusion' (CSI Mission, 2009). Reasons behind the relative novelty of 'social inclusion' in the American vocabulary can be identified in the varying traditions of social policy and daily political discourse. The 'Republican Revolution' that began in the mid-1990s was influential in at least setting the tone of the debate with regard to such issues as community and morality. As Newt Gingrich put it in 1994, the fundamental social issues in the United States concerned not money or the lack of it, but

> Twelve-year-olds having babies, with fifteen-year-olds killing each other, with seventeen-year-olds dying of AIDS, and with eighteen-year-olds ending up with diplomas they can't even read. What is at issue is literally not Republican or Democrat or liberal or conservative, but the question of whether or not our civilization will survive. (Gingrich, 1994: 182)

Such moral and moralistic issues have been identified as key themes in, for example, George W. Bush's presidential campaigns.

Even though the politicians of the American centre–left have differed from Gingrich or Bush in many ways, they have still had to respond to the claims regarding the loss of community or the fragmentation of a shared morality. Thus, in the presidential campaign of 1996, Bill Clinton made a point of demonstrating that the responsibility for maintaining the moral fabric of society cannot rest on the shoulders of the government only. In a way reminiscent of the social conservatives for example, he took sexual ethics as one of the key areas of his doctrine: 'Teen pregnancy is not simply foolish and costly, it is destructive to children, to families, to our society. It is *wrong*' (Clinton, 1996: 71, emphasis in original). Nevertheless, he attempted to present his vision of the good society (and 'community') as substantially less authoritarian and more tolerant to diversity than that of the hard-line Republicans.

It is precisely in contexts such as these where communitarianism has been able to enter political discourse as a middle-way public philosophy. In spite of the considerable areas of disagreement, encouraging responsible behaviour, empowering local communities, and getting people from welfare to work is the common ground elaborated by communitarian thinkers and shared by influential parts of the American centre–left and right. The influence of communitarianism on public policy has been more visible in North America than on the other continents, with the possible exception of the UK. The best-known communitarian philosophers are Anglo–American, and when speaking about 'community', a particular form of life, they often discuss small-town traditions, neighbourhoods and associations that may not make an immediate appeal to others. But it has also been suggested that the disintegrating forces of liberal modernity have torn traditional social fabric much more in the United States than in most other countries, thus also provoking the most recognizably communitarian counter-reaction (Walzer, 1990). However, the general idea of 'balancing rights with responsibilities', now influential in many European countries as well, has its strongest origins in communitarianism.[4]

CONCLUSIONS

If we centre our attention on those countries where social inclusion has been recently adopted as an organizing principle for social policy, the concept and practices of social inclusion will appear as relatively new. However, the modern history of addressing related problems, such as poverty, social marginalization and the lack of education or healthcare, is much longer. Nevertheless, the contemporary policies of social inclusion contain aspects that differentiate them from the policies that were predominant in the welfare states of the 1970s or 1980s. One of the key differences is that whereas the production of social equality and cohesion used to be perceived as mainly a duty of the government and the public sector, much more responsibility is nowadays allocated to the

third sector, voluntary associations, public–private partnerships, and to the individuals themselves.

It is also claimed by the proponents of the social inclusion approach that while poverty was earlier recognized in economic terms only, the present approach can perceive social disadvantage as a substantially more multidimensional phenomenon. Hence, social inclusion is a typical example of a new institutionalist 'joined-up service', that addresses a social problem too complex for any single government agency to deal with alone. In some countries and organizations, to achieve the necessary level of coordination, social inclusion has entered the top or 'strategic' level of policymaking, as seen in the examples of the Social Exclusion Unit in Tony Blair's Cabinet Office in 1997–2002, the Second Pillar of the EU's Lisbon Strategy for the years 2000–10, and the Social Inclusion Unit in Australia's Department of the Prime Minister and Cabinet since 2007.

It has been suggested in this chapter that exploring the theories of governance behind public policy can help understand the reasons for such changes. The critiques against the welfare model gained strength during the 1970s and 1980s as they pointed out the deficiencies in the ability of public policy to identify and alleviate the problems of the most seriously underprivileged groups. The most fundamental critiques against the welfare model emerged from the neoliberal right. They were highly influential in changing the general context of the debate, even if policymakers and academics not nearly always adopted the policies promoted by the New Right.

The contemporary mainstream notions of 'social inclusion', as observed in the public policy of the EU and the UK, represent a blend of different theoretical concepts. With regard to the conceptualization of 'society' and its internal dynamics, the new institutional impetus has probably been the strongest. At least indirect evidence of this is provided by the global spread of concepts such as network, partnership, trust and social capital. The new institutionalist (and to some degree communitarian) terms have managed to maintain an air of political neutrality, and therefore they can be used for a very wide range of purposes. They also constitute a key element of the expert language spoken by government administrators, and as such they shape the terms of self-identification of NGOs and voluntary associations when they are applying for external funding, as well as the self-identification of individuals when they are seeking social aid.

The communitarian influence can be detected in politicians' commitment to (non-state) 'communities' and the need to reconsider the balance of rights and responsibilities between government, communities and individuals. The traditional welfarist values are evoked in the commitment to maintain a 'dynamic' or 'economically feasible' welfare society with the help of the social protection and social inclusion programmes. In recent public policy, social inclusion has been approached increasingly from the direction of economy and employment. This has been highlighted in the EU and its efforts to coordinate policies of social protection and inclusion that would contribute to sustained economic growth and the creation of new jobs.

NOTES

1   Government agrees upon the main lines of economic and social policy together with the employees' and employers' unions. Tripartite corporatism as a decision-making procedure is sometimes perceived as a rival or threat to parliamentarianism.

2   In this chapter, the term neoliberal refers to the new wave of economic liberalism and associated political ideas after the early 1970s.

3   The most famous example being the 'Chicago boys', a group of about 25 young Chilean economists trained under Milton Friedman at the University of Chicago. Greenspan was Chairman of the US Federal Reserve in the period 1987–2006; Laffer was member of Ronald Reagan's Economic Policy Advisory Board during 1981–89.

4   See, for example, the current Finnish Government Programme: 'A new sense of community is required. As it continues to build Finland's

welfare society, the Government will seek to clarify the division of responsibilities between individuals, communities and society as a whole' (Finnish Government, 2007).

REFERENCES

Arendt, Hannah (1959) *The Human Condition.* Garden City, NY: Doubleday.

Bellah, R.N., Madsen, R., Sullivan, W.M., Swidler, A. and Tipton, S.M. (1985) *Habits of the Heart: Individualism and Commitment in American Life.* Berkeley, CA: University of California Press.

Bevir, Mark (2005) *New Labour: A Critique.* London: Routledge.

Burchardt, T., Le Grand, J. and Piachaud, D. (2002) 'Degrees of Exclusion: Developing a Dynamic, Multidimensional Measure', in J. Hills, J. Le Grand and D. Piachaud (eds), *Understanding Social Exclusion.* Oxford: Oxford University Press; pp. 30–43.

Clinton, Bill (1996) *Between Hope and History: Meeting America's Challenges for the 21st Century.* New York: Random House.

CSI Mission (2009) Mission Statement of the Center of Social Inclusion: A Project of the Tides Center, New York. Retrieved 23 August 2009, from http://www.centerforsocialinclusion.org/about_mission.html.

Ervasti, H., Fridberg, T., Hjerm, M., Kangas, O. and Ringdal, K. (2008) 'The Nordic Model', in H. Ervasti, T. Fridberg, M. Hjerm and K. Ringdal (eds), *Nordic Social Attitudes in a European Perspective.* Cheltenham: Edward Elgar; pp. 1–21.

Esping-Andersen, Gøsta (1990) *The Three Worlds of Welfare Capitalism.* Princeton, NJ: Princeton University Press.

Esping-Andersen, Gøsta (1996) 'After the Golden Age? Welfare State Dilemmas in Global Economy', in Gøsta Esping-Andersen (ed.), *Welfare States in Transition: National Adaptations in Global Economics.* London: Sage; pp. 1–31.

Etzioni, Amitai (1993) *The Spirit of Community: The Reinvention of American Society.* New York: Touchstone.

Etzioni, Amitai (1997) *The New Golden Rule: Community and Morality in a Democratic Society.* London: Profile Books.

EU Lisbon Strategy (2000) *Lisbon European Council 23 and 24 March Presidency Conclusions.* Retrieved 15 August 2009, from http://www.europarl.europa.eu/summits/lis1_en.htm.

EUROPA (2008) Employment, Social Affairs & Equal Opportunities (European Commission), keywords 'Social Inclusion'; 'Social Protection'. Retrieved 15 August 2009, from http://ec.europa.eu/employment_social/spsi/index_en.htm.

Finnish Government (2007) *A Responsible, Caring and Rewarding Finland.* The Government Programme, Prime Minister Matti Vanhanen's Second Cabinet.

Finnish Ministry of Justice (2003) *Citizen Participation Policy Programme: Towards a Mature Democratic Culture – Promoting Active Citizenship, a Lively Civil Society, Interaction between Citizens and Government, and Representative Democracy.* Helsinki: Ministry of Justice.

Finnish Ministry of Social Affairs and Health (2008) *Kansallinen sosiaalisen suojelun ja osallisuuden strategiaraportti vuosille 2008–2010* (National Strategy Report on Social Protection and Social Inclusion 2008–2011).

Gingrich, Newt (1994) 'Remarks in Washington Research Group Symposium, Washington, DC, November 11, 1994', in *Contract With America: The Bold Plan by Rep. Newt Gingrich, Rep. Dick Armey and the House Republicans to Change the Nation.* New York: Random House; pp. 181–96.

Granovetter, Mark (1973) 'The Strength of Weak Ties', *The American Journal of Sociology* 78(6): 1360–80.

Granovetter, Mark (1985) 'Economic Action and Social Structure', *The American Journal of Sociology* 91(3): 481–510.

Hayes, A., Gray, M. and Edwards, B. (2008) *Social Inclusion: Origins, Concepts and Key Themes.* Paper prepared by the Australian Institute of Family Studies for the Social Inclusion Unit for the Australian Department of the Prime Minister and Cabinet.

Kangas, Olli and Palme, Joakim (2005) 'Coming Late – Catching Up: The Formation of a "Nordic Model"', in Olli Kangas and Joakim Palme (eds), *Social Policy and Economic Development in the Nordic Countries.* Houndmills: Palgrave Macmillan; pp. 17–59.

Laslett, Peter (1960) '"Introduction" to John Locke', *Two Treatises of Government: A Critical Edition with an Introduction and Apparatus Criticus by Peter Laslett.* Cambridge: Cambridge University Press; pp. 3–120.

MacIntyre, Alasdair (1981) *After Virtue: A Study in Moral Theory.* London: Duckworth.

Marcuse, Herbert (1964) *One-Dimensional Man.* Boston, MA: Beacon.

Nozick, Robert (1974) *Anarchy, State, and Utopia.* Oxford: Basil Blackwell.

Nozick, Robert (1997) 'On the Randian Argument', in Robert Nozick, *Socratic Puzzles.* Cambridge, MA: The Belknap Press of Harvard University Press; pp. 249–64. (First published in 1971.)

NZ Treasury (1987) *Government Management: Brief to the Incoming Government 1987.* Wellington: The Treasury.

Oakeshott, Michael (1956) 'Political Education', in Peter Laslett (ed.), *Philosophy, Politics and Society.* First Series. Oxford: Basil Blackwell; pp. 1–21.

Powell, Walter W. (1990) 'Neither Market Nor Hierarchy: Network Forms of Organization', *Research in Organizational Behavior* 12: 295–336.

Putnam, Robert S. (2000) *Bowling Alone: The Collapse and Revival of American Community.* New York: Simon & Schuster.

Rand, Ayn (1957), *Atlas Shrugged.* New York: Random House.

Rand, Ayn (1959), 'Ayn Rand Television Interview with Mike Wallace, CBS'. Retrieved 20 April 2009, from http://video.google.com/videoplay?docid=8572902747504405420.

Rand, Ayn and Branden, Nathaniel (1964) *The Virtue of Selfishness: A New Concept of Egoism.* New York: New American Library.

Rawls, John (1971) *A Theory of Justice.* Cambridge, MA: The Belknap Press of Harvard University Press.

Rescher, Nicholas (1967) *Distributive Justice.* Lanham, MD: University Press of America.

Sandel, Michael (1982) *Liberalism and the Limits of Justice.* Cambridge: Cambridge University Press.

Sandel, Michael (1996) *Democracy's Discontent: America in Search of a Public Philosophy.* Cambridge, MA: Harvard University Press.

Silver, Hilary (1994) 'Social Exclusion and Social Solidarity', *International Labour Review* 133(5–6): 531–78.

Stephens, John D. (1996) 'The Scandinavian Welfare States: Achievements, Crisis, and Prospects', in Gøsta Esping-Andersen (ed.), *Welfare States in Transition: National Adaptations in Global Economics.* London: Sage; pp. 32–65.

Swedish Government Offices (2008) *Sveriges strategirapport för social trygghet och social delaktighet 2008–2010* [Sweden's Strategy Report for Social Protection and Social Inclusion 2008–2010].

Taylor, Charles (1989) *Sources of the Self.* Cambridge, MA: Harvard University Press.

Taylor, Charles (1991) *The Ethics of Authenticity.* Cambridge, MA: Harvard University Press.

UK Labour Party (1997) *New Labour: Because Britain Deserves Better.* Labour Party Manifesto, General

Election 1997. Retrieved 15 April 2008, from http://www.psr.keele.ac.uk/area/uk/man/lab97.htm

UK Social Exclusion Unit (1997) *Social Exclusion Unit: Purpose, Work Priorities and Working Methods.* London: The Stationery Office.

Walzer, Michael (1990) 'The Communitarian Critique of Liberalism', *Political Theory* 18(1): 6–23.

Wolin, Sheldon (1960) *Politics and Vision: Continuity and Innovation in Western Political Thought.* Boston: Little, Brown & Co.

30

Capacity Building

Hok Bun Ku and
Angelina W.K. Yuen-Tsang

INTRODUCTION

In the past 20 years, capacity building has fast become a major topic among governmental, non-governmental, non-profit and management support organizations. Its perspective and model of practice has also become important in helping professions such as social work and nursing. No United Nations (UN) conferences and other non-governmental orgainzation (NGO) meetings go by without ritual calls for capacity building programmes. Capacity building is seen as an essential element if development is to be sustainable and people-centred, and hence becomes a key term in funding application proposals as well as an important indicator for measuring the effectiveness and performance of development programmes (James, 1994).

While the concept of capacity building is widely accepted, it seems that there are a variety of definitions of capacity building in different fields and disciplines. Capacity building therefore remains vague as a concept. As Moor points out, 'What is "capacity building?" That is the problem. It includes everything that was covered by the different definitions of "institution building", and

much more besides ...' (Moore, 1995: 90). Even when most would agree on capacity building as a people-centred instrument to strengthen civil society, thereby fostering democratization and building strong, effective and accountable institutions of government, few can define what it means in practice.

To get away from the jargon, we would like to introduce what we consider capacity building to be, and how it integrates with our own practice in rural social work. In this chapter, we outline the theoretical roots of the capacity building model and introduce our understanding of capacity building based on our actual experience in community development. We use an example from China to illustrate how we built the capacity of a local community while practising community development.

DEFINING CAPACITY BUILDING

Like most academic jargon, capacity building is now used so indiscriminately that it can have almost any meaning. The vague and inconsistent definitions give rise to nothing but confusion and controversy. Worse, they undermine the core concept and lower the morale of people concerned with capacity building by weakening their sense that they have a clear mission (Moore, 1995: 92). As far as we are concerned, capacity building hardly means anything in itself. However, it has core values and focuses that should not be lost. We should also understand that the content of the capacity building approach is not static, rather, it is defined based on a specific context. Given that every organization needs a clear conceptual framework for its activities, formulating such a framework requires an organization to identify and define the ideas and values that it finds most meaningful. Below, we introduce some UN agencies' and NGOs' definitions of capacity building.

In the field of development and international assistance, capacity building is generally defined as activities that strengthen the knowledge, abilities, skills and behaviour of individuals, and improve institutional structures and processes, so that the organization can efficiently meet its goals in a sustainable way. It also often refers to assistance which is provided to entities, usually societies in developing countries, which need to develop a certain skill or competence, or for general upgrading of performance (United Nations, 1999). It emphasizes community participation, meaning that most capacity is built by societies themselves, sometimes in the public sector, and other times in the non-governmental and the private sectors. Many international organizations, often from the UN family, have provided capacity building as part of their programmes of technical cooperation with their member countries. Most local NGOs which offer capacity building services are themselves recipients of capacity building.

The lead within the UN system for action and thinking in this area was given to The United Nations Development Programme (UNDP), and it has offered instruction to its staff and governments on what was then called institution building since the

early 1970s. This involved building up the ability of basic national organizations, in areas such as civil aviation, meteorology, agriculture, health and nutrition, to carry out their tasks well. The UNDP defined capacity building as

> The creation of an enabling environment with appropriate policy and legal frameworks, institutional development, including community participation (of women in particular), human resources development and strengthening of managerial systems. The UNDP also recognizes that capacity building is a long-term, continuing process, in which all stakeholders participate (ministries, local authorities, non-governmental organizations, water user groups, professional associations, academics and others). (UNDP, 2009)

All UN specialized agencies were supposed to be active in support of capacity building in the areas for which they were technically qualified, and to have their own definition of capacity building as well. For example, as UNCED indicates,

> Specifically, capacity building encompasses the country's human, scientific, technological, organizational, institutional and resource capabilities. A fundamental goal of capacity building is to enhance the ability to evaluate and address the crucial questions related to policy choices and modes of implementation among development options, based on an understanding of environment potentials and limits and of needs perceived by the people of the country concerned. (UNCED, 1992)

Meanwhile, the Food and Agricultural Organization (FAO) states,

> In its broadest interpretation, capacity building encompasses human resource development (HRD) as an essential part of development. It is based on the concept that education and training lie at the heart of development efforts and that without HRD most development interventions will be ineffective. It focuses on a series of actions directed at helping participants in the development process to increase their knowledge, skills and understandings and to develop the attitudes needed to bring about the desired developmental change. (FAO, 2009)

Needless to say, different NGOs, too, have their own definitions of capacity building. For instance, Counterpart International sees partnership development in capacity building as 'another essential mechanism', since partnerships

> give a local NGO access to knowledge and skills; innovative and proven methodologies; networking and funding opportunities; replicable models for addressing community needs and managing resources; options for organizational management and governance; and strategies for advocacy, government relations and public outreach. (Counterpart International, 2009)

The Catholic Relief Service (CRS), in its turn, defines capacity building as 'an ongoing process through which individuals, groups, organizations and societies enhance their ability to identify and meet development challenges', and the CRS's capacity building activities are based on three key elements: partnership, organizational development and strengthening of civil society. Thus, the CRS's 'guiding partnership principles emphasize the importance of building just relationships with local partners and strengthening their skills in areas such as strategic planning, advocacy, organizational management, and project development and management' (CRS, 2009).

Oxfam has its own clear definition of capacity building as well, which is guided by its fundamental beliefs that

> All people have the right to an equitable share in the world's resources, and to be the authors of their own development; and that the denial of such rights is at the heart of poverty and suffering. Strengthening people's capacity to determine their own values and priorities, and to act on these, is the basic of development. It follows, then that for Oxfam, capacity building is an approach to development rather than a set of discrete or prepackaged intervention. So while there are certain basic capacities (social, economic, political, and practical) on which development depends, Oxfam seeks to support organizations working for sustainable social justice. (Eade, 1997: 2–3)

We basically share Oxfam's view of capacity building in social development.

While the definitions of capacity building vary, there is a common focus on the positives, including the strength perspective, empowerment models and the social development approach. Capacity building signifies

a paradigm shift 'from problems to challenges, pathology to strengths, preoccupation with the past to an orientation to the future, and the practitioner's role as an expert professional to that of collaborative partner' (O'Mela and DuBois, 1994:168). Within the same time frame, other disciplines such as psychology, developmental economics, management and political science have rediscovered the power of the positives. It is critical to understand the historical background and theoretical roots of the capacity building approach, so that we can make sense of its core values.

HISTORICAL AND THEORETICAL ROOTS OF CAPACITY BUILDING

Today's thinking on capacity building is influenced by earlier ideas concerning empowerment, civil society, social movement and participation (e.g. Escobar and Alvarez, 1992; Eade and Williams, 1995; Rowland, 1997), and these ideas have in fact been largely shaped by the work of the Brazilian educationalist Paulo Freire and the impact of liberation theology (Freire, 1972). The idea of conscientization, or the awareness-creation approach to adult literacy, of Paulo Freire and liberation theology emerged in Latin America during the 1970s and 1980s, and went on to become the intellectual and moral framework for defining human development and empowerment. These concepts grew during a period when political and military repression was at its height in Latin America. Many leftist intellectuals were forced into political exile, while many hundreds of priests and religious communities were persecuted by right-wing forces in many Latin American countries. The involvement of the proponents of these ideas with the daily struggle of poor people to resist oppression, and to achieve social justice, helped to make these ideas profoundly influential. Today, the ideas of Paulo Freire and the Latin American movement still inspire the development of the capacity building approach.

Freire's works *Pedagogy of the Oppressed* (1972) and *Education for Critical Consciousness* (1973) argue that, in a sense, the process of learning to read and the act of reading are deeply political, as our reading of the word is shaped by our reading of the world. Rather than seeing education as a means by which knowledge is handed down from an omniscient teacher to ignorant students, Freire argued that education for liberation must be a process of problem solving and dialogue among equals. These ideas contributed to the development of the capacity building approach in three ways: first, that the learner and the learner's own experience and knowledge are of crucial importance; secondly, that awareness, learning, self-esteem and the capacity for action and change are key points; and thirdly, that poor and marginalized people have the right and the capacity to organize and challenge authority in order to create a new society without exploitation and oppression.

Liberation theology, which called for a new interpretation of the Bible and sought to rediscover Christ's authentic 'gospel of the poor', is another historical source of the capacity building approach. In the new interpretation of the Bible, those committed to personal, collective and even national liberation would challenge injustice and poverty in the real world, even at the expense of their own lives. Feminist theologians have expanded the meaning and scope of liberation theology, making it a powerful tool for working with poor women (Eade, 1997 :12). These ideas challenge the power of those Whites who control wealth and biblical interpretation. They give emphasis to the power of the poor and the marginalized, and encourage peoples' movements and empowerment.

In short, the current emphasis on empowerment and participation has been deeply influenced by the experiences of the Latin American movement. In the past two decades, the development of the capacity building model has enabled us to replace previous practice models based on problems and personal weaknesses.

The strengths perspective

The strengths perspective was developed by faculty members at the University of Kansas School of Social Work (Weick et al., 1989; Saleeby, 1997; Morris, Sherraden and McMillen, 2002). It is different from the problem-based approach, which focuses on the limitations and problems that clients face (Scales and Streeter, 2003). This perspective taught us how to recognize and assess local communities' and people's strengths (Cowger, 1997; Sherraden, 1991). It also sees people as possessing the capacity to grow and thus redirect the focus of our work and discover and mobilize people's strengths (including their internal resources, past successes and positive qualities), to help them reach their development goals. It is argued that intervention strategies are discovered through identifying resources within the client and the client's associated systems. Locke, Garrison and Winship (1998: 11) added that clients' strength-based resources 'may contribute to the development of capacities for managing the issue(s) of concern'. Thus, the strengths perspective is at the core of the capacity building model, which draws our attention to discovering local capacity based on strengths, as opposed to weaknesses.

Empowerment

Integrating elements of feminist theory and liberation theory (Freire, 1973; Lee, 2001), empowerment has also been proposed as an alternative to the problem-solving model (O'Mela and DuBois, 1994). The empowerment model emerged at the same time as the birth of the strengths perspective in the late 1980s, largely as a method for working with women, people of colour and other oppressed groups (Gutierrez, 1990, 1994). The goal of the empowerment model is to create empowered people. According to Lee (2001), there are three dimensions of empowerment: (1) the development of a more positive and potent sense of self; (2) the construction of knowledge and capacity for more critical comprehension of the web of social and political realities of one's environment; and (3) the cultivation of resources and strategies, or more functional competence, for attainment of personal and collective goals (Lee, 2001: 34).

In other words, empowerment practice aims to increase the personal, interpersonal and political power of clients so that they can take action to improve their own situation (Gutierrez, Delois and GlenMaye, 1995). It suggests that once clients are empowered, they then have the capacity to improve multiple domains of their lives.

The premise of the empowerment model is that any crucial problem that people face arises from a lack of access to resources, power and control, rather than from bad choices and pathological behaviour by clients. The model acknowledges the social, political and economic forces that constrain people's choice and participation. It rejects the problem-based model that considers the poverty or tragedies of local people to be due to personal problems or pathological behaviour. Thus, it calls for practice that promotes both change of the individual and of social systems and institutions. To achieve the objective of empowerment, we should provide practices that will create awareness by clients of the personal and interpersonal, as well as the environmental, aspects of their situation. We should also endeavour to guide clients in understanding the links between the personal, interpersonal and sociopolitical aspects of a problem, as well as the power dynamics that create and keep them in their problem situations.

Social development

The strengths perspective and empowerment practices have primarily been aimed at those who work with micro- and mezzo-level interventions in mind. The social development approach is explicitly macro, which shifts the capacity building model to tackle the macro concern of development. According to Midgley (1995), the overall goal of the development approach is to ensure that social and economic policies are inclusive and bring benefits to all levels of society, and promote social welfare policies. Any development programmes should be investment-oriented and sustainable, as well as people-centred (e.g. Chambers, 1984; Eade, 1997; Plummer, 2000). We should seek to enhance human capabilities so that individuals can participate in and be productive in social and economic development (Midgley, 1995; Torczyner, 2000). The fundamental belief is also that the poor and the marginalized are endowed with considerable capacities and assets. Strengthening people's capacity to make choices, determine their own priorities, and take action to achieve their goals are the bases of development (Ginsberg, 2005; Lohmann and Lohmann, 2005; Collier, 2006).

Another fundamental belief is that all people have the right to share in the world's resources equally and to be masters of their own development and destiny, and that the denial of such rights is a root cause of poverty and suffering. A better way towards social development is to build the capacity of the local community. Over the last two decades, capacity building has been widely adopted by community service providers to strengthen and support the ability of communities to grow and change (e.g. Moyer et al., 1999; Li et al., 2001). Participation is probably the most essential element of capacity building, because we believe that non-participation by the local community is one of the main factors contributing to the failure of community development. Thus, a key task for community development workers is to enhance the capacity of the local community, be it on an individual or collective level.

WORKING PRINCIPLES OF CAPACITY BUILDING

Having introduced the theoretical roots of capacity building based on the wide-ranging literature, we synthesize the utility of this information for practice into a set of general working principles for capacity building practice.

- We agree with Eade (1997) that the capacity building approach cannot be employed or undertaken in isolation, as it is deeply embedded in the social, economic and political environment. Understanding the complexity of the environment is critical to understanding who lacks what capacity, in any given context.
- We also believe that the local poor and marginalized are invariably endowed with considerable capacities, a fact that may not be obvious to outsiders, and even not be recognized by themselves. We view the local community and people as capable of extraordinary growth and change given the right circumstances. However, it may take time for them to discover these capacities and potentialities.
- It is important for the local community to identify their own needs, including both the problems they want to solve, and their dreams and aspirations beyond problem solving.
- It is also important to raise the consciousness of the local people and help them situate themselves as agents of transformative action. In Freire's words, it is an educational process 'through which men and women can become conscious about presence in the world. The way they act and think when they develop all of their capacities, taking into consideration their needs, but also the needs and aspirations of others' (Freire, 1998: p xiii).
- We should help the local community to identify personal and institutional constraints in order to develop intervention options.
- Partnership and collaboration are emphasized in the process. Participatory methods are adopted to ensure that locals are involved in all efforts towards the planned change.
- We should make efforts to develop the knowledge, skills and resources that will make it possible for the local community to pursue their aspirations and solve their problems.
- In collaborating with the local community in choosing intervention options, we should endeavour to lead towards the development of personal, social, economic and political competence, and the expansion of opportunity, choice and power.
- We have to understand that an individual's capacities and needs depend on the myriad factors that differentiate human beings from each other, and shape social identities, relationships and life experiences: most obviously gender, age and disability, as well as cultural identity and socioeconomic status.
- While capacity building is designed to promote individual and communal change, interventions themselves take place within far wider processes of social and economic transformation. Hence, the importance of being flexible enough to respond to a changing situation, while maintaining a sense of direction.
- We not only work to enhance the capacity of the local community but also we need to create the conditions and contexts that can be put in place that allow people to enhance their capacities.
- We have the responsibility to expand the social capital of the local community as well as to develop their skill in accessing resources and capital through social networking.
- Finally, we understand that capacity building is not about carrying out individual and communal development on the cheap or against the clock; nor is it risk-free. It implies a long-term investment in people and their organizations, and commitment to the various processes through which they can better shape the forces that affect their lives (Eade, 1997).

In short, the main objective of capacity building should be to empower the local community to become the subject of and take control of their development. The above principles are not mutually exclusive, but interwoven in capacity building practice. In the following section, we will demonstrate how we practise capacity building in a Chinese village.

AN ILLUSTRATION OF PRACTISING CAPACITY BUILDING IN A CHINESE VILLAGE

Since the rural reform in the late 1970s, Chinese villages have experienced remarkable transformation in terms of dismantling the commune system and the Maoist way of life. Agricultural production has been organized on an individual or household basis. Villagers seldom communicate with each other except at weddings, funerals or important festivals like New Year's holidays. Each household works on its own piece of contracted land, and there are no collective projects for public affairs (Ku, 2003, 2007). We discovered that there had also been a loss of social capital, as reflected by a steady decline in civic participation. This, in turn, had resulted in the loss of trust and reciprocity, eventually undermining communities' capacities to solve problems and sustain economic prosperity.

We also found that the most acute social problem in China is rural poverty, which causes severe tension between the state/local state and villagers. Increasing incidents of popular resistance have undermined the authority of rural cadres, and further weakened the social fabric and long-standing mechanisms for social control.

On the other hand, poor governance has threatened the stability and harmony of the vast rural population in China. While the Chinese government has already launched macro-level anti-poverty programmes to combat rural poverty,[1] most of its efforts are directed towards economic development and income generation, and relatively little attention has been devoted to improving the capacities of the community. Little wonder then that the poverty reduction programme itself becomes a source of rural conflict between the local state and villagers, rendering the economic programme unsustainable.

Based on these observations, the capacity of the local people and the community – including officials – needs to be enhanced before community development can become successful. Hence, in this section we use our community development project in a Chinese ethnic minority village in Yunnan province in Southwest China to illustrate how capacity building was able to break down the barriers established by household individualism and overcome sociocultural hostilities and suspicions towards collectivism in the village, resulting in improved community capacity and promotion of social development.

Stage I: mapping the existing problem of community governance

The core objective of our project is to build the capacity of the local community. With this in mind, how to transform the conventional practice of community development became our main task. In authoritarian states, development policymaking and implementation are often top-down in nature. The local people and community are constrained in expressing their opinions, and the policymaking process is not transparent as it is decided by the government or external experts. The problem with this practice is that policy is unable to meet the needs of the local community, and then faces resistance from the bottom. To solve this problem and transform the conventional practice of community development, we need to find ways of getting the local community involved in the new form of practice. To achieve this, we repeatedly reminded ourselves at every stage not to be domineering, but to let the local participants become owners and leaders of the project. Before implementing any concrete project in the village, it is important for the local people to identify their needs and articulate their desired outcome, including both the problems they want to solve and their dreams and aspirations beyond problem solving.

The focus of the first stage of development was to invite the participation of the villagers, listen to their voices, understand their concerns and problems, and identify their capacity for development. We did not come with preconceived ideas and a fixed agenda for intervention prior to our entry into the village. Instead, we partnered with the local people to discover their needs, to map the existing approaches that they used to deal with their problems, and to reflect on the strengths and weaknesses of existing local practices.

While there are many methods of participatory needs assessment in rural community development, we ended up choosing oral testimony. Our purpose was to transform the existing top-down approach of development in rural China. More than a simple method of collecting data, oral testimony provides us with voices beyond that of mainstream discourse, and uncovers personal testimonies and aspects of life that are buried or hidden from the public realm. It is a tool to encourage participation and inclusion, and to facilitate the analytical abilities of local peoples and empower them to plan and undertake sustainable action (Campbell, 2001; Slim and Thompson, 1995). Through collecting the oral testimony of the local people, hidden experiences would be exposed, enabling us to acquire greater understanding and facilitate dialogue between people of different ages, genders and backgrounds.

The process of collecting oral testimony was that of mobilizing the community, building up capabilities, empowering and participating. It gave us a chance to build up capabilities alongside the villagers, through mobilizing them to establish communal relationships, strengthening social cohesion and producing a community leader from among them. It was also a catalyst for the birth of organization, making it possible for us to integrate ourselves into the community through direct interaction with the villagers, so as to deepen our partnership with them and to allow them to understand us, as well as to trust us.

The process of oral testimony was roughly divided into several phases. We first openly recruited local people as our project partners from various natural villages,[2] and finally 42 people indicated their willingness to participate in oral testimony collection. These local participants were young and middle-aged men and women. Some of them were married; some were junior secondary school graduates. Seven teams were formed to carry out the oral testimony interviews in seven natural villages. The team members also selected their team leader in their own way, such as by drawing lots, which meant that everyone had an opportunity to become team leader. Following this, several workshops on oral testimony were organized for the local villagers. We used different participatory methods, such as drawing, dramas and games, to help the local villagers understand the meaning of oral testimony and be willing to take the initiative to find out the life situations of their fellow villagers, as well as what they desired. Moreover, we worked alongside the participants to formulate the interview questions. We discussed the interview topics together by drawing life-course maps.

As we did not understand the local dialect, we had to collaborate with local villagers to collect the stories, and these villagers became our interviewers and translators. We provided the local participants with tape recorders and they mastered the tool very quickly, although they had not been familiar with such machines before. After the training workshops, each team, led by their team leader, had to collect oral testimonies in different villages. Finally, we had different stories from the elderly, young schoolgirls, middle-aged women, husbands and wives.

Guided by the basic principles of the capacity building approach, we emphasized the participation of local people in collecting life stories. As the local participants collected stories in the local dialect, they took the leading role. Through collecting stories, the villagers became the experts, for what they told were their own stories, and they surely knew more about their own affairs than did the outsiders. Given this fact, we, the so-called 'experts', became students, as we would have to listen carefully to the stories told by the interviewees, and it was the villagers who would tell us about their life courses, their life experiences, and what life strategies they adopted to deal with the hardships of earning a living. In this sense, we exchanged roles with the locals, and the power relationship was reversed, giving the right to speak back to the local people. Oral testimony is therefore a channel of empowerment for locals in terms of development. Oral testimony is also a more democratic method of conducting research, in that it stresses showing respect for the experience and knowledge of the villagers, and requires the interviewer to take the role of listener (Slim and Thompson, 1995; Perks and Thompson, 1998).

To achieve the objectives of capacity building, equity and inclusiveness are important principles. Oral testimony is a good way to promote community inclusiveness. For example, in working with us, the young villagers who participated in collecting oral histories also had an opportunity to listen to the stories of their fellow villagers and to read the testimonies of those 'marginalized' individuals. In the process of collecting oral histories, the young and the old were able to find common topics of conversation and to bridge the generation gap between them. Moreover, elderly villagers were also included in the project. Telling their stories helped them rebuild their confidence and rediscover their abilities, which encouraged them to participate in the community once again. It was therefore a process of social inclusion and empowerment for them (Yow, 1994; Slim and Thompson, 1995; Perks and Thompson, 1998; Portelli, 1998).

In short, oral testimony was only a start for us in terms of implementing participatory development and capacity building. During this stage, we were able to build trust and rapport with the local villagers, discover the needs and problems of the local community, and map the existing practice approaches used by local villagers. As oral testimony covered different aspects of people's lives

and focused in on community governance, we began to narrow down the issues into the following questions:

How do the villagers perceive their development?
Do residents in rural communities affect collective well-being through self-governance, and production of public goods and services?
In what ways are villages and local governments collaborating in the planning, implementation and provision of much-needed social services?
How should community-based development strategies be designed to address the needs of villages, based on understanding of the communities' capabilities and on acting collectively in collaboration with local governments?

Stage II: constructing a rural capacity building practice framework through community participation and partnership

Following the principle of capacity building and participation, the villagers and our community workers collaborated in a reciprocal process of analysing and reflecting on the oral history testimonies collected. We organized sharing sessions, and went through the stories together with the local participants. We sought to examine the capability of the communities, discover the needs of the villagers, plan future village development programmes, and encourage the villagers to take control of the decision-making process. This was a deliberate process intended to involve the active local villagers in community analysis, so as to build their capacity for critical reflection and for future leadership.

Developing local leadership is crucial in sustainable community development. We selected 30 active villagers and developed different working groups by employing some social work techniques. During the group work, we began to discuss the problem of poverty with local villagers and identified barriers to their participation and to inclusive governance in local development. We organized them to visit local villagers, local cadres and stakeholders, and discussed with them issues of concern identified through analysis of the oral testimonies.

Different workshops and focus groups were organized to raise the awareness of the villagers of their life situation. We also guided them in understanding the links between the personal, interpersonal and sociopolitical aspects of a problem, as well as the power dynamics that create their problem situations, and keep them in poverty. In the group discussions, villagers found that they were not alone in facing the problem, as poverty was common in rural China. This created a sense of solidarity and led to self-help, mutual support and collective action. As Gutierrez, Parsons and Cox state, helping villagers to articulate the political nature of their personal problems and to develop ways to affect change is a key process in capacity building (Gutierrez, Parsons and Cox, 1998).

Attempts were also made to facilitate discussion by the villagers of their vision of the desired community and their suggestions for preliminary steps to achieve their goals through realistic community involvement projects. The villagers participated enthusiastically in the discussions and developed a strong sense of ownership of the problems identified and the concrete suggestions made. The discussion and analysis with the villagers also helped us to develop a preliminary scope and plan for the community development project, through which we hoped we could find ways to enable local government agencies and communities to collaborate and innovate in the planning and implementation of critical public goods and social services. In the process, different local leaders, local networks and small groups such as youth groups, women's groups and groups of elderly people gradually emerged. The small groups also started to propose different concrete development projects. Though there was disagreement on the proposals at the beginning, it was important for the groups to learn how to achieve consensus through democratic decision-making.

Different from conventional NGO iniatives, the projects per se are not only intended to improve the livelihoods of the locals but also to build up the capacity and confidence of the local people, and, in the process, change local power relationships. Equity and inclusiveness were advocated. The marginalized were included in the projects and became active participants in community development. Consensus has also been developed during the process.

Stage III: implementing the rural capacity building practice framework

Having developed the rural capacity building practice framework, it was implemented through the use of the participatory method. We facilitated the villagers to work on the ideas that they had proposed in the previous stage, and helped them to actualize their plans through group work and community organization strategies.

Concrete projects were carefully deliberated and subsequently implemented, taking into consideration the realities and constraints of the local context. Projects that were put into practice included:

- the generation of methane gas for fuel
- the formation of support groups for women and the elderly
- the provision of adult education programmes for the illiterate
- leadership training for young villagers
- training programmes for children and young people on ethnic songs and dances by elderly villagers in order to preserve the cultural heritage
- the construction of a local museum of ethnic history and culture
- the development of income-generating handicraft projects.

All these projects were discussed, planned and implemented collectively, by involving the villagers and local stakeholders concerned. The local people also proposed building an integrated community service centre to serve as a hub for local villagers to meet and to engage in communal activities. With funding for the building materials raised in Hong Kong, the community centre was planned, designed and built by villagers.

The villagers involved in the project were transformed from pessimistic and passive recipients into active participants. Many of them were previously very pessimistic and hopeless because of the grave poverty in their village. Their only way out had been to leave their village and seek jobs in urban factories. With the development of the rural capacity building project, e.g. the women's handicraft project, many of them realized that they could find ways to enhance their social and economic well-being through collective efforts. Moreover, instead of despising their traditional ethnic culture, many of them began to discover the richness of their cultural heritage, and were keen to preserve it and pass it on to future generations.

In addition, at the outset, the women thought that they were working for the project organizers: their only concern was the daily allowance they received from us. This view has changed now that they clearly understand it is their own project. Any development of the group is the responsibility of its members. In establishing the group, the women discovered their own capacity and potential. At first, they wanted professional experts to teach them product design or give them a sample to copy. However, when they had the opportunity to observe handicraft markets and compare their skills with those of other ethnic minorities, their confidence was increased. Their potential creativity and design capacity became fully realized, and the intervention of professional designers was no longer necessary. The women became designers, experimenting with patterns, colours and types of products.

Another important aspect of capacity building in community development is to enable the local people to develop the knowledge, skills and resources that will make it possible for them to pursue their aspirations

and solve their problems. For example, in the women's handicraft project, the women were also trained in basic business knowledge (e.g. cost calculations, price setting and merchandising). Now, rules and regulations are in place and there is a clear division of labour in the group, as each woman has duties according to her particular talents and abilities (e.g. pattern and product design, material acquisition, marketing, quality control and bookkeeping).

Similarly, in an education project, a management committee was formed by the villagers, who learned how to manage the collective education fund donated by external foundations to support students from poor families. Initially, they had arguments when setting the criteria for financial difficulty and the amount of support. The chair of the committee learned to listen to different opinions from the committee members and also sought second opinions from schoolteachers and villagers. In the end, a consensus was obtained and the final decision was made in a collective manner. In the process, we employed a capacity building approach and tried to take the role of facilitators rather than experts in community development.

We pushed the villagers to learn project planning, budgeting, financial reporting and democratic decision-making. From both the women's project and the education project, villagers learned to implement the principles of good governance, consensus building, equity and inclusiveness. Transparency and accountability of their finances were also included in the capacity building process.

A cultural identity crisis was another obstacle to development in rural China. Under the influence of the market economy, the value of a product was measured by its market price. Villagers no longer treasured their traditional culture, because their skills and knowledge appeared to have no market value. Traditional customs had become unpopular: for example, young people preferred to wear T-shirts and jeans, and many men chose to wear T-shirts to work since they were comfortable. Young girls were reluctant to learn embroidery skills because the process was time-consuming and the products seemed to have no market value.

However, good community development also emphasizes producing a result that meets the needs of the community while making the best use of the resources at their disposal. Our commitment to implementing the project helped lead to a renewed appreciation of the value of traditional culture.

For example, after several years of implementing the women's handicraft project, the villagers recognized that their traditional customs and linens could be a source of supplementary income and decided to revitalize their skills. The women are now aware of the importance of cultural preservation. They have begun to collect old embroidery and fabrics in preparation for their museum. They also cooperate with the older women in the village's seniors' association and have restarted traditional fabric production and colouring practices. They want to ensure that their traditional embroidery skills will be preserved, revitalized and improved.

Stage IV: reflecting on the experiment and ensuring sustainable efforts for change

Besides engagement in continuous reciprocal reflection-in-action throughout the entire process, a major evaluation was carried out in the summer of 2005 to reflect on the whole project since its inception in 2000. The purpose of the evaluation was to reflect on experiences, to identify the gaps and limitations of the approach, to refine and improve the rural capacity building practice framework, and to ensure the long-term sustainability of the project. Project staff, villagers and local officials involved in the project over the past five years were invited to attend the meeting and to share their views on the project.

The most critical problem confronting us during the process was the difficulty of changing the mindset of the people, especially the local government officials. Even though the project emphasized social development and had adopted a capacity building approach, most of us involved in the project found it extremely difficult to practise their values and beliefs in the real-life context. While we advocated equity, justice and fairness, we found that we were often the ones who violated such principles and asserted our power and domination in the decision-making process. While we were educating the villagers to exercise gender equality, some of the male students and teachers could be exhibiting chauvinistic behaviour towards their female colleagues, which had caused much embarrassment and unhappiness. While we were zealously promoting social change and social development, we could be using methods and strategies which, though seemingly efficient and effective, were contradictory to the core beliefs of social development. Fortunately, the use of the reciprocal reflection paradigm has helped in minimizing blind spots, sharpening critical reflection, and creating an environment for open dialogue and mutual support among key players involved in the project.

Another issue of concern was the sustainability of the changes. The project had started many worthwhile initiatives at the community level, but it was not at all easy to sustain these initiatives on a long-term basis. While it was relatively easy to sustain the involvement of the villagers in the various interest groups and support groups, it was extremely difficult to maintain the momentum of the income-generating projects. For instance, the handicrafts project was developed with a view to helping local women to generate income through production of local handicrafts and cloths. However, it was difficult to secure a market for the project, and it could only provide minimal supplementary income for a few families. The team reflected on the underlying causes of the problems and discussed ways to enhance the sustainability of the income-generating projects. The core issue was again related to the mindset of the people. It was felt that some of the women involved in the project were only concerned about generating income from the project to improve their own household income, and were not concerned about improvement of the collective good and social development. The team found that they had not done enough preparation to educate the women and to enhance their knowledge and understanding about social development before the commencement of the project. It was therefore suggested that more efforts should be made not only to enhance the capacity of the participants to generate income but also more importantly, to promote the collective good through mutual support. Moreover, it was suggested that efforts should be made to involve local and provincial officials as partners in the projects, so that government resources and support could be drawn upon to help the villagers. The team also suggested that we had been overemphasizing the 'social' aspect of development, and not paying adequate attention to the 'economic' and other related aspects of development. Therefore, it was suggested that we should strengthen our team by drawing upon the help of economists, designers, natural scientists, health professionals and others so that we could provide a holistic and inter-disciplinary approach to social development.

Another major challenge for us at this stage was, again, to make a shift from the familiar expert-oriented approach to a collaborative and facilitative approach. This problem became more apparent when we had to work closely with the villagers to develop concrete plans for action. We were used to consulting and giving expert advice in our normal roles as university professors and researchers. We had great difficulty in holding back from making suggestions in a directive manner, and instead to listen to the voices of the people in a humble and empathetic manner. However, we were alerted to our blind spots through continuous reciprocal reflection-in-action processes.

Continual reflexivity and self-critique is an essential component of capacity building and participatory development (Chambers, 1997; Cooke and Kothari, 2001), as McGee has suggested, 'ongoing dialogue between practitioners on quality, validity and ethics of what they are doing, ... is intended to guard against slipping standards, poor practice, abuse or exploitation of the people involved' (McGee, 2002: 105). This intrinsic facet of capacity building in fact is also crucial for good practice in community development.

CONCLUSION

The capacity building approach emphasizes strengths and assets. It helps us to understand that the poor and the marginalized are endowed with considerable capacities, which may not be obvious to outsiders and which even they, themselves, may not recognize (Sherraden, 1991; Saleebey, 1997; Templeman, 2005; Tice, 2005). It also allows us to see that local communities possess a wide range of resources and strengths, and discourages us from dwelling on deficiencies, problems or disabilities. As Scales and Streeter note, the role of the community development worker is to 'seek to uncover and reaffirm people's abilities, talents, survival strategies, and aspiration, and community's assets and resources' (Scales and Streeter, 2003: 2). We are committed to empowering rural communities so that they can use their resources in innovative ways to create new assets. We also need to help them to determine their own direction, set their own priorities, and leverage both internal and external resources.

Our experience has shown us that the people in a community are actually full of ideas and have great capacity for development despite their lack of education, resources and experience. Given opportunities and encouragement, people can become highly motivated and can join together to do amazing things to improve the quality of life, not only for themselves and their families but also for the collective good of their community.

Moreover, we found that transforming the conventional practice of community development is possible if we can build up the capacity of the locals, and involve them in the process of conceptualizing, planning and implementing social change and social development.

Capacity building is a good strategy for enhancing good community development. It transforms the mindset of the local community as well as the practice of following a top-down approach in community development. However, capacity building involves a long-term investment in people and their organizations, and a commitment to changing the various processes and forces that negatively affect people's lives. Capacity building is not just on the individual level but also on the collective level. We need to make efforts to break down the barriers established by individualism, and overcome sociocultural hostilities and suspicions towards collectivism in the community.

NOTES

1   The Chinese government has made impressive progress in rural poverty reduction in terms of economic indicators. According to the World Bank (2004), China has made the largest single contribution to global poverty reduction of any country in the last 20 years. Using the official poverty figures, the number of poor people is estimated to have decreased from about 200 million in 1981 to 28 million in 2002.

2   In China, villages can be classified according to two levels – administrative villages and natural villages. An administrative village is defined by the government and normally includes several natural villages.

REFERENCES

Campbell, John R. (2001) 'Participatory Rural Appraisal as Qualitative Research: Distinguishing Methodological Issues from Participatory Claims', *Human Organization* 60(4): pp. 380–9.

Chambers, R. (1984) *Rural Development: Putting the Last First.* London: Longman Group.

Chambers, R. (1997) *Rural Development: Putting the First Last.* London: Intermediate Technology Publications.

Coleman, J.S. (1998) 'Social Capital in the Creation of Human Capital', *American Journal of Sociology* 94(Suppl): 95–120.

Collier, K. (2006) *Social Work with Rural Peoples.* Vancouver: New Star Books.

Cooke, B. and Kothari, U. (2001) *Participation: The New Tyranny?* London: Zebs Books.

Counterpart International (2009). 'Defining Capacity Building. Global Development', Research Centre (internet). Available at: http://www.gdrc.org/uem/capacity-define.html.

Cowger, C. (1997) 'Assessing Client Strengths: Assessment for Client Empowerment', in D. Saleeby (ed.), *The Strengths Perspective in Social Work Practice.* (pp. 59–73). New York: Longman.

CRS (2009) 'Capacity Building'. CRS (internet). Available at: http://crs.org/capacity-building.

Eade, D. (1997) *Capacity-Building: An Approach to People-Centred Development.* Oxford: Oxfam.

Eade, D. and Williams, S. (1995) *The Oxfam Handbook of Development and Relief.* Oxford: Oxfam.

Escobar, A. and Alvarez, S. (1992) *The Making of Social Movements in Latin America: Identity, Strategy and Democracy.* Boulder, CO: Westview Press.

FAO (2009) 'Capacity Building'. FAO (internet). Available at: ftp://ftp.fao.org/docrep/fao/011/i0765e/i0765e15.pdf.

Freire, P. (1972) *Pedagogy of the Oppressed.* Harmondsworth: Penguin Books.

Freire, P. (1973) *Education for Critical Consciousness.* London: Sheed and Ward.

Freire, P. (1998) *Teachers as Cultural Workers: Letters to Those Who Dare Teach.* Boulder, CO: Westview Press.

Ginsberg, L.H. (2005) *Social Work in Rural Communities.* Virginia: CSWE Press.

Gutierrez, L. (1990) 'Working with Women of Color: An Empowerment Perspective', *Social Work* 35, 149–54.

Gutierrez, L. (1994) 'Beyond Coping: An Empowerment Perspective on Stressful Life Events', *Journal of Sociology and Social Welfare* 21, 201–20.

Gutierrez, L., Delois, K. and GlenMaye, L. (1995) 'Understanding Empowerment Practice: Building on Practitioner Based Knowledge', *Family in Society* 76, 4–542.

Gutierrez, L.M., Parsons, R.J. and Cox, E.O. (1998) *Empowerment in Social Work Practice: A Sourcebook.*

Pacific Grove, CA: Brooks/Cole Publishing Company.

James, R. (1994) *Strengthening the Capacity of Southern NGO Partners.* Occasional Paper Series Number 5. Oxford: INTRAC.

Ku, H.B. (2003) *Moral Politics in a South Chinese Village: Responsibility, Reciprocity and Resistance.* Lanham, MD: Rowman & Littlefield.

Ku, H.B. (2007) 'Bypassing Government/Reconstructing the Village: Formation of Self-organization in a Hakka Community in South China', *Taiwan: A Radical Quarterly in Social Studies* 66: 195–229 [in Chinese].

Lee, J.A. (2001) *The Empowerment Approach to Social Work Practice: Building the Beloved Community,* New York: Columbia University Press.

Li, V.C., Wang, S., Wu, K., et al. (2001) 'Capacity Building to Improve Women's Health in Rural China', *Social Science and Medicine* 52(2): 279–92.

Locke, B., Garrison, R. and Winship, J. (1998) *Generalist Social Work Practice: Context, Story and Partnerships.* Pacific Grove, CA: Brooks/Cole.

Lohmann, N. and Lohmann, R.A. (2005). *Rural Social Work Practice.* New York: Columbia University Press.

Midgley, J. (1995) *Social Development: The Developmental Perspective in Social Welfare.* New York: Sage Publications.

Moore, M. (1995) 'Promoting Good Government by Supporting Institutional Development', *IDS Bulletin* 26(2): 89–96.

Morris, L., Sherraden, M. and McMillen, C. (2002) 'Integrating Capacity Building Approaches to Social Work Practice'. Working paper of George Warren Brown School of Social Work, Washington University in St. Louis.

Moyer, A., Coristine, M., Maclean, L. and Meyer, M. (1999) 'A Model for Building Collective Capacity in Community-based Programs: The Elderly in Need Project', *Public Health Nursing* 16(3): 205–14.

O'Melia, M. and DuBois, B. (1994) 'From Problem-Solving to Empowerment Based Social Work Practice' in L. Gutierrez and P. Nurius (Eds.) *The Education and Research for Empowerment Based Practice* (pp. 161–70). Seattle, WA: Center for Social Policy and Practice, University of Washington.

Perks, R. and Thompson, A. (1998) *The Oral History Reader.* New York: Routledge.

Plummer, J. (2000) *Municipalities and Community Participation.* London & Sterling: Earthscan.

Portelli, A. (1998) *Narrative and Genre.* London: Routledge.

Rowland, J. (1997) *Questioning Empowerment: Working with Women in Honduras.* Oxford: Oxfam.

Saleebey, D. (1997) *The Strengths Perspective in Social Work Practice.* New York: Longman.

Scales, T. L. and Streeter, C.L. (2003) *Rural Social Work: Building and Sustaining Community Assets.* Belmont, CA: Brooks/Cole/Thomson Learning.

Sherraden, M. (1991) *Assets and the Poor: A New American Welfare Policy.* Armonk, NY: M.E. Sharpe.

Slim, H. and Thompson, P. (1995) *Listening for a Change: Oral Testimony and Community Development.* London: New Society Publishers.

Templeman, S.B. (2005) 'Building Assets in Rural Communities through Service Learning', in L.H. Ginsberg (ed.), *Social Work in Rural Communities.* Virginia: CSWE Press.

Tice, C.J. (2005) 'Celebrating Rural Communities: A Strengths Assessment', in L.H. Ginsberg (ed.), *Social Work in Rural Communities.* Virginia: CSWE Press.

Torczyner, J. (2000) 'Globalization, Inequality and Peace Making: What Social Work Can Do', *Canadian Social Work* 2, 123–46.

United Nations (1999) *Capacity-Building Supported by the United Nations: Some Evaluations and Some Lessons.* United Nations.

UNCED (1992) *Results of the World Conference on Environment and Development: Agenda 21.* UNCED United Nations Conference on Environment and Development, Rio de Janeiro, United Nations, New York.

UNDP (2009) 'Capacity for Development: New Solutions to Old Problems'. UN (internet). Available at: http://www.undp.org/capacity/resources.shtml.

Weick, A. Rapp, C.A., Sullivan, W.P. and Kirsthardt, W. (1989) 'A Strengths Perspective for Social Work Practice', *Social Work* 344, 350–54.

World Bank (2004) *China's (Uneven) Progress against Poverty.* Washington D.C.: World Bank.

Yow, V.R. (1994). *Recording Oral History.* London: Sage.

31

Decentralization

Fumihiko Saito

INTRODUCTION

Decentralization is a process through which subnational governments increasingly partake in deciding on and administering essential public policies. Various decentralization measures are currently being implemented in many parts of the world, primarily because it is hoped that decentralized states will fulfill high expectations reflecting the diverse demands of our time. Decentralization reforms have become particularly popular since the 1980s. These measures are expected to make states both democratic and developmental. As regards democratization, decentralization is intended to widen the opportunities for citizens to participate in local decision-making processes. As for economic development, it is anticipated that decentralized states will improve general welfare by making public services more responsive to the different needs of people. Therefore, decentralization has often been regarded almost as a 'panacea' – a policy that is indisputably and normatively justified, even if nobody has officially proclaimed decentralization as such.

In federal states (already a decentralized polity), the intermediate tier is becoming more important than previously (states in the United States, provinces in Canada, and regional governments in Spain). In unitary states (often thought of as the opposite of federal states), decentralization is also often pursued. Various indicators, such as elected subnational governments (as in Wales and Scotland in the United Kingdom) as well as the size of fiscal expenditures by subnational governments (Stegarescu, 2006), show a clear general tendency towards decentralization. International organizations are increasingly involved in assisting decentralization programs in developing countries (World Bank, 2008).

Moreover, decentralization reforms are often pursued along with other initiatives, such as marketization and corporate management. As a result, there has been a significant increase in the numbers of non-state actors involved in local service delivery in the last couple of decades. The newly emerged collaborative networks between public and private entities may give hope for better services and possibly more efficient institutions. However, they raise a critical challenge of coordination: (local) governments have to oversee non-state actors. Today, this kind of public–private partnership (PPP) is rapidly proliferating, and it even appears as if PPPs have almost become the new pattern for institutions and rules, although contradictions may arise in attaining both political legitimacy and economic efficiency.

It may, therefore, not be an exaggeration to say that both such excessive expectations and uncritical approval initially made critical scrutiny of decentralization very difficult. In the 1980s analysts tended to overlook the historical, political, and socioeconomic contexts in which this complex reform has to take place. In the 1990s more empirical investigation started to report that decentralization sometimes is implemented in a half-hearted way, and often results in unsatisfactory outcomes. While the good intentions behind decentralization can be appreciated, the important point is to examine whether such noble intentions can actually be realized in the harsh realities of today's world, especially in developing countries. The crucial question is under what conditions decentralization measures can be successful both politically and economically (Cheema and Rondinelli, 2007). These critical reflections helped a 'second generation of decentralization theory' to emerge, which has important implications for democratic governance.

Because decentralization is a very popular item on the policy agenda, having an adequate understanding of the subject is of utmost importance, not only for researchers but also for practitioners. Indeed, various local government associations around the globe are adopting declarations that usually emphasize more participatory and inclusive governance, democratic renewal, revitalization of the local economy, and environmental conservation. In short, their declarations represent an attempt to achieve sustainable communities through decentralization (United Cities and Local Governments, 2008).

However, the characteristics of the subject pose a very serious dilemma. On the one hand, precisely because decentralization is not a monolithic notion, it is necessary to cover multiple aspects in a balanced way to achieve adequate understanding. While in the past, for instance, economists tended to pay attention to fiscal and taxation issues and public administration experts almost exclusively dealt with institutional design, today much more inter-disciplinary research is needed (Smoke et al., 2006).

On the other hand, conducting such holistic examination is extremely demanding and faces methodological difficulties. The challenge to satisfactory research is increased by the diversity of forms, scopes, and issues associated with decentralization. Even in one country, variations in local government functions and responsibilities exist. Attempts at comparative cross-national analyses have been further fragmented by specific regional focuses. For instance, while Western Europe has been relatively well studied (e.g. Denters and Rose, 2005), only recently have limited pioneering attempts been made to integrate assessments of industrialized countries with those of developing countries (e.g. Wibbels, 2005; Rodden, 2006).

This chapter attempts a comparative assessment across countries and regions by relying on existing knowledge.[1] The fact that researching decentralization reforms is demanding should not deter us from engaging in further discussion. On the contrary, with the insights of the 'second generation theory', which is essentially oriented towards a political economy approach and to moving beyond normative and idealized assumptions, it is clear that more research is needed for systematic understanding of this popular policy. This necessity should be emphasized because decentralization is now associated with a number of diverse goals and motivations, encompassing, *inter alia*, economic growth, conflict mitigation, community-based resource management, and nurturing civic values and social capital.

BACKGROUND OF DECENTRALIZATION

It is important to understand why decentralization measures have become so widespread.

As Treisman points out (2007: p.6), 'The question of how governments should be organized must be as old as the study of politics'. Yet classic thinkers on politics did not pay much attention to how diverse functions should be divided between central and subnational governments (hereafter 'subnational' and 'local' are used interchangeably in this chapter). Modern states that evolved first in Europe were characterized by a monopoly of forces (standing armies and police), the expansion of state administration (bureaucracy), territorial rule, and the diplomatic system for interstate relations (Held, et al., 1999, Chapter 1; Loughlin, 2004). Even if subsequent political developments in various regions and countries differed, modern statehood has been closely associated with centralization of power. Centralized states continued through the middle of the twentieth century. Centralization, even around the 1950s and 1960s, was closely associated with the welfare state in achieving improved living standards for populations.

However, around the world, centralized states now face enormous challenges to meet the expectations of them. There are several important background reasons why centralized states are not fulfilling popular expectations. First, citizens in both rich and poor countries have become more demanding of their governments for provision of the services that they desire. Secondly, such demands are often heterogeneous, which derives from many factors, including improved access to information through urbanization and globalization, as well as increasingly divergent lifestyles (especially in industrialized countries) (Denters and Rose, 2005). Thirdly, because people, goods, services, and information cross national borders more rapidly than before, management of social issues can no longer be handled effectively within one country alone. Fourthly, globalization has been transforming significantly the nature of the state, which has been the fundamental institution both domestically and internationally in the modern period (Held et al., 1999). Fifthly, the states of today face serious legitimacy problems. In the developing South, for example, Somalia and Afghanistan are typically considered as 'failed states' where sovereignty is not effectively exercised (Rotberg, 2004). In the industrialized North, low voter turnouts in elections highlight the crisis of democracy. While it is debatable whether the role of the state is more or less important than before, it is unquestionable that states are struggling to meet the expectations of them.

A shift from centralized to decentralized states is proposed in the search for an alternative mode of problem-solving. This shift is further supported by the romantic image of small communities where direct participation was possible (Treisman, 2007: Chapter 12). Often decentralized states are thought to embody the ideal polity that would serve the needs of its citizens. 'Nation-states exist to provide a *decentralized* method of delivering political (public) goods to persons living within designated parameters (borders)' (Rotberg, 2004: p.2, emphasis added).[2]

PROS AND CONS OF DECENTRALIZATION

Pro-decentralization arguments

Among the many reasons for decentralization, economic efficiency is at the heart of the debate between supporters and opponents of decentralization policies. The efficiency argument constitutes the core of the 'first generation theory' of decentralization that started to emerge around the 1950s and 1960s, and culminated in a seminal *Fiscal Federalism* by Wallace Oates (1972). Decentralists argue that because local governments are located closer to people, they are better suited than central government to identify what kinds of services people need. This *information* advantage in identifying public needs suggests that local governments can produce services that are more *responsive* to public aspirations (Hayek, 1948). This is often called *the principle of subsidiarity*: 'provision of public services should be located at the lowest level of government, encompassing, in a spatial sense, the relevant benefits and costs' (Oates, 1999: p.1122). In addition, public needs differ from one locality to another. Local governments can provide 'tailor-made' solutions in each locality, whereas the central government tends to impose standardized services across the country. Accordingly, a certain *allocative efficiency* is attained (Oates, 1972, 1999).

Local revenue raising is another economic issue. Decentralists maintain that service improvement is highly appreciated by citizens at the grassroots, and that this appreciation leads to an increased willingness to share the costs of services. Experience, especially in many developing countries, suggests that even the poor become more willing to pay for the services as long as the payment is used to provide more satisfactory services. This is much more easily established with local than with centralized taxes, since at local levels people can more easily see the connection between taxes and services. As a result, the revenue available to local governments from user contributions is increased (Bräutigam et al., 2008).

Participation of citizens in local decision making is also an important advantage claimed by decentralists. Participation signifies that people have the legitimate right to voice their concerns in affairs which affect their lives. If and when the socially marginalized – the poor, the young, women, ethnic minorities, etc. – can participate in designing and implementing public policies, the socially weak can reflect critically on their current situation, which may lead to possible solutions. This process is itself *empowering* to the marginalized, both in the North and in the South. The consultative processes provide opportunities to overcome social isolation and exclusion (Crook and Manor, 1998).

In addition, such consultative processes provide valuable opportunities for disseminating critical government *information* which was not easily accessible before. Since local governments are close to the people, this kind of information can be more readily disseminated locally. Decentralists thus believe that people can scrutinize local governments more closely than central governments. Accordingly, decentralized states reduce corruption and misappropriation of public funds by political representatives and administrators. Furthermore, if officials are elected by popular mandate, relations between leaders and the population become more intense, which in turn contributes to more trusting and accountable relations between leaders and followers. Through these processes civil values are nurtured, which is quite important in young democracies. In short, decentralists often consider that locality is a 'school for democracy', as earlier argued by John Stuart Mill.

This desirable outcome is reinforced by the notion of *competition* in which local governments are engaged, with central as well as with other local governments, in order to attract resources. This 'yardstick competition' makes voters more motivated to learn which localities are performing better than others (Bordignon et al., 2004). Competition also induces local governments to become more honest, efficient, and responsive. Here, the analogy of decentralization with markets is obvious; participation of numerous local governments in competition with each other will result in better allocation of resources. Weingast (1995) has suggested that decentralization and federalism are 'market preserving' arrangements.

Pro-decentralists also insist that decentralization helps to achieve *ethnic harmony* and *national unity*. They argue that local democratization is a prerequisite for building national unity in multi-ethnic and multi-religious societies in both industrialized and developing countries. They argue that increased local autonomy can better accommodate the competing interests of diverse social groups, including ethnic and religious minorities. Unless the legitimate political claims of the local population are reasonably satisfied, national unity and harmony cannot be established. Local governments are in a better position than central governments to facilitate diverse claims by their populations. These considerations particularly apply to Africa, where the states are formed on the basis of colonial legacies (Crawford and Hartmann, 2008).

Last but not least, among pro-decentralists decentralized states are considered to be less bureaucratic and smaller than centralized ones. They argue that decentralization measures make the public sector *smaller*, as more functions are delegated to local authorities with improved inter-office coordination. Improved efficiency and effectiveness of public resource management at the local level means that large bureaucracies are no longer required at the center (World Bank, 1999).

Counterarguments by critics

Skeptics of decentralization measures provide counterarguments to all the claims made by pro-decentralists. In order for *economic efficiency* to be gained, local governments are urged to translate their claimed information advantage of proximity into practice. In reality, this translation is often difficult. Local people do not necessarily know local issues well. In addition, if proximity is to result in knowledge, attitudes of government officials, who tend to be authoritative, have to be changed in order to facilitate interactions with people at the grassroots, especially the poor and the marginalized (Chambers, 1997). Furthermore, proximity does not mean that knowledge is acquired with less cost or is used more effectively. It depends on how data are collected, processed, and used for policymaking (Treisman, 2007: Chapter 9).

In addition, whereas local governments may enjoy an information advantage, decentralized governments often face an increased cost of *coordination*. Critics argue that precisely because many tasks are devolved from the central to different local governments, and even to non-governmental organizations

(NGOs) and others, coordination becomes a critical issue that consumes much more energy than centralization. Managing complex coordination in fact inevitably demands more sophisticated skills at the center in order to secure national integrity (Tendler, 1997: p.143). This is called a 'paradox of decentralization'; i.e. decentralizing measures may require more effective and possibly *bigger* central governments. According to Prud'homme (1996: p.357, quoted in Treisman, 2007: p.282), 'Where decentralization is needed (because central governments are corrupt and inefficient), it cannot be implemented. Where it can be implemented, it is not needed'.

Furthermore, critics point out that the closeness between local governments and people does not always yield positive results. Local governments are more prone to interference by the locally powerful. The newly available opportunities of local autonomy are often abused by local leaders. Unless this *élite capture* problem is avoided, decentralized states are far from achieving more efficient and effective outcomes (Platteau, 2004). On the contrary, attempts at decentralization may undermine the aim that traditional administration should be operated objectivity and rationally, as idealized by Max Weber and in his legacies.

While pro-decentralists emphasize the potential for *revenue enhancement*, skeptics of decentralization refute such a claim. The critics argue that limitations on various resources do not allow improvement of services. Instead, they maintain that economic improvement is better attained by applying *economy of scale* nationally. Furthermore, they argue that implementing decentralization is too complicated for the limited resources, skills, and knowledge available to local governments, particularly in the developing world. Furthermore, central government is often unwilling to relinquish the necessary political, administrative, financial, and technical resources to local governments, which are then left to struggle without resources and support. This particularly applies to *fiscal decentralization* (Ahmand and Brosio, 2006). When central government is reluctant to hand over valuable tax revenue to local governments, local governments must either depend on grants transferred from the center or attempt to implement additional but not promising taxation measures. Consequently, the intended result, that people become more willing to pay for services, is not achieved. If so, the critics continue, it is preferable that such limited resources should be utilized more effectively, being concentrated at the center instead of thinly spread in diverse localities.

Critics disagree with the merits of *participation* as well. The local population is not necessarily accustomed to participation. The grassroots poor are usually not used to being consulted by government officials. Local officials are often not favorable toward facilitating popular participation either. Political and administrative leaders often unmistakably look down upon the socially weak and the disadvantaged. This attitudinal problem, in part due to élitist education, clearly hampers the evolution of consultative processes. Newly granted local autonomy may indeed reinforce this tendency by 'élite capture'. In addition, participation is costly to organize. Inclusive processes require a lot of time and energy in order to be properly managed. Often, the required skills are not available locally. In this situation, some may be easily frustrated by the gap between the rhetoric and realities of participation (Chambers, 1997).

The democratic effects stressed by decentralists receive criticism as well. While supporters of decentralization insist that decentralized states are more transparent, less corrupt, and more accountable, the critics disagree. Localities are not homogeneous and local communities display inequality in power as well. Even if it is essential to avoid élite capture for many of the benefits of decentralization to be realized, there is no logical proof that local political leaders are more benevolent than their central counterparts. Élites may simply take advantage of

the new opportunities of autonomy, and consequently corruption may also be 'decentralized' (Bardhan, 1997). Furthermore, as long as central government retains control of budgeting and financial controls, local leaders may look for central government to improve 'upward' accountability, at a cost to the 'downward' accountability to local residents that is often expected as a democratization effect by pro-decentralists. Accordingly, critics continue, decentralization does not nurture civic values and is not a 'school for democracy'.

Furthermore, while pro-decentralists argue that *inter-jurisdictional competition*, like markets, yields more efficient and responsive government, critics argue that the conditions needed for such realization are rarely seen on the ground. In order for competition to be achieved, people should be able to move reasonably freely from one place to another, to find the best match between their preferences and local services. Yet, this 'voting with their feet' (Tiebout, 1956) is not possible for those who depend on livelihoods in certain locations, for instance. It is also unrealistic to expect that there is no cost to such mobility (Treisman, 2007: Chapter 4).

As regards *ethnic harmonization* and *national unity*, disagreement also unfolds. It may be possible to envisage a situation in which certain ethnic minorities are clustered geographically, and whereby it would be possible to clearly demarcate areas by ethnicity. However, such clear zonal 'homogeneity' rarely exists in reality. Thus, granting regional autonomy to subnational governments simply shifts ethnic tensions from national to local levels. If this is mingled with political interference by local élites, achieving ethnic harmony becomes more problematic. In addition, critics continue, decentralization measures tend to jeopardize equity among different localities. Resource-rich areas may take advantage of the opportunities of autonomy created by decentralizing, leaving relatively poor areas behind unless remedial measures are taken (usually by central government). Additionally, decentralizing attempts may foster greater attachment to regional identities, rather than to national unity, in multi-ethnic and multi-religious societies in many countries. As a result, national integrity becomes threatened, instead of decentralization serving as a 'peace preserving' process (Bermeo, 2002: p.108)

If decentralization signifies weakened functioning of central government, then decentralization is not only misleading but dangerous. Of particular importance are redistributional and stabilizing functions, usually carried out by central government. It is normally the responsibility of the central government to ensure, through redistribution of revenues, that people in poorer parts of the country enjoy a reasonable standard of living. Stabilization functions for the macroeconomy, through monetary and fiscal policies, should also be undertaken by the national government (Oates, 2005).

Diverse issues in decentralization

As becomes obvious, decentralization measures have been associated with a number of diverse issues. Different political and economic groups support decentralization for different reasons. Those who emphasize economic efficiency (neoliberalists) support decentralized states, with their emphasis on markets and small governments. They advocate swift marketization and increased reliance on private service providers. For those who appreciate democratization (what might be termed 'neopopulists'), decentralization is a promising avenue because it enlarges the scope for citizen participation. They thus call for enhanced democratic control of both the state and the private sector which have tended to marginalize the socially weak. Neoliberalists are inclined to be politically conservative, while neopopulists tend to be liberal. Pro-decentralization advocacy, thus, originates from diverse reasons and conflicting arguments, and does not necessarily have a single consolidated justification.

Moreover, historically, different themes have been discussed in different times.

Decentralization in the 1980s was initially associated with neoliberal reforms, in both industrialized and developing countries, in order to reduce the size of the state, especially in the forms of deconcentration and privatization. The Regan administration in the United States and the Thatcher government in the United Kingdom spearheaded this trend. The trend was also reflected in the structural adjustment programs of the International Monetary Fund (IMF) and the World Bank. Then, in the 1990s, with the end of the cold war, the relative emphasis shifted to global democratization. Next, decentralization, especially in the form of devolution, became increasingly associated with governance reform to achieve social inclusion in rich countries and participatory development in poor nations (Smith, 2007).

Perhaps more importantly, what becomes evident from the decentralization debate is that the same rationales are used toward their own ends by both supporters and opponents. Larmour and Qalo (1985) stated that 'arguments for and against decentralisation are often "like proverbs" with most principles answerable by an equally plausible and acceptable contradictory principle …. Decentralisation promotes efficiency and reduces it. Decentralisation enhances national unity and inhibits it' (quoted in Regan, 1995: p.279). Studying decentralization is, therefore, essentially empirical. As the debate demonstrates clearly, criticism of decentralization consists largely of empirical arguments rather than theoretical ones. Even the critics tend not to deny totally the good intentions of pro-decentralists. In short, 'anti-decentralists' are not really pro-centralists.

DEFINITION AND TYPOLOGY OF DECENTRALIZATION

Because decentralization measures are related to diverse goals and issues, finding a coherent definition becomes close to a nightmare (Schneider, 2003). Conventionally, decentralization is defined as a process through which central government transfers various forms of authority and functions to subnational governments for timely adaptation to locally specific conditions. This is a broad definition, and usually suitable for accessing the degree of autonomy and authority granted to local governments, including planning, financing, and implementing their policies. Yet, a more nuanced understanding is essential. Transferring various kinds of authority and functions from central to local governments does not have to be zero sum. Indeed, what is commonly practiced is a kind of *joint* decision-making by central and subnational governments in deciding important pubic policies. Relatively, the influence of local governments, as co-managers of (local) public goods, becomes more important than before (Rodden, 2006).

What is equally difficult is to devise a coherent typology to classify the diverse forms of decentralization initiatives. Different classifications are often used for different reasons.

One common classification is to distinguish deconcentration, delegation, and devolution (e.g. World Bank, 2008). *Deconcentration* refers to a situation whereby certain responsibilities are assigned and services transferred from central government to its regional offices and branches. *Devolution* normally indicates a situation in which authority for decision-making and finance is transferred from central to subnational governments, which enjoy a reasonably high degree of autonomy. Deconcentration takes place normally within administrative structures, while devolution mainly centers around political bodies. In short, while deconcentration simply relocates authority at different levels of government, devolution removes authority from central to subnational governments. Another crucial difference between deconcentration and devolution is the way in which accountability works. In deconcentration, even though decision makers are located in local offices, they are still held accountable to central authorities. In contrast, in devolution, locally-based decision-makers are accountable to the public on a local level (Uphoff, 1986: p.221–2).[3]

Defining *delegation* tends to be problematic in relation to deconcentration and devolution. Some analysts tend to define delegation as something in between deconcentration and devolution, according to the extent of autonomy transferred from central to subnational governments. But delegation is often related to both political and administrative spheres. One of the main reasons why delegation is defined as a form of decentralization derives from *new public management* reform, especially that initiated in the United Kingdom. While previously, government offices themselves provided services, special agencies were created, particularly in the 1980s, for service delivery. The intention was to apply business practices to bureaucracies to improve economic efficiency and to reduce the size of the government. By extending this reasoning, privatization also becomes a type of decentralization (Turner and Hulme, 1997). However, privatization (and marketization) is usually not equated with decentralization, which is primarily understood as a division of tasks among different political offices.

In order for subnational governments to discharge newly assigned responsibilities, *fiscal decentralization* is also often implemented. It transfers authorities in revenue-raising and expenditure decision-making from central to local governments. Issues related to fiscal decentralization are diverse, including inter-governmental transfer of grants, the possibility for local governments to borrow money from financial markets by issuing bonds, and reforming the entire tax policy in line with decentralization. Of particular importance is an articulated mechanism for settling local governments' debt, if needed, since it is usually the responsibility of central government to maintain macroeconomic stability. If central government bails out local governments without strict conditions, this would create moral hazard for local governments spending their budgets without strict control. This is often called 'soft budget constraint' (Kornai et al., 2003; Rodden et al., 2003). Contrarily, if the center does not rescue local governments with financial problems, the local governments bear the final responsibility; this constitutes 'hard budget constraint'. Fiscal autonomy and political decentralization (devolution) should go hand in hand, if decentralization is really to transfer authority from central to subnational governments. Without financial authority, decision-making autonomy is incomplete (Ahmand and Brosio, 2006).

Furthermore, *federalism* and decentralization often tend to be used interchangeably. While in a large body of literature (e.g. public finance) this usage is not considered a problem, for political scientists, federalism and decentralization are not the same. Rodden (2006) emphasizes that federalism is not so much about how authority institutionally is distributed between federal and subnational governments, but rather an ongoing political bargaining process through which authority is distributed, contested, and renegotiated. Federalism is a kind of contractual arrangement in which at least two tiers of government have obligations to each other. Federal constitutions usually specify:

1 Two tiers of government rule the same territories and people.
2 Each tier has some autonomous policy arenas.
3 A constitutional guarantee of respective autonomy in explicit clauses (Riker, 1964).
4 Regions are normally represented in the national legislature in order to create 'shared rule' (Wibbels, 2006: Chapter 2).

The language of federalism is about fragmented sovereignty, which is usually not the case in decentralization discussions. Nonetheless, recent discussion of federalism re-emphasizes that the distinction between unitary and federal political systems should not be treated in a dichotomous way. On the contrary, as federalism shares sovereignty between two tiers of government, our concern is the extent of authority shared to resolve various issues.[4]

Furthermore, some analysts, have attempted to create models for mapping out the diverse goals of decentralization in a coherent way (von Braun and Grote, 2002; Jütting et al., 2005). These models are primarily concerned with the possible paths by which decentralization measures can produce desired outcomes. Steiner (2007), following the World Bank model of poverty reduction, presented an idealized vision of such pro-poor channels. What becomes complicated is that the diverse goals associated with decentralization are sometimes mutually reinforcing, and at other times contradictory. Thus, while it is useful to devise idealized models, the reality surrounding decentralization is profoundly complex and 'messy', and the decentralization debate and issues related to its typology still remain essentially empirical questions.

What becomes problematic empirically, furthermore, is that because decentralization entails complex processes, usually a country's experiences demonstrate more than one aspect at the same time: for instance, politically devolved but fiscally recentralized. It tends, therefore, to be useless to try to fit one country's decentralization measures into a single category, such as either devolution or deconcentration.

EMPIRICAL INVESTIGATIONS

What then would be the empirical evidence that may either support or refute decentralists' visions? Although the voluminous literature discusses diverse goals, two broad categories are highlighted for comparative analysis here: improving living conditions and reviving (local) democracy. While these categorizations are most obvious in transitional and developing countries (e.g. Smoke et al., 2006), they can be analytically applied to industrialized countries as well.[5] The empirical studies are largely divided into two types: one applies statistical methods to data sets to see correlation and/or causality; and the other relies more on qualitative case studies through observation and interviews.

Decentralization and economic performance

What are the effects of decentralization on economic performance? The existing literature is inconclusive. Wibbels (2005: pp.75–6) compared federations and unitary states among 83 developing countries during the period 1978–2000. His finding is that federations increase budget deficits by 8.8% compared with unitary polity, have more than twice the impact on the recorded inflation rate than on growth, and that the effect of federalism on national debt is insignificant.

Similarly, Rodden (2006: Chapter 4) also finds, based on 1986–1996 data for 43 developed and developing countries, that when subnational governments depend on intergovernmental fiscal transfers and when central government allows subnational borrowing, statistically there is a significantly greater chance of macroeconomic instability.

Both of these findings mean that decentralization and federalism are 'market distorting' rather than 'market preserving' as argued by Weingast (1995), and contradict the results predicted by fiscal decentralization theory. One suggestion by Treisman (2007: p.206) is that decentralized countries – either in the North or in the South – tend to maintain the same economic performances (either good or bad) for years and decades.

Clearly, the empirical agenda is far from complete. Whereas it is right to measure the effects of decentralization on macroeconomic (in)stability, little research has been done into how decentralization raises *local* income levels (Crawford and Hartmann, 2008: p.18). Thus, several case studies employ more qualitative methods for diagnosing the path from decentralization to pro-poor outcomes. For instance, in Africa, Crawford and Hartmann (2008: Chapter 9) conclude that the results are generally less positive in Ghana, Uganda, and Malawi, but more positive in Tanzania. However, this may be too general a conclusion. In Uganda, one of the most decentralized countries in Sub-Saharan Africa, poverty trends have been more complicated in recent times, and public satisfaction differs from one service to another as well as from one region to another (Saito, 2003, 2008).

Thus, it would be difficult to be sure whether decentralization brings much of the poverty reduction anticipated, especially in developing countries. Yet, this inconclusiveness derives, not so surprisingly, from the intricate nature of economic change. Economic growth and poverty reduction may be realized, as fiscal federalists such as Wallace Oates have been arguing. However, in reality many other policies are launched to accelerate growth and improve welfare in addition to decentralization. Conceptually as well as methodologically, it becomes difficult to isolate decentralization from many other factors. Furthermore, decentralization may relate to economic growth directly and indirectly (through allocative efficiency, improved services, etc.). Thus, it is necessary to deconstruct the overall question about decentralization and economic performance, and much more methodological sophistication is needed, especially for comparative analyses (Martine-Vazquez and McNab, 2003).

Decentralization and democracy

Does decentralization foster democracy, or does it lead to more corruption and élite capture? The recently growing literature is again inconclusive. Treisman (2007) demonstrates that when the proportion of subnational spending in total government expenditure during 1985–1995 is plotted on an x-axis and the World Bank corruption score of countries for 1996–2002 on a y-axis, a C-shaped curve appears. Curiously, Treisman continues, a high proportion of fiscally decentralized governments are either very clean or very corrupt, but rarely in the middle. He suggests that once income level is controlled, the C-shape turns into an upward slope, signifying that more fiscally decentralized means more corruption (Treisman, 2007: pp.252–253).

Lederman et al. (2005), on the other hand, using the International Country Risk Guide (ICRG) during 1984–1999, found that democracies, parliamentary systems, political stability, and freedom of the press are all associated with less corruption. Fisman and Gatti (2002) also conclude, based on the ICRG and other data from 59 countries during 1980 to 1995, that, generally, fiscal decentralization is strongly associated with less corruption. But, Treisman (2007: p.254) interprets that result as being partly due to missing data from three notoriously corrupt federal states: Nigeria, Pakistan, and Russia.

Enikolopov and Zhuravskaya (2007), using panel data from 75 developing and transitional countries during 1975–2000, found that well-organized national political parties significantly improve the outcomes of fiscal decentralization, such as economic growth, quality of government, and public goods provision. But when local politicians are appointed and not elected, such administrative subordination causes the opposite effect.

Grindle (2007) offers a more nuanced explanation from Mexican municipalities, combining both quantitative and qualitative methods. She concludes that, because local governance institutions are weak, newly elected officials can introduce significant changes, but find it difficult to sustain them due to the same weakness. Likewise, while constituencies welcome increased opportunities for political participation, they try to extract more resources from leaders instead of trying to hold them accountable for their actions.

This kind of observation, of 'decentralization as a double-edged sword', is often found in case studies, including my own study results from Uganda (Saito, 2003, 2008). Local elections and devolution have increased the local decision-making autonomy of local governments, but election campaigns have raised consciousness of ethnic origins, which resulted in the election as well as the appointment of officials considered to adequately represent 'sons and daughters of the soil'.

In summary, what becomes apparent from the literature relates to fundamental methodological issues. Obviously, results of quantitative research differ depending on panel data (which countries are used for what period). The question whether decentralization leads to more democracy or not tends to be too broad to be discussed. We need a more fine-tuned analysis of the ways relationships between elected leaders and constituencies have been affected by decentralization reforms. As Grindle and my studies suggest, often subtle and even contradictory forces are unfolding, and blunt judgments such as 'decentralization leads to more democratic practices' would likely to be too simplistic.

'SECOND GENERATION THEORY' AND LOCAL GOVERNMENT IN THE 21ST CENTURY

The inconclusive literature from empirical studies is a part of the reason why the 'second generation theory' (SGT) of decentralization has recently emerged, especially in the last five years or so. This new theory has the following characteristics, though the 'new' does not totally deny the 'old':

1 It emphasizes political economy in its approach, whether or not incentives for diverse stakeholders are congruent in order to attain common objectives.
2 It acknowledges that information is not equitably shared among these stakeholders.
3 It goes beyond the idealized normative assumptions by paying relatively more attention to empirical results.
4 It moves beyond North America and industrialized countries to global comparisons.

In short, efforts are made to understand very complex political as well as socioeconomic relations between national and subnational governments (Oates, 2005).

The SGT is much welcomed for various reasons. Decentralization is not an end itself but usually a means toward a range of broader objectives, encompassing democratic deepening and economic progress. Placing decentralization in diverse contexts is more useful than a static analysis treating decentralization per se as either right or wrong.

Furthermore, the SGT is very suited in diagnosing contradiction inherent in decentralization. For Rodden (2006), this dilemma was at the heart of Alexander Hamilton's writings (especially his *Federalist* 7 and 19). The dilemma is 'how to create a central government that is simultaneously strong and limited. The center must be strong enough to achieve the desired collective goods – free trade, common defense, and the like – but weak enough to preserve a robust sense of local autonomy' (Rodden, 2006: p.17). Thus, decentralization is an ongoing process to find an optimal balance for each country between democratic autonomy for subnational entities and effective control by central government, in unique historical, geographical, and other important circumstances. Today, this dilemma is highlighted even more in the context of decentralization being more often implemented together with marketization and PPP.

Another important reason why the SGT is welcomed is that local governments are now situated at a strategic crossroads. They are the indispensable actors for both vertical (central–local relations) and horizontal (public–private) coordination . Both are more fluid and dynamic than ever before. Furthermore, it is at the local level that *three rather distinct reform agendas* need to be integrated: decentralization for administrative reform; expansion of markets for economic transactions; and empowerment for civil society, including the weak and the less privileged. Local leaders need to integrate these three reforms coherently, which is no trivial task. For any partnerships to realize their objectives, effective engagement of local government leaders and staff is essential.

Furthermore, focusing on divergent incentives helps to achieve governance as a coordination mechanism. While 'inputs' such as sufficient financial resources, tax revenues, facilitative leaders and support personnel, and a clear legal framework are all obviously needed, something more is necessary to put these inputs together to generate synergetic effects. We need to pay sufficient attention to the changing dynamics of essential stakeholders who attempt to create rules in their favor, interpret laws and legislations for their advantage, and mobilize all sorts of resources from finance to symbolic figures to support their claims. While the involvement of private entities in service delivery may enhance economic efficiency, it tends to fragment democratic control by the state. Devising workable coordination mechanisms satisfying both political legitimacy and economic rationality is no trivial task. The 'new' perspective is thus illuminating in order to examine how interrelations among diverse stakeholders change over time for key issues, including resource allocation.[6]

Finally, as our attention shifts from comparing local *governments* to local *governance* (Kjaer, 2004), the scope for investigation is significantly widened, encompassing not only formal structures but also informal coordination, as both attempt to produce the intended outcomes (better services and/or strengthened democracy). Widespread reliance on markets and networks again further blurs the boundary between formal and informal mechanisms in both rich and poor countries. Particularly in developing countries, the spread of user committees further complicates the development of formal and informal institutions. While these committees are usually for short-term project management purposes with single-issue orientation, decentralized local governments under the auspices of elected local councils exist as more durable and multi-dimensional decision-makers. The new theory helps us address several critical imbalances of power and resources among diverse participants in governance arrangements (Manor, 2004).

FOR SYNERGISTIC EXCELLENCE

It has become abundantly clear that decentralization initiatives relate to a wide range of issues and subjects. Even if successful decentralization is very demanding, there are some 'good practices' that are informative about how different 'inputs' can be fused together to produce much-desired synergistic effects. Three examples merit brief description as they are illuminating from the perspective of the SGT, and also because they have affected not only their home locality but also have gained international reputation as well.

The first example is Kerala State, located at the southern end of India. When local educationalists established a community organization in the 1960s, this ushered in a series of social movements. The state government then realized that for effective development it is prudent to collaborate with civic leaders. In 1993 constitutional amendments formally started to implement decentralization. In 1996, People's Plan and Campaign was introduced as a new policy, and the prior collaborative experiences helped the Campaign to evolve into a new participatory exercise in which a proportion of the state budget is reserved for bottom-up activities (Sandbrook et al., 2007). Kerala is often considered an exceptional success, not only in India but also in South Asia and the developing world in general.

Porto Alegre, Brazil is our second example. The 1988 constitution allowed municipalities to have autonomous governments. Then the leftist mayor exercised leadership in promoting direct citizen engagement in participatory budgeting (PB) processes, which allowed each 'community area' to have a voice in determining the allocation of capital investments. Although, initially, participation was not very widespread, as the effects of PB became evident in the form of improved neighborhood conditions, participation in PB processes increased. PB was subsequently emulated in other Brazilian and Latin American cities, and then elsewhere. Simply put, PB aims to increase democratic control of public resources through citizens' direct engagement in budgeting processes (Bruce, 2004).

Our final example is the One Village and One Product movement in Oita Prefecture in Japan, which started in 1979 with the inauguration of a new governor. The local residents often complained about insufficient support by the central government as a main cause of their poverty. The new governor transformed this situation by a series of initiatives that can be characterized not only as economic regeneration by emphasizing locally made produce but also as a broader social–cultural movement that nurtured civic values and provided unconventional training for the next generation of new local leaders. This success was subsequently emulated in other areas of Japan and then by Thailand, Malawi, and other countries (Oita OVOP International Exchange Committee, 2006).

All these examples demonstrate that decentralization measures form a part of a much larger overall sociopolitical reform agenda. 'Putting the decision making closer to people' alone may not result in sustainable communities and democratic governance, unless it is implemented together with political, economic, and social reforms. If decentralization replaces low-quality public services provided by central government with similarly unsatisfactory services managed by local governments, the public is far from satisfied with such a change. In order to realize the claimed advantages of decentralization, broader improvements are indispensable. The SGT highlights both the importance and difficulties of such broad reforms in conjunction with decentralization.

Moreover, paying sufficient attention to political dynamics among diverse stakeholders is a necessity, as the SGT insists. Decentralization measures without an articulated political reform agenda will never succeed. As the recent literature abundantly demonstrates, there are a number of political issues. Political parties play crucial roles. Party functions range from commitment to/ interference in appointment of local officials to the possibility of aggregating diverse interests of the population in different settings, and even to creating desirable incentive mechanisms linking policy reforms at both national and subnational levels. Establishing a viable local legislature and electoral governance mechanisms are also essential, because elections form the core of democracy. Moreover, creating effective links between different levels of (global, national, and subnational) democracies is much desired, even though this subject is not sufficiently understood (Loughlin, 2004).

Of equal importance is that all best practices demonstrate that facilitative leadership and deliberative democracy mutually reinforce each other. Put differently, 'top-down' and 'bottom-up' initiatives neatly mesh together to address common objectives without aggravating equity concerns. Fung and Write call this 'empowered participatory governance'; all the examples started out to address specific practical public concerns; decision-making relied on empowered involvement of ordinary citizens and officials; and all attempted to solve the problems through reasoned deliberation (Fung and Wright, 2003). It needs to be added hastily that the local decision-making process is not free from problems. In order to overcome dangers of élite capture and misuse of patronage, possibly in the form of PPPs, *inter alia*, it is essential to take remedial action: critical information should be disseminated widely; negotiation and bargaining should be widened to broaden coalitions in support of reform; and policy experiments and public feedback can create institutionalization, which if supported widely, can no longer be hijacked by a small number of élite and private service providers at a cost to the public at large. The SGT reaffirms that these remedies reduce the risk of reformers themselves becoming predatory and starting to prevent reforms from deepening (Bebbington and McCourt, 2007).

Of course, the lessons from these 'best practices' cannot be applied to all conditions. Each locality has its unique historical and cultural background. Administrative boundaries determine the size of subnational governments and if their size is too large

(even though economies of scale yield greater efficiency), effective participatory governance may not be realized (Alesina and Spolaore, 2003). Nonetheless, the SGT helps us to confirm that 'best practices' are still informative. If newly granted autonomy is anchored by both upward and downward accountability mechanisms encompassing diverse entities, and officials and citizens share common visions and information on public matters, there is some prospect that decentralization measures can achieve much-needed outcomes. In addition, if decentralization adequately improves coordination through mentoring and support of local actions by national actors, as well as through public scrutiny of ever-proliferating markets and networks, there would be more interesting results. Examples demonstrate that successful decentralization is well coordinated rather than fragmented around the boundaries of subnational governments.

CONCLUSIONS

In governance studies, decentralization is an excellent topic, since the various issues and discussions are relevant both theoretically and practically. This is our first conclusion. Generally much of the debate related to decentralization involves significant issues in coordinating diverse stakeholders in realizing political and socioeconomic common goods, and often at local levels in the middle of ever-changing circumstances, which are due to, *inter alia*, marketization and globalization. Thus, it is no wonder that the very recent discourse in the literature has moved from 'decentralization' to 'comparative local governance' studies (Stoker, 2006). Whether this shift is more than discursive, it may remain to be seen. But a recent theoretical deepening, in the form of the SGT, is probably very helpful.

Secondly, diverse arguments including both pros and cons helped the SGT of decentralization to emerge, although the 'first' and 'second' generation theories are not entirely mutually exclusive. This evolution is a desirable step forward: to move from the normatively idealized notions of decentralization to a more realistic assessment of the difficulties in implementing the complex policy agenda of decentralization. With the SGT, we have moved a step closer to a standpoint that enables us to devise policies more suited to each country's situation, without depending on a simplistic belief that the experiences of advanced countries should be transferable to the developing world.

Thirdly, decentralization is essentially a political question (Smoke et al., 2006; Saito, 2008), and the SGT pays close attention to the intricate relations between national and subnational politics, through the diverse interactions of legislators, political party officials, voters, and others. These diverse channels work sometimes in harmony with and at other times in conflict with each other in attempting to aggregate the heterogeneous citizens' preferences for social services. It becomes of utmost important to understand this complicated dynamism.

Fourthly, however, the study of decentralization reforms faces enormous conceptual and methodological difficulties. As highlighted in this review, scholars have not yet agreed upon a common definition and typology, which makes comparative assessment troublesome, if not impossible. Unless future research activities are carefully designed, they may invite the risks of concept-stretching and miscomparison (Satori, 1991). But, as all second generation theorists maintain, this challenge should not deter us from embarking on further clarification of the ways in which our normative vision of decentralization can be made workable in the diverse realities of the world.

NOTES

1   This chapter builds on my earlier publications (Saito, 2003, 2008).

2   See Treisman (2007: Chapter 12) for more reasons for the popularity of decentralization.
3   To further complicate the matter, political decentralization sometimes means not political aspects of intergovernmental relations but a change in how local government leaders are appointed, from central appointment to elections (Rodden, 2006: p.25).
4   The fiscal federalism literature is not about the political dimension of fiscal decentralization, but is almost purely economic-focused. Indeed, it does not address the issue of political incentives for subnational politicians in federations (Wibbels, 2006: p.63).
5   In addition, studies have accumulated on the impacts of decentralization on, *inter alia*, ethnic conflicts and natural resource management. For the former, see, for instance, Treisman, 2007: Chapter 11; Crawford and Hartmann, 2008. For the latter, see Ribbot et al., 2008.
6   The SGT is somewhat similar to network management. It reminds us that similar to failures of the command-and-control approach applied in government, and market failures through imperfect competitions, networks of collaborators may collapse as well.

REFERENCES

Ahmand, Ehtisham and Brosio, Giorgio (eds) (2006) *Handbook of Fiscal Federalism*. Cheltenham: Edward Elgar.
Alesina, Alberto and Spolaore, Enrico (2003) *The Size of Nations*. Cambridge, MA: MIT Press.
Bardhan, Pranab (1997) 'Corruption and Development: A Review of Issues', *Journal of Economic Literature* 35(3): 1320–46.
Bebbington, Anthony and McCourt, Willy (eds) (2007) *Development Success: Statecraft in the South*. Basingstoke: Palgrave Macmillan.
Bermeo, Nancy (2002) 'The Import of Institutions', *Journal of Democracy* 35(2): 96–110.
Bordignon, Massimo, Cerniglia, Floriana and Revelli, Federico (2004) 'Yardstick Competition in Intergovernmental Relationships: Theory and Empirical Predictions', *Economics Letters* 83(3): 325–33.
Bräutigam, Deborah, Fjeldstad, Odd-Helge and Moore, Mick (eds) (2008) *Taxation and State-Building in Developing Countries: Capacity and Consent*. Cambridge: Cambridge University Press.
Bruce, Iain (edited and translated) (2004) *The Porto Alegre Alternative: Direct Democracy in Action*.

London: Pluto Press with the International Institute for Research and Education.

Chambers, Robert (1997) *Whose Reality Counts?: Putting the First Last.* London: Intermediate Technology Publications.

Cheema, G. Shabbir and Rondinelli, Dennis A. (eds) (2007) *Decentralizing Governance: Emerging Concepts and Practices.* Washington, DC: Brookings Institution Press.

Crawford, Gordan and Hartmann, Christof (eds) (2008) *Decentralisation in Africa: A Pathway Out of Poverty and Conflict?* Amsterdam: Amsterdam University Press.

Crook, Richard and Manor, James (1998) *Democracy and Decentralisation in South Asia and West Africa: Participation, Accountability and Performance.* Cambridge: Cambridge University Press.

Denters, Bas and Rose, Lawrence E. (eds) (2005) *Comparing Local Governance: Trends and Developments.* Basingstoke: Palgrave Macmillan.

Enikolopov, Ruben and Zhuravskaya, Ekaterina (2007) 'Decentralization and Political Institutions', *Journal of Public Economics* 91(11–12): 2261–90.

Fisman, Raymond and Gatti, Roberta (2002) 'Decentralization and Corruption: Evidence across Countries', *Journal of Public Economics* 83(3): 325–45.

Fung, Archon and Wright, Erik O. (eds) (2003) *Deepening Democracy: Institutional Innovations in Empowered Participatory Governance.* London: Verso.

Grindle, Merilee S. (2007) *Going Local: Decentralization, Democratization, and the Promise of Good Governance.* Princeton NJ: Princeton University Press.

Hayek, Friedrich A. (1948) *Individualism and Economic Order.* London: Routledge and Kegan Paul.

Held, David, McGrew, Anthony, Goldblatt, David and Perraton, Jonathan (1999) *Global Transformations: Politics, Economics and Culture.* Cambridge: Polity Press.

Jütting, Johannes, Corsi, Elena, Kauffmann, Celine, et al. (2005) 'What Makes Decentralisation in Developing Countries Pro-poor?', *The European Journal of Development Research* 17(4): 626–48.

Kjaer, Anne Mette (2004) *Governance.* Cambridge: Polity Press.

Kornai, János, Maskin, Eric and Roland, Gérard (2003) 'Understanding the Soft Budget Constraint', *Journal of Economic Literature*, 41(4): 1095–136.

Larmour, P. and Qalo, R. (1985) *Decentralisation in the South Pacific: Local, Provincial, and State Government in Twenty Countries.* Suva: University of South Pacific.

Lederman, Daniel, Loayza, Norman V. and Soares, Rodrigo R. (2005) 'Accountability and Corruption: Political Institutions Matter', *Economics & Politics* 17(1): 1–35.

Loughlin, John (ed.) (2004) *Subnational Democracy in the European Union: Challenges and Opportunities.* Oxford: Oxford University Press.

Manor, James (2004) 'User Committees: A Potentially Damaging Second Wave of Decentralization?', *European Journal of Development Research* 16(1): 192–213.

Martine-Vazquez, George and McNab, Robert M. (2003) 'Fiscal Decentralization and Economic Growth', *World Development* 31(9): 1597–616.

Oates, Wallace E. (1972). *Fiscal Federalism.* New York: Harcourt Brace Jovanovich.

Oates, Wallace E. (1999) 'An Essay on Fiscal Federalism', *Journal of Economic Literature* 37(3):1120–49.

Oates, Wallace E. (2005) 'Toward a Second-Generation Theory of Fiscal Federalism' *International Tax and Public Finance* 12(4): 349–73.

Oita OVOP International Exchange Committee, Japan (2006) 'Proceedings of the One Village One Product International Seminar in Oita: *"One Village, One Product"* Spreading throughout the World'. Oita: Oita OVOP International Exchange Committee, Japan.

Platteau, Jean-Philippe (2004) 'Monitoring Elite Capture in Community-Driven Development', *Development and Change* 35(2): 223–46.

Prud'homme, Remy (1996) "Comment on 'Conflicts and Dilemmas of Decentralization', by Rudolf Hommes", in *Annual World Bank Conference on Development Economics 1995* Washington DC; World Bank; pp. 354–9.

Regan, Anthony (1995) 'A Comparative Framework for Analysing Uganda's Decentralisation Policy', in P. Langseth, J. Katorobo, E. Brett, and J. Munene (eds) *Uganda: Landmarks in Rebuilding a Nation.* Kampala: Fountain Publishers.

Ribbot, Jesse C., Chhatre, Ashwini and Lankia, Tomila (2008) 'Introduction: Institutional Choice and Recognition in the Formation and Consolidation of Local Democracy', *Conservation and Society* 6(1): 1–11.

Riker, William (1964) *Federalism: Origin, Operation, Significance.* Boston MA: Little, Brown, and Company.

Rodden, Jonathan A. (2006) *Hamilton's Paradox: The Promise and Peril of Fiscal Federalism.* Cambridge: Cambridge University Press.

Rodden, Jonathan, Eskeland, Gunnar S. and Litvack, Jennie (eds) (2003) *Fiscal Decentralization and the*

Challenge of Hard Budget Constraints. Cambridge, MA: MIT Press.

Rotberg, Robert I. (2004) *When States Fall: Causes and Consequences.* Princeton, NJ: Princeton University Press.

Saito, Fumihiko (2003) *Decentralization and Development Partnerships: Lessons from Uganda.* Tokyo: Springer-Verlag.

Saito, Fumihiko (ed.) (2008) *Foundations for Local Governance: Decentralization in Comparative Perspective.* Heidelberg, Germany: Physica-Verlag.

Sandbrook, Richard, Edelman, Marc, Heller, Patrick and Teichman, Judith (2007) *Social Democracy in the Global Periphery: Origins, Challenges, Prospects.* Cambridge: Cambridge University Press.

Satori, Giovanni (1991) 'Comparing and Miscomparing', *Journal of Theoretical Politics* 3(3): 243–57.

Schneider, Aaron (2003) 'Decentralization: Conceptualization and Measurement', *Studies in Comparative International Development* 38(3): 32–56.

Smith, B.C. (2007) *Good Governance and Development.* Basingstoke: Palgrave Macmillan.

Smoke, Paul, Gomez, Eduarado J. and Peterson, George E. (eds) (2006) *Decentralization in Asia and Latin America.* Northampton, MA: Edward Elgar.

Stegarescu, Dan (2006) *Decentralised Government in an Integrating World: Quantitative Studies for OECD Countries.* Heidelberg, Germany: Physica-Verlag.

Steiner, Susan (2007) 'Decentralisation and Poverty: Conceptual Framework and Application to Uganda', *Public Administration and Development* 27(2): 175–85.

Stoker, Gerry (2006) 'Comparative Local Governance', in R.A.W. Rhodes, Sarah A. Binder, and Bert A. Rockman, (eds) *The Oxford Handbook of Political Institutions.* Oxford: Oxford University Press.

Tendler, Judith (1997) *Good Government in the Tropics.* Baltimore, MD: the Johns Hopkins University Press.

Tiebout, Charles M. (1956) 'A Pure Theory of Local Expenditures', *The Journal of Political Economy* 64(5): 416–24.

Treisman, Daniel (2007) *The Architecture of Government: Rethinking Political Decentralization.* Cambridge: Cambridge University Press.

Turner, M., and Hulme, D. (1997) *Governance, Administration and Development: Making the State Work.* London: Macmillan.

United Cities and Local Governments (2008) *Decentralization and Local Democracy in the World: First Global Report.* Washington, DC: World Bank.

Uphoff, N. (1986) *Local Institutional Development: An Analytical Sourcebook with Cases.* West Hartford, CO.: Kumarian Press.

von Braun, Joachim and Grote, Ulrike (2002) 'Does Decentralization Serve the Poor?', in E. Ahmad, and Vito Tanzi, (eds) *Managing Fiscal Decentralization.* London: Routledge.

Weingast, Barry R. (1995) 'The Economic Role of Political Institutions: Market-Preserving Federalism and Economic Development', *The Journal of Law, Economics, & Organization* 11(1): 1–31.

Wibbels, Erik (2005) *Federalism and the Market: Intergovernmental Conflict and Economic Reform in the Developing World.* Cambridge: Cambridge University Press.

World Bank (1999) *World Development Report 1999/2000.* Washington, DC: World Bank.

World Bank (2008) *Decentralization in Client Countries: An Evaluation of World Bank Support, 1990–2007.* Washington, DC: World Bank.

32

Governing the Commons

Wai Fung Lam

INTRODUCTION

In his famous article in *Science*, Garret Hardin (1968) challenged readers to envision a hypothetical situation in which a pasture is open to all; an individual herder is free to decide the size of the herd he will bring in to graze in the pasture. In such a 'state of nature' situation, the incentive facing the herders is simple and straightforward. A rational herder will maximize his benefit by bringing in as large a herd as possible until the marginal cost of bringing in an additional animal is equal to the marginal benefit. Such a strategy will maximize the individual's short-term benefit, but it is not consistent with the pasture's maximum sustainable yield. If every herder adopts the strategy, the collective outcome will be overgrazing and eventually a total depletion of the pasture. The herder is surely aware of the predicament coming, but he has no incentive to restrain himself because his individual behavior by itself will not help preserve the pasture but will only permit other herders to bring in more of *their* animals and render his restraint foolish and self-destructive. Garrett Hardin vividly names the situation 'the tragedy of the commons' to denote both its unhappy ending and the remorselessness of the process involved.

Hardin's article triggered substantial interest in the commons in both practical policy and academic circles. For policymakers and policy analysts, the tragedy of the commons provides a neat metaphor that presumably captures the crux of the problem of resource management (Dasgupta, 1982; Hardin, 1998); it also hints at a simple diagnosis, which comes with clear and unambiguous policy implications (Munger, 2000; Weimer and Vining, 1999). As I shall elaborate in the following sections, the development of resource management policy around the world in the past few decades, particularly in the less-developed countries, has largely been informed by and hence has mirrored a search for solutions to the tragedy of the commons. Policy analysts also recognize that the commons problem pertains not only to resource management but also to a large array of policy problems involving goods or services that have the characteristics of a common-pool resource (CPR). A CPR is a natural or man-made resource from which it is difficult and costly to exclude potential users, and from which the units are subtractable in the sense that the units a user consumes will not be available to others (Oakerson, 1992; V. Ostrom and Ostrom, 1991). In addition to the more traditional CPRs, such as irrigation, pastures, fishery, and groundwater, the problem of the commons holds the key to addressing policy issues such as public budgets (Baden and Fort, 1980; Shepsle, 1983), transport systems (Waller, 1986), the atmosphere (Barnes, 2001; Harrison and Matson, 2001), and even the Internet (Hess and Ostrom, 2003; Kollock and Marc, 1996).

In academic circles, social scientists regard the commons problem as a conceptual window through which to visualize a question most fundamental to social sciences and the study of governance: How do individuals cope with problem-solving in the context of interdependency? The tragedy of the commons is in fact a specific type of social dilemma in which interdependent individuals are faced with incentives to choose independent actions that maximize their individual benefit but generate inefficient aggregate outcomes collectively (R. Hardin, 1982; E. Ostrom, 1990). This social dilemma is not necessarily the result of intentional malicious acts; as long as human interdependency exists, social dilemmas are always a possibility.

Building on the concept of social dilemmas as a theoretical foundation, research on the commons has explicitly or implicitly taken on an individualistic conception of human order. By an individualistic conception, I refer to the use of methodological individualism to explain macro-social phenomena in terms of the micro motives that activate individual action and interaction (Schelling, 1960). Governance, thus, is concerned with constituting rule–ruler–ruled relationships for collective action to cope with problems affecting the collective interest of communities of individuals (V. Ostrom, 1990, 1991, 1997). The process of governing is to arrive at collective choices that are authoritative and regarded as legitimate by members of the relevant community (Young, 2002). While governance in many circumstances involves the use of governmental

authority, it is not confined to government or the public sector. Very often it pertains to collective action beyond the governmental domain, involving actors in the private and non-profit sectors. Milward and Provan (2000) argue that the essence of governance is its focus on governing mechanisms that do not rest solely on the authority and sanctions of government.

An individualistic conception of governance is based on three premises.

First, because social phenomena are constituted by the action and interaction of individuals, a theory of governance has to take into account individual choices and actions and, more importantly, the ways they are aggregated into macro patterns.

Secondly, given that collective action and the process of governing are founded on individual choices and actions, a theory of governance must necessarily be grounded upon a set of assumptions about the cognitive architecture of human beings. These assumptions are indispensable to theoretical inference because they activate the causal link between the incentives embedded in a governing mechanism on the one hand, and individual action and interaction on the other.

Thirdly, collective action can take place in diverse settings at different jurisdiction levels, as well as at different spatial and temporal scales. Understanding how different contextual variables pose as opportunities and constraints to individual actors is of major importance. These contextual variables may pertain to the biophysical world, which is often composed of both natural and artificial elements; they may also pertain to social infrastructure, including institutions and communities of common understanding.

A research program regarding the commons thus has three major building blocks – a model of rationality, assumptions about the nature of the biophysical world, and a process of aggregation. In the remainder of this chapter, I trace the evolution and development of commons research with a view to reporting the major research findings and also deciphering the evolving theoretical foundation of the research. In particular, I identify key lessons that the research has offered to the daunting task of governing the commons, with a focus on the institutional design of governing mechanisms. To provide a more solid, focused discussion, I draw upon research on irrigation, a prototype CPR, to illustrate the applications and utilities of various theories of the commons.

A SEARCH FOR BENEVOLENT GOVERNMENT INTERVENTION

Theoretical foundation: rational men in a social dilemma

Conventional theories of the commons are constructed along the lines of Hardin's conception of the commons (Gordon, 1954; Hardin and Baden, 1977). Individuals are assumed to have clear and stable preferences, command good information about the resource and the environment, and have superb cognitive capacity in calculation and information-processing. These rational individuals will maximize their individual benefit by engaging in a meticulous cost–benefit calculus that takes into account the incentives embedded in a choice situation. These individuals are, however, assumed to be asocial; they see one another as no more than competing strangers in a maximization game.

The conventional theories make simplifying assumptions about the CPRs and the biophysical settings in which the rational individuals find themselves. They often presuppose that the particular commons problems at issue are well understood by these rational individuals, that the operation of the biophysical world can be adequately described and captured by a limited number of variables, that these variables are minimally related to one another in a linear manner, and that the configurations of these variables are relatively stable over time (Walker and Salt, 2006; Wilson, 2002; Winter, 2004). For the hypothetical pasture described by Hardin,

for example, all that we know is that the pasture is of a finite size, a renewable resource open to all, and that there are a large number of herders, who live in an institutional vacuum and make choices upon the sole motive of maximizing their short-term gain from grazing on the pasture. With such assumptions, Hardin presents a very thin model, one for which the tragedy of commons is probably the best prediction of what the collective outcome will be.

Analytically, the conventional theories focus on explicating the incentives embedded in social dilemmas, identifying the best strategies for the rational individuals in the dilemmas, and examining variables that may affect the incentives and hence the probability of success of collective action. Variables that have been studied in detail in commons research include the number of resource users, the degree of user heterogeneity, the production function of the resource, the ways that users relate to and communicate with one another, and the degree of closure of users' interactions (Agrawal, 2001; Baland and Platteau, 1996).

Theory in practice: a bureaucratic mode of governance

Policymakers of resource management were quick to embrace the conventional theories of the commons as the theoretical foundation for policy panaceas. Given that the users of a commons would only consider individual short-term benefit and be oblivious of long-term collective interest, governing the commons would require a government to impose ownership on the resource and regulate the behaviors of resource users (Ophuls, 1977). Presumably, a clear ownership structure would help specify who would receive the residual benefit of the resource; government regulation, on the other hand, would allow the internalization of the costs and benefits of the users' behavior. The broad assumption underlying the conventional theories is that users are unable to get out of social dilemmas by themselves, without help from a government. The bureaucratic approach to governance overlapped with mainstream social science and its view of the state in the postwar years (Jessop, 2006).

In irrigation management in the 1970s and 1980s, for example, the policy recipe for governing irrigation was to have governmental authorities play the benevolent roles of provider, regulator, and promoter of irrigation development (Barker et al., 1984; Coward, 1980). In practice, the policy recipe meant billions of dollars of investment by international donors and national governments, particularly in much of the less-developed world, to construct brand new large-scale irrigation infrastructure and to replace primitive systems in use by modern infrastructure and management (Easter, 1986; E. Ostrom, Schroeder and Wynne, 1993). Parallel to the infrastructure investment were programs of outright nationalization of the existing irrigation systems, the establishment of a strong, centralized irrigation bureaucracy, and the development of sophisticated technical guidelines for system operation and water delivery and allocation (Ascher and Healy, 1990; Chambers, 1988; Lam, 1996b).

By the early 1980s the viability of the bureaucratic mode of governance was subject to serious challenge. There was strong evidence it was not performing to expectations. In a study of more than 150 irrigation systems in Nepal, for example, Lam found that systems managed by government agencies were outperformed by systems run by farmers in terms of the physical condition of the infrastructure, water-delivery efficiency, and agricultural productivity (Lam, 1998; Lam, Lee, and Ostrom, 1997). Such patterns are not confined to Nepal but have been found repeatedly in many other countries. Research has identified the ineffectiveness and lack of motivation of irrigation officials to be the major reasons for the underperformance (Chambers, 1988; Lam, 2006b; Tang, 1992; Wade, 1982b). As Chambers (1988) pointed out perceptively, the theories that underlie a bureaucratic mode of irrigation governance

focused mainly on what governments should do to provide for irrigation and to regulate water users; the question as to the kind of incentive required to motivate irrigation officials to do their job is missing. Research has also found that a bureaucratic mode of governance, with its top-down focus, often contributes to the demise of social capital that farmers have accumulated through years of interaction (Hunt, 1989; Lam, 1996b; Uphoff, 1991; Wade, 1982b, 1987). It is a commonplace that well-intentioned efforts to introduce modern irrigation management have been followed by the rapid unraveling of local communities (Lam, 1998; Ostrom and Gardner, 1993).

The disappointing performance of the bureaucratic mode of irrigation governance led many to conclude that government is inherently inconsistent with effective irrigation governance. Some have gone so far as to argue that government is irrelevant and should be excluded from irrigation governance to the extent possible. Many studies of social capital and development, however, suggest that a state–society synergy is instrumental to materializing development potentials in various domains of collective action (Evans, 1996; Putnam, 1993); empirical studies of irrigation management in East Asia also suggest that synergy between farmers and government officials can improve irrigation performance (Dasgupta and Serageldin, 2000; Lam, 1996a, 2006a, 2006b; Moore, 1989; Wade, 1982a). In fact, in countries that have gone through the process of industrialization and become new members of the developed world, the role of the state in irrigation management has become even more important (Lam, 2001, 2006a). So perhaps the study of the governance of irrigation, and of the commons in general, should not center around the dichotomous choice of whether a bureaucratic mode of governance will work or not; rather, more attention should be given to the kinds of working relationships among resource managers and users that will be more likely to bring about good performance and the kinds of governing mechanisms needed to sustain the productive relationships (Curtis, 1991).

GETTING PROPERTY RIGHTS RIGHT

Creating the market

The crux of the commons problem is a discrepancy between individual rationality and aggregate efficiency. While advocates for a bureaucratic mode of governance focus their attention on how governments, by nationalization and regulation, can help align individual behavior to aggregate efficiency, policy analysts trained in economics, in particular property rights economics, have advocated a market approach that strives to cope with the discrepancy by internalizing the costs and benefits of a user's action in relation to the commons (Randall, 1981; Smith, 1981). The rise of the market approach to governance owed to rational-choice theory and, more generally, the application of ideas from neoclassical economics to solve problems in non-market settings (Friedman, 1996; Green and Shapiro, 1994). Like the bureaucratic approach, the market approach offers a simple, straightforward analytic solution: by putting in place private property rights that will in turn facilitate some sort of (pseudo-) market exchange, the owners of a CPR will have the incentive to make the best use of the resource they own. By internalizing externalities, the maximizing behavior of the owners will be aggregated into collective efficiency (Baumol and Oates, 1988).

As neat as it seems, the literature does not provide very clear guidance as to how this analytic solution can be translated into concrete policy or programs. In particular, what kind of governing mechanisms would be necessary for introducing and sustaining the pseudo market? Is it practicable – or even possible – to divide up a commons? If so, how can it be done? Theoretically, it is very easy to argue for privatizing a CPR and then assigning the ownership, but privatization is possible only if one assumes that the owner has the necessary technology and resources to fence and defend the resource and that the private property rights do not affect the operation of the resource. These assumptions, however, are questionable because they assume away the very problematics that a governing mechanism is supposed to cope with; they beg the question of how governance can be designed to cope with the problems of exclusion and appropriation inherent in a CPR (Rosegrant and Binswagner, 1994). In irrigation, for example, an owner of an irrigation system can theoretically fence the canals to prevent water theft; yet one will rarely find such complete fencing in the real world because putting up and maintaining a fence is simply not cost-effective. In fact, a CPR usually operates in a functionally intact manner where it is impossible to separate the resource from the broader environment or to divide the resource meaningfully. In an irrigation system, for example, it does not make much sense to divide an irrigation system and assign individual users private property rights to pieces of the system. The system is of value only if it functions as a coherent whole. In fact, in many circumstances the CPRs are considered so essential to the well-being of the larger community that privatizing the resource is deemed socially and politically unacceptable.

Theory in practice

Instead of privatizing the commons per se, most of the applications of the market approach have emphasized privatizing the rights of appropriation from the resources. A market-oriented governance structure usually combines governmental ownership with a system of exchange of the rights of appropriation (Dinar, Rosegrant and Meinzen-Dick, 1997). Governmental authorities play two important roles. First, by owning the resource, at least nominally, they are the ones who decide the maximum level of appropriation allowed and the initial allocation of the rights of appropriation to different users. Secondly, the governmental authorities serve as an arbitrator to monitor and enforce the exercise and exchange of the rights of appropriation among the users. Once an individual user is given rights, he is allowed to exercise them for his own use or to trade them to other actors who may value them more. The governmental authorities are there to make sure that the user can actually do what the rights entitle him to do. Presumably, such a combined governance structure can ensure the sustainability of the resource on the one hand, yet attain allocation efficiency on the other. In Taiwan, for example, all water resources are owned by the national government. Every year the government first determines the sectoral allocation of water on the basis of criteria that include the estimates of water availability, policy priorities and commitments, and prior norms; it then assigns water rights to various (corporate) water users such as the parastatal Irrigation Associations, city and township governments, and businesses and industrial corporations. While formally these corporate users cannot trade their rights (as they all belong to the government, at least *de jure*), they often engage in transfers of rights so as to maximize their benefit; these transfers constitute an informal water market.

Practical experience suggests that a market mode of governance is possible only if it is supported by an efficient use of governmental authority (Easter, Becker and Tsur, 1997; Gardner and Fullerton, 1968; Hartman and Seastone, 1970). In fact, a market mode of governance shares remarkable similarities with a bureaucratic mode of governance in several important aspects – both modes (1) make external governmental authorities the single owner of the resource, (2) rely on governmental authorities to determine the overall sustainable level of appropriation, and (3) portray resource users as a group of atomistic individuals striving to maximize individual short-term benefits. Given the similarities, it is not surprising that many problems that plague the bureaucratic mode of governance can also be found in the market mode.

Specifically, having a government serve as an guardian of collective interests – in many CPRs, it refers to the long-term sustainability of the resource – assumes a rather utopian degree of impartiality and autonomy in government policymakers. Such an assumption, however, is dubious. As many researchers and practitioners have observed, introducing a market mode of governance is itself a complicated process involving negotiation within wider contexts and preconditions such as political choices and cultural practices (Bauer, 1997; Mackenzie, 2008; Whitford and Clark, 2007). Maintaining the long-term sustainability of a resource is but one of the many concerns that policymakers take into account when they decide on the level of appropriation allowed and the ways the water rights are initially allocated (Dinar, Rosegrant and Meinzen-Dick, 1997; Randall, 1981). Even if the policymakers are all well-intentioned and act in good faith, they often do not have the information necessary to determine the sustainable level of appropriation (Marino and Kemper, 1999).

Another problem in introducing a market mode of governance concerns how to keep the transaction costs involved in the exchange of rights at a reasonably low level. In irrigation management, for example, practical experience suggests that a water market requires not only effective infrastructure allowing for efficient transfers of resource units (Tsur and Dinar, 1998) but also sufficient monitoring and enforcement by government officials or owner-users, as well as a clear common understanding among owner-users about the proper functioning of the market. Assuming that a water market can be created simply by having a government assign property rights to users begs the question of how a governing mechanism should be designed for collective action. As Marino and Kemper (1999) argue, a governing mechanism that provides a high degree of transparency and accountability among users is a necessary condition for a market mode of governance. An effective governing mechanism has to be able to provide proper facilities and venues with which water rights can be accurately measured and enforced, and knowledge and information about the resource can be effectively generated (Easter, Becker and Tsur 1997).

GOING BEYOND THE TRAGEDY OF THE COMMONS

By the early 1980s, it had become obvious that neither a bureaucratic mode nor a market mode of governance could serve as a policy panacea for governing the commons. The unsatisfactory performance of both modes prompted researchers and policy analysts to systematically take stock of existing ethnographic evidence as to what was actually happening in the field and to re-examine the theoretical foundation upon which the policy recommendations were made.

What is happening in the field?

Extensive empirical research on the commons challenged Hardin's pessimistic prediction and questioned whether the dichotomous choice between the state versus markets provides an adequate basis for understanding the governance of the commons.

First, there is substantial evidence that while the tragedy of the commons does happen in some circumstances, it is by no means the only possible outcome. Cases of success abound where resource users and managers are able to govern their resource in a most sustainable manner. These success stories can be found in a wide variety of policy domains ranging across irrigation, fisheries, groundwater, forestry, and grazing lands (Agrawal, 2001; National Research Council, 2002; V. Ostrom, 1990; Tang, 1992; Wade, 1988).

Secondly, in almost all of the successful cases, one can find a set of well-designed institutional arrangements that enable resource users and managers to engage in the process of governing – making rules that stipulate the actions and interactions pertaining to the use of the resource (Agrawal and Gupta, 2005; Lam, 1998; E. Ostrom, Gardner and Walker, 1994; V. Ostrom, 1990). The open-access situation that characterizes Hardin's hypothetical pasture is more an exception than a norm. More important, there is considerable diversity in the design of institutional arrangements; the simple dichotomy of the state versus markets can never hope to capture the diversity of these arrangements adequately.

Thirdly, while both the bureaucratic and market modes of governance are based upon the assumption that the users of a CPR are unable to cope with social dilemmas and have to be helped by an external authority (who either directly regulates the users' behavior or initiates and enforces a system of private property rights), evidence from many communities of resource users around the world has suggested that resource users not only cope with collective action problems but also are capable of crafting rules to govern their own systems. The potential of self-governance is by no means trivial. In irrigation, for example, some of the oldest, most long-enduring systems have been constructed, governed, and maintained by farmers themselves for long periods of time (Cernea, 1987; Shivakoti et al., 2005; Yoder, 1992). Research also suggests that, even in irrigation systems that are governed and managed under a bureaucratic mode, a certain degree of self-governance among farmers at the field level is essential to effective operation of the systems (Chambers, 1988; Lam, 1996a; Uphoff, 1991; Wade and Seckler, 1990).

From rational fools to fallible human beings

Hardin's analysis of the commons and conventional CPR theories are grounded on the assumption of a neoclassical rational man who is portrayed as having clear, definite preferences and possessing excellent information-processing capabilities. Recent research, however, has found that the neoclassical model is only one of the many possible portraits of a rational man (Ostrom, 2005). The model works well only in circumstances where the information required for decision-making is minimal; for an analysis of decision-making in a highly fluid, uncertain situation like a commons situation, whether and how individuals are able to learn is an important parameter that cannot simply be assumed away (Jones, 2003; Simon, 1962, 1986). A model of bounded rationality grounded upon an appreciation of the cognitive limitations of human beings would be more appropriate.

Instead of portraying the users of a commons to be a group of rational fools who have superb computational capacity for meticulous calculation but not the foresight to see beyond short-term individual benefit, the model of bounded rationality portrays fallible individuals who continuously struggle to learn from their mistakes to improve their understanding of their action situations and who always try to do the best they can. Fallible individuals have the capacity to change the structure of situations leading to social dilemmas, and they also have the foresight to develop institutional arrangements to attain mutual betterment (Ostrom, 2005).

GOVERNING THE COMMONS AS A SEARCH FOR EFFECTIVE DESIGN OF INSTITUTIONS

An Institutional Analysis and Development framework

Building upon a model of a boundedly rational, fallible man and a better appreciation of institutional diversity, the focus of the commons research in the last two decades has shifted towards explicating a theoretical logic of how institutions may help boundedly rational individuals cope with social dilemmas and identifying design principles for institutions that are conducive to effective governance of the commons. Like many important

concepts in social sciences, there are different definitions of the concept of institutions and hence contending approaches to institutional analysis and institutionalism (Bevir and Rhodes, 2001; Peters, 1999). Among these approaches, in the CPR literature, the Institutional Analysis and Development (IAD) framework developed by Elinor Ostrom and her colleagues at Indiana University has provided a particularly useful analytical basis for research and has been most influential. There are already excellent overviews of the IAD framework in the literature (Oakerson, 1992; Ostrom, 1986a, 1986b, 1999, 2005; Sproule-Jones, 1993); therefore, instead of repeating in detail what others have said about the IAD framework, it is sufficient here to highlight the major premises of the IAD framework that, in my judgment, constitute a useful way of looking at the issue of governing the commons.

In the IAD framework, institutions are defined as rules-in-use adopted by a community of individuals to regulate their repetitive interactions pertaining to the biophysical world of which a CPR is part. The rules-in-use are linguistic prescriptions that require, prohibit, or permit a range of action for individuals under particular situations. When individuals ponder their actions and strategies in relation to one another, they take the rules into their calculus. A focus on rules-in-use has several advantages. First, by differentiating behavioral patterns from the rules that give rise to them, an analyst is provided with an analytical leverage point at which he can explain patterns of behavior by examining how the rules affect individual action and interaction. From the IAD perspective, 'governance' is the aggregate patterns of rules–ruler–ruled relationships; to improve governance requires that appropriate rules are in place to get the relationships right.

Secondly, a focus on rules-in-use helps shift the analytical focus of governance from a choice of discrete types of governing mechanisms (the state versus markets) to an analysis of configurations of rules. An analyst is hard pressed to unpack such big concepts as the state and the market, which are often construed very differently by different researchers. But by focusing on the rules-in-use that constitute one mode of governance, the analyst is able to decipher the processes through which the governing mechanisms affect individual incentives and behaviors. Moreover, a focus on rules-in-use also provides a useful analytic scheme to describe and analyze institutional diversity within a particular type of governing mechanism. As irrigation specialists have long recognized, for example, a water market can be designed in different ways depending on specific circumstances; different designs will, in turn, bring about very different outcomes.

In the IAD framework, the unit of analysis is an action situation in which individuals make choices. Unlike some other approaches to institutional analysis that seek to identify and establish deterministic causal relationships between particular types of institutions and behavioral outcome, the IAD framework focuses on the incentives offered to individuals, which are constituted by a configuration of the rules-in-use, the biophysical world, and the communities of common understanding. Instead of trying to discover a panacea, or a blueprint, of institutional design, the IAD framework focuses on a logic of collective action and on how different designs of institutions, as rules-in-use, may impact on incentives and hence collective action. A particular rule that works well in one setting may not work at all in another circumstance.

Another major premise of the IAD framework is that rules are nested within one another. There are two types of 'nesting'. The first is analytical. Rules that stipulate opportunities and constraints for individual decision-making are operational rules. Operational rules are nested within a set of collective-choice rules that stipulate how the operational rules are made, amended, or abolished. The collective-choice rules are in turn nested within a set of constitutional-choice rules, which define the basic terms and conditions of the collective entity of individuals (Kiser and Ostrom, 1982; Sproule-Jones, 1993).

Taking a self-governing water-user group as an example, an allocation rule that says the amount of water distributed to a particular farmer is determined by the size of his field is an operational rule. Rules that describe the procedures through which the water allocation rule can be changed are collective-choice rules. A rule specifying that only individuals with particular attributes are allowed to join the water-user group is a constitutional-choice rule because it stipulates the basic terms and conditions of the collective endeavor. These rules operate in a configural way; an analyst will need to understand the rules and conditions of a particular situation well enough to decipher how the rules are nested within one another functionally.

It is a commonplace that the three levels of rules exist in a collective endeavor at a particular jurisdiction level. In the example of the water-user group, for example, it is the three layers of rules together that activate the operation of the group, a collective endeavor, at the local level. In any collective endeavor, individuals can make collective and constitutional choices; hence, the process of governing – crafting rules that stipulate the interaction of individuals – is not necessarily a government prerogative (Lam, 1998; Ostrom, 1989). Obviously, governing the commons concerns more than having an external authority impose rules on the users, whether it is government regulations or a private property rights system. Instead, it pertains to how institutions can be designed to enable the users to engage in the process of governing at different nodes of collective action.

The second type of nesting is concerned with how collective entities at different jurisdiction levels or scales of activities relate to one another. In irrigation, for example, while a water-user group is a collective entity around which water users organize collective action at the local level to deal with irrigation operation and maintenance at the field level, the group is usually nested within the larger water-management regime that attends to the broader watershed. The ways that institutions at different jurisdiction levels and scales are nested within one another affect not only the operation of the collective entities embedded therein but also the overall performance of the configuration of institutions.

A logic of institutional effect and principles of institutional design

Unlike the conventional theories of the commons that mainly focus on how users choose strategies of action in response to a given incentive structure, the IAD framework looks at the governance of the commons as an ongoing process that requires continual contribution from the users and recognizes the possibility of the users developing and modifying institutions to govern the resource. Based upon careful theoretical analysis and meta-analysis of a large number of empirical case studies, Elinor Ostrom and her colleagues have identified eight principles of institutional design for robust governance of CPRs: (1) clearly defined boundaries, (2) congruence between rules and physical conditions, (3) collective-choice arrangements, (4) monitoring, (5) graduated sanctions, (6) conflict-resolution mechanisms, (7) minimal recognition of rights to organize, and (8) nested enterprises (Ostrom, 1990, 2005).

Research has shown that institutions that are characterized by some or all of these design principles are better able to provide incentives for users of a commons to engage in collective action and, more important, to craft and continuously re-craft institutions (rules-in-use) to govern the commons. The theoretical logic underlying these design principles pertains to conditions that are conducive to collective action, which I now turn to.

Relating individual interest to collective interest

Collective actions among individuals are mostly grounded upon the furtherance of mutual interests; finding a common ground for mutual interests is a prerequisite to collective action. Whether a common ground can be attained depends, to a large extent, upon whether and how institutional arrangements relate the individuals' self-interests to collective action. The more gain an individual perceives that he will receive by participating in a collective effort, the more likely the individual is to contribute to the effort. In irrigation management, for example, it has been found that the existence of rules that clearly stipulate *how* consequences of collective endeavors will impact on *whom* have major significance in encouraging individuals to contribute to collective action. Many studies have found that well-defined boundary rules are a major component of irrigation governance and account for high levels of system performance (Ostrom, 1990, 1992; Tang, 1992; Yoder, 1986).

Awareness of interdependence

Individuals in an interdependent situation are not always able to see that they are interdependent, and more important, to understand the implications of interdependencies. Making interdependencies as conspicuous to individuals as possible is a necessary condition for encouraging individuals to contribute to collective action. Institutions affect the levels of awareness of interdependencies among individuals. Whether individuals are given opportunities to communicate, reason, and share information with one another on matters of mutual concerns is, to a significant extent, determined by the design of institutions. Users of a CPR are more likely to understand how their individual actions may affect others in the system if they are provided with an arena for discussion and resolving disagreement.

Shared mental models

Even in situations where individuals are aware of their interdependence, problems may still arise when the individuals have different cognitive orientations about how their individual interests can be best served in the interdependent situations. In a village where irrigation water is badly needed, for example, some farmers may consider the best way out is waiting for external assistance to construct a system for them. Others may prefer to organize themselves in order to construct a new irrigation system. Problems involved in the convergence of cognitive orientations and in relating cognitive orientations to problem-solving activities are not simply those of limited information, but of differences in the cognitive lenses adopted by individuals to make sense of the world (Denzau and North, 1993). Institutional arrangements that provide opportunities and channels for discourse can help bring individuals together to achieve a higher level of common understanding and hence to achieve a common ground for mutual interests. Such a common ground can then serve as the foundation for collective action.

Effective use of information

One major source of uncertainty in human interaction is the limited capability of human beings to gather and process information. Institutions can generate information that helps individuals to decipher their environment. In addition to information about the biophysical and technological aspects of the environment, information about possible actions is also of major importance. In an interdependent situation where the choice of each individual depends on the choices of others, a large repertoire of potential actions implies a high degree of uncertainty when individuals make choices. Institutions, by prescribing what kinds of actions are obliged, permitted, and forbidden in a particular setting, relate the actions of individuals to those of one another in a coordinated manner. By ruling in certain actions and ruling out certain others, institutions provide individuals with opportunities to cooperate with one another by restricting the range of strategies available for individual action (Ostrom, 1986a, 1986b). Such information allows individuals to form expectations about the actions of one another. These expectations, in turn, enable individuals to make better choices by taking the possible choices of others into consideration. In situations where

multiple equilibrium patterns of interaction exist, institutions enhance the predictability of individual actions by allowing the development of mutual expectations among individuals, These, in turn, decrease the uncertainty faced by individuals.

Coping with opportunism

Another source of uncertainty pertaining to human cooperation is the propensity of human beings to behave in an opportunistic manner. All kinds of institutional arrangements and agreements are by nature 'soft' constraints, meaning that their effects come about through their impact on the actions of individuals who can withdraw their adherence to these constraints if they choose to do so. To counteract the threat of opportunism, institutions can be crafted in such a way that the actions of individuals are made as visible to one another as possible. For instance, using a sequential rotation system in water distribution can make the actions of farmers taking water visible to those who are next in line (Ostrom, 1992); the existence of records showing the contributions of each farmer to maintenance can also expose any free-riding behavior to others.

Monitoring and sanctioning

Strategies available to individuals that are ruled in by institutions are usually the ones that maximize collective outcomes, but not individual payoffs. Consequently, the equilibrium pattern of interaction brought about by institutions usually hinges on quasi-voluntary compliance, where the compliance of an individual is contingent upon the compliance of others (Levi, 1988). Quasi-voluntary compliance can be sustained only if individuals expect gains from complying with the rules and perceive some likelihood that violators of the rules will be sanctioned. Under such a situation, the enforcement of rules needs to be supported by monitoring and sanctioning, which adds to the costs of violating the rules in the calculus of individuals. Elinor Ostrom (1990, 1992) finds that effective monitoring and sanctioning arrangements exist in most successful cases of irrigation governance and management. In these successful cases, sanctioning is usually not intended so much to punish as to assure individuals that their compliance will be consistent with the compliance of others.

Monitoring and punishing rule violations are always costly for punishers. To reduce the costs of monitoring and sanctioning, institutions can be so designed that individuals are able to engage in mutual monitoring and sanctioning activities in their daily interactions. When the scope of monitoring is diffused in this manner, the opportunities for violating rules without being detected can be greatly reduced.

Problem-solving in multiple levels

Due to the limited cognitive capability of human beings, no set of rules can take all future exigencies into consideration ahead of time. Unexpected contingencies may arise that make ineffective a set of rules that once produced productive relationships among individuals. Intelligent human beings are able, however, to learn continuously through acting and interacting with one another. This learning process enables them to gain experiences and information about the advantages and disadvantages of various institutional arrangements. Only when individuals are allowed to craft and modify institutional arrangements in light of what they have learned about existing institutional arrangements can they integrate new knowledge and information into their efforts to establish and maintain productive working relationships with one another. The question, then, turns to whether the collective-choice arrangements in a community can serve as arenas for individuals to engage in rule-crafting and rule-modifying activities.

Problems involved in irrigation governance and management are often very complex, and *a single* collective-choice arrangement is seldom able to carry out the 'tuning' process all by itself. Effective rule-crafting and rule-modifying activities usually involve *multiple* collective-choice arrangements at *multiple*

levels that correspond to multiple communities of interests. The existence of multiple collective-choice arrangements at multiple levels will not produce favorable outcomes, however, unless the relationships among the arrangements are designed to be complementary (Berkes, 2002; Lam, 1996a). Each collective-choice arrangement must possess a certain degree of autonomy so that individuals are given opportunities to utilize problem-solving capabilities and to integrate local time-and-place-specific information into collective-choice making.

THE WAY FORWARD: COPING WITH COMPLEXITY

Decades of research on the commons have accumulated a rich body of knowledge. We have not only gained a better understanding of the problems involved but also we have come a long way in studying institutions for governing the commons. We know what 'good' institutions look like and why, and we have in hand a set of principles of institutional design that can enhance good governance of the commons (Agrawal, 2001; Auer, 2006). In recent years there has been a growing appreciation of the dynamic complexity involved in the commons, which has prompted some scholars to adopt a social–ecological system (SES) approach to the study of the governance of the commons.

An SES is a system composed of biophysical and social components where individuals have self-consciously invested time and effort to develop some type of physical and institutional infrastructure that affects the way a system functions over time in coping with diverse external disturbances and internal problems (Anderies, Janssen and Ostrom, 2004; Berkes and Folke, 1998). For instance, an irrigation system composed of a resource (sources of water), physical infrastructure (storage and canals), actors who manage and appropriate from the resource (farmers and irrigation managers), and a governance structure that regulates the action and interaction of the actors (irrigation institutions) is an SES. An SES has several interesting features and characteristics. First, an SES is a complex system composed of many mutually adapting actors and biophysical elements whose patterns of interaction produce emergent systemic properties and behavior (Camazine et al., 2001; Carlson and Doyle, 2002). Secondly, the process of aggregation of the behavior of individual units into systemic behavior is often non-linear and combinatorial. Trivial changes at the individual level may trigger chains of effects that lead to substantive transformation and even surprises at the systemic level. Thirdly, an SES is activated by human beings who have the ability to think and foresee action-outcome links, acquire and appreciate the value and meaning of action, and learn and conduct trial-and-error experiments. The architecture of human cognition takes on an important role in understanding human choice and action in a complex system (Jones, 2003). Fourthly, an SES is a hierarchical system, which is defined by Simon (1962) as composed of interrelated subsystems, each of which is hierarchic in structure until some lowest level of elementary subsystem is reached. Structures and processes of different scales on different levels tend to have very different spatial and temporal attributes, and they tend to affect one another. Fifthly, a dynamic SES defies a static assessment of its performance. The continual evolution of an SES, generated by the changing environment and also its own internal dynamics, suggests that the viability of the SES can be assessed and construed only in a dynamic manner. Instead of focusing on an SES's performance, however it is defined, at a particular point in time, it is more appropriate to look at its robustness, the system's ability to continue to attain some desired outcomes.

These features of an SES point to a new direction in thinking about how to govern the commons. Instead of striving for policy panaceas that presumably can cure all, efforts to understand and govern the commons should be based on a diagnostic approach that focuses on identifying variables that affect the incentives for the interaction among the individuals involved and on the interplay between the social and ecological components of the particular system (Dietz, Ostrom and Stern, 2003; Ostrom, Janssen and Anderies, 2007). Recent research has identified six broad variables that affect the interaction and hence outcomes: the attributes of the resource system, the attributes of the resource units, the characteristics of resource users, the governance structure (particularly the design of the institutions governing the behavior of the users), the macro social–political systems, and the broader ecological system in which the resource is nested. Depending on particular situations, the analyst may focus on some of these broad variables and further unpack them to identify lower-tier variables for more in-depth analysis and empirical research (Lam and Ostrom, 2010; Ostrom, 2007). For example, the lower-tier variables for 'characteristics of resource users' may include the number of and degree of heterogeneity among the resource users. In an overview of the extant CPR literature, Agrawal (2001) has identified more than 30 of these lower-tier variables.

Conceptualizing a CPR as an SES, research on the commons has focused on how institutions can be designed to allow resource users and managers to cope with the dynamics in the SES and thereby contribute to the robustness of the system. Several lessons from the research are particularly important.

First, the robust governance of a CPR is built upon institutions that allow effective coordination of the activities of a multitude of resource users, enhance the development and sustenance of a repertoire of ideas, and nest the problem-solving efforts of various scopes and scales in a complementary manner. These institutions enable individuals and organizations at different levels to engage in continuous learning and adaptation that, in turn, facilitates the adaptation of the systems to the changing environment.

Secondly, institutions exist at particular historical junctures characterized by specific temporal and contextual features. They are a product not only of rational institutional choices but also of the opportunities and constraints embedded in particular historical contexts. Any efforts to create institutional recipes for effective management of the commons that operate on the assumption that the recipes can be easily transplanted to other settings are doomed to fail (Evans, 2004; Meinzen-Dick, 2007).

Thirdly, the SES approach argues that the process of institutional change and development can be an emergent process over which individual agents have very little control. The trajectory of institutional change is highly sensitive to the initial condition of the institutions, the combinatorial nature of the factors, and the way that units are linked to one another temporally and laterally.

REFERENCES

Agrawal, A. (2001) 'Common Property Institutions and Sustainable Governance of Resources', *World Development* 29: 1649–72.

Agrawal, A. and Gupta, K. (2005) 'Decentralization and Participation: The Governance of Common Pool Resources in Nepal's Terai', *World Development* 33(7): 1101.

Anderies, J., Janssen, M. and Ostrom, E. (2004) 'A Framework to Analyze the Robustness of Social-Ecological Systems from an Institutional Perspective', *Ecology and Society* 9(1): 18. http://www.ecologyandsociety.org/vol9/iss1/art18.

Ascher, William and Healy, Robert (1990) *Natural Resource Policy Making in Developing Countries*. Durham, NC: Duke University Press.

Auer, M. (2006) 'Contexts, Multiple Methods, and Values in the Study of Common-pool Resources', *Journal of Policy Analysis and Management* 25(1): 215.

Baden, J. and Fort, R.D. (1980) 'The Federal Budget as a Common Pool Resource: The Development of a Predatory Bureaucracy', in J. Baden (ed), *Earth Day Reconsidered*. Washington, DC: The Heritage Foundation.

Baland, Jean-Marie and Platteau, Jean-Phillipe (1996) *Halting Degradation of Natural Resources: Is There a Role for Rural Communities?* Oxford: Clarendon Press.

Barker, Randolph, Coward, E. Walter, Jr, Levine, Gilbert, and Small, Leslie E. (1984) *Irrigation Development in Asia: Past Trends and Future Directions*. Ithaca, NY: Cornell University Press.

Barnes, P. (2001) *Who Owns the Sky? Our Common Assets and the Future of Capitalism*. Washington, DC: Island Press.

Bauer, C.J. (1997) 'Bringing Water Markets Down to Earth: The Political Economy of Water Rights in Chile, 1976–95', *World Development* 25(5): 639–56.

Baumol, William J. and Oates, W.E. (1988) *The Theory of Environmental Policy*. Cambridge: Cambridge University Press.

Berkes, F. (2002) 'Cross-scale Institutional Linkages: Perspectives from the Bottom Up', in E. Ostrom, T. Dietz, N. Dolsak, et al. (eds), *The Drama of the Commons*. Washington, DC: National Academy Press.

Berkes, F. and Folke, C. (1998) *Linking Social and Ecological Systems: Management Practices and Social Mechanisms for Building Resilience*. Cambridge: Cambridge University Press.

Bevir, M. and Rhodes, R.A.W. (2001) 'A Decentered Theory of Governance: Rational Choice, Institutionalism, and Interpretation', *Institute of Governmental Studies* Paper WP 2001-10.

Camazine, S., Deneubourg J.L., Franks, N.R., et al. (2001) *Self-Organization in Biological Systems*. Princeton, NJ: Princeton University Press.

Carlson, J.M. and Doyle, J. (2002) 'Complexity and Robustness', *Proceedings of the National Academy of Science* 99(Suppl 1): 2538–45.

Cernea, Michael M. (1987) 'Farmer Organization and Institution Building for Sustainable Development', *Regional Development Dialogue* 8(2):1–24. Nagoya, Japan: United Nations Center for Regional Development.

Chambers, Robert (1988) *Managing Canal Irrigation: Practical Analysis from South Asia*. Cambridge: Cambridge University Press.

Coward, E. Walter, Jr (ed.) (1980) *Irrigation and Agricultural Development in Asia*. Ithaca, NY: Cornell University Press.

Curtis, Donald (1991) *Beyond Government: Organisations for Common Benefit*. London: Macmillan.

Dasgupta, P.S. (1982) *The Control of Resources*. Oxford: Blackwell.

Dasgupta, P.S. and Serageldin, I. (2000) *Social Capital: A Multifaceted Perspective*. Washington, DC: The World Bank.

Denzau, Arthur T. and North, Douglass C. (1993) 'Shared Mental Models: Ideologies and Institutions'.

Working Paper. Center for the Study of Political Economy. Washington University (St. Louis).

Dietz, T., Ostrom, E. and Stern, P.C. (2003). 'The Struggle to Govern the Commons', *Science* 302: 1907–12.

Dinar, A., Rosegrant, M.W. and Meinzen-Dick, R. (1997) 'Water Allocation Mechanisms: Principles and Examples'. World Bank, Agriculture and Natural Resources Department.

Easter, K. William (1986) *Irrigation Investment, Technology, and Management Strategies for Development.* Studies in Water Policy and Management, No. 9. Boulder, CO: Westview Press.

Easter, K.W., Becker, N. and Tsur, Y. (1997) 'Economic Mechanisms for Managing Water Resources: Pricing, Permits, and Markets', in A.K. Biswas (ed.), *Water Resources: Environmental Planning, Management and Development.* New York: McGraw-Hill.

Evans, Peter B. (1996) 'Government Action, Social Capital and Development: Reviewing the Evidence on Synergy', *World Development* 24(6): 1119–32.

Evans, Peter B. (2004) 'Development as Institutional Change: The Pitfalls of Monocropping and the Potentials of Deliberation', *Studies in Comparative International Development* 39(4): 30–52.

Friedman, Jeffrey (ed.) (1996) *The Rational Choice Controversy.* New Haven, CT: Yale University Press.

Gardner, B.D. and Fullerton, H.H. (1968) 'Transfer Restrictions and Misallocations of Irrigation Water', *American Journal of Agricultural Economics* 50: 556–71.

Gordon, H. Scott (1954) 'The Economic Theory of a Common Property Resource: The Fishery', *Journal of Political Economy* 62: 124–42.

Green, Donald P. and Shapiro, Ian (1994) *Pathologies of Rational Choice Theory: A Critique of Applications in Political Science.* New Haven, CT: Yale University Press.

Hardin, Garrett (1968) 'The Tragedy of the Commons', *Science* 162 (December): 1243–8.

Hardin, Garrett (1998) 'Extensions of "The Tragedy of the Commons"', *Science* 280: 682–3.

Hardin, Garrett and Baden, John (1977) *Managing the Commons.* San Francisco, CA: W.H. Freeman.

Hardin, Russell (1982) *Collective Action.* Baltimore, MD: Johns Hopkins University Press.

Harrison, J. and Matson, P. (2001) 'The Atmospheric Commons', in J. Burger, E. Ostrom, R.B. Norgaard, D. Policansky and B.D. Goldstein (eds), *Protecting the Commons: A Framework for Resource Management in the Americas.* Washington, DC: Island, Press.

Hartman, L.M. and Seastone, D. (1970) *Water Transfer: Economic Efficiency and Alternative Institutions.* Baltimore, MD: Johns Hopkins Press.

Hess, C. and Ostrom, E. (2003) 'Artifacts, and Facilities: Information as a Common-pool Resource', *Law and Contemporary Problems* 66(1/2): 111–45.

Hunt, Robert (1989) 'Appropriate Social Organization? Water User Associations in Bureaucratic Canal Irrigation Systems', *Human Organization* 48(1): 79–90.

Jessop, Bob (2006) 'The State and State-Building', in R.A.W. Rhodes, Sarah A. Binder and Bert A. Rockman (eds), *The Oxford Handbook of Political Institutions.* Oxford: Oxford University Press; pp. 111–30.

Jones, Bryan D. (2003) 'Bounded Rationality and Political Science: Lessons from Public Administration and Public Policy', *Journal of Public Administration Research and Theory* 13(4): 395–412.

Kiser, Larry L. and Ostrom, Elinor (1982) 'The Three Worlds of Action: A Metatheoretical Synthesis of Institutional Approaches', in Elinor Ostrom (ed.), *Strategies of Political Inquiry.* Beverly Hills, CA: Sage; pp. 179–222.

Kollock, P. and Marc, S. (1996) 'Managing the Virtual Commons: Cooperation and Conflict in Computer Communities', in S. Herring (ed.), *Computer-Mediated Communication: Linguistic, Social, and Cross-cultural Perspectives.* Amsterdam: John Betjamins.

Lam, Wai Fung (1996a) 'Institutional Design of Public Agencies and Coproduction: A Study of Irrigation Associations in Taiwan', *World Development* 24(6): 1039–54.

Lam, Wai Fung (1996b) 'Improving the Performance of Small-Scale Irrigation Systems: The Effects of Technological Investments and Governance Structure on Irrigation Performance in Nepal', *World Development* 24(8): 1301–15.

Lam, Wai Fung (1998) *Governing Irrigation Systems in Nepal: Institutions, Infrastructure, and Collective Action.* Oakland: CA: Institute for Contemporary Studies (ICS) Press.

Lam, Wai Fung (2001) 'Coping with Change: A Study of Local Irrigation Institutions in Taiwan', *World Development* 29(9): 1569–92.

Lam, Wai Fung (2006a) 'Foundations of a Robust Social–Ecological System: Irrigation Institutions in Taiwan', *Journal of Institutional Economics* 2(2): 1–24.

Lam, Wai Fung (2006b) 'Designing Institutions for Irrigation Management: Comparing Irrigation Agencies in Nepal and Taiwan', *Property Management* 24(2): 162–78.

Lam, Wai Fung and Ostrom, Elinor (2010). 'Analyzing the Dynamic Complexity of Development Interventions: Lessons from an Irrigation Experiment in Nepal', *Policy Sciences* 43: 1–25.

Lam, Wai Fung, Lee, Myungsuk and Ostrom, Elinor (1997) 'The Institutional Analysis and Development Framework: Application to Irrigation Policy in Nepal', in Derek W. Brinkerhoff (ed.), *Policy Analysis Concepts and Methods: An Institutional and Implementation Focus*. JAI Policy Studies and Developing Nation Series, Vol 15. Greenwich, CT: JAI Press; pp. 53–85.

Levi, Margaret (1988) *Of Rule and Revenue*. Berkeley, CA: University of California Press.

Mackenzie, J. (2008) 'Watered Down: The Role of Public Participation in Australian Water Governance', *Social Alternatives* 27(3): 8.

Marino, M. and Kemper, K.E. (1999) *Institutional Frameworks in Successful Water Markets: Brazil, Spain, and Colorado, USA*. Washington, DC: The World Bank.

Meinzen-Dick, R. (2007) 'Beyond Panaceas in Water Institutions', *Proceedings of the National Academy of Sciences* 104(39): 15200–5.

Milward, H. Brinton and Provan, Keith G. (2000) 'Governing the Hollow State', *Journal of Public Administration Research and Theory* 10(2): 359–79.

Moore, M. (1989) 'The Fruits and Fallacies of Neoliberalism: The Case of Irrigation Policy', *World Development* 17(11): 1733–50.

Munger, Michael C. (2000) *Analyzing Policy: Choices, Conflicts, and Practices*. New York: W.W. Norton.

National Research Council (2002) *The Drama of the Commons*. Washington, DC: National Academy Press.

Oakerson, Ronald J. (1992) 'Analyzing the Commons: A Framework', in Daniel W. Bromley (ed.), *Making the Commons Work: Theory, Practice, and Policy*. San Francisco, CA: ICS Press; pp. 41–59.

Ophuls, W. (1977) *Ecology and the Politics of Scarcity*. San Francisco, CA: Freeman.

Ostrom, Elinor (1986a) 'A Method of Institutional Analysis', in Franz-Xaver Kaufmann, Giandomenico Majone and Vincent Ostrom (eds), *Guidance, Control, and Evaluation in the Public Sector*. Berlin: de Gruyter; pp. 459–75.

Ostrom, Elinor (1986b) 'An Agenda for the Study of Institutions', *Public Choice* 48: 3–25.

Ostrom, Elinor (1989) 'Microconstitutional Change in Multiconstitutional Political Systems', *Rationality and Society* 1(1): 11–50.

Ostrom, Elinor (1990) *Governing the Commons: The Evolution of Institutions for Collective Action*. Cambridge: Cambridge University Press.

Ostrom, Elinor (1992) *Crafting Institutions for Self-Governing Irrigation Systems*. San Francisco, CA: ICS Press.

Ostrom, Elinor (1999) 'Institutional Rational Choice: An Assessment of the Institutional Analysis and Development Framework', in Paul A. Sabatier (ed.), *Theories of the Policy Process*. Boulder, CO: Westview Press; pp. 35–71.

Ostrom, Elinor (2005) *Understanding Institutional Diversity*. Princeton, NJ: Princeton University Press.

Ostrom, Elinor (2007) 'A Diagnostic Approach for Going Beyond Panaceas', *Proceedings of the National Academy of Sciences* 104: 15181–7.

Ostrom, Elinor and Gardner, Roy (1993) 'Coping with Asymmetries in the Commons: Self-governing Irrigation Systems Can Work', *Journal of Economic Perspectives* 7(4): 93–112.

Ostrom, Elinor, Schroeder, Larry and Wynne, Susan (1993) *Institutional Incentives and Sustainable Development: Infrastructure Policies in Perspective*. Boulder, CO: Westview Press.

Ostrom, Elinor, Gardner, Roy and Walker, James (1994) *Rules, Games, and Common-Pool Resources*. Ann Arbor, MI: University of Michigan Press.

Ostrom, Elinor, Janssen, M. and Anderies, J. (2007) 'Going beyond Panaceas', *Proceedings of the National Academy of Sciences* 104: 15176–8.

Ostrom, Vincent (1990) 'Problems of Cognition as a Challenge to Policy Analysts and Democratic Societies', *Journal of Theoretical Politics* 2 (July): 243–62.

Ostrom, Vincent (1991) 'Some Ontological and Epistemological Puzzles in Policy Analysis'. Working paper. Bloomington, IN: Indiana University, Workshop in Political Theory and Policy Analysis.

Ostrom, Vincent (1997) *The Meaning of Democracy and the Vulnerability of Democracies: A Response to Tocqueville's Challenge*. Ann Arbor, MI: University of Michigan Press.

Ostrom, Vincent and Ostrom, Elinor (1991) 'Public Goods and Public Choices: The Emergence of Public Economies and Industry Structures', in Vincent Ostrom (ed.), *The Meaning of American Federalism*. Oakland, CA: ICS Press; pp. 163–98.

Peters, B. Guy (1999) *Institutional Theory in Political Science: The 'New Institutionalism'*. London: Pinter.

Putnam, Robert D. (1993) *Making Democracy Work: Civic Traditions in Modern Italy*. Princeton, NJ: Princeton University Press.

Randall, A. (1981) 'Property Entitlements and Pricing Policies for a Maturing Water Economy', *Australian Journal of Agricultural Economics* 25: 195–212.

Rosegrant, M.W. and Binswanger, H.P. (1994) 'Markets in Tradable Water Rights: Potential for Efficiency Gains in Developing Country Water Resource Allocation', *World Development* 22(11): 1613–25.

Schelling, Thomas C. (1960) *The Strategy of Conflict.* Oxford: Oxford University Press.

Shepsle, K.A. (1983) 'Overgrazing the Budgetary Commons: Incentive-Compatible Solutions to the Problem of Deficits', in L. Meyer (ed.), *The Economic Consequences of Government Deficits.* Boston: Kluwer-Nijhoff.

Shivakoti, Ganesh, Vermillion, Douglass, Lam, Wai Fung, et al. (eds) (2005) *Asian Irrigation Systems in Transition: Responding to the Challenges Ahead.* New Dehli: Sage.

Simon, H. (1962) 'The Architecture of Complexity', *Proceedings of the American Philosophical Society* 106: 467–82.

Simon, H. (1986) 'Rationality in Psychology and Economics', in Robin M. Hogarth and Melvin W. Reder (eds), *Rational Choice: The Contrast between Economics and Psychology.* Chicago: University of Chicago Press; pp. 25–40.

Smith, Robert J. (1981) 'Resolving the Tragedy of the Commons by Creating Private Property Rights in Wildlife', *CATO Journal* 1: 439–68.

Sproule-Jones, Mark (1993) *Governments at Work: Canadian Parliamentary Federalism and Its Public Policy Effects.* Toronto: University of Toronto Press.

Tang, Shui Yan (1992) *Institutions and Collective Action: Self-Governance in Irrigation.* San Francisco, CA: ICS Press.

Tsur, Y. and Dinar, A. (1998) 'On the Relative Efficiency of Alternative Methods for Pricing Irrigation Water and Their Implementation', *World Bank Economic Review* 11.

Uphoff, Norman (1991) *Managing Irrigation: Analyzing and Improving the Performance of Bureaucracies.* New Delhi: Sage.

Wade, Robert (1982a) *Irrigation and Agricultural Politics in South Korea.* Boulder, CO: Westview Press.

Wade, Robert (1982b) 'The System of Administrative and Political Corruption: Canal Irrigation in South India', *Journal of Development Studies* 18(3): 287–328.

Wade, Robert (1987) 'Managing Water Managers: Deterring Expropriation or Equity as a Control Mechanism', in W.R. Jordan (ed.), *Water and Water Policy in World Food Supplies.* College Station, TX: Texas A&M University Press; pp. 177–83.

Wade, Robert (1988) *Village Republics: Economic Conditions for Collective Action in South India.* Cambridge: Cambridge University Press.

Wade, Robert and Seckler, David (1990) 'Priority Issues in the Management of Irrigation systems', in R.K. Sampath and Robert A. Young (eds), *Social, Economic, and Institutional Issues in Third World Irrigation Management.* Boulder, CO: Westview Press; pp. 13–30.

Walker, Brian and Salt, David (2006) *Resilience Thinking: Sustaining Ecosystem and People in a Changing World.* Washington, DC: Island Press.

Waller, P.F. (1986) 'The Highway Transportation System as a Commons: Implications for Risk Policy', *Accident Analysis and Prevention* 18(5): 417–24.

Weimer, David and Vining, Aiden (1999) *Policy Analysis: Concepts and Practice*, 3rd edn. Upper Saddle River, NJ: Prentice Hall.

Whitford, A.B. and Clark, B.Y. (2007) 'Designing Property Rights for Water: Mediating Market, Government, and Corporation Failures', *Policy Science* 40: 335–51.

Wilson, James (2002) 'Scientific Uncertainty, Complex Systems, and the Design of Common-pool Institutions', in National Research Council (ed.), *The Drama of the Commons.* Washington, DC: National Academy Press; pp. 327–60.

Winter, Sidney G. (2004) 'The "Easy Problem" Problem', in Mie Augier and James G. March (eds), *Models of a Man: Essays in Memory of Herbert A. Simon.* Cambridge, MA: MIT Press; pp. 297–303.

Yoder, Robert (1992) *Performance of the Chhattis Mauja Irrigation System: A Thirty-five Hundred Hectare System Built and Managed by Farmers in Nepal.* Colombo, Sri Lanka: International Irrigation Management Institute.

Young, Oran R. (2002) 'Institutional Interplay: The Environmental Consequences of Cross-scale Interactions', in National Research Council (ed.), *The Drama of the Commons.* Washington, DC: National Academy Press; pp. 263–92.

33

Regulation

Marian Döhler

INTRODUCTION

At first sight, regulation appears to be a fairly simple concept of authoritative rules, imposed on businesses to correct market failures of various kinds (Mitnick, 1980). More generally, it could be regarded as an alternative to public ownership. Both were true for its early incarnation in the late nineteenth-century United States, when the Interstate Commerce Commission was founded to regulate commercial trade between the states. Ever since, regulation has expanded into new economic and social domains, travelled even into countries with a more activist state (ownership) tradition, and gone beyond its command-and-control image into a mixture of government-enforced rules, and economic and social self-regulation. It has also evolved from a purely national into a transnational activity, involving large numbers of public and private actors. Nowadays, regulation is part of a complex web of transnational governance in which nation-states, inter-national organizations, and private actors – ranging from multinational firms to non-governmental organizations (NGOs) – participate to set standards and enforce rules to regulate markets, as well as technical or product-related risks. Despite its spread,

the concept has never been exempt from criticism. Since scientific interest in regula-tion gained momentum in the 1950s, political scientists, and economists on a broader scale, have pointed out shortcomings, unintended consequences, and inefficiencies. This debate came to full force with the rise of the 'Reagan revolution' that promised to cut down big government and to achieve regulatory 'relief'. However, instead of reducing or even elimi-nating regulation, additional layers of cost–benefit analysis and external scrutiny were imposed on agencies, thus giving rise to a new debate. The goal is no longer restricted to scaling-down the size of regulation, but rather has expanded to making it more effi-cient. 'Regulatory reform' has itself evolved into a new intellectual growth industry, including lobby groups, international organizations – the European Union (EU), Organization for Economic Co-operation and Development (OECD), International Monetary Fund (IMF), and the World Bank – independent and partisan think-tanks, as well as the economics press. The story to be unfolded in this chapter is therefore about the evolution of regulation, not necessarily to domination, but from a simple policy tool to a complex public–private affair, from a national to a transnational policy, and from

straightforward criticism to more complicated economic and political pay-offs.

REGULATION AS A CONCEPT

For almost a century, regulation was associated with politics in the United States.
Regulation appeared as a form of state
intervention, enforced by specialized agencies, situated 'at arm's length' from direct
political control. The special relevance
assigned to regulatory agencies stems from
their broad discretionary mandate, including
a rule-making competence (Kerwin, 1999)
which in the European model of separation
of powers would be reserved for parliament
(Pünder, 2009). Typical examples are the
Securities and Exchange Commission (SEC),
created in 1934 to control the conduct of
traders, especially to prevent insider trading,
or the Food and Drug Administration (FDA),
created in 1938 and charged with authorizing
pharmaceutical drugs and controlling drug
risks. No wonder that most scholars doing
research on this subject were Americans and,
therefore, reinforced the 'born in the
USA' image of regulation. Eminent political
scientists such as Pendleton Herring (1936),
Samuel P. Huntington (1952), or Marver H.
Bernstein (1955) contributed to the first wave
of research. Huntington and Bernstein, in
particular, offered rather critical views.
Bernstein introduced a highly influential
theorem known as the 'life cycle' of regulatory agencies. As 'a general pattern of evolution' (Bernstein, 1955: 74), four stages in the
historical development of regulatory agencies are identified: gestation, youth, maturity,
and old age. During this life cycle an agency
is transformed from hopeful expectations of
serving the public interest into a passive
underperforming bureaucracy that is losing
political support and thus triggering a new
drive for regulation. The life cycle concept
gave birth to several 'capture' theories,
according to which regulators are pressured
by external groups until they move away

from their original role and please the
industry they were supposed to regulate in
the first place.

This rather disappointing perception was
based on sketchy empirical data (cf. Sabatier,
1975), but also reflects the fact that regulation is often regarded as a less-than-ideal
solution for correcting market failures.
Regulatory measures are under constant
pressure to justify their very existence, and
therefore generate political conflict in the
United States. There is a different attitude in
Europe concerning the level of conflict as
well as the role of administrative law. This is
reflected in the US Administrative Procedure
Act (APA) of 1946 which provides the basic
information, participation, and accountability rules all agencies have to comply with.
The APA resulted from the political struggle
between Democratic New Deal proponents
and Republican opponents, both of whom
tried to hardwire their contradictory preferences into law (McCubbins, Noll and
Weingast 1999). More generally, administrative procedures, especially if stipulating participation and hearing rights for external
groups, evolved as equivalents to the
more detailed European style of legislative
programming. This also explains why administrative law in Europe is perceived as a set of
purely legal provisions securing judicial
protection for individuals, and remains at a
clear distance from politics.

Whereas the early contributions on agency
capture remained influential, Theodore
Lowi's famous typology of policies became
equally important for a grasp of the meaning
of regulation. According to Lowi there are
three types of public policies: distributive,
redistributive, and regulatory (1964: 713).[1]
Among the distinguishing features are the
degree of conflict between political actors
and the likelihood of coercion being necessary to enforce a policy. In political science
the legacy of this typology was to compare
regulation with distributive and redistributive
policies, i.e. to focus on rule enforcement aiming at controlling the behavior
of business firms and other private actors.

As opposed to other scientific accounts, this typology contained no criticism per se. Regulation could be perceived as a 'business as usual' category of public policy. But the continuing distrust of the results brought in a more powerful group of analysts whose impact went far beyond academics.

Since the early 1970s liberal-market economists have become highly influential, especially in explaining the origins and shortcomings of regulation. In contrast to Bernstein, who focused on the internal sphere of agencies, scholars linked to the law and economics school of thought at the University of Chicago put economic self-interest at the heart of a new theory of regulation. Nobel Prize winner George J. Stigler rejected the idea that regulation could serve the public interest, because 'as a rule, regulation is acquired by the industry and is designed and operated primarily for its benefits' (Stigler, 1971: 3). Whereas Bernstein's life cycle attributes an effective regulatory mandate to agencies at least during their 'youth', the Chicago School regards the lawmaking process as already being captured by industry interests. Regulation is wrongly programmed from the outset. Richard A. Posner, another eminent Chicago scholar who later became a judge in the US court of appeals, continued this line of thought by applying the economic theory of cartels to explain regulatory origin (Posner, 1974). Examples are the motor carrier industry or licensed occupations, who both manage to control market entry, resulting in protection from competitors. Suffice it here to mention that this family of theories is still popular among economists, although nowadays based on more sophisticated assumptions and modeling.[2] The mixture of economic reasoning and – if only implicit – distrust of government intervention in business produced the intellectual context for debating regulation as 'a system of public, bureaucratic coercion deliberately sought by firms to consolidate cartelization and market power' (Schneiberg and Bartley, 2008: 34). This shaped its image even outside the United States.

During the 1970s, regulatory policies took a new direction that did not fit easily into the previous wisdom. Contrary to theoretical expectations, many agencies and commissions reversed their policies and injected heavy doses of competition into economic sectors such as air travel, telephony, and electricity, and even more surprisingly, they enforced consumer-friendly regulations against the resistance of industry. In a widely-quoted book, edited by James Q. Wilson, the central message was 'that there *is* a politics of regulation' (Wilson, 1980: 357). This may sound trivial, but in fact was a rejection of a then-prevailing view of regulation as a predetermined government activity that inevitably ends with business or industry dominance. The case studies in the book showed a much more varied picture, and supported the assumption that there is no single path into which regulation is locked, but rather a variety of political contests with different results. Instead of imposing new rules and restrictions on industry, some agencies even started to 'deregulate' formerly uncompetitive sectors. Among the prominent cases was the deregulation of air travel, leading to more competition and lower air fares. This was probably one of the triggering events adding a 'regulation *for* competition' to the already existing 'regulation *of* competition'; the former not only became a central idea in creating a single European market (Young, 2006) but also made pro-activism an attribute of regulation. The turn to deregulation was not a death blow to capture theories, mainly because contrary cases persisted, but it demonstrated that regulation is not simply motivated by one category of interests and beneficiaries. It still has various tasks and is open to various interests, and thus to fluctuating fortunes.

Aside from these rather historical traits of the concept, a peculiarity of the American regulatory style was aptly described as 'adversarial legalism' (Kagan, 2001). Robert Kagan, who coined this phrase, stresses four distinct characteristics: (1) due to complicated and thus contestable rules, regulation in the United States is heavily legalistic; (2) it is strongly based on formal sanctions for enforcement; (3) it is adversarial, as both regulators and the regulated strive for judicial dispute settlement; and (4) each step of regulatory politics (lawmaking, appointing regulators, monitoring, etc.) is vulnerable to political conflict, because all participants try to hardwire their political preferences (cf. Kagan, 2001: 187). It is still common for US regulators to measure their success in numbers of legal actions taken or the amount of fines. Kagan's observation supports previous research on policy styles, pointing to clear differences between the old and the new world. The adversarial and litigious style of enforcement stood in contrast to the European style, which relies much more on cooperation and negotiation during implementation – a term preferred in Europe over the adversarial-sounding 'enforcement'.

For a long time, regulation was seen as a rival concept to antitrust policy. Stigler even regarded them as 'deadly enemies' (Stigler, 1975: 183). Both concepts are designed to deal with market failures, but in different ways. Antitrust policy aims at competition across economic sectors, and tends to use universal rules to prevent anti-competitive behavior, thus preventing the favoring of special interests or particular sectors of the economy over others. Regulation, by contrast, aims at specific industries or products, uses more fine-grained rules such as rate-setting, licensing, and technical or safety norms, and thereby tends to be selective in allocating costs and benefits. Whether this leads to rivalry or to complementarity is still debated (Petit, 2005; Carlton and Picker, 2006). In the early stage of market regulation in Europe it was a popular idea that regulatory agencies could be phased out as soon as their mission was fulfilled and that antitrust authorities would take over – which did not happen anywhere. Nonetheless, economists are still predisposed towards antitrust policy, not least because its more general and thus clientele-resistant goals are considered

to be a more reliable protection against capture. However, as will be shown in the next section, regulation is by no means restricted to moderating or even subverting competition.

EXPANDING THE REALM OF REGULATION

The above-mentioned policy change among established regulatory agencies was accompanied by the creation of new agencies that ventured into formerly underdeveloped regulatory fields in the late 1960s and early 1970s. In a nutshell, whereas the beneficiaries of the old regulation tended to be corporations, the new regulation was aptly described as 'compensating for capitalism' (Eisner, 1993: 118). Three elements distinguish the 'old' economic regulation from the 'new' social regulation (Vogel, 1981).

First, the focus expanded from rules addressed at firms in a single sector of the economy to problems cutting across sectors such as environmental protection, occupational health and safety, toxic substances and waste, consumer product safety, etc. Whether this transition in policy could be attributed to the rise of the New Left or the ascendance of the consumer movement is not entirely clear. In any case, it could be argued that 'concerns about the power of the corporate state; visions of a participatory democracy consisting of multiple grass-roots organizations, and the salience of so-called quality-of-life issues motivated individuals to create, join, and support advocacy groups' (Eisner, 1993: 125).

Secondly, these new public interest groups became political actors in their own right, and gained influence not only in the legislative process but also in agency rule-making. Thanks to a series of court rulings, standing requirements were eased, thus allowing greater access to judicial review; a fair representation of interests during agency rule-making was required, and much more emphasis was put on justifying decisions by disclosing that alternatives, pros and cons, had been thoroughly examined. This increased the amount of judicial review of agency decisions. However, not only courts gained influence; interest groups also, especially those excluded under the old regime, achieved influence through a whole new array of litigation-based strategies. The rise of public interest groups as new constituencies could be interpreted as the deliberate result of political decision-makers nurturing supportive groups – a strategy that fits with Lowi's (1972: 300) constituent policy. Certainly, this became another source of the adversarial legalism described above.

Thirdly, the new regulation tended to be more science-based than its predecessor. In part this was caused by new regulatory objects such as the environment, toxic substances or product safety, all of which require expert knowledge to define health or environmental risks, measure limits or conduct impact assessments (Eisner, 1993: 129; Merrill, 2003). The increasing role of science did not remain restricted to natural sciences or engineering. Economics, especially the pro-market schools, gained perceptible influence in regulatory thinking. Emission trading has to be mentioned as one of the influential innovations in environmental regulation. Furthermore, the 'hard look' doctrine, developed by US courts during the 1970s, created strong incentives for agencies to rely on scientific standards, because they proved to be a decisive prerequisite for judicial deference (Merrill, 2003: 2). To be sure, science-based strategies for influencing regulation also emerged in relations between agencies and interest groups, the latter generating an expertise of their own. Through the rise of the 'counter-expert', formerly almost sacrosanct scientific authority became contestable. All in all, at the end of the 1970s, regulation had become more wide-ranging, more inclined towards underprivileged groups, and more scientific.

The type of market and risk regulation described above would probably have been restricted to the United States, if another transformation under the banners 'deregulation' and 'regulatory reform' were not taking place. The APA was the first systematic effort to control regulation, especially with procedures and control mechanisms imposed on agencies (McCubbins, Noll and Weingast, 1999: 186), and could be perceived as a harbinger for future political struggles. As cross-sectoral regulation increased during the 1970s, so did the political incentives to take a broader look instead of examining sector by sector. The first steps to centralize political control over agencies were taken during the Carter presidency, but to coordinate rather than to suppress regulatory activities. It was the Reagan era that unleashed a much more vigorous and overtly critical approach. The new philosophy is reflected in a famous executive order from 1981 stipulating that 'regulatory action shall not be taken unless the potential benefits to society for the regulation outweigh the potential costs to society' (quoted in Eisner, 1993: 189). What might sound like a balanced approach at first sight, in fact was bowing in one direction, which soon became the trademark of the Reagan presidency: deregulation. This policy was realized through new requirements imposed on agencies, often expressed in cost–benefit terms, as well as tough centralized control. An institutional legacy of the Reagan era is the Office of Information and Regulatory Affairs (OIRA), launched in 1980 inside the White House to review agencies. Most recently, President Obama appointed Cass Sunstein, an eminent law scholar, as OIRA administrator. Despite his liberal reputation, Sunstein is also well-known as an ardent critic of risk regulation (Sunstein, 2005), especially if it is instructed by the precautionary principle which, in his opinion, inflates public expectations beyond rational reasoning (see also Vogel, 2003: 566). The 'clash of culture' undertones, typical of US regulatory politics, are one of the few aspects of the concept that stayed at home.

In the 1980s regulation started to travel across the world. This policy diffusion probably had the greatest impact in Europe, not only in single member states but also at the European Union level. Regulation, of course, had been practised in Europe long before, even though under a different designation. The long-dominant German equivalent, for example, is 'Aufsicht' (oversight). Despite a good dose of legalism, oversight remains more distanced, less contested,[3] and less pro-active than regulation. It is based on a rather paternalistic approach towards business and society, aiming at the prevention of hazards ('Gefahrenabwehr') and creating an institutional order ('Ordnungsrahmen') prior to the existence of markets (Dyson, 1980: 222, 270). Oversight aims at controlling market *behavior* and not at *creating* markets. Another fundamental difference is the broad acceptance of the state as an 'architect of political order' in Germany, and in continental Europe as well. For the most part, therefore, state intervention can draw on a pre-existing legitimacy that is not challenged case by case. Whereas it is only a small step from regulation to over-regulation, oversight was rarely discussed in terms of doing too much. No wonder that it took until 1996 for the term regulation to be introduced into German legal language, through the – then almost revolutionary – Telecommunications Act (Coen, Héretier and Böllhoff, 2002: 7). Other sectors such as rail or financial services remained more hesitant (Coen, Héretier and Böllhoff, 2002: 18), obviously because the pro-active, pro-competition template did not fit with established policy patterns. In a legalized culture like Germany, it is not without relevance that legal scholars still argue about regulation as a generic concept or a subcategory of administrative law (Schorkopf, 2008: 27–9). The later interpretation would allow regulation to be subordinated under a set of tried and tested legal doctrines, thus not only avoiding uncertainty but also reducing the costs of adaptation.

As regulation has diffused to Europe, different political contexts have to be considered. Prior to the 1990s, the term had no specific meaning in Europe. Basically, regulation was equated with state intervention in general (Jordana and Levi-Faur, 2004: 4). The narrower meaning was adopted in the late 1990s, but remains more challenged by rival types of policy, especially the stronger European welfare state policy, with its redistributive focus, as well as the stronger tradition of public ownership. Another important difference is the political decision to delegate regulatory competencies, which has received much more attention in the United States than in Europe (Epstein and O'Halloran, 1999). This could be explained by the broader mandate of US agencies, which goes beyond the regular European separation-of-power model. Regulatory agencies and commissions in the United States are not only charged with broad executive discretion but also perform court-like functions and have a rule-making authority, based on an open-ended mandate, which makes 'agencies act like legislatures' (Kerwin, 1999: 51).

The policy transfer was characterized by two peculiarities. The first is that regulation traveled to Europe in its deregulation incarnation. But things differed in one important aspect. In most European countries, key sectors of the economy were locked in public or quasi-public ownership. Thus, privatization was a logical requirement prior to any deregulation, although both terms are often used interchangeably. The first EU member state to adopt this idea was the United Kingdom during the Thatcher government. Even if the hyperactivism of British liberalization (Moran, 2003) was not exactly emulated by other EU member states, it evolved into a benchmark, not least for the European Commission, that could not simply be argued away by referring to national traditions or other peculiarities. Since the early 1990s, the European Commission's increasingly stringent privatization policy has forced member states to deregulate their public utility monopolies in telecommunications, energy, and rail (Coen, Héretier and Böllhoff, 2002). This was not only the decisive opening for US style of regulation in Europe but also opened the door for market creation as a completely new field of state intervention: confusingly enough, enabled only through a preceding privatization.

The second peculiarity is a growing concern with the quality and performance of regulation, not so different from in the United States, but with a different focus: namely, privatized industries. To prevent former monopolists from undermining competition, facilitated through continuing grid ownership, special agencies were created and charged with a regulation *for* competition mandate. This 're-regulation' policy (Majone, 1990) has to cope with a new set of problems, such as constructing regulatory agencies and insuring their credibility, coordination with antitrust policy, or establishing 'level playing fields', i.e. creating equal conditions for all competitors. Simultaneous with EU liberalization, the OECD (2002, 2005) promoted a more general debate about regulatory quality. The targets were the problems arising from an uncoordinated and fragmented regulation of privatized sectors. The notion of 'regulatory governance', used in OECD documents since the 1990s, thus refers to policy initiatives aimed at optimizing the institutional and procedural framework that could affect the performance of regulation (OECD, 2005)[4]. According to OECD-speak, regulatory reform is the process which should lead to high-quality regulatory governance. In addition to numerous 'how-to-regulate' books, the OECD also publishes country reports in which the OECD-defined 'progress' of national regulatory systems is reported. The reasons why even notoriously reluctant countries like France and Germany eventually considered taking part in these benchmark activities are twofold: one is the growing reputation of international organizations for ranking countries according to economic or quality-of-life indicators, which almost automatically are used to judge the performance of incumbent governments; the second reason is the growing awareness that poorly performing national regulations might discourage foreign investment or create other comparative disadvantages. No wonder therefore, that most OECD countries have adopted some sort of quality-of-regulation policy (Wegrich, 2009: 58).

The EU is an active participant in this debate. Based on the 'Mandelkern report' of 2001, the EU has developed its own reform program called 'Better Regulation' (EU, 2006; Radaelli and Meuwese, 2009). The motivation is to increase international competitiveness. The means to achieve this goal are often expressed in the formula 'less red tape = more growth' (quoted in Hardacre, 2008: 7). The EU initiative stresses three instruments to improve regulatory performance: ex ante impact assessments, simplification of rules, and 'consultation with all interested parties' (Hardacre, 2008: 7). The third instrument, especially, reflects a typical European policy style which could be labeled as a multi-stakeholder approach. The aim is not only to reconcile government–business relations but also to include consumer/citizen interests in the regulatory process. From a comparative perspective, the Better Regulation concept of – and inside[5] – the EU tries to moderate the most obvious conflicts, which in the United States are carried out openly via legislative struggles over agency competencies and design, or inside the courtroom.

If the scientific community is inclined to emphasize the shift from government to governance (van Kersbergen and van Waarden, 2004: 152), this is of course triggered by the denationalization of regulatory policies, giving birth to more non-state actors, as well as the public (think tank) demand for a 'multi-tasking' upgrade of regulation by imposing a reform layer on an already complicated policy tool. Both developments tend to reduce governmental control over regulatory policies. Whether this justifies the – normatively inspired – widespread replacement of government with governance is an open question. From an analytical point of view, this is one reason why it is difficult to exactly reconstruct the fusion between regulation and governance into a new concept.

However, since the EU has gained a prominent role in regulatory affairs, it makes sense to treat both as being interconnected. Even if some authors regard regulation 'as a mode of governance' (Jordana and Levi-Faur, 2004: 1) from the outset, at least two additional arguments deserve mention. At a more general level, policymaking in the EU is often characterized as 'network governance', mainly because of the 'comitology' system. In this arcane arrangement for policy formation, which brings together government bureaucrats and experts from various non-state backgrounds, 'expertise and persuasion are the currencies of influence' (Young, 2006: 385), not simply power and resources. Thus, neither pluralism nor corporatism can be applied as descriptive or even explanatory categories to European policymaking. A second and more specific justification for using the governance concept is the rise of European – and increasingly – 'transnational regulatory networks' (Eberlein and Grande, 2005: 101; Coen and Thatcher, 2008), consisting of national experts, not necessarily government officials, who develop regulatory standards which are transformed into national law in a second step. As opposed to comitology, they are not part of an international organization but form international organizations of their own. The Florence Forum for Electricity and the Independent Regulators' Group (for telecommunications) are two European examples (Eberlein and Grande, 2005: 99); at the transnational level the Basel Committee on Banking Supervision (still not 'on Regulation') is the most prominent case. According to the criteria developed by Coen and Thatcher (2008: 50) – i.e. linking different institutional levels, shifting power to actors who coordinate others, and consultation instead of hierarchical decision-making – all the above-mentioned committees could be regarded as prototypes of network governance. The implications for regulation are severe: it is no longer a purely national affair, it is no longer exclusively state-driven, and it is no longer mainly hierarchical.

Quite similar to in the United States, regulatory policy in the EU started with market regulation first and embraced 'risk regulation', the equivalent of social regulation, later. Risk regulation gained ground first, and most prominently, in environmental policy (Héritier, Knill and Mingers, 1996). A driving force behind making this policy domain the most Europeanized was the integration of the precautionary principle into the EU treaty in 1993 (Vogel, 2003: 566). Even without the inherent expansionary tendency of this principle, the EU enlarged their risk regulation activity throughout the 1990s, for example in occupational safety and health, genetically modified organisms (GMOs), often linked to food safety, or pharmaceuticals, the latter supported by its own agency (Young, 2006: 379). This was mainly perceived as a step towards positive integration, i.e. creating common rules and standards instead of only removing trade barriers. Thus, risk regulation was already on track when the bovine spongiform encephalopathy (BSE) crisis, culminating in the early 2000s, served as a catalyst for a far-reaching overhaul of food safety competencies and institutions. The subsequent creation of the European Food Safety Agency and the reform of national food safety arrangements injected a new degree of conflict into European regulatory policies, described as 'contested governance', i.e. when 'day-to-day battles are displaced by more widespread public debate about the fundamentals of governance' (Ansell and Vogel, 2006: 11). Ansell and Vogel mention several controversial issues in food safety regulation, two of which seem to carry special weight for other sectors as well. One issue is the question of at which level regulatory power should be located. So far, EU agencies have no or only very limited enforcement functions. But there is perceptible pressure to upgrade their mandate (e.g. Majone, 2003: 31). The second issue is to what extent regulatory action should rest upon precaution, or to be more precise: upon the aim of preventing *potential* hazards. If an aggressive reading of the precautionary principle – which has more than lukewarm support – would prevail, risk regulation, if anything, could become infinite.

REGULATORS AND REGULATORY INSTITUTIONS

So far, regulation has been reviewed on the policy dimension. In addition, there are two important institutional dimensions, both of which have their own dynamic: the regulatory state and regulatory agencies which enforce the law. The term 'regulatory state' is ambiguous as it is applied to different things. A wider definition refers to the rise and growth of regulation as a central state function (Glaeser and Shleifer, 2003), often linked with an anti-state undertone. One problem with this label is the bias toward an understanding of regulation as the dominant type of public policy. The idea of 'the regulatory state as *the* major aspect in transformation of the governance of capitalist economies since the 1980s' (Jordana and Levi-Faur, 2004: 9) is contestable, because it tends to confuse a heuristic perspective with a description of an empirical phenomenon. A second more restricted definition, therefore, tries to fill out the blanks. Majone, for example, contrasts the regulatory state with the postwar 'positive' or 'Keynesian welfare state' (Majone, 1997: 141), the main functions of which were public spending, state-owned enterprises, and welfare provision.[6] By contrast, the regulatory state, regarded as a response to the deficiencies of the welfare state, focuses on rule-making (Majone, 1997: 143). The welfare state was the producer of a wide range of social services; the regulatory state provides and enforces standards for private service producers. In this perspective, the regulatory state almost supersedes the postwar welfare state.

However solid the empirical evidence for this observation may be, the contrast between the welfare and the regulatory state refers to another important aspect. Even if there is a growth of regulatory norms, the attribute 'regulatory' is not referring to *expanding* state functions; rather, it denotes a *change* of policy instrumentation, associated with the idea of a 'disaggregated' state at the institutional level.[7] Slaughter, who stressed this term most prominently, defines the disaggregated state as an extension of the unitary state. Disaggregation takes place because of 'the rising need and capacity of different government institutions to engage in activities beyond their borders' (Slaughter, 2004: 12). Of course, the result is not a new (regulatory) state at the transnational level. The new creature is called 'horizontal government networks' (Slaughter, 2004: 13), populated – depending on their function – by legislators, judges or regulators. Majone has a stronger focus on the Europeanization of policymaking, which, in turn, is supposed to have a disaggregating impact on national polities. Instead of stressing the 'going transnational' of regulators, he regards governmental decentralization as 'the breakdown of formerly monolithic entities into single-purpose units with their own budgets [...] operating outside the normal executive branch framework' (Majone, 1997: 146; see also Jayasuriya, 2001) as being of prime importance. Both views suggest that the institutional dimension of the regulatory state should be analyzed at the national as well as at the transnational levels, the latter being discussed further below.

The European debate differs from that in the United States in general because regulation in the United States has been a fact of political life for more than a century. No wonder, therefore, that the arrival of regulation in Europe has been perceived as a critical juncture. Again, it is not always clear whether the notion of the regulatory state serves heuristic purposes or should describe an empirical phenomenon. Obviously, the latter perspective is used when terms like 'revolutionary' (Sturm, et al., 2002: 3) are attached to it. Beyond queries about the proper classification, there can be no doubt that the EU has arrived in the real world of regulatory politics as an actor in its own right. This was demonstrated, for example, through a directive issued by the European Commission in 2003 which obliged all member states to set up a separate agency for energy regulation (Eberlein, 2008: 81). Although targeted to drive France and Germany into a liberalized energy market, this move has not only endorsed the EU as an actor in regulatory politics[8] but also has shown that the European Commission is able to influence domestic administrative structures.

Whatever perspective the regulatory state is analyzed under, one element can be found in almost every account: the rise and diffusion of regulatory agencies. This type of state bureaucracy is seen as both an innovation and as a contradiction to the parliamentary model of most European governments. Whereas in the positive state, functions were hierarchically integrated into centralized ministerial departments, the regulatory state 'is characterized by pluralism, diffusion of power, and extensive delegation of tasks to non-majoritarian institutions like agencies or commissions' (Majone, 1997: 159). The underlying motive for promoting agencies, which is also valid in public management reform (Pollitt and Talbot, 2004), is to separate policies from operations, or – more bluntly – to keep politics away from law enforcement. By creating single-purpose organizations, detached from party politics, and staffed with experts, the expectation is that the performance of policy implementation will be improved (Schick, 2002: 36). Within the context of regulation, agency autonomy, also referred to as *non-majoritarian*, has attracted special attention. One reason is that 'the diffusion of the regulatory agency model has challenged the structure of power in many countries, often reducing centralization in the governance of many policy sectors' (Jordana and Sancho, 2004: 307; Jayasuriya, 2001). The other reason is that agency independence is seen as a protection against capture by politicians,

who are suspected of letting short-term considerations dominate over long-term administrative expertise. This idea has gained ground throughout Europe, even if the degree of autonomy granted to agencies still varies (Gilardi, 2005; Petit, 2005; Christensen and Lægreid, 2006).

Agency independence raises the problem of accountability. How can elected politicians be accountable to their voters if vital state functions are delegated to agencies outside their reach? Majone gives a straightforward answer. The question itself rests on doubtful normative assumptions, because politicians are inclined to interfere in agency decisions. Even policy guidance based on constitutional doctrines such as ministerial responsibility is assumed to have 'perverse effects on public accountability. Because such interventions were usually exercised through informal and even secret processes, rather than by official directions, accountability was almost eliminated' (Majone, 2005: 128; Majone, 1997: 161). Agencies, by contrast, draw their credibility from neutral expertise and political independence. Their legitimacy rests on their regulatory output and not – as in the positive state – on the input side, i.e. a chain of accountability from voters, to legislators, and finally, to a hierarchically controlled executive. By and large this could be seen as a contest between hierarchy and transparency as competing techniques for governing agencies. To be sure, public administration will never be de-hierarchized across the board. However, in important domains of public policy, regulatory agencies have served to facilitate a more transparent approach to administrative action. Relying on public reporting, benchmarking, and an open, participative decision-making process, rather than on hierarchical guidance, seems to be the most important contribution of regulatory agencies to modern governance.

The concurrent switch from input- to output-legitimacy has another important implication for the way agencies enforce rules and standards. Agencies within the EU in particular are increasingly obliged to follow US-like hearing and consultation procedures: for example, in drug licensing or the authorization of GMOs (Cananea, 2004: 205). On balance, a positive interpretation dominates according to which these procedures will lead to greater 'procedural legitimacy' (Majone, 1997: 160) or will help regulators learn how to cope with clients (Coen, 2005). But some doubts remain, in particular when considering that regulation is designed to force private actors to comply with rules which, in the absence of regulation, would not be observed (Alford and Speed, 2006: 314). The suspicion that consultative or cooperative regulation only works if regulators are willing to cede concessions is reinforced when the issue of global regulatory competition is taken into account (see below). In any case, it is getting more difficult to properly ascribe the costs and benefits of regulation to a particular constituency.

FROM NATIONAL TO TRANSNATIONAL GOVERNANCE

Since the 1990s, globalization, its origins, nature, and consequences have become the major theme of social science. In their seminal book on the subject, Braithwaite and Drahos make a distinction between the globalization of firms, of markets, and of regulation (Braithwaite and Drahos, 2000: 8). Despite regulation is conceived as 'the norms, standards, principles and rules that govern commerce' (Braithwaite and Drahos, 2000: 10), the authors also include objects such as labor standards, the environment or food safety in their list of case studies which, in the present context, would be subsumed under the narrower label of risk regulation. This lack of differentiation is worth mentioning because it indicates that Braithwaite and Drahos consider regulation to be a transnational contest about regulatory standards driven by the process of globalization.

Owing to this perspective, their interest in the national causation and specification of regulation is low. In the globalized world, described by Braithwaite and Drahos (2000: 551, 553, 557), regulation occurs in transnational 'webs of influence', 'webs of dialogue', and "webs of reward and coercion'. Slaughter makes a quite similar distinction between three types of 'executive transgovernementalism' (Slaughter, 2004: 41): information networks, enforcement networks, and harmonization networks (Slaughter, 2004: 51–2), all of which are mainly populated with 'regulocrats' (Levi-Faur, Gilardi and Jordana, 2005), whose technocratic expertise dominates over the 'democratic policy outcome' (Slaughter, 2004: 63) of government officials. These writings depict a new way of thinking about regulation: power and enforcement are still out there, but are almost softened away by expertise, dialogue, and negotiation.

Although at first sight, the global governance debate has not changed the meaning of regulation dramatically, as is shown in the definition by the editors of the new *Regulation & Governance* journal. Regulation is seen 'as a large subset of governance that is about steering the flow of events and behavior, as opposed to providing and distributing' (Braithwaite, Coglianese and Levi-Faur, 2007: 3). The upshot is that regulation is not swept away, but rather is conceptualized as part of a more encompassing 'regulatory governance' in which regulation is one of several ingredients. Interestingly, the authors nonetheless regard regulation as 'the expanding part of governance' (Braithwaite, Coglianese and Levi-Faur, 2007: 1). What does this mean for regulation? On a very abstract level, governance could be regarded as a great softener for the erstwhile clear-cut concept. The softening takes places at three levels.

The first concerns the role of the state. Global governance rules out an all-dominating state that is able to impose its prerogatives on business and other non-state actors. There are two consequences. The first is that persuasion and voluntary action, rather than hierarchy, becomes the new currency of regulatory success (Abbott and Snidal, 2008: 506). The second consequence is the growing relevance of 'regulatory coordination' (Drezner, 2007: 11), which presumably becomes as important as regulatory enforcement. This also means that national regulations will continue to exist, probably not even subordinated to transnational regimes. The main challenge is to make national regulations interact at the transnational level. The near meltdown of the global financial system in late 2008 is likely to lead to an upgrade of already existing transnational agreements. But they will be based on 'soft power' (Slaughter, 2004: 169) and not on coercion. It is in this context in which the shift from government to governance is often emphasized, based on the assumption that governments are no longer able to act unilaterally.

This leads to the second point. Transnational 'webs' and 'networks' become the new location for manufacturing regulatory rules and standards. Agencies no longer form the center of action; rather, they serve as suppliers of personnel. National interests are thereby not crowded out. Often enough, regulatory networks are initiated, promoted, and/or orchestrated by national governments (Slaughter, 2004: 171; Drezner, 2007; Abbott and Snidal, 2008: 521). Nonetheless, their grip is loosening to the extent to which the interactive dynamics inside transnational networks are getting stronger.[9] Even if national representatives feel loyalty to their home country, the fact of becoming a member of a transnational epistemic community, upgraded by group dynamics and temporary detachment from domestic influence, is likely to switch national interest defenders into 'double-hatted' (Egeberg, 2004: 17) regulators.

Thirdly, globalization not only creates new market opportunities but also a growing demand to cope with the negative externalities of trade liberalization. Thus, the number of constituencies in the regulatory process grows.

In an optimistic version, this increases the relevance of civil society and its representatives in NGOs, and consumer and labor organizations. In a pessimist version, non-state actors are equated with business interests who capture regulatory networks, making them 'instruments of private interests rather than of public good' (Underhill and Zhang, 2008: 542). Leaving aside the question, 'Which of the two is the more appropriate perspective to characterize globalization?', it seems to be clear that globally organized regulation is demanded by business as well as by public interest groups to a similar extent (Braithwaite and Drahos, 2000; Slaughter, 2004; Abbott and Snidal, 2008). Having more constituencies inevitably leads to more complicated regulatory goals and, as a consequence, to more 'please-all' policies.

Globalization, however, not only softens regulation but also creates a new dimension of political competition and probably of conflict. Two of the most debated consequences for regulation are the contradictory concepts of the 'race to the bottom' and the 'race to the top' (Vogel, 2003; Schnaiberg and Bartley, 2008: 36). The first is the more prominent, because it was frequently used to corroborate a pessimistic view of globalization. The basic idea is that liberalized trade will force one country after another to comply with less regulation in trade-sensitive domains such as labor standards, environmental protection or financial services. A similar apprehension was expressed in the early days of the EU single market. However, on balance, there is only scant empirical evidence for races to the bottom (Schnaiberg and Bartley, 2008: 37). Rather, the opposite can be observed. Even though the evidence for the 'California effect' as the main factor determining the intensity of regulation is contestable as well (Drezner, 2007: 17), the bulk of research sides with the race to the top concept (Radaelli, 2004: 7). Again, an optimistic version, trusting in more public interest-based regulations, can be distinguished from a pessimistic version, arguing that multinational firms like

Monsanto exploit patent laws or GMO regulations to support their business model (Braithwaite and Drahos, 2000: 526).

Whereas both concepts could be interpreted as rather passive aquiescence to external pressure, the notion of regulatory competition has a clearly proactive undertone. The focus is not primarily on more or less stringent regulations, but rather on the question of who is able to dominate over global regulatory standards. Not surprisingly, the sources of regulatory competition, in other words the major beneficiaries, are seen to be either business interests (Murphy, 2004) or national governments engaging in 'regulatory export' (Slaughter, 2004: 172–7). Few observers would dispute that this is a typical American strategy to get a competitive advantage. A third hypothesis is provided by Jonathan Macey, who argues that the driving forces are regulators themselves. If political conditions at home make them feel 'the threat of irrelevance', regulators 'respond by banding together with their international colleagues to increase their regulatory reach' (Macey, 2003: 1354). Each of the three concepts has some empirical evidence on its side. More generally, this demonstrates that regulation is no longer a bilateral political game between governments and business firms, but, in fact, has become a multidimensional phenomenon.

SUMMARY

Compared to previous decades, regulation today undoubtedly has become a more complex technique for problem-solving. Starting as an authoritative policy instrument to correct market failures in single sectors of the economy, regulation has gradually expanded into environmental and consumer affairs. As social consciousness of risks reaches into a wider universe of technologies, substances, and products, there can be few doubts that political demand for risk regulation will continue, probably even at a

faster pace. Something similar could be said about market regulation. The seeming paradox that freer markets need more rules to prevent economic and social distortions (Vogel, 1996) is a driving force not only behind new regulations but also behind regulatory reform. The current state of the art could be summarized as follows. Market and risk regulation, regulatory reform (better regulation), and regulatory governance are the four pillars on which the concept rests today. Each has several dimensions but can be distinguished through focal points. Market and risk regulation have their focus on particular subjects: the former deals with market imperfections in general; the latter with all types of hazards emanating from production processes and modern lifestyles. Regulatory reform, by contrast, has no substantial or sectoral focus, but is concerned with regulation itself. Spawned by criticism from different constituencies about regulatory 'burden' as well as the fear of comparative disadvantages, regulatory reform today is differentiated into a family of concepts such as deregulation, better regulation, higher-quality regulation, red tape reduction, etc. Finally, the focal point of regulatory governance is most difficult to discern because its definition(s) tend to broaden rather than to circumscribe the concept. It has a threefold focus: first, the shift from national to transnational regulation and regulatory institutions; second, the increasing integration of non-state actors; and third, the multiplication of stakeholders and thus of interest-based demands addressed at regulatory outcomes.

This is reflected in the range of regulatory issues, which vary from rain forest conservation, product labeling in order to ban child labor on the one side, to accounting rules or capital-to-lending ratios on the other side of the spectrum. The consequences for regulation as a concept and as a policy instrument are profound. By expanding through a wide range of policies, from the new to the old world, and from national to transnational levels, not least due to the rise of regulation as an attribute of state functions and structures, the concept has been loaded up with numerous new obligations and expectations, both in the real world of politics and in the analytic world of scientific observers. This has decreased the erstwhile sharp contours and easy-to-observe interests and constituencies. In addition, the intersection between regulation and governance has shifted research interest away from nation-state-rooted institutions towards deliberation-based transnational networks. This requires more research to explain the driving forces, the aims, and the impact of regulation. However, at the core, regulation remains a concept and a tool to change the behavior of private actors by means of authoritative state action. Even in an age of governance this should be kept in mind, to save regulation from conceptual overstretch.

NOTES

1   Lowi later added 'constituent' policy as a fourth type. It was somewhat vaguely described as 'reapportionment' (Lowi, 1972: 300). What Lowi had in mind was a sort of policy that accommodated constituencies with more power or influence in the political process.

2   A good overview of recent research is provided by Holburn and Vanden Bergh (2008). The two main strategies for influencing regulation are either lobbying legislators or influencing regulators, both of which may be used over time, depending on the perceived 'hostility' of the regulator towards business preferences.

3   In German banking oversight, 'soft regulation' (Sturm et al., 2002: 35) was practised long before the term was introduced into the debate on regulation.

4   Another term is 'meta-regulation', denoting 'the process of regulation itself becomes regulated' (Jordana and Levi-Faur, 2004: 6). See also Wegrich (2009: 37–42).

5   At the national level, not only governments but also a growing private think tank and consulting industry have embraced the Better Regulation initiative. In Germany, for example, the Bertelsmann Foundation, belonging to the homonymous multinational media corporation, has succeeded in establishing itself as an authority inside the reducing-red-tape community. Despite a plethora of 'improving regulation' rhetoric, the border to anti-regulation

is pervious. Thus, it could be not excluded that business firms exploit this sort of policy initiatives to get rid of undesired rules and obligations. A good discussion of the tensions inherent in the Better Regulation ideology can be found in Radaelli and Meuwese (2009: 649).

6   One should admit that Majone adds a good dose of advocacy to most of his publications. His perspective is not primarily that there *is* a regulatory state, but that there *should* be one or, at least, what could be achieved if a fully-fledged regulatory state did exist in Europe.

7   'Regulatory capitalism' is a close but nonetheless rival concept. Proponents claim that, due to the growth of non-state regulation, it is more appropriate to talk about regulatory capitalism than about the regulatory state (cf. Braithwaite, 2005).

8   And, of course, as an additional level of politics, which could be exploited by national governments and interest groups. The ensuing 'multilevel governance' in the EU must be regarded as a two-way street of influence and policymaking.

9   Schnaiberg and Bartley (2008: 40) emphasize that the network image as a 'fragmented, neomedieval patchwork of authority' is increasingly replaced by the idea of a more coherent, organized and rational mode of governance. This is consistent with the observation that inside the EU networks of regulators are flourishing as a governance technique. But they are still a good way away from being equivalent to regulatory agencies at the domestic level (Coen and Thatcher, 2008: 67).

REFERENCES

Abbott, K.W. and Snidal, D. (2008) 'Strengthening International Regulation through Transnational New Governance', *Vanderbilt Journal of Transnational Law* 42(2): 501–78.

Alford, J. and Speed, R. (2006) 'Client Focus in Regulatory Agencies. Oxymoron or Opportunity?', *Public Management Review* 8(2): 313–31.

Ansell, C. and Vogel, D. (eds) (2006) *What's the Beef: The Contested Governance of European Food Safety.* Cambridge, MA: MIT Press.

Bernstein, M.H. (1955) *Regulating Business by Independent Commission.* Princeton, NJ: Princeton University Press.

Braithwaite, J. (2005) 'Neoliberalism or Regulatory Capitalism?', *RegNet Occasional Paper No 5.* Canberra: Australian National University.

Braithwaite, J. and Drahos, P. (2000) *Global Business Regulation.* Cambridge, MA: Cambridge University Press.

Braithwaite, J., Coglianese, G. and Levi-Faur, D. (2007) 'Can Regulation and Governance Make a Difference?', *Regulation & Governance* 1(1): 1–7.

Cananea, G. (2004) 'The European Union's Mixed Administrative Proceedings', *Law & Contemporary Problems* 67(1): 197–217.

Carlton, D.W. and Picker, R.C. (2006) 'Antitrust and Regulation', *Olin Working Paper* No. 312. University of Chicago Law & Economics.

Christensen, T. and Lægreid, P. (eds) (2006) *Autonomy and Regulation. Coping with Agencies in the Modern State.* Cheltenham, UK: Edward Elgar

Coen, D. (2005) 'Business-Regulatory Relations: Learning to Play Regulatory Games in European Utility Markets', *Governance* 18(3): 375–98.

Coen, D. and Thatcher, M. (2008) 'Network Governance and Multi-level Delegation: European Networks of Regulatory Agencies', *Journal of Public Policy* 28(1): 49–71.

Coen, D., Héritier, A. and Böllhoff, D. (2002) *Regulating the Utilities: Business and Regulator Perspectives in the UK and Germany.* Anglo-German Foundation.

Drezner, D.W. (2007) *All Politics is Global: Explaining International Regulatory Regimes.* Princeton, NJ: Princeton University Press.

Dyson, K.H.F. (1980) *The State Tradition in Western Europe.* Oxford: Oxford University Press.

Eberlein, B. (2008) 'The Making of the European Energy Market: The Interplay of Governance and Government', *Journal of Public Policy* 28(1): 73–92.

Eberlein, B. and Grande, E. (2005) 'Beyond Delegation: Transnational Regulatory Regimes and the EU Regulatory State', *Journal of European Public Policy* 12(1): 89–112.

Egeberg, M. (2004) 'Organising Institutional Autonomy in a Political Context: Enduring Tensions in the European Commission's Development'. *Arena Working Paper 2/2004*, Oslo.

Eisner, M.A. (1993) *Regulatory Politics in Transition.* Baltimore, MD: Johns Hopkins University Press.

Epstein, D. and O'Halloran, S. (1999) *Delegating Powers: A Transaction Cost Politics Approach to Policy Making under Separate Powers.* Cambridge, MA: Cambridge University Press.

European Commission (2006) 'A Strategic Review of Better Regulation in the European Union'. COM(2006)689.

Gilardi, F. (2005) 'The Institutional Foundations of Regulatory Capitalism. The Diffusion of Independent Regulatory Agencies in Western Europe', *Annals of the American Academy of Social and Political Sciences* 598: 84–101.

Glaeser, E.L. and Shleifer, A. (2003) 'The Rise of the Regulatory State', *Journal of Economic Literature* 41(2): 401–25.

Hardacre, A. (2008) 'Better Regulation – What Is at Stake?', *Eipascope* 2: 5–10.

Héritier, A., Knill, C. and Mingers S. (1996) *Ringing the Changes in Europe: Regulatory Competition and the Transformation of the State.* Berlin: de Gruyter.

Herring, E.P. (1936) *Public Administration and the Public Interest.* New York: McGraw-Hill.

Holburn, G.L.F. and Vanden Bergh, R. (2008) 'Making Friends in Hostile Environments: Political Strategy in Regulated Industries', *The Academy of Management Review* 33(2): 521–40.

Huntington, S.P. (1952) 'The Marasmus of the ICC', *Yale Law Journal* 61(4): 467–509.

Jayasuriya, K. (2001) 'Globalization and the Changing Architecture of the State: The Regulatory State and the Politics of Negative Co-ordination', *Journal of European Public Policy* 8: 101–23.

Jordana, J. and Levi-Faur, D. (2004) 'The Politics of Regulation in the Age of Governance', in J. Jordana and D. Levi-Faur (eds), *The Politics of Regulation. Institutions and Regulatory Reforms for the Age of Governance.* Cheltenham, UK: Edward Elgar; pp. 1–28.

Jordana, J. and Sancho, D. (2004) 'Regulatory Design, Institutional Constellations and the Study of the Regulatory State', in J. Jordana and D. Levi-Faur (eds), *The Politics of Regulation. Institutions and Regulatory Reforms for the Age of Governance.* Cheltenham, UK: Edward Elgar.

Kagan, R.A. (2001) *Adversarial Legalism. The American Way of Law.* Cambridge, MA: Harvard University Press.

Kersbergen, K. van and Waarden, F. van (2004) 'Governance as a Bridge between Disciplines: Cross-disciplinary Inspiration Regarding Shifts in Governance and Problems of Governability, Accountability and Legitimacy', *European Journal of Political Research* 43(1): 143–71.

Kerwin, C.M. (1999) *Rulemaking: How Government Agencies Write Law and Make Policy*, 2nd edn. Washington, DC: Congressional Quarterly Press.

Levi-Faur, D., Gilardi, F. and Jordana J. (2005) 'Regulatory Revolution by Surprise: On the Citadels of Regulatory Capitalism and the Rise of Regulocracy'. Paper prepared for the 3rd ECPR Conference, Budapest, 8–10, September. http://galactus.upf.edu/regulation/reg-gov/ecpr-05-papers/dlevifaur.pdf

Lowi, T.J. (1964) 'American Business, Public Policy, Case Studies, and Political Theory', *World Politics* 16(4): 677–93.

Lowi, T.J. (1972) 'Four Systems of Policy, Politics, and Choice', *Public Administration Review* 32(7/8): 298–310.

McCubbins, M.D., Noll, R.G. and Weingast, B.R. (1999) 'The Political Origins of the Administrative Procedure Act', *Journal of Law, Economics, and Organization* 15(Spring): 180–217.

Macey, J.R. (2003) 'Regulatory Globalization as a Response to Regulatory Competition', *Emory Law Journal* 52(3): 1353–80.

Majone, G. (ed.) (1990) *Deregulation or Re-regulation? Regulatory Reform in Europe and the United States.* London: Francis Pinter.

Majone, G. (1997) 'From the Positive to the Regulatory State: Causes and Consequences of Changes in the Mode of Governance', *Journal of Public Policy* 17(2): 139–67.

Majone, G. (2003) 'Foundations of Risk Regulation: Science, Decision-Making, Policy Learning and Institutional Reform', in G. Majone (ed.), *Risk Regulation in the European Union: Between Enlargement and Internationalization,* Florence: European University Institute; pp. 9–32.

Majone, G. (2005). 'Strategy and Structure: The Political Economy of Agency Independence and Accountability', in *Designing Independent and Accountable Authorities for High Quality Regulation.* Paris: OECD; pp. 126–55.

Merrill, R.A. (2003) Foreword (special issue on 'Science in the Regulatory Process'), *Law & Contemporary Problems* 66(August): 1–6.

Mitnick, B. (1980) *The Political Economy of Regulation.* Cambridge, MA: Cambridge University Press.

Moran, M. (2003) *The British Regulatory State: High Modernism and Hyper-innovation.* Oxford: Oxford University Press.

Murphy, D.D. (2004) *The Structure of Regulatory Competition: Corporations and Public Policies in a Global Economy.* Oxford: Oxford University Press.

OECD (2002) *Regulatory Policies in OECD Countries. From Interventionism to Regulatory Governance.* Paris: OECD.

OECD (2005) *Guiding Principles for Regulatory Quality and Performance.* Paris: OECD.

Petit, N. (2005) 'The Proliferation of National Authorities alongside Competition Authorities: A Source of Jurisdictional Confusion?', in D. Geradin, R. Muñoz and N. Petit (eds), *Regulation through Agencies in the EU: A New Paradigm of European Governance.* Cheltenham, UK: Edward Elgar; pp. 180–212.

Pollitt, C. and Talbot, C. (eds) (2004) *Unbundled Government. A Critical Analysis of the Global Trend to Agencies, Quangos and Contracturalisation.* London: Routledge.

Posner, R.A. (1974) 'Theories of Economic Regulation', *Bell Journal of Economics and Management Science* 5(Autum): 337–52.

Pünder, H. (2009) 'Democratic Legitimation of Delegated Legislation – A Comparative View on the American, British and German Law', *International and Comparative Law Quarterly* 58(April): 353–78.

Radaelli, C.M. (2004) 'The Puzzle of Regulatory Competition', *Journal of Public Policy* 24(1): 1–23.

Radaelli, C.M. and Meuwese, A.C.M. (2009) 'Better Regulation in Europe: Between Public Management and Regulatory Reform', *Public Administration* 87(1): 639–54.

Sabatier, P.A. (1975) 'Social Movements and Regulatory Agencies', *Policy Sciences* 6(September): 301–42.

Schick, A. (2002) 'Agencies in Search of Principles', in OECD (ed.), *Distributed Public Governance: Agencies, Authorities and other Autonomous Bodies.* Paris: OECD; pp. 25–38.

Schneiberg, M. and Bartley, T. (2008) 'Organizations, Regulation and Economic Behavior: Regulatory Dynamics and Forms from the Nineteenth to Twenty-First Century', *Annual Review and Law and Society* 4: 31–61.

Schorkopf, F. (2008) 'Regulierung nach den Grundsätzen des Rechtsstaats', *Juristen-Zeitung* 63(1): 21–9.

Slaughter, A.-M. (2004) *A New World Order,* Princeton; NJ: Princeton University Press.

Stigler, G.J. (1971) 'The Theory of Economic Regulation', *Bell Journal of Economics and Management Science* 2(Spring): 3–21.

Stigler, G.J. (1975) *The Citizen and the State: Essays on Regulation.* Chicago: Chicago University Press.

Sturm, R., Wilks, S., Müller, M.M. and Bartle, I. (2002) 'Der regulatorische Staat in Deutschland und Großbritannien: Konvergenz und Divergenz im inter-sektoralen Vergleich'. Anglo-German Foundation.

Sunstein, C.R. (2005) *Laws of Fear: Beyond the Precautionary Principle.* Cambridge, MA: Cambridge University Press.

Underhill, G.R.D. and Zhang, Z. (2008) 'Setting the Rules: Private Power, Political Underpinning, and Legitimacy in Global Monetary and Financial Governance', *International Affairs* 84(3): 535–54.

Vogel, D. (1981) 'The "New" Social Regulation in Historical and Comparative Perspective', in T. McGraw (ed.), *Regulation in Perspective: Historical Essays.* Cambridge, MA: Harvard University Press; pp. 155–85.

Vogel, D. (2003) 'The Hare and the Tortoise Revisited: The New Politics of Consumer and Environmental

Regulation in Europe', *British Journal of Political Science* 33(4): 557–80.

Vogel, S.K. (1996) *Freer Markets, More Rules: Regulatory Reform in Advanced Industrial Countries.* Ithaca, NY: Cornell University Press.

Wegrich, K. (2009) *Better Regulation. Grundmerkmale moderner Regulierungspolitik im internationalen Vergleich.* Gütersloh: Bertelsmann Stiftung.

Wilson, J.Q. (ed.) (1980) *The Politics of Regulation.* Cambridge, MA: Cambridge University Press.

Young, A.R. (2006) 'The Politics of Regulation and the Internal Market', in K.E. Joergensen, M.A. Pollak and B. Rosmund (eds), *Handbook of European Union Politics.* London: Sage; pp. 374–94.

34

Sustainable Development

James Meadowcroft

Over the past half century one of the more significant changes to political life in developed countries has been the emergence of the environment as a central focus for societal argument and government action. The increasing political salience of environmental issues has been driven by long-term development trends, including rising pressures on natural systems from increasingly potent and widespread technologies, growing human numbers, and higher levels of material consumption. Ideas have played a central role in defining emerging problems and legitimating government intervention for environment-related ends. Among the more influential of these ideas has been the notion of 'sustainable development'. This chapter will explore tensions surrounding the notoriously slippery concepts of 'governance' and 'sustainable development' (Adger and Jordan, 2009). It will argue that their intersection defines a crucial area for societal concern and for academic investigation. After reviewing the main themes that have emerged so far in discussions of governance and sustainable development, it will examine two particular approaches in more detail, before setting out a broad agenda for future inquiry. At the core of the argument is the contention that the emerging literature has focused too much on the details of policy, and the provision of expert advice, and has not addressed adequately broader issues related to politics, democracy, distribution and power.

The discussion is organized into four parts:

1 A short introduction to governance and sustainable development.
2 A brief overview of current research.
3 An introduction to two prominent perspectives on governance for sustainable development – transition management and adaptive management/ resilience.
4 An agenda for the future.

SUSTAINABLE DEVELOPMENT AND GOVERNANCE FOR SUSTAINABLE DEVELOPMENT

The Report of the World Commission on Environment and Development first propelled the idea of sustainable development to international prominence more than 20 years ago (WCED, 1987). Concerned with both the plight of the world's poor and the increasing pace of environmental destruction, the Commission called for reorienting the international development trajectory to enhance equity within and between generations and to protect environmental life support systems. Sustainable development was intended to capture this image of genuine societal advance and, over time, the idiom of sustainable development has been incorporated increasingly into international political discourse.

Perhaps the most straightforward way to understand sustainable development is as a political concept that denotes a basket of normative concerns, including the welfare of present and future generations, attention to the basic needs of the poor, protection of the natural environment, and public participation in environment and development decision-making (Lafferty, 1996; Meadowcroft, 2007 a). In this sense it is much like other value-laden political concepts (consider 'justice', 'freedom' and 'democracy'), which have determinate meanings, and provide an essential common vocabulary through which we think and talk about politics, but which are subject to constant reinterpretation, and about which we argue continuously.

Sustainable development has been subject to many criticisms: that it does too much, or alternatively not enough, to preserve the environment; that it is too vague, or little more than a slogan, that can mean all things to all people; or that it lumps together different sorts of issues that are best managed apart (Meadowcroft and Toner, 2009). Nevertheless, the concept has proven relatively resilient. This is because it speaks to an essential dilemma confronting the modern world – how to continue the quest for progress in a context where the basic needs of much of the world's population are not being met, while the pressures humankind is imposing on the global environment *are already* having grave and irreversible consequences – while leaving relatively open the precise definition of the problems and their solutions.

As other chapters in this volume have made clear, 'governance' can be understood in various ways. For the discussion here it is helpful to recall a simple distinction (made in Chapter 1 of this book) between wider and narrower usages, where governance is associated either with a broad range of practices and institutions whereby order in maintained in human social systems, or with a more specific set of mechanisms (including market-based and network approaches) whose significance came to be appreciated particularly during the final decades of the twentieth century (Pierre and Peters, 2000). For convenience the latter will be referred to as 'new governance'.

Starting with the broader conception, there are several things to be said at the outset. First, sustainable development is really all about governance. The idea was formulated because of dissatisfaction with existing ('unsustainable') development patterns. And the assumption was that conscious and collective – i.e. *political* – intervention would be required to shift the societal development trajectory on to more sustainable lines. Flawed governance practices encourage unsustainable development, so improved governance is required to put things right. Secondly, sustainable development embodies an implicit perspective on societal steering. It suggests that it is possible for human societies to orient long-term social development in desirable directions. So while it is admitted that we cannot predict the future, there is also a belief that we can positively influence the way in which it unfolds (Meadowcroft, 1999). Thirdly, sustainable development implies a change agenda. It is about encouraging the transformation of existing institutions. And we are talking not about a few minor administrative reforms, but rather about a profound transformation of current practices. For example, recent scientific assessments suggest that greenhouse gas emissions will have to decline by 80% in developed countries by mid century if the more serious risks of climate change are to be avoided (IPCC, 2007). This will require dramatic changes in key economic sectors, including energy, agriculture, construction, and transportation. So, sustainable development is about governing long-term socioeconomic change.

Fourthly, such deep-seated reform requires collaboration among all sorts of societal actors, including businesses, civil society organizations, and ordinary citizens. It is not just a question of applying known solutions to fully characterized problems, but rather one of continuously developing knowledge to refine the understanding of problems and encourage social innovation. And this is a challenge that requires participation from society as a whole. Fifthly (and notwithstanding the importance of societal mobilization), governments at all levels – from local authorities, through regional and national governments, to international institutions – will be expected to play an active role, as they have the financial, organizational, and legal resources to backstop such an ambitious change agenda. And finally, the democratic dimension is critical. Sustainable development involves choices about basic values, about defining the kind of lives citizens wish to live, and the sort of society they wish to build and leave for posterity. So it is only right that the voice of each citizen be heard in the processes of environment and development decision-making that render sustainable development concrete. Sustainable development is not a technocratic project that can be realized by experts, but a political project that requires decisions by implicated communities (Meadowcroft, 1999). It is concerned not just with the governance of change, but ultimately with *democratic* governance.

Turning next to the perspective of *new* governance, a number of additional points can be made. To start with, issues related to sustainability can be cited as typical of the kind of complex and deep-seated societal problems which traditional – state-centred and hierarchical – modes of governance are ill equipped to handle (Kooiman, 2003). Environmental issues cut across established ministerial mandates, spill over jurisdictional frontiers, and their successful resolution involves interactions among many kinds of social actors. They involve complex causal chains and pervasive uncertainties. They provide evidence of the increasing interdependence of social subsystems, the prevalence of unintended consequences, and

the impossibility of controlling from a single centre. Moreover, the persistence of environmental problems and their increasing scope – despite decades of regulation and expenditure – suggest that alternative approaches to governance are required to manage these challenges more successfully (Durant, Fiorino and O'Leary, 2004).

It is striking that sustainable development and ideas about new governance rose to prominence at more or less the same time. Indeed, there is substantial evidence of mutual influence between the two currents. Just as sustainability provides one of the core challenges which new governance approaches must address (and contexts to which they must adapt), new governance perspectives have coloured visions of what sustainable development would actually entail, and what sorts of mechanisms should be put into place to pursue it. Many of the policy tools most closely associated with new governance (such as negotiated agreements and market-based instruments) were trialed in the environmental sector. Think of environmental agreements in the Netherlands, the involvement of not-for-profit organizations in managing nature conservation in the UK, or carbon pricing through taxation or cap and trade systems across Europe. And there is no doubt that the 'network-governance' ideal that has figured prominently in new governance literatures has resonated strongly in the sustainable development file, where 'multi-stakeholder' processes have been at the core of national and international initiatives.

Yet this linkage between sustainable development and non-regulatory policy approaches that has been so evident over the past 15 years reflects contingent as well as substantive affinities. Substantively, there has been dissatisfaction with the results of environmental regulation (duplication, bureaucracy, endlessly proliferating rules, costs, and so on) and profound doubts that a 'compliance mentality' will ever encourage the innovation required to develop a truly sustainable way of doing things. Hence there has been openness to alternative policy instruments. And yet during much of the 1990s and 2000s there was also a belief that – given the dominant pro-market orientation of most political cultures – 'soft' measures were about the best that advocates of improved environmental stewardship could expect.

Most observers would now agree that experience over the past two decades suggests that while one can't make progress towards sustainability without new governance mechanisms, there is also a critical place for good old-fashioned – regulative and redistributive – state action.

CRITICAL LITERATURES

Literatures which engage with the problematic of sustainability governance are extremely diverse, with contributions coming from varied sources (universities, thinktanks, government agencies, international bodies, business organizations) and many disciplines (political studies, sociology, economics, geography, development and/or environmental studies, and so on). Focusing only on the more politically and analytically sophisticated of these contributions, it is possible to sort them into four rough categories, depending on whether they approach the issue from the perspective of (1) specific environment or development problems, (2) a particular scale of governance, (3) the issue of policy instruments or (4) the general requirements of governance for sustainable development. Work of the first type starts from particular problems, examining causes, implications and potential solutions. Problems of climate change, the management of water, forests, and fisheries, and the loss of biodiversity are typical frames for such investigations. And the focus is the governance mechanisms required to address these dilemmas. The second group involves work that privileges a particular governance 'level' – whether that may be a specific organization (a firm or agency) or cities, regional or national

governments, international organizations, and so on (Pattberg, 2007). The third category – which is most closely linked to new governance literatures – concentrates on policy instruments. The concern is with the design and selection of instruments, and the assessment of their relative performance (Dietz and Stern, 2002; Fiorino, 2006). Thus there is a great deal of writing on 'negotiated' or 'voluntary' instruments and on 'market-friendly' approaches such as cap and trade systems (Mol, Lauber and Liefferink, 2000; Cashore, Auld and Newsom, 2004). Finally, there is writing concerned with the overall project of governance for sustainable development – with its functional requirements, and with the character of the reforms required to ensure movement towards sustainability (Lafferty and Meadowcroft, 2000; Lafferty, 2004a; Lundqvist, 2004; Meadowcroft, 2007 a; Newig, Voss and Monstadt, 2008; Adger and Jordan, 2009).

This general literature has enumerated a series of challenges which sustainable development presents to contemporary governance systems (Meadowcroft and Bregha, 2009). These are understood to include the following difficulties.

- Drawing together decision-making about economic, social and environmental affairs. Modern states have typically decomposed problems, assigning responsibilities for economic, social and environmental policy to different agencies. But it is argued that sustainability demands a more holistic approach that can balance different kinds of societal goals.
- Working with multiple time frames. Environmental impacts are often manifest over the long term; the benefits of protective measures may only be felt in the future, while costs are carried today, and the short-term horizons of political interactions clash with the need for longer-term (multi-generational) planning perspectives.
- Coordinating files across a functionally differentiated bureaucracy. Issues like climate change demand action in many societal sectors and require coordination among multiple ministries (energy, agriculture, transport, urban affairs, education, and so on). But this collides with established administrative routines.

- Assigning appropriate responsibilities and integrating action at different scales. Environment and development problems are manifest at many different levels, often cutting across existing political/administrative boundaries. Sense must somehow be made of the array of overlapping jurisdictions from local communities to international organizations.
- Taking reasonable decisions in the face of persistent uncertainty. Again, climate change provides an illustration here. Despite years of research, great uncertainty remains about the pace and scale of climate change and the regional distribution of impacts. Policy must be developed today, even though uncertainties are likely to persist for decades into the future. And such uncertainty is a characteristic of many sustainable development-related issues.
- Integrating different kinds of knowledge in decision-making, including scientific, lay and traditional knowledge.
- Developing appropriate participatory mechanisms that can involve citizens meaningfully in key sustainability-related choices.
- Mediating complex conflicts of interest. Sustainable development requires radical change to existing patterns of production and consumption. But the most powerful groups in society have done well from existing arrangements. And the development of reform coalitions and the neutralization of opponents is critical.
- Escaping technological and societal 'lock-in', which reinforce path dependence, in order to develop innovative technical and social approaches.

Of course, such difficulties are not for the most part unique to the environment and sustainable development: however, in this sphere, they are found frequently, and in particularly challenging combinations.

Four elements which have featured prominently in these discussions are: 'integration'; 'measurement'; 'participation' or 'partnerships'; and 'reflexivity'. The critical importance of the *integration* of environment and development decision-making was emphasized by the Report of the WCED back in 1987. The argument was that environmental policy would never succeed if it was essentially devoted to post hoc clean up, while development decisions remained in the hands of production-oriented ministries (energy, natural resources, transport, industry, etc.). Instead, environmental considerations should be included from the outset. Thus, it would be possible to 'change the quality of growth' and avoid unwanted environmental damage. The goal was to 'integrate' environment into development decision-making – within government, but also in society more generally. By 'factoring-in' environmental dimensions from the outset, problems could be avoided and a more balanced development model could be implemented.

'Integration' has long been identified as a worthy goal in the policy and administrative sciences (Lafferty, 2004b). Fragmented, disjointed and/or partially contradictory policy initiatives waste resources and can jeopardize the attainment of priority objectives. The search for 'integration' – for coordination among administrative levels, harmonization among goals, and mutual support among policy initiatives – has been understood as a hallmark of rational policy design and implementation. But from the mid-1980s this traditional integrative preoccupation was reinterpreted, first as a call for 'integrated pollution control', and then more generally under the banner of 'environmental policy integration' (EPI). And there has been substantial discussion about different forms of 'integration' (across governance levels, among ministries, within each sector, and so on), the mechanisms to achieve integration, and the potential gains and/or costs/risks of integration (Lenschow 2002; Lafferty, 2004b; Nilsson and Eckerberg, 2007; Jordan and Lenschow, 2008). So far the basic insight seems to be that while the importance of integration is now formally recognized by many governments, practical achievements are harder to identify. There is a risk that 'integration' of environment into the activities of sectoral ministries degenerates into an exercise in box-ticking, while established production-oriented groups continue to dominate major policy decisions. Links between environmental policy and social policy remain especially weak in most contexts.

Measurement is another critical dimension of governance for sustainable development. The old adage that you can't manage what you can't measure is certainly pertinent, and the problem here is that sustainable development is a broad normative objective that can only be translated into a set of quantifiable objectives through analysis, value judgement and debate (Gibson et al., 2005). Among the more influential approaches are indicator sets that measure specific dimensions of sustainable development (environment, economic or social dimensions); ecological footprint analysis (that assess total imposed environmental burden of an individual, household, city or region by converting resource use and waste generation into a land area required to sustain those activities); sustainability assessment that evaluates the all-rounds effects of plans, policies and programmes; and indexes that rank countries according to their sustainability. Enormous progress has been made over the past two decades in collecting environmental information and developing reliable indicators for many environmental issues (see, for example, the work of the European Environment Agency). Consider also the measurement and monitoring programme linked to the Swedish system of National Environmental Objectives (EOC, 2008). But there is still much debate about how specific indicators and indicator sets relate to sustainable development, and a tension between the need for detailed tracking of specific issues and the desire for aggregative 'headline indicators'. Comparative international sustainability indexes are also under development but results remain highly dependent on the issues chosen for inclusion and their relative weighting. For instance, Canada ranks high on measures that attach greater significance to low population density (ESI, 2008).

Participation and *partnerships* have been another focus of research. Here long-standing concerns with civic and community participation have merged with more recent interest in 'stakeholder' participation and partnerships which can launch sustainability initiatives to achieve objectives that are beyond the reach of actors taken individually. Everyone agrees sustainability requires 'participation'. But what kind of participation, and how should it be organized? Attention has been directed to new forms of cooperative or joint governance, and various multi-stakeholder process, and to the analysis of the relative environmental performance of such institutions (Glasbergen, Biermann and Mol, 2007; Huijstee, Francken and Leroy, 2007).

With respect to *reflexivity*, the argument is that sustainable development requires societies to acquire a critical self-awareness of their development trajectories and to deploy mechanisms to modify those trajectories so as to avoid undesirable futures. Thus 'reflexivity' – the capacity to reflect on performance and to change behaviour in order to alter anticipated outcomes – is critical to governance for sustainable development. But where and how is this reflexivity to occur? How can 'society' take stock of current trends, evaluate existing practices, experiment with alternative ways of doing things, and encourage a shift to more desirable alternatives? The issue is one of institutionalizing reflexive governance – the way it can be embedded in specific structures and processes (Grin, 2006; Voss and Kemp, 2006). Discussion here has focused on two complementary tracks: first, the creation of specific mechanisms to encourage reflexive governance for sustainability (i.e. the construction of dedicated sites or processes that encourage the analysis of experience and the drawing of lessons about sustainability); and secondly, reform of the more general institutions of political decision-making so that reflexivity is enhanced. An example of the first track is provided by national sustainable development strategies. Encouraged by international processes such as the 1992 Rio Earth Summit (and more recently by the European Union), most developed states have initiated processes to prepare such strategies (Volkery et al., 2006; Bregha, 2008). In many cases these strategies are little more than glossy restatements of established government priorities, but in some countries they have prompted periodic reflection and public debate about progress towards sustainability, and there have been suggestions that such strategy processes can contribute to reflexive governance (Steurer and Martinuzzi, 2005; Meadowcroft, 2007b). Institutional innovations such as the creation of the UK Climate Change Committee, which monitors UK climate change policy and reports annually to Parliament (DEFRA, 2008), may also contribute in this direction. The second tack requires more general reforms to political systems and societal institutions to promote reflexivity, and suggestions here cover topics as wide as electoral system reform (especially in 'first-past-the-post' countries), campaign expenditure limits, media ownership, civic education, science communication and public participation.

TWO SAMPLE APPROACHES

To gain additional insights into recent thinking about governance and sustainable development, we now turn to two prominent currents which engage with different elements of the sustainability problematic: first, the 'transition' approach, which deals with change processes in large socio-technical systems (such as the energy or agricultural systems) (Rotmans, Kemp and van Asselt, 2001; Geels and Schot, 2007); and secondly, the 'adaptive management'/'resiliency' perspective, which is focused on the governance of specific locales or ecosystems, and on the management of biological resources (Gunderson and Holling, 2002).

Transition management and the evolution of large socio-technical systems

Developed by researchers in the Netherlands concerned with technological innovation, the transition approach draws on the experience of Dutch environmental policy, and applies insights from the study of historical 'transitions' between dominant socio-technical regimes (from sailing ships to steam ships; from outhouses to modern sewage systems; from coal to gas for domestic heating; and so on). Such 'transitions' are understood as structural changes in major societal subsystems (Geels 2005). They involve a shift in the dominant 'rules of the game', a transformation of established technologies and societal practices, typically stretching over several generations (25–50 years). The idea is that by understanding the dynamics of transition processes governments can intervene deliberately to influence societal development trajectories. Some authors in this tradition have referred to 'transition management' as a distinct approach to governance, or as 'a different type of governance model' (Kemp and Rotmans, 2005: 54).

Aware that the policy agenda is typically dominated by short-term considerations and that in established technological fields incumbents are focused principally on incremental improvements to dominant designs, transition management theorists are concerned to open the door to broader possibilities for innovation. The problems that particularly exercise them relate to the unsustainability of current production/consumption complexes, and the transformation of critical systems (energy, mobility, agriculture, and so on) to radically reduce their environmental impacts. Kemp and Rotmans define transition management as 'a deliberate attempt to bring about structural change in a stepwise manner' (Kemp and Rotmans, 2005: 42).

Two devices which figure prominently in this approach are 'transition visions' and 'transition experiments'. Transition visions are inspiring images of the future, and an evolving basket of such visions can draw different actors into the transition process. Transition experiments are the central practical focus for engaged stakeholders, for it is here they can work with others to implement innovative projects. Experiments may involve novel technologies, processes, networks, and practices; and they may be located at different points in production/consumption cycles. By developing a broad portfolio of experiments, steps along alternative transition pathways can be explored and new connections and opportunities for change opened up to society.

Transition management has been proposed to help policymakers confront persistent problems. It is not about 'planning', in the sense of realizing a predetermined blueprint. But neither is it about 'incrementalism', if this is understood to mean no more than continuous small adjustments to the status quo. Rather, it represents a form of 'goal-oriented modulation' (Kemp and Loorbach, 2007) that attempts to realize socially determined objectives by altering existing trajectories in small steps. The notion of 'evolution' has been present since the outset – consider the title of the classic essay by Rotmans, Kemp and van Asselt (2001): 'More evolution than revolution: transition management in public policy' – but recent discussions have tended to emphasize 'coevolution' and to make explicit the deliberate encouragement of variation (through experimentation) and the use of selective pressures (both markets and politics) to influence development trajectories. Indeed, the writers most closely associated with this approach have now described transition management as 'a new steering concept that relies on "Darwinistic" processes of guided variation and selection instead of planning' (Kemp, Rotmans and Loorbach, 2007: 7.)

It is worth emphasizing the close linkage between theoretical discussion of transition management and the practical development of Dutch environmental policy. The writers who pioneered the approach were involved in preparing the Netherlands Fourth National Environmental Policy Plan. The plan made explicit reference to the need to rectify 'design flaws' in societal subsystems, and emphasized the importance of managing societal transitions over periods of a generation or more (NEEP4, 2002). In subsequent years the Dutch government initiated a variety of programmes inspired by transition management, with the Ministry of Economic Affairs playing a particularly active role with respect to energy matters (Kemp, Rotmans and Loorbach, 2007).

From the perspective of governance for sustainable development, transition management possesses a number of appealing features. Of particular note is the emphasis the approach places on:

- *making the future more clearly manifest in current decisions*, by adopting longer time frames, exploring alternative trajectories, and opening avenues for system innovation (as well as system improvement)
- *transforming established practices in critical societal* subsystems within which unsustainable practices are deeply embedded
- *developing interactive processes* where networks of actors implicated in a particular production/consumption nexus can come together, develop shared problem definitions, appreciate differing perspectives and, above all, develop practical activities
- *linking technological and social innovation*, because both sorts of change are necessary if society is to move on to a more sustainable pathway
- *'learning-by-doing'*, developing experiments with novel practices and technologies, because it is only by initiating change that we can learn the potential (and the limits) of different approaches
- *tailoring support for technologies to the different phases of the innovation cycle*
- *encouraging a diversity of innovations ('variation') and competition among different approaches (selection)* to fulfill societal needs
- *assigning an active role to government* in mobilizing society to orient change in desired directions.

Adaptive management and resilience

'Adaptive management' has its origins in modern ecological science and attempts to understand persistent failures in the governance of biological resource systems such as forests or fisheries. It points to the complex, dynamic and interconnected character of ecosystems, and the limits to scientific capacities to predict the future. Its central critique is that human agents are typically interested in managing natural systems to maximize one resource output (e.g. the timber harvest or fish catch). But activities to promote this end reduce ecosystem resilience – making ecological and social–ecological systems more brittle – and thus open the way to dramatic change (collapse of the existing system) in the future.

This tradition emphasizes a number of key features of ecosystem processes, including that:

- ecosystem 'change is neither continuous and gradual nor consistently chaotic' (rather, processes function at different rates and episodic change is caused by interaction between slow and fast processes)
- spatial scale matters – the natural world is 'lumpy' and non-linear processes abound
- ecosystems can have multiple equilibrium states.

Thus, the management of ecosystems has to be 'flexible, adaptive and experiment at scales compatible with the scales of critical ecosystem functions' (Gunderson and Holling, 2002: 26).

Gunderson and Holling have proposed a four-stage heuristic to capture the nature of change in ecosystems and in eco–social systems. It comprises phases of 'exploitation', 'conservation', 'release' and 'reorganization' and is represented by the image of a twisting loop mapping different degrees of 'connectedness' and 'potential'. For example, forests often experience a cycle where fire or insect predation periodically destroys mature stands, but this destruction also opens the way for regeneration and new growth. Such cycles – where the ecosystem passes through distinct phases – are connected to similar cycles at larger and smaller scales. Thus, change and renewal take place at different rhythms up and down the twisted links of this chain. Rather than understanding ecosystems as undergoing a linear ascent, that tends towards a 'climax' state of maximum

diversity and interdependence, this vision is dynamic and cyclical, emphasizing ecosystem change and continuity at different rates and scales. And researchers working in this tradition have applied the four-stage heuristic in diverse contexts, including ecosystems, political and economic systems, and eco–social systems.

'Panarchy' is the term Gunderson and Holling have invoked to denote the multiscale regulatory cycles that govern the development of adaptive systems. It 'captures the adaptive and evolutionary nature of adaptive cycles that are nested one within the other across space and time scales'. 'Panarchy' emphasizes on the one hand that there is an adaptive *cycle* where the 'reorganization' phase plays a critical role in promoting variety and regeneration and on the other hand that there are multiple connections among levels (cross-scale interactions) especially at the 'revolt' and 'remember' phases of the cycle. Turbulence at smaller scales ('revolt') can spread up the chain (e.g. a small fire spreading to wider areas), while stability at the larger scale ('remember') can assist local regeneration (e.g. the influx of seeds from undisturbed areas). And this applies as much to human social systems as to natural ecosystems. The twisting loop therefore captures the 'essence of a theory of change'. It shows the importance of stability, conservation and remembrance as well as of turbulence, collapse and creative destruction.

As a management approach, 'adaptive management' presents policy as an experiment. Since it is not possible to predict complex ecosystem interactions, policy should be framed cautiously. Results should be closely monitored, lessons drawn on the basis of experience and actions adjusted in light of that experience. Adaptive management rejects the notion of managing resource systems to generate 'maximum sustainable yields' because it is in principle impossible to determine what this might be, and efforts to sustain such yields will increase the vulnerability of ecosystems and social systems.

'Resilience' can be understood as a more appropriate focus for management efforts. It defines both a property of eco–social systems and a goal of intervention. With enhanced resilience, eco–social systems can respond to unexpected circumstances, read-just, and remain productive. In their writing, Holling and Gunderson emphasize two understandings of resilience: resilience as flexibility about an equilibrium (the ability to return to the equilibrium point after a distur-bance); and resilience as the capacity to maintain function while cycling through multiple equilibriums. Both are important, but the second is more fundamental, as the system retains the capacity to reorganize to preserve function in the face of significant change. With respect to eco-social systems, 'resilience' relates to the capacity to adjust to changing circumstances, to learn from expe-rience, and enhance adaptive capacity. 'Diversity' is typically taken as critical to maintaining and enhancing resilience both for ecosystems and eco–social systems. Diversity provides a rich foundation for adaptation when confronted with unexpected changes.

The extension of this work into economics and politics has been carried out in slightly different ways. Social science collaborators of Gunderson and Holling developed models of economic and political practices, explor-ing application of the 'twisted loop' in social systems and in linked social and ecological systems. Researchers linked into the broader Resilience Alliance and groups such as the Stockholm Resilience Centre have adopted a variety of approaches, often emphasizing the resilience of specific human communities and social institutions. Resilience is seen as critical to promoting long-term sustainabil-ity. 'Resilience' serves as a focal point for examining eco–social linkages, for enhanc-ing learning about ecological and social interdependencies, for encouraging commu-nication and strengthening capacities to respond to changing circumstances. A slightly different approach has been taken by other analysts – for example, Swanson in a project

organized by IISD and the Indian TERI (and financed by Canada's IDRC) has examined 'adaptive policies'. The concern is the design of policies that can adapt to anticipated changes and to unanticipated changes. Key mechanisms to implement adaptive policies include: 'automatic adjustment', 'integrated assessment to inform policy parameters', 'multi-perspective deliberation', 'formal review and continuous learning', 'encourag-ing self-organization and networking', 'subsidiarity', and 'promoting variation' (Swanson, 2009). The difference here is the switch away from the place-, resource- and ecosystem-based frames out of which 'adap-tive management' first emerged to a concern with more general policy domains.

Juxtaposing these two approaches: What is the role of politics?

Previous discussions of the relationship between transition management and adaptive management/resilience have pointed to a number of similarities. Van der Brugge and van Raak cite four important 'commonalities':

- both approaches 'have roots in complex adaptive system theory'
- they are concerned with similar objects of study – 'namely, the dynamics and governance of [socio–ecological systems]'
- both 'address multi-scale dynamics' ('panarchy' in the case of adaptive management/resilience and the 'multi-level perspective' in transition management)
- both explore '"self-organizing regimes" and the possibility of regime shifts' (Van der Brugge and van Raak, 2007: 4).

Foxon, Reed and Stringer (2009) emphasize that these approaches 'have their roots in thinking that recognizes the complexity of, and interactions between, social, economic and ecological systems' and suggest a gov-ernance philosophy for complex adaptive systems that is 'iterative' and 'learning-based'. They both embrace 'experiments', and the 'involvement of a wide range of stakeholders'. Smith and Stirling allude to 'generic similarities' between the approaches, including the emphasis on 'evolutionary, path dependent change', on 'flexible and learning-oriented approaches for modulating those changes', and on 'diversity' (to promote resilience in adaptive management/resilience and to provide niches for innovative technologies in transition management). (Smith and Stirling, 2009.)

Foxon, Reed and Stringer (2009) point to a number of differences between the approaches, including that while transition management seeks to orient 'long-term changes in functioning of socio-technical systems', adaptive management is more concerned with 'the accretion of adaptive capacity in order to absorb and manage rather than to *direct* change'. For their part, Smith and Stirling argue that 'socio-ecological systems research and socio-technical research have different aims. Socio-ecological systems research (no matter how sophisticated its treatment of interacting scales and levels) is concerned about the services flowing from a socio-ecological system rooted in a particular spatial context'. In contrast, 'socio-technical research is not so place-bound'; it concerns regimes that 'operate simultaneously across multiple (often quite unconnected) loci', involving 'patchworks of socio-ecological systems in resource extraction and waste assimilation' (Smith and Stirling, 2009: 19). Thus 'Social-ecological systems research takes a social-ecological system as its basic unit of analysis', and technology is 'not central' and 'is rarely unpacked and considered dynamically'. On the other hand, 'socio-ecological processes are not integrated centrally into transition studies' (Smith and Stirling, 2009: 18). Smith and Sterling also point out that, for transition management, 'resilience' can be as much a problem as a solution because socio-technical regimes that resist reform ('lock-in') can hamper progress towards sustainability. And when 'structural socio-technical resilience militates against delivery of sustainability function' (e.g. the fossil-fuel energy system), the governance

challenge 'is to erode the structural resilience of incumbent socio-technical regimes in order to promote socio-ecological systems resilience.'

These discussions point to some of the parallels and contrasts between these two approaches to governing for sustainable development. Both start from a recognition of the failures of existing environmental policy and are understood as governance projects oriented towards sustainability. Both adopt a systems perspective and an evolutionary orientation – they are concerned with patterns of change and continuity in complex dynamic systems, and with the potential for human agents to intervene to influence these patterns. Understanding the interactions among different temporal and spatial scales is a critical concern in each case, and there are significant similarities between the 'multi-level framework' of transition management and the three interconnected twisted loops that express the essence of 'panarchy'. The convergence of 'governance' prescriptions is particularly striking (as Smith and Stirling note): with a rejection of formal planning, sympathy for aspects of 'incrementalism' as a management strategy (albeit with longer-term objectives in view), an emphasis on iterative policy design, and experiments and learning.

But the similarities are connected to important differences. The most obvious relates to the systems with which they are concerned. Adaptive management/resilience deals with socio-ecological systems, highlighting complex interdependencies between society and ecology. It emerged from a concern with the management of biological resources in ecological systems, and retains its place-based orientation, although developments at the base locale are linked to wider social and ecological processes. Typically, the starting points are areas where the connection between the social economy and ecosystems remains relatively direct (communities dependent on flows of biological resources) rather than major metropolitan areas. Transition management is concerned with socio-technical systems, and the mutual shaping of society and technology. It emerged from environmental assessment, innovation and science and technology studies, and starts from particular societal subsystems. Interestingly, the two approaches may be able to meet at the community level, as transition management is being applied to address persistent problems at the local level (local subsystems) and of course the application of adaptive management/resilience is well suited to such contexts.

Transition management and adaptive management/resilience both embody theories of change. The ideal model of transition management focuses on movement from one equilibrium to another (hence, the need for a 'transition'), while adaptive management refers to cycles of growth and decay. This contrast may appear to be grounded in the subject matter from which the theories first developed. In the broad sweep of history (especially over the past three centuries), and in the life experience of people in contemporary developed states, socio-technical systems display a clear pattern of succession: one set of technologies replaces another. For example, the age of sailing ships gives way to the era of steam. But of course societies have known technological regression and stagnation as well as linear advance. Ecological systems are understood to change at multiple scales and to experience cycles of renewal. But of course there is a more linear way to understand their development and, until challenged by theorists such as Holling, such views prevailed. And to some extent, whether history is an ascending line, a cycle or spiral depends on when and where one chooses to start and end the story.

But there is an important difference in emphasis with regards to the way conscious intervention relates to change. Smith and Stirling refer to this as the greater 'directionality' of transition management. It is focused on effecting a particular change (transition), while adaptive management/resilience concentrates on enhancing a community's capacity to adapt to a turbulent environment. Transition management seeks to prise open technological 'lock in', to weaken path dependence and open up new development trajectories. Adaptive management/resilience tries to broaden opportunities to adjust, given evolving circumstances. Thus, evolution plays a different role in the two theories – with one current equipping communities to deal with evolving conditions, while the other tries to harness selective pressures to improve social-technological practices.

Each of these approaches has been subject to lively debate and criticism, but the first point to which attention should be drawn here is the extent to which both address limited portions of the field marked out by governance for sustainable development. Adaptive management/resilience seems pertinent in contexts where the linkages between communities and resources are reasonably straightforward, but appears less relevant elsewhere – e.g. in a complex modern national economy or a globally connected city. Of course, 'resilience' provides an anchor for policy. Sustainable development suggests there is also a normative and transformative agenda that has to do not just with making communities more able to adapt – but with making them better places in which to live. And it is not clear that the reactive focus of adaptive management/resilience expresses this well. Transition management is supposed to apply to social practices as well as to technologies, to consumption as well as to production. But in practice, transition experiments have focused on the technological side as this seems far easier for officials and politicians to accommodate (Kemp, Rotmans and Loorbach, 2007; Kern and Smith, 2008). Here, transition management is linked to the idea of growing green businesses and export markets, which is much more appealing than talk of frugality, simplicity, managed consumption and post-consumer lifestyles. Even on the production side the transition approach has in practice been adopted more as an add-on to traditional modes of policymaking rather than marking a more fundamental shift.

Approaching this from a slightly different angle, one could ask 'Is there something that these two approaches do not do?' Are there 'systems' with which they do not engage? And the answer here must have something to do with politics, political action and political institutions. Each of these approaches got its initial impetus in the sphere of *expert* management. Adaptive management/resilience started with ecological scientists concerned with the systematic failures of biological resource management. And it was first trialled by entrepreneurial resources managers attempting to improve the management of fisheries, forests, lakes and rivers. Coupled with resilience, it becomes applicable to communities and their interdependent eco–social systems. Transition management started with environmental managers and technology experts identifying structural obstacles to resolving persistent problems and focuses on the transformation of social–technical regimes. In both cases the political and the political system are exogenous. Indeed part of the management strategy consists of deliberately 'depoliticising' these issues – trying to take them out of the political arena. But of course 'depoliticising' topics is in one sense the grandest political move of all! It 'normalizes' them as part of everyday administration and business. And yet despite their non-political focus, each approach depends heavily on the involvement of societal stakeholders, and ultimately on the approbation of political authorities, who grant support and funding for adaptive management and transition management experiments.

AN AGENDA FOR THE FUTURE

To this point we have considered the general problem raised by governance and sustainable development, touched upon some recent literatures, and explored two particular approaches in more detail. The threads of this discussion will now be drawn together.

A good starting point is the admission that the critique presented above of transition management and adaptive management/resilience for side-stepping politics is a little unfair: not because it is untrue, but rather because a similar criticism could be levelled at much of recent thinking about governance for sustainable development. For the most part, this discussion has concentrated on the details of policy and process: on what governments, communities and businesses are actually doing, and what they should be doing, if their formal commitment to sustainable development is to be consequent. But the *politics* of these issues – why they are doing what they are doing – is relatively neglected. Above all, the attention of researchers has seldom been directed at the critical problem of exploring how political conditions might be altered, so that the sustainability problematic could shift closer towards the heart of policymaking.

To put this another way, we have lots of work on policies that would generate better environmental outcomes, and some studies of what happens when governments do attempt sustainability-related reforms, but far less reflection on the political changes that might motivate governments to take all this more seriously. On climate change, for example, discussion of policy instruments abound: there is an ever-accumulating mass of proposals for tweaking established instruments or switching to new ones. But there is very little written on approaches to institutionalizing climate policy within democratic political systems. And there is even less work on the politics of climate policy (the formation of public opinion, the creation of winning coalitions, the role of veto blocks, and so on), particularly the analysis of how this politics might be transformed. But that too is part of governance for sustainable development; indeed, it is perhaps the most critical part. After all, at the core of movement towards sustainable development lie political processes – processes of collective decision-making; mechanisms for selecting and renewing leaders; and cycles of defining, assessing and changing policy orientations.

The problem of governance for sustainable development links up to broad challenges facing contemporary polities (and contemporary political analysts), including the development of effective international governance mechanisms, designing public policy in a context of increased complexity and interdependence, and the renewal of democratic systems. But it also focuses attention on a particular set of problems now confronting human societies: where the existing development trajectory is increasingly undermining the ecological foundations on which it has been predicated. And the ramifications of these problems potentially cut to the heart of established economic and political practices.

Looking at the current state of the debate around sustainability governance in developed countries, three inter-related issues appear of particular theoretical and practical salience: moving beyond the expansionist material economy; rethinking the environmental state/welfare state linkage; and reforming representative democracy.

First, The continuing rise in human numbers, and the growth in levels of material consumption, is placing ever greater strains upon the biosphere (MEA, 2006; IPCC, 2007; OECD, 2008). Sustainable development suggests that we should be concerned not so much with economic growth but rather with human 'development', and that the 'quality of growth' should be adjusted to avoid damage to critical environmental systems. But two decades of 'sustainable development' and four decades of modern environmental policy have not succeeded in significantly displacing the overall development trajectory. Ensuring good old-fashioned economic growth remains the foundation of government policy around the world, and gains in material and energy efficiency are regularly swamped by rises in absolute consumption. It may in principle be possible for an entire economy to shift to a green track – where environmental loadings (linked to resource extraction, consumption and waste emission) fall, even as well-being rises – but so far no one has done it. Of course, a few decades is not much time when one is dealing with fundamental structural reform. However, experience does suggest that a lot more work is needed to understand pathways to change, to appreciate what a 'green growth' or 'low material growth' economy really implies, and to take on issues such as population growth rates and levels as well as consumption more directly. For the most part, academic analysts (much like activists and politicians) have shied away from these issues, convinced perhaps that they go so much against the grain of conventional thinking that they are not fruitful avenues around which to campaign for reform. But it seems hard to imagine how one can have a serious discussion about governance for sustainability unless the potential for the conscious and collective management of population and consumption can be explored (Victor, 2008).

Second, existing welfare states have been predicated on the continuous expansion of material consumption that provides the foundation for trickle down and for (strictly limited and highly variable) redistributive mechanisms (Pierson, 1998; Meadowcroft, 2005). But how are welfare models to be adjusted to accommodate a different – non-expansionist – economic paradigm? Moreover, environmental problems are bringing to the fore new distributive issues, including the sharing of increasingly scare resources (e.g. water), sinks (the ecosystem's capacity to absorb pollutants) and the costs of remedial action (climate change mitigation and adaptation). Any significant move towards a low-carbon economy will generate winners and losers, just as the shift to the oil-based economy did over the past century. How are these distributive challenges to be managed? Exploring such welfare and redistributive dimensions is therefore a critical challenge for sustainability governance.

Third, there is the operation of representative democratic systems themselves. The political systems that we have inherited in developed states have been passed down from an earlier era and, to the extent that they were consciously designed (rather than representing a contingent accumulation of partial reforms), they were designed to address different problems. These institutions (imperfectly) embody a valuable heritage – including responsible government, representative government, the rule of law, universal suffrage, federalism, and so on – that allows some measure of protection for individual rights, popular input to political decision-making, an accommodations of interests, the undertaking of collective projects, pluralism and peaceful and ordered governance. Modern governments are also economic actors and maintain welfare programmes. They also protect privilege and are rife with inconsistencies and injustices. All this is the result of acute and protracted political struggles. However, they bear the mark of being born in an expansionist economic era, where there appeared no practical limits to the environment's capacity to accommodate human desires. Moreover, most polities display some signs of sclerosis as public participation in the formal political system (parties and elections) continues to decline. Some green thinkers have discussed the environmental deficits of contemporary democracy (Dryzek, 2002; Eckersley, 2004; Meadowcroft, 2004), and considered the prospects for deliberative or discursive reform, but there is much more to be done to explore avenues for change in democratic polities: for example, in relation to public education, the building of reform coalitions and institutional innovation.

Each of these three issues is linked to the others. And each is also fundamentally a problem of governance, in the broad sense of having to do with the way order, but also change, can be structured in human societies. Moreover, each relates also to the challenges raised by the new governance literatures. The issues of moving beyond the expansionist growth economy, rethinking distributive and welfare issues, and recasting democratic governance all suggest that the old governance models of the twentieth century have had

their day. The point is not that the state has been hollowed out, but rather that it will have to respond to new challenges, be recast in new institutional forms, and act more cooperatively with a complex array of social forces if it is to handle the challenges of the future.

REFERENCES

Adger, Neil and Jordan, Andrew (2009) *Governing Sustainability*. Cambridge: Cambridge University Press.

Bregha, Francois (2008) 'Missing the Opportunity: A Decade of Sustainable Development Strategies', in G. Toner (ed.), *Innovation, Science, Environment 2008–2009: Canadian Policies and Performance*. Montreal: McGill-Queen's University Press.

Cashore, B., Auld, G. and Newsom, D. (2004) *Governing through Markets*. New Haven, CT: Yale University Press.

DEFRA (2008) see: http://www.defra.gov.uk/environment/climatechange/uk/legislation/.

Dietz, Thomas and Stern, Paul (eds.) (2002) *New Tools for Environmental Protection*. Washington, DC: National Academy Press.

Dryzek, John (2002) *Deliberative Democracy and Beyond*. Oxford: Oxford University Press.

Durant, R., Fiorino, D. and O'Leary, R. (eds) (2004) *Environmental Governance Reconsidered: Challenges, Choices and Opportunities*. Cambridge, MA: MIT Press; pp. 183–218.

Eckersley, Robyn (2004) *The Green State*. Cambridge, MA: MIT Press.

Environmental Objectives Council (EOC) (2008) see: http://www.miljomal.nu/english/english.php.

ESI (2008) 'Environmental Sustainability Index'. Yale Center for Environmental Law & Policy, available at http://sedac.ciesin.columbia.edu/es/esi/.

Fiorino, Daniel (2006) *The New Environmental Regulation*. Cambridge, MA: MIT Press.

Foxon, T., Reed, M. and Stringer, L. (2009) 'Governing Long-term Social-Ecological Change: What Can the Adaptive Management and Transition Management Approaches Learn from Each Other?', *Environmental Policy and Governance* 19: 3–20.

Geels, Frank (2005) *Technological Transitions and System Innovations: A Co-evolutionary and Sociotechnical Analysis*. Cheltenham: Edward Elgar.

Geels, Frank and Schot, Johan (2007) 'Typology of Sociotechnical Transition Pathways', *Research Policy* 36: 399–417.

Gibson, R., Hassan, S., Holtz, S., Tansey, J. and Whitelaw, G. (2005) *Sustainability Assessment*. London: Earthscan.

Glasbergen, P., Biermann, F. and Mol, A. (eds) (2007) *Partnerships, Governance and Sustainable Development: Reflections on Theory and Practice*. Cheltenham: Edward Elgar.

Grin, John (2006) 'Reflexive Modernization as a Governance Issue, or Designing and Shaping Restructuration', in J. Voss, D. Bauknecht and R. Kemp (eds), *Reflexive Governance for Sustainable Development*. Cheltenham: Edward Elgar; pp. 54–81.

Gunderson, Lance and Holling, Crawford (eds) (2002) *Panarchy: Understanding Transformations in Human and Natural Systems*. Washington, DC: Island Press.

Huijstee, M. van, Francken, M. and Leroy, P. (2007) 'Partnerships for Sustainable Development: A Review of Current Literature', *Environmental Sciences* 4(2): 75–89.

IPCC (2007) *Climate Change 2007: Synthesis Report*. Intergovernmental Panel on Climate Change.

Jordan, Andrew and Lenschow, Andrea (eds) (2008) *Innovation in Environmental Policy? Integrating the Environment for Sustainability*. Cheltenham: Edward Elgar.

Kemp, Rene and Loorbach, Derk (2007) 'Transition Management: A Reflexive Governance approach', in Jan-Peter Voss, Dierk Bauknecht and Rene Kemp (eds.). Cheltenham: Edward Elgar.

Kemp, Rene and Rotmans, Jan (2005) 'The Management of the Co-evolution of Technical, Environmental and Social Systems', in Matthias Weber and Jens Hemmelskemp (eds), *Towards Environmental Innovation Systems*. Berlin: Springer.

Kemp, R., Rotmans, J. and Loorbach, D. (2007) 'Assessing the Dutch Energy Transition Policy: How Does It Deal with Dilemmas of Managing Transitions?', *Journal of Environment Policy and Planning* 9(3): 315–31.

Kern, Florian and Smith, Adrian (2008) 'Restructuring Energy Systems for Sustainability? Energy Transition Policy in the Netherlands', *Energy Policy* 36: 4093–103.

Kooiman, Jan (2003) *Governing as Governance*. London: Sage.

Lafferty, William (1996) 'The Politics of Sustainable Development: Global Norms for National Implementation', *Environmental Politics*, 5: 185–208.

Lafferty, William (2004a) *Governance for Sustainable Development: The Challenge of Adapting Form to Function*. Cheltenham: Edward Elgar.

Lafferty, William (2004b) 'From Environmental Protection to Sustainable Development: The Challenge of Decoupling through Sectoral Integration', in W. Lafferty (ed.), *Governance for Sustainable Development*. Cheltenham: Edward Elgar.

Lafferty, William and Meadowcroft, James (eds) (2000) *Implementing Sustainable Development*. Oxford: Oxford University Press.

Lenschow, Andrea (2002) *Environmental Policy Integration: Greening Sectoral Policies in Europe*. London: Earthscan.

Lundqvist, Lennart (2004) *Sweden and Ecological Governance: Straddling the Fence*. Manchester: Manchester University Press.

MEA (2006) *Ecosystem and Human Well-being: General Synthesis*. Millennium Ecosystem Assessment. Washington, DC: Island Press.

Meadowcroft, James (1999) 'Planning for Sustainable Development: What Can Be Learned from the Critics?', in M. Kenny and J. Meadowcroft (eds), *Planning for Sustainability*. London: Routledge; pp. 12–38.

Meadowcroft, James (2004) 'Deliberative Democracy', in R. Durant, D. Fiorino and R. O'Leary (eds), *Environmental Governance Reconsidered: Challenges, Choices and Opportunities*. Cambridge, MA: MIT Press.

Meadowcroft, James (2005) 'From Welfare State to Ecostate?', in J. Barry and R. Eckersley (eds), *The State and the Global Ecological Crisis*. Cambridge, MA: MIT Press; pp. 3–23.

Meadowcroft, James (2007a) 'Who Is in Charge Here? Governance for Sustainable Development in a Complex World', *Journal of Environment Policy and Planning* 9: 299–314.

Meadowcroft, James (2007b) 'National Sustainable Development Strategies: A Contribution to Reflexive Governance?', *European Environment* 17: 152–63.

Meadowcroft, James and Bregha, Francois (2009) 'Governance for Sustainable Development: Meeting the Challenge Ahead', a scoping paper prepared for the Policy Research Initiative, Ottawa.

Meadowcroft, James and Toner, Glen (2009) 'Engaging with Sustainable Development: Setting the Canadian Experience in Context', in G. Toner and J. Meadowcroft (eds), *Innovation Science and Environment, Charting Sustainable Development in Canada, 1987–2007*. Montreal: McGill-Queens University Press.

Mol, A., Lauber, V. and Liefferink, D. (2000) *The Voluntary Approach to Environmental Policy.* Oxford: Oxford University Press.

NEEP4 (2002) *Where There's a Will There's a World.* The Netherlands Fourth National Environmental Policy Plan. Ministry of Housing Spatial Planning and the Environment.

Newig, J., Voss, J.-P. and Monstadt, J. (2008) *Governance for Sustainable Develoment: Coping with Ambivalence, Uncertainty and Distributed Power.* London: Routledge.

Nilsson, Mans and Eckerberg, Katarina (2007) *Environmental Policy Integration in Practice: Shaping Institutions for Learning.* London: Earthscan.

OECD (2008) *OECD Environmental Outlook to 2030.* Paris: OECD.

Pattberg, Philipp (2007) *Private Institutions of Global Governance.* Cheltenham: Edward Elgar.

Pierre, Jon and Peters, Guy (2000) *Governance, Politics and the State.* London: Palgrave.

Pierson, Christopher (1998) *Beyond the Welfare State: the New Political Economy of Welfare,* 2nd edn. Cambridge: Polity Press.

Rotmans, J., Kemp, R. and van Asselt, M. (2001) 'More Evolution than Revolution: Transition Management in Public Policy', *Foresight,* 3: 15–31.

Smith, Adrian and Stirling, Andrew (2008) 'Social-Ecological Resilience and Socio-Technical Transitions: Critical Issues for Sustainability Governance'. STEPS Centre Working Paper.

Steurer, Reinhard and Martinuzzi, Andre (2005) 'Towards a New Pattern of Strategy Formation in the Public Sector: First Experiences with National Strategies for Sustainable Development in Europe', *Environment and Planning C: Government and Policy* 23: 455–72.

Swanson, Darren (2009) 'Adaptive Policies: Seven Things Policymakers Should Know to Craft Better Policies in Today's Dynamic and Uncertain World'. Available at: https://policyresearch.gc.ca/doclib/PS_04022009_AdaptivePolicies.pdf.

Van der Brugge, R. and van Raak, R. (2007) 'Facing the Adaptive Management Challenge: Insights from Transition Management, *Ecology and Society* 12(2): 33. [Online URL: http://www.ecologyandsociety.org/vol12/iss2/art33/

Victor, P. (2008) *Managing without Growth: Slower by Design, Not Disaster.* Cheltenham: Edward Elgar.

Volkery, A., Swanson, D., Jacob, K., Bregha, F. and Pinter, L. (2006) 'Coordination, Challenges, and Innovations in 19 National Sustainable Development Strategies', *World Development* 34: 2047–63.

Voss, Jan-Peter and Kemp, Rene (2006) 'Sustainability and Reflexive Governance: Introduction', in J.-P. Voss, D. Bauknecht and R. Kemp (eds), *Reflexive Governance for Sustainable Development.* Cheltenham, UK: Edward Elgar; pp. 3–28.

WCED (1987) *Our Common Future.* World Commission on Environment and Development. Oxford: Oxford University Press.

Name Index

Subject Index